INTERNATIONAL ENCYCLOPEDIA OF

Marriage and Family

INTERNATIONAL ENCYCLOPEDIA OF

Marriage and Family

SECOND EDITION

Volume 1: Ab–Du

James J. Ponzetti, Jr
Editor in Chief

**MACMILLAN
REFERENCE
USA**™

THOMSON
GALE

New York • Detroit • San Diego • San Francisco • Cleveland • New Haven, Conn. • Waterville, Maine • London • Munich

THOMSON
GALE

International Encyclopedia of Marriage and Family

James J. Ponzetti, Jr.

Macmillan Reference USA
300 Park Avenue South, 9th Floor
New York, NY 10010

Macmillan Reference USA
27500 Drake Road
Farmington Hills, MI 48331-3535

LIBRARY OF CONGRESS CATALOGING-IN-PUBLICATION DATA

International encyclopedia of marriage and family / James J. Ponzetti, Jr.,
editor in chief. — 2nd ed.
p. cm.
Rev. ed. of: Encyclopedia of marriage and the family. c1995.
Includes bibliographical references and index.
ISBN 0-02-865672-5 (set : alk. paper) — ISBN 0-02-865673-3 (v. 1 : alk.
paper) — ISBN 0-02-865674-1 (v. 2 : alk. paper) — ISBN 0-02-865675-X
(v. 3 : alk. paper) — ISBN 0-02-865676-8 (v. 4 : alk. paper)
1. Marriage—Encyclopedias. 2. Family—Encyclopedias. I. Ponzetti,
James J. II. Encyclopedia of marriage and family.

HQ9 .E52 2003
306.8'03—dc21

2002014107

Printed in the United States of America
10 9 8 7 6 5 4 3 2

CONTENTS

Preface . . . . *vii*

List of Articles . . . . *xi*

List of Contributors . . . . *xxi*

INTERNATIONAL ENCYCLOPEDIA OF MARRIAGE AND FAMILY
1

Index *1745*

PREFACE

People everywhere form bonds of friendship, develop close intimate relationships, cohabit, and raise children, but each of these acts is conditioned by cultural expectations, customs, norms, rules, mysteries, and ceremonies. Of all the institutions that have shaped human life, marriages and families have been the most important. While marriage and family relationships constitute basic institutions, both for the individuals involved in them and for society as a whole, they are neither simple nor static. On the contrary, they are constantly changing, evolving with time, and adapting to place. It is in these relationships that many of the most distinctive features of human life are most clearly and unambiguously illustrated.

Love, sex, marriage, and families are subjects of intrinsic interest to nearly everyone. Perhaps this is so because they represent common experiences that are given special favor and protection in one way or another by all societies. Familial activities and relations are intertwined with many other kinds of activities and relations. Accordingly, marriage and family relationships must be understood as part of the cultural life as a whole.

Different societies have different conceptions of what constitutes a marriage or family, but in all societies the relations between the sexes and the generations have an identifiable pattern. Marriage and family life are so decisive in the formation of personality and the shaping of people's most intimate feelings that as they evolve, surely personal habits, social arrangements, quotidian emotions, and even one's innermost thoughts will also change. This diversity and malleability make it difficult to comprehend contemporary marriages and families, yet it is the very reason understanding is necessary.

The literature on marital and family relations is fragmented and diverse, "running all the way from superstition-based folklore, to imaginative fiction, to poetic outpourings, to philosophical speculation, to popularized magazine articles and advice columns, and finally to reports of scientific investigations" (Christensen 1964, p. x). Yet, the multidisciplinary study of these relationships has only just been recognized as a distinct area of study (Burr and Leigh 1983). Over the past two decades, Family Science has emerged as a significant and burgeoning field of study in the social and behavioral sciences (Hollinger 2003). Unfortunately, much of the scholarship has been limited to English-speaking, Western, industrialized countries, and little work has taken an international perspective.

The purpose of the *International Encyclopedia of Marriage and Family, Second Edition,* is to peruse the current state and panoramic diversity of marriage and family life in an international context. The basic aim of this encyclopedia is to make information that is often difficult to find and analyze available to students, scholars, journalists, and other interested readers in an easy-to-use reference source. This information is vital to contemporary life in a global society because modernization and globalization continue to alter the way people live. These social forces and the change they inevitably bring about weaken the foundations of the old norms and customs without creating any consensus on new ones. Instead of living in small towns where surveillance by family and friends is ubiquitous, people now live mostly in cities where anonymity is the rule and few care about what they do.

That new conditions engender new attitudes is indisputable, but the salient question is not change per se but the response to it. Many people expect marriage and family relations to respond to changes due to globalization by providing the emotional nurturance that is not easily attained in other, more impersonal social contexts. In order to address this expectation, greater understanding and mutual respect for diverse arrangements and behaviors is essential.

The *International Encyclopedia of Marriage and Family* is a significant expansion and revision of the *Encyclopedia of Marriage and the Family* published in 1995. This project began in 2000 with the goal of creating a focal reference source on the diverse marriage and family lifestyles evident around the world. An exceptional group of scholars representing different disciplines and perspectives was invited to serve on the Editorial Board, which met in Denver to plan the scope of the project. All the entries from the *Encyclopedia of Marriage and the Family* were reviewed in light of the present edition's strong international focus: Some were updated, others substantively revised, and still others deleted. Additional topics, issues, and countries were identified for the new edition, scholars were commissioned to contribute to the project, completed entries were carefully reviewed by the Editorial Board for readability and content, and final entries were compiled.

Format of the Encyclopedia

The expanded *International Encyclopedia of Marriage and Family* comprises four volumes and is a compendium surveying the shared patterns and amazing variation in marriage and family life in a rapidly changing multicultural world. These volumes, as in the first edition, present "knowledge about marriages, families, and human relationships and about the psychological, cultural, and societal forces that influence them" (Levinson 1995, p. x). One critical addition justifies the doubling in length of the second edition, namely, the integration of a global perspective.

The incorporation of an international focus was not an easy one to bring to fruition. As noted above, marriage and family scholarship is multidisciplinary and thus not confined to scholars in a single academic discipline. Further, the study of marriage and family is not pervasive in all countries; that is, more research is available on the industrialized West than on developing countries. The inconsistent coverage presented a significant obstacle to overcome, making the *International Encyclopedia of Marriage and Family* an impressive accomplishment indeed.

In keeping with the inclusive and multidisciplinary definition used in the first edition, the terms *marriage* and *family* are used in the broadest sense, not just to include socially approved, durable heterosexual unions that beget children, but also to encompass a wide variety of topics and issues pertinent to these relations and contemporary variations that may be less traditional such as abortion, gay and lesbian parenting, infidelity, and spouse abuse. However, this second edition significantly differs from the first in its deliberate attention to marriage and family in an international context. Given global diversity and the lack of scholarly attention to marriage and family in many nations worldwide, a representative rather than comprehensive selection of countries and ethnic groups was identified.

Fifty countries representing the regions of the world from Africa, Asia and the Pacific, Europe, the Middle East, the Americas, and the Caribbean were selected. Every attempt was made to identify scholars from within (rather than outside) the countries, to write about family life in their nations. Twelve entries on unique racial/ethnic groups were also included. These groups were selected because they were either indigenous (e.g., First Nations families in Canada, Yoruba families) or prominent (e.g., Basque families, African-American families) in heterogeneous nations and research was available about their distinct family patterns. In addition, eleven entries on specific religions or belief systems (e.g., Catholicism, Evangelical Christianity, Islam, Confucianism) were included because of the profound impact these systems have in guiding and supporting lifestyle choices and patterns.

The contributors are family scholars with particular expertise on the topic or country on which they are writing. They represent numerous disciplines such as family studies, psychology, sociology, social work, gerontology, history, home economics, law, medicine, and theology. A concerted effort, which achieved significant success, was made to solicit scholars from outside the United States. Contributors from Europe, Africa, Asia and the Pacific, and the Americas strengthened the overall presentation. A more competent and internationally representative group of scholars has yet to be convened in this field. Accordingly, readers can be assured of the veracity of the close to four hundred entries.

Use of the Encyclopedia

The *International Encyclopedia of Marriage and Family* is designed for use by general readers interested in the dynamics of marriage and family around the world, as well as students and scholars seeking a unique source of information regarding global family lifestyles. This extensive reference work serves as a springboard to new insight and understanding. In fact, it is the first comprehensive publication to focus on marriage and relationships from an international perspective.

Readers will find detailed entries that integrate often discrete information into a concise, readable review. Entries are cogent, carefully documented, and accompanied by a bibliography incorporating cited works and suggestions for further reading. All entries are signed and include cross references to related content. These cross references facilitate the use of the multi-volume set and make the content more accessible. Thus, a reader may begin reading an entry on one aspect of his or her field of inquiry and move easily to other entries on related aspects of the subject. For example, after reading the entry on godparents, one might consult the entries on extended families and kinship, and then move on to consider particular countries where godparents are important, such as Mexico and the Philippines, or even look at the entry on Catholicism because of the salient role of godparents within this religion. Someone who is interested in chronic illness could examine the entry on that topic, and then read about specific illnesses (e.g., Alzheimers, AIDS, depression, schizophrenia) or find more generic discussions on health and families, caregiving, death and dying, and grief.

At the beginning of the first volume, alphabetical lists of entries and contributors with affiliations are presented. A notation of (1995) after an entry title in the lists indicates that the entry has been essentially reprinted from the first edition, with an updated bibliography. A comprehensive index of concepts, names, and terms at the end of volume four is designed to assist readers in locating topics throughout the *Encyclopedia* and directs readers to the discussion of these subjects. Many subjects are not treated in separate entries but instead appear within the context of more comprehensive articles.

Acknowledgments

In a project of this magnitude, there are many people to acknowledge and thank for their contribution. I am grateful to David Levinson for his invitation, almost a decade ago, to join him in working on the *Encyclopedia of Marriage and the Family*. His phenomenal intellect and energy have remained an inspiration. Of course, the numerous contributors must be acknowledged as vital to this project. Their willingness to share their expertise was requisite for the project's fulfillment. The professional staff of Macmillan Reference USA—Elly Dickason, Jill Lectka, and Dawn Cavalieri—have gone "above and beyond" in their unfailing assistance throughout the planning and editorial process that produced this second edition. Thank you.

I am indebted as well to the Associate Editors—Raeann Hamon, Yvonne Kellar-Guenther, Patricia Kerig, Laine Scales, and James White—for the privilege of working with such committed and competent scholars. In addition, the University of British Columbia provided an environment conducive to and supportive of this endeavor. My colleagues on the Family Studies faculty—Phyllis Johnson, Sheila Marshall, Anne Martin-Matthews, Daniel Perlman, and James White—encouraged me and offered their considerable expertise to this project.

Finally, I owe everything to my family who tolerated my preoccupation with this project. My wife, Rosanne, and our children—Caitlin, Nicholas, Olivia, and Bridget—provide a personal and professional *raison d'etre*.

JAMES J. PONZETTI, JR.

References

Burr, W., and Leigh, G. (1983). "Famology: A New Discipline." *Journal of Marriage and the Family* 45:467–480.

Christensen, H. (1964). *Handbook of Marriage and the Family*. Chicago: Rand McNally and Co.

Hollinger, M. (2003). "Family Science." In *International Encyclopedia of Marriage and Family,* 2nd edition, ed. J. Ponzetti. New York: Macmillan Reference USA.

Levinson, D. (1995). Preface to *Encyclopedia of Marriage and the Family,* ed. D. Levinson. New York: Macmillan Library Reference USA.

LIST OF ARTICLES

Abortion
  Warren M. Hern
Abstinence
  Terrance D. Olson
Academic Achievement
  Kevin Marjoribanks
Acculturation
  Bilge Ataca
  John W. Berry
Acquired Immunodeficiency Syndrome (AIDS)
  Hope Haslam Straughan
Adolescent Parenthood
  Ted G. Futris
  Kay Pasley
Adoption
  David S. Rosettenstein
Adulthood
  Judith G. Gonyea
Affection
  Jennifer M. Keithley
Afghanistan
  Shahin Gerami
African-American Families
  Oscar A. Barbarin
  Terry T. McCandies
Alzheimer's Disease
  Jon C. Stuckey
American-Indian Families
  Le Anne E. Silvey
Anabaptists (Amish, Mennonite)
  Thomas J. Meyers
Ancestor Worship
  Masako Ishii-Kuntz
Annulment (1995)
  Warren Schumacher
Anxiety Disorders
  Lissette M. Saavedra
  Wendy K. Silverman

Argentina
  Alicia Itatí Palermo
Asian-American Families
  Susan Matoba Adler
Assisted Reproductive Technologies
  Carl H. Coleman
Attachment
  Couple Relationships
    Brooke C. Feeney
    Nancy L. Collins
  Parent-Child Relationships
    Karen S. Rosen
    Fred Rothbaum
Attention Deficit/Hyperactivity Disorder (ADHD)
  Stephen P. Hinshaw
Attraction
  Michael R. Cunningham
  Lara K. Ault
  Anita P. Barbee
Attribution in Relationships
  Hyungshim Jang
  John H. Harvey
Aunt
  Nijole V. Benokraitis
Australia
  Ruth E. Weston
  Robyn Parker
  Lixia Qu
Austria
  Josef Hörl
Basque Families
  Linda White
Bedouin-Arab Families
  Alean Al-Krenawi
Birth Control
  Contraceptive Methods
    Stephanie B. Teal
  Sociocultural and Historical Aspects
    Vern L. Bullough

Birth Order
Gloria M. Montes de Oca
Alan E. Stewart

Boundary Ambiguity
Carla M. Dahl

Boundary Dissolution
Patricia K. Kerig

Brazil
Gláucia Diniz

Bride-Price
Usher Fleising

Buddhism
F. Matthew Schobert, Jr.
Scott W. Taylor

Bundling
Bron B. Ingoldsby

Canada
Tracy Matsuo
Lorne Tepperman

Canada First Nations Families
Charles R. Menzies

Caregiving
Formal
Ellie Brubaker
Timothy H. Brubaker

Informal
David E. Biegel
Barbara L. Wieder

Caribbean Families
Winston Seegobin

Catholicism
David Michael Thomas

Child Abuse
Physical Abuse and Neglect
Beth M. Schwartz-Kenney
Michelle McCauley

Psychological Maltreatment
Stuart N. Hart
Marla R. Brassard
Nelson J. Binggeli
Howard A. Davidson

Sexual Abuse
Kathleen Kendall-Tackett

Childcare
Alice M. Atkinson

Child Custody
Marygold S. Melli

Childhood (1995)
Stevi Jackson

Childhood, Stages of
Adolescence
Ronda Copher
Jeylan T. Mortimer

Infancy
M. G. Carelli
M. Cusinato

Middle Childhood
M. Cusinato
M. G. Carelli

Preschool
M. G. Carelli
M. Cusinato

Toddlerhood
M. Cusinato
M. G. Carelli

Childlessness
D. T. Rowland

Children of Alcoholics
Tony D. Crespi

Children's Rights
Virginia Murphy-Berman
Howard A. Davidson

China
Hsiang-Ming Kung

Chronic Illness
Shirley A. Hill

Circumcision
Paul J. Ford

Clan
John Barker

Codependency
Douglas J. Scaturo

Cohabitation
Zheng Wu
Christoph M. Schimmele

Colic
Ian St. James-Roberts

Communication
Couple Relationships
Tara M. Emmers-Sommer

Family Relationships
Kathleen M. Galvin

Commuter Marriages
Elaine A. Anderson

Comparative Analysis
William H. McKellin

Computers and Family
James M. White

Conduct Disorder
Bernadette Marie Bullock
Thomas J. Dishion

Conflict
Couple Relationships
William R. Cupach
Daniel J. Canary

Family Relationships
Sam Vuchinich

Parent-Child Relationships
Susan J. Messman

Confucianism
Douglas K. Chung

Coparenting
Melanie C. McConnell
Easter Dawn Vo
James P. McHale
Cousins
John Barker
Czech Republic
Marie Čermáková
Dating
Mary Riege Laner
Death and Dying
Kathleen R. Gilbert
Decision Making
Lynn H. Turner
Dementia
Rona J. Karasik
Depression
Adults
Ian H. Gotlib
Karen L. Kasch
Children and Adolescents
Judith Semon Dubas
Anne C. Petersen
Development
Cognitive
Usha Goswami
Emotional
Susanne A. Denham
Anita Kochanoff
Karen Neal
Teresa Mason
Hideko Hamada
Moral
Silvia Koller
Angela M. B. Biaggio
Self
Susan Harter
Lisa Kiang
Developmental Disabilities
Cordelia Robinson
Developmental Psychopathology
Patrick T. Davies
E. Mark Cummings
Susan B. Campbell
Dialectical Theory
Leslie A. Baxter
Disabilities (1995)
Joän M. Patterson
Discipline
Robert E. Larzelere
Brett R. Kuhn
Division of Labor
Scott Coltrane
Michele Adams
Divorce
Effects on Children
David H. Demo
Andrew J. Supple

Effects on Couples
Kari Henley
Kay Pasley
Effects on Parents
Colleen L. Johnson
Divorce Mediation
David M. Kleist
Dowry
John Barker
Dual-Earner Families
Shannon N. Davis
Barbara J. Risman
Eating Disorders
Bryan Lask
Egypt
Bahira Sherif
Elder Abuse
Rosalie S. Wolf†
Elders
Enid Opal Cox
Pamela Metz
Equity
Alaina M. Winters
Ethnic Variation/Ethnicity
Deborale Richardson-Bouie
Euthanasia
Robert Kastenbaum
Evangelical Christianity
Les Parrott
Extended Families
Amy E. Wagner
Failure to Thrive
Peter Dawson
Lynne Sturm
Familism
Adela Garzón Pérez
Family, Definition of
Brenda Munro
Gordon Munro
Family, History of
Cynthia Comacchio
Family and Relational Rules
Yvonne Kellar-Guenther
Family Assessment
Gary E. Stollak
Family Business
Michael A. Gross
Family Development Theory
James M. White
Family Diagnosis/DSM-IV
Lynelle C. Yingling
Family Diagrammatic Assessment
Ecomap
T. Laine Scales
Renee H. Blanchard

Genogram
J. Phillip Stanberry

Family Folklore
Jill Terry Rudy

Family Law
John Dewar

Family Life Education
Margaret Edwards Arcus

Family Literacy
Jim Anderson
Suzanne Smythe
Jacqueline Lynch

Family Loyalty
Karen M. Kobayashi

Family Ministry
Diana R. Garland

Family Planning
Vern L. Bullough

Family Policy
Maureen Baker

Family Rituals
Barbara H. Fiese
Kimberly Howell

Family Roles
Laurence L. Falk

Family Science
Mary Ann Hollinger

Family Stories and Myths
James J. Ponzetti, Jr.
Yvonne Kellar-Guenther

Family Strengths
John DeFrain
Nick Stinnett

Family Systems Theory
William M. Fleming

Family Theory (1995)
David M. Klein

Family Values
Barbara A. Arrighi

Fatherhood
Ross D. Parke
David J. McDowell

Favoritism/Differential Treatment
Shirley McGuire

Fertility
Maili Malin

Fictive Kinship (1995)
Richard A. Wagner

Filial Responsibility
Raeann R. Hamon
Keli R. Whitney

Food
Renee A. Oscarson

Forgiveness
Susan D. Boon
Stacey L. Nairn

Foster Parenting
Elisabeth Kenny

France
Didier Le Gall

French Canadian Families
Évelyne Lapierre-Adamcyk
Céline Le Bourdais
Nicole Marcil-Gratton

Friendship
Paul H. Wright

Gangs
Bill McCarthy
Monica J. Martin

Gay Parents
Todd A. Savage
Marc E. Frisiello
Sharon Scales Rostosky

Gender
Kelly Rice Wood
Sharon Scales Rostosky
Pam Remer

Gender Identity
Gregory K. Lehne

Genealogy (1995)
Alice Eichholz

Genetic Counseling (1995)
Alicia Craffey

Germany
Klaus Peter Strohmeier
Johannes Huinink

Ghana
Baffour K. Takyi

Gifted and Talented Children
Miraca U. M. Gross

Global Citizenship
Judith A. Myers-Walls

Godparents
Rozzana Sánchez Aragón

Grandparenthood
Yoshinori Kamo
Chizuko Wakabayashi

Grandparents' Rights
Tammy L. Henderson

Great Britain
Jane Millar

Greece
Aphrodite Teperoglou

Greenland
Mark Nuttall

Grief, Loss, and Bereavement
Colleen I. Murray

Guardianship
David M. English

Health and Families
Yvonne Kellar-Guenther

Hinduism
  Laju M. Balani
  Scott W. Taylor

Hispanic-American Families
  Graciela M. Castex

Home
  Sheila K. Marshall

Home Economics
  Virginia Vincenti

Homeless Families
  Irene Glasser

Homeschooling
  Brian D. Ray

Honeymoon
  Kris Bulcroft
  Linda Smeins
  Richard Bulcroft

Hospice
  Robert Kastenbaum

Housework
  Michele Adams
  Scott Coltrane

Housing
  Sheila K. Marshall

Human Ecology Theory
  Ruth E. Berry

Hungary
  Olga Tóth

Husband
  John Barker

Hutterite Families
  Bron B. Ingoldsby

Immigration
  Phyllis J. Johnson

Incest
  Jennifer L. Matheson

Incest/Inbreeding Taboos
  Gregory C. Leavitt

India
  Nilufer P. Medora

Indonesia
  Clark E. Cunningham

Industrialization
  Elinor Accampo

Infanticide (1995)
  Leigh Minturn†

Infidelity
  Judith Treas

In-Law Relationships (1995)
  Rhonda J. V. Montgomery

Intentional Communities
  William L. Smith

Interfaith Marriage
  Mary Helène Rosenbaum

Intergenerational Programming
  Sally Newman

Intergenerational Relations
  Adam Davey
  Jyoti (Tina) Savla
  Lisa M. Belliston

Intergenerational Transmission
  Anne Martin-Matthews
  Karen M. Kobayashi

Interparental Conflict—Effects on Children
  Kristin Lindahl

Interparental Violence—Effects on Children
  B. B. Robbie Rossman

Interracial Marriage
  Richard C. Henriksen, Jr.
  Richard E. Watts

Intimacy
  Karen Jean Prager

Iran
  Mohammadreza Hojat
  Amir H. Mehryar

Ireland
  Gabriel Kiely

Islam
  Marsha T. Carolan
  Monica Mouton-Sanders

Israel
  Orna Cohen

Italy
  Luisa Leonini

Japan
  Junko Kuninobu

Jealousy
  Gary L. Hansen
  Zheng Zeng

Judaism
  Steven Weiland

Juvenile Delinquency
  Joan McCord

Kenya
  Salome Nasiroli Wawire

Kinship (1995)
  Gwen J. Broude

Korea
  Hyunsook Chung

Kurdish Families
  Mihri İnal Çakir

Kyrgyzstan
  Kunduz Asanova

Later Life Families
  Laura Hurd Clarke

Latin America
  Bron B. Ingoldsby

Latvia
  Parsla Eglite

Learning Disorders
 Margaret Semrud-Clikeman
 Kellie Higgins

Leisure
 Valeria J. Freysinger

Lesbian Parents
 Gina Owens
 Ashley Reed
 Sharon Scales Rostosky

Life Course Theory
 Barbara A. Mitchell

Loneliness
 Daniel Perlman

Love
 Clyde Hendrick
 Susan S. Hendrick

Malaysia
 Sunil Kukreja

Marital Quality (1995)
 Norval D. Glenn

Marital Sex
 Pamela C. Regan

Marital Typologies
 Edgar C. J. Long
 Jeffrey J. Angera

Marriage Ceremonies
 Marilyn Ihinger-Tallman
 Debra A. Henderson

Marriage, Definition of (1995)
 Marilyn Ihinger-Tallman
 David Levinson

Marriage Enrichment
 Britton Wood

Marriage Preparation
 Benjamin Silliman

Marriage Squeeze
 Jean E. Veevers

Mate Selection
 Douglas T. Kenrick
 Susan Ledlow
 Josh Ackerman

Menarche
 Lana Thompson

Menopause
 Marcia K. Spira

Menstrual Taboo
 Elizabeth Arveda Kissling

Mexico
 Rozzana Sánchez Aragón

Migration
 Zheng Wu

Missing Children
 Tillman Rodabough
 Elizabeth Kelly

Mormonism
 Dennis T. Haynes
 Mark O. Jarvis

Motherhood
 Masako Ishii-Kuntz

Munchausen Syndrome by Proxy
 Christopher N. Bools

Nagging and Complaining
 Jess K. Alberts
 Christina Granato Yoshimura

Names for Children
 Richard Alford

Neighborhood
 Robyn Bateman Driskell

New Zealand
 Maureen Baker

Nigeria
 Julia O. Omokhodion

Nonmarital Childbearing
 Brent C. Miller
 Kyung-Eun Park
 Anne Thomas

Nuclear Families (1995)
 Arlene Skolnick

Only Children (1995)
 Toni Falbo

Oppositionality
 Joseph M. Rey
 Se-fong Hung

Orphans
 Kim MacLean

Parenting Education
 H. Wallace Goddard
 Steven A. Dennis

Parenting Styles
 Judith G. Smetana
 Nicole Campione

Peer Influence
 Peter T. Haugen
 Sharon C. Risch
 Deborah P. Welsh

Peru
 Myrian Carbajal Mendoza

Phenomenology
 Stan J. Knapp

Philippines, The
 Kathleen Nadeau

Play
 Dorothy G. Singer

Poland
 Barbara Łobodzińska

Portugal
 Shawn S. Parkhurst

Postpartum Depression
 Peter J. Cooper
 Lynne Murray

Posttraumatic Stress Disorder (PTSD)
Betty Pfefferbaum

Poverty
Gaynor Yancey

Power
Family Relationships
Brian Jory
Marital Relationships
Carrie L. Yodanis

Pregnancy and Birth
Jacqueline Fawcett
Cynthia Aber
Virginia Bowen Silva

Premarital Agreements
Judith T. Younger

Primogeniture
John Barker

Problem Solving
Sam Vuchinich

Protestantism
John Witte Jr.

Rape
Zoë D. Peterson
Charlene L. Muehlenhard

Relationship Dissolution
Steve Duck
Stephanie Rollie

Relationship Initiation
Anita L. Vangelisti
John A. Daly

Relationship Maintenance
Daniel J. Canary
Elaine D. Zelley

Relationship Metaphors
Leslie A. Baxter

Relationship Theories—Self-Other Relationship
William W. Wilmot
Mark J. Bergstrom

Religion
Ruth Cordle Hatch
Walter R. Schumm

Remarriage
Margaret Crosbie-Burnett
Katrina McClintic

Renewal of Wedding Vows (1995)
Dawn O. Braithwaite

Research
Family Measurement (1995)
Murray A. Straus
Susan M. Ross
Methodology
Alan Acock
Yoshie Sano

Resource Management
Elizabeth Beard Goldsmith

Respite Care
Adult
Karen A. Roberto
Child
Stephen R. Block
April W. Block

Retirement
Maximiliane E. Szinovacz

Rich/Wealthy Families
Frank S. Pittman III
Frank S. Pittman IV

Rites of Passage
Bruce Freeman
Usher Fleising

Role Theory
Carrie L. Yodanis

Romania
Mihaela Robila

Runaway Youths
Sarah Michelle Stohlman
Robyn Bateman Driskell

Rural Families
Linda B. Morales
Sam Copeland

Russia
Jean M. Ispa
Julian G. Elliott

Sandwich Generation
Christine A. Price

Scandinavia
Jan Trost

Schizophrenia
Monica E. Calkins
William G. Iacono

School
Mitzi A. Lowe

School Phobia and School Refusal
Ximena Franco
Wendy K. Silverman

Self-Disclosure
Sandra Petronio
Jack Sargent

Self-Esteem
Viktor Gecas
Monica Longmore

Senegal
Pierre Ngom

Separation Anxiety
Diane E. Wille

Separation-Individuation
Meryl J. Botkin

Sexual Communication
Couple Relationships
Sandra Metts
Parent-Child Relationships
James Jaccard

Sexual Dysfunction
  A. R. Allgeier
Sexuality
  John DeLamater
  Janet Shibley Hyde
Sexuality Education
  Elias J. Duryea
  Kari L. Kuka
  Denise E. Herrera
Sexuality in Adolescence
  Brent C. Miller
  Spencer C. Leavitt
Sexuality in Adulthood
  Phyllis A. Greenberg
Sexuality in Childhood
  Sara Moorhead Phillips
  Debra L. Berke
Sexually Transmitted Diseases
  Ronald R. Fichtner
Sexual Orientation
  Barbara Ryan
  Joseph R.G. DeMarco
Shyness
  Warren H. Jones
Sibling Relationships
  Marilyn Ihinger-Tallman
  Ying-Ling (Amy) Hsiao
Sikhism
  Pashaura Singh
Single-Parent Families
  Kathryn M. Feltey
Singles/Never Married Persons
  Lori D. Campbell
Slovakia
  Bernardína Bodnárová
  Jarmila Filadelfiová
Social Exchange Theory
  Ronald M. Sabatelli
Socialization
  Hilary A. Rose
Social Networks
  Catherine H. Stein
  Marcia G. Hunt
Socioeconomic Status
  Neil Guppy
South Africa
  Abraham P. Greeff
Spain
  J. Roberto Reyes
Spanking
  John A. Addleman
Spouse Abuse
  Prevalence
    Orsolya Magyar
  Theoretical Explanations (1995)
    Richard J. Gelles

Stepfamilies
  Mark A. Fine
  Jean A. McBride
Stress
  Elizabeth G. Menaghan
Structural-Functional Theory
  John Scanzoni
  Nancy Kingsbury
Substance Abuse
  Mark J. Macgowan
  Christopher P. Rice
Substitute Caregivers
  Theodore N. Greenstein
Sudden Infant Death Syndrome (SIDS)
  Marianne Arnestad
Suicide
  David Lester
Surrogacy
  Heléna Ragoné
Switzerland
  Beat Fux
Symbolic Interactionism
  Viktor Gecas
  Teresa Tsushima
Television and Family
  Alison Alexander
  Yeora Kim
Temperament
  Mary K. Rothbart
  Jennifer Simonds
Therapy
  Couple Relationships
    Lorelei E. Simpson
    Krista S. Gattis
    Andrew Christensen
  Family Relationships
    Linda Berg-Cross
    Michelle Morales
    Christi Moore
  Parent-Child Relationships
    Marian J. Bakermans-Kranenburg
    Marinus H. van Ijzendoorn
    Femmie Juffer
Time Use
  Kerry J. Daly
Togo
  Koffi Ekouevi
Transition to Parenthood
  Glen H. Stamp
Triangulation
  Kristin Lindahl
Trust
  John K. Rempel
Turkey
  Akile Gursoy

Uncle
Nijole V. Benokraitis

Unemployment
Anb T. Le
Paul W. Miller

United States
Stephanie Coontz
Mary Beth Ofstedal

Urbanization
Larry S. Bourne

Venezuela
Samuel Hurtado Salazar

Vietnam
Steven K. Wisensale

War/Political Violence
Karen S. Myers-Bowman

Wedding Ring
Bron B. Ingoldsby

Widowhood
Felix M. Berardo
Donna H. Berardo

Wife
John Barker

Women's Movements
Lynn Walter

Work and Family
Debra L. Berke

Yoruba Families
Emmanuel D. Babatunde
Kelebogile V. Setiloane

Zambia
Vijayan K. Pillai

LIST OF CONTRIBUTORS

CYNTHIA ABER
University of Massachusetts, Boston
Pregnancy and Birth

ELINOR ACCAMPO
University of Southern California
Industrialization

JOSH ACKERMAN
Arizona State University
Mate Selection

ALAN ACOCK
Oregon State University
Research: Methodology

MICHELE ADAMS
University of California, Riverside
Housework

JOHN A. ADDLEMAN
Messiah College
Spanking

SUSAN MATOBA ADLER
University of Illinois at Urbana-Champaign
Asian-American Families

JESS K. ALBERTS
Arizona State University
Nagging and Complaining

ALISON ALEXANDER
University of Georgia
Television and Family

RICHARD ALFORD
East Central University
Names for Children

ALEAN AL-KRENAWI
Ben Gurion University of the Negev
Bedouin-Arab Families

A. R. ALLGEIER
Allgeier & Associates, Bowling Green, Ohio
Sexual Dysfunction

ELAINE A. ANDERSON
University of Maryland
Commuter Marriages

JIM ANDERSON
University of British Columbia
Family Literacy

JEFFREY J. ANGERA
Central Michigan University
Marital Typologies

MARGARET EDWARDS ARCUS
University of British Columbia
Family Life Education

MARIANNE ARNESTAD
University of Oslo
Sudden Infant Death Syndrome (SIDS)

BARBARA A. ARRIGHI
Northern Kentucky University
Family Values

KUNDUZ ASANOVA
Kyrgyz State National University
Kyrgyzstan

BILGE ATACA
Boğaziçi University
Acculturation

ALICE M. ATKINSON
University of Iowa
Childcare

LARA K. AULT
University of Louisville
Attraction

EMMANUEL D. BABATUNDE
Lincoln University
Yoruba Families

MAUREEN BAKER
University of Aukland
Family Policy
New Zealand

MARIAN J. BAKERMANS-KRANENBURG
Leiden University
Therapy: Parent-Child Relationships

LAJU M. BALANI
Baylor University
Hinduism

OSCAR A. BARBARIN
University of North Carolina
African-American Families

ANITA P. BARBEE
University of Louisville
Attraction

JOHN BARKER
University of British Columbia
Clan
Cousins
Dowry
Husband
Primogeniture
Wife

LESLIE A. BAXTER
University of Iowa
Dialectical Theory
Relationship Metaphors

LISA M. BELLISTON
University of Georgia
Intergenerational Relations

NIJOLE V. BENOKRAITIS
University of Baltimore
Aunt
Uncle

DONNA H. BERARDO
University of Florida
Widowhood

FELIX M. BERARDO
University of Florida
Widowhood

LINDA BERG-CROSS
Howard University
Therapy: Family Relationships

MARK J. BERGSTROM
University of Utah
Relationship Theories—Self-Other Relationship

DEBRA L. BERKE
Messiah College
Sexuality in Childhood
Work and Family

JOHN W. BERRY
Queen's University
Acculturation

RUTH E. BERRY
University of Manitoba
Human Ecology Theory

ANGELA M. B. BIAGGIO
Universidade Federal de Rio Grande do Sul, Brazil
Development: Moral

DAVID E. BIEGEL
Case Western Reserve University
Caregiving: Informal

NELSON J. BINGGELI
Georgia State University
Child Abuse: Psychological Maltreatment

RENEE H. BLANCHARD
Baylor University
Family Diagrammatic Assessment: Ecomap

APRIL W. BLOCK
University of Northern Colorado
Respite Care: Child

STEPHEN R. BLOCK
Denver Options, Inc., Denver, Colorado, and University of
Colorado at Denver
Respite Care: Child

BERNARDÍNA BODNÁROVÁ
Bratislava International Centre for Family Studies
Slovakia

CHRISTOPHER N. BOOLS
Avon and Wiltshire Mental Health Partnership NHS Trust;
Chippenham Family Health Centre, Wiltshire, UK
Munchausen Syndrome by Proxy

SUSAN D. BOON
University of Calgary
Forgiveness

MERYL J. BOTKIN
University of California, San Francisco
Separation-Individuation

LARRY S. BOURNE
University of Toronto
Urbanization

DAWN O. BRAITHWAITE
University of Nebraska–Lincoln
Renewal of Wedding Vows

MARLA R. BRASSARD
Columbia University
Child Abuse: Psychological Maltreatment

GWEN J. BROUDE
Vassar College
Kinship (1995)

ELLIE BRUBAKER
Miami University
Caregiving: Formal

TIMOTHY H. BRUBAKER
Miami University
Caregiving: Formal

KRIS BULCROFT
Western Washington University
Honeymoon

RICHARD BULCROFT
Western Washington University
Honeymoon

BERNADETTE MARIE BULLOCK
University of Oregon
Conduct Disorder

VERN L. BULLOUGH
University of Southern California and State University
of New York
Birth Control: Sociocultural and Historical Aspects
Family Planning

MIHRI İNAL ÇAKIR
Binghamton University
Kurdish Families

MONICA E. CALKINS
University of Minnesota, Twin Cities
Schizophrenia

LORI D. CAMPBELL
McMaster University
Singles/Never Married Persons

SUSAN B. CAMPBELL
University of Pittsburgh
Developmental Psychopathology

NICOLE CAMPIONE
University of Rochester
Parenting Styles

DANIEL J. CANARY
Arizona State University
Relationship Maintenance
Conflict: Couple Relationships

M. G. CARELLI
Umeå University
Childhood, Stages of: Infancy
Childhood, Stages of: Middle Childhood
Childhood, Stages of: Preschool
Childhood, Stages of: Toddlerhood

MARSHA T. CAROLAN
Michigan State University
Islam

GRACIELA M. CASTEX
Lehman College
Hispanic-American Families

MARIE ČERMÁKOVÁ
Adademy of Sciences of the Czech Republic
Czech Republic

ANDREW CHRISTENSEN
University of California, Los Angeles
Therapy: Couple Relationships

DOUGLAS K. CHUNG
Grand Valley State University
Confucianism

HYUNSOOK CHUNG
Sangmyung University
Korea

LAURA HURD CLARKE
University of British Columbia
Later Life Families

ORNA COHEN
Tel-Aviv University
Israel

CARL H. COLEMAN
Seton Hall Law School
Assisted Reproductive Technologies

NANCY L. COLLINS
University of California, Santa Barbara
Attachment: Couple Relationships

SCOTT COLTRANE
University of California, Riverside
Division of Labor
Housework

CYNTHIA COMACCHIO
Wilfrid Laurier University
Family, History of

STEPHANIE COONTZ
The Evergreen State College
United States

PETER J. COOPER
University of Reading
Postpartum Depression

SAM COPELAND
Stephen F. Austin State University
Rural Families

RONDA COPHER
University of Minnesota
Childhood, Stages of: Adolescence

ENID OPAL COX
University of Denver
Elders

ALICIA CRAFFEY
University of Connecticut Health Center
Genetic Counseling (1995)

TONY D. CRESPI
University of Hartford
Children of Alcoholics

MARGARET CROSBIE-BURNETT
University of Miami
Remarriage

E. MARK CUMMINGS
University of Notre Dame
Developmental Psychopathology

CLARK E. CUNNINGHAM
University of Illinois, Urbana-Champaign
Indonesia

MICHAEL R. CUNNINGHAM
University of Louisville
Attraction

WILLIAM R. CUPACH
Illinois State University
Conflict: Couple Relationships

M. CUSINATO
Università degli Studi di Padova
Childhood, Stages of: Infancy
Childhood, Stages of: Middle Childhood
Childhood, Stages of: Preschool
Childhood, Stages of: Toddlerhood

CARLA M. DAHL
Bethel Seminary Marriage and Family Therapy Program
Boundary Ambiguity

JOHN A. DALY
University of Texas at Austin
Relationship Initiation

KERRY J. DALY
University of Guelph
Time Use

ADAM DAVEY
University of Georgia
Intergenerational Relations

HOWARD A. DAVIDSON
American Bar Association Center on Children and the Law
Child Abuse: Psychological Maltreatment
Children's Rights

PATRICK T. DAVIES
University of Rochester
Developmental Psychopathology

SHANNON N. DAVIS
North Carolina State University
Dual-Earner Families

PETER DAWSON
University of Colorado School of Medicine
Failure to Thrive

JOHN DeFRAIN
University of Nebraska–Lincoln
Family Strengths

JOHN DeLAMATER
University of Wisconsin–Madison
Sexuality

JOSEPH R. G. DeMARCO
Widener University
Sexual Orientation

DAVID H. DEMO
The University of North Carolina at Greensboro
Divorce: Effects on Children

SUSANNE A. DENHAM
George Mason University
Development: Emotional

STEVEN A. DENNIS
University of Arkansas
Parenting Education

JOHN DEWAR
Griffith University
Family Law

GLÁUCIA DINIZ
Universidade de Brasília
Brazil

THOMAS J. DISHION
University of Oregon
Conduct Disorder

ROBYN BATEMAN DRISKELL
Baylor University
Neighborhood
Runaway Youths

JUDITH SEMON DUBAS
Utrecht University
Depression: Children and Adolescents

STEVE DUCK
University of Iowa
Relationship Dissolution

ELIAS J. DURYEA
University of New Mexico, Albuquerque
Sexuality Education

PARSLA EGLITE
Institute of Economics, Riga, Latvia
Latvia

ALICE EICHHOLZ
Union Institute & University/Vermont College
Genealogy (1995)

KOFFI EKOUEVI
Annandale, Virginia
Togo

JULIAN G. ELLIOTT
Sunderland University
Russia

TARA M. EMMERS-SOMMER
University of Arizona
Communication: Couple Relationships

DAVID M. ENGLISH
University of Missouri–Columbia
Guardianship

TONI FALBO
University of Texas, Austin
Only Children (1995)

LAURENCE L. FALK
Concordia College
Family Roles

JACQUELINE FAWCETT
University of Massachusetts, Boston
Pregnancy and Birth

BROOKE C. FEENEY
Carnegie Mellon University
Attachment: Couple Relationships

KATHRYN M. FELTEY
University of Akron
Single-Parent Families

RONALD R. FICHTNER
Statistics Research Division/SSCS,
RTI International, Atlanta, Georgia
Sexually Transmitted Diseases

BARBARA H. FIESE
Syracuse University
Family Rituals

JARMILA FILADELFIOVÁ
Bratislava International Centre for Family Studies
Slovakia

MARK A. FINE
University of Missouri, Columbia
Stepfamilies

USHER FLEISING
University of Calgary
Bride-Price
Rites of Passage

WILLIAM M. FLEMING
University of Northern Iowa
Family Systems Theory

PAUL J. FORD
The Cleveland Clinic Foundation, Cleveland, Ohio
Circumcision

XIMENA FRANCO
Florida International University
School Phobia and School Refusal

BRUCE FREEMAN
University of Calgary
Rites of Passage

VALERIA J. FREYSINGER
Miami University of Ohio
Leisure

MARC E. FRISIELLO
University of Kentucky
Gay Parents

TED G. FUTRIS
The Ohio State University
Adolescent Parenthood

BEAT FUX
University of Zurich
Switzerland

KATHLEEN M. GALVIN
Northwestern University
Communication: Family Relationships

DIANA R. GARLAND
Baylor University
Family Ministry

KRISTA S. GATTIS
University of California, Los Angeles
Therapy: Couple Relationships

VIKTOR GECAS
Washington State University
Self-Esteem
Symbolic Interactionism

RICHARD J. GELLES
University of Pennsylvania
Spouse Abuse: Theoretical Explanations (1995)

SHAHIN GERAMI
Southwest Missouri State University
Afghanistan

KATHLEEN R. GILBERT
Indiana University
Death and Dying

IRENE GLASSER
Brown University
Homeless Families

NORVAL D. GLENN
University of Texas, Austin
Marital Quality (1995)

H. WALLACE GODDARD
University of Arkansas
Parenting Education

ELIZABETH BEARD GOLDSMITH
Florida State University
Resource Management

JUDITH G. GONYEA
Boston University
Adulthood

USHA GOSWAMI
University College London
Development: Cognitive

IAN H. GOTLIB
Stanford University
Depression: Adults

ABRAHAM P. GREEFF
University of Stellenbosch
South Africa

PHYLLIS A. GREENBERG
St. Cloud State University
Sexuality in Adulthood

THEODORE N. GREENSTEIN
North Carolina State University
Substitute Caregivers

MICHAEL A. GROSS
Colorado State University
Family Business

MIRACA U. M. GROSS
University of New South Wales
Gifted and Talented Children

NEIL GUPPY
University of British Columbia
Socioeconomic Status

AKILE GURSOY
Yeditepe University
Turkey

HIDEKO HAMADA
George Mason University
Development: Emotional

RAEANN R. HAMON
Messiah College
Filial Responsibility

GARY L. HANSEN
University of Kentucky
Jealousy

STUART N. HART
Indiana University–Purdue University
Child Abuse: Psychological Maltreatment

SUSAN HARTER
University of Denver
Development: Self

JOHN H. HARVEY
University of Iowa
Attribution in Relationships

RUTH CORDLE HATCH
Indianapolis, Indiana
Religion

PETER T. HAUGEN
University of Tennessee
Peer Influence

DENNIS T. HAYNES
University of Texas at Austin
Mormonism

DEBRA A. HENDERSON
Ohio University
Marriage Ceremonies

TAMMY L. HENDERSON
Virginia Polytechnic Institute and State Universitfy
Grandparents' Rights

CLYDE HENDRICK
Texas Tech University
Love

SUSAN S. HENDRICK
Texas Tech University
Love

KARI HENLEY
University of North Carolina at Greensboro
Divorce: Effects on Couple

RICHARD C. HENRIKSEN, JR.
Western Illinois University
Interracial Marriage

WARREN M. HERN
Boulder Abortion Clinic
University of Colorado
Abortion

DENISE E. HERRERA
University of New Mexico, Albuquerque
Sexuality Education

KELLIE HIGGINS
University of Texas at Austin
Learning Disorders

SHIRLEY A. HILL
University of Kansas
Chronic Illness

STEPHEN P. HINSHAW
University of California, Berkeley
Attention Deficit/Hyperactivity Disorder (ADHD)

MOHAMMADREZA HOJAT
Jefferson Medical College of Thomas Jefferson University
Iran

MARY ANN HOLLINGER
Messiah College
Family Science

JOSEF HÖRL
University of Vienna
Austria

YING-LING (AMY) HSIAO
Shih-Chien University
Sibling Relationships

JOHANNES HUININK
University of Rostock
Germany

SE-FONG HUNG
Kwai Chung Hospital, Hong Kong
Oppositionality

MARCIA G. HUNT
Bowling Green State University
Social Networks

SAMUEL HURTADO SALAZAR
Caracas, Venezuela
Venezuela

JANET SHIBLEY HYDE
University of Wisconsin, Madison
Sexuality

WILLIAM G. IACONO
University of Minnesota, Twin Cities
Schizophrenia

MARILYN IHINGER-TALLMAN
Washington State University
Marriage Ceremonies
Marriage, Definition of (1995)
Sibling Relationships

MARINUS H. VAN IJZENDOORN
Leiden University
Therapy: Parent-Child Relationships

BRON B. INGOLDSBY
Brigham Young University
Bundling
Hutterite Families
Latin America
Wedding Ring

MASAKO ISHII-KUNTZ
University of California, Riverside
Ancestor Worship
Motherhood

JEAN M. ISPA
University of Missouri—Columbia
Russia

JAMES JACCARD
University of Albany, State University of New York
Sexual Communication: Parent-Child Relationships

STEVI JACKSON
The University of York
Childhood (1995)

HYUNGSHIM JANG
University of Iowa
Attribution in Relationships

MARK O. JARVIS
University of Texas at Austin
Mormonism

COLLEEN L. JOHNSON
University of California, San Francisco
Divorce: Effects on Parents

PHYLLIS J. JOHNSON
University of British Columbia
Immigration

WARREN H. JONES
University of Tennessee
Shyness

BRIAN JORY
Berry College
Power: Family Relationships

KIMBERLY JOSEPHS
Syracuse University
Family Rituals

FEMMIE JUFFER
Leiden University
Therapy: Parent-Child Relationships

YOSHINORI KAMO
Louisiana State University
Grandparenthood

RONA J. KARASIK
St. Cloud State University
Dementia

KAREN L. KASCH
Stanford University
Depression: Adults

ROBERT KASTENBAUM
Arizona State University
Euthanasia
Hospice

JENNIFER M. KEITHLEY
Lewis & Clark Community College
Affection

ELIZABETH KELLY
Baylor University
Missing Children

YVONNE KELLAR-GUENTHER
University of Colorado Health Sciences Center
Family and Relational Rules
Family Stories and Myths
Health and Families

KATHLEEN KENDALL-TACKETT
University of New Hampshire
Child Abuse: Sexual Abuse

ELISABETH KENNY
Stephen F. Austin State University
Foster Parenting

DOUGLAS T. KENRICK
Arizona State University
Mate Selection

PATRICIA K. KERIG
University of North Carolina at Chapel Hill
Boundary Dissolution

LISA KIANG
University of Denver
Development: Self

GABRIEL KIELY
University College Dublin
Ireland

YEORA KIM
University of Georgia
Television and Family

NANCY KINGSBURY
Georgia Southern University
Structural-Functional Theory

ELIZABETH ARVEDA KISSLING
Eastern Washington University
Menstrual Taboo

DAVID M. KLEIN
University of Notre Dame
Family Theory

DAVID M. KLEIST
Idaho State University
Divorce Mediation

STAN J. KNAPP
Brigham Young University
Phenomenology

KAREN M. KOBAYASHI
University of British Columbia
Family Loyalty
Intergenerational Transmission

ANITA KOCHANOFF
George Mason University
Development: Emotional

SILVIA KOLLER
Universidade Federal de Rio Grande do Sul, Brazil
Development: Moral

BRETT R. KUHN
University of Nebraska Medical Center
Discipline

KARI L. KUKA
University of New Mexico, Albuquerque
Sexuality Education

SUNIL KUKREJA
University of Puget Sound
Malaysia

HSIANG-MING KUNG
Shih Hsin University
China

JUNKO KUNINOBU
Aichi Shukutoku University
Japan

MARY RIEGE LANER
Arizona State University
Dating

ÉVELYNE LAPIERRE-ADAMCYK
Université de Montréal
French Canadian Families

ROBERT E. LARZELERE
University of Nebraska Medical Center
Discipline

BRYAN LASK
St George's Hospital Medical School, University of London
Eating Disorders

ANH T. LE
University of Western Australia
Unemployment

GREGORY C. LEAVITT
Idaho State University
Incest/Inbreeding Taboos

SPENCER C. LEAVITT
Utah State University
Sexuality in Adolescence

CÉLINE LE BOURDAIS
INRS-Urbanisation Culture Société, Montreal
French Canadian Families

SUSAN LEDLOW
Arizona State University
Mate Selection

DIDIER LE GALL
Université de Caen Basse-Normandie
France

GREGORY K. LEHNE
The Johns Hopkins University School of Medicine
Gender Identity

LUISA LEONINI
Milan University
Italy

DAVID LESTER
Richard Stockton College of NJ
Suicide

DAVID LEVINSON
Berkshire Publishing Group, Great Barrington, MA
Marriage, Definition of (1995)

KRISTIN LINDAHL
University of Miami
Interparental Conflict—Effects on Children
Triangulation

BARBARA ŁOBODZIŃSKA
New Brighton, Minnesota
Poland

EDGAR C. J. LONG
Central Michigan University
Marital Typologies

MONICA LONGMORE
Bowling Green State University
Self-Esteem

MITZI A. LOWE
California State University, Fresno
School

JACQUELINE LYNCH
University of British Columbia
Family Literacy

MARK J. MACGOWAN
Florida International University
Substance Abuse

KIM MACLEAN
St. Francis Xavier University
Orphans

ORSOLYA MAGYAR
University of British Columbia
Spouse Abuse: Prevalence

MAILI MALIN
STAKES, Evaluation of Health Services, Helsinki, Finland
Fertility

NICOLE MARCIL-GRATTON
Université de Montréal
French Canadian Families

KEVIN MARJORIBANKS
University of Adelaide
Academic Achievement

SHEILA K. MARSHALL
University of British Columbia
Home
Housing

MONICA MARTIN
University of California, Davis
Gangs

ANNE MARTIN-MATTHEWS
University of British Columbia
Intergenerational Transmission

TERESA MASON
George Mason University
Development: Emotional

JENNIFER L. MATHESON
Virginia Polytechnic Institute and State University
Incest

TRACY MATSUO
University of Toronto
Canada

JEAN A. MCBRIDE
Fort Collins, Colorado
Stepfamilies

TERRY T. MCCANDIES
University of North Carolina at Chapel Hill
African-American Families

BILL MCCARTHY
University of California, Davis
Gangs

MICHELLE MCCAULEY
Middlebury College
Child Abuse: Physical Abuse and Neglect

KATRINA MCCLINTIC
University of Miami
Remarriage

MELANIE C. MCCONNELL
Clark University
Coparenting

JOAN MCCORD
Temple University
Juvenile Delinquency

DAVID J. MCDOWELL
University of Rochester
Fatherhood

SHIRLEY MCGUIRE
University of San Francisco
Favoritism/Differential Treatment

JAMES P. MCHALE
Clark University
Coparenting

WILLIAM H. MCKELLIN
University of British Columbia
Comparative Analysis

NILUFER P. MEDORA
California State University
India

AMIR H. MEHRYAR
Institute for Research in Planning and Development, Tehran, Iran
Iran

MARYGOLD S. MELLI
The University of Wisconsin Law School
Child Custody

ELIZABETH G. MENAGHAN
The Ohio State University
Stress

MYRIAN CARBAJAL MENDOZA
University of Fribourg
Peru

CHARLES R. MENZIES
University of British Columbia
Canada First Nations Families

SUSAN J. MESSMAN
Arizona State University
Conflict: Parent-Child Relationships

SANDRA METTS
Illinois State University
Sexual Communication: Couple Relationships

PAMELA METZ
University of Denver
Elders

THOMAS J. MEYERS
Goshen College
Anabaptists (Amish, Mennonite)

BRENT C. MILLER
Utah State University
Nonmarital Childbearing
Sexuality in Adolescence

JANE MILLAR
University of Bath
Great Britain

PAUL W. MILLER
University of Western Australia
Unemployment

LEIGH MINTURN†
Infanticide (1995)

BARBARA A. MITCHELL
Simon Fraser University
Life Course Theory

GLORIA M. MONTES DE OCA
University of Florida
Birth Order

RHONDA J. V. MONTGOMERY
University of Kansas
In-Law Relationships (1995)

CHRISTI MOORE
Howard University
Therapy: Family Relationships

LINDA B. MORALES
Stephen F. Austin State University
Rural Families

MICHELLE MORALES
Howard University
Therapy: Family Relationships

JEYLAN T. MORTIMER
University of Minnesota
Childhood, Stages of: Adolescence

MONICA MOUTON-SANDERS
Michigan State University
Islam

CHARLENE L. MUEHLENHARD
University of Kansas
Rape

BRENDA MUNRO
University of Alberta
Family, Definition of

GORDON MUNRO
Alberta Alcohol and Drug Abuse Commission, Edmonton
Family, Definition of

VIRGINIA MURPHY-BERMAN
Skidmore College
Children's Rights

COLLEEN I. MURRAY
University of Nevada, Reno
Grief, Loss, and Bereavement

LYNNE MURRAY
University of Reading
Postpartum Depression

KAREN S. MYERS-BOWMAN
Kansas State University
War/Political Violence

JUDITH A. MYERS-WALLS
Purdue University
Global Citizenship

KATHY NADEAU
California State University, San Bernadino
Philippines, The

STACEY L. NAIRN
University of Calgary
Forgiveness

KAREN NEAL
George Mason University
Development: Emotional

SALLY NEWMAN
University of Pittsburgh
Intergenerational Programming

PIERRE NGOM
African Population and Heath Research Center, Nairobi, Kenya
Senegal

MARK NUTTALL
University of Aberdeen
Greenland

MARY BETH OFSTEDAL
University of Michigan
United States

TERRANCE D. OLSON
Brigham Young University
Abstinence

JULIA O. OMOKHODION
Lagos State University
Nigeria

RENEE A. OSCARSON
South Dakota State University
Food

GINA OWENS
University of Kentucky
Lesbian Parents

ALICIA ITATÍ PALERMO
National University of Lujan
Argentina

KYUNG-EUN PARK
Utah State University
Nonmarital Childbearing

ROSS D. PARKE
University of California, Riverside
Fatherhood

ROBYN PARKER
Australian Institute of Family Studies, Melbourne
Australia

SHAWN S. PARKHURST
University of Louisville
Portugal

LES PARROTT
Seattle Pacific University
Evangelical Christianity

KAY PASLEY
The University of North Carolina at Greensboro
Adolescent Parenthood
Divorce: Effects on Couples

JOÄN M. PATTERSON
University of Minnesota
Disabilities (1995)

DANIEL PERLMAN
University of British Columbia
Loneliness

ADELA GARZÓN PÉREZ
Valencia University
Familism

ANNE C. PETERSEN
WK Kellogg Foundation, East Battle Creek, Michigan
Depression: Children and Adolescents

ZOË D. PETERSON
University of Kansas
Rape

SANDRA PETRONIO
Wayne State University
Self-Disclosure

BETTY PFEFFERBAUM
University of Oklahoma Health Sciences Center
Posttraumatic Stress Disorder (PTSD)

SARA MOORHEAD PHILLIPS
Messiah College
Sexuality in Childhood

VIJAYAN K. PILLAI
University of Texas at Arlington
Zambia

FRANK S. PITTMAN III
Atlanta, Georgia
Rich/Wealthy Families

FRANK S. PITTMAN IV
Atlanta, Georgia
Rich/Wealthy Families

JAMES J. PONZETTI, JR.
University of British Columbia
Family Stories and Myths

KAREN JEAN PRAGER
The University of Texas at Dallas
Intimacy

CHRISTINE A. PRICE
The Ohio State University
Sandwich Generation

LIXIA QU
Australian Institute of Family Studies
Australia

HELÉNA RAGONÉ
University of Massachusetts Boston
Surrogacy

BRIAN D. RAY
National Home Education Research Institute, Salem, Oregon
Homeschooling

ASHLEY REED
University of Kentucky
Lesbian Parents

PAMELA C. REGAN
California State University—Los Angeles
Marital Sex

PAM REMER
University of Kentucky
Gender

JOHN K. REMPEL
St. Jerome's University
Trust

JOSEPH M. REY
University of Sydney
Oppositionality

J. ROBERTO REYES
Messiah College
Spain

CHRISTOPHER P. RICE
Florida International University
Substance Abuse

DEBORALE RICHARDSON–BOUIE
Messiah College
Ethnic Variation/Ethnicity

SHARON C. RISCH
University of Tennessee
Peer Influence

BARBARA J. RISMAN
North Carolina State University
Dual-Earner Families

KAREN A. ROBERTO
Virginia Polytechnic Institute and State University
Respite Care: Adult

MIHAELA ROBILA
Syracuse University
Romania

CORDELIA ROBINSON
University of Colorado Health Sciences Center
Developmental Disabilities

TILLMAN RODABOUGH
Baylor University
Missing Children

STEPHANIE ROLLIE
University of Iowa
Relationship Dissolution

HILARY A. ROSE
Washington State University
Socialization

KAREN S. ROSEN
Boston College
Attachment: Parent-Child Relationships

MARY HELÉNE ROSENBAUM
Dovetail Institute for Interfaith Family Resources
Interfaith Marriage

DAVID S. ROSETTENSTEIN
Quinnipiac University School of Law
Adoption

SUSAN M. ROSS
University of New Hampshire
Research: Family Measurement (1995)

B. B. ROBBIE ROSSMAN
University of Denver
Interparental Violence—Effects on Children

SHARON SCALES ROSTOSKY
University of Kentucky
Gay Parents
Gender
Lesbian Parents

MARY K. ROTHBART
University of Oregon
Temperament

FRED ROTHBAUM
Tufts University
Attachment: Parent-Child Relationships

D. T. ROWLAND
The Australian National University
Childlessness

JILL TERRY RUDY
Brigham Young University
Family Folklore

BARBARA RYAN
Widener University
Sexual Orientation

LISSETTE M. SAAVEDRA
Florida International University
Anxiety Disorders

RONALD M. SABATELLI
University of Connecticut
Social Exchange Theory

ROZZANA SÁNCHEZ ARAGÓN
National Autonomous University of Mexico
Godparents
Mexico

YOSHIE SANO
Oregon State University
Research: Methodology

JACK SARGENT
Kean College
Self-Disclosure

TODD A. SAVAGE
University of Kentucky
Gay Parents

JYOTI SAVLA
University of Georgia
Intergenerational Relations

T. LAINE SCALES
Baylor University
Family Diagrammatic Assessment: Ecomap

JOHN SCANZONI
University of Florida
Structural-Functional Theory

DOUGLAS J. SCATURO
Syracuse VA Medical Center, Syracuse, New York
Codependency

CHRISTOPH M. SCHIMMLLL
University of Victoria
Cohabitation

F. MATTHEW SCHOBERT, JR.
Baylor University
Buddhism

WARREN SCHUMACHER
University of Massachusetts, Amherst
Annulment

WALTER R. SCHUMM
Manhattan, Kansas
Religion

BETH M. SCHWARTZ-KENNEY
Randolph-Macon Woman's College
Child Abuse: Physical Abuse and Neglect

WINSTON SEEGOBIN
Messiah College
Caribbean Families

MARGARET SEMRUD-CLIKEMAN
University of Texas at Austin
Learning Disorders

KELEBOGILE V. SETILOANE
University of Delaware
Yoruba Families

BAHIRA SHERIF
University of Delware
Egypt

BENJAMIN SILLIMAN
North Carolina State University
Marriage Preparation

VIRGINIA BOWEN SILVA
Brigham and Women's Hospital, Boston
Pregnancy and Birth

WENDY K. SILVERMAN
Florida International University
Anxiety Disorders
School Phobia and School Refusal

LE ANNE E. SILVEY
Michigan State University
American-Indian Families

JENNIFER SIMONDS
University of Oregon
Temperament

LORELEI E. SIMPSON
University of California, Los Angeles
Therapy: Couple Relationships

DOROTHY G. SINGER
Yale University
Play

PASHAURA SINGH
University of Michigan, Ann Arbor
Sikhism

ARLENE SKOLNICK
University of California, Berkeley
Nuclear Families (1995)

LINDA SMEINS
Western Washington University
Honeymoon

JUDITH G. SMETANA
Univerisity of Rochester
Parenting Styles

WILLIAM L. SMITH
Georgia Southern University
Intentional Communities

SUZANNE SMYTHE
University of British Columbia
Family Literacy

MARCIA K. SPIRA
Loyola University Chicago
Menopause

IAN ST. JAMES-ROBERTS
University of London
Colic

GLEN H. STAMP
Ball State University
Transition to Parenthood

J. PHILLIP STANBERRY
The University of Southern Mississippi
Family Diagrammatic Assessment: Genogram

CATHERINE H. STEIN
Bowling Green State University
Social Networks

ALAN E. STEWART
University of Georgia
Birth Order

NICK STINNETT
University of Alabama at Tuscaloosa
Family Strengths

SARAH MICHELLE STOHLMAN
Baylor University
Runaway Youths

GARY E. STOLLAK
Michigan State University
Family Assessment

HOPE HASLAM STRAUGHAN
Wheelock College
Acquired Immunodeficiency Syndrome (AIDS)

MURRAY A. STRAUS
University of New Hampshire
Research: Family Measurement (1995)

KLAUS PETER STROHMEIER
Universität Bochum
Germany

JON C. STUCKEY
Messiah College
Alzheimer's Disease

LYNNE STURM
Indiana University School of Medicine
Failure to Thrive

ANDREW J. SUPPLE
The University of North Carolina at Greensboro
Divorce: Effects on Children

MAXIMILIANE E. SZINOVACZ
Eastern Virginia Medical School
Retirement

BAFFOUR K. TAKYI
University of Akron
Ghana

SCOTT W. TAYLOR
Baylor University
Buddhism
Hinduism

STEPHANIE TEAL
New York, NY
Birth Control: Contraceptive Methods

APHRODITE TEPEROGLOU
National Center for Social Research, Athens, Greece
Greece

LORNE TEPPERMAN
University of Toronto
Canada

ANNE THOMAS
Utah State University
Nonmarital Childbearing

DAVID MICHAEL THOMAS
Bethany Family Institute, Ireland, United Kingdom, and
United States; Benziger Publishing Co., Woodland Hills,
California
Catholicism

LANA THOMPSON
Florida Atlantic University
Menarche

OLGA TÓTH
Hungarian Academy of Sciences
Hungary

JUDITH TREAS
University of California, Irvine
Infidelity

JAN TROST
Uppsala University
Scandinavia

TERESA TSUSHIMA
Washington State University
Symbolic Interactionism

LYNN H. TURNER
Marquette University
Decision Making

ANITA L. VANGELISTI
University of Texas at Austin
Relationship Initiation

JEAN E. VEEVERS
Victoria, British Columbia
Marriage Squeeze

VIRGINIA VINCENTI
University of Wyoming
Home Economics

EASTER DAWN VO
Clark University
Coparenting

SAM VUCHINICH
Oregon State University
Conflict: Family Relationships
Problem Solving

AMY E. WAGNER
University of Iowa
Extended Families

RICHARD A. WAGNER
Smith College
Fictive Kinship (1995)

CHIZUKO WAKABAYASHI
Louisiana State University
Grandparenthood

LYNN WALTER
University of Wisconsin—Green Bay
Women's Movements

RICHARD E. WATTS
Baylor University
Interracial Marriage

SALOME NASIROLI WAWIRE
African Population and Heath Reseach Center, Nairobi, Kenya
Kenya

STEVEN WEILAND
Michigan State Universty
Judaism

DEBORAH P. WELSH
University of Tennessee
Peer Influence

RUTH E. WESTON
Australian Institute of Family Studies, Melbourne, Australia
Australia

JAMES M. WHITE
University of British Columbia
Computers and Family
Family Development Theory

LINDA WHITE
University of Nevada
Basque Families

KELI R. WHITNEY
Messiah College
Filial Responsibility

BARBARA L. WIEDER
Case Western Reserve University
Caregiving: Informal

DIANE E. WILLE
Indiana University Southeast
Separation Anxiety

WILLIAM W. WILMOT
University of Montana
Relationship Theories—Self-Other Relationship

ALAINA M. WINTERS
Heartland Community College
Equity

STEVEN K. WISENSALE
University of Connecticut
Vietnam

JOHN WITTE JR.
Emory University
Protestantism

ROSALIE S. WOLF†
Elder Abuse

BRITTON WOOD
Association for Couples in Marriage Enrichment
Marriage Enrichment

KELLY RICE WOOD
University of Kentucky
Gender

PAUL H. WRIGHT
University of North Dakota
Friendship

ZHENG WU
University of Victoria
Cohabitation
Migration

GAYNOR YANCEY
Baylor University
Poverty

LYNELLE YINGLING
J&L Human Systems Development
Family Diagnosis/DSM-IV

CARRIE L. YODANIS
University of Fribourg
Power: Marital Relationships
Role Theory

CHRISTINA GRANATO YOSHIMURA
Arizona State University
Nagging and Complaining

JUDITH T. YOUNGER
University of Minnesota Law School
Premarital Agreements

ELAINE D. ZELLEY
La Salle University
Relationship Maintenance

ZHENG ZENG
University of Kentucky
Jealousy

ABORTION

Abortion is one of the most difficult, controversial, and painful subjects in modern society. The principal controversy revolves around the questions of who makes the decision concerning abortion, the individual or the state; under what circumstances it may be done; and who is capable of making the decision. Medical questions such as techniques of abortion are less controversial but are sometimes part of the larger debate.

Abortion is not new in human society; a study by the anthropologist George Devereux (1955) showed that more than 300 contemporary human nonindustrial societies practiced abortion. Women have performed abortions on themselves or experienced abortions at the hands of others for thousands of years (Potts, Diggory, and Peel 1977), and abortions continue to occur today in developing areas under medically primitive conditions. However, modern technology and social change have made abortion a part of modern health care. At the same time, abortion has become a political issue in some societies and a flash point for disagreements about the role of women and individual autonomy in life decisions.

Definition Of Abortion

The classic definition of abortion is "expulsion of the fetus before it is viable." This could include spontaneous abortion (miscarriage) or induced abortion, in which someone (a doctor, the woman herself, or a layperson) causes the abortion. Before modern methods of abortion, this sometimes meant the introduction of foreign objects like catheters into the uterus to disrupt the placenta and embryo (or fetus) so that a miscarriage would result. In preindustrial societies, hitting the pregnant woman in the abdomen over the uterus and jumping on her abdomen while she lies on the ground are common techniques used to induce an abortion (Early and Peters 1990). Although these methods can be effective, they may also result in the death of the woman if her uterus is ruptured or if some of the amniotic fluid surrounding the fetus enters her bloodstream. From the colonial period to the early twentieth-century in America, primitive methods such as these were used along with the introduction of foreign objects into the uterus (wooden sticks, knitting needles, catheters, etc.) to cause abortion, frequently with tragic results (Lee 1969).

In modern society, abortions are performed surgically by physicians or other trained personnel experienced in this technique, making the procedure much safer. The goal of induced abortion remains the same: to interrupt the pregnancy so that the woman will not continue to term and deliver a baby.

One problem with the classical definition of abortion is the changing definition of viability (the ability to live outside the womb). Premature birth is historically associated with high death and disability rates for babies born alive, but medical advances of the twentieth century have made it possible to save the lives of babies born after only thirty weeks of pregnancy when the usual pregnancy lasts forty weeks. Some infants born at twenty-six to twenty-seven weeks or younger have even survived through massive intervention and support. At the same time, abortions are now routinely performed up to twenty-five to twenty-six weeks of pregnancy. Therefore, the old definition of viability is not helpful in determining whether an abortion has been or should be performed (Grobstein 1988).

Reasons for Abortions

There are probably as many reasons for abortions as there are women who have them. Some pregnancies result from rape or incest, and women who are victims of these assaults often seek abortions. Most women, however, decide to have an abortion because the pregnancy represents a problem in their lives (Bankole et al. 1998, 1999; Alan Guttmacher Institute 1999).

Some women feel emotionally unprepared to enter parenthood and raise a child; they are too young or do not have a reliable partner with whom to raise a child. Many young women in high school or college find themselves pregnant and must choose between continuing the education they need to survive economically and dropping out to have a baby. Young couples who are just starting their lives together and want children might prefer to become financially secure first to provide better care for their future children.

Sometimes people enter into a casual sexual relationship that leads to pregnancy with no prospect of marriage. Even if the sexual relationship is more than casual, abortion is may be sought because a woman decides that the social status of the male is inappropriate. Abortion is reported to be sought by some women because of popular beliefs that forms of modern contraceptives are more dangerous than abortion (Otoide et al. 2001).

Some of the most difficult and painful choices are faced by women who are happily pregnant for the first time late in the reproductive years (thirty-five to forty-five) but discover in late pregnancy (twenty-six or more weeks) that the fetus is so defective it may not live or have a normal life. Even worse is a diagnosis of abnormalities that may or may not result in problems after birth. Some women and couples in this situation choose to have a late abortion (Kolata 1992; Hern et al. 1993).

In some cases, a woman must have an abortion to survive a pregnancy. An example is the diabetic woman who develops a condition in pregnancy called hyperemesis gravidarum (uncontrollable vomiting associated with pregnancy). She becomes malnourished and dehydrated in spite of intravenous therapy and other treatment, threatening heart failure, among other things. Only an abortion will cure this life-threatening condition.

In certain traditional or tribal societies, either the decision to end a pregnancy by abortion or the method of doing so is determined by the group. John Early and John Peters (1990) described a method used by the Yanomami of the Amazon of hitting or jumping on a pregnant woman's abdomen to cause an abortion. A similar method has been described in other tribal societies in Africa and South Asia. Among the Suraya of seventeenth-century Taiwan, a woman under the age of thirty was required to end all pregnancies by abortion by forceful uterine massage (Shepherd 1995).

Studies done in Chile in the 1960s showed that the majority of women who sought abortions at that time were likely to be married, to have the approval of the husband, and were having the abortion for economic reasons (Armijo and Monreal 1965; Requena 1965). This pattern has been observed in many other countries.

In certain Muslim societies, a young couple from feuding families must wait five years or more to have a child, with the result of numerous abortions in order to observe this family rule.

When and How Abortions Are Performed

In the United States and in European countries such as the Netherlands, more than 90 percent of all abortions are performed in the first trimester of pregnancy (up to twelve weeks from the last normal menstrual period). Most take place in outpatient clinics specially designed and equipped for this purpose. Nearly all abortions in the United States are performed by physicians, although two states (Montana and Vermont) permit physicians' assistants to do the procedure. A limited number of physicians in specialized clinics perform abortions during the second trimester of pregnancy, but only a few perform abortions after pregnancy has advanced to more than twenty-five weeks. Although hospitals permit abortions to be performed, the number is limited because the costs to perform an abortion in the hospital are greater and hospital operating room schedules do not allow for a large number of patients. In addition, staff members at hospitals are not chosen on the basis of their willingness to help perform abortions, while clinic staff members are hired for that purpose.

Most early abortions (up to twelve to fourteen weeks of pregnancy) are performed with some use of vacuum aspiration equipment. A machine or specially designed syringe is used to create a vacuum, and the suction draws the contents of the uterus into an outside container. The physician then checks the inside of the uterus with a *curette,* a spoon-shaped device with a loop at the end and sharp edges to scrape the wall of the uterus (Hern 1990).

Before the uterus can be emptied, however, the *cervix* (opening of the uterus) must be dilated, or stretched, in order to introduce the instruments. There are two principal ways this can be done. Specially designed metal *dilators,* steel rods with tapered ends that allow the surgeon to force the cervix open a little at a time, are used for most abortions. This process is usually done under local anesthesia, but sometimes general anesthesia is used. The cervix can also be dilated by placing pieces of medically prepared seaweed stalk called Laminaria in the cervix and leaving it for a few hours or overnight (Hern 1975, 1990). The Laminaria draws water from the woman's tissues and swells up, gently expanding as the woman's cervix softens and opens from the loss of moisture. The Laminaria is then removed, and a vacuum cannula or tube is placed into the uterus to remove the pregnancy by suction (Figure 1). Following this, the walls of the uterus are gently scraped with the curette.

After twelve weeks of pregnancy, performing an abortion becomes much more complicated and dangerous. The uterus, the embryo or fetus, and the blood vessels within the uterus are all much larger. The volume of amniotic fluid around the fetus has increased substantially, creating a potential hazard. If the amniotic fluid enters the woman's circulatory system, she could die instantly or bleed to death from a disruption of the blood-clotting system. This hazard is an important consideration in performing late abortions.

Ultrasound equipment, which uses sound waves to show a picture of the fetus, is used to examine the woman before a late abortion is performed. Parts of the fetus such as the head and long bones are measured to determine the length of pregnancy. The ultrasound image also permits determination of fetal position, location of the placenta, and the presence of any abnormalities that could cause a complication.

Between fourteen and twenty weeks of pregnancy, Laminaria is placed in the cervix over a period of a day or two, sometimes changing the Laminaria and replacing the first batch with a larger amount in order to increase cervical dilation (Hern 1990). At the time of the abortion, the Laminaria is removed, the amniotic sac (bag of waters) is ruptured with an instrument, and the amniotic fluid is allowed to drain out. This procedure reduces the risk of an *amniotic fluid embolism,* escape of the amniotic fluid into the bloodstream, and allows the uterus to contract to make the abortion safer. Using an ultrasound real-time image, the surgeon then places special instruments such as grasping forceps into the uterus and removes the fetus and placenta (Hern 1990). This has proven to be the safest way to perform late abortions, but it requires great care and skill.

Other methods of late abortion include the use of *prostaglandin* (a naturally occurring hormone), either by suppository or by injection (Hern 1988). Other materials injected into the pregnant uterus to effect late abortion include hypertonic (concentrated) saline (salt) solution, hypertonic urea, and hyperosmolar (concentrated) glucose solution.

Injections are also used with late abortions, especially those performed at twenty-five weeks or more for reasons of fetal disorder. The lethal injection into the fetus is performed several days prior to the abortion, along with other treatments that permit a safe abortion (Hern et al. 1993; Hern 2001).

Although surgical abortion is still performed outside the United States, *medical abortion* is growing in use in Europe and in the United States following the introduction in France in 1988 of mifepristone (also known as RU-486) and misoprostol, a synthetic prostaglandin. Mifepristone works by blocking the hormonal receptors in the placenta from receiving progesterone, which is necessary for continuation of the pregnancy. Along with misoprostol, mifepristone may cause a complete abortion in 95 percent of early pregnancies within a few days. Most patients do not require a surgical treatment for completion of the abortion.

Risks Of Abortion

In the United States, Canada, and Western Europe, abortion has become not only the most common but also one of the safest operations being performed. This was not always the case. In the nineteenth and early twentieth centuries, abortion was quite dangerous, and many women died as a result.

Pregnancy itself is not a harmless condition; women can die during pregnancy. The *maternal mortality rate* (the proportion of women dying from pregnancy and childbirth) is found by dividing the number of women dying from all causes related to pregnancy, childbirth, and the puerperium (the six-week period following childbirth) by the total number of live births and then multiplying by a constant factor such as 100,000. For example, the maternal mortality rate in the United States in 1920 was 680 maternal deaths per 100,000 live births (Lerner and Anderson 1963). It had fallen to 38 deaths per 100,000 live births by 1960 and 8 deaths per 100,000 live births by 1994. Illegal abortion accounted for about 50 percent of all maternal deaths in 1920, and that was still true in 1960. By 1980, however, the percentage of deaths due to abortion had dropped to nearly zero (Cates 1982). The difference in maternal mortality rates due to abortion reflected the increasing legalization of abortion from 1967 to 1973 that permitted abortions to be done safely by doctors in clinics and hospitals. The changed legal climate also permitted the prompt treatment of complications that occurred with abortions.

The complication rates and death rates associated with abortion itself can also be examined. In 1970, Christopher Tietze of the Population Council began studying the risks of death and complications due to abortion by collecting data from hospitals and clinics throughout the nation. The statistical analyses at that time showed that the death rate due to abortion was about 2 deaths per 100,000 procedures compared with the current maternal mortality rate exclusive of abortion of 12 deaths per 100,000 live births. In other words, a woman having an abortion was six times less likely to die than a woman who chose to carry a pregnancy to term. Tietze also found that early abortion was many times safer than abortion done after twelve weeks of pregnancy (Tietze and Lewit 1972) and that some abortion techniques were safer than others. The Centers for Disease Control

in Atlanta took over the national study of abortion statistics that had been developed by Tietze, and abortion became the most carefully studied surgical procedure in the United States. As doctors gained more experience with abortion and as techniques improved, death and complication rates due to abortion continued to decline. The rates declined because women were seeking abortions earlier in pregnancy, when the procedure was safer. Clinics where safe abortions could be obtained were opened in many U.S. cities across the country, improving access to this service.

By the early 1990s in the United States, the risk of death in early abortion was less than 1 death per 1 million procedures, and for later abortion, about 1 death per 100,000 procedures (Koonin et al. 1992). The overall risk of death in abortion was about 0.4 deaths per 100,000 procedures compared with a maternal mortality rate (exclusive of abortion) of about 9.1 deaths per 100,000 live births (Koonin et al. 1991a, 1991b).

Incidence Of Abortion

Although the exact number may never be known, it is estimated that between 20 million and 50 million abortions are performed each year (World Health Organization 1994). The proportion of women having abortions and the proportion of pregnancies terminated vary widely from country to country. In the past, the highest rates have been observed in the Soviet Union and eastern European countries where abortion is more socially acceptable than in other regions and where contraceptive services have been scarce or unreliable.

According to Singh and Henshaw (1996), about half of all abortions in 1990 occurred in Asia, with almost one-fourth occurring in the former USSR. Approximately 3 percent occurred in Canada and the United States. In Colombia during the 1980s, according to unofficial reports, it appeared that one out of every two pregnancies ended in abortion.

The highest abortion rates recorded have been in Romania in 1965, where, among women in the reproductive age from fifteen to forty-four, one in four had an abortion each year (Henshaw and Morrow 1990). The abortion rate in Romania plummeted in 1966 when Romanian dictator Nicolau Ceaucescu banned abortion in an attempt to increase population growth rates. Police surveillance of women included mandatory pelvic examinations and pregnancy tests. This action resulted in higher birth rates, but it was also accompanied by skyrocketing maternal mortality rates including a dramatic increase in deaths from abortion, which caused approximately 85 percent of all maternal deaths. The Romanian maternal mortality rate went from 86 per 100,000 live births in 1966 to 170 per 100,000 live births in the late 1980s—the highest in Europe.

Approximately 10,000 excess maternal deaths due to abortion occurred during the period from 1966–1989 (Serbanescu et al. 2001). Romanian abortion rates again became the highest in the world after Ceaucescu was overthrown in 1989, and abortion mortality rates dropped (Joffe 1999; Henshaw 1999). Within one year after the fall of the Ceaucescu regime, the maternal mortality rate dropped by 50 per cent. By 1997, there were 21 abortion-related deaths per 100,000 live births (Serbanescu et al. 2001).

In other countries such as Canada and the Netherlands, where abortion is legal and widely available, but where other means of fertility control are easily available, abortion rates are sometimes quite low (Henshaw 1999). In the Ukraine, the abortion rate in women in the reproductive age range of fifteen to forty-four years fell 50 percent from 77 abortions per 1,000 women to 36 per 1,000 in the interval from 1990 to 1998 (Goldberg et al. 2001).

It appears that, when abortion is both legal and widely available but is not the only means of effective fertility control, about one-fourth of all pregnancies will end in abortion. Lack of access to contraception may result in higher abortion rates. The principal effect of laws making abortion illegal appears to be to make abortion more dangerous but not less common.

Physical And Psychological Effects of Abortion

Studies of the long-term risks of induced abortion, such as difficulties with future pregnancies, show that these risks are minimal. A properly done early abortion may even result in a lower risk of certain obstetrical problems with later pregnancies (Hern 1982; Hogue, Cates, and Tietze 1982). An uncomplicated early abortion should have no effect on future health or childbearing. If the abortion permits postponement of the first term pregnancy to after adolescence, the usual risks associated with a

Strong emotional support and a knowledgable physician can ease the difficulties women face when dealing with abortion. JENNIE WOODCOCK; REFLECTIONS PHOTOLIBRARY/CORBIS

first term pregnancy are actually reduced. Psychological studies consistently show that women who are basically healthy can adjust to any outcome of pregnancy, whether it is term birth, induced abortion, or spontaneous abortion (miscarriage) (Adler et al. 1990). It is highly desirable, however, to have strong emotional support not only from friends and family but also from a sympathetic physician and a lay abortion counselor who will be with the woman during her abortion experience.

Denial of abortion can have serious adverse consequences for the children who result from the pregnancies their mothers had wanted to terminate. A long-term study in Czechoslovakia of the offspring of women who were denied abortions showed a range of adjustment and developmental difficulties in these children (David et al. 1988).

Social Responses To Abortion

The various social responses to abortion range from those of the individual and her immediate circle of family and friends to the organizational, community, and even national levels. Each culture and society has specific ways of dealing with unplanned or unwanted pregnancy and with abortion. These traditions are changing rapidly in the modern world.

See also: BIRTH CONTROL: CONTRACEPTIVE METHODS; BIRTH CONTROL: SOCIOCULTURAL AND HISTORICAL ASPECTS; FAMILY PLANNING; FERTILITY; GENETIC COUNSELING;

INFANTICIDE; NONMARITAL CHILDBEARING; PREGNANCY
AND BIRTH; RAPE; RELIGION

Bibliography

Adler, N. E.; David, H. P.; Major, B. N.; Roth, S. H.; Russo, N. F.; and Wyatt, D. E. (1990). "Psychological Responses after Abortion." *Science* 248:41–44.

Alan Guttmacher Institute. (1999). *Sharing Responsibiity: Women, Society and Abortion Worldwide.* New York: Alan Guttmacher Institute.

Armijo, R., and Monreal, T. (1965). "The Epidemiology of Provoked Abortion in Santiago, Chile." In *Population Dynamics,* ed. M. Muramatsu and P. A. Harper. Baltimore: Johns Hopkins University Press.

Bankole, A.; Singh, S.; and Haas, T. (1998). "Reasons Why Women Have Induced Abortions: Evidence from 27 Countries." *International Family Planning Perspectives* 24(3):117–127.

Bankole, A.; Singh, S.; and Haas, T. (1999). "Characteristics of Women Who Obtain Induced Abortion: A Worldwide Review." *International Family Planning Perspectives* 25(2):68–77.

Cates, W., Jr. (1982). "Abortion: The Public Health Record." *Science* 215:1586.

David, H. P.; Dytrych, Z.; Matejcek, Z.; and Schuller, V. (1988). *Born Unwanted: Developmental Effects of Denied Abortion.* New York: Springer.

Devereux, G. (1955). *A Study of Abortion in Primitive Society.* New York: Julian Press.

Early, J. D., and Peters, J. F. (1990). *The Population Dynamics of the Mucajai Yanomama.* San Diego: Academic Press.

Goldberg, H.; Melnikova, N.; Buslayeva, E.; and Zakhozha, V. (2001). *1999 Ukraine Reproductive Health Survey. Final Report, September, 2001.* Atlanta: U.S. Centers for Disease Control and Prevention.

Grobstein, C. (1988). *Science and the Unborn.* New York: Basic Books.

Handwerker, W. P. (1990). *Births and Power: Social Change and the Politics of Reproduction.* Boulder, CO: Westview Press.

Henshaw, S. K. (1999). "Unintended Pregnancy and Abortion: A Public Health Perspective." In *A Clinician's Guide to Medical and Surgical Abortion,* ed. M. Paul, E. S. Lichtenberg, L. Borgatta, D.A. Grimes, and P.G. Stubblefield. New York: Churchill.

Henshaw, S. K., and Morrow, E. (1990). "Induced Abortion: A World Review," 1990 supplement. New York: Alan Guttmacher Institute.

Henshaw, S. K., and Van Vort, J. (1992). *Abortion Factbook, 1992 Edition: Readings, Trends, and State and Local Data to 1988.* New York: Alan Guttmacher Institute.

Hern, W. M. (1975). "Laminaria in Abortion: Use in 1368 Patients in First Trimester." *Rocky Mountain Medical Journal* 72:390–395.

Hern, W. M. (1982). "Long-term Risks of Induced Abortion." In *Gynecology and Obstetrics,* ed. J. J. Sciarra. Philadelphia: Harper and Row.

Hern, W. M. (1988). "The Use of Prostaglandins as Abortifacients." In *Gynecology and Obstetrics,* ed. J. J. Sciarra. Philadelphia: Harper and Row.

Hern, W. M. (1990). *Abortion Practice.* Boulder, CO: Alpenglo Graphics.

Hern, W. M. (2001). "Laminaria, Induced Fetal Demise, and Misoprostol in Late Abortion." *International Journal of Gynecology and Obstetrics* 75:279–286.

Hern, W. M.; Zen, C.; Ferguson, K. A.; Hart, V.; and Haseman, M. V. (1993). "Late Abortion for Fetal Anomaly and Fetal Death: Techniques and Clinical Management." *Obstetrics and Gynecology* 81:301–306.

Hodgson, J. (1981). *Abortion and Sterilization: Medical and Social Aspects.* London: Academic Press.

Hogue, C. J. R.; Cates, W., Jr.; and Tietze, C. (1982). "The Effects of Induced abortion on Subsequent Reproduction." *Epidemiologic Reviews* 4:66.

Joffe, C. (1999). "Abortion in Historical Perspective." In *A Clinician's Guide to Medical and Surgical Abortion,* ed. M. Paul, E. S. Lichtenberg, L. Borgatta, D. A. Grimes, and P. G. Stubblefield. New York: Churchill Livingstone.

Kolata, G. (1992). "In Late Abortions, Decisions Are Painful and Options Few." *New York Times,* January 5.

Koonin, L. M.; Atrash, H. K.; Lawson, H. W.; Smith, J. C. (1991b). *Maternal Mortality Surveillance, United States, 1979–1986. CDC Surveillance Summaries, July, 1991,* MMWR 40(No. SS-2):1–13.

Koonin, L. M.; Kochanek, K. D.; Smith, J. C.; Ramick, M. (1991a). *Abortion Surveillance, United States, 1988. CDC Surveillance Summaries, July, 1991,* MMWR 40(No. SS-2):15–42.

Koonin, L. M.; Smith, J. C.; Ramick, M.; and Lawson, H. W. (1992). *Abortion Surveillance, United States, 1989. CDC Surveillance Summaries, September 4, 1992,* MMWR 41(No. SS-5):1–33.

Lee, N. H. (1969). *The Search for an Abortionist.* Chicago: University of Chicago Press.

Lerner, M., and Anderson, O. W. (1963). *Health Progress in United States: 1900–1960.* Chicago: University of Chicago Press.

Otoide, V.O.; Oronsaye, F.; and Okonofua, F.E. (2001). "Why Nigerian Adolescents Seek Abortion Rather Than Contraception: Evidence From Focus-Group Discussions." *International Family Planning Perspectives* 27(2):77–81.

Potts, M.; Diggory, P.; and Peel, J. (1977). *Abortion*. Cambridge, UK: Cambridge University Press.

Requena, M. (1965). "Social and Economic Correlates of Induced Abortion in Santiago, Chile." *Demography* 2:33.

Serbanescu, F.; Morris, L.; and Marin, M. (2001). *Reproductive Health Survey, Romania, 1999*. Atlanta, GA: U.S. Centers for Disease Control & Prevention.

Shepherd, J. R. (1995). *Marriage and Mandatory Abortion Among the 17th Century Suraya*. Arlington, VA: American Anthropological Association.

Singh, S., and Henshaw, S. K. (1996). "The Incidence of Abortion: A World-wide Overview Focusing on Methodology and on Latin America." In *International Union for the Scientific Study of Population: Sociocultural and Political Aspects of Abortion in a Changing World*. Liège, Belgium: International Union for the Scientific Study of Population.

Tietze, C., and Lewit, S. (1972). "Joint Program for the Study of Abortion (JPSA): Early Complications of Medical Abortion." *Studies in Family Planning* 3:97.

World Health Organization, Maternal Health and Safe Motherhood Programme (1994). *Abortion: A Tabulation of Available Data On The Frequency and Mortality of Unsafe Abortion*. 2nd edition. Geneva: World Health Organization.

Other Resources

Alan Guttmacher Institute. Available from http://www.agi-usa.org.

International Society of Abortion Doctors. Available from http://www.isad.org.

National Abortion Federation. Available from http://www.prochoice.org.

WARREN M. HERN

ABSTINENCE

Historically and culturally, sexual relationships rarely have been granted a place independent of the social, emotional, familial, generational, economic, and spiritual dimensions of human experience. That may be why the idea of premarital abstinence will continue to be a feature of philosophy and practice, even though many avenues of sexual involvement seem to be expanding in contemporary Western societies. Both sexual involvement and abstinence can be expressions of religious beliefs and traditions, the meanings of marriage and family relationships, contemporary cultural philosophies, and features of one's personal identity, commitments, and beliefs. These sources of sexual practices are intertwined, and produce norms and exceptions to any given culture's stance on what is acceptable in sexual expression. Specifically, sexual involvement can be seen by religions, cultures, families and individuals as inherently wrong, as a necessary evil, as an amoral inevitability fundamental to human nature, as an act that can be engaged in morally or immorally, or as a sacred act reserved for specific contexts or persons.

Sexual expression always has been a concern in religious traditions, and has included boundaries usually concerning marriage and family relationships. Although premarital sexual abstinence is frequently central to religious practices, permanent sexual abstinence within marriage is certainly not the norm across religions or cultures. Yet, some couples practice "marital celibacy" for a variety of reasons.

One rendition of early Christian doctrine suggests a fundamental incompatibility between sexual involvement and being "good." Not only was premarital abstinence expected to be the norm, but to marry and thus participate in conjugal relationships was to choose worldliness over godliness. Sexuality was seen as basic evidence of human kind's fallen nature, while abstinence or celibacy was seen as the ultimate sign of spirituality (Elliott 1993). Such a dichotomy creates an inescapable moral conflict between the meaning of sexual participation—marital or premarital—and abstinence. This may have prompted some couples, from the time of Christ to the sixteenth century, to practice various forms of "spiritual marriage," meaning to live in a marital, but nonsexual, relationship. But there is a difference between a culture advocating abstinence as the prelude to marriage, and installing the practice of abstinence in the marriage itself.

Some religious groups, such as the "Shaking Quakers" (Shakers) in the late 1700s, also extended sexual abstinence to the marital relationship. Not surprisingly, this doctrine undermines a fundamental feature of marriage, rarely questioned in history or in general practice. In fact, with this doctrine, the Shakers "abolished . . . the very heart of orthodox society: the traditional family" (Abbott 2000, p.152). Some feminist critics point out that abstinence in marriage, especially in earlier centuries, could serve to liberate the woman from the threat of disease, death, childbirth, and the sexual demands of the male in nonegalitarian cultures.

Not all Christian or religious groups view sexuality as irrevocable evidence of being fallen or depraved, and some philosophies grant sexuality a positive or even celebrated place in human experience. Some religious groups and cultures do formally declare abstinence to be appropriate until marriage, without invoking an antisexual moral doctrine. The Islamic world and Mormon doctrine, for example, do not see marital sexual involvement as a moral compromise, but as an essential or even higher good. In such philosophies, the purposes of premarital abstinence are not grounded in the idea of sexuality as inherently evil, but as a gift not to be used whimsically. In Islamic belief, celibacy in a marital context is forbidden (see Rizvi 1994). Non-Western and religious cultures are more likely to have normative beliefs in favor of premarital abstinence, while Western and secular cultures are more likely to have specific, even pragmatic reasons for promoting premarital abstinence.

Sometimes due to, or in spite of, specific cultural, personal, or religious philosophies, sexual expression does occur outside of marital boundaries, and in Western cultures, has steadily increased in frequency among both unmarried adults and adolescents. While the premarital rate of sexual participation has expanded, a philosophy of sexual exclusivity is still the norm for married couples. Moreover, sexual expression is still defined by its relationship to marriage. For example, Western culture describes participation outside of marriage not as "nonmarital," but as "premarital" sex. Rationales for such behavior seem to have moved from "sex with commitment" (as in the case of historic betrothal practices or contemporary boundaries defined by "being engaged") to "sex with affection," where mutual, voluntary attraction seems to be the fundamental justification for sexual participation.

In spite of data showing public disapproval of premarital sexual involvement among adolescents, there is debate regarding why the majority of teens (typically sexually abstinent until at least age seventeen) abstain. Reasons for premarital sexual abstinence in the West seem related to four factors:

(1) personal beliefs about marriage, family, and sexuality; (2) practical concerns about physical consequences, such as the avoidance of STDS, AIDS, or pregnancy; (3) specific moral or religious considerations (usually defining the meaning and value of marriage and family across generations); and (4) the desire to preserve or not jeopardize opportunities for additional education, financial well-being, or the future capacity for establishing stable family lives (see Davidson and Moore 1996).

These factors are expressions of personal beliefs and cultural contexts, and generally are not evidence of an extensive antisexual philosophy. Rather, individuals can articulate a philosophy of sexual involvement that takes into account the time, place, and person—all contextual factors—with whom sexual involvement would be appropriate. Western media (television, movies, pop magazines) unfold stories, plots, and advice that, at the least, presents sexual abstinence among unmarried adults as atypical. Given the data on adolescent behavior, the media seems to ignore or discount a view of abstinence or celibacy subscribed to behaviorally by the young. Personal beliefs about sexual expression may be more conservative than media philosophies, but personal practices can be more liberal than personal beliefs—given the sexual participation rates of those who express a belief in abstinence before marriage, for example (Miller and Olson 1988). Moreover, beliefs and practices about sexual involvement in any culture are not necessarily congruent, and often include a double standard by gender. Nevertheless, in cultures worldwide, there seems to be a link between one's philosophy of sexual involvement (including the options of abstinence or celibacy), and one's philosophy of marriage and family relationships.

Most studies in the United States show that, generally, the majority of adolescents (junior high and high school age) were sexually abstinent until the 1970s. In this decade, some research samples obtained self-reports from the majority of adolescent males that they had been involved in sexual intercourse. By the 1980s, more research studies obtained reports of involvement by a majority of adolescent females, although few studies indicated the frequency of participation. Clearly, premarital sexual abstinence is less a norm than prior to the 1970s (Davidson and Moore 1996).

In assessing both broad cultural beliefs and an individual's commitments, sexual abstinence or engagement is grounded in more than mere physical satisfaction. Especially in egalitarian cultures, the meaning of sexual participation is grounded in the quality of the relationship itself, and takes on the meaning of that relationship. In exploitive relationships, sexual involvement becomes an expression of that exploitation. In relationships characterized by mutuality, equality, and commitment, sexual involvement becomes an expression of these characteristics. Similarly, in cultures where sexual abstinence is recommended before or even during marriage, it is often linked to issues of mutuality, equality, and commitment. As examples, consider that sexual abstinence can become a recommended (and usually temporary) course of action when relationships are not mutual, not equal, and not in a context of commitment. Voluntary sexual abstinence, however temporary, is also dictated within marital relationships for a variety of other reasons. In a 1987 survey (Pietropinto 1987), stress and work pressures were cited as the most common reasons, but illness, marital discord, and decreased personal interest were reasons also given.

A resurgence in calls for sexual abstinence prior to marriage has taken place in Africa, where the threat of AIDS threatens to decimate whole populations. In 2002, King Goodwill Zwelithini of the Zulu tribe in South Africa used a major tribal gathering to appeal to young people, "male and female, to abstain from sex until they get married or until they decide to raise their families." He "called for a revival of the traditions and culture of the tribe, once the most powerful in Southern Africa. . . . The spread of HIV/AIDS and other associated problems, such as drug-taking and promiscuity, reinforced the need for traditional values and unity" (Unruh 2002). His words are similar to that of Janet Museveni, the first lady of Uganda, who has issued calls to the youth of her country.

This plea from Africa integrates traditional religious beliefs, a philosophy of marriage and family relationships, cultural practices, and pragmatic concern for the physical well-being of the population into a stance in support of abstinence. It is not the only view or even a prevailing one, but it illustrates an attempt to acknowledge abstinence as a historic and contemporary foundation for sexual relationships.

Similar arguments and calls to abstinence are a feature of dialogue in the West, and often also include assumptions or research about the impact of premarital sexual involvement on the stability of later marital relationships and the cohesiveness of a pluralistic society (Gallagher 1999). Non-Western cultures that mandate or prefer premarital abstinence or marital celibacy usually match Western cultures in that they do so for religious reasons, out of culture-wide norms and beliefs, or as prevention strategies for the preservation of a generation in the face of life-threatening sexually transmitted diseases.

Bibliography

Abbott, E. (2000). *A History of Celibacy*. New York: Scribner.

Davidson, J. K., Sr., and Moore, N. B. (1996). *Marriage and Family: Change and Continuity*. Boston, MA: Allyn & Bacon.

Elliott, D. (1993). *Spiritual Marriage: Sexual Abstinence in Medieval Wedlock*. Princeton, NJ: Princeton University Press.

Gallagher, M. (1999). *The Age of Unwed Mothers: Is Teen Pregnancy the Problem?* New York: Institute for American Values.

Miller, B. C., and Olson, T. D. (1988). "Sexual Attitudes and Behavior of High School Students in Relation to Background and Contextual Factors." *The Journal of Sex Research* 24:194–200.

Pietropinto, A. (1987). "Survey: Sexual Abstinence." *Medical Aspects of Human Sexuality* 21(7):115–118.

Rizvi, S. M. (1994). *Marriage and Morals in Islam*, 2nd edition. Scarborough, Ontario: Islamic Education and Information Centre.

Other Resources

Unruh, J. (2002). "Good News from Africa." Abstinence Clearinghouse web site. Available from http://www.abstinence.net.

TERRANCE D. OLSON

ABUSE AND NEGLECT

See CHILD ABUSE: PHYSICAL ABUSE AND NEGLECT; CHILD ABUSE: PSYCHOLOGICAL MALTREATMENT; CHILD ABUSE: SEXUAL ABUSE; ELDER ABUSE;

INTERPARENTAL VIOLENCE—EFFECTS ON CHILDREN;
SPOUSE ABUSE: PREVALENCE; SPOUSE ABUSE:
THEORETICAL EXPLANATIONS

ACADEMIC ACHIEVEMENT

It is generally accepted that the quality of family interactions has important associations with children's and adolescents' academic motivation and achievement, and with young adults' eventual educational and occupational attainments. Thomas Kellaghan and his colleagues (1993) claim, for example, that the family environment is the most powerful influence in determining students' school achievement, academic motivation, and the number of years of schooling they will receive. Similarly, James S. Coleman (1991) states that parents' involvement in learning activities has substantial emotional and intellectual benefits for children. He observes, however, that because supportive and strong families are significant for school success, teachers confront increasing challenges as many children experience severe family disruption and upheaval. Although it is acknowledged that families are perhaps the most substantial influence on children's school success, it is not always clear which family influences are the most important. In addition, research findings are inconclusive about the extent to which relationships between family interactions and academic performance are independent of a child's family background and family structure.

Family Influences

Coleman (1997) proposes that family influences can be separated into components such as economic, human, and social capital. *Economic capital* refers to the financial resources and assets available to families, whereas *human capital* provides parents with the knowledge resources necessary to create supportive learning environments for their children. In contrast, *family social capital* is defined by the relationships that develop between family members. It is through these relationships that children gain access to the economic, human, and cultural resources of their families. Similarly, Pierre Bourdieu (1998) suggests that children in families from various social status and ethnic/racial groups have differing degrees of access to those forms of cultural capital that support academic success. Bourdieu claims that within social groups, parents provide experiences that result in children developing similar tastes, preferences, academic motivation, and preferences. Eventually, these attributes are related to social status and ethnic/racial group differences in academic and occupational outcomes. A number of theories have been developed to examine those parent-child interactions that provide children with differential access to family resources.

Steinberg's family model. In a set of investigations, Laurence Steinberg (1996) proposes that to understand family influences, it is important to disentangle three different aspects of parenting. These include: (1) parenting style, which provides the emotional context in which parent-child interactions occur; (2) the goals that parents establish for their children; and (3) the practices adopted by parents to help children attain those goals. It has been shown, for example, that a parenting style defined as authoritative is related to positive academic motivation and successful academic achievement (Darling and Steinberg 1993). Such a style creates a context in which parents encourage their children's independence and individuality, provide opportunities for children to be involved in family decision making, expect high standards for their children, and have warm relationships with their children.

Family achievement syndrome. In one of the most significant attempts to construct a framework for the study of family influences, Bernard C. Rosen (1959, 1973) developed the concept of the family achievement syndrome. He proposes that achievement-oriented families can be characterized by variations in the interrelated components of: achievement training, independence training, achievement-value orientations, and educational-occupational aspirations. Whereas achievement training aims at getting children to do things well, independence training attempts to teach children to do things on their own. Rosen indicates that achievement and independence training act together to generate achievement motivation, which provides children with the impetus to excel in situations involving standards of excellence. In the achievement syndrome, it is proposed that achievement values help to shape children's behavior so that achievement motivation can be translated into successful academic achievement. Rosen states, however, that unless parents express high aspirations for their children, other family influences may not necessarily be associated with academic success. In analyses of social mobility, it has been shown that families from various social status and ethnic/racial groups place different emphases on the dimensions of the family achievement syndrome, and that variations in mobility are related to these group differences in family-achievement orientations.

Bloom's subenvironment model. It was not until Benjamin S. Bloom (1964) and a number of his students examined the family correlates of children's affective and academic outcomes, that a school of research emerged to investigate the relationships between family influences and academic outcomes. Bloom defines family environments as the conditions, forces, and external stimuli that impinge on children. He proposes that these forces, which may be physical or social as well as intellectual, provide a network that surrounds, engulfs, and plays on the child. The Bloom model suggests that the total family context surrounding a child may be considered as being composed of a number of subenvironments. If the development of particular characteristics, such as academic motivation and academic achievement, are to be understood, then it is necessary to identify those subenvironments that are potentially related to the characteristics. The analyses guided by the subenvironment model indicate that it is possible to measure family influences that, when combined, have medium associations with children's academic motivation and large associations with their academic achievement.

Alterable family influences. In an extension of his family model, Bloom (1980) proposes that the objective of family research should be to search for those variables that can be altered, and therefore make a difference in children's learning. The findings from family learning environment research suggest that children's academic success is influenced by the interrelationships among high parental educational and occupational aspirations; a language environment that is characterized by strong reading habits and rich parent-child verbal interactions; academic involvement and support, where parents become actively involved in their

children's schooling; an intellectually stimulating home setting, in which parents provide opportunities for children to explore ideas and encourage their children to become involved in imagination-provoking activities; and parent-child interactions that support the pursuit of excellence in academic and cultural experiences, and that allow independent-oriented behavior. It is important, therefore, that when attempts are made to help families develop more enriched learning environments, the strategies adopted acknowledge the significance of the interrelationships among such influences.

Family Background and Family Structure

Investigations that have adopted refined measures of family influences have tended to show that they are related more strongly to academic outcomes than are more global measures of family background. Kellaghan and this colleagues (1993) conclude, for example, that family social status or cultural background need not determine a child's achievement at school. They propose that for academic success, it is what parents do in the home, and not children's family background, that is significant. Similarly, Sam Redding (1999) indicates that in relation to academic outcomes, the potential limitations associated with poor economic circumstances can be overcome by parents who provide stimulating, supportive, and language-rich experiences for their children.

It is important, however, to recognize the nature of the interrelationships between family background characteristics and more refined family influences. In the development of a model of human development, for example, Stephen J. Ceci and his colleagues (1997) propose that the efficacy of a family influence for academic success is determined to a large degree by a child's family background. They observe that parent-child interactions are the forces that lead to academic performance. In addition, they claim that academic success is achieved only if family background resources can be accessed to maximize the association between family influences and outcomes: relationships between family influences and academic achievement need to take into account the potentially constraining or expanding opportunities provided by children's family backgrounds. Analyses of the relations between families and academic achievement also need to consider children's family structures,

A mother does homework with her children. It is generally acknowledged that family environment is the most powerful influence in determining a child's academic motivation and achievement. HUREWITZ CREATIVE/CORBIS

such as the influence of single-parent families and the effect of sibling structures.

Single-parent families. Research that has examined relationships between changing family structures and students' school-related outcomes, has tended to show that in relation to two-parent families, children in single-parent families have lower academic performance, are more susceptible to peer pressure to engage in deviant behavior, have higher dropout rates from high school, and have greater social and psychological problems. Although the differences are generally small, a number of theories have been proposed to explain the variations. The *no-impact* perspective claims, for example, that the association between changing family structures and children's academic outcomes can be attributed to a combination of family background factors such as parents' education and incomes and the ethnicity/race of the family. Further, some researchers propose that much family structure research is inconclusive because it has failed to differentiate among various types of single-parent families such as whether they result from marital

disruption (divorce or separation), parental death, or a never-married parent. In addition, it is suggested that many studies fail to take into account the timing in a child's life of a family disruption, the duration of the effects of that disruption, and whether the lone parent is the father, mother, or a guardian. An *economic deprivation theory* suggests that economic hardship in single-parent families is likely to require adolescents to work long hours and to take greater responsibility for younger brothers and/or sisters. As a result, these time-consuming activities are likely to be related to lower school achievement. In a *family socialization perspective,* it is proposed that the absence of a parent is probably associated with a decrease in total parental involvement, which in turn is related to poorer school outcomes. It is often claimed that the absence of fathers has particularly negative socialization influences, which may be especially detrimental for boys.

In general, research suggests that differences in the academic achievement of children from single- and two-parent families can be related to changes in the economic circumstances of families and to variations in the quality of parent-child interactions in the different family structures.

Sibling structure. There has been a long-standing fascination with exploring associations between sibling variables, such as the number of children in a family and a child's birth-order position in the family, and children's academic achievement. Typically, these sibling variables have small but significant inverse associations with academic outcomes, especially verbal measures of achievement. A number of theoretical perspectives have been proposed to explain these relationships, including the resource dilution hypothesis and the confluence model.

The *resource dilution hypothesis* proposes that sibling variables are related to the quality and quantity of parent-child interaction in families, and that such variations in parent resources are associated with sibling differences in academic achievement. That is, the greater the number of children in a family or the later the birth-order position, the more those children have to share family resources. As a result, children have lower scores on those academic outcomes affected by the diluted family influences. An alternate perspective is the *confluence model* which proposes that children's academic development is affected by the number of children in families, the age-spacing among children, and whether children are only, first, or last born in families. The model claims, for example, that with short birth intervals between children, increasing birth order is related to lower academic performance. In contrast, with sufficiently large intervals, the birth-order pattern may be mitigated or even reversed.

Generally, sibling research suggests that relationships between sibling structure variables and children's academic performance can be attributed to differences in family background, variations in family economic resources, and variations in the quality of parent-child interactions.

International Research

International research is increasingly examining relationships among family background, family influences, and children's academic outcomes. Kevin Marjoribanks (1996), for example, adopted the Steinberg family model and indicated that measures of family human capital, independent-oriented parenting styles, and parental involvement in children's learning accounted for ethnic group differences in Australian adolescents' academic achievement. In an investigation of U.S. students, Vincent J. Roscigno and James W. Ainsworth-Darnell (1999) show that in relation to academic performance, low social status and African-American students receive less return for family investment in cultural trips and educational resources than do their higher social status and white counterparts. In the Netherlands, Nan Dirk De Graaf and his colleagues (2000) examined associations between parental cultural capital and academic performance. They demonstrate that parents' reading behavior is particularly important in low social status families if their children are to be academically successful. In an analysis in the former Czechoslovakia, Raymond S-K. Wong (1998) concludes that parents use a combination of family resources to affect their children's academic outcomes. As a result, he suggests that it is necessary to include both family background and refined family influence measures when attempting to explain differences in children's achievement outcomes. Kevin Marjoribanks and Mzobanzi Mboya (2000) used such a combination of family measures to examine differences in the academic goal orientations of African students in South Africa. The findings indicate that while measures of refined family influences are related to goal orientations, there continue to be unmediated differences for students from various social status backgrounds and from urban-rural locations. In an examination of differences in the academic performance of U.S. children from immigrant families, Lingxin Hao and Melissa Bonstead-Bruns (1998) investigated within- and between-family influences. They demonstrate that parents in immigrant groups provide differing within-family opportunities and support for their children. In addition, families in some groups are able to use the economic and educational resources of their communities. These between-family factors can have a large impact on children's achievement, even when parents within families are unable to provide appropriate support. These studies reflect the diversity of family research in various international settings, and emphasize the complex nature of the relations between families and academic outcomes.

Future Family Research

The complexity of relationships between family background, family structure, parent-child interactions, and academic achievement indicates the difficult task confronting parents and teachers when attempting to design and implement programs to enhance children's academic outcomes. Parents and teachers may, for example, construct what they consider to be supportive and harmonious learning environments. Children's perceptions of those environments, however, may be affected adversely by experiences related to their family backgrounds and family structures. What is needed are investigations that examine how refined measures of within- and between-family cultural and social capital are related to the academic motivation and achievement of children with different family structures and from various social status and ethnic/racial group backgrounds. Only after such inclusive studies are completed—including a number of international contexts—will there be an advance in understanding of the relationships between families and academic achievement.

See also: BIRTH ORDER; CHILDREN OF ALCOHOLICS; COMMUNICATION: PARENT-CHILD RELATIONSHIPS; DEVELOPMENT: COGNITIVE; FAMILY LITERACY; GIFTED AND TALENTED CHILDREN; HOMESCHOOLING; LEARNING DISORDERS; ONLY CHILDREN; PARENTING STYLES; SCHOOL; SCHOOL PHOBIA AND SCHOOL REFUSAL; SIBLING RELATIONSHIPS; SINGLE-PARENT FAMILIES; SOCIOECONOMIC STATUS

Bibliography

Bloom, B. S. (1964). *Stability and Change in Human Characteristics*. New York: Wiley.

Bloom, B. S. (1980). "The New Directions in Educational Research: Alterable Variables in Education," In *The State of Research on Selected Alterable Variables in Education,* ed. K. D. Sloane and M. L. O'Brien. Chicago: University of Chicago, Department of Education.

Bourdieu, P. (1998). *Practical Reason: On the Theory of Action*. Cambridge, UK: Polity Press.

Ceci, S. J.; Rosenblum, T.; de Bruyn, E.; and Lee, D. Y. (1997). "A Bio-Ecological Model of Human Development." In *Intelligence, Heredity, and Environment,* ed. R. J. Sternberg and E. L. Grigorenko. New York: Cambridge University Press.

Coleman, J. S. (1991). *Parental Involvement in Education*. Washington, DC: U.S. Department of Education.

Coleman, J. S. (1997). "Family, School, and Social Capital." In *International Encyclopedia of the Sociology of Education,* ed. L. J. Saha. Oxford, UK: Pergamon.

Darling, N., and Steinberg, L. (1993). "Parenting Style as Context: An Integrative Model." *Psychological Bulletin* 113:487–496.

De Graaf, N. D.; De Graaf, P. M.; and Kraaykamp, G. (2000). "Parental Cultural Capital and Educational Achievement in The Netherlands." *Sociology of Education* 73:92–111.

Hao, L., and Bonstead-Bruns, M. (1998). "Parent-Child Differences in Educational Expectations and the Academic Achievement of Immigrant and Native Students." *Sociology of Education* 71:175–198.

Kellaghan, T.; Sloane, K.; Alvarez, B.; and Bloom, B. S. (1993). *The Home Environment and School Learning: Promoting Parental Involvement in the Education of Children*. San Francisco: Jossey-Bass.

Marjoribanks, K. (1996). "Ethnicity, Proximal Family Environment, and Young Adolescents' Cognitive Performance." *Journal of Early Adolescence* 16:340–359.

Marjoribanks, K., and Mboya, M. (2000). "Family and Individual Correlates of Academic Goal Orientations: Social Context Differences in South Africa." *Psychological Reports* 87:373–380.

Redding, S. (1999). *Parents and Learning*. Brussels: International Academy of Education.

Roscingo, V. J., and Ainsworth-Darnell, J.W. (1999). "Race, Cultural Capital, and Educational Resources: Persistent Inequalities and Achievement Returns." *Sociology of Education* 72:158–178.

Rosen, B. C. (1959). "Race, Ethnicity, and Achievement Syndrome." *American Sociological Review* 24:47–60.

Rosen, B. C. (1973). "Social Change, Migration and Family Interaction in Brazil." *American Sociological Review* 38:198–212.

Steinberg, L. (1996). *Beyond the Classroom*. New York: Simon & Schuster.

Wong, R. S-K. (1998). "Multidimensional Influences of Family Environment in Education: The Case of Czechoslovakia." *Sociology of Education* 71:1–22.

KEVIN MARJORIBANKS

ACCULTURATION

The term *acculturation* was first used to refer to the changes that take place in cultural groups as a result of contact between them: "Acculturation comprehends those phenomena which result when groups of individuals having different cultures come into continuous first-hand contact, with subsequent changes in the original culture patterns of either or both groups" (Redfield, Linton, and Herskovits 1936). Later, recognizing that there are psychological changes among the group to which they belong, Graves (1967) coined the term *psychological acculturation*. At both the cultural and psychological levels, the term has become widely used to refer to both the *process* of change (over time) and to the longer-term *outcomes* (often termed "adaptation") of the contact.

Acculturation is different from both *enculturation* and *socialization*. The latter terms refer to the process of initial incorporation into one's primary cultural group through an informal enfolding of the individual (enculturation), or by more formal and deliberate teaching (socialization). The former refers to a later involvement with a second culture, which may or may not lead to the incorporation of individuals into it.

Contemporary Issues

Current work on acculturation deals with several issues. First, the process is highly variable and has a number of possible outcomes (Berry 1980) depending on whether we focus on dominant (numerical, powerful) groups or non-dominant ones. One possibility is that the groups and individuals will merge to form a new culture that combines elements of both cultures (usually by the non-dominant group changing to become more like the dominant culture): this possibility has been termed *assimilation*. A second possibility is that the non-dominant group seeks to maintain its culture and avoids further contact with dominant group (termed *separation*). A third way (*integration*) occurs when both groups maintain their own cultures, adapting them so that their continuing contacts enable them to live together in a culturally plural society. The fourth possibility (*marginalization*) occurs when individuals and groups no longer value their own culture and do not seek to participate in the larger society. For many years, it was assumed that assimilation was the only and inevitable way for acculturation to take place; however, the continued existence of many cultural communities within diverse societies demonstrates that the other three ways are also possible. Integration is often the preferred way of acculturating (Berry 2002).

A second issue is whether change following contact will be only in the non-dominant group or will also be evident in the dominant group. Acculturative change is clearly underway in both groups: massive changes have occurred in immigrant-receiving societies, as well as among immigrant groups themselves. Increasingly, acculturation is recognized as a process of mutual accommodation, in which both (all) groups in contact change in the various ways outlined above.

A third issue is whether the process is a short-term one that is over and done with in few years. Historical and current evidence shows that changes continue over generations, starting with those first in contact, and continuing for their children and later generations. Cultural groups often do maintain themselves by way of the process of enculturation, and then continue to adapt to their ongoing intercultural contact, by way of acculturation.

Fourth is the distinction between process and outcome. Acculturation (the process) clearly takes place over time and has a complex course as groups and individuals try out the various ways of acculturating. However, at any one time, groups and individuals can be understood as acculturating in a particular way, with certain consequences. A distinction has been made between two forms of adaptation (Ward 1996): *psychological* and *sociocultural*. The former refers to internal personal qualities (e.g., self-esteem, good mental health, a clear identity); the latter refers to relationships between the individual and the new sociocultural context (e.g., competence in living interculturally, in daily interactions in school and work). Successful acculturation requires both forms of adaptation evidenced by positive psychological and sociocultural adaptation. Integration is not only the most preferred way, but it is also the most successful (Berry 1997).

Family Acculturation

Beyond cultural groups and individuals, acculturation processes and outcomes also take place in families, often with evidence of differences between spouses and between parents and children, in both their preferred ways of acculturating and in the adaptations that are achieved.

Acculturation constitutes a double transition for married immigrants in that both the individuals and the marriage need to adapt to the new culture.

In this context, marital adaptation relates to the mutual accommodation of spouses when each is faced with a new culture, new forms of behavior, and different ways of acculturating. Marital and acculturation problems may be closely linked with each other. Marital problems constitute a major source of stress leading to disagreement between spouses. These problems can make life more difficult in the new culture, or conversely, a happy marriage can lead to a successful adaptation. Marital strain was found to have an impact on both the marital distress and the depressive and psychosomatic symptoms of Indo-Canadian women (Dyal, Rybensky, and Somers 1988). Josephine Naidoo (1985) found that South Asian women in Canada who had supportive husbands experienced fewer feelings of stress. Among Muslim Moroccan immigrants in Montreal, those who were more satisfied in their marriages had less psychological stress (El Haïli and Lasry 1997).

Research suggests that marital conflict does not necessarily increase due to immigration. Immigrant Jewish couples in Israel were found not to experience more marital tension than Israeli-born couples. In fact, couples who stayed in their native land expressed more conflict than immigrant couples in domains such as whether the wife should work outside the home and the division of labor in the home; the two groups did not differ in terms of decision making in the home (Hartman and Hartman 1986). Hispanic American couples also did not differ from European American couples in the frequency of major marital conflict (Lindahl and Malik 1999).

In a study on the acculturation and adaptation of married Turkish immigrants in Toronto, Canada, Bilge Ataca (1998) introduced marital adaptation as a separate facet of the overall adaptation of immigrants. The findings showed that the marital relationship did not experience more difficulty due to the problems of living in a new culture. Immigrant couples were not found to be different from Turkish couples in Turkey and European Canadian couples in terms of marital adaptation. Hence, it seems as if immigration increases solidarity between spouses by leaving them to resolve problems on their own, thereby, improving the marital relationship (Hartman and Hartman 1986).

Overall, Turkish immigrant couples strongly adopted the separation strategy more than other acculturation strategies. They placed high value on maintaining their cultural identity and characteristics, and resisted relations with the larger society. Couples of high and low socioeconomic status (SES), however, showed different preferences. Those of high SES preferred integration and assimilation to a greater, and separation to a lesser extent than those of low SES (Ataca 1998).

When marital adaptation was examined in light of acculturation attitudes, marginalization showed a significant impact on psychological and marital adaptation (Ataca and Berry under review). Marginalization brought about not only negative psychological outcomes, but also impeded the couple's adaptation. When alienated from both the culture of origin and the culture of settlement, individuals may develop a marginal state of mind in which it is cumbersome to accommodate the spouse. However, the established link in the literature between marginalization and psychological difficulty held true only for those of lower SES. Adopting the marginalization strategy (as defined above), only when coupled with low levels of education, produced a negative effect on psychological and marital well-being. The feelings of not belonging to either culture, loss, isolation, and loneliness, coupled with few resources such as low proficiency in English, low wages, and few appropriate skills in the new cultural context, may trigger feelings of helplessness and hopelessness, and thereby lead to the most adverse effects. This state of mind may also promote more marital discord.

Ataca's (1998) study also revealed a major effect of SES on the marital relationship. Immigrant couples of low SES had better marital adaptation than those of high SES (Ataca and Berry 2002). Because most high SES women are employed outside the home, they can be more independent and enjoy greater autonomy and freedom than their counterparts in the low SES group. This may cause conflicts between spouses in the high SES group because it weakens the husband's traditional authority. In contrast, the traditional roles are the norm and, therefore, are more prevalent in the low SES group. Most women are not employed outside the home; they are dependent on and submissive to their husbands. They do not challenge the husbands' authority; this prevents tension in the marital relationship. In general, with networks of friends and relatives less available, the spouses depend more on each other for support as they become acculturated. Marital support and adaptation in this context were also related to acculturation attitudes. The stronger the bond between spouses with greater support and satisfaction in marriage, the more they chose to cherish the culture of origin and resist relations with the larger society (Ataca 1998).

Intergenerational conflicts and acculturation preferences of parents and children have also attracted attention in the area of family acculturation. One study found that young Cuban Americans adopted the values of the larger American society more than their parents, whereas the parents remained more attached to their heritage cultures. These differences in acculturation led to greater intergenerational conflicts; parents lost control over their adolescents who strived for autonomy and rejected the traditional Cuban ways (see Szapocznik and Kurtines 1993). Jean S. Phinney, Anthony Ong, and Tanya Madden (2000) studied intergenerational value discrepancies in family obligations among both immigrant and nonimmigrant families in the United States. In the Armenian and Vietnamese families, the intergenerational discrepancy was greater in families who had longer residence and a U.S.-born adolescent, while Mexican families did not show such a difference. The Vietnamese had the largest discrepancy compared to the other immigrant groups. Such discrepancies, however, were not found to be greater in immigrant families; European and African American families did not differ from Armenian and Mexican American families. Phinney and colleagues (2000) concluded that value discrepancies between parents and adolescents are not necessarily related to immigration, but may reflect a universal tendency in which parents strive to maintain the existing norms, and adolescents question their obligations.

Andrew J. Fuligni and colleagues studied attitudes toward authority, autonomy, family obligations, and perceptions of family conflict and cohesion among American adolescents with Filipino, Chinese, Mexican, Central and South American, and European backgrounds (Fuligni 1998; Fuligni, Tseng, and Lam 1999). Asian and Latin American adolescents had stronger beliefs and greater expectations about their obligation to assist, respect, and support their families than did European American adolescents. This finding was consistent across the adolescents' generation; the same ethnic differences held true for the third-generation adolescents (Fuligni et al. 1999). However, in terms of beliefs

and expectations about parental authority and autonomy, Fuligni (1998) found that only Chinese, Filipino, and Mexican American adolescents who come from immigrant families followed traditional norms of agreeing with parents and placing less emphasis on behavioral autonomy. Adolescents from native-born families were similar to European American adolescents in their beliefs and expectations. Hence, over generations, Asian and Latin American adolescents displayed influences of both their culture of origin by the endorsement of family obligations and of the American culture by the desire for greater autonomy (Fuligni et al. 1999).

Conclusion

Acculturation is a highly variable process for both the cultural groups in contact and for their individual members; it is also a complex situation for spouses and for parents and their children. Thus, no easy generalizations can be made. However, in most studies, people tend to prefer to acculturate first by integrating and then by separation. Both of these involve the maintenance, to some extent, of their heritage culture. This pattern of preference is also the most successful for couples and families, especially when spouses and parents and children agree on how to acculturate. At the same time, some evidence supports involvement with, and acquisition of competence in the larger society. However, if this is done at the expense of heritage culture loss, it can be personally maladaptive and disruptive to marital and family relationships.

See also: IMMIGRATION; INTERGENERATIONAL TRANSMISSION; SOCIALIZATION; SOCIOECONOMIC STATUS

Bibliography

Ataca, B. (1998). "Psychological, Sociocultural, and Marital Adaptation of Turkish Immigrants in Canada." Ph.D. dissertation. Kingston: Queen's University.

Ataca, B., and Berry, J. W. (2002). "Psychological, Sociocultural, and Marital Adaptation of Turkish Immigrants." *International Journal of Psychology* 37:13–26.

Ataca, B. and Berry, J. W. (under review). "Comparative Study of Acculturation and Adaptation Among Turkish Immigrants in Canada." *Journal of Cross-Cultural Psychology.*

Berry, J. W. (1980). "Acculturation as Varieties of Adaptation." In *Acculturation: Theory, Models, and Some New Findings,* ed. A. Padilla. Boulder, CO: Westview Press.

Berry, J. W. (1997). "Immigration, Acculturation and Adaptation." *Applied Psychology: An International Review* 46:5–8.

Berry, J. W. (2002). "Conceptual Approaches to Acculturation." In *Acculturation,* ed. G. Marin, P. Balls-Organista, and K. Chung. Washington, DC: APA Books.

Dyal, J. A.; Rybensky, L.; and Somers, M. (1988). "Marital and Acculturative Strain Among Indo-Canadian and Euro-Canadian Women." In *Ethnic Psychology: Research and Practice with Immigrants, Refugees, Native Peoples, Ethnic Groups, and Sojourners,* ed. J. W. Berry and R. C. Annis. Lisse, Netherlands: Swets and Zeitlinger.

El Haïli, S., and Lasry, J. (1998). "Pouvoir Conjugal, Roles Sexuels, et Harmonie Maritale Chez des Couples Immigrants Marocains a Montreal." *Revue Quebecoise de Psychologie* 19:1–18.

Fuligni, A. J. (1998). "Authority, Autonomy, and Parent-Adolescent Conflict and Cohesion: A Study of Adolescents from Mexican, Chinese, Filipino, and European Backgrounds." *Developmental Psychology* 34:782–792.

Fuligni, A. J.; Tseng, V.; and Lam, M. (1999). "Attitudes Toward Family Obligations Among American Adolescents with Asian, Latin American, and European Backgrounds." *Child Development* 70:1030–1044.

Graves, T. (1967). "Psychological Acculturation in a Tri-Ethnic Community." *Southwestern Journal of Anthropology* 23:337–350.

Hartman, M., and Hartman, H. (1986). "International Migration and Household Conflict." *Journal of Comparative Family Studies* 17:131–138.

Lindahl, K. M., and Malik, N. M. (1999). "Marital Conflict, Family Processes, and Boys' Externalizing Behavior in Hispanic American and European American Families." *Journal of Clinical Child Psychology* 28:12–24.

Naidoo, J. C. (1985). "A Cultural Perspective on the Adjustment of South Asian Women in Canada." In *From a Different Perspective: Studies of Behavior Across Cultures,* ed. I. R. Lagunes and Y. H. Poortinga. Lisse, Netherlands: Swets and Zeitlinger.

Phinney, J. S.; Ong, A.; and Madden T. (2000). "Cultural Values and Intergenerational Value Discrepancies in Immigrant and Nonimmigrant Families." *Child Development* 71:528–539.

Redfield, R.; Linton, R.; and Herskovits, M. J. (1936). "Memorandum for the Study of Acculturation." *American Anthropologist* 38:149–152.

Szapocznik, J., and Kurtines, W. M. (1993). "Family Psychology and Cultural Diversity: Opportunities for Theory, Research, and Application." *American Psychologist* 48:400–407.

Ward, C. (1996). "Acculturation." In *Handbook of Intercultural Training,* ed. D. Landis and R. Bhagat. Thousand Oaks, CA: Sage.

BILGE ATACA
JOHN W. BERRY

ACQUIRED IMMUNODEFICIENCY SYNDROME (AIDS)

Acquired Immunodeficiency Syndrome (AIDS) is caused by the human immunodeficiency virus (HIV), which destroys the cells in the human body that combat infections. Although recent medical advances have caused a shift from the mindset of a terminal disease to one of a chronic, manageable condition in some areas of the world, this new approach brings challenges of its own, as the disease is eventually fatal (Ferri et. al 1997). HIV has brought about a global epidemic far more extensive than what was predicted even a decade ago. The issue of HIV/AIDS is not only relevant to medical documentation, but is complex and highly politically charged, affecting all communities regardless of race, age, or sexual orientation (Ginsberg 1995). At the end of the year 2000, it was estimated that there were 36.1 million adults and children living with HIV/AIDS, the vast majority of whom live in the developing world, with more than twenty-five million living in the continent of Africa ("Global Summary of the HIV/AIDS Epidemic, 2000" 2001).

History

The epidemic began in the late 1970s and early 1980s in sub-Saharan Africa, Latin America, the Caribbean, Western Europe, North America, Australia, and New Zealand. In the late 1980s, the epidemic continued to spread to North Africa and the Middle East, South and Southeast Asia, East Asia, and the Pacific. Only in the late 1990s did the epidemic spread significantly to Eastern Europe and Central Asia. (See Table 1 for a summary of HIV/AIDS statistics and features, including the primary mode(s) of transmission in each region.) Since 1981, the AIDS pandemic has brought sexually transmitted diseases to the center of medical

TABLE 1

HIV/AIDS statistics and features		
Region	Main mode(s) of transmission* for adults # living with HIV/AIDS	Epidemic started
Australia & New Zealand	MSM	Late 1970s – Early 1980s
Caribbean	hetero, MSM	Late 1970s – Early 1980s
East Asia & Pacific	IDU, hetero, MSM	Late 1980s
Eastern Europe & Central Asia	IDU	Early 1990s
Latin America	MSM, IDU, hetero	Late 1970s – Early 1980s
North Africa & Middle East	hetero, IDU	Late 1980s
North America	MSM, IDU, hetero	Late 1970s – Early 1980s
South & South-East Asia	hetero, IDU	Late 1980s
Sub-Saharan Africa	hetero	Late 1970s – Early 1980s

*Hetero (heterosexual transmission), IDU (transmission through intravenous drug use), MSM (sexual transmission among men who have sex with men).
The proportion of adults (15 to 49 years of age) living with HIV/AIDS.

and social consciousness. Indeed, "not since the world-wide pandemic of swine influenza in 1918 have we faced a public health emergency of such tragic magnitude" (Brandt 1988, p. 151).

In response to this mysterious ailment, articles began to appear in newspapers and magazines in the United States that described an illness unofficially identified as gay-related immunodeficiency (GRID). As early as 1982, however, it became clear to the researchers at the Centers for Disease Control (CDC), that the disease was not exclusively a gay syndrome. Other groups began to get the disease: heterosexuals from sub-Saharan Africa, Haitians, prostitutes, and women who had sex with bisexual males (Tebble 1986).

The human T-cell lymphotropic virus (HTLV-III) was isolated as the retrovirus responsible for causing AIDS in 1984 (Getzel 1992; Levenson 1996). A retrovirus is a type of virus that replicates mutant strains, and then infects other cells (Gant 1998). "The virus, called HTLV-III by the Americans and LAV by the French—would eventually be designated as HIV" (Bethel 1995, p. 69). HIV-I (the most common type found worldwide) and HIV-II (found mostly in West Africa), both responsible for AIDS, are rapid replicators. The newer strains of HIV that were identified in the late 1990s are stronger and more resistant to medications.

Modes of Transmission

HIV is transmitted only through the intimate exchange of body fluids, specifically blood, semen, vaginal fluid, and mother's milk (Dane and Miller

1990). HIV is sometimes passed perinatally from mother to fetus, or through breastfeeding (Mulvihill 1996). HIV levels in the bloodstream are typically highest when a person is first infected and again in the late stages of the illness. High-risk behaviors include unprotected anal and vaginal intercourse (without condom) and intravenous drug use. Before blood screening began in 1986, the virus was also being contracted from transfusions and blood-clotting agents.

Testing and Diagnosis

One year after the isolation of HIV, the ELISA (enzyme-linked immunosorbent assay) test was developed, allowing detection of HIV antibodies well before the onset of any clinical manifestations, creating an opportunity for preventive therapy against opportunistic infections (Bellutta 1995). The required pre- and post-test counseling for the ELISA tests has been shown to help people to make informed decisions, cope better with their potential health condition, lead more positive lives, and prevent further transmission of HIV. Because the number of false positives is high, a positive ELISA test must be confirmed by a more specific test, the Western blot, which detects specific antibodies to a particular pathogen (Gant 1998). In many countries, home tests were approved in mid-1990s, and the oral collection (OraSure) for HIV antibody test was approved by the Food and Drug Administration (FDA) in the United States in 1996. These tests are not very reliable, and support such as pre- and post-test counseling is not available ("Fact Sheet 1 HIV/AIDS: The Infection" 2000).

The advent of HIV testing brought with it the need for guidelines surrounding the confidentiality of test results and anonymity of the individual during the testing process to protect that person against social stigmatization and economic exploitation. These measures are also intended to encourage widespread testing, so that medical care and support services can be instituted early in the process.

HIV attacks and destroys CD4 T-lymphocytes, which assist in the regulation of the entire immune system. CD-4 lymphocytes, also called CD-4 cells, T4cells, and CD-4 lymphocytes, are a type of blood cell important to the immune system. The loss of these cells reduces the system's ability to fight infection, increasing the risk of opportunistic infections, or infections that can take hold because a person's immune system is weak (Gant 1998). AIDS can be described as a continuum that begins with infection by the HIV virus leading to decreasing numbers of CD-4 cells and eventual progress to opportunistic diseases (Bellutta 1995).

Symptoms

HIV ranges from asymptomatic infection to severe forms of the disease (Aronstein and Thompson 1998). There is no dormant phase of the HIV infection. Rather, the body and the virus are locked in a pitched battle from the beginning. Every day the viral intruder produces a billion copies of itself, all intent on the destruction of CD-4 cells (Gorman 1996). With immune deficiency, the HIV-infected person becomes susceptible to opportunistic organisms that normally would be harmless (Aronstein and Thompson 1998).

Kaposi's sarcoma is a malignant tumor affecting the skin and mucous membranes and is usually characterized by the formation of pink to reddish-brown or bluish patches. In general, these tumors are quite rare, slow-growing, vascular in nature, and most commonly affect elderly men of Mediterranean descent. In the early AIDS cases, however, the tumors affected young white males in the United States and were found to grow and disseminate rapidly. Overwhelming infection and respiratory failure due to pneumocystis carinii pneumonia (PCP), a form of pneumonia caused by a microorganism that attacks the inner fibrous tissues of the lungs, were the leading causes of death in early AIDS cases (Bellutta 1995).

HIV-infected persons often experience acute symptoms including night sweats, sore throat, headache, fever, muscular pains, thrush, wasting, and rashes. It is estimated that more than half of the people diagnosed with AIDS at some time will display central nervous system dysfunction resulting from HIV infiltration of brain structures. The growing crisis of AIDS-related cognitive impairment ranges from mild cognitive disturbance to moderate and severe AIDS dementia complex (ADC).

Neuropsychological symptoms are typically more pronounced in the end stage of the disease; however, decreased concentration, memory loss, and confusion may be the first symptoms of AIDS.

Treatment

Researchers persist in their attempts to develop effective medical treatments to reduce the suffering of those who are HIV-infected or seriously ill with AIDS. Encouraging early treatment is crucial for persons that test HIV positive (Levenson 1996). HIV treatments include two components: first, prophylactic drugs to prevent and treat opportunistic infections, and, second, combination or three-drug combinations (also known as drug cocktails) to directly reduce replication of the virus (Linsk and Keigher 1997). Where available, the antiretroviral drug combinations (protease inhibitor combined with two or more Reverse Transcriptase inhibitors) require strict adherence to a complex drug regimen. The potential benefits and risks of the combinations are great. Many people taking drug combinations have been found to have reduced viral load to levels below the detection limits of current viral load tests, therefore appearing to be no longer HIV positive. However, the virus can easily become resistant to the medications if the regimen is not followed, often causing the viral load to increase. Many people infected with HIV are finding that eating a healthful diet, getting sufficient rest, and drinking little alcohol increase their level of functioning.

HIV/AIDS prevention through education, as well as safe-sex information, distribution of condoms, and needle exchange programs worldwide have greatly decreased the transmission of new HIV cases in many parts of the world since 1990. In addition, officials from many health organizations, including the World Health Organization (WHO), and governments from various countries, have been collaborating in an effort to address the urgent need for an HIV vaccine. Since 1991, these constituents have worked to prepare for HIV vaccine efficacy trials. In February of 1999, Thailand became the first developing nation to announce a three-year, Phase III vaccine field trial, AIDSVAX. A Phase III trial is done to determine if a vaccine is effective in protecting against infection or disease and is an important step in the evaluation process leading to licensure.

Psychosocial Issues

In the initial years of the epidemic, the complex clinical treatment dynamics, negative public attitudes, and limited personal and community resources available to people with AIDS challenged the advocacy and discharge-planning skills of many professionals (Mantell, Shulman, Belmont, and Spivak 1989). Repeated exposure to death, homophobia, negative attitudes about addictive lifestyles, antisocial behaviors, and fear of AIDS contagion have added stress to professionals employed in the health arena and supporting services (Wade, Stein, and Beckerman 1995).

Partially because disadvantaged populations are disproportionately affected by HIV/AIDS, there is often a stigma attached to the diagnosis (Diaz and Kelly 1991; Reamer 1993). People within the United States have been victims of hate crimes due to their HIV positive status. Within many countries in Africa, people have been stoned to death, or disowned when an HIV positive status was disclosed ("Fact Sheet 6 HIV/AIDS: Fear, Stigma, and Isolation" 2000). Fear and prejudice have been an integral part of this epidemic since its inception, often exacerbating already difficult situations for those dealing with the diagnosis of HIV/AIDS (Ryan and Rowe 1988). Responses to this difficult reality include depression, claiming illness is something other than HIV/AIDS, withdrawal from loved ones and work environments, and even suicide (Ellenberg 1998).

Global Implications

The challenges of HIV vary enormously from place to place, depending on how far and fast the virus is spreading, whether those infected have started to fall ill or die in large numbers, and what sort of access they have to medical care. In all parts of the world except sub-Saharan Africa, more men than women are infected with HIV and dying of AIDS. Men's behavior—often influenced by harmful cultural beliefs about masculinity—makes them the prime casualties of the epidemic. Male behavior also contributes to HIV infections in women, who often have less power to determine where, when, and how sex takes place ("Global Summary of the HI/AIDS Epidemic" 2001). Men's enormous potential to make a difference when it comes to curbing HIV transmission, caring for infected family members, and looking after orphans and other survivors of the epidemic has been noted in many countries.

As the number of children orphaned by HIV/AIDS rises, some calls have been heard for an increase in institutional care for children. This solution is impracticably expensive. In Ethiopia, for example, keeping a child in an orphanage costs about U.S. $500 a year, more than three times the national income per person. One solution developed by church groups in Zimbabwe is to recruit community members to visit orphans in the homes where they live—either with foster parents, grandparents or other relatives, or in child-headed households. Households caring for orphans are provided with clothing, blankets, school fees, seeds, and fertilizer as necessary, and communities contribute to activities such as farming communal fields and generating income to support the program. This community-driven approach to orphan support has been reproduced all over Zimbabwe, and replicas are now sprouting up in other African countries ("Global Summary of the HIV/AIDS Epidemic, 2000" 2001).

Internationally, a campaign by AIDS activists succeeded in 2000 in getting drug companies to lower prices for the antiretroviral medications. But even at prices 90 percent lower than in the United States, drugs are still beyond the reach of most Africans. There is a debate among those working on AIDS in Africa and elsewhere about whether the current emphasis on drugs is taking the spotlight off prevention, where many feel it should be. Apart from the staggering costs of drugs, world health leaders say huge sums of money are needed just for basic AIDS prevention and care in Africa and other developing nations ("Confronting AIDS" 2001).

UNAIDS and WHO now estimate that the number of people living with HIV or AIDS at the end of the year 2000 stands at 36.1 million, 50 percent higher than what the WHO's Global Programme on AIDS projected in 1991 ("Global Summary of the HIV/AIDS Epidemic, 2000" 2001). The unique situation in various countries and parts of the world will be presented in order to catch a glimpse of the diverse face of HIV/AIDS in the early twenty-first century. In each area, access to health care and medication, HIV transmission, and political responses will be considered.

Botswana. The first AIDS cases in Botswana were reported in 1985. An estimated 36 percent of adults were HIV positive as of 2000. The highest HIV prevalence rate is among twenty to thirty-nine year olds. An estimated 300,000 adults and 26,000 children under age five are living with HIV/AIDS. The mean age of death due to AIDS in Botswana is twenty-five in females and thirty-five in males, the reproductive and economically productive years.

Unlike many other African countries, Botswana has a strong and developed infrastructure that provides people with such social services as education and health care. The government, as well as many companies, are trying to provide antiretrovirals to all who need them, regardless of their ability to pay. Well-supplied hospitals and adequate foreign reserves make it easier for Botswana than for other African countries to provide the drugs. But even here, where the annual per capita income is $3,700 a year (high for Africa), many people remain poor. In the next ten years AIDS will slice 20 percent off the government budget, erode development gains, and bring about a 13 percent reduction in the income of the poorest households ("Global AIDS Program Countries" 2001).

The hope of treatment encourages people to be tested, and testing is considered crucial for prevention. Even as efforts to treat people get underway, prevention remains the highest priority, including visits to local bars to show people how to prevent HIV using male and female condoms and going to schools to keep the next generation HIV-free.

Brazil. HIV began to spread in Brazil in the 1980s. At of the end of the year 2000, slightly more than 196,000 cases of AIDS had been reported in Brazil, the largest number in South America. Brazil is unique among the Latin American countries in that it provides those people with HIV infection antiretroviral therapy free of charge if they meet the national medical guidelines for treatment.

An estimated 12,898 pregnant women had HIV infection in 1998, while 536,920 people between the ages of fifteen and twenty-nine were infected with HIV. Between the years 1978 and 1999, 29,929 children were orphaned in Brazil due to AIDS. Although rates of AIDS are decreasing among men who have sex with men and injection drug users, the rate of heterosexual transmission of AIDS is increasing. In many municipalities, especially along the coast, the ratio of AIDS between men and women is approaching 1:1 ("Global AIDS Program Countries" 2001).

South Africa. The HIV/AIDS epidemic started in sub-Saharan Africa in the late 1970s and early 1980s. Half of all HIV positive people in the nine southern African countries hardest hit by the pandemic live in South Africa. The government estimates that 4.2 million persons, and 19.9 percent of the adult population, are infected with HIV, and by 2010 adult HIV prevalence could reach 25 percent, similar to infection rates in neighboring Zimbabwe and Botswana. In 1998 South Africa had approximately 100,000 AIDS orphans, and by 2008, 1.6 million children will have been orphaned by AIDS ("Global AIDS Program Countries" 2001).

Reasons cited for high rates of HIV/AIDS in South Africa are the realities of migrant labor, high prevalence of sexually transmitted disease, and presence of multiple strains of the disease. Exacerbating factors include a society in denial about an overwhelming epidemic that is ravaging the lives and bodies of many persons within a context of poverty and a thriving commercial sex work industry.

Families are especially hard hit by HIV/AIDS in South Africa. One in five pregnant women in South African clinics is HIV positive. Studies have shown that treating pregnant African women with the drug AZT significantly reduced the risk that they would transmit the virus to their babies. However, if these women then breastfed their infants, the risks of transmission rebounded, making it more urgent than ever to find acceptable alternatives to breastfeeding among infected African women. The AIDS virus accounts for most pediatric cases in hospitals. The worst is yet to come because most of the infected have not yet developed AIDS symptoms, and many still feed an infection spiral that is creating about 1,700 new cases every day.

Thailand. Thailand has experienced a rapidly escalating and severe HIV epidemic since 1988. Among the sixty million inhabitants of Thailand, as many as 800,000 people are currently believed to be living with HIV. Despite innovative and persistent prevention efforts, HIV continues to spread rapidly, particularly among Thailand's population of injection drug users (IDUs). Methadone treatment, education, counseling on HIV prevention, and easy access to sterile needles have helped to slow the epidemic. Yet, among IDUs in Bangkok, 6 percent continue to become infected each year.

As part of the Thai National Plan for HIV vaccine research, the Bangkok Metropolitan Administration is leading the three-year collaborative research trial to evaluate the ability of AIDSVAX to prevent HIV infection among uninfected IDUs in Bangkok, Thailand. For people infected with HIV, the Thai government and health officials feel very strongly that treatment should follow the protocols that they have established for their country. Therefore, the triple drug therapies currently being used elsewhere are not considered feasible for use in Thailand, not only because of cost constraints, but also because of issues related to the complexity of the regimen, the necessary follow-up and monitoring of patients, and tolerance to the therapies.

United States. In the early 1980s, a number of unexplainable phenomena began to surface across the United States. As the incidents of pneumocystic pneumonia and Kaposi's sarcoma were reported to the Center for Disease Control, a pattern began to emerge. The CDC first published a report reflecting these observations in June of 1981, identifying all of the people demonstrating these symptoms as gay men (Black 1985). In the absence of services in established medical centers and social agencies, many gay men and lesbians joined with activists to establish community-based AIDS service organizations to meet the needs of people affected by HIV. The Names Project Quilt, or AIDS Quilt, has been an important mechanism for people within the United States to recognize the lives of those who have died of HIV/AIDS. The quilt was first displayed in Washington, DC, in 1987, and then in its entirety for the last time in October of 1996, with more than 30,000 panels.

In the United States, as of December 2000, 774,467 AIDS cases had been reported including

A Thai toddler orphaned by AIDS. Many communites are struggling with how to care for the rising number of children orphaned by AIDS. JEREMY HORNER/CORBIS

640,022 cases among men and 134,441 among women. The main modes of transmission for adults living with HIV/AIDS were men having sex with men, intravenous drug users, and heterosexual transmission. In the United States HIV and AIDS have disproportionately affected the most disadvantaged and stigmatized groups in American society (Barbour 1994). Analyzed by race, 330,160 AIDS cases have been reported among whites, 292,522 among blacks, and 141,694 among Hispanics.

In early 1998, AIDS deaths in the United States dropped by 47 percent. "In recent years, the rate of decline for both cases and deaths began to slow, and in 1999, the annual number of AIDS cases appears to be leveling, while the decline in AIDS deaths has slowed considerably" ("A Glance at the

HIV Epidemic" 2001, p. 3). Overall, HIV prevalence rose risen slightly, mainly because antiretroviral therapy is keeping HIV positive people alive longer. Thousands of infections are still occurring through unsafe sex between men. In this era in which few young gay men have seen friends die of AIDS, and some mistakenly view antiretrovirals as a cure, there is growing complacency about the HIV risk, judging from reports of increased sexual risk behavior among this population.

Conclusion

The family is greatly affected in all cases of HIV/AIDS, regardless of where the person might live. Issues such as safe sex practices, planning for care of children during parents' illness and after death, dealing with prejudices and unmet expectations within the family unit, coming out as a homosexual, admitting to intravenous drug use, or to sexual activity with multiple partners, are often on the forefront during this difficult time. Until a vaccine is approved and widely disseminated, people must avoid risky behaviors in order to curb the spread of this devastating disease. One of the primary issues is to support extended family members who are taking in children orphaned by AIDS, while grieving the great loss of loved ones.

See also: CHRONIC ILLNESS; DEATH AND DYING; DEMENTIA; FAMILY PLANNING; HOSPICE; SEXUALITY; SEXUALITY EDUCATION; SEXUALLY TRANSMITTED DISEASES; STRESS

Bibliography

Aronstein, D. M., and Thompson, B. J., eds. (1998). *HIV and Social Work: A Practitioner's Guide.* Binghamton, NY: The Harrington Park Press.

Barbour, R. S. (1984). "Social Work Education: Tackling the Theory-Practice Dilemma." *The British Journal of Social Work* 14:557–577.

Bellutta, H. P. (1995). "AIDS." In *Encyclopedia of Marriage and the Family,* ed. D. Levinson. New York: Simon and Schuster Macmillan.

Bethel, E. R. (1995). *AIDS: Readings on a Global Crisis.* Boston: Allyn and Bacon.

Black, D. (1985). *The Plague Years: A Chronicle of AIDS the Epidemic of our Times.* New York: Simon and Schuster.

Brandt, A. (1988). "The Approaching Epidemic." *Journal of Social Work and Human Sexuality* 6:151–154.

Broder, S., and Gallo, R. C. (1984). "A Pathogenic Retrovirus (HTLV-III) Linked to AIDS." *New England Journal of Medicine* 311:1292–1297.

Dane, B. O., and Miller, S. O. (1990). "AIDS and Dying: The Teaching Challenge." *Journal of Teaching in Social Work* 4:85–100.

Diaz, Y. E., and Kelly, J. A. (1991). "AIDS-Related Training in United States Schools of Social Work." *Social Work* 36(1):38–42.

Ellenberg, L.W. (1998). "HIV Risk Assessment in Mental Health Settings." In *HIV and Social Work: A Practitioner's Guide,* ed. David M. Aronstein and Bruce J. Thompson. New York: The Harrington Park Press.

Ferri, R.; Fontaine, M.; Gallego, S. M.; Grossman, H. A.; Lynch, V. J.; Shiloh-Cryer, A.; Zevin, B.; and Zizzo, W., eds. (1997). "AIDS Deaths Drop 19% in United States, in Part from New Treatment." *HIV Frontline: A Newsletter for Professionals who Counsel People Living with HIV* 30:6.

Gant, L. M. (1998). "Essential Facts Every Social Worker Needs to Know." In *HIV and Social Work: A Practitioner's Guide,* ed. David M. Aronstein and Bruce J. Thompson. New York: The Harrington Park Press.

Getzel, G. S. (1992). "AIDS and Social Work: A Decade Later." *Social Work in Healthcare* 17(2):1–9.

Ginsberg, L. (1995). "AIDS." *Social Work Almanac,* 2nd edition. Washington, DC: NASW.

Gorman, C. (1996). "The Exorcists." *Time* 148:64–66.

Levenson, D. (1996). "Home Testing: Boon to the AIDS Battle?" *NASW Press* (September):3.

Linsk, N. L., and Keigher, S. M. (1997). "Of Magic Bullets and Social Justice: Emerging Challenges of Recent Advances in AIDS Treatment." *Health and Social Work* 22:70–74.

Mantell, J. E.; Shulman, L. C.; Belmont, M. F.; and Spivak, H. B. (1989). "Social Workers Respond to the AIDS Epidemic in an Acute Care Hospital." *Health and Social Work* 14:41–51.

Mulvihill, C. K. (1996). "AIDS Education for College Students: Review and Proposal for Research-Based Curriculum." *AIDS Education and Prevention* 8:11–25.

Reamer, F. G. (1993). "AIDS and Social Work: The Ethics and Civil Liberties Agenda." *Social Work,* 38(4): 412–419.

Ryan, C. C., and Rowe, M. J. (1988). "AIDS: Legal and Ethical Issues." *Social Casework,* 69(6):324–333.

Tebble, W. E. M. (1986). "AIDS and AIDS Related Conditions: Effects on Gay Men and Issues for Social Workers." *Australian Social Work* 39:13–18.

Wade, K.; Stein, E.; and Beckerman, N. (1995). "Tuberculosis and AIDS: The Impact on the Hospital Social Worker." *Social Work in Health Care* 21:29–41.

Other Resources

"Confronting AIDS." (2001). NewsHour with Jim Lehrer Transcript Online Focus. Available from http://www.pbs.org/newshour/bb/health/jan-june01/aids_2-21.html.

"Fact Sheet 1 HIV/AIDS: The Infection." (2000). World Health Organization. Available from http://www-int/whosis/statistics/factsheets-hiv-nurses/fact-sheet-1/index.html.

"Fact Sheet 6 HIV/AIDS: Fear, Stigma and Isolation." (2000). World Health Organization. Available from http://www-int/whosis/statistics/factsheets-hiv-nurses/fact-sheet-6/index.html.

"A Glance at the HIV Epidemic." (2001). Centers for Disease Control, Atlanta, Georgia. Available from http://www.cdc.gov/hiv/aidsupdate.htm.

"Global AIDS Program Countries." (2001). Center for Disease Control, Atlanta, Georgia. Available from http://www.cdc.gov/nchstp/od/gap/text/countries/south_africa.htm.

"Global AIDS Program Countries." (2001). Center for Disease Control, Atlanta, Georgia. Available from http://www.cdc.gov/nchstp/od/gap/text/countries/brazil.htm.

"Global Summary of the HIV/AIDS Epidemic, 2000." (2001). Joint United Nations Programme on HIV/AIDS and World Health Organization, Geneva, Switzerland. Available from http://www.unaids.org/was/2000/wad00/files/WAD_epidemic.html.

HOPE HASLAM STRAUGHAN

ADOLESCENT PARENTHOOD

Adolescent parenting refers primarily to women and men nineteen years or younger who give birth to and elect to parent a child. Although most adolescent pregnancies are unintended, an increasing number of pregnant adolescents choose to continue the pregnancy and become parents. Estimates suggest that each year, slightly more than 10 percent of all births worldwide—almost 15 million—are to adolescent women (Alan Guttmacher Institute 1996). Adolescent childbearing is more common in developing countries, where about one in every six births is to women under twenty.

At any age, pregnancy and first parenthood produce changes that require adaptation. For adolescents, three transitions occur simultaneously. They must adjust to changes in their family-of-origin relationships during adolescence, changes in their physical and cognitive abilities, and changes in their social reality. Add to this the changes caused by premature parenthood, and the potential for stress increases. Typically, adolescent parents experience stress from five sources: relationships with the self, partners, parents, nonfamily institutions, and intergenerational relations. Thus, the adolescent parent faces a series of competing developmental tasks that increase the likelihood of stress.

Trends in the United States

Despite a modest reduction in the pregnancy rate among sexually experienced fifteen- to nineteen-year-olds since the late 1980s, nearly one-fifth of sexually active adolescent females become pregnant each year in the United States (Darroch and Singh 1999). Nationwide, the estimated adolescent pregnancy rate in 1996 (the most recent year for which adolescent pregnancy rates can be computed) was 98.7 pregnancies per 1,000 women aged fifteen through nineteen, down 15 percent since peaking in 1991 at 116.5 and lower than in any year since 1976 (Ventura et al. 2000). Although about 25 percent of the overall decline in the pregnancy rate resulted from increased abstinence, approximately 75 percent was due to more effective contraceptive practice. Nevertheless, nearly one million adolescents between fifteen and nineteen become pregnant each year, and nearly two-thirds of these pregnancies are to eighteen to nineteen year olds (Alan Guttmacher Institute 1999).

Among those girls aged fifteen to nineteen who become pregnant, just over half give birth annually (Darroch and Singh 1999). Consistent with the steady decline in the pregnancy rate, a parallel drop was observed in the birthrate. For example, 51.1 per 1,000 women in this age group years gave birth in 1998, 18 percent lower than in 1991 when the rate reached its recent peak of 62.1 (Ventura et al. 2000). This declining birthrate represents a smaller decrease for those eighteen to nineteen

(13% drop to 82 per 1,000) than for women aged fifteen to seventeen (21% drop to 30.4 per 1,000). Overall, nearly two-thirds of births to teenagers occur in the later years of adolescence.

Although the prevalence of adolescent pregnancy and childbearing in the United States declined in the 1990s, substantial racial variations exist. In 1996, whites were nearly 2.5 times less likely to become pregnant (66.1 per 1,000 fifteen-to nineteen-year-olds) than Hispanics (164.6) or African Americans (178.9). Differences in pregnancy rates among racial groups persisted across the 1990s, and sharper drops in the birthrates among African Americans than among whites narrowed the gap between these groups. For example, the birthrates per 1,000 African-American adolescents declined 26 percent from 1991 (115.5) to 1998 (85.4), whereas the rates for whites declined 19 percent (43.4 to 35.2). A modest but steady decline in the birthrates for Hispanic adolescents occurred between 1994 (107.7) and 1998 (93.6), resulting in Hispanic adolescents now having the highest birthrate. Importantly, despite the overrepresentation of adolescent pregnancy and childbearing among minority groups, the actual number of births to whites is nearly double that of births to both African-American and Hispanic adolescents (Ventura et al. 2000).

Detailed and thorough information on the fathers of children born to adolescent mothers is scarce. However, the general consensus is that these fathers are less likely to be adolescents. In the mid-1990s, slightly over half of adolescent mothers reported that their child's father was at least three years older (e.g., Darroch, Landry, and Oslak 1999). In fact, sexually experienced adolescent women with much older partners were more likely to conceive than were young women whose partners were closer in age. Overall, 30 to 50 percent of pregnancies to an adolescent mother involved a father younger than twenty at the time of the child's birth. Unlike the birthrate trends for adolescent mothers, rates for adolescent fathers grew substantially between 1986 and 1996, when 23 of every 1,000 males age fifteen to nineteen became fathers (Thornberry et al. 2000).

International Trends

Consistent with the trends in the United States, declines in pregnancy rates and birthrates to women

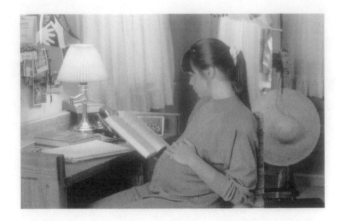

Each year nearly 15 million babies are born to teenage women worldwide. PALMER/KANE, INC./CORBIS

age fifteen to nineteen occurred in the majority of industrialized countries and in many developing countries (Singh and Darroch 2000). Among the more developed regions (i.e., Australia, New Zealand, Europe, North America, and Japan), the lowest adolescent birthrates (ten or fewer per 1,000) in 1995 were in ten countries, nine of which were western, northern, and southern European countries that experienced at least a 70 percent decline since 1970: Belgium, Denmark, Finland, France, Italy, Slovenia, Spain, Sweden, and Switzerland. Japan experienced little change (12% drop) since 1970 and reported the lowest birthrate (3.9) in 1995. In contrast, birthrates increased substantially (35% or more) between 1970 and 1995 in seven countries—all were eastern European countries that also reported high birthrates (35 or more per 1,000) in 1995: Armenia, Belarus, Georgia, Lithuania, Macedonia, the Russian Federation, and Ukraine. Still, the number of industrialized countries with high adolescent birthrates has fallen from twenty-nine countries in 1970 to twelve countries in 1995. Overall, the United States continues to have the highest premarital pregnancy rate and correspondingly one of the highest rates of births to young, unmarried women in the industrialized world.

Similar declining trends in birthrate among adolescents have occurred in many countries of developing regions (i.e., Asia, North Africa, and the Middle East), while little change has occurred in Latin America and the Caribbean and sub-Saharan Africa (Alan Guttmacher Institute 1996). For example, nearly 35 percent of young women in Latin America and the Caribbean, and an even higher proportion (50–60%) in most countries in sub-Saharan Africa have their first child before the age of twenty.

Antecedents of Adolescent Pregnancy

Research consistently shows that there is no single factor associated with the specific behaviors that lead to adolescent pregnancy (e.g., early initiation of sexual intercourse, lack of access to information and services, nonuse or inconsistent use of contraception). Instead, multiple factors place adolescents at risk for pregnancy, including family structure, economic disadvantage, community disadvantage, family, peer, and partner attitudes and behavior, and characteristics of teens themselves (e.g., Coley and Chase-Lansdale 1998). Like adolescent mothers, the fathers appear to exhibit many of the same risk factors (e.g., Thornberry et al. 1997). Studies on non-U.S. samples of adolescent parents suggest similar findings (e.g., Dearden et al. 1995; Gupta and Leite 1999; Lee et al. 1997; Olenick 1999).

For instance, living in a lower socioeconomic household, being raised in poverty by a single parent, having older and sexually active or pregnant/parenting siblings, and residing in rural settings and communities with high rates of poverty, welfare use, and single-mother households place teens at elevated risk of early pregnancy. These same adolescents exhibit certain behaviors and hold particular attitudes that also elevate their risk for pregnancy, such as having lower self-esteem, doing less well in school, having low educational aspirations, and perceiving lower educational, career, and economic opportunities. The early onset of adolescent sexual behavior and pregnancy also is linked to other problem behaviors (e.g., use of alcohol, tobacco, and/or drugs, delinquency, violence); in the United States, these linkages tend to be stronger for whites than for African Americans. Also, findings show that parent-child connectedness, parental supervision, monitoring, or regulation of children's activities, and parents' values against teen intercourse or unprotected intercourse decrease the risk of adolescent pregnancy.

Adoption, Marriage, and Single Parenthood

Fewer than 4 percent of U.S. adolescents place their child for adoption (Bachrach et al. 1992). Adoption is less common among African-American or Hispanic unmarried mothers, whose extended family members have traditionally played an important role in helping to raise children born outside of marriage. Also, compared to adolescent mothers who keep their infants, those who choose adoption are more likely to be in school at the time, younger, come from higher socioeconomic status households, have more favorable attitudes toward adoption, hold more realistic expectations of and understanding about the consequences of parenthood, and perceive having more alternatives to early parenthood. Findings suggest that compared to those who keep their child, those who give their child for adoption are more likely to experience both short- and long-term socioeconomic benefits, even after controlling for preexisting differences (e.g., Donnelly and Voydanoff 1996). Overall, the latter are more successful in achieving a higher education, avoiding rapid subsequent pregnancy, and securing employment, and are less likely to be receiving welfare support than are those who keep the child. Although giving a child for adoption is associated with experiences of greater sorrow or regret concerning her parenting decision, adoption does not result in significant negative psychological consequences for the young mother.

Marriage is an alternative response to placing the child for adoption. In fact, in developing countries (e.g., Central and West Africa, South Asia) over half of all women under eighteen are married, often in response to out-of-wedlock pregnancy. In contrast, fewer adolescent pregnancies in industrialized countries result in marriage. For example, less than one-third of such births in the United States occur or result in marriage; young white mothers are most likely to marry, followed by Hispanics and African Americans. In general, studies suggest that the immediate benefits of early marriage for adolescent mothers include financial support from her husband and an expanded familial support system. These benefits tend to be outweighed by a truncated education for both young mothers and fathers that leads to underemployment and future economic hardship. Also, adolescent marriages are less stable and more prone to divorce than other marriages. The risk of dissolution of subsequent marriages also is higher when the first marriage occurs during adolescence.

Overall, the low incidence of adoption among adolescent parents and the disproportionate number of those who marry means that an increasing number of unmarried adolescents are raising children. In lieu of the general decline in the adolescent birthrate since the late 1950s, the proportion of nonmarital adolescent births has risen steeply. In 1998, nearly eight out of ten adolescent births in the United States occurred outside marriage. Still, the total number of births to unmarried women under twenty years represents less than one-third of the total number of births to all unmarried women—a shift since 1970, when half of nonmarital births occurred to adolescents. A similar pattern exists for adolescent fathers. When compared to all fathers of children born out-of-wedlock, estimates are that less than one-fifth of all nonmarital births are to young men under age twenty and slightly more than 60 percent are to men age twenty to twenty-nine. Similarly, estimates suggest large percentages of teen births occur outside marriage in other Western and European industrialized countries as well.

The consequences of nonmarital childbearing are discussed below. Although the research available has been predominantly based on U.S. samples, findings from non-U.S. samples suggest that these consequences are shared worldwide.

Adolescent Mothers

Compared to adolescents who delay parenthood, those who become mothers experience elevated risks for negative outcomes (e.g., Coley and Chase-Lansdale 1998; Herdman 1997; Maynard 1997). Adolescent mothers are less likely to complete high school, avoid welfare, be employed, have stable employment, and earn adequate incomes. Longitudinal research shows that for many adolescent mothers, some of these negative consequences may be short term, as many are able to eventually complete school and become economically self-sufficient. However, they are likely to experience numerous stressful life events, adverse family functioning, and low levels of life satisfaction.

There is a great variability among adolescent mothers in the likelihood of becoming socioeconomically disadvantaged. For example, having parents with more education, attending a special school for pregnant youth, having high aspirations at the time of birth, finishing high school within five years of the birth of a first child, limiting subsequent childbearing, and growing up in a family that did not receive welfare promoted economic

well-being (Brooks-Gunn and Chase-Lansdale 1995). Some findings also suggest that the economic disadvantages of early parenting may be more prevalent among African Americans than among whites. Although being a young mother seems to influence later experiences, the contextual precursors (e.g., poverty) associated with adolescent parenthood explain much of the deleterious effects.

Effects of Adolescent Parenthood on Children

Overall, research shows that children of adolescent parents are at greater risk for health, developmental, and behavioral problems compared to children born to older mothers (e.g., Alonso and Moreno 2000; Maynard 1997). Compared to older mothers, adolescent mothers are more likely to experience pregnancy and delivery problems and have less healthy babies overall (e.g., low birth weight, high infant morbidity), but these negative health consequences are becoming less common in industrialized countries because of increased health services for young mothers. Few differences in cognitive functioning are found in infancy, but small and consistent differences are detected in preschool children that continue into middle childhood. Also, preschool children of adolescent mothers tend to show more behavior problems (e.g., aggressive, less self-control) than children of older mothers, a finding especially pronounced for boys. During adolescence, problems begin to show up, such as grade failure, delinquent acts, and early sexual activity and pregnancy.

Research finds that the health of infants is affected more by family background characteristics (e.g., race, residence, mother's education) and mother's health-related behavior (e.g., smoking, drinking, prenatal care) than by mother's age (Geronimus and Korenman 1993; Roy et al. 1999). Other factors that place these offspring at greater risk include the adverse social and economic effects associated with early parenthood, the emotional immaturity of a younger mother, and less experienced and/or less adequate parenting. Although adolescent mothers tend to be as warm toward their young child as older mothers, research shows that they are less verbal, sensitive, and responsive, provide a less stimulating home environment, perceive their infants as being more difficult, and have more unrealistic expectations (Coley and Chase-Lansdale 1998). Fewer differences are typically found when adolescent mothers are compared to mothers in their early twenties who also live in poverty (e.g., Lacroix et al. 2001). Also, differences are typically not found in infant health outcomes of unmarried versus married adolescent mothers. Despite consistent evidence of greater risk, findings show more variability in whether children exhibit these problem behaviors and that many children develop normally.

Societal Costs of Adolescent Parenting

In the United States, and most other countries too, adolescent mothers have a high probability of raising their children in poverty and relying on public assistance. More than one-half of all U.S. adolescent mothers and about three-fourths of all unmarried adolescent mothers receive welfare support (Moore et al. 1993). Whereas they represent only a minority of all welfare cases, 53 percent of welfare funding is to families formed by adolescent births (Alan Guttmacher Institute 1994). Also, adolescent mothers are most likely to have long careers on public assistance, as more than 40 percent report living in poverty at age twenty-seven.

Although the children of adolescent mothers visit medical providers less frequently and have lower total medical expenses, more of their expenses are paid by others than is true among children of older mothers. Estimates suggest that the expenses paid by others would decrease by nearly half if adolescent mothers postponed childbearing until at least age twenty-two (Maynard 1997). Overall, best estimates indicate that adolescent childbearing coupled with the other disadvantages faced by adolescent mothers costs U.S. taxpayers a total of $13 to $19 billion annually.

Adolescent Fathers

For adolescent fathers, much of their stress involves vocational/educational issues, interpersonal relationships, health, and concern over future parenting competence. Like adolescent mothers, fathers obtain less education and, thus, have lower long-term labor market and earning potential than their counterparts who delay fathering. Whether these deficits predate the pregnancy or are a result of the pregnancy (e.g., drop out of school to provide support), these young fathers are generally disadvantaged.

The involvement of fathers with their children is higher than expected, at least in the first few years. Research shows that almost half of young nonresident fathers visit their children weekly, and almost 25 percent have daily contact. However, contact with the child typically diminishes over time, such that fewer than 25 percent see their school-age children weekly. Lack of contact is related to economic status; those fathers with more resources (e.g., education, income) are more involved. Financial support follows a similar pattern, although when support is provided, it is often modest. Estimates project that U.S. fathers who do not marry the adolescent mothers have incomes sufficient to expect them to contribute support at a level that would offset as much as 40 to 50 percent of welfare costs (Maynard 1997).

Grandparenting

Because the majority of adolescent mothers do not marry, they likely spend the first few years after the child's birth in a multigenerational household. Findings suggest that the presence of a grandmother in the home appears to be both beneficial and harmful to the adolescent parent and her child. Grandmothers often assist the adolescent mother with childcare responsibilities and provide additional financial resources. Their presence in the home is beneficial to the health and development of low birth weight infants born to young mothers (Pope 1993). Grandmother support for older adolescent mothers also is associated with the mother completing her education, especially if the grandmother provides childcare.

However, coresidence with a grandmother may not always foster optimal childrearing environments. The competing developmental needs of young mothers (e.g., autonomy, school, work, childcare) and young grandmothers (e.g., adult midlife, work, relationships, parenting, unanticipated childcare demands) combined with their likely economic struggle often result in stressful living arrangements and consequently less supportive and beneficial environments for the adolescent and her offspring. In some cases, an adolescent mother may assume less responsibility for the care of her child, leaving an already overburdened grandmother in charge. As the grandmother's stress increases, the quality of the care she provides may diminish. Yet studies show that when young mothers have mature, flexible, and autonomous interactions with their own mothers, they are more likely to be emotionally supportive, affective, and authoritative parents to their own child (Brooks-Gunn and Chase-Lansdale 1995).

Policy Related to Adolescent Parenting

There are several policy concerns around the economic, social, and psychological burdens of adolescent parenting for individuals and the broader society. Many adolescent parenting programs attempt to address these concerns by providing services to adolescents with the goal of decreasing the likelihood of second births, increasing self-sufficiency through vocational training, and enhancing parenting skills through parent education. Additional policy concerns focus on the provision of child support. Shirley L. Zimmerman (1992) argued that adolescent parenting must be examined in the larger context in which it occurs, because regions where there are higher poverty rates, higher unemployment rates, higher divorce rates, and low rates of school completion report higher rates of births to teens. She suggested that policy must address the forces that "give rise to high birthrates among the young, cultural norms, family instability, academic failure, and individual motivation within the context of persistent inequality and growing social isolation of the poor" (p. 428). Although the occurrence of adolescent parenthood will not completely disappear, multifaceted strategies are warranted to facilitate the transition out of poverty or at least minimize the hardships imposed by social disadvantage on adolescent parents.

See also: ADOPTION; BIRTH CONTROL: SOCIOCULTURAL AND HISTORICAL ASPECTS; CHILDHOOD, STAGES OF: ADOLESCENCE; FATHERHOOD; GRAND-PARENTHOOD; MOTHERHOOD; NONMARITAL CHILDBEARING; PARENTING EDUCATION; PREGNANCY AND BIRTH; POVERTY; SEXUALITY EDUCATION; SEXUALITY IN ADOLESCENCE; SINGLE-PARENT FAMILIES

Bibliography

Alan Guttmacher Institute. (1994). *Sex and America's Teenagers.* New York: Author.

Alan Guttmacher Institute. (1996). *Risks and Realities of Early Childbearing Worldwide.* New York: Author.

Alan Guttmacher Institute. (1999). *Teenage Pregnancy: Overall Trends and State-by-State Information.* New York: Author.

Alonso, C. R., and Moreno, R. (2000). "Maternidad adolescente: Consecuencias." *Revista de Psiquiatria Infanto-Juvenil* 1:6–11.

Bachrach, C. A.; Stolley, K. S.; and London, K. A. (1992). "Relinquishement of Premarital Births: Evidence from National Survey Data." *Family Planning Perspectives* 24(1):27–33.

Brooks-Gunn, J., and Chase-Lansdale, P. L. (1995). "Adolescent Parenthood." In *Handbook of Parenting, Vol. 3: Status and Social Conditions of Parenting,* ed. M. H. Bornstein. Mahwah, NJ: Lawrence Erlbaum Associates.

Coley, R. L., and Chase-Lansdale, P. L. (1998). "Adolescent Pregnancy and Parenthood: Recent Evidence and Future Direction." *American Psychologist* 53:152–160.

Darroch, J. E.; Landry, D. J.; and Oslak, S. (1999). "Age Differences Between Sexual Partners in the United States." *Family Planning Perspectives* 31(4):160–167.

Darroch, J. E., and Singh, S. (1999). *Why is Teenage Pregnancy Declining? The Roles of Abstinence, Sexual Activity, and Contraceptive Use (Occasional Report No. 1).* New York: The Alan Guttmacher Institute.

Dearden, K. A.; Hale, C. B.; and Woolley, T. (1995). "The Antecedents of Teen Fatherhood: A Retrospective Case-control Study of Great Britain Youth." *American Journal of Public Health* 58(4):551–554.

Donnelly, B. W., and Voydanoff, P. (1996). "Parenting versus Placing for Adoption: Consequences for Adolescent Mothers." *Family Relations* 45:427–434.

Geronimu, A. T., and Korenman, S. (1993). "Maternal Youth or Family Background? On the Health Disadvantages of Infants with Teenage Mothers." *American Journal of Epidemiology* 137:213–225.

Gupta, N., and Leite, I. C. (1999). "Adolescent Fertility Behavior: Trends and Determinants in Northeastern Brazil." *International Family Planning Perspectives* 25(3):125–130.

Herdman, C. (1997). *The Impact of Early Pregnancy and Childbearing on Adolescent Mothers and Their Children in Latin America and the Caribbean.* Washington, D.C.: Advocates for Youth.

Lacroix, V.; Pomerieau, A.; Malcuit, G.; Seguin, R.; Lamare, G. (2001). "Development langagier et cognitive de l'enfant durant les trois premieres annees en relation avec la duree des vocalizations maternelles et les jouets presents dans l'environnement: Etude longitudinale aupres de populations a risqué." *Canadian Journal of Behavioral Science* 33(2):65–76.

Lee, M.; Lu, T.; and Chou, M. (1997). "Characteristics of Adolescent Pregnancy in Taiwan." *International*

Journal of Adolescent Medicine and Health 9(3):213–216.

Maynard, R. A. (1997). *Kids Having Kids: Economic Costs and Social Consequences of Teen Pregnancy.* Washington, D.C.: The Urban Institute Press.

Moore, K. A.; Myers, D. E.; Morrison, D. R.; Nord, C. W.; Brown, B.; and Edmonston, B. (1993). "Age at First Childbirth and Later Poverty." *Journal of Research on Adolescence* 3(4):393–422.

Olenick, I. (1999). "Among Young Jamaicans, Sex and Childbearing Often Begin During Adolescence." *International Family Planning Perspective* 25:206–207.

Pope, S. K. (1993). "Low-Birth-Weight Infants Born to Adolescent Mothers: Effects of Coresidency with Grandmother on Child Development." *Journal of the American Medical Association* 269:1396–1400.

Roy, E.; Schapira, I. T.; Cortigiani, M. R.; Oiberman, A.; Parisi, N.; and Szapu, B. (1999). "Atencion pediatrica primaria para hijos de madres adolescents: Seguimento durante los primeros 24 meses de vida." *Interdisciplinaria* 16(2):99–121.

Singh, S., and Darroch, J. E. (2000). "Adolescent Pregnancy and Childbearing: Levels and Trends in Developed Countries." *Family Planning Perspectives* 32(1):14–23.

Thornberry, T. P.; Smith, C. A.; and Howard, G. J. (1997). "Risk Factors for Teenage Fatherhood." *Journal of Marriage and the Family* 59(3):505–522.

Thornberry, T. P.; Wei, E. H.; Stouthamer-Loeber, M.; and Dyke, J. V. (2000). *Teenage Fatherhood and Delinquent Behavior.* U.S. Department of Justice: Office of Juvenile Justice and Delinquency Prevention.

Ventura, S. J.; Curtin, S. C.; and Mathews, T. J. (2000). "Variations in Teenage Birth Rates, 1991–1998: National and State Trends." *National Vital Statistics Reports* 48(6). Hyattsville, MD: National Center for Health Statistics.

Zimmerman, S. L. (1992). "Family Trends: What Implications for Family Policy?" *Family Relations* 41:423–429.

Other Resources

The Alan Guttmacher Institute. Available from http://www.agi-usa.org.

Bridges for Adolescent Pregnancy, Parenting, and Sexuality Web Site. Available from http://www.nnh.org.

National Organization on Adolescent Pregnancy, Parenting, and Prevention. Available from http://www.noappp.org.

TED G. FUTRIS
KAY PASLEY

ADOPTION

Adoption is a process in which a person (the adoptee) acquires the rights and duties of a biological child with respect to an individual who is not the adoptee's biological parent. The process is usually legal in character, but in some cultures adoption occurs by social ritual. As part of the process of adoption, the adoptee's legal relationship with his or her biological parents may be terminated.

Common events triggering the possibility of adoption are the death of a biological parent; the termination of a biological parent's rights following the abuse, neglect or abandonment of the adoptee; or the divorce of the biological parents followed by the remarriage of the custodial parent and a loss of contact with the noncustodial biological parent.

Legal Consequences and Availability

Two standard models of adoption exist. In one model, found in Anglo-American jurisprudence and other legal systems, the effect of adoption is that the biological parent's rights and duties end with respect to the adoptee (Cretney and Masson 1997). These rights and duties are acquired by the adoptive parents (Hampton 2000). Thus, the biological parents cease to owe the adoptee a duty of support, and this duty is imposed on the adoptive parents. Similarly, normally the adoptee loses the right to inherit from a biological parent who dies leaving no will, but acquires such a right to inherit from the adoptive parent. In the second model, a complete severance of the legal relationship between the adoptee and his or her biological parent does not occur. Instead, as in Turkey (Örücü 1999), the adoptee acquires some rights and duties with respect to the adoptive parent, but retains others with respect to a biological parent.

In some countries, both models may co-exist. This occurs notably in Europe, as in Bosnia and Herzegovina (Bubic 1998) and Portugal (De Oliveira and Cid 1998), and in those countries whose legal traditions flow from Europe, as in Argentina (Grosman 1998), Colombia, and other countries in Central and South America (Monroy 1998). The model used in any given adoption may depend on the purpose behind the adoption or the circumstances of the adoptive and biological parents and the adoptee. For example, in Scotland

(Sutherland 1997), when a biological parent remarries and the adoption is by the stepparent, the legal relationship with the other biological parent may not terminate completely even though a legal relationship with the adoptive parent is established. This approach is often followed in the United States (Hampton 2000). Thus, the adoptee may be entitled to support from both the biological parents and the adoptive parent. Similarly, the adoptee may be entitled to inherit from both the adoptive parent and perhaps his or her relatives, as well as from the biological parents and their relatives.

Islamic jurisprudence generally does not permit formal adoption. However, some Islamic countries such as Somalia and Tunisia permit adoption. Adoption is also possible in some circumstances among Muslims in South Asia (Pearl and Menski 1998).

In some countries, the applicable family law rules may be determined by factors such as the individual's citizenship, clan membership, or religion. Accordingly, in a given country, adoption rules may vary with the individuals involved, and indeed, may not be available to some individuals at all. Thus, in India, the availability of adoption is controlled by an individual's religion. Statute permits adoption among a broadly defined group of Hindus. The law, however, does not apply to those who are Muslim, Christian, Parsi, or Jew by religion (Pant 1994). Ordinarily, these individuals cannot formally adopt a child, although some of the objectives of adoption can be achieved using the laws of guardianship or the rules regulating the distribution of property by will (Manooja 1993).

History and Purpose

Adoption has been known from biblical times and in many cultures (Goody 1969). In Europe, the roots of modern law lie with the Greeks and Romans. Similarly, in the East, adoption has a long tradition. In Hindu literature, discussions of adoption go back more than 5,500 years (Pant 1994). Common themes dominate the purposes behind adoption in ancient times. Some of these themes are still relevant today.

To the early Greeks and Romans, the goal of adoption was to perpetuate the family based on the male line of descent and to ensure the continuation of the family's religious practices. Thus, the adopter originally had to be a male without a legitimate son (Harrison 1968; Hornblower and Spanforth 1996). Adoption also served the purpose of cementing political alliances between families and continuing political dynasties (Gager 1996). Later Roman emperors, however, did permit adoption by women to "console them for the loss of children" (Moyle 1912). Similarly, early Chinese tradition was primarily concerned with the goals of family continuity and preserving the cult of the ancestors. The object of adoption was to produce a legal successor, and the process was governed by strict rules. For example, the adoptee had to be from the same clan as the adopter, or at least have the same surname and be younger than the adopter so as to maintain order in the family genealogy (Bodde and Morris 1967). However, Chinese tradition also permitted the adoption of a *charity son* who was supported by the family but acquired no rights in it and did not participate in family religious rituals.

With time, the Roman concept of adoption migrated through Europe where it encountered local customs and codes, such as those found among the Germanic peoples. The use of formal adoption floundered in Europe, and notably in France, during the seventeenth century, chiefly as a result of the disapproval of the church (Gager 1996). Adoption survived, however, due to existing practices of custom, coupled with the needs of the elderly who, after depopulation following the plague epidemic, were willing to trade inheritances for security in old age—as the elderly still do in Turkey (Örücü 1999). One form of adoption practice employed during the seventeenth century involved the use of notarized contracts of adoption. This form is still found in some countries. Postrevolutionary France saw adoption as a means to break down class barriers and redistribute wealth, as well as being a remedy for childless households and children without families. Even so, the Napoleonic Code imposed strict limitations aimed at protecting legitimate biological heirs and the institution of marriage. As a result, ordinarily, only married couples could adopt (Gager 1996).

In contrast, Roman adoption practices never took hold in England. Statute law first introduced adoption to England in 1926 (Cretney and Masson 1997). English concerns with the integrity of blood lines and the desire to ensure that property was inherited by legitimate biological descendants meant that there was no adoption law to be received in postrevolutionary America. In the United States, adoption laws developed in response to the needs of dependent children, not infrequently poor, orphaned, or handicapped. Statutory schemes regulating adoption were first enacted by the states after the middle of the nineteenth century, the earliest probably being in Massachusetts in 1851.

The English and their European neighbors took their adoption practices to their colonies. For example, French and Spanish principles found their way to Central and South America (Monroy 1998). Imperial rules often encountered customary practices. Accordingly, current adoption law sometimes reflects a blend of the European roots and local tradition, as in New Zealand (Atkin 1997), Uganda (Okumu Wengi 1997), and Zambia (Munalula 1999).

In relatively recent times there has been a significant worldwide shift to recognizing the role adoption should play in advancing the interest of the individual adoptee, rather than the goals of broader elements of society or the interests of would-be adopters. This process has been enhanced by the evolution of global standards as reflected, for example, in the United Nations Convention on Rights of the Child. In some countries, for example, Argentina (Grosman 1998) and Uganda (Okumu Wengi 1997), this Convention is an integral part of the country's adoption law. In others, as in Scotland (Sutherland 1997), the Convention is highly influential.

Process

There are three basic types of adoption processes: direct placement by the biological parent or parents, placement through a state agency, or placement through a private agency licensed by the state. Direct placement is often found where the adopter is a stepparent or close relative, as in Germany (Deliyannis 1997). Where direct placement by a biological parent is permitted, there is increasing concern to ensure that the adoptive parents are subjected to a screening process if they are not related to the adoptee (Boskey and Hollinger 2000). Any such screening is usually conducted by a state agency or an entity or individual approved by the state. However, screening does not occur in all countries (Manooja 1993).

Countries such as Argentina (Grosman 1998), China (Palmer 2000), and Latvia (Vebers 1999), or

sometimes adoption agencies themselves, often impose extensive conditions on the eligibility of people to adopt and the children who may be placed with particular adoptive parents. As far as adoptive parents are concerned, conditions may include requirements relating to their ages and the age difference between them and the adoptee, their physical and mental health, their financial resources, and their community reputation. Adoption by unmarried couples, couples of the same sex, single individuals, and couples whose infertility is not established, may also be precluded (Forder 2000; Cretney and Masson 1997; Kounougeri-Manoledaki 1995). Traditionally, attention was paid to matching the physical characteristics of adoptive parents and the adoptee, as well as their socioeconomic backgrounds, religion, and race. Eligibility for adoption also might be affected by clan, tribal, or caste membership (Okumu Wengi 1997). Sometimes, as in Colombia (Monroy 1998), the concern is that neglecting race or tribal membership, for example, will adversely affect the adoptee and lead to the erosion of the relevant group and its culture. For these reasons, in the United States, the federal Indian Child Welfare Act of 1978 places control of the adoption of children eligible for tribal membership in the hands of the tribe and the tribal courts (Hollinger 2000a). In contrast, although a child's race may be taken into account for placement purposes, federal law does not permit the adoption placement to be delayed unduly while a same-race placement is sought.

In some countries, adoption can occur in a relatively informal way by mere agreement between the adoptive parents and the biological parents. This agreement may be reflected in some symbolic way in the form of a more or less public ceremony or ritual, as in India (Manooja 1993; Pant 1994), or by written contract, or by registration, as in China (Zhang 1997) and Rwanda (Ntampaka 1997). In other countries, adoption requires a decree by a court, as in Argentina (Grosman 1998), the United States (Hollinger 2000b), and Russia (Khazova 2000), or a decision by an administrative agency, as in Hungary (Dóczi 1997).

In many countries, the adoption process involves three phases: termination of parental rights; placement of the adoptee with an adoptive family; and finalization of the adoption. Sometimes, as in England (Cretney and Masson 1997), the state obtains the termination of the rights of a biological parent over the opposition of that parent. This may be due to the parent's abuse, neglect, or abandonment of the child, or due to a failure to support the child, or because the parent is mentally or physically ill, or imprisoned, or otherwise unfit. Where the biological parent favors the adoption, parental rights usually are relinquished either by surrender of the adoptee to an agency, or by the formal consent of the parent to the adoption. To help ensure that the biological parent is willing to surrender the child for adoption, many countries, as in Poland (Stojanowska 1997), specify that consent to the adoption cannot be given before the birth of the child. Also, formal procedures are employed to reduce the risk that the biological parent will be pressured into giving consent (Melli 1996). In this regard, generally, a biological parent cannot be paid for consenting to adoption. However, adoptive parents routinely pay for expenses associated with birth, as well as paying agencies and other intermediaries for their services (Melli 1996; Somit 2000). Despite these rules, there is concern that economic circumstances in some countries drive parents to give up their children, sometimes for compensation. Many countries require that children above a certain age must consent to their adoption, or, at least, be consulted regarding it.

Some countries, for example Argentina (Grosman 1998), Japan (Oda 1999), and the United States (Melli 1996), often impose a delay between the time when the adoptee is placed with the adoptive parents and the point where the adoption becomes final. This delay, as in Switzerland (Graham-Siegenthaler 1995), is to enable an investigator to conduct a home study and report to the relevant court or administrative agency on the success of the placement before the court or agency grants the final order of adoption.

Procedurally, difficulties can arise with respect to the biological father of the adoptee. His identity or location may be unknown, or may be known to the adoptee's mother, who conceals the information from the adoption authorities. Moreover, the father may be unaware of the mother's pregnancy, or he may know of the birth but have played no active role in either supporting the child or developing a social relationship with it. In such contexts, countries are reluctant to put the father in a position to block the adoption or delay it. To address these concerns, modern law tends to require that a biological father who has acknowledged his paternity or had it determined (Frank 1997) or who has been socially or financially active in the adoptee's life must give his consent to the adoption, or, if grounds exist, have his rights terminated on an involuntary basis (Cretney and Masson 1997). Where the father's identity is unknown or where he played a passive role in the adoptee's life, his consent to adoption is not required. At best, as in the Republic of Ireland (Ward 2000), an effort will be made to find the father and notify him of the proposed adoption and receive his input without giving him the ability to control the process.

In some cultures, adoption is a public event. Both the fact of adoption and the identity of the birth parents are known. In other traditions, the fact of adoption and related issues are kept secret. This might be because adoption is a means of dealing with children born out of wedlock or because secrecy and anonymity are seen as devices producing greater integration of the adoptee into the adoptive family, while shielding the biological parents. This approach requires adoption records to be sealed and placements to occur through intermediaries. Increasingly, health concerns and other considerations have led to requirements, as for example in the United States (Melli 1996), that nonidentifying background information be made available to adoptive parents. Beyond this, some countries, such as Argentina (Grosman 1998), are willing to allow access to background information, even if the effect is to reveal the fact of the adoption and the identities of the biological and adoptive families. In England, an adoptee, upon adulthood, may obtain a copy of the original birth certificate (Cretney and Masson 1997). In some countries, this access is possible only if good cause can be shown for disclosing the information. In other instances, a register is maintained of biological and adoptive parents who are willing to have their identities revealed if an inquiry is made. Even in countries where secret adoptions were the norm, there is increasing interest, as in New Zealand (Atkin 1997), in *open* adoptions, that is adoptions where contact is maintained between the biological parents and the adoptive family. These contacts may range from limited written communication to formal arrangements for physical contact. Such arrangements may even extend to more remote family members such as biological grandparents. The maintenance of contacts is seen as a way of helping biological parents deal with a sense of grief while facilitating the adoption process. However, concerns exist that open adoptions risk disrupting the adoptive family (Cretney and Masson 1997). Open adoptions are particularly favored in the context of adoptions by stepparents or adoptions of older children, that is, in circumstances where the adoptee already has an established relationship with the biological parents.

International Adoptions

Concern with an increasing incidence of children from one country being adopted in another led, in 1993, to the Hague Convention on Protection of Children and Co-operation in Respect of Intercountry Adoption (Pfund 1993). The increase in international adoptions in recent times is due to a decline in the birth rate in certain countries, coupled with relatively high fertility rates in other countries, possibly accompanied by social disruption because of war, disease, famine, and poverty. The Convention attempts to address a number of concerns. First, it seeks to ensure that the children are legitimately available for adoption. Second, the Convention requires reasonable efforts to find a permanent placement in the child's country of origin. Finally, the Convention aims to ensure that the placement in the receiving country is one that will benefit the child, and, in particular, that the adoptive parents are suitable (Bartholet 2000; Rosettenstein 1995). Many countries have ratified the Convention and modified their laws to meet its requirements.

See also: ADOLESCENT PARENTHOOD; CHILDREN'S RIGHTS; FAMILY LAW; GAY PARENTS; LESBIAN PARENTS; ORPHANS; SINGLE-PARENT FAMILIES

Bibliography

Atkin, B. (1997). "Dealing With Family Violence: Family Law in New Zealand." In *The International Survey of Family Law 1995,* ed. A. Bainham. The Hague, Netherlands: Kluwer Law International.

Bartholet, E. (2000). "International Adoption: Overview." In *Adoption Law and Practice,* ed. J. Heifetz Hollinger. New York: LEXIS Publishing.

Bodde, D., and Morris, C. (1967). *Law in Imperial China.* Philadelphia: University of Pennsylvania Press.

Boskey, J. B., and Hollinger, J. (2000). "Placing Children for Adoption." In *Adoption Law and Practice,* ed. J. Heifetz Hollinger. New York: LEXIS Publishing.

Bubic, S. (1998). "Family Law in Bosnia and Herzogovina." In *The International Survey of Family Law 1996,* ed. A. Bainham. The Hague, Netherlands: Kluwer Law International.

Cretney, S. M., and Masson, J. M. (1997). *Principles of Family Law,* 6th edition. London: Sweet and Maxwell.

Deliyannis, I. (1997). "Reforming the Law of Adoption." In *The International Survey of Family Law 1995,* ed. A. Bainham. The Hague, Netherlands: Kluwer Law International.

De Oliviera, G., and Cid, N. de S. (1998). "Family Law in Portugal." In *The International Survey of Family Law 1996,* ed. A. Bainham. The Hague, Netherlands: Kluwer Law International.

Dóczi, M. (1997). "Family Law in Hungary." In *The International Survey of Family Law 1995,* ed. A. Bainham. The Hague, Netherlands: Kluwer Law International.

Forder, C. (2000). "Opening Up Marriage to Same Sex Partners and Providing for Adoption by Same Sex Couples, Managing Information on Sperm Donors, and Lots of Private International Law." In *The International Survey of Family Law 2000 Edition,* ed. A. Bainham. Bristol, UK: Jordan.

Frank, R. (1997). "The Need for Reform in Parentage Law." In *The International Survey of Family Law 1995,* ed. A. Bainham. The Hague, Netherlands: Kluwer Law International.

Gager, K. E. (1996). *Blood Ties and Fictive Ties.* Princeton, NJ: Princeton University Press.

Goody, J. (1969). "Adoption In Cross-Cultural Perspective." *Comparative Studies in Society and History* 11:55–78.

Graham-Siegenthaler, B. (1995). "Family Law In Switzerland." In *Family Law In Europe,* ed. C. Hamilton and K. Standley. London: Butterworths.

Grosman, C. P. (1998). "The Recent Reform of Argentine Adoption Law." In *The International Survey of Family Law 1996,* ed. A. Bainham. The Hague, Netherlands: Kluwer Law International.

Harrison, A. R. W. (1968). *The Law of Athens.* Oxford, UK: Clarendon Press.

Hampton, L. P. (2000). "The Aftermath of Adoption: Support, Inheritance and Taxes." In *Adoption Law and Practice,* ed. J. Heifetz Hollinger. New York: LEXIS Publishing.

Hollinger, J. H. (2000a). "Adoption of Native American Children." In *Adoption Law and Practice,* ed. J. Heifetz Hollinger. New York: LEXIS Publishing.

Hollinger, J. H. (2000b). "Adoption Procedure." In *Adoption Law and Practice,* ed. J. Heifetz Hollinger. New York: LEXIS Publishing.

Hornblower, S., and Spanforth, A. (1996). *The Oxford Classical Dictionary.* New York: Oxford University Press.

Khazova, O. (2000). "Three Years After the Adoption of the New Russian Family Code." In *The International Survey of Family Law 2000 Edition,* ed. A. Bainham. Bristol, UK: Jordan.

Kounougeri-Manoledaki, E. (1995). "Family Law in Greece." In *Family Law In Europe,* ed. C. Hamilton and K. Standley. London: Butterworths.

Manooja, D. C. (1993). *Adoption Law and Practice.* New Delhi, India: Deep and Deep Publications.

Melli, M. S. (1996). "Focus on Adoption." In *The International Survey of Family Law 1994,* ed. A. Bainham. The Hague, Netherlands: Kluwer Law International.

Moyle, J. B. (1912). *Imperatoris Iustiniani Istitutionum.* Oxford, UK: Clarendon Press.

Monroy, P. A. (1998). "Adoption Law in Colombia." In *The International Survey of Family Law 1996,* ed. A. Bainham. The Hague, Netherlands: Kluwer Law International.

Munalula, M. (1999). "Family Law in Zambia." In *The International Survey Of Family Law 1997,* ed. A. Bainham. The Hague, Netherlands: Kluwer Law International.

Ntampaka, C. (1997). "Family Law in Rwanda." In *The International Survey of Family Law 1995,* ed. A. Bainham. The Hague, Netherlands: Kluwer Law International.

Oda, H. (1999). *Japanese Law,* 2nd edition. Oxford, UK: Oxford University Press.

Okumu Wengi, J. (1997). *Weeding the Millet Field: Women's Law and Grassroots Justice in Uganda.* Kampala: Uganda Law Watch Center.

Örücü, E. (1999). "Improving the Lot of Women and Children." In *The International Survey of Family Law 1997,* ed. A. Bainham. The Hague, Netherlands: Kluwer Law International.

Palmer, M. (2000). "Caring for Young and Old: Developments in the Family Law of the People's Republic of China, 1996–1998." In *The International Survey of Family Law 2000 Edition,* ed. A. Bainham. Bristol, UK: Jordan.

Pant, P. C. (1994). *The Hindu Adoptions and Maintenance Act, 1956,* 4th edition. Allahabad, India: The Law Book Company.

Pearl, D., and Menski, W. (1998). *Muslim Family Law,* 3rd edition. London: Sweet and Maxwell.

Pfund, P. H. (1993). "Introductory Note." *International Legal Materials* 32:1134–1146.

Rosettenstein, D. S. (1995). "Trans-Racial Adoption in the United States and the Impact of Considerations Relating to Minority Population Groups on International Adoptions in the United States." *International Journal of Law and the Family* 9:131–154.

Somit, J. (2000). "Independent Adoptions in California; Dual Representation Allowed." In *Adoption Law and Practice,* ed. J. Heifetz Hollinger. New York: LEXIS Publishing.

Stojanowska, W. (1997). "Adoption: Revision of the Family and Custody Code." In *The International Survey of Family Law 1995,* ed. A. Bainham. The Hague, Netherlands: Kluwer Law International.

Sutherland, E. E. (1997). "Child Law Reform—At Last!" In *The International Survey of Family Law 1995,* ed. A. Bainham. The Hague, Netherlands: Kluwer Law International.

Vebers, J. (1999). "Family Law in Latvia: From Establishment of the Independent State of Latvia in 1918 to Restoration of Independence in 1993." In *The International Survey of Family Law 1997,* ed. A. Bainham. The Hague, Netherlands: Kluwer Law International.

Ward, P. (2000). "Judicial and Legislative Family Law Developments." In *The International Survey of Family Law 2000 Edition,* ed. A. Bainham. Bristol, UK: Jordan.

Zhang, X. (1997). "Family Law." In *Introduction to Chinese Law,* ed. C. Wang and X. Zhang. Hong Kong-Singapore: Sweet and Maxwell.

DAVID S. ROSETTENSTEIN

ADULTHOOD

Interest in adult development and the aging experience is a relatively new area of inquiry. Throughout the first half of the twentieth century, the study of human development was largely the study of child development. Growing awareness of the dramatic global growth in the older population and rising life expectancies led to the emergence of the field of *social gerontology.* In 1900 people over sixty-five accounted for approximately 4 percent of the U.S. population—less than one in twenty-five. At that time, the average life expectancy (i.e., the average length of time one could expect to live if one were born that year) was forty-seven years. In 2000 adults between twenty and forty-four years of age comprised 36.9 percent of the U.S. population; adults between forty-five and sixty-four made up 22 percent; and those over the age of sixty-five represented 12.8 percent. Today, life expectancy at birth in the United States has risen to 72.5 years for men and 79.3 years for women (U.S. Census Bureau 2000a).

All world regions are experiencing an increase in the absolute and relative size of their older populations. There are, however, substantial differences in the current numbers and expected growth rates of the older population between industrialized and developing countries. For example, 15.5 percent of the population of Europe is aged sixty-five and older. In contrast, only 2.9 percent of sub-Saharan Africa's population is over age sixty-five. The less-developed regions of the world, however, are expected to show significant increases in the size of their older populations in the upcoming decades. For example, the size of the elderly population in sub-Saharan Africa is expected to jump by 50 percent, from 19.3 million to 28.9 million people between 2000 and 2015 (U.S. Census Bureau 2000b).

The *democratization of the aging experience* or the *longevity revolution* has also led to a *life course revolution* (Treas and Bengtson 1982; Skolnick 1991). The changes in mortality have had a profound impact on the concept of *adulthood*. The odyssey from youth to old age—or the concept of adulthood—can be viewed through many different lens, including chronological, biological, psychological, social, cultural, economic, and legal perspectives.

Life Stages

The distinction between childhood and adulthood varies considerably among cultural and social groups and across historical periods. Aging is not only a biological process; it is also a social process. The personal and social significance of the passage of years is shaped by the cultural age system. All societies divide the life span into recognized stages. These life stages or periods are marked by certain physical, psychological, and/or social milestones. Privileges, obligations, rights, and roles are assigned according to culturally shared definitions of periods of life (Fry 1980; Hagestad and Neugarten 1990). In Western industrialized societies, the life stages are commonly identified as: *prenatal* stage (from conception until birth); *infancy*

(from birth to the end of the second year of life); *early childhood* (ages three to six years); *middle childhood* (six years until puberty); *adolescence* (start of puberty to adulthood); *young adulthood* (ages twenty to forty); *middle adulthood* (ages forty to sixty-five); and *later adulthood* or *old age* (sixty-five and older).

These socially constructed life stages are not fixed; rather, they have expanded and contracted in length and new ones have emerged in response to broader social changes. For example, Jeffrey Jensen Arnett (2000) proposes *emerging adulthood* as a new conception of development for the period from the late teenage years through the twenties (with a focus on the ages of eighteen to twenty-five) in industrialized societies that allow young people a prolonged period of independent role exploration (Arnett 2000). In doing so, he draws parallels between his conception of emerging adulthood to Erik Erikson's concept of *prolonged adolescence* in industrialized society in which "young adults through role experimentation may find a niche in some section of his society" (Erikson 1968, p. 156).

Arnett (2000) argues that emerging adulthood is distinct demographically. It is the "only period of life in which nothing is normative demographically" (p. 471). Almost all of U.S. adolescents from twelve to seventeen years of age live at home with one or more parents, are enrolled in school, and are unmarried and childless. In contrast, emerging adults' lives are characterized by diversity. About one-third of young persons in the United States go off to college after high school, another 40 percent move out of their parental home for independent living and work, and about 10 percent of men and 30 percent of women remain at home until marriage. About two-thirds of emerging adults experience a period of cohabitation with an intimate partner (Michael et al. 1995). These emerging adults often change residences, including temporarily moving back into their parents' home. It is estimated that about 40 percent of recent cohorts of young adults have returned to their parent's home after moving away (Goldscheider and Goldscheider 1994). Arnett notes that it is with the transition to young adulthood, as more stable choices in love and work are made, that the diversity narrows. As further evidence of emerging adulthood as a distinct life stage, Arnett (2000) cites a survey in which the majority of people in the United

States in their late teens and early twenties indicated "somewhat yes and somewhat no" versus an absolute "yes" or "no" to whether they felt they had reached adulthood.

Changes are occurring not only in the social construction of entry to adulthood but also in the social conception of the late stage of adulthood, or old age. The definition of *old age* as beginning at age sixty-five is a relatively recent phenomenon. It reflects primarily the decision of European countries and the United States, in their creation of their old-age social insurance programs (i.e., national retirement or pension systems) during the first half of the twentieth century, to establish this chronological age as determining eligibility. More recently, the growing numbers of older adults, especially those age eighty and older, has resulted in the redefining of later adulthood into the two distinct life stages or age groups: the *younger-old* (ages sixty-five to seventy-five) and the *older-old* or *oldest-old* (older than seventy-five). Indeed, in many countries, the oldest-old are now the fastest growing portion of the total population. Persons aged eighty and older represented 17 percent of the world's elderly in 2000: 23 percent in developed countries and 13 percent in developing countries (U.S. Census Bureau 2000b). Stressing the relative newness of the oldest-old phenomenon, Richard Suzman and Matilda White Riley (1985, p. 177) emphasized that "less is known about it than any other age group" and that there "is little in historical experience that can help in interpreting it."

Approximately a decade later, similar claims were asserted about *middle age*. Orville G. Brim, Jr. (1992, p. 171) referred to the middle years as the "last uncharted territory in human development." Concern about the status and welfare of children and the elderly contributed to the scientific study of the biological, psychological, and social development of these two vulnerable populations. This concern led to the enactment of federal and state statutes to protect children and elders. Many researchers' lack of interest in the midlife reflected the predominant view that personality is stable during adulthood. Moreover, from a public policy perspective, adults were not viewed as a vulnerable population requiring protection of "their best interests" by the state.

Bernice L. Neugarten and Nancy Datan (1974) noted that researchers and clinicians constructed dissimilar images of the understudied middle years of adulthood. Whereas researchers characterized young adulthood as a period of major transitions, middle adulthood was often viewed as a plateau with little of significance occurring until old age. In contrast, clinicians often portrayed middle age as a time of crisis. The aging of the baby boomer generation and the sheer number of this cohort entering midlife have had a profound impact on the current interest in this life stage. In 2000 more than 80 million members of the baby boomer generation were between the ages of thirty-five and fifty-four (U.S. Census Bureau 2000a). The interest in middle age spurred the MacArthur Foundation Research Network on Successful Midlife Development (MIDMAC); one of the most significant interdisciplinary research endeavors devoted to the study of midlife. The studies emerging from the MIDMAC large representative survey of midlife in the United States are reshaping our understanding of these middle years. It was only in 2001 that the first *Handbook of Midlife Development*, one of the most significant contributions to the field, was published (Lachman 2001).

The period called middle age lacks well-defined boundaries. Michael P. Farrell and Stanley Rosenberg (1981, p. 16) note "like defining a period of history, no one quite agrees when middle age begins or ends." Margie E. Lachman and her colleagues (1994) found that the subjective boundaries of middle age vary positively with age. The older an individual is, the more likely she or he will be to report later entry and exit years as demarcating middle age. Although the ages of forty to sixty are typically considered to be middle-aged, for some persons middle age begins as young as thirty and for others middle age is not perceived as ending until age seventy-five. Middle-aged persons typically report feeling about ten years younger than their chronological age (Montepare and Lachman 1989). As life expectancy increases, the boundaries of middle age may also shift. A National Council on Aging (2000) survey revealed that one-third of Americans in their seventies perceive of themselves as middle-aged. Midlife or middle age does not exist as a concept in all cultures; there is also considerable cultural variation in the social construction of this life stage. Usha Menon (2001) illustrates this variation through a comparative analysis of the conception of middle age and the social roles associated with this stage of life in three societies—middle-class Japan, upper-caste Hindu in rural India, and middle-class Anglo-America.

Whereas childhood and adolescence are often marked by formal rites of passage, the transition from young adult to middle-aged adult is marked neither by special rites of passage nor by predictable chronological events. The transition from young adulthood to middle adulthood is often a gradual one. Social cues, especially changes in family and work domains, may be better indicators of developmental change than chronological age alone.

The midlife research of the past decade has dispelled many of the myths and negative stereotypes of middle age. For most middle-aged adults, their physical health is good, although concerns are expressed about being overweight and future declining health (American Board of Family Practice 1990). Only 7 percent of adults in their early forties, 16 percent of adults in their early fifties, and 30 percent of adults in their early sixties have a disabling health condition (Bumpass and Aquilino 1995). Although middle-aged adults often face a number of family and work stresses, for both men and women there is evidence of a decrease in negative emotions and an increase in positive mood in the middle adult years (Mroczek and Kolarz 1998).

Despite the pervasive and persistent societal view of menopause as a stressful life experience, research has consistently documented that most women pass through menopause with little difficulty. In a longitudinal study of the menopausal transition, Nancy E. Avis and Sonja M. McKinley (1991) found that more than two-thirds of women report relief or neutral feelings about the cessation of menses and that over a four-year period changes in attitudes toward menopause are in a positive or neutral direction. Rather than a crisis, the majority of women viewed their post-menopausal period as a new and fulfilling stage of life. The loss of fertility in menopause is sometimes experienced as a gain in freedom in sexual expression. It is important to stress that there is wide cultural variation in the menopausal experience. For example, Japanese women do not view menopause as a distinct event or a disease; rather it is seen as part of the general aging process. Thus, the physiological changes Japanese women

identify as associated with menopause—stiff shoulders, dizziness, headaches, and dry mouth—are changes identified more broadly with growing older. In contrast to U.S. women, few Japanese women identify hot flashes or sweats as symptoms of menopause (Lock 1994).

Adaptation to Aging

To understand adaptation to aging, Laurie Russell Hatch (2000) proposes the adoption of a *multilevel life course model* organized around four interrelated levels of human experience: personal biographies, social location and membership in social groups, birth cohort, and social context. *Personal biography* or history encompasses our personal characteristics (i.e., cognitive abilities, personality, health), our patterns of coping and adaptation, and events of our lives.

Social location and membership in social groups recognizes the variability between individuals in human development, both within cultures and across cultures. For example, middle-aged adults from lower socioeconomic groups are more likely to have chronic health conditions. Social location and group membership recognizes the hierarchies of privileges (i.e., gender, social class, sexual orientation, ethnicity) that shape individuals' life experiences and determine the life chances available to them.

Birth cohort and social context analysis recognizes the impact of generational differences. As Matilda White Riley, Anne Foner, and John W. Riley, Jr. (1999) emphasize, changing societies change the life course of individuals, who then during their lives modify society. Cohort variances are particularly relevant to adult development. As Klaus Werner Schaie (2000, p. 262) notes, cohort variance in infancy and childhood studies may be only a "minor disturbance unlikely to overshadow or hide universal developmental laws." In contrast, Schaie stresses cohort variance has "a substantively meaningful role" in the study of adult development. Individual differences in adulthood, prior to old age, are largely modified by environmental context. Examples cited as major contexts that differ dramatically for successive generations include shifts in educational attainment, changes in diet and exercise, and advances in life expectancy.

Although social scientists increasingly emphasize the link between *social history and context* and adult development, few empirical studies have explored this connection. An exception is Lauren E. Duncan and Gail S. Agronick's (1995) study of the intersection of life stage with the experience of social events. Their research, using three age-cohorts of college-educated women, revealed that social events (i.e., World War II, the Eisenhower and Kennedy presidencies, social protests, the women's movement) that coincided with early adulthood were more salient than events that occurred at other life stages.

Duncan and Agronick (1995) also examined more closely the impact of one specific social event, the women's movement. They were particularly interested in a comparative analysis of the effects of the women's movement on college-educated women who experienced this event in early and middle adulthood. Their findings not only underscored that the women's movement was more personally meaningful to women who experienced this event in early adulthood, but also revealed that women of both age cohorts who found the movement important were likely to have higher educational, career, and income attainment, and be more assertive and externally oriented at midlife. Studies, such as the one conducted by Duncan and Agronick (1995), underscore the importance of a multilevel approach to understanding adult development.

Adult and Family Development

Human development occurs within the context of family. Individuals' lives are intertwined with families. It is useful therefore to consider individual development and family development simultaneously, focusing upon the intersection of *individual time, family time,* and *historical time* (Hareven 1978). Change occurs at three different levels: the developing individual, dyadic relationships within the family, and the institution of the family (Jerrome 1994). The family as a social group or institution moves through time in a constantly changing social and cultural environment. The family has a culture of its own that is sustained and elaborated upon by generations of members. Dyadic relationships within the family (i.e., parent and child, siblings) typically last across multiple decades and provide horizontal and vertical linkages in the family system. Change in individual family members, involving personality and family roles, are connected to their own (and other relatives') aging

process. As Dorothy Jerrome (1994, p. 8) notes: "The family of childhood becomes the family of middle adulthood, which is replaced by the family of old age. The overlap in membership gradually diminishes until in the end the former group of relatives is completely replaced. Arguably, it is still the same family, though, through the handing down of traditions, family 'ways' and items or objects which link present generations to previous ones."

Within industrialized societies, demographic and social changes of the twentieth century have had profound effects on the family as an institution, dyadic relationships, and members' roles. The shift from *high mortality–high fertility* to *low mortality–low fertility* has heightened interest in adult intergenerational relationships. Increased life expectancy coupled with declining fertility has led to the *verticalization* of the family—a pattern of an increasing number of generations in a family accompanied by a decreasing number of members within a single generation (Bengtson, Rosenthal, and Burton 1990). Thus, family relationships are of unprecedented duration. Parents and children now share five decades of life, siblings may share eight decades of life, and the grandparent-grandchild bond may last two or three decades. Increases in life expectancies have led to middle age becoming the life stage in which adult children typically confront parental declining health and death. About 40 percent of Americans enter midlife with both parents alive, whereas 77 percent leave midlife with no parents alive.

The verticalization of the family in developed countries has also been accompanied by increased educational and labor force opportunities for women, technological advances in reproductive choice, and greater public acceptance of diverse lifestyles and family choices. Adults face unprecedented choices about whether and when to marry, whether to remain married, divorce, or remarry, and whether and when to have children. There is a growing heterogeneity in life course transitions as both men and women move in and out of cohabitation, marriage, parenthood, school, employment, and occupational careers at widely disparate ages and in different sequences. Phenomena that were once clear markers of young adulthood, such as marriage and parenthood, are therefore less predictable and there is greater diversity in the structure of families.

One phenomenon of the changing age structure of families that has received growing attention is the *sandwich generation,* those adults who find themselves caring for aging parents while still caring for their own children. Recent studies have raised questions, however, about the size of this phenomenon. A study of twelve European Union countries found that only 4 percent of men and 10 percent of women aged forty-five to fifty-four had overlapping responsibilities for children and older adults who required care (Hagestad 2000). Yet, others stress that the definition of caring that is employed greatly influences the obtained percentage of sandwiched adults. For example, the previously described emerging adult life stage (a prolonged period of independent role exploration) has led to a prolonged parenting phase for many midlife adults. Approximately one-third of U.S. parents aged forty to sixty currently coreside with an adult child (Ward and Spitze 1996).

Conclusion

The beginning of the twenty-first century will mean continued heterogeneity in the timing and sequencing of adult life course transitions. There are also reasons to believe that multigenerational bonds will be more important in the upcoming decades. First, the demographic changes of the aging population mean more years of shared living between generations. The impacts of this demographic shift will be particularly profound in developing countries. More than half (59%) of the world's elderly people now live in the developing nations and this proportion is expected to increase to 71 percent by 2030 (U.S. Census Bureau 2002b). Second, we have witnessed a growing importance in the roles of grandparents and other kin in supporting family functioning and well being. Middle-aged and older adults worldwide are increasingly parenting grandchildren and other young kin in families devastated by social problems such as substance abuse, the HIV/AIDs epidemic, civil war, forced migration, and poverty. Finally, despite popular rhetoric in a number of developed nations that the "nuclear family is in decline," research has consistently demonstrated the strength and resilience of family members' bonds across the generations.

See also: CHILDHOOD; ELDERS; FAMILY DEVELOPMENT THEORY; FILIAL RESPONSIBILITY; GRANDPARENTHOOD; INTERGENERATIONAL RELATIONS; LATER LIFE FAMILIES; LIFE COURSE THEORY; MENOPAUSE; RETIREMENT; SANDWICH GENERATION; SEXUALITY IN ADULTHOOD; SIBLING RELATIONSHIPS; TRANSITION TO PARENTHOOD

Bibliography

American Board of Family Practice. (1990). *Perspectives on Middle Age: The Vintage Years.* Princeton, NJ: New World Decisions.

Arnett, J. J. (2000). "Emerging Adulthood: A Theory of Development from the Late Teens through the Twenties." *American Psychologist* 55:469–80.

Avis, N. E., and McKinlay, S. M. (1991). "A Longitudinal Analysis of Women's Attitudes Toward the Menopause." *Maturitas* 13:65–79.

Bengtson, V.; Rosenthal, C.; and Burton, L. (1990). "Families and Aging: Diversity and Heterogeneity." In *Handbook of Aging and the Social Sciences,* 3rd edition, ed. R. H. Binstock and L. K. George. New York: Academic Press.

Brim, O. G. (1992). "Theories of Male Mid-Life Crisis." *Counseling Psychologist* 6:2–9.

Bumpaoo, Larry L., and Aquilino, William S. (1995). *A Social Map of Midlife: Family and Work over the Middle Life Course.* Madison, WI: Center for Demography and Ecology.

Duncan, L. E., and Agronick, G. S. (1995). "The Intersection of Life Stage and Social Events: Personality and Life Outcomes." *Journal of Personality and Social Psychology* 69:558–68.

Erikson, E. (1968). *Identity: Youth and Crisis.* New York: Norton.

Farrell, M. P., and Rosenberg, S. D. (1981). *Men at Midlife.* Boston: Auburn House.

Fry, C. L. (1980). *Aging in Culture and Society: Contemporary View Points and Strategies.* New York: Praeger.

Goldscheider, F. K., and Goldscheider, C. (1994). "Leaving and Returning Home in 20th-Century America." *Population Bulletin* 48:2–33.

Hagestad, G. O. (2000). "Intergenerational Relations." Paper prepared for the United Nations Economic Commission for Europe Conference on Generations and Gender, Geneva, July 3.

Hagestad, G. O., and Neugarten, B. L. (1990). "Age and the Life Course." In *Handbook on Aging and the Social Sciences,* 3rd edition, ed. R. H. Binstock and L. K. George. New York: Academic Press

Hareven, T. K. (1978). *Transitions: The Family and the Life Course in Historical Perspective.* New York: Academic Press.

Hatch, L. R. (2000). *Beyond Gender Differences: Adaptation to Aging in Life Course Perspective*. Amityville, NY: Baywood.

Jerrome, D. (1994). "Time, Change and Continuity in Family Life." *Ageing and Society* 14:1–27.

Lachman, M. E. (2001). *Handbook on Midlife Development*. New York: Wiley.

Lachman, M. E.; Lewkowicz, C.; Marcus, A.; and Peng, Y. (1994). "Images of Midlife Development among Young, Middle-Aged, and Older Adults." *Journal of Adult Development* 1:201–11.

Lock, M. (1994). "Encounters with Aging: Mythologies of Menopause in Japan and North America." Berkeley: University of California Press.

Menon, U. (2001). "Middle Adulthood in Cultural Perspective: The Imagined and Experienced in Three Cultures." In *Handbook on Midlife Development,* ed. M. E. Lachman. New York: Wiley.

Michael, R. T.; Gagnon, J. H.; Laumann, E. O.; and Kolata, G. (1995). *Sex in America: A Definitive Survey*. New York: Warner Books.

Montepare, J., and Lachman, M. E. (1989). "You're Only As Old As You Feel: Self-Perceptions of Age, Fears of Aging, and Life Satisfaction from Adolescence to Old Age." *Psychology and Aging* 4:73–78.

Mroczek, D. K., and Kolarz, C. M. (1998). "The Effects of Age on Positive and Negative Affect: A Developmental Perspective on Happiness." *Journal of Personality and Social Psychology* 75:1333–49.

National Council on Aging. (2000). *Myths and Realities: 2000 Survey Results*. Washington DC: Author.

Neugarten, B., and Datan, N. (1974). "The Middle Years." In *American Handbook of Psychology,* ed. S. Arieti. New York: Basic Books.

Riley, M. W.; Foner, M. A.; and Riley J. W., Jr. (1999). "The Aging and Society Paradigm." In *Handbook of Theories of Aging,* ed. J. E. Birren and K. W. Schaie. New York: Van Nostrand Reinhold.

Schaie, K. W. (2000). "The Impact of Longitudinal Studies on Understanding Development from Young Adulthood to Old Age." *International Journal of Behavioral Development* 24:257–66.

Skolnick, A. (1991). *Embattled Paradise*. New York: Basic Books.

Suzman, R., and Riley, M. W. (1985). "Introducing the Oldest-Old." *Milbank Quarterly* 63:177–86.

Treas, J., and Bengtson, V. L. (1982). "The Demography of Mid- and Late-Life Transitions." *Annals of the American Academy of Political and Social Science* 464:11–21.

Ward, R. A., and Spitze, G. (1996). "Will the Children Ever Leave? Parent-Child Coresidence History and Plans." *Journal of Family Issues* 17:514–39.

Other Resources

U.S. Census Bureau. (2000a). "Population Projections of the United States by Age, Sex, Race, Hispanic Origin, and Nativity: 1999 to 2000." Available from www.census.gov/population/www/projections/natproj.html.

U.S. Census Bureau. (2000b). "International Database." Available from www.census.gov/ipc/www/idbnew.html.

JUDITH G. GONYEA

AFFECTION

In the hit 1978 song, "You Don't Bring Me Flowers," Neil Diamond and Barbra Streisand sing of two lovers' sadness over their dying relationship.

The two lovers in this song notice that doing such things as bringing flowers, touching each other, and even chatting about the day's events, do not appear to be the priorities that they had once been. These *expressions of affection* (various means by which love is communicated to another person) contribute to the overall atmosphere of love in a given relationship. In fact, research suggests that the informed and deliberate use of expressions of affection has a profound impact on marital satisfaction. In the song above, the couple could, as a result of a failure to express affection, feel the relationship falling apart. Many people, particularly married couples, relate to this song because they have experienced this tragic loss of relational satisfaction on some level.

John Gottman has researched this phenomenon of relationship dissolution for over twenty years. He has predicted (1994), with 94 percent accuracy, whether or not a couple will stay together. According to Gottman, the main indicator of whether or not a couple will stay together is what he calls a 5:1 ratio between *positive moments* and *negative moments. Positive moments* are those subjective feelings of love experienced by one spouse that are directly due to the actions of the other spouse. *Negative moments* are those occasions when one of the partners feels unloved due to the actions (or inactions) of their spouse.

Gottman suggests that the people who are dissatisfied with their relationships and wish to dissolve them do so because they find that the negative moments in the relationship have more impact than the positive moments. Even if there are more positive than negative moments, if the ratio is not great enough, the relationship will be strained. This is primarily the result of the greater impact that unexpected negative moments have on a spouse as opposed to expected positive moments. After all, who marries anticipating feeling unloved? People expect the positive moments and relish the expressions of affection that they receive from their partners, and reel from the negative moments that appear to come, seemingly, out of nowhere. Therefore, according to Gottman, each person needs to experience a larger percentage of positive moments to negative moments in order to feel a sense of satisfaction in the relationship and a desire to maintain it. This is exemplified in the song quoted above.

Expressions of Affection

Given this positive moment–negative moment phenomenon, how can people maximize the positive moments and thereby keep not only their relationship intact, but also their relational partner satisfied? Two studies have addressed this to some degree by considering how one relational partner expresses love to the other (i.e., how to give positive moments through various expressions of affection). Kenneth Villard and Leland Whipple (1976) suggested ways that people express affection to each other. Gary Chapman (1997) followed the same vein, in his book entitled *The Five Love Languages*. Chapman developed categories of expressions of affection strikingly similar to Villard and Whipple's, including verbal expressions, quality time, gifts, service, and touch. Villard and Whipple had a sixth category, acts of aggression. Even these two lists may not provide an exhaustive understanding of how people express affection, but they do give a general framework for understanding tendencies in this area of relationships.

Verbal expressions. A verbal expression of affection is anything that could be said to or about the other person that could cause them to feel encouraged, loved, or validated. This includes, but is not limited to, the obvious statement "I love you." Many people long for this direct verbal expression of their spouse's feelings (Chapman 1997). The person who looks for verbal expressions of affection is happy with a compliment on appearance, a positive comment about a tasty meal, praise of victories achieved, or verbal support of a spouse's goals or dreams. Public praise or admiration of the spouse, even if it is not said directly to the spouse (either it is overheard or relayed by a third party), enhances the feelings of love felt by the recipient.

Quality time. Whereas some people feel loved when their spouse says positive things about them, others appreciate the second type of expression, *quality time.* For example, a husband who feels most loved through quality time, feels important when his wife takes time away from her other duties to spend time with him. Or a wife might feel loved through a silent walk on the beach. The quality time does not need to be spent with the couple in seclusion, although it could be spent that way. The most important element in quality time is togetherness. This might mean something as mundane as washing dishes together. While one washes and one dries, they could share stories about their day, dreams about life, or quietly go about the work in front of them with no words exchanged at all. Some research even suggests that such quality time is essential for development and maintenance of relationships (Baxter and Bullis 1986).

Gifts. Although some people see quality time as the primary expression of affection, others enjoy receiving gifts. Research indicates that there are many reasons why a person likes to receive gifts (Areni, Kieckner, and Palan 1998). A wife who feels loved by receiving gifts might be pleased because her husband spent money when it was totally out of character for him to do so. The giving of flowers to signify that the spouse remembered a special day (Mother's Day, birthday, or anniversary) could speak volumes to some partners. A gift could provide a positive moment because it indicates that the spouse thought of the other person when he or she was not present and that thought motivated the gift. Something as simple as picking up a candy bar can express affection.

Acts of service. Many people would say that gifts are perfectly fine, but "the clothes aren't going to fold themselves!" *Acts of service,* the fourth type of expression of affection, involves one partner performing specific actions for their spouse. The exertion of time and energy for the other's benefit is key. A husband who feels loved by what his wife does for him would experience the greatest feeling of love when his wife fixes dinner or surprises him by mowing the lawn. Likewise, a husband might express affection by changing soiled diapers or doing the laundry. These actions are not always the most wonderful or desirable things to do. Most people do not jump at the chance to clean the toilet or wash the car. However, the thought that a spouse would do something like this, even though he or she does not particularly like to, would make the other spouse feel loved. One researcher has indicated that supportive behaviors include *tangible support* (i.e., acts of service) through "offering assistance or resources" (Cutrona 1996). By offering time and energy through serving one another, marriage partners are likely to experience positive moments.

Touch. In addition to acts of service, many have the primary need for the fifth type of expression of affection, touch. Physical touch is *positive touching*. Positive touching does not necessarily have sexual overtones, though it does include this. Rather it is physical touch done for the purpose of showing positive feelings for someone. For instance, cuddling, hugging, an arm around the shoulder, or even holding hands fulfills a person's desire to be touched without a sexual level of involvement. These instances of touch let the other person know that he or she is loved. Touch is a *symbolic behavior* that sends several different messages. Researchers have outlined four particular categories of touch as a symbolic behavior: support, appreciation, inclusion, and sexual touch (Jones and Yarbrough 1985). *Supportive touch* happens when one spouse shows care and concern for the other such as through a hug. *Appreciation touching* usually occurs with verbalized statement of gratitude. The touch might be a pat on the back or a kiss on the cheek accompanying "Thank you!" *Inclusion touching* is reserved for intimate friends, spouses, or other family members. It involves such behaviors as holding hands and sitting on laps to suggest special inclusion of deliberately chosen individuals. Sexual touch is designed to indicate sexual attraction and intent toward and including sexual intercourse. Although these are different types of touch, they all could signify a positive moment for some spouses.

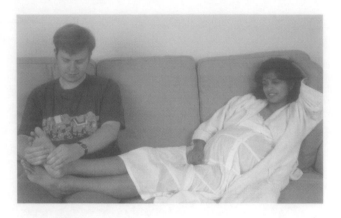

A pregnant woman enjoys a foot massage from her partner. Research indicates that selfless gestures of affection are related to the degree of marital satisfaction. JENNIE WOODCOCK; REFLECTIONS PHOTOLIBRARY/CORBIS

Aggression. The final category, which could arguably fall under physical touch, has been separated out because some of its distinct qualities. Aggression, as Villard and Whipple (1967) use it, seems paradoxical. The goal of *aggressive touch* is not to injure or cause harm to a person (the very antithesis of love). Instead, aggression is affection that might best be described as "horse-play" or "rough-housing." This is the playful pinching, wrestling, or soft punching on the arm that are indicative of many friendships. It differs from physical touch in that it can often be misconstrued by outsiders or even by the recipient of this affection. A specific example of this is playfully wrestling the remote control from a reluctant spouse's hand (with more interest in the wrestling than in the remote control). Messing up a spouse's hair or tugging at their clothing can likewise send signals of affection. Certainly, acts of aggression come in various forms and cease to express love if the other spouse feels, in any way, violated as a result.

Sex Differences and Expressions of Affection

There is an ongoing debate as to whether or not there is a difference between how men and women exhibit these various expressions of affection and how they desire to receive it. For example, Deborah Tannen (1990) suggests there is a difference in how men and women desire to communicate verbally with each other. Although both spouses are capable of utilizing supportive verbal behaviors, men tend to use *report speaking,* and women tend to use *rapport speaking.* Report speaking is a type of verbal interaction where the whole purpose is to inform. A husband might organize his thoughts into a list of things that he intends to communicate to his wife. He tells her the items on his list and feels that he has communicated. According to Tannen, this tends to frustrate women who use a rapport type of verbal communication style, in which the whole purpose is to build relationships and share meanings. Tannen argues that, in general, women are more emotionally expressive and feel hurt by men who do not talk about everything on their minds.

Some argue that men and women are predisposed toward particular expressions of affection. Men, it is suggested, are more likely to remember the occasion and effort that they put into giving a gift while women are more likely to remember receiving a gift (Areni, Kieckner, and Palan 1998). If a wife brings her husband a collectible item, he might appreciate it. However, when questioned about gifts, he would be more likely to say that he enjoyed giving her a gift, than receiving one himself. Men, on the other hand, might be more likely to desire physical touch.

As appealing as these differences may sound, and however they may accord with the experience of many, researchers have begun to think that, in general, sex differences in communication are minimal (Canary and Dindia 1998; Canary, Emmers-Sommer, and Faulkner 1997). At issue is not so much how different genders express affection but how individual spouses in a given marriage relationship express it.

Marital Satisfaction

The categories of how people express love to each other are potentially helpful. These expressions of affection suggest a framework for understanding how different people view positive moments. Unfortunately, each spouse has a tendency to expect others to act, think, and desire things the way they do (Knapp and Vangelisti 1996). They focus on how they would like to receive affection. As a result, husbands and wives tend to express love to each other the way that they would like to receive it, thus neglecting to express love the way that the other person would feel the most loved. Examples of this confusion include a wife who feels love through the reception of gifts and who, in turn, gives gifts to her spouse to express affection to him. Little does she realize that he most feels loved

through words of affirmation and encouragement. What should have been a positive moment turns into a negative one when a fight ensues because "You don't sing me love songs!" Consequently, spouses become dissatisfied and the relationship dissolves without either party really knowing what happened. Their main explanation is that they no longer feel loved.

Research suggests that a spouse who receives the type of love that he or she desires has higher levels of marital satisfaction than a spouse who does not (Keithley 2000). Each person in the relationship can directly influence the level of satisfaction that the other person experiences. This has profound implications for a relationship.

Knowing that a relational partner might not fully appreciate or feel loved by a certain action makes it clear that communication on this topic between spouses is essential. Likewise, it requires communication to know what positively increases a spouse's sense of satisfaction. If the two people in the relationship take the time to talk about the expressions of affection that the other spouse could perform to make them feel loved (i.e., increase their positive moments), they could specifically attempt to meet their spouse's needs in an informed and deliberate manner. This, of course, demands a certain degree of selfless behavior by both partners in the marriage. But doing so would increase each person's good moments, which, in turn, gives the relationship a greater degree of satisfaction. The song then changes, "You buy me flowers, you sing me love songs, you talk to me all the more, when you walk through the door at the end of the day."

See also: COMMUNICATION: COUPLE RELATIONSHIPS; FRIENDSHIP; INTIMACY; LOVE; MARITAL QUALITY; RELATIONSHIP MAINTENANCE; RENEWAL OF WEDDING VOWS

Bibliography

Areni, C. S.; Kieckner, P.; and Palan, K. M. (1998). "Is It Better to Give than to Receive? Exploring Gender Differences in the Meaning of Memorable Gifts." *Psychology and Marketing* 15:81–109.

Baxter, L. A., and Bullis, C. (1986). "Turning Points in Developing Romantic Relationships." *Communication Research* 12:469–493.

Canary, D. J., and Dindia, K., eds. (1998). *Sex Differences and Similarities in Communication: Critical Essays and Empirical Investigations of Sex and Gender in Interaction.* Mahwah, NJ: Lawrence Erlbaum Associates.

Canary D. J.; Emmers-Sommer, T. M.; and Faulkner, S. (1997). *Sex and Gender: Differences in Personal Relationships.* New York: Guilford Press.

Chapman, G. (1997). *The Five Love Languages: How to Express Heartfelt Commitment to Your Mate.* Chicago: Northfield Publishing.

Cutrona, C. E. (1996). "Social Support as a Determinant of Marital Quality: The Interplay of Negative and Supportive Behaviors." In *Handbook of Social Support and the Family,* ed. G. R. Pierce, B. R. Sarason, and I. G. Sarason. New York: Plenum Press.

Diamond, N.; Bergman, A.; and Bergman, M. (1978). "You Don't Bring Me Flowers." Stonebrige Music (ASCAP) and Threesome Music (ASCAP).

Gottman, J. M. (1994). "Why Marriages Fail." In *Making Connections: Readings in Relational Communication,* ed. K. M. Galvin and P. J. Cooper. Los Angeles: Roxbury.

Jones, S. E., and Yarbrough, A. E. (1985). "A Naturalistic Study of the Meanings of Touch." *Communication Monographs* 52:19–55.

Keithley, J. M. (2000). "How Do I Love Thee? Let Me Count the Ways: The Impact of Affection on Marital Satisfaction." Unpublished master's thesis. Macomb: Western Illinois University.

Knapp, M. L., and Vangelisti, A. L. (1996). *Interpersonal Communication and Human Relationships,* 3rd edition. Boston: Allyn and Bacon.

Tannen, D. (1990). *You Just Don't Understand: Women and Men in Conversation.* New York: Ballantine Books.

Villard, K. L., and Whipple, L. J. (1967). *Beginnings in Relational Communication.* New York: John Wiley and Sons.

JENNIFER M. KEITHLEY

AFGHANISTAN

Afghanistan lies in Central Asia between Iran on the west, Pakistan on the east and south, and Turkmenistan, Uzbekistan, and Tajikistan on the north side. The Afghani population in the early twenty-first century is estimated at about 22 million people living in Afghanistan and as refugees in Iran and Pakistan. There are more than forty ethnic groups in Afghanistan. Pushtuns are the largest ethnic group, about 40 percent of the population, living in the south and southeast parts of the country. Tajiks make up about 35 percent and live in central and eastern parts of the country. The next two groups are Hazarahs, minority Shiite Muslims who represent about 8 percent, and Uzbeks, who represent about 9 percent of the population, respectively. The dominant religion is Sunni Islam, and most Afghanis are bilingual in Duri and Pushtu. The mountainous terrain of Afghanistan has created a sociogeography of isolation, ethnic conflict, and tribal alliances. To discuss any aspect of family life in Afghanistan requires a brief recount of modern history of the country.

Historical Background

In 1919, Afghanistan gained independence from Britain and adopted a constitution in 1964. Tribalism and a pastoral economy dominated Afghanistan's socioeconomic structure until the 1970s. In 1978, a series of upheavals called the Saour Revolution led to a leftist government in Kabul. Legal measures such as land reform and family laws were introduced to modernize and unify the country. However, factional conflicts in the ruling party and tribal disputes with the central government led to Soviet intervention in 1979. In response to the Soviet intervention, the United States, Saudi Arabia, and Pakistan joined to help the opposition, which consisted of a loose federation of resistance groups called the *Mujahidins.* In 1989, the Soviet army left Afghanistan, and the American aid stopped. In 1992, several Mujahidin factions entered Kabul and removed President Najibullah. Between 1992 and 1994, power changed hands in violent clashes between Mujahidin factions with an estimated fifty thousands civilians killed. A less known faction of the Mujahidin, called the *Taliban*—meaning students of Islamic seminaries—took control of 90 percent of Afghanistan in 1994. Between 1994 until September 2001, the Taliban established order, although at great cost to many segments of the population. Meanwhile, they battled an opposition group called the Northern Alliance. Civil war, refugee status, and extreme economic conditions have changed the family structure in Afghanistan.

Continuity and Change in Traditional Afghani Family

Family and tribal identity have encompassed Afghan women's lives. Marriages were endogamous based on family considerations, tribal lineage, and geographical location. Nancy Tapper (1991) writes about Pushtuns' tribal system in pre-1970 Afghanistan as patrilineal and endogamous. Property inheritance was patrilineal (through the male line), and women did not inherit property except their trousseau given by their birth family. The Hazarahs and some of the Tajiks followed the inheritance requirements of the Islamic law of Shari'at, in which daughters inherit half and wives one-fourth of the property. Divorce was rare, and polygamous marriages were common.

As in many North African and Middle Eastern societies, an Afghan man's honor is closely linked to the behavior of his female relatives. A woman's indiscretion could directly affect a man's social standing. Consequently, men controlled women's behavior in public and monitored their interaction in private. This control was rarely complete, and women could subvert men's control and exert influence in family relationships.

Marriages, until legal reforms in family law, were arranged in three forms: among equals for the bride-price given to the father of the bride, as an exchange of brides between families for the bride-price, and as the giving of the bride for blood money (i.e., the victim's family would agree to receive a girl from the accused's family instead of avenging their member's blood by killing the accused) or as compensation for stolen or destroyed property (Tapper 1991). These forms of marriages are less common today, and giving women for blood money has been banned completely. As in many Muslim countries, family is still the locus of social relationships, ethnic identity is strong, and for the most part marriages take place within the same tribal lineage.

Many aspects of family relations changed after the leftist government of Mohammad Saoud came to power in 1973. Women were allowed into the National Assembly; forced marriages were banned; a minimum age for marriage was established; and women gained the right to employment. The socialist government established a national educational system for all children; schools were co-ed,

and 70 percent of teachers and 50 percent of civil service employees were women. These changes were voluntary, and many urban families supported a gradual change of gender roles. After the Soviet army left and the Mujahidin took power, many of these rights were canceled, although haphazardly.

In 1994, when the Taliban came to power, they officially rescinded all previous reforms and launched a campaign of terror against ethnic minorities, especially Shiite Hazarahs and some Tajiks. They imposed a strict gender code based on their interpretation of Islamic law of Shari'at. Immediately after takeover, on September 26, they issued an edict that banned women from working, closed girls' schools, and required women to wear *Borqa*—a full body covering with a meshed section for the eyes—and to be accompanied outside home by a male guardian. Women's access to health care was restricted and female health care workers and aid workers were either purged or had their activities constrained. As a result, women's health has suffered. In a 1998 survey, Zohra Rasekh and colleagues reported that women living in camps in Pakistan had a high rate of depression, displacement hardship, and other health-related problems.

Initially, Afghani women's oppression received world attention that condemned Taliban policies. Simplistically, these policies were attributed to the extreme Islamic fundamentalism that disregarded Pushtuns' ideals regarding family honor and tribal identity. The Taliban forces consisted of Pushtun boys trained by conservative mullahs in *madrasses,* or Islamic seminaries, in Pakistan. They had minimum contact with any women, including female family members. In the seminaries, they were taught a potent revolutionary ideology constructed of Pushtun notions of shame and honor based on men's control of women's sexuality, combined with Pushtuns' perception of their ethnic superiority. In madrasses, this ethnic and gender supremacy was cast into conservative Islamic theology to create the Taliban's notion of pure society and women's place in it.

The fate of women received world attention, but at the same time, all family members suffered. Men paid heavily for the war and Taliban domination. The few who were employed were mindful of their family's security, faced harassment by morality police, and looked to protect their sons from a

A group of children read in a school located within a mosque in Afghanistan. When the Taliban came into power in 1994, they closed many schools and prohibited education for females. These restrictions were lifted in September 2001. CARO-LINE PENN/CORBIS

military draft that had no age limit or required consent. Those unemployed tried to support their family without the safety net of the extended family. In rural areas, drought limited pastures for herders and made farming less predictable. The only income left was from smuggling and poppy cultivation. If they moved their families, men went back and forth to care for elderly parents or other relatives. They faced capture or bandits, and in the host countries performed the most undesirable manual work. For urban families, women's confinement meant closure of schools and loss of women's income. Many families, including some Taliban officials, who did not support school closure moved their families out of the country to secure education of their children, both boys and girls, and keep them away from the clashes.

The Afghani Family in the Early Twenty-First Century

The status of contemporary Afghani families is a patchwork of displacement, poverty, war, unemployment, and lack of basic necessities. As of spring 2002, the United Nations and aid agencies report 5.3 million very vulnerable people at risk of severe malnutrition. Families struggle to survive in an agricultural economy dependent on opium cultivation ravaged by war and drought. Approximately 350,000 internally displaced individuals and an estimated five million refugees in Iran and Pakistan suggest profound structural changes for Afghani families. The majority of refugees in Pakistan are Pushtuns, and most refugees in Iran are Tajiks and Hazarahs.

In Iran, only a small fraction of refugees live in camps. The early refugee families are intact and, despite economic difficulties, are living together. Some are second generation and have never been to Afghanistan. The majority are integrated in three areas in central and eastern cities. This group benefits from the national health care, and their children attend public schools. The government and aid agencies provide health screening and vaccination for children and free reproductive health services for women. Distrustful of madrasses, the Iranian government frowns upon private Afghani schools and provides public education as much as possible.

The refugees arriving after 1995 face more problems. They came in small groups and have had trouble joining other family members. Accordingly, female-headed households are more common among the later refugees. Another incoming group consists of unmarried young men attracted to the booming construction industry.

The Pakistani government has taken a different approach to Afghan refugees. Pakistan helped the Taliban faction and was one of the three countries recognizing them as a legitimate government (the other two being Saudi Arabia and the United Arab Emirates). Although some of the early refugees to Pakistan became integrated into society, many live in about 300 refugee villages set up by the United Nations High Commissioner for Refugees (UNHCR). The early refugees in Pakistan, like those in Iran, consist of more intact families. Unlike Iran, the Pakistani government encouraged madrasses and military camps to train Taliban fighters. There they absorbed a potent revolutionary ideology constructed of Pushtun ethnic supremacy, Sunni Islam, and traditional patriarchy.

On September 11, 2001, terrorist attacks against the United States led to massive destruction and fatalities in New York City and Washington, DC. The group responsible was perceived to be hiding in Afghanistan. The U.S.-led bombing of Afghanistan caused the massive movement of people at borders to enter Iran or Pakistan. As of spring 2002, the Taliban had been removed, the U.S. forces were in the country, and a new interim government had taken office. Two women serve as cabinet members of this new government. A voluntary repatriation program arranged by the UNHCR and the Iranian and Pakistani governments is underway. About half million refugees from Pakistan and approximately 80,000 from Iran have returned.

The picture of Afghani family is one of individuals holding to extended family and lineage when possible, but less than half of the Afghani population can do so. The UNHCR is involved in the largest human assistance program, started on September 24, 2001. Life expectancy is forty-four years, and one out of four children dies before reaching the age of five. Afghanistan has the highest density of landmines of any country in the world. Both the Taliban and the Northern Alliance recruited, sometimes by force, young boys into their armed forces.

The unintended consequence of the war has been the broadening of women's views about their roles. By various accounts, there are close to one million widows or separated women who are the heads of households. Afghani women refugees, witnessing Iranian and Pakistani women's educational and occupational achievements, have acquired new expectations for their daughters and themselves. In Iran, Afghani girls attending primary school outnumber Afghani boys. The aid agencies' policies are a factor in this: For example, under the Oil for Girls program, a family receives a gallon of cooking oil for every month that a girl stays in school. Afghani women have acquired a sense of autonomy by dealing on their own with aid agencies or government bureaucracies of the host nations.

Intratribal or bicultural marriages have increased. Nevertheless, this is particularly problematic when Afghani men marry Iranian or Pakistani women. Because a woman carries her husband's legal status, these men do not become citizens of their wives' respective countries, though their children are registered to both parents. This creates problems for Iranian families when women unfamiliar with the law marry Afghani men. In contrast, Afghani women marrying Iranian or Pakistani men do not face such a problem. The latter is less common.

Conclusion

For Afghanis, family life continues to function as a paramount social institution. However, in the face of war and the refugee situation, families have experienced change and disruption. Afghani refugee women in Iran deeply regret the loss of family support, but governments and aid agencies have replaced some of this support. Refugee girls born or raised outside Afghanistan may not return, and some of those who have remained in the country are traumatized by chronic problems of displacement and famine. Further, there is a generation of young men and boys raised on the streets or in training camps and madrasses away from extended family's support and removed from its code of responsibility and rights. Despite the historic resilience of the people, this combination does not bode well for the future of Afghan family.

See also: ISLAM; WAR/POLITICAL VIOLENCE

Bibliography

Benjamin, J. (2000) "Afghanistan: Women Survivors of War under the Taliban." In *War's Offensive on Women:*

The Humanitarian Challenge in Bosnia, Kosvo, and Afghanistan, ed. J. A Mertus. Bloomfield. CT: Kumarian Press.

Gerami, S. (1996). *Women and Fundamentalism: Islam and Christianity.* New York: Garland.

Gregorian, V. (1969). *The Emergence of Modern Afghanistan: Politics of Reform and Modernization 1880–1946.* Stanford, CA: Stanford University Press.

Hatch Dupree, N. (1998). "Afghan Women under the Taliban." In *Fundamentalism Reborn? Afghanistan and Taliban,* ed. William Maley. New York: New York University Press.

Rasekh, Z., et al. (1998). "Women's Health and Human Rights in Afghanistan." *Journal of the American Medical Association* 5:449–455.

Rubin, B. R. (1995). *The Fragmentation of Afghanistan: State Formation and Collapse of the International System.* New Haven, CT: Yale University Press.

Squire, C. (2000). "Education of Afghan Refugees in the Islamic Republic of Iran." Tehran: UNHCR and UNICEF.

Tapper, N. (1991). *Bartered Brides: Politics, Gender and Marriage in an Afghan Tribal Society.* Cambridge: Cambridge University Press.

United Nations High Commissioner for Refugees (2001a). *Background Paper on Refugees and Asylum Seekers from Afghanistan.* Geneva: Center for Documentation and Research.

Other Resources

United Nations High Commissioner for Refugees (2001). "UN Prepares for Massive Humanitarian Crisis in Afghanistan." Available from http://www.unhcr.ch/cgi-bin/texis/vtx/home.

SHAHIN GERAMI

AFRICAN–AMERICAN FAMILIES

In 1998, there were approximately 8.4 million African-American households in the United States. With a total population of approximately 34.5 million, African Americans made up 13 percent of the population of U.S. families. African-American families are not very different from other U.S. families; they, too, are chiefly responsible for the care and development of children. However, African-American family life has several distinctive features related to the timing and approaches to marriage and family formation, gender roles, parenting styles, and strategies for coping with adversity.

Historical and Cultural Influences on African-American Family Life

These explanations include contemporary economic hardship, the historic constraints of slavery, and integration of African culture in American life. Accordingly, three sets of forces account for the forms and manifestation of African-American family life as it exists in the contemporary United States. These forces include (1) integration into family life of cultural practices adapted from West Africa; (2) structural adaptations to slavery, especially the disruptions of family ties and the overall lack of control over life; and (3) past and current discrimination and economic inequality.

Pre-slavery influences: culture and family life in West Africa. Over the years, fierce intellectual struggles have been waged over the extent to which Africans brought to the United States as slaves were able to retain their culture. That debate has largely been settled by a preponderance of evidence demonstrating structural, linguistic, and behavioral parallels between African Americans and West Africans. Most African Americans are descended from people brought to the United States as slaves from West Africa after a period of reprogramming in the Caribbean. Their families in Africa were tightly organized in extended family units, which by most historical accounts were social units that functioned effectively. Their marriages involved contractual agreements between families as much as agreements between the men and women. What is most distinctive about family life in West Africa is that individuals traced their ancestral lineage not through their fathers, but through their mothers. The matrilineal organization of family was evidenced by the practice of children belonging solely to the family of the mother, and by the role accorded to the mother's oldest brother, who was the most responsible for his sister's children. In these families, mothers' brothers were accorded the same respect as a father; maternal cousins were regarded as siblings. Unlike patriarchal societies, marriage did not sever the ties between a woman and her family, nor did it end the obligation of the mother's family to her and her offspring.

The West African family, viewed as a clan, is arguably a predecessor or model for the extended family structures found in contemporary African-American communities. During slavery, the family remained a principal base for social affiliation, economic activity, and political organization. Family traditions in Western Africa served as the model for family life during the period of slavery. The family lives of Africans brought to the American colonies as slaves retained some of the same qualities particularly the matriarchal focus (Franklin and Moss 1988). Nevertheless, the biological father was responsible for ensuring physical and psychological well-being. In West Africa, ties to a common female ancestor bound members of a clan to one another. Indentured servants brought this template of family life, with its mores, customs, and beliefs to the New World, and retained them during the long period of slavery to pass them on to their children.

Family life during slavery. Although some early ancestors of African Americans came to the United States as free or indentured servants and maintained their free status over the generations, the majority were forced into a long life of servitude. To exact involuntary labor from African slaves, European Americans used generous portions of both physical and psychological violence. However, European Americans understood that they would only be able to consolidate their control if they stripped Africans of their identity, language, and the culture that bound them to their past in Africa (Franklin and Moss 1988). This was accomplished by undermining and replacing family structures with transient relationships built around identity as slaves owned by others, rather than with a family unit. These efforts were not entirely successful. In spite of the obstacles, many slaves organized themselves into family structures remarkably similar to nuclear family structures in the rest of America. Intact and committed marital relationships were commonplace among slaves. Men and women joined in monogamous relationships through explicit ceremonies. The children born of these relationships had paternal and maternal relationships, even when the parents could not exercise complete control over their children's lives. Throughout the period of slavery in the United States, strong family ties and committed marital relationships were evident even among couples forced to live apart. When men and women were able to purchase their freedom or to secure it through the beneficence of the slave owner, they would work for money to purchase the freedom of their spouses and their

children. These and many other efforts to bring family to live in the same household suggest strongly that African Americans strove to create the ideals of family life made difficult by the institution of slavery (Gutman 1977).

Contemporary Social Influences

Historical and cultural forces cannot account for every aspect of African-American family life. Contemporary social forces exert very powerful influences over the formation and nature of family life in black America today. For example, successive waves of migration from rural to urban areas during the twentieth century, racism, poverty, urbanization, segregation, and immigration from outside the United States have profoundly reshaped family life.

Rural to urban migration. When the Civil War ended, and former slaves were free to move, an overwhelming majority of African Americans resided in the rural South. In later decades, however, in response to economic downturns and the absence of opportunity in rural areas, African Americans moved to cities in the northeast and to urban midwestern areas to seek economic advancement. This twentieth century wave of migration out of the rural South was so massive that by 1998, only 55 percent of African Americans lived in the South. They make up one-fifth of that region's population. Nationwide, 54 percent resided in the central cities of metro areas. Half of the ten states with the largest African-American populations were outside of the deep South. New York (3.2 million) tops the list of states with the largest African-American population, followed by California (2.4 million).

As a consequence of these migrations, families moved from relatively cohesive rural communities to cities where they were anonymous. Not all families were able to re-create networks by moving close to relatives and people they had known in the South or to establish new ones with fictive kin. Urbanization with its fast-paced life, long work hours, multiple jobs, and neighborhoods, proved destructive to family life. Because women had access to the labor market, men assumed domestic responsibilities and shared in the care of children. African Americans encountered new and virulent forms of racism and discrimination, which were less obvious in the northeast, midwest, and west than those of the South. This new racism, however, had more subtle and deleterious effects. Residential segregation was enforced not by law, but by informal covenants and economic discrimination. Although many families had access to better paying jobs than were available in the South, their ability to advance their socioeconomic status (SES) on the basis of merit was often limited by the same racial discrimination they had experienced in the South.

Poverty. The transition from the rural South to urban life, often in northern cities, offered no guarantee of relief from poverty for African-American families. Poverty has remained the most pressing issue adversely affecting family life among African-Americans. Family life among African Americans is adversely affected by a tightly related set of adverse social conditions. These conditions include low SES and educational achievement, underemployment, teenage pregnancy, patterns of family formation, divorce, health problems, and psychological adjustment. In 1998, 88 percent of African Americans ages twenty-five to twenty-nine had graduated from high-school, continuing an upward trend in the educational attainment of African Americans that began in 1940. Despite this increased achievement, however, the median income for African-American households in 1997 was $25,050. Thus, the number of African-American families living below the poverty level stood at 26.5 percent in 1998. Poverty is important in its own right for the material hardship it brings. It has multiple adverse effects because it is implicated in marital distress and dissolution, health problems, lower educational attainment and deficits in psychological functioning, and prospects for healthy development over the life course (Barbarin 1983).

Immigration. Beginning in the 1990s and stretching into the twenty-first century, African-American family life has been subject to an influx of new immigrants from the Caribbean and parts of Africa. This movement is oddly reminiscent of the immigration pattern three centuries earlier. Arrivals from the Caribbean and East and West Africa have expanded the diversity of African-American families as they reconnect African Americans with their distant relatives who themselves have been transformed by modernity and urbanization. These new immigrants make for an African-American community that is even more diverse in language. The range of languages spans from the Creole patois of Haiti and French-speaking Africa to the Spanish of Panama.

Immigrants of African descent give new meaning and flavor to the American melting pot as they create their own blend of lilting cadences of Caribbean English, plus an added spice of French-speaking Senegalese. In one manner, these new groups of voluntary immigrants represent assimilation without accommodating the customs of American mainstream values and beliefs. While Africans and West Indians come to the United States to seek opportunities and freedom, they retain national pride and also the languages and customs associated with their countries of origin. As the issue of assimilation into the African-American community takes place, new tensions and promises will arise, as newcomers and long-time residents establish their relationships with one another and grope to find their areas of common ground.

African-American Families in the New Millennium

Historical and cultural influences, racism, urbanization, migration, discrimination, segregation, and immigration have profoundly shaped contemporary African-American family functioning. The new millennium brings with it striking differences in contemporary African-American functioning families and those of the past. These differences are specifically marked by the timing of family formation and stability of marriages, the flexibility of its gender roles, patterns of paternal involvement in child care, the fluidity of household composition, and the cultural resources the family has available to cope with adversity.

Timing of the formation of African-American households. The formation of African-American households often originates not in marriage but in the birth of a child. Fifty-six percent of African-American children were born in families in which the mother was not married to the biological father. Of 8.4 million African-American households, slightly less than half are presided over by a married couple. About 4 million African-American children (36 percent) reside with both their parents. Not surprisingly, women head a majority of the families formed by unmarried parents. For example, in 1998, single women headed 54 percent of African-American households. Unfortunately, mothers living with their children without ever having been married face decreasing prospects of marriage and thus look to a future in which they will spend much of their adult lives as unmarried caregivers of their children and their children's children. However, such demographic data taken alone paint a misleading portrait of African-American families.

Marriage. Historically, strong marriages and commitment to family life have been central features of African-American families. In the last decade of the twentieth century, however, marriage rates among African Americans declined significantly. In 1998, for example, 41 percent of all African-American men over the age of eighteen had never been married and 37 percent of African-American women over the age of eighteen had never married (U.S. Bureau of the Census, 1999). Experts on the African-American family have attributed the declining rates to the shortage of marriageable African-American males (Wilson 1987) and to structural, social, and economic factors (Tucker and Mitchell-Kernan 1995).

Throughout history, the population of African-American women has outnumbered the population of African-American men. By 1990, there were only 88 males for every 100 females (Tucker and Mitchell-Kernan 1995). The shortage of African-American males is further exacerbated by the large percentage of men who are unemployed, underemployed, users of narcotic drugs, or mentally ill, and thus fall into the undesirable category (Chapman 1997). That is, few African-American women would consider these men suitable for marriage. Thus, the chances of ever getting married are dramatically reduced by the overall sex-ratio imbalance among African Americans and the relatively low percentage of available marriageable males.

Although the basic determinants underlying the high rates of singlehood among African Americans are structural and ideological preferences, definite patterns also exist along class and gender lines (Staples 1997). For low-income African Americans, the structural constraints appear to be primarily that of unavailability and undesirability. However, among middle-class African Americans, the desire not to marry is more prevalent. Because African-American women have long been in the workforce, their earning power is similar to that of African-American men, and thus many African-American females do not feel a need to marry for economic support. Staples (1997) believes the greater a woman's educational level and income, the less desirable she is to many African-American men.

Despite the problematic aspect of finding a mate, many single African Americans continue to dream of marrying and living happily. However, the probability of staying together in a marital relationship is low because of the high divorce rate among African Americans. Although African Americans continue to have higher divorce rates than those in the general population, there was a slight decrease in divorce rate from 1990 to 1998 (U.S. Bureau of Census 1999).

For new immigrants and for those who have been in the United States for generations, family units retain important parental functions to care for, socialize, and nurture dependent children and to provide social intimacy that protects adults against loneliness and alienation. In many societies, this latter goal is often carried out through some form of marital relationship. Family units also have an important role in helping individuals to cope with the vicissitudes of life, the adverse life events both expected and unexpected. Thus, the importance of extended family and kin in reinforcing and maintaining connective and strong supportive ties among family members is often overshadowed by these negative portrayals of contemporary African-American family life.

Extended family structure. Census data on the composition of African-American households often overlook the functional and adaptive importance of the extended family structure and supportive kin networks. This is especially true of households headed by single mothers. Even when single mothers and their children do not reside with other kin, the money, time, childcare, and emotional support that family members lend substantially enriches single-parent households. Exchanges across households also mean that membership in a given household may fluctuate as children and adult kin move for a time from one household to another. Although single mothers and children live in close proximity to extended family members, frequent phone calls and face-to-face contact reinforce connections that often involve exchanges across households of social and material resources needed to meet the demands of daily living. Consequently, a majority of African-American family structures are more accurately depicted as extended family units rather than single adult nuclear family units. Snapshots of households from survey studies reveal more than seventy different family structures based on the number of generations and the relationship of people living in a single house. This compares to about forty structures for whites and certainly underscores the variability of African-American family structure and the flexible roles family members typically engender (Barbarin and Soler 1993).

Fathers. Even with the high proportion of single adult households headed by women, men continue to play key roles in the African-American family and contribute significantly to the effectiveness of family functioning. In African-American families, men adopt more flexible gender roles and take on a much broader array of household duties and responsibility for the care of children than is true in other groups. The relationship between mothers and the biological fathers who do not reside with their children often dictates the level of involvement that noncustodial fathers have with their children. When the relationships with mothers are good, fathers regularly visit or care for children and provide consistent financial support. Even if the biological father is not involved, other men such as stepfathers, grandparents, uncles, cousins and nonmarried partners may be instrumentally and regularly involved with the children.

Parenting and discipline. Another way in which African-American families tend to differ from other ethnic groups is in their style of discipline and parenting. African-American parents tend to be more hierarchical in relationships with their children. They are more likely to be strict, to hold demanding standards for behavior, and to use physical discipline more frequently in enforcing these standards. However, in African-American families the high use of physical punishment occurs within a context of strong support and affection. This combination of warmth with strictness tends to mediate negative impact of physical punishment delivered in other circumstances. Consequently, physical punishment does not result in the same adverse developmental outcomes for African-American children that it does for European-American children (McLoyd, Cauce, Takeuchi, and Wilson 2000).

Grandparents. Grandparents—particularly grandmothers—play an especially important role in African-American families in providing support for mothers and care for children. When mothers are not able to carry out their roles, grandmothers are the surrogate parents of choice. In 1998, 1.4 million African-American children (12%) lived in a grandparent's home (with or without their parents present). Grandparents' contribution to the care of young children is reciprocated at the end of life. Many African-American families care for relatives at the end of their lives in family settings. Rather than to relying on nursing homes or paid live-in care, African-American adult family members are more likely to bring their aging parents into their homes to care for them. Indeed, studies of the burden and psychological results of caring for the elderly show that African-American families are affected less negatively than any other ethnic group that cares for elderly and dying family members.

Siblings. Older siblings also play an important role in African-American families particularly households. When partners, grandmothers, or other adults from the extended kin network are not available in the household, older siblings, especially female siblings, are pressed into service to assist the mother. When single parents are required to work and to be away from home for extended times, older children are asked to monitor, feed, and discipline younger siblings. The placement of older children in these roles is both a source of early maturation and strain for older siblings, who more often than not are the oldest female siblings in the household.

Cultural resources for families. Since their introduction to North America as indentured servants and slaves, African-American families have transcended adversity in part by relying on important cultural and social resources such as spirituality, mutual support, ethnic identity, and adaptive extended family structures. Religious institutions, particularly Christian churches, have been important in the African-American community both for the religious ideology that gives meaning to uncontrollable and distressing life events and for the emotional support and practical aid they often provide. (Lincoln and Mamiya 1990). Also important to coping is the strength of ethnic identity through which African Americans maintain a favorable view of self and a strong group affiliation. These cultural resources, spirituality, ethnic identity, and mutual support contribute greatly to the resilience African-American families.

Resilience and coping. To appreciate how African-American families survived slavery, rampant racial discrimination, and chronic poverty, it is helpful to focus on several cultural resources they

The extended family structure, in which members of a family provide assistance in the form of the money, time, childcare, and emotional support to each other, is an important characteristic of many African-American families. BILL BACHMANN/ INDEX STOCK IMAGERY

have historically counted upon in the face of adversity. These resources include culturally based spirituality, strong ethnic identity, social support from extended kin and community, and the capacity to apply externalizing interpretive frameworks to problems in daily living (Barbarin 1983). African-American families are grounded, and extended family and communities' social support systems provide resources, both emotional and practical, to assist in coping with life problems. Moreover, religion and spirituality provide a foundation for coping by extending to them a providential and protective God with whom they developed a personal relationship (Taylor and Chatters 1991). In addition, religion provides additional benefits through participation in a social network of church members who became important sources of practical aid and emotional support. The development of strategies for coping with racial slights and discrimination also forms an important part of children's socialization experiences. By knowing that they are identifying strongly with their ethnic group African-American family members, children forge a strong sense of identity by

which they buttress themselves and see themselves as part of a larger group that must face and overcome the challenges of racism. With a keen awareness of the reality of racism in their lives, African-American children are exhorted to recognize what they are working against and understand the necessity of working twice as hard as European Americans to get what they want and need. This perspective on the self and sensitivity to discrimination helps them to sustain efforts when times are difficult. Cultural resources such as kin support, spirituality, and ethnic identity over time have been important factors in protecting and strengthening African-American families in coping with their lion's share of adversities—before, during, and after slavery.

See also: ETHNIC VARIATION/ETHNICITY; UNITED STATES

Bibliography

Barbarin, O. (1983). "Coping with Ecological Transitions by Black Families: A Psycho-social model." *Journal of Community Psychology* 11:308–322.

Chapman, A. B. (1997). "The Black Search for Love and Devotion: Facing the Future Against All Odds." In *Black Families,* 3rd edition, ed. H. P. McAdoo. Newbury Park, CA: Sage.

Franklin, J. H. and Moss, A. A. (1988). *From Slavery to Freedom: A History of Negro Americans,* 6th edition. New York: Alfred A. Knopf.

Gutman, H. G. (1977). *The Black Family in Slavery and Freedom: 1750–1925.* New York: Vintage Books

Lincoln, C. E., and Mamiya, L. H. (1990). *The Black Church in the African American Experience.* Durham, NC: Duke University Press.

McLoyd, V. C.; Cauce, A. M.; Takeuchi, D.; and Wilson, L. (2000). "Marital Processes and Parental Socialization in Families of Color: A Decade Review of Research." *Journal of Marriage and the Family* 62:1070–1093.

Staples, R. (1997). "An Overview of Race and Marital Status." In *Black Families,* 3rd edition, ed. H. P. McAdoo. Newbury Park, CA: Sage.

Taylor, R. J., and Chatters, L. M. (1991). "Religious Life of Black Americans." In *Life in Black America,* ed. J. S. Jackson. Newbury Park, CA: Sage.

Tucker, M. B., and Mitchell-Kernan, C. (1995). *The Decline in Marriage Among African Americans.* New York: Russell Sage Foundation.

U.S. Bureau of the Census. (1999). *Selected Social Characteristics of the Population by Region and Race.* Washington, DC: Author, April.

Wilson, W. J. (1987). *The Truly Disadvantaged: The Inner City, the Underclass, and Public Policy.* Chicago: University of Chicago Press.

OSCAR A. BARBARIN
TERRY MCCANDIES

AFRICAN FAMILIES

See AFRICAN-AMERICAN FAMILIES; CARIBBEAN FAMILIES; EGYPT; ETHNIC VARIATION/ETHNICITY; GHANA; KENYA; NIGERIA; SENEGAL; SOUTH AFRICA; TOGO; YORUBA FAMILIES; ZAMBIA

AGING

See ADULTHOOD; ALZHEIMER'S DISEASE; DEATH AND DYING; DEMENTIA; DEPRESSION: ADULTS; ELDER ABUSE; ELDERS; GRANDPARENTHOOD; GRANDPARENTS' RIGHTS; GRIEF, LOSS, AND BEREAVEMENT; INTERGENERATIONAL PROGRAMMING; INTERGENERATIONAL RELATIONS; INTERGENERATIONAL TRANSMISSION; LATER LIFE FAMILIES; LONELINESS; MENOPAUSE; RESPITE CARE: ADULT; RETIREMENT; WIDOWHOOD

AIDS

See ACQUIRED IMMUNODEFICIENCY SYNDROME (AIDS); SEXUALLY TRANSMITTED DISEASES

ALZHEIMER'S DISEASE

Alzheimer's disease (AD) is a progressive and irreversible neurological disorder that results in significant memory loss and behavioral and personality changes. It is the most common form of *dementia,* which is a category of diseases characterized by serious memory loss and other neurological symptoms. The two hallmarks of Alzheimer's disease are the amyloid plaques and neurofibrillary tangles that are found in the brain cells of those with a diagnosis of Alzheimer's disease. The *amyloid plaques* are abnormal clusters of dead nerve cells and amyloid proteins. The *neurofibrillary tangles* are twisted protein fragments inside the nerve cells. These plaques and tangles "clog" the messaging system in the brain and prevent neurons from communicating with each other and, hence, prevent the brain from functioning normally.

Symptoms

The Alzheimer's Association (2001) has developed a document entitled the *10 Warning Signs of Alzheimer's Disease.* Forgetting names or past events is not necessarily a sign of Alzheimer's disease. However, when the memory loss is significant, such as familiar names or frequently used telephone numbers, then it may be a sign of illness. A person with Alzheimer's disease may find even the easiest tasks, such as tying one's shoes or setting the table for dinner, too hard to complete. Similarly, difficulty may arise with job performance, even if the person has been working in the same job for many years.

Word-finding difficulties or becoming easily tongue-tied are characteristics of Alzheimer's disease. Moreover, new nonsense words may be used when the correct words cannot be remembered. Having Alzheimer's disease may mean becoming easily lost, even in one's own neighborhood, or not knowing the accurate day of the week. Someone with Alzheimer's disease may wear winter clothes in the summer or make poor decisions regarding money, such as entrusting a total stranger with large sums of cash.

It is very easy to lose eyeglasses or misplace keys. However, individuals with Alzheimer's disease will lose many items, often placing them in inappropriate places, such as clothes in the freezer or milk in the cedar chest. Mood swings are common in individuals with Alzheimer's disease and often occur for no apparent reason. Someone may become quickly enraged and then immediately calm down.

Perhaps one of the most disturbing symptoms of Alzheimer's disease is the change that may occur in personality. A normally happy person may become chronically depressed or a mild-mannered person may become rude and easily agitated. Another symptom of Alzheimer's disease is excessive sleeping or unusual passivity. The individual may become chronically fatigued and uncooperative.

Causes

The cause of Alzheimer's disease remains a mystery. However, on-going research has provided clues as to possible underlying causes of the disease. Alzheimer's disease is usually categorized into two types: familial and sporadic onset (National Institute on Aging 2000). *Familial Alzheimer's disease,* where the cause of the disease is linked to heredity, is most often associated with an early onset of symptoms (under the age of sixty-five). Early onset cases only account for about 5 to 10 percent of the total number of Alzheimer's cases. Defects in three different genes have been linked to familial Alzheimer's disease: chromosomes 21, 14, and 1.

The most prevalent type of Alzheimer's disease is *sporadic onset,* which is often linked to an onset of symptoms beginning after the age of sixty-five. Indeed, increased age is one of the largest risk factors of developing Alzheimer's. During the aging process, neurons in the brain may die or shrink and lose their ability to maintain functioning. On-going research is looking for reasons why these changes in the brain lead to Alzheimer's disease in some people but not others. Other risk factors associated with sporadic onset Alzheimer's disease are head trauma and lesions on the brain.

Diagnosis

It is important to note that Alzheimer's disease is not a normal part of the aging process—it is a disease. Moreover, many illnesses that cause symptoms similar to Alzheimer's are treatable. Clinical depression, for example, will cause dementia-like symptoms, but is an illness that can be treated effectively with medication and other types of therapy. Consequently, it is vitally important to receive a complete neurological examination as soon as symptoms arise.

No one test serves as a definitive indicator for Alzheimer's disease. However, when administered together, a full medical history, a mental status examination, physical and neurological examinations, neuropsychology tests, and laboratory tests help physicians determine a diagnosis with a high rate of accuracy. The only way to be one hundred percent certain that a person has Alzheimer's disease is to examine brain tissue at autopsy.

When receiving a diagnosis of Alzheimer's disease, individuals are usually placed in one of two categories: probable AD and possible AD. *Probable AD* is an indication that the physician has eliminated other possible causes of dementia and that the symptoms are most likely caused by Alzheimer's disease. *Possible AD* implies that although Alzheimer's is most likely the primary reason for the dementia, other disorders, such as *Parkinson's disease,* may be affecting the disease's progression.

Treatments

Although there is, at present, no cure for Alzheimer's disease, a class of medications has been approved for the treatment of Alzheimer's disease in the United States, Japan, England, Italy, Canada, and many other countries. These medications are known as *cholinesterase inhibitors.* They improve memory by increasing levels of the chemical *acetylcholine,* which helps transmit messages in the brain. Another treatment for Alzheimer's disease is *Vitamin E.* In a widely cited study (Sano et al. 1997), results suggest that Vitamin E helps to delay the onset of symptoms. Research is also looking into the roles that other drug therapies may play in treating

Alzheimer's disease, such as *hormone replacement therapy* and *anti-inflammatory medications*. The results of these research studies, however, have been inconclusive.

There are nonpharmacological treatments that can help both the person diagnosed with Alzheimer's disease and family members. These include personal and family counseling, making modifications to living arrangements, and remaining active. There is evidently some truth to the old "use it or lose it" adage. Research has consistently shown that maintaining mental activity can help stave off Alzheimer's disease. For example, in a study of older nuns (Wilson et al. 2002), results suggest that active participation in cognitively stimulating activities reduces the risk of developing Alzheimer's disease.

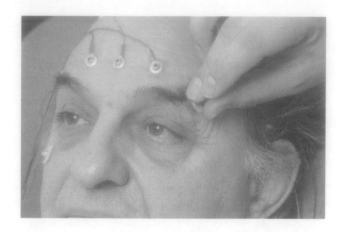

Electrodes are placed on the head of an Alzheimer's patient. This form of treatment may help improve memory or slow the progression of symptoms. CUSTOM MEDICAL STOCK PHOTO, INC.

World Prevalence

The worldwide rates of Alzheimer's disease continue to rise. Alzheimer's Disease International, a voluntary health organization that supports a network of member associations from fifty countries, estimates that over 18 million people worldwide have dementia; two-thirds of those cases are likely Alzheimer's disease. It is projected that by 2025, 34 million will develop dementia. Of that number, over two-thirds will be from developing countries—countries that will have poor access to treatments and adequate health care.

Impact on the Family

Research has consistently shown that providing care for a family member with Alzheimer's disease is one of the most stressful of life events, particularly for women, who are more likely than men to be primary caregivers. The majority of people with Alzheimer's disease are cared for in the home, which may affect the work situation of the caregivers, their own health, and their finances. In the United States alone, direct-care costs for people with Alzheimer's disease are over $50 billion per year (Leon, Cheng, and Neumann 1998). That figure does not include billions of dollars that businesses lose each year because of productivity losses and absenteeism of caregivers.

Further Information

Several organizations are focused on providing support and education to the topic of Alzheimer's disease. Three of the most prominent are the Alzheimer's Association, Alzheimer's Disease International (ADI), and the Alzheimer's Disease Education and Referral Center (ADEAR).

Alzheimer's Association. Through its national network of chapters, the Alzheimer's Association offers a broad range of programs and services for diagnosed persons, their families, and caregivers. The Association is also the largest private funder of research directed at the cause and cure of Alzheimer's disease.

Alzheimer's Disease International. ADI is an umbrella organization for Alzheimer's Associations throughout the word. The essential role of ADI is to strengthen this network of associations so that each is better able to support families living with dementia.

Alzheimer's Disease Education and Referral Center. ADEAR is an official site of the National Institute on Aging of the U.S. Department of Health and Human Services. ADEAR provides information about the latest research breakthroughs in federally funded Alzheimer's research and about ongoing clinical trials. It is also a resource for family caregivers.

See also: CAREGIVING: FORMAL; CAREGIVING: INFORMAL; CHRONIC ILLNESS; DEMENTIA; DISABILITIES; ELDERS; HEALTH AND FAMILIES; RESPITE CARE: ADULT

Bibliography

Alzheimer's Association. (2001). *10 Warning Signs of Alzheimer's Disease.* Chicago: Author.

Leon, J.; Cheng, C.; and Neumann, P. (1998). "Alzheimer's Disease Care: Costs and Potential Savings." *Health Affairs* 17: 206–216.

National Institute on Aging. (2000). *Progress Report on Alzheimer's Disease.* Bethesda, MD: National Institutes of Health.

Sano, M.; Ernesto, C; Thomas, R. G.; Klauber, M. R.; Schaffer, K.; Grundman, M.; Woodbury, P.; Growdon, J.; Cotman, C. W.; Pfeiffer, E.; Schneider, L. S.; Thal, L. J.; and Member of the Alzheimer's Disease Cooperative Study. (1997). "A Controlled Trial of Selegiline, Alpha-Tocopherol, or Both as Treatment for Alzheimer's Disease." *New England Journal of Medicine* 336: 1216–1222.

Shirey, L.; Summer, L; and O'Neill, G. (2000). *Alzheimer's Disease and Dementia: A Growing Challenge.* Washington, DC: National Academy on an Aging Society.

Wilson, R. S.; Mendes de Leon, C. F.; Barnes, L. L.; Schneider, J. A.; Bienias, J. L.; Evans, D. A.; and Bennett, D. A. (2002). "Participation in Cognitively Stimulating Activities and Risk of Incident Alzheimer Disease." *Journal of the American Medical Association* 287: 742–748.

Other Resources

Alzheimer's Association. Available from http://www.alz.org.

Alzheimer's Disease Education and Referral Center. Available from http://www.alzheimers.org.

Alzheimer's Disease International. Available from http://www.alz.co.uk.

JON C. STUCKEY

AMERICAN–INDIAN FAMILIES

American Indians are the indigenous peoples of the United States. According to archeological estimates, bronze-skinned women and men from northern Asia had been exploring and settling the Americas for 10,000 to 50,000 years. By the fifteenth century, descendants of these women and men from northern Asia had spread southward to populate both continents (Nabokov 1999). When Christopher Columbus arrived in 1492, North America had already been home to an estimated two million to ten million people. These Native-American peoples had developed over 300 distinct cultures and had the equivalent of some two hundred distinct languages. The majority of these peoples had settled along the western coastal strip known today as California. The second most populated region was the southwest, followed by regions east of the Mississippi.

By the time Columbus arrived, an array of Native-American civilizations existed, exhibiting a variety of lifestyles and practices among them. For example, the groups had different methods of gathering food, different dwellings, and different cultural and religious patterns, as well as population sizes. All this changed once the Europeans arrived and began to establish their own settlements.

American-Indian groups had established their own forms of tribal or group government for keeping order among themselves and as a means to interrelate among and between each other. When Europeans first arrived in the northeast, they came into contact with the five Iroquoian tribes that had established a permanent political union. Known as the Great League, their style of government was so formidable that the British and French had no choice but to deal with these Indian groups as separate but equal sovereign entities. When Europeans ventured into the southeast, they encountered the Creek Confederacy, which was made up of thousands of Muskogean-speaking Indians (Nabokov 1999). Some of the more well known among the Muskogean-speaking tribes were the Creek, Choctaws, Chickasaws, and the Seminoles (Beach 1910). In Louisiana, European settlers met up with the aristocratic Indian group known as the Natchez. The Natchez had a hierarchical type of society and were ruled by a monarch called The Sun. The Powhatan Confederacy was based in Virginia and consisted of two hundred villages and thirty different tribes, while in California, European settlers found numerous independent and isolated Indian groups who had different dialects and varied greatly in size.

It is important to bear in mind that *first contact,* a term used by anthropologists, between American Indians and Europeans occurred at different times and in different regions of the country. For example, first contact was earlier in the more eastern and southern locales. Accordingly, the Hopi Indians of Arizona and the Hurons of eastern Canada both had experienced their initial contact with the Europeans by the 1540s. Conversely, the Sioux Indians of the Dakota plains would not have their first encounter with Europeans until the 1690s, about 150 years later than the Hopi and Huron, while the Wintu tribe of northern California did not have their first contact with Europeans until the mid-1700s. Finally, the last known first contact occurred in 1818, when the polar Eskimos encountered a British naval expedition. It was then that the Eskimos learned that they were not the only humans on earth. By this time, virtually every American-Indian tribal group had made some form of contact with and accommodation to the European settlers and traders. Some American-Indian–European relations fared well while others were extremely hostile and ended in tragedy for the American-Indian men, women, and children.

General Points of Interest

Today, the total population for American Indians alone is 1,865,118, a figure that increases to 2,475,956 after combining the total population for American Indians and Alaska Natives. The average family size for American Indians across the fifty states ranges from a low of 2.99 in West Virginia to a high of 4.18 in South Dakota (U.S. Census Bureau 2000). As far as birth rates, the American-Indian and Alaska Native birth rate for 1994–1996 (the latest available) of 24.1 births per 1,000 population was 63 percent greater than the United States in general, all races birth rate for 1995 of 14.8, and 70 percent greater than the rate for the U.S. white population of 14.2 (Indian Health Service 1998–99).

In terms of health-related concerns, statistics show that the top leading health problem areas among American Indians are: diseases of the heart, malignant neoplasms, accidents, diabetes mellitus, and chronic liver disease and cirrhosis. The two leading causes of death for American Indians and Alaska Natives (1994–1996) and the United States, all races and white populations (1995) were diseases of the heart and malignant neoplasms. Conversely, the ten leading causes of death for decedents of all ages among American Indians and Alaska Natives within the Indian Health Services (HIS) area, from 1994–1996 based on a rate per 100,000 population, were: (1) diseases of the heart, (2) malignant neoplasms, (3) accidents, with motor vehicle accidents having the largest number, (4) diabetes mellitus, (5) chronic liver disease and cirrhosis, (6) cerebrovascular diseases, (7) pneumonia and influenza, (8) suicide, (9) chronic

obstructive pulmonary diseases, and (10) homicide and legal intervention (Indian Health Service 1998–99).

Boarding Schools

There have been several generations of both physical and psychological parental loss affecting American-Indian families. This parental loss has occurred across tribal communities, whether on reservations or in urban centers, in which a large percentage of American-Indian families live. There have been three primary contributing factors that can be attributed to this parental loss for American-Indian families: the abrupt removal and placement of Indian children in foster and adoptive homes, the education of Indian children in boarding schools, and the impact of alcohol on American-Indian families.

The forced removal of Indian children from their families of origin by Bureau of Indian Affairs agents, and later missionaries acting on behalf of the government, was the single most damaging action taken against American-Indian families. Boarding schools were initially established in the late nineteenth century and continued to exist throughout the mid- to late 1960s. These schools were meant to educate American-Indian children in the European-American tradition.

The government's strategy was to remove American-Indian children from their families of origin and place them in boarding schools, sometimes hundreds of miles away from their families and communities, with the goal of breaking up the traditional family as well as the transmission of their cultural way of life. If the children were not around for the parents to teach cultural ways, then slowly, over time, the government would achieve its goal of exterminating American-Indian culture and traditional family life and replace it with total assimilation to European-American society. Parents had sporadic or virtually no contact with their children while they were in the boarding schools.

Over the years, the impact of the boarding school experience on American-Indian families and their children has been of interest to researchers, educators, family scholars, and the more than five hundred tribes in the United States. Families were tragically disrupted; the children were raised in an institutional setting that promoted isolation and lack of appropriate interaction between females and males, as well as various methods of assimilation tactics. Often, when children were released from the boarding school environment they had no knowledge or skills to survive in the larger society. If they did find their way back to their families or tribal communities, they often experienced ostracism and feelings of not belonging due to perceptions of being a "red apple"—red on the outside for Indianness and white on the inside for acting according to the ways of the European-American society. Parents of these children did not know how to deal with them and often could not communicate with their children because they did not speak English, and their children no longer spoke their native dialect.

The end result was loss of family, parents suffering from unresolved grief and loss, high incidence of mental health problems and alcoholism, children who grew up not knowing their culture or how to parent when they became adults, identity struggles, and generational transmission of the ramifications of boarding school experiences from fear or shame about identifying as an American Indian to an inability to be good parents to their children through healthy and nurturing relationships.

Family Life Today

In many respects, the history of the past has influenced and helped to shape the structure, roles, and meaning of family to American Indians today. American Indians would define family as members made up of fictive and nonfictive kin (blood related and non-blood related), extended family, tribal community, and the nation of American Indians as a whole today. In this regard, one is never alone or without family, a kinship network. Some tribes are patriarchal and patrilocal; others are matriarchal and matrilocal in structure.

The structural context of the family is immersed in history and traditional cultural values (Red Horse, Lewis, Feit, and Decker 1978; Red Horse 1980). For example, American-Indian women were often viewed in the context of expressive roles; namely, childrearing, domestic tasks, and the overall concerns of the family (Hanson 1980; John 1988). American-Indian men were often cast in roles of leadership outside the home; as medicine men and spiritual guides, and as leaders in tribal community matters.

Today, some believe that the centrality of the culture is maintained in American-Indian women (Allen 1986). This is a progressive and feminist view that does not apply across all tribes in the United States. For example, women of tribes in the west and southwest have lower status than those from tribes from the east and south. Others view the role of women as based on an ethic of care (Gilligan 1993) in which women are principally concerned with the responsibility and activity involved in the care of others and their development. In essence, American-Indian women see themselves as providing an integral role centered around an ethic of care that is the connection between relationship and responsibility.

The contemporary role of American-Indian women is very much rooted in their role historically, but in a more modernized version due to the changing times.

Women's activity—in relation to others—is more aptly depicted in language such as "being able to encompass the experiences and well-being of the other" (Miller 1986, p. x). What American Indian women have been doing in life is best described as "active participation in the development of others" (p. xx).

This active participation occurs daily; as the women interact with adults and children they engage in a relational connection. By looking at the conventional ways women have been socialized to carry out the expressive activities and functions of the so-called female role—that is, wife, mother, nurturer, responsible for child rearing and the private sphere of home—it is clear that these expressive activities are focused on serving others' needs. For American-Indian women, then, ties to others represent affiliations based on an ethic of care: the connection between relationship and responsibility (Silvey 1997).

In their role as American-Indian women, women are viewed as the carriers of culture, or put another way, keepers of the culture. As such, the women are not suppressed in their role, but the same cannot be said for American-Indian men. The cultural context of the outside, larger society has negatively affected the role and status of the American-Indian male compared to that of the American-Indian female. From a historical perspective, the net result over time has evinced a cultural context of adaptation and evolution in the role and status of American-Indian women and men, as opposed to tradition.

American-Indian men have a harder time finding their niche in contemporary society. The status of the Indian male has not risen anywhere near that of the Indian female. It is much harder for men to find employment that has the opportunity for career advancement. American-Indian males have been known to be great on their feet and have been sought out as ironworkers and for various jobs in the construction field. More often than not, the Indian male will find himself relegated to providing for his family through various means of manual labor and work in blue-collar industries. It is rare that American-Indian men can be found working in white-collar occupations and jobs that tend to hold status and prestige, all symbols of very successful and upwardly mobile men by today's standards. Many American-Indian men are in prominent roles within their tribal communities as tribal judges, tribal chairmen and administrators, and in mental health and casino positions. Some men have gone on to become lawyers and work for their tribe or types of Indian legal services. Others have very strong creative and artistic abilities and have become entrepreneurs.

However, it is still far easier for American-Indian women to find jobs that enable them to provide for their families and establish a career ladder at the same time than it is for American-Indian men. Historically, the role of American-Indian men as providers for their family was much easier, and held more status, than it is or does in contemporary society.

The structure of American-Indian families is often misunderstood and confusing to non-American-Indian people. The expansive nature of the family structure, inclusive of extended family systems, is confusing because of the number of non-blood-related members inherent in the family. Not all members may be primarily of American-Indian descent or of the same tribal affiliation. A nonblood or fictive member may be an elder who is referred to by other members as an uncle, but who in fact has no biological relationship to other members.

Confusing to the non-American Indian is the number of people who reside together and that it is not always possible to tell by looking at members which ones are fictive and nonfictive (Red Horse 1980; Silvey 1997).

The goal of family and parental support, within the context of the American-Indian family of origin, is to foster interdependence. The family serves as a facilitator in the development of its members and does so according to family or cultural role, not necessarily according to age (Red Horse 1980). Family and parental support encompasses cultural and spiritual maintenance, satisfaction of physical and emotional needs, and the themes of providing care, being cared for, and preparing to care for, throughout the lifespan. In this regard, the family is strengthened and lifelong interdependence among members is fostered. This approach to familial support contrasts with European-American family support in that the goal of the latter is independence of members rather than interdependence among members.

American-Indian Child Welfare

One of the most heart-wrenching legacies from the past was the effect of the boarding schools on American-Indian families and children. In part, the unwarranted removal of children from their family of origin by missionaries and the U.S. government helped to bring about activism and outcry from American-Indian communities for something to be done to save their children, families, and tribes. In 1978, Congress enacted P.L. 95-608, which has come to be known as the Indian Child Welfare Act of 1978 (George 1997). The legislative intent behind this law was to stop the unwarranted removal of American-Indian children from their families and to set minimum standards for the removal and placement of the children in the event removal was necessary (Myers 1981). From oral and written testimony given before Congress, it was determined that American-Indian children were being removed at an alarmingly high rate—a rate five times higher than any other group of children. It took action by the U.S. federal government to intervene in the form of passing this statute to help ameliorate the large rate of unwarranted removal of Indian children. This federal law is still in effect and governs how social service agencies remove children if necessary, what services are to be provided and by Indian providers and/or organizations where possible, and stringent placement guidelines for Indian child welfare cases in the event removal is necessary. As a federal law, this statute takes precedence over all state laws in child custody matters involving American-Indian children, except in the case of divorce and delinquency matters unless termination of parental rights occurs at the same time in the case of the latter.

In the case of foster care, it has long been a tradition among American-Indian families to care for the children of other families should the need arise. It is a system that operates much like an informal fostering or adoption network, wherein arrangements are made privately between the families without involving a lawyer or court system. One could liken it to practices in today's society where grandparents are often raising their grandchildren, not only within the American-Indian culture, but also across various cultures in the United States, on an informal basis. The Indian Child Welfare Act (ICWA) requires that social service agents find clear and convincing evidence for removal of an Indian child, whereas state standards require a lesser burden of proof based on the preponderance of the evidence. No longer may Indian children be removed solely on the basis of environmental poverty or alcoholism, as was frequently done in the past. There must be clear and convincing evidence that some type of abuse or neglect has occurred.

The ICWA sets minimum standards and guidelines for the placement of American-Indian children once removal is indicated. These placement priorities apply to foster care and adoption procedures. The first placement priority is always with a relative or extended family member. If this cannot be achieved, which in the majority of cases it can be, then the second placement priority is placement with an American-Indian family of the same tribal affiliation as the child; for example, a child of Ottawa or Odawa descent is placed with a family of the same descendency. If this priority cannot be achieved, then the third and final placement priority is for the Indian child to be placed with an Indian family of a different tribal affiliation than the child; for example, a child of Ottawa or Odawa descent with a family of Chippewa or Ojibwa lineage. It is only as a last resort, and only after placement in one of the first three priorities cannot be met, that an Indian child may be open to placement with any family of any descent as long as it is in the best interests of the Indian child. To date, this is the only federal law in place that affords children the rights and protections of being placed with families, and receiving services from providers, who are of the same racial ethnic heritage—the American Indian. There is no other federal law that affords the same rights and protections to any other group of children in the United States. Children are viewed as the most valuable resource while American-Indian elderly are revered and accorded honor, within the context of the family. American-Indian children are reared with the mindset that there is no gender inequality within the family. For example, Indian males learn to be self-reliant in tasks that are typically considered in the domain of the female role, such as cooking, rearing children, doing laundry and grocery shopping, and cleaning house. American-Indian females are raised knowing how to mow the lawn, perform various mechanical repairs around the home and on their own vehicles, and in other tasks typically regarded as belonging to men. What is most important in raising male and female children is that they learn to be self-reliant and self-sufficient in a variety of tasks so that they are able to take care of themselves in the event that they do not marry, or there is no one else around to help them. For example, among some Woodland Indian tribes, males are taught how to cook, clean, do laundry, and be self-reliant without a female, whereas females are taught how to do basic mechanical maintenance on cars or household items, as well as to paint and perform general repair work (Silvey 1997).

American-Indian families may be found to consist of all types of family forms, as is the case with other populations. There are two-parent, single-parent, and blended families, families without children, live-together partners, foster and adoptive families, and lesbian and gay family members. American-Indian lesbian and gay members, also known as two-spirit people, are accepted and often extolled by Indian tribal groups. The families of American-Indian lesbian and gay persons do not usually abandon or ostracize them, thus helping them face a generally unaccepting American society (Brown 1997).

American-Indian families are not immune from divorce. It is not the preferred family dynamic but it is also not discouraged in the case of domestic violence, substance abuse, abandonment, or irreconcilable differences, for example. Among American Indians, it is not uncommon to hear a divorce or relationship breakup spoken of in terms of "split the blanket," meaning a couple has split up.

Throughout life, American-Indian families have various rituals or ceremonial practices. However, these ritual and ceremonial practices are not universally accepted or practiced by all American Indian tribal families. For example, the southwest Navajo tribe has a practice of using cradleboards for their infants. They also have a ritual wherein the person who is the first to make a newborn or infant smile is then honored by throwing a special feast for the child. Among the eastern and woodland tribes, the firstborn daughter becomes the keeper of the culture, keeper of the family, and in charge of the overall responsibility for their family members when in need, as she advances in life. Additionally, many American-Indian tribes partake in a naming ceremony where an individual tribal member is given his or her Indian name. Usually, a revered elder or spiritual guide is the person who bequeaths the Indian name to the individual based on what is known about the individual's character and potential.

Conclusion

The interrelationships between European Americans and American Indians have sometimes been smooth and sometimes conflicted. American Indian families are very diverse according to which tribe they belong to. In fact, it can safely be said that there is as much diversity within American Indians as there is between American Indians and other groups. There are more than 500 federally recognized tribes in the United States, and families are very diverse according to which tribe they belong to. Despite the lack of universal practices and dialects, there are some commonalities among the various tribes and American-Indian families. For example, there is a shared history of oppression that still affects contemporary families in the United States, much as it affected earlier generations.

See also: CANADA FIRST NATIONS FAMILIES; UNITED STATES

Bibliography

Allen, P. G. (1986). *The Sacred Hoop.* Boston: Beacon Press.

Beach, F. C. (1910). *The Americana.* Vol. 8. New York: Scientific American Compiling Department.

Brown, L. B. (1997). *Two Spirit People: American Indian Lesbian and Gay Men.* Binghamton, NY: Harrington Park Press/Haworth Press.

George, L. J. (1997). "Why the Need for the Indian Child Welfare Act?" *Journal of Multicultural Social Work* 5(3/4):165–175.

Gilligan, C. (1993). *In a Different Voice: Psychological Theory and Women's Development,* rev. edition. Cambridge, MA: Harvard University Press.

Hanson, W. (1980). "The Urban Indian Woman And Her Family." *Social Casework* (October) 476–483.

John, R. (1988). "The Native American Family." In *Ethnic Families In America,* ed. C. Mindel, R. Habenstein, and R. Wright. New York: Elsevier.

Kawamoto, W. T., ed. (2001). "Understanding American Indian Families." *American Behavioral Scientist* 44(9):1443–1535.

Miller, J. B. (1986). *Toward a New Psychology of Women,* 2nd edition. Boston: Beacon Press.

Myers, Joseph A., ed. (1981). *They Are Young Once But Indian Forever.* Oakland, CA: American Indian Lawyer Training Program, Inc.

Nabokov, P. (1999). *Native American Testimony,* rev. edition. New York: Penguin.

Red Horse, J. G.; Lewis, R.; Feit, M.; and Decker, J. (1978). "Family Behavior of Urban American Indians." *Social Casework* (February):67–72.

Red Horse, J. G. (1980). "Family Structure and Value Orientation in American Indians." *Social Casework* (October):462–467.

Silvey, L. E. (1997). "Ordinal Position and Role Development of the Firstborn Daughter Within Her Family of Origin." Dissertation. Lansing: Department of Family and Child Ecology, Michigan State University.

Other Resources

Indian Health Service. (2002). *Trends in Indian Health 1998-99.* Available from http://www.his.gov/PublicInfo/Publications/trends98/trends98.asp.

U.S. Government. (2001). *2000 Decennial Census.* Available from http://www.census.gov/Press-Release/www.2001/raceqandas.html.

LE ANNE E. SILVEY

AMISH FAMILIES

See ANABAPTISTS (AMISH, MENNONITE)

ANABAPTISTS (AMISH, MENNONITE)

The Amish and Mennonites stem from the Anabaptist movement of the sixteenth-century Reformation. Members of the Anabaptist movement insisted that church membership involve a fully informed adult decision, hence many of them requested a second baptism that symbolically superceded their infant baptism. As a result of this practice their opponents called them *rebaptizers* or *Anabaptists*. The first adult baptism was performed in January 1525 in Zurich (Snyder 1995).

In addition to adult baptism the Anabaptists proposed a complete separation of church and state, including refusing to participate in the military or swearing oaths of allegiance; a nonhierarchical church wherein clergy and laity formed a priesthood of believers; and a commitment against any use of force. These beliefs caused Anabaptists to be persecuted, and many died a martyr's death for their faith. An important book for all of the heirs of the Anabaptists is *The Bloody Theater; or Martyrs' Mirror* by Thieleman van Braght ([1660] 1990). This collection of accounts of persecution, torture, and death, first published in Holland in 1660, continues to be part of the collective memory of the descendents of these people.

For the Anabaptists, the call to discipleship often took precedence over family. There are many stories where men and women willingly gave their lives for the sake of their beliefs and left spouses and children behind to fend for themselves. In the Anabaptist tradition a believer was a follower of Christ first, and loyalty to family took second place (Graber-Miller 2001; Roth 2001).

The Anabaptists produced three groups: the Mennonites, Hutterites, and Amish. The Mennonites take their name from a Dutch Catholic priest, Menno Simons, who joined the movement in 1530. The earliest groups of Anabaptists were established in Zurich, the cantons of Appenzell, Bern, and St. Gall, and the northern Dutch province of Friesland where Menno lived and worked. The groups in the south were known initially as the *Swiss Brethren* and later broke into two groups: the Mennonites and the Amish. The faction known as Mennonite had formed alliances with the *Dutch Mennonites* by the end of sixteenth century (Redekop 1989).

The Amish emerged at the end of the seventeenth century when a young Mennonite minister, Jacob Ammann, became embroiled in a controversy with his fellow ministers in the Alsace, the Palatinate, and the canton of Bern (Meyers 1996). The heart of the argument concerned the degree of discipline that should be applied to a church member who violated accepted standards of behavior. Ammann insisted that the deviant should be excommunicated and subsequently shunned by all other members of the church, including members of the individual's family. When the two sides could not reconcile their differences, a division occurred in 1693, and Ammann and his followers broke away from the larger group of Mennonites. Those who sided with Ammann are now known as the Amish (Nolt 1992).

Because of persecution in Europe many Mennonites fled their homelands and moved east as far as Russia, while others fled west to North America. Although a small number of Mennonites remained in Europe, the majority have emigrated. The first wave of Mennonite migration to North America began in 1683. The Amish began to leave Europe in the 1820s. Many of the so-called *Russian Mennonites* left the Ukraine in 1874 for new homes in North America (Redekop 1989). The decision to leave Russia followed two problematic pieces of legislation implemented by the government: In 1864 a law required that all schools' primary language of instruction was to be Russian, and in 1871 compulsory military service was introduced. Rather than give up their German language and their pacifist position, the Mennonites decided to emigrate.

No Amish remain in Europe. Today there are nearly 200,000 Amish in North America, with more than 250 communities in twenty U.S. states and the province of Ontario, Canada (Kraybill and Bowman 2001).

In the four centuries since the beginning of the Anabaptist movement there have been many schisms among the Mennonites and they form a continuum from the most conservative, *Old Order Mennonites* (Scott 1996; Kraybill and Bowman 2001) to progressive groups (Kauffman and Dreidger 1991) that have been almost completely acculturated into the mainstream of society. The various factions of Mennonites are spread throughout the world. The fastest growing membership is in the Southern Hemisphere. Of the estimated 1,203,995 Mennonites worldwide, 702,000 church members can be found in Africa, Asia, the Caribbean Islands, and Central and South America. (Mennonite World Conference 2000).

The discussion of family life will focus on the two largest groups, the Old Order Amish and the most progressive Mennonites. The term Old Order is used to describe the Amish who retain a traditional lifestyle that includes the retention of a dialect of the German language, horse and buggy as primary form of transportation, nineteenth-century dress and hairstyle, and a resistance to organizing human beings in hierarchical organizations. Progressive Mennonites have retained an emphasis on believer's baptism, nonviolence, and the separation of church and state. However, in contrast to the Old Orders they have become increasingly urban, emphasize higher education and employment in professions, and have developed an elaborate denominational bureaucracy (Kauffman and Dreidger 1991).

Amish Community and Family Life

The two basic units in Amish society are church and family, and these institutions intersect at a number of levels. Amish churches are defined geographically, that is, all church members within a square mile or several square miles form a church district. The size of a church (160 or fewer persons) is usually described in terms of the number of families rather than the number of individual members. The Amish do not construct church buildings, but meet for worship in members' homes. A church will divide into two geographic units, or two new districts, when there are too many families to fit comfortably in any individual member's home (Hostetler 1993).

Family life is inextricably related to the life of the church. Among other things, a child learns early in life to submit to the authority of the adults in his or her life. Respecting the authority of elders in childhood is assumed to lead to a life of submission to the rules of the church. When an Amish young person begins to think about marriage this issue is often related to a decision about church membership. Marriage within the Amish church is only permitted after an individual is baptized and may only occur with another Amish person.

Stages of Amish Family Life

Infancy and early childhood. Amish children are received by their parents and the community with a great deal of joy. Because contraception is rarely used it is assumed that when a couple marries children will be born within a year or two. The infant is assumed to be innocent until he or she becomes self-aware. At this point adults consider it their responsibility to begin to "break the will of the child." At approximately age two a child must begin to learn the meaning of discipline. They are beginning a period of preparation for church membership that will continue until they are sixteen years of age.

Children begin to help with farm or household chores at a very young age. They are encouraged to begin by helping to gather eggs, feed chickens, pull weeds, and sweep floors. As time progresses they will be expected to do more sophisticated work, but they are rarely pushed to do more than they are capable of at a particular age.

Parents expect conformity; they have relatively little tolerance for disobedience or defiance. They have no time for modern permissive childrearing and will not hesitate to use corporal punishment if needed (Hostetler and Huntington 1992).

Scholars. Typically, Amish children do not go to preschool or kindergarten. At the age of six or seven they begin to go to school and become *scholars.* Most Amish children attend one- or two-room Amish parochial schools. All children go to school through the age of fifteen at which point they are free to leave school. Most do so, because the Amish believe that a child has learned enough, at that point, of basic mathematics, English reading, and writing skills to function as an adult. Furthermore, Amish children are not permitted to go to high school or university. Higher education is perceived as threatening and may lead to critical thinking (Hostetler and Huntington 1992; Meyers 1993).

Youth. A child leads a fairly controlled life until he or she is sixteen. At this age there is a period of latitude, where some of the restrictions on a child's behavior are removed.

Many boys acquire their first horse and buggy at sixteen. At this point, they have the freedom to come and go from their home. Some teens begin to experiment with aspects of the non-Amish world. They may wear non-Amish clothes, put a radio in the buggy, and in some cases secure a driver's license and purchase a car.

What is the meaning of this period of latitude? Why do some parents overlook the indiscretions of

An Amish family rides in a horse-drawn wagon. Amish males usually receive their first horse and buggy at the age of sixteen THOMAS B. HOLLYMAN/SCIENCESOURCE/PHOTO RESEARCHERS

their children? Although few parents will say so, they allow some experimentation with the world so that when a child makes his or her decision to join the church he or she will have some knowledge about what is being rejected in the membership commitment.

In the late teens two critical events typically occur in a young person's life. The youth must make a decision about whether to be baptized and to become a church member. The young person is also searching for a marriage partner. Baptism and marriage often, but not always, occur in a relatively short period of time. An Amish man or woman may not marry in the Amish church unless he or she is a baptized member. Furthermore, a member of the church is only permitted to marry another member. Since more than 80 percent of Amish young people choose to remain in the faith of their parents (Meyers 1994a), marriage is almost always endogamous.

Amish courtship tends to be very serious. There is much less casual dating than in the dominant culture. Dates are often limited to a young man taking a young woman home in his buggy after a Sunday evening singing service. When a couple decides to marry there is a process of permission that must be sought from parents and church leaders. When all agree that a wedding may take place, the Bishop will announce at the end of a regular church service that two individuals will be married at a designated time and place in the coming weeks. At that moment the couple has been *published*.

Married Couples. A wedding is one of the most important days in an Amish person's life. It is one of the few opportunities to be the center of attention. The couple stands before the congregation and exchanges vows, and then elaborate meals are prepared for them. There is a special table set in a corner of a main room, known as *the Eck.* (*Eck* is the German word for corner.) The bride and groom choose some of their best friends to be the table waiters for the meal. These people leave the service about a half-hour before it is over to make the final preparations for the meal, which has been in the works for days.

Once married the couple establishes their own home and typically begins to assume fairly traditional roles. Men work in the fields, the shop, or the factory, and women work in the home, cooking, cleaning, and occasionally assisting their husband with outside work. Although in the past farming was synonymous with the Amish way of life, farmers are now in the minority in the largest Amish settlements in Indiana, Ohio, and Pennsylvania. (Meyers 1994a; Kraybill and Nolt 1995).

A father in the Amish home is the religious leader. He may read the Bible in the morning or read prayers from their prayer book before and after meals. Both parents, however, teach their children, by example, how to be men and women.

Aging. Amish people tend to retire in their late fifties or early sixties. A farmer, in particular, may allow a son or son-in-law to take over the farm at this age. He may still have an active role on the farm but the next generation assumes the major responsibility for the farm operation.

Elderly people are rarely put in nursing homes. They are usually maintained at home in a separate room, apartment, or a smaller building on the property of one of their adult children. Smaller homes for the elderly are known as the *grandfather* or *dawdy house.* Older people are respected, and members of their community treat them with a great deal of kindness and affection.

Mennonite Families

In the twentieth century Mennonite community and family life changed in some significant ways. At the beginning of the century they were primarily an agrarian people who lived in homogenous rural communities. By the close of the century less than 7 percent of Mennonites were still on the farm (Kauffman and Dreidger 1991). For the most part they have given up traditional dress, have left the agrarian way of life, have moved into most professions, and are much more involved in the life of the dominant culture. They have developed their own institutions of higher education, an insurance industry, an international mission and service organization, retirement communities for the elderly, and many other formal organizations.

Within families there has been an increasing emphasis on egalitarian childrearing and a trend toward a balance of power between husband and wife. This change is probably associated with the increasing emphasis on employment for women. The majority of married Mennonite women are employed full-time outside of the home (Kauffman and Meyers 2001).

The average number of children in Mennonite families also approaches the national norm. In contrast to the Amish who continue to have large families, with the average family including 7 children (Hostetler 1993), Mennonites average 2.3 children per family among couples under the age of 49 (Kauffman and Driedger 1991).

Although Mennonite families are similar in many ways to families in the larger society, there are some unique characteristics of this population. Mennonites continue to place great value on marriage. Ninety-one percent of women and 98 percent of men marry. The majority of Mennonites prefer to marry within their religious tradition. Furthermore, in the United States Mennonites tend to marry earlier than the rest of the population. The average age at marriage for men in 1989 was 23.2 and women 21.3 (Kauffman and Meyers 2001). In contrast the average for males and females in the general population was 26.2 and 23.9 (Eshleman 1997).

Mennonite families also tend to have higher incomes and lower rates of divorce than the dominant culture. The most recent comprehensive survey of Mennonites was taken in 1989 and in that year divorce rates were less than half of the non-Mennonite population in the United States. Only five percent of the respondents over the age of thirty who had married at some point in their life were divorced or separated (Kauffman and Meyers 2001).

Finally, progressive Mennonites tend to be less sexually active prior to marriage than the larger society. Approximately one-third of Mennonites admit to premarital intercourse, which is less than half the incidence in the general population (Lauman et al. 1994).

See also: HUTTERITE FAMILIES; PROTESTANTISM; RELIGION

Bibliography

Braght, T. van. [1660] (1990). *The Bloody Theater; or Martyrs' Mirror*, trans. J. F. Sohm. Scottdale, PA: Herald Press.

Eshleman, J. R. (1997). *The Family*, 8th edition. Needham Heights, MA: Allyn & Bacon.

Graber-Miller, K. (2001). "Innocence, Nurture and Vigilance: The Child in the Work of Menno Simons." *Mennonite Quarterly Review* 25(2):173–198.

Hostetler, J. A. (1993). *Amish Society*. Baltimore: Johns Hopkins University Press.

Hostetler, J. A., and Huntington, G. E. (1992). *Amish Children*. Fort Worth, TX: Harcourt Brace Jovanovich.

Kauffman, J. H., and Dreidger, L. (1991). *The Mennonite Mosaic*. Scottdale, PA: Herald Press.

Kauffman, J. H., and Meyers, T. J. (2001). "Mennonite Families: Characteristics and Trends." *Mennonite Quarterly Review* 25(2):199–210.

Kraybill, D. B. (1989). *The Riddle of Amish Culture*. Baltimore, MD: Johns Hopkins University Press.

Kraybill, D. B., and Bowman, C. F. (2001). *On the Backroad to Heaven*. Baltimore, MD: Johns Hopkins University Press.

Kraybill, D. B., and Nolt, S. M. (1995). *Amish Enterprise: From Plows to Profits*. Baltimore, MD: Johns Hopkins University Press.

Laumann, E. O.; Gagnon, J. H.; Michael, R. T.; and Michaels, S. (1994). *The Social Organization of Sexuality: Sexual Practices in the United States*. Chicago: University of Chicago Press.

Meyers, T. J. (1993). "Education and Schooling." In *The Amish and the State*, ed. D. Kraybill. Baltimore: Johns Hopkins University Press.

Meyers, T. J. (1994a). "Lunch Pails and Factories." In *The Amish Struggle with Modernity*, ed. D. B. Kraybill and M. A. Olshan. Hanover, NH: University Press of New England.

Meyers, T. J. (1994b). "The Old Order Amish: To Remain in the Faith or to Leave." *Mennonite Quarterly Review* 68(3):378–395.

Nolt, S. M. (1992). *A History of the Amish*. Intercourse, PA: Good Books.

Redekop, C. W. (1989). *Mennonite Society*. Baltimore, MD: Johns Hopkins University Press.

Roth, J. D. (2001). "Family, Community and Discipleship in the Anabaptist-Mennonite Tradition." *Mennonite Quarterly Review* 75(2):147–160.

Scott, S. (1996). *An Introduction to Old Order and Conservative Mennonite Groups*. Intercourse, PA: Good Books.

Snyder, C. A. (1995). *Anabaptist History and Theology: An Introduction*. Kitchener, Ont.: Pandora Press.

Other Resources

Mennonite World Conference. (2000). "Mennonite and Brethren in Christ World Membership Totals for 2000." Available from http://www.mwc-cmm.org/Directory/mbictotal.html.

THOMAS J. MEYERS

ANCESTOR WORSHIP

The term *ancestor worship,* coined in 1885 by the British philosopher and sociologist Herbert Spencer, refers to a ritualized invocation of dead kin. It is based on the belief that the spirits of the dead have the power to influence the affairs of the living. Ancestors who are respected and remembered by elaborate rites include members of the family, clans, and tribes. Ancestral spirits that are worshiped also vary in distance of time from the living. In some societies, only the spirits of the recently deceased are worshiped, while in others, all ancestors are included.

The practice of ancestor worship is not universal, but exists or formerly existed in many countries including those in West Africa, Europe, the Pacific, and East Asia. Information is most abundant on traditional practices of familial ancestor worship in China (Thompson 1973) and Japan (Yanagita 1970).

Ancestor Worship in China

In China, the practice of ancestor worship has existed since ancient times, and it emphasized continuity of family lines. *Filial piety,* advocated by the Confucian teachings of the sixth and fifth centuries B.C.E., emphasized respect for senior family members (Granet 1975). The practice of ancestor worship, therefore, can be seen as an extension of this reverence. Additionally, the family was viewed as a closely united group of living and dead relatives. Unity of the entire kin group was also reinforced through religious acts at temples that honored all ancestral spirits.

Photos offered in a Malaysian temple illustrate a form of ancestor worship. Ancestor worship is based on the belief that spirits of the dead can influence the affairs of the living. SIMON ARNOLD; EYE UBIQUITOUS/CORBIS

Rites of reverence were also held at home and gravesites. Ancestral shrines containing tablets bearing the names of recently deceased ancestors were maintained in homes, and rites were observed before them. The ancestral tablets, which are the locus of worship for the deceased, operate in two ways within the practice of ancestor worship. In one way they are like the ancestral hall, showing outsiders the public face of the lineage. In another way, they represent the lineage as a body of individual members. Ancestor festivals occur around the fifteenth of July, during which items such as fruit, preserves, candies, two or more bowls containing fragrant wood, some lotus or other flowers in the vase, and a number of dishes or bowls of cooked food are placed in front of the shrine. If the family can afford it, one or more priests are invited to read scriptures and perform certain rituals before the shrine during this period (Hsu 1948).

Emily Ahern (1973) emphasizes that the reciprocal obligation between the living and the dead is an important element in Chinese family life. For example, in a Chinese village that Ahern studied, the living are expected to care for the dead in payment of the debts they owe them, and, in turn, the living hope to obtain the good life as they perceive it: wealth, rich harvests, and offspring who will ensure undying memory and sustenance in the afterlife.

The state of ancestor worship in modern China is unclear, but it was reported to be disappearing (Welch 1969) under the Communist regime. Rennselaer Lee (1964) argues that the Chinese Communists have been fundamentally hostile towards religion, but the government solicited the cooperation of religious leaders in an attempt to create the new China. Others, however, are more cynical of these governmental efforts (Levenson 1965) and report that religious repression has been severe (Welch 1969).

Ancestor Worship in Japan

Most of the historically known practices of ancestor worship in Japan are adaptations of Chinese customs. With the passage of time and in coexistence with the Shinto religion, Japanese Buddhism began to emphasize death rites and commemorative ceremonies. Although Confucianism was never fully developed in Japan, quasi-religious Confucian ideals of filial piety became important and were sometimes incorporated in the teachings of Japanese Buddhist sects, thereby reinforcing respect for ancestors (Tamaru 1972).

Japanese rites, like those of China, consist of elaborate funerals and many commemorative rites at home, temple, and gravesites. A *Butsudan* (family altar to ancestors), which displays tablets with inscribed ancestors' names, is present in many Japanese households. An annual ancestral ceremony, *Bon*, takes place in either July or August and along with the New Year's celebration, is considered to be one of the two most important observances in Japan (Yanagita 1970). During Bon ceremony, family members return to their parental homes to honor all spirits of the dead who are believed to return to their homes at that time. As was the case in China, fresh fruit, flowers, and cooked rice are offered on the family altar. Many family members go to meet the souls of their ancestors in the cemetery or at the temple. In many neighborhoods, an annual Bon dance is held to celebrate this special observance in which adults and children dance to Japanese folk music. In addition to the annual ancestral festival, ancestors are remembered and worshipped through the purification rituals that take place seven days, forty-nine days, and one hundred days after the death of a family member, during the first Bon, and the first, third, seventh, thirteenth, seventeenth, twenty-third, twenty-seventh, thirty-third, fiftieth, and one hundredth year anniversaries of their death.

In modern Japan, ancestors have declined in importance, and Buddhist ritual tends to emphasize funerals, giving less attention than formerly to commemorative ceremonies.

To many Japanese, the ancestral festival, Bon, has become nothing more than a few days of rest. In a 1968 survey of religious attitudes of Japanese men, Fernando Basabe found that one in four Japanese men believed that the spirits of the ancestors return to their homes during the Bon festival. Although the lives of most Japanese are intertwined with religious observances such as Bon, and most have Buddhist altars in the homes, the majority of Japanese do not consider themselves

believers in any religion (Reischauer 1981). This suggests that Japanese people are slowly losing interest in the worship of ancestral spirits.

Despite these modern trends, ancestor worship continues to be an important mechanism through which the living feel that they are spiritually connected to the deceased family members, thereby ensuring the continuity of family lineage.

See also: BUDDHISM; CHINA; CONFUCIANISM; JAPAN

Bibliography

Ahern, E. M. (1973). *The Cult of the Dead in a Chinese Village.* Stanford, CA: Stanford University Press.

Basabe, F. M. (1968). *Religious Attitudes of Japanese Men: A Sociological Survey.* Tokyo: Sophia University Press.

Granet, M. (1975). *The Religion of the Chinese People.* Oxford: Blackwell.

Hsu, L. K. (1948). *Under the Ancestors' Shadow.* New York: Columbia University Press.

Lee, R. W., III. (1964). "General Aspects of Chinese Communist Religious Policy, with Soviet Comparison." *China Quarterly* 19:16–173.

Levenson, J. (1965). "The Communist Attitude towards Religion." In *The Chinese Model; A Political, Economic, and Social Survey.* Hong Kong: University of Hong Kong Press.

Reischauer, E. O. (1981). *The Japanese.* Cambridge, MA: Harvard University Press.

Tamaru, N. (1972). "Buddhism." In *Japanese Religion: A Survey by the Agency for Cultural Affairs,* ed. I. Hori, F. Ikado, T. Wakimoto, and K. Yanagawa. Tokyo: Kodansha.

Thompson, L. G. (1973). *The Religious Life of Man: The Chinese Way in Religion.* Belmont, CA: Wadsworth.

Welch, H. (1969). "Buddhism Since the Cultural Revolution." *China Quarterly* 40:127–136.

Yanagita, K. (1970). *About Our Ancestors: The Japanese Family System.* Tokyo: Japan Society for the Promotion of Science.

MASAKO ISHII-KUNTZ

ANNULMENT

Annulment is the judicial pronouncement declaring a marriage invalid. A few ideas must be kept in mind in order to understand the concept of annulment and how it differs from divorce:

(1) Every society establishes rules of conduct for its members relating to behavior that affects the common good. Marriage is an institution designed to enable people to establish stable primary intimate relationships that potentially involve the procreation and rearing of children. While the right to marry is fundamental, each society passes legislation to control and restrict the exercise of this right.

(2) The rules governing the valid contracting of legal obligations are not necessarily shared by other social units and vary from society to society. If an individual belongs to multiple social units, the validity of contracts entered into by persons who choose to remain part of that social unit is governed by the laws passed by the legitimate authority of that unit.

(3) If the requirements that have been established by the legally binding authority of the social unit and that are in existence at the time of entering the contract are not fulfilled, the contract is considered null and void from its outset.

(4) The marriage ceremony takes place in a specific geographic locale. The requirements and regulations established by the state where the exchange of vows takes place may refer to the radical capacity or ability of persons entering marriage to take on the responsibilities and enjoy the rights of marriage (i.e., age and mental competence), the specific form that must be followed (i.e., valid license and official minister who is to witness the exchange of vows), or other regulations that fall into a questionable area between the basic ability or capacity to enter marriage and the format required (i.e., gender of the contracting parties). Whatever the category of requirement or regulation, if *all* norms so determined by the state are not followed, the contract is null and void, invalid; no marriage exists and no rights or obligations are incurred.

Divorce Versus Annulment

Before persons can enter another marriage after they have exchanged vows in a marriage ceremony, the prior marriage must be liquidated. To sever the chains of matrimony or "untie the knot," the case must be adjudicated in a civil court that handles either divorce or annulment.

Divorce presupposes that a valid marriage was entered into by the parties involved and ends a marriage as of the date the divorce decree becomes final. Divorce per se has no effect on the legitimacy of children born of this union or on a claim for alimony.

Annulment implies that a valid marriage never took place because of the inability to perform the responsibilities of marriage. The parties are considered to lack the ability to give valid consent if, at the time and in the place where the marriage ceremony was performed, there was some defect, impediment, or lack of capacity preventing a legal marriage between the parties concerned. When this fact is so judged by legal authority (adjudicated), the legal judgment implies that the marriage is voided *from its inception*. Unless altered by statute, annulment has the legal effect of rendering the children born of this union "illegitimate." A claim for alimony would also be invalid unless the rule is changed by statute or judicial decision.

State legislatures have tended to confuse the distinction between divorce and annulment as they enact divorce statutes. Divorce serves as a substitute for annulment in those jurisdictions that have no statutes allowing courts to grant annulments and becomes a catchall for cases involving such issues as bigamy and impotency.

Grounds for Annulment

The statutes or legislation that determine the impediments to a valid marital contract are not uniform from state to state, and the grounds for annulment vary from one jurisdiction to another. In every case, however, these grounds must be clear, strong, and convincing before an annulment court will issue a decree of nullity following legal proceedings to liquidate a marriage. While the rule of law changes from one jurisdiction to another, some reasons why parties are unable to exchange marital consent include:

(1) failure to follow legal format, such as not obtaining a marriage license or neglecting to fulfill other statutory prohibitions;

(2) being underage—there is a fixed marriageable age that must be respected;

(3) gender—most societies permit only heterosexuals to marry;

(4) consanguinity—a marriage would be considered "incestuous and void" if the parties were related by blood, that is, ancestors and

descendants such as father and daughter, brothers and sisters, uncles and nieces, aunts and nephews;

(5) affinity—a relationship established by marriage, such as stepbrother and stepsister;

(6) impotency—the incapacity to perform the act of sexual intercourse;

(7) duress (force and fear)—a valid marriage requires free and willing consent of both male and female;

(8) fraud (deception)—both parties must intend to assume the contractual obligations; and

(9) mental disorder or mental deficiency—persons must possess the ability to understand the nature and consequences of the marriage ceremony.

If any of these impediments were present at the time of the marriage and proven in a court of law, a decree of nullity would be issued indicating that no marriage existed.

Historical Link with Church Law

The concept of annulment draws its heritage from the ecclesiastical courts of England and canon law of the Roman Catholic church. In sharp contrast to Roman law, which considered marriage and its dissolution to be determined by the free will of the parties concerned, the Catholic church believes that a valid marriage entered into by two baptized Christians (classified as "sacramental") cannot be dissolved by any human power. Consequently, if a valid marriage is sacramental and consummated through sexual intercourse, it can be dissolved only by the death of one spouse. Hence the focus on annulment to prove some impediment or defect that would render the contract itself invalid from the outset; this would prove that the marriage never existed.

When an individual falls under the jurisdiction of both state and church law because of an affiliation with a specific religious denomination, the rules of law of both state and church become significant.

For those religious organizations that permit divorce, the usual procedure is to recognize the legal authority of the state to dissolve the marriage in civil court. The denominations would then accept the decree of divorce as valid, thereby freeing both parties to remarry according to the rules of both state and church.

The Roman Catholic church does not allow its members to divorce. If Catholics who previously had exchanged marital vows wish to marry a different partner, a lengthy annulment procedure in the ecclesiastical tribunal is usually required. While the state may allow an individual to remarry within its jurisdiction, the church would forbid a new marriage within the church until an annulment procedure had declared the previous marriage null and void. On the other hand, even though the church has issued a "decree of nullity," the state would require a civil procedure to be completed within the divorce court of the state before allowing either of the parties to enter a new marriage.

See also: CATHOLICISM

Bibliography

Anderson, E. A. (1989). "An Exploration of a Divorce Statute: Implications for Future Policy Development." *Journal of Divorce* 12(4):1–18.

Bassett, W. (1968). *The Bond of Marriage.* Notre Dame, IN: University of Notre Dame Press.

Burd, J. (1991). "Splitting the Marriage in More Ways Than One: Bifurcation of Divorce Proceedings." *Journal of Family Law* 30:903–917.

Freed, D. J. (1991). "Family Law in the Fifty States: An Overview." *Family Law Quarterly* 24:309–405.

Jenks, R. J., and Woolever, C. A. (1999). "Divorce and Annulment Among American Catholics." *Journal of Divorce and Remarriage* 30:45–55.

Kelleher, S. (1973). *Divorce and Remarriage for Catholics.* Garden City, NY: Doubleday.

Nadelson, C., and Polonsky, D. (1984). *Marriage and Divorce.* New York: Guilford.

Parkman, A. M. (1992). *No-Fault Divorce: What Went Wrong?* Boulder, CO: Westview Press.

Phillips, R. (1991). *Untying the Knot: A Short History of Divorce.* New York: Cambridge University Press.

"Same Sex Couples and the Law." (1989). *Harvard Law Review* 102:1603–1628.

Siegle, B. (1986). *Marriage According to the New Code of Canon Law.* New York: Alba House.

Steinbock, B. (1992). "The Relevancy of Illegality." *Hastings Center Report* 22:19–22.

Sugarman, S. D. (1990). *Divorce Reform: At the Crossroads.* New Haven, CT: Yale University Press.

Wisensale, S. K. (1992). "Toward the 21st Century: Family Change and Public Policy." *Family Relations* 41:417–422.

Zimmerman, S. L. (1989). "Comparing the Family Policies of Three States." *Family Relations* 38:190–195.

WARREN F. SCHUMACHER (1995)
BIBLIOGRAPHY REVISED BY JAMES J. PONZETTI, JR.

ANOREXIA NERVOSA

See EATING DISORDERS

ANXIETY DISORDERS

Anxiety disorders include *separation anxiety disorder, social phobia, specific phobia, generalized anxiety disorder, agoraphobia, panic disorder* with and without agoraphobia, *obsessive-compulsive disorder, posttraumatic stress disorder, acute stress disorder,* anxiety disorder due to a general medical condition, *substance-induced anxiety disorder,* and anxiety disorder not otherwise specified. Common features shared across anxiety disorders include (1) avoidance of feared objects, situations, or events, or enduring such objects, situations, events with severe distress; (2) maladaptive thoughts or cognitions, typically regarding harm or injury to oneself or loved one; and (3) physiological arousal or reactions (e.g., palpitations, sweating, irritability). According to the *Diagnostic and Statistical Manual of Mental Disorders* (DSM-IV) (American Psychiatric Association 1994), with the exception of the anxiety disorder specific to childhood, separation anxiety disorder, the same criteria are applied for diagnosing anxiety disorders in adults and children. For all anxiety disorders, symptoms must be present for a specific time period (at least four weeks for separation anxiety disorder; six months for all other anxiety disorders), be age inappropriate, and interfere with an individual's functioning.

Ethnic and Cultural Variations

Epidemiological studies of anxiety disorders in children have rarely been conducted using diverse ethnic or racial groups. Hector R. Bird and his colleagues (1988) conducted a community study of behavioral and emotional problems in youth aged four to sixteen years in Puerto Rico. Prevalence rates for the most common anxiety disorders were 2.6 percent for specific phobia and 4.7 percent for separation anxiety disorder.

Glorisa Canino and her colleagues (1986) compared rates of anxiety symptoms (not diagnoses) in an outpatient clinic sample of African-American and Hispanic youth (aged five to fourteen years). Hispanic children were found to present with more symptoms of fears, phobias, anxiety, panic, school refusal, and disturbed peer relationships than African-American children. C. G. Last and S. Perrin (1993) compared African-American and Euro-American children (aged five to seventeen years) who were referred to a childhood anxiety disorders specialty clinic, and found no significant differences between the two groups in lifetime prevalence rates of anxiety diagnoses. Golda Ginsburg and Wendy Silverman's (1996) comparison of Hispanic and Euro-American children (aged six to seventeen years) who were referred to a childhood anxiety disorders specialty clinic indicated that the two groups were more similar than different on the main variables examined, including mean age at intake, family income, mean ratings of impairment of diagnoses (0-9 point scale), school refusal behavior, and number of co-occurring diagnoses. More research is needed on the expression of anxiety disorders using ethnically and culturally diverse samples of children.

Biological Factors

Evidence for biological factors that predispose children to anxiety disorders is based largely on findings from family aggregation, twin, behavioral genetic, and behavioral inhibition studies. Family aggregation studies suggest that children whose parents have an anxiety disorder are at risk for developing an anxiety disorder themselves (Biederman et al. 2001). Similarly, parents whose children have an anxiety disorder are likely to show anxiety disorders or symptoms themselves. Research on family aggregation also suggests that when parents have an anxiety disorder, mothers are more often associated with familial transmission of anxiety than fathers. Also, children of anxious parents are likely to have an earlier onset for anxiety disorders than their parents.

Twin studies also suggest a familial transmission. For example, concordance rates from different *monozygotic* (identical) and *dizygotic* (fraternal) twin pairs suggest a strong genetic basis for *anxiety neurosis*. Thalia C. Eley's (1999) review of behavioral genetic research concluded that factors in shared and nonshared environments of parents with anxiety disorders have an important influence on the development and maintenance of most anxiety disorders in their children and adolescents.

Recent research on behavioral inhibition and anxiety has provided important neurobiological insights regarding correlates in the etiology of anxiety disorders (Sallee and Greenawald 1995). *Behavioral inhibition* refers to the temperamental style of approximately 10 to 15 percent of Euro-American infants who are predisposed to being irritable, shy, and fearful as toddlers, and cautious, quiet, and introverted as school-aged children (e.g., Kagan 1989).

Although family, twin, behavioral genetic, and behavioral inhibition investigations all provide empirical support for biological dispositional factors in the etiology of anxiety disorders in children, the specific mechanism of transmission are unclear. This represents a critical area for further research.

Family Environment and Parenting Factors

Parenting styles of anxious children have been described as *overprotecting, ambivalent, rejecting,* and *hostile* (See Ginsburg, Silverman, and Kurtines 1995). Retrospective reports of adults with anxiety disorders show that these adults view their parents as overcontrolling and less affectionate. Studies of families of *school-refusing/anxious* children indicate that these families score lower on indices of child independence and participation in recreational activities, and higher on indices of hostility/conflict than families of non-school-refusing/anxious children (Kearney and Silverman 1995). These families also have been found to be more overprotective and disturbed in role performance, communication, affective expression, and control relative to families of children with nonanxiety psychiatric disorders (e.g., Bernstein and Garfinkel 1986). In a review of the parenting and child-rearing practices research literature, Ronald Rapee (1997) concluded that rejection and excessive parental control were related to the development and maintenance of anxiety disorders in children.

An observational study conducted by Paula Barrett and her colleagues (1996) found that children with anxiety disorders and their parents generated more avoidant solutions in problem-solving situations relative to aggressive and nonclinical controls. These parents also modeled caution, provided information about risks, expressed doubts about child competency, and rewarded avoidant behavior. Moreover, having an anxious family member (e.g., parent) also has been shown to increase risk for distress and dysfunction in family relationships (Bruch and Heimberg 1994). Given the consistency of findings showing the role of the family environment and parenting factors, interventions have been aimed at incorporating these factors in treating children with anxiety disorders.

Family-Focused Interventions

Considerable evidence has accumulated demonstrating the efficacy of individual *child cognitive behavior therapy* (CBT) for reducing anxiety disorders in children (see Silverman and Berman 2001, for review). In consideration of the accumulating evidence (summarized above), highlighting the importance of the familial context in the development and maintenance of anxiety disorders, early twenty-first century clinical research was directed toward evaluating whether CBT, when used with anxious children, also is efficacious when family parenting variables are targeted in the treatment program. Such work also is a response to increasing interest among practitioners in having available alternative treatment approaches that draw on supplementary therapeutic resources, especially when individual child therapy does not seem sufficient.

As a result, empirical evidence from clinical trials as well as single case study designs suggests that childhood anxiety disorders can be reduced when exposure-based cognitive behavioral treatments target family/parent variables. For example, in a sample of seventy-nine children (ages seven to fourteen years old) and their parents, Paula Barrett, Mark Dadds, and Ronald Rapee (1996) demonstrated that *individual cognitive behavioral treatment* (ICBT) might be enhanced by parental involvement in the treatment of childhood anxiety disorders when compared to a wait-list comparison group. Results indicated that a large percentage (69.8%) of children who received ICBT, either with or without a parenting component, no longer met diagnostic criteria for an anxiety disorder. Moreover, children who received ICBT with a parenting component had significantly higher treatment success rates (84%) than children who received ICBT without the parenting component (57.1%). Improvement also was evident on child and parent rating scales, though statistically significant differences between the treatment conditions (i.e., ICBT with parent involvement vs. ICBT without parent involvement) were not as apparent on these measures. An interesting age/treatment interaction was observed in that younger children showed more improvement in ICBT with the parenting component than older children who received ICBT without the parenting component.

Barrett and colleagues (2001) reported long-term (five to seven years post-treatment) maintenance of treatment gains from Barrett, Dadds, and Rapee's (1996) study. For both treatment conditions (i.e., ICBT with parental involvement vs. ICBT without parental involvement), treatment gains were maintained for this period as shown by continued absence of the targeted anxiety disorder diagnosis as reported by the child, and on all the child and parent rating scales. The only exception was levels of self-rated fear: children who received ICBT with parental involvement rated significantly less fear at long-term follow-up in comparison to children who received ICBT without parental involvement.

Findings from Vanessa Cobham, Mark Dadds, and Susan Spence (1998) provide additional evidence for ICBT as well as for the involvement of parents in intervention. In this study parental involvement included not only parental management of the child's anxiety, but also parental management of their own anxiety. Children (N=67; ages seven to fourteen years old) with anxiety disorders were assigned to conditions according to whether parents were anxious or not. Treatment success rates for ICBT among children with nonanxious parents were similar to those children with anxious parents who received ICBT plus a parental anxiety management component. Thus, the addition of a parent anxiety management component to ICBT was important for diagnostic recovery for those children with anxious parents.

Barrett (1998) evaluated the effectiveness of including a family component to group CBT. Participants consisted of sixty children (ages seven to fourteen years old) and their parents. Treatment conditions were: (1) child group CBT, (2) child group CBT plus a family management component, and (3) a wait-list control condition. The family management component consisted of parent training of contingency management techniques for their child's anxiety and for any anxiety that parents may experience themselves. Results indicated that children in both group CBT and group CBT plus the family component showed positive treatment in comparison to the wait-list condition. However, children in the group CBT plus family component condition showed somewhat better improvement than children in the group CBT condition as evident in less family disruption, greater parental perception of ability to deal with child's behaviors, and lower child's reports of fear. At one-year follow-up, children in the group CBT plus family maintained lower scores for internalizing and externalizing behaviors as reported by parents. Overall, however, both treatment conditions produced significant change in terms of successful treatment outcome relative to the waitlist condition.

Sandra Mendlowitz and colleagues (1999) conducted a clinical trial examining group CBT for anxiety in children (N=68; ages seven to twelve years old). Three conditions were compared: (1) group CBT for children only, (2) group CBT for children and parents, and (3) group CBT for parents only. A wait-list control condition also was included. Improvement was noted for all treatment conditions in terms of reduction in anxiety symptoms; however, children in the group CBT for children and parents condition showed significantly greater improvement in their coping strategies relative to children in the other conditions.

Susan Spence, Caroline Donovan, and Margaret Brechman-Toussaint (2000) conducted a clinical trial for children with social phobia (N=50; ages seven to fourteen years old) in which group CBT was compared to group CBT with parental involvement, and a wait-list control. Parental involvement consisted mainly of enhanced contingency management techniques taught to parents during therapy sessions. Results indicated that both treatment conditions (i.e., ICBT and ICBT with the parental component) showed significant improvements at post-treatment and twelve-month follow-up when compared to the wait-list condition. It is interesting, however, that comparisons between the two treatment conditions did not show statistically significant differences, suggesting both conditions were efficacious in reducing symptoms of social phobia.

Two late-twentieth-century studies reported on parent and family factors that may be related to treatment success or failure (Berman et al. 2000). Steven L. Berman and his colleagues (2000) found that child symptoms of depression as well as parent self-reported symptoms of depression, fear, hostility, and/or paranoia were predictive of treatment failure. Melissa Crawford and Katharina Manassis (2001) found that child, maternal, and paternal reports of family dysfunction and maternal frustration were significant predictors of a less favorable outcome in child's anxiety and overall functioning. Also, paternal reports of multiple physiological symptoms for which no medical cause was evident were predictive of a less favorable outcome in terms of overall child functioning.

In sum, there is strong and consistent evidence showing a familial influence in the development and maintenance of anxiety disorders. This evidence supports both a biological and psychosocial influence. The intervention research literature further suggests strong evidence for the efficacy of ICBT for reducing anxiety disorders in children. Although the effects might be enhanced when including a family component to the intervention, further research on this issue is needed.

See also: ATTACHMENT; PARENT-CHILD RELATIONSHIPS; CHRONIC ILLNESS; CODEPENDENCY; DEVELOPMENTAL PSYCHOPATHOLOGY; DISABILITIES; PARENTING STYLES; POSTTRAUMATIC STRESS DISORDER (PTSD); SCHOOL PHOBIA AND SCHOOL REFUSAL; SEPARATION ANXIETY; SHYNESS; SUBSTITUTE CAREGIVERS; THERAPY: COUPLE RELATIONSHIPS

Bibliography

American Psychiatric Association. (1994). *Diagnostic and Statistical Manual of Mental Disorders,* 4th edition. Washington, DC: Author.

Barrett, P. M.; Dadds, M. R.; and Rapee, R. M. (1996). "Family Treatment of Childhood Anxiety: A Controlled Trial." *Journal of Consulting and Clinical Psychology* 64:333–342.

Barrett, P. M.; Duffy, A. L.; Dadds, M. R.; and Rapee R. M. (2001). "Cognitive-Behavioral Treatment of Anxiety Disorders in Children: Long-Term (6-Year) Follow-Up." *Journal of Consulting and Clinical Psychology* 69:135–141.

Berman, S. L.; Weems, C. F.; Silverman, W. K.; and Kurtines, W. M. (2000). "Predictors of Outcome in Exposure-Based Cognitive and Behavioral Treatments for Phobic and Anxiety Disorders in Children." *Behavior Therapy* 31:713–731.

Bernstein, G. A., and Garfinkel, B. D. (1986). "School Phobia: The Overlap of Affective and Anxiety Disorders." *Journal of the American Academy of Child and Adolescent Psychiatry* 25:235–241.

Biederman, J.; Rosenbaum, J. F.; Hirshfeld, D. R.; and Faraone, S. V. (1990). "Psychiatric Correlates of Behavioral Inhibition in Young Children of Parents with and without Psychiatric Disorders." *Archives of General Psychiatry* 47:21–26.

Biederman, J.; Faraone, S. V.; Hirshfeld-Becker, D. R.; Friedman, D.; Robin, J. A.; and Rosenbaum, J. F. (2001). "Patterns of Psychopathology and Dysfunction in High-Risk Children of Parents with Panic Disorder." *American Journal of Psychiatry* 158:49–57.

Bird, H. R.; Canino, G.; Rubio-Stipec, M.; and Gould, M. S. (1988). "Estimates of the Prevalence of Childhood Maladjustment in a Community Survey in Puerto Rico: The Use of Combined Measures." *Archives of General Psychiatry* 45:1120–1126.

Bruch, M. A., and Heimberg, R. G. (1994). "Differences in Perceptions of Parental and Personal Characteristics between Generalized and Nongeneralized Social Phobics." *Journal of Anxiety Disorders* 8:155–168.

Canino, I. A.; Gould, M. A.; Prupis, S.; and Schaffer D. (1986). "A Comparison of Symptoms and Diagnoses in Hispanic and Black Children in an Outpatient Mental Health Clinic." *Journal of the American Academy of Child Psychiatry* 25:254–259.

Cobham, V. E.; Dadds, M. R.; and Spence, S. H. (1998). "The Role of Parental Anxiety in the Treatment of Childhood Anxiety." *Journal of Consulting and Clinical Psychology* 66:893–905.

Eley, T. (1999). "Behavioral Genetics As a Tool for Developmental Psychology: Anxiety and Depression in Children and Adolescents." *Clinical Child and Family Psychology Review* 2:21–36.

Ginsburg, G. S., and Silverman, W. K. (1996). "Phobic and Anxiety Disorders in Hispanic and Caucasian Youth." *Journal of Anxiety Disorders* 10:517–528.

Ginsburg, G. S.; Silverman, W. K.; and Kurtines, W. K. (1995). "Family Involvement in Treating Children with

Phobic and Anxiety Disorders: A Look Ahead." *Clinical Psychology Review* 15: 457–473.

Kagan, J. (1989). "Temperamental Contributions to Social Behavior." *American Psychologist* 44:668–674.

Kearney, C. A., and Silverman, W. K. (1995). "Family Environment of Youngsters with School Refusal Behavior: A Synopsis with Implications for Assessment and Treatment." *American Journal of Family Therapy* 23:59–72.

Last, C. G., and Perrin, S. (1993). "Anxiety Disorders in African-American and White Children." *Journal of Abnormal Child Psychology* 21:153–164.

Mendlowitz, S. L.; Manassis, K.; Bradley, S.; Scapillato, D.; Miezitis, S.; and Shaw, B. F. (1999). "Cognitive-Behavioral Group Treatments in Childhood Anxiety Disorders: The Role of Parental Involvement." *Journal of the American Academy of Child and Adolescent Psychiatry* 38:1223–1229.

Rapee, R. (1997). "Potential Role of Childrearing Practices in the Development of Anxiety and Depression." *Clinical Psychology Review* 17:47–67.

Sallee, R., and Greenawald, J. (1995). "Neurobiology." In *Anxiety Disorders in Children and Adolescents,* ed. J. S. March. New York: Guilford Press.

Silverman, W. K., and Berman, S. L. (2001). "Psychosocial Interventions for Anxiety Disorders in Children: Status and Future Directions." In *Anxiety Disorders in Children and Adolescents: Research, Assessment and Intervention,* ed. W. K. Silverman and P. D. A. Treffers. Cambridge, UK: Cambridge University Press.

Spence, S. H.; Donovan, C.; and Brechman-Toussaint, M. (2000). "The Treatment of Childhood Social Phobia: The Effectiveness of a Social Skills Training-Based, Cognitive Behavioural Intervention, with and without Parent Involvement." *Journal of Child Psychology and Psychiatry and Allied Disciplines* 41:713–726.

LISSETTE M. SAAVEDRA
WENDY K. SILVERMAN

ARGENTINA

Argentine families are a heterogeneous result of the many changes that have had an impact on their *structures* and *dynamics*. These changes have taken place both in Argentina and other Latin American and Caribbean countries in the last few decades.

The socioeconomic crisis that has affected Latin America since the 1970s aroused a growing interest in the study of its impact on family structures and dynamics. In Latin America, research has been undertaken from two different perspectives. The first emphasizes the study of the variations in sociodemographic indicators (marriages, fecundity, aging, divorce, etc.) and the extent to which they have influenced *family structures*. It also stresses the coexistence of various family patterns.

The second perspective focuses on the relations within the family group. These relations can be analyzed from two stances. The first is a theoretical stand favoring the convergence of the goals of the different family members and the different tasks or roles assigned to each of them. The second is a perspective that emphasizes the idea that the family is a microcosm where authority and power relations interact and where conflict is present.

This kind of research, regardless of which perspective it is based on, explores the distribution of tasks within families, the relation between the sexes and generations, the responsibilities and personal projects of each family member, and the strategies devised by families throughout their different stages. The research contributes to the study of *family dynamics.*

What is Meant by Family?
Proposed Definition

The wide variety of existing definitions of family is the product of the different disciplinary perspectives and of the various theoretical conceptions. However, it is also a reflection of the difficulty that arises in explaining the diversity of family structures and dynamics. Each of them emphasizes one or many aspects or dimensions it deems central to the family concept. These dimensions are: kinship and marriage or common-law marriage; sexuality and reproduction; social acceptance and marriage or common-law marriage stability; household or domestic unit; common residence or cohabitation; social group and interactions within it; family group relations with society and the state, and history, origin, and evolution of family structures.

At present, defining and understanding the family necessarily presupposes an approach from different disciplines and theoretical stances. The definition of the family concept confronts one with a sociopolitical debate that transcends the limits of the private world to constitute a unit that continuously interacts with the sociopolitical sphere (Colombo, Palermo, and Schmukler 1994).

Social links between the sexes and among generations, and production and reproduction relations can be observed within the family. In it, there are common interests and affection, but there are also individual interests and conflict elements. The family represents an authority and power system. In this regard, the family constructs ideology because it does not only receive ideological influences from the outside world, but it also reconstructs those messages and values and answers from its own specific perspective.

This way of conceiving families allows an explanation of not only its various structures but also its dynamics.

Main Transformations in Argentine Society in the Second Half of the Twentieth Century

Below are listed the main transformations that the Argentine society has undergone as of the second half of the twentieth century and that have had an impact on family structures and dynamics.

Autonomization processes and the end of the patriarchal family. One of the most significant changes is related to the emergence of processes of individualization and achievement of autonomy, first, in young generations and, second, of women. These processes are part of a movement towards the modernization of societies and are related to the loss of father's authority within the family.

The most outstanding feature of these processes is "the tendency of young people from middle and high sectors, mainly men, to live on their own, regardless of the process of forming a couple." (Jelin 1994, p. 38).

However, this process of achieving autonomy has been affected by the economic crisis that started in the mid-1970s and the concurrent high level of unemployment among young people in Argentina—not being able to find a job or losing it "interrupts the expected progression towards young people['s] independence" (Allat and Yeandle 1992, p. 83).

Changes in women's situation. The condition of women in Argentine society experienced important changes throughout the twentieth century,

This Argentinian family gathers for a Sunday dinner. Because of socioeconomic changes, family dynamics in Argentina have become more democratic and less patriarchal. PABLO CORRAL V/CORBIS

most of which began in the 1960s. Women are now more involved in education, in the labor market, in politics and in other areas of social, cultural, and political life.

In turn, "due to technological changes linked to birth control and changes in interpersonal relations, the place of marriage as a privileged space for sexuality has also changed, as has the identification of sexuality with reproduction" (Jelin 1994, p. 33).

Feminist movements also played an important part in leading women to question traditional roles and struggling to achieve equal rights for men and women. The legal system has formalized these changes by subsequently modifying the legal status of women within the family and society.

Beginning in the mid-1970s, Argentina experienced a deep economic crisis that led to a recession. This crisis had different effects on men and women. As a result of the recession more women entered the workforce, and there was a rise in unemployment for men, particularly for heads of households. Women whose participation in the labor market increased were those "married and cohabiting, mostly those whose partner was household head, and those who were relatively better educated, having a middle and in most cases, high level of formal education, i.e., society's middle and high sectors" (Wainerman and Geldstein 1994, p. 199). More divorced and separated women also entered the workforce.

Sociodemographic changes. The birth rate in Argentina began to drop at the end of the nineteenth century, as occurred in other industrialized nations. The birth rate had both increases and decreases through the twentieth century, but it stabilized as of 1982, affecting the reduction in the size of families. However, since 1970, there has been an increase in teenage fertility, primarily among lower-class women.

Another important change in sociodemographic indicators is an uninterrupted decrease in mortality rate during the second half of the twentieth century, mainly of women, together with an increase in life expectancy. This directly affects the potential duration of marital life, the probability of divorce and separation, and, certainly, of widowhood.

An overview of the main changes in family structures and dynamics that have taken place in Argentina in the last decades appears below.

Family structures. Table 1 shows the different lifestyles in Argentina at two different times: 1986 and 1997 (complete data from the Population and Households National Census conducted in 2001 is not yet available).

As shown on the table, the nuclear family is the most common household structure in Argentina. However, between 1986 and 1997, the number of nuclear families has decreased, compared to individual households, the number of which increased. The same is true with extended and compound families, but to a lesser extent. However, research (2001) by the Information, Evaluation and Monitoring System of Social Programs of the Ministry of Social Development showed that in that year, the percentage of extended and compound families increased by 15 percent, with a tendency to further increase as a result of Argentina's economic crisis.

This heterogeneous overview also shows differences within each of the categories. Although the number of complete nuclear families has increased, this group includes legal marriages, common-law marriages, and reconstituted families (families formed in a second, subsequent union, often involving children of previous unions). At the same time, it also includes complete families, couples, and one-parent households (mainly mothers living with their children).

Extended or compound families are also diverse. Generally, they are households in which the head, her/his partner, and unmarried children reside with other people, whether relatives or not.

TABLE 1

Types of households and families in Argentina

Types of households and families	1986	1997
Individual	11.3 %	15.3 %
Nuclear	71.9 %	65.9 %
Extended and compound	12.7 %	13.7 %
Without nucleus	4.1 %	4.7 %

SOURCE: Based on data collected from Instituto Nacional de Estadística y Censos. Household Surveys Initiative (MECOVI).

Two-thirds of these households are from low social strata and one-third from middle-class families.

One-person households also show differences: among the young, individual men living by themselves are most common, while among the elderly, separated women and widows are more common.

These diverse family structures reflect a set of changes that have taken place in Argentina during the second half of the twentieth century regarding guidelines for family formation, and which can be summarized as follows:

- An increase in common-law marriages and a decrease in legal marriages.
- Common-law marriages increased in all age sectors. In terms of socioeconomic status, however, they have increased among the youngest in low sectors and among older people in high sectors.
- An increase in the age in which the first marriage takes place, whether common-law or legal.
- Family formation standards differ between sexes and among social strata. Men get married—whether legally or by common-law—at an older age, mainly, in higher social sectors. In contrast, women marry at younger ages, but they follow the pattern described for starting a family, mainly those who are more educated. Couples who are legally married are less likely to have children, and if they do, they do so at an older age.
- An increase in the number of children born out of wedlock.
- An increase in the number of separations.
- An increase in the number of reconstituted families, families without children, and female-headed families.

- An increase of one-person households, more as a consequence of marriage break-ups than of failure to marry (Wainerman and Geldstein 1994).

- Nuclear families, while decreasing in number, are still the most frequent household type. However, these families' characteristics have changed; many of them are common-law marriages or reconstituted families. The size of these families is smaller, and they tend to be unstable.

Family dynamics in Argentina. Most of the research on family dynamics is conducted from a qualitative and microsocial approach. It contributes evidence of important trends in family dynamics, most of which are the result of the economic crisis and the high unemployment rates. They are:

- The emergence of new income providers in households, which implies that men are no longer the only—nor, frequently, the main—provider of family income.

- An increase in the number of female-headed households.

- Changes in patterns of domestic life. Although women's work outside the home does not necessarily result in a reorganization of tasks within households (existence of a double working day), it has in some cases led to a new awareness on the part of women and a more equitable distribution of power in the family environment. When, at the same time, men are out of work for a prolonged period of time, women's outside employment may have different consequences, such as the reorganization of tasks and loss of authority or conflicts, the effects of which may include domestic violence or marital separation.

- Crisis and unemployment seem to have different effects on men and women. Women seem to manage crises better, implementing a set of strategies for the survival of the family group. At the same time, they are the ones that absorb more of the effects of the crisis, regarding both the redistribution of responsibilities and their role of protection and emotional support (Merlinsky 2001; Sagot; and Schmukler 2001).

- A marked increase in the number of poor families—according to data from research (2001) by the Information, Evaluation and Monitoring System of Social Programs of the Ministry of Social Development, almost half of Argentine households are poor.

In summary, the beginning of the twenty-first century brought new standards for family formation. They include different domestic arrangements and changes in both male and female gender-linked behavior and attitudes, which can be interpreted as a tendency towards democratization of family bonds—there is clearly a greater equality between men and women, as well as a fairer distribution of tasks and power within families. According to Beatriz Schmukler (2001), this trend is part of a broader democratizing process at a sociopolitical level.

At the beginning of the third millenium, Argentina faces great diversity in family life. Family formation and dissolution vary according to social sectors, gender, and area of residence. These changes, however, should not be interpreted as a crisis of the family institution or as evidence of its disappearance, in spite of the evident loss of its social functions (Jelin 1994). Marital unions survive, although they are less stable and less formal (Wainerman and Geldstein 1994).

Research findings by CEPAL (1994) suggest that different types of families can look after the well-being of their members and contribute to fair and democratic family development, provided there is a family project, that is, a common life plan in which goals and priorities are established. At a time of a deep social, political, and economic crisis, family life will adapt.

See also: LATIN AMERICA

Bibliography

Agnés, M., and Barrére, M. (1999). *La división familiar del trabajo. La vida doble.* Buenos Aires: Editorial Lumen/Humanitas.

Allat, P., and Yeandle, S. (1992). *Youth Unemployment and the Family. Voices of Disordered Times,* London: Routledge.

Borsotti, C. (1981). *La organización social de la reproducción de los agentes sociales, las unidades familiares y sus estrategias.* Buenos Aires: CENEP.

CEPAL. (1994). *Familia y Futuro.* Author: Santiago de Chile.

Colombo, G., and Palermo, A. (1994). *Madres de sectores populares y escuela*. Buenos Aires: CEPAL.

Chapp, M., and Palermo, A. (1994). *Autoridad y roles sexuales en la familia y la escuela*. Buenos Aires: CEAL.

Geldstein, R. (1994). *Los roles de fénero en la crisis. Mujeres como principal sostén económico del hogar*. Buenos Aires: CENEP.

Gil Lozano, F.; Pita, V.; Ini, M. (2000). *Historia de las mujeres en la Argentina. Siglo XX*. Buenos Aires: Taurus.

Instituto nacional de estadistica y censos. Household Surveys Initiative (MECOVI).

ISIS Mudar. (1988). *Mujeres, crisis y movimientos*. Santiago: ISIS International.

Jelin, E. (1994). "Familia: Crisis y después." In *Vivir en Familia*. Buenos Aires: Losada.

Jelin, E., and Feijoó, M. del C. (1980). *Trabajo y familia en el ciclo de vida femenino. El caso de los sectores populares de Buenos Aires*. Buenos Aires: CEDES.

Levi Strauss, C. (1976). "La familia." In *Polémica sobre el origen y universalidad de la familia*. Barcelona: Anagrama.

López Hernández, G.; Loira Saviñón, C.; and Cervera, J. (1995). *Familias con futuro. Derecho a una sociedad más justa*. México, D.F.: Grupo de Educación Popular con Mujeres.

Merlinsky, M. G. (2001). "Desocupación y crisis en las imágenes de género." In *Mujeres en América Latina transformando la vida*. San José, Costa Rica: Universidad de Costa Rica.

Palermo, A. (2001). "La educación universitaria de la mujer. Entre las reivindicaciones y las realizaciones." In *Revista alternativas. Serie historia y prácticas pedagógicas*. Año III, No. 3:175–191. San Luis, Argentina: Publicación Internacional del LAE.

Schmukler, B., and Di Marco, G. (1997). *Las madres y la democratización de la familia en la Argentina contemporánea*. Buenos Aires: Biblos.

Schmukler, B., coordinator. (1999). *Familias y relaciones de género en transformación*. México, D.F.: Edamax, S.A. de C.V. y The Population Council, Inc.

Torrado, S. (1993). *Procreación en la Argentina. Hechos e ideas*. Buenos Aires: Edición de la Flor.

Wainerman, C., and Geldstein, R. (1994). "Viviendo en familia: Ayer y Hoy." In *Vivir en familia*. Buenos Aires: Losada.

Other Resource

Arriagada, I. (1999). "¿Nuevas Familias para un nuevo siglo?" In *Revista de la CEPAL* No. 65. Available from http://www.socwatch.org.uy/2000/esp/tematicos/nuevasfamilias.htm.

ALICIA ITATÍ PALERMO

ARMENIA

See ETHNIC VARIATION/ETHNICITY

ARRANGED MARRIAGE

See ASIAN-AMERICAN FAMILIES; BRIDE-PRICE; DATING; DOWRY; HINDUISM; HUSBAND; INDIA; IRAN; MARRIAGE, DEFINITION OF; MATE SELECTION; WIFE

ASIAN-AMERICAN FAMILIES

Asian Americans in the United States are a heterogeneous group of many ethnicities, including Japanese, Chinese, Korean, Filipino, Asian (East) Indians, and Southeast Asians. They are neither a single identity group nor a monolithic culture; therefore it is more accurate to speak of Asian-American cultures (Zia 2000). Early Asian groups were voluntary immigrants, but after the Vietnam War, Southeast Asians were primarily refugees (Ng 1998). Although immigration policies historically limited or even barred entry of Asians into the United States, eventually a 1965 amendment to the Immigration and Nationality Act promoted family unification, allowing spouses and parents of Asians legally residing in the United States not to be counted in the established yearly quotas (Ng 1998). Pacific Islanders are also included in this group, creating an APA or Asian and Pacific Americans category. The term *Asian American* identifies people with origins in twenty-six countries, including Bangladesh, Bhutan, Burma, Cambodia, China, Hong Kong, India, Indonesia, Japan, Laos, Macao, Malaysia, the Maldives, Mongolia, North Korea, South Korea, Nepal, Pakistan, the Philippines, Singapore, Sri Lanka, Taiwan, Thailand, and many Pacific Islands (Hildebrand, Phenice, Gray, and Hines 2000).

This population also includes Amerasians (children of U.S. servicemen during the Vietnam War and their Indochinese mothers), adopted Asian children (a large number from Korea), and multiracial children of mixed Asian and European or African-American marriages. Originally this mixed-heritage group included the children of *war brides* (wives of U.S. soldiers stationed abroad) primarily from Korea, Japan, and the Philippines. Currently, it also includes children of interracial Asian-American marriages and intra-ethnic Asian-American marriages, more commonly found in places like California and Hawaii, where there are large Asian populations.

During the pre–World War II period, ethnic groups such as the Japanese named their generations starting with immigrants as the first, or Issei generation, followed by the second, or Nisei, born in the United States generation, and their American children, the third, or sansei generation. The fourth generation, the yonsei, included biracial children. By the third and fourth generations, after the war, children did not speak Japanese and were culturally assimilated (Adler 1998). New Japanese immigrants arriving after 1946 were referred to as Shin-Issei (or new immigrants). This post–World War II immigrant group and their children do not share the negative legacy of internment and racial segregation, although they may also experience discrimination. As new immigrants arrived in the United States, Asian-American ethnic groups created categories relevant to their immigration patterns. For some groups, first generation meant foreign-born adolescents thirteen years or over, 1.5 generation referred to foreign-born ages five through twelve, and second generation include United States–born or arriving at preschool age, zero to four years.

Varied Immigration Histories

The immigration of Asians to America can be divided into several distinct waves prompted by different political events. Early Asian immigrants provided cheap labor for the Hawaiian sugar plantations and California factories and fruit growers. Japanese laborers were listed along with supplies (bonemeal, canvas, macaroni) and "Chinamen" on company purchase orders (Takaki 1989). Chinese were imported as cheap contract labor, as *coolies,* and as strikebreakers to replace white workers (Chow 1998). The hope of finding gold in California, striking it rich, and returning to their Asian homeland became unrealistic goals upon arriving in the West. Chinese men outnumbered women and the lack of marriageable Chinese

women created a lucrative market for prostitution, until immigration of single women was barred in the 1850s (Chow 1998). The 1882 Chinese Exclusion Act established a European racial preference for immigration, thus eliminating the development of Chinese-American families and the growth of their communities in the United States.

The 1908 Gentleman's Agreement with Japan restricted immigration of laborers, but a loophole allowed entry of parents, wives, and children of those already in the United States, thus influencing the rise of *picture brides* from Japan and Korea (Takaki 1989). The Picture Bride System was a modification of the arranged marriages by families or professional go-betweens. In these arranged marriages, sometimes older bachelors would send pictures of themselves as younger men, and when young brides-to-be arrived in the United States, they found their husbands-to-be nothing like what they expected. Sometimes the women refused to marry them. Some women became *picture brides* not only out of filial duty, but also as a strategy to start a new life for themselves (Hune 2000). Picture brides tended to be better educated than their husbands, and by the time the practice was curtailed in 1920, there were almost 30,000 American-born children from these marriages (Chan 1991). The 1945 War Brides Act allowed GIs to reunite with their Asian wives, which brought more immigrants to the United States. But it was not until the McCarran-Walter Act of 1952 that race was eliminated as a category for immigration (Takaki 1989).

Early Filipino immigrants were predominantly male students, *pensionados,* or those individuals sponsored by the territorial government, and those who chose to remain became unskilled laborers because they could not become naturalized citizens. The Immigration Act of 1965 gave preference to, in order: (1) unmarried children of U.S. citizens; (2) spouses and children of permanent residents; (3) professionals and scientists or artists of exceptional ability; (4) married children of U.S. citizens; (5) brothers and sisters of U.S. citizens; and (6) skilled and unskilled workers in occupations for which labor is in short supply. But most important for Asian families, the exemptions, for which there was no numerical limit, included: spouses of U.S. citizens, children (under twenty-one) of U.S. citizens, and parents of U.S. citizens (Ng 1998). This facilitated chain migration of Filipinos joining other family members between 1966 and 1970.

Migrations of highly educated Asians began in the 1960s. Between 1972 and 1988, approximately 200,000 Asians with training in the science-based professions entered the United States from the four major sending countries. Engineers and physicians came primarily from India, health practitioners from the Philippines and Korea, and scientists from China (Ng 1998). East Indians were the wealthiest, most highly educated, and most English-proficient of the Asian immigrants (Bacon 1996). As professionals with middle- and upper-class occupations, this group contributed to the stereotypic myth of the "model minority" who have assimilated and produced well-educated, high-achieving offspring.

After the fall of Saigon in April 1975, and the communist victory in Indochina, the Orderly Departure Program was established to facilitate the removal of refugees to the "first-asylum" countries of Thailand, Malaysia, Singapore, Indonesia, and the Philippines. These camps began to overflow with refugees from Vietnam and Laos (including the Hmong), and the Khmer from Cambodia (Suhrke 1998). The U.N. Convention and clauses from the 1980 U.S. Refugee Act defined who counted as a refugee and eventually resulted in either repatriation or settlement in the United States providing there were sponsors. Settlement patterns in the United States led to the dispersal of 130,000 first-wave refugees (1975) throughout the country. The second wave of refugees (1981) were predominantly family-reunification cases sponsored by relatives (Ng 1998).

The nationwide dispersal and diffusion of Indochinese refugees mirrored the governmental dispersion of Japanese Americans from internment camps after World War II, using the same rationale of preventing ethnic enclaves and not overburdening any single locale (Chan 1994; Zhou and Gatewood 2000). Ironically, the refugees came to the United States for political freedom and asylum, while the Nisei evacuees, citizens by birth, were denied their constitutional rights, though they eventually received an apology and reparations in 1988 (Takaki 1989). The effects upon families and ethnic communities due to this dispersion contributed to the diversity of experiences of Asian-American groups. Japanese-American families in the Midwest tended to transform their culture (Adler 1998), while the Hmong relied upon secondary and tertiary migration to reunite families and clans (Chan 1994). Secondary migration

brought many Indochinese to California, settling in Los Angeles, Orange and San Diego counties, and in the Silicon Valley of San Jose. The dispersement of Hmong and Cambodians to frostbelt locations in northern states required major adjustment to a climate different from that of Asia.

Family Structures and Gender Roles

The vertical family structure of patriarchal lineage and hierarchal relationships is common in traditional Asian-American families, but there is diversity in practice across cultures. Based on the teachings of Confucius, responsibility moves from father to son, elder brother to younger brother, and husband to wife. Women are expected to be passive, and nurture the well-being of the family. A mother forms a close bond with her children, favoring her eldest son over her husband (Hildebrand, Phenice, Gray, and Hines 2000). On rural farms in the west, where Japanese women were isolated and saw other women only once a year, they often became extremely close to their children (Chan 1991). Thus, cultural tradition and living conditions both fostered this close relationship.

Over the generations, as in the case of the Japanese Americans, this pattern changed from the linear male-oriented pattern of kinship to a stem pattern of shared responsibility and inheritance for both sons and daughters (Adler 1998). In contrast to the patriarchal and patrilineal structure of Japanese, Chinese, and Korean societies, the gender structure in the Philippines is more egalitarian, and kinship is bilateral. In employment, women had and continue to have equal status with men (Espiritu 1995). Women held high positions and were role models in all aspects of Filipino society.

For Southeast Asian refugee families, the change in gender relations was a function of the changing gender roles upon relocation. Older men lost their traditional roles as elders who solved problems, adjudicated quarrels, and made important decisions, when they became powerless without fluency in English and understanding of Western culture. Hmong parents found their children were serving as cultural brokers, which undermined the father's ability to support his family, thus reducing his status. Hmong women, on the other hand, discovered that they had more rights and protection from abuse, which made their adjustment easier than their husbands'. In addition, they sold their intricate needlework, providing family income (Chan 1994).

Structurally, Asian-American families historically included split-household families, transnational families, extended families, nuclear families, and multiple nuclear family households. Evelyn Nakano Glen (1983) described Chinese split-household families as part production or income earning by men sojourning abroad, and part reproduction or maintaining the family household, including childrearing and caring for the elderly by wives and relatives in China. Split-household families were common for Chinese between 1850 and the 1920s. In the 1930s Filipino families also had split-household families since men far exceeded women on the mainland. Gender roles became reversed when Filipina women migrated to become domestic workers and nurses in the health care system, becoming family breadwinners with children and spouses in the homeland. Transnational (split-household) families grew out of economic necessity, and transcended borders and spatial boundaries to take advantage of the lower cost of living for families in a developing country (Zhou and Gatewood 2000). Filipina women preferred having kin, rather than strangers, provide childcare, especially during infancy, even if that meant living away from their children. But this arrangement was considered a *broken home* because the ideal family was the nuclear family, and there was an emotional cost of not being able to supervise one's own children. These kinship patterns reinforced the cultural value of familism, or mutual cooperation, collectivism, and mutual obligation among kin (Zhou and Gatewood 2000).

There are a variety of reasons for the creation of extended family households, including the desire for children to support their parents and grandparents, the inculcation of language and culture, economic stability, cultural obligation, and family reunification patterns. Extended families living in the same household was a function of cultural norms, economic needs, and a process of migration. Discrimination in housing and economic necessity after World War II often brought a variety of Japanese family (and nonfamily) members together in one household. In addition, older Issei, who could not speak English, relied upon their children, the Nisei, to help them negotiate daily living in mainstream society (Adler 1998). Households might include parents, children, unmarried siblings, and grandparents. Traditional Asian-Indian families live in a joint family, which includes a married couple, their unmarried children, and their married sons with their spouses and children. Thus, three or more generations may reside in the same household.

Economic opportunities and upward mobility caused younger professionals to move their nuclear families away from parents, who may have preferred to remain in their familiar ethnic communities. Some Filipino families combined nuclear families into multiple family households for economic reasons. But for Indochinese families who were dependent upon welfare, social service agencies defined their family for them as nuclear, not extended, for the purposes of distribution of assistance. Rather than the family being a unit of production, as in Laos, families became a unit of consumption in the United States (Chan 1994). Regardless of how families were defined legally, Vietnamese families pooled and exchanged material resources within family groups, building a cooperative family economy. Informal women-centered social groups and community networks were established to regulate the exchange of resources among households, and to mediate domestic tensions and disputes (Zhou and Gatewood 2000).

Religion and Cultural Values

Asian immigrants arrive in the United States with many religions, including Buddhism, Confucianism, Hinduism, Islam, and Christianity. The kinds of interpretive frameworks provided by religion, as a central source of cultural components, become particularly important when people are coping with changing environments (Zhou and Gatewood 2000). Immigrants make sense out of their new environment by utilizing cultural components from traditional religion and subtly altering them to reflect the demands of the new environment. The diversity of Asian immigrant religions include Theravada Buddhism, Mahayana Buddhism, Shamanism (Hmong), Christianity (primarily Koreans and Filipinos), and forms of Hinduism, Sikhism, Jainism, Sunni and Shiite Islam, and Syro-Malabar Catholicism (primarily Asian-Indian and Pakistani) (Zhou and Gatewood 2000).

It is through organized religion and family modeling that values and beliefs are inculcated in the younger generation. Although there are distinct differences among the Asian ethnic groups, some of the commonalities in worldview include: group orientation (collectivity); family cohesion and responsibility; self-control and personal discipline; emphasis on educational achievement; respect for authority; reverence for the elderly (filial piety); the use of shame for behavioral control; and interdependence of families and individuals (Hildebrand, Phenice, Gray, and Hines 2000).

In the East Asian Indian worldview there are no individuals; rather, each person is born with a distinctly different nature or essence, based upon his or her parents and the specific circumstances of birth. This makes people fundamentally different, rather than same (or equal), and this nature changes over time (Bacon 1996). This holistic worldview makes Asian-Indian identity tied to social relationships, and the inherent inequality gives rise to social rankings based upon social relations. The caste system can be visualized as a system of concentric circles in which the social groups that encompass others are ranked higher than those they encompass, rather than a ladder system of inequality. As a result of this traditional worldview, for Asian Indians social relationships are the building blocks of society. In the Western perspective, individual choice is the foundation of group affiliation (Bacon 1996).

Traditionally, ethnic enclaves such as Chinatowns served as self-defense mechanisms to insulate the Chinese from racial conflicts, and were home to *tongs,* or tight-knit fraternal organizations, which provided justice, economic stability, and social services (Chow 1998). Thus, Chinese culture was maintained. Later, in contemporary settings, the ethnic churches are where culture and language are passed on through language schools, summer camps, youth groups, and conferences. The ethnic church is also the place where the development of ethnic identity and socialization of peers (and future mates) play important roles. In some Asian cultures where intermarriage is taboo, or at least greatly discouraged, ethnic churches become the primary venue for friendship and dating.

In the United States, the church has become a major and central anchoring institution for Korean immigrant society. Facing discrimination, Korean Americans find in the close-knit religious community a place where their bruised identity can be healed and affirmed (Ryu 1992). Korean churches, whether they are Christian, Buddhist, or based on Confucianism, provide for the holistic needs of their members, including social services, education, language classes, or simply socialization in an accepting environment. Approximately 78 percent of Korean Americans belong to a church, making it a social evangelism. Well-to-do Koreans come to the English-language services and feel a sense of belonging that they do not feel in the corporate world of their daily lives. Whether they belong to an organized religion or not, Koreans have always seen their lives in somewhat religious terms (Ryu 1992).

The cultural differences and difficulty of the Hmong to adjust to Western society illustrate the diversity of life experiences and traditions of Asian Americans. The Hmong were slash-and-burn farmers in Laos and came to the United States with few skills for urban living. What was legal and socially acceptable in Laos, such as opium production, polygamy, bride kidnapping, coining, and wife beating, is condemned and illegal in Western society. Values based upon the worldview that what is good for the family supersedes individual interest, and what is good for the spirit supersedes material interest, need to be altered to adapt to the individualism and materialism of American society (Faderman 1998; Hones and Cha 1999). Voluntary placement agencies called *Volags* received $500 for each refugee they aided and included many Christian religious organizations (Chan 1991). Thus, many of these refugees found themselves being inculcated by well-meaning sponsors with religious beliefs that contradicted their native religions, such as belief in the power of Shamanism for the Hmong. For some, elements of the traditional beliefs such as Chao Fa, or Angel of the Sky, and new religions are creating a Christian religion with a distinctive Hmong flavor (Hones and Cha 1999).

Regional and Generational Differences

Historically, Asian immigrants were concentrated in Hawaii and in states along the Pacific coast, settling in segregated ethnic enclaves such as Chinatowns, Little Tokyos, and Little Manilas (Zhou and Gatewood 2000). As the population began to disperse throughout the Northeast, the Midwest, and the South, sizable ethnic communities developed in cities such as Saint Paul and Minneapolis (Hmong), New York (Chinese and Asian Indians), New Orleans (Vietnamese), and Houston (Vietnamese and Chinese). Recent trends of Asian Americans moving into white middle-class suburban areas have been strong, thus decreasing residential segregation.

Generational differences and regional differences both contributed to the increase of out-marrying among Asian Americans. Third and fourth generations, as well as ethnics living in predominately European-American neighborhoods, tend to out-marry more than do recent immigrants or those living in segregated ethnic communities. Interracial marriages were considered illegal in some states until 1967, at the height of the civil rights movement, when the U.S. Supreme Court declared all anti-miscegenation laws unconstitutional. It was believed that intermarriage was concentrated disproportionately among higher classes of Asian Americans to more advantaged European Americans for upward mobility (Zhou and Gatewood 2000). More children of Japanese-American heritage are born to interracial couples than same-race couples. Higher cross-cultural marriages for Japanese-American women may be the result of preference for a more equitable marriage over the traditional Japanese patriarchal family, and the importance of family continuity pressuring Japanese men to marry within their race and ethnic group (Ishii-Kuntz 1997).

The ethnic dynamics in Hawaii and the mainland are quite different, and intra-ethnic acceptance of *Hapas,* or people of mixed ancestry, appears to be inverted. In Hawaii, Chinese Hapa are more acceptable than Japanese Hapa, while in west coast cities such as San Francisco and Seattle, Japanese Hapa are more accepted in the ethnic communities than Chinese Hapa (Zhou and Gatewood 2000).

In the early 1900s, East Asian Indians settling in California remained isolated on small farms, and few were able to bring wives from India. Family life was restricted by prejudice against dark-skinned people, though Indians were considered Caucasian and even attained citizenship at the time. As intermarriage with African Americans was discouraged, Mexican-American women became the most acceptable and accessible mates (Hess 1998). The children of these marriages were called Mexican-Hindu (Chan 1991). Naturalization of Asian Indians was reversed in 1923 by the Thind case, and citizenship was not restored until 1946. Studies conducted in the 1950s and 1960s indicated that East Indian men preferred to remain single rather than out-marry, and that the shortage of eligible Indian women contributed to the breakdown of the caste system in the United States, as marriages, by necessity, occurred between castes (Hess 1998).

In the Midwest, Minnesota's *Land of 10,000 Lakes* has become the land of 10,000 to 15,000 Korean adoptees. Nationwide, 140,000 Korean-born children have been adopted by American families (mostly European American) since adoption began after the end of the Korean War in 1953 (Zia 2000). The identity development of these Asian adoptees depended on their access to Korean culture and language, the beliefs of the adoptive parents regarding their race and ethnicity, and their acceptance into Korean communities (Mullen 1995). Now, becoming adults, these adoptive children find that they, like some Hapas, or mixed-race Asian Americans, find it difficult to become integrated into their ethnic communities. After adoption from Korea tapered off in 1998, each year approximately 1,000 children (mostly girls) have been adopted from China. By 1998, the total of Chinese adoptees had risen to 15,000.

Asian-American parent-child relationships have changed across generations for a variety of reasons. For Vietnamese-American families, better language skills, opportunities for education and job training, and familiarity with Western cultural norms have given children greater advantages over their parents for dealing with American institutions. Early Vietnamese immigrants, with higher social status, have attained economic success, but later refugees have less economic capital. Vietnamese youth migrating without older family members and the small number of Vietnamese elders in the United States have contributed to the lack of guardianship for some youth. But generally, traditional family values of collectivism and family hierarchy have remained strong. Interdependence within Asian-American families and communities has continued on some level, while emphasis on independence in American culture has influenced Asian-American youth. Cultural agents, such as television and its emphasis on materialism, popular music with the free expression of crude language, and schools promoting individualism, have been serious concerns that can erode authority and power of Asian-American parents.

Effects of Oppression on Family Life

Stereotyping, racism, discrimination, and racial profiling have a long history of oppression of Asian Americans in the United States and appear to continue today. Hate crimes against Asians and *glass ceilings* preventing upward mobility in employment have been well documented. Asian Americans have the worst chance of advancing into management positions and the U.S. Commission on Civil Rights cited the glass ceiling as one of the major types of discrimination faced by Asian Americans (Zia 2000). Asian-American families attempt to socialize their children to cope with these realities, while retaining a sense of cultural integrity and ethnic identity. Asian-Pacific American children should not accept that they are inferior or less deserving of civil rights because of their race and ethnicity. The United States of America is their home and they need not feel like outsiders (Pang and Cheng 1998). American-born and mixed-race Asian Americans develop their identities as Asian-derived people with sensitivities to where they are living, in this case the United States. Thus, it is important to understand the sociopolitical climate of American society and to study one's heritage and family roots.

One overt example of institutional racism came in the 1940s as part of the U.S. government's response to Pearl Harbor. The internment of Japanese and Japanese Americans during World War II dismantled the family structure by eliminating traditional parental roles, thus weakening parental authority. Everyone ate in mess halls, so adolescent Nisei often ate with their friends rather than with their families. Children joined their peers for recreational activities rather than staying in the crowded barracks with their siblings and parents. Nisei sons, who could gain employment in camp, sometimes replaced their Issei fathers as heads-of-the-household. Issei women were relieved of their cooking and farm labor responsibilities and gained more free time to socialize (Adler 1998). Thus, the institutionalization of families destroyed the Asian lifestyle of working together in small businesses or on the farm.

For Koreans, the small retail business became a lifeline when language barriers and job discrimination gave them few options for livelihood. There is a high degree of ethnic homogeneity in that they tend to service co-ethnics, and the owners/managers tend to be college educated and held professional or managerial positions prior to immigration (Chung 1997). Immigration laws gave health care professionals, such as physicians, dentists, nurses, and pharmacists, preference for entry into the United States, but upon arrival, their educational training, certifications, and credentials were deemed unacceptable. Thus, the labor-intensive family-owned business became the only option, and family members, elderly, women, and children, became the employees. Chung (1997) maintains that the unusually high propensity of Asian immigrants' businesses should be regarded as a form of underemployment and a source of cheap labor.

Although there has always been tension when Korean business owners were located in predominantly African-American neighborhoods, this tension escalated to racial animosity after the acquittal of the white police officers in the Rodney King beating. In April 1992, a three-day uprising in Los Angeles left fifty-four people dead and 4,500 shops in ashes, more than half of which were Korean-run businesses. Koreans and other ethnic minorities lost their livelihood in the event termed *sa-i-gu* (pronounced sah-ee-goo), a defining moment of economic devastation for the Korean community, nationwide (Zia 2000). It took years for families to rebuild and major adjustments in family life to cope with the physical and psychological loss.

Asian Americans have been subjects of stereotypes, or group definition by others, depending upon the sociopolitical context of the time. Early stereotypes of immigrants described Japanese and Chinese as *Orientals* who could not be assimilated. Then, during wartime hysteria, Japanese and Japanese Americans were characterized as the *yellow peril* (although this label had been prominent since their arrival in the 1800s) and any Asian in the United States was still considered a *perpetual foreigner*. Postwar years and the impact of higher education on Asian Americans brought the stereotype of the overachieving *model minority* (Chan 1991). Geishas, gooks, and geeks have been the major staple of Asian stereotypes, with men portrayed as untrustworthy, evil, or ineffectual, emasculated nerds, and women cast as subservient, passive females, or the seductive, malicious dragon lady (Zia 2000). Although stereotyping clearly remains, the desire to be *politically correct* and not offend minorities has tempered the overt expression of group labels and stereotypes.

Asian parents, who had experienced name-calling and stereotyping throughout their lives, advised their children to ignore the comments, or to rise above them by being better (wiser, stronger,

A Japanese family awaits internment in 1942. The U.S. government placed all Japanese and Japanese-American citizens in internment camps during World War II. NATIONAL ARCHIVES AND RECORDS ADMINISTRATION

smarter) than their tormentors. Some Asian-American parents did not discuss prejudice and discrimination directly with their children, though it was acknowledged as part of life. Children were expected to endure and persevere, which would make them mentally stronger (Adler 1998). This approach also applied to academic success, which brings *face* to their families. These high expectations of Asian-American parents sometimes appear to be unrealistic to the children, but are founded upon the sacrifices families endured for their children's education (Pang and Cheng 1998).

Hate crimes, such as the killing of five Southeast Asian children in a Stockton, California, schoolyard by a gunman wearing military fatigues, and the murder of a Filipino postal worker, Joseph Ileto, because of his Asian ethnicity, have become too common (Zia 2000). Racial profiling in the Wen Ho Lee case, the Taiwanese-American scientist at Los Alamo who was accused of being a Chinese spy, is clear evidence that even high-level white collar Asian-American employees can become targets of racism at any time. There was mounting evidence that Lee was scapegoated and accused of espionage because of his ethnicity (Zia 2000).

Future of Asian-American Families

The future of each group will indeed be as complex and diverse as the ethnic groups themselves. When asked what Asian-American parents fear the most for their children, common responses include: the loss of ethnic culture and language; poor self-concept and identity development; the alienation of adolescents resulting in their association with gangs; the ability to get into a good college; and the need to find a good, stable job. But there is a sense of hope, an expectation that hard work and perseverance will bring success, and for some, the belief in meritocracy. Others believe that Asian Americans still have to work 200 percent to get to the same place as their white peers, and that the playing field is still not level for people of color. Nathan Caplan, Marcellea Choy, and John Whitmore (1994) identified six factors that best characterize the value system of Southeast Asian refugees, the latest and poorest group: cultural foundation, family-based achievement, hard work, resettlement and commonality of the family, self-reliance and family pride, and coping and integration. In terms of priority, parents indicated that education and achievement ranked first, followed by cooperative and harmonious family, while children ranked respect for family members first and education and achievement second. The lowest values, ranking twenty-fifth and twenty-sixth for both parents and children, were desire for material possessions and for seeking fun and excitement (Caplan, Choy, and Whitmore 1994). This seems to indicate that the inculcation of what earlier Asian immigrants viewed as Asian values has been perpetuated through the generations.

See also: BUDDHISM; CHINA; CONFUCIANISM; ETHNIC VARIATION/ETHNICITY; EXTENDED FAMILIES; HINDUISM; INDIA; INDONESIA; JAPAN; KOREA; PHILIPPINES, THE; UNITED STATES; VIETNAM

Bibliography

Adler. S. M. (1998). *Mothering, Education, and Ethnicity: The Transformation of Japanese American Culture.* New York: Garland.

Bacon, J. (1996). *Life Lines: Community, Family, and Assimilation among Asian Indian Immigrants.* New York: Oxford University Press.

Caplan, N.; Choy, M. H.; and Whitmore, J. K. (1994). *Children of the Boat People: A Study of Educational Success.* Ann Arbor: University of Michigan Press.

Chan, S. (1991). *Asian Americans: An Interpretive History.* New York: Twayne Publishers.

Chan, S. (1994). *Hmong Means Free: Life in Laos and America.* Philadelphia: Temple University Press.

Chow, E. N. (1998). "Family, Economy, and the State: A Legacy of Struggle for Chinese American Women." In *Shifting the Center: Understanding Contemporary Families,* ed. S. J. Ferguson. Mountain View, CA: Mayfield Publishing Company.

Chung, J. S. (1997). "Korean American Entrepreneurship Is an Indication of Economic Exploitation." In *Asian Americans: Opposing Viewpoints,* ed. B. Leone, San Diego, CA: Greenhaven Press.

Espiritu, Y. L. (1995). *Filipino American Lives.* Philadelphia: Temple University Press.

Faderman, L. (1998). *I Begin My Life All Over: The Hmong and the American Immigrant Experience.* Boston: Beacon.

Glenn, E. N. (1983). "Split Household, Small Producer and Dual Wage Earners: An Analysis of Chinese-American Family Strategies." *Journal of Marriage and Family* 45:35–46.

Hess, G. R. (1998). "The Forgotten Asian Americans: The East Indian Community in the United States." In *The History and Immigration of Asian Americans,* ed. F. Ng. New York: Garland.

Hildebrand, V.; Phenice, L. A.; Gray, M. M.; and Hines, R. P. (2000). *Knowing and Serving Diverse Families,* 2nd edition. Columbus, OH: Merrill.

Hones, D. F., and Cha, C. S. (1999). *Educating New Americans: Immigrant Lives and Learning.* Mahwah, NJ: Lawrence Erlbaum Associates.

Hune S. (2000). "Doing Gender with a Feminist Gaze: Toward a Historical Reconstruction of Asian America." In *Contemporary Asian America: A Multidisciplinary Reader,* ed. M. Zhou and J. V. Gatewood. New York: New York University Press.

Ishii-Kuntz, M. (1997). "Japanese American Families." In *Families in Cultural Context: Strengths and Challenges in Diversity,* ed. M. K. DeGenova. Mountain View, CA: Mayfield Publishing Company.

Mullen, M. (1995). "Identity Development of Korean Adoptees." In *Re-Viewing Asian America: Locating Diversity,* ed. F. Ng et al. Seattle: University of Washington Press.

Ng, F. (1998). *The History and Immigration of Asian Americans.* New York: Garland.

Pang, V. O., and Cheng, L. L. (1998). *Struggling to Be Heard: The Unmet Needs of Asian Pacific American Children.* Albany: State University of New York Press.

Root, M. P. (1995). "The Multiracial Contribution to the Psychological Browning of America." In *American Mixed Race: The Culture of Microdiversity,* ed. N. Zack. Lanham, MD: Rowman & Littlefield.

Ryu, C. (1992). "Koreans and Church." In *Asian Americans: Oral Histories of First to Fourth Generation Americans from China, the Philippines, Japan, India, the Pacific Islands, Vietnam and Cambodia,* ed. J. F. Lee. New York: The New Press.

Takaki, R. (1989). *Strangers from a Different Shore: A History of Asian Americans.* Boston: Little, Brown.

Zhou, M. (2000). "Social Capital in Chinatown: The Role of Community-Based Organizations and Families in the Adaptation of the Younger Generation." In *Contemporary Asian America: A Multidisciplinary Reader,* ed. M. Zhou and J. V. Gatewood. New York: New York University Press.

Zhou, M., and Gatewood, J. V. (2000). *Contemporary Asian America: A Multidisciplinary Reader.* New York: New York University Press.

Zia, H. (2000). *Asian American Dreams: The Emergence of an American People.* New York: Farrar, Straus and Giroux.

SUSAN MATOBA ADLER

ASIAN FAMILIES

See ASIAN-AMERICAN FAMILIES; CARIBBEAN FAMILIES; CHINA; ETHNIC VARIATION/ETHNICITY, INDIA, INDONESIA, JAPAN; KOREA; PHILIPPINES, THE; VIETNAM

ASSISTED REPRODUCTIVE TECHNOLOGIES

The term *assisted reproductive technologies* (ARTs) refers to a variety of procedures that enable people to reproduce without engaging in genital intercourse. Most people who use ARTs do so because they are infertile and other methods of treating their infertility have proven unsuccessful. Some people without fertility problems also use ARTs to minimize the risk of transmitting certain genetic disorders or to reproduce without a partner of the opposite sex.

Basic ART Procedures

The most commonly used type of ART is *assisted insemination* (also known as *artificial insemination*). With assisted insemination, sperm is obtained from the male through masturbation and then placed in the woman's vagina, cervix, or uterus with a syringe or similar device. Assisted insemination is used to overcome medical conditions that interfere with the ability of sperm to reach and fertilize an egg.

In-vitro fertilization (IVF), a more complex and expensive procedure than assisted insemination, is used for a variety of diagnoses, including unexplained infertility. With IVF, physicians surgically retrieve eggs from the woman's body (in most cases, following a series of hormonal treatments that stimulate the production of multiple eggs), fertilize the eggs in a petri dish, culture the resulting embryos in the laboratory for several days, and then transfer some or all of the embryos back into the woman's uterus for implantation.

Two procedures related to IVF are *gamete intrafallopian transfer* (GIFT) and *zygote intrafallopian transfer* (ZIFT). With GIFT, as with IVF, physicians remove eggs from the woman's body, but instead of fertilizing the eggs in a petri dish they transfer the unfertilized eggs, along with sperm, back into the woman's fallopian tubes. With ZIFT, the eggs are fertilized in a petri dish before they are transferred, but instead of transferring the embryos directly into the uterus (as they are in IVF), the embryos are inserted into the fallopian tubes. GIFT and ZIFT were developed as potentially more effective alternatives to IVF, but since success rates with IVF have improved, the popularity of GIFT and ZIFT has declined.

The likelihood that IVF, GIFT, or ZIFT will succeed varies considerably, depending on factors such as the woman's age, the nature of her infertility, and the skills and experience of the practitioners performing the procedures. In 1999, approximately 25 percent of these procedures led to a live birth (Center for Disease Control and Prevention 2002).

IVF is sometimes performed in conjunction with *intracytoplasmic sperm injection* (ICSI), a procedure in which fertilization is achieved by injecting a single sperm directly into each egg. Because only a few normal sperm are required to perform the procedure, ICSI can be used for men who have poor-quality sperm or extremely low sperm counts. The first successful pregnancy resulting from ICSI was reported in 1992, marking a milestone in the treatment of male infertility.

Variations on the Procedures

Although ARTs are usually performed with the gametes (i.e., sperm and eggs) of the intended parents, in some cases gametes of one of the intended parents are combined with *donor gametes*. Gamete donors may be friends or relatives of the intended parents, or they may be individuals who have been recruited by the ART program and paid for their services. In the latter situation, the identity of the donor is usually not disclosed to the recipients, although nonidentifying medical and personal information may be made available.

Sperm donation is used for a variety of purposes. First, it may be used when the male partner is unable to produce a sufficient amount of viable sperm. It is a far less expensive treatment for this purpose than ICSI and, because it can be used in conjunction with assisted insemination, the woman does not have to undergo the medical risks and burdens of IVF. Second, sperm donation may be used by couples at risk of transmitting certain genetic diseases. For example, if both partners are carriers of a recessive genetic disorder, such as *sickle-cell disease,* using sperm from a donor who is not a carrier will ensure that the resulting child is not born with the disease. Finally, sperm donation may be used by single women or lesbian couples who seek to reproduce without a male partner. Sperm donation is a simple process that involves no physical risks to the donor.

Although sperm donation has been available since the 1950s, *egg donation* is a relatively new procedure, available only since the early 1980s. It is used by women who are unable to produce eggs of their own or, as with sperm donation, by couples who want to avoid transmitting certain genetic diseases. Egg donation enables women to have children long after they have passed menopause; in 1997, physicians reported a successful pregnancy in a 63-year-old woman who had used egg donation (New York State Task Force on Life and the Law 1998). Unlike sperm donation, being an egg donor is time consuming and involves medical risks, primarily those associated with ovarian stimulation and egg retrieval. Donors are generally college-age women, and they are typically paid several thousand dollars for each cycle of donation.

Depending on applicable state law, some ART programs offer the option of *surrogate parenting* (also known as *surrogacy*). Surrogacy does not refer to a specific type of ART, but rather to a social arrangement in which a woman agrees to become pregnant and relinquish the child to the intended parents after birth. Surrogacy is used by couples in which the female partner is unable to gestate a pregnancy, or by single men or gay male couples who want to reproduce without a female partner. With *genetic-gestational surrogacy* (sometimes referred to as *traditional surrogacy*), the surrogate becomes pregnant by undergoing assisted insemination with the intended father's sperm. With *gestational surrogacy,* the intended parents create an embryo through IVF (using their own gametes, donor gametes, or a combination), and the embryo is then transferred into the surrogate to establish a pregnancy.

The ability to *cryopreserve,* or freeze, gametes and embryos is an important part of many ART procedures. Both sperm and embryos can be cryopreserved. Some success has been achieved with freezing unfertilized eggs, although the cryopreservation of eggs is still considered experimental. One of the benefits of cryopreservation is that it can preserve the reproductive capacity of individuals about to undergo chemotherapy or other medical treatments that might impair their fertility. In addition, for couples undergoing IVF, the ability to cryopreserve extra embryos makes it possible to engage in additional attempts at pregnancy without having to undergo ovarian stimulation and egg retrieval each time. If couples have excess frozen embryos after they are finished with their treatment, they can keep them in storage indefinitely, destroy them, donate them to other patients, or make them available to researchers (Coleman 1999).

Some people use ARTs in order to take advantage of *pre-implantation genetic diagnosis* (PIGD). With PIGD, physicians create embryos through IVF, remove one or more cells from each embryo (a process that does not harm the embryos), and then perform genetic testing on the removed cells.

PIGD enables individuals at risk of transmitting serious genetic disorders to select for implantation only those embryos found not to be affected. It also permits prospective parents to determine the sex of their children by transferring embryos of only one sex. In addition to PIGD, individuals who want to increase the likelihood of having a child of a particular sex can do so before conception through the use of *sperm-sorting* technologies, although, unlike PIGD, these techniques cannot guarantee the birth of a child of a particular sex.

In the future, it may be possible to go beyond the process of genetic screening to affirmative genetic manipulation of embryos. Such techniques could give individuals significant control over their children's genetic makeup by enabling physicians to eliminate traits considered undesirable, or to add traits considered desirable.

Medical Risks of ARTs

Like any medical procedure, ARTs involve both benefits and risks. Fertility drugs, whether used alone or in conjunction with IVF, can lead to a condition known as *ovarian hyperstimulation syndrome,* which, in rare cases, can be life threatening. This risk extends not only to women taking the fertility drugs for their own benefit, but also to egg donors who take fertility drugs to increase the number of eggs they will be able to donate.

One of the most serious risks associated with ARTs is the significantly increased likelihood of *multiple gestation*. About one-third of all IVF-generated pregnancies result in multiple births; approximately one-fifth of these multiple pregnancies are triplets or higher-order multiples. The use of fertility drugs without IVF also is associated with an increased risk of multiple pregnancies.

Multiple pregnancies involve significant risks. A woman pregnant with multiples is more likely to develop diseases like *anemia, high blood pressure* (*hypertension*), and *pre-eclampsia*. In addition, approximately 10 percent of children in multiple births die before their first birthday, and the surviving children are at significantly increased risk of lifelong disability. To reduce these risks, some women who have high-order multiple pregnancies undergo *multifetal reduction,* a procedure in which one or more of the fetuses are aborted. Although this procedure increases the likelihood that the remaining fetuses will be born healthy, it does not eliminate the risks associated with multiple gestation. Moreover, it is emotionally difficult and ethically problematic for many patients.

The high rate of multiple gestation associated with IVF is a result of efforts to increase the likelihood of pregnancy by transferring multiple embryos into the uterus in a single cycle. Physicians have been criticized for failing to adequately inform patients of the risk of multiple gestation (New York State Task Force on Life and the Law 1998). In the United States, professional organizations have recommended limits on the number of embryos transferred per cycle, although physicians are not legally required to adhere to these limits. Some European and Asian countries have imposed mandatory limits on the number of embryos physicians may transfer in each cycle.

Ethical and Religious Perspectives on ARTs

Commentators have taken widely differing positions on the appropriateness of having children through ARTs. Some commentators embrace these technologies with few reservations, emphasizing the benefits they offer both infertile couples and women who want to reproduce without a partner of the opposite sex. Supporters of ARTs argue that society should defer to individual decisions about reproductive matters, citing the legal and ethical principle of individual autonomy and the absence of evidence that ARTs result in tangible harm (Robertson 1994).

Other commentators, although generally supportive of at least some forms of ARTs, have expressed concerns about certain aspects of these technologies. Some commentators worry that, as the use of ARTs becomes more routine, children will come to be seen as products to be manufactured according to parents' specifications, rather than as unique individuals to be accepted and loved unconditionally (Murray 1996). As an example of this phenomenon, some gamete donation programs that allow prospective parents to select donors based on personal characteristics like SAT scores, athletic ability, or physical appearance. Similarly, some disability rights activists worry that technologies designed to avoid the birth of children with genetic disorders send a negative message about the value of people with disabilities who are already alive (Asch 1989). Many commentators express particular concern about the prospect of germ-line modification, particularly if it is used for nondisease related reasons, such as controlling a child's hair or eye color or enhancing athletic ability or other personal characteristics (Mehlman 2000).

The danger that ARTs will change the way that children are valued also underlies some commentators' objections to the increasing commercialization of reproductive services. For example, some commentators decry the high fees paid to egg donors and surrogate mothers, based partly on their fear that purchasing an individual's reproductive capacity inappropriately *commodifies* the process of reproduction—in other words, that it turns reproduction into a commodity for sale in the market, rather than a private activity motivated solely by love. Some commentators find it difficult to distinguish between paid surrogate parenting and baby selling, as both practices involve the payment of money to obtain a child (New York State Task Force on Life and the Law 1998).

For some commentators, the acceptability of ARTs turns in part on the environment in which the resulting child will be raised. Thus, some commentators support the use of ARTs by married couples unable to reproduce through sexual intercourse but object to the provision of IVF to single women or lesbian couples (Lauritzen 1993). Others oppose the use of egg donation in postmenopausal women, given the possibility that older women might die while their children are still young (Cohen 1996). By contrast, many commentators believe that children can thrive in a variety of environments, and that efforts to restrict reproduction to young married couples are motivated primarily by ignorance or bias (Murphy 1999).

The use of third-party participants in ARTs—particularly egg donors and surrogate mothers—has generated significant controversy. These women undergo significant medical and psychological risks, often at young age, and usually for a considerable amount of money. Many commentators have expressed concern about the potential for exploitation as young women in need of money undergo risks to benefit older, wealthier couples who want to reproduce (Rothman 1989). With surrogate parenting, commentators also argue that a birth mother cannot make an informed and voluntary decision to give up her child before she has gone through pregnancy and childbirth (Steinbock 1988).

Feminist commentators disagree about many of the ethical issues surrounding ARTs (Warren 1988). Some feminists believe that ARTs are a positive development for women because they give women greater control over the timing and manner of reproduction. Others, by contrast, maintain that the increasing medicalization of infertility reinforces the view of women as primarily mothers, making it more difficult for women to choose to remain childless.

Feminists are particularly divided over the practice of surrogate parenting. Some believe that surrogacy, especially paid surrogacy, exploits women by treating them as mere "incubators" (New York State Task Force on Life and the Law 1988, p. 85). Others maintain that efforts to restrict surrogate parenting are based on misguided paternalism, and that women have a right to use their bodies as they see fit.

Religious perspectives on ARTs are as varied as the positions of secular commentators. At one extreme, the Roman Catholic Church has consistently opposed all forms of ARTs, based on its belief that reproduction must remain inextricably linked to sexual intimacy within a marital relationship (Congregation for the Doctrine of the Faith 1987). The Church has expressed particular concern about ARTs that result in the creation of multiple embryos, as some of these embryos will ultimately be destroyed. Because the Church believes that embryos are persons from the moment of conception, it regards the destruction of an embryo as morally equivalent to killing a person who has already been born.

In most other religious traditions, however, the use of at least some forms of ARTs is considered ethically acceptable (New York State Task Force on Life and the Law 1998). Most Protestant denominations, as well as Jewish, Islamic, Hindu, and Buddhist authorities, support the use of ARTs using gametes from a married couple. Indeed, some Jewish and Islamic theologians suggest that infertile married couples have a duty to use ARTs, given the importance of procreation in these religious traditions. Many of these religions, however, are opposed to the use of donor gametes.

Legal Considerations

ARTs raise a variety of complex legal issues. For example, with ARTs it is now possible for a child to have three biologically related parents—the man who provides the sperm, the woman who provides the egg, and the woman who gestates the child and gives birth—as well as one or more additional *social parents* who intend to raise the child after it is born. If conflicts arise among these individuals, how should the law apportion their respective rights and responsibilities? Some courts have held that parental rights should be based on the intent of the parties at the time of conception; thus, when one woman gives birth to a child conceived with another woman's egg, the woman who intended to act as the child's parent will be considered the mother. Other courts have rejected this intent-based approach in favor of clear rules favoring either genetic or gestational bonds. In many jurisdictions, the law in this area remains unsettled (Garrison 2000).

Disputes also can arise over the disposition of cryopreserved gametes and embryos. When individuals die before their frozen gametes or embryos have been used, should a surviving spouse or partner have the right to use the frozen specimens without the donor's explicit consent? When a couple freezes their embryos for future use and then divorces, may one partner use the embryos to have a child over the other partner's objection? Internationally, courts have taken widely differing approaches to these issues. To avoid disputes over frozen gametes and embryos, many authorities suggest that people should leave written instructions regarding their future disposition wishes. However, some courts have suggested that, even when such instructions exist, individuals retain the right to change their minds at a later date (Coleman 1999).

The law also governs the relationship between ART practitioners and the patients they serve. Physicians have been accused of understating the risks associated with ARTs, particularly the likelihood and consequences of multiple gestation, as well as overstating the likelihood that treatment will result in a live birth. Such practices may form the basis for legal claims of misrepresentation or failure to obtain informed consent. The law also may constrain the exercise of discretion by physicians in their selection of patients. For example, physicians who are unwilling to provide ARTs to unmarried women or HIV-positive patients may find their decisions challenged under antidiscrimination laws (New York State Task Force on Life and the Law 1998).

Conclusion

ARTs have helped numerous individuals overcome physiological or social barriers to reproduction that, in previous generations, would have made it impossible for them to have children. At the same time, they have generated significant ethical, religious, and legal issues about which no societal consensus yet exists. As developments in ARTs continue to proceed, the challenge will be to promote the beneficial use of technology while minimizing the social harms.

See also: BIRTH CONTROL: CONTRACEPTIVE METHODS; BIRTH CONTROL: SOCIOCULTURAL AND HISTORICAL ASPECTS; FAMILY PLANNING; FERTILITY; SEXUALITY EDUCATION; SEXUALITY IN ADULTHOOD; SURROGACY

Bibliography

Andrews, L. B. (1999). *The Clone Age: Adventures in the New World of Assisted Reproductive Technology.* New York: Henry Holt.

Asch, A. (1989). "Reproductive Technology and Disability." In *Reproductive Laws for the 1990s,* ed. S. Cohen and N. Taub. Clifton, NJ: Humana Press.

Cohen, C. B., ed. (1996). *New Ways of Making Babies: The Case of Egg Donation.* Bloomington: Indiana University Press.

Coleman, C. H. (1999). "Procreative Liberty and Contemporaneous Choice: An Inalienable Rights Approach to Frozen Embryo Disputes." *Minnesota Law Review* 84:55–127.

Congregation for the Doctrine of the Faith. (1987). "Instruction on Respect for Human Life in Its Origin and on the Dignity of Procreation." *Origins* 16:697–711.

Dolgin, J. L. (1997). *Defining the Family: Law, Technology, and Reproduction in an Uneasy Age.* New York: New York University Press.

Garrison, M. (2000). "Law Making for Baby Making: An Interpretive Approach to the Determination of Legal Parentage." *Harvard Law Review* 113:835–923.

Lauritzen, P. (1993). *Pursuing Parenthood: Ethical Issues in Assisted Reproduction.* Bloomington: Indiana University Press.

McGee, G. (2000). *The Perfect Baby: Parenthood in the New World of Cloning and Genetics.* Lanham, MD: Rowman and Littlefield.

Mehlman, M. J. (2000). "The Law of Above Averages: Leveling the New Genetic Enhancement Playing Field." *Iowa Law Review* 85:517–593.

Murphy, J. S. (1999). "Should Lesbians Count as Infertile Couples? Antilesbian Discrimination in Assisted Reproduction." In *Embodying Bioethics: Recent Feminist Advances,* ed. A. Donchin and L. M. Purdy. Lanham, MD: Rowman and Littlefield.

Murray, T. H. (1996). *The Worth of a Child.* Berkeley: University of California Press.

New York State Task Force on Life and the Law. (1988). *Surrogate Parenting: Analysis and Recommendations for Public Policy.* New York: Author.

New York State Task Force on Life and the Law. (1998). *Assisted Reproductive Technologies: Analysis and Recommendations for Public Policy.* New York: Author.

Peters, P. G. (1989). "Protecting the Unconceived: Nonexistence, Avoidability, and Reproductive Technology." *Arizona Law Review* 31:487–548.

Roberts, D. E. (1996). "Race and the New Reproduction." *Hastings Law Journal* 47:935–949.

Robertson, J. A. (1994). *Children of Choice: Freedom and the New Reproductive Technologies.* Princeton: Princeton University Press.

Rothman, B. K. (1989). *Recreating Motherhood: Ideology and Technology in a Patriarchal Society.* New York: Norton.

Steinbock, B. (1988). "Surrogate Motherhood as Prenatal Adoption." *Law, Medicine and Health Care* 16 (Spring/Summer):40–50.

Warren, M. A. (1988). "IVF and Women's Interests: An Analysis of Feminist Concerns." *Bioethics* 2:37–57.

Other Resources

American Society for Reproductive Medicine. (2002). *Ethical Considerations of Assisted Reproductive Technologies: ASRM Ethics Committee Reports and Statements.* Available from www.asrm.org/Media/ Ethics/ethicsmain.html.

Centers for Disease Control and Prevention. (2002). *Assisted Reproductive Technology Reports.* Available from www.cdc.gov/nccdphp/drh/art.htm.

Human Fertilisation and Embryology Authority. (2001). *HFEA Code of Practice.* Available from www.hfea. gov.uk/frame.htm.

CARL H. COLEMAN

ATTACHMENT

COUPLE RELATIONSHIPS *Brooke c. Feeney, Nancy L. Collins*

PARENT-CHILD RELATIONSHIPS *Karen S. Rosen, Fred Rothbaum*

COUPLE RELATIONSHIPS

Attachment bonds refer to the relatively enduring and emotionally significant relationships that develop, first between children and parents, and later between adult mated pairs. The propensity to form intimate bonds is considered to be a basic component of human nature that continues throughout the lifespan. Although attachment theory was first formulated to explain the bond that develops between infants and their primary caregivers, John Bowlby, the British psychiatrist responsible for pioneering the theory, asserted that attachment is an integral part of human behavior "from the cradle to the grave" (Bowlby, 1979). This entry focuses on the role of attachment processes in adult intimate relationships.

Normative Attachment Processes in Adulthood

Attachment refers to a specific type of bond that has four defining features:

(1) *proximity maintenance*—the attached individual wishes to be in close proximity to the attachment figure;

(2) *separation distress*—the attached individual experiences an increase in anxiety during unwanted or prolonged separation from the attachment figure;

(3) *safe haven*—the attachment figure serves as a source of comfort and security such that the attached individual experiences diminished anxiety when in the company of the attachment figure; and

(4) *secure base*—the attachment figure serves as a base of security from which the attached individual engages in explorations of the social and physical world.

Bonds of attachment are found in some, but not all, relationships of emotional significance— only those that are critical to an individual's sense of security and emotional stability (Weiss 1982). Adult pair bonds, in which sexual partners mutually provide security to one another, are presumed to be the prototypical attachment relationship in adulthood (see Hazan and Zeifman 1999 for a review).

John Bowlby (1969/1982, 1973, 1980, 1988) proposed that attachment bonds involve two behavioral systems—an attachment system and a caregiving system. First, individuals come into the world equipped with an attachment behavioral system that is prone to activation when they are distressed and that serves a major evolutionary function of protection and survival (Bowlby 1969; Bretherton 1987). The attachment system is, thus, a safety-regulating system that solidifies enduring emotional bonds between individuals that contribute to reproductive success. Although there are normative developmental changes in the expression of the attachment system across the lifespan, the basic function of the attachment system remains constant (Hazan and Zeifman 1999). Adults as well as children benefit from having someone looking out for them—someone who is deeply invested in their welfare, who monitors their whereabouts, and who is reliably available to help if needed. Consistent with this idea, research indicates that intimate relationships play a critical role in promoting health and well-being in adulthood, and that relationship disruption in adulthood is associated with a wide range of adverse health outcomes (see Uchino, Cacioppo, and Kiecolt-Glaser 1996 for a review).

Second, attachment theory stipulates that the caregiving system is another normative, safety-regulating system that is intended to reduce the risk of a close other coming to harm (Bowlby 1969/1982, 1988). *Caregiving* refers to a broad array of behaviors that complement a partner's attachment behavior, and may include help or assistance, comfort and reassurance, and support of a partner's autonomous activities and personal growth (Collins and Feeney, B., 2000; Kunce and Shaver 1994). Responsive caregiving in situations of distress restores feelings of security and gives the attached individual confidence to explore the environment and productively engage in social and achievement activities. Unlike parent-child relationships, which have clearly defined caregiving and care-seeking roles, adult intimate relationships are reciprocal and mutual. Therefore, in well-functioning attachment bonds, adult partners should be able to comfortably rely on one another in times of need, sometimes as care-seekers and sometimes as caregivers (Collins and Feeney, B., 2000).

Individual Differences in Adult Attachment Styles

Although the need for security is believed to be universal, adults differ systematically in their beliefs regarding attachment relationships and in the way they maintain and regulate feelings of security. Differences in *attachment style* are thought to be rooted in underlying differences in *internal working models* of self (as worthy or unworthy of love) and others (as responsive or unresponsive). Working models are thought to develop, at least in part, from interactions with important attachment figures and, once formed, are presumed to guide social interaction and emotion regulation in childhood and adulthood (Ainsworth et al. 1978; Bowlby 1973; Collins and Read 1994; Main, Kaplan, and Cassidy 1985).

Although the basic tenets of attachment theory argue for the existence of attachment bonds throughout the lifespan, the systematic investigation of attachment processes in adult couple relationships did not begin until Cindy Hazan and Philip Shaver (1987) identified styles of attachment in adulthood that parallel those observed among infants. Subsequent advances in the conceptualization and measurement of these styles have led adult attachment researchers to recognize four prototypic *attachment styles,* which are derived from two underlying dimensions. These dimensions are referred to as *anxiety* and *avoidance,* and they are most often assessed through self-report questionnaires (for reviews, see Brennan, Clark, and Shaver 1998; Crowell, Fraley and Shaver 1999). The anxiety dimension refers to the degree to which an individual is worried about being rejected or unloved; the avoidance dimension refers to the degree to which an individual avoids (versus approaches) intimacy and interdependence with others. The four attachment styles derived from these two dimensions are:

(1) *Secure* adults are low in both attachment-related anxiety and avoidance; they are comfortable with intimacy, willing to rely on others for support, and are confident that they are loved and valued by others.

(2) *Preoccupied* (anxious-ambivalent) adults are high in anxiety and low in avoidance; they have an exaggerated desire for closeness and dependence, coupled with a heightened concern about being rejected.

(3) *Dismissing avoidant* adults are low in attachment-related anxiety but high in avoidance; they view close relationships as relatively unimportant, and they value independence and self-reliance.

(4) Finally, *fearful avoidant* adults are high in both anxiety and avoidance; although they desire close relationships and the approval of others, they avoid intimacy because they fear being rejected.

Consistent with the major tenets of attachment theory, adult attachment researchers have argued that these different styles of attachment can be understood in terms of rules that guide individuals' responses to emotionally distressing situations (Fraley and Shaver 2000), which have evolved, at least in part, in the context of parental responsiveness to signals of distress (Kobak and Sceery 1988). For example, secure attachment is organized by rules that allow acknowledgment of distress and turning to others for support. In contrast, avoidant attachment is organized by rules that restrict acknowledgment of distress, as well as any attempts to seek comfort and support from others, whereas preoccupied attachment is organized by rules that direct attention toward distress and attachment figures in a hypervigilant manner that inhibits autonomy and self-confidence.

Although most of the empirical work on adult couple relationships (summarized below) utilizes self-report measures of adult attachment style, several interview measures have also been developed (Bartholomew and Horowitz 1991; Crowell and Owens 1996; George, Kaplan, and Main 1985) and are increasingly used to study adult intimate relationships (e.g., Cohn et al. 1992; Crowell et al., in press). However, these measures are not yet widely used in couples research, in part because they are time-consuming to administer and difficult to code (all require specialized training). Moreover, several studies have found relatively weak convergence between some self-report and interview measures of adult attachment (e.g., Shaver, Belsky, and Brennan 2000). The reasons for these modest effects are not well understood, and researchers continue to debate a variety of unresolved measurement and conceptual issues regarding the assessment of attachment adult style (see Crowell, Fraley, and Shaver 1999, for an overview).

Stability and Change in Adult Attachment Styles

Attachment theory argues that individual differences in attachment style will be relatively stable over time in part because working models tend to function automatically and unconsciously, and because they serve to direct attention, as well as organize and filter new information (Bowlby 1988; Bretherton 1985, 1987; Collins and Read 1994; Shaver, Collins, and Clark 1996). However, it cannot be assumed that the attachment styles observed in adulthood (between romantic partners) are identical to those formed in infancy (between children and parents). Longitudinal studies have obtained mixed results regarding the stability of attachment styles from infancy to early adulthood (for reviews, see Allen and Land 1999; Crowell, Fraley, and Shaver 1999). Although there is some evidence for the importance of family experiences in the development of adult attachment processes, there is little evidence of a simple or direct relationship between childhood attachment style and adult romantic attachment style.

Although there is little evidence of direct continuity from childhood to adulthood, there is evidence for stability across adulthood (see Feeney J., 1999 for a review). Studies of adult romantic attachment have shown moderate to high stability of attachment style over intervals ranging from one week to four years (e.g., Baldwin and Fehr 1995; Collins and Read 1990; Davila, Burge, and Hammen 1997; Fuller and Fincham 1995; Scharfe and Bartholomew 1994). Of course, some observed instability may reflect problems in measurement. Nonetheless, it is also the case that some instability reflects actual change in working models over time and appears to be shaped by changing interpersonal circumstances (e.g., Davila, Karney, and Bradbury 1999; Fuller and Fincham 1995). Attachment researchers are continuing to investigate the continuity and the lawful discontinuity of attachment patterns over time. Adult attachment style is best considered a relatively stable personal characteristic that is sensitive to current relationship experiences and open to change over time.

Studies of Adult Romantic Attachment

Since Hazan and Shaver's (1987) seminal study of adult romantic attachment, there has been a burgeoning of research on this topic within social, personality, and clinical psychology. Studies of adult romantic attachment have generally focused on the examination of attachment style differences in overall relationship quality and in specific relationship processes involving emotion, behavior, cognition, and psychophysiology. Although it is not possible to review all of these studies in this entry, some important findings to emerge from the adult romantic attachment literature are highlighted.

Relationship quality and stability. With regard to overall relationship quality, a large body of research indicates that secure adults develop relationships that are happier and better functioning than their insecure counterparts (e.g., Bartholomew and Horowitz, 1991; Collins and Read 1990; Feeney , J., and Noller, 1990; Hazan and Shaver 1987; Simpson 1990). Secure adults tend to be involved in relationships characterized by frequent positive emotion and high levels of interdependence, commitment, trust, and satisfaction. These individuals have high self-esteem, are generally positive and self-assured in their interactions with others, and report an absence of serious interpersonal problems. Anxious/preoccupied adults, on the other hand, tend to be involved in relationships characterized by jealousy, frequent negative affect, and low levels of trust and satisfaction. They report a strong desire for commitment in relationships and exhibit a controlling (over-dominating) interpersonal style. Avoidant adults tend to be involved in relationships characterized by low levels of interdependence, commitment, trust, and satisfaction. They also report low levels of distress following relationship breakup. Similar to anxious/preoccupied individuals, their relationships tend to involve more frequent negative emotions and less frequent positive emotions; however, the negative nature of their relationships stems from discomfort with intimacy rather than obsessive preoccupation with partners.

Although insecure adults tend to have less satisfying relationships, their relationships are not always less stable. For example, in a four-year prospective study, Lee Kirkpatrick and Cindy Hazan (1994) found that the relationships of anxious/ambivalent (preoccupied) respondents were quite stable over time despite their initial, negative ratings of relationship quality (see also Kirkpatrick and Davis 1994). Likewise, in a four-year prospective study of newlyweds, Joanne Davila and Thomas Bradbury (2001) found that insecure individuals were more likely to be involved in unhappy but stable marriages over time. These studies suggest that insecure adults may be more willing than secure adults to tolerate unhappy relationships, perhaps because they are less confident about their available alternatives.

Interpersonal behavior. In addition to studying attachment style differences in relationship quality, a growing body of research examines how secure and insecure adults differ in their interpersonal behavior in a variety of relationship contexts. Although some of this research relies on self-reported behavior, many studies utilize observational methods to examine behavior in laboratory and field settings. These studies have revealed that (a) secure individuals tend to be more effective support-providers and support-seekers than insecure adults (e.g. Carnelley, Pietromonaco, and Jaffe 1996; Collins and Feeney, B., 2000; Feeney, J., 1996; Feeney, B., and Collins, 2001; Kobak and Hazan 1991; Kunce and Shaver 1994; Simpson, Rholes, and Nelligan 1992); (b) secure adults tend to use more constructive strategies for dealing with conflict than insecure adults (e.g. Pistole 1989; Simpson, Rholes, and Phillips 1996); (c) secure adults exhibit more effective communication styles (Feeney, J., Noller, and Callan 1994) and more adaptive patterns of self-disclosure (Mikulincer and Nachshon 1991) than insecure adults; (d) secure individuals tend to respond more adaptively than insecure adults to separations from their partner (Cafferty et al. 1994; Feeney, J., 1998; Fraley and Shaver 1998); and (e) relative to secure and anxious/ambivalent individuals, avoidant individuals experience lower levels of intimacy, enjoyment, and positive emotion, and higher levels of negative emotion, in their daily interactions with others (Tidwell, Reis, and Shaver 1996).

Attachment style differences in adult sexual behaviors have also been documented. For example, avoidant individuals are more likely than secure individuals to engage in "one-night stands" (Brennan and Shaver 1995; Hazan, Zeifman, and Middleton, 1994 as cited in Feeney, J., 1999) and have more accepting attitudes toward casual sex (Feeney, J., Noller, and Patty 1993). Relative to secure and avoidant individuals, anxious/ambivalent individuals (especially women) tend to engage in intercourse at a younger age and to report a larger number of lifetime sexual partners (Bogaert and Sadava 2002); they are also more likely to experience unwanted pregnancy (Cooper, Shaver, and Collinsand 1998). Relative to their insecure counterparts, secure adults are less likely to have sex outside their primary relationship, more likely to be involved in mutually initiated sex, and more likely to enjoy physical contact that is both intimate and sexual (Hazan, Zeifman, and Middleton 1994, as cited in Feeney, J., 1999).

Cognition and perception. Research on interpersonal perception in couples indicates that secure and insecure adults differ in the way that they construe their relationship experiences (see Collins and Allard 2001 for a review). For example, secure adults are more likely than insecure adults to make benign (relationship-protective) attributions for their partners' transgressions (Collins 1996) and to change their perceptions of relationship partners after receiving information that disconfirmed their expectations (Mikulincer and Arad 1999). Attachment models also appear to shape memories of daily social interactions (Pietromonaco and Barrett 1997). Other research shows that avoidant adults tend to suppress their attachment systems by restricting the encoding and accessibility of attachment-related thoughts and memories (Fraley, Garner, and Shaver 2000; Fraley and Shaver 1997; Mikulincer and Orbach 1995). However, psychophysiological studies reveal that although avoidant individuals may report that relationships are unimportant to them, they exhibit elevated physiological responses when separated from their partner in stressful situations (Feeney, B., and Kirkpatrick 1996), and they are just as physiologically stressed as other individuals when they discuss losing their partners (Fraley and Shaver 1997).

Adult Attachment Processes Across Cultures

Research on adult attachment processes has been conducted all over the world and measures of adult attachment style have been translated into many different languages. Nevertheless, most of the empirical work reviewed above comes from industrialized countries, with predominantly Western cultures including Australia, Canada, Germany, Israel, Italy, Portugal, The Netherlands, the United Kingdom, and the United States. There is a growing interest in attachment processes in countries with predominantly Eastern cultures (including China, Japan, and Korea), but this early research has not yet been published in English language journals. In addition, to our knowledge, there is no published research on adult romantic attachment in nonindustrialized societies. Thus it is not possible in this entry to draw conclusions regarding similarities or differences in adult attachment processes between Western and non-Western cultures, or between industrialized and nonindustrialized societies. However, across a variety of Western, industrialized countries, there appears to be a great deal of convergence in normative attachment processes and in the consequences of secure and insecure attachment styles for relationship outcomes.

Conclusion

In conclusion, theoretical and empirical work in the study of attachment indicates that feelings of security are maintained and regulated, at least in part, through the development of intimate relationships with significant others who can serve as a reliable safe haven in times of need. Thus, understanding adult relationships requires an understanding of attachment dynamics, which have been shown to have important implications for personal health and well-being, as well as for relationship functioning.

Bibliography

Ainsworth, M.; Blehar, M.; Waters, E.; and Wall, S. (1978). *Patterns of Attachment.* Hillsdale, NJ: Erlbaum.

Allen, J. P., and Land, D. (1999). "Attachment in Adolescence." *Handbook of Attachment Theory and Research: Theory, Research, and Clinical Applications,* ed. J. Cassidy and P. Shaver. New York: Guilford Press.

Baldwin, M., W. and Fehr, B. (1995). "On the Instability of Attachment Style Ratings." *Personal Relationships* 2:247–261.

Bartholomew, K., and Horowitz, L. M. (1991). "Attachment Styles Among Young Adults: A Test of a Four-Category Model". *Journal of Personality and Social Psychology* 61:226–244.

Bogaert, A. F. and Sadava, S. (2002). "Adult attachment and sexual behavior." *Personal Relationships* 9:191–204.

Bowlby, J. (1969/1982). *Attachment and Loss,* Vol. 1: *Attachment.* New York: Basic Books.

Bowlby, J. (1973). *Attachment and Loss,* Vol. 2: *Separation.* New York: Basic Books.

Bowlby, J. (1979). *The Making and Breaking of Affectional Bonds.* London: Tavistock.

Bowlby, J. (1980). *Attachment and Loss,* Vol. 3. *Loss.* New York: Basic Books.

Bowlby, J. (1988). *A Secure Base.* New York: Basic Books.

Brennan, K. A.; Clark, C. L.; and Shaver, P. R. (1998). "Self-Report Measurement of Adult Attachment: An Integrative Overview." In *Attachment Theory and Close Relationships,* ed. J. A. Simpson and W. S. Rholes. New York: Guilford Press.

Brennan, K. A., and Shaver, P. R. (1995). "Dimensions of Adult Attachment, Affect Regulation, and Romantic Relationship Functioning." *Personality and Social Psychology Bulletin* 21:267–283.

Bretherton, I. (1985). "Attachment Theory: Retrospect and Prospect." In *Growing Points in Attachment Theory and Research, Monographs of the Society for Research in Child Development* 50(1–2, Serial No. 209):3–38.

Bretherton, I. (1987). "New Perspectives on Attachment Relations: Security, Communication, and Internal Working Models." In *Handbook of Infant Development,* 2nd edition, ed. J. Osofsky. New York: Wiley.

Cafferty, T. P.; Davis, K. E.; Medway, F. J.; O'Hearn, R. E.; and Chappell, K. D. (1994). "Reunion Dynamics among Couples Separated During Operation Desert Storm: An Attachment Theory Analysis." In *Advances in Personal Relationships, Vol 5: Attachment Processes in Adulthood,* ed. K. Bartholomew and D. Perlman. London: Jessica Kingsley.

Carnelley, K. B.; Pietromonaco, P. R.; and Jaffe, K. (1996). "Attachment, Caregiving, and Relationship Functioning in Couples: Effects of Self and Partner." *Personal Relationships* 3:257–278.

Cohn, D. A.; Silver, D. H.; Cowan, C. P.; Cowan, P. A.; and Pearson, J. (1992). "Working Models of Childhood Attachment and Couple Relationships." *Journal of Family Issues* 13:432–449.

Collins, N. L. (1996). "Working Models of Attachment: Implications for Explanation, Emotion, and Behavior." *Journal of Personality and Social Psychology* 71:810–832.

Collins, N. L., and Allard, L. M. (2001). "Cognitive Representations of Attachment: The Content and Function of Working Models." In *Blackwell Handbook of Social Psychology,* Vol. 2: *Interpersonal Processes,* ed. G. J. O. Fletcher and M. S. Clark. Oxford, UK: Blackwell Publishers.

Collins, N. L., and Feeney, B. C. (2000). "A Safe Haven: An Attachment Theory Perspective on Support Seeking and Caregiving in Intimate Relationships." *Journal of Personality and Social Psychology* 78:1053–1073.

Collins, N. L., and Read, S. J. (1990). "Adult Attachment, Working Models, and Relationship Quality in Dating Couples." *Journal of Personality and Social Psychology* 58:644–663.

Collins, N. L., and Read, S. J. (1994). "Cognitive Representations of Attachment: The Structure and Function of Working Models." In *Advances in Personal Relationships, Vol 5: Attachment Processes in Adulthood,* ed. K. Bartholomew and D. Perlman. London: Jessica Kingsley.

Cooper, M. L.; Shaver, P. R.; and Collins, N. L. (1998). "Attachment Styles, Emotion Regulation, and Adjustment in Adolescence." *Journal of Personality and Social Psychology* 74:1380–1397.

Crowell, J. A.; Fraley, R. C.; and Shaver, P. R. (1999). "Measurement of Individual Differences in Adolescent and Adult Attachment." In *Handbook of Attachment: Theory, Research, and Clinical Applications,* ed. J. Cassidy and P. R. Shaver. New York: Guilford Press.

Crowell, J. A., and Owens, G. (1996). *Current Relationships Interview and Scoring System.* Unpublished manuscript, State University of New York at Stony Brook.

Crowell, J. A.; Treboux, D.; Gao, Y.; Pan, H.; Fyffe, C.; and Waters, E. (in press). "Secure Base Behavior in Adulthood: Measurement, Links to Adult Attachment Representations, and Relations to Couples' Communication Skills and Self-Reports." *Developmental Psychology.*

Davila, J., and Bradbury, T. N. (2001). "Attachment Insecurity and the Distinction between Unhappy Spouses Who Do and Do Not Divorce." *Journal of Family Psychology* 15:371–393.

Davila, J.; Burge, D.; and Hammen, C. (1997). "What Does Attachment Style Change?" *Journal of Personality and Social Psychology* 73:826–838.

Davila, J.; Karney, B. R.; and Bradbury, T. N. (1999). "Attachment Change Processes in the Early Years of Marriage." *Journal of Personality and Social Psychology* 76:783–802.

Feeney, B. C., and Collins, N. L. (2001). "Predictors of Caregiving in Adult Intimate Relationships: An Attachment Theoretical Perspective." *Journal of Personality and Social Psychology* 80:972–994.

Feeney, B. C., and Kirkpatrick, L. A. (1996). "Effects of Adult Attachment and Presence of Romantic Partners on Physiological Responses to Stress." *Journal of Personality and Social Psychology* 70:255–270.

Feeney, J. A. (1996). "Attachment, Caregiving, and Marital Satisfaction." *Personal Relationships* 3:401–416.

Feeney, J. A. (1998). "Adult attachment and relationship-centered anxiety: Responses to physical and emotional distancing." In *Attachment Theory and Close Relationships,* ed. J. A. Simpson and W. S. Rholes. New York: Guilford Press.

Feeney, J. A. (1999). "Adult Romantic Attachment and Couple Relationships." In *Handbook of Attachment: Theory, Research, and Clinical Applications, ed.* J. Cassidy and P. R. Shaver. New York: Guilford Press.

Feeney, J. A., and Noller, P. (1990). "Attachment Style as a Predictor of Adult Romantic Relationships." *Journal of Personality and Social Psychology* 58:281–291.

Feeney, J. A., Noller, P., & Callan, V. J. (1994). "Attachment Style, Communication and Satisfaction in the Early Years of Marriage." In *Attachment processes in adulthood: Vol. 5. Advances in personal relationships,* ed. K. Bartholomew, and D. Perlman. London: Jessica Kingsley.

Feeney, J. A.; Noller, P.; and Patty, J. (1993). "Adolescents' Interactions with the Opposite Sex: Influence of Attachment Style and Gender." *Journal of Adolescence* 16:169–186.

Fraley, R. C.; Garner, J. P.; and Shaver, P. R. (2000). "Adult Attachment and the Defensive Regulation of Attention and Memory: Examining the Role of Preemptive and Postemptive Defensive Processes." *Journal of Personality and Social Psychology* 79:1–11.

Fraley, R. C., and Shaver, P. R. (1997). "Adult Attachment and the Suppression of Unwanted Thoughts." *Journal of Personality and Social Psychology* 73:1080–1091.

Fraley, R. C., and Shaver, P. R. (1998). "Airport Separations: A Naturalistic Study of Adult Attachment Dynamics in Separating Couples." *Journal of Personality and Social Psychology* 75:1198–1212.

Fraley, R. C., and Shaver, P. R. (2000). "Adult Romantic Attachment: Theoretical Developments, Emerging Controversies, and Unanswered Questions." *Review of General Psychology* 4:132–154.

Fuller, T. L., and Fincham, F. D. (1995). "Attachment Style in Married Couples: Relation to Current Martial Functioning, Stability Over Time, and Method of Assessment." *Personal Relationships* 2:17–34.

George, C.; Kaplan, N.; and Main, M. (1985). *Adult Attachment Interview,* 2nd edition. Unpublished manuscript, University of California at Berkley.George, C. and Solomon, J. (1999). "Attachment and Caregiving: The Caregiving Behavioral System." In *Handbook of Attachment: Theory, Research, and Clinical Applications,* ed. J. Cassidy and P. R. Shaver. New York: Guilford Press.

Hazan, C., and Shaver, P. R. (1987). "Romantic Love Conceptualized as an Attachment Process." *Journal of Personality and Social Psychology* 52:511–524.

Hazan, C., and Zeifman, D. (1999). "Pair Bonds as Attachment: Evaluating the Evidence." In *Handbook of Attachment: Theory, Research, and Clinical Applications,* ed. J. Cassidy and P. Shaver. New York: Guilford Press.

Kirkpatrick, L. A., and Davis, K. E. (1994). "Attachment Style, Gender, and Relationship Stability: A Longitudinal Analysis." *Journal of Personality and Social Psychology* 66:502–512.

Kirkpatrick, L. E., and Hazan, C. (1994). "Attachment Styles and Close Relationships: A Four–Year Prospective Study." *Personal Relationships* 1:123–142.

Kobak, R., and Hazan, C. (1991). "Attachment and marriage: Effects of security and accuracy of working models." *Journal of Personality and Social Psychology* 60:861–869.

Kobak, R. R., and Sceery, A. (1988). "Attachment in Late Adolescence: Working Models, Affect Regulation, and Representations of Self and Other." *Child Development* 59:135–146.

Kunce, L. J., and Shaver, P. R. (1994). "An Attachment-Theoretical Approach to Caregiving in Romantic Relationships." In *Advances in Personal Relationships,* Vol. 5, ed. K. Bartholomew and D. Perlman. London: Jessica Kingsley.

Main, M.; Kaplan, N.; and Cassidy, J. (1985). "Security in Infancy, Childhood, and Adulthood: A Move to the Level of Representation." In *Growing Points in Attachment Theory and Research, Monographs of the Society for Research in Child Development* 50:66–106.

Mikulincer, M., and Arad, D. (1999). "Attachment Working Models and Cognitive Openness in Close Relationships: A Test of Chronic and Temporary Accessibility Effects." *Journal of Personality and Social Psychology* 77:710–725.

Mikulincer, M., and Nachshon, O. (1991). "Attachment Styles and Patterns of Self-Disclosure." *Journal of Personality and Social Psychology* 61:321–331.

Orbach, I. (1995). Attachment styles and repressive defensiveness: The accessibility and architecture of affective memories. *Journal of Personality and Social Psychology,* 68:917–925.

Pietromonaco, P. R., and Barrett, L. (1997). "Working Models of Attachment and Daily Social Interactions." Journal of Personality and Social Psychology 73:1409–1423.

Pistole, M. C. (1989). "Attachment in Adult Romantic Relationships: Style of Conflict Resolution and Relationship Satisfaction." *Journal of Social and Personal Relationships* 6:505–510.

Scharfe, E., and Bartholomew, K. (1994). "Reliability and Stability of Adult Attachment Patterns." *Personal Relationships* 1:23–43.

Shaver, P. R.; Belsky, J.; and Brennan, K. A. (2000). "The Adult Attachment Interview and Self–Reports of Romantic Attachment: Association across Domains and Methods." *Personal Relationships* 7: 25–43.

Shaver, P. R.; Collins, N. L.; and Clark, C. L. (1996). "Attachment Styles and Internal Working Models of Self and Relationship Partners." In *Knowledge Structures in Close Relationships: A Social Psychological Approach,* ed. G. J. O. Fletcher and J. Fitness. Mahwah, NJ: Erlbaum.

Simpson, J. A. (1990). "Influence of Attachment Styles on Romantic Relationships." *Journal of Personality and Social Psychology* 59:971–980.

Simpson, J. A.; Rholes, W. S.; and Nelligan, J. S. (1992). "Support Seeking and Support Giving within Couples in an Anxiety-Provoking Situation: The Role of Attachment Styles." *Journal of Personality and Social Psychology* 62:434–446.

Simpson, J. A.; Rholes, W. S.; and Phillips, D. (1996). "Conflict in Close Relationships: An Attachment Perspective." *Journal of Personality and Social Psychology* 71:899–914.

Tidwell, M. O.; Reis, H. T.; and Shaver, P. R. (1996). "Attachment, Attractiveness, and Social Interaction: A Diary Study." *Journal of Personality and Social Psychology* 71:729–745.

Uchino, B. N.; Cacioppo, J. T.; and Kiecolt-Glaser, J. K. (1996). "The Relationship between Social Support and Physiological Processes: A Review with Emphasis on Underlying Mechanisms and Implications for Health." *Psychological Bulletin* 119: 488–531.

Weiss, R. S. (1982). "Attachment in Adult Life." In *The Place of Attachment in Human Behavior,* ed. C. M.

Parkes and J. Stevenson-Hinde. New York: Basic Books.

BROOKE C. FEENEY
NANCY L. COLLINS

PARENT-CHILD RELATIONSHIPS

During the first year of life, infants develop a deep emotional connection to those adults who are involved regularly in their care. *Attachment* is the term used to describe this special relationship between infants and their caregivers. The history of infants' interactions with their caregivers, and the infants' emerging affective and cognitive capacities, provides the context within which patterns of emotional and behavioral responses become organized and the attachment relationship develops. For most infants, their primary attachment is to their mother. But young infants also form attachments with their fathers and with other consistently available and responsive caregivers.

Attachment theorists believe that infants are biologically predisposed to develop attachments. Infants rely on the attachment figure as a protector in the face of danger and as a secure base for exploration. Except in extreme cases where no stable interactive person is present (e.g., institutional care), all infants, even those who are diagnosed with developmental disorders or who have a history of abuse or neglect, will form an attachment relationship with their primary caregivers. How attachment relationships unfold, what factors influence qualitative differences in the patterning of these relationships, and how early attachments influence children's evolving sense of self, as well as their functioning in school, with peers and partners, and as parents, are questions that attachment researchers have been exploring for decades. More recently, contextual factors influencing attachment, such as the cultural context of caregiving, have been explored. Considered together, what has emerged is a rich and complex portrait of the infant's early attachment experiences, of the developmental significance of attachments, and of the continuities and discontinuities of attachments across time and relational contexts.

Attachment Theory

John Bowlby was a psychoanalytically trained clinician who integrated several theoretical perspectives, including ethology (Lorenz 1935; Tinbergen 1951), psychoanalysis (especially object relations theory [Fairbairn 1952; Klein 1932; Winnicott 1958]), general systems theory (Bertalanfly 1968), and cognitive psychology (Erdelyi 1985), into his theory of attachment (Bowlby 1969). Bowlby originally described attachment as a dynamic behavioral system and delineated the set goals and functions of the system within a context of natural selection and survival. He highlighted the ways in which the attachment system is related to the exploratory, fear, and affiliative behavioral systems. Because these systems are organized and in balance, the activation of one is related to activation of the others (Bowlby 1969).

Bowlby delineated several stages in the development of attachment to the mother. During the stage of *indiscriminate sociability* (birth to six weeks), infants respond to a variety of social and nonsocial cues without showing a preference for a particular person. During the phase of *discriminating sociability* (six weeks to six or seven months), infants begin to show a preference for the mother, smiling and vocalizing more readily in her company. They learn the contingencies of this relationship, developing expectations about the mothers' response to particular signals and cues. During the stage of *attachment* (seven months to two years), infants are able to use the mother as a secure base for exploration and to return to her for comfort when distressed. Infants prefer to be in the company of their mother and seek proximity to her, but are able to venture away to explore their environment. Once an attachment has developed, infants are more likely to protest when with an unfamiliar person (*stranger anxiety*) or when separated from the mother (*separation anxiety*). Finally, after two years of age, children move into the stage of *goal-corrected partnership*. At this point, children are able to recognize that the mother may have needs or goals that are different from their own. The developing capacity for tolerating frustration while delaying the gratification of needs marks this shift in the attachment relationship. There is a new understanding of reciprocity and turn-taking, thereby allowing each partner to modify his or her goals in the service of strengthening the attachment relationship.

Though Bowlby described the goal-corrected partnership as the last phase in the development of attachments, he also acknowledged that attachments remain important throughout the life span and continue to undergo profound changes. Significant organizational shifts may occur within the attachment system, and between the attachment, exploratory, fear, and affiliative systems, and new individuals (in addition to the mother) may serve as attachment figures. As attachments become more abstract and sophisticated, and less dependent on behavioral indices of contact maintenance and proximity seeking, they are also more difficult to measure (Bowlby 1969). Still, attachment behaviors will be evident even during childhood and adolescence, particularly when individuals are afraid, sick, distressed, or reunited with an attachment figure following a long absence (Ainsworth 1990).

Other theorists built on Bowlby's writings in important ways. Mary Ainsworth, a developmental psychologist, identified individual differences in patterns of attachment and studied maternal caregiving behaviors during the first year that contribute to these different attachment patterns at one year of age. Ainsworth's contributions to the development of attachment theory are so significant that the theory is often referred to as the Bowlby-Ainsworth theory of attachment (see, for example, Vaughn and Bost 1999). L. Alan Sroufe and Everett Waters (1977) incorporated motivational and affective components into attachment theory, describing attachment within an organizational perspective. Still others expanded Bowlby's description of multiple attachments (Cassidy 1999) and of developmental changes in attachments beyond the infancy period (Greenberg, Cicchetti, and Cummings 1990).

The Assessment of Attachment in Infancy, Childhood, Adolescence, and Adulthood

When the construct of attachment was originally introduced, attachment relationships were conceptualized as being critical throughout the life span (Bowlby 1969). However, the research that followed Bowlby's original ideas focused initially on the infancy period. This was because of the theoretical framework out of which attachment theory emerged, the developmental perspective within which attachment research evolved, and the underlying assumptions made regarding the situations that activate attachment behaviors and enable the classification of attachment patterns (see Schneider-Rosen 1990 for an elaboration of these ideas). Since 1980, conceptual models and new methodologies have been introduced that have expanded the field of attachment (Bretherton 1985; Cassidy and Shaver 1999; Greenberg, Cicchetti, and Cummings 1990). The result of these efforts is that there are now several classification schemes available to assess individual differences in attachment relationships in infancy, childhood, adolescence, and adulthood.

The most popular and commonly used measure to assess patterns of attachment is Mary Ainsworth and Barbara Wittig's *Strange Situation* (1969). Indeed, it was the introduction of this standardized procedure that led to the explosion of research on individual differences in attachment patterns and enabled questions regarding the precursors to, and consequences of, these different patterns to be explored. The *Strange Situation* relies on the use of a series of increasingly stressful situations during which infant behaviors towards the caregiver are observed and coded. Infant-caregiver dyads are then assigned into one of three attachment patterns (Ainsworth et al. 1978) based on the organization of specific infant behaviors throughout the Strange Situation.

Securely attached infants (representing approximately 65% of those classified by the Strange Situation) seek interaction with their caregiver, although not always in close proximity. If they are upset by their caregiver's departure, they are easily calmed and well able to return to exploration upon their caregiver's return to the playroom. *Anxious-avoidant* infants (20% of those classified) show little or no tendency to interact with or maintain contact to their caregiver in the Strange Situation. They show little or no distress upon separation, avoid the caregiver upon reunion by ignoring, looking away, or moving past the caregiver rather than approaching, and are more inclined to interact with the stranger. *Anxious-resistant* infants (10% of those classified) show little exploratory behavior and are wary of the stranger. They demonstrate a strong desire to maintain proximity to the caregiver following separation combined with an angry resistance to the caregiver upon reunion. They are unable to be comforted or calmed by their caregiver. Their ambivalence toward the caregiver is reflected in both seeking contact and then angrily resisting it once it is achieved. The percentages of infants classified in each of the attachment categories vary across groups and (in particular) cultures.

A couple cuddles with their infant son. Infants as young as six weeks old show attachment to their caregivers and develop expectations about their caregivers' response and affection. ARIEL SKELLEY/CORBIS

Many researchers found that there were some infants who did not fit into any of these three attachment categories. The introduction of the *disorganized/disoriented* (Main and Solomon 1990) category (5% of those classified) was based on the observation of contradictory, misdirected, stereotypical, frozen, dazed, or rapidly changing affective behavior in the Strange Situation (Lyons-Ruth and Jacobvitz 1999). Infants classified as disorganized/disoriented show a combination of both avoidant and resistant behaviors, reflecting an apparent confusion about whether to avoid or approach the caregiver. They fail to exhibit a clear or consistent strategy for coping with separation. These infants appear to be most stressed by the Strange Situation and may be the most insecure (Hertsgaard et al. 1995).

Although the Strange Situation has been used extensively in attachment research and a clear majority of infants can be classified into one of the four attachment categories, there are some who remain critical of this laboratory-based procedure. Michael Lamb and Alison Nash (1989) argue that the Strange Situation lacks ecological validity; in other words, it does not occur in natural surroundings. Ross Thompson (1988) claims that independent behavior in the Strange Situation is often mistakenly interpreted as reflective of the insecure/avoidant attachment pattern. And temperament researchers (e.g., Kagan 1995) challenge the use of the Strange Situation by arguing that individual differences in behavioral inhibition can explain the behaviors characteristic of children assigned to the attachment categories.

A second widely used measure is the *Attachment Q-set* (Waters and Deane 1985), which is appropriate for use with one- to five-year-olds. The Q-set involves either a parent or a trained rater observing the child-caregiver dyad in and around the home and sorting ninety-one cards containing attachment-related statements into nine piles ranging from most to least descriptive of the child. The score derived from the Q-set reflects the degree to which the attachment relationship is secure. The Q-set measure was designed as an ecologically valid alternative to the Strange Situation in that the behaviors that are rated are those that occur in more natural settings. However, critics of the Q-set methodology argue that the instrument may not be measuring attachment behaviors (those that are elicited in response to stressful circumstances) but rather correlates of those behaviors. Moreover, attachment theory pertains to the quality of attachment, whereas the Q-set method provides a quantitative, continuous measurement of attachment security (Schneider, Atkinson, and Tardif 2001). Only modest convergence has been found in a recent meta-analysis between the Strange Situation and the Attachment Q-set ($r = 0.26$; IJzendoorn, Vereijken, and Ridsen-Walraven in press).

There are several other techniques that have been developed to assess attachment security for preschoolers, children, adolescents, and adults (see Solomon and George 1999). The proliferation of new instruments suggests the many directions in which attachment theory has been applied, as well as the need for integrative approaches to assessment in the future.

Parental Caregiving, Infant Temperament, and the Development of Attachment Relationships

One of the assumptions pervading attachment theory and research is that variations in maternal responsiveness to the child's needs lead to individual differences in attachment security (Ainsworth et al. 1978). Early work, which obtained the strongest associations between maternal responsiveness and child security, focused on maternal sensitivity, availability, acceptance, and cooperation (Ainsworth et al. 1978). Since then, research on the association between maternal responsiveness and

quality of attachment has yielded mixed results (see Rosen and Rothbaum 1993 for a review). Although many studies have found higher quality caregiving in dyads that are classified as secure, the magnitude of the effects in most of these studies is small (DeWolff and IJzendoorn 1997; Rosen and Rothbaum 1993). The failure to account for a larger portion of the variance in attachment security has led some to conclude that a move to the contextual level is essential in future studies of the caregiving antecedents of attachment security (IJzendoorn and De Wolff 1997). Researchers could consider, for example, the conditions under which caregiving influences attachment (Belsky 1997) or a more complex family systems analysis of the dynamics involved in attachment patterns (Cowan 1997).

The modest associations between caregiving and attachment security have led investigators to look beyond caregivers' influence on attachment patterns (Sroufe 1985). Many researchers have studied temperamental characteristics as potential determinants of individual differences in attachment. Complex and interesting associations have been found for certain temperamental qualities, for specific age groups, and for particular high-risk populations (Vaughn and Bost 1999). The link between temperament and attachment security may not be direct (Belsky and Rovine 1987; Seifer et al. 1996). Rather, although some of the behaviors seen in the Strange Situation may be related to temperament, the preponderance of evidence indicates that the attachment relationship and the confidence of the infant in the caregiver's responsiveness are not determined by temperament alone but by a complex interactional history (Vaughn and Bost 1999). It is most likely that a secure attachment will evolve in relationships where there is a "good fit" between the infants' temperament and the caregiving they are provided, whereas insecure attachments are more likely to develop when highly stressed or insensitive caregivers fail to accommodate to their infants' particular temperamental qualities (Boom 1994).

Consequences of Attachment for Children's Emotional Development and Social Relationships beyond the Family

John Bowlby (1973) and Mary Ainsworth and her colleagues (1978) maintained that the assessment of individual differences in infant-caregiver attachment would be critical not only to better understand the antecedents of attachment relationships but also to identify the consequences of variations in attachment security for the child's later development. To date, there are dozens of studies that have explored the longitudinal associations between early mother-child attachment and later functioning. For example, securely attached infants are more curious and persistent in toddlerhood, more empathic with peers, and show higher levels of self-esteem than children with insecure attachments. Securely attached infants are also more likely to be curious, self-directed, sensitive to others, and eager to learn in preschool at three-and-a-half years. Significant associations have been found between attachment security and children's interactions with unfamiliar age-mates and adults (see reviews by Thompson 1998, 1999; Weinfield et al. 1999).

At six years of age, securely attached infants engage in more positive interactions with peers in school. In middle childhood and adolescence, children with a history of secure attachment have been found to be more ego resilient and socially competent and to display better cognitive functioning. A follow-up in a camp setting at eleven and twelve years found that those who were securely attached as infants displayed better social skills and had closer friends than their age-matched peers who were insecurely attached as infants (reviewed in Thompson 1999). Children with insecure attachments during infancy are more likely than those with secure attachments to have poor peer relations (see Schneider, Atkinson, and Tardif 2001 for a meta-analysis) and to display deviant behavior in adolescence (Allen et al. 1998; Carlson 1998). Moreover, infant attachment classifications predict later adult attachment categories on the *Adult Attachment Interview* (Hesse 1999).

There has been considerable controversy as to what factors contribute to the predictive power of attachments. Some theorists believe that children develop internal working models of their early relationships and that these models mediate between early attachment experiences and later social competence. Based on the early relationship with their attachment figures, infants begin to develop expectations for their caregivers' behavior in response to their signals and cues. Infants create representations or models of what to expect from their world and of how they can expect to be treated by

others. If infants are treated in a responsive and consistently sensitive manner, then they develop models of the world as good and of the self as deserving and valued. If, on the other hand, infants are responded to inconsistently or in a rejecting manner, or if infants are ignored, the world is seen as insensitive and unpredictable and the self is viewed as unworthy. These "internal working models" (Bowlby 1969, 1973) of self and relationships are carried forward into new experiences with new interactional partners, influencing children's subsequent behavior and their expectations regarding the sensitivity and contingent responsiveness of others (Waters et al. 1995).

Internal models become more sophisticated and stable with age (Bowlby 1969; DeWolff and IJzendoorn 1997). They are amenable to change (with consistent or life altering changes in the environment) but cannot be modified easily. The developmental processes involved in the elaboration and consolidation of working models are far from understood (Thompson 1999). Understanding these processes is important for comprehending the role of internal models in the continuity between early attachment and later functioning.

Not all theorists agree that internal working models are adequate for explaining the link between early attachment security and subsequent child adjustment. Several other mechanisms have been implicated, such as emotional security, the continuity of caregiving experiences, and the mediating effect of basic features of the child's affective functioning (Kochanska 2001). Jerome Kagan (1995) suggests that other nonattachment constructs such as temperament might account for this association. Michael Lewis and Candice Feiring (1989) maintain that there are many important socialization agents (other than parents) that influence children's social relationships and may account for the associations between attachment and later social functioning.

Attachment and Culture

Attachment theory is often assumed to have universal applicability. To test the universality of four critical hypotheses of the theory, Marinus van IJzendoorn and Abraham Sagi (1999) reviewed studies from a variety of non-Western cultures—including Africa, China, Israel, and Japan. Given the diversity of cultures and the complexity of the attachment behaviors examined, there was impressive support for the universality of the first hypothesis examined. Specifically, there are similar patterns of *proximity seeking, proximity maintaining,* and *separation protest* by infants in relation to their primary caregivers in stressful situations. The second hypothesis, that most children are securely attached, received "rather strong" support as well. In the eleven non-Western cultures (the African societies of Dogon, Efe, Ganda, Gusil, Hausa, and !Kung San; China; Israel [Kibbutz and city]; and Japan [Tokyo and Sappora]) for which data are available, between 56 percent and 80 percent of children are securely attached. Although there were fewer direct tests of the third hypothesis (i.e., the *sensitivity hypothesis*: that security is fostered by sensitive responsiveness to infants' signals) and the fourth hypothesis (i.e., the *competence hypothesis*: that security in infancy is associated with later social competence), IJzendoorn and Sagi (1999) conclude that "the universal validity of attachment theory appears to be confirmed in the cross-cultural research" (p. 730).

A somewhat different portrait of cultural differences is provided by Robin Harwood and her colleagues (Harwood, Miller, and Irizarry 1995). These authors suggest that Euro-American, as compared to Puerto Rican, mothers were more likely to evaluate toddler behavior in terms of the development of independence and self-confidence, whereas the Puerto Rican mothers placed more emphasis on the development of respectfulness. These findings highlight the existence of cultural variation in the meaning of social competence, as well as in the meaning of behaviors characterized as secure (at least in the eyes of their caregivers). In a recent study, Vivian Carlson and Robin Harwood (in press) found differences between Puerto Rican and Euro-American mothers that "call into question a single universal definition of maternal sensitivity, instead providing evidence that sensitive caregiving behaviors may be culturally constructed . . ." (p. 17).

Fred Rothbaum and his colleagues (Rothbaum et al. in press; Rothbaum et al. 2000; Rothbaum et al. 2001) maintain that extant notions of attachment are infused with Western ideals and preconceptions because attachment theory has been championed by Western thinkers and the studies have overwhelmingly involved Western samples.

Although most attachment theorists acknowledge that culture influences specific attachment behaviors, they tend to view culture as an overlay on biologically determined human behavior. By contrast, Jerome Bruner (1990) views culture and biology as inseparable aspects of the attachment system. Rothbaum and his colleagues (2000, 2001) call into question the universality of the sensitivity and competence hypotheses for the same reasons as Harwood—what constitutes sensitive caregiving and social competence are culturally constructed. Because Rothbaum and his colleagues focus on findings from Japan rather than Puerto Rico, their concerns add to those raised by Harwood. The evidence from Japan indicates that behavior that is highly valued in the United States, such as autonomy and self-assertion, is seen as immature in Japan.

Beneath the debate over the universality of attachment lie important points of agreement. First, all of the investigators would agree that: (a) there are propensities for attachment behaviors by caregivers and children that are common to all humans; (b) there are important cultural differences in how these propensities are manifested; (c) the final verdict has not yet been reached as to whether there are fundamental cultural differences in attachment because much more cross-cultural evidence is needed. The disagreement revolves around what constitutes a "fundamental" difference in attachment. We should probably avoid such debatable labels and focus instead on the ways in which key attachment constructs are conceptualized and manifested in different cultures. This would lead to research that does not simply rely on Western based measures of attachment (as did most of the studies reviewed by IJzendoorn and Sagi 1999) but focuses as well on widely accepted concepts and beliefs from the cultures being examined and devises measures to explore them. This process would lead to a much more inclusive theory of attachment that embraces cultural differences.

Conclusion

The research generated by attachment theory has yielded an impressive array of studies providing considerable support for many of the theory's underlying premises. It is clear that early attachments have a profound impact on young children's developmental trajectories and on the intergenerational transmission of attachment patterns. Researchers have increasingly highlighted assumptions and biases of attachment theory that pose difficulties when applying the theory to non-Western cultures. The recent focus on context (including, for example, inter- and intracultural differences) and the study of multiple attachments across the life span reflect new directions that are important for the theory's development.

It is undeniable that attachment theory has had a profound impact on the field of developmental psychology. Its continued growth speaks, in part, to the intellectual breadth of its founders (John Bowlby and Mary Ainsworth), to the talented group of investigators who have continued in their tradition, to the enormous wealth of data generated by questions evolving from attachment theory, and to the theory's flexibility in accommodating new and unanticipated research findings while remaining clear about, and committed to, the central tenets of the theory.

See also: ATTACHMENT: COUPLE RELATIONSHIPS; ANXIETY DISORDERS; BOUNDARY DISSOLUTION; CHILDCARE; CHILDHOOD, STAGES OF: INFANCY; CHILDHOOD, STAGES OF: TODDLERHOOD; DEPRESSION: CHILDREN AND ADOLESCENTS; DEVELOPMENT: EMOTIONAL; DEVELOPMENT: SELF; DEVELOPMENTAL PSYCHOPATHOLOGY; DISCIPLINE; FATHERHOOD; INTERPARENTAL CONFLICT: EFFECTS ON CHILDREN; MOTHERHOOD; PARENTING EDUCATION; PARENTING STYLES; POSTPARTUM DEPRESSION; POSTTRAUMATIC STRESS DISORDER (PTSD); SEPARATION ANXIETY; SEPARATION-INDIVIDUATION; SUBSTITUTE CAREGIVERS; THERAPY: PARENT-CHILD RELATIONSHIPS; TRUST

Bibliography

Ainsworth, M. D. S. (1990). Epilogue to "Some Considerations Regarding Theory and Assessment Relevant to Attachments Beyond Infancy." In *Attachment in the Preschool Years,* ed. M. T. Greenberg, D. Cicchetti, and E. M. Cummings. Chicago: University of Chicago Press.

Ainsworth, M. D. S.; Blehar, M.; Waters, E.; and Wall, S. (1978). *Patterns of Attachment: A Psychosocial Study of the Strange Situation.* Hillsdale, NJ: Lawrence Erlbaum Associates.

Ainsworth, M. D. S., and Wittig, B. A. (1969). "Attachment and Exploratory Behavior of One-Year-Olds in a Strange Situation." In *Determinants of Infant Behavior IV,* ed. B. M. Foss. London: Methuen.

Allen, J. P.; Moore, C.; Kuperminc, G.; and Bell, K. (1998). "Attachment and Adolescent Psychosocial Functioning." *Child Development* 69:1406–1419.

Belsky, J. (1997). "Theory Testing, Effect-Size Evaluation, and Differential Susceptibility to Rearing Influence: The Case of Mothering and Attachment." *Child Development* 64:598–600.

Belsky, J., and Rovine, M. (1987). "Temperament and Attachment Security in the Strange Situation: An Empirical Rapprochement." *Child Development* 58:787–795.

Bertalanffy, L. von. (1968). *General Systems Theory: Foundations, Development, Applications.* New York: George Braziller.

Boom, D. van den. (1994). "The Influence of Temperament and Mothering on Attachment and Exploration: An Experimental Manipulation of Sensitive Responsiveness among Lower-Class Mothers with Irritable Infants." *Child Development* 65:1457–1477.

Bowlby, J. (1969). *Attachment and Loss,* Vol. 1: *Attachment.* New York: Basic Books.

Bowlby, J. (1973). *Attachment and Loss,* Vol. 2: *Separation.* New York: Basic Books.

Bretherton, I. (1985). "Attachment Theory: Retrospect and Prospect." In *Growing Points of Attachment Theory and Research,* ed. I. Bretherton and E. Waters. Chicago: University of Chicago Press for the Society for Research in Child Development. 50 (1–2, Serial No. 209).

Bruner, J. (1990). *Acts of Meaning.* Cambridge, MA: Harvard University Press.

Carlson, E. A. (1998). "A Prospective Longitudinal Study of Attachment Disorganization/Disorientation." *Child Development* 69:1107–1128.

Carlson, V., and Harwood, R. (in press). "Attachment, Culture, and the Caregiving System: The Cultural Patterning of Everyday Experiences among Anglo and Puerto Rican Mother-Infant Pairs." *Infant Mental Health Journal.*

Cassidy, J. (1999). "The Nature of the Child's Ties." In *Handbook of Attachment: Theory, Research, and Clinical Applications,* ed. J. Cassidy and P. Shaver. New York: Guilford Press.

Cassidy, J., and Shaver, P. R. (1999). *Handbook of Attachment: Theory, Research, and Clinical Applications.* New York: Guilford Press.

Cowan, P. (1997). "Beyond Meta-Analysis: A Plea for a Family Systems View of Attachment." *Child Development* 68:601–603.

DeWolff, M. S., and IJzendoorn, M. H. van. (1997). "Sensitivity and Attachment: A Meta-Analysis on Parental Antecedents of Infant Attachment." *Child Development* 68:571–591.

Erdelyi, H. M. (1985). *Psychoanalysis: Freud's Cognitive Psychology.* San Francisco: W. H. Freeman.

Fairbairn, W. R. D. (1952). *An Object-Relations Theory of the Personality.* New York: Basic Books.

Greenberg, M. T.; Cicchetti, D.; and Cummings, E. M. (1990). *Attachment in the Preschool Years: Theory, Research, and Intervention.* Chicago: University of Chicago Press.

Harwood, R. L.; Miller, J. G.; and Irizarry, N. L. (1995). *Culture and Attachment: Perceptions of the Child in Context.* New York: Guilford Press.

Hertsgaard, L.; Gunnar, M.; Erickson, M. F.; and Nachmias, M. (1995). "Adrenocortical Responses to the Strange Situation in Infants with Disorganized/Disoriented Attachment Relationships." *Child Development* 66:1100–1106.

Hesse, E. (1999). "The Adult Attachment Interview: Historical and Current Perspectives." In *Handbook of Attachment: Theory, Research, and Clinical Applications,* ed. J. Cassidy and P. Shaver. New York: Guilford Press.

IJzendoorn, M. H. van, and DeWolff, M. S. (1997). "In Search of the Absent Father–Meta-Analysis of Infant-Father Attachment: A Rejoinder to Our Discussion." *Child Development* 68:604–609.

IJzendoorn, M. H. van, and Sagi, A. (1999). "Cross-Cultural Patterns of Attachment: Universal and Contextual Dimensions." In *Handbook of Attachment: Theory, Research, and Clinical Applications,* ed. J. Cassidy and P. Shaver. New York: Guilford Press.

IJzendoorn, M. H. van; Vereijken, C. M. J. L.; and Ridsen-Walraven, J. M. A. (in press). "Is the Attachment Q-sort a Valid Measure of Attachment Security in Young Children?" In *Patterns of Secure Base Behavior: Q-sort Perspectives on Attachment and Caregiving,* ed. B. E. Vaughn and E. Waters. Mahwah, NJ: Lawrence Erlbaum Associates.

Kagan, J. (1995). "On Attachment." *Harvard Review of Psychiatry* 3:104–106.

Klein, M. (1932). "The Psychoanalysis of Children." In *The Writings of Melanie Klein.* London: Hogarth Press.

Kochanska, G. (2001). "Emotional Development in Children with Different Attachment Histories: The First Three Years." *Child Development* 72:474–490.

Lamb, M. E., and Nash, A. (1989). "Infant-Mother Attachment, Sociability, and Peer Competence." In *Peer Relationships in Child Development,* ed. T. J. Berndt and G. W. Ladd. New York: Wiley.

Lewis, M., and Feiring, C. (1989). "Infant, Mother, and Infant-Mother Interaction Behavior and Subsequent Attachment." *Child Development* 60:831–837.

Lorenz, K. E. (1935). "Der Kumpan in der Umvelt des Vogels." In *Instinctive Behavior,* ed. C. H. Schiller. New York: International Universities Press.

Lyons-Ruth, K., and Jacobvitz, D. (1999). "Attachment Disorganization: Unresolved Loss, Relational Violence, and Lapses in Behavioral and Attentional Strategies." In *Handbook of Attachment: Theory, Research, and Clinical Applications,* ed. J. Cassidy and P. Shaver. New York: Guilford Press.

Main, M., and Solomon, J. (1990). "Procedures for Identifying Infants as Disorganized/Disoriented during the Ainsworth Strange Situation." In *Attachment in the Preschool Years,* ed. M. T. Greenberg, D. Cicchetti, and E. M. Cummings. Chicago: University of Chicago Press.

Rosen, K. S., and Rothbaum, F. (1993). "Quality of Parental Caregiving and Security of Attachment." *Developmental Psychology* 29:358–367.

Rothbaum, F.; Rosen, K. S.; Ujiie, T.; and Uchida, N. (in press). "Family Systems Theory, Attachment Theory, and Culture." *Family Process.*

Rothbaum, F.; Weisz, J.; Pott, M.; and Miyake, K. (2000). "Attachment and Culture: Security in the United States and Japan." *American Psychologist* 55:1093–1104.

Rothbaum, F.; Weisz, J.; Pott, M.; Miyake, K.; and Morelli, G. (2001)."Deeper into Attachment and Culture." *American Psychologist* 56(10):827–829.

Schneider, B. H.; Atkinson, L.; and Tardif, C. (2001). "Child-Parent Attachment and Children's Peer Relations: A Quantitative Review." *Developmental Psychology* 37:86–100.

Schneider-Rosen, K. (1990). "The Developmental Reorganization of Attachment Relationships: Guidelines for Classification beyond Infancy." In *Attachment in the Preschool Years,* ed. M. T. Greenberg, D. Cicchetti, and E. M. Cummings. Chicago: University of Chicago Press.

Seifer, R.; Schiller, M.; Sameroff, A.; Resnick, S.; and Riordan, K. (1996). "Attachment, Maternal Sensitivity, and Infant Temperament during the First Year of Life." *Developmental Psychology* 32:12–25.

Solomon, J., and George, C. (1999). "The Measurement of Attachment Security in Infancy and Childhood." In *Handbook of Attachment: Theory, Research, and*

Clinical Applications, ed. J. Cassidy and P. Shaver. New York: Guilford Press.

Sroufe, L. A. (1985). "Attachment Classification from the Perspective of Infant-Caregiver Relationships and Infant Temperament." *Child Development* 56:1–14.

Sroufe, L. A., and Waters, E. (1977). "Attachment as an Organizational Construct." *Child Development* 48:1184–1199.

Thompson, R. A. (1988). "The Effects of Infant Day Care through the Prism of Attachment Theory: A Critical Appraisal." *Early Childhood Research Quarterly* 3:273–282.

Thompson, R. A. (1998). "Early Sociopersonality Development." In *Social, Emotional, and Personality Development,* Vol. 3 of *Handbook of Child Psychology,* 5th edition, ed. N. Eisenberg and W. Damon. New York: Wiley.

Thompson, R. A. (1999). "Early Attachment and Later Development." In *Handbook of Attachment: Theory, Research, and Clinical Applications,* ed. J. Cassidy and P. Shaver. New York: Guilford Press.

Tinbergen, N. (1951). *The Study of Instinct.* London: Oxford University Press.

Vaughn, B. E., and Bost, K. K. (1999). "Attachment and Temperament: Redundant, Independent, and Interacting Influences on Interpersonal Adaptation and Personality Development?" In *Handbook of Attachment: Theory, Research, and Clinical Applications,* ed. J. Cassidy and P. Shaver. New York: Guilford Press.

Waters, E., and Deane, K. E. (1985). "Defining and Assessing Individual Differences in Attachment Relationships: Q-Methodology and the Organization of Behavior in Infancy and Early Childhood." *Monographs of the Society for Research in Child Development* 50 (1–2, Serial No. 209).

Waters, E.; Vaughn, B. E.; Posada, G.; and Kondo-Ikemura, K., eds. (1995). "Caregiving, Cultural, and Cognitive Perspectives on Secure-Base Behavior and Working Models: New Growing Points of Attachment Theory and Research." *Monographs of the Society for Research in Child Development* 60 (2–3, Serial No. 244).

Weinfield, N. S.; Sroufe, L. A.; Egeland, B.; and Carlson, E. (1999). "The Nature of Individual Differences in Infant-Caregiver Attachment." In *Handbook of Attachment: Theory, Research, and Clinical Applications,* ed. J. Cassidy and P. Shaver. New York: Guilford Press.

Winnicott, D. W. (1958). *Collected Papers: Through Paediatrics to Psycho-Analysis.* London: HarperCollins.

KAREN S. ROSEN
FRED ROTHBAUM

ATTENTION DEFICIT/ HYPERACTIVITY DISORDER (ADHD)

Attention Deficit/Hyperactivity Disorder (ADHD) is the diagnostic term used to describe patterns of behavior, beginning in childhood, related to deficient self-regulation. In the course of the twentieth century, ADHD has been called *minimal brain dysfunction, hyperkinesis,* or *attention deficit disorder.* The core symptoms include (a) difficulties in paying *attention,* particularly in situations that demand concentration, like school classes and homework sessions; (b) *impulsivity* or *poor impulse control—* in other words, "acting before thinking"—and behavior that ranges from the annoying to the physically dangerous; and (c) *hyperactivity,* including fidgetiness, motor restlessness, and actions such as running through a classroom. Given that close attention is demanded from students, ADHD became an important issue with the advent of compulsory education. Considerable notoriety currently surrounds ADHD; there is an ongoing debate over its status as a legitimate diagnosis as opposed to an excuse for the overzealous use of pharmacological treatments or a "medicalized" label for problems that actually result from discordant family interactions, poor schooling, or increasing societal demands for educational attainment (DeGrandpre and Hinshaw 2000).

Part of the reason for the intensity of this debate is that the constituent behaviors are part of normal development. Indeed, inattention, impulsivity, and overactivity are ubiquitous in children—particularly boys—during the preschool or early elementary years, when the frontal lobes of the brain have not fully matured yet demands for compliance and socialization increase markedly. To make an accurate diagnosis, clinicians must document that the behavior patterns are (a) developmentally extreme (i.e., statistically rare for children of the same age); (b) of early onset (aged 6 years or younger); (c) present in both home and school situations (or, for adults, in home and work settings); and (d) impairing with respect to family interactions, educational achievement, friendships, and the attainment of independence (American Psychiatric Association 1994).

In fact, despite the contention that ADHD is a mythical condition, children who meet stringent diagnostic criteria are often severely impaired. School failure is common, despite average or above-average intelligence; discordant parent-child relationships are commonplace; rejection from the peer group is common, as youth with ADHD are almost universally disliked by their peers; self-concept and self-esteem suffer, particularly as development progresses; and the risk of serious accidental injury—ranging from burns and falls in childhood to serious automobile accidents in adolescence and adulthood—is striking (Hinshaw 1999). Thus, despite allegations that ADHD is a convenient diagnostic term for children who are simply exuberant or bothersome to adults, careful assessment can warn of significant developmental failures and impairments.

A brief office visit is insufficient for a proper diagnostic work-up. A complete evaluation must include parent and teacher ratings of the constituent behaviors (with scales that are carefully normed), a careful history gathered from caregivers, conversations with teachers (and classroom observations), a physical examination (to rule out various medical and neurological conditions that can mimic ADHD), and appraisal of the presence of co-occurring learning and behavioral difficulties. In fact, there are many reasons why a child or adolescent could display symptoms related to ADHD, including life stress, child abuse, depression or various neurological conditions, unstructured family configurations, or grossly disorganized classroom settings (Barkley 1998). Thus, assessment must use multiple sources of information and transcend brief observations of the child in the office, where the novelty of the situation may temporarily suppress the ongoing behavior patterns.

Demographics, Developmental Course, and Etiology

ADHD occurs in about 3 to 7 percent of the general population. As is the case with nearly all developmental disorders, it is more common in boys than girls, with a male to female ratio of about 3:1 in community settings and even higher in clinical settings. An exception is that individuals displaying the Inattentive type of ADHD—formerly termed *attention deficit disorder without hyperactivity* and distinguished by inattention but without noteworthy hyperactivity and impulsivity—has a male to female ratio closer to 1.5:1 or 2:1.

Longitudinal studies demonstrate that ADHD almost always persists into adolescence, and in a plurality of cases impairment lasts into adulthood (Mannuzza and Klein 1999). Although the motor overactivity per se dissipates with time, inattention, disorganization, impulsivity, and academic and social difficulties are likely to persist well beyond childhood.

Regarding etiology, ADHD is one of the most heritable conditions in all of psychopathology. Seventy to 80 percent of the individual differences in ADHD-related symptoms are attributed to genetic rather than environmental factors. Thus, ADHD's genetic liability is higher than that for *depression* or *schizophrenia,* and roughly equal to that for *bipolar disorder* or *autistic disorder* (Tannock 1998). Although ADHD is not a simple, single-gene condition, recent discoveries at the molecular genetic level implicate genes related to dopamine neurotransmission. Note that, because ADHD persists throughout development and because it is strongly familial, a high proportion (30–40%) of the biological parents of children with ADHD will have clinically significant symptoms themselves, whether or not formally diagnosed. Thus, the new generation often suffers from both genetic and psychosocial risk, the latter related to being raised by parents who are themselves not fully self-regulated.

Other biological (but non-genetic) risk factors for ADHD include low birthweight, several types of prenatal and perinatal complications, and maternal use of substances such as nicotine, alcohol, or illicit drugs during pregnancy (Tannock 1998). Although these risk factors are not inevitable causes of ADHD—and most cases of ADHD do not show associations with these risks—they do play a role in many individuals with the disorder. Overall, ADHD has strong psychobiological origins.

Can ineffective parenting cause ADHD? Most experts say no, because (a) many discordant family characteristics appear to result from (rather than predispose to) having a child with the difficult behavioral pattern demarcated by ADHD and (b) children with ADHD do not show higher than expected rates of insecure attachment in infancy and toddlerhood (Hinshaw 1999). Nevertheless, there some evidence for family "causation" with respect to children from impoverished backgrounds: In a high-risk sample, Elizabeth Carlson and colleagues

(1995) found that unresponsive and overly stimulating parenting styles during the first two years of life could be used to predict ADHD-related symptomatology years later, over and above indicators of early temperament and biological dysfunction. In most cases, however, parenting may serve to accentuate or exacerbate difficult temperament or other signs of early biological risk.

Family Processes and ADHD

As reviewed by Johnston and Mash (2001), families of children and adolescents with ADHD experience a number of difficulties, in contrast to families who do not have offspring with this diagnosis. First, caregivers report higher levels of family conflict and stress and lower levels of perceived competence in the parenting role. They also report lower rates of *authoritative parenting,* a style blending warmth, limit setting, and autonomy encouragement typically associated with the child's attainment of social and academic competence (Hinshaw et al. 1997). Second, parents of children with ADHD experience greater marital conflict and less marital satisfaction than families of comparison children. Third, direct observations of parent-child interaction (an important area of research, given the potential for biases in self-reports from parents) have reported high levels of parental negativity and *harsh/directive parenting* to characterize family interchanges, particularly for mothers interacting with their sons who have ADHD. Fourth, children with ADHD are overrepresented in the population of children who have been adopted (Simmel et al. 2001). As in all aspects of research regarding ADHD, however, far more is known about boys than girls; more is known about mothers than fathers; more is known about majority than ethnic minority children (because of a dearth of research on the latter group); and more is known about youth in middle childhood than in adolescence. Nonetheless, this disorder is clearly characterized by family stress and distress and negative parent-child interactions.

Two issues require comment. First, the family variables noted above may pertain as much to aggressive behavior patterns that frequently accompany ADHD as to the core symptoms of ADHD itself. Harsh and unresponsive parenting, in particular, is causally related to the development of aggressive behavior in children (Patterson, Reid,

and Dishion 1992); negative parenting and family variables may therefore pertain more to noncompliance, aggression, and covert antisocial behaviors like stealing than to inattention, impulsivity, and hyperactivity per se (Johnston and Mash 2001). Insecure attachment in early development predicts subsequent aggression but not ADHD. Second, the processes and mechanisms responsible for the associations between family distress and ADHD remain elusive. Indeed, instead of the usual supposition that negative parenting influences difficult child behavior, it is conceivable (given ADHD's strong heritability) that the same genes are responsible for (a) impulsive, harsh parenting behaviors and (b) noncompliant and negative behaviors in the child. In addition, many of the negative behaviors displayed by parents could be a reaction to, rather than a cause of, the child's noncompliant, difficult temperamental and behavioral style. The chains of risk and causation are likely to be *reciprocal* (with negative parenting triggered by child impulsivity and defiance but also fueling further difficulty in the child) and *transactional* (with reciprocal chains of influence proceeding through development). Thus, the picture is of a child with early temperamental difficulties and behavior problems, with less-than-optimal parenting serving to amplify problem behavior and set the stage for further negativity and even aggression.

Culture and Ethnicity

Research indicates that ADHD exists in multiple cultures, societies, and nations. Not only has ADHD been diagnosed in various ethnic groups within the United States, but it has been documented in China, South America, Europe, India, and Japan, as well as other regions (Hinshaw and Park 1999). Thus, ADHD is not simply a product of Western industrialized societies, although its visibility and detection are bound to be far greater in cultures and societies with compulsory education. Considerably more research is needed if we are to understand whether the prevalence of ADHD is equal across nations and cultures or whether, as might be predicted, different styles of child temperament (known to display differing rates in different nations) or different childrearing styles (also known to vary across nations and cultures) could influence symptoms (Hinshaw and Park 1999). In other words, ADHD appears to be a universal—rather than culturally specific—disorder, but we still have much to learn about the influence of culture, schooling practices, and nationality on its prevalence and presentation.

Treatment

Only two intervention strategies have shown research-based evidence for the treatment of ADHD: (a) stimulant medications, such as methylphenidate or dextroamphetamine, which regulate dopamine neurotransmission and (b) *behavioral strategies* such as *parent management training, school consultation,* and *direct contingency management* in classroom or special educational settings (Pelham, Wheeler, and Chronis 1998). Indeed, individual therapies that do not directly target the child's social, behavioral, and academic problems have not yielded clear support regarding intervention for ADHD. Medication typically yields stronger effects than behavioral interventions in terms of improving core symptomatology, but (a) psychosocial treatments may be preferable for some families (who may be philosophically opposed to medication); (b) perhaps as many as 20 percent of the youths with ADHD either do not respond optimally to medication or show prohibitive side effects; (c) medication alone is typically insufficient for helping the child learn new academic or social skills or for the family to learn and practice new management skills; and (d) combining well-delivered pharmacological intervention with systematic behavioral family and school treatment is most likely to yield normalization of behavioral, social, and academic targets (Pelham, Wheeler, and Chronis 1998). It is important to note that both pharmacological and behavioral treatments for ADHD share a common limitation: their benefits tend to persist only as long as the intervention is delivered. ADHD is a chronic condition and may well require chronic treatment.

Unfortunately, in light of the strongly heritable nature of ADHD and the documented success of pharmacological interventions, it could be concluded that family and school environments are not particularly important and that psychosocial interventions have limited potential for success. Such thinking fails to take into account the demonstrated facts that (a) conditions with clear psychosocial etiology may respond to biological treatment regimens and (b) conditions with strong psychobiological underpinnings may respond to

A mother dispenses stimulant medication to her son. Although medication is the most effective form of treatment for ADHD, it is not always the preferred form of treatment. Research has shown behaviorial therapy to be an effective form of treatment as well. STOCK BOSTON, INC.

treatments emphasizing skill enhancement or environmental manipulation. In fact, recent evidence suggests that even for a condition as heritable as ADHD a combination of treatments may be the answer: when combined pharmacological and behavioral treatments produce optimal benefits for youth with ADHD, a key explanatory factor is the family's reduction of harsh and ineffective discipline strategies at home (Hinshaw et al. 2000). Thus, the family's learning of more productive management strategies at home and their coordination of intervention efforts with the school are necessary components of a viable treatment plan for ADHD. The development of self-regulation requires active teaching by parents and teachers, often in concert with pharmacological interventions to enhance attention and regulate impulse control. Such consistent intervention from families appears necessary to break the intergenerational cycle that is often found with ADHD.

See also: CHRONIC ILLNESS; CONDUCT DISORDER; DEVELOPMENTAL PSYCHOPATHOLOGY; PARENTING STYLES; SCHOOL; TEMPERAMENT

Bibliography

American Psychiatric Association. (1994). *Diagnostic and Statistical Manual of Mental Disorders,* 4th edition. Washington, DC: American Psychiatric Press.

Barkley, R. A. (1998). *Attention Deficit Hyperactivity Disorder: A Handbook for Diagnosis and Treatment,* 2nd edition. New York: Guilford.

Carlson, E. A.; Jacobvitz, D.; and Sroufe, L. A. (1995). "A Developmental Investigation of Inattentiveness and Hyperactivity." *Child Development* 66:37–54.

DeGrandpre, R., and Hinshaw, S. P. (2000). "Attention-Deficit Hyperactivity Disorder: Psychiatric Problem or American Cop-Out?" *Cerebrum* 2:12–38.

Hinshaw, S. P. (1999). "Psychosocial Intervention for Childhood ADHD: Etiologic and Developmental Themes, Comorbidity, and Integration with Pharmacotherapy." In *Rochester Symposium on Developmental Psychopathology,* Vol. 9: *Developmental Approaches to Prevention and Intervention,* ed. D. Ciccehetti and S. L. Toth. Rochester, NY: University of Rochester Press.

Hinshaw, S. P.; Owens, E. B.; Wells, K. C.; Kraemer, H. C.; Abikoff, H. B.; Arnold, L. E.; Conners, C. K.; Elliott, G.; Greenhill, L. L.; Hechtman, L.; Hoza, B.; Jensen, P. S.; March, J. S.; Newcorn, J.; Pelham, W. E.; Swanson, J. M.; Vitiello, B.; and Wigal, T. (2000). "Family Processes and Treatment Outcome in the MTA: Negative/Ineffective Parenting Practices in Relation to Multimodal Treatment." *Journal of Abnormal Child Psychology* 28:555–568.

Hinshaw, S. P., and Park, T. (1999). "Research Issues and Problems: Toward a More Definitive Science of Disruptive Behavior Disorders." In *Handbook of Disruptive Behavior Disorders,* ed. H. C. Quay and A. E. Hogan. New York: Plenum.

Hinshaw, S. P.; Zupan, B. A.; Simmel, C.; Nigg, J. T.; and Melnick, S. M. (1997). "Peer Status in Boys With and Without Attention-Deficit Hyperactivity Disorder: Predictions from Overt and Covert Antisocial Behavior, Social Isolation, and Authoritative Parenting Beliefs." *Child Development* 64:880–896.

Johnston, C., and Mash, E. J. (2001). "Families of Children with Attention-Deficit/Hyperactivity Disorder: Review and Recommendations for Future Research." *Clinical Child and Family Psychology Review* 4:183–207.

Mannuzza, S., and Klein, R. G. (1999). "Adolescent and Adult Outcomes in Attention-Deficit/Hyperactivity Disorder." In *Handbook of Disruptive Behavior Disorders,* ed. H. C. Quay and A. E. Hogan. New York: Plenum.

Patterson, G. R.; Reid, J.; and Dishion, T. (1992). *Antisocial Boys.* Eugene, OR: Castalia.

Pelham, W. E.; Wheeler, T.; and Chronis, A. (1998). "Empirically Supported Psychosocial Treatments for ADHD." *Journal of Clinical Child Psychology* 27:189–204.

Simmel, C.; Brooks, D.; Barth, R. P.; and Hinshaw, S. P. (2001). "Externalizing Symptomatology Among Adoptive Youth: Prevalence and Preadoption Risk Factors." *Journal of Abnormal Child Psychology* 29:57–69.

Tannock, R. (1998). "Attention Deficit Hyperactivity Disorder: Advances in Cognitive, Neurobiological, and Genetic Research." *Journal of Child Psychology and Psychiatry* 39:65–99.

STEPHEN P. HINSHAW

ATTRACTION

Attraction is an interactive process that involves one person who transmits verbal, visual, or other stimuli, and another who responds more or less positively to those stimuli. Early research viewed the *attraction response* as an attitude toward the target person that included favorable evaluations and the expectation that *approach behaviors,* such as a willingness to work with or date the person, were likely to be rewarding. Later, attraction was seen as having emotional components, which included the possibility of ambivalent feelings of simultaneous liking and disliking (Berscheid and Reis 1998). Recently, it was recognized that attraction also involves motivational qualities, such as a yearning or desire for connection with a person, based on the perception that he or she is fit to satisfy one or more of the perceiver's needs. The motivational analysis of attraction suggests that satisfaction is produced if a relationship with an attractive person is established, disappointment occurs if the other person rejects the relationship, and sadness or anger follows if a relationship is first formed, then broken (Baumeister and Leary 1995).

The motivational analysis also notes that the perceiver's motives determine the criteria used for judging the attractiveness of the other person, and such criteria may vary depending on whether the perceiver needs a long-term romantic partner, friend, mentor, employee, or a child to adopt (Cunningham et al. 1995). Thus, the motivational analysis suggests that attraction is influenced by characteristics of the target person being evaluated as attractive; by the perceiver's needs, feelings and traits; and by the situation in which the perceiver is exposed to the target, which may influence both the perception of the stimulus and the positivity of the response. Much of the research on interpersonal attraction focused on evaluations of potential romantic partners, but many of the variables are relevant to other forms of relationships as well.

Situational Factors in Attraction

The first step in attraction is being aware of the people to whom one might be attracted. Attraction is remarkably easy to stimulate; the more likely there is contact between people, the more likely they are to become attracted. A classic study by Leon Festinger and his associates (1950) demonstrated that the number of friends that a person had in college was best predicted by proximity, or a person's accessibility for interaction. The researchers found that students whose dorm rooms were centrally located made more friends than those whose rooms were isolated. Accessibility increased the opportunity both for positive social contact and for familiarity. Research on familiarity demonstrated that people reported greater liking for others the more that they were shown the other people's photographs, even when the exposures were brief and not consciously noted. This *mere exposure effect* is quite powerful, but only works if the stimuli initially evoke either neutral or positive feelings, which can produce a sense of comfort and security. If someone is repeatedly exposed to an obnoxious person, then repulsion may increase disproportionately, in a process termed a *social allergy* (Cunningham, Barbee, and Druen 1997).

Physical proximity is not the only basis of interaction accessibility. People can become attracted to people whom they encounter on television, and can now meet people from other countries almost as easily as they can meet people from their own neighborhoods using e-mail and the Internet. Nor is it necessary to meet someone in order to be attracted to the person. Sometimes, simply being aware of the prospect of future interaction with a target person can increase liking. Ellen Berscheid and her colleagues (1976) found that research participants increased their liking for an individual after learning that they would be going out on a blind date with the person, compared to people whom they believed they would not meet. Most people seem inclined to like those whom they encounter in their social environment.

Attraction also may be increased as a function of the time of night that one is making an evaluation. Susan Sprecher (1984) found that the later in the evening that people were asked to evaluate members of the opposite sex in a bar, the more positively the people were rated. Apparently, standards go down as the prospect of loneliness goes up. This tendency was more evident for working people than for college students, perhaps because the latter may have more chances to meet members of the opposite sex.

Situational factors that alter the emotional and motivational state of the perceiver may increase attraction to another person, if the other person seems appropriate for the way that the individual is feeling. For example, men who were instructed to read a sexually arousing passage from a novel rated pictures of women, especially ones whom the men thought might be their blind dates, as more attractive than did men who were not sexually aroused (Stephan, Berscheid, and Walster 1971). Although positive feelings often generalize to create more positive evaluations of other people, there are times when negative feelings can induce attraction. Individuals who are experiencing anxious arousal, such as before a dental exam or prior to crossing a high, scary bridge, often respond more positively to friendly and attractive people than they do at other times (Foster et al. 1998). For example, men who were induced to feel depressed by watching sad movies were particularly attracted to women who appeared warm and supportive, even if the women were not particularly beautiful. By contrast, men who were induced to feel elated by watching an upbeat movie were particularly attracted to a beautiful but cool woman, who presented an intriguing challenge (Cunningham, Druen, and Barbee 1997).

Target Factors in Attraction

The way that a potential target of attraction introduces him- or herself, and communicates personality and intentions, can affect whether attraction occurs. Men have traditionally been more likely than women to make the first overt move in relationship initiation. Although this may be changing, much of the research on attraction has focused on men as the initiators and women as the targets of romantic overtures. People are attracted to people who express liking for them; just knowing that someone is attracted to oneself tends to induce reciprocal interest. Reciprocal self-disclosure, in the form of taking turns in revealing details about oneself, can foster attraction. Reciprocal liking can also be indicated nonverbally (e.g., Grammer, Kruck, and Magnusson 1998). Women who maintain eye contact with a man, for example, or flip their hair, or lean towards him, may communicate their interest. Unfortunately, men may sometimes misinterpret casual female friendliness for sexual interest.

In first encounters, people often ingratiate, flatter, and praise people whose favor they are trying to win, and modify their self-presentations to be what the other person seeks (Rowatt, Cunningham, and Druen 1998). Although most people enjoy hearing praise, ingratiation can backfire and produce dislike if the flattered person suspects that the flatterer is self-serving rather than sincere. A second exception to the rule that people like compliments and flattery was offered by Ellen Berscheid and her associates. An evaluator who was initially critical of a target, and later changed his or her mind and expressed approval, was rated more positively than was an evaluator who was consistently positive to a target. The attraction to the re-evaluator may have been due to a sudden reduction of tension, because the effect was not observed when the same person was simultaneously exposed to a consistently positive evaluator, along with a second evaluator who shifted from negative to positive. Such complexities may help explain why "playing hard to get" does not reliably increase attraction.

A sense of humor is a positively rated quality, and being perceived as humorous can increase attraction. This is especially true for men. Duane Lundy and colleagues (1998) found that women rated physically attractive men who expressed humor as more desirable than they rated physically attractive non-humorous men. Physically attractive men who expressed self-deprecating humor were seen as more cheerful, and perhaps more humane and less threatening, than non-humorous handsome men. But, humor that people perceive as threatening can backfire. Michael Cunningham studied opening lines in bars. Humorously flippant comments (e.g., "You remind me of someone I used to date") were least effective in generating attraction, whereas direct (e.g., "I'm a little embarrassed about this, but I'd really like to meet you") or innocuous lines (e.g. "What do you think of the music?") were more successful. Such outcomes are consistent with research that indicated that women are attracted to dominant men only when the men are also agreeable and nice (Jensen-Campbell, Graziano, and West 1995). Extremely dominant behavior, without kindness and gentleness, can be intimidating rather than attractive to women.

Physical attractiveness has a tremendous influence on first encounters, perhaps because it appears to convey a great deal of information about the person. The *Multiple Fitness* model of physical attractiveness, advanced by Cunningham and his colleagues (1995), suggests that five categories of features influence social perception and attraction. *Babyish features,* such as large eyes, a small nose, smooth skin, and light coloration suggest youthful openness. By contrast, *sexual maturity features* suggest strength, dominance, and fitness to perform sex-role tasks. Such maturity features include high cheekbones, narrow cheeks, prominent breasts, and a 0.70 ratio of waist to hips in women, and a wide chin, thick eyebrows, evidence of facial hair, a prominent chest, and a 1.0 ratio of waist to hips in men. Sexual maturity features that are asymmetrical, or that deviate substantially from the population average, may indicate low biological fitness. However, *biological qualities,* such as youthfulness, fertility, or virility, are not the only determinants of physical attractiveness. *Expressive features,* such as highly set eyebrows and a large smile, are attractive by conveying friendliness and supportiveness.

A combination of exceptional features, including ideal babyish, sexually mature, and expressive characteristics, were seen as attractive by whites, blacks, Asians, and Hispanics. By contrast, the desirability of grooming features tends to be seen differently across cultures. *Grooming features,* such as body weight, hairstyle, cosmetics, and tattoos, may be attractive in themselves, or may accentuate other attractive qualities. In addition, some grooming features may reflect a learned desire for status symbols or novelty, whereas other grooming features may reflect adaptations to the local ecology. Analyses of sixty-two cultures indicated that preferences for slenderness, for example, were associated with a reliable food supply and greater female social power (Anderson et al. 1992). Finally, senescence features, such as gray hair or baldness, reduced romantic attractiveness, but increased perceived social maturity, wisdom, and attractiveness as a mentor.

Early research observed that favoritism to the physically attractive extended beyond romantic dating to teacher evaluations, friendship choices, employment decisions, and jury verdicts. Subsequent research indicated that different dimensions of physical attractiveness may be responsible for such preferences. Individuals who frequently smile may make better friends than their gloomy counterparts (Harker and Keltner 2001).

Perceiver Factors in Attraction

Response to attractive stimuli depends on the perceiver as well as the stimulus. People's response to a target's physical attractiveness, for example, is influenced by the number of strikingly attractive people that they have recently viewed, by the opinions of other people, and by how invested they are in their current relationship.

Similarity involves a match between the target and the perceiver. People tend to like others who seem similar to themselves in attitudes and beliefs and, to a much lesser extent, in personality and physical attractiveness (Byrne 1971). Similarity in attitudes helps to avoid conflict, and the agreement of others helps to validate one's own opinions. Such validation is particularly attractive when people feel threatened or insecure.

One exception to the similarity-attraction rule is that women are often initially attracted to men who are the opposite of themselves, by being stereotypically masculine and task-focused. Conversely, men are attracted to women who are stereotypically feminine, expressive, and relationship-focused. William Ickes (1993) suggested that this opposites-attract tendency is ironic, because relationships between people who have traditional gender roles are typically less satisfying and more problematic than are relationships between people

who are androgynous, having both masculine and feminine qualities.

Some of the cause of attraction to sex-role typical mates may be due to hormones. Researchers who study the effects of hormones on attraction, such as Ian Penton-Voak and his associates (1999), found that women who were at the midpoint of their menstrual cycle, and experiencing higher levels of hormones, rated ruggedly masculine men as more attractive than women who were at other points in their menstrual cycle, who preferred a less masculine male appearance. Further, women at the midpoint of their cycle displayed strongest attraction to t-shirts that had been worn by more robust and symmetrical men, which presumably contained the men's pheromones. Men did not display such olfactory sensitivity (Thornhill and Gangestad 1999).

Sociobiological theory (Cunningham 1981) interpreted attraction in terms of evolutionary dynamics, such as the differential mating requirements of males and females. Men may have greater need than women for a young, healthy, fertile partner, which may be suggested by a partner's physical attractiveness, whereas women may need someone with resources to invest in their offspring, which may be indicated by a partner's wealth and status. Research conducted in thirty-seven cultures suggested that men are more interested than women in potential partners' physical attractiveness, whereas women are more interested than men in potential partners' wealth and status (Buss 1989). Although physical attractiveness and wealth influence attraction, the results of over one hundred studies about what people are looking for in long-term relationships indicated that mate qualities that indicate caring, such as being kind, supportive, and understanding, are more important in attraction to both males and females than material qualities such as physical attractiveness or wealth (Cunningham, Druen, and Barbee 1997).

Attachment theory suggested that an individual's disposition to be kind and caring may begin in childhood, as a result of the responsiveness and affection shown by the parents. A *secure attachment style* involves a positive attitude about oneself and other people, and is characterized by happiness, trust, and comfort with closeness. Rand Conger and his associates (2000) reported that when individuals had nurturing and involved parents in the seventh grade, they turned out to be warm, supportive, and low in hostility when they were in romantic relationships in their twenties.

Individuals with a *preoccupied attachment style* have positive attitude about others, but low self-esteem and anxious attitudes about themselves. They tend to experience emotional extremes in their relationships, to crave closeness but have a fear of rejection. Individuals with such low self-esteem may underestimate their partner's attraction, and eventually may cause the rejection that they fear. Individuals with a *dismissive attachment style* have high self-esteem, but are negative toward other people, whereas those with a *fearful attachment style* are both anxious about themselves and avoidant toward others. Bruce Ellis and associates (1996) reported that people who grow up in a stressful environment, and develop a dismissive or fearful attachment style, may initiate sexual activity at an earlier age. Such individuals may seek short-term relationships due to their fear of intimacy, according to Pilkington and Richardson, and may emphasize physical attractiveness and wealth when choosing such a short-term partner (Kenrick et al. 1990).

People generally are attracted to potential partners with secure attachment styles, who make them feel loved and cared for, despite the fact that the other person is dissimilar to their own attachment style (Chappell and Davis 1998). Individuals who are themselves insecure, however, may inaccurately see insecure people as being secure. In addition, such variables as familiarity, physical attraction, or similarity in attitudes also may cause individuals to become attracted to insecure partners.

When the object of evaluation is a stranger, a low rating of interpersonal attraction usually means neutrality or indifference. But when the target is a close associate, low levels of attraction usually mean hatred or disgust. It is unclear whether changes in the positive qualities of another person, such as decreases in their supportiveness, generosity, or beauty, cause a substantial change in attraction, or whether increases in negative behavior, such as criticism, unfairness, or withdrawal, are primarily responsible for disaffection (Huston et al. 2001). It is likely, however, that attraction is a function of the perceiver's motivation that is most acute at the time of evaluation of the other person. If the

perceiver is feeling a need for respect, and the other person is derogatory, then attraction is likely to be low. But if the two break up, and the perceiver is feeling lonely, then the perceiver may become attracted again to the former partner, as a familiar conversationalist. If the two get back together, however, then loneliness will recede as a motive, and other needs will return to influence attraction or repulsion. Thus, interpersonal attraction, from the beginning to the end of a relationship, may be influenced by characteristics of the target person being evaluated as attractive; by the perceiver's needs, feelings and traits; and by the situation in which the perceiver is exposed to the target.

See also: ATTACHMENT: COUPLE RELATIONSHIPS; COMMUNICATION: COUPLE RELATIONSHIPS; DATING; FRIENDSHIP; MATE SELECTION; RELATIONSHIP INITIATION; RELATIONSHIP MAINTENANCE; SELF-ESTEEM; SEXUAL COMMUNICATION: COUPLE RELATIONSHIPS; SEXUALITY

Bibliography

Anderson, J. L.; Crawford, C. B.; Nadeau, J.; and Lindberg, T. (1992). "Was the Duchess of Windsor Right? A Cross-Cultural Review of the Socioecology of Ideals of Female Body Shape." *Ethology and Sociobiology* 13(3):197–227.

Baumeister, R. F., and Leary, M. R. (1995). "The Need to Belong: Desire for Interpersonal Attachments as a Fundamental Human Motivation." *Psychological Bulletin* 117:497–529.

Berscheid, E., and Reis, H. (1998). "Attraction and Close Relationships." In *The Handbook of Social Psychology,* 4th edition, Vol. 2D, ed. T. Gilbert, S. T. Fiske, and G. Lindzey. New York: McGraw-Hill.

Berscheid, E.; Brothen, T.; and Graziano, W. (1976). "Gain-Loss Theory and the 'Law of Infidelity': Mr. Doting versus the Admiring Stranger." *Journal of Personality and Social Psychology* 33(6):709–718.

Buss, D. M. (1989). "Sex Differences in Human Mate Preferences: Evolutionary Hypotheses Tested in 37 Cultures." *Behavior and Brain Sciences* 12:1–49.

Byrne, D. (1971). *The Attraction Paradigm.* New York: Academic Press.

Chappell, K. D., and Davis, K. E. (1998). "Attachment, Partner Choice, and Perception of Romantic Partners: An Experimental Test of the Attachment-Security Hypothesis." *Personal Relationships* 3(2):117–136.

Conger, R. D.; Cui, M.; Bryant, C. M.; and Elder, G. H. (2000). "Competence in Early Adult Romantic Relationships: A Developmental Perspective on Family Influences." *Journal of Personality and Social Psychology* 79(2):224–237.

Cunningham, M. R. (1981). "Sociobiology as a Supplementary Paradigm for Social Psychological Research." In *Review of Personality and Social Psychology,* Vol. 2, ed. L. Wheeler. Beverly Hills, CA: Sage Publications.

Cunningham, M. R.; Barbee, A. P.; and Druen, P. B. (1997). "Social Antigens and Allergies: The Development of Hypersensitivity in Close Relationships." In *Aversive Interpersonal Behaviors,* ed. R. Kowalski. New York: Plenum.

Cunningham, M. R.; Druen, P. B.; and Barbee, A. P. (1997). "Angels, Mentors, and Friends: Trade-Offs among Evolutionary, Social, and Individual Variables in Physical Appearance." In *Evolutionary Social Psychology,* ed. J.A. Simpson and D.T. Kenrick. Mahwah, NJ: Erlbaum.

Cunningham, M. R.; Roberts, A. R.; Barbee, A. P.; Druen, P. B.; and Wu, C. (1995). "'Their Ideas of Beauty Are, on the Whole, the Same as Ours': Consistency and Variability in the Cross-Cultural Perception of Female Physical Attractiveness." *Journal of Personality and Social Psychology* 68:261–279.

Ellis, B. J. (1996). "Quality of Early Family Relationships and Individual Differences in the Timing of Pubertal Maturation in Girls: A Longitudinal Test of an Evolutionary Model." *Journal of Personality and Social Psychology* 71(2):387–401.

Festinger, L.; Schacter, S.; and Back, K. W. (1950). *Social Pressures in Informal Groups.* New York: Harper.

Foster, C. A.; Witcher, B. S.; Campbell, W. K.; and Green, J. D. (1998). "Arousal and Attraction: Evidence for Automatic and Controlled Processes." *Journal of Personality and Social Psychology* 74(1):86–101.

Grammer, K.; Kruck, K. B.; and Magnusson, M. S. (1998). "The Courtship Dance: Patterns of Nonverbal Synchronization in Opposite-Sex Encounters." *Journal of Nonverbal Behavior* 22(1):3–29.

Harker, L., and Keltner, D. (2001). "Expressions of Positive Emotion in Women's College Yearbook Pictures and Their Relationship to Personality and Life Outcomes across Adulthood." *Journal of Personality and Social Psychology* 80(1):112–124.

Huston, T. L.; Caughlin, J. P.; Houts, R. M.; Smith, S. E.; and George, L. J. (2001). "The Connubial Crucible: Newlywed Years as Predictors of Marital Delight, Distress, and Divorce." *Journal of Personality and Social Psychology* 80(2):237–252.

Ickes, W. (1993). "Traditional Gender Roles: Do They Make, and Then Break, Our Relationships?" *Journal of Social Issues* 49(3):71–86.

Jensen-Campbell, L. A.; Graziano, W. G.; and West, S. G. (1995). "Dominance, Prosocial Orientation, and Female Preferences: Do Nice Guys Really Finish Last?" *Journal of Personality and Social Psychology* 68:427–440.

Kenrick, D. T.; Sadalla, E. K.; Groth, G.; and Trost, M. R. (1990). "Evolution, Traits, and the Stages of Human Courtship: Qualifying the Parental Investment Model." *Journal of Personality* 58:97–116.

Lundy, D. E; Tan, J.; and Cunningham, M. R. (1998). "Heterosexual Romantic Preferences: The Importance of Humor and Physical Attractiveness for Different Types of Relationships." *Personal Relationships* 5:311–325.

Penton-Voak, I. S.; Perrett, D. I.; Castles, D. L.; Kobayashi, T.; Burt, D. M.; Murray, L. K.; and Minamisawa, R. (1999). "Menstrual Cycle Alters Face Preference." *Nature* 399:741–742.

Rowatt, W. C.; Cunningham, M. R.; and Druen, P. B. (1998). "Deception to Get a Date." *Personality and Social Psychology Bulletin* 24(11):1228–1242.

Sprecher, S. (1984). "Asking Questions in Bars: The Girls (and Boys) May Not Get Prettier at Closing Time and Other Results." *Personality and Social Psychology Bulletin* 10:482–488.

Stephan, W.; Berscheid, E.; and Walster, E. (1971). "Sexual Arousal and Heterosexual Perception." *Journal of Personality and Social Psychology* 20:93–101.

Thornhill, R.; and Gangestad, S.W. (1999). "The Scent of Symmetry: A Human Sex Pheromone that Signals Fitness?" *Evolution and Human Behavior* 20(3):175–201.

MICHAEL R. CUNNINGHAM
LARA K. AULT
ANITA P. BARBEE

ATTRIBUTION IN RELATIONSHIPS

The term *attribution* refers to the interpretation of an event by inferring what caused the event to occur. This interpretation may also extend to inference of responsibility for an event and judgment about the trait qualities of another person, or of oneself. As an illustration of a common situation involving attribution activity, a husband may ask why his wife left the room with a sudden burst of tears in the middle of what he perceived to be an innocent conversation about their respective days at the office (i.e., where does responsibility lie?) or whether her emotional display pertains to something about her personality (i.e., her trait to readily exhibit emotional outbursts).

The concept of attribution was developed by Fritz Heider (1958) and articulated into testable theories by Edward Jones and Keith Davis (1965) and Harold Kelley (1967). Also, in his self-perception theory, Daryl Bem (1972) extended attributional theorizing to encompass self-attributions. Bem posited that people take some meaningful form of action and then, in forming a perception about that action, use their own behavior and the context in which it occurs to judge their attitudes, beliefs, and other internal states. For example, a husband whose wife has suddenly, and in tears, ended their conversation may look back at his behavior and conclude, "I was being insensitive in those remarks I made about our friends. No wonder she was upset."

For the situation involving a wife's sudden emotional outburst, these theories suggest that observers infer the bases for the wife's behavior by logical analysis of such information as: (1) her behavior in previous similar situations (i.e., consistency information—is it common for her to show her emotions in this way?); (2) the husband's insensitive behavior toward his wife (i.e., consensus information—does she often become upset in talking with him?); (3) any specific events that distinguish this circumstance for her (i.e., distinctiveness information—something unusual and highly embarrassing happening a the office that day); and/or (4) the wife's intention to show her hurt about some past concern, or the husband's intent to upset his wife, and whether either type of intention reveals something about the wife's or husband's personality.

Attribution theory in social psychology became a prominent topic for examination in the 1970s. As early as the mid-1970s, an extension of attributional theorizing focused on heterosexual, close relationships (relationships in which two people's lives reflect strong and regular interconnections in

their thoughts, feelings, and behavior). A major theoretical analysis that contributed to this extension was Edward Jones and Richard Nisbett's 1972 divergent perceptions hypothesis. This hypothesis pertains to a situation in which an actor and an observer come to different explanations for the same action. It stated that the actor would attribute her behavior to the forces in the situation, while the observer would attribute the same behavior to personality characteristics of the actor.

Jones and Nisbett's explanation for why the divergent perspective tendency occurs emphasized cognitive-perceptual dynamics, namely that: (1) the actor perceptually views the situation as central in his or her field of thought and perception, whereas the observer views the actor as central, and (2) the actor will have evidence that she has shown variation in behavior across different situations, whereas the observer often will not have access to that evidence. Another type of explanation, one that is quite germane to the situation that couples often encounter, is that actors are motivated to protect their self-esteem in situations in which their behavior leads to questionable outcomes. Actors may be inclined to attribute their behavior to the situation to better protect their self-esteem, while observers may be motivated to attribute bad outcomes to the actor's personality as a means of punishing or controlling the actor. Heider's (1958) conception of attributional phenomena emphasized this type of integration of cognitive and self-esteem or motivational elements.

Extending Attribution Research to Close Relationships

The first investigation to study connections between attributions and close relationships was conducted by Bruce Orvis, Harold Kelley, and Deborah Butler (1976). They asked college-age couples to list examples of behavior, for oneself and one's partner, for which each had a different explanation. Several categories of behavior yielded divergent attributions (e.g., "Actor criticizes or places demands upon the partner"). More generally, for behavior resulting in negative outcomes, respondents exonerated themselves and blamed their partners. Later work suggests that this egocentric bias in attribution by close relationship partners holds mainly for couples experiencing distress. For those who are less distressed, they attribute bad outcomes to the situation and good outcomes to their partner or to their collaboration with their partner (see below).

An important implication of the results of Orvis and colleagues' investigation is that attributions made directly to one's partner, or indirectly in public and available to one's partner, may represent an attempt to influence the partner about why problematic events are occurring. For example, a spouse may say, "Our problems have been caused mainly by his inability to break the controlling influence his parents have over what he does." Whether or not the spouse believes that this control factor is critical, she may be making the attribution in an attempt to influence the partner to sever the control his parents have in his life. Helen Newman (1981) elaborated on attribution as a form of persuasion and ongoing communication in close relationships.

This early work by Orvis and colleagues confirmed the value of Jones and Nisbett's (1972) divergent perspectives hypothesis, with the important qualification that attributions often reflect self-esteem motivation when couples are making attributions about their relationships. Another amplification of this hypothesis was revealed in a study by John Harvey, Gary Wells, and Marlene Alvarez (1978). They showed that relationship partners who are distressed not only diverge in their attributions about relationship problems, but also cannot readily predict one another's attributions about the sources of the problems.

Attributional Biases in Relationships

During the 1980s and 1990s, the predominant research on attributions in close relationships has focused on attributional biases of partners. The aforementioned egocentric bias has been repeatedly found in different relationship situations (e.g., Fincham 1985). Theorists have suggested that this bias may have affect satisfaction in relationships, or it could serve as a secondary indicator that the relationship is already distressed. In an impressive program of research, Frank Fincham, Thomas Bradbury, and colleagues (e.g., Bradbury and Fincham 1992) have presented evidence that attributions play a causal role in both the development and the breakdown of close relationships. Their theoretical analysis, referred to as a contextual model, emphasizes that context always must be taken into account in understanding relationships.

An argument erupts between this couple during breakfast. Attribution, or the interpretation of an event based on what caused it to occur, is a factor in understanding and solving such disagreements. SIE PRODUCTIONS/CORBIS

They argue that behaviors exchanged in an interaction can have different meanings, depending on other events occurring in the interaction.

Another interesting track for work on attributions in relationships concerns gender differences. Amy Holtzworth-Munroe and Neil Jacobson (1985) found that in general during the course of relationships, women tend to do more processing and analyzing of the causes of issues and events than do men. In contrast, men appear to become quite active in their analysis when the relationship begins to encounter serious turmoil. This finding, therefore, suggests that a man's involvement in extensive attributional work in a relationship may be a good barometer of the seriousness of distress being jointly experienced in the relationship. It also is consistent with earlier work on possible gender differences in how women and men experience relationship breakdown (e.g., Weiss 1975).

New Directions

Later work has extended attributional perspectives to a variety of relationship phenomena, including: (1) linking attributions, communications, and affect in ongoing relationships (Vangelisti 1992); (2) the types of attributions made by violent men regarding their marriages (Holtzworth-Munroe 1988); and (3) attributions made by women who are victims of marital violence (Andrews 1992). A primary conclusion of these extrapolations is that attributions play a key role in relationship events, often being implicated in causal sequence.

A further new direction that shows promise views attribution as part of people's natural stories, narratives, or accounts relating to their relationships. According to this approach, in their daily lives, people often form understandings and make attributions about their relationships in the form of storylike constructions that usually are privately developed initially and then are communicated to other people. Such diverse writings as those of Robert Weiss (1975) and John Harvey, Ann Weber, and Terri Orbuch (1990) may be interpreted as embracing this approach. Illustrative research stresses the collection of people's naturalistic attributional accounts and the linking of those accounts to relationship behavior.

In the early twenty-first century, a blossoming area of work concerned the interface of close relationships, attribution, and communication behavior. A recent edited book by Valerie Manusov and John Harvey (2001) documents work at this interface. An interesting line of work that illustrates this area was carried out by Manusov and Koenig (2001). They have examined the attributions that couples provide for nonverbal interaction behaviors as the meanings that these couples have ascribed to the communication cues. These authors are operationalizing the attribution as the message. In a similar research program, Alan Sillars, Linda Roberts, Tim Dun, and Kenneth Leonard (2001) also focus on attributions as communication. In their extensive coding of real-time interactions, Sillars and colleagues accessed the attributions that people gave to what they or their partners were likely thinking at the time of the interaction. Individual members of couples stated what they thought that they and their partner were attempting to communicate or what was probably going on in their minds as they interacted. Thus, the attributions reflected the couples' assessments of the

meanings for the communication behaviors in which they or their partner engaged.

As Manusov (2001) argues, attributions may be seen as a form of communication that involves explanations for behaviors or events. Attributions may be viewed as necessary for communication cues (i.e., causal or other explanations are given for why someone communicated what or how he or she did). Attributions may be seen as an important part of the communicated message itself, with causal explanations becoming the meaning ascribed to or communicated by behaviors.

A plethora of other strands of work are evolving with attribution as a central construct. As Catherine Surra and colleagues have shown, attributions and communications help establish relational identity (Surra and Hughes 1997). Individuals in close relationships have identities connected to those relationships that presumably are cultivated over time through interaction and attributions held in private and sometimes communicated to the partner. These identities are fashioned and refined in accounts people develop about relationships and their own personal relationships in particular. Accounts, or storylike constructions containing attributions, remain a viable way for studying attributions in relationships.

A new theory of how relationships are maintained and enhanced argues that people take care in making attributions about their partners, emphasizing positive attributions but moreover accurate attributions (Harvey and Omarzu 1999). This theory, called minding the close relationship, also embraces the idea that a mutual, never-ending knowing process, involving self-disclosure and soliciting self-disclosures from other, is critical to relationship enhancement. Minding is the act of using one's mind purposefully in thinking and acting relevant to one's close relationship. Attributions about one's partner and the events unfolding in the relationship are assumed to be pervasive in ongoing flow of close relationships. Since this theory pivots around the attribution concept, we will outline aspects of the theory below.

According to minding theory, attributional activity is a central way in which we develop a sense of meaning about our relationships. Attributional activity reflects our trust and belief in our partners. When we attribute our partners' negative behaviors, such as rudeness or insensitivity, to outside causes we are essentially telling ourselves that they are *not* really insensitive; it is the situation. We believe better of them. However, if we attribute our partners' positive, caring acts to outside events or to self-interest, we are convincing ourselves not to believe in their love, not to trust their sincerity.

Minding theory stresses relationship-enhancing attributions. Relationship-enhancing attributions tend to be those that attribute positive behaviors to dispositional causes: "He came home early to spend time with me." "She called me at work because she cares about me." Negative behaviors, in contrast, are attributed more often to external causes: "She yelled at me because she's stressed at work." "He is late for our date because his car broke down." Attribution theorists such as Heider recognized that people's attributions of causality and responsibility often are mixtures of internal and external attribution. For example, the husband in the foregoing example may emphasize his wife's stress at work, but also attribute part of her temper display to her susceptibility to such stresses. In well-minded relationships, these attributional activities will be carefully carried out, which includes working to develop fair mixtures of internal and external attributions.

In well-minded relationships, partners will recognize how easy it is to be mistaken about a partner's behavior, feelings, intentions, and motivations, and how important it is to feel firm about attributions regarding behavior of their partner in different situations. Flexibility and willingness to reexamine attributions about one's partner and the relationship characterize well-minded relationships. Partners also will understand the value of honest, carefully developed attributions about their partner and relationship events. Not all attributions about one's partner or the relationship can be positive. On occasion, negative attributions can be used in redressing relationship problems and negotiating stronger relationships.

Partners who are minding well can use the knowledge that they have gained about each other to help ensure that they do not blindly attribute all good, or all bad, to their partners. Parts of the minding process build on each other. The knowledge and attribution components work together to help couples build trust and positive beliefs that are based in real knowledge and that they can feel confident about relying on.

Another prominent program of work on maintenance of close relationships that emphasizes attributions is being implemented by Benjamin Karney and colleagues. Benjamin Karney, James McNulty, and Nancy Frye (2001) pinpoint a specific mechanism at work in the maintenance and enhancement of close relationships that involves the extent to which individuals hold positive beliefs about their partner. Karney and his colleagues make the intriguing suggestion that relationship satisfaction may not necessarily result from the *content* of cognitions, but it may be more related to the manner in which the valence of cognitions at various levels (e.g., global vs. specific) are integrated. Because couples are likely to experience some adversity in their relationship, it is posited that their relationship satisfaction can be maintained to the extent to which individuals can separate cognitions associated with specific events from global beliefs about their partner. Attributions, the most widely studied cognitive process in the literature about close relationships, are proposed to affect relationship satisfaction by influencing the extent to which perceptions of specific behaviors modify global beliefs about one's partner. In all, Karney and his colleagues constructed an impressive model of the interplay between cognitive content, process, and structure. They believe that it will be important to link such results with other important variables, such as personality and life stress, to formulate a comprehensive model to characterize satisfaction in close relationships over time.

International Research

Increasingly, attribution is being applied in understanding close relationships by scholars who represent diverse countries and cultures. A small sampling of representative work will be reviewed here.

In one study, seventy-four French-Canadian couples reported on attributions for global marital conflict and marital adjustment (Sabourin, Lussier, and Wright 1991). It was found that the more likely individuals were to attribute their marital conflicts to global or stable causes and to assign blame to their partners, the more likely they were to report marital dissatisfaction. Global attributions for marital conflicts were the most consistent predictors of marital satisfaction scores.

A study of attribution and marital distress in China and the United States was carried out by

Daniel Stander, Donald Hsiung, and Donald Mac-Dermid (2001). In this work, thirty-six couples from China and thirty-two couples from the United States reported attributions associated with various types of conflict they had indicated to be occurring in their relationships. It was found that marital attributions were correlated with marital distress for both groups. However, the Chinese spouses tended to report more relationship-enhancing causal attributions than did spouses in the United States. There also were some differences in attributions of responsibility and blame across cultures.

Garth Fletcher (1993) has carried out a substantial program of work in New Zealand concerned with attribution and close relationships. He argues that the standard close relationship attribution model, which is concerned with connections between relationship satisfaction and causal attributions, is silent about the information processing involved in the links between dispositional structures, such as relationship satisfaction, and cognition, affect, and behavior. His model encompasses the outcomes when eliciting events during an interaction between partners are subjected to automatic/controlled processing. He studies close relationships beliefs, specific relationship knowledge structures, affect, and behavioral interactions in his program. Fletcher's work has not suggested major differences in information-processing tendencies for attributions in relationships across comparisons of couples in New Zealand, the United States, and Europe.

Other representative work has focused on attributions and self-serving biases in attributions among persons in relationships in India (Higgins and Bhatt 2001) and attributional style and self-concept among people in relationships in Hong Kong (Poon and Lau 1999). These studies showed that people in India and Hong Kong used attributions in ways found in previous studies in the United States (e.g., higher self-esteem for respondents shown for the Hong Kong study if the respondents attributed relationship problems to outside forces affecting their relationships).

More work is necessary to investigate attribution-relationship linkages in cultures not influenced by Western mores. A major difficulty facing this type of cross-cultural work is to be able to translate standardized instruments into different languages in a way that is both meaningful to the respondents and, at the same time, consistent with the intent of the questions and measures used.

Conclusion

As is clear in theories such as minding theory, attributions increasingly are seen as mediators of relationship events. Attributions are often seen as representing the process activities between social perception of close others and behavior directed toward them. This view of attribution is wed with a vibrant field of work on social cognition, or how people perceive others. In the early twenty-first century, attribution is alive and well, but mainly plays a major role in interdisciplinary work, such as that occurring in relationship theory and research.

See also: SELF-ESTEEM; THERAPY: COUPLE RELATIONSHIPS

Bibliography

Andrews, B. (1992). "Attribution Processes in Victims of Marital Violence." In *Attributions, Accounts, and Close Relationships,* ed. J. H. Harvey, T. L. Orbuch, and A. L. Weber. New York: Springer-Verlag.

Bem, D. J. (1972). "Self-Perception Theory." In *Advances in Experimental Social Psychology,* Vol. 6, ed. L. Berkowitz. New York: Academic Press.

Bradbury, T. N., and Fincham, F. D. (1992). "Attributions and Behavior in Marital Interaction." *Journal of Personality and Social Psychology* 63:613–628.

Fincham, F. D. (1985). "Attributional Processes in Distressed and Nondistressed Couples." *Journal of Abnormal Psychology* 94:183–190.

Fletcher, G. J. O. (1993). "Cognition in Close Relationships." *New Zealand Journal of Psychology* 22:69–81.

Harvey, J. H., and Omarzu, J. (1999). *Minding the Close Relationship.* New York: Cambridge University Press.

Harvey, J. H.; Weber, A. L.; and Orbuch, T. L. (1990). *Interpersonal Accounts.* Oxford: Basil Blackwell.

Harvey, J. H.; Wells, G. L.; and Alvarez, M. D. (1978). "Attribution in the Context of Conflict and Separation in Close Relationships." In *New Directions in Attribution Research,* Vol. 2, ed. J. H. Harvey, W. J. Ickes, and R. F. Kidd. Hillsdale, NJ: Erlbaum.

Heider, F. (1958). *The Psychology of Interpersonal Relations.* New York: John Wiley and Sons.

Higgins, N. C., and Bhatt, G. (2001). "Cultural Moderates the Self-Serving Bias: Etic and Emic Features of Causal Attributions in India and in Canada." *Social Behavior and Personality* 29:49–61.

Holtzworkth-Munroe, A. (1988). "Causal Attributions in Marital Violence." *Clinical Psychology Review* 8:331–334.

Holtzworkth-Munroe, A., and Jacobson, J. J. (1985). "Causal Attributions of Married Couples." *Journal of Personality and Social Psychology* 48:1398–1412.

Jones, E. E., and Davis, K. E. (1972). "The Actor and the Observer: Divergent Perceptions of the Causes of Behavior." In *Attribution: Perceiving the Causes of Behavior,* ed. E. E. Jones, D. Kanouse, H. Kelley, R. Nisbett, S. Valins, and B. Weiner. Morristown, NJ: General Learning Press.

Karney, B. R.; McNulty, J. K.; and Frye, N. (2001). "A Social-Cognitive Perspective on the Maintenance and Deterioration of Relationship Satisfaction." In *Close Romantic Relationships: Maintenance and Enhancement,* ed. J. H. Harvey and A. Wenzel. Mahwah, NJ: Erlbaum.

Kelley, H. H. (1967). "Attribution Theory in Social Psychology." In *Nebraska Symposium on Motivation,* Vol. 15, ed. D. Levine. Lincoln: University of Nebraska Press.

Manusov, V. (2001). "Introduction." In *Attribution, Communication Behavior, and Close Relationships,* ed. V. Manusov and J. H. Harvey. New York: Cambridge University Press.

Manusov, V., and Harvey, J. H., eds. (2001). *Attribution, Communication Behavior, and Close Relationships.* New York: Cambridge University Press.

Manusov, V., and Koenig, J. (2001). "The Content of Attributions in Couples' Communication." In *Attribution, Communication Behavior, and Close Relationships,* ed. V. Manusov and J. H. Harvey. New York: Cambridge University Press.

Newman, H. (1981). "Communication Within Ongoing Intimate Relationships: An Attributional Perspective." *Personality and Social Psychology Bulletin* 7:59–70.

Orvis, B. R.; Kelley, H. H.; and Butler, D. (1976). "Attributional Conflict in Young Couples." In *New Directions in Attribution Research,* Vol. 1, ed. J. Harvey, W. Ickes, and R. Kidd. Hillsdale, NJ: Erlbaum.

Poon, W-T., and Lau, S. (1999). "Coping with Failure: Relationship with Self-Concept Discrepancy and Attributional Style." *Journal of Social Psychology* 139:639–653.

Sabourin, S.; Lussier, Y.; and Wright, J. (1991). "The Effects of Measurement Strategy on Attributions for Marital Problems and Behaviors." *Journal of Applied Social Psychology* 21:734–746.

Sillars, A.; Roberts, L. J.; Dun, T.; and Leonard, K. (2001). "Stepping into the Stream of Thought: Cognition During Marital Conflict." In *Attribution, Communication Behavior, and Close Relationships,* ed. V. Manusov and J. H. Harvey. New York: Cambridge University Press.

Stander, V.; Hsiung, P-C.; and MacDermid, S. (2001). "The Relationship of Attributions to Marital Distress: A Comparison of Mainland Chinese and U.S. Couples." *Journal of Family Psychology* 15:124–134.

Surra, C. A., and Hughes, D. K. (1997). "Commitment Processes Accounts of the Development of Premarital Relationships." *Journal of Marriage and the Family* 59:5–21.

Vangelisti, A. L. (1992). "Communication Problems in Committed Relationships: An Attributional Approach." In *Attributions, Accounts, and Close Relationships,* ed. J. H. Harvery, T. L. Orbuch, and A. L. Weber. New York: Springer-Verlag.

Weiss, R. S. (1975). *Marital Separation.* New York: Basic Books.

HYUNGSHIM JANG
JOHN H. HARVEY

AUNT

Aunt refers to a sister of one's mother or father or the wife of one's uncle. In different cultures, both the terminology and the social significance of an aunt's role in a kinship network vary considerably. In English-speaking countries, the word aunt is typically used for the mother's sister, the father's sister, and an uncle's wife. The lack of distinction between these three kinds of relatives may reflect the structure and organization of modern industrial societies. In Western countries, kinship systems are *bilateral*: Family members trace descent through both females and males, and both parents have equal social weight in determining kinship. In bilateral kinship, neither side of the family has economic or social control over relatives. As a result, for instance, both nieces and nephews have equal inheritance rights (Farber 1966; Radcliffe-Brown 1950). Some families in the United States do not use the *uncle-aunt* terms at all but refer to these relatives by their first names (Coombs 1980).

In contrast to English-speaking countries, many other societies differentiate aunts on the mother's side and on the father's side. The terms also specify whether the relationship is through blood or marriage and indicate the gender of the person through whom a relationship exists. In

Denmark and Sweden, for example, families distinguish between maternal and paternal kinship relations: A *moster* is the mother's sister (and usually also the wife of the mother's brother); a *faster* is a father's sister (and usually also the wife of a father's brother). According to anthropologists, kinship terminology provides guides for proper behavior and usually has social significance (Linton 1964; Schusky 1983). It is not clear, however, why the kin terms of some Western countries refer to aunts (and uncles) more precisely than others.

In many nonindustrialized cultures, distinctions between a paternal aunt and a maternal aunt are important because they reflect authority, ties to the mother's clan, or close kinship bonds. Whether the kinship system is *matrilineal* (descent is traced through females) or *patrilineal* (descent is traced through males), the father's sister is treated as a sort of female father. Among the Bunyoro, Swazi, and Ashanti in Africa, as well as Australian aboriginal tribes, for example, the father's sister may discipline her brothers' children, commands the same respect and authority as her brother, and arranges her nephew's marriage or may forbid it if the nephew chooses an unacceptable mate (Beattie 1960; Fortes 1969; Hart and Pilling 1960; Kuper 1950; Reed 1975).

See also: COUSINS; KINSHIP; SIBLING RELATIONSHIPS; UNCLE

Bibliography

Beattie, J. (1960). *Bunyoro: An African Kingdom.* New York: Holt, Rinehart, and Winston.

Coombs, G. (1980). "Variant Usage in American Kinship: The Nomenclator Effect." In *The Versatility of Kinship,* ed. L. S. Cordell and S. Beckerman. New York: Academic Press.

Farber, B., ed. (1966). *Kinship and Family Organization.* New York: John Wiley & Sons.

Fortes, M. (1969). *Kinship and the Social Order: The Legacy of Lewis Henry Morgan.* Chicago: Aldine Publishing.

Hart, C. W. M., and Pilling, A. R. (1960). *The Tiwi of North Australia.* New York: Holt, Rinehart, and Winston.

Kuper, H. (1950). "Kinship among the Swazi." In *African Systems of Kinship and Marriage,* ed. A. R. Radcliffe-Brown and D. Forde. New York: Oxford University Press.

Linton, R. (1964). *The Study of Man.* 1936. Reprint, New York: Appleton-Century-Crofts.

Radcliffe-Brown, A. R. (1950). "Introduction." In *African Systems of Kinship and Marriage,* ed. A. R. Radcliffe-Brown and D. Forde. New York: Oxford University Press.

Reed, E. (1975). *Woman's Evolution: From Matriarchal Clan to Patriarchal Family.* New York: Pathfinder Press.

Schusky, E. L. (1983). *Manual for Kinship Analysis,* 2nd edition. Lanham, MD: University Press of America.

NIJOLE V. BENOKRAITIS

AUSTRALIA

As in most Western countries, family life in Australia has changed dramatically over the last few decades. Some changes in family trends—including increases in divorce, more cohabitation, and the falling fertility rate—have sparked misgivings about the direction that marriage and family life is heading. Such issues are best understood within a historical framework. Is today different from earlier periods of Australia's history of white settlement? Was the post-World War II period an aberration? Before attempting to answer these questions, it is important to recognize that family life before white settlement was markedly different from any period thereafter.

Indigenous Australian Families

For many thousands of years before white settlement, virtually all aspects of life for the indigenous Australians—including relationships—were regulated by a complex kinship system in which children were the responsibility of the entire system rather than only the biological parents.

This complex kinship system lost prominence in Australia during the first forty years of white settlement, when the size of the indigenous population declined rapidly (Jackson 1988). Today, indigenous Australians represent about 2 percent of the total population. The kinship system continues in varying degrees—along with a strong social identity (Bourke 1993; Kolar and Soriano 2000). Thus, indigenous Australians may define family very broadly, for example, as "various arrangements people make to ensure that the young are nurtured and people looked after" (O'Donoghue 1993).

White Settlement

Marriage and family life among the early white settlers were very much shaped by the circumstances of their settlement and laws of their country of origin. White settlement began in 1788 with the arrival of convicts transported from Great Britain to penal colonies in Australia, along with officials and military personnel. In the early days men dramatically outnumbered women. By 1836 around 100,000 convicts had arrived, of whom only 13,000 were female.

During this time, no provisions were made for a wife and family to follow male convicts except for those with life sentences. In 1812, however, an experimental group of ten women who were seen as industrious and of good character were sent out to join their convict husbands (Jose and Carter 1925). Married convicts who had been separated from their spouses for seven years were permitted to remarry. As the demand for labor increased, convicts were sent out more frequently, with the numbers peaking in 1833. All transportation had ceased by 1868.

From the 1830s onwards, free immigrants became the dominant source of population growth. The gold rushes of the 1850s extended this period of rapid population growth until the late 1850s (Jackson 1988). Although more men than women were free immigrants, the imbalance was not as great as it had been for the convict population.

In the nineteenth century migrants were mostly from Britain and Ireland. To exclude non-Europeans, the Immigration Restrictions Act was introduced soon after Federation (in 1901). A strict English-language dictation test was used to retain the Anglo-Celtic profile. A surge of European migrants after World War II sparked the beginning of ethnic diversity. Gradually, the government relaxed the rules on the migration of non-Europeans. Nevertheless, it was not until the early 1970s that the *White Australia Policy* was formally abolished. Australia has since become one of the most ethnically diverse countries in the world, although the proportion of Australians who were born overseas was exactly the same in 1901 and 1996 (22.8 percent) (Hartley 1995; Hugo 2001).

Families in the twentieth century were affected by other significant demographic and economic changes. For example, urbanization continued throughout the century. The rural population fell from about 40 percent to less than 15 percent, with a concomitant fall in the proportion of workers in agriculture—from around 33 percent to less than 5 percent. The proportion of workers in the manufacturing industry began to fall in the second half of the century from nearly 30 percent to around 13 percent at the close of the century (Hugo 2001).

Family Trends: A Long-Term Perspective

Recent family-related trends that seem alarming today may seem less so if viewed in the context of changes that have occurred over the last 200 years. Key areas of change in family life in Australia include family formation, dissolution, and reformation; family diversity; and gender roles. These trends not only interact with each other but also represent outcomes of, and factors contributing to, other social developments.

Cohabitation. One issue that has led to misgivings about the future of marriage concerns the rising proportion of couples who are living together without having married (here called *cohabiting*). The proportion of all couples who were cohabiting almost doubled from 5 percent in 1982 to 9 percent in 1997. Although the increase was significant, these figures nevertheless still indicate that the overwhelming majority of couples who live together are married.

However, cohabitation in the early nineteenth century was even more common, with one 1806 report about Sydney suggesting that only 28 percent of adult women were married, and most of the rest were cohabiting. Incumbent governors resolved to restore the regulation of partnerships through marriage—an objective that was substantially achieved by 1860 (Carmichael 1988).

Cohabitation now takes many forms, including unions without commitment, replacements for marriage, and trial marriages. More and more couples are living together before they get married, apparently part of other dramatic changes in social attitudes (McDonald 1995). By the late 1990s around two-thirds of couples who married had already been living together—a situation that applied to less than one-quarter of marrying couples some twenty years earlier (ABS 2000a).

Marriage. Couples are now marrying later because increasing numbers are living together before marriage or advancing their educations. Between 1971 and 1999, the median age at first marriage increased from 21.1 to 26.4 for women and 23.4 to 28.2 years for men (Hugo 2001). In addition, the last few decades have seen a progressive rise in the proportion of men and women who never marry. In the 1950s and 1960s fewer than 10 percent of men and women never married (McDonald, Ruzicka, and Pyne 1987). Today, this applies to around 25 percent of men and women (ABS 2000a).

Although the magnitude of the modern swing from early to late marriages has no historical precedent (McDonald 1995), some of these trends are by no means new. In the second half of the nineteenth century, the proportion of women who married declined, and age at first marriage rose for both men and women (Carmichael 1988; Jackson 1988).

In the 1950s and 1960s early marriage was associated with leaving the parental home to form a new household and establish independence from parents, thus symbolizing the transition to adulthood. However, this tendency to marry early weakened in the 1970s, in line with the increasing emphasis placed on individual growth and freedom (Carmichael 1988; Gilding 1997).

Since the 1970s, dramatic changes have occurred in the education and employment of young people, with increasing numbers completing high school and going on to post-secondary education, and decreasing numbers of early school leavers finding full-time paid work. Few now leave the family home to marry, and more and more young people are living with their parents for support while studying. At the same time, many, particularly Anglo-Australians, also live independently in various arrangements (Hartley and de Vaus 1997; McDonald 1995).

Having children. While out-of-wedlock births were more common during the early period of white settlement than they are today (Carmichael 1995), the rate has risen with the increasing popularity of cohabitation—from about 5 percent of all births in the 1950s and 1960s to around 30 percent by the end of the 1990s. Paternity is now acknowledged on the birth certificates of almost 90 percent of babies born out of wedlock (ABS 2000b), compared to 68 percent in 1980 (ABS 1997).

Most births occur within marriage, but the total fertility rate is falling. While this trend has occurred before, the recent fall in fertility is unprecedented. Fertility fell in the second half of the nineteenth

century first in response to the decline in marriage rates, and later though increasing knowledge and acceptance of contraception, a period of massive unemployment (in the 1890s), and gradual implementation of compulsory schooling and abolition of child labor—leading children to become an expense rather than economic asset (Gilding 1991; Caldwell, McDonald, and Ruzicka 1982).

Figure 1 shows the trends in fertility across the twentieth century, where troughs and peaks reflect socioeconomic forces of the time. The Great Depression marked an early low point in fertility, with 2.1 babies per woman born in 1934. The end of World War II sparked the baby boom years, with the fertility rate peaking at 3.5 in 1961. An overall downward trend then reappeared, hitting a low of 1.75 babies per woman in 1999 (ABS 2000).

Specifically, the proportion of women between the ages of forty and forty-four who gave birth to at least four children has decreased (from 26 percent for those born in the late 1930s to 13 percent for those born in the early to mid-1950s), while the proportion of women who never had children increased (from 8 percent to 12 percent for the same generations) (ABS 1999). Furthermore, it is estimated at least one in five women who are currently in their early childbearing years will not have children. This, too, represents a recurring trend. Thirty-one percent of all women born at the turn of the twentieth century had not given birth by the time they were forty-five (Merlo and Rowland 2000).

Contemporary falls in fertility can be explained by multiple interacting factors, including the introduction of the contraceptive pill and the increased availability of legal abortion, improvements in the education levels of young women, and the increasing participation of married women in paid employment. Women also face substantial opportunity costs if they leave work to care for a child (Gray and Chapman 2001), and, conversely, some lose the chance to have children if they delay childbearing and then separate from their partner (Qu, Weston, and Kilmartin 2000). Some evidence also suggests a decline in the perceived importance attached to having children (de Vaus 1997), although most young people apparently intend to marry and have children (McCabe and Cummins 1998).

The combination of falling fertility and increasing longevity is creating an aging of the population

FIGURE 1

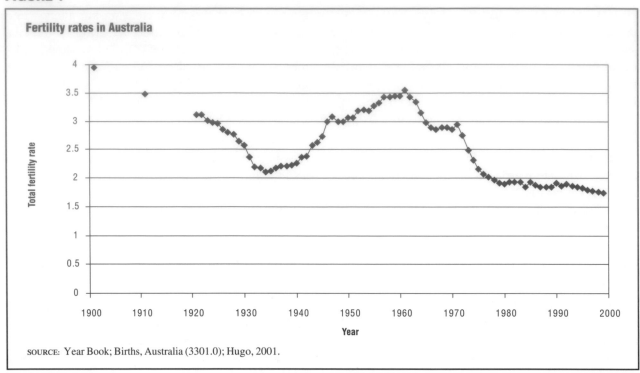

Fertility rates in Australia

SOURCE: Year Book; Births, Australia (3301.0); Hugo, 2001.

that carries with it economic and social challenges (e.g., the difficulties of supporting a burgeoning retired population and demands on health care and other needs of the elderly).

Divorce. In the early years of white settlement, divorce was difficult to obtain, expensive, and rare. Divorce legislation was not introduced by individual colonies until between 1858 and 1873, with matrimonial misconduct (which includes adultery, cruelty, or desertion, and acts such as incest, bigamy, or rape) being the key grounds. Over the years, the forms of misconduct accepted as grounds for divorce widened in all states (Carmichael and McDonald 1986).

The divorce rate rose slightly in the 1920s to early 1940s, then peaked in 1947, as some hasty wartime marriages were dissolved (Carmichael and McDonald 1986). A further rise followed the introduction of a uniform law across the states and territories in 1959, which allowed couples to divorce after five years of separation.

However, the most dramatic increase occurred when the Family Law Act (1975) was introduced. "Irretrievable breakdown," as evidenced by one year of separation after filing for divorce, became the only ground for divorce. Prior long-term separations were thus formalized, and some divorces

were brought forward, contributing to a peak of almost nineteen divorces per 1,000 married men and women in 1976. More recently, the rate has increased from 10.6 per 1,000 married men and women in 1987 to 12.7 in 1999. Now more than 40 percent of marriages are expected to end in divorce. Figure 2 shows that the number of children under eighteen years old who are involved in divorce has also increased (from 13,000 in 1966 to 53,000 in 1999) (ABS 1994, 2000a).

Although many people remarry after divorce, remarriage rates have declined in all age groups, mostly by more than 50 percent (ABS 1998)—a trend that is likely to reflect a preference for cohabitation. Remarriages tend to be less stable than first marriages, particularly for those who are quite young when they remarry (de Vaus 1997).

Family Diversity

Together, these trends indicate that Australians at the end of the 1990s had a far greater choice of lifestyles regarding forming relationships, having children, and leaving marriages. This has led to an increase in the diversity of family types. Changes in the labor market and the increase in ethnic diversity in Australia have also expanded the variety of family lifestyles in Australia today—although once

FIGURE 2

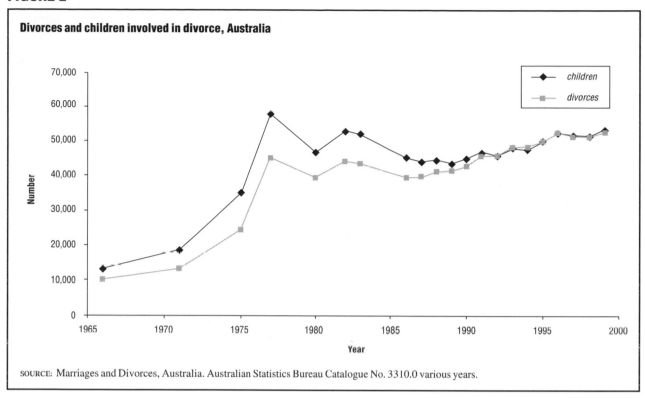

Divorces and children involved in divorce, Australia

SOURCE: Marriages and Divorces, Australia. Australian Statistics Bureau Catalogue No. 3310.0 various years.

again, some areas of current diversity (for example, lone-parent families) were apparent more than a century ago despite the limited choice available then. A few examples of the diversity characterizing Australian families are provided below.

Family types. With the increase in relationship breakdown, the proportion of families with dependent children that are headed by one parent has increased progressively (from 15% in 1986 to 21% today). However, sole-parent families were relatively common 100 years ago. For instance, in 1891 in the state of Victoria, this circumstance represented nearly 17 percent of all families with dependent children (McDonald 1995). Nevertheless, *sole father* families with dependent children are less common today (6% in 2000) than in 1891 (38%), reflecting the high levels of maternal mortality in the nineteenth century (ABS 2000; McDonald 1995).

As more couples dissolve their relationship and acquire new partners, many children are being raised in stepfamilies for varying lengths of time. Around 9 percent of couple families with children under eighteen are stepfamilies (ABS 1998). However, stepparents were even more common 100 years ago than they are today, although the leading cause underlying stepparenting has changed from death of natural parent to divorce (McDonald 1995).

Multicultural families. Increasing cultural diversity in Australia has expanded the range of family lifestyle patterns and religious affiliations. For example, while the vast majority of family households in Australia comprise only one family, disproportionate numbers in some cultural groups, including Southern European, Middle Eastern, and Asian groups as well as indigenous Australians live in extended family households (Millward and de Vaus 1997). Approximately 28 percent of all marriages are intermarriages—mostly involving Australian-born men and women marrying partners born overseas (ABS 1999).

The numbers of Buddhists, Hindus, and Muslims increased by the end of the 1990s, although less than 3 percent of the total population identify with these religions (Bouma 1997). Although Christianity continues to predominate, the percentage of the population describing themselves as Christian fell from 96 percent in 1901 to 71 percent in 1996. During the same period, the percentage describing themselves as not religious increased from 0.4 percent to 17 percent.

Work and family. The percentage of married women aged twenty to twenty-four and twenty-five to thirty-four in the labor force increased from 4 to 5 percent in 1933 to 57 and 49 percent, respectively, in 1981. Today, around two-thirds of married women in these age groups are employed outside the home. This dramatic change has led to increased concern about balancing work and family life (Wolcott and Glezer 1995). Although surveys repeatedly show that domestic tasks are shared along gender lines, some evidence suggests that this division of gender roles is weakening (Wolcott 1997).

The marked increase in the labor force participation of women has led to an increase in the number of children being cared for by people other than their parents, in both formal (regulated, paid care) and informal (provided by family or unrelated others, usually unpaid) situations. Today, half of children under age twelve use some type of childcare (ABS 2000c). Since the late 1980s, the proportion of children using formal care has increased progressively, while the proportion of children using informal care has changed little. Of the children using informal care, nearly 60 percent are cared for by grandparents alone or in combination with other forms of care.

Conclusion

The traditional family as we tend to understand it today has not been with us throughout history. Prior to white settlement, complex kinship systems regulated virtually all aspects of life of aborigines in Australia. Although many aspects of this management have eroded, a distinctive aboriginal family form continues to exist today, reflecting the resilience of this form of family system—a point noted by McDonald (1995).

The 200 years of white settlement in Australia have seen huge changes in the population and land use. As wave after wave of new settlers reached Australia's shores, the makeup of Australian families underwent dramatic transformations. But in some respects, the wheel has turned full circle. For instance, high rates of cohabitation and sole-parent families—which are sometimes seen as threats to the survival of the family—were also quite common in the pioneering period, although the circumstances surrounding them are different than they were then.

Many of the modern changes have created misgivings about the future of the family, but its failure to change can be a bigger threat to survival than change itself. The pattern of fluctuations across the past century reflects the capacity of the family to enact and respond to change, and in doing so, reflects the resilience of the family as an institution.

See also: KINSHIP

Bibliography

ABS. (1997). *Births, Australia 1995,* Catalogue No. 3301.0. Canberra, ACT: Australian Bureau of Statistics.

ABS. (1998). *Marriages and Divorces, Australia 1997,* Catalogue No. 3310.0. Canberra, ACT: Australian Bureau of Statistics.

ABS. (1999). *Marriages and Divorces, Australia 1999,* Catalogue No. 3310.0. Canberra, ACT: Australian Bureau of Statistics.

ABS. (2000a). *Marriages and Divorces, Australia 1999,* Catalogue No. 3310.0. Canberra, ACT: Australian Bureau of Statistics.

ABS. (2000b). *Births, Australia 1999,* Catalogue No. 3301.0. Canberra, ACT: Australian Bureau of Statistics.

ABS. (2000c). *Child Care, Australia 1999,* Catalogue No. 4402.0. Canberra, ACT: Australian Bureau of Statistics.

Bouma, G. D. (1997). "Increasing Diversity in Religious Identification in Australia: Comparing 1947, 1991, and 1996 Census Reports." *People and Place* 5(3):12–18.

Bourke, E. (1993). "The First Australians: Kinship, Family and Identity." *Family Matters* 35 (August):4–6.

Caldwell, J. C.; McDonald, P. F.; and Ruzicka, L. T. (1982). "Nuptiality and Fertility in Australia, 1921–1976." In *Proceedings of a Seminar Held in Bruges, Belgium, 8–11 January 1979,* ed. L. T. Ruzicka. Liege: International Union for the Scientific Study of Population.

Carmichael, G. A. (1988). *With This Ring: First Marriage Patterns, Trends, and Prospects in Australia.* Canberra: Department of Demography, Australian National University and Australian Institute of Family Studies.

Carmichael, G. A., and McDonald, P. F. (1986). "The Rise and Fall (?) of Divorce in Australia, 1968–1985." In *Australian Population Association. Conference Proceedings.* Adelaide, SA: Flinders University of South Australia.

de Vaus, D. (1997). "Family Values in the Nineties." *Family Matters* 48 (Spring-Summer):5–10.

Gilding, M. (1991). *The Making and Breaking of the Australian Family*. North Sydney, NSW: Allen and Unwin.

Gilding, M. (1997). *Australian Families: A Comparative Perspective*. Melbourne, VIC: Addison, Wesley, and Longman.

Gray, M., and Chapman, B., (2001). "Forgone Earnings from Child Rearing." *Family Matters* 58 (August):4–9.

Hartley, R. (1995). "Families, Values and Change: Setting the Scene." In *Families and Cultural Diversity in Australia*, ed. R. Hartley. St. Leonards, NSW: Allen and Unwin in Association with Australia Institute of Family Studies.

Hartley, R., and de Vaus, D. (1997). "Young People." *Australian Family Profile*, ed. D. de Vaus and I. Wolcott. Melbourne, VIC: Australian Institute of Family Studies.

Hugo, G. (2001). "Centenary Article—A Century of Population Change in Australia." In *Year Book Australia 2001*. Canberra, ACT: Australian Bureau of Statistics.

Jackson, R. V. (1988). *Population History of Australia*. Fitzroy, VIC: McPhee Gribble/Penguin Books.

Jose, A. W., and Carter, H. J. (1925). *Australian Encyclopaedia*. Sydney: Angus and Robertson.

Kolar, V., and Soriano, G. (2000). *Parenting in Australian Families: A Comparative Study of Anglo, Torres Strait Islander, and Vietnamese Communities*. Melbourne, VIC: Australian Institute of Family Studies.

McDonald. P. (1995). *Families in Australia: A Socio-Demographic Perspective*. Melbourne, VIC. Australian Institute of Family Studies.

McDonald, P.; Ruzicka, L.; and Pyne, P. (1987). "Marriage, Fertility, and Mortality." In *Australians: Historical Statistics*, ed. W. Vamplew. Broadway, NSW: Fairfax, Syme and Weldon.

Merlo R., and Rowland, D. (2000). "The Prevalence of Childlessness in Australia." *People and Place* 8(2):21–32.

O'Donoghue, L. (1993). " Aboriginal Families and ATSIC." *Family Matters* 35 (August):14–15.

Qu, L.; Weston, R.; and Kilmartin, C. (2000). "Children? No Children? The Effect of Changing Personal Relationships on Decisions about Having Children." *Family Matters* 57 (Spring-Summer):44–49.

Wolcott, I., and Glezer, H. (1995). *Work and Family Life: Achieving Integration*. Melbourne, VIC: Australian Institute of Family Studies.

Wolcott, I. (1997). "Work and Family." In *Australian Family Profile,* ed. D. de Vaus and I. Wolcott. Melbourne, VIC: Australian Institute of Family Studies.

RUTH E. WESTON
ROBYN PARKER
LIXIA QU

AUSTRIA

The Republic of Austria is one of Europe's smaller countries, covering a landlocked area somewhat less than that of Hungary or Portugal. The 2001 census population of the country was 8.0 million, approximately the same as that of Sweden or Bulgaria.

Family Values

Abundant evidence suggests that the family and family-related values enjoy approval in all social groups and age cohorts. Three-quarters of Austrians hold that they need a family to be happy (Schulz 1996); results from the Family and Fertility Survey 1996 indicate that nine out of ten Austrians (but only three-fourths of Germans) between the ages of twenty-one and thirty-nine would like to see more weight given to family life in the future (Fux and Pfeiffer 1999). Austrians also view the traditional nuclear family as the standard, that is, *family* defined as a social group consisting of a man and a woman (married to each other) as parents and their children. Asked about the ideal family size, almost two-thirds of Austrians prefer two children, with almost another third favoring three children; only 1 percent consider childlessness as the best way of life. Around 80 percent in the Population Policy Acceptance Survey view the increasing number of divorces as a negative trend in society. However, Austrians view divorces between childless couples much less negatively, and a great majority opposes more restrictive divorce laws.

Compared to other European societies, Austrians appear to hold conservative attitudes toward abortion and divorce. Furthermore, according to the European Value Study, they give greater support to the traditional separation of gender roles and the homemaker role for mothers. At the same time, they highly appreciate the financial aspect of women's contribution to household income. There seems to be broad agreement—even among the older generation—that married women should be working outside home in the period between the wedding and the birth of the first child, as well as in the period after the children have left school. However, Austrians remain conservative about employment outside the home for women with small children. More than 80 percent agree that preschool children suffer when their mothers are employed for pay (Fux and Pfeiffer 1999).

A large majority of Austrians disapprove of abortion (between 83% and 67% in various surveys)—which can be legally performed within the first three months of pregnancy if the mother is unmarried or the couple does not want any more children. A minority of one-third oppose abortion in case of an expected birth defect.

Thus, Austrians' subjective attitudes could not be much more positive toward marriage and family, albeit defined in a rather traditional mode. At the same time, the evidence suggests a wide variety of existing living arrangements, including consensual unions and couples living apart together—i.e., married couples and families maintaining separate households. It also points to a growing number of more complex family forms, including continuation marriages—i.e., remarriage and the formation of a new family following divorce and family disruption—and middle-aged unmarried couples with children from previous relationships.

Sociodemographic Trends

In general, trends in Austria parallel those in most other (Western) European countries (Kytir and Münz 1999). Couples delay the birth of the first child; childlessness is increasing, but most women do become mothers; out-of-wedlock births are increasing; the age at first marriage is rising; a growing proportion of people do not marry at all; the number of divorces is growing; and life expectancy is higher than ever.

After an extended period of nearly zero population growth between the early 1970s and the late 1980s, the population increase accelerated again when a large group of females reached childbearing age, and a growing number of immigrant foreign workers and refugees and their families entered the country. In the foreseeable future, a long period of stable or even reduced population is projected.

Since 1963, fertility has declined more or less continuously. In 1999, the birth rate reached an all-time low of 1.31 children per woman—one of the lowest in the world, only slightly higher than in Spain, Italy, Greece, and the Czech Republic. In 2000 there was a slight increase to 1.34 children per woman. Families with four or more children have almost completely disappeared among groups born after 1940. The mean age of mothers at first birth (twenty-seven years in 1998) is still low, for example, two years younger than in the Netherlands.

Obviously, ideal and actual family sizes differ greatly. This discrepancy can partly be explained because women and couples postpone their desire to have children. Women want to enter the labor force or remain there, and they view successful parenthood as difficult to combine with gainful employment. In multiple cases, what were intended to be temporary postponements result in lifelong childlessness (Lutz 2000).

With 31 percent of births by unmarried women, Austria ranks lower than Scandinavian countries, but higher than Southern Europe. Distinct regional differences in attitudes toward out-of-wedlock births are reflected in ancient rural inheritance patterns and religious traditions. In some parts of Austria, it is traditional and acceptable for single women to have children, and the percentage of illegitimate first-borns may be as high as 75 percent. The mother's chances of later marriage are not seriously affected. The social pattern whereby women consciously reject marriage but not motherhood is found only in small, urban, progressive groups.

Despite the widespread use of birth control, 40 percent of all first births are described in retrospect as "unplanned" (Family Fertility Survey 1996, cited in Kytir and Münz 1999). In any case, the transition to parenthood is a critical life event; currently, almost all mothers of a newborn child—including those with higher levels of education—leave their paid employment at least temporarily (for one year or longer). At the same time, couples often return to a gender-oriented traditional division of labor with fathers assuming responsibility for supporting the family financially (Beham 1999).

Living Arrangements

Marriage as a legal institution is losing ground. Since the 1960s, age-specific marriage rates (taking

A family in the yard of a farmhouse in Hunspach, Austria. Traditional family structures and values are held in high regard among a majority of Austrians. Seventy-five percent of the population considers a family to be essential to happiness.
MARC GARANGER/CORBIS

into account the age structure of the population) have dropped by a half. This trend signals profound structural and behavioral changes: extended education; more insecure part-time and flexible jobs; and new self-fulfillment values that do not promote early commitment. It is estimated (Kytir and Münz 1999) that among the younger generation now in their late teens or early twenties, the number of life-long never married men and women could reach 30 and 25 percent, respectively.

The divorce rate has increased steadily since the end of the 1960s. As of the early twenty-first century, statistics suggested that four out of ten marriages would end in divorce, up from only two in the early 1970s. There is a clear relationship between the number of children in a marriage and the probability of divorce—more than one-third of all terminated marriages were childless as of 2000. The most frequently cited reasons for divorce are unfulfilled demands for personal happiness, harmony, and sexual fulfillment (Benard and Schlaffer 1995).

At least among young people, other forms of cohabitation are replacing legally authorized marriage. A large majority of all childless young couples start their conjugal life in consensual unions. As standard behavior, this is accepted even by a majority of elderly people (Prinz 1998). At the same time, more people in their twenties are remaining in the parental household. Consequently, the life phase of postadolescence (from nineteen to under thirty years) has changed in character. Since the mid-1970s the mean age at first marriage has increased considerably and was as of 2000 over twenty-seven years for women and thirty for men (which is still low by Scandinavian standards). However, the birth of a child still leads to marriage in many cases; three-fourths of all one-year-old children live with both parents. Rosemarie Nave-Herz (1989) speaks of a "child-oriented marriage pattern."

The most striking feature of household composition is the high rate of intergenerational co-residence: 22 percent of Austrians live in households consisting of at least three adults (usually parents and grandparents) plus children; this is approximately the same rate as in Ireland, Portugal, and Spain, and three times higher than in Germany, Denmark, the United Kingdom, and the Netherlands (European Commission household panel 1995, cited in Fotakis 2000).

The family life of the various ethnic groups (Turks, Serbs, Croats, etc.) living in Austria probably deviates from the social patterns described above. Unfortunately, this research area has been neglected, although foreign families make up an increasing proportion of the population: The proportion of marriages including at least one non-Austrian partner is around 20 percent (2000); one out of five newborn babies has at least one foreign parent.

Consequences of Increased Life Expectancy

The enormous reduction in mortality in the course of the twentieth century has had massive repercussions on family life: The survival of all newborn children is practically guaranteed; the smaller number of children reduces drastically the life phase dominated by childcare; and despite the rising divorce rate, more couples than ever remain married for many years. Furthermore, Austrians now may well live for thirty or so years in a three- or even four-generation family.

This development has sparked a debate on the effects of these longstanding multigenerational constellations, such as money transfers and assistance patterns (Rosenmayr 1999). For instance, the popular belief is that many women between forty and sixty are caught between competing responsibilities for children and grandchildren and their aging parents (*sandwich generation*). Empirically, however, only about one-fourth of middle-aged women are actually in this situation (Hörl and Kytir 1998).

Family and Social Policy

In comparison with most other European countries, Austria's family-related social policy expenditures are generous. The European Commission household panel (1996, cited in Giorgi 1999) found that for the poorest households, family and other transfer payments contribute a substantial part (31%) of household income. Moreover, kindergartens (where available) are highly subsidized or free. Education (including schoolbooks and travel expenses) is free up through the secondary level; university fees were not collected until 2001.

A key question in modern family policy is how women are able to combine parenthood with participation in the labor market. Few possibilities are available for flexible labor arrangements for mothers, and deficits remain in the supply of kindergartens, particularly for children under five years old and in rural areas.

In January 2002 a new type of child allowance (*Kinderbetreuungsgeld*) became available. The allowance (amounting to 436 euro per month, per child) is not conditional on prior employment of the parents and will be paid for three years (provided that both parents share childcare responsibilities; otherwise for two-and-a-half years). In addition, the parent (usually the mother) may be employed out of the home. The goal of this new legislation is to improve the flexibility in combining work and family tasks.

Quality of Marital and Family Relations

The dominant pattern of family life is still a household of parents and one or more children, at least until parents reach the age of fifty. However, many scholars have observed that people are more freely defining the family as a group and personalizing the conjugal relationship at the same time that traditional roles are changing (Beck-Gernsheim 1998; Goldberg 1998; Schulz 1996; Weiss 1995). Each family member demands that others recognize his or her very own concept of what a family is. Individual claims for happiness are considered normal. Thus, marital partners most frequently mention as central gratifications in relationships sexuality, communication, and the feelings of security, protection, and of being loved.

Likewise, the wish to have children is rooted in the desire to be needed and to give life a deeper meaning. In the past several decades emotional bonding between fathers and children seems to have become more intense, resulting, for example in increased joint leisure activities (Werneck 1996).

A change towards more egalitarian sex-role attitudes has taken place, too. Men's daily behavior reflects this shift only slightly because women still perform the major proportion of domestic work (Bacher and Wilk 1996).

Intergenerational relationships are characterized by more emotional and nonhierarchical interactions and self-determination on the part of children, who are allowed to make their own decisions regarding clothing, hairstyle, leisure activities, and other areas. Grandparents and grandchildren have regular contact, highly valued by both sides (Wilk 1993). Little is known, however, about the impact of these relationships in such areas as the transfer of values.

Despite the emphasis on highly individualized and emotionalized family relations, long-term intergenerational solidarity is unbroken. Providing care, support, and shelter for the young, the old, the sick, and the disabled remains one of the most important tasks that families fulfill for society.

Bibliography

Bacher, J., and Wilk, L. (1996). "Geschlechtsspezifische Arbeitsteilung—Ausmaß und Bedingungen männlicher Mitarbeit im Haushalt." In *Österreich im Wandel: Werte, Lebensformen und Lebensqualität 1986 bis 1993,* ed. M. Haller, K. Holm, K. M. Müller, W. Schulz, and E. Cyba. Vienna: Verlag für Geschichte und Politik.

Beck-Gernsheim, E. (1998). *Was kommt nach der Familie? Einblicke in neue Lebensformen.* Munich. Beck.

Beham, M. (1999). "Übergang zur Elternschaft." In *4. Österreichischer Familienbericht,* ed. Bundesministerium für Umwelt, Jugend und Familie. Vienna.

Benard, C., and Schlaffer, E. (1995). *Sind Sie noch zu retten? Warum Ihre Ehe schief ging.* Vienna: Deuticke.

Fotakis, C. (2000). "Wie sozial ist Europa?" *Family Observer* 2:32–40.

Fux, B., and Pfeiffer, C. (1999). "Ehe, Familie, Kinderzahl: Gesellschaftliche Einstellungen und individuelle Zielvorstellungen." In *4. Österreichischer Familienbericht,* ed. Bundesministerium für Umwelt, Jugend und Familie. Vienna.

Giorgi, L. (1999). "Über die soziale Lage österreichischer Familien." In *4. Österreichischer Familienbericht,* ed. Bundesministerium für Umwelt, Jugend und Familie. Vienna.

Goldberg, C. (1998). "Familie in der Post-Moderne." In *Postmodernes Österreich?,* ed. M. Preglau and R. Richter. Vienna: Signum.

Hörl, J., and Kytir, J. (1998). "Die 'Sandwich-Generation': Soziale Realität oder gerontologischer Mythos? Basisdaten zur Generationenstruktur der Frauen mittleren Alters in Österreich." *Kölner Zeitschrift für Soziologie und Sozialpsychologie* 50:730–741.

Kytir, J., and Münz, R. (1999). "Langfristige demografische Entwicklungen und aktuelle Trends." In *4. Österreichischer Familienbericht,* ed. Bundesministerium für Umwelt, Jugend und Familie. Vienna.

Lutz, W. (2000). "Determinants of Low Fertility and Ageing Prospects for Europe." In *Family Issues between Gender and Generations,* ed. European Commission. Luxembourg: Office for Official Publications of the European Communities.

Nave-Herz, R. (1989). "Zeitgeschichtlicher Bedeutungswandel von Ehe und Familie in der Bundesrepublik Deutschland." In *Handbuch der Familien- und Jugendforschung, Band 1,* ed. R. Nave-Herz and M. Markefka. Neuwied: Luchterhand.

Prinz, C. (1998). "Lebensgemeinschaften mit Kindern in europäischer Perspektive." In *Lebens- und Familienformen—Tatsachen und Normen,* ed. L. A. Vaskovics and H. Schattovits. Vienna: Österreichisches Institut für Familienforschung.

Rosenmayr, L. (1999). "Über Generationen. Begriffe, Datenbezug und sozialpolitische Praxisrelevanz." In *Sozialpolitik und Ökologieprobleme der Zukunft,* ed. H. Löffler and E. W. Streissler. Vienna: Verlag der Österreichischen Akademie der Wissenschaften.

Schulz, W. (1996). "Wertorientierungen im Bereich von Ehe und Familie." In *Österreich im Wandel: Werte, Lebensformen und Lebensqualität 1986 bis 1993,* ed. M. Haller, K. Holm, K.M. Müller, W. Schulz, and E. Cyba. Vienna: Verlag für Geschichte und Politik.

Weiss, H. (1995). "Liebesauffassungen der Geschlechter. Veränderungen in Partnerschaft und Liebe." *Soziale Welt* 46:119–137.

Werneck, H. (1996). "Übergang zur Vaterschaft. Eine empirische Längsschnittstudie auf der Suche nach den 'Neuen Vätern'." Ph.D. diss. University of Vienna.

Wilk, L. (1993). "Großeltern und Enkelkinder." In *Generationsbeziehungen in postmodernen Gesellschaften,* ed. K. Lüscher and F. Schultheis. Constance: Universitätsverlag.

JOSEF HÖRL

B

BASQUE FAMILIES

Any discussion of the Basque family must begin by acknowledging that Basque families can and do exist outside the Basque country. They differ even within the Basque country because sociological and political definitions are framed by the influence of two different states, Spain and France. The region known as the Basque country comprises an area of a hundred square miles (about the size of the state of Rhode Island) historically divided into seven provinces. Three of the provinces are in France (Behe-Nafarroa, Lapurdi, and Zuberoa), and four are in Spain (Araba, Bizkaia, Gipuzkoa, and Navarra). The provinces in France are contained within the official Département des Pyrénées-Atlantiques.

Political changes in Spain since the death of Francisco Franco in 1975 have affected the names used to refer to the provinces there. With the Spanish Constitution of 1978, Araba, Bizkaia, and Gipuzkoa became the Autonomous Community of Euskadi, and Navarra became the Autonomous Community of Navarra. In the Basque language, Euskara, the provinces on the French side of the border are called Iparralde "the north side," and those in Spain are Hegoalde, "the south side." Many Basques refer to the Basque country as a whole (the traditional seven provinces) as Euskal Herria, the Basque Country. The variation in the spelling of Navarra (the Spanish spelling) and Nafarroa (the Basque spelling in Behe-Nafarroa) is representative of political differences of opinion that have long existed between Navarra and the provinces now known as Euskadi.

Euskara has played an important role in many aspects of Basque life and politics, but the language had no standardized spelling for many centuries. During the mid-twentieth century, the process of standardization began in earnest. As a result, any search for information about the Basque provinces must take into account the variable spellings for each: Araba (Alava); Behe-Nafarroa (Basse-Navarre); Bizkaia (Vizcaya, Biscay); Gipuzkoa (Guipúzcoa); Lapurdi (Laburdi, Labourd); Navarra (Nafarroa, Navarre); and Zuberoa (Xiberoa, Soule).

The Basque history of migration means that there are also populations in the Americas, the Philippines, Australia, and other parts of the world who identify themselves as Basque. However, after the second generation, many of the family traits of these groups are strongly influenced by the culture in which they are living. The Basque provinces in rural agricultural Iparralde are very small, and the population is about one-tenth that of the provinces in Spain. For that reason, the Basque family described here is assumed to dwell in Hegoalde, unless otherwise noted.

Family Size

Basque families are predominantly Catholic, and because of this many people are surprised to learn that the Basque country has the lowest birth rate in Spain, which in turn has one of the lowest fertility rates in the world (Reher 1997). During the regime

A Basque family works together processing cheese. Families in rural households of the Basque country are typically multigenerational, sometimes including live-in grandparents. GALEN ROWELL/CORBIS

of Francisco Franco, several laws were passed that affected families in many ways. The 1938 Labor Charter prohibited married women from working outside the home, so couples got in the habit of postponing marriage so that the woman might continue to earn an income. The right to work outside the home was restored in 1961 (Jones 1997), but the tendency to marry late remained. At the same time, social pressures strongly discouraged having children out of wedlock.

Educational practices were also changing throughout the twentieth century, and as people became more educated, the birth rate experienced a significant decline. The level of illiteracy in Spain was cut by more than one-half between 1970 and 1992 (Reher 1997; Boyd 1997). Perhaps the biggest impact of education on Basque families at the beginning of the twenty-first century is the decision about which schools the children should attend, a question that often revolves around whether the parents want the children educated in Spanish or in Euskara.

Although families have few children, rural households are still multigenerational, including grandparents, parents, and children. Often, unmarried siblings remain at home until they either marry or seek work elsewhere. This rural model has become less common since the end of the twentieth century, when the majority of the Basque population shifted to urban centers. However, the rural model has great cultural significance in the Basque

country and has not lost all of its influence on the modern family.

Gender Roles

During the 1940s, Franco's Falangist ideology was transformed into laws that denied women the right to work outside the home, did away with divorce, established severe penalties for female adultery, and discriminated against children unfortunate enough to be born out of wedlock (Astelarra 1995). Changes to these laws emerged slowly from the 1960s through the 1980s. Women's right to work was restored in 1961, access to an abortion if the health of the mother is at risk was granted in 1985, and divorce became legal in 1981 (Jones 1997), although separation is much more popular than divorce. Gender roles in Basque families are slowly being transformed by these legal changes and by the impact of globalization on regional cultures. However, these changes are difficult to measure and vary from family to family.

Traditional gender roles continued to predominate throughout the 1990s, so much so that the Women's Municipal Service of Bilbao launched a program in 1994 to cross-train women and men in certain elementary tasks that were considered the domain of the opposite sex. Women were trained to replace washers, change light bulbs, paint a wall, and fix a flat tire, while men were taught to sew on a button, prepare a simple meal, and do the laundry (Ostolaza 1997).

Gender roles are a facet of Basque family life that appear highly resistant to change. The overall impression is still one of traditional gender roles, with women responsible for housework and childcare while men work outside the home. If a woman takes advantage of the opportunity to earn extra income outside the home, she is still expected to fulfill her duties at home. Studies assert that Basque women continue to feel responsible for domestic tasks and teach their daughters to feel the same way, while men continue to distance themselves from housework and childcare (Pérez de Lara 1995; Rodríguez 1996). Girls are expected to help their mothers, while boys are generally free from such obligations.

Daily Life

The school day for Basque children allows for a lengthy midday break during which the students are bused home for lunch, then bused back to school for the rest of the afternoon. The elementary schedule can vary from school to school, but two examples from the Bilbao area are typical. On one schedule, students are in class from 9:30 A.M. to 12:30 P.M., followed by a two-hour break, then back to school from 2:30 P.M. until 4:30 P.M. Another schedule from the same area has children in class from 10:15 A.M. until 1:15 P.M., followed by a two-hour break, and then back to class from 3:15 P.M. until 5:15 P.M.

This traditional custom of a long midday break for what historically was the main meal of the day is slowly giving way in the business world to a schedule more typical of the United States because of the influx and influence of international corporations such as IBM, but such changes have not yet taken effect in the schools. Although some schools offer lunch programs, most children still go home for lunch. Women are expected to prepare the midday meal. Many small shops in the Basque country still maintain business hours from eight to one and four to eight in the evening (with some variations), making shopping a challenge for working women whose breaks in the day coincide with the closing of the shops.

Basque families watch less television than do North American families. Prime time begins at 10:00 P.M. and extends to 1:00 A.M. The hours after work, weather permitting, are more likely to be spent strolling along the avenues with family and friends. Parents with children are a common sight in parks and town squares, where they visit or read or take in the air while the little ones play. Older children spend long hours in the company of their *cuadrillas,* a Spanish term referring to one's closest friends. Adults often move from tavern to tavern, sipping a single small beverage at each one before moving on. The crowds in these taverns are predominantly male, but with each new generation, more and more women take part.

Language in the Family

Not all Basque families speak Euskara, and in many families, some members speak it, while others do not. In these cases, families conduct conversations in the language understood by all. Situations are common where one parent speaks Euskara, and the other speaks only Spanish. Since monolingual speakers of Euskara have disappeared, those who speak the Basque language are also bilingual in either Spanish or French. As a result, a household with linguistically mixed parents will generally communicate in Spanish. Even in homes where Euskara is spoken, Spanish is so prevalent in the surrounding society and in the media that the children will pick it up from their friends and by watching television. By the end of the twentieth century, there were several Basque-language radio stations and one Basque-language television channel, but channels that broadcast in Spanish and French far outnumbered them.

Some Basques feel that Euskara defines who they are. They believe that the only true Basque is one who speaks the language. This point of view has its basis in the preeminent role that language played in the definition of Basque nationalism generated by the founders of ETA (*Euzkadi ta Askatasuna,* "Basque Country and Freedom") in 1959 (Tejerina 1992). Other Basques feel that it is more important to be born and raised in the Basque country, whether one speaks the language or not. From this point of view, a family can be completely Basque and speak nothing but Spanish.

The language question has great importance in the Basque country. Many families quit speaking Euskara when Francisco Franco came to power after the Spanish Civil War. Franco made it illegal to speak any language but Spanish. Since the Basque country was on the losing side of the Civil War conflict, Basques felt particularly targeted and threatened by these prohibitions against minority languages. To protect their children, many parents insisted that only Spanish be spoken in the home. In these families, Euskara was lost.

After Franco's death, the establishment of a new Spanish constitution (in 1978) allowed Euskadi and Navarra (and the other autonomous communities of Spain) to have control over their own school systems. It then became necessary for Basque parents to decide whether their children would be educated in Spanish or in Euskara. Since fluency in Euskara is often required to obtain employment, especially for government jobs and teaching positions, many parents choose the Euskara option for schooling their children. Sometimes even parents who speak no Euskara choose to send their children to an *ikastola,* a school were all the subjects are taught in Euskara. Many others choose schools that teach half the day in Euskara and half in

Spanish. The least favorite option in the Basque country is that of education in the Spanish language with Euskara treated as just another subject.

In Iparralde, Basque parents have four educational options. The most popular, with 85.5 percent of elementary school children enrolled, is the all-French option. Until the late 1970s, this was the only option available. Since 1983, students have been offered four options: the original all-French option; all-French with the exception of a class for learning Euskara; half of the instruction in French, the other half in Euskara; and all-Euskara in preschool with the introduction of French in elementary school, increasing the amount of French to nine hours out of twenty-eight (Jauréguiberry 1993).

At the end of the twentieth century, despite a quarter century of efforts to reclaim Euskara, in Hegoalde three out of four residents over the age of fifteen indicated that Spanish was their first language, and in Iparralde, three out of four claimed French (*Euskal Herriko* 1996). Whether a family speaks Euskara or not, there has been a widespread movement during the last twenty-five years of the twentieth century to give children Basque names on their official papers. As a result, there is now an entire generation of sonorous first names such as: Gorka, "George"; Gotzon, "Angel"; Iker, "Visitation"; Koldo, "Louis;" and Unai, "Shepherd"; for boys; and Edurne, "Snow"; Maite, "Darling" or "Darlene"; Nere, "Mine" or "Mia"; Nekane, "Dolores"; and Itxaso, "Sea" for girls.

Families and Political Prisoners

For more than a century, tension has existed between the Basque country and the central government of Spain. As a result of the radical Basque nationalist activities of the middle and late twentieth centuries, most families in the Basque country either know someone who is in prison or have had a family member incarcerated. These prisoners are often housed far from the Basque country, and families must make special efforts to stay in touch. A simple visit may require a lengthy trip across Spain or north to Paris. Even if they have no personal experience of the situation of political prisoners, Basques write much graffiti and put up many posters declaring support for these individuals, especially in the cities. Even in a family-oriented event such as the *Korrika,* a long-distance walk/run fundraiser for Basque-language literacy

efforts, the absent prisoners are represented by participants who carry their photographs on posters as they run their leg of the course (del Valle 1994). The question of whether or not to become involved in activities that support the movement to free these prisoners, or to take part in political activities that could result in such imprisonment, has the potential to tear a family apart. To make matters more complex, not all Basques see these prisoners as different from criminals. The question of the Basque prisoners is one of the issues that affect Basque families every day.

Although living in the Basque country ensures that a Basque family must think about the issue of nationalism and what it means to their lives, not all Basques are nationalists, and even among those who demonstrate pronationalist sentiment, there exists a sliding scale that extends from lip service to radical activism. At the beginning of the twenty-first century, a conservative political movement began gaining strength in Euskadi, and in the Basque context "conservative" usually translates as antinationalist.

Basque Families in North America

For American Basques, especially those in the United States, Euskara is peripheral to Basque identity (Urla 1987; Urla 2000). Close-knit family groups are an important part of Basque-American culture. Basqueness is very much a family issue, and in families where only one parent is of Basque descent, the children are often raised with a high consciousness of their Basque ancestry. The families most actively involved in maintaining their ethnic heritage belong to Basque clubs where they meet regularly with other Basques in their community to enjoy traditional foods, encourage their children to learn Basque dancing, and celebrate their ethnicity. The North American Basque Organizations, Inc. (NABO) is a federation of the Basque clubs of North America and a group with liaisons to similar federations elsewhere and to the Basque government. Children can attend the NABO-sponsored *Udaleku* summer camp to improve their dance skills, study Euskara, learn to play traditional musical instruments, participate in Basque games and sports (such as the card game *mus* or the handball relative *pelota*), and sing Basque songs. These families consider Basqueness something to be worked at and sought after.

Outside the Basque country, European politics and issues such as the state of political prisoners are generally not a family concern. Catholicism remains the predominant religion among Basque emigrant families and their descendants. Gender roles in these families tend to resemble those of the surrounding majority culture.

Not all emigrant Basques have maintained the link to their ethnicity. Many descendants of early settlers in Latin America and some descendants of more recent emigrants to other parts of the world no longer identify themselves as Basque. Conversely, there are also many families who still consider themselves Basque although their children may only be one-half, one-fourth, or even one-eighth Basque.

See also: SPAIN

Bibliography

Astelarra, J. (1995). "Women, Political Culture, and Empowerment in Spain." In *Women in World Politics: An Introduction,* ed. F. D'Amico and P. R. Beckman. Westport, CT and London: Bergin & Garvey.

Boyd, C. (1997). *Historia Patria: Politics, History, and National Identity in Spain, 1875-1975.* Princeton, NJ: Princeton University Press.

Bullen, M. (2000). "Gender and Identity in the *Alardes* of Two Basque Towns." In *Basque Cultural Studies,* ed. W. A. Douglass, C. Urza, L. White, and J. Zulaika. Reno, NV: Basque Studies Program.

del Valle, T. (1994). *Korrika: Basque Ritual for Ethnic Identity,* trans. L. White. Reno: University of Nevada.

Echeverria, J. (1999). *Home Away from Home: A History of Basque Boardinghouses.* Reno and Las Vegas: University of Nevada.

Escario, P. (1992). "El ama de casa, consumidora y prescriptora del consumo" (The housewife, consumer and prescriber of consumption). In *El Ama de Casa, Hoy* (The Housewife, Today). Elorrio: Eroski.

Euskal herriko soziolinguistikazko inkesta 1996 (Sociolinguistic survey of the Basque country). (1996). 4 volumes. Vitoria-Gasteiz: Eusko Jaurlaritza Kultura Saila; Gobierno de Navarra; Institut Culturel Basque. Vol. 1, *Euskal herria* (The Basque country).

Jauréguiberry, F. (1993). *Le Basque à l'école maternelle et elémentaire* (Basque in pre-school and elementary school). Pau: Université de Pau et des Pays de l'Adour.

Jones, A. B. (1997). *Women in Spain.* Manchester and New York: Manchester University.

MacKinnon, K. (1997). "Minority Languages in an Integrating Europe: Prospects for Viability and Maintenance." In *Language Minorities and Minority Languages in the Changing Europe,* ed. B. Synak and T. Wicherkiewicz. Gdansk, Poland: Widawnictwo Uniwersytetu Gdanskiego.

Mar-Molinero, C. (1995). "The Politics of Language: Spain's Minority Languages." In *Spanish Cultural Studies: An Introduction: The Struggle for Modernity.* Oxford and New York: Oxford University Press.

Morcillo Gómez, A. (1999). "Shaping True Catholic Womanhood: Francoist Educational Discourse on Women." In *Constructing Spanish Womanhood: Female Identity in Modern Spain,* ed. V. L. Enders and P. B. Radcliff. Albany: State University of New York Press.

Ostolaza, A. (1997). "Reparto de tareas domésticas" (Division of Domestic Tasks). *Emakunde* 28:52–55.

Pérez de Lara, N. (1995). "La Situación de las mujeres universitarias y los cambios sociales" (The situation of university women and social changes). In *As mulleres e os cambios sociais e económicos,* ed. R. R. Philipp and M. Carme García Negro. Santiago de Compostela: Universidade de Santiago de Compostela.

Reher, D. S. (1997). *Perspectives on the Family in Spain, Past and Present.* Oxford: Clarendon Press.

Rodríguez, A. (1996). "Las mujeres cambian los tiempos" (Women Change the Times) *Hika* 52–53.

Tejerina Montaña, B. (1992). *Nacionalismo y lengua: Los procesos de cambio lingüístico en el país vasco* (Nationalism and language: The processes of linguistic change in the Basque country). Madrid: Centro de Investigaciones Sociológicas.

Tovar, A. (1957). *The Basque Language,* trans. H. P. Houghton. Originally published as *La lengua vasca.* Philadelphia: University of Pennsylvania.

Urla, J. (1987). "Being Basque, Speaking Basque: The Politics of Language and Identity in the Basque Country." Ph.D. dissertation, University of California, Berkeley.

Urla, J. (2000)."Basque Language Revival and Popular Culture." In *Basque Cultural Studies,* ed. W. A. Douglass, C. Urza, L. White, and J. Zulaika. Reno: Basque Studies Program.

White, L. (2001). "Basque Identity, Past and Present." In *Endangered Peoples of Europe: Struggles to Survive and Thrive,* ed. J. S. Forward. Westport, CT and London: Greenwood.

Zulaika, J., and Douglass, W. A. (1996). *Terror and Taboo: The Follies, Fables, and Faces of Terrorism.* New York and London: Routledge.

Other Resource

North American Basque Organizations, Inc. (2002). Available from http://www.naboinc.com/.

LINDA WHITE

BEDOUIN–ARAB FAMILIES

The word *Bedouin* is the Western version of the Arabic word *badawiyin,* which means "inhabitants of the desert," the *badia.* Technically, the term refers only to the camel-herding tribes of desert dwellers, but it has been applied in English to all nomadic Arabs (Kay 1978). The Bedouin-Arab presence extends to Egypt, Israel, Jordan, Lebanon, Saudi Arabia, Syria, and elsewhere in the Middle East and North Africa (Barakat 1993).

Traditionally, the Bedouin lived by raising camels, sheep, and goats and followed their herds in search of grazing areas. Beginning in the latter third of the twentieth century, pastoral nomadism became increasingly rare because of nation-states with closed borders and the rapid urbanization of the region's populations (Sharabi 1988; Fabietti 1991; Al-Krenawi 2000). As a result, the Bedouin have become increasingly sedentary. Only 5 percent of Bedouin still live as pastoral nomads; the remainder have settled in villages and towns (Al-Khatib 2000).

The Bedouin family, like other Arab families, is anchored in a culture-bound socioeconomic and political network. The largest unit in the Bedouin network is the Qabilah, or nation, consisting of several tribes (*ashira,* plural *ashir*) each with its own land and leader. The tribe is a union of extended families, or *hamula* (plural *hamail*). The *hamula* constitutes the major family unit. It is a patrilineal kinship structure of several generations that encompasses a wide network of blood relations descended through the male line. In the past, the hamula provided its members, who lived and wandered together and shared land and labor, with economic security and protection. With the loss of the Bedouin's traditional livelihoods, the hamula is less able to fulfill these functions. It still serves, however, as major source of identity and psychosocial support and social status. The nuclear family of parents and children is the smallest family unit. The nuclear family, hamula, and tribe are closely bound by extensive mutual commitments and obligations.

This social network is underpinned and maintained by a deeply ingrained system of values and expectations that govern the behavior and the relationships of the members. The key values are harmony, kinship solidarity, and hierarchy. The Bedouin emphasize cooperation, adaptation, accommodation, and family cohesion. Individuals are expected to show loyalty and responsibility to the collective, to place its good above their own, and to follow the rules and commands of those above them in the hierarchy (Al-Krenawi 1999).

Marriage and Divorce

Marriage for Bedouins has both religious and social significance. From an Islamic perspective, marriage legalizes sexual relations and provides the framework for procreation. From a social perspective, it brings together not only the bride and groom but also their nuclear families and *hamail.*

Parents or parent substitutes arrange most marriages, sometimes without prior consultation with the prospective spouses or over their objections. Since Islam encourages early marriage and childbearing, marriages may be arranged when the future bride and groom are in their early teens and, sometimes, when they are still children. There is no dating or courtship. A girl or young woman suspected of contact with a boy will be physically punished and have her freedom of movement and communication severely curtailed (Mass and Al-Krenawi 1994).

Romantic love is regarded as a feeble basis for marriage. Muslims believe that love should grow out of marriage (Denny 1985). The main factors considered in the selection of a mate are the character, reputation, and economic and social status of the prospective in-laws, followed by the character and reputation of the spouses-to-be. Preference is usually given to relatives. First-degree relatives receive first choice of a prospective bride, followed by other members of the *hamula* and tribe. Hence, many Bedouin marriages are endogamous.

In some cases, exchange marriages (*badal*) are made. These are marriages in which two men marry one another's sisters. Among the purposes of such marriages is to obtain a mate for a boy or girl with poor marital prospects. Often at least one of the parties in such unions agrees to it out of family pressure or a sense of duty.

The boy's family initiates marriage. It may be arranged directly by the families themselves or through mediators (Hana 1984; Moors 1995). In Islam, marriage is effected through a legal contract, which stipulates, among other things, the amount of the *mahr*, the dower, that the groom's family must pay. In Bedouin-Arab families, the mahr is given to the bride's guardian, usually her father, to purchase clothing and jewelry for her to start her married life. The jewelry serves as economic security for the wife in case of mishap. The mahr consists of a sum paid before the marriage and a larger sum to be paid only if the husband initiates a divorce. The latter sum is meant to discourage him from casting off his wife lightly (Moors 1995). The sum of the mahr varies with the families' blood relations and is lower for relatives than for outsiders.

Polygamy, which is permitted by the Qur'an (4:3), is practiced by a certain percentage of Bedouin-Arabs. Reasons for polygamy include pressure to take part in an exchange marriage; the illness or infertility of the wife, or her failure to bear sons or to meet her husband's sexual needs (Al-Krenawi 1998b). Among some Bedouin, polygamy confers prestige as a sign of wealth and prowess (Abu-Lughod 1986). Traditionally, polygamy served as a way to enlarge the family labor pool and also as a way of providing the protection of marriage for women when there was a shortage of men (Al-Krenawi 1998b). Its negative consequences include the unequal distribution of resources among rival households, and jealousy and acrimony among the co-wives and among the children of different wives (Al-Krenawi 1998b; Al-Krenawi and Lightman 2000).

Divorce is stigmatized and rare in Bedouin society. Unhappily married women are deterred from seeking divorce because the father is entitled to custody, whatever the child's age, and by the poor prospects of remarriage for divorcees, other than to an older man or as a second, third, or fourth wife in a polygamous household (Al-Krenawi 1998a, 1998b).

Family Dynamics in Bedouin-Arab Society

The traditional Bedouin-Arab family mirrors the structure and dynamics of Bedouin society. Like the society as a whole, the Bedouin family is authoritarian, hierarchical, dominated by males, and oriented to the group (Al-Krenawi 1998a, 2000).

The identity and self-concept of the individuals in the family are inextricably linked with the collective identity of the family, hamula, and tribe (Al-Krenawi 2000). The Western ideal of an autonomous, individualized self bears little relevance to the pattern of psychosocial development in the traditional Bedouin family (Al-Krenawi 1998a). Conversely, the honor and reputation of the family are reflected in the behavior of its members. Thus, if a family member is successful, the entire family enjoys the credit. If the family member violates social norms, the entire family loses honor and feels shame (Al-Krenawi 2000).

This interdependency at these basic psychological and social levels necessitates considerable self-sacrifice on the part of all family members and issues in a strong system of family control over all aspects of the members' lives. Major life decisions, such as who to marry, where to live, what occupation to pursue, and so forth, are determined with strong reference to, and often by, the nuclear and extended family (Al-Krenawi 2000).

Emotional expression is also controlled. Individuals are not permitted to express negative emotions, such as anger and jealousy, towards family members (Al-Krenawi 1998a). Unacceptable emotions are generally expressed indirectly: through metaphoric speech, acting out, or the development of physical symptoms that have no organic basis. Intrafamily communication styles tend to be restrained, impersonal, and formal.

Family roles and relationships are governed by gender and age, with males taking precedence over females (Al-Krenawi 1998a). At the same time, the honor of the family is also reflected in the behavior of its females. Because Bedouin-Arab view women as temptresses, women are closely supervised in order to preserve the family's honor. Their social contacts are traditionally confined to the family circle and, within the family, they are subjected to various degrees of segregation (Mass and Al-Krenawi 1994; Abu-Lughod 1986).

Interpersonal Dynamics

The father leads the Bedouin family. His roles are to control and punish, to maintain harmony and cohesion among the family members, and to represent his family to the outside world (Ginat 1987). He is expected to be a charismatic figure who commands subordination and respect as the legitimate authority in all family matters (Al-Krenawi 1999).

In contrast, the mother is perceived as the emotional hub of the nuclear family. Her role is to nurture and bring up the children and to take care of her husband. She often wields tremendous emotional power and may serve as a conduit between the children and their more forbidding father, conveying their messages and requests to him. Nonetheless, she has little public power or authority and is expected to defer in most matters to her husband, his parents, and the elders in his hamula (Al-Krenawi 2000). Her status in the family is strongly contingent on her bearing sons, who are viewed as valuable contributors to the family's economic and political strength. Bedouin culture holds the woman responsible for any lack of sons (Al-Krenawi 1998b).

Children are expected to show respect and obedience to their parents and other relatives, who, as in other Arab families, generally play a substantial part in raising them. Boys and girls are socialized separately into their future roles by the parent and relatives of the same gender. Girls are taught from earliest childhood to be submissive to male authority and to conduct themselves with the modesty and restraint required to preserve the family honor. In preparation for their future as wives and mothers, they are enlisted in helping their mothers in the home.

Boys are taught to be strong and brave, not to show weakness, to maneuver effectively within the social system, and to treat visitors with due hospitality. They are also taught their obligations to preserve the family honor, by guarding their sisters and by undertaking blood vengeance when so required (Al-Krenawi and Graham 1999). Although boys are given more responsibility than girls, the rules governing their behavior are more flexible. For example, boys are more readily permitted to socialize with peers outside of the home than are their sisters.

Alongside the stringent rules governing father-child relations, mediating mechanisms provide flexibility. Male relatives or grandmothers, whose age bestows respect and frees them from the constraints on younger women, may intervene in intergenerational disagreements.

Sibling relationships are also governed by the hierarchies of age and gender. Boys are viewed as more valuable to the family than girls and thus have more prestige and power than their sisters. The eldest brother has authority over and responsibility for his younger siblings. He is expected to serve as a role model for them and to assume the role of the father when the father is away. He is also expected to take care of his younger brothers and sisters throughout their lives. The other brothers are similarly expected to protect their sisters throughout their lives.

The Impact of Societal Change

The rapid shift within Bedouin-Arab society from a nomadic to a sedentary life in the last three decades of the twentieth century has resulted in sweeping social, economic, and political changes (Al-Krenawi 2000; Hana 1984). Bedouin men have left the traditional economic pursuits that kept them dependent on their families; Bedouin women have joined the labor force outside the home; and men and women both are becoming increasingly educated.

As of the end of the twentieth century, these changes have not substantially affected the values or the structure of the Bedouin family. Bedouin society remains a high context society, which means that it tends to emphasize the collective over the individual, and has a slower pace of societal change and greater social stability (Al-Krenawi 1998a). Thus, for example, despite the increased education of Bedouin women and their entry into the labor force, their social status in the home remains subordinate (Al-Krenawi 1999).

The changes, however, are opening up the once closed Bedouin family and giving rise to tension and conflicts. Sons and daughters who watch television and go to school are more exposed to the modern world than are their elders. When they bring home modern ideas, whether of freedom, self-expression, or dress, they often meet with strong disapproval and punishment. Young Bedouin are increasingly caught between the social demands for conformity to the community and family norms with which they were raised and their desire to pursue their own personal goals and aspirations. The price of the pursuit of self-actualization may be well be reduced family support and increased social isolation (Al-Krenawi 1998b).

See also: Islam; Israel

Bibliography

Abu-Lughod, L. (1986). *Veiled Sentiments: Honor and Poetry in a Bedouin Society.* Cairo: The American University in Cairo Press.

Al-Khatib, M. (2000). "The Arab World: Language and Cultural Issues." *Language, Culture and Curriculum* 13(2):121–125.

Al-Krenawi, A. (1998a). "Reconciling Western Treatment and Traditional Healing: A Social Worker Walks with the Wind." *Reflections: Narratives of Professional Helping* 4(3):6-21.

Al-Krenawi, A. (1998b). "Family Therapy with a Multiparental/Multispousal Family." *Family Process* 37(1):65-81.

Al-Krenawi, A. (1999). "Social Workers Practicing in their Non-Western Home Communities: Overcoming Conflict between Professional and Cultural Values." *Families in Society* 80(5):488–495.

Al-Krenawi, A. (2000). "Bedouin-Arab Clients' Use of Proverbs in the Therapeutic Setting." *International Journal for the Advancement of Counselling* 22(2):91–102.

Al-Krenawi, A., and Graham, J. R. (1999). "Social Work Intervention with Bedouin-Arab Children in the Context of Blood Vengeance." *Child Welfare* 78(2):283–296.

Al-Krenawi, A., and Lightman, E. S. (2000). "Learning Achievement, Social Adjustment, and Family Conflict among Bedouin-Arab Children from Polygamous and Monogamous Families." *Social Psychology* 140(3):345–355.

Barakat, H. (1993). *The Arab World: Society, Culture and State.* Berkeley: University of California Press.

Denny, F. (1985). *An Introduction to Islam.* New York: Macmillian.

Fabietti, U. (1991). "Control of Resources and Social Cohesion. The Role of the Bedouin Domestic Group." *Nomadic Peoples* 28:18–27.

Ginat, J. (1987). *Blood Disputes among Bedouin and Rural Arabs in Israel: Revenge, Mediation, Outcasting, and Family Honor.* Pittsburgh, PA: University of Pittsburgh Press.

Hana, N. S. (1984). *The Desert Societies in the Arab World.* Cairo: Daar Al-Marif (in Arabic).

Kay, S. (1978). *The Bedouin.* New York: Crane Rvssak.

Mass, M., and Al-Krenawi, A. (1994). "When a Man Encounters a Woman, Satan Is Also Present: Clinical Relationships in Bedouin Society." *American Journal of Orthopsychiatry* 64(3):357–367.

Moors, A. (1995). *Women, Property, and Islam Palestinian Experiences, 1920–1990.* Cambridge, UK: Cambridge University Press.

Sharabi, H. (1988). *Neopatriarchy: A Theory of Distorted Change in Arab Society.* New York: Oxford University Press

ALEAN AL-KRENAWI

BEHAVIOR PROBLEMS

See: ATTENTION-DEFICIT HYPERACTIVITY DISORDER (ADHD); CHILD ABUSE: PHYSICAL ABUSE AND NEGLECT; CHILD ABUSE: PSYCHOLOGICAL MALTREATMENT; CHILD ABUSE: SEXUAL ABUSE; CHILDHOOD, STAGES OF: ADOLESCENCE; CHILDREN OF ALCOHOLICS; CONDUCT DISORDER; DEVELOPMENTAL PSYCHOPATHOLOGY; DISCIPLINE; FAMILY DIAGNOSIS/DSM-IV; GANGS; JUVENILE DELINQUENCY; OPPOSITIONALITY; PARENTING STYLES; RUNAWAY CHILDREN; SPANKING; SUBSTANCE ABUSE

BIRTH CONTROL

CONTRACEPTIVE METHODS *Stephanie B. Teal*
SOCIOCULTURAL AND HISTORICAL ASPECTS *Vern L. Bullough*

CONTRACEPTIVE METHODS

Contraception has been used worldwide since ancient times. Writings in Egyptian papyri, the Bible, and Greek and Roman texts indicate the usage of various herb and root preparations for contraception and abortion (Riddle 1992). Decisions regarding the timing of pregnancy and control over family size continue to be important issues for all adults.

An average woman in the developing world who wants four children must use effective contraception for sixteen years. The average U.S. woman who wants two children needs to effectively use contraception for twenty years to achieve her desired family size (Alan Guttmacher Institute 1999).

Worldwide, many contraceptive methods are available. Factors influencing the choice of method include availability, cost, reversibility, ease of use, cultural preferences, privacy, side effects, and medical risks. When evaluating risk, it is important to note that all available birth control methods carry lower risk of death than pregnancy, even in developed countries where maternal death rates are already low.

Patterns of use differ significantly internationally. The oral contraceptive pill accounts for 34 percent of contraceptive use in the Netherlands, but only 2 percent in Japan. The intrauterine device provides contraception for 19 percent of French women, but only 1 percent of U.S. women (Senanayake and Potts 1995). Conversely, the United States has the highest rate of female sterilization in the developed world.

Contraceptive methods have many different mechanisms of action, but may be generally grouped into *hormonal* or *nonhormonal* classes.

Hormonal Methods

Hormones are the chemical messengers the body uses to control and coordinate various physical processes. The major hormones influencing the female reproductive organs are *estrogen* and *progesterone*. Manipulation of these hormones may disrupt the normal processes required for fertility, such as *ovulation*, transport of egg and sperm in the Fallopian tubes, thinning of cervical mucus, and preparation of the uterine lining (*endometrium*) for implantation. Hormonal methods of contraception must affect these processes enough to prevent fertility, without causing too many other bothersome side effects or risks.

Combination oral contraceptive pills. The *combination oral contraceptive* (COC) pill is a highly effective, reversible female contraceptive. It contains both estrogen and *progestin* (a compound that mimics natural progesterone). Taken every day for three out of four weeks, it prevents ovulation by inhibiting the secretion of two regulatory hormones from the brain's pituitary gland. The estrogen suppresses *follicle stimulating hormone* (FSH) and thus prevents preparation of an egg for ovulation. The main contraceptive effect, however, is from the *progestin*, which suppresses *luteinizing hormone* (LH). The lack of the *LH surge* prevents ovulation. The progestin also has effects on the endometrium and cervical mucus. The endometrium becomes much less favorable to implantation due

to thinning. Meanwhile, the cervical mucus becomes thick, limiting sperm penetration and transport into the uterine cavity. Even if ovulation occasionally occurs, these other effects contribute to the overall high contraceptive efficacy of 98 percent (Trussell and Vaughan 1999).

The COC pill has significant noncontraceptive benefits, including reduction of menstrual blood loss, reduction of cramps, and improved regularity of the menstrual cycle. It also significantly reduces the risks of ovarian and endometrial cancer, pelvic inflammatory disease, breast cysts, and endometriosis. Both acne and excessive hair growth are improved by COC pill use.

Although the COC pill has many contraceptive and noncontraceptive benefits, it is not appropriate for everyone. Contraindications include breast cancer, severe liver disease, and uncontrolled hypertension. Blood clots in the deep veins are a rare but sometimes serious risk associated with the pill. Women who smoke are already at higher risk of blood clots and heart attack due to their cigarette usage, and smokers are discouraged from COC use. In nonsmokers, however, the pill is safe to use through the age of menopause.

Depo-Provera. Depo-Provera (*depot medroxyprogesterone acetate*) is a long-acting, reversible injectable contraceptive available in many countries since the late 1970s and in the United States since 1992. It results in initially high progestin levels which taper off over the following weeks. It is given as an injection every twelve to thirteen weeks. The progestin dose results in thickening of cervical mucus and thinning of the endometrium, but also is high enough to suppress ovulation, leading to a high efficacy rate of 99 percent (Trussell and Vaughan 1999). Because of the lack of estrogen with this method, a common side effect is unscheduled irregular bleeding. This usually resolves over several months, and 50 percent of women have no bleeding at all after one year of use (Kaunitz 2001). In fact, this method may be beneficial to women who are troubled by heavy, prolonged menstrual periods. Depo-Provera is also an excellent contraceptive for those who cannot use estrogen, want a private method whose timing is not related to intercourse, or do not want to take a pill every day. Because it can have a prolonged effect on a woman's return to fertility, Depo-Provera is not a good option for women planning

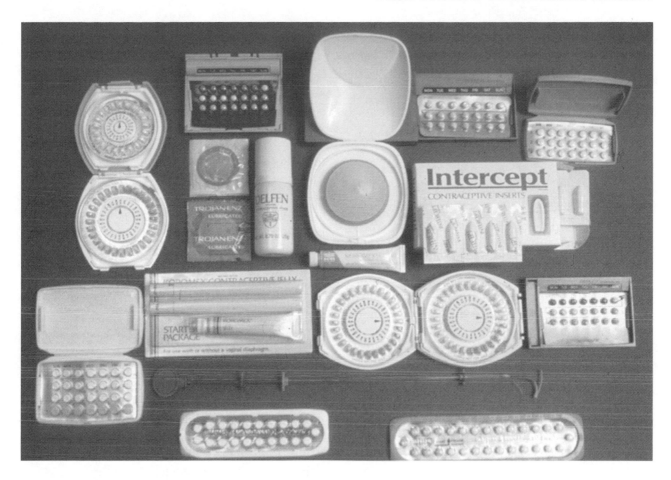

Worldwide, many contraceptive methods are available. Factors influencing the choice of method include availability, cost, reversibility, ease of use, cultural preferences, privacy, side effects, and medical risks. RAY ELLIS/PHOTO RESEARCHERS, INC.

pregnancy within the next year. It is still controversial whether it promotes weight gain: this effect has only been noted in U.S. trials of this internationally popular method (Kaunitz 2001).

Lunelle. Lunelle, an injectable monthly contraceptive, contains one-sixth the dose of medroxyprogesterone acetate as Depo-Provera, and also contains estrogen. Lunelle is given by injection every twenty-three to thirty-three days. Like Depo-Provera, the progestin in Lunelle inhibits the secretion of the hormone LH, preventing ovulation. Because of the estrogen the bothersome unscheduled bleeding of Depo-Provera is much improved. In the first ninety days of use, 57 percent of Lunelle users report variations in their bleeding patterns, compared with 91 percent of Depo-Provera users (Hall 1998). However, long-term Lunelle users tend to see normalization of their bleeding patterns, and after a year, 70 percent report normal monthly bleeding. Lunelle is highly effective. In studies conducted by the World Health Organization, over 12,000 women in nine countries were followed for a total of 100,000 woman-months use: five pregnancies occurred (Hall 1998). The formulation in Lunelle has been used in some countries for twenty years prior to FDA (Food and Drug Administration) approval in the United States.

Implantables. Several *sustained-release* progestin-only contraceptives have been developed to reduce the frequency of administration and decrease the high progestin levels associated with Depo-Provera. *Norplant* consists of six capsules filled with the progestin *levonorgestrel* that are placed under the skin of the upper arm. The capsules release the hormone at a constant low rate, resulting in a daily dose about 25 to 50 percent that of low-dose COCs. Unscheduled bleeding does occur, especially during the first year, but women often return to a normal menstrual pattern thereafter. Norplant may be used for up to five years.

Implanon. A single capsule system which is effective for three years, Implanon's major benefit over Norplant is the ease of insertion and removal, which can be difficult if the capsules are placed too deeply or irregularly. One of the most obvious benefits of these implants is the low demand on the contraceptive user, especially as compared to daily pill use. Efficacy is also extremely high, with a failure rate of less than 1 percent per year.

Progestin Intrauterine Device. Widely used in Europe, the progestin intrauterine device (IUD) is a low-maintenance method that has high efficacy, rapid reversibility, and reduction of menstrual blood loss. The *Mirena progestin IUD* is a small, T-shaped flexible plastic device that slowly releases levonorgestrel contained in the long stem of the T. The contraceptive effect is primarily from the thickening of cervical mucus and alteration of sperm motility and function. Although ovulation is not usually inhibited, the failure rate is only 0.14 percent. After placement, the progestin IUD may be left in place up to five years, or removed when pregnancy is desired.

Nonhormonal Methods

Nonhormonal methods rely on prevention of contact of the egg and sperm. Many nonhormonal methods require implementation around the time of intercourse, or place restrictions on when or how intercourse may occur, whereas others require little maintenance. Because of this, these methods have a much wider range of contraceptive failure than the hormonal methods, ranging from as high as 25 percent for withdrawal and natural family planning, to as low as 0.5 to 1 percent for the IUD and sterilization.

Intrauterine Device. The intrauterine device is a highly effective, reversible, long-acting, nonhormonal method of contraception. It is popular in Europe, Asia, and South America. Nonhormonal IUDs come in many different forms, but the most common type in the United States is the TCu-380A, also known as *Paraguard.* The Paraguard IUD is a small plastic "T" wrapped with copper. It exerts its effect through several mechanisms: first, the copper significantly decreases sperm motility and lifespan, second, the IUD produces changes in the endometrium that are hostile to sperm. The IUD does not affect ovulation, nor does it cause abortions. The overall failure rate of the IUD is less than 1 percent per year, which is comparable to female sterilization (Meirik et al. 2001). After removal, a woman can become pregnant immediately. Despite its benefits, its popularity in the United States waned in the mid-1970s due to a rash of litigation related to reports of increased pelvic infection and infertility related to its use. Later studies largely refuted these concerns, but the bad publicity has lingered (Hubacher et al. 2001). Although slowly increasing, U.S. use rate of the IUD still lags far behind the rest of the world.

Condom: male and female. The male condom is a sheath of latex or polyurethane that is placed over the penis prior to intercourse as a barrier to sperm. It is inexpensive, readily available, and has the added health benefit of providing protection against sexually transmitted diseases, including HIV. Condoms may also be lubricated with a spermicide.

The female condom is a polyurethane sheath with two rings attached, which is placed in the vagina prior to intercourse. In clinical trials it has had high patient acceptance, and has the benefit of being a woman-controlled method of sexually transmitted disease protection. Couples should not use both a male and a female condom during an act of intercourse, as this increases the risk of breakage. The failure rate of condoms is 12 to 20 percent (Fu et al. 1999).

Diaphragm. The diaphragm is a rubber cup-shaped device which is filled with spermicide and inserted into the vagina, creating a barrier in front of the cervix. Like the condom, the efficacy rate of the diaphragm is dependent on the user, but ranges from 80 to 90 percent. The diaphragm does provide some protection against *gonorrhea* and pelvic inflammatory disease, but has not been shown to reduce transmission of HIV or other viral sexually transmitted infections. Although it must be obtained by prescription, a diaphragm is relatively inexpensive, and with proper care lasts for several years. It may be combined with condom use for greater contraceptive efficacy and disease prevention.

Withdrawal. Also known as *coitus interruptus,* withdrawal requires the male partner to remove his penis from the woman's vagina prior to ejaculation. Although theoretically sperm should not enter the vagina and fertilization should be prevented, this method has a failure rate of up to 25 percent in typical use (Trussell and Vaughan 1999). Withdrawal is probably most useful as a back-up method for couples using, for example, periodic abstinence.

Natural family planning. Periodic abstinence, also known as natural family planning, depends on determining *safe periods* when conception is less likely, and using this information to avoid pregnancy. The various methods of natural family planning include the *calendar, thermal shift, symptothermal,* and *cervical mucus methods.* All of these methods require training in the recognition of the fertile phase of the menstrual cycle, as well as a mature commitment by both partners to abstain from intercourse during this time. If the woman does not have a predictable menstrual cycle, some of these methods are more difficult to use effectively. Although with perfect use the failure rate could be as low as 5 percent, actual failure rates are closer to 25 percent and above (Fu et al. 1999; Trussell and Vaughan 1999).

Female sterilization. Female sterilization is the most common method of birth control for married couples in the United States. The technique is performed surgically, through one or two incisions in the abdomen. The Fallopian tubes may be tied, cut, burnt, banded with rings, or blocked with clips. Sterilization should be considered final and irreversible, although expensive microsurgery can sometimes repair the tube enough to allow pregnancy. Some couples assume that because this method is irreversible, it has a perfect efficacy rate, but this is not true. Each method has a slightly different rate of failure or complication, but the overall failure rate for female sterilization is about 1 percent (Peterson et al. 1996). The failure rate of sterilization is also dependent on the age of the patient, with younger patients more likely to experience an unplanned pregnancy up to ten years after the procedure. Younger patients are also more likely to experience regret in the years following sterilization.

Male sterilization. Male sterilization (*vasectomy*) is also a highly effective, permanent method of contraception. It is accomplished by making a small hole on either side of the scrotum and tying off the spermatic cord which transports sperm into the semen just prior to ejaculation. Compared to female sterilization, it is less expensive, more effective, easier to do with less surgical risk, and is easier to reverse if necessary. Vasectomy has no effect on male sexual function, including erectile function, ejaculation, volume of semen, or sexual pleasure. However, vasectomy rates consistently lag far behind those of female sterilization in all parts of the world, due mainly to cultural factors.

Emergency Contraception

Emergency contraception, also known as *post-coital contraception,* includes any method that acts after intercourse to prevent pregnancy. The *Yuzpe method* uses COC pills to deliver two large doses of hormones, twelve hours apart. These must be taken within seventy-two hours of the unprotected intercourse to be effective. A prepackaged emergency contraceptive kit called *Preven* is also available. The kit contains a pregnancy test, instructions, and two pills with the appropriate doses of estrogen and progestin. Studies show a pregnancy rate of 3.2 percent for the cycle in which the woman took the emergency contraception, which is a 75 percent reduction of the 8 percent expected pregnancy rate per unprotected cycle (Ho 2000). The main side effects are nausea and possibly vomiting from the high dose of estrogen. Emergency contraception using a special progestin-only pill containing levonorgestrel avoids this side effect. It is marketed as *Plan B.* A study of 967 women using Plan B showed a pregnancy rate of 1.1 percent, or an 85 percent reduction. Both methods cause a 95 percent reduction in the risk of pregnancy if taken within the first twelve hours after unprotected intercourse (Nelson et al. 2000). The mechanism of action of the hormonal pills is probably the prevention of ovulation, with some contribution of changes in the endometrium. They do not cause abortion.

Conclusion

Control of family size is an important consideration for all adults, in every country. Many different contraceptive methods exist, and no single method is appropriate for all couples. When choosing a contraceptive method, factors such as effectiveness, reversibility, side effects, privacy, cost, and cultural preferences should be considered.

See also: ABORTION; ABSTINENCE; ASSISTED REPRODUCTIVE TECHNOLOGIES; BIRTH CONTROL: SOCIOCULTURAL AND HISTORICAL ASPECTS; CHILDLESSNESS; FAMILY LIFE EDUCATION; FAMILY

PLANNING; FERTILITY; INFANTICIDE; SEXUALITY
EDUCATION

Bibliography

Alan Guttmacher Institute. (1999). "Sharing Responsibility: Women, Society and Abortion Worldwide." New York: Author.

Fu, H.; Darroch, J. E.; Haas, T.; Ranjit, N. (1999). "Contraceptive Failure Rates: New Estimates from the 1995 National Survey of Family Growth." *Family Planning Perspectives* 31(2):56–63.

Hall, P. E. (1998). "New Once-a-Month Injectable Contraceptives, with Particular Reference to Cyclofem/Cyclo-Provera." *International Journal of Gynaecology and Obstetrics* 62:S43–S56.

Hatcher, R. A.; Trussel, J.; Stewart, F., and Cates, W. (1998). *Contraceptive Technology,* 17th edition. New York: Irvington.

Ho, P. C. (2000). "Emergency Contraception: Methods and Efficacy." *Current Opinion in Obstetrics and Gynecology.* 12(3):175–179.

Hubacher, D.; Lara-Ricalde, R.; Taylor, D. J.; Guerra-Infante, F.; and Guzman-Rodriguez, R. (2001). "Use of Copper Intrauterine Devices and the Risk of Tubal Infertility among Nulligravid Women." *New England Journal of Medicine* 345(8):561–567.

Kaunitz, A. M. (2001). "Injectable Long-Acting Contraceptives." *Clinical Obstetrics and Gynecology* 44(1):73–91.

Meirik, O.; Farley, T. M. M.; and Sivin, I. (2001). "Safety and Efficacy of Levonorgestrel Implant, Intrauterine Device, and Sterilization" *Obstetrics and Gynecology* 97(4):539–547.

Nelson, A. L.; Hatcher, R. A.; Zieman, M.; Watt, A.; Darney, P. D., Creinin, M. D. (2000). *Managing Contraception,* 3rd edition. Tiger, GA: Bridging the Gap Foundation.

Peterson, H. B.; Xia, Z.; Hughes, J. M.; Wilcox, L. S.; Tylor, L. R.; and Trussell, J. (1996). "The Risk of Pregnancy after Tubal Sterilization: Findings from the U.S. Collaborative Review of Sterilization." *American Journal of Obstetrics and Gynecology* 174:1161–1170.

Riddle, J. M. (1992). *Contraception and Abortion from the Ancient World to the Renaissance.* Cambridge, MA: Harvard University Press.

Senanayake, P., and Potts, M. (1995). *An Atlas of Contraception.* Pearl River, NY: Parthenon.

Trussell, J., and Vaughan, B. (1999) "Contraceptive Failure, Method-Related Discontinuation and Resumption of Use: Results from the 1995 National Survey of Family Growth." *Family Planning Perspectives* 31(2):64–72.

Other Resource

Alan Guttmacher Institute. (2000). "Contraceptive Use." Available from www.agi-usa.org/pubs/fb_contr_use.html.

STEPHANIE B. TEAL

SOCIOCULTURAL AND HISTORICAL ASPECTS

Birth control (a term popularized by Margaret Sanger, 1876–1966) refers to control over and decisions about the timing and number of births that a woman or couple has; it is a part of family planning and includes more than contraception.

People have used various forms of birth control throughout history, including abstinence (both short-term and, for some individuals, lifetime continence), abortion (abortifacients are common in both historical and oral sources), infanticide (disposing of unwanted infants), and surgical intervention (ranging from castration to creating a hypospadias condition in the male by making an exit for sperm and urine at the base of the penis). Forms of contraception have ranged from "natural" means, such as withdrawal or use of other orifices, to a variety of mechanical means including intrauterine devices (IUDs) and various barriers such as the condom or vaginal inserts.

Historically, however, birth control was not a general matter for public discourse. Although various medical writers described methods, some more effective than others, and theologians took conflicting stands about non-procreative sexual activities, most of the information was passed on informally among women themselves, some of it more accurate than others. Historians believe that the first really measurable efforts toward some form of fertility control, probably *coitus interruptus,* took place in France in the eighteenth century. Full scale debate on the issue, however, did not take place until the nineteenth century.

Widespread Public Discussion

Key to the emerging public discussion about birth control was concern with overpopulation, and only later did the feminist issue of right to plan families emerge. The population issue was first put before the public by the Reverend Thomas Robert Malthus (1766–1834) in his *Essay on the Principle of Population* (1708). The first edition was published anonymously, but Malthus signed his name to the second, expanded edition published in 1803. Malthus believed that human beings were possessed by a sexual urge that led them to multiply faster than their food supply, and unless some checks could somehow be applied, the inevitable results of such unlimited procreation were misery, war, and vice. Population, he argued, increased geometrically (1, 2, 4, 8, 16, 32 . . .) whereas food supply only increased arithmetically (1, 2, 3, 4, 5, 6, . . .) Malthus's only solution was to urge humans to exercise control over their sexual instincts (i.e., to abstain from sex except within marriage) and to marry as late as possible. Sexually, Malthus was an extreme conservative who went so far as to classify as vice all promiscuous intercourse, "unnatural" passions, violations of the marriage bed, use of mechanical contraceptives, and irregular sexual liaisons.

Many of those who agreed with Malthus about the threat of overpopulation disagreed with him on the solutions and instead advocated the use of contraceptives. Those who did so came to be known as *neo-Malthusians*. Much of the debate over birth control, however, came to be centered on attitudes toward sexuality. Malthus recognized the need of sexual activity for procreation but not for pleasure. The neo-Malthusians held that continence or abstinence was no solution because sex urges were too powerful and nonprocreative sex was as pleasurable as procreative sex.

To overcome the lack of public information about contraception, the neo-Malthusians felt it was essential to spread information about the methods of contraception. The person in the English speaking world generally given credit for first doing so was the English tailor, Francis Place (1771–1854). Place was concerned with the widespread poverty of his time, a poverty accentuated by the growth of industrialization and urbanization as well as the breakdown of the traditional village economy. Large families, he felt, were more likely to live in poverty than smaller ones, and to help overcome this state affairs, Place published in 1882 his *Illustrations and Proofs of the Principle of Population*. He urged married couples (not unmarried lovers) to use "precautionary" means to plan their families better, but he did not go into detail. To remedy this lack of instruction, he printed handbills in 1823 addressed simply *To the Married of Both Sexes*. In it he advocated the use of a dampened sponge which was to be inserted in the vagina with a string attached to it prior to "coition" as an effective method of birth control. Later pamphlets by Place and those who followed him added other methods, all involving the female. Pamphlets of the time, by Place and others, were never subject to any legal interference, although they were brought to the attention of the attorney general who did not take any action. Place ultimately turned to other issues, but his disciples, notably Richard Carlile (1790–1843), took up the cause. It became an increasingly controversial subject in part because Place and Carlile were social reformers as well as advocates of birth control. Carlile was the first man in England to put his name to a book devoted to the subject, *Every Woman's Book* (1826).

Early U.S. Birth Control Movement

In the United States, the movement for birth control may be said to have begun in 1831 with publication by Robert Dale Owen (1801–1877) of the booklet *Moral Physiology*. Following the model of Carlile, Owen advocated three methods of birth control, with *coitus interruptus* being his first choice. His second alternative was the vaginal sponge, and the third the condom. Ultimately far more influential was a Massachusetts physician, Charles Knowlton (1800–1850) who published his *Fruits of Philosophy* in 1832. In his first edition, Knowlton advocated a policy of douching, a not particularly effective contraceptive, but it was the controversy the book caused rather than its recommendation for which it is remembered. As he lectured on the topic through Massachusetts, he was jailed in Cambridge, fined in Taunton, and twice acquitted in trials in Greenfield. These actions increased public interest in contraception, and Knowlton had sold some 10,000 copies of his book by 1839. In subsequent editions of his book, Knowlton added other more reliable methods of contraception.

Once the barriers to publications describing methods of contraception had fallen, a number of other books appeared throughout the English-speaking world. The most widely read material was probably the brief descriptions included in *Elements of Social Science* (1854), a sex education book written by George Drysdale (1825–1901).

Drysdale was convinced that the only cause of poverty was overpopulation, a concept that his more radical freethinking rivals did not fully accept. They were more interested in reforming society by eliminating the grosser inequities, and for them contraception was just one among many changes for which they campaigned.

Influence of Eugenics

Giving a further impetus to the more conservative voices in the birth control movement was the growth of the eugenics movement. The eugenicists, while concerned with the high birthrates among the poor and the illiterate, emphasized the problem of low birthrates among the more "intellectual" upper classes. Eugenics came to be defined as an applied biological science concerned with increasing the proportion of persons of better than average intellectual endowment in succeeding generations. The eugenicists threw themselves into the campaign for birth control among the poor and illiterate, while urging the "gifted" to produce more. The word *eugenics* had been coined by Francis Galton (1822–1911), a great believer in heredity, who also had many of the prejudices of an upper-class English gentleman in regard to social class and race. Galton's hypotheses were given further "academic" respectability by Karl Pearson (1857–1936), the first holder of the Galton endowed chair of eugenics at the University of London. Pearson believed that the high birthrate of the poor was a threat to civilization, and if members of the "higher" races did not make it their duty to reproduce, they would be supplanted in time by the members of the "lower races."

When put in this harsh light, eugenics gave "scientific" support to those who believed in racial and class superiority. It was just such ideas that Adolph Hitler attempted to implement in his "solution" to the "racial problem." Although Pearson's views were eventually opposed by the English Eugenics Society, the U.S. eugenics movement, founded in 1905, adopted his view. Inevitably, a large component of the organized family planning movement in the United States was made up of eugenicists. The fact that the Pearson-oriented eugenicists also advocated such beliefs as enforced sterilization of the "undesirables" inevitably tainted the group in which they were active even when they were not the dominant voices.

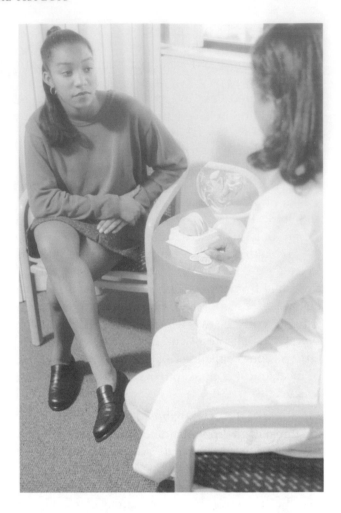

With legal obstacles to the dissemination of contraceptive information removed, the remaining challenges are to distribute information and encourage people to use contraceptives for effective family planning. Teenagers are one of the more difficult audiences to reach. PHOTODISC, INC.

Dissemination of Information and Censorship

Population studies indicate that at least among the upper-classes in the United States and Britain, some form of population limitation was being practiced. Those active in the birth control movement, however, found it difficult to contact the people they most wanted to reach, namely the poor, overburdened mothers who did not want more children or who, in more affirmative terms, wanted to plan and space their children. The matter was complicated by the enactment of anti-pornography and anti-obscenity legislation which classed birth control information as obscene. In England, with the passage of the first laws on the subject in 1853, contraception was interpreted to be pornographic since of necessity it included discussion of sex. Books on contraception that earlier had been widely sold and distributed were seized and condemned. Such seizures were challenged in England in 1877 by Charles Bradlaugh (1833–1891) and Annie Besant (1847–1933). Bradlaugh and Besant were convicted by a jury that really wanted to acquit them, but the judgement was overturned on a technicality. In the aftermath, information on contraception circulated widely in Great Britain and its colonies.

In the United States, however, where similar legislation was enacted by various states and by the federal government, materials that contained information about birth control and that were distributed through the postal system or entered the country through customs ran into the censoring activities of Anthony Comstock (1844–1915) who had been appointed as a special postal agent in 1873. One of his first successful prosecutions was against a pamphlet on contraception by Edward Bliss Foote (1829–1906). As a result, information about contraceptives was driven underground, although since state regulations varied some states were more receptive to information about birth control. Only those people who went to Europe regularly kept up with contemporary developments such as the diaphragm, which began to be prescribed in Dutch clinics at the end of the nineteenth century. The few physicians who did keep current in the field tended to restrict their services to upper-class groups. The dominant voice of the physicians in the increasingly powerful American Medical Association was opposed to the use of contraceptives and considered them immoral. That this situation changed is generally credited to Sanger, a nurse.

In 1914, Sanger, then an active socialist, began to publish *The Woman Rebel,* a magazine designed to stimulate working women to think for themselves and to free themselves from bearing unwanted children. To educate women about the possibilities of birth control, Sanger decided to defy the laws pertaining to the dissemination of contraceptive information by publishing a small pamphlet, *Family Limitation* (1914), for which she was arrested. Before her formal trial, she fled to England, where she spent much of her time learning about European contraceptive methods, including the diaphragm. While she was absent her husband, William Sanger (1873–1961), who had little to do with his wife's publishing activities, was tricked into giving a copy of the pamphlet to a Comstock agent, and for this was arrested and convicted, an act that led to the almost immediate return of his wife. Before she was brought to trial, however, Comstock died. The zealousness of his methods had so alienated many prominent people that the government—without Comstock pushing for a conviction—simply decided not to prosecute Sanger, a decision which received widespread public support.

In part through her efforts, by 1917 another element had been added to the forces campaigning for more effective birth control information, namely the woman's movement (or at least certain segments of it). Women soon became the most vocal advocates and campaigners for effective birth control, joining "radical" reformers and eugenicists in an uneasy coalition.

Sanger, though relieved at being freed from prosecution, was still anxious to spread the message of birth control to the working women of New York. To reach them, she opened the first U.S. birth control clinic, which was patterned after the Dutch model. Since no physician would participate with her, she opened it with two other women, Ethel Byrne, her sister and also a nurse, and Fania Mindell, a social worker. The well-publicized opening attracted long lines of interested women—as well as several vice officers—and after some ten days of disseminating information and devices, Sanger and her two colleagues were arrested. Byrne, who was tried first and sentenced to thirty days in jail, promptly went on a hunger strike, attracting so much national attention that after eleven days she was pardoned by the governor of New York. Mindell, who was also convicted, was only fined $50. By the time of Sanger's trial, the prosecution was willing to drop charges provided she would agree not to open another clinic, a request she refused. She was sentenced to thirty days in jail and immediately appealed her conviction. The New York Court of Appeals rendered a rather ambiguous decision in acquitting her, holding that it was legal to disseminate contraceptive information for the "cure and prevention of disease," although they failed to specify the disease. Sanger, interpreting unwanted pregnancy as a disease, used this legal loophole and continued her campaign unchallenged.

New York, however, was just one state; there were many state laws to be overcome before information about contraceptives could be widely disseminated. Even after the legal barriers began to fall, the policies of many agencies made it difficult to distribute information. Volunteer birth control clinics were often prevented from publicly advertising their existence. It was not until 1965 that the U.S. Supreme Court, in *Griswold v. Connecticut,* removed the obstacle to the dissemination of contraceptive information to married women. It took several more years before dissemination of information to unmarried women was legal in every state.

In Europe, the battle, led by the Netherlands, for the dissemination of information about birth control methods took place during the first half of the twentieth century. It was not until after World War II when, under Sanger's leadership, the International Federation for Planned Parenthood was organized, that a worldwide campaign to spread the message took place. At the beginning of the twenty-first century two major countries, Japan and Russia, still used abortion as a major means of family planning. In many countries, more than 60 percent of women of childbearing age are using modern contraceptives, including Argentina, Australia, Austria, the Bahamas, Belgium, Brazil, Canada, China, Costa Rica, Cuba, Denmark, Finland, France, Hungary, Italy, Jamaica, Korea, New Zealand, Netherlands, Norway, Spain, Sweden, Switzerland, Singapore, Thailand, the United Kingdom, and the United States. Many other nations are approaching this rate of success, but much lower rates exist throughout Africa (where Tunisia seems to the highest at 49 percent), in most of the former areas of the Soviet Union and the eastern block countries, and in much of Asia and Latin America. The International Planned Parenthood Federation does periodic surveys of much of the world which are regularly updated on its website (see also Bullough 2001).

Teenagers and Birth Control

With legal obstacles for adults removed, and a variety of new contraceptives available, the remaining problems are to disseminate information and encourage people to use contraceptives for effective family planning. One of the more difficult audiences to reach has been teenagers. Many so-called family life or sex education programs refuse to deal with the issue of contraceptives and instead emphasize abstinence from sex until married. Unfortunately, abstinence—or continence as it is sometimes called—has the highest failure rate of any of the possible means of birth control since there is no protection against pregnancy if the will power for abstinence fails. The result was a significant increase in the 1990s of unmarried teenage mothers, although not of teenage mothers in general. The highest percentage of teenage mothers in the years the United States has been keeping statistics on such matters came in 1957, but the overwhelming majority of these were married women. Although the number of all teenage mothers has been declining ever since, reaching new lows in 1999–2000, an increased percentage of them are unmarried. In fact, it is the change in marriage patterns and in adoption patterns, more than the sexual activity of teenagers, that led to public concern over unmarried teenage mothers. Since societal belief patterns have increasingly frowned upon what might be called "forced marriages" of pregnant teenagers, and the welfare system itself was modified to offer support to single mothers, at least within certain limits, teenagers who earlier might have given up their children for adoption decided to keep them.

Many programs have been introduced since the federal government in 1997 created the abstinence-only-until-marriage program to teach those teenagers most at-risk to be more sexually responsible. Only a few of the programs included a component about contraceptives since the federally funded programs do not provide for it, and only a few states such as California have provided funds to do so. Most of the programs emphasize self-esteem, the need for adult responsibility, and the importance of continence, all important for teenage development, but almost all the research on the topic, summaries of which are regularly carried in issues of *SIECUS Report,* has found that the lack of specific mention of birth control methods has handicapped their effectiveness in curtailing teenage pregnancy. This deficiency has been somewhat compensated for by the development of more efficient and easy-to-use contraceptives and availability of information about them from other sources.

Still, although contraception and family planning increasingly have come to be part of the belief structure of the U.S. family, large segments of the population remain frightened by, unaware of, or unconvinced by discussion about birth control.

Unfortunately, because much of public education about birth control for much of the twentieth century was aimed at the poor and minorities, some feel that birth control is a form of racial suicide. It takes a lot of time and much education to erase such fears and success can only come when such anxieties can be put to rest.

See also: ABORTION; ABSTINENCE; ADOLESCENT PARENTHOOD; ASSISTED REPRODUCTIVE TECHNOLOGIES; BIRTH CONTROL: CONTRACEPTIVE METHODS; CHILDLESSNESS; FAMILY LIFE EDUCATION; FAMILY PLANNING; FERTILITY; INFANTICIDE; SEXUALITY EDUCATION; WOMEN'S MOVEMENTS

Bibliography

Bullough, V. L., and Bullough, B. *Contraception*. (1997) Buffalo, NY: Prometheus.

Bullough, V. L. (2001). *Encyclopedia of Birth Control*. Santa Barbara, CA: ABC-Clio.

Chandrasekhar, S. (1981). *A Dirty, Filthy Book: The Writings of Charles Knowlton and Annie Besant on Reproductive Physiology and Birth Contol and An Account of the Bradlaugh-Besant Trial*. Berkeley and Los Angeles: University of California Press.

Fryer, P. (1965). *The Birth Controllers*. London: Secker & Warburg.

Grossman, Atina. (1995). *Reforming Sex: The German Movement for Birth Control and Abortion Reform*. New York: Oxford University Press.

McLaren, Angus. (1990). *A History of Contraception*. London: Blackwell.

New York University. *Margaret Sanger Papers Project*. New York: New York University Department of History.

Population Information Program. *Population Reports*. Baltimore, MD: Johns Hopkins University School of Public Health.

Reed, J. (1978). *From Private Vice to Public Virtue: The Birth Control Movement and American Society Since 1830*. New York: Basic Books.

Riddle, John M. (1997). *Eve's Herbs: A History of Contraception and Abortion in the West*. Cambridge, MA: Harvard University Press.

Solway, R. A. (1982). *Birth Control and the Population Question in England, 1877–1930*. Chapel Hill: University of North Carolina Press.

Case

Griswold v. *Connecticut*, 381 U.S. 479, 85 S.Ct. 1678, 14 L.Ed.2d 510 (1965).

Other Resource

International Planned Parenthood Federation. "Country Profiles." Available from http://www.ippf.org/regions/country.

VERN L. BULLOUGH

BIRTH ORDER

Birth order refers to the order in which siblings are born into a family. Although siblings may be ranked numerically according to their order of appearance, four positions typically are recognized: first, middle, youngest, and only child. Only one sibling may occupy the first, youngest or only positions, but many children can be classified as middle.

Alfred Adler (1927, 1956) was the first psychologist to theorize about the effects of birth order on personality development (Stewart and Stewart 1995). Adler (1927) believed that parents' responses to their children were affected by the order of each child's birth into the family. This differential treatment of each child based on birth order position was believed to influence the child's developing personality. Since the inception of Adler's theories, more than 1,700 journal articles and dissertations have been written about birth order and its relationship to a wide variety of psychological topics. Two of the most popular areas of inquiry include personality traits and intellectual achievement (Rodgers et al. 2000; Stewart and Stewart 1995).

Birth Order and Personality

Birth order theories enjoy popular appeal because they provide an intuitive and commonsense explanation for the personality differences between siblings of different birth ranks. Additionally, the publication of popular resources, such as Kevin Leman's *Birth Order Book* (1985), that attribute myriad individual differences to birth order can create the impression that birth order plays a very significant role in personality development.

From 1976 to the end of the twentieth century researchers conducted more than 141 studies of the relationship between birth order and personality. The methodologically sound studies among this number generally have revealed few reliable differences in personality variables due to birth order

Research suggests that siblings' roles in families depend more on gender, differing ages, and other variables than on actual birth order. DEAN CONGER/CORBIS

(Dunn and Plomin 1990; Ernst and Angst 1983; Jefferson, Herbst, and McCrae 1998; Parker 1998; Phillips 1998; Stewart, Stewart, and Campbell 2001).

Frank Sulloway's book *Born to Rebel* (1996) generated renewed interest in birth order and personality research by contending that firstborn children are more responsible, competitive, and conventional, while laterborns are more playful, cooperative, and rebellious. Although Sulloway's rationale of niche-picking within the family is compelling, the hypothesized relationships have received only marginal support using the big-five model of personality, which comprises the traits of neuroticism, extraversion, openness, agreeableness, and conscientiousness (Jefferson et al. 1998). Within-family studies have yielded slightly more support for Sulloway's theory (Paulhus, Trapnell, and Chen 1999). Overall, studies of the relationship between birth order and personality have yielded very small effect sizes at best. Consequently, one can question whether birth order and

personality effects either are noticeable in everyday life or possess significance for clinical practice. It is likely that birth order and personality effects are more apparent than they are real.

Psychological Birth Order

Adlerian psychology and contributions from developmental psychology and role theory suggest that personality variables may relate more meaningfully to the roles that siblings construct or are ascribed rather than to actual birth order (Adler 1927; Hoffman 1991). That is, although a child may be the youngest, the gender mix of the siblings, the differences in ages, and other unique variables may combine to create a firstborn role for the youngest child.

Studies that have measured the perceived or psychological birth order of young adults revealed that 45 percent of men and 52 percent of women have a distinctive sibling role in their families and that psychological and actual birth order is in agreement for 19 percent of people (Campbell, White, and Stewart 1991; Stewart and Campbell 1998). Further, sibling roles may mediate the effects of actual birth order and family atmosphere on personality traits (Stewart, Stewart, and Campbell 2001). Consequently, research using sibling or family roles may be more revealing than studies relying upon actual birth order, especially those that simply split participant samples into firstborn versus laterborn; this may mask the important effects of the nonshared family environment.

Birth Order and Intellectual Achievement

In addition to personality, birth order research has also largely focused on its relation to intelligence and scholastic achievement. The literature in this area reveals inconsistent results that have stemmed largely from confounding variables present in many birth order studies, including socioeconomic status, race and ethnicity, and age of participants (Rodgers et al. 2000; Steelman 1985; Sulloway 1996). Additionally, much of the research in this area indicates that birth order effects are inextricably related to family size, with stronger effects appearing in larger families (Heer 1985; Sputa and Paulson 1995).

Even studies of the effects of family size have been equivocal. Joseph Rodgers and colleagues (2000) analyzed the relationships of birth order and family size to the intelligence quotient (IQ) within families using data from the National Longitudinal Survey of Youth. Their results suggest that neither birth order nor family size directly affects IQ; rather, it is the parents' IQ that is more likely to influence both family size and children's IQ levels.

Several studies found achievement motivation, rather than intelligence, to be associated with ordinal position in the family (Vandergriff and Rust 1985). Later research on birth order and achievement began to focus on aspiration levels and achievement attributions more than simply on academic achievement. Firstborns attribute success or failure to internal causes and may even underestimate how their situations might have affected success, compared to laterborns (Phillips and Phillips 1994).

Toni Falbo (1981) observed a significant relationship between birth order and competitiveness. First and middle children scored significantly higher than lastborns on competitiveness. Only children did not differ significantly from any of the other groups on this variable. William Snell, Linda Hargrove, and Toni Falbo (1986) explored the relationship between birth order and achievement motivation and found a significant correlation between birth order and one specific facet of achievement motivation, competitiveness. It may be that the presence of competitiveness mediates the relationship between birth order and achievement.

See also: ACADEMIC ACHIEVEMENT; FAVORITISM/DIFFERENTIAL TREATMENT; PRIMOGENITURE; SELF-ESTEEM; SIBLING RELATIONSHIPS

Bibliography

Adler, A. (1927). *Understanding Human Nature.* Garden City, NY: Garden City Publishers.

Adler, A. (1956). "The Origin of the Neurotic Disposition." In *The Individual Psychology of Alfred Adler,* ed. H. L. Ansbacher and R. R. Ansbacher. New York: Basic Books.

Campbell, L. F.; White, J.; and Stewart, A. E. (1991). "The Relationship of Psychological Birth Order to Actual Birth Order." *Individual Psychology* 47:380–391.

Falbo, T. (1981). "Relationships between Birth Category, Achievement, and Interpersonal Orientation." *Journal of Personality and Social Psychology* 41:121–131.

Heer, D. M. (1985). "Effects of Sibling Number on Child Outcome." *Annual Review of Sociology* 11:27–47.

Hoffman, L. W. (1991). "The Influence of the Family Environment on Personality: Accounting for Sibling Differences." *Psychological Bulletin* 110:187–203.

Leman, K. (1985). *The Birth Order Book: Why You Are the Way You Are.* Grand Rapids, MI: Spire Books.

Paulhus, D. L.; Trapnell, P. D.; and Chen, D. (1999). "Birth Order Effects on Personality and Achievement within Families." *Psychological Science* 10:482–488.

Phillips, A. S., and Phillips, C. R. (1994). "Birth Order and Achievement Attributions." *Individual Psychology* 50:119–124.

Rodgers, J. L.; Cleveland, H. H.; van den Oord, E.; and Rowe, D. C. (2000). "Resolving the Debate over Birth Order, Family Size, and Intelligence." *American Psychologist* 55:599–612.

Snell, W. E.; Hargrove, L.; and Falbo, T. (1986). "Birth Order and Achievement Motivation Configurations in

Women and Men." *Individual Psychology: Journal of Adlerian Theory, Research, and Practice* 42:428–438.

Sputa, C. L., and Paulson, S. E. (1995). "Birth Order and Family Size: Influences on Adolescents' Achievement and Related Parenting Behaviors." *Psychological Reports* 76:43–51.

Steelman, L. C. (1985). "A Tale of Two Variables: A Review of the Intellectual Consequences of Sibship Size and Birth Order." *Review of Educational Research* 55:353–386.

Stewart, A. E., and Campbell, L. F. (1998). "Validity and Reliability of the White-Campbell Psychological Birth Order Inventory." *Journal of Individual Psychology* 54:41–60.

Stewart, A. E., and Stewart, E. A. (1995). "Trends in Birth Order Research: 1976–1993." *Individual Psychology: Journal of Adlerian Theory, Research and Practice* 51:21–36.

Stewart, A. E.; Stewart, E. A.; and Campbell, L. F. (2001). "The Relationship of Psychological Birth Order to the Family Atmosphere and to Personality." *Journal of Individual Psychology* 57:363–387.

Sulloway, F. J. (1996). *Born to Rebel: Birth Order, Family Dynamics, and Creative Lives.* New York: Pantheon Books.

Vandergriff, L., and Rust, J. O. (1985). "The Relationship between Classroom Behavior and Self-concept." *Education* 106:172–178.

GLORIA M. MONTES DE OCA

ALAN E. STEWART

BOUNDARY AMBIGUITY

On September 11, 2001, four commercial airliners were deliberately crashed—two into the World Trade Center in New York City, one into the Pentagon in Washington, DC, and one into a field in Pennsylvania—and more than 4,000 families from over eighty countries were simultaneously plunged into uncertainty. Relatively few of these families knew with certainty whether their loved ones on the planes or in the buildings were dead or alive; even those who did know had no information about why or how this tragedy had happened. These families—and, to a lesser degree, millions of eyewitnesses around the world—began an unprecedented journey of meaning-making characterized in great measure by a concept known as *boundary ambiguity.*

Every family, at many points in the life-cycle, must deal with changes in its boundaries: the symbolic markers between itself and its environment and among its members. Exits and entries are inevitable. Some are expected: Children are born into the family, adolescents leave for college or military service or just "their own place," couples marry, aging members die. Others are unpredictable and sometimes shocking: An aging parent demonstrates signs of dementia, a child is kidnapped, infertility changes a couple's dreams for their family, a family emigrates from their war-torn country with few resources or options. At any transition point, normative or nonnormative, a family must renegotiate its internal and external boundaries. These exits and entries constitute a challenge to the family's primary task of boundary maintenance and create stress for the family.

Since the 1940s, sociologists and family researchers have studied the ways families experience and manage stress. Boundary ambiguity has become a valuable concept in understanding why even healthy families sometimes struggle to do this well. Researcher and family therapist Pauline Boss defines boundary ambiguity as a state, resulting from either nonnormative or normative stressor events, in which family members are uncertain about who is in the family and who is out, or about who is performing which roles and tasks within the family system (Boss 1977, 1987, 2002). In some stressful situations, the family cannot obtain the facts surrounding the troubling event. This degree of uncertainty—Is a missing member dead or alive? What will the course of a terminal illness be?—prevents the family from defining the situation clearly enough to know how to respond to it (Boss 1993).

In other stressful situations, the facts are available to the family but the members ignore, deny, or distort those facts. Therapists, researchers, and other outside observers may believe they are able to objectively identify who is in the family and in what capacity, but *the family's perception of the event and the meaning they give it comprise the critical variable in determining family membership*

In some stressful situations, such as those faced by individuals who had family members in the World Trade Center towers when they were attacked, uncertainty about the fate of loved ones prevents the family from knowing how to respond to the event. A/P WIDE WORLD PHOTOS

and, therefore, the existence and degree of boundary ambiguity" (Boss 1987, p. 709, emphasis in the original). In other words, the discrepancy between an observer's perception and the family's perception cannot be resolved by emphasizing facts, as long as the family assigns a different meaning to those facts.

Definitions of boundaries in the family are further complicated by any incongruence between a family's perception of a member's *physical* presence or absence and his or her *psychological* presence or absence. One may not be synonymous with the other. Adoption researcher Debra Fravel and her colleagues (2000) describe physical presence as the literal, bodily existence of a person in the family and psychological presence as the symbolic existence of that person in the hearts and minds of family members in a way that affects their

emotions, thoughts, and sense of identity as individuals and as a family. In cases of a soldier missing in action or of a kidnapped child, for example, remaining family members may be emotionally preoccupied with the missing member and have a strong sense that he or she is still part of the family, still influences decisions, still deserves loyalty. The person is physically absent but psychologically present. A different discrepancy is present when a member has a disease such as Alzheimer's disease or is preoccupied with work problems. The member is physically present but psychologically absent. Both kinds of incongruence create boundary ambiguity and challenge the family's ability to manage the stressful event that resulted in the incongruence.

The basic premise is that a system needs to be sure of its components, that is, who is inside system boundaries physically and psychologically, and who is outside, physically and psychologically. Furthermore, that knowledge must be based on congruence between reality and perceptions. It is suggested that a major consequence of an ambiguous system, that is, a system that is not sure of its components, is that systemic communication, feedback and subsequent adjustment over time are curtailed. The system cannot subsequently adapt to the stress of inevitable developmental changes throughout the family life cycle nor to stress from equally inevitable unpredicted crises. (Boss 1977, p. 142).

Boundary ambiguity as a variable in family stress research has been studied in families of soldiers missing in action; families of corporate executives; families launching adolescents; couples dealing with infertility; elderly widows; families with kidnapped children; clergy families; farm families transferring farm ownership; divorced and remarried families; adoptive families, adopted children, and birthmothers; and families providing care to members with Alzheimer's disease. Some of these families are managing relatively normative stressors; others are faced with unexpected, unusual life circumstances. In some of these situations, members' physical absence is incongruent with their psychological presence; in others, their physical presence is incongruent with their psychological absence. Nevertheless, in all, the perceptions of the remaining family members are the critical factor in whether the family is able to define and maintain the boundaries of the family and thus manage the stress more effectively.

Coping with Boundary Ambiguity: Two Approaches

The family gamble. When boundary ambiguity is created by a lack of clear facts about the event, some families resolve the ambiguity by arbitrarily deciding on a perception of the event that makes the most sense given the available information. Boss refers to this as the *family gamble* (1987, 2002). Indeed, it does lower the degree of boundary ambiguity, but only as long as the chosen perception is not threatened by new information. For example, a family may decide, based on limited medical information, that a member in a coma is not going to wake up. This decision lowers the ambiguity and allows the family to reorganize their boundaries, but if a nurse reports that the member showed some signs of regaining consciousness, the ambiguity will likely rise. Even though the new information is positive, it again has a disorganizing influence on the family boundaries. Although this constant renegotiation of family membership and interaction is stressful—from high ambiguity to low and back again over time—Boss's research suggests that, "despite the uncertainty of their decision . . . a family is always better off making an educated guess about the status of their loss rather than continuing indefinitely in limbo" (1999, p. 94). Long-term, chronic ambiguity is almost impossible for even healthy families to tolerate.

Denial. Related to the family gamble is the place of denial in managing boundary ambiguity. Families may refuse to acknowledge a physical reality or the facts about a stressor event. Although denial is often labeled as an unhealthy response, it actually may be either functional or dysfunctional in dealing with boundary ambiguity. Particularly in the early stages of a stressful event, a cognitive decision to deny a negative outcome may allow a family to maintain morale while they wait for further evidence. In the wake of the September 11 tragedy, for example, relatives of possible victims who were interviewed by reporters consistently used the phrase, "Till we know for sure. . . ." One woman said, "Even if there are only two more hours of this hope, I'll take those two hours."

As the event unfolds, however, or if the situation remains ambiguous over a long period of time, denial becomes increasingly dysfunctional as a means of coping with the stress, because it becomes a barrier to reorganizing the family structure and interaction. The family instead defends itself against feeling the emotion of the possible negative reality.

Other families, in a kind of *reverse denial,* also defend against experiencing the painful loss of a member by prematurely closing out the one whose membership in the family is ambiguous. A parent with a terminal illness, for example, might be excluded from his or her former decision-making role; perhaps other family members stop confiding in him or her about emotional or relational concerns. Both extremes of denial, although understandable in their attempts to reduce the pain of the loss inherent in the boundary ambiguity, serve to increase the family's dysfunction.

Cultural Differences in the Experience of Boundary Ambiguity

Although all families face the challenge of boundary maintenance, cultural value orientations affect how they perceive and respond to ambiguity and even how they may practice denial. First, families from different cultures hold different values about exits and entries themselves. In some cultures, for example, parents see themselves as failures if their children do not move away and become independent; in others, parents consider themselves failures if their children do. In some cultures, family interaction is relatively democratic; in other, hierarchy and parent-child distance are valued more highly than is open intergenerational communication. Exits and entries thus are assigned different meanings from one culture to another, and what may be considered ambiguous in one may not be in another.

Cultures also hold differing values about time, relationships, and nature (Kluckhohn and Strodt-beck 1961), and these values will affect a family's response to ambiguity. For example, in cultures oriented toward submission to or harmony with nature more than mastery over nature, a socially appropriate response to incomplete information may be resignation. In a culture that more highly values mastery over nature, an aggressive search for the missing facts may be expected by both the family and others around them.

Another example may be found in cultures that value the past more highly than the future. In such cultures, members who have died or disappeared are often kept psychologically present. In China, Africa, and India, for example, ancestor worship is one means of the ongoing integration and unity of the family. Departed members have an ongoing role in family decisions and behavior, and living members can, in some cases, influence the peace of their ancestors by their own present behavior (Augsburger 1986). In such families, maintaining psychological presence of an absent member may be much more functional than it would in a culture more oriented to the future.

Even denial may be influenced by cultural values. Our cultural context teaches us what we should and should not notice and how to interpret what we do see. Families do not respond to ambiguity in a vacuum. Perhaps families who are able to incorporate elements of other value orientations do best. Boss found, in her research with families coping with dementia, that "both mastery and a spiritual acceptance of the situation are highly functional for caregiving families as they live with the ambiguous loss of Alzheimer's disease. Indeed, those who use only mastery manifest the most anxiety and depression" (Boss 1999, p. 116; see also Kaplan and Boss 1999).

A special case of boundary ambiguity related to cultural value orientations is that of immigrant families. When a family must flee a dangerous situation in their home country, they may come to a new country with few economic and sociocultural resources. Family members may be left behind, and the new context may hold no familiar traditions or rituals. Parents may be homesick and emotionally preoccupied with the well-being of loved ones far away and therefore be psychologically absent for their children.

Monica McGoldrick and Joe Giordano note that "migration is so disruptive that it seems to add an entire extra stage to the life cycle for those who must negotiate it. Adjusting to a new culture is not a single event, but a prolonged developmental process that affects family members differently, depending on their life cycle phase" (1996, pp. 17–18). The normative boundary ambiguity that all families face is exacerbated by the additional stressors of immigration and adaptation to a new culture. Families who migrate with adolescents may face some of the most daunting challenges: They will soon be launching children, with the attending ambiguity of that exit, and they may not be able to honor the family obligations expected of them by absent members still in the home country. Thus, immigration creates a kind of boundary ambiguity in which the family may wonder whether they themselves are in or out: in or out of their extended family, in or out of their home culture, in or out of the new culture.

Helping Families Manage Boundary Ambiguity

Strategies for helping stressed families may be more effective if the initial focus is on clarifying the perception of who is in and who is out of the family. Because family members of different ages and genders will often vary in how they interpret an unclear loss, a primary goal might be to help a family achieve some degree of agreement in their definition of the situation (Boss 1999).

As this redefinition and reorganization of the family occurs, helpers may find the use of appropriate rituals—borrowed from others or created by the family members themselves—to be a powerful expression of both the ambiguity itself and the resolution of that ambiguity. Rituals can help families make the transition to their new identity even as they honor the missing member(s). The ultimate goal for families is to find some way to change even though the ambiguity of their situation might remain.

Every family will at some point face a situation that represents an irrevocable change in the family's structure and interaction. Adapting to these changes in the family system is an important coping strategy for all families and their members. "Whether these changes result in relief or sadness, they represent the loss of something irretrievable. Families cannot go back to the way things were. Human development brings inevitable change; hence family boundaries also change. The perception of who is in and who is out must match those changes if family boundaries are to be maintained." (Boss 2002, p. 106)

See also: BOUNDARY DISSOLUTION; DISABILITIES; GRIEF, LOSS, AND BEREAVEMENT; STRESS

Bibliography

Augsburger, D. W. (1986). *Pastoral Counseling Across Cultures.* Philadelphia: Westminster Press.

Boss, P. (1977). "A Clarification of the Concept of Psychological Father Presence in Families Experiencing Ambiguity of Boundary." *Journal of Marriage and the Family* 39:141–151.

Boss, P. (1987). "Family Stress." In *Handbook of Marriage and the Family,* ed. M. B. Sussman and S. K. Steinmetz. New York: Plenum Press.

Boss, P. (1993). "The Reconstruction of Family Life with Alzheimer's Disease: Generating Theory to Lower Family Stress from Ambiguous Loss." In *Sourcebook of Family Theories and Methods: A Contextual Approach,* ed. P. G. Boss, W. J. Doherty, R. LaRossa, W. R. Schumm, and S. K. Steinmetz. New York: Plenum Press.

Boss, P. (1999). *Ambiguous Loss: Learning to Live with Unresolved Grief.* Cambridge, MA: Harvard University Press.

Boss, P. (2002). *Family Stress Management: A Contextual Approach,* 2nd edition. Thousand Oaks, CA: Sage Publications.

Boss, P., and Greenberg, J. (1984). "Family Boundary Ambiguity: A New Variable in Family Stress Theory." *Family Process* 23(4):535–546.

Boss, P.; Pearce McCall, D.; and Greenberg, J. (1987). "Normative Loss in Mid-Life Families: Rural, Urban, and Gender Differences." *Family Relations* 36(4):437–443.

Fravel, D. L.; McRoy, R. G.; and Grotevant, H. D. (2000) "Birthmother Perceptions of the Psychologically Present Adopted Child: Adoption Openness and Boundary Ambiguity." *Family Relations* 49:425–433.

Kaplan, L., and Boss, P. (1999). "Depressive Symptoms among Spousal Caregivers of Institutionalized Mates with Alzheimer's: Boundary Ambiguity and Mastery as Predictors." *Family Process* 38(1):85–103.

Kluckhohn, F. R., and Strodtbeck, F. L. (1961). *Variations in Value Orientations.* Reprint, Westport, CT: Greenwood Press, 1973.

McGoldrick, M., and Giordano, J. (1996). "Overview: Ethnicity and Family Therapy." In *Ethnicity and Family Therapy,* 2d edition, ed. M. McGoldrick, J. Giordano, and J. K. Pearce. New York: Guilford Press.

CARLA M. DAHL

BOUNDARY DISSOLUTION

Boundary dissolution, also termed boundary confusion, distortion, diffusion, or violation, refers to a failure to recognize the psychological distinctiveness of individuals or a confusion of their interpersonal roles. The concept of boundaries has a rich history in family systems theory but also is important to psychodynamic explanations of childhood psychopathology. Indeed, the concept itself might be said to stand at the boundary between psychodynamic and family systems perspectives.

Salvador Minuchin (1974) argues that the maintenance of psychological boundaries in the family, particularly between children and their parents, is crucial to healthy development. Boundaries define appropriate family roles (e.g., by clarifying who is the parent and who is the child); demarcate developmental differences (e.g., by defining the special responsibilities or privileges of the eldest child); and ensure that parents meet their adult emotional needs in the marital relationship rather than through their children (e.g., by turning to the spouse for nurturance rather than the child). Ideally, boundaries are flexible, allowing family members to be close to one another and yet to have a sense of separateness. Kenji Kameguchi (1996) likens boundaries to a "membrane" that surrounds each individual and subsystem in the family. Like the membrane around a cell, boundaries need to be firm enough to ensure the integrity of the cell and yet permeable enough to allow communication between cells. Overly rigid boundaries might constrict family relationships and limit family members' access to one another (e.g., "children should be seen and not heard"), whereas overly permeable or blurred boundaries might lead to confusion between the generations (e.g., "who is the parent and who is the child?" [Hiester 1995]).

There are many different ways in which the psychological boundaries between one person and another might be blurred. Therefore, boundary dissolution is best conceptualized as a multifaceted phenomenon. The literature provides evidence for four dimensions of boundary dissolution—*enmeshment, intrusiveness, role-reversal,* and *spousification*—that research shows to have different correlates and consequences for child development (Brown and Kerig 1998; Rowa, Kerig, and Geller 2001).

Dimensions of Boundary Dissolution

Enmeshment. At the extreme of boundary dissolution is *enmeshment,* a lack of acknowledgement of the separateness between the self and other. Minuchin (1974) described the enmeshed family as one in which family members are overly involved with and reactive to one another, such that "a sneeze brings on a flurry of handkerchief offers." On the positive side, such families may provide feelings of mutuality, belonging, and emotional support. However, at the extreme, enmeshment interferes with the child's development of autonomy and individual agency. Changes in one family member quickly reverberate throughout the entire family system and may be perceived as threats to

the family togetherness. For example, adolescence may precipitate a crisis when a young person begins to assert his or her own independence, such as by expressing the desire to go away for college (Kerig, in press-a).

In *psychodynamic theory* enmeshment is the initial state of being from which all children must wrest their sense of individual selfhood. According to separation-individual theory (Mahler, Pine, and Bergman 1975), infants originally experience themselves as part of a symbiotic relationship with their mothers. Over the course of infant development, inevitable failures in perfect empathy and wish-fulfillment help children to recognize that their mother is a separate individual with her own thoughts and feelings. However, in pathological development, emotionally deprived mothers may feel threatened by the infant's emergent sense of individuality and act in ways so as to promote and prolong this sense of parent-infant oneness. The consequences to the child can be severe, interfering with the ability to forge and assert a separate sense of identity. For example, enmeshment in the parent-child relationship is believed to be central to the development of *borderline personality disorder,* a syndrome characterized by the inability to preserve a cohesive sense of self and to maintain emotional boundaries between the self and other (Pine 1979). At a lesser extreme, childhood enmeshment predicts young adults' attachment insecurity and preoccupation with their families of origin (Allen and Hauser 1996).

Intrusiveness. Intrusiveness, also termed *psychological control,* is characterized by overly controlling and coercive parenting that intrudes into the child's thoughts and emotions and is not respectful of the autonomy of the child (Barber 1996). Whereas enmeshment is characterized by a seamless equality ("we feel alike"), the intrusive relationship is a hierarchical one in which the parent attempts to direct the child's inner life ("you feel as I say"). Psychological control may be carried out in ways that are more subtle than overt behavioral control. Rather than telling the child directly what to do or think, the parent may use indirect hints and respond with guilt induction or withdrawal of love if the child refuses to comply. In short, a psychologically controlling parent strives to manipulate the child's thoughts and feelings in such a way that the child's psyche will conform to the parent's wishes. Longitudinal data show that infants of intrusive mothers later demonstrate problems in academic, social, behavioral, and emotional adjustment in first and second grades (Egeland, Pianta, and O'Brien 1993). Psychological control also is predictive of anxiety and depression in children (see Barber 2002) and of delinquency, particularly in African-American youth (Walker-Barnes and Mason 2001).

Role-reversal. Role-reversal, also termed *parentification,* refers to a dynamic in which parents turn to children for emotional support (Boszormenyi-Nagy and Spark 1973; Jurkovic 1997). Although learning to be responsive and empathic to others' needs is a healthy part of child development, parentification involves an exploitative relationship in which the parents' expectations exceed the child's capacities, the parent ignores the child's developmental needs, or the parent expects nurturance but does not give it reciprocally (Chase 1999). A parent engaged in role-reversal may be ostensibly warm and solicitous to the child, but the relationship is not a truly supportive one because the parents' emotional needs are being met at the expense of the child's. Further, children are often unable to meet these developmentally inappropriate expectations, which may lead to frustration, disappointment, and even anger (Zeanah and Klitzke 1991). In fact, parents' inappropriate expectations for children, such that they provide nurturing to their parents, are a key predictor of child maltreatment (Azar 1997).

Research shows that, over the course of childhood, young children who fulfill their parents' need for intimacy have difficulty regulating their behavior and emotions (Carlson, Jacobvitz, and Sroufe 1995) and demonstrate a pseudomature, emotionally constricted interpersonal style (Johnston 1990). In the longer term, childhood role reversal is associated with difficulties in young adults' ability to individuate from their families (Fullinwider-Bush and Jacobvitz 1993) and adjust to college (Chase, Deming, and Wells 1998). Parent-child role reversal also is associated with depression, low-self esteem, anxiety (Jacobvitz and Bush 1996), and eating disorders (Rowa, Kerig, and Geller 2001) in young women. Due to cultural expectations that associate caregiving with the feminine role, daughters may be particularly vulnerable to being pulled into the role of "mother's

little helper" (Brody 1996; Chodorow 1978). Consistent with *family systems theory* (Minuchin 1974), boundary violations also are more likely to occur when the marital relationship is an unhappy one and the parent turns to the child for fulfillment of unmet emotional needs (Fish, Belsky, and Youngblade 1991; Jacobvitz and Bush 1996).

Role-reversal may take different forms, depending on the role the child is asked to play. Parents might behave in a child-like way, turning to the child to act as a parenting figure, termed *parentification* or *child-as-parent* (Walsh 1979; Goglia et al. 1992); or they may relate to the child as a peer, confidante, or friend (Brown and Kerig 1998), which might be termed *adultification* or *child-as-peer.* Although providing a parent with friendship, emotional intimacy, and companionship ultimately interferes with the child's individuation and social development outside the home, the negative implications of a peer-like parent-child relationship may be less severe than a complete reversal of roles in which the parent relinquishes all caregiving responsibilities. Role reversal can also occur between adults, such as when an adult turns to the spouse to act as a parent, seeking guidance and care instead of a mutually autonomous relationship, termed *spouse-as-parent* (Boszormenyi-Nagy and Spark 1973; Chase 1999). Another form of role reversal occurs when the parent behaves in a seductive manner toward the child, placing the child not in the role of parent or peer, but of romantic partner.

Spousification. Of particular concern to Minuchin (1974) was the blurring of the boundary between the marital and child subsystem, which can lead children to become inappropriately involved in their parents' marital problems. This may take the form of a *compensatory closeness* between an unhappily married parent and a child of the other sex, termed *spousification* (Sroufe and Ward 1980) or *child-as-mate* (Walsh 1979; Goglia et al. 1992). Although spousification is often considered to be a form of role-reversal, it is distinguished by the fact that the parent is seeking a special kind of intimacy—perhaps even including sexual gratification (Jacobvitz, Riggs, and Johnson 1999). For example, Sroufe and colleagues (1985) found that emotionally troubled mothers, many of whom were survivors of incest, engaged in seductive behaviors with their young sons while responding in a hostile way toward daughters. However, the relationship between spousification and gender may be more complex. When marital conflict spills over onto parent-child relationships it also may take a hostile form, termed *negative spousification* or *spillover* (Kerig, Cowan, and Cowan 1993). Spillover of marital tensions may cause a parent to view a child in the same negative terms as the spouse, thus blurring the boundaries between them (e.g., "You sound just like your father"; "You're your mother's daughter, aren't you?") (Kerig, in press-b). Research has shown that maternal stress and depression increase the risk of negative spousification that, in turn, predicts anxiety and depression in school-age children (Brown and Kerig 1998).

Is Boundary Dissolution a Whole-Family or Dyadic Phenomenon?

Minuchin (1974) proposed that entire families could be characterized with qualities such as enmeshment. However, although the whole family system might be characterized by a particular type of boundary rigidity or permeability, it is also possible for there to be multiple kinds of boundaries in a family. Philip and Carolyn Cowan (1990) point out that an enmeshed mother-child relationship, for example, is usually counterbalanced by detachment in the relationship between father and the child. If different forms of boundaries exist simultaneously, Cowan and Cowan ask, "How, then, are we to describe *the family*?" (p. 42).

To address the dilemma of multiple relationships, many family systems investigators assess the boundaries between each dyad in the family (Kerig 2001b). For example, a commonly used clinical method of assessing multiple relationships in the family is the *genogram* (McGoldrick, Gerson, and Shellenberger 1997), which depicts the quality of the relationship between each pair of family members. A dotted line may be used to depict a disengaged relationship, a solid line a close relationship, and a double line an enmeshed relationship. By examining the constellation of relationships within a family, a clinician is able to discern where boundary violations have occurred and whether enmeshment in one relationship interferes with closeness between other family members. By the same token, the majority of questionnaire measures used to assess boundary dissolution inquire separately about the mother-child and father-child relationships.

Is Boundary Dissolution a Culturally Bounded Phenomenon?

Western psychology has been criticized for treating psychological constructs derived from the standards of industrialized, European societies as normative (Anderson 1999). A number of critics have argued that Western psychology promotes a highly individualistic, autonomous self as the ideal, whereas other societies value a more communal and interdependent sense of self (Markus and Kitayama 1991; Sampson 1993). Therefore, Western psychologists might perceive pathological boundary dissolution among family members who are reflecting their own culture's healthy norms of communality.

For example, Nancy Boyd-Franklin (1989) argues that African-American families developed flexible roles in order to respond to the challenges of poverty and racism. Extended kinships involve many different, sometimes biologically unrelated, adults in the rearing of children, so that there is role diffusion in parenting. Additionally, the common necessity for both parents to work outside the home has meant that "Black women have sometimes had to act as the 'father' and Black men as the 'mother' . . . while children are often required to assume 'parental child' roles necessary for family survival" (p. 64). Boyd-Franklin identifies the "parental child" as a common experience in the African-American family, where working single mothers often assign the task of caring for younger children to the oldest child, placing that child in a parental role. As long as the responsibilities assigned to the eldest are clear and well-defined, with the parent remaining "in charge" and parenting functions "delegated and not abdicated," the parental child family structure may be adaptive. However, a mother who is so overburdened that she begins to rely on her eldest child as her "right-hand man" places unreasonable responsibilities on the child, interfering with the child's social and emotional development. In addition, high rates of teenage pregnancy require many older women to take on the burden of caring not only for their children but for the children of their children. With the blurring of family roles in the three-generational family, "the mother of the female adolescent with a baby never fully becomes a grandmother while her daughter is never allowed to fully function as a mother to her own child" (p. 74). Therefore, although flexible boundaries can be a source of strength, they also can leave families vulnerable to role confusion and boundary dissolution.

Louis Anderson (1999) also acknowledges the negative implications of a reversal of roles in the African-American family, such as when the child is forced to "parent the parent." However, in the context of African-American culture, flexible family roles and interdependence are the norm, and children are socialized to advance quickly through development in order to become contributors to the family's welfare. Anderson argues that, before taking on responsibilities such as the care of younger siblings, African-American children go through an extended apprenticeship and are provided with supervision and instruction so that they are developmentally prepared for the tasks they are to assume. What most clearly differentiates pathological parentification from healthy socialization is that, although children are given responsibilities in the normative African-American family, they are still allowed to be children and "are not elevated to the executive structure of the household" (p. 164).

The concept of boundary dissolution also has been found to be relevant in family research outside the United States. For example, Kenji Kameguchi and Stephen Murphy-Shigetmatsu (2001) use the concept of boundary dissolution to understand the pervasive problem of Japanese children refusing to go to school. Following Minuchin (1974), they argue that a strong *membrane* around the parental subsystem is essential to the healthy organization of the family. However, among Japanese families of school-refusing children, Kameguchi and his colleagues observe a common pattern of boundary dissolution characterized by an undifferentiated mother-child relationship. The membrane separating the mother and child is diffuse, whereas the mother-father and father-child relationships are disengaged and easily disrupted. "Weakness in a parental membrane leads to vague generational boundaries between a parental dyad and a child [and] interferes with the developmental tasks of adolescen[ce]. . . . The child is thus deprived of experiences that accelerate his or her psychological separation from the parents and that also assist the parents in separating from the adolescent" (Kameguchi and Murphy-Shigetmatsu 2001, p. 68). Ultimately, both parents and child collude in behaviors that interfere with individuation, such as the child's staying home from school.

Interventions for Boundary Dissolution

Interventions may focus on the individual parent, the marital relationship, the family system, or the child. For example, Ivan Boszormenyi-Nagy and Geraldine Spark (1973) recommend helping individual parents to resolve issues from their own childhoods so as to refrain from attempting to redress old grievances in their relationship with their children. In her work with divorcing parents, Janet Johnston (1999) averts role reversal by encouraging parents to seek sources of social support outside of their relationships with children. Family systems therapists, in turn, focus on strengthening the parental coalition so as to help parents get their needs met in the marital relationship or else attempt to directly change the dynamics of the parent-child relationship. Boyd-Franklin (1989) uses Minuchin's (1974) family systems approach as an intervention for boundary dissolution in the African-American family, as does Kameguchi (1998) in the Japanese context. For example, in the case of the multigenerational family, a new *alliance of executives* can be fostered between the grandmother and her daughter that encourages the grandmother to support her daughter's learning to be an effective parent. In the case of the parentalized child in a single mother household, the goal is to allow the child to continue being helpful to the mother, but to return the child to the sibling subsystem in which he or she can exercise a developmentally appropriate level of leadership and *junior executive power*. Using *strategic family therapy techniques,* Helen Coale (1999) describes techniques for countering boundary dissolution such as creating rituals that shift parents and children into more appropriate roles. In turn, individual work with children can provide better coping strategies that *de-triangulate* the child from parental or interparental problems (Kerig 2001a). In psychoanalytic treatment, Marolyn Wells and Rebecca Jones (1999) provide a corrective emotional experience to help adults who were parentified as children to overcome their shame, defensiveness, difficulty tolerating interpersonal disappointments, and compulsion to recreate in the present the kinds of relationships they experienced in the past.

See also: ATTACHMENT: PARENT-CHILD RELATIONSHIPS; BOUNDARY AMBIGUITY; DEVELOPMENT: SELF; FAMILY DIAGRAMMATIC ASSESSMENT: GENOGRAM; FAMILY SYSTEMS THEORY; PARENTING STYLES; SEPARATION-INDIVIDUATION; THERAPY: FAMILY RELATIONSHIPS; THERAPY: PARENT-CHILD RELATIONSHIPS; TRIANGULATION

Bibliography

Allen, J. P., and Hauser, S. T. (1996). "Autonomy and Relatedness in Adolescent-Family Interactions as Predictors of Young Adults' States of Mind Regarding Attachment." *Development and Psychopathology* 8:793–809.

Anderson, L. P. (1999). "Parentification in the Context of the African American Family." In *Burdened Children,* ed. N. D. Chase. Thousand Oaks, CA: Sage.

Azar, S. T. (1997). "A Cognitive Behavioral Approach to Understanding and Treating Parents Who Physically Abuse Their Children." In *Child Abuse: New Directions in Prevention and Treatment across the Lifespan,* ed. D. A. Wolfe, R. J. McMahon, and R. D. Peters. Thousand Oaks, CA: Sage.

Barber, B. K. (1996). "Parental Psychological Control: Revisiting a Neglected Construct." *Child Development* 67: 3296–3319.

Barber, B. K., ed. (2002). *Intrusive Parenting: How Psychological Control Affects Children and Adolescents.* Washington, DC: American Psychological Association.

Boszormenyi-Nagy, I., and Spark, G. (1973). *Invisible Loyalties: Reciprocity in Intergenerational Family Therapy.* New York: Harper and Row.

Brody, L. R. (1996). "Gender, Emotional Expression and Parent-Child Boundaries." In *Emotion: Interdisciplinary Perspectives,* ed. R. D. Kavenaugh, B. Zimmerberg, and S. Fein. Hillsdale, NJ: Lawrence Erlbaum Associates.

Brown, C. A., and Kerig, P. K. (1998). "Parent-Child Boundaries as Mediators of the Effects of Maternal Distress on Children's Adjustment." Paper presented at the annual meeting of the American Psychological Association, San Francisco, August.

Carlson, E. A.; Jacobvitz, D.; and Sroufe, L. A. (1995). "A Developmental Investigation of Inattentiveness and Hyperactivity." *Child Development* 66:37–54.

Chase, N. D. (1999). "Parentification: An Overview of Theory, Research, and Societal Issues." In *Burdened Children,* ed. N. D. Chase. Thousand Oaks, CA: Sage.

Chodorow, N. J. (1978). *The Reproduction of Mothering.* Berkeley: University of California Press.

Coale, H. W. (1999). "Therapeutic Rituals and Rites of Passage: Helping Parentified Children and Their Families." In *Burdened Children,* ed. N. D. Chase. Thousand Oaks, CA: Sage.

Cowan, P. A., and Cowan, C. P. (1990). "Becoming a Family: Research and Intervention." In *Normal Families,* Vol. 1: *Methods of Family Research: Biographies of Research Projects,* ed. I. E. Sigel and G. H. Brody. Hillsdale, NJ: Lawrence Erlbaum Associates.

Egeland, B. R.; Pianta, R. C.; and O'Brien, M. A. (1993). "Maternal Intrusiveness in Infancy and Child Maladaptation in Early School Years." *Development and Psychopathology* 5:359–370.

Fish, M.; Belsky, J.; and Youngblade, L. (1991). "Developmental Antecedents and Measurement of Intergenerational Boundary Violation in a Nonclinical Sample." *Journal of Family Psychology* 4:278–297.

Fulliwider-Bush, N., and Jacobvitz, D. B. (1993). "The Transition to Young Adulthood: Generational Boundary Dissolution and Female Identity Development." *Family Process* 32:87–103.

Goglia, L. R.; Jurkovic, G. J.; Burt, A. M.; and Burge-Callaway, K. G. (1992). "Generational Boundary Distortions by Adult Children of Alcoholics: Child-as-Parent and Child-as-Mate." *American Journal of Family Therapy* 20:291–299.

Hiester, M. (1995). "Who's the Parent and Who's the Child: Generational Boundary Dissolution between Mothers and Their Children." Paper presented at the biennial meeting of the Society for Research in Child Development, Indianapolis, IN, March.

Jacobvitz, D. B., and Bush, N. F. (1996). "Reconstructions of Family Relationships: Parent-Child Alliances, Personal Distress, and Self-Esteem." *Developmental Psychology* 32:732–743.

Jacobvitz, D. B.; Morgan, E.; Kretchmar, M. D.; and Morgan, Y. (1991). "The Transmission of Mother-Child Boundary Disturbances across Three Generations." *Development and Psychopathology* 3:513–528.

Jacobvitz, D. B.; Riggs, S.; and Johnson, E. (1999). "Cross-Sex and Same-Sex Family Alliances: Immediate and Long-Term Effects on Sons and Daughters." In *Burdened Children,* ed. N. D. Chase. Thousand Oaks, CA: Sage.

Johnston, J. R. (1990). "Role Diffusion and Role Reversal: Structural Variations in Divorced Families and Children's Functioning." *Family Relations* 39:405–413.

Jurkovic, G. J. (1997). *Lost Childhoods: The Plight of the Parentified Child.* Philadelphia: Brunner/Mazel.

Jurkovic, G. J. (1998). Destructive Parentification in Families: Causes and Consequences. In *Family Psychopathology: The Relational Roots of Dysfunctional Behavior,* ed. L. L'Abate. New York: Guilford.

Kameguchi, K. (1996). "Chaotic States of Generational Boundaries in Contemporary Japanese Families." In *Research on Family Resources and Needs across the World,* ed. M. Cusinato. Milan: Edizioni Universitarie di Lettere Economia Diritto.

Kameguchi, K. (1998). "Family Therapy with Japanese Families." In *The Family and Family Therapy in International Perspective,* ed. U. Gielen. Trieste: Edizioni Lint Trieste.

Kameguchi, K., and Murphy-Shigetmatsu, S. (2001). "Family Psychology and Family Therapy in Japan." *American Psychologist* 56:65–70.

Kerig, P. K. (2001a). "Children's Coping with Interparental Conflict." In *Interparental Conflict and Child Development,* ed. J. H. Grych and F. D. Fincham. Cambridge, UK: Cambridge University Press.

Kerig, P. K. (2001b). "Conceptual Issues in Family Observational Research." In *Family Observational Coding Systems: Resources for Systemic Research,* ed. P. K. Kerig and K. M. Lindahl. Hillsdale, NJ: Lawrence Erlbaum Associates.

Kerig, P. K. (in press-a). *Developmental Psychopathology: From Infancy through Adolescence,* 5th edition. New York: McGraw-Hill.

Kerig, P. K. (in press-b). "In Search of Protective Processes for Children Exposed to Violence." *Journal of Emotional Abuse.*

Kerig, P. K.; Cowan, P. A.; and Cowan, C. P. (1993). "Marital Quality and Gender Differences in Parent-Child Interaction." *Developmental Psychology* 29:931–939.

Mahler, M. S.; Pine, F.; and Bergman, A. (1975). *The Psychological Birth of the Human Infant.* New York: Basic Books.

Markus, H. R., and Kitayama, S. (1991). "Culture and the Self: Implications for Cognition, Emotion, and Motivation." *Psychological Review* 98:224–253.

McGoldrick, M.; Gerson, R.; and Shellenberger, S. (1997). *Genograms: Assessment and Intervention.* New York: Norton.

Minuchin, S. (1974). *Families and Family Therapy.* Cambridge, MA: Harvard University Press.

Pine, F. (1979). "On the Pathology of the Separation-Individuation Process as Manifested in Later Clinical Work: An Attempt at Delineation." *International Journal of Psychoanalysis* 60:225–242.

Rowa, K.; Kerig, P. K.; and Geller, J. (2001). "The Family and Anorexia: Examining Parent-Child Boundary Problems." *European Eating Disorders Review* 9:97–114.

Sampson, E. E. (1993). "Identity Politics: Challenges to Psychology's Understanding." *American Psychologist* 48:1219–1230.

Sroufe, L. A.; Jacobvitz, D.; Magelsdorf, S.; DeAngelo, E.; and Ward, M. J. (1985). "Generational Boundary Dissolution between Mothers and Their Preschool Children: A Relationship Systems Approach." *Child Development* 56:317–325.

Sroufe, L. A., and Ward, M. J. (1980). "Seductive Behavior of Mothers of Toddlers: Occurrence, Correlates and Family Origins." *Child Development* 51:1222–1229.

Walker-Barnes, C. J., and Mason, C. A. (2001). "Ethnic Differences in the Effect of Parenting on Gang Involvement and Gang Delinquency: A Longitudinal, Hierarchical Linear Modeling Perspective." *Child Development* 72:1814–1831.

Wells, M., and Jones, R. (1999). "Object Relations Therapy for Individuals with Narcissistic and Masochistic Parentification Styles." In *Burdened Children,* ed. N. D. Chase. Thousand Oaks, CA: Sage.

Zeanah, C. H., and Klitzke, M. (1991). "Role Reversal and the Self-Effacing Solution: Observations from Infant-Parent Psychotherapy." *Psychiatry: Interpersonal and Biological Processes* 54:346–357.

PATRICIA K. KERIG

BRAZIL

Brazil is the fifth largest country in the world, with 170 million inhabitants distributed throughout twenty-six states and the Federal District. The official language is Portuguese. When the Portugueses arrived in 1500, there were between two and five million Indians living in the territory. They spoke around one thousand different languages (UnB revista 2001). As frequently happens with those who are colonized, Indians were seen as inferior and became objects of acculturation. However, the Indians' rich languages, costumes, and way of life influenced the new "owners" of the land and their culture.

A native Brazilian family waits to see a doctor at one of few government health clinics available in a remote area of Estado do Rondonia. STEPHANIE MAZE/CORBIS

The Portuguese colonization was marked by depredation. The Portuguese exploited the riches of the land and exported them to Europe. During this period Brazil used slaves from different African countries for the sugar cane trade. Brazilian culture is therefore a peculiar mixture of three peoples—native Indians, Africans, and Portuguese.

A Historical Perspective on Family Life

The colonization of Brazil started on the shores of the Atlantic, in the northeast region of the country. During early colonial times, the economy was agrarian, based on the cultivation of single crops. This economic pattern depended upon control exerted by the social structure on the family system and on Indian and slave labor. The family was the center of life as it fulfilled both economical and political roles (Bruschini 1993).

Families, especially in the northeast where sugar cane grew, and in the southeast where coffee was the predominant crop, were composed of married couples, their children, and many aggregated persons—relatives, godchildren, workers, Indians, and slaves. These two groups—the nuclear family and all who lived around them—held in common a strong sense of commitment and obedience to the head of the household. The head of the household held personal and social authority and power. As the political chief and holder of all economic resources, he was called *colonel,* and was revered and feared by his family and those who worked for, served, and depended on him. Any act seen as disloyal to him was met with severe punishment.

Family life was based on strong patriarchal values. Roles were extremely hierarchical and rigid. Women cared for the house, raised the couple's many children, and zealously protected family traditions and social customs. Female authority was only shown in the absence of the husband. Men, on the other hand, were socially and sexually free (Bruschini 1993).

Marriages in the upper class were usually arranged. Building alliances between families to maintain power and economic interests was a priority. Love and affection were not usually the basis for unions and men used this as an "excuse" to seek lovers on their properties and often had children with other women. In this way the three cultures began a complex process of integration.

Consensual unions were common in other social classes. In such family systems, men tended not to feel obliged to assume patriarchal roles, and therefore many women became heads of households. Slaves were not allowed to stay together as families. Family members were separated among different properties in order to undermine the strength and cohesion of the African group to which the slave belonged (Brushini 1993).

The colonial patriarchal family structure became the symbol of family life in Brazil. The seminal work of Brazilian anthropologist Gilberto Freyre, particularly *Casa Grande e Senzala* (1943), helped consolidate this representation. Critics of Freyre's work argue that this social representation of family life should not be seen as the prevailing model for all areas of the country or for all social groups. It could be seen as an ideological construction, or ideal myth, of the integration of roles and relationships between unequal people and social groups—e.g., men/women, parents/children, master/slave or other laborers, white/Indian, white/Negro (Samara 1983; Almeida, Carneiro, and Silvana de Paula 1987).

Freyre's ideas have had a tremendous impact on how family and social life are thought of in Brazil. Angela M. de Almeida, Maria Jose Carneiro, and Silvana G. de Paula (1987) recognize that this model served as a blueprint for a set of values and ethics that has influenced all other forms of family life in Brazil. It may also have influenced other social spheres, such as politics, labor relations, and philosophies of citizenship and civil rights.

The colonization of southern Brazil presented distinctive features when compared to the northeast. The militaristic colonization, especially of São Paulo, and the movement called *Entradas e Bandeiras*—the male-dominated expeditions to map inland regions and claim ownership of the land—forced women to administer farms and control workers, including slaves (Neder 1998). Taking an active role in society, however, did not liberate women from submissiveness and subordination to male authority. Family structure remained extremely repressive, faithfully reproducing rules and norms of discipline and social control dictated by the Catholic faith brought from Portugal.

Research done by Eni de M. Samara (1983, 1987) shows that families in the São Paulo area were smaller, as couples had fewer children. Also, fewer extended family members lived with the nuclear family. Married children usually left their parents' house to build an independent life. Samara (1983) also found a peculiar trend—a great number of informal unions. Many men and women remained legally single but had as may as eight children with one or more partners. Society's acceptance of these children varied, depending on sex, race, and the socioeconomic status of the father.

During the nineteenth century, the agrarian, family-centered social organization began to change drastically. Urbanization, industrialization, and later, the end of slavery (1888) and Proclamation of the Republic (1889) were some of the forces of change. The Republican project included a revision and reorganization of roles both within the family and in society. The modern family was composed of the couple and their children. Marriages were no longer prompted solely by financial or political interests. The emotional and sexual needs of spouses were now considered (Corrêa 1982). The role of women changed drastically. They were to be mothers and supporters to their husbands. Women gained access to education in order to be educators of their children. This process targeted mainly white families of European descent (Neder 1998).

Aspects of the Contemporary Family

The dominant social representation of family in Brazil is the traditional family, comprised of a couple and their children, with an emphasis on the psychological and emotional bond (Bruschini and Ridenti 1994). Another important characteristic is the connection with extended families: Although the individuality of the couple is respected, spouses are expected to maintain close ties with families of origin. The degree of closeness, as well as the amount of participation of the extended family in the couple's daily life, varies with social, economical, and relational factors.

Family life in Brazil underwent major changes during the last three decades of the twentieth century. More diverse and complex forms emerged. The number of dual-worker, single-parent, and remarried families increased. Regardless of social class, families became smaller (Goldani 1994).

On the political level, movements to increase democracy and build citizenship raised feminist consciousness. Women have entered the work force and are seeking better education and equality in the workplace. Dual-career and dual-worker marriages have become common in urban areas. In the capital city, Brasilia, a vast number of man and women are employed full-time in public offices and in the administrative service sector.

Approximately five hundred men and women living in this area participated in a study regarding dual-career/dual-worker marriages (Diniz 1999). Men and women in the study agreed that work allows women to enjoy greater independence and freedom. Work, besides a source of financial success, is valued as a means to obtain personal and relational benefits, an increased sense of competency and self-esteem, and a social network. Discrimination in payment and sexual harassment were mentioned as disadvantages for women.

Women felt that the burden of traditional role expectations exacerbated work stress; they continue to be responsible for the majority of domestic activities. However, 35 percent of the men said that they perform approximately half or more of the household tasks. A cultural factor—easy access to hired help—probably mitigates role overload for women. Men and women are happy with their marriages and are willing to make efforts for the relationship to work (Diniz 1999).

The number of families living in poverty has increased dramatically. The main reasons for this are decreased spending power due to high inflation rates, increased unemployment rates, and political and economic policies that deprive access to social benefits. Many male and female heads of households have resorted to an informal job market and now depend on unstable income (Carvalho 1995).

Women have had a major role in guaranteeing the maintenance of the family. In an informal economy it is easier for them to become nannies, maids, and house cleaners. They also perform in-home activities such as sewing, embroidery, and handcrafting. Many have started small businesses, absorbing other family members' labor. Minors commonly quit school to help support the family. Family roles and distribution of power have been reorganized. Many men, ashamed with the inversion of roles flee their homes. Excessive idle time boosts alcoholism, often precipitating the woman or the rest of the family to expel the alcohol dependent man. Due to the mobility of the male population, women have become the stable reference around which family life revolves.

Massive migration from rural to urban areas has also influenced poverty levels. Lack of formal education, poor job skills, and inadequate governmental support make everyday living a challenge for migrant families, who largely dwell in urban slums. Leaning on group resources is a major survival strategy for this population. Many share their small houses or lots with extended family members or acquaintances from their places of origin. Their lives are bound together by mutual dependency, solidarity, and a shared value in family and friendship ties (Mello 1995).

Silvia L. de Mello (1995) and Maria do Carmo B. de Carvalho (1995) call attention to the process of deprivation and discrimination imposed by the larger society upon impoverished families. The enormous difficulties these families face are often underestimated and attributed to personality deformities or characteristics such as laziness or incompetence. These families are also seen as disorganized, an idea based on myths of how a normal or good family should live. The gravity of their social situation defies simplistic normative explanations of a psychological, sociological, or political nature. Jerusa V. Gomes (1995) proposes a larger concept—abandoned families—rather than abandoned children, irresponsible parents, or other similar classifications. She calls for an awareness of the social violence and institutionalization enforced upon the unprivileged.

Perspectives of the Future

Brazil faces many challenges in the age of globalization. Old problems have gained new dimensions, and many new ones have been added to compound an already complex situation. Among these difficulties, the crises of the welfare state and its repercussions on social and family life, such as the institutionalization of individual and group necessities, deserve further attention. Furthermore, Brazilian social policies have not addressed factors that promote exclusion or limited access to social benefits. There is a great degree of inequality between the rich and poor, and the concentration of liquid wealth in the hands of few remains an important social issue. The middle class continues to shrink, and poverty continues to increase. Carvalho (1995) appropriately named this process *social apartheid*. Its impact on family structure, function, and roles needs to be researched.

The indigenous population. Brazil has neglected to care for its original inhabitants. The Indian population has dropped to 510,000 including those located on reservations and in cities. The majority of Indians (58%) live in the Amazon region, divided into 230 nations (UnB revista 2001). During the 1988 constitutional revision, the Indians fought for recognition of ethnic differences and for better access to land, healthcare, education, and other social benefits. After a successful campaign, the Indians gained full civil rights as citizens (Ramos 2001).

The African population. Africans have been victims of policies that maintained their exclusion. The Republican project sustained racism, ideas of inferiority, and the biological determinism of colonial times, and prohibited Africans from property ownership. The implicit belief was that Africans lacked the ability to become educated and socially successful (Neder 1998). During the constitutional revision the black movement organized politically to ensure their rights. As in the case of the Indians, much needs to be done to repair the losses brought about by the continued denial of Brazilian-African civil rights and by the minimization of their contribution to the economic, social, political, and cultural fabric of the nation.

Traditional vs. modern family structures. The diversity of family life in Brazil has yet to be represented in the legal discourse about the family. Leila L. Barsted (1987) focuses on the distance between law and social reality. The family form generally considered is nuclear, patriarchal, hierarchical, and monogamic. It reflects a vision of the dominant elite and the value the elite place on family lineage. Although Brazil revised the Constitution in 1988, civil, penal, criminal, and family law codes date back to 1916. Conservatism is apparent in issues of women's legal rights and citizenship. The 1988 constitution did grant legitimacy to informal unions and to children born out of them. Men and women that opt for consensual relationships now have the same rights and obligations of those legally married. Gay and lesbian families have not yet been socially recognized. In the early 1990s, Congressperson Marta Suplicy advocated for formal unions between gay partners. After much debate and revisions the resolution passed, due largely to pressure from gay and lesbian groups and from intellectual circles.

Attention must be given to the paradox created by the existence of opposing forces in society. Gizlene Neder (1998) argues that acknowledgment of these forces has two major impacts. First, it necessitates a rethinking of the notion of family to include other family forms besides the traditional Brazilian patriarchal family. These other families have always been present in society, but until very recently have been ignored. Second, it challenges the social-political establishment to take into consideration the complex racial and familial background of the country. Policies need to be sensitive to and respectful of the rich cultural thread. They also need to take into consideration differences in power and access to social resources.

In 1889, when the Proclamation of the Republic took place, issues of nationality and citizenship were discussed. This political event, like the constitutional revision of 1988, forced the nation to review ideas and concepts long held and unquestioned. This process of revision must continue to ensure that the Brazilian family can be thought of in the plural form. As Brazilian society faces transformations at the social, economic, cultural, legal, and ethical levels, family life must remain a fundamental topic of reflection and social concern. Plurality and differences must be respected, encouraged, and protected if the country wishes to value the lessons from its past in order to ensure a better future for all its citizens and families.

Bibliography

Almeida, A. M.; Carneiro, M. J.; and de Paula, S. G. (1987). "Introdução." In *Pensando a família no Brasil: Da colônia a modernidade,* ed. A. M. de Almeida, M. J. Carneiro, and S. G. de Paula. Rio de Janeiro, RJ: Espaç e Tempo/Editora da UFRJ.

Barsted, L. L. (1987). "Permanência ou mudança? O discorso legal sobre a família." In *Pensando a família no Brasil: Da colônia a modernidade,* ed. A. M. de Almeida, M. J. Carneiro, and S. G. de Paula. Rio de Janeiro, RJ: Espaç e Tempo/Editora da UFRJ.

Bruschini, C. (1993). "Teoria crítica da família." In *Infância e niolência doméstica: Fronteiras do conhecimento,* ed. M. A. Azevedo and V. N. de A Guerra. São Paulo, SP: Editora Cortez.

Bruschini, C., and Ridenti, S. (1994). "Família, casa e trabalho." *Cadernos de pesquisa* 88:30–36.

Carvalho, M. do C. B. (1995). "A priorização da família na agenda da politica social." In *A família contemporânea em debate,* ed. M. do C. B. de Carvalho. São Paulo, SP: EDUC—Editora da PUC/SP.

Corrêa, M. (1982). "Repensando a família patriarcal Brasileira." In *Colcha de retalhos: estudos sobre a família no Brasil.* São Paula, SP: Editora Brasilience.

Diniz, G. (1999). "Homens e mulheres frente a interação casamento-trabalho: aspectos da realidade Brasileira." In *Casal e familia: entre a tradição e a transformação,* ed. T. F. Carneiro. Rio de Janeiro, RJ: NAU Editora.

Freyre, G. (1933). *Casa grande e sanzala.* Buenes Aires: Emecé editores.

Goldani, A. M. (1994). "As famílias Brasileiras: mudanças e perspectivas." *Cadernos de Pesquisa,* 91:7–22.

Gomes, J. V. (1995). "Família: cotidiano e luta pela sobrevivência." In *A família contemporânea em eebate,* ed.

M do C. B. de Carvalho. São Paulo, SP: EDUC—Editora da PUC/SP.

Mello, S. L. (1995). "Família: perspectiva teórica e observação factual." In *A família contemporânea em debate,* ed M. do C.B. de Carvalho. São Paulo, SP: EDUC—Editora da PUC/SP.

Neder, G. (1998). "Ajustando o foco das lentes: um novo olhar sobre a organização das famílias no Brasil." In *Família Brasileira, a base de tudo,* 3d edition, ed. S. M. Kaloustian. São Paulo, SP: Cortez Editora/UNICEF.

Ramos, A. R. (2001). "O futuro do Brasil indigena." *UnB revista* 1(2):85-86.

Samara, E. de M. (1983). *A família Brasileira.* São Paulo, SP: Brasiliense.

Samara, E. de M. (1987). "Tendêcias atuais da história da família no Brasil." In *Pensando a família no Brasil: da colônia a modernidade,* ed. A. M. de Almeida, M. J. Carneiro, and S. G. de Paula. Rio de Janeiro, RJ: Espaç e Tempo/Editora da UFRJ.

UnB revista (2001). "Povos indígenas." *UnB revista* 1(2):29.

GLÁUCIA DINIZ

BRIDE-PRICE

In many societies where the economic aspects of life are intimately associated with group interests, bride-price is present as an arrangement between corporate groups that negotiate transfers of wealth and rights. *Bride-price,* sometimes referred to as *bride-wealth,* is a form of marriage payment in which the bride's group receives a payment of goods, money, or livestock to compensate for the loss of a woman's labor and the children she bears. These exchange relations between families may persist over many years and in some societies constitute the chief means for the circulation of wealth. In these situations, marriage is a corporate enterprise in which control over prestige valuables is exercised by an older generation of men. Marriage payments are thus a way of establishing and securing alliances and for allocating women's labor power and fertility.

Bride-price is not a payment for women, but rather is seen as a way of valuing the labor of women, the effort involved by the bride's family in raising the female, and the labor value of a woman's offspring. The payment is a way of securing the rights of the husband's group over the woman's children. Although women are valued in such societies, their status relative to men's is lower because it is the men who make the corporate household decisions. Often, payments are made in installments in case the couple divorces or fails to produce a child.

A cluster of variables has been identified as being associated with bride-price. It is more common in descent systems that are patrilineal, although when it is found in a matrilineal system, it is the case that the wife moves to the residence of the husband's group. Subsistence economies that are horticultural or pastoral and marked with a relative absence of social stratification also feature bride-price, and there is evidence that it is common where land is abundant and the labor of women and children contributes to group welfare.

In societies that have some type of economic transaction with marriage, bride-price accounts for almost half the cases, making it the most common form of marriage payment arrangement. Often bride-price is contrasted with a rarer form of marriage payment, *dowry,* which is a transfer of wealth by the relatives of the bride to her and her husband and which operates in stratified societies. It has been noted that shifts from bride-price to indirect dowry (a contribution by the groom to the bride for her use) have occurred in African society in response to shifts in economic behavior.

Bride-price is an important variable that is particularly useful for charting social change, broad patterns of cultural evolution, the economics of inheritance, and the status of women. Studies of bride-price also shed light on strategies for bargaining and negotiation because these are important dynamics in setting the level of bride-price payment that in turn is dependent on local economic conditions, such as the availability of land.

Because the transfer of wealth has implications for status and power, the study of the mechanisms and variables associated with bride-price is an important topic of study for anthropologists, demographers, and social historians. Evolutionary ecological studies have also examined bride-price because of the significance of women's labor and reproductive value to evolutionary hypotheses. In this area of study, researchers make assumptions about maximizing the material, social, or political value of the exchange.

See also: DOWRY; HUSBAND; KINSHIP; MARRIAGE CEREMONIES; MATE SELECTION; WIFE

Bibliography

Borgerhoff Mulder, M. (1995). "Bridewealth and its Correlates: Quantifying Changes over Time." *Current Anthropology* 36:573–603.

Cronk, L. (1991). "Wealth Status and Reproductive Success among the Mukogodo of Kenya." *American Anthropologist* 93:345–360.

Ensminger, J., and Knight, J. (1997). "Changing Social Norms: Common Property, Bridewealth, and Clan Exogamy." *Current Anthropology* 38:1–24.

Goody, J. (1976). *Production and Reproduction: A Comparative Study of the Domestic Domain.* Cambridge, UK: Cambridge University Press.

Tambiah, S. J. (1989). Bridewealth and Dowry Revisited: The Position of Women in Sub-Saharan Africa and North India. *Current Anthropology* 30:413–435.

USHER FLEISING

BUDDHISM

Buddhism, one of the world's major religious traditions, originated, as did Jainism, in northeastern India in the sixth century B.C.E. Both religious movements arose in response to discontent with the prevailing religion of Hinduism. Buddhism derives its name from its founder, Siddhartha Gautama, known as the Buddha. Buddha is not a name, but an earned title meaning Enlightened or Awakened One. Following the Buddha's death, Buddhism developed into two major traditions, Theravada and Mahayana. Over the next several centuries, Buddhism spread throughout Southeast and Central Asia and Japan. During the late nineteenth century, it was introduced into Europe and North America through immigration, missionary activity, and a growing interest among Westerners in Eastern religions.

Buddhist History and Overview

The life of Siddhartha Gautama. Although precise dates for Siddhartha Gautama's life are disputed, most scholars accept 560–480 B.C.E. as rough approximations. Siddhartha was the son of a local ruler of the Sakyas clan, located on the Indian-Nepalese border. At his birth, it was prophesied that he would fulfill one of two destinies. Either he would become a great conqueror and unite all of India into one kingdom, or he would assume a religious vocation and become a world redeemer. Siddhartha's father preferred the destiny of a great conqueror and encouraged his son toward this destiny by surrounding him with worldly pleasures and shielding him from all of life's suffering.

Siddhartha grew up in luxury, married a beautiful princess, and fathered a son. Then, in his late twenties, on three successive trips into the city, Siddhartha saw an elderly man, a diseased person, and a corpse. Shocked by life's afflictions, Siddhartha fell into despair until a fourth excursion into the city when he encountered a monk seeking enlightenment. These confrontations with old age, disease, death, and the monastic life are known as the Four Passing Sights. They culminated in the Great Going Forth, a night in Siddhartha's twenty-ninth year when he abandoned his princely and family life for the religious pursuit of enlightenment.

Siddhartha spent the next six years seeking to understand suffering and the nature of existence. Initially, he studied under two prominent Hindu sages. After extensive learning from these teachers, he joined a band of wandering ascetics and assumed practices of extreme self-mortification, depriving his body of food and comfort. After reaching the point of death, yet without achieving enlightenment, he abandoned his companions and seated himself beneath a pipal tree to meditate, vowing not to rise until attaining enlightenment. For forty-nine days, Mara, an evil deity embodying death and desire, tempted Siddhartha to abandon his quest. Resisting all temptations, Siddhartha conquered Mara and awoke to the true nature and meaning of life. For the next forty-five years, until his death at the age of eighty, he taught others the path to enlightenment.

Basic Buddhist teachings. Buddhism's basic teachings are properly understood in light of several prevailing Hindu beliefs, that is, *samsara, karma,* and *nirvana.* Samsara is the Wheel of Life and refers to the cyclical stages of existence that are characteristic of reincarnation or transmigration: birth-death-rebirth. Integral to samsara is the role of karma, or the consequences of one's deeds and actions. Committing good acts merits one good karma that results in a higher rebirth in the realms of existence. Committing evil acts, however, accrues bad karma and subjects one to rebirth in a lower level of existence. Six realms of existence compose samsara. The three higher realms are the realms of the *devas* (gods), of the *asuras* (jealous gods), and of humans. The three lower realms are the realms of animals, of the *pretas* (hungry ghosts), and of hell. Of these six realms, only the human realm offers the possibility of achieving nirvana and escaping the continuous cycle of rebirths. Nirvana is the extinction of all desire and corresponds to the liberation of the individual from the Three Marks of Existence: suffering, impermanence, and the doctrine of no-self. Achieving nirvana is the Buddhist goal.

Siddhartha preached his first sermon at Deer Park near Benares (Sarnath). Known as the First Turning of the Wheel of the Dharma (Dharma is the Sanskrit word for *truth* or *law* and refers to the Buddha's teachings), the Buddha proclaimed to his former band of ascetics the Four Noble Truths: The Truth of Suffering, The Truth of the Origin of Suffering, The Truth of the Cessation of Suffering, and The Truth of the Path to the Cessation of Suffering.

The First Noble Truth is the Buddha's observation that life is fundamentally characterized by suffering (*dukkha*). This should not be mistaken as a pessimistic interpretation of life; rather it displays a realistic awareness that life is filled with sorrow. Sorrow results from life's impermanence (*anicca*). Life is transitory, continually traversing the processes of change and becoming. Since humans are trapped in the continual cycle of birth-death-rebirth, the Buddha taught the doctrine of no-self (*anatta*), meaning that there is no abiding, enduring essence, such as a self or a soul, inherent in human existence. Instead of a permanent self or essence, human beings consist of five aggregates: (1) matter or form, (2) sensation or feeling, (3) perception, (4) mental formations, and (5) consciousness.

The Second Noble Truth identifies the origin or cause of suffering. Suffering is the result of human cravings or desires for fulfillment and contentment. These desires give rise to suffering not because the desires are evil, but because of life's impermanence, they are never sated. Although humans do experience moments of happiness or pleasure, these moments are necessarily fleeting, leaving people mired in a continual state of desire and suffering.

The first two Noble Truths describe and diagnose life. The Third Noble Truth prescribes a cure for life's dis-ease. To overcome suffering and desire, one must control and ultimately eliminate all cravings and attachments to worldly matters. The extinction of cravings or desires produces a state free from attachments to the world and therefore free from suffering. This state is nirvana.

The Fourth Noble Truth, also known as the Middle Way, teaches one how to extinguish desire and achieve enlightenment by avoiding the extremes of self-indulgence (hedonism) and self-mortification (asceticism). Traveling the Middle Way requires practicing the Eightfold Path. This path consists of eight practices that one must master to awaken to the true nature of the world and enter nirvana. These practices are organized into three categories: (1) wisdom, which includes the practices of right view/understanding and right intention/thought; (2) ethical conduct, which includes right speech, right action, right livelihood, and right diligence/effort; and (3) mental discipline, which includes right mindfulness and right concentration. These categories are interdependent, requiring one to practice wisdom, ethical conduct, and mental discipline simultaneously. By deliberately engaging in these practices, one travels the Path of Liberation to nirvana.

Development and diversity of Buddhist traditions. Following the Buddha's death, a council was called at Rajagrha to codify his teachings. Five hundred monks attended the meeting. The council produced two authoritative, oral traditions of the Buddha's teachings, the *Vinaya* and the *Sutta*. The *Vinaya* described disciplines and rules for the monastic life, and the *Sutta* contained the Buddha's basic teachings. Over the course of the next several centuries, several other great councils were held. Each council addressed the gradual development of diverging ideological interpretations and religious practices within Buddhism. The result was a process of fragmentation that eventually produced eighteen different Buddhist schools. One of the first, and most prominent, schools to emerge was the conservative school of Theravada (Way of the Elders). Theravada contains the earliest collection of Buddhist scriptures, the *Pali Tipitaka* (The

Three Baskets). The elements of the *Pali* canon are the *Vinaya* (monastic codes), *Sutta* (basic teachings), and *Abhidhamma* (philosophical doctrines).

Theravada Buddhism emphasized the monastic lifestyle. The Theravada ideal was the *arhat,* an accomplished monk who achieved nirvana through wisdom, meditation, and self-effort. Within this tradition, the laity's primary purpose was to provide for the physical and material needs of the monastics. This arrangement produced a symbiotic relationship in which monastics carried on the Buddha's spiritual work while the laity supported the religious community. Theravada Buddhism flourished in India, reaching its zenith under the patronage of King Ashoka in the third century B.C.E. During Ashoka's reign, Buddhist missionaries introduced Theravada to Sri Lanka. Eventually, Theravada Buddhism spread throughout all of Southeast Asia. It remains the dominant Buddhist tradition in these countries. Geographically, it is designated Southern Buddhism.

The second major Buddhist tradition is the more diverse and liberal Mahayana (Great Vehicle). Mahayana developed in India in the first century B.C.E. Its adherents, competing with Theravada Buddhism for legitimacy, pejoratively dubbed the Theravada tradition, Hinayana, meaning the Lesser Vehicle. For the Mahayana, the ideal Buddhist was the *bodhisattva,* one who, having reached nirvana, chooses to return to the world to assist others on the path to enlightenment. The example of the bodhisattva promotes compassionate actions toward others. Eventually, both the Buddha and the bodhisattva came to be regarded as beings worthy of devotion. The bodhisattva model of compassion toward others and the development of acts of devotion towards the Buddha and the bodhisattvas empowered the laity to work towards nirvana through acts of compassion and devotion.

The Mahayana tradition spread from India northward and eastward into China, Tibet, Korea, and Japan. Geographically, this tradition is known as Northern Buddhism. As it encountered new cultures and pre-existing religious and philosophical traditions, such as Taoism, Confucianism, and Shinto, it generated several different forms of Mahayana. This religious diversity produced a vast quantity of sacred texts recognized by various Mahayana schools. Three of the more well-known Mahayana schools are Pure Land Buddhism, Chinese Ch'an or Japanese Zen Buddhism, and Tibetan Vajrayana or Tantric Buddhism. Amongst Western Europeans and North Americans, Ch'an/Zen and Tibetan/Tantric Buddhism are more commonly known and practiced.

Originating in China in the fifth and sixth centuries C.E., Pure Land Buddhism differed from other Buddhist schools by emphasizing faith as the means of entering the Pure Land, a "salvific paradise," or "paradise of salvation" where one could be saved and free from suffering. Ch'an or Zen Buddhism developed in China and Japan in the sixth century C.E. and sought enlightenment through practicing seated meditation (*zazen*) on paradoxical problems (*koan*) under a master's guidance (*sanzen*). Often considered a third Buddhist tradition, Vajrayana (Thunderbolt or Diamond Vehicle) or Tantric Buddhism developed in India and Sri Lanka in the seventh century C.E. and spread into Tibet. Vajrayana is also known as Esoteric Buddhism because it claims it originated with secret teachings of the Buddha that were passed down orally. Vajrayana teaches rapid and sudden enlightenment by using all of the body's latent energy. This is accomplished through the use of carefully choreographed body movements and posturing (*mudras*), repetitive recitation of chants and formulas (*mantras*), and meditation on religious icons and symbols (*mandalas*). The use of these methods earned this school yet another name, Mantrayana (Vehicle of the Sacred Formula).

Buddhism and the Family

Marriage and family relationships. Buddhism is not a family-centered religion. For a variety of reasons, it does not possess doctrinal standards or institutionalized models of the family. Some of these reasons include the role of renunciation, detachment, and the individual's pursuit of enlightenment. The virtue of renunciation derives from Siddhartha's Great Going Forth, at which point he forsook his family and familial obligations as son, husband, and father. The monastic lifestyle and the role of the religious community (*sangha*) formalized the renouncing of familial relationships. The goal of detachment also impinges negatively upon family life. The inherent nature of families and family relationships produces attachments that constitute formidable obstacles to achieving detachment from worldly affairs and desires. Finally, the practices for pursuing enlightenment are adult-oriented disciplines requiring significant amounts of time and effort in solitary study and meditation. Although these three factors adversely affect the role of family life, the vast majority of Buddhists are lay people with immediate and extended families.

Because Buddhism does not espouse any particular form of the family or family relationships, Buddhist family life generally reflects pre-existing cultural and religious values, customs, and socially sanctioned modes of expression. Within Asian Buddhist cultures, this typically translates into a traditional, patriarchal family structure with clearly defined familial roles. Buddhism's primary contribution to the family consists of five ethical prescriptions that inform all aspects of family life, including marriage, roles and expectations, sexuality, children, and divorce. Originally composed by the Buddha for families and laity not capable of adopting monasticism, the Five Precepts are binding ethical mandates promoting personal virtues. They are (1) abstaining from harming living beings; (2) abstaining from taking what is not given; (3) abstaining from sexual misconduct; (4) abstaining from false speech; and (5) abstaining from intoxicants. Although none of these precepts directly addresses the family, by governing social and interpersonal relationships they provide an ethical framework for family life.

Buddhism does not regard marriage as a religious act, duty, or obligation. Instead, marriage is viewed as a civic or secular matter. Therefore, wedding ceremonies are not considered religious events, and Buddhist monks do not officiate during the service. Monks may, however, attend weddings, and they often pronounce blessings and recite protective rites for the couple. Depending upon cultural traditions, marriages are either arranged between two families, as in many Eastern cultures, or decided upon and entered into between two consenting adults, as in the West. While monogamy is the principle form of marriage, Buddhism does not prohibit other forms, such as polygamy, polyandry, and group marriages. In fact, although not common, marriages of each of these types have existed within Asian cultures. Again, it is important to remember that the mode of marriage depends not upon a particular Buddhist ideal or teaching but upon pre-existing and prevailing cultural attitudes.

Neither the Buddha nor Buddhist texts give specific instructions on marriage and family life. There is, however, a great deal of commentary offering advice on how marital and family life can be lived happily. The emphasis within family life in Buddhist ethics rests upon the proper roles and responsibilities that characterize the husband-wife relationship and the parent-child relationship. Husbands and wives are to cultivate respect, honor, and faithfulness towards one another. Parents are responsible for inculcating Buddhist ethics and practices in their children and, in turn, children are expected to be obedient and to preserve the traditions of the family.

One of the primary means by which parents teach their children Buddhist beliefs and values is through participation in the life of religious community (*sangha*). Typically, in Buddhist homes, families erect a small shrine displaying a statue of the Buddha. Some families set aside an entire shrine room. Before the Buddha shrine, families conduct daily, short religious services, especially on full moon and festival days. During these services, members of the family make devotional offerings of food, flowers, candles, and incense to the Buddha. They also, through recitation, commit themselves to the Three Refuges ("I take refuge in the Buddha. I take refuge in the Dharma. I take refuge in the Sangha.") and to Buddhist ethical precepts. Outside of the home, religious instruction consists of regular attendance at religious services and participation in religious festivals.

Divorce, although uncommon for Buddhists, is not prohibited. It is expected, however, that if a couple enters into marriage and adheres to Buddhism's ethical prescriptions for marital and family life, that divorce becomes a non-issue. If, however, a couple refuses to follow the ethical prescriptions, is unable to live in peace, harmony, and mutuality with one another, or in the event of extreme circumstances, such as adultery or violence, it is preferable for the marriage to be broken than for the marriage to destroy the couple or the family.

Although Buddhism is generally viewed as fairly permissive in terms of marriage, sexuality (non-procreative sex, including homosexuality, is not condemned), and divorce, it is important to note that Buddhism condemns abortion as the taking of life. Although abortion is not absolutely forbidden, Buddhism generally considers life to begin at conception and views terminating pregnancy as a violation of the first ethical principle.

Rites of passage. Buddhism possesses few official rites of passage. Most often such events are cultural rituals with little distinctive Buddhist presence or involvement. Like marriage, this characteristic is due to the perception that many rites of passage are social, civic, or secular affairs. For example, Buddhist monks may attend birthing or naming ceremonies; however their role rarely extends beyond reading sacred texts or making blessing pronouncements. There are two noteworthy exceptions to this general rule: ordination and death.

Buddhist males and females may seek ordination for life or, more commonly, for briefer designated periods of time. Ordination ceremonies and vows serve several purposes. They bestow the ordinand's family with karmic merit and honor, they reflect the highest aspirations of Buddhist life, and they signify entrance into adulthood and the larger society.

No rite of passage, however, is more significant than death. Death and funeral rituals, unlike other rites of passage, are distinctively Buddhist. Death's association with rebirth produced highly ritualistic and elaborate ceremonies to prepare for death and to ensure that the deceased enters into nirvana after death (*paranirvana*). To prepare for death, monks recite religious texts to the dying, creating and maintaining for them a state of peace and tranquility in which they can enter into death. Funeral rituals also involve reciting sacred texts. They include other religious practices as well, especially merit ceremonies designed to bestow additional karma upon the dead and protective rites to exorcise evil influences. These two features of death and funeral rites are crucial to ensure that the deceased is either liberated from the cycle of reincarnation or receives a meritorious rebirth.

Religious festivals. Religious festivals play important roles in preserving basic Buddhist beliefs, practices, and teachings. Because of Buddhism's vast religious and cultural diversity, there is a multitude of diverse religious festivals. There are, however, three principle festivals within Buddhism that celebrate the Three Jewels of Buddhism: the Buddha, the Dharma (the Buddha's teachings), and the Sangha (the religious community). The Three Jewels are also known as the Three Refuges. *Wesak,* the most important Buddhist festival, celebrates the Buddha's birth, enlightenment, and death (*paranirvana*), all of which, according to tradition, occurred on the same day of the year. *Wesak* is celebrated on the full moon day in late May or early June. *Dharma Day,* celebrated on the full moon in July, commemorates the Buddha's teachings, particularly his first sermon in which he taught the Four Noble Truths. Finally, *Sangha Day,* which is held on the full moon day in November, celebrates the founding of the monastic and religious community.

See also: ANCESTOR WORSHIP; ASIAN-AMERICAN FAMILIES; CHINA; INTERFAITH MARRIAGE; JAPAN; KOREA; RELIGION

Bibliography

Canda, E. R., and Phaobtong, T. (1992). "Buddhism as a Support System for Southeast Asian Refugees." *Social Work* 37:61–67.

Erricker, C. (1995). *Buddhism.* Lincolnwood, IL: NTC/Contemporary Publishing.

Fujii, M. (1983). "Maintenance and Change in Japanese Traditional Funerals and Death-Related Behavior." *Japanese Journal of Religious Studies* 10:39–64.

Gross, R. M. (1985). "The Householder and the World-Renunciant: Two Modes of Sexual Expression in Buddhism." *Journal of Ecumenical Studies* 22:81–96.

Gross, R. M. (1998). *Soaring and Settling: Buddhist Perspectives on Contemporary Social and Religious Issues.* New York: Continuum.

Harvey, P. (1990). *An Introduction to Buddhism: Teachings, History, and Practices.* Cambridge: Cambridge University Press.

Karetzky, P. E. (1992). *The Life of the Buddha: Ancient Scriptural and Pictorial Traditions.* Lanham, MD: University Press of America.

Mizuno, K. (1996). *Essentials of Buddhism: Basic Terminology and Concepts of Buddhist Philosophy and Practice,* trans. Gaynor Sekimori. Tokyo: Kosei Publishing.

Nishiyama, H. (1995). "Marriage and Family Life in Soto Zen Buddhism." *Dialogue and Alliance* 9:49–53.

Noss, D. S., and Noss, J. B., eds. (1990). "Buddhism." In *A History of the World's Religions,* 8th edition. New York: Macmillan.

Reader, I. (1989). "Images in Soto Zen: Buddhism as a Religion of the Family in Contemporary Japan." *Scottish Journal of Religious Studies* 10:5–21.

Reynolds, F. E., and Carbine, J. A., eds. (2000). *The Life of Buddhism.* Berkeley: University of California Press.

Skilton, A. (1997). *A Concise History of Buddhism*. Birmingham, UK: Windhorse Publications.

Smith, H. (1991). "Buddhism." In *The World's Religions: Our Great Wisdom Traditions*. New York: HarperCollins.

Snelling, J. (1991). *The Buddhist Handbook: A Complete Guide to Buddhist Schools, Teaching, Practice, and History*. Rochester, VT: Inner Traditions.

Stevens, J. (1990). *Lust for Enlightenment: Buddhism and Sex*. Boston: Shambhala.

F. MATTHEW SCHOBERT JR.

SCOTT W. TAYLOR

BULIMIA NERVOSA

See EATING DISORDERS

BUNDLING

Bundling is probably the best known courtship practice of colonial America, even though very little research on the topic has ever been published. It appears to contradict the otherwise sexually strict mores of the Puritans. It meant that a courting couple would be in bed together, but with their clothes on. With fuel at a premium, it was often difficult to keep a house warm in the evenings. Since this is when a man would be visiting his betrothed in her home, they would bundle in her bed together in order to keep warm. A board might be placed in the middle to keep them separate, or the young lady could be put in a bundling bag or duffel-like chastity bag. The best protection against sin were the parents, who were usually in the same room with them. It may not have been good enough, however, as records indicate that up to one-third of couples engaged in premarital relations in spite of the public penalties, such as being fined and whipped, that often resulted (Ingoldsby 1995).

There was no dating per se in colonial times. A man would ask the parents for a young woman's hand in marriage and once they agreed courting could begin. The young couple had already determined that they were in love, of course. Parents would approve of bundling for their daughter with the man she intended to marry. Although it was not always this strictly controlled, it is clear that the women determined when and with whom bundling occurred. It provided the opportunity for some physical closeness in an otherwise strict society.

The beginning of bundling is unclear, though it does seem certain that it was a practice brought by the Puritans from Europe. Some feel that its origin can be traced to the Biblical story of Ruth and Boaz, where she laid at his feet and he invited her to "Tarry this night" (Ruth 3:6–13). Bundling was occasionally referred to as *tarrying*.

Historian Henry Reed Stiles railed against the practice:

> This amazing increase may, indeed, be partly ascribed to a singular custom prevalent among them, commonly known by the name of bundling—a superstitious rite observed by the young people of both sexes, with which they usually terminated their festivities, and which was kept up with religious strictness by the more bigoted and vulgar part of the community. This ceremony was likewise, in those primitive times, considered as an indispensable preliminary to matrimony. . . . To this sagacious custom do I chiefly attribute the unparalleled increase of the Yankee tribe; for it is a certain fact, well authenticated by court records and parish registers, that wherever the practice of bundling prevailed, there was an amazing number of sturdy brats annually born unto the state (Stiles 1871, p. 50–53)

Some of the New England ministers defended the practice and saw no harm in it. Others condemned it as inappropriate. The Reverend Samuel Peters opined:

> Notwithstanding the modesty of the females is such that it would be accounted the greatest rudeness for a gentleman to speak before a lady of a garter, knee, or leg, yet it is thought but a piece of civility to ask her to bundle, a custom as old as the first settlement in 1634. It is certainly innocent, virtuous and prudent, or the puritans would not have permitted it to prevail among their offspring. . . . People who are influenced more by lust, than a serious faith in God, ought never to bundle. . . . I am no advocate for temptation; yet must

say, that bundling has prevailed 160 years in New England, and, I verily believe, with ten times more chastity than the sitting on a sofa.

A Reverend James Haven is given credit by Stiles for helping to end the practice. He urged his congregation to abandon a practice which placed many in too much temptation and they were apparently shamed into more proper behavior:

Mr. Haven, in a long and memorable discourse, sought out the cause of the growing sin, and suggested the proper remedy. He attributed the frequent recurrence of the fault to the custom then prevalent, of females admitting young men to their beds, who sought their company with intentions to marriage. And he exhorted all to abandon that custom, and no longer expose themselves to temptations which so many were found unable to resist. . . . The females blushed and hung down their heads. The men, too, hung down their heads, and now and then looked out from under their fallen eyebrows, to observe how others supported the attack. If the outward appearance of the assembly was somewhat composed, there was a violent internal agitation in many minds. . . .The custom was abandoned. The sexes learned to cultivate the proper degree of delicacy in their intercourse, and instances of unlawful cohabitation in this town since that time have been extremely rare. (Laurer and Laurer 2000, p. 145)

In spite of such opposition, many women supported the practice, as evidenced by this poem from the period:

Some maidens say, if through the nation,
Bundling should quite go out of fashion,
Courtship would lose its sweets; and they
Could have no fun till wedding day.

It shant be so, they rage and storm,
And country girls in clusters swarm,
And fly and buzz, like angry bees,
And vow they'll bundle when they please.
Some mothers too, will plead their cause,
And give their daughters great applause,
And tell them, 'tis no sin nor shame,
For we, your mothers, did the same.
(Kephart and Jedlicka 1991, p. 63–64)

Courtship must adjust to environmental conditions, and young women were given greater freedom in frontier settlements than their parents had in Europe. Limited space in living quarters may explain the revival of the folk custom of bundling. It became common in New England in spite of being frowned upon by many community leaders. Eventually the advent of singing schools and other opportunities for young people to gather provided other settings for courtship (Groves 1934). After colonial youth returned from the French and Indian wars, bundling was attacked as immoral and became a vice rather than a simple custom, and it appears to have withered away over time.

Bibliography

Groves, E. (1934). *The American Family*. Chicago: Lippincott.

Ingoldsby, B., and Smith, S. (1995). *Families in Multicultural Perspective*. New York: Guilford Press.

Kephart, W., and Jedlicka, D. (1991). *The Family, Society, and the Individual*. New York: HarperCollins.

Laurer, R., and Lauer, J. (2000). *Marriage and Family: The Quest for Intimacy*. Boston: McGraw-Hill.

Stiles, H. (1871). *Bundling: Its Origin, Progress and Decline in America*. New York: Book Collectors Association.

BRON B. INGOLDSBY

C

CAMBODIA

See ETHNIC VARIATION/ETHNICITY

CANADA

Families in Canada—more so than in Britain, France, or even the Americas—are characterized by enormous diversity, especially regional and ethnic diversity. Canada has historically been a society of immigrants and of regions. First, the Aboriginal, or native people, arrived from Asia about ten thousand years ago. They organized into complex national groups with their own distinct cultures, economic bases, and languages. Norsemen explored but did not settle Canada in the years before 1500. French explorers and colonists arrived in the early seventeenth century and continued to settle throughout the first half of the next. The British began arriving in the early eighteenth century. After skirmishes and a decisive battle between the French and British armies in 1763, the British came to dominate the part of North America that is today Canada. In 1867 Confederation—Canada's founding event—set the groundwork for provincial differentiation (Quebec versus the rest), two official languages (French and English), two privileged religions (Protestantism and Catholicism), and what became known in the late twentieth century as "multiculturalism."

Varied timetables of immigration, economic opportunities, and demographic mixes caused Canada's regions to develop differently from one another. Their lack of similarity was largely due to Canada's enormous size, disparate economic development, and the distances between communities. Unequal educational opportunities and social mobility maintained the ethnic and class distinctions that made Canada what the sociologist John Porter came to call a "vertical mosaic."

Today, with more postsecondary education, travel, and mass communication, these ethnic and regional variations have begun to shrink. In this entry we will emphasize similarities and general tendencies. The theme of diversity remains important, though, as it is essential to understanding Canadian family life.

Defining Families

Canadians generally derive a great deal of pleasure from their families. In a 1994 Angus Reid opinion poll, two-thirds of Canadians strongly agreed with the statement that their families are "the greatest joy in their lives." Yet the meaning of *family* varies from one person to the next. Statistics Canada, the branch of the Canadian government responsible for collecting and analyzing national data, defines the family as

> a now-married couple (with or without never-married sons and/or daughters of either or both spouses), a couple living common-law (with or without never-married sons and/or daughters of either or both partners), or a lone parent of any marital status, with at least one never-married son or daughter living in the same dwelling. (Statistics Canada, 1999, p. 119)

They call this family form the *census family* and it is the basic unit upon which the agency collects its family data. Unless otherwise noted, the statistics discussed throughout this article will refer to this family arrangement.

Although a majority of Canadians live in census families—83 percent in 1996—a significant proportion do not (Gee 2000). In 1996 just under a quarter (24.1%) of households were made up of a single person, and 4 percent consisted of people who were either unrelated, or related but did not meet the census definition of a family. The agency also overlooks relations of affection and support that occur outside the immediate household (e.g. relations between absent parents and their children, and between elderly parents living independently from their adult children). Thus, the fairly narrow definition held by Statistics Canada fails to portray accurately the variety of Canadian family and household forms.

Trends in Marriage

More than one hundred years ago, settlers from northern and western Europe brought norms that dictated that young people establish independent homes upon marriage (Gee 1982). As a result, many people did not marry, or they married late in life because they did not have the financial resources to support a household. In 1921 the average age of marriage for men was twenty-eight years and for women it was just under twenty-five. In some ethnic groups—for example, those descended from Highland Scots—the average age of marriage was even higher.

Historically, marriage rates in Canada have fluctuated with the state of the country's economy. In the 1930s, while Canada experienced the Great Depression, many couples refrained from marrying due to economic uncertainty and high unemployment. Marriage rates decreased from 7.5 marriages per 1,000 people in 1928 to 5.9 in 1932 (Milan 2000). It was not until World War II that Canadians began to marry again in large numbers. New employment opportunities stimulated the increased rate of matrimony, as did the possibility of conscription. Single men were being called to wartime service, and many couples tried to prevent this through marriage. As a result, in 1942 there were almost eleven marriages per 1,000 people—nearly twice the marriage rate of a decade earlier. The rate declined while the men were at war, but it returned to its 1942 level when couples were reunited in 1946.

By the late 1940s marriage rates began to drop again and continued to decline until the 1970s, when children of the postwar marriages, called the *baby boom generation,* were themselves ready to marry. However, in the 1980s marriage rates returned to a downward trend, and in 1998 they reached an unprecedented low of five marriages per 1,000 people. Fewer Canadians were choosing to marry than ever before, although the economy was not a major influence in this decline.

Typically, nations with low marriage rates are late marrying populations, so along with the fluctuations in the incidence of marriage rates came a variation in the average age of first marriage. During the early twentieth century, couples married late in life. This changed in the years following World War II, as marriage rates increased and the average age at first marriage declined steadily. By 1962 the average age had dropped to 25.2 years for men and 22.5 for women. The increased affluence following World War II contributed to lowering the age at first marriage because couples could then afford to marry earlier.

Since the late 1960s, the age at first marriage has risen again. In 1997, for example, first-time brides were, on average, 27.4 years old and grooms were 29.5 year old (The Vanier Institute 2000). This increase has been associated with, among other factors, greater acceptance of cohabitation without marriage, as well as more education and economic independence for women. So paradoxically, though current figures are similar to those earlier in the century, the reasons behind them are quite different.

Cohabitation versus Marriage

Most Canadian families, 74 percent, were based in married couple unions in 1996. However, membership in this group had declined since 1986, when 80 percent of all couples were legally married. The decreased rate of marriage has been associated with a corresponding increase in common-law unions. Statistics Canada defines a common-law couple as "two persons of opposite sex who are not legally married to each other, but live together as husband and wife in the same dwelling." Although historically Canadians frowned on couples who lived together before marriage, more recently the stigma against nonmarital cohabitation has diminished, if not disappeared. By the end of the millennium, the common-law union was the fastest-growing family category. In 1996 one in seven couples in Canada was living common law, compared with one in nine in 1991. Nonmarital cohabitation was most prevalent in the province of Quebec, where one in four couples live common-law and 43 percent of all such relationships in Canada occurred (Bélanger et al. 2001).

For some Canadians, nonmarital cohabitation is a temporary state that precedes a legal marriage, but for others it is a permanent substitute for marriage. There are important differences between legal marriage and cohabitation, despite their perceived interchangeability in some quarters (Baker 2001). Canadian society provides less protection for the property rights of partners in common-law relationships than those of legally married partners. Common-law relationships are typically shorter, produce fewer children, and have a greater tendency towards spousal abuse. They are also particularly vulnerable to changes in economic circumstances (Wu and Pollard 2000). Finally, cohabiting relationships and post-cohabiting marriages are at greater risk of dissolution than are marriages not preceded by cohabitation. The last factor is likely due to what researchers call *adverse selectivity*. That is, these relationships attract people who are more willing to dissolve unsatisfactory relationships, rather than remain in them unhappily.

However, marriage is not necessarily better than cohabitation. Once other factors (including adverse selectivity) are controlled, physical and mental health differences between cohabiters and the currently married disappear, and both categories are better off than the divorced, separated, and single/never married.

Divorce

At the beginning of the twentieth century, divorce was rare in Canada. In 1900 a mere eleven divorces were registered. People widely disapproved of divorce, and the law restricted it. Until 1968, adultery was the only grounds for divorce. Families did dissolve during this period: Some spouses canceled their spousal and parental responsibilities by simply abandoning their families. However,

they remained married under law, and this prevented remarriage and the legal establishment of a new family.

The introduction of the Divorce Act in 1968 led to a massive change in family behaviors. This law allowed judges to grant divorces on the grounds of "marriage-breakdown," after a couple had been separated for at least three years. Between 1968 and 1970, the number of divorces nearly doubled. A subsequent amendment to the Divorce Act in 1986 reduced the minimum period of separation to one year. Again, this modification resulted in a huge increase in divorce, with the number peaking at 90,900 divorces in 1987 (Oderkirk 1994).

Between 1965 and 1988, Canada's divorce rate went from being one of the lowest among industrialized nations to being one of the highest, surpassing even the divorce rates in progressive countries such as France and Sweden. In 1991, once divorce rates had leveled off, there were still 2.8 divorces per 1,000 people in Canada, compared with 1.9 in France and 2.5 in Sweden (in 1992). However, the American divorce rate surpassed that of Canada. In 1992 there were 4.8 divorces per 1,000 people in the United States—nearly twice the Canadian rate (Dumas 1994).

Variations on the Dominant Pattern

Immigrant families. In the years following Confederation, wave upon wave of immigrants arrived in Canada, often "imported" into particular regions to carry out specific economic tasks: from China to construct the railroad, from Eastern Europe to settle the prairie wheatlands, from Southern Europe to build the central cities. Yet government legislation at the time effectively prevented the development of certain ethnic communities, especially among Asian and black immigrants (Das Gupta 2000). For instance, in the early twentieth century, Chinese immigrants had to pay a "head tax" to gain entrance to Canada. Since most men could not afford to bring their wife and children into the country, this law systematically prevented the creation of Chinese Canadian families.

Before the mid-twentieth century, Canadian immigration policy favored European settlement in hopes of maintaining a predominantly Anglo-Saxon society (Richard 1991). Immigration from non-European countries was severely restricted. This changed as popular opinion in the early 1960s turned against restrictions on nonwhite immigration. In 1968 a new immigration policy was set up that based admission eligibility not on ethnicity or race, but on broader criteria such as education and training, skills, personal attributes (such as adaptability, motivation, and initiative), demand for the applicant's occupation in Canada, arranged employment, and knowledge of English or French. In the decades that followed, the numbers of British and American immigrants to Canada decreased, and immigration from Asian countries increased substantially.

Many immigrants came from cultures in which men subordinate women, and their elders subordinate young people. Migration creates profound changes in the relationship between men and women, as well as between generations; it disrupts traditional expectations and supports the possibility of individuation (Shahidian 1999).

Women's experience of cultural displacement through immigration may be more positive than that of men because women may be less inclined to resist the women-friendlier dominant culture. For example, more Iranian men retained the socially conservative nature of their patriarchal home culture after immigration than did Iranian women, and they also experienced more problems in adjusting to Western social and economic trends, and to changes in gender roles that augment women's notions of self and female sexuality (Moghissi and Goodman 1999). On the other hand, institutional racism may counterbalance women's positive experiences (Moghissi 1999).

Migration can lead to generational conflict as young people attempt to embrace North American society (Tirone and Pedlar 2000). Young immigrants, or the children of immigrants, may have problems adjusting to school life, have strained family relationships, and experience issues of ethnic identity and minority status. Often community organizations help young people—especially women—develop an awareness of their condition, a new identity, and a measure of control over their lives (Ralston 1998).

In the new cultural environment, families become more nuclear, with the result that extended families loosen their grip, and a cultural distance builds up between members of the diaspora and members of the homeland (Chan and Dorais 1998). Some communities, such as the Asian Indians in Toronto, modify traditional patterns of arranged marriage to give the young more freedom while at the same time enforcing traditional group expectations.

The post-1960s amendments to the Immigration Act have led to greater ethnic diversity in Canada, especially among nonwhite groups. While one might expect this to have increased in-marriage (or endogamy) among newly enlarged minority groups, paradoxically, the opposite has occurred. The postwar "merit-point system" created a stream of affluent and highly educated new entrants. People with higher levels of education are more exogamous: that is, they show a greater tendency to marry outside their group (Richard 1991). It is therefore not surprising that ethnic exogamy has been increasing.

However, Canadians have always practiced ethnic intermarriage, and this trend has been on the rise since the time of Confederation. In 1991 Canada-born husbands and wives were more exogamous than their foreign-born counterparts, and higher proportions of males married out of their ethnic group than females. Groups who have had high rates of immigration—such as Asian Indians and Chinese—showed the lowest rates of exogamy. Canadians of French and English descent also have low levels of ethnic out-marriage, probably because their large numbers in the Canadian population make it easier to find a spouse of the same ethnic group. Overall, members of the British and French "charter groups" are a popular choice of mate. Both men and women tend to marry members of these groups, if they do not marry people of their own ethnic background (Kalbach 2000).

Same-sex unions. Although fewer social barriers prevent marriage between people of different ethnic groups, the same is not true for same-sex partners. Although Canadians are more liberal in their views on homosexuality than Americans or Mexicans (Tepperman and Curtis 2002)—religious ideas continue to fuel discrimination against homosexuals and their right to form families. In Canada, as in most nations, gays and lesbians are unable to legally marry because marriage continues to be defined as a union between a man and a woman. Gays and lesbians are often portrayed as being outside of and excluded from family social relations. In reality, many are deeply embedded in familial structures as partners, parents, children, siblings, aunts, uncles, and grandchildren.

At the start of the twenty-first century, same-sex couples had gained some of the recognition and benefits automatically granted to heterosexual couples. In February 1998 the province of British Columbia became the first jurisdiction in North America to redefine the term "spouse" in its Family Relations Act to include same-sex couples. The amendment gave gay and lesbian partners the same privileges and obligations held by those in heterosexual unions, including: custody of children, access, and child support (O'Brian and Goldberg 2000). In 1999 and 2000 Quebec, Ontario, and the federal government adopted omnibus bills granting same-sex common-law spouses almost all the same rights as heterosexual couples under the tax system, social security programs, and family law (Rose 2000). Additionally, in 2001 Statistics Canada included questions about same-sex unions for the first time in the national census.

These changes showed the growing acceptance of gay and lesbian couples in Canadian society. Public opinion polls confirmed that Canadians are becoming more accepting of same-sex unions. In a 2001 Leger Marketing poll, 65.4 percent of those surveyed agreed that Canada should grant same-sex couples the right to legally marry and 75.7 percent felt that Canada should give homosexuals the same rights as heterosexuals.

However, these tolerant attitudes do not extend to the issue of childcare. For example, only 53.1 percent of those surveyed agreed that Canada should permit homosexuals to adopt children. This disapproval of adoption by gays and lesbians likely reflects the belief that homosexual parenting will have a harmful influence on the child's sexual development. By contrast, research on the topic shows that children raised by gays and lesbians exhibit neither a greater tendency toward homosexuality nor significant differences in gender identity or gender behaviors than children raised by heterosexual parents (O'Brien and Goldberg 2000).

Families with Children

The addition of a child has an enormous impact on any family. Family dynamics and relations are often altered to accommodate the new member. Typically, a woman's dependence on her partner's earnings, and thereby her vulnerability within the family, increases with the presence of young children and relative to the number of children. This pattern is similar—indeed, deeply entrenched—across Western industrial countries, and continues even in the face of active social policies to minimize their effects (Bianchi, Casper, and Peltola 1999). From this standpoint, fertility and fertility decline play important roles in changing gender relations and family life, in Canada and elsewhere.

Fertility Decline

The average size of the Canadian family has dropped since the 1970s. In 1971 families had an average of 3.7 persons; since 1986, the average has remained constant at 3.1 persons. Contemporary Canadian families are similar in size to those in the United States, where an average of 3.2 persons made up the American family in 2000 (Fields and Casper 2000). These small family sizes are mainly a result of lower fertility and reduced childbearing, as showed by lower birth rates.

In fact, birth rates have been dropping in most industrialized countries since the latter part of the nineteenth century. These rates have fluctuated slightly over that period. For instance, after World War II (roughly 1946–1966), both Canada and the United States experienced high birth rates in what people refer to as the *postwar baby boom*. During this boom, the total fertility rate (TFR)—the average number of children a woman is likely to bear in her lifetime—peaked at 3.94 children in 1959, and actual birth rates peaked in 1957 (Péron et al. 1999).

The Canadian TFR dropped dramatically from its height in the 1960s, and fertility remained fairly stable through the mid-1970s to the end of the millennium. After 1976, the rate fluctuated between 1.8 and 1.6, although 1998 saw a slight drop in TFR to 1.55 births (Bélanger et al. 2001). These rates have varied across the country, illustrating Canada's regional and ethnic diversity. In 1998 Newfoundland had the lowest fertility rate in Canada, at 1.2 births per woman. In the same year Nunavut, a region with a high proportion of Aboriginal peoples, had a fertility rate of three births per woman.

Canadian women give birth to more children than do women in many European countries. This is largely because of high rates of immigration from high-fertility countries. Still, the Canadian fertility rate is below that of the United States, where in 1997 American women were estimated to bear 2.06 children in their lifetimes (Bélanger 1999).

Not only are Canadian couples having fewer children than in the past; they are also having children later in life. Many Canadian women now wait until they are in their late twenties or early thirties before having their first child. The mother's age at childbirth, which varies by region and ethnicity, also varies according to social and economic status. Women who have children early typically have less education and fewer job skills (therefore, lower job possibilities and less income potential). Young mothers are also more likely to be unmarried, so many must deal with the economic difficulties associated with single parenthood.

Single-Parent Families

Among those Canadian marriages that dissolved in 1995, child custody was a concern in approximately 70 percent of these cases. In more than two-thirds of these divorces, the courts granted mothers sole custody of their offspring. Thus, many women in Canada who experienced divorce also became single parents.

Of the 1.1 million single parents enumerated in 1996, 58 percent were separated or divorced, 22 percent were single or never married, and 20 percent were widows. The vast majority, 83 percent, were women (The Vanier Institute 2000). This gender difference is significant because female-headed single-parent families are more likely to suffer from lower incomes—indeed, poverty—than male-headed single-parent families. In 1998 single-parent families headed by women made up the largest fraction of all low-income families. Women-headed families were more than twice as likely as male-headed families to be living in poverty (42% versus 17.5%).

The number of Canadian single-parent families increased dramatically since the 1970s: almost 250 percent between 1971 and 1996, compared with an overall increase of only 55 percent in the total number of Canadian families. These rates mark a return to proportions seen in the early decades of the twentieth century. In 1931, for example, 13.6 percent of Canadian families were headed by one parent; this is compared to 15 percent in 1996. However, the reasons for single parenthood have changed during this century. Whereas in the first half of the twentieth century, most single-parent households were a result of the death of a spouse, in the second half of the century

they were mainly the result of separation, divorce, or nonmarriage (Oderkirk and Lochhead 1992).

Families over the Life Course

Canada's population is aging. This results from a combination of lowered fertility and general increases in life expectancy among both men and women. In 1999 12.4 percent of the Canadian population was sixty-five years of age or older (Bélanger et al. 2001). By the year 2001, it was projected that this portion will have risen to 14 percent, and with continued declines in fertility, this fraction will continue rising. These are trends common to other Western societies, especially those throughout Europe.

With the graying of the population, concerns about the costs of treating an aging population have increased. Recently, there has been a trend to move elder care outside institutional settings, and it has increasingly become the responsibility of informal caregivers, most frequently female family members. Health care services that were previously offered in institutional settings are now being performed in community health centers, day clinics, and people's own homes. This has created a difficult situation for elderly people, especially in rural Canada. Alongside limited formal health care supports in these areas, depopulation, aging communities, smaller family sizes, limited community resources, and volunteer burnout have resulted in fewer informal community supports (Blakley 1999).

This, in turn, led to widespread unease that the middle-aged children of elderly parents will be squeezed or sandwiched by the multiple roles and obligations associated with dependent children, elderly parents, and work obligations (McDaniel 2001). Elder care involvement can significantly reduce the amount of time available for other family relationships, as well as for work and leisure; yet research has shown that, so far, this has not occurred among the vast majority of middle-aged Canadians. Few Canadians provide frequent help to their elderly parents (Rosenthal et al. 1996). In fact, until parents reach the age of seventy-five, the flow of support favors the children: they receive more help from parents than they give to them.

The majority of Canadian seniors continue to live on their own well into advanced age, and most of the care they receive comes not from their children, but from other members of the same generation, usually a spouse. Friends and neighbors may, however, provide essential help when seniors live alone (Martel and Legare 2000).

Ethnicity influences the amount of assistance provided to older relatives. Asians, East Indians, and southern Europeans provide higher levels of help than British respondents; for example *Oya koh koh* (filial obligation in Japanese) has a significant effect on *nisei* (second generation) and *sansei* (third generation) children's provision of emotional support to older parents in British Columbia (Kobayashi 2000). However, structural factors (like living arrangement and age) rather than cultural factors (like filial obligation) are stronger predictors of assistance and involvement (Keefe, Rosenthal, and Beland 2000). Even among *nisei* and *sansei* children, financial and service support are more affected by such material conditions as socioeconomic status, child's availability, and parent's health (Kobayashi 2000.)

Conclusion

This chapter has provided an illustration of the diversity of Canadian families over time and space. We have seen that government policies sometimes shape Canadian families, and sometimes people form their families despite such policies. Families grow out of past traditions and new perspectives. Relations within and between families will often differ, depending on gender, race, ethnicity, economic situation, and sexual orientation.

Changes in Canadian families since the mid-1970s include fewer children, more working mothers, more divorces, and more people cohabitating. Exogamy has increased even among traditional endogamous people such as Jewish Canadians. In many respects, Canadian families are similar to families in other Western societies, such as the United Kingdom, France, and the United States. Households have shrunk throughout the West. Marriages are expressive and companionate, and though they may have an instrumental component, they are not formed for instrumental reasons alone. Women will often leave marriages that do not provide what they require. Family members, generally, are mobile and often distant. Overall, people's lives are more individualized: more fluid, varied,

and idiosyncratic (see Jones, Marsden, and Tepperman 1992).

Enormous diversity has always characterized families in Canada, although the nature of this diversity has changed over the years. Canada has historically been a society of immigrants and a society of regions. The new immigration policy has increased the ethnic mélange of the Canadian population and in so doing dramatically shifted the variety of Canadian families. It also increased exogamy and mixing, leading to the creation of new, blended cultures, in an already multicultural population.

See also: CANADA FIRST NATIONS FAMILIES; FRENCH CANADIAN FAMILIES; UNITED STATES

Bibliography

Baker, M. (2001). "Definitions, Cultural Variations and Demographic Trends." In *Families: Changing Trends in Canada,* 4th edition, ed. M. Baker. Toronto: McGraw-Hill.

Bélanger, A. (1999). *Report on the Demographic Situation in Canada 1998–1999.* Ottawa: Statistics Canada, cat no. 91–209XPE.

Bélanger, A. et al. (2001). *Report on the Demographic Situation in Canada 2000.* Ottawa: Statistics Canada, cat. no. 91–209.

Bianchi, S. M.; Casper, L. M.; and Peltola, P. K. (1999). "A Cross-National Look at Married Women's Earnings Dependency." *Gender Issues* 17(3):3–33.

Blakley, B. M. (1999) "The Impact of Health Care Reforms on Elderly Caregivers in Rural Canada." Conference Paper, Society for the Study of Social Problems.

Chan, K. B., and Dorais, L.-J. (1998). "Family, Identity, and the Vietnamese Diaspora: The Quebec Experience." *Journal of Social Issues in Southeast Asia* 13(2):285–308.

Das Gupta, T. (2000). "Families of Native People, Immigrants, and People of Colour." In *Canadian Families: Diversity, Conflict, and Change,* ed. N. Mandell and A. Duffy. Toronto: Harcourt Canada.

Dumas, J. (1994). *Report on the Demographic Situation in Canada 1993.* Ottawa: Statistics Canada. Catalogue no. 91–209E

Gee, E. M. (1982). "Marriage in Nineteenth-Century Canada." *Canadian Review of Sociology and Anthropology* 19(3):311–325.

Gee, E. M. (2000). "Contemporary Diversities." In *Canadian Families: Diversity, Conflict, and Change,* ed. N. Mandell and A. Duffy. Toronto: Harcourt Canada.

Jones, C.; Marsden, L.; and Tepperman, L. (1990). *Lives of Their Own.* Toronto: Oxford University Press.

Kalbach, M. A. (2000). "Ethnicity at the Altar." In *Perspectives on Ethnicity in Canada: A Reader,* ed. M. A. Kalbach and W. E. Kalbach. Toronto: Harcourt Canada.

Keefe, J.; Rosenthal, C.; and Beland, F. (2000). "The Impact of Ethnicity on Helping Older Relatives: Findings from a Sample of Employed Canadians." *Canadian Journal on Aging* 19(3):317–342.

Kobayashi, K. M. (2000). "The Nature of Support from Adult Sansei (Third Generation) Children to Older (Second Generation) Parents in Japanese Canadian Families." *Journal of Cross-Cultural Gerontology* 15(3):185–205.

Martel, L., and Legare, J. (2000). "L'orientation et le contenu des relations reciproques des personnes agees." *Canadian Journal on Aging* 19(1):80–105.

McDaniel, S. A. "The Family Lives of the Middle-Aged and Elderly in Canada." In *Families: Changing Trends in Canada,* 4th edition, ed. Maureen Baker. Toronto: McGraw-Hill.

Milan, A. (2000). "One Hundred Years of Families." *Canadian Social Trends* 56(Spring):2–12. Cat no. 11-008.

Moghissi, H. (1999). "Away from Home: Iranian Women, Displacement, Cultural Resistance and Change." *Journal of Comparative Family Studies* 30(2):207–217.

Moghissi, H., and Goodman, M. J. (1999). "'Cultures of Violence' and Diaspora: Dislocation and Gendered Conflict in Iranian-Canadian Communities." *Humanity and Society* 23(4):297–318.

O'Brien, C.-A., and Goldberg, A. (2000). "Lesbians and Gay Men Inside and Outside Families." In *Canadian Families: Diversity, Conflict, and Change,* ed. N. Mandell and A. Duffy. Toronto: Harcourt Canada.

Oderkirk, J. (1994). "Marriage in Canada: Changing Beliefs and Behaviours, 1600–1990." *Canadian Social Trends* 33 (Summer):3–7. Cat no. 11–008E.

Oderkirk, J., and Lochhead, C. (1992). "Lone Parenthood: Gender Differences." *Canadian Social Trends* 27 (Winter):16–19. Cat no. 11–008E.

Péron, Y., et al. (1999). *Canadian Families at the Approach of the Year 2000.* Ottawa: Statistics Canada. Cat no. 96-321–MPE No. 4.

Ralston, H. (1998). "South Asian Immigrant Women Organize for Social Change in the Diaspora: A Comparative Study." *Asian and Pacific Migration Journal* (7)4:453–482.

Richard, M. A. (1991). *Ethnic Groups and Marital Choices.* Vancouver: UBC Press.

Rose, R. (2000). "Les droits des lesbiennes au Quebec et au Canada." *Recherches feministes* 13(1):145–148.

Rosenthal, C. J., et al. (1996). "Caught in the Middle? Occupancy in Multiple Roles and Help to Parents in a National Probability Sample of Canadian Adults." *Journal of Gerontology: Social Sciences* 51(6):S274–S283.

Shahidian, H. (1999) "Gender and Sexuality among Immigrant Iranians in Canada." *Sexualities* 2(2):189–222.

Tepperman, L., and Curtis, J. (2003). "Patterns of Homophobia in Canada, Mexico, and the US." In *Exploring Myths: Historical and Sociological Perspectives in Canadian Culture,* ed. J. Curtis, E. Grabb, and D. Baer. Toronto: Oxford University Press.

Tirone, S., and Pedlar, A. (2000). "Understanding the Leisure Experiences of a Minority Ethnic Group: South Asian Teens and Young Adults in Canada." *Loisir et Societe/Society and Leisure* 23(1):145–169.

Vanier Institute of the Family. (2000). *Profiling Canada's Families II.* Ottawa.

Wu, Z., and Pollard, M. S. (2000). "Economic Circumstances and the Stability of Nonmarital Cohabitation." *Journal of Family Issues* 21(3):303–328.

Other Resources

Fields, J., and Casper, L. M. (2000). "America's Families and Living Arrangements: Population Characteristics." *Current Population Reports,* P20–537. U.S. Census Bureau, Washington, DC. Available from http://www.census.gov/prod/2001pubs/p20–537.pdf.

Statistics Canada. (1999). *1996 Census Dictionary Final Edition Reference.* Ottawa: Statistics Canada, cat. No. 92–351-UIE. Available from *http://www.statcan.ca/english/IPS/Data/92-351-UIE.htm.*

TRACY MATSUO
LORNE TEPPERMAN

CANADA FIRST NATIONS FAMILIES

To discuss *First Nations families* in Canada is to simultaneously learn about a core concept of indigenous social organization and to come to terms with the legacy of several centuries of colonialism.

The common sense notion of family—a social unit comprised of husband and wife/parent(s) and child—is full of cultural connotations that render it ineffective as a way of understanding First Nations societies. However, this does not mean that families do not exist nor that families have no meaning for First Nations peoples: families, groups of people related by marriage, birth, and history, are in fact at the core of First Nations societies. It is important to pay attention to the local, historical, and cultural manifestation and structure of what a particular culture or society call a family. In First Nations societies families are best understood in the context of social networks of related people, called *kinship* in anthropological studies, in which an individual's identity, rights, and responsibilities are defined and given meaning. Historically, these networks were also the basis of First Nations economies. Membership in family groups determined ownership of territories, access to knowledge, and defined local systems of production and consumption.

When colonizers arrived in North America they realized this essential truth, and the ensuing generations of colonial policy have been targeted at undermining the strength and vitality of indigenous families through polices ranging from direct genocide, to forced assimilation in residential schools, to child apprehension policies of the 1960s and 1970s in which indigenous children were taken from their home communities and raised in nonaboriginal foster homes, "for their own good." Although the specific histories of colonialism vary across Canada, the underlying process has been one in which outsiders have invaded, disrupted, stolen, and denigrated indigenous experiences, ways of life, and societies.

Since the late 1880s the Canadian government regulated indigenous people under an act of Parliament referred to as the *Indian Act*. Among other things, this act was designed to enforce a Eurocentric concept of family on First Nations people. This was most evident in the provisions of the Indian Act that defined an individual's legal status as *Indian*. Until 1985, when this clause was repealed by Bill C-31, a status Indian women would lose her status upon marrying a nonstatus man. However, if a status Indian man married a nonstatus woman, he would not lose his status and his nonstatus wife actually gained status. Losing status under the Indian act resulted in many women being expelled from their home communities and losing access to important social and educational programs. These women were also prohibited from owning land in their home communities. Their forced expulsion contributed to undermining the social fabric of indigenous communities. The impact was particularly severe in matrilineal communities in which family membership was defined by one's mother.

Family ties continue to be important in maintaining the well-being of indigenous communities. Thus, when families are broken down the implications can be far more severe than might otherwise be expected in surrounding nonindigenous communities. Although there may be utilitarian value in repeating the cold numbers and describing the harsh trend lines of domestic abuse, child neglect, or lone-parent families in indigenous societies, dwelling on the symptoms of a cancer will not lead to a cure. There is, in fact, much to celebrate about First Nations families that should not be overshadowed by the troubles and difficulties that too often feed the prurient interests of tabloid and broadsheet journalism.

As discussed above, family or kinship ties set the limits of an individual's rights and responsibilities within the indigenous community. These ties also provide access to important food gathering areas, create opportunities to share responsibility for raising and caring for children, and play a critical role in contemporary politics. In First Nations communities more emphasis is placed on large multigenerational families than on nuclear families. How this is manifest in each First Nations community varies greatly. Some First Nations, such as the *Tsimshian* emphasize the matrilineal line. Others, such as the *Mi'kmaqs,* reckon descent bilaterally. Still others highlight the importance of the patrilineal line. In every case family networks of sharing and reciprocity continue as a crucial aspect of First Nations society. The following examples highlight some of the complexity of First Nations family organization.

Amongst the Tsimshian of the Pacific Northwest, for example, membership in a matrilineal extended family grouping, called a *walp,* confers specific rights of access to rich food gathering areas. The *walp* is critical in the maintenance of Tsimshian social structure and ownership even in the face of colonial incursions. Ceremonial feasts, known as *potlatches* to nonaboriginal peoples, are held to officially recognize the transfer of leadership and social rights to territory and hereditary names. Current efforts to reaffirm Tsimshian authority over their territories are being propelled by the *walps* as they reassert their control over tribal politics and local economics.

Mi'kmaqs family structure has adapted to their contemporary role in seasonal and off-reserve wage labor. Historically, Mi'kmaqs's family size alternated between small groups of closely related kin and larger, extended household groups during the spring and summer months in accordance with cycles of hunting, gathering, and fishing. Membership in these family groups was more fluid than amongst the Tsimshian, for example, in that it is determined bilaterally; that is, an individual had membership in both their father and mother's family group. In the contemporary world this flexibility is relied upon to provide care and support for children. Adults engaged in off-reserve labor can leave their children with relatives on reserve. The experience of growing up on reserve in an extended family headed by their grandmother or aunt provides Mi'kmaqs children with an important opportunity to develop a sense of their identity. This is an important point of difference between most Euro-Canadian families who tend to value the direct role of parents, over grandparents, as primary caregivers.

Throughout the Canadian Arctic and sub-Arctic regions few First Nations or Inuit peoples have adopted a Euro-Canadian nuclear family pattern. Instead, the most important social units remain extended family groups or alliances of associated family groups. These groups are the essential social units of production, consumption, cooperation, and reciprocity. Amongst the *Innu* of eastern Quebec, for example, social life is organized around flexible household units based on bilateral principles of kinship. Even with the growing importance of a wage economy, coupled with social assistance programs, critical networks of sharing and reciprocity continue to play an important role in social life. Families returning from extended hunting or fishing trips share food with members of their extended families and with community members in need.

The different types of First Nations families are linked in their common history as the social and economic backbone of indigenous society. From the complex social organization of the Tsimshian on the Pacific to small, mobile communities of *Cree* or Innu peoples everyday needs were produced and consumed by groups of people connected by kinship. A person who had no relations was not a person in First Nations society. First Nations families also share a common colonial experience in which outsiders attempted to eradicate local family forms and recast indigenous society in the image of Euro-Canadian desires. Although the impact has been devastating, First Nations people have found power in their relations and are today looking to the past to find solutions with which to overcome the legacy of colonialism. Many of the social problems can only be solved by a reaffirmation and reestablishment of the power of First Nations families and kinship networks. Although there is no one single solution, there is a common theme: *all my relations*.

See also: AMERICAN INDIAN FAMILIES; CANADA

Bibliography

DeMallie, R. J. (1998). "Kinship: The Foundation for Native American Society." In *Studying Native America: Problems and Prospects,* ed. R. Thornton. Madison: The University of Wisconsin Press.

Fiske, J.-A., and Johnny, R. (1996). "The Nedut'en Family: Yesterday and Today." In *Voices: Essays on Canadian Families,* ed. M. Lynn. Scarborough, Canada: Nelson Canada.

Fourniers, S., and Crey, E. (1997). *Stolen from Our Embrace: The Abduction of First Nations Children and the Restoration of Aboriginal Communities.* Vancouver: Douglas and McIntyre.

Frideres, J., and Gadacz, R. (2001). *Aboriginal Peoples in Canada: Contemporary Conflicts.* Toronto: Prentice-Hall.

CHARLES R. MENZIES

CAREGIVING

FORMAL *Ellie Brubaker, Timothy H. Brubaker*

INFORMAL *David E. Biegel, Barbara L. Wieder*

FORMAL

Formal caregiving services for elderly individuals are those services bureaucratically provided by nonfamilial and noninformal social systems. Although families provide the majority of care to their older members who require aid with activities of daily living, formal services exist to support both the older individual and the family.

When the United States enacted the Social Security Act in 1935, it was intended to provide resources for older adults. With the 1965 Older American's Act and subsequent amendments, attempts were made to increase the well-being of elderly persons in the United States. The Older Americans Act authorized to Area Agencies on Aging to support programs which provide a variety of formal services to older Americans (Ozawa and Tseng 1999). Numerous other formal service policies and programs exist for older individuals and their families.

Internationally, various pension and retirement systems exist for aging individuals. For example, in Chile, a pension system is in place which allows each Chilean citizen to choose the age at which she or he will retire with the retirement pension based on that individual's contribution throughout his or her work life (Dychtwald 1999). Canada, Sweden, and United Kingdom are among other countries with pension systems for their citizens. In Switzerland, a national pension system exists with workers and employers each paying half the contribution to the pension system (Dychtwald 1999).

Variety of Services Available

Formal care to older adults includes care provided in the home and care away from the home. In-home services include, but are not limited to, visiting nurse services, homemaker services, respite care, and home health aide services. Care away from the home involves services such as care provided in a physician's office, day care provided in a nursing facility or other bureaucratic facility, congregate housing, senior center activities, nursing care provided in residential settings, and transportation.

Individuals receiving formal services may be provided with just one service, such as meals on wheels, or may receive a variety of services at any given time. An older individual living in his or her own home might be visited weekly by a visiting nurse, receive homemaker services, and have family members who shop for groceries, mow the lawn and provide transportation when needed, while carrying out tasks to care for her/himself as well. The recipient of formal services may work with a social worker who acts as a liaison between the recipient and providers of informal services and formal services. This social worker would be a formal service provider as well.

One family caregiver related the combination of services provided to her elderly mother. The adult daughter provided emotional support, transportation, and brought food she had cooked to the home. Physicians and nurses provided medical care. Several different types of homemaker services were used but none satisfied the mother. Finally, the mother and daughter agreed upon having the woman who had cleaned the mother's home for years come to the home for an hour each day to help with bathing and other personal tasks. This combination of informal, formal, and semiformal services met the mother's needs and allowed the daughter to remain involved as a partner in planning and providing care.

Factors Influencing Utilization of Formal Resources

Each older individual and later life family is unique. Throughout the elderly population, there are significant variations in the amount of dependency experienced as well as in the amount of care received (Uhlenberg 1996). In a study of 18,136 older adults, it was found that various factors influenced the utilization of formal resources, including marital status, race, age, and education (Ozawa and Tseng 1999). Younger, well educated, single, or widowed adults were more likely to utilize out of home services. White, as opposed to nonwhite, older adults were more likely to subscribe to in-home services. Married adults were less likely to receive formal services than nonmarried, due to the informal supports more available to married adults (Ozawa and Tseng 1999).

An individual's geographic location is also a factor in relation to use of formal services. In some countries, formal services are not as readily available as in the United States, or family members are expected to meet the service needs of their older relatives. Misa Izuhara (2000), for example, notes that in Japan although family relationships may have become less dependent, the government has not developed necessary services to meet the needs of the older population. In the United Kingdom, surveys have found that older individuals are supported by their families when needed, but that informal social supports often provide for the older

A geriatric social worker kneels beside a patient at an adult daycare facility for Alzheimer's patients. Although families provide the majority of care to their older members, formal services such as this program exist to support both the individual and the family. MARTHA TABOR/ WORKING IMAGES PHOTOGRAPHS

individual also (Botelho and Thane 2001). Paul B. Baltes and Karl Ulrich Mayer (1999) report on findings that in Berlin, Germany, formal care is associated with older elders who experience lack of physical mobility, who are educated, and live alone.

Several studies have found that having adult children is not a predictor of use of formal services. Spouses are a more likely resource than are children (Cicirelli 1981; Ozawa and Tseng 1999). Consequently, older, divorced, or widowed individuals with children may use formal resources to a greater extent than older, married persons without children.

Availability and Prevalence of Formal Services

Little information is available concerning the extent to which older individuals utilize the vast array of formal services available (Ozawa and Tseng 1999). Frequently, older persons are unaware of formal services available to them and "some studies have found that the level of use is even lower than the level of awareness of services" (Ozawa and Tseng 1999, p. 5). One factor which increases the difficulty of gaining information regarding service use is the fact that information about the prevalence of home care services is dependent upon data reported by the recipients of those services and their families (Diwan, Berger, and Manns 1997).

Little information exists regarding the ways in which formal services and programs are provided or how various racial and ethnic populations respond to those services and programs. However, what research does exist in this area indicates that older individuals of color are less likely to utilize formal services than are white elderly. It has been suggested that for some individuals and families of color, acceptance of formal services has been influenced by experiences of discrimination and a lack of input into the development of formal services (Toseland and McCallion 1997).

The lack of specific information concerning the prevalence of formal services has a direct influence on the ability of social policy to provide for programs and services to meet the needs of later life families. In the same way, needs assessments of the later life families would provide rich data from which policies and programs could be developed.

Policies and Programs Related to Formal Services

Policies and programs established to meet the needs of the elderly population exist at the federal, state, and local levels. The gerontological literature both describes policy regarding social services as well as makes recommendations for policy development in areas which research has found lacking.

In the United States, the older population with developmental disabilities serves as an example of the ability of policies and programs to provide formal services for caregivers and recipients of care alike. As individuals with developmental disabilities age, the need for formal services for this population has increased. "The increased life expectancy of persons with developmental disabilities between 1970 and the present accounts for a significant percentage, perhaps as much as 20% or more, of the long-term care resources now being consumed by such persons in the formal out-of-home long term care system" (Braddock 1999, p. 158).

As this population ages, so do their caregivers. Older individuals with developmental disabilities may outlive their parents who have been their lifelong caregivers. Sibling caregivers will age correspondingly with the recipients of their care. The need for formal services will dramatically increase as these families of caregivers and recipients enter later life.

The demand for long-term care for this population of elderly has exceeded the available placements. The state of New Jersey responded to this by designating $30 million during the 1999 fiscal year to help reduce its waiting list for community based residential services (Braddock 1999).

Policy directed toward racially and ethnically diverse older populations has been successful in California. Policy in the state of California was developed to increase the participation of ethnically diverse elderly in a dementia-specific program. Due to underutilization of services by ethnically diverse populations, the California Department of Health Services developed an outreach program to overcome barriers to utilization of Alzheimer's disease diagnostic centers. In addition to the development of an outreach manual distributed to its community centers, this policy provided for education and linkages with established community agencies already engaged with the populations to be served. The result of these efforts is that Hispanic, African-American, and Asian populations in California "are utilizing the network of state diagnostic centers at a rate proportional to their representation in the population" (Hart et al. 1996, p. 259).

The success of a policy funded to train home-care workers providing services to American Indians is described by Robert John and his colleagues (1996). This policy directed funds to a community college in Minnesota to develop a curriculum that would train students, including American-Indian students, as home-care workers with information about aging American Indians. John and his colleagues (1996) speak to the success of this program, which has provided jobs for American Indians; supported frail, elderly American Indians so that they may remain in their own homes; and enhanced the community's knowledge about the needs of elderly American Indians.

The gerontological literature provides numerous recommendations for policy related to formal caregiving services and family caregivers. The need for policy makers and service providers to view family members as partners in the provision of services to older clients is suggested repeatedly in the literature. Family members may have been providing services before formal service providers became involved. The caregiving ethos that family caregivers and older recipients have provided will benefit from formal service provision that supports

that ethos and the family's established values and traditions. Formal services that incorporate the wishes of the elderly recipient and involved family members are more likely to be successful and garner continued participation. Karen D. Pyke and Vern L. Bengston stress that "it is incumbent on researchers and policymakers to consider the ways that families organize their response to needy members" (1996, p. 390).

In an article written for practitioners providing formal care to elderly clients and their family caregivers Judy M. Zarit (1999) states, "the nature of family caregiving is so diverse that it lends itself to endless variation, and it takes practice and skill to come up with solutions that speak to the obvious demands of problems while simultaneously addressing the underlying family dynamics . . ." (p. 430). Zarit's (1999) advice to practitioners is also beneficial for policy makers: ignoring the aging-family ethos may result in disruptions of formal services at a later date. Service delivery does not occur in a vacuum, but interacts with the overt and underlying interactions and dynamics of the families served. Developing policies that attend to the idiosyncrasies of each family will allow programs and services to function more successfully.

One study of later life families caring for older members with developmental disabilities reported on focus groups with American Indian, Hispanic/Latino-American, Korean-American, Haitian-American, African-American, and Chinese-American communities (McCallion, Janicki, and Grant-Griffin 1997). The study stressed the need to understand the older family's caregiving history and to create a partnership with family members. Margaret B. Neal, Berit Ingersoll-Dayton, and Marjorie Starrels (1997) suggest that social service programs located in the community should increase the hours in which they are available to family members and elders so that later life families can more effectively become involved with formal services in the provision of care.

It is frequently suggested that policies should provide for formal caregiving to the family caregivers themselves. For example, it has been suggested that counseling services be specifically tailored to meet the needs of caregiving daughters and sons (Mui 1995). Wives who are caregivers would benefit from policies and programs that function to enhance the ways in which the husbands receiving care and the wives providing care emotionally support one another (Wright and Aquilino 1998).

The gerontological literature suggests that older elderly clients and their families, the consumers of formal services, be educated to maximize their utilization of those services. For Hispanic elderly, a language barrier may deny access to programs available to them. The differing cultural backgrounds of Hispanic consumers and service providers may prevent successful delivery of services and, in effect, deny services to that population (Hildreth and Williams 1996). The literature suggests that culturally sensitive policies will incorporate training for both consumers (Dilworth-Anderson and Williams 1996) and formal service providers. The literature calls for policies attentive to the unique and diverse perspectives of older recipients and their families.

Costs and/or Benefits for Families

Families are involved in providing care to their elderly members. In the United States, family members provide for the majority of care for elderly individuals who live in noninstitutionalized settings (Choi and Wodarski 1996). Karen D. Pyke and Vern L. Bengtson (1996) report that family members provide more care for their older relatives than ever before in our history. Informal care provided to older individuals is a typical occurrence in the United States, and that family members incur great economic, emotional, and time-related costs.

Alun E. Joseph and Bonnie C. Hallman (1996) note that in Canada, families are decreasing in size whereas more elderly individuals are living longer. In the United States and Canada, women who have traditionally been informal caregivers are in the workforce. The benefits of formal services to female caregivers in Canada are similar to those in the United States. Caregivers of older individuals have role requirements beyond caring for an older family member. Many caregivers of older individuals are employed and have families of their own. Women in particular provide a disproportionate amount of care to families' elders. For women who have been traditionally viewed as the family caregivers the demands of children, careers, spouses, and caregiving tasks may prevent them from full participation in the roles they have chosen. Jean Pearson Scott (1996) states, "the significant amount of unpaid care women provide to their families

often removes them from the paid workforce and jeopardizes their financial security in the later years" (p. 26). The benefits of formal services for family members include the provision of services which family members cannot provide themselves, a sense of shared burden, and a respite from care which is too demanding.

When an elderly relative requires services that are more extensive than family members can offer, the provision of formal services does not mean the end of informal services provided by family members. For some families, lifting an elderly family member or providing medical services is beyond their ability. When an older relative enters a nursing home, many families stay involved in caregiving activities. "A growing body of research . . . suggests that responsibilities of family members continue after an elderly member has been admitted to a ltc [long-term care] facility" (Keefe and Fancey 2000).

Clearly the benefits of formal caregiving can extend to both the caregivers and to the recipients of care as well. Formal care that exists in partnership with the family and the care recipient will most likely benefit those individuals. Formal care provided without familial and recipient input and investment may be contrary to the expectations and wishes of the family and recipient, confounding rather than minimizing caregiving issues. In these situations, family members may find that the costs of care outweigh the benefits. The reality that someone outside of the family is making decisions for their loved one or that someone unrelated to the family has taken control over tasks the family wishes to carry out may be perceived as a disadvantage by family members.

A U.S. study of family members with elderly relatives in long-term care found that the staff of those facilities did not include families in decision making. The authors of the study suggest that involvement of family members be encouraged and that staff educate family members about the resident's needs. As a result, family visits can be beneficial to the family and to the elderly resident (Keefe and Fancey 2000). The manner in which formal care is provided is important in its influence on the well-being of the family and care recipient.

The Future of Formal Care

Paul S. Haggen (1998) views future changes in the aging landscape as a challenge for formal services providers. With a growing aging population and smaller families to provide care, he suggests that adult children will be "grossly unprepared to meet both personal needs and the developmental needs of their parents. This creates an opportunity for mental health professionals to assist in changes with societal implications that may enrich the lives of many generations" (p. 333).

The changes occurring in society will require more complex service provision to meet the needs of families as they age. Mental health care is just one aspect of those requirements. "Policies and programs are needed which strengthen the ability of formal service caregivers to effectively provide services and empower families and older individuals to determine the types and quality of services provided" (Brubaker 1996, p. 10).

Although the outcomes of current political discussions about changes in Medicaid and Medicare will affect all the elderly, some older populations will be influenced more than others. Elderly African Americans and Hispanic families, more than white elderly, are dependent upon formal support systems (Hildreth and Williams 1996) and federal programs such as social security, Medicare, and Medicaid. Reductions in those federal programs greatly disadvantage those populations (Dilworth-Anderson and Williams 1996). Future formal care policies will determine the well-being of both elderly recipients and their later life family members.

See also: ALZHEIMER'S DISEASE; CAREGIVING: INFORMAL; CHRONIC ILLNESS; DEMENTIA; DISABILITIES; ELDERS; HOSPICE: LATER LIFE FAMILIES; RESPITE CARE: ADULT; SUBSTITUTE CAREGIVERS

Bibliography

Baltes, P. B., and Mayer, K. U. (1999). *The Berlin Aging Study: Aging from 70 to 100.* Cambridge, UK: Cambridge University Press.

Botelho, L., and Thane, P. (2001). *Women and Ageing in British Society Since 1500.* Harlow, UK: Longman.

Braddock, D. (1999). "Aging and Developmental Disabilities: Demographic and Policy Issues Affecting American Families." *Mental Retardation* (April):155–161.

Brubaker, E. (1996). "Families and Nursing Homes." In *Vision 2010: Families and Aging,* ed. T. H. Brubaker. Minneapolis, MN: National Council on Family Relations.

Choi, N. G., and Wodarski, J. S. (1996). "The Relationship Between Social Support and Health Status of Elderly People: Does Social Support Slow Down Physical and Functional Deterioration?" *Social Work Research* 20:52–63.

Cicirelli, V. G. (1981). "Kin Relationships of Childless and One-Child Elderly in Relation to Social Services." *Journal of Gerontological Social Work* 4:19–33.

Dilworth-Anderson, P., and Williams, S. W. (1996). "African American Elderly." In *Vision 2010: Families and Aging,* ed. T. H. Brubaker. Minneapolis, MN: National Council on Family Relations.

Diwan, S.; Berger, C.; and Manns, E. K. (1997). "Composition of the Home Care Service Package: Predictors of Type, Volume, and Mix of Services Provided to Poor and Frail Older People." *Gerontologist* 17:169–181.

Dychtwald, K. (1999). *Age Power: How the 21st Century Will Be Ruled by the New World.* New York: Putnam.

Hart, V. R.; Gallagher-Thompson, D; Davies, H. D.; DiMinno, M.; and Lessin, P. J. (1996). "Strategies for Increasing Participation of Ethnic Minorities in Alzheimer's Disease Diagnostic Centers: A Multifaceted Approach in California." *Gerontologist* 36:259–262.

Hildreth, G. J., and Williams, N. (1996). "Older Hispanic Families." In *Vision 2010: Families and Aging,* ed. T. H. Brubaker. Minneapolis, MN: National Council on Family Relations.

Izuhara, M. (2000). *Family Change and Housing in Post-War Japanese Society. The Experiences of Older Women.* Aldershot, UK: Ashgate.

John, R.; Salvini, M. L.; Dietz, T. L.; Gittings; R.; and Roy, L. (1996). "Training in Support of the American Indian Eldercare Campaign: Replication of an American Indian Home-Care Training Program." *Educational Gerontology* 22:723–734.

Joseph, A. E., and Hallman, B. C. (1996). "Caught in the Triangle: The Influence of Home, Work and Elder Location on Work-Family Balance." *Canadian Journal on Aging* 15:393–412.

Keefe, J., and Fancey, P. (2000). "The Care Continues: Responsibility for Elderly Relatives Before and After Admission to a Long Term Care Facility." *Family Relations* 49:235–244.

McCallion, P.; Janicki, M.; and Grant-Griffin, L. (1997). "Exploring the Impact of Culture and Acculturation on Older Families Caregiving for Persons with Developmental Disabilities." *Family Relations* 46:347–357.

Mui, A. C. (1995). "Caring for Frail Elderly Parents: A Comparison of Adult Sons and Daughters." *Gerontologist* 35:86–93.

Neal, M. B.; Ingersoll-Dayton, B.; and Starrels, M. E. (1997). "Gender and Relationship Differences in Caregiving Patterns and Consequences among Employed Caregivers." *Gerontologist* 37:804–816.

Ozawa, M. N., and Tseng, H. (1999). "Utilization of Formal Services during the 10 Years after Retirement." *Journal of Gerontological Social Work* 31:3–20.

Pyke, K. D., and Bengston, V. L. (1996). "Caring More or Less: Individualistic and Collectivist Systems of Family Eldercare." *Journal of Marriage and the Family* 58:379–392.

Scott, J. P. (1996). "Women in Later Life." In *Vision 2010: Families and Aging,* ed. T. H. Brubaker. Minneapolis, MN: National Council on Family Relations.

Toseland, R., and McCallion, P. (1997). "Trends in Caregiving Intervention Research." *Social Work Research* 21:154–164.

Uhlenberg, P. (1996). "The Burden of Aging: A Theoretical Framework for Understanding the Shifting Balance of Caregiving and Care Receiving as Cohorts Age." *Gerontologist* 36:761–767.

Wright, D. L., and Aquilino, W. S. (1998). "Influence of Emotional Support Exchange in Marriage on Caregiving Wives' Burden and Marital Satisfaction." *Family Relations* 47:195–204.

Zarit, J. M. (1999) "Caring for the Caregivers of the Elderly: Having Fun While Doing Good." *Family Relations* 48:429–431.

ELLIE BRUBAKER
TIMOTHY H. BRUBAKER

INFORMAL

There has been increasing awareness in both the popular and scientific literatures about the roles that families play in providing care to a relative with a chronic illness and/or a functional impairment. About three-quarters of caregivers are women who tend to provide hands-on care as compared to men who provide *care management* (Hooyman and Gonyea 1995). Such *informal caregiving* often allows ill family members to remain at home or to live in a community residence rather than be hospitalized or institutionalized. The value of such care to society has been estimated to be significant and without its provision, professional care would be needed. Although families report many positive effects of their caregiving experience, including feelings of satisfaction, effectiveness, gratification, and love (Veltman,

Cameron, and Stewart 2002; Walker, Shin, and Bird 1990), caregiving can also be a source of stress for family caregivers and can result in negative health and mental health outcomes for the caregivers (Friesen 1996).

Definition of Family Caregiving

The provision of assistance and support by one family member to another is a regular and usual part of family interactions, and is in fact a normal and pervasive activity. Thus, caregiving due to chronic illness and disability represents something that, in principle, is not very different from traditional tasks and activities rendered to family members. This is especially true for women, who, across cultures, have traditionally shouldered a disproportionate amount of family caregiving responsibility (McGoldrick 1989). The difference, however, is that caregiving in chronic illness often represents an increase in care that surpasses the bounds of normal or usual care.

Caregiving in chronic illness involves a significant expenditure of time and energy over extended periods of time, involves tasks that may be unpleasant and uncomfortable, is likely to be non-symmetrical, and is often a role that had not been anticipated by the caregiver. When these unanticipated roles are incongruent with stereotypical gender expectations (e.g., when a male caregiver must attend to a disabled relative's bathing or laundry or when a female caregiver is responsible for controlling a mentally ill relative's troublesome or dangerous behavior), the stress can be exacerbated (Tessler and Gamache 2000).

Although much of the empirical research on caregiving limits the definition of family caregivers to blood relatives, factors such as families' nationality and race/ethnicity, and the sexual orientation of the ill relative may dictate broader conceptualizations. These may include more extended kin and non-kin relationships (Tessler and Gamache 2000).

Extent of Family Caregiving

The expectation and prevalence of caregiving in families is high. As social welfare costs rise in many nations, there are increasing obligations placed on family members, primarily females, to undertake caregiving responsibilities (Barusch 1995; Olson 1994). One might argue that a caregiver is needed for every person with health-related mobility and self-care limitations that make it difficult to take care of personal needs, such as dressing, bathing, and moving around the home. Current estimates indicate that 4 percent of the noninstitutionalized U.S. population under the age of fifty-five meet these criteria. Over the age of fifty-five, the proportion of persons with mobility or self-care limitations, or both, increases dramatically; fully half of the population falls into this category after the age eight-five (U.S. Bureau of the Census 1990). If it is assumed that each of these individuals requires a minimum of one caregiver, such an estimate would yield over 15 million caregivers in the United States alone. Added to this number would be persons with, by and large, no mobility problems and who are able to perform most self-care tasks, but who require vigilance and supervision, such as adults with severe and persistent mental illness. Indeed, a recent national survey of caregivers reported that there were 22.4 million households meeting broad criteria for the presence of a caregiver in the past twelve months. Of course, not all persons who need assistance from family caregivers actually receive this help for a variety of reasons, including a lack of family members or unwillingness or inability of family members to provide care.

The provision of care by family members to other family members who become dependent due to physical and/or mental effects of chronic illness is not a new phenomenon. In fact, families have always provided care to their dependent family members (Lefley 2001; Olson 1994). However, there is now growing recognition among service providers and researchers that family caregiving will become more significant in the future because of demographic, economic, and social changes in the late twentieth century that are anticipated to continue into the next century.

A number of important trends are likely to shape the future of informal caregiving. Life expectancy and the aging of the population have increased dramatically during this century with the world's population aging at a fast rate, especially in developing countries. A shift in the epidemiology of disease from acute to chronic diseases and also a decrease in accidental deaths in developed countries has resulted in an increase in the number of persons in the population with functional activity and mobility limitations. The number of multigenerational families has increased, resulting in a

growing number of elderly caregivers as well as increased numbers in the *sandwich generation*. With greater numbers of women, the traditional caregivers, in the labor force in the United States and in developed countries, the combination of working outside the home and providing care for dependent family members has become increasingly more difficult. The search for alternatives to institutional care due to financial considerations and efforts to reduce unnecessary institutionalization in the United States and in other countries have led to more community-based treatment options and therefore have placed more demands on family caregivers. Increases in the divorce rate have weakened caregiving ties. Changes in health care reimbursement and medical technology in developed countries have shifted the burden of post-acute care to family caregivers. Increased geographic mobility in the United States and the movement of youth from rural to urban areas in developing countries has distanced adult children from chronically ill siblings and/or parents (Barusch 1995; Levkoff, Macarthur, and Bucknall 1995; Olson 1994).

Nature of Family Caregiving

The roles and functions of family caregivers vary by type and stage of illness and include both direct and indirect activities. Direct activities can include provision of *personal care tasks,* such as helping with bathing, grooming, dressing, or toileting; *health care tasks* such as catheter care, giving injections, or monitoring medications; and *checking and monitoring tasks,* such as continuous supervision, regular checking, and telephone monitoring. Indirect tasks include *care management,* such as locating services, coordinating service use, monitoring services, or advocacy, and *households tasks,* such as cooking, cleaning, shopping, money management, and transportation of family members to medical appointments and day care programs (Noelker and Bass 1994). The intensity with which some or all of these caregiving activities are performed varies widely; some caregivers have only limited types of involvement for a few hours per week whereas other caregivers might provide more than forty hours a week of care and be on call twenty-four hours per day. There are, for example, significant differences in caregiving responsibilities and tasks for caregivers of elderly persons as compared to caregivers of persons with mental illness, with the former involving more *hands-on* care, in other words, personal care and households tasks and the latter potentially carrying social stigma and pervasive worry about the relative's safety.

Caregiver Burden and Effects of Caregiving

Although the literature on caregiver burden tends to highlight the negative effects on persons in the caregiver role, numerous studies have investigated the positive impact of tending to an ill relative's needs. Findings from a Swedish study, for example, suggest that satisfaction from caregiving derives from varied sources and that most caregivers do experience some kind of benefit (Lundh 1999). Some families of adults with severe mental illness report instrumental as well as psychological reward, notably when the care recipient is able to reciprocate with both concrete and emotional contributions to the family (Tessler and Gamache 2000). Elderly spousal caregivers of persons with Alzheimer's disease studied in a cross-national study were found to derive satisfaction from doing their job well, experiencing affection and companionship from the care recipient, and fulfilling a perceived dutiful role (Murray et al 1999).

Nevertheless, many families report caregiving to be an emotional, physical, and at times, financial burden. However, the caregiving literature contains little consensus as to the conceptualization and measurement of caregiver burden, with criteria for defining burden ranging from care-recipient behaviors to caregiver tasks to general caregiver well-being. Although the definition of what constitutes caregiving and the caregiving experience varies widely among studies (Malone, Beach, and Zarit 1991), it is generally agreed that a conceptualization of caregiver burden contains both objective and subjective dimensions.

Objective burden can be defined as the time and effort required for one person to attend to the needs of another. Thus, it might include the amount of time spent in caregiving, the type of caregiving services provided, and financial resources expended on behalf of the dependent elder. Subjective burden refers to perceived beliefs and feelings by the caregiver about the performance of caregiver tasks and assumptions of the caregiver role. Definitions of subjective burden are more varied than those of objective burden and

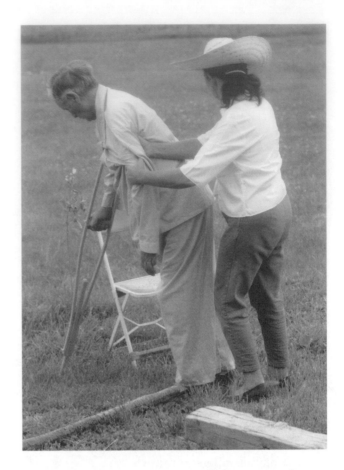

Informal caregiving—assistance and support given by one family member to another—enables an individual with a chronic illness or functional impairment to remain at home or live in a community residence rather than an institution or hospital. About three-quarters of informal caregivers are women. JEFF ALBERTSON/CORBIS

studies have included such elements as the extent to which caregiving causes strain with regard to work, finances, well-being, family relationships and social life, or emotional distress associated with caregiving. Some researchers have suggested that specific burdens are linked to specific types of impairment (Rolland 1994); caregivers of persons with mental illness and Alzheimer's disease report that disruptive or bizarre behaviors are especially troubling. In addition, caregivers' perceptions that ill relatives are increasingly dependent and that other family members are not contributing assistance and support may increase the burden.

Significant effects of family caregiving include: restrictions on social and leisure activities; infringement upon privacy; disruption of household and work routines; conflicting multiple role demands, and disruption of family roles and relationships. Because of the emotional, physical, and at times, financial burden reported by many family caregivers, these effects may be salient in the decision to institutionalize an elderly parent. Data indicate that almost one-third of caregivers do not receive any assistance in their caregiving functions from other informal or formal providers; further, family caregivers are more likely to have lower income and lower self-reported health than the population at large. Research shows that the burden of caring for a relative with severe mental illness or Alzheimer's disease can contribute to caregivers' depressive symptomatology and that, in turn, as caregivers are less able to provide support for their ill relatives, their relatives' well-being, and ability to remain in the community suffer (Song, Biegel, and Milligan 1997).

Factors Affecting Caregiver Burden

When the relationships between caregiver burden and a range of caregiver and care-recipient demographic, socioeconomic, and illness characteristics are examined, the results across studies are consistent for some variables and inconsistent for others. Generally, findings concerning the role of objective stressors, such as illness-related variables, are more consistent than findings concerning contextual variables such as caregiver demographic and socioeconomic characteristics and social support.

A number of variables pertaining to the nature of chronic illness affect the type and level of burden that will be experienced by family members. John Rolland's (1994) psychosocial typology of chronic illness gauges the influence of illness on caregivers using four criteria:

(1) *Onset,* in other words, whether the illness begins gradually, as in Alzheimer's and Parkinson's diseases, or suddenly, as in stroke and myocardial infarction;

(2) *Disease course,* of which there are three types—*progressive,* such as in Alzheimer's disease and cancer, with increased severity and continual adaptations over time; *constant,* as in stroke, where an initial acute event stabilizes and persists over time; or *relapsing/episodic,* as in severe and persistent mental illness and certain cancers, where periods of remission from acute illness provide relief for caregivers only to be followed by repeated, often unpredictable, acute exacerbations;

(3) *Outcome,* in other words, whether the illness diagnosis carries a prognosis of fatality, or shortening of the lifespan; and

(4) *Incapacitation,* in other words, whether the ill family member experiences short- or long-term cognitive, movement, or speech impairment, social impairment such as stigma, or incapacitating effects of medical intervention, for example, chemotherapy, as well as the degree of that impairment or incapacitation.

Additional variables pertaining to the illness that affect family caregivers are: the *stage of illness* (i.e., onset, long haul, end stage, etc.), and the *duration of illness* (i.e., lifetime vs. old age). There is also a strong relationship between care-recipient behaviors and caregiver burden. Care-recipient behaviors that are known to be especially burdensome include: incontinence, severe functional impairments, hallucinations, suspiciousness, agitation, wandering, catastrophic emotional reactions, disruptiveness at night, behaviors dangerous to the patient, and the need for constant supervision. Because many of these characteristics are common among dementia patients, it is believed that caregiving for an elderly person with dementia is more difficult than providing care to an elderly person with physical rather than mental limitations (Ory et al. 1999).

The structure of the family providing care for an ill relative (e.g., child[ren] of divorce providing care for aging, chronically ill parents in geographically disparate sites) as well as the life stage of the family (e.g., elderly parent[s] caring for an adult child with severe mental illness, or a mid-life mother of teenaged children caring for her husband, former family breadwinner, incapacitated by multiple sclerosis) can present different challenges to caregivers (Pot, Deeg, and Knipscheer 2001). Added to the interface of illness type and stage and family life stage and functioning, caregivers' interactions with health care providers and the health care system can have an important impact on their perceptions of caregiver distress (Friesen and Huff 1996). Research studies have shown that for family caregivers of persons with severe and persistent mental illness, dissatisfaction with their interactions with mental health providers (i.e., they perceive the interactions to be inadequate, exclusionary, or negative) are associated with higher levels of caregiver burden and depressive symptomatology (Song, Biegel, and Milligan 1997).

Although the literature shows a moderate relationship between the level of patient disability and psychological distress of the caregiver, there is considerable variability in caregiver outcomes. Such outcomes are thought to be mediated and/or moderated by a variety of factors including the viability of relationships between caregiver and ill relative that predate the illness, as well as the quality of individuals'—both caregivers' and care recipients'—pre-existing emotional resources. The availability of economic and social supports and a host of individual factors, such as gender, personality attributes (optimism, self-esteem, self-mastery), caregiving beliefs and values (guilt, stigma), and coping strategies used, have been found to be significant. Reliance on religious beliefs and faith has been shown to be an important coping strategy, particularly among African-American caregivers (Adler 2001; Songwathana 2001; Yates, Tennstedt, and Chang 1999).

Researchers have further extended basic stress-coping models to include examination of secondary stressors, such as the number and variety of the caregivers' other roles and role conflict engendered by caregiving demands, and have applied a number of additional theoretical perspectives borrowed from social and clinical psychology, sociology, and the health and biological sciences to help understand specific aspects of the caregiving situation (Pearlin, Aneshensel, and LeBlanc 1997).

Female caregivers show higher levels of caregiver burden than males (Miller and Cafasso 1992). Spousal caregivers have higher burden levels than nonspousal caregivers, but this finding may be confounded with age, since spousal caregivers are more likely to be elderly. Eileen Malone Beach and Steve Zarit (1991) believe that some of the inconsistencies in the effects of caregiver characteristics on caregiver burden are due to a failure to disentangle caregiver gender, age, and relationship, which can interact to cause confounding effects.

This complexity is compounded if ethnic identity is added to this mix. For example, data indicate that African-American caregivers do not have the same levels of stress and depressive symptomatology as white caregivers, that African-American and Latino/a caregivers are more likely to provide more challenging personal care and experience

greater financial hardship when compared to Asians or whites, and that culture and ethnicity affect access to and use of professional services, with caregivers from minority groups often indicating problems in these areas (Aranda and Knight 1997; Martin 2000; Song, Biegel, and Milligan 1997).

As stated previously, caregiving can have positive effects for the caregiver as well (Beach et al. 2000; Bulger, Wandersman, and Goldman 1993). For example, Steve Beach and his colleagues found that elderly spousal caregivers demonstrated improved mental and physical health as caregiving activity increased. Adult children who are caregivers to elderly parents report that they find caregiving gratifying because they can "pay back" the care that their parents provided to them when they were young. In addition, caregivers report that being a caregiver helps them gain inner strength or learn new skills. Michael Bulger, Abraham Wandersman, and Charles Goldman (1993) found that parents caring for adult children with schizophrenia report that the caregiving experiences aided their personal growth and increased their understanding of family problems.

Policy and Program Support for Family Caregivers

A number of countries provide tax relief and/or direct payments to family members who care for family members with disabilities (Barusch 1995). In addition, a range of programmatic interventions have been developed to address the needs of families with a member who has a chronic illness and/or a functional disability. The availability of particular interventions varies greatly by country and by location within a given country (i.e., urban vs. rural areas). However, even where interventions are offered, caregivers' ethnicity and socioeconomic status can act as barriers to access and utilization of services (Biegel, Johnsen, and Shafran 1997; Bruce and Paterson 2000; Olson 1994). Interventions for families can be conceptualized as falling into the following categories:

Support groups. A group-based intervention intended to provide families and family caregivers with social and psychological support, and in most instances with varying amounts of information about a particular chronic illness, as well as suggestions for coping with that illness. Support groups may be professionally led (usually time-limited) or peer led (usually open-ended and on-going). The former are often conducted in facilities such as hospitals or clinics, whereas the latter are typically held in community meeting places such as churches, libraries, or social centers. Although support groups can be found in many countries in addition to the United States, they are more likely to be found in developed than in developing countries.

Education. An individual- or group-based intervention for families of persons with chronic illness, usually of short duration (less than six months) focusing on provision of information about the chronic illness and its management, including advice for family members. This intervention may be led by either mental health professionals or by trained, lay group leaders. A newer implementation of educational support is computer-based and may include websites, chat rooms, listservs, and e-mail services. This approach is particularly useful for caregivers living with their ill family members who have may not have back-up care for their family member that would enable them to participate in an agency-based intervention program. This latter type of educational support, which requires access to advanced technology, is less widespread than other types of educational interventions.

Psychoeducation. Psychoeducational interventions have, as a principal component, a focus on changing family coping behaviors and attitudes. In addition to the presentation of information, they typically include skills training for families in communication and problem-solving. Although the designated target of change is the family, the ultimate impact of psychoeducation is on the patient's symptoms and functioning. Psychoeducational interventions are provided in both multi-family and single family formats and are most likely to be found in developed rather than developing countries.

Counseling and family support. Counseling, therapy, and/or other direct family support services are provided to individual family units or their members by professionals. This category consists of a wide variety of services, the most prominent of which are *family therapy, individual supportive therapy, family consultation,* and *case management.* Counseling and family support services are often provided on an open-ended, as-needed

basis, with the option of becoming long term. Such services are most likely to be founded in developed countries.

Respite and day care services. These are services that although designed for the family member with chronic illness and/or disability, are offered in part to give the family caregiver a break from caregiver responsibilities. Services offered are both in-home and in-agency institutional settings for short periods of time ranging from a few hours per day to a week or two while the caregiver may be out of town. These services are being provided in both developed and developing countries (Levkoff, Macarthur, and Bucknall 1995).

There is usually some overlap among intervention categories, particularly between education and support groups. For example, most support groups do contain an education component, although generally informal in nature, and many education groups attempt to provide social support for their participants.

There have been several studies of the outcomes of interventions for family caregivers of particular chronic illnesses (Biegel, Robinson, and Kennedy 2000; Kennet, Burgio, and Schulz 2000). In general, interventions that are comprehensive, intensive, long-term, and individually tailored are likely to be more effective than those that are not (Mittleman et al. 1996).

Despite the availability of an increasing range of intervention programs for family caregivers of persons with a variety of chronic illnesses, significant gaps in services exist. There is considerable unevenness in the degree to which interventions for family caregivers of particular chronic illnesses have been implemented. For example, even those interventions for family caregivers of persons with serious mental illness that have demonstrated effectiveness have not been widely adopted as standard practice by most mental health systems in the United States (Lehman et al. 1998).

Conclusion

Although the activity of tending to the needs of an ill relative by another member of the family is surely as old as the institution of the family itself, many factors throughout history have influenced the nature, extent, and cost, as well as the inevitability of such activity. The surge in awareness and study of informal family care to persons with chronic illnesses and impairments points to the recognition that family caregivers provide services to their relatives that are beyond the capacity of the formal system of care, both structurally and financially. Recent research has also highlighted the need to pay attention to the well-being of these caregivers so that their ability to continue to provide support for their ill family members is not compromised. It appears that the necessity for ongoing attention to and inquiries about the many factors that affect the viability of family caregiving will increase as the social, political, economic, and cultural currents of world society ebb and flow.

See also: ALZHEIMER'S DISEASE; CAREGIVING: FORMAL; CHRONIC ILLNESS; DEMENTIA; DISABILITIES; DIVISION OF LABOR; ELDER ABUSE; ELDERS; FILIAL RESPONSIBILITY; HEALTH AND FAMILIES; HOSPICE; HOUSEWORK; RESPITE CARE: ADULT; STRESS; SUBSTITUTE CAREGIVERS

Bibliography

Adler, L. L. (2001). "Women and Gender Roles." In *Cross-Cultural Topics in Psychology,* ed. L. L. Adler and U. P. Gielen. Westport, CT: Praeger.

Aranda, M. P., and Knight, B. G. (1997). "The Influence of Ethnicity and Culture on the Caregiver Stress and Coping Process: A Sociocultural Review and Analysis." *Gerontologist* 37(3):342–354.

Barusch, A. S. (1995). "Programming for Family Care of Elderly Dependents: Mandates, Incentives, and Service Rationing." *Social Work* 40(3):315–322.

Beach, S. R.; Schulz, R.; Yee, J. L.; and Jackson, S. (2000). "Negative and Positive Health Effects of Caring for a Disabled Spouse: Longitudinal Findings from The Caregiver Health Effects Study." *Psychology and Aging* 15(2):259–271.

Biegel, D. E.; Johnsen, J. A.; and Shafran, R. (1997). "Overcoming Barriers Faced by African-American Families with a Family Member with Mental Illness." *Family Relations* 46(2):163–178.

Biegel, D. E.; Robinson, E. M.; and Kennedy, M. (2000). "A Review of Empirical Studies of Interventions for Families of Persons with Mental Illness." In *Research in Community Mental Health,* Vol. 11, ed. J. Morrisey. Greenwich, CT: JAI Press.

Bruce, D. G., and Patterson, A. (2000). "Barriers to Community Support for the Dementia Carer: A Qualitative Study." *International Journal of Geriatric Psychiatry* 15(5):451–457.

Bulger, M. W.; Wandersman, A.; and Goldman, C. R. (1993). "Burdens and Gratifications of Caregiving: Appraisal of Parental Care of Adults with Schizophrenia." *American Journal of Orthopsychiatry* 63(2):255–265.

Friesen, B. J. (1996). "Family Support in Child and Adult Mental Health." In *Redefining Family Support: Innovations in Public-Private Partnerships,* ed. G. H. S. Singer, L. E. Powers, and A. L. Olson. Baltimore, MD: Paul Brookes.

Friesen, B. J., and Huff, B. (1996). "Family Perspectives on Systems of Care." In *Children's Mental Health: Creating Systems of Care in a Changing Society,* ed. B. A. Stroul. Baltimore, MD: Paul Brookes.

Hooyman, N. R., and Gonyea, J. (1995). *Feminist Perspectives on Family Care.* Newbury Park, CA: Sage.

Kennet, J.; Burgio, L.; and Schulz, R. "Interventions for In-Home Caregivers: A Review of Research 1990 to Present." In *Handbook of Dementia Caregiving: Evidence-Based Interventions for Family Caregivers,* ed. R. Schulz. Newbury Park, CA: Sage.

Lefley, H. (2001). "Mental Health Treatment and Service Delivery in Cross-Cultural Perspective." In *Cross-Cultural Topics in Psychology,* ed. L. L. Adler and U. P. Gielen. Westport, CT: Praeger.

Lehman, A. F.; Steinwachs, D. M.; Dixon, L. B.; Goldman, H. H.; Osher, F.; Postrado, L.; Scott, J. E.; Thompson, J. W.; Fahey, M.; Fischer, P.; Kasper, J. A.; Lyles, A.; Skinner, E. A.; Buchanan, R.; Carpenter, W. T., Jr.; Levine, J.; McGlynn, E. A.; Rosenheck, R.; and Zito, J. (1998). "Translating Research into Practice: The Schizophrenia Patient Outcomes Research Team (PORT) Treatment Recommendations." *Schizophrenia Bulletin* 24(1):1–10.

Levkoff, S. E.; Macarthur, I. W.; and Bucknall, J. (1995). "Elderly Mental Health in the Developing World." *Social Science and Medicine* 41(7):983–1003.

Lundh, U. (1999). "Family Carers: Sources of Satisfaction among Swedish Carers." *British Journal of Nursing* 8(10):647–652.

Malone Beach, E. E.; and Zarit, S. H. (1991). "Current Research Issues in Caregiving to the Elderly." *International Journal of Aging and Human Development* 32(2):103–114.

Martin, C. D. (2000). "More Than the Work: Race and Gender Differences in Caregiving Burden." *Journal of Family Issues* 21(8):986–1005.

McGoldrick, M. (1989). "Women and the Family Life Cycle." In *The Changing Family Life Cycle: A Framework for Family Therapy,* 2nd edition, ed. B. Carter and M. McGoldrick. Boston: Allyn and Bacon.

Miller, B., and Cafasso, L. (1992). "Gender Differences in Caregiving: Fact or Artifact?" *Gerontologist* 32:498–507.

Mittleman, M. S.; Ferris, S. H.; Shulman, E.; Steinberg, G.; and Levin, B. (1996). "A Family Intervention to Delay Nursing Home Placement of Patients with Alzheimer's Disease." *Journal of the American Medical Association* 276:1725–1731.

Murray, J.; Scheider, J.; Banerjee, S.; and Mann, A. (1999). "Eurocare: A Cross-National Study of Co-Resident Spouse Carers for People with Alzheimer's Disease." *International Journal of Geriatric Psychiatry* 14(8):662–667.

Noelker, L. S., and Bass, D. M. (1994). "Relationships between the Frail Elderly's Informal and Formal Helpers." In *Family Caregiving across the Lifespan,* ed. E. Kahana, D. E. Biegel, and M. L. Wykle. Family Caregiver Applications Series, Vol. 4. Newbury Park, CA: Sage.

Olson, L. K., ed. (1994). *The Graying of the World: Who Will Care for the Frail Elderly.* New York: Haworth Press.

Ory, M. G.; Hoffman III, R. R.; Yee, J. L.; Tennstedt, S.; and Schultz, R. (1999). "Prevalence and Impact of Caregiving: A Detailed Comparison between Dementia and Nondementia Caregivers." *The Gerontologist,* 39:117–185.

Pearlin, L. I.; Aneshensel, C. S.; and LeBlanc, A. J. (1997). "The Forms and Mechanisms of Stress Proliferation: The Case of AIDS Caregivers." *Journal of Health and Social Behavior* 38(3):223–236.

Pot, A. M.; Deeg, D. J. H.; and Knipscheer, C. P. M. (2001). "Institutionalization of Demented Elderly: The Role of Caregiver Characteristics." *International Journal of Geriatric Psychiatry* 16(3):273–280.

Rolland, J. S. (1994). *Families, Illness and Disability: An Integrated Treatment Model.* New York: Basic Books.

Song, L.; Biegel, D. E.; and Milligan, E. (1997). "Predictors of Depressive Symptomatology among Lower Social Class Caregivers of Persons with Chronic Mental Illness." *Community Mental Health Journal* 33(4):269–286.

Songwathana, P. (2001). "Women and AIDS Caregiving: Women's Work?" *Health Care for Women International* 22(3):263–279.

Tessler, R., and Gamache, G. (2000). *Family Experiences with Mental Illness.* Westport, CT: Auburn House.

U.S. Bureau of the Census. (1990). *The Need for Personal Assistance with Everyday Activities: Recipients and Caregivers.* Current Populations Reports: Household Economic Studies (Series P-70, No. 19). Washington, DC: Government Printing Office.

Veltman, A.; Cameron, J.; and Stewart, D. E. (2002). "The Experience of Providing Care to Relatives with Chronic Mental Illness." *Journal of Nervous and Mental Disease* 190(2):108–114.

Walker, A. J.; Shin, H.; and Bird, D. N. (1990). "Perceptions of Relationship Change and Caregiver Satisfaction." *Family Relations* 39(2):147–152.

Yates, M. E.; Tennstedt, S.; and Chang, B. H. (1999). "Contributors to and Mediators of Psychological Well-Being for Informal Caregivers." *Psychological and Social Sciences* 54B(1):P12–P22.

DAVID E. BIEGEL
BARBARA L. WIEDER

CARIBBEAN FAMILIES

The Caribbean, with a population of about 50 million, consists of a series of countries stretching from the Bahamian Islands and Cuba in the north, to Belize in the west, to Guyana on the coast of South America (Barrow 1996). The region can be divided by language with some of the countries speaking Spanish (e.g., Puerto Rico), some French (e.g., Martinique), some Dutch (e.g., Curacao), and others English (e.g., Trinidad and Tobago). The focus of this entry is on the English-speaking Caribbean, with particular emphasis on the countries of Jamaica, Trinidad and Tobago, Guyana, and Barbados, where approximately five million people dwell (Evans and Davies 1996).

The Caribbean countries were originally inhabited by the Caribs and Arawaks. The Caribs were fierce and aggressive whereas the Arawaks were peaceful. When Christopher Columbus and the Spanish came to the Caribbean countries in the fifteenth century, the Caribs and Arawaks were enslaved and put to work in the gold mines. As a result of brutal treatment and diseases, the Arawaks died rapidly. The Caribs tried to resist enslavement by the Spaniards, but were eventually overcome, and most of them died. As the European invasion and settlement in these countries continued, slaves from Africa were brought to the Caribbean to work on the plantations, especially under British rule. After the abolition of slavery in 1833, indentured laborers from India were brought to work on the plantations (Gopaul-McNicol 1993). Most of them settled in Trinidad and Tobago and Guyana. It is estimated that 238,960 Indians arrived in Guyana between 1838 and 1917 (Roopnarine et al. 1996); between 1815 and 1917, 150,000 Indians came to Trinidad and Tobago (Barrow 1996). However, small groups of Indians are scattered across the Caribbean and can be found in other countries such as Jamaica and St. Vincent. The Chinese, Lebanese, and Syrians make up a small percentage of the population in the Caribbean.

Family Structure

The role of family members is different in Caribbean families. The father's principal role is economic provider and protector of the family. They are also involved in the discipline of the children, especially the males, and often have a distant relationship with their daughters. In general, they are not actively involved in day-to-day childcare, especially for young infants. This should not be construed as not caring for their children; they tend to feel that women are better with children at this stage. However, the late twentieth century saw some men becoming more involved in their children's lives, spending more time playing and talking with them (Roopnarine et al. 1996).

The mother's principal role is to take care of the children and be the primary nurturer in the family. They are also the primary caretakers of the home. Children are required to be obedient, respectful, and submissive to their parents. Girls are expected to help with domestic chores around the house, whereas boys are expected to do activities outside the house, such as taking care of the yard and running errands (Evans and Davies 1996).

There is much diversity in Caribbean families. They are, in some ways, a distinct group because of their multiethnic composition. Although the majority of the families have an African background, which sometimes causes people from the Caribbean to be identified as such, there are families from Indian, Chinese, Middle Eastern, and European backgrounds who identify themselves as Caribbean. The family structure of Caribbean families will be discussed within the context of three of the primary ethnic groups in the region (African, Indian, and Chinese). Although there are some similarities in family structures, each group has

unique customs and traditions. Yogendra Malik (1971) noted that although East Indians and Africans have been living in close proximity for more than a century, each group possesses distinct values, institutions, authority patterns, kinship groups, and goals.

African-Caribbean families. Approximately 80 to 90 percent of families in the Caribbean are from an African background, and came as slaves to the region. Most of them settled in Jamaica, Barbados, and other Caribbean islands. Almost half of the population in both Trinidad and Tobago and Guyana is of African descent (Barrow 1996).

The African-Caribbean family has unique mating and childrearing patterns. Some of these patterns include absent fathers, grandmother-dominated households, frequently terminated common-law unions, and *child-shifting,* where children are sent to live with relatives because the parents have migrated or have begun a union with another spouse. Families tend to have a *matrifocal* or *matricentric* structure. Jacqueline Sharpe noted that, "To say that African Caribbean fathers and other men are fundamental to the socialization of children and to an understanding of African Caribbean family life is putting it mildly. That Caribbean men care for their family and provide for them economically has been demonstrated. . . . However, their emotional availability and their social ties to children are unclear" (Sharpe 1996, p. 261–262). A study conducted with students from the University of the West Indies suggested that Caribbean men have poor emotional relationships with their children. As a result, young boys may view family patterns such as matriarchal households, male absenteeism, and extramarital relationships as norms and continue them as adults (Sharpe 1996).

There are four basic types of family structures that affect childrearing, values, and lifestyles. Hyacinth Evans and Rose Davies (1996) describe these as (1) *the marital union*; (2) the *common-law union* (the parents live together, but are not legally married); (3) the *visiting union* (the mother still lives in the parents' home); and (4) the *single parent family*. Relationships often start as a visiting union, change to a common-law union, and culminate in a marital union. Approximately 30 to 50 percent of African-Caribbean families are headed by a female (Jamaica: 33.8%; Barbados: 42.9%;

Grenada: 45.3%) (Massiah 1982). It is estimated that 60 percent of children grow up in two-parent homes, and 30 percent live in households where they are raised exclusively by their mothers. Children born to couples in the later stages of family development usually have two parents in the home (Powell 1986).

Being a majority in the Caribbean, African-Caribbean families have significantly influenced the culture and political climate of the region. For instance, the celebration of Carnival in Trinidad and Tobago, the introduction of *reggae* and *calypso,* and the invention of the steel pan all originated in African-Caribbean families. In addition, most of the political leaders are from an African background. It is also evident that African-Caribbean families have shaped the history of the region in significant ways.

Indian-Caribbean families. The family structure of Indian-Caribbean families is in many ways similar to their Indian counterparts. In the traditional Indian-Caribbean family, the roles of family members are clearly delineated. The father is seen as the head of the family, the authority figure, and the primary breadwinner. He has the final authority in most matters. In general, males are valued more than females and are seen as the primary disciplinarians and decision makers (Seegobin 1999).

The mother has a nurturing role in the family, and is usually responsible for taking care of the children and household chores. In general, women are taught that their major role is to get married and contribute to their husband's family. From a traditional Hindu religious perspective, women are seen as subordinate and inferior to men (Seegobin 1999).

The principal role of children is to bring honor to their families by their achievements, good behavior, and contribution to the family's well-being. As such, characteristics such as obedience, conformity, generational interdependence, obligation, and shame are highly valued. Children are seen as parents' pride and the products of their hard work. One of the primary goals of marriage in Hindu families is to have children. It is assumed that children will be cared for by their parents as long as is necessary with the understanding that children will take care of parents when they grow old (Seegobin 1999).

Indian-Caribbean families usually share their resources and have mutual obligations to each other. It is not unusual to see several generations living in the same house or in houses built close to each other, even after marriage.

Marriage is an important event for girls, because they are groomed for it from childhood (Leo-Rhynie 1996). At marriage, the woman leaves her family and becomes a part of her husband's family and is expected to be submissive to her husband as well as his family. Men in these families have more privileges and respect, and women are expected to cater to their needs and desires.

However, there have been some significant changes in Indian-Caribbean families. More women are going to high school and university, and hold prestigious jobs (Sharpe 1996). Marriages are also becoming more egalitarian. Fewer of these families are headed by females when compared with African-Caribbean families (Guyana: 22.4%; Trinidad and Tobago: 27%), and when it does occur, these households are usually headed by widows and not single mothers (Massiah 1982).

Chinese-Caribbean families. The Chinese-Caribbean family may be called the "missing minority" because so little is written or researched about them. The Chinese were brought to the Caribbean as indentured laborers between 1853 and 1866. In the late nineteenth century and the first half of the twentieth century, they came as entrepreneurs and were involved in businesses such as laundries, restaurants, and supermarkets (Brereton 1993). Since that time, they have become involved in several sectors in the society, and some hold prestigious jobs in areas such as medicine, sales, management, and politics. The Chinese-Caribbean families try to keep much of the traditions and customs of China, especially in the preservation of their language. They often identify with the districts from which they came in China, and have close associations with people from these districts. Families from the districts usually get together for the Chinese New Year celebration.

Although they provide education for all their children, parents still tend to favor their sons, and push them to accomplish as much as they can. Family problems are usually kept private and only talked about within the family. As a result, these families may appear to be more stable. In general, they are less emotionally expressive, although they more easily show anger than love. Physical demonstrations of love in public are rare. Although many of them identify with religions such as Anglicanism and Catholicism, they continue their Buddhist traditions such as lighting incense, and some have Buddhist shrines at home. They also seem to trust herbal medicine more than traditional medicine. Even though Chinese-Caribbean families have lived in the Caribbean for many years, they are still perceived by some people as an exclusive group because of their lighter skin color.

Extended Family

The role of extended family is significant in Caribbean families. For many, family does not mean only the nuclear family, but includes aunts, uncles, cousins, nieces, nephews, and grandparents. Childcare is often provided by extended family when parents work or are away from home, and they sometimes assume as much responsibility for raising the children as the parents. Families also get considerable support and assistance from their relatives. In the case where adult children live away from their parents, it is not unusual for parents to visit them for extended periods of time. Often siblings may also visit for long periods. Relatives also help each other financially.

Extended family may not only include biological relatives, but other adults in the community. Rita Dudley-Grant (2001) cites the case of a single, elderly grandmother who might take care of seven to ten children. She commands respect from the children, not necessarily by her discipline of the children, but by the cultural value that children should respect older adults, even calling her "granny." In the Caribbean, community involvement plays a major role in childrearing.

Mate Selection and Marriage

For the most part, marriage is taken seriously, and as a result, divorce is less frequent. Most people choose their own mates. However, parental approval, especially from the mother, is still valued. As in the United States, marriages are occurring at a later age and families also tend to be smaller, consisting of one or two children. Many people have a traditional church marriage, because the predominant religions in the Caribbean are Christian.

In general, Caribbean marriages tend to follow a patriarchal pattern where the men are considered the head of the household, and the wife is expected to submit to her husband. However, changes in the status of women—such as accomplishments in higher education and careers—have meant that women have more authority in the home.

Legal marriages are more frequent than common-law relationships within Indian-Caribbean families compared to African-Caribbean families. Traditionally, in Indian-Caribbean families parents arranged marriages for their children. Marriage was seen as not only the joining of two persons, but also the joining of two families and two communities. In such marriages, individuals married at an earlier age. Even in the late twentieth century in Trinidad and Tobago, according to the Hindu Marriage Act, a girl may marry at fourteen and a boy at eighteen, and under the Moslem Marriage Act, both girls and boys may marry at twelve. One of the reasons for early marriages was to prevent the daughter from getting into relationships where she might become pregnant and bring disgrace to the family.

Interracial or mixed marriages have been unusual. However, these marriages slowly became more common toward the end of the 1990s. Most of the marriages occur between the Indian-Caribbean and African-Caribbean families, and to a lesser extent between these families and Chinese-Caribbean families.

Role of Religion

Religion has played a significant role in family life in the Caribbean. Initially, religion was closely associated with education; thus, many of the schools have a religious affiliation. Most families from an African background identify with one of the Christian denominations. Although most families from an Indian background are Hindus or Moslems, there are increasing numbers who identify themselves as Christian. Religion continues to serve a vital function in preserving family stability and marriages. For many families, religion helps them to cope with difficult situations and crises, and provides hope in times of desperate economic need. As a whole, Caribbean people cherish their religion.

Parent-Child Relationships

Children are seen as desirable and highly valued in Caribbean society. Parental success is measured by children's ability to sit still and listen and be clean and tidy, and by their helpfulness and cooperation.

Many Caribbean parents adhere to the biblical teaching to not "spare the rod and spoil the child," and feel that "children should be seen and not heard." In general, parents use a punitive approach to discipline. As a result, qualities such as obedience and submission are valued, especially with girls. Parents are often extremely protective (possibly over-protective) of girls and restrict their activities outside the home, for fear that they might get romantically involved with the wrong person, or get involved in sex which may result in pregnancy and shame to the family. Boys, on the other hand, are encouraged to become involved in activities outside of the home (Evan and Davies 1996).

Although corporal punishment is given to both boys and girls, boys usually receive harsher punishment. Punishment is used to curb inappropriate behaviors, and may be over-used because other forms of discipline have not been learned or are thought to be ineffective. In low-income families, especially where the parents are absent because of work situations, communication with children is limited and punishment may be used to gain control. Parents who are more educated use a variety of disciplinary measures, and are usually more communicative with their children and reason with them more. Children who have lighter skin complexion are favored and treated better than children with darker skin, irrespective of their sex (Leo-Rhynie 1996).

Children may sometimes be conceived for the wrong reasons, such as to enhance the image of the parent, and not for the welfare of the child. In 1984, 28 percent of all live births in Jamaica were to girls who were sixteen years or younger. A 1988 survey reported that 50 percent of Jamaican males and 15 percent of Jamaican females were sexually active by age fourteen. In some rural communities in Jamaica, girls who do not produce a child by age seventeen are called *mules* and are pressured to not use contraceptives (Leo-Rhynie 1996).

The practice of shifting the responsibilities of childrearing from the biological mother or parents to relatives, close friends, or neighbors is an established pattern of family life in the Caribbean, and is known as child-shifting. The shift may be permanent or temporary; it may last anywhere from a few days to several years (Russell-Brown, Norville, and Griffith 1996). It usually occurs because of the inability of the parents to take care of the children, and is more common among low-income African-Caribbean families. It is estimated that approximately 15 to 30 percent of children grow up with relatives or neighbors and not their parents (Evans and Davies 1996).

The child may be shifted for a variety of reasons. These include: migration of the biological parent; death of the biological parent or other caretaker; birth of another child (or pregnancy); formation of a new union where the child is not wanted; or the individual receiving the child having no children of her own, being more economically capable, or being able to provide a better life for the child (Barrow 1996; Evans and Davies 1996). In most cases, the child is not shifted because the mother has a lack of affection for the child, but because she recognizes her inability to effectively care for the child, and wants the child to be in a relationship where there is better care and support. The experience is often painful for the mother because of the separation from the child, but she is willing to make that sacrifice in order for the child to have a better future (Russell-Brown, Norville, and Griffith 1996).

Child shifting occurs most frequently with teenage mothers and the children are often shifted to grandparents, aunts, or uncles (i.e., someone within the extended family): individuals who share similar values to the mother, and who are more competent in raising children. A child-shifting study conducted in Barbados found that fathers were actively involved in both the decision-making process and the outcome (Russell-Brown, Norville, and Griffith 1996).

Conclusion

As a result of U.S. influence, primarily through the media, the values of Caribbean families are changing. For instance, the nuclear family is now considered the ideal (Dudley-Grant 2001). The Caribbean had been a community where extended family played a significant role. Extended family included not only immediate relatives (e.g., aunts, cousins), but also godparents and neighbors. Children were raised by communities, and children were disciplined by almost any adult member of the community. Children were also more respectful of adults calling them "auntie or uncle" instead of their name. Although this still happens to some degree, the nuclear family remains the site of primary caretaking.

Caribbean families are complex because of their multiple races, traditions, and structures. However, there is considerable unity among Caribbean people. Regardless of their ethnic backgrounds or unique family patterns, they identify themselves as people from the Caribbean and often see their roots as Caribbean. This is clearly seen in the development of practices which are uniquely Caribbean. For instance, in the area of music, the Caribbean is known for its distinctive taste in reggae (Jamaica), calypso, and chutney (both from Trinidad). There is distinct Caribbean cuisine, including dishes such as ache and saltfish, or callaloo. The motto of the Jamaican people captures, to some extent, the spirit of all Caribbean people: "Out of many, one."

See also: ETHNIC VARIATION/ETHNICITY; EXTENDED FAMILIES

Bibliography

Barrow, C. (1996). *Family in the Caribbean: Themes and Perspectives.* Kingston, Jamaica: Ian Randle.

Brereton, B. (1993). "Social Organization and Class, Racial and Cultural Conflict in Nineteenth-Century Trinidad." In *Trinidad Ethnicity,* ed. K. Yelvington. London: Macmillan.

Dudley-Grant, G. R. (2001). "Eastern Caribbean Family Psychology with Conduct-Disordered Adolescents from the Virgin Islands." *American Psychologist* 56:47–57.

Evans, H., and Davies, R. (1996). "Overview Issues in Child Socialization in the Caribbean." In *Caribbean Families: Diversity among Ethnic Groups,* ed. J. L. Roopnarine and J. Brown. Greenwich, CT: Ablex.

Gopaul-McNicol, S. (1993). *Working with West Indian Families.* New York: Guilford Press.

Leo-Rhynie, E. A. (1996). "Class, Race, and Gender Issues in Child Rearing in the Caribbean." In *Caribbean Families: Diversity among Ethnic Groups,* ed. J. L. Roopnarine and J. Brown. Greenwich, CT: Ablex.

Malik, Y. K. (1971). *East Indians in Trinidad: A Study in Minority Politics.* Oxford, UK: Oxford University Press.

Massiah, J. (1982). "Women Who Head Households." In *Women and the Family,* ed. D. Massiah. Cave Hill, Barbados: Institute of Social and Economic Policy.

Powell, D. (1986). "Caribbean Women and Their Response to Familial Experiences." *Social and Economic Studies* 35:83–130.

Roopnarine, J. L.; Snell-White, P.; Riegraf, N. B.; Wolfsenberger, J.; Hossain, Z.; and Mathur, S. (1996). "Family Socialization in an East Indian Village in Guyana: A Focus on Fathers." In *Caribbean Families: Diversity among Ethnic Groups,* ed. J. L. Roopnarine and J. Brown. Greenwich, CT: Ablex.

Russell-Brown, P. A.; Norville, B.; and Griffith, C. (1996). "Child Shifting: A Survival Strategy for Teenage Mothers." In *Caribbean Families: Diversity among Ethnic Groups,* ed. J. L. Roopnarine and J. Brown. Greenwich, CT: Ablex.

Seegobin, W. (1999). "Important Considerations in Counseling Asian Indians." In *Counseling Asian Families from a Systems Perspective,* ed. K. S. Ng. Alexandria, VA: American Counseling Association.

Sharpe, J. (1996). "Mental Health Issues and Family Socialization in the Caribbean." In *Caribbean Families: Diversity among Ethnic Groups,* ed. J. L. Roopnarine and J. Brown. Greenwich, CT: Ablex.

WINSTON SEEGOBIN

CASTE

See ASIAN-AMERICAN FAMILIES; HINDUISM; INDIA

CATHOLICISM

The Catholic Church traces its origins directly to the person and life of Jesus Christ. Therefore, any historical presentation of family life as it relates to the Catholic Church must go back two thousand years to the very dawn of Christianity. Scholars of this early period point to a major role played by the family in the life and expansion of Christianity.

During the first three centuries of its existence, Christianity not only lacked public approval, but its followers also experienced regular persecution by secular powers. The early Christian church was an assemblage of families who met together for prayer and worship in homes, rather than in public church buildings. Such gatherings contributed to the spirit of church life by having an important family dimension. Roman society failed to value the importance of women and children. The early church took a strong position on the dignity and value of all people. Some historians claim that the church's valuing of everyone, its openness to all regardless of gender, age, or social class, was partly the reason Christianity was persecuted by the state. Its openness to all people was deeply at odds with the hierarchical values and social structures supported by the reigning authorities.

Christian families were sometimes referred to as *households of faith* in the writings of the early church. Both the celebration of the Eucharist, sometimes called the *agape* or love feast, along with the celebration of baptism, were events directly involving the family. Occasionally, whole families were baptized into the church. Further, local church leaders, both bishops and presbyters, were chosen in part because of their proven leadership of a Christian household.

Two influential church theologians and leaders, St. Augustine (354–430) and St. John Chrysostom (347–407), both referred to the family as *a domestic church* in their writings. Although this language was not taken up by the church in subsequent centuries until the Second Vatican Council (1961–1965), the apparent high regard for the family was nevertheless an essential dimension of church life. That their language seemed all but forgotten indicates that soon after this early period, the family seems to recede into the background as a major setting for the Christian life. Family life was no longer a central interest of the church.

Its place as the primary small community of the church was replaced by the creation of monasticism, especially through the efforts of St. Benedict (480–550) and his sister St. Scholastica (480–543). In the rule written for monastic life, they borrowed language inherent to family life. The head of the monastery was to be called the abbot (a derivation of the word for father) while abbesses headed the convents for religious women. The members of the monastic community were to be called brothers and sisters. Entrance into the monastic community was akin to being brought into a new family. Often one's name was changed to underscore a new identity and a new set of familial relationships.

From the inception of the monastic movement, the quest for spiritual perfection within the Catholic Church was largely considered a matter for vowed monks and nuns. Those who lived in ordinary families were implicitly considered second-class members of the church. As the Christian Church became more of a public institution after Emperor Constantine's Edict of Milan (313), Christian families blended in with all the other families of the west. For the next 1,400 years, there is a loud silence in the writings and teaching of the Catholic Church about the role of family life. There is no mention of the importance of family life as significant either for salvation or sanctification.

The Beginnings of a Social Concern for Families

In 1891 Pope Leo XIII initiated a new interest in the church about family life with his pioneering social encyclical called *Rerum Novarum (On New Things)*. The primary focus of this letter concerned the state of labor particularly as it was being influenced by the socialist revolution of the times. As the pope considered the condition of the typical worker, he also took the opportunity to comment on the state of the worker's family. Here he noted the right of families, especially poor families, to adequate food, clothing, shelter, and protection. His interest was primarily on the material or social needs of the family.

The issuance of that encyclical began a pattern of church support for the social welfare of the family. Especially in the United States there developed a group of major church agencies whose primary purpose was assistance to families, especially economic assistance. The St. Vincent de Paul Society, along with many diocesan programs under what was usually called Catholic Charities, sought to meet the needs of families and children. Catholic hospitals and schools, while attending primarily to the sick and to children, often included an interest in the families of those they served. Starting with a huge influx of Irish immigrants in the mid-nineteenth century, the number of needy Catholic families has remained high.

Toward the end of the twentieth century, many Catholic families came to the United States from Latin America and Asia. Helping these families remains a high priority for the Catholic Church. A similar effort toward helping needy families occurs around the world though a variety of international Catholic agencies like Catholic Relief Services and various international organizations sponsored by such religious communities as the Jesuits, Franciscans, and Maryknoll.

Catholic Teachings on Marriage and Family Life

Catholic teaching about marriage was minimal until the Catholic Church formally taught that

A Roman Catholic priest sprinkles holy water on children taking their first communion in the Philippines. The Catholic Church affirms that the family is an essential life-giving part of the church and that it is a source of on-going vitality for the entire church. BULLIT MARQUEZ/A/P WIDE WORLD PHOTOS

Christian marriage or matrimony was one of the seven sacraments of the church. This was officially declared at the Council of Trent (1545–1563). This teaching was partly to counteract Martin Luther's claim that there were only two sacraments: baptism and eucharist. Theologians from the thirteenth century on had made mention of the sacramental nature of Christian marriage, but it was not made part of official church teaching until the above-mentioned council.

Naming Christian marriage as one of the seven sacraments of the church meant that the act of marrying another, with the intent that the marriage be faithful, exclusive, and open to the creation of new life, creates a sacramental relationship between the wife and husband that participates through the working of grace. Marriage was not only a human or secular relationship. It was part of the dynamic life of being a Christian. It was drawn into the energizing presence of God's spirit that continuously breathes life into the church. Marriage is a sanctified state of life. It renders the wife and husband holy through all those acts that constitute the marriage. This graced dynamic begins with the exchange of marriage vows and through the consummation of the marriage in sexual intercourse. The process of sanctification continues though their life together.

After Christian marriage was officially incorporated as part of church life, there followed a whole series of changes in church practice. These changes happened slowly. In fact, some four hundred years later, there still remain further opportunities on the part of the church to enrich the graced state of marriage and the spiritual lives of families. First of all, the Catholic Church established rather detailed laws concerning who could marry, what dispositions or attitudes were required for marriage, how the sacramental ritual of marriage should be enacted (before a priest and two witnesses), and when and where marriages should take place when celebrated in the church.

Because of these church requirements, the church involved itself in the period before marriage to insure that all its requirements for Christian marriage were satisfied. From the sixteenth until the middle of the twentieth century, this requirement was usually met by a meeting with a priest right before the wedding.

In the middle of the twentieth century, the Catholic Church, especially in the United States and Canada, developed a variety of educational programs for engaged couples. They were designed to help couples enter Christian marriage more knowingly and more personally. These marriage preparation programs were usually given by a priest with the assistance of qualified laity.

As the Catholic Church found itself in situations where the population was religiously diverse, it also faced the issue of marriages between Catholics and non-Catholics. These were commonly referred to as mixed marriages. Up until the Second Vatican Council, these marriages were clearly thought of as second class. Usually they were not celebrated in the church building, and the non-Catholic party had to promise that any children from their marriage would be baptized and raised Catholic.

After the Second Vatican Council, the church took a more pastoral approach to these marriages, sometimes creating special programs for marriage preparation and enrichment. Also, the non-Catholic partners are no longer required to promise that children of the marriage become Catholic. Nevertheless, the Catholic partners are asked to promise to do all within their power to ensure this result. At the beginning of the twenty-first century, just under one half of the marriages that are celebrated in the church are mixed. Sometimes leaders of each one's respective religious community jointly celebrate the weddings of these people.

There are various programs and movements within the Catholic Church to enrich marriages. Many Catholic parishes and dioceses sponsor educational programs for the married. Deserving special mention are the various marriage encounter retreats or experiences that have helped thousands of Catholics gain skills in communication and insights into the sacramental and holy or sacred dimension of Christian marriage.

At the other end of the spectrum, laws and procedures were created to deal with ways the church could accept that a marriage had ended. Up until the Second Vatican Council, there were few justifying causes for a marriage to be declared ended. In brief, this could be accomplished only when the marriage partners had not consummated their union or if one of the parties decided to enter religious life. Courts were established both at the Vatican and in Catholic dioceses to deal with these cases.

Around the time of the Second Vatican Council, a new set of criteria for dissolving marriages was established by the marriage court of the Vatican, which is called the Rota. It allowed the church to declare that a given marriage lacked certain essential qualities that the church held as necessary for the existence of a Christian marriage. If the marriage lacked certain essential qualities, then the parties were given an annulment, which indicates that a Christian marriage was not canonically valid. Essential qualities may be absent in the intention of one or both parties at the time of the wedding, for example, an unwillingness to have children. Or one or both parties may have a personal psychological predisposition that makes them incapable of establishing a lifelong union of life and love.

Catholic Teachings on Human Sexuality

For most of its history, the Catholic Church taught that the primary purpose of God's gift of sexuality was the procreation and education of children. Occasionally other purposes of sexuality were noted, such as deepening the friendship of the married couple and helping to control excessive sexual desire. During the twentieth century biological science and technology made it possible to more effectively control the process of fertilization and the question arose whether Catholics might use these new methods of fertility control.

After extensive discussion involving bishops, theologians, and lay people, Pope Paul VI issued the encyclical letter, *Humanae Vitae* (On Human Life) in 1968. Before the issuance of that letter, many Catholics expected that the Catholic Church would change its rule of fertility control, which up to that time included only the use of *natural methods*. In brief, these methods allowed a couple to engage in sexual intercourse during infertile or safe times of the woman's cycle. Various methods of determining the precise time of infertility were developed to assist the couple in their quest for being responsible in the use of their procreative powers. New methods of fertility control developed in the years immediately preceding *Humanae Vitae*, the most well known being a pill that prevented ovulation. One of its developers was D. John Rock, who was a Catholic doctor.

The pope responded to this by saying that each and every act of sexual intercourse must be open to the creation of new life. In practice, that meant that the couple could not actively prevent possible fertilization from taking place. This teaching has been controversial for many Catholics. Nevertheless Pope John Paul II has strongly maintained the teaching of Pope Paul VI.

The Second Vatican Council reformulated and updated many teachings and practices of the church. In its document called *Gaudium et Spes (The Pastoral Constitution on the Church in the Modern World)* it devoted a lengthy section on what it labeled *The Dignity of Marriage and the Family*. Here it expanded on the meaning of human sexuality in marriage by saying that it is both an expression of marital love, and it is an act that potentially could generate new human life. The church left behind any language of primary or secondary meaning to marital sex. It took a "both-and" approach in affirming two essential purposes of human sexuality. Many pastors, theologians, and married couples welcomed this broader understanding, which clearly valued human sexuality as essentially expressive of marital love.

The 1980 Vatican Synod on Family and *Familiaris Consortio*

As the Second Vatican Council adjourned, many church leaders felt that the ancient practice of holding regular church meetings or synods would be useful in implementing the reforms of Vatican II and for dealing with pressing issues facing the church. The Vatican has convened synods in roughly three-year intervals since 1965. In 1980, the first synod was held in the pontificate of Pope John Paul II. Its topic was the role of the Christian family in the modern word.

More than 200 bishops representing the Catholic Church from around the world met for five weeks of discussion. In general, the concerns of the bishops were divided into two sets of issues.

For bishops from developing countries, there were many issues raised dealing with such matters as family survival under difficult political and economic circumstances, the role of the state in determining family size, and the survival of the Christian family where Christians were a minority of the population.

For industrialized countries, the concerns were more concerned with internal family issues. Bishops focused the challenges of maintaining intimacy in marriage, the church's response to divorce, the need for family spirituality, and the roles of women and men in the family. The results of all these deliberations were handed over to Pope John Paul II, who then responded in a major teaching document. A year after the synod on the family adjourned, he issued *Familiaris Consortio (On the Family)*. It was easily the lengthiest treatise on marriage and family ever created in the Catholic Church.

The papal document was divided into four sections. The first section of this apostolic exhortation (its official church designation as a document) deals with the realities of family life today. Based on the testimony of bishops from around the world, the pope notes that there are both positive and negative forces that influence family life. Like other parts of human life, the family is a mixture of the light and darkness.

The second section notes that the family must affirm and respect the full personhood of every family member. No other community can value the individual person more than can the family. The depersonalizing forces of society can be countered by an acceptance and love that is a primary part of the God-given role of the family.

Section three presents the heart of the document when it describes the comprehensive role of the Christian family. It divides the family's role into four parts. First, it is to form a community of people, bound together for life while enriching each other, especially through acts of care, kindness, compassion, forgiveness, and love. Its second role is to serve life from its beginning in the mother's womb until death. The family is to be a community of life, protecting life from all that diminishes it, supporting life in all circumstances. Third, the role of the family in society is developed by comparing families to cells that contributes directly to the life and health of the whole body. A strong message of interconnectedness and interdependency comes forth in this part of the pope's exhortation. The last aspect mentioned is the family's role in the life of the church. Here new theological ground is created by showing that the family is not just served by the church or contributes to the church, but rather that the life of the family itself is a significant part of the church's life. This teaching reaches back to the notion of the family as the domestic church, language first expressed in the early church and recaptured in the documents of the Second Vatican Council.

Section four of *Familiaris Consortio* calls for a comprehensive plan of support for family life from all the other sectors of church life. It calls for a pastoral outreach to all the types of family structures. It requests that local churches serve the needs of single parents, the widowed, the divorced, and the separated. In other words, there is an acknowledgement and respect given to people in a variety of family structures, which is clearly the trend that has developed in contemporary times.

The basic message of this extensive document on the family is that the church must respect and assist Christian families in whatever way it can. Clearly, the family stands at the crossroads of change in modern life. The Catholic Church is called to see that the future of the family is its own future. This perspective comes from both a sense of crisis and an awareness of a pastoral opportunity for church renewal. A family-sensitive approach to church life has roots going back to the beginning of the Christian era. In brief, the Catholic Church now affirms that the family is an essential life-giving part of the church and that it is a source of on-going vitality for entire church.

See also: ANNULMENT; FAMILY MINISTRY; GODPARENTS; INTERFAITH MARRIAGE; MARRIAGE PREPARATION; PROTESTANTISM; RELIGION

Bibliography

Barton, S. C., ed. (1996). *The Family in Theological Perspective*. Edinburgh: T and T Clark.

Cahill, L. S. (2000). *Family: A Christian Social Perspective*. Minneapolis, MN: Fortress Press.

Foley, G. (1995). *Family-Centered Church: A New Parish Model*. Kansas City, MO: Sheed and Ward.

John Paul II. (1981). *Familiaris Consortio—On the Family*. Washington, DC: Office of Publishing Services, United States Catholic Conference.

Kasper, W. (1980). *Theology of Christian Marriage*. New York: Crossroad.

Lawler, M. G. (1998). *Family: American and Christian*, Chicago: Loyola Press.

Lawler, M. G., and Roberts, W. P., eds. (1996). *Christian Marriage and Family: Contemporary Theological and Pastoral Perspectives*, Collegeville, MN: The Liturgical Press.

Mackin, T. (1982). *What is Marriage?* Ramsey, NJ: Paulist Press.

Mackin, T. (1989). *The Marital Sacrament*. Mahwah, NJ: Paulist Press.

Ruether, R. R. (2000). *Christianity and the Making of the Modern Family*. Boston: Beacon Press.

Schillebeecky, E. (1986). *Marriage, Human Reality, and Saving Mystery*. London: Sheed and Ward.

DAVID MICHAEL THOMAS

CHILD ABUSE

PHYSICAL ABUSE AND NEGLECT *Beth M. Schwartz-Kenney, Michelle McCauley*

PSYCHOLOGICAL MALTREATMENT *Stuart N. Hart, Marla R. Brassard, Nelson J. Binggeli, Howard A. Davidson*

SEXUAL ABUSE *Kathleen Kendall-Tackett*

PHYSICAL ABUSE AND NEGLECT

Child abuse and neglect is a social problem faced by individuals and societies around the world; however, few works exist that compare this problem across national boundaries. The International Society for the Prevention of Child Abuse and Neglect (IPSCAN) is an international organization focused on prevention and treatment issues associated with child abuse and neglect, and provides researchers in a number of disciplines with the opportunity to communicate about global issues of child abuse. One forum for this communication is *Child Abuse and Neglect: The International Journal*. One text, *Child Abuse: A Global Perspective*, by Beth Schwartz-Kenney, Michelle McCauley, and Michelle Epstein (2001), takes an extensive global view of all areas of child abuse among sixteen countries worldwide. This comparative perspective describes the nature of child abuse within each country and the countries' responses to abuse with regard to prevention and treatment.

Defining Child Physical Abuse and Neglect

The definition of abuse and neglect is difficult to determine even within a particular country. For example, Joaquín De Paúl and Olaya González (2001) note that before 1987 professionals in Spain could not reach an agreement concerning how one should classify child maltreatment cases: There was no commonly used definition of child abuse and neglect. Given the many cultural and societal influences affecting the way in which a country defines abuse, defining abuse globally is obviously a formidable task, although definitions of abuse and neglect do contain commonalities across countries. Child maltreatment includes both the abuse and neglect of a child, two different types of problems with slightly different causes, perpetrators, and outcomes. Furthermore, abuse occurs in a number of different forms including physical abuse, psychological maltreatment, and sexual abuse. These categorizations of abuse are fairly common across cultures.

Physical abuse often is described as a situation in which a child sustains injury due to the willful acts of an adult. This type of abuse can be defined very loosely, where abuse is defined as the ill-treatment of children. However, the definition may be as specific as stating that the injuries are inflicted by particular acts such as hitting, biting, kicking, or slapping; and/or occur through the use of objects such as belts, sticks, rods, or bats. These more specific definitions are usually the result of laws created to protect children. For instance in Spain the 21/87 Act improved the consistency of definitions used throughout the country in identifying child abuse (De Paúl and González 2001). In Israel in 1989 an amendment was passed known as the Law for the Prevention of Abuse of Minors and the Helpless. Specific types of abuse were defined within this amendment, creating a more definitive classification of each type of abuse in Israel (Cohen 2001). In many countries, the definition of physical abuse involves the presence of a physical mark created by intentional physical contact by an adult. One advantage of clear definitions is that they result in a more accurate reporting of physical abuse to authorities (Kasim 2001).

Physical abuse occurs more often in families with female children and in those with four or more children. Child victims are more likely than nonvictims to experience post-traumatic stress disorder, depression, attachment difficulties, and low self-esteem. ROY MORSCH/CORBIS

Physical abuse can also be a result of parental and/or school discipline in which a child is punished by beating or other forms of corporal punishment. It should be noted, however, that there are large cultural differences in the interpretation of corporal punishment as abuse. Many Western countries classify corporal punishment of any kind as physical abuse, although this is not true for the United States or Canada. In fact, twenty-three U.S. states allow corporal punishment in the public school system (National Coalition to Abolish Corporal Punishment in Schools 2001). Corporal punishment of children is also accepted in other countries. In Sri Lanka, caning a child is still a permitted form of punishment in government schools, and parents and teachers believe they have the right to impose corporal punishment (de Silva 2001). This is also the case in Kenya, where physical punishment is an acceptable way of disciplining children (Onyango and Kattambo 2001). In Romania 96 percent of the population are comfortable with beating a child as a form of discipline and do not feel that this beating would have any negative impact on the child's development (Muntean and Roth 2001). In India, Uma Segal (1995) examined the incidence of physical abuse defined as "discipline." Her results indicate that 57.9 percent of parents stated that they had engaged in "normal" corporal punishment, 41 percent in "abusive" discipline, and 2.9 percent in "extreme" discipline.

Physical abuse also includes acts of *exploitation*. This type of physical abuse is prevalent in a number of countries such as Sri Lanka, the Philippines, and Thailand where sexual exploitation of children is well documented (de Silva 2001). Exploitation is also seen in the form of child labor in a number of countries, such as India (Segal 2001), and in the conscription into the military of children in Sri Lanka (de Silva 2001). Finally, one less common form of psychical abuse results when a caretaker fabricates a child's illness, known as *Munchausen Syndrome by Proxy*. The pattern of events accompanying this syndrome often results in physical injury to the child (Wiehe 1996). Munchausen Syndrome by Proxy has been identified in a number of different countries (Schwartz-Kenney, McCauley, and Epstein 2001).

In the United States, following C. Henry Kempe and his colleagues' (1962) identification of *battered-child syndrome,* physical abuse was identified more objectively through the use of medical definitions. The Child Abuse Prevention and Treatment Act of 1974 led to a federal definition of child abuse and neglect. This Act provided definitions for all types of abuse and led to greater public awareness and response to problems associated to child maltreatment. This federal definition was changed in 1996 by the U.S. Congress. Child abuse and neglect in the United States is now defined as ". . . any recent act or failure to act on the part of a parent or caretaker, which results in the death, serious physical or emotional harm, sexual abuse or exploitation, or an act or failure to act which present an imminent risk of serious harm" (42 U.S.C. §5106g[2] [1999]). This change gave greater

discretion to the states, allowing each state to define abuse more broadly.

Child neglect also can take on a number of different forms. For instance a child's nutritional needs can be ignored, resulting in a deficient diet and, in turn, a "failure to thrive." This *nutritional neglect* is not necessarily intentional and may result from a parent's lack of knowledge regarding a healthy diet or from poverty. *Physical neglect* results when a child is not provided with adequate food, shelter, and clothing. Neglect can also come in the form of inadequate medical care, lack of proper supervision, and lack of educational opportunities. Finally, neglect also includes inadequate emotional care, where a child experiences a continuous lack of response to his or her crying or any other behavior in need of a response.

The type of neglect experienced by children is dependent upon the culture in which one lives. For instance, in India one problem still faced by many young women is *child marriage.* Due to extreme poverty, many girls are perceived as a financial burden to their families and are in turn forced to marry in exchange for money. In some cases, young women are sold to brothels. As Segal (2001) notes, under both circumstances these children are inevitably physically abused.

A very distinct type of neglect occurs in Japan, where coin-operated lockers have been a part of the problem. For years, unwanted children were placed in these lockers and, in many cases, died when not found in time. This became a serious social problem in the mid-1970s. According to Akihisa Kouno and Charles Felzen Johnson (1995), approximately 7 percent of infanticides in Japan during this period were of coin-operated locker babies. Since that time, this type of neglect has dropped dramatically due to an increase in locker inspection and relocation and to educational programs on contraception.

Abuse and neglect in Romania often takes the form of child abandonment, believed to be due to poverty, lack of education, and lack of assistance to families in need (Muntean and Roth 2001). Additional abuse and neglect takes place within the family given the existing living conditions. Ana Muntean and Maria Roth state that the "emotional, physical, and even sexual abuse is quite frequent within the Romanian-family system, as well as neglect" (p. 185).

Differences in prevalence of particular subtypes of abuse are therefore evident when examining child maltreatment from an international perspective. Although evidence of abuse can be found in all countries, how abuse is defined, prevented, and treated is often determined by social agencies such as the U.S. Department of Health. The definition itself is dependent upon the national boundaries in which the agency exists. One common thread within the prevalence data in most countries is that the individuals responsible for collecting these data often state that it is likely that the numbers underestimate the degree of child abuse due to the underreporting of incidents to legal authorities (Schwartz-Kenney, McCauley, and Epstein 2001).

Prevalence of Abuse and Neglect

Internationally, child abuse is more common than previously acknowledged. Historically, it was hard for many to believe that parents or caregivers would intentionally inflict harm towards their children. Thus, in many countries child abuse and neglect were often ignored or denied as a result of people's acceptance of violence in a given culture or due to their belief that the culture must focus on preserving the family (Schwartz-Kenney, McCauley, and Epstein 2001). Some cultures simply denied that child neglect or abuse occurred. For example, Mohd Sham Kasim (2001) states that in Malaysia the problem of abuse was at one time believed to be a problem only for Western cultures. This stemmed from the idea that the strong family ties and assistance from the extended family prevalent in Malaysia prevented the problem from occurring.

Internationally, it has always been the case that the culture had to acknowledge the problem of neglect and abuse before national organizations concerned with prevention and treatment could be created. Unfortunately, it took many years (often decades) before many societies recognized it as a problem worthy of governmental resources. As mentioned above, the noted physician C. Henry Kempe dramatically increased many countries' public awareness regarding the abuse and neglect of children in his lectures on the battered-child syndrome (Kempe et al. 1962).

The prevalence of each type of maltreatment is a question that can be answered in some countries but not others. For example, this type of data is available in the United States, Australia, Malaysia, and Ireland. Other countries, such as Canada, are studying this question, whereas others, such as Mexico and Romania, are grappling with how to identify children in need rather than placing their resources in the assessment of prevalence rates for each type of abuse. When comparing countries in which the numbers are available, it is evident that there are differences with regard to the prevalence of each type of abuse. For instance, in Australia, 31 percent of reports were of emotional abuse, 28 percent included physical abuse, 16 percent consisted of sexual abuse, and 24 percent represented neglect (Hatty and Hatty 2001). This is compared to the prevalence reports in Ireland, where 34 percent of reports involved sexual abuse, 8 percent included emotional abuse, 11 percent were identified as physical abuse, and 47 percent were of neglect (Ferguson 2001). In the United States, the Child Protective Services (CPS) state that neglect is the most prevalent type of maltreatment, accounting for 45 percent of all reports, followed by physical abuse in 25 percent of cases, sexual abuse in 16 percent of cases, and finally psychological abuse in 6 percent of all reports (Briere et al. 1996).

Thus, cultural differences significantly influence the way in which forms of abuse are defined and in turn the prevalence rates that result. Given differences in defining abuse, it is not surprising that the prevalence numbers such as those reported above differ dramatically from one country to the next. For instance, as Kouno and Johnson (2001) indicate, "the disparity between prevalence rates of report abuse cases in the United States and Japan may be the result of differences in lifestyle and reporting laws between Western countries and Japan" (pp. 102–103). Comparing abuse from one country to the next is a difficult task given the differences in definition, lifestyle, and legal system. In all cases, authorities believe the prevalence rates represent approximately one-third of all cases of child abuse because these statistics are based only on reported cases and therefore ignore the remaining two-thirds of all occurrences of maltreatment. With the introduction of mandatory reporting laws in numerous countries, however, these numbers are rising. In addition, an increase in public awareness of the problem of abuse and neglect directly relates to an increase in reporting of abuse to authorities.

Perpetrators and Families in which Neglect Occurs

Who is more likely to neglect a child? Researchers have examined the characteristics of families often associated with neglect. One finding is that the perpetrator of neglect in the United States and other Western countries is likely to be female (Ferguson 2001; Juvenile Justice Bulletin 1999). This may be a function of the fact that neglect is more likely to occur in single-parent families and homes in which the mother is young. Children born to women under the age of twenty in the United States are 3.5 times more likely to experience neglect and abuse than children born to older mothers (Lee and Goerge 1999). In addition, neglect occurs more often in families with mothers who are child-like in nature—for instance, those who are more dependent on others, act more impulsively, cannot assume responsibility for themselves or others, and show poor judgment. These mothers often receive very little social support, were neglected as children themselves, have higher rates of depression than the overall population, experience high degrees of stress, and were part of families that lived in environments that did not provide adequate mental and health services or educational facilities (Wiehe 1996). Domestic abuse has also been found related to maternal neglect in Western countries such as Ireland (Ferguson 2001) and the United States (Briere et al. 1996). Researchers have also found that children born to substance abusers are more likely to experience neglect and injury compared to children of non-substance abusers (Bijur et al. 1992). Concerning family factors, children of neglect were most often from families living in poverty, families without a father present (Ferguson 2001; Polansky et al. 1981) or with an unemployed male adult (Hawkins and Dunkin 1985), families with four or more children (Juvenile Justice Bulletin 1999), and families in which the interaction between the children and adults was primarily negative (Wiehe 1996). All of these factors often lead to a parent's inability to adequately parent, resulting in neglect of one form or another.

Perpetrators and Families in which Physical Abuse Occurs

Researchers have identified a number of factors associated with the physical abuse of a child, such as the characteristics of individuals who abuse and the characteristics of families in which child abuse occurs. In the United States less than 10 percent of child abuse is committed by non-family members (Juvenile Justice Bulletin 1999). Obviously, the non-family abuse rate may be higher in countries such as Sri Lanka where conscription into the military and child prostitution are greater problems (de Silva 2001). In addition, in the United States only 3 percent of child maltreatment occurs at day care facilities or other institutions (Prevent Child Abuse America 1997). This rate may be higher in countries such as Romania (Muntean and Roth 2001) and Russia where institutional abuse of children has been identified as a serious problem (Berrien, Safonova, and Tsimbal 2001).

In general, there are a number of individual perpetrator differences that predict abuse in the West. For instance, individuals who were abused as children are believed to be more at risk to become abusers as adults (Straus, Gelles, and Steinmetz 1980). Physical abuse is also more likely to occur in family situations in which parental knowledge of parenting skills is inadequate, when high levels of stress are present, when parents are very young, when parental expectations are too high regarding a child's behaviors, when substance abuse is present, and/or when adults in the family have low levels of empathy towards a child (Kolko 1996). Abuse is found more often in families with female children (Sedlack and Broadhurst 1996) and in families with four or more children (Juvenile Justice Bulletin 1999). Finally factors such as economic distress, lack of social support, and cultural or religious values have been linked to incidences of physical abuse in most countries that have addressed this problem (Schwartz-Kenney, McCauley, and Epstein 2001).

Effects of Abuse and Neglect: Long-Term and Short-Term Effects

There is little cross-cultural data on differences in harm to victims of child neglect and abuse in different countries. However, when one looks at studies from different countries there are a number of similarities. In general, empirical studies indicate that various forms of child maltreatment negatively affect the victim's development physically, intellectually, and psychosocially (Kempe and Kempe 1978; Mullen et al. 1993). Child victims of neglect and/or abuse are 1.75 times more likely to experience *posttraumatic stress disorder* as adults compared to individuals who did not experience neglect and/or abuse (Widom 1999). In addition, child victims are more likely to experience depression, attachment difficulties, and low self-esteem (Kolko 1996). A Canadian study found that a history of child abuse was one of the leading predictors of psychological problems in adulthood (Mian, Bala, and MacMillan 2001). Many studies also indicate the long-term effects of maltreatment given the carry-over from one generation to the next (Zuravin et al. 1996).

Furthermore, there are particular risks and harm associated with certain types of abuse, which are more prevalent in certain countries. For example, in addition to the negative outcomes discussed above, conscription into the military carries with it the risk of physical injury or death. Being forced to work as a prostitute significantly increases the chance of becoming infected with HIV or other sexually transmitted diseases. In India, which has a very high rate of child labor, children are often forced to work in dangerous conditions at exhausting hours (Segal 2001).

Finally, in addition to the harm of neglect and abuse to the individual child, there is also a broader harm or cost to society as a whole. Researchers have established a link between experiencing neglect and abuse as a child and engaging in illegal and delinquent behaviors as a teenager and adult (Widom 2001).

Cultural Differences

One must take into account the vast cross-cultural differences that exist when defining any type of child maltreatment. By examining comparative data from a diverse group of cultures, perhaps cultural factors and social structures can be identified to help us gain a better understanding of factors that contribute to abuse and factors that might assist in effectively preventing abuse. Simple definitions of child abuse and neglect do not exist, although there are a number of similarities in definitions even across cultures. Regardless of the differences in how abuse is defined, the number of reports of abuse has risen dramatically in the last decade without the needed growth in staff to respond to this increase in reports. This clearly indicates the need for greater prevention, resources dedicated to staffing, and effective treatment of this worldwide social problem.

See also: CHILD ABUSE: PSYCHOLOGICAL

MALTREATMENT; CHILD ABUSE: SEXUAL ABUSE;

CHILDHOOD; CHILDREN OF ALCOHOLICS; CHILDREN'S RIGHTS; CONDUCT DISORDER; DEPRESSION: CHILDREN AND ADOLESCENTS; DISCIPLINE; FAILURE TO THRIVE; INFANTICIDE; JUVENILE DELINQUENCY; MUNCHAUSEN SYNDROME BY PROXY; PARENTING STYLES; POSTTRAUMATIC STRESS DISORDER (PTSD); POWER: FAMILY RELATIONSHIPS; RUNAWAY YOUTHS; SPANKING; SUBSTANCE ABUSE

Bibliography

Berrien, F. B.; Safanova, T. Y.; and Tsimbal, E. I. (2001). "Russia." In *Child Abuse: A Global View,* ed. B. M. Schwartz-Kenney, M. McCauley, and M. Epstein. Westport, CT: Greenwood.

Bijur, P. E.; Kurzon, M.; Overpeck, M. D.; and Scheidt, P. C. (1992). "Parental Alcohol Use, Problem Drinking and Child Injuries." *Journal of the American Medical Association* 23:3166–3171.

Briere, J.; Berliner, L.; Bulkley, J. A.; Jenny, C.; and Reid, T. (1996). "Child Neglect." In *The APSAC Handbook on Child Maltreatment,* ed. J. Briere, L. Berliner, J. A. Bulkley, C. Jenny, and T. Reid. Thousand Oaks, CA: Sage.

Child Abuse and Prevention and Treatment Act of 1974, P.L. 93–247 (renamed Child Abuse Prevention and Treatment and Adoption Reform Act), codified at 42 U.S.C. §510, *et seq.*

Cohen, T. (2001). "Israel." In *Child Abuse: A Global View,* ed. B. M. Schwartz-Kenney, M. McCauley, and M. Epstein. Westport, CT: Greenwood.

De Paúl, J., and González, O. (2001). "Spain." In *Child Abuse: A Global View,* ed. B. M. Schwartz-Kenney, M. McCauley, and M. Epstein. Westport, CT: Greenwood.

de Silva, D. G. H. (2001). "Sri Lanka." In *Child Abuse: A Global View,* ed. B. M. Schwartz-Kenney, M. McCauley, and M. Epstein. Westport, CT: Greenwood.

Ferguson, H. (2001). "Ireland." In *Child Abuse: A Global View,* ed. B. M. Schwartz-Kenney, M. McCauley, and M. Epstein. Westport, CT: Greenwood.

Hatty, S. E., and Hatty, J. (2001). "Australia." In *Child Abuse: A Global View,* ed. B. M. Schwartz-Kenney, M. McCauley, and M. Epstein. Westport, CT: Greenwood.

Hawkins, W., and Dunkin, D. (1985). "Perpetrator and Family Characteristics Related to Child Abuse and Neglect: Comparison of Substantiated and Unsubstantiated Reports." *Psychological Reports* 56:407–410.

Kasim, M. S. (2001). "Malaysia." In *Child Abuse: A Global View,* ed. B. M. Schwartz-Kenney, M. McCauley, and M. Epstein. Westport, CT: Greenwood.

Kempe, C.; Silverman, F.; Steele, B.; Droegemueller, W.; and Silver, H. (1962). "The Battered-Child Syndrome." *Journal of American Medical Association* 181:17–24.

Kempe, R., and Kempe, C. H. (1978). *Child Abuse*. London: Fontana Open Books.

Kolko, D. J. (1996) "Child Physical Abuse." In *The APSAC Handbook on Child Maltreatment,* ed. J. Briere, L. Berliner, J. A. Bulkley, C. Jenny, and T. Reid. Thousand Oaks, CA: Sage.

Kouno, A., and Johnson, C. F. (1995). "Child Abuse and Neglect in Japan: Coin-Operated Locker Babies." *Child Abuse and Neglect* 19:25–31.

Kouno, A., and Johnson, C. F. (2001). "Japan." In *Child Abuse: A Global View,* ed. B. M. Schwartz-Kenney, M. McCauley, and M. Epstein. Westport, CT: Greenwood.

Lee, B. J., and Goerge, R. M. (1999). "Poverty, Early Childbearing, and Child Maltreatment: A Multinominal Analysis." *Children and Youth Services Review* 21:755–780.

Mian, M.; Bala, N.; and MacMillan, H. (2001). "Canada." In *Child Abuse: A Global View,* ed. B. M. Schwartz-Kenney, M. McCauley, and M. Epstein. Westport, CT: Greenwood.

Mullen, P. E.; Martin, J. L.; Anderson, J. C.; Romans, S. E.; and Hubison, G. J. (1993). "Childhood Sexual Abuse and Mental Health in Adult Life." *British Journal of Psychiatry* 163:721–732.

Muntean, A., and Roth. M. (2001). "Romania." In *Child Abuse: A Global View,* ed. B. M. Schwartz-Kenney, M. McCauley, and M. Epstein. Westport, CT: Greenwood.

Onyango, P. P. M., and Kattambo, V. W. M. (2001). "Kenya." In *Child Abuse: A Global View,* ed. B. M. Schwartz-Kenney, M. McCauley, and M. Epstein. Westport, CT: Greenwood.

Polansky, N.; Chalmers, M.; Buttenweiser, E.; and Williams, D. (1981). *Damaged Parents: An Anatomy of Child Neglect*. Chicago: University of Chicago Press.

Schwartz-Kenney, B. M.; McCauley, M.; and Epstein, M. (2001). *Child Abuse: A Global View*. Westport, CT: Greenwood.

Sedlack, A. J., and Broadhurst, D. D. (1996). *The Third National Incidence Study of Child Abuse and Neglect*. Washington, DC: Government Printing Office.

Segal, U. A. (2001). "India." In *Child Abuse: A Global View,* ed. B. M. Schwartz-Kenney, M. McCauley, and M. Epstein. Westport, CT: Greenwood.

Segal, U. A. (1995). "Child Abuse by the Middle Class? A Study of Professionals in India." *Child Abuse and Neglect* 19:213–227.

Straus, M. A.; Gelles, R.; and Steinmetz, S. (1980). *Behind Close Doors: Violence in the American Family*. Garden City, NY: Doubleday.

Widom, C. S. (2001). "Child Abuse and Neglect." In *Handbook of Youth and Justice,* ed. S. O. White. New York: Plenum.

Widom, C. S. (1999). "Posttraumatic Stress Disorder in Abused and Neglected Children Grown-Up." *American Journal of Psychiatry* 156:1223–1229.

Wiehe, V. R. (1996). *Working with Child Abuse and Neglect: A Primer*. Thousand Oaks, CA: Sage.

Zuravin, S.; McMillan, C.; DePantilis, D.; and Risley-Curtis, C. (1996). "The Intergenerational Cycle of Child Maltreatment: Continuity versus Discontinuity." *Journal of Interpersonal Violence* 7:471–489.

Other Resources

Juvenile Justice Bulletin. (1999). Available from http://www.ncjrs.org/html/ojjdp/2000_5_2/child_09.html.

National Coalition to Abolish Corporal Punishment in Schools. (2001). "Facts about Corporal Punishment." Available from http://www.stophitting.com/disatschool/facts.php.

Prevent Child Abuse America. (1997). *Current Trends in Child Abuse. 1997 Annual 50 State Survey*. Available from http://www.childabuse.com/50data97.htm.

BETH M. SCHWARTZ-KENNEY
MICHELLE MCCAULEY

PSYCHOLOGICAL MALTREATMENT

Children should be protected against all forms of child maltreatment, including physical or mental violence, injury, abuse, or neglect. Children who have been maltreated should be given all necessary support to achieve recovery. These principles now have nearly universal acceptance by virtue of the standards of Articles 3, 19, 34, and 39 of the United Nations Convention on the Rights of the Child (United Nations General Assembly 1989), a treaty ratified by 191 of the 193 recognized nations of the world.

There are two major types of child maltreatment: physical and psychological. Sexual abuse, generally a combination of the two major types, is primarily psychological in the nature of its acts and consequences. Psychological maltreatment is understood to occur alone as psychological abuse or

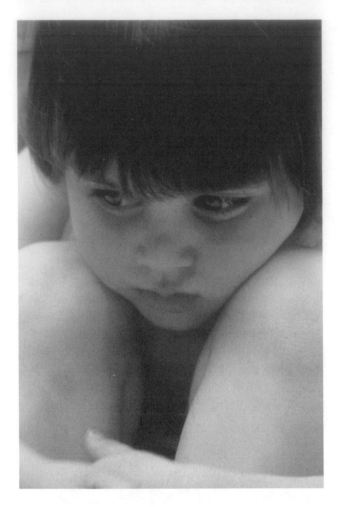

Studies have documented that psychological abuse is a stronger predictor than physical abuse of both depression and low self-esteem and, in particular, is strongly related to anxiety, depression, interpersonal sensitivity, dissociation, and low self-esteem. CRAIG HAMMELL/CORBIS

neglect, to occur in association with other forms of abuse and neglect, and to be the embedded psychological context and meanings of other forms of abuse and neglect.

The present empirical and theoretical knowledge base for child maltreatment supports the view considering psychological maltreatment to be the unifying concept embodying many of the most significant components of child abuse and neglect (Binggeli, Hart, and Brassard 2001). Essential aspects of this knowledge base are presented in this entry.

Definition

The lack of an adequate definition of psychological maltreatment was a major obstacle to making progress dealing with the issue during the first decades of serious societal consideration of child maltreatment (1960–1990). Since the early 1980s recognizable advances have been made in articulating rationally defensible definitions of psychological maltreatment that have substantial professional and public support.

The first U.S. law on child abuse—Public Law 93–247, originally passed in 1974—included attention to psychological maltreatment under the category of "mental injury." Early attempts to elaborate this ambiguous category in national policy and state law were not adequate and resulted in a confusing diversity of terms and standards. Significant progress toward a useful definition occurred through the processes and outcomes of the International Conference on Psychological Abuse of the Child (Office for the Study of the Psychological Rights of the Child 1983); through conceptual and empirical research (Baily and Baily 1986; Brassard, Germain, and Hart 1987; Garbarino, Guttman, and Seely 1986; Hart and Brassard 1989–1991); and through the development of related standards by the American Professional Society on the Abuse of Children (APSAC) (1995). Concern about psychological maltreatment internationally is displayed in the laws of Sweden prohibiting emotional psychological abuse of children, and in the expansion of child protection law in Singapore to include "emotional injury" in the definition of when a child or young person needs care and protection (Children and Young Persons [Amendment] Act 2001; source: Ministry for Community Development and Sports, Singapore).

The term *psychological maltreatment* has come to be preferred to other labels (e.g., emotional abuse and neglect, mental abuse or injury). It includes both the cognitive and affective (psychological) meanings of maltreatment as well as perpetrator maltreatment acts of both commission and omission.

The strongest expert-supported definition of psychological maltreatment is presently in the APSAC *Guidelines for Psychosocial Evaluation of Suspected Psychological Maltreatment of Children and Adolescents* (1995). These guidelines include the following conceptual statement and psychological maltreatment categories:

- Psychological maltreatment means a repeated pattern of caregiver behavior or extreme incident(s) that convey to children that

CHILD ABUSE: PSYCHOLOGICAL MALTREATMENT

they are worthless, flawed, unloved, un-wanted, endangered, or only of value in meeting another's needs (p. 2).

- Psychological maltreatment includes: (1) *spurning* (i.e., hostile rejecting/degrading verbal and nonverbal caregiver acts that reject and degrade a child); (2) *terrorizing* (i.e., caregiver behavior that threatens or is likely to physically hurt, kill, abandon, or place the child or child's loved ones or objects in recognizably dangerous situations); (3) *isolating* (i.e., caregiver acts that consistently deny the child opportunities to meet needs for interacting or communicating with peers or adults inside or outside the home); (4) *exploiting/corrupting* (i.e., modeling, permitting, or encouraging antisocial behavior); (5) *denying emotional responsiveness* (i.e., caregiver acts that ignore the child's attempts and needs to interact and show no emotion in interactions with the child); and (6) *mental health, medical, and educational neglect* (i.e., ignoring the need for, failing, or refusing to allow or provide treatment for serious emotional/behavioral, physical health, or educational problems or needs of the child).

These six categories of psychological maltreatment are further delineated through detailed subcategories that clarify their meanings (APSAC 1995). Empirical and conceptual support for these categories and definitions will be found in child-study research (Rohner and Rohner 1980; Claussen and Crittenden 1991; Egeland and Erickson 1987; Binggeli, Hart, and Brassard 2001); and in expert- and public-opinion research (Burnett 1993; Portwood 1999).

Incidence and Prevalence

Incidence of maltreatment generally refers to the number of new cases coming to the attention of authorities within a given year. *Prevalence* represents the total number of people in a sample who have ever experienced the maltreatment.

The true incidence of psychological maltreatment is unknown. The best available estimates of the incidence of psychological maltreatment come from findings of the National Incidence Study and research on verbal aggression. The National Incidence Study of the Federal Office on Child Abuse

and Neglect (Sedlak and Broadhurst 1996) applies both an existing *Harm Standard* and a projected *Endangerment Standard* in gathering data from local social service, health and law enforcement professionals, and child welfare agencies. Data for 1993 supported estimates of more than 1.5 million children abused or neglected under the Harm Standard and three million under the Endangerment Standard, with approximately 532,000 of these children emotionally abused and 585,100 emotionally neglected. High annual levels of verbal/symbolic aggression (defined as "communication intended to cause psychological pain to another person, or a communication perceived as having that intent," [Vissing et al. 1991, p. 224]) were found in a telephone survey of the tactics used by a national sample of 3,458 parents to deal with conflicts in relations with their children. Over 11 percent if the children were reported to have experienced an average of more than two such incidents per month, whereas 63 percent experienced at least one such incident per year (Vissing et al. 1991).

Prevalence estimates can be made from data collected in studies of the childhood-experience histories of adults, retrospectively surveyed, using definitions similar to those in the APSAC *Guidelines* (1995). Nelson Binggeli, Stuart Hart, and Marla Brassard (2001) concluded, from reviews of such studies, that over one-third of the adult population has had significant psychological maltreatment experiences and that 10 to 15 percent of the adult population has suffered chronic or severe psychological maltreatment. Confidence in these estimates is further supported by the facts that the definitions used in these studies were fairly conservative, the types were considered appropriate by both researchers and community representatives, and it is more likely that the subjects minimized rather than exaggerated their maltreatment histories.

Evidence of Impact

Evidence that psychological maltreatment is a threat and destructive to the well-being and development of children is vital to producing the societal concern and interventions necessary to combat it. Until recently, however, the relationship between psychological maltreatment and negative developmental consequences for victims have had to be accepted as somewhat speculative because the construct was not well defined.

The existence of the broadly supported definitions for spurning, terrorizing, isolating, corrupting/exploiting, and denying emotional responsiveness has made it possible to carry out more rigorous reviews of related research literature. The available knowledge base indicates that psychological maltreatment probably has the most severe, longest lasting, and broadest range of negative developmental consequences of any form of child abuse or neglect (with the exception of the killing of a child), and that it is the core component in child abuse (Hart, Brassard, and Binggeli 1998).

Longitudinal and cross-cultural research has identified psychological maltreatment as a significant contributor to the following conditions: children who become angry, assaultive, or aggressive; delinquent, criminal, and/or substance abusers; persons who feel unloved and inadequate; and persons who develop negative feelings and perspectives about the purposes and possibilities for enjoyment of life, including having a happy marriage and being a good parent (Egeland and Erickson 1987; Rohner and Rohner 1980). Studies comparing the effects of various forms of child maltreatment have documented that (a) combinations of verbal abuse and emotional neglect tend to produce the most powerfully negative outcomes; (b) psychological maltreatment is a better predictor of detrimental developmental outcomes for young children than is the severity of physical injury experienced by children; (c) psychological maltreatment is the indicator most related to behavior problems for children and adolescents, and is more strongly related to physical aggression, delinquency, or interpersonal problems than parental physical aggression; (d) psychological abuse is a stronger predictor than physical abuse of both depression and low self-esteem and, in particular, is strongly related to anxiety, depression, interpersonal sensitivity, dissociation (disruption in usually integrated functions of consciousness, identity, or perception of the environment), and low self-esteem; and (e) psychologically unavailable caretaking is the most devastating of all maltreatment forms (Briere and Runtz 1990; Claussen and Crittenden 1991; Egeland and Erickson 1987; Vissing et al. 1991).

Numerous studies have identified the possible effects of psychological maltreatment within families. This evidence found through these studies fits nicely within the conceptual framework used by the nation's schools to guide identification of child "emotional disturbance" (federal *Individuals with Disabilities Act* Law 94–142). Findings indicate relationships between psychological maltreatment and problems with *intrapersonal* thoughts, feelings, and behaviors (e.g., anxiety, depression, low self-esteem, negative life views, post-traumatic symptoms and fears, and suicidal thinking); *emotional problem symptoms* (e.g., emotional instability, impulse control problems, unresponsiveness, substance abuse, and eating disorders); *social competency problems* and anti-social functioning (e.g., attachment problems, self-isolating behavior, low social competency, low empathy, non-compliance, dependency, sexual maladjustment, aggression and violent behavior, and delinquency or criminality); *learning problems* (e.g., decline in mental competence, lower measured intelligence, non-compliance, lack of impulse control, impaired learning, academic problems and lower achievement test results, and impaired development of moral reasoning); and *physical health problems* (e.g., allergies, asthma and other respiratory ailments, hypertension, somatic complaints, physical growth failure, physical and behavioral delay, brain damage, and high mortality rates) (Hart, Brassard, and Binggeli 1998).

Theoretical Perspectives

Psychological maltreatment is an interpersonal experience. The essential role of interpersonal relations in human development and need fulfillment establishes an inherent vulnerability to psychological maltreatment. Many of the major theories in psychology contain constructs that are related to psychological maltreatment, particularly in the way they describe critical factors of the developmental process susceptible to the influences of various kinds of interpersonal experiences. *Human needs theory, psychosocial stage theory, attachment theory, parental acceptance-rejection theory,* the *coercion model* and the *prisoner of war model* each have value for psychological maltreatment research and interventions. They clarify the ways in which psychological maltreatment interferes with need fulfillment and development processes and produce retardation and/or distortions in growth and behavior (Binggeli, Hart, and Brassard 2001).

Psychological Maltreatment and the Law

In general, psychological maltreatment has not led to coercive or punitive governmental intervention, unless it accompanied other forms of maltreatment. Judicial precedents on psychological maltreatment are, for most part, unavailable to courts because there have been few reported appellate court decisions on stand-alone psychological maltreatment. Child protection officials and judges must largely be guided by the relevant language in state laws. Current state laws indicates that the federal "mental injury" principle has proven difficult for many legislatures to define.

Some states have simply used the term mental injury—or some similar term—without further explanation. Other states have incorporated one or more of the following standards or requirements:

- The child has experienced serious psychological or mental injury caused by recognizable acts;

- Injuries must be observable, substantial, sustained, and identifiable impairments of the child's intellectual or psychological capacity or emotional stability;

- A child displays substantially diminished psychological or intellectual functioning;

- Failure to provide for a child's "mental or emotional needs";

- Application of a list of problem-related symptoms (see earlier lists of impact);

- Failure to provide needed health services;

- Expert witness opinion (e.g., a licensed physician or qualified mental health professional);

- Specific recognition of certain forms of psychological maltreatment (e.g., isolation through use of mechanical devices to physically restrain).

The psychological maltreatment experienced by children due to exposure to domestic violence in the home is an emerging area of concern. Evidence of negative child-impact from observed domestic violence is growing (Hughes and Graham-Bermann 1998). California (Domestic Violence Unit 1999) has taken deliberate efforts to work toward identifying and serving domestic violence–exposed children as abused.

Despite the myriad of potential statutory variations for legal intervention where psychological harm has been inflicted upon children by their parents, it should be possible for judicial and CPS agency efforts to be applied to psychological maltreatment cases. For this to occur, it will require a change from the status quo: child welfare agency personnel, attorneys, and juvenile court judges will need to be educated on psychological maltreatment (Hart et al. 2001).

Interventions for Psychological Maltreatment

Substantial progress has been made in guiding assessments in cases of suspected psychological maltreatment of children, whereas only small beginnings have been made in developing effective correction and prevention strategies. The APSAC *Guidelines* (1995) provides the best available framework for professionals in evaluations of suspected psychological maltreatment. The guidelines were designed to assist in case planning, legal decision making, and treatment planning for psychological maltreatment that occurs as a powerful single instance or continual pattern, and maltreatment that occurs in isolation from as well as in conjunction with other forms of abuse and neglect. The *Guidelines* assist in making determinations of the nature and severity of psychological maltreatment, including extant or predicted developmental impact, through direct observation, interviews, review of records and collateral reports, and consultation. The *Guidelines* also help professionals apply ethical standards, weigh cultural factors, and report findings.

In general, the development of effective strategies for prevention and treatment of child maltreatment has been elusive, and psychological maltreatment has received relatively little direct attention in this regard. Intervention models applied to perpetrators and families that have shown improved outcomes have devoted resources (e.g., reduced client load, highly trained and well-supervised therapists, and many client contact hours) well beyond those usually available to child protective services or contracted private agencies. Although the development and study of specific treatments for children has genuine potential, according to existing research findings, it remains uncommon. Available research does indicate that children generally experience greater treatment gains than adults and provides unquestionable evidence of intergenerational transmission of child maltreatment.

It appears wise to give prevention the top intervention priority for child maltreatment, and particularly for psychological maltreatment because it is such a pervading, insidious, and powerfully destructive force. Studies of resilience have identified affiliation and self-efficacy (i.e., realistic confidence in one's competence to deal effectively with life's challenges and opportunities) as necessary to support healthy development under difficult conditions. Prevention *and* correction are well served by programs supporting development of secure attachment to adult caretakers through sensitive, responsive parenting and pre-school and elementary school teacher-student relations; through modeling and promoting appropriate childcare and interpersonal skills for parents and children; and through helping children develop a genuine sense of practical competence in school and community play and work, including problem solving and conflict resolution. Progress can be made if high quality intervention research and effective programs are supported through societal commitment and funding.

See also: CHILD ABUSE: PHYSICAL ABUSE AND NEGLECT; CHILD ABUSE: SEXUAL ABUSE; CHILDHOOD; CHILDREN'S RIGHTS; CONDUCT DISORDER; DEPRESSION: CHILDREN AND ADOLESCENTS; INTERPARENTAL VIOLENCE—EFFECTS ON CHILDREN; MUNCHAUSEN SYNDROME BY PROXY; PARENTING STYLES; POWER: FAMILY RELATIONSHIPS; RUNAWAY YOUTHS; SPANKING

Bibliography

American Professional Society on the Abuse of Children (APSAC). (1995). *Guidelines for the Psychosocial Evaluation of Suspected Psychological Maltreatment in Children and Adolescents.* Chicago: Author.

Baily, T. F., and Baily, W. H. (1986). *Operational Definitions of Child Emotional Maltreatment: Final Report.* Washington, DC: Government Printing Office.

Binggeli, N. J.; Hart, S. N.; and Brassard, M. R. (2001). *Psychological Maltreatment: A Study Guide.* Thousand Oaks, CA: Sage.

Brassard, M. R.; Germain, R.; and Hart, S. N., eds. (1987). *Psychological Maltreatment of Children and Youth.* New York: Pergamon.

Briere, J., and Runtz, M. (1990). "Differential Adult Symptomology Associated with Three Types of Child Abuse Histories." *Child Abuse and Neglect* 14:357–364.

Burnett, B. B. (1993). "The Psychological Abuse of Latency Age Children: A Survey." *Child Abuse and Neglect* 17:441–454.

Claussen, A. H., and Crittenden, P.M. (1991). "Physical and Psychological Maltreatment: Relations among Types of Aaltreatment." *Child Abuse and Neglect* 15:5–18.

Daro, D. (1988). *Confronting Child Abuse: Research for Effective Program Design.* New York: Free Press.

Domestic Violence Unit. (1999). *It Shouldn't Hurt To Go Home: The Domestic Violence Victim's Handbook.* Los Angeles: Author.

Egeland, B., and Erickson, M. (1987). "Psychologically Unavailable Caregiving." In *Psychological Maltreatment of Children and Youth,* ed. M. R. Brassard, R. Germain, and S. N. Hart. New York: Pergamon Press.

Garbarino, J.; Guttman, E.; and Seeley, J. (1986). *The Psychologically Battered Child: Strategies for Identification, Assessment and Intervention.* San Francisco: Jossey-Bass.

Hart, S. N.; Binggeli, N. J.; and Brassard, M. R. (1998). "Evidence of the Effects of Psychological Maltreatment." *Journal of Emotional Abuse* 1(1):27–58.

Hart, S. N., and Brassard, M. R. (1989–1991). Final report (stages 1 and 2). *Developing and Validating Operationally Defined Measures of Emotional Maltreatment: A Multimodal Study of the Relationship between Caretaker Behaviors and Children Characteristics across Three Developmental Levels* (Grant No. DHHS90CA1216). Washington, DC: Department of Health and Human Services and National Center for Child Abuse and Neglect.

Hart, S. N.; Brassard M. R.; Binggeli, N. J.; and Davidson, H. A. (2002). "Psychological Maltreatment." In *The APSAC Handbook on Child Maltreatment,* 2nd edition, ed. J. E. B., Myers, L. Berliner, J. Briere, C. T. Hendrix, C. Jenny, and T. A. Reid. Thousand Oaks, CA: Sage Publications.

Hughes, H. M.; and Graham-Bermann, S.A. (1998). "Children of Battered Women: Impact of Emotional Abuse on Adjustment and Development." *Journal of Emotional Abuse* 1(2):23–50.

Office for the Study of the Psychological Rights of the Child (1983). *Proceedings Summary of the International Conference on Psychological Abuse of Children and Youth (Indiana University Purdue University Indianapolis).* Indianapolis: Author, Indiana University.

Portwood, S. G. (1999). "Coming to Terms with a Consensual Definition of Child Maltreatment." *Child Maltreatment* 4(1):56–68.

Rohner, R. P., and Rohner, E. C. (1980). "Antecedents and Consequences of Parental Rejection: A Theory of Emotional Abuse." *Child Abuse and Neglect* 4:189–198.

Sedlak, A. J., and Broadhurst, D. D. (1996). *The Third National Incidence Study of Child Abuse and Neglect.* Washington, DC: U. S. Department of Health and Human Services, Administration for Children, Youth, and Families.

United Nations General Assembly. (1989). *Adoption of a Convention on the Rights of the Child.* New York: Author.

Vissing, Y. M.; Straus, M. A.; Gelles, R. J.; and Harrop, J. W. (1991). "Verbal Aggression by Parents and Psychosocial Problems of Children." *Child Abuse and Neglect* 15:223–238.

STUART N. HART
MARLA R. BRASSARD
NELSON J. BINGGELI
HOWARD A. DAVIDSON

SEXUAL ABUSE

Each year, thousands of boys and girls are sexually abused. The effects of this abuse can last a lifetime. The American Academy of Pediatrics (1991) defines sexual abuse as "engaging of a child in sexual activities that the child cannot comprehend, for which the child is developmentally unprepared and cannot give informed consent, and/or that violate the social and legal taboos of society" (p. 254).

Sexual abuse accounts for 12 percent of the one million substantiated cases of child abuse and neglect annually (Reece 2000). Approximately 20 percent of adult women, and 5 to 10 percent of men have been sexually abused as children. The peak age of vulnerability to sexual abuse is between seven and thirteen years of age, but children older or much younger have been abused (Finkelhor 1994). Girls are approximately three times more likely to be sexually abused than boys (Sedlak and Broadhurst 1996). The overwhelming majority of victims know their abusers. Girls are more likely to be abused by family members, and boys by friends of the family (Kendall-Tackett and Simon 1992).

The Effects of Sexual Abuse

The effects of sexual abuse are its most highly studied aspect—and its most political. Some claim sexual abuse is *always* harmful. Others maintain that some children actually *benefit* from these sexual experiences. And some children show no symptoms at all (Kendall-Tackett, Williams, and Finkelhor 1993). Allegations of abuse also raise legal and custody issues.

Short-term effects. Children experience a wide range of symptoms after they have been sexually abused. Some symptoms show up immediately, and others appear as delayed responses. Still others get better over time. Traumatic events, including sexual abuse, can alter the brains of children, and the effects may not be obvious for several years (Perry 2001).

Posttraumatic stress disorder (PTSD) is common, but not specific to sexual abuse. Sexualized behavior is the most characteristic symptom, but not one that every child manifests. It is also one of the more disturbing symptoms and includes public masturbation, sexual play with dolls, and asking other children and adults to participate in sexual activity.

Symptoms by age of child. The symptoms that children manifest also vary by age of the child. For example, preschool-age children are more likely to experience anxiety, nightmares, or sexual acting out. Common symptoms for school-age children include fear, aggression, school problems, hyperactivity, and regressive behaviors. Adolescents are more likely to be depressed, attempt suicide, abuse substances, or participate in illegal behaviors. Symptoms often change over time. For example, a preschooler who is sexually acting out may become an adolescent with multiple sexual partners (Kendall-Tackett et al. 1993).

Long-term effects. The effects of child sexual abuse can continue well into adulthood. Symptoms adult survivors manifest are often logical extensions of dysfunctional coping mechanisms developed during childhood. While these dysfunctional behaviors may have helped the child cope with on-going abuse, they have a negative impact on adult functioning. Long-term effects can be divided into seven categories (Briere and Elliot 1994; Kendall-Tackett and Marshall 1998):

- *Posttraumatic stress disorder (PTSD)*. Posttraumatic stress disorder (PTSD) is a commonly occurring symptom among adult survivors of sexual abuse. According to John Briere and Diana Elliot (1994), 80 percent of abuse survivors have symptoms of PTSD, even if they do not meet the full diagnostic criteria. These reactions include hypervigilance, sleep disturbances, startle responses, intrusive thoughts, and flashbacks.

- *Cognitive distortions*. Sexual abuse survivors often learn to perceive the world as a dangerous place. These cognitive distortions make them more vulnerable to both re-victimization and depression because they believe they are powerless to change their lives.

- *Emotional distress*. Emotional distress is another common symptom among adult survivors. Sexual abuse survivors have a lifetime risk of depression that is four times higher than their nonabused counterparts. They may also experience mild-to-severe anxiety and anger on a regular basis.

- *Impaired sense of self*. Survivors may have difficulty separating their moods and emotional states from the reactions of others. If their partners are depressed or angry, survivors are too, without necessarily considering whether they really feel the same way. Impaired sense of self can also inhibit self-protection, increasing survivors' risk of re-victimization.

- *Avoidance*. Avoidance includes some of the more serious sequelae of past abuse. Survivors may experience dissociation, which includes feeling separated from their bodies, emotional numbing, amnesia for painful memories, and multiple personality disorder. Other types of avoidant behavior are substance abuse, suicidal ideation and attempts, and *tension-reducing activities,* including indiscriminate sexual behavior, bingeing and purging, and self-mutilation.

- *Interpersonal difficulties*. Adult survivors may have problems with interpersonal relationships. They may adopt an avoidant style, characterized by low interdependency, self-disclosure, and warmth. Or they may adopt an "intrusive" style, characterized by extremely high needs for closeness, excessive self-disclosure, and a demanding and controlling style. Both styles result in loneliness (Becker-Lausen and Mallon-Kraft 1997).

- *Physical health problems*. Adult survivors have substantially higher rates of health care use than their nonabused counterparts. Pain syndromes are the most common type of illness and include irritable bowel syndrome, fibromyalgia, headache, pelvic pain, and back pain. Adult survivors also had overall lower satisfaction with their physical health than their nonabused counterparts (Kendall-Tackett 2000).

Differences in Response to Sexual Abuse

Reactions to child sexual abuse can vary tremendously depending on the child, the family, whether it was reported to law enforcement, and the types of support that were available after disclosure. Responses can also vary by both characteristics of the abuse and ethnicity of the child.

Characteristics of the abuse. Characteristics of the abuse itself can also exert an influence on how people react. Some people are more seriously affected by abuse because their experiences were more severe. In general, abuse will be more harmful if the abuser is someone the child knows and trusts, and the abuse violates that trust. Abuse that includes penetration (oral, vaginal, or anal) often leads to more symptoms. Abuse that occurs often and lasts for years will typically be more harmful than abuse that happens only sporadically and over less time. The exception is the one-time violent assault (Berliner and Elliot 1996; Kendall-Tackett et al. 1993).

Differences among ethnic groups. Researchers have identified some specific ethnic-group differences in both characteristics of abuse and in reactions to it. Although no clear patterns have emerged, there are enough differences for professionals to understand the importance of ethnic group identity and meaning of sexual abuse in a culture.

Asian children tend to be older at the onset of victimization than non-Asians. African-American children tend to be younger at onset than either their Asian or Caucasian counterparts (Berliner and Elliot 1996). African-American victims have approximately the same rates of victimization as Caucasian children, but are more likely to experience penetration as part of their victimization experience (Wyatt 1985). The overall rates of sexual abuse are lowest for Asian women, but high for Hispanic women, when reported retrospectively (Russell 1984). In a sample of 582 Southwestern American Indians, rates of sexual abuse were high, especially among females. Forty-nine percent of females in the sample and 14 percent of males reported a history of sexual abuse. Seventy-eight percent reported intrafamilial abuse (Robin et al. 1997). Worldwide, rates of child sexual abuse have similar ranges (from low to high). According to the World Health Organization (1999), in studies from nineteen countries, including South Africa, Sweden, and the Dominican Republic, rates of sexual abuse range from 7 percent to 34 percent for girls, and from 3 percent to 29 percent for boys. Some of these differences in range are due to varying definitions of sexual abuse from country to country and the accuracy of the reporting system.

Culture and ethnicity also appear related to how symptomatic abuse survivors become in the wake of their abuse experiences. Ferol Mennen (1995) found that Latina girls whose abuse included penetration were more anxious and depressed than African-American or white girls who experienced penetration. The author explains these findings in part as due to the emphasis on purity and virginity in Latino communities. When virginity is lost, the trauma of sexual abuse is compounded because the Latina girls feel that they are no longer suitable marriage partners.

Another ethnic-group difference appeared in rates of re-victimization. In a sample drawn from a community college, black women who were sexually abused in childhood were more likely to be raped as adults than their white, Latina, or Asian counterparts (Urquiza and Goodlin-Jones 1994).

Gordon Nagayama Hall and Christy Barongan (1997) speculated that these differences in rates of sexual aggression might be due to characteristics of specific cultures. For example, cultures with a collectivist orientation, where the group is more important than the individual, tend to have lower rates of sexual aggression. Asian cultures often have a collectivist orientation. Crimes against a single person are perceived as crimes against the entire culture. Shame also keeps these behaviors in check. However, as Catherine Koverola and Subadra Panchandeswaran (in press) describe, shame may not keep the behaviors in check, but may

keep people from acknowledging these crimes outside the community. Thus, it is at least possible that even in cultures where the rates appear low, abuse may simply be hidden from view.

How Sexual Abuse Compares with Other Types of Child Maltreatment

Although researchers have focused predominantly on sexual abuse, it is not the most common type of maltreatment. In the *Third National Incidence Study of Child Abuse and Neglect,* the rate of sexual abuse per 1,000 children was 4.9 for females and 1.6 for males. For physical abuse the rate was 5.6 per 1,000 for females and 5.8 for males. For neglect, the rate was 12.9 per 1,000 for females and 13.3 for males. Physical abuse and neglect are much more common for both boys and for girls. Girls and boys have approximately the same rates of fatal injuries (.01/1000 and .04/1000 for females and males respectively). Sexual abuse can certainly be harmful, but the plight of the physically abused or neglected child also deserves the attention of professionals (Sedlak and Broadhurst 1996).

Conclusion

Abuse experiences vary in their severity, as do reactions of those who are sexually abused. Even when the experience is severe, however, there is hope for healing. In one study, survivors reported that good came from the tragedy of their abuse (McMillen, Zuravin, and Rideout 1995). They described how their abusive pasts made them more sensitive to the needs of others. Many felt compelled to help others who had suffered similar experiences.

See also: CHILD ABUSE: PHYSICAL ABUSE AND NEGLECT; CHILD ABUSE: PSYCHOLOGICAL MALTREATMENT; CHILDHOOD; CHILDREN'S RIGHTS; CONDUCT DISORDER; DEPRESSION: CHILDREN AND ADOLESCENTS; INCEST; INCEST/INBREEDING TABOOS; MUNCHAUSEN SYNDROME BY PROXY; PARENTING STYLES; POSTTRAUMATIC STRESS DISORDER (PTSD); POWER: FAMILY RELATIONSHIPS; RAPE; RUNAWAY YOUTHS; SUBSTANCE ABUSE

Bibliography

American Academy of Pediatrics. (1991). Committee on Child Abuse and Neglect Policy Statement. "Guidelines for the Evaluation of Sexual Abuse of Children (RE 9202)." *Pediatrics* 87:254–260.

Becker-Lausen, E., and Mallon-Kraft, S. (1997). "Pandemic Outcomes: The Intimacy Variable." In *Out of Darkness: Current Perspectives on Family Violence,* ed. G. K. Kantor and J. S. Jasinski. Newbury Park, CA: Sage.

Berliner, L. and Elliot, D. (1996). "Sexual Abuse of Children." In *The APSAC Handbook on Child Maltreatment,* ed. J. Briere, L. Berliner, J. A. Bulkley, C. Jenny, and T. Reid. Newbury Park, CA: Sage.

Briere, J. N., and Elliot, D. M. (1994). "Immediate and Long-Term Impacts of Child Sexual Abuse." *The Future of Children* 4:54–69.

Finkelhor, D. (1994). "Current Information on the Scope and Nature of Child Sexual Abuse." *The Future of Children* 4:31–53.

Kendall-Tackett, K. A. (2000). "The Long-Term Health Effects of Victimization." *Joining Forces* 5(1):1–4.

Kendall-Tackett, K. A., and Marshall, R. (1998). "Sexual Victimization of Children: Incest and Child Sexual Abuse." In *Issues in Intimate Violence,* ed. R. K. Bergen. Newbury Park, CA: Sage.

Kendall-Tackett, K. A., and Simon, A. F. (1992). "A Comparison of the Abuse Experiences of Male and Female Adults Molested as Children." *Journal of Family Violence* 7:57–62.

Kendall-Tackett, K. A.; Williams, L. M.; and Finkelhor, D. (1993). "The Effects of Sexual Abuse on Children: A Review and Synthesis of Recent Empirical Studies." *Psychological Bulletin* 113:164–180.

McMillen, C.; Zuravin, S.; and Rideout, G. (1995). "Perceived Benefit from Child Sexual Abuse." *Journal of Consulting and Clinical Psychology* 63:1037–1043.

Mennen, F. E. (1995). "The Relationship of Race/Ethnicity to Symptoms of Childhood Sexual Abuse." *Child Abuse and Neglect* 19:115–124.

Nagayama Hall, G. C., and Barongan, C. (1997). "Prevention of Sexual Aggression: Sociocultural Risk and Protective Factors." *American Psychologist* 52:5–14.

Perry, B. D. (2001). "The Neuroarcheology of Childhood Maltreatment: The Neurodevelopmental Costs of Adverse Childhood Events." In *The Cost of Child Maltreatment: Who Pays? We All Do,* ed. K. Franey, R. Geffner, and R. Falconer. San Diego, CA: Family Violence and Sexual Assault Institute.

Reece, R. M. (2000). *Treatment of Child Abuse: Common Ground for Mental Health, Medical, and Legal Practitioners.* Baltimore, MD: The Johns Hopkins University Press.

Robin, R. W.; Chester, B.; Rasmussen, J. K.; Jaranson, J. M.; and Goldman, D. (1997). "Prevalence, Characteristics, and Impact of Childhood Sexual Abuse in a Southwestern American Indian Tribe." *Child Abuse and Neglect* 21:769–787.

Russell, D. E. H. (1984). "The Prevalence and Seriousness of Incestuous Abuse: Stepfathers vs. Biological Fathers." *Child Abuse and Neglect.* 8:15–22.

Sedlak, A., and Broadhurst, D. D. (1996). *Third National Incidence Study of Child Abuse and Neglect.* Final Report. Washington, DC: U.S. Department of Health and Human Services.

Urquiza, A. J., and Goodlin-Jones, B. L. (1994). "Child Sexual Abuse and Adult Revictimization with Women of Color." *Violence and Victims* 9:223–232.

Wyatt, G. E. (1985). "The Sexual Abuse of Afro-American and White-American Women in Childhood." *Child Abuse and Neglect* 9:507–519.

Other Resource

World Health Organization. (1999). "WHO Recognizes Child Abuse as a Public Health Problem." Available from http://www.who.org/PR-99-20.

KATHLEEN KENDALL-TACKETT

CHILDCARE

Broadly defined, the term *childcare* includes all types of education and care provided for young children. The term is also used more specifically for the supplemental care of children from birth to age eight years by persons other than parents. Childcare is used for a variety of reasons, and programs vary by the number and age of children, the reason care is used, the preparation and status of caregivers, and the location of the care. Terminology varies in different countries although there may be similar concerns of low pay and status, and insufficient training for teachers (Katz 1999; Woodill, Bernhard, and Prochner 1992).

The two major purposes of early childhood programs are care and education. A majority of families today use childcare while they are employed or engaged in other activities. Many programs include an educational component, based on a growing body of research that documents the importance of children's early experiences for their healthy development and academic success. A large number of programs have originated through concern for children living in poverty and who may be at risk for success in school and later life. Programs may also include a parent component designed to educate parents through their participation in children's activities. In some countries, such as the People's Republic of China, programs are used to instill societal values in young children such as working together in a collective tradition. The childcare used for short-term activities such as shopping, appointments, and leisure activities has been less well studied (Cochran 1993; Feeney 1992).

Why is Childcare Important?

The economic structure of society has significantly influenced how families care for their children. Because women are usually the primary caregivers, the nature of their work roles has an important effect on childcare. In some societies, mothers as well as fathers can provide childcare, food, clothing, and shelter for their families through work located in or near the family home. In other situations, men are employed away from home and the daily care of children becomes the primary responsibility of women (Carnoy 2000).

Some women work only before marriage, before children are born, or after children are mature enough to care for themselves. However, for a variety of personal and economic reasons, including single parenthood, many mothers with young children today work outside the home and can no longer fill the traditional responsibilities of home and childcare. Because children's early experiences and relationships with caregivers have a significant influence on their future development and achievements, the quality of their care is an important concern for all.

Societal response to these changes in family structure and roles has varied. Some countries, such as Hungary, Brazil, and Russia, have highly centralized patterns of authority and provide universal support of childcare. In other countries, such as the United States, Britain, and Canada, family and childcare policies and standards are created at state, province, or local levels and childcare is the responsibility of the family. The questions of what the purpose of childcare should be and who it should serve are simple, but the answers are complex and have varied over time and from one culture to another (Cochran 1993).

Many childcare programs include an educational component. The role of teacher varies by culture. Data show that a low teacher-child ratio and a language-based curriculum are essential parts of an effective program. TERRY WILD STUDIO

Available Childcare

Childcare primarily occurs in three locations: care in the child's home by relatives or nonrelatives; care in a home outside the child's home by relatives or nonrelatives; and center-based care. There are significant variations within and between these categories, including the time that care is available, the cost and quality of care, the professional status of the caregiver, and the relationship between the caregiver and the family. The age of the child, marital status, race and national origin, and family income are also major influences on the care arrangements used by parents.

Some employed mothers do not use supplemental childcare because they work at home, they are able to alternate childcare with their spouses, older siblings care for younger children, or the children care for themselves. Relatives (often grandparents) may provide a great deal of care for children, ranging from occasional to full-time, regular care while the parents are employed. Care may occur in the parental home, especially if relatives live with the family or in the relative's home. Relatives are especially important caregivers for infants and toddlers, and as a supplement to school attendance for school-aged children, both times when other caregivers are difficult to find. The relationship between relatives and children may be especially strong as relatives have a past and anticipated future relationship and commitment to the family. However, the use of relatives as caregivers may occur because of limited options for childcare due to low income and poverty. Interest in care by relatives has increased in the United States and Canada since the passage of national welfare reforms requiring mothers of young children to enter the workplace. This has led to concerns about the quality of care provided by relatives and the use of public subsidies for caregivers who may work from a sense of duty rather than choice.

Individuals unrelated to the family also provide care in the child's home. Caregivers (nannies) may live in the family home and perform other household duties, whereas baby-sitters (often teenagers) provide occasional care for only a few hours. Sitters have been a common form of childcare in Canada and the United States when other alternatives were limited. Some families jointly hire and share the services of an in-home caregiver or trade childcare on a regular basis.

Children also receive significant amounts of care in other homes. In the United States, 21 percent of the care of children age five years and under was provided in another home by a nonrelative (U.S. Bureau of Census 2000). *Family day care* (also called *home childcare, day mothers,* or *child minding*) involves the care of a small number of children, usually six or fewer, in a private home. Care is provided for a fee unless the caregiver is a relative. In the United States and Canada, family day care is primarily regulated by states or provinces through licensing or registration, although many homes are unregulated.

The small number of children in day-care homes produces a desirable adult-child ratio, although the quality and the stability of the care depend on the characteristics of the caregiver. Although most providers have experience with young children, few may have formal training in child development. Providers may find home day care a positive way to combine care of their own children with the ability to earn income, but the presence of young nonfamily children in the home is stressful and the turnover rate of providers is high (Atkinson 1992; Nelson 1991).

The use of *center-based childcare* (also described as a *nursery school, kindergarten, crèche, community-based care,* or *child development center*) has generally increased over time. These programs are often staffed with professionally trained directors and teachers, and enrollment may range from fifteen to more than a hundred children, often organized by age of children. Some programs, initially designed for middle- and upper-class homes, provide a part-day program of cognitive enrichment and socialization. Other programs provide full-day care and have evolved from child welfare programs created to care for children from poor families whose mothers were employed outside the home. Today the differences between these two types of programs have lessened as many centers provide full-day care as well as educational programs. Although childcare centers have typically provided services for children from two and five years of age, there is a growing demand for center-based programs for infants and toddlers.

Some centers operate as for-profit businesses, whereas other centers are not-for-profit and may be sponsored by community organizations and social agencies. Cooperative programs have paid professional head teachers but use parent volunteers for the rest of the teaching staff. A small but growing number of employers support childcare by providing on-site care, information and referral services, flexible financial benefits, and/or flexible work schedules for parents.

Older children also need care when school hours do not mesh with parental hours of employment. The term *latchkey child* reflects concern for children who spend significant amounts of time without adult supervision. The descriptions of *self-care* or *out of school care* are now used as more positive terms. Parents may supervise children from work by checking periodically in person or by telephone. Other parents use programs that have been developed to provide care before and after school, usually at the school itself, offering breakfast and snacks as well as supervision until parents can pick up their children. Programs vary in whether the emphasis is placed on academic activities such as homework or on free time and recreational programs. Children may spend a significant amount of time outside of school in activities such as lessons and clubs regardless of whether their parents are employed.

Many programs have been developed to provide services for children with special needs. *At-risk* programs provide comprehensive services for children considered to have high risk of failure in school. The goal of these programs is to give young children a boost that will help them succeed in school and life. Activities are designed for cognitive stimulation, socialization, and emotional support and also provide comprehensive services for parents and health and nutrition programs for children. These programs may be in cooperation with public schools, with programs available to provide parents with support services. *Head Start* is the best-known program in the United States, beginning in 1965 as part of the *War on Poverty and the Great Society*. A more recent component called *Early Head Start* serves children from birth to age three and has shown promising results (Gilliam and Ziglar 2000). Children with atypical development may receive care in separate facilities or, more commonly, are included in programs for typically developing children.

Although many educational philosophies exist, programs are often child-centered and based on hands-on learning experiences that encourage children to learn about the world through play and experimentation with materials and ideas. Another common goal is to help children learn how to function within a group and to successfully work with peers and adults. European educators have had an important influence on developing curriculum for young children. Johann Pestalozzi, a Swiss educator, and Friedrich Froebel, a German founder of the kindergarten movement, developed the basic ideas of a child-centered curriculum. Other important innovators included Maria Montessori, an Italian physician, and John Dewey, an American philosopher. Important theorists of the late twentieth century include Jean Piaget, a Swiss epistemologist, Lev Vygotsky, a Russian psychologist, and the community-based approach found in Reggio Emilia, an area in northern Italy (Prochner and Howes 2000). Many of these original ideas changed over time as they were adapted in different countries.

The curriculum generally includes periods of free-choice play, planned activities, rest periods, and meals and snacks. Governmental agencies often set basic standards for the centers' programs, buildings and equipment, and staff certification. Some centers and caregivers meet even higher standards through accreditation by professional organizations such as the National Association for the Education of Young Children (Breddecamp and Copple 1997; Swiniarski, Breitborde, and Murphy 1999).

The professional role of the teacher varies between countries. A summary of European Union countries identified four broad typologies: early childhood pedagogues serving children from birth to compulsory school age; preschool specialists serving children in the two to three years preceding school entry; teachers involved with children from age three to eleven-and-a-half; and social pedagogues involved in various work fields including early childhood education (Oberhuemer 2000). Because of cultural differences, it is difficult to compare the effectiveness of programs in countries that have different needs, resources, and philosophies (Feeney 1992; Katz 2000). Projects such as the *Effectiveness Initiative* sponsored by the Bernard van Leer Foundation are attempts to cross-culturally compare what works in early childhood development programs and the barriers to success. (Early Childhood Matters 2000)

Effects of Childcare

Much research has been done on the positive and negative effects that extensive hours of childcare may have on children. When mothers began entering the labor force in large numbers in the 1960s, experts in child development expressed concern about the effect of mothers' absences on the emotional relationship between children and parents. Attachment, the emotional bond that begins early in life, is considered to have a critical influence on a child's social, emotional, and cognitive development. Most experts agree that children need a stable and continuous relationship with a sensitive and responsive caregiver in order to develop a secure emotional attachment.

Concern that this bond would be weakened when the child attended day care grew from previous studies of short- and long-term parent-child separations during war time and hospitalizations. Some researchers are concerned that children with extensive nonparental care in their first year of life may be negatively affected by the quality of the care (Shonkoff and Phillips 2000). Other research has examined the effect of day care on children's social development. Children enrolled in childcare typically have more experience interacting with peers than children raised at home, creating both positive and negative results. These children typically show greater independence, self-confidence, and social adeptness, but they may also show evidence of greater aggression and noncompliance to adult requests (Booth 1992). The cultural context of childcare may have a significant influence on children. For example, research has shown significant differences in the effects of childcare on children living in the United States as compared to children living in Sweden (Lamb et al. 1992).

Initial research with childcare in high-quality university day-care centers found little evidence that day care produced damage to children. In fact, this childcare often provided important benefits for children with restricted home environments. Current research suggests that the *quality* of childcare is a critical factor determining how children are influenced by childcare.

The long-term impact of extended early intervention programs on children's success in school and life is now being documented in the United States through longitudinal studies (Schweinhart and Weikart 1997). Data collected for thirty-three years from the Chicago Child-Parent Centers (Reynolds 2000) suggests several principles to guide early intervention programs. Preference in enrollment in such programs should be given to children with the greatest learning needs, as the effects of participation are greatest for children living in the highest poverty neighborhoods. Both early intervention and extensive participation in a program appear to be important in influencing children's development. Comprehensive programs that focus on the "whole child" and assist families in meeting health and nutritional needs are important components, as is active parent involvement in the program. Small class sizes, low teacher-child ratios, and a language-based curriculum are critical components of an effective program as is continual training for program staff. Continuing research and evaluation are vital components for program improvement.

The relationship between maternal employment and children's development is complex with many indirect linkages. Research studies have been limited in the scope of questions asked, and care must be taken in generalizing between cultures. However, mothers' employment status by itself does not appear to create a negative experience for children. To predict the effect of childcare accurately, the characteristics of the child, the child's family, the childcare program, parental employment, and the context of the society must all be considered (Prochner and Howe 2000).

Availability, Cost, and Quality of Childcare

Unless care is subsidized on a national level, childcare is a major expenditure for many families. For low-income families, the cost of childcare may be similar to the cost of food and housing and require a significant portion of family income. Some low-income families can find good quality care that is subsidized by government programs, although this care is often limited. Families with higher incomes may spend a small percent of their total income on childcare, but families with moderate incomes who are ineligible for subsidies may be least able to afford good quality childcare. The cost of childcare also differs by the type of care used. In-home care, such as that provided by a nanny, is generally the most expensive care; center-based care and family day care are usually in between; and care provided by relatives the least expensive (Giannarelli and Barsimantov 2000).

The quality of the childcare is critically important when children spend many hours away from home. Experts define quality in different ways but generally agree on several important factors. The easiest aspects of quality to identify are those associated with the structure of the childcare. These include items that can easily be regulated such as the caregiver to child ratio, group size, caregiver education and training, and the size of the program. Process or interactive dimensions of quality may be even more important but are more difficult to measure. These include the relationship between the child and the caregiver; learning activities; the physical environment, including the organization of equipment and space; and the child's relationship with peers. To be effective, programs and activities should be sensitive to children's cultural experiences and fit their level of development and interests (Prochner and Howe 2000; Breddecamp and Copple 1997).

Evaluation of care may vary depending on the experience of the person doing the evaluation. One may view care from a top-down perspective (characteristics of the setting, equipment, and the programs as seen by adults) or from the bottom up (how children experience care). Quality may also be viewed from the inside (staff) or from the outside (parents). A societal perspective may also be used to view childcare, assessing how programs serve the community and the larger society. In a comparison of childcare in different countries,

Michael E. Lamb and his associates (1992) have documented how interpretations of quality differ according to the context and values of the community and family.

Parents generally indicate that they are satisfied with the childcare they use, although some would prefer other care and may become more critical when they are no longer using the care. Parents say that the quality of the care is the characteristic most valued when selecting childcare, and the most important aspect of quality is the nature of the provider-child relationship.

Selection of Childcare

Parents' actions and decisions are critical in the selection of childcare. The search for good-quality childcare requires an investment of parental time and energy and often begins with an assessment of family needs and values. How many hours a day is care needed and during which days in the week? Most childcare used to meet employment needs is available weekdays, and it may be difficult to find care on weekends, at night, or for irregular time periods. The child's age is also important as it is usually easier to find care for preschoolers than infants and toddlers.

With this knowledge, parents can explore available childcare arrangements. Most parents report that they learn about their childcare from friends, coworkers, and relatives. Regulated family day care and day-care centers are often listed with governmental agencies, and information and referral centers can provide personalized information and listings of caregivers.

Most parents need backup arrangements for times when the main caregiver is unavailable or the child is sick. Although the turnover rate of individual caregivers in center-based care is high, the service is usually continuous. However, if an individual caregiver is unable to work, the parent must find a replacement. This problem is most severe for mothers with jobs that allow little or no leave time for childcare emergencies. Finding suitable childcare involves consideration of parental and child needs as well as the supply of childcare and the demands of a job. Many families report that no one type of care is sufficient to meet all their childcare needs.

Childcare Policy Issues

The care and education of young children is a primary responsibility of parents; however, the well-being of children is also an important concern for the whole society. What rights and responsibilities should parents, employers, schools, community groups, and the society have for children? If governments certify that childcare meets basic standards, what should these standards be? Should parents who do not work outside the home receive support for the care they provide for children?

Childcare has become an important business (more than $40 billion is spent annually for childcare in the United States), and a central component of the economic and social goals of many countries. In some countries, such as France and Taiwan, curriculum and standards for the professional preparation of caregivers are established at a national level and childcare is universally available. In other countries, such as the United States and Canada, the responsibility for finding high-quality childcare is primarily a parental responsibility (Brennan 1998; Prochner and Howe 2000). Standards are usually the most rigorous for center-based care although little formal preparation may be required for family day-care providers, relatives, or caregivers in the child's home.

Childcare has become an accepted part of life for many families in the world and its use is linked with a variety of purposes, national priorities, and policies. However, the lack of adequate funding to meet the demands of the childcare system appears to be a worldwide constant (Feeney 1992). A second universal challenge is to find ways to ensure that children receive high-quality care in all settings and that the care also meets the needs and concerns of family members, employers, caregivers, schools, and society in general (Swaminathan 1998).

See also: ATTACHMENT: PARENT-CHILD RELATIONSHIPS; CHILD CUSTODY; CHILDHOOD; COLIC; DISABILITIES; DISCIPLINE; DIVISION OF LABOR; DUAL-EARNER FAMILIES; FAMILY PLANNING; FAMILY POLICY; FATHERHOOD; GAY PARENTS; GRANDPARENTHOOD; HOUSEWORK; INTERGENERATIONAL PROGRAMMING; LESBIAN PARENTS; MOTHERHOOD; RESPITE CARE: CHILD; SINGLE-PARENT FAMILIES; SIBLING RELATIONSHIPS; SPANKING; SUBSTITUTE CAREGIVERS; TIME USE; TRANSITION TO PARENTHOOD; WORK AND FAMILY

Bibliography

Atkinson, A. M. (1992). "Stress Levels of Family Day Care Providers, Mothers Employed Outside the Home, and Mothers at Home." *Journal of Marriage and the Family* 54:379–386.

Boocock, S. S.; Barnett, W. S.; and Frede, E. (2001). "Long-Term Outcomes of Early Childhood Programs in Other Nations: Lessons for Americans." *Young Children* 56(5):43–50.

Booth, A., ed. (1992). *Childcare in the 1990s: Trends and Consequences.* Hillsdale, NJ: Lawrence Erlbaum Associates.

Breddecamp, S., and Copple, C., eds. (1997). *Developmentally Appropriate Practice in Early Childhood Programs.* Washington, DC: National Association for the Education of Young Children.

Brennan, D. (1998). *The Politics of Australian Childcare,* rev. edition. Cambridge, UK: Cambridge University Press.

Cochran, M., ed. (1993). *International Handbook of Childcare Policies and Programs.* Westport, CT: Greenwood Press.

Carnoy, M. (2000). *Sustaining the New Economy.* Cambridge, MA: Harvard University Press.

Dewey, J. (1900). *The School and Society.* Chicago: University of Chicago Press.

Edwards, C.; Gandini, L.; and Forman, G., eds. (1998). *The Hundred Languages of Children: The Reggio Emilia Approach—Advanced Reflections,* 2nd edition. Greenwich, CT: Ablex.

Feeney, S. (1992). *Early Childhood Education in Asia and the Pacific.* New York: Garland.

Froebel, F. (1896). *Pedagogics of the Kindergarten,* trans. J. Jarvis. New York: Appleton.

Gilliam, W., and Ziglar, E. F. (2000). "A Critical Meta-Analysis of All Evaluations of State Funded Preschool from 1977 to 1998: Implications for Policy, Service Delivery and Program Evaluation." *Early Childhood Research Quarterly* 15(4):441–73.

Lamb, M. E.; Steinberg, K. J.; Hwang, C. P; and Broberg, A. G., eds. (1992). *Childcare in Context.* Hillsdale, NJ: Lawrence Erlbaum Associates.

Montessori, M. (1936). *The Secret of Childhood.* Bombay, India: Orient Longman.

Nelson, M. K. (1991). *Negotiated Care: The Experience of Family Day Care Providers.* Philadelphia: Temple University Press.

Pestalozzi, J. H. (1900). *How Gertrude Teaches Her Children.* Syracuse, NY: Bardeen.

Piaget, J. (1952). *The Origins of Intelligence in Children.* New York: International Universities Press.

Prochner, L., and Howe, N., eds. (2000) *Early Childhood Care and Education in Canada.* Vancouver: University of British Columbia Press.

Reynolds, A. (2000). *Success in Early Intervention.* Lincoln: University of Nebraska Press.

Schweinhart, L., and Weikart D. P. (1997). "The High/Scope Preschool Curriculum Comparison Study through Age 23." *Early Childhood Research Quarterly* 12(2):117–43.

Shonkoff, J., and Phillips, D. (2000). *From Neurons to Neighborhoods.* Washington, DC: National Academy Press.

Swaminathan, M. (1998). *The First Five Years: A Critical Perspective on Early Childhood Care and Education in India.* New Delhi: Sage.

Swiniarski, L. A.; Breitborde, M.; and Murphy, J. (1999). *Educating the Global Village: Including the Young Child in the World.* Upper Saddle River, NJ: Prentice Hall.

U.S. Bureau of the Census. (2000). *Who's Minding the Kids? Child-Care Arrangements, 1995.* Current Population Report. Washington, DC: Government Printing Office.

Vygotsky, L. S. (1962). *Mind in Society.* Cambridge, MA: Harvard University Press.

Woodill, G.; Bernhard, J; and Prochner, L. (1992). *International Handbook of Early Childhood Education.* New York: Garland.

Yánez, L.(2000). "Reflections on Dynamics, Process, and Initial Findings." *Early Child Matters* 96:17-25.

Other Resources

Giannarelli, L., and Barsimantov, J. (2000). "Childcare Expenses of America's Families." The Urban Institute. Available from http://www.urban.org.

Katz, L. (1999). "International Perspectives on Early Childhood Education: Lessons from My Travels." *Early Childhood Research and Practice* 1(1). Available from http://www.ecrp.uiuc.edu.

Oberhuemer, P. (2000). "Conceptualizing the Professional Role in Early Childhood Centers: Emerging Profiles in Four European Countries." *Early Childhood Research and Practice* 2(2). Available at http://www.ecrp.uiuc.edu.

ALICE M. ATKINSON

CHILD CUSTODY

Child custody is the term used by most legal systems to describe the bundle of rights and responsibilities that parents have regarding their biological or adopted children under the age, usually, of eighteen. Custody includes the right to have the child live with the parents and to make decisions about the health, welfare, and lifestyle of the child.

Issues about custody arise in three distinct contexts: when government proposes to interfere with parental custody in an intact family; when parents live separately and a decision about custody must be made between them; and when third parties seek custody in preference to parents.

These custody issues arise throughout the world, and there is widespread agreement on how to treat them in the law of different legal systems, particularly countries whose legal structures are based on Western concepts. Consequently, the focus of the discussion in this entry is on the law of the United States as representative of the law internationally.

Intact Families

In most Western countries, parents in an intact family make decisions for the children in their custody with relatively little interference from government. Western law accords great deference to family autonomy and privacy. When governmental interference does occur, it is focused on and initiated by concern about harm to children.

Abuse and neglect situations are the most important areas in which government interferes with parental custody. Most jurisdictions authorize an agency, often a juvenile court, to remove children from the custody of their parents if parents fail to meet minimal societal norms of parenting. Although the laws differ considerably from state to state and country to country, they typically authorize intervention because the child is physically or sexually abused or because the parent fails to provide necessary care, food, clothing, medical care, or shelter so that the health of the child is endangered (Clark 1988).

In the United States allegations of parental misconduct are processed by the juvenile court. Unlike other courts, the juvenile court is charged with investigating and evaluating the charges for the purpose of initially providing services to the family so the child remains in the home if possible. These treatment and preventive services may interfere with parental custodial decision making by requiring certain conduct or providing supervision, but they do not remove the child from the residential custody of the parents.

If parental failure continues in spite of limited state intervention, the court, after a hearing, may order the child removed from the home and custody transferred to a public or licensed private social agency to provide care and treatment of the child. Although the legal process is a transfer of custody to an agency, the actual physical care of the child is then placed with foster parents (Wald 1976).

A transfer of custody by a juvenile court is a limited type of custody. It means that the physical care of the child is removed from the parental residence and decisions about the daily care of the child are made by the agency or by the foster parents; the child's parents, however, retain the right to make major decisions, such as decisions about religious training, surgery or other significant medical treatment, or consent to adoption by a new set of parents. The term used to describe the right to make these major decisions is that of *parental rights*.

The purpose of removing a child from the custody of parents in a juvenile court proceeding is to protect and provide for the child, with the ultimate objective of returning the child to a parental home that is adequate to meet at least minimal parenting requirements. Therefore, in addition to providing care for the child, the state is required by juvenile court statutes to attempt to rehabilitate the parents so they can adequately care for the child.

Parents Who Live Separately

The concept of child custody receives its major attention in the law when parents live separately. In these situations, it is necessary to determine what living arrangements will be made for the children and how parents will exercise their custodial rights and responsibilities. Although the most common situation in which this occurs is when parents divorce, and the family dissolves as an entity, the issue of parental custodial rights between the parents of children born outside of marriage is growing in importance.

Custody between unmarried parents. Changes in family patterns are greater in some countries than in others, but throughout the world, increasing numbers of children are born to parents who are not married to each other and who may not even live together. In those cases, the custodial rights of the father are dependent, first of all, on the establishment of paternity. Historically, even after paternity was established, the mother had a superior right to custody of the child. Today, there appears to be a trend—at least in the United States and many European countries—to apply the same rules to custody disputes between unmarried parents as between married parents, particularly in cases where the unmarried father has lived with and cared for the child. However, even in those jurisdictions that accord rights to unmarried fathers, the one who has never lived with the child or established a parent-child relationship in some other way will find his custody rights to be much more limited than those of the mother.

Types of custody. When parents do not live together, the possible custodial arrangements available can be described as sole custody, split custody, joint legal custody, and joint legal and physical custody.

Sole custody means that the child resides with the parent awarded sole custody, and that parent has authority to make decisions for the child on lifestyle issues, such as education, religion, medical treatment, and general welfare. The other parent has the right of visitation but limited authority. Historically, this was the only kind of custodial arrangement provided by the law when parents separated. It continues to be the most common custodial form and, in some countries, the only form.

Split custody is really a form of sole custody, with the sole custody of the children divided between the parents; each parent has sole custody of one or more of the children. A very small number of custody arrangements involve split custody.

Joint custody is a relatively new custody form, dating from the 1970s. Although the exact meaning of joint custody is not clear, the term usually refers to two types of custodial arrangements. One form that has become popular is known as joint legal custody. In joint legal custody, the decision-making aspect of custody is separated from the physical care aspect. Both parents exercise decision-making authority for the child, but the child resides with one parent, usually the mother. Joint legal custody

with physical custody to one parent, usually the mother, is the most common form of joint custody.

The other type of joint custody is joint legal and physical custody, where the parents share decision-making authority, and the child resides in both households. This arrangement is sometimes referred to as dual residence. The amount of time the child spends may be equally divided between parental homes, or the child may spend a majority of time with one parent and a lesser amount with the other parent.

Interest in joint custody as a parenting arrangement is most widespread in the United States, Canada, and the countries of Western Europe. As parenting roles change in those areas and fathers assume more custodial duties in intact families, shared time or dual residence seems to grow in popularity. One study in the United States found that, over a twelve-year period from 1980 to 1992, shared physical custody increased from 2.2 percent to 14.2 percent of the cases (Melli, Brown, and Cancian 1997).

Standards for awarding custody. The universal rule that guides the courts in deciding which parent should have custody is *the best interests of the child*. Although historically the father had a superior right to custody of his children and in some societies still has that right, the best interests of the child has become the polestar in custody decisions in most countries. The best interests of the child are frequently equated with mothers' custody, particularly for young children. However, in recent years, the preference for mothers has begun to disappear formally from the law. In the United States it has been abolished by statute or case law in the wake of concerns about gender equity. Since then, the assessment of what is in the best interests of the child has been greatly influenced by *Beyond the Best Interests of the Child* (Goldstein, Freud, and Solnit 1979), a book that stressed the importance of the relationships, particularly the psychological ties that children have with their parents.

Application of the best interests of the child criterion implies that the court's decision will provide the very best possible solution for the child. Unfortunately, as numerous critics have pointed out, obtaining the best possible solution is more illusory than real. Human knowledge is too limited and problematic to give clear guidance when making decisions that will be affected by unpredictable future events. In addition, the courts often lack the time and staff to gather sufficient information with which to determine the best possible solution (Erlanger, Chambliss, and Melli 1987; Melli 1993; Mnookin 1975). Scholars have also expressed concern that the lack of predictability on what constitutes the best interests of the child encourages litigation—a result that is universally regarded as undesirable (Mnookin and Kornhauser 1979). Considerable attention has been devoted to searching for some limiting preference that would reflect the best interests of most children. In the United States, the influential American Law Institute has recommended that custodial responsibility be allocated in rough proportion to the share each parent assumed before the divorce (Bartlett 1999).

Regardless of the standard applied, the great majority of children in single-parent families live with their mothers. Most studies show mother custody at about 70 to 80 percent, with father custody, split custody, and shared custody accounting for the rest (Maccoby and Mnookin 1993; Melli, Brown, and Cancian 1997).

The role of the court. A custody arrangement is made by an order of the court as part of the divorce proceeding. However, in the great majority of cases, the parents, not the court, make the actual decision. Most estimates are that 95 percent of the custody orders are based on parental agreement. One study in California found that only 3.5 percent of the cases required a decision by the court; the rest were arranged by the parents themselves or, if the parents were in disagreement, were negotiated and settled with the aid of their lawyers (Maccoby and Mnookin 1993).

Unfortunately, those few cases that are litigated are often high-conflict ones that may seriously harm the children involved (Elrod and Ramsay 2001).

The role of the child. Given the importance of a custody determination to a child, several issues arise as to the role of the child in such a proceeding. Most judges view the child's preference as relevant to a custody decision (Scott, Reppucci, and Aber 1988). The weight to be given to the child's wishes usually depends on the child's age and maturity of judgment.

A related issue is whether a child has a right to be represented in the custody proceedings. This issue recognizes the concern that custody litigation may lose sight of the best interests of the child. Hostile parents and their lawyers may fail to inform courts about issues important to the well-being of the child. The U.N. Convention on the Rights of the Child (1989) provides in Article 12 that states should assure a child the right to be heard in custody proceedings either directly or through a representative.

The role of mediation. When parents are in conflict about the custodial arrangements, there is substantial agreement that the traditional dispute resolution process of the law, litigation, is not suited for the problem. The most frequently suggested alternative is mediation (Milne and Folberg 1988). The research on mediation is very limited, but it appears to result in more user satisfaction than do litigation experiences (Pearson and Thoennes 1988). However, its use is controversial. Critics claim that mediation results in undesirable shared custody arrangements (Bruch 1988), and feminists express concern about unfair pressures on mothers in the process (Grillo 1991).

Modification of custody. Custody arrangements are not final; they may be changed by the parties or modified by the court. One study found that over a period of three-and-a-half years, there was a fair amount of change in the residential arrangements of the children. Mother sole custody was the most stable arrangement, with 81 percent of the children who lived with their mothers at the time of the first interview still living there at the time of the third interview. The other two types of physical custody arrangements, father custody and dual residence, were much less stable, with 51 percent of the children in those arrangements making at least one change (Maccoby and Mnookin (1993).

In addition to informal changes made by the parties themselves (these are often not ratified by a change in the formal court order), the court may modify the custody award because it is never considered a final order and is, therefore, subject to modification. This nonfinality for custody orders reflects concern about the need to protect children from harmful circumstances, but it conflicts with an equally important policy favoring stability for children. For this reason there has been a clear trend in the law toward making changes difficult, discouraging parents from relitigating custody decisions. For example, the consideration of a custodial change may be limited to situations where it can be shown that there has been a change in circumstances since the date of the custody decree, or where evidence not considered by the court in granting the decree is now presented for the first time. Some jurisdictions are even more restrictive, prohibiting the consideration of requests for changes for a set period of time, such as two years after the entry of the original order, unless the existing physical custody arrangement seriously endangers the child.

Once the set of conditions for considering a custody change has been established, the issue is whether a change in custody is in the best interests of the child. Again, concern that custodial change is not good for the child is an important consideration. The usual presumption is that staying in the present placement is in the child's best interest. Apart from concerns about changing children's living situations, courts consider the same kinds of issues on modification as they do in making the original order.

Joint physical custody poses particular problems of modification because any change in parental circumstances can easily upset a complicated dual residence arrangement. Therefore, courts are more willing to consider requests to change dual residence arrangements. Usually, for example, a prohibition against change in custody for the first two years after the original order is not applied to joint physical custody situations.

Other Custody Issues between Parents Who Live Separately

Parental child abduction. Parental child abduction is an international child custody problem of major proportions. The problem of child abduction may arise in a variety of situations. A parent dissatisfied with a custody decision may take the child to another country. Often that parent may be a national of the country to which he takes the child. Also common is when a noncustodial parent who lives in another country may refuse to return a child after authorized visitation in that country.

Historically, the parent violating the custody order often prevailed: a child custody order is not final and, therefore, may be modified. Because jurisdiction is based on the presence of the child, the court where the noncustodial parent lives has jurisdiction to redetermine the issue of custody. Sometimes that court, based on incomplete information provided by the absconding parent or applying standards different from those of the jurisdiction where custody between the parents was

determined originally, has changed the custodial determination to favor the absconding parent.

In 1988, to remedy this situation, the Hague Convention on the Civil Aspects of International Child Abduction (Hague Convention) was completed. It has been ratified by more than sixty nations. It is modeled after United States legislation that requires a state to honor the custody award of the child's home state. The Hague Convention is actively used, but the numbers of children abducted to foreign countries continues to grow, partly because of the increase in binational marriages.

One of the major criticisms of the Hague Convention is that it does not protect mothers who are victims of domestic violence who flee a country for safety (Sapone 2000). Changes to remedy this problem are being considered (Weiner 2000).

Visitation. When one parent has sole physical custody, which is the situation in the majority of the cases, the other parent is entitled to spend time with the child during what is usually called *visitation*. Visitation is usually regarded as a right of the noncustodial parent to which that parent is entitled unless visitation would seriously harm the child. Therefore, a custodial parent who objects to visitation by the noncustodial parent has the burden of showing that the child would be harmed by contact with the child's other parent.

Difficult situations are presented to those who must make decisions when the conflict between the parents is so great that the children are drawn into it and object to seeing a parent because they have, in effect, taken the view of the parent with whom they live. However, even when children object to seeing their noncustodial parent, most courts will order visitation.

The prevailing rule that the noncustodial parent has a right to see and spend time with the child, absent a showing of some type of harm to the child, reflects a public policy recognizing that continued contact with both parents is desirable. It has been argued that stability and a positive relationship with one parent are the most important factors in the development of a child and that parental conflict over the noncustodial parent's time with the child is so divisive that it ought to be controlled by the custodial parent (Goldstein, Freud, and Solnit 1979). Nevertheless, the weight of social science research supports the value of continued association with both parents (Maccoby et al. 1993; Kelly and Lamb 2000). Continued contact with a noncustodial parent is important to a child in terms of both social and financial support. Evidence suggests, for example, that noncustodial parents who visit their children more frequently also pay more child support (Anditti 1991; Dudley 1991; Seltzer, Schaeffer, and Charng 1989).

Enforcement of visitation. When the custodial parent interferes with or prevents visitation by the noncustodial parent, the principal remedy of the law is contempt of court with a fine or imprisonment. Such a severe remedy against a custodial parent is rarely used. In the United States, some courts and legislatures have provided for the reduction or withholding of child support in response to visitation infractions (Czapanskiy 1989). Unfortunately, such a remedy primarily affects the child.

Third-Party Disputes

A child custody dispute may arise between a parent and a nonparent in a variety of contexts. One type of case that has received considerable comment involves the same-gender partner of the child's parent. Other situations involve a stepparent, probably the most common case of a nonparent seeking custody; a relative, including a grandparent; or a third party with whom a parent has placed the child during an extended period. In all of these cases, the child may have lived with the nonparent for most of the child's life, and the nonparent may have been the primary caretaker of the child, forming a very close psychological parent-child bond.

In these types of custodial disputes, the nonparent seeking custody is faced with the traditional rule that the parent is entitled to custody unless that parent is found to be unfit (Buser 1991; Clark 1988). The effect of giving primacy to the interests of the biological parent when the other choice is a nonparent means that the best interests of the child may be disregarded.

Legal scholars have puzzled over the persistence of a rule that seems to place the child's best interests after those of the parent. Some scholars speculate that these cases reflect a concern about the importance of blood ties and a belief that the child's biological parent will in the long run be the most successful caretaker for the child. In addition, courts often show sympathy for a biological parent who has, perhaps after a period of years, now realized how important the child is (Chambers 1990). Finally, in the case of the same-gender partner, the court may express some of the societal ambivalence toward that family form.

Custody for nonparents is an area in which the law is developing and in which changing values and attitudes may result in changes in the law. The American Law Institute's Principles of Family Dissolution treat nonparents who have lived with and cared for a child as *de facto parents* and authorizes the award of custody to them.

Nonparents often seek another custodially related right, that of visitation. Here they have been more successful, perhaps because one of the major nonparent groups interested in securing visitation rights has been grandparents, who have shown themselves to be very effective lobbyists (Clark 1988). In the United States, although all states have adopted statutes authorizing courts to grant visitation rights—if in the best interests of the child—to grandparents and often to other nonparents, in *Troxell v. Granville* (2000) the United States Supreme Court struck down a broadly worded Washington statute authorizing the court to grand visitation to "any person." Although the Supreme Court indicated that this did not affect other nonparent visitation statutes, some states have held their statutes to be unconstitutional under *Troxell* (Bobroff 2000).

See also: CHILDCARE; CHILDHOOD; CHILDREN'S RIGHTS; DIVORCE: EFFECTS ON CHILDREN; DIVORCE MEDIATION; FAMILY LAW; GAY PARENTS; GRANDPARENTS' RIGHTS; GUARDIANSHIP; IN-LAW RELATIONSHIPS; LESBIAN PARENTS; STEPFAMILIES

Bibliography

Arditti, J. A. (1991). "Child Support Noncompliance and Divorced Fathers: Rethinking the Role of Parental Involvement." *Journal of Divorce and Remarriage* 14:107–120.

Bartlett, K. T. (1999). "Child Custody in the 21st Century: How The American Law Institute Proposes To Achieve Predictability and Still Protect the Individual Child's Best Interests." *Willamette Law Review* 35:467–476.

Bobroff, R. (2000). "The Survival of Grandparent Visitation Statutes." *Clearinghouse Review* 34:284–288.

Bruch, C. S. (1988). "And How Are the Children? The Effects of Ideology and Mediation in Child Custody Law and the Children's Well-Being in the United States." *International Journal of Law and the Family* 2:106–126.

Buser, P. J. (1991). "The First Generation of Stepchildren." *Family Law Quarterly* 25:1–18.

Chambers, D. L. (1990). "Stepparents, Biologic Parents, and the Law's Perception of 'Family' After Divorce." In *Divorce Reform at the Crossroads,* ed. S. D. Sugarman and H. H. Kay. New Haven, CT: Yale University Press.

Charlow, A. (1987). "Whose Child Is It Anyway? The Best Interests of the Child and Other Fictions." *Yale Law and Policy Review* 5:267–290.

Clark, H. H., Jr. (1988). *The Law of Domestic Relations in the United States,* 2nd edition. St. Paul, MN: West Publishing.

Czapanskiy, K. (1989). "Child Support and Visitation: Rethinking the Connections." *Rutgers Law Journal* 20:619–665.

Dudley, J. R. (1991). "Exploring Ways to Get Divorced Fathers to Comply Willingly with Child Support Agreements." *Journal of Divorce and Remarriage* 14:121–135.

Elrod, L. D. and Ramsay, S. H. (2001). "High-Conflict Custody Cases: Reforming the System for Children—Conference Report and Action Plan." *Family Law Quarterly* 34:589–606.

Erlanger, H. S.; Chambliss, E.; and Melli, M. S. (1987). "Participation and Flexibility in Informal Processes: Cautions from the Divorce Context." *Law and Society Review* 21:585–604.

Goldstein, J.; Freud, A.; and Solnit, A. J. (1979). *Beyond the Best Interests of the Child,* 2nd edition. New York: Free Press.

Grillo, T. (1991). "The Mediation Alternative: Process Dangers for Women." *Yale Law Journal* 100:1545–1610.

Kelly, J. B., and Lamb, H. E. (2000). "Using Child Development Research to Make Appropriate Custody and Access Decisions for Young Children." *Family and Conciliation Courts Review* 38:297–311.

Maccoby, E. E.; Buchanan, C. M.; Mnookin, R. H.; and Dornbusch, S. M. (1993). "Postdivorce Roles of Mothers and Fathers in the Lives of Their Children." *Journal of Family Psychology* 7:24–38.

Maccoby, E. E., and Mnookin, R. H. (1993). *Dividing the Child.* Cambridge: Harvard University Press.

Melli, M. S. (1993). "Toward a Restructuring of Custody Decision Making at Divorce: An Alternative Approach to the Best Interests of the Child." In *Parenthood in Modern Society,* ed. J. M. Eekelaar and P. Sarcevic. Dordrecht, Netherlands: Martinus Nijhoff.

Melli, M. S.; Brown, P. R.; and Cancian, M. (1997). "Child Custody in a Changing World: A Study of Postdivorce Arrangements in Wisconsin." *University of Illinois Law Review* 1997:773–800.

Milne, A., and Folberg, J. (1988). "The Theory and Practice of Divorce Mediation: An Overview." In *Divorce Mediation,* ed. J. Folberg and A. Milne. New York: Guilford.

Mnookin, R. H. (1975). "Child Custody Adjudication: Judicial Functions in the Face of Indeterminacy." *Law and Contemporary Problems* 39:226–293.

Mnookin, R. H., and Kornhauser, L. (1979). "Bargaining in the Shadow of the Law: The Case of Divorce." *Yale Law Journal* 88:950–997.

Pearson, J., and Thoennes, N. (1988). "Divorce Mediation Results." In *Divorce Mediation,* ed. J. Folberg and A. Milne. New York: Guilford.

Sapone, A. I. (2000). "Children as Pawns in Their Parents' Fight for Control: The Failure of the United States to Protect Against International Child Abduction." *Women's Rights Reporter* 21:129–138.

Schepard, A. (1985). "Taking Children Seriously: Promoting Cooperative Custody After Divorce." *Texas Law Review* 64:687–788.

Scott, E. S.; Reppucci, N. D.; and Aber, M. (1988). "Children's Preference in Adjudicated Custody Decisions." *Georgia Law Review* 22:1035–1050.

Seltzer, J. A.; Schaeffer, N. C.; and Charng, H. (1989). "Family Ties After Divorce: The Relationship Between Visiting and Paying Child Support." *Journal of Marriage and the Family* 51:1013–1031.

Weiner, M. (2000). "International Child Abduction and the Escape from Domestic Violence." *Fordham Law Review* 69:593–706.

Case

Troxell v. Granville, 120 S. Ct. 2054 (2000).

Treaties

Hague Convention on the Civil Aspects of International Child Abduction. (1980).

United Nations Convention on the Rights of the Child. (1989). *International Legal Materials,* Vol. 48. New York: United Nations.

MARYGOLD S. MELLI

CHILDHOOD

Childhood is usually defined in relation to adulthood: the condition of being an immature person, of having not yet become an adult. In some societies, physical or reproductive maturity marks the transition to adulthood, but in modern Western societies full adult status is not usually achieved until several years after puberty. Childhood is legally defined here as a state of dependency on adults or as the status of those excluded from citizenship on the grounds of their youth. Dependence and exclusion from citizenship are in turn justified in terms of young people's incapacity to look after themselves or their emotional and cognitive unfitness for adult rights and responsibilities. Hence, psychological immaturity becomes a further criterion for deciding who counts as a child. The definition of childhood, then, involves complex cultural judgments about maturity and immaturity, children's assumed capabilities, and their difference from adults. Therefore, childhood is a social category, not merely a natural one.

Modern legal systems institutionalize childhood by setting an age of majority at which persons become legal subjects responsible for their own affairs and able to exercise citizenship rights. The United Nations Convention on the Rights of the Child defines a child as anyone under the age of eighteen unless, under the laws of his or her country, the age of majority comes sooner. Even with such legalistic dividing lines, there are still areas of ambiguity. Within any one country there may be various markers of adult status, so that one ceases to be a child for some purposes while remaining one for others. For example, the right to vote and the right to marry without parental consent may be acquired at different times.

Modern Western Conception of Childhood

Childhood has not been defined and experienced in the same ways in all societies at all times. The modern Western conception of childhood is historically and culturally specific. Philippe Ariès (1962) was one of the first to suggest that childhood is a modern discovery. He argued that in medieval times children, once past infancy, were regarded as miniature adults; they dressed like adults and shared adult's work and leisure. Children were not assumed to have needs distinct from those of adults, nor were they shielded from any aspects of adult life. Knowledge of sexual relations was not considered harmful to them and public executions were a spectacle attended by people of all ages. In claiming that there was no concept of childhood prior to modern times, however, Ariès overstated his case (see Pollock 1983; Archard 1993). Shulamith Shahar (1990) suggests that medieval thinkers did see young children as being less developed in their mental and moral capacities than adults. It is clear from Ariès's own evidence that children did not always do the same work as adults and that they occupied a distinct place within society.

David Archard (1993) makes a useful distinction here between a concept of childhood and a conception of childhood. A concept of childhood requires only that children are in some way distinguished from adults; a conception entails more specific ideas about children's distinctiveness. The existence of a concept of childhood in the past does not mean that those people shared the modern conception of childhood. Medieval writers thought of childhood rather differently from how it is viewed today. They dwelt on the status and duties of children and on the rights accorded them at various stages of maturity (Shahar 1990). Childhood was defined primarily as a social status rather than as a psychological, developmental stage. Attitudes toward children began to change, very slowly, in the sixteenth and seventeenth centuries, affecting upper-class boys first, then their sisters (Ariès 1962; Pinchbeck and Hewitt 1969). By the nineteenth century, middle-class children were confined to home and school, but many working-class children continued to work and contribute to the support of their families (see Davin 1990; Pinchbeck and Hewitt 1973). Gradually, however, children as a whole were excluded from the adult world of work and the period of dependent childhood lengthened.

Both historians and anthropologists have argued that modern Western societies make an unusually sharp distinction between childhood and adulthood (Ariès 1962; Benedict: 1938; Mead and Wolfenstein 1955). Western children are excluded by law and convention from many aspects of adult social life. They spend most of their time either within their families or within institutions designed to care for, educate, or entertain them separately from adults. They therefore have little contact with adults outside the circle of family and friends apart from childcare professionals. Many of the special arrangements made for children serve to emphasize their difference from adults: their clothes, toys, games, songs and books, even the colors of their bedrooms. Children are treated not simply as inexperienced members of society, but as qualitatively different from adults.

Childhood is also conceptualized as a process of development toward adulthood. In the nineteenth century, childhood began to be mapped out as a series of developmental stages that determined the character of the adult individual. Both Archard (1993) and Nikolas Rose (1989) accord a decisive role at this time to the emerging discipline of psychology. Rose argues that, in making it the object of scientific inquiry, psychology constructed or invented childhood and claimed a particular expertise in categorizing children, measuring their aptitudes, managing and disciplining them—and has done so ever since (Rose 1989).

Living in a society where childhood is thought of as a series of developmental stages has specific effects on children. For example, schooling is organized as a series of age-graded progressions, which means that children are not only relatively segregated from adults but also from children of different ages. Children themselves acquire ideas about what is appropriate for people of their own age and may try to negotiate specific freedoms or privileges on this basis. Ordering children's lives in this way also influences what they are capable of achieving. It has been argued that the restriction of children to age-graded institutions may help to construct the very developmental stages that are seen as universal features of childhood (Skolnick 1980; Archard 1993). For a child to behave in the manner of someone older is often thought inappropriate, so the term *precocious* has become an insult. Age-grading may help to keep children childish. Historical and anthropological evidence suggests that children in other societies and in the past were far more independent and capable of taking care of themselves than Western children are today (Jackson 1982).

The idea of childhood as a developmental phase means that childhood is usually seen as important largely in terms of its consequences for adulthood. This is, as a number of researchers have pointed out, a very adult-centered view (Leonard 1990; Thorne 1987; Waksler 1986). Children are thought of as incomplete adults whose experiences are not worth investigating in their own right, but only insofar as they constitute learning for adulthood. Developmental theories presuppose that children have different capacities at different ages, yet children are frequently characterized as the polar opposites of adults: children are dependent, adults are independent; children play, adults work; children are emotional, adults are rational. The definitions of both childhood and adulthood are, moreover, gendered. Models of ideal adulthood are frequently in effect models of manhood, so that there is often a correspondence between attributes deemed childish and those deemed feminine—such as emotionality—and conversely those deemed adult and masculine—such as rationality (Jackson 1982; Thorne 1987).

The definition of childhood as a developmental stage and psychological state masks the fact that it is still a social status. Because childhood is defined as a stage or state of incapacity, children are thought to be incapable of exercising adult rights. There is considerable debate about whether this assumption is justified or not and about what rights are appropriate to children (see Thorne 1987; Archard 1993). Childhood is an exclusionary status (Hood-Williams 1990) in that children are neither citizens nor legal subjects and are under the jurisdiction of their parents. Their subordinate position is also evident in their interaction with adults. A child is expected to be deferential and obedient; a "naughty" child is one who defies adult authority.

Children Within Families

Within families, children are defined as dependents, subject to parental authority. Economic dependence is a crucial, and often neglected, aspect of children's status within families (see Leonard 1990; Hood-Williams 1990; Delphy and Leonard 1992). Children's lifestyles are dependent on their parents' income and their parents' decisions about how that income should be spent. The goods children receive come in the form of gifts or maintenance; they have things bought for them rather than buying them for themselves. Children can exercise choice over these purchases only if their parents allow them to choose. A child may well receive pocket money, or money as gifts, but this too is given at adults' discretion and adults may seek to influence how it is spent. Dependent, adult-mediated consumption is one facet of the power that parents have over children.

It has been argued that parents today have less power and autonomy than in the past because childrearing is now policed and regulated by experts and state agencies (Donzalot 1980; Ehrenreich and English 1978). Nonetheless, parents have a great deal of latitude in rearing their children as they wish, in setting acceptable standards of behavior, and in deciding what their children should eat and wear and how they should be educated and disciplined. Others' interference in these matters is regarded as violation of family privacy and an assault on parents' rights. Because modern families are seen as private institutions, state or public regulation generally only intrudes where parents are deemed to have abused their power or not exercised it effectively enough—where children are abused, neglected, or delinquent. As Barrie Thorne (1987) points out, the situation of children enters the public domain only when they are seen as victims of adults or a threat to adult society. Children also come into public view if their parents separate and contest custody, asserting the primacy of his or her rights over those of the other. Only during the late twentieth century have children been accorded any rights in deciding with which parent they prefer to live.

John Hood-Williams (1990) argues that children's lives within families are regulated in unique ways. Confinement to highly localized, restricted social spaces is part of the everyday parameters of childhood, as is the ordering of children's time by others. Childhood is also remarkable, says Hood-Williams, for the degree of control exercised over the body by others. Children's deportment, posture, movement, and appearance are regulated; they are touched, kissed, and fussed over to a degree unparalleled in any other social relationship. Children are also the people most likely to be subject to corporal punishment; many U.S. and U.K. parents hit their children on occasion (Gelles 1979; Newsom and Newsom 1965, 1968).

Styles of childrearing, however, have become undoubtedly less authoritarian than they were in the late nineteenth century. Increased concern about children's special needs has resulted in more emphasis on the quality of childcare, and each new model of child development has involved changes in standards of ideal parenting, especially mothering (see Hardyment 1983). Families are often described as child-centered. Certainly children's needs are given a high priority, but these are defined for them by adults, tied in part to the responsibility placed on parents to raise children who will conform to wider social norms. It is widely recognized that socialization, or the social construction of subjectivity, of identities, desires, and aptitudes begins with early experience of family life.

An important aspect of this process is the reproduction of family members, of each new generation of adults who will marry and have children. Although family structures are changing, the majority of the Western population still fulfills these expectations. To take up positions as husbands and wives, fathers and mothers, individuals are required to be identifiably masculine or feminine and to be predominantly heterosexual. Despite opposition from feminist, lesbian, and gay activists, the family remains a heterosexual institution founded on hierarchies of age and gender (see Delphy and Leonard 1992).

This raises questions about how childhood experiences influence sexual and romantic desires and expectations of marriage and family life. Much of what children learn derives from their experience of family life and the sense they make of it. This is evident, for example, in the way young children play house, recreating the patterns of relationships they see around them. The single most important factor in the shaping of future sexual and familial identities and experiences is gender. To enter into any social relationships whatsoever, children must be defined, and must position themselves, as girls or boys; there is no gender-neutral option. Gender then becomes an organizing principle around which sexual, emotional, and romantic desires are ordered (Jackson 1982; Davies 1989; Crawford et al. 1992).

Sexual learning in early childhood, for both sexes, is limited by adults' concealment of sexual knowledge from children. Children usually first learn about sexual relations as a reproductive, heterosexual act, but this does not mean that children learn nothing else of sexual significance. They learn, for instance, about bodily attractiveness, deportment, and modesty in a way that is shaped by adult sexual assumptions and impinges particularly on girls (Jackson 1982; Haug 1987). They become acquainted with codes of romance from such sources as fairy tales (Davies 1989). This is true of both sexes, but again it is girls who are encouraged to take part in feminine romantic rituals and to become more fluent in discourses of love and emotion (Jackson 1993). Numerous researchers suggest that romantic ideals profoundly affect the way in which young women later come to terms with their sexuality (Lees 1993; Thompson 1989; Thomson and Scott 1991). Boys, on the whole, become less emotionally fluent, find intimacy problematic, and make sense of sexuality through a language of masculine bravado (Seidler 1989; Wood 1984). This may help set the pattern, so often observed in studies of marriage, where women seek forms of emotional closeness that men are unable to provide (Cancian 1989).

Nancy Chodorow (1978) argues, from a psychoanalytic perspective, that this pattern of heterosexual incompatibility is reproduced because women care for children. Girls grow up in a close identificatory relationship with their mothers and so develop the desire to nurture and be nurtured. Boys can establish their masculinity only by distancing themselves from the feminine, becoming more autonomous and less able to establish emotional closeness with others. This process is envisaged as occurring largely at an unconscious level. Other perspectives suggest that children's emotional and sexual desires develop through their active negotiation of gendered positions within the social world (Davies 1989; Haug 1987; Jackson 1993; Crawford et al. 1992). In either case, the experiences of children have an effect on their later lives and on the expectations they bring to adult sexual, marital, and family relationships.

See also: ADULTHOOD; CHILD ABUSE: PHYSICAL ABUSE AND NEGLECT; CHILD ABUSE: PSYCHOLOGICAL MALTREATMENT; CHILD ABUSE: SEXUAL ABUSE; CHILDCARE; CHILD CUSTODY; CHILDHOOD, STAGES OF: ADOLESCENCE; CHILDHOOD, STAGES OF: INFANCY; CHILDHOOD, STAGES OF: MIDDLE CHILDHOOD; CHILDHOOD, STAGES OF: PRESCHOOL; CHILDHOOD, STAGES OF: TODDLERHOOD; CHILDREN'S RIGHTS; DEVELOPMENT: COGNITIVE; DEVELOPMENT: EMOTIONAL; DEVELOPMENT: MORAL; DEVELOPMENT: SELF; DISCIPLINE; FAMILY DEVELOPMENT THEORY; FAMILY, HISTORY OF; FAMILY POLICY; FAMILY ROLES; GENDER; GENDER IDENTITY; ONLY CHILDREN; OPPOSITIONALITY; PLAY; SEXUALITY IN CHILDHOOD; SCHOOL; SOCIALIZATION

Bibliography

Archard, D. (1993). *Children: Rights and Childhood.* London: Routledge & Kegan Paul.

Ariès, P. (1962). *Centuries of Childhood.* London: Jonathan Cape.

Benedict, R. (1938). "Continuities and Discontinuities in Cultural Conditioning." *Psychiatry* 1:161–167.

Cancian, F. (1989). *Love in America.* Cambridge, UK.: Cambridge University Press.

Chodorow, N. (1978). *The Reproduction of Mothering.* Berkeley: University of California Press.

Crawford, J.; Kippax, S.; Onyx, J.; Gault, U.; and Benton, P. (1982). *Emotion and Gender: Constructing Meaning from Memory.* Newbury Park, CA: Sage Publications.

Davies, B. (1989). *Frogs and Snails and Feminist Tales.* Sydney: Allen and Unwin.

Davin, A. (1990). "When Is a Child Not a Child?" In *The Politics of Everyday Life,* ed. H. Corr and L. Jamieson. London: Macmillan.

Delphy, C., and Leonard, D. (1992). *Familiar Exploitation.* Oxford: Polity.

Donzalot, J. (1980). *The Policing of Families: Welfare Versus the State.* London: Hutchinson.

Ehrenreich, B., and English, D. (1978). *For Her Own Good: 150 Years of Experts' Advice to Women.* New York: Doubleday.

Gelles, R. (1979). *Family Violence.* Newbury Park, CA: Sage Publications.

Hardyment, C. (1983). *Dream Babies: Child Care from Locke to Spock.* London: Jonathan Cape.

Haug, F., ed. (1987). *Female Sexualization.* London: Verso.

Hernandez, D. J. (1997). "Child Development and the Social Demographics of Childhood." *Child Development* 68(1):149–169.

Hood-Williams, J. (1990). "Patriarchy for Children: On the Stability of Power Relations in Children's Lives." In *Childhood, Youth, and Social Change: A Comparative Perspective,* ed. L. Chisholm, P. Buchner, H.-H. Kruger, and P. Brown. London: Falmer.

Jackson, S. (1982). *Childhood and Sexuality.* Oxford: Basil Blackwell.

Jackson, S. (1993). "Even Sociologists Fall in Love: An Exploration in the Sociology of Emotions." *Sociology* 27:201–220.

Jenks, C. (1996). *Childhood*. New York: Routledge.

Kagan, J., and Gall, S. B., eds. (1998). *The Gale Encyclopedia of Childhood and Adolescence*. Detroit: Gale.

Lees, S. (1993). *Sugar and Spice: Sexuality and Adolescent Girls*. London: Penguin Books.

Leonard, D. (1990). "Persons in Their Own Right: Children and Sociology in the UK." In *Childhood, Youth, and Social Change: A Comparative Perspective*, ed. L. Chisholm, P. Buchner, H.-H. Kruger, and P. Brown. London: Falmer.

Mansfield, P., and Collard, J. (1988). *The Beginning of the Rest of Your Life*. London: Macmillan.

Mead, M., and Wolfenstein, M. (1955). *Childhood in Contemporary Cultures*. Chicago: University of Chicago Press.

Newsom, J., and Newsom, E. (1965). *Patterns of Infant Care in an Urban Community*. London: Penguin Books.

Newsom, J., and Newson, E. (1968). *Four Years Old in an Urban Community*. London: Penguin Books.

Pinchbeck, I., and Hewitt, M. (1969). *Children in English Society*, Vol. 1. London: Routledge & Kegan Paul.

Pinchbeck, I., and Hewitt, M. (1973). *Children in English Society*, Vol. 2. London: Routledge & Kegan Paul.

Pollock, L. A. (1983). *Forgotten Children: Parent-Child Relations from 1500–1900*. Cambridge, UK: Cambridge University Press.

Rose, N. (1989). *Governing the Soul: The Shaping of the Private Self*. London: Routledge & Kegan Paul.

Seidler, V. (1989). *Rediscovering Masculinity*. London: Routledge & Kegan Paul.

Shahar, S. (1990). *Childhood in the Middle Ages*. London: Routledge & Kegan Paul.

Skolnick, A. (1980). "Children's Rights, Children's Development." In *Children's Rights and Juvenile Justice*, ed. L. T. Empey. Charlottesville: University of Virginia Press.

Thompson, S. (1989). "Search for Tomorrow: On Feminism and the Reconstruction of Teen Romance." In *Pleasure and Danger*, ed. C. Vance. London: Pandora.

Thomson, R., and Scott, S. (1991). *Learning About Sex: Young Women and the Social Construction of Sexual Identity*. London: Tufnell Press.

Thorne, B. (1985). "Revisioning Women and Social Change: Where Are the Children?" *Gender and Society* 1:85–109.

Waksler, F. C. (1986). "Studying Children: Phenomenological Insights." *Human Studies* 91:71–82.

Wood, J. (1984). "Groping Towards Sexism: Boys' Sex Talk." In *Gender and Generation*, ed. A. McRobbie and M. Nava. London: Macmillan.

STEVI JACKSON (1995)
BIBLIOGRAPHY REVISED BY JAMES J. PONZETTI, JR.

CHILDHOOD, STAGES OF

ADOLESCENCE *Ronda Copher, Jeylan T. Mortimer*
INFANCY *M. G. Carelli, M. Cusinato*
MIDDLE CHILDHOOD *M. Cusinato, M. G. Carelli*
PRESCHOOL *M. G. Carelli, M. Cusinato*
TODDLERHOOD *M. Cusinato, M. G. Carelli*

ADOLESCENCE

First recognized at the beginning of the twentieth century, adolescence is defined as the stage of the life-course between childhood and adulthood. Adolescence is a time of pubertal change, identity formation, social development, and the acquisition of experiences and credentials promoting entry to adult roles. Adolescence and early adulthood are also critical periods for the development of psychological attributes, such as political attitudes and work orientations, that tend to persist through adulthood.

Although it is a recognized stage in most parts of the world, adolescence involves different experiences for youth depending upon where they live. In Western countries such as the United States and parts of Europe, the adolescent is thought to be relatively free of adult responsibilities; lacking in long-term commitments; oriented to fun, sports, popular music, and peers; receptive to change; and ready to experiment with alternative identities. Adolescence in other parts of the world can be far less carefree, and decisions made during this time are fraught with more definitive long-term consequences. Families make crucial decisions that affect youth, such as in sub-Saharan Africa, where adolescents are placed in the homes of relatives, friends, or others so that they may provide services; sometimes they receive apprentice training or education. These youth become separated from their immediate family, parents, and siblings, potentially weakening familial ties. Yet, in India, adolescents spend much more time with their families than with friends; the family has priority over time spent with peers (see Verma and Saraswathi in Brown, Larson, and Saraswathi 2002). Whether a youth leads a carefree adolescence depends upon social norms and the needs of their families.

Attitudes formed during adolescence have marked consequences for subsequent attainments. Research on adolescence in the United States demonstrates that early orientations about efficacy and competence influence later adaptations and goal attainment. John A. Clausen (1993) finds that adolescent planful competence, denoting self-confidence, intellectual investment, and dependability, positively influences men's adult occupational status. Adults question whether the adolescents from single-child families in China and Japan, labeled as the "me" generation for their emphasis on their own satisfaction, will possess the self-discipline required to maintain adult employment. Indian adolescents learn that male supremacy reigns, making gender important to their identity and future social status.

Multiple transitions designating adult status mark the end of adolescence—the completion of formal education, obtaining economic self-sufficiency, independent residence, marriage, parenthood, or entry into full-time work. The ages at which young people typically acquire adult roles, the character of marking events, and the availability of opportunities to assume adult statuses vary by country, within countries, by socioeconomic origin, and by other background characteristics. For example, initiation into adulthood for the Nso boys of Cameroon begins with moving from associating with women and children to the company of men, but full adult status is not achieved until marriage and parenthood (Nsamenang 1992). Although for many youth worldwide, marriage is the marker of adulthood, movement out of the parental household does not usually follow marriage. At least partial economic dependence on the family characterizes more advantaged young people in developing societies as they extend their educations into their twenties or even early thirties. For poor areas in the United States, as well as in other countries, economic conditions prevent substantial proportions of youth from acquiring adult-like economic roles.

Changing Identities

The establishment of identity is widely viewed as the key developmental task of adolescence, sometimes accompanied by emotional strain as adolescents grapple with the question of who they are and what they want to become. Identities can be based on roles, relationships, status in an organization, or those related to character traits (psychological and behavioral attributes). Westerners conceptualize adolescents as playful, experimental, carefree, even reckless, while adults, in contrast, are thought to be independent, productive, hardworking, and responsible. Yet the experiences of many youth worldwide differ from these ideals; many quickly assume adult role identities. Issues of adolescent identity are further complicated by diverse legal definitions. For example, in Japan, the ceremony of *seijinshiki* occurs when a youth reaches twenty years of age and indicates legal adult status. However, this ceremony does not necessarily mean that the youth has the social status of an adult.

Given asynchronies in the age-grading systems of different societal institutions, the adolescent (and youth) is subject to recurring status inconsistencies and identity conflicts. Independent, autonomous character identities, characteristic of adulthood, are confirmed in some contexts, but not in others. As a result, it is widely believed that adolescence and youth are stressful life stages, and that problems diminish with the successful entry into adult roles. Characteristic of one-third of American adolescents at any given time is a "mid-adolescence peak" of depressed mood (Petersen; Compas; Brooks-Gunn; Stemmler; Ey; and Grant 1993). Researchers in other countries, such as Canada and Germany, have reported similar findings. Moreover, depressive affect and disorder show marked increases in adolescence, especially among girls (see Marcotte, Alain, and Gosselin 1999). Adolescent well-being overall tends to be lower in those countries where the standards of living are poor (Grob, Stetsenko, Sabatier, Botcheva, and Macek 1999).

Because of their capacity to engage in formal operational thought, adolescents may recognize

A Muslim Palestinian woman and her adolescent daughter prepare traditional foods during the Muslim holy month of Ramadan. How much time adolescents spend with their families and their expected contributions to the family varies according to social norms and family needs. ANNIE GRIFFITHS BELT/CORBIS

the multiplicity of choices available to them, and the likelihood that their choices may not be optimal. This process of identity exploration is more highly differentiated and sophisticated in areas salient to adult possible selves, such as the domain of work and family. Further, the resolution of important identity issues facilitates career choice, the formation of stable intimate relationships, and political-religious ideologies. Optimally, those identities sought by adolescents will foster a coherent, unified set of self-images and activities, congruent with social niches.

Yet the multiplicity of options is problematic for many adolescents as they attempt to manage their lives in a changing world of sociopolitical as well as economic upheaval. Adolescents must navigate between traditional expectations and contemporary conditions. For example, despite their patriarchal culture, many adolescents in India think that all family members, including women, should be involved in decision making (Verma and Saraswathi

in Brown et al. 2002). In particular, changes such as women's participation in paid employment have altered family life by requiring more help within the home and increasing young women's expectations. Although not all change is positive, as in Southeast Asia; the disruption to family life by women taking paid employment and migration into urban areas are seen as precursors to increased sexual activity for youth (Santa Maria in Brown et al. 2002). Ideas about premarital sex further illustrate the conflict of past and present beliefs, as more adolescents are sexually active despite traditional social views to the contrary. Moreover, at least two-thirds of young adults in the United States and northern European countries are avoiding conventional marriage, choosing instead to cohabitate (Hurrelmann and Settertobulte 1994).

Educational Attainment

Considerable attention has been directed to adolescent educational attainment, given its clear link to socioeconomic standing in adulthood. For youth worldwide, education is of central importance for occupational attainment, a critical component of adult status. Many countries have multiple secondary education institutions to assist adolescents in achieving occupational success: for example, college preparatory or vocational, where students learn trades like carpentry or auto mechanics. Apprenticeships combine occupational training in the context of work organizations and educational training for youth in Europe. By age fifteen or sixteen, adolescents in Germany select their apprenticeships, and thus their occupational destinations (see Mortimer and Kruger 2000). For better placement into secondary education institutions, students in China and Japan spend extra time after school preparing for entrance exams (Stevenson and Zusho in Brown et al. 2002).

The prolonged character of educational preparation is a worldwide trend. Currently in Europe 20 to 40 percent of young people are attending institutions of higher education (Lagree 1995). In the United States, more than 60 percent of high school graduates enter college, yet less than 30 percent of recent cohorts complete a four-year degree. Jeffery J. Arnett (1998) argues that continued participation in education extends the transition to adult status, thus creating an emerging adulthood period. Current market conditions favor the more highly educated. Adolescents may be pursuing further education for better jobs, but it also prolongs their pre-adult status. Barbara Schneider and David Stevenson (1999) maintain that the exclusive emphasis on attaining higher education in the American high school provides little vocational direction for young people, contributing to "floundering" and the less-than-optimal utilization of educational resources.

Education offers opportunities for improving the conditions of youth worldwide, but there are inequities based on social class. For example, in India, those in the lower castes are disadvantaged by their class position, limiting their social mobility. Adolescents from families with fewer resources are unable to continue their educations due to cost, which is increasingly problematic in Latin America (Welti in Brown et al. 2002). Adolescents of higher social class background in the United States have higher educational and occupational aspirations, which, in turn, foster higher attainments. The more socioeconomically advantaged

parents also engage in more supportive childrearing behavior, fostering personality traits that are conducive to occupational attainment. Geographic location also affects the availability of education. In Southeast Asia, 70 percent of out-of-school youth reside in rural areas (Saint Marie in Brown et al. 2002) where educational facilities are often more limited than in urban areas.

Increasingly throughout the world, women receive more formal education than was previously allowed. Despite having the highest illiteracy rates among females, in Latin American countries, more young women are given access to education than in prior years. In China and Japan, families are more likely to provide resources for men to attend school because sons perpetuate the family name and are expected to contribute to the support of their parents (Soled 1995).

Work

Most adolescents work while they are attending school to obtain spending money; many save at least part of their earnings for higher education and other goals. This is the normative pattern in the United States and Canada. Parents typically hold quite favorable opinions about their adolescent children's work, believing that this experience will help them to become responsible and independent, to learn to handle money, and to manage time. Yet Ellen Greenberger and Laurence Steinberg (1986) alleged that employed adolescents have more cynical attitudes toward work than those who are not employed. Employment during high school predicts more stable work histories and higher earnings in the years immediately following (see Chapter 4, National Academy Press 1998). David Stern and Yoshi-Fumi Nakata (1989), using data from noncollege youth in the National Longitudinal Survey of Youth in the United States, reported that more complex work in adolescence predicts lower incidence of unemployment and higher earnings three years after high school. Furthermore, evidence from the Youth Development Study, a longitudinal investigation of a representative panel of urban high school students, suggests that in the United States, the quality of adolescent work matters for psychological outcomes that could influence adult attainment, such as a sense of competence or personal efficacy, depressive affect, and occupational reward values (see Grabowski, Call, and Mortimer 2001). The most beneficial pattern, with respect to educational attainment, is for youth to engage in stable employment of low intensity (Mortimer and Johnson 1998), allowing them to participate in diverse, developmentally beneficial activities in their schools, families, and peer groups. Whereas middle-class white youth have the most bountiful work opportunities, minority youth, particularly those who reside in inner cities, are less likely to be employed. Given the benefits to be drawn from youth employment experience, the lack of job opportunities for minority teenagers is cause for concern (Newman 1999).

Upon completion of secondary schooling, youth in the United States who do not go on to college obtain jobs that are usually in the secondary sector of the economy. They experience high unemployment and job instability. At the same time, employers express preference for low-wage workers who do not require fringe benefits and are not likely to unionize. When filling adultlike primary jobs, employers seek evidence of stability or settling down. The absence of a clear channel of mobility from education to work in the United States, unlike Germany and Japan (Hamilton 1990), reduces the level of human capital investment (e.g., in the form of job training and continuous work experience) of noncollege young people in the years after high school.

In other countries, there are stronger bridges from education to work. In Germany, part-time adolescent work is tied institutionally to the apprentice system, which influences later employment. In Japan, linkages between schools and employers provide another kind of institutional bridge, though this is weakening with economic decline (Brinton 2000).

The majority of adolescents worldwide seek employment after leaving school in order to contribute to their families' resources or to satisfy their own immediate needs, as Lewis Aptekar (1994) describes among street children in Africa. When working, adolescents are often underemployed and receive low wages in comparison to adult laborers in similar jobs. Employers in India rely on young labor as an inexpensive and compliant source of workers (Burra 1997). Yet, as in Africa, some countries are attempting to create more gainful and sustainable employment for adolescents.

Despite the low wages that are available to them, adolescents often migrate to urban areas in search of employment. In the Philippines, Indonesia, and Zambia, adolescents leave rural areas in hopes of increased employment in urban environments. Latin American adolescents relocate to the cities to work, sharing residence with other working teens. Although migration may result in employment, there are also substantial costs involved. It is estimated that upwards of eleven million youth live on the streets of India (Phillips 1992). Separation from family disrupts transmission of important cultural values and mores, disadvantaging adolescents. Further, many youth are denied formal education, which limits their skills and available human capital. These adolescents are also at risk from poor nutrition and various environmental hazards.

Youth Problem Behaviors

For many youth, adolescence is a period of increased risk taking that later declines with age. Sometimes youth problem behaviors, such as delinquency and substance use, are attributed to the absence of meaningful, valued adult social roles, despite adolescents' growing capacity to fill them. Some behaviors that are considered problematic or even legally prohibited when engaged in by minors (e.g., smoking, alcohol use, and sexual activity) are legitimate in adulthood. Over 40 percent of high school seniors in the United States have experimented with illicit drugs, though the numbers are declining (Monitoring the Future 2000). These behaviors are seen as attempts to affirm maturity or to negotiate adult status. In addition, adolescents worldwide are using tobacco and alcohol in record numbers. The potential consequences of substance use and abuse (e.g., addiction, automobile accidents, crime, and health problems) make this quite prevalent behavior problematic.

Although there is continuity in conduct problems in childhood, adolescent delinquency, and adult criminality, adolescents, particularly males of lower socioeconomic background, have distinctly high rates of criminal behavior. These are not always reflected in conviction rates because of the tendency to dispose of adolescent arrests informally. Juvenile delinquency has multifaceted causes: macrostructural (e.g., the failure of the society to provide opportunities to obtain widespread success goals legitimately); familial (e.g., indifferent or inconsistent parental monitoring and discipline or parental criminality); network-related (e.g., involvement with delinquent peer subcultures); personal (e.g., low levels of moral development, low IQ; see Hirschi and Hindelang 1977); and other biological or genetic deficits.

Drug use, whether criminal or conventional, poses serious health risks for youth worldwide. Adolescent drug use is more legally problematic in the United States than, for example, in Switzerland, where drug use has been decriminalized (Buchmann 1994). Only 25 percent of Swiss youth, aged fifteen to twenty-five, report ever smoking marijuana, compared to over 36 percent of twelfth graders in the United States (Monitoring the Future 2000). Canadian adolescent drug use is also higher than in European countries (Galambos and Kolaric 1994), while narcotic drug use by Arab adolescents is less frequent than in Western countries. The most prevalent use of drugs by adolescents involves alcohol and tobacco. Tobacco is used by between 20 to 50 percent of adolescents in Western countries. Tobacco smoking by Russian youth is widespread (Prokhorov and Alexandrov 1992); the average age of onset of smoking by boys has decreased to eleven years, by girls to thirteen (World Health Organization 2000).

Adolescent experiences vary throughout the world, yet these years in the life-course provide the foundation for adult roles and responsibilities. Youth in Westernized countries enter into the arena of adulthood relatively late, while in developing nations, formal assumption of adult responsibilities occurs at a much younger age. Clearly, cultural, social, and economic variations across nation-states affect the definition and the experiences of adolescents. There are opportunities for intervention during the period of adolescence, to encourage and improve the outcomes for youth throughout the world. In 1996, the United Nations created a set of goals for youth worldwide. Its policy recommendation addresses basic human rights of health and freedom, and importantly calls attention to the need for access to education, sustainable employment, and participation in decisions that affect young people's lives (see Sarawathi and Larson in Brown et al 2002). Enacting these principles would offer youth the opportunity to develop the skills necessary for adulthood, engage productively in their constantly changing environments, and develop healthier and more satisfying lives.

See also: ADOLESCENT PARENTHOOD; CHILDHOOD; CONDUCT DISORDER; DEPRESSION: CHILDREN AND ADOLESCENTS; DEVELOPMENT: SELF; EATING DISORDERS; FAMILY LIFE EDUCATION; JUVENILE DELINQUENCY; MENARCHE; OPPOSITIONALITY; PEER INFLUENCE; RITES OF PASSAGE; RUNAWAY YOUTHS; SCHOOL; SEXUALITY IN ADOLESCENCE; SUBSTANCE ABUSE; SUICIDE

Bibliography

Aptekar, L. (1994). "Street Children in the Developing World: A Review of their Condition." *Cross-Cultural Research* 28:195–224.

Archer, S. L. (1991). "Gender Differences in Identity Development." *Encyclopedia of Adolescence,* ed. by R. M. Lerner, A. C. Petersen, and J. Brooks-Gunn. Vol. 1: 522–524.

Arnett, J. J. (1998). "Learning to Stand Alone: The Contemporary American Transition to Adulthood in Cultural and Historical Context." *Human Development* 54:317–326.

Brinton, M. C. (2000). "Social Capital in the Japanese Youth Labor Market: Labor Market Policy, Schools, and Norms." *Policy Sciences* 33:289–306

Brown, B. B.; Larson, R.; and Saraswathi, T. S. (2002). *The World's Youth: Adolescence in Eight Regions of the Globe.* New York: Cambridge University Press.

Buchmann, M. (1994). "Switzerland." In the *International Handbook of Adolescence,* ed. K. Hurrelmann. Westport, CT: Greenwood Press.

Burra, N. (1997). *Born to Work: Child Labor in India.* Delhi: Oxford University Press.

Clausen, J. (1993). *American Lives.* New York: Free Press.

Galambos, N., and Kolaric, G. C. (1994). "Canada." In the *International Handbook of Adolescence,* ed. K. Hurrelmann. Westport, CT: Greenwood Press.

Grabowski, L. S.; Call, K. T.; and Mortimer, J. T. (2001). "Global and Economic Self-Efficacy in the Educational Attainment Process." *Social Psychology Quarterly* 64:164–179.

Greenberger, E., and Steinberg, L. (1986). *When Teenagers Work.* New York: Basic Books.

Grobb, A.; Stetsenko, A.; Sabatier, C.; Botcheva, L.; and Macek, P. (1999). "A Cross-National Model of Subjective Well-being in Adolescence." In the *Adolescent Experience: European and American Adolescents in the 1990s,* ed. F. D. Alsaker and A. Flammer. Mahwah, NJ: Erlbaum.

Hirschi, T., and M. J. Hindelang. (1977). "Intelligence and Delinquency: A Revisionist Review." *American Sociological Review* 42:571–587.

Hurrelmann, K. and Settertobulte, W. (1994). "Germany." In the *International Handbook of Adolescence,* ed. K. Hurrelmann. Westport, CT: Greenwood Press.

Lagree, J. C. (1995). "Young People in the European Community: Convergence or Divergence?" In *Growing Up in Europe: Contemporary Horizons in Childhood and Youth Studies,* ed. L. Chisholm; P. Buchner; H. H. Kruger; and M. du Bois-Reymond. New York: Walter de Gruyter.

Marcotte, D.; Alain, M.; and Gosselin, M. J. (1999). "Gender Difference in Adolescent Depression: Gender-Typed Characteristics or Problem-Solving Skill Deficits?" *Sex Roles* 41:31–48.

Mortimer, J. T., and Johnson, M. K. (1998). "Adolescent Part-Time Work and Educational Attainment." In *The Adolescent Years: Social Influences and Educational Challenges,* ed. K. Borman and B. Schneider. Chicago: National Society for the Study of Education.

Mortimer, J. T., and Kruger, H. (2000). "Pathways from School to Work in Germany and the United States." In the *Handbook of Education,* ed. M. T. Hallinan. New York: Kluwer Academic/Plenum Press.

National Academy Press. (1998). *Protecting Youth at Work: Health, Safety, and Development of Working Children and Adolescents in the United States.* Washington, DC: National Academy Press

Newman, K. S. (1999). *No Shame in My Game: The Working Poor in the Inner City.* New York: Alfred A. Knopf and the Russell Sage Foundation.

Nsamenang, A. B. (1992). *Human Development in Cultural Context: A Third World Perspective.* Newbury Park, CA: Sage.

Petersen, A. C.; Compas, B. E.; Brooks-Gunn, J.; Stemmler, E.; Ey, S.; and Grant, K. E. (1993). "Depression in Adolescence." *American Psychologist* 48:155–168.

Phillips, W. S. K. (1992). *Street Children of India.* Noida: Child Labor Cell.

Prokhorov, A. V., and Alexandrov, A. A. (1992). "Tobacco Smoking in Moscow School Students." *British Journal of Addiction* 87:1469–1476.

Schneider, B., and Stevenson, D. (1999). *The Ambitious Generation: America's Teenagers, Motivated but Directionless.* New Haven, CT: Yale University Press.

Schraedley, P. K.; Gotlib, I. H.; and Hayward, C. (1999). "Gender Differences in Correlates of Depressive Symptoms in Adolescents." *Journal of Adolescent Health* 25:98–108.

Soled, D. E. (1995). *China: A Nation in Transition.* Washington, DC: Congressional Quarterly.

Stern, D., and Nakata, Y. F. (1989). "Characteristics of High School Students' Paid Jobs and Employment Experience After Graduation." In *Adolescence and Work: Influences of Social Structure, Labor Markets, and Culture,* ed. D. Stern and D. Eichorn. Hillsdale, NJ: Erlbaum.

Other Resources

Monitoring the Future. (2000). Trends in the Lifetime Prevalence of Use of Various Drugs for Eighth, Tenth, and Twelfth Graders. Available from http://www.monitoringthefuture.org/data/00data/pr00t1.pdf.

World Health Organization. (2001). Highlights on the Health in the Russian Federation. Available from http://www.who.dk/country/rus01.pdf.

RONDA COPHER
JEYLAN T. MORTIMER

INFANCY

According to the ancient Romans, an infant is "one who does not speak" (*infans* in Latin means speechless). Modern developmental psychologists still consider the ability to speak to be an important sign that the infancy has come to an end.

Infancy refers to the period of child development that begins at birth and ends at about eighteen months to two years of age. Despite the fact that it comprises a very short period of the individual life span, infancy is one of the most fascinating times of development.

Cognitive Development

The aim of research on infant cognitive development is to describe how babies think and how and why thought processes change with age. In the view of Jean Piaget, one of the most prominent cognitive developmentalists of the twentieth century, children are active participants in the development of knowledge. In constructing their own understanding, children try to impose order on the information they receive through their senses and to adapt to the world around using sensorimotor schemas (such as grasping, throwing, sucking, banging, and kicking). These are representations of a class of sensory or motor actions used to attain a goal. For example, the actions of holding, touching, and throwing are children's schemas for round objects. Twelve-month-old children spend most of their playtime exploring and manipulating objects by using different sensor motor schemas, putting things in their mouths, shaking them, and moving them along the floor. Infants acquire knowledge about objects through their actions with them. Children learn, for example, that an object is a thing that tastes and feels a certain way when it is touched, or has a particular color. This wholly practical, action-bound kind of intellectual functioning is acquired through a sequence of stages, which together make up what Piaget termed the sensorimotor period, extending from birth until about two years of age (Piaget and Inhelder 1969).

One way of summarizing cognitive development in infancy is to say that the infant "knows" in the sense of recognizing or anticipating familiar, recurring objects and events, and "thinks" in the sense of behaving toward them with mouth, hand, eye, and other sensory-motor instruments in predictable and organized ways (Flavell 1985).

As infants near their first birthdays, they show important changes in their cognitive skills. They learn more rapidly and remember what they have learned for longer periods of time. They are able to anticipate the course of simple familiar routines (or scripts), and they act surprised if their expectations are violated. They have expanded the rudimentary categories they use to interpret their experiences and guide their actions. These new achievements make it possible for them to play simple games such as "peekaboo."

Developmental research has shown, however, that infants are more competent than what traditional theories indicated, and that they seem to display certain cognitive capacities much sooner than Piaget believed. Piaget thought that as early as the first months of life, infants could imitate their own actions, such as hand gestures, but could not imitate other people's facial gestures until late in the first year. Later research has shown that newborn babies can imitate certain facial gestures, such as tongue protrusion (Anisfeld 1991). Furthermore, nine-month-old babies can defer their imitation over a period as long as twenty-four hours, and can keep several actions in mind at the same time (Meltzoff 1988). Babies as young as two months also show preferences for attractive faces (Langlois et al 1991).

Even infants younger than six months are skilled at categorization—the ability to mentally sort objects by their properties. With increasing experience, both the categories and the properties used for categorizing grow in complexity. Research on memory development indicates that infants easily forget, but their implicit memory can be reactivated with reminder sessions of past events. Carolyn Rovee-Collier (1993) has found that babies as young as three months of age demonstrate implicit memory for actions with specific objects over periods of as long as a week (see Rovee-Collier 1999 for a review of infant memory).

In summary, Piaget seems to have underestimated the ability of infants to store, remember, and organize sensory and motor information. Very young babies pay much more attention to patterns, sequences, and prototypical features than Piaget thought, and can apparently represent them over at least short intervals. Many later theorists have concluded that babies come equipped with a range of built-in knowledge on their ways of understanding the world (Mandler 1997; Spelke and Newport 1997).

Language Development

In the early stage of language acquisition children are able to discriminate sounds, learn to segment and produce the basic sounds of language, and show a predisposition to respond to language as a unique auditory stimulus. Many of the developments during the *prelinguistic* (before the first word) phase are significant precursors to language. Around two months of age babies begin to make vowel-like noises called *cooing*; gradually, at around six months of age, they add consonants and start babbling. During this phase of language development infants repeat consonant-vowel combinations in long strings, such as "bababa" and "nanana."

At about one year of age the earliest words appear. Some of these early words are combined with gestures to convey whole sentences of meaning, a pattern called *holophrase*. During this one-word period infants spend several months expanding their vocabularies one word at the time. They talk mostly about moving or manipulating objects that interest them and show a vocabulary spurt or *naming explosion* between eighteen and twenty-four months of age. The first two-word sentences normally appear between eighteen and twenty-four months and are short and grammatically simple, lacking the various grammatical inflections. The child at this age can nonetheless convey many different meanings, such as location, possession, and agent-object relationships.

From a cross-cultural point of view there is some evidence of large similarities in early vocabularies. For example, the prelinguistic phase seems to be identical in all language communities. All babies coo, then babble, and the babbling stream resembles the sounds of the child's language community (at around one year of age). All babies understand language before they can speak it, and babies in all cultures begin to use their first words at about twelve months. In all language communities studied, a one-word phase precedes the two-word phase, with the latter beginning at about eighteen months. The functions of the first combinations of words seem to be present in infants in all language communities, and prepositions describing locations are added essentially in the same order. Finally, children in all cultures studied seem to pay more attention to the ends of words than to the beginnings, and thus learn suffixes before they learn prefixes (see Mohanty and Perregaux 1997 for a review).

Emotional Development

Do babies experience and display specific emotions such as happiness or sadness? At birth, infants have different facial expressions associated with several emotions, including interest, pain, disgust, joy, and surprise. By the time babies are two to three months old, adult observers can also distinguish expressions of anger and sadness, with expressions of fear appearing by six or seven months (Izard and Harris 1995). Early in the second year of life, at about the same time that children show self-recognition in the mirror, there is the emergence of self-conscious emotional expressions such as embarrassment, pride, and shame, all of which involve some aspects of self-evaluation. Infants are not only able to show emotions, then, but they also seem to be able to discriminate other people's emotional expressions. Haviland and Lelwica (1987) found that when mothers expressed happiness, their ten-week-old babies looked happy and gazed at them. However, when the mothers expressed sadness, babies showed increased mouth movements or looked away; when the mothers expressed anger, some babies cried vigorously, while others showed a kind of "frozen" look.

As early as five months of age infants associate emotional meaning with different tones of voice, such as encouraging or disapproving intonations. A father's expression of alarm can tell an infant how to react to an unfamiliar event. At about six months of age, infants begin to use social referencing—searching the expressions of others for emotional cues. Social referencing becomes increasingly distinct and important when crawling (at about nine months) and walking (at about twelve months) make infants independent and the active period of exploration begins. A detailed longitudinal study by Malinda Carpenter, Katherine Nagell, and Michael Tomasello (1998) has shown that nine- to fifteen-month-olds follow a standard sequence: They follow their parents' expressions and gestures, then they actively share in mutual emotional experiences, and finally they are able to lead the process by using their own words and gestures to engage their parents' attention.

From a cross-cultural perspective, "the available evidence is that emotion[s] exist in all cultures . . . events considered relevant to major concerns are seen to elicit emotional responses, including facial expressions, physiological changes, hedonic experiences, and important shifts in the control of behavior pertinent to interactions with the environment. . . . [Nevertheless] there is evidence of consistent cultural differences as well as similarities in each component of emotions" (Mesquita, Frijda, and Scherer 1997, p. 287).

Parent-Child Relationships

Modern theories in developmental psychology conceive the interaction between the caregiver and the child as crucial to all psychological growth. A child's parents and the emotional atmosphere of the home greatly influence the kind of person the infant will become. During the early years parental attitudes toward the infant are critical: The infant may receive feelings that will foster a sense of love and security or those that will promote anxiety and mistrust. Infants are interested in social interaction virtually from birth—voices and faces are among the first stimuli to capture a newborn's attention.

By the age of two to three months, babies start to respond to parents in a special way: they smile, show wider grins, coo, and show other reactions that signify special status in their unique worlds. Many parents report that their own affection for their babies deepens at this time, in a sense that parents proceed from a newborn phase of caregiving to a family phase in which the child becomes a social partner who reciprocates their love (Berger 2001). Progressively that initial face-to-face play becomes a more coordinated interaction. This synchrony helps the infant to develop some of the basic skills of social interaction, such as taking turns, which they will use throughout life.

Cross-culturally, these episodes of face-to-face play are a universal feature of the early interaction between caregivers and infants. However, the frequency, duration, and goals of these episodes differ among cultures. For example, U.S. mothers employ more social overtures (such as tickling) that stimulate and excite their babies; mothers in Kenya are more soothing and quieting in their initiatives (LeVine et al. 1994); while Japanese mothers typically focus on establishing mutual intimacy by maintaining eye contact with their infants as well as kissing and hugging (Bornstein and Lamb 1992). Fathers seem to be active partners, and older siblings and other adults also assume active roles in infant care and participate in social play with babies in many non-Western cultures (Tronick, Morelli, and Ivey 1992).

Attachment

In John Bowlby's (1958) view, attachment is the affectionate bond between infant and caregiver, and is a vital component of healthy functioning. Bowlby believed that every infant, like the young of the other animal species, is endowed with a set of built-in behaviors (e. g., smiling, grasping, crying, gazing) that help to keep the parent nearby and thereby increase the chances that the infant will be protected from danger. Contact with the parent also ensures that the baby will be fed, but Bowlby was careful to point out that feeding is not the basis for attachment. Instead the attachment bond has strong biological roots, and can best be understood within an evolutionary framework in which survival of the species is of utmost importance.

The development of attachment takes place in three phases. During the first phase (from birth to two to three months), very young babies cannot identify their mothers and therefore cannot exhibit differential emotional responses to them. Infants do, however, recognize their own mother's smell and voice, but they are not yet attached to her, and they do not mind being left with an unfamiliar adult. By three months of age babies begin to respond differently to a familiar caregiver than to a stranger. For example, they smile more freely when interacting with the mother and become calm more quickly when picked up by her. As infants engage in face-to-face interaction with the parent and experience relief from distress, they learn that their own actions affect the behavior of those around them. As a result, they begin to develop an expectation that the caregiver will respond when signaled. At that stage babies still do not protest when separated from the parent, despite the fact that they can recognize and distinguish her from unfamiliar people. During the third phase (between six to eight months and eighteen months to two years) the attachment to the familiar caregiver is evident. Babies of this age show separation anxiety in that they become very upset when the adult on whom they have come to rely leaves.

Cross-cultural comparisons indicate that separation distress is a universal feature of the attachment process. It emerges in the second half of the first year, increasing until about fifteen months, and then starts to decline. Infants construct enduring affective ties to caregivers out of their experiences during the developmental course of attachment. This inner representation of the parent-child bond serves as an internal working model, or set of expectations concerning the availability of attachment figures, a model that serves as a guide for all future close relationships (see Waters et al. 1995 for a review).

Research on what leads to variations in patterns of attachment has focused on several factors: the infant's temperament and capacities, the mother's responsiveness, stresses within the family, and the child-rearing patterns of the cultural group to which the mother and the child belong. Many theorists believe that the major influence on the quality of the infant-caregiver attachment relationship appears to result primarily from the caregiver's responsiveness. Mothers who are more sensitive to their babies' signals and who adjust their behavior to that of their children are more likely to develop secure attachment relationships (Ainsworth 1983).

Family Environment

The specific family environment in which child-rearing takes place also affects infants' development. The belief that the family environment has a great impact on the characteristics that infants will have as adults has led many researchers to try to identify the optimal conditions for infant development. Ideas about the nature of optimal environment depend on the historical and cultural values of the society into which a child is born. In Western societies it is commonly held that the ideal conditions should include a variety of objects for the baby to investigate, some free opportunity to explore, and loving, responsive, and sensitive adults who talk to their infant often and respond to the infant's cues (Bradley et al. 1989). Different cultures value different strategies for achieving their optimal pattern. Japanese mothers, for example, seem very responsive to their children, to the point of encouraging considerable emotional dependence (Miyaki et al. 1986). In contrast to U.S. society, which values self-determination and independence, Japanese society fosters interdependence and cooperation.

A different set of conditions prevails in areas in which children are born into very poor and hostile environments. Mothers of children living, for example, in the areas of northeastern Brazil have different beliefs about childrearing that seem uncaring by the standards of middle-class Western societies (Scheper-Hughes 1992). They view children who are developmentally delayed or who have quiet temperaments as weak and unlikely to survive and as a consequence might neglect these children. Further, mothers expect five- to six-year-old children to start contributing to the family's livelihood. But as the research by Nancy Scheper-Hughes points it out, these mothers are doing the best they can to prepare their children to survive and successfully adapt to their environment.

Cross-cultural studies of this kind are becoming increasingly important. They indicate that any final statements about the optimal conditions for infant development must take into account the actual circumstances in which children in different cultures live (Cole and Cole 2001).

The End of Infancy

Between the second and the third birthdays, children complete the period of infancy. The end of this important part in their lives is marked by changes in biological processes, by expanding physical and mental abilities, and by the appearance of a new relationship with themselves and the social world. Significant changes combine to produce a transition to a new stage evidenced by a new self-concept and autonomy (including the decline in the level of separation distress that children show when they are separated from their caregivers). The increased abilities to think and play in symbolic ways, to engage in more complex problem solving, and to express themselves in elementary phrases make infants ready to enter a new distinctive stage of development.

See also: ATTACHMENT: PARENT-CHILD RELATIONSHIPS; CHILDHOOD; COLIC; DEVELOPMENT: COGNITIVE; DEVELOPMENT: EMOTIONAL; DEVELOPMENT: MORAL; DEVELOPMENT: SELF; FAILURE TO THRIVE; PLAY; SEPARATION-INDIVIDUATION; SUDDEN INFANT DEATH SYNDROME (SIDS); TEMPERAMENT

Bibliography

Ainsworth, M. D. S. (1983). "Patterns of Infant-Mother Attachment as Related to Maternal Care: Their Early History and Their Contribution to Continuity." In *Human Development: A Interactional Perspective,* ed. D. Magnusson and V. Allen. New York: Academic Press.

Anisfeld, M. (1991). "Neonatal Imitation." *Developmental Review* 11:60–97.

Berger, K. S. (2001). *The Developing Person Through the Life Span.* New York: Worth Publishers.

Bowlby, J. (1958). "The Nature of the Child's Tie to His Mother." *International Journal of Psychoanalysis* 39:350–373.

Bornstein, M. H., and Lamb, M. E. (1992). *Development in Infancy,* 3rd edition. New York: McGraw-Hill.

Bradley, R. H.; Caldwell, B. M.; Rock, S. L.; Barnard, K. E.; Gray, C.; Hammond, M. A.; Mitchell, S.; Siegel, L.; Ramey, C. D.; Gottfried, A. W.; Siegel, L.; and Johnson, D. L. (1989). "Home Environment and Cognitive Development in the First 3 Years of Life: A Collaborative Study Involving Six Cities and Three Ethnic Groups in North America." *Developmental Psychology* 25:217–235.

Carpenter, M.; Nagell, K.; and Tomasello, M. (1998). "Social Cognition, Joint Attention, and Communicative Competence from 9 to 15 Months of Age." *Monographs of the Society for Research in Child Development* 63.

Cole, M., and Cole, S. (2001). *The Development of Children.* New York: W. H. Freeman and Company.

Flavell, J. (1985). *Cognitive Development.* Englewood Cliffs, NJ: Prentice Hall.

Haviland, J. M., and Lelwica, M. (1987). "The Induced Affect Response: 10-Week-Old Infants' Responses to

Three Emotional Expressions." *Developmental Psychology* 23:97–104.

Izard, C. E., and Harris, P. (1995). "Emotional Development and Developmental Psychopathology." In *Developmental Psychopathology*, Vol. 1: *Theory and Methods*, ed. D. Cicchetti and D. J. Cohen. New York: Wiley.

Langlois, J. H.; Ritter, J. M.; Roggman, L. A.; and Vaughn, L. S. (1991). "Facial Diversity and Infant Preferences for Attractive Faces." *Developmental Psychology* 27:79–84.

LeVine, R.; Dixon, S.; LeVine S.; Richman, A.; Leiderman, P. H.; Keeferk C. H.; and Brazelton, B. (1994). *Child Care and Culture: Lessons from Africa*. New York: Cambridge University Press.

Mandler, J. (1997). "Representation." In *Handbook of Child Psychology*, gen. ed. W. Damon, Vol. 2: *Cognition, Perception and Language*, ed. D. Kuhn and R. S. Siegler. New York: Wiley.

Meltzoff, A. N. (1988). "Infant Imitation and Memory. Nine-Month-Olds in Immediate and Deferred Tests." *Child Development* 59:217–225.

Mesquita, B.; Frijda, N.; and Scherer, K. (1997). "Culture and Emotions." In *Cross-Cultural Psychology*, Vol. 2: *Basic Processes and Human Development*, ed. J. W. Berry, P. R. Dasen, and T. S. Saraswathi. Boston: Allyn and Bacon.

Miyaki, K.; Campos, J.; Bradshaw, D. L.; and Kagan, J. (1986). "Issues in Socio-Emotional Development." In *Child Development and Education in Japan*, ed. H. Stevenson, H. Azuma, and K. Hakuta. New York: W. H. Freeman.

Mohanty, A. K., and Perregaux, C. (1997). "Language Acquisition and Bilingualism." In *Cross-Cultural Psychology*, Vol. 2: *Basic Processes and Human Development*, ed. J. W. Berry, P. R. Dasen, and T. S. Saraswathi. Boston: Allyn and Bacon.

Piaget, J., and Inhelder, B. (1969). *The Psychology of the Child*. New York: Basic Books.

Rovee-Collier, C. (1993). "The Capacity for Long-Term Memory in Infancy." *Current Directions in Psychological Science* 2:130–135.

Rovee-Collier, C. (1999). "The Development of Infant Memory." *Current Directions in Psychological Science* 8:80–85.

Scheper-Hughes, N. (1992). *Death without Weeping: The Violence of Everyday Life in Brazil*. Berkeley: University of California Press.

Spelke, E. S., and Newport, E. S. (1997). "Nativism, Empiricism, and the Development of Knowledge." In *Handbook of Child Psychology*, gen. ed. W. Damon, Vol. 1: *Theories of Development*, ed. R. Lerner. New York: Wiley.

Tronick, E. Z.; Morelli, G. A.; and Ivey, P. K. (1992). "The Efe Forager Infant and Toddler's Pattern of Social Relationships: Multiple and Simultaneous." *Developmental Psychology* 28:568–577.

Waters, E. ; Vaughn, B. E.; Posada, G.; and Kondo-Ikamura, K. (1995). "Caregiving, Cultural, and Cognitive Perspectives on Secure-Base Behavior and Working Models: New Growing Points of Attachment Theory and Research." *Monographs of the Society for Research in Child Development* 60:2–3, Serial No. 244.

M. G. CARELLI
M. CUSINATO

MIDDLE CHILDHOOD

Middle childhood is the period of the child's life that spans ages six to twelve years. It is a developmental stage referred to as *the school years,* because almost every culture worldwide considers these children ready and eager to learn. In fact, children in this age span are able, from a mental point of view, to deal systematically with many variables simultaneously. Speed and distance, for instance, can be successfully manipulated, so that mathematical problems can be solved. School-age children possess more refined levels of linguistic proficiency, develop new abilities to think more deeply and logically, and are more consistent and perseverant when they try to solve a problem. This is also the period of the emergence of a global sense of self-worth, and the period in which gender segregation in peer relationships becomes virtually complete. The fact that schooling begins at this age seems to reflect an implicit or explicit recognition of this essential shift in the period of the child's development.

Cognitive Development

The most important achievement of cognitive development during middle childhood is the attainment of the *concrete operational* stage. According to Jean Piaget and Bärbel Inhelder (Piaget and Inhelder 1969), concrete operational reasoning is far more logical, flexible, and organized than cognition was during the preschool period. Children between seven and eleven years understand logical principles, and they apply them in concrete situations. They are able to engage in mental operations that have *reversibility*. For example, a child understands that subtracting a few coins from a jar of coins can be reversed by adding the same number of coins to the jar. Another important cognitive acquisition is the capacity of *decentration,* that is, children can focus their attention on several attributes of an object or event simultaneously and understand the relations among dimensions or attributes.

Concrete operational thinkers understand that objects have more than one dimension (e.g., "A car is both large and heavy") and that these dimensions are separable. The physical world becomes more predictable because children come to understand that certain physical aspects of objects, such as length, size, density, and number, remain the same even when other aspects of the object's appearance have changed. However, school-age children cannot think abstractly. That is, they are able to think in an organized, logical fashion only when dealing with concrete information they can directly perceive. Thus, youngsters cannot truly analyze their own thoughts or think about problems in the future.

Are these characteristics of the concrete operational thinking universal? According to Piaget, brain maturation with experience in a stimulating environment should lead children in every culture to reach the concrete operational stage. However, cross-cultural research has shown that specific cultural practices have a great deal to do with children's mastery of Piagetian tasks (Dasen 1994; Rogoff 1990), and that concrete operational reasoning may not be a form of logic that emerges universally during middle childhood, but it may be a product of direct training, context, and cultural conditions (Light and Perret-Clermont 1989). Marshall Segall and his colleagues (1999) argued that when Piaget's clinical procedures are applied appropriately, by using contents with which people have extensive experience, the concrete operational thought is a universal cognitive achievement of middle childhood, just as predicted by Piaget.

Although all developmental psychologists do not agree with Piaget's theory, there is general consensus that children's thinking during middle childhood becomes more *two sided,* in that the children can think about objects from more than one perspective and are able to hold one aspect of a situation while comparing it with another. There is also a general agreement that this special characteristic of concrete operational thought is due to an increased memory capacity and abilities. Important memory changes seem to be characteristic of this period, including an increase in the knowledge about the things one is trying to remember (Chi and Koeske 1983), the acquisition of more effective strategies for remembering (Schneider and Bjorklund 1998; see also Rogoff and Mistry 1990 for a cross-cultural perspective), an increase in the speed of memory processing and memory capacity (Kail and Park 1994), and the emergence of *metamemory,* or the ability to think about one's own memory processes (Schneider and Pressley 1997).

In addition to the two-sidedness of thought and more powerful memory abilities, there is another important milestone in children's cognitive development during the school years. They become aware that the content of their thinking is partly under their conscious control. Children develop *metacognition,* which means "thinking about thinking" (Flavell, Green, and Flavell 1995). The ability to control one's mental processes emerges during the preschool years, but it is only during the school years that control processes become markedly better, especially in regard to intellectual efforts. It is difficult for preschoolers to judge, for example, whether a problem is difficult or easy, whereas children in the school years know how to identify challenging tasks, and how to evaluate their learning progress.

The Influence of Schooling

Schooling during middle childhood is available in every nation. Where it varies considerably is in who receives instructions, in what subjects, and with which teaching techniques. There is some sort of inequality in the distribution of formal schooling in developing countries, so that more boys than girls attend elementary school (58% versus 42%); and in most Western countries, less is generally demanded of poor children and girls, specifically in science and mathematics (Unesco 1997, cited in Berger 2001). There are many ways to assess the cognitive impact of schooling (see Morrison, Griffith, and Alberts 1997 for a review). One of the most interesting lines of evidence for the way in which schooling affects development comes from Robert LeVine and his colleagues, who have studied the impact of schooling on the childrearing practices of parents who have, or have not, gone to

Middle childhood is a developmental stage referred to as the school years. Across cultures, children in this stage show an ability and eagerness to learn. Gender segregation in peer relations becomes virtually complete at this stage. FRANK GRIZZAFFI/TEXAS CATHOLIC HERALD

school (LeVine et al. 1996). This study shows that mothers who had several years of education talked more with their children and used less directive childrearing methods, and most significantly, their children performed better in school and on standardized tests of cognitive development.

Overall, research on cognitive consequences of schooling has produced a mixed picture. A wide variety of studies have led to the conclusion that school experiences improve cognitive performances, by teaching specific information-processing strategies that are relevant primarily to school itself, by increasing children's knowledge base, including ways to use language, and by changing children's overall life situations and attitudes.

On the other hand, there is only minimal support for the idea that schooling is directly responsible for broad changes in the way the mind works (Cole and Cole 2001). Perhaps the most important aspect of schooling is at the social level, so that success in school seems to be an important contributor to children's later economic well-being, at least in literate societies.

Emotional Development

During middle childhood, the child becomes emotionally more flexible and acquires a greater emotional differentiation. Comparing with infants and preschoolers, school-age children's range of emotions becomes more specific, diverse, and sophisticated. Also evident at this time is the child's growing ability to detect and understand the emotions expressed by others. During middle childhood, there is a decline in fears related to body safety (such as sickness and injury) and in the fear of dogs, noises, darkness, and storms. However, there is no significant decline in fears of supernatural forces, such as ghosts and witches. Most of the new fears emerging at this age are related to school and family, in accordance with children's expanding social boundaries. Fears of ridicule by parents, teachers, and friends also increase, as do fears of parental rejection and disapproval. Many school-aged children also report fearing that their parents will die (DeSpelder and Strickland 1992).

One of the skills that appears later in childhood is the ability to *mask* or fake an emotional state. By this time, children understand behaviors prescribed by cultural rules (for example, you are supposed to look happy when you are given a gift even if you do not like it). By the middle school years, children have developed a broad understanding of the social norms and expectations that surround the display of feelings or emotional display rules (Harris 1989).

In summary, emotional development in older children is closely related to advances in cognition that allow children to think in more abstract and complex terms. In addition, it is apparent that the way in which children express and understand emotions can be a major component in their success with social relationships. Children who are popular with their peers know how to deliver positively toned messages to their playmates. Similarly, the emergence of guilt and shame is related to moral development and altruism, two other important aspects of social development.

Self-Concept

The self-perceptions of preschool children are tied to visible concrete characteristics, such as what they look like, whom they play with, rather than to more inner qualities, such as personality traits or basic abilities. During the school-age period, this concrete self-concept gradually shifts toward a more generalized self-definition, to a more abstract categorical self. A five-year-old might describe himself as "smart" or "nice," but a nine-year-old is more likely to say she is "not as good at volleyball as my friends." School-age children's self-concept is less based on external aspects and more focused on stable, internal qualities and, for the first time, they develop a global sense of their own self-worth. They begin to measure themselves in terms of a variety of competencies; they can, for example, realize that they are weak at playing a musical instrument, talented at playing sports, or basically good at making friends. This increased self-understanding brings automatically self-criticism and self-worth. According to Susan Harter (1999), the child experiences some degree of discrepancy between what he or she would like to be (or thinks he or she ought to be) and what he or she thinks he or she is. When that discrepancy is high, the child's self-esteem will be much lower, and vice versa.

A school-age child often abandons the imagery, rosy self-evaluation that he or she had during early childhood, and is more able to evaluate him- or herself through social comparison. They also are more sensitive to how parents, teachers and peers look at their actual behavior (Grolnick, Deci, and Ryan 1997; Pomerantz et al. 1995).

Social Development

One of the most important shifts in children's social development in the years of middle childhood is the increasing centrality of the peer group. In this period of life children prefer to play with other kids, and playing (along with watching television) takes up virtually all their free time (Timmer, Eccles, and O'Brien 1985). Shared play interests continue to form the major basis of these school-age peer relationships. Furthermore, children of this age define play groups in terms of common activities, rather than in terms of common attitudes or values (see O'Brien and Bierman 1988). The rise of the peer group as a major context for development seems to be a rather general characteristic of middle childhood. For the first time, children must define their status within a group of relative equals without the intervention of adults. In many cultures, interactions with peers become coordinated with games governed by rules serving as surrogates for adult control. The experience of negotiating these interactions and comparing themselves with peers contributes to children's mastery of the social conventions and moral rules that regulate their communities. Peer interactions also provide crucial contexts within which children arrive at a new, more complex and global sense of themselves (Cole and Cole 2001).

Another important feature of social development at this age is the emergence of *gender segregation,* that is, children's tendency to play with peers of the same sex, so that boys play with boys and girls play with girls, each in their own areas and at their own kinds of games. They avoid interacting with one another and show strong preference for their own gender and negative stereotyping of the opposite gender (Powlishta 1995). An interesting study by Eleanor Maccoby and Carol Jaklin (1987) showed that given a forced choice between playing with a child of the opposite gender or a child of a different race, elementary school-age children will make the cross-race choice rather than the cross-gender choice. Gender segregation in the elementary school seems also to be a universal pattern of peer-group interactions that occurs in every culture in the world (Archer 1992).

During middle childhood, children's concepts of friendship also become more complex and psychologically based. Friendship is no longer simply a matter of engaging in the same activities, but is a relationship based on mutual trust and assistance, in which children like each other's personal qualities and respond to one another's needs and desires. As a consequence, events that break up a friendship are different than they were during the preschool years. School-age children regard violations of trust, such as not helping when others need help, breaking promises, and gossiping behind the other's back as serious breaches of the friendship.

Family Influences

Parent-child relationships. The fact that children now attend school, have greater interaction with their peers, and display heightened levels of independence places the family in a new perspective. School children continue to use their parents as a safe base, they continue to rely on their presence, support, and affection (Buhrmester 1992), and they continue to be strongly influenced by their parents' judgments. What does change is the agenda of issues between parents and children. Parents no longer act as if their children are adorable; school-aged children are expected to behave appropriately and to do regular chores. The children, for their part, are often embarrassed when their parents do show them affection in public, and tend to argue with their parents and point out their parents' inconsistencies or mistakes. In general, they also are more severe and more critical of parents' mistakes than when they were preschoolers.

In many non-Western countries, parents also must now begin to teach children specific tasks, such as agricultural work and care of younger children (or animals), all of which may be necessary for the survival of the family. In these cultures, children of six to seven years are considered intelligent and responsible, and are given almost adult-like roles. In some Polynesian and West African cultures, it is also common for children of this age to be sent out to apprentice with skilled tradespersons or to foster care with relatives (Bee 1998).

Despite cultural variation in the precise age at which the various competencies are expected to be achieved, most parents expect their children to attain competence in activities that contribute to the families' means of subsistence during middle childhood. In economically developed countries, school is a prominent arena in which children's achievement is judged by parents. Parents worry about how involved they should become in their children's schoolwork and other school-related problems. On the other hand, in less economically developed countries, where a family's survival often depends on putting children to work as early as possible, parents worry about their children's ability to take care of younger kin in the absence of adult supervision, and to carry out important economic tasks such as caring for livestock or hoeing weeds (Weisner 1996).

As children grow older, parents try to influence their behavior by reasoning with them, arousing their sense of guilt, or appealing to their self-esteem or to their sense of humor. Maccoby (1984) introduced the term *coregulation* by indicating the share of responsibility between the parents and children over the children's lives. Coregulation is a cooperative process from both sides: Children must be willing to inform their parents of their activities and problems; parents, in turn, must monitor, guide, and support their children, using the time they are together to reinforce their children's understanding of right and wrong. Shared responsibility seems to be a critical ingredient behind healthy family relations. By sharing responsibility, children learn to believe in their capacity to make contributions, to be responsive to other family members' feelings. They also learn to breed other important positive traits, such as affirmation, respect, and trust.

Family support and favorable environment. Children need to experience a favorable climate throughout all of childhood, but this is especially true during the school years. Children need the support of parents as they seek to meet the challenges of this age. Favorable home environments are those capable of providing warmth and acceptance to children. Positive home climates usually employ consistent measures of discipline, encourage social and emotional competence, and are responsive to the child's growing needs. Furthermore, positive home environment encourages learning, develops self-esteem, and provides harmony and stability. Given these qualities, children are apt to become emotionally stable, cooperative, and happy. The rejected child, on the other hand, often becomes withdrawn, resentful, lonely, and insecure (Holcomb and Kashani 1991).

Conclusion

Despite the differences in the lives of Western and non-Western children, there are interesting similarities among children in the school-age period. In many cultures, children in middle childhood develop the cognitive underpinnings of *reciprocity,* learn the beginnings of what Piaget called concrete operations. They also develop individual friendships, segregate their play groups by gender, and acquire some of the basic skills that will be required for adult life. The overall pattern of changes associated with middle childhood seems to be consistent, and thus suggests a distinctive stage of children's life.

See also: CHILDHOOD; DEVELOPMENT: COGNITIVE; DEVELOPMENT: EMOTIONAL; DEVELOPMENT: MORAL; DEVELOPMENT: SELF; OPPOSITIONALITY; SCHOOL; SEPARATION-INDIVIDUATION

Bibliography

Archer, J. (1992). "Childhood Gender Roles: Social Context and Organization." In *Childhood Social Development: Contemporary Perspectives,* ed. H. McGurk. Hove, UK: Lawrence Erlbaum Associates.

Bee, H. (1998). *Lifespan Development.* New York: Longman

Berger, K. S. (2001). *The Developing Person Through the Life Span.* New York: Worth.

Buhrmester, D. (1992). "The Developmental Courses of Siblings and Peers Relationships." In *Children's Siblings Relationships: Developmental and Clinical Issues,* ed. F. Boer and J. Dunn. Hillsdale, NJ: Lawrence Erlbaum Associates.

Cole, M., and Cole, S. (2001). *The Development of Children.* New York: Freeman.

Chi, M. T. H., and Koeske, R. D. (1983). "Network Representation of a Child's Dinosaur Knowledge." *Developmental Psychology* 19:29–39.

Dasen, P. R. (1994). "Culture and Cognitive Development from a Piagetian Perspective." In *Psychology and Culture,* ed. W. J. Lonner and R. S. Malpass. Needham Heights, MA: Allyn and Bacon.

DeSpelder, L., and Strickland, A. L. (1992). *The Last Dance: Encountering Death and Dying,* 3rd edition. Palo Alto, CA: Mayfield.

Flavell, J. H.; Green, F. L.; and Flavell, E. R. (1995). "Young Children's Knowledge about Thinking." *Monographs of the Society for Research in Child Development* 60:1–95.

Grolnick, W. S.; Deci, E. L.; and Ryan, R. M. (1997). "Internalization within the Family: The Self-Determination Theory Perspective." In *Parenting and Children's Internalization of Values: A Handbook of Contemporary Theory,* ed. J. E. Grusec and L. Kuczynski. New York: Wiley.

Harris, P. (1989). *Children and Emotions: The Development of Psychological Understanding.* Oxford: Blackwell.

Harter, S. (1999). *The Construction of the Self: A Developmental Perspective.* New York: Guilford.

Holcomb, W. R., and Kashani, J. H. (1991). "Personality Characteristics of a Community Sample of Adolescents with Conduct Disorders." *Adolescence* 26(103):579–586.

Kail, R., and Park, Y.(1994). "Processing Time, Articulation Time, and Memory Span." *Journal of Experimental Child Psychology* 57:281–291.

LeVine, R. A.; Miller, P.; Richman, A.; and LeVine, S. (1996). "Education and Mother-infant Interaction: A Mexican Case Study." In *Parents' Cultural Belief Systems: Their Origins, Expressions, and Consequences,* ed. S. Harkness and C. Super. New York: Guilford.

Light, P., and Perret-Clermont, A. (1989). "Social Context Effects in Learning and Testing." In *Cognition and Social Worlds,* ed. A. R. H. Gellatly, D. Rogers, and J. Sloboda. Oxford: Clarendon Press.

Maccoby, E. E. (1984). "Middle Childhood in the Context of the Family." In *Development During Middle Childhood: The Years from Six to Twelve,* ed. W. A. Collins. Washington, DC: National Academy Press.

Maccoby, E. E., and Jaklin, C. N. (1987). "Gender Segregation in Childhood." In *Advances in Child Development and Behavior,* Vol. 20, ed. H. W. Reese. Orlando, FL: Academic Press.

Morrison, F. J.; Griffith, E. M.; and Alberts, D. M. (1997). "Nature-Nurture in the Class-Room: Entrance Age, School Readiness, and Learning in Children." *Developmental Psychology* 33:254–262.

O'Brien, S. F., and Bierman, K. L. (1988). "Conceptions and Perceived Influence of Peer Groups: Interviews with Preadolescents and Adolescents." *Child Development* 9:1360–1365.

Piaget, J., and Inhelder, B. (1969). *The Psychology of the Child.* New York: Basic Books.

Pomerantz, E. M.; Ruble, D. N.; Frey, K. S.; and Greulich, F. (1995). "Meeting Goals and Confronting Conflicts: Children's Changing Perceptions of Social Comparisons." *Child Development* 66:723–738.

Powlishta, K. K. (1995). "Intergroup Processes in Childhood: Social Categorization and Sex Role Development." *Developmental Psychology* 31:781–788.

Rogoff, B. (1990). *Apprentice in Thinking: Cognitive Development in Social Context.* New York: Oxford University Press.

Rogoff, B., and Mistry, J. (1990). "The Social and Functional Context of Children's Remembering." In *Knowing and Remembering in Young Children,* ed. R. Fives and J. A. Hudson. New York: Cambridge University Press.

Schneider, W., and Bjorklund, D. F. (1998). "Memory." In *Cognition, Perception, and Language,* Vol. 2: *Handbook of Child Psychology,* 5th edition, ed. D. Kuhn and R. S. Siegler. New York: Wiley.

Schneider, W., and Pressley, M. (1997). *Memory Development between Two and Twenty,* 2nd edition. Mahwah, NJ: Lawrence Erlbaum Associates.

Segall, M. H.; Dasen, P. R.; Berry, J. W.; and Poortinga, Y. H. (1999). *Human Behavior in Global Perspective: An Introduction to Cross-Cultural Psychology,* 2nd edition. New York: Pergamon.

Timmer, S. G.; Eccles, J.; and O'Brien, K. (1985) "How Children Use Time." In *Time, Goods, and Well Being,* ed. F. T. Juster and F. P. Stafford. Ann Arbor, MI: Institute for Social Research.

Weisner, T. S. (1996). "The 5-to-7 Transition as an Ecocultural Project." In *Reason and Responsibility: The Passage Through Childhood,* ed. A. J. Sameroff and M. M. Haith. Chicago: University of Chicago Press.

M. CUSINATO
M. G. CARELLI

PRESCHOOL

The period from ages two to six is usually called *early childhood,* or the *preschool period.* It is also referred as the *play years,* because the preschool period is considered as the most playful of all. Young children spend most of their time at playing. They play with words and ideas, developing their minds; they invent new games and dramatize fantasies; but they also acquire new social skills and learn moral rules (Berger 2001).

Cognitive Development

Cognitive development enables preschoolers to think in qualitatively different ways than infants or toddlers do. Preschoolers' thinking is more advanced, especially in regard to the refinement and elaboration of concepts. Their thinking becomes more systematic and deliberate, and they do not become discouraged as easily with cognitive challenges, so they become motivated to do tasks at hand.

Moreover, there is an important cognitive advance in this period: a rapid development of a more sophisticated *theory of mind.* The term refers to children's understanding of the mental world—what they think about other people's intentions, thoughts, beliefs, and desires—and the theories they form about how they think (Frye and Moore 1991). Jean Piaget's position on this topic was clear: "The child knows nothing about the nature of thought. . . ." (Piaget 1929, p. 37). Piaget stated that children are not capable of distinguishing between mental and physical entities until the school years. To the child under the age of eight, dreams and mental images are as real as any events in waking, conscious life.

Despite Piaget's claims, research has shown considerable evidence to the contrary. By the age of three, children begin to understand for the first time that others not only think and believe differently from themselves, but that others act on the basis of their beliefs and can even have false beliefs (Lewis and Mitchell 1994). In addition, they understand that thoughts (as well as dreams and memories) are not physical entities. A common interpretation of this achievement is that children begin to think of themselves and others as acting on the basis of representations of the world, in other words, *mental events,* rather than as acting directly on the world. From the age of three, children's ideas about how the mind works are more differentiated, organized, and accurate enough to qualify as a "theory" (Wellman 1990). Older preschoolers know that both beliefs and desires determine actions, and they understand the relationship among these three constructs. Children apparently have well-articulated theories of mind by the time they are ready to enter school.

Children from different cultures including China (Flavell et al. 1983), Japan (Gardner et al. 1988), and the preliterate Baka society of Cameroon (Avis and Harris 1991) show similar developmental changes in their understanding of beliefs. A provocative possibility is that, even if there is a universal pattern in the emergence of the theory of mind (but see also Vinden 1996), this concept may have distinct biological roots. Nevertheless, researchers disagree on the extent to which this early understanding is due to maturation or social experiences common to most young children.

The acquisition of theory of mind has important implications for social development: The child is now able to predict, explain, and influence others' intentions, thoughts, and beliefs. Without a theory of mind children would never be able to understand the social world, just as they cannot make sense of the physical world without a grasp of time, space, and the permanence of objects.

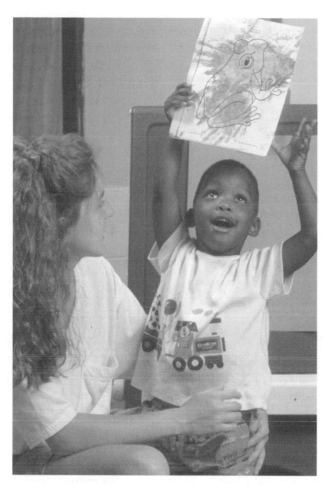

The period from ages two to six is referred to as the play years. *Children in this stage spend most of their time at play—playing with words and ideas as well as developing new games.* TERRY WILD STUDIO

Emotional Development

A process that is linked to the emerging theory of mind and that expands greatly in the preschool years is the child's ability to understand emotions. To become a socioemotionally competent individual, young children must learn to interpret the emotional states of those around them, to be able to modify their own emotions, and to learn how to mask their true emotions when it is necessary. By age four, children's emotional vocabulary has expanded enough that they can recognize facial expressions on other' faces and situations that convey the emotions happy, sad, mad, loving, and scared. Furthermore, preschoolers begin to understand the links between other people's emotions and their circumstances. The preschool-aged child also begins to figure out that particular emotions occur in situations involving specific relationships between desire and reality.

During preschool years, the child also learns to regulate his or her own expression of emotions (Dunn 1994; Saarni 1999). Part of this process is the development of *impulse control,* the growing ability to inhibit a response, to wait rather than to cry, to protest verbally rather than to hit. When an infant is upset, it is the parents who help to regulate that emotion by cuddling or soothing. Over the preschool years, this regulation process is gradually taken over more and more by the child. Two-year-olds are only minimally able to modulate their feelings in this way, but by ages five or six, most children have made great strides in controlling the intensity of their expression of strong feelings. They can avoid or reduce emotionally charged information, for example, by closing their eyes, turning away, and putting their hands over their ears.

Another important aspect of this regulation of emotion is the ability to display emotions in a socially appropriate way. Cross-cultural research has shown (see Thompson 1998) that during early childhood children in different cultures acquire the ability to recognize when people are masking their feelings. Furthermore, learning the social rules of emotional expressions seems to be gender related, in that girls are generally better able to display and recognize a masked emotion than boys. Finally, there is a great cultural variation in the age at which children learn to display emotions appropriately and the conditions under which it is expected. For example, four-year-old girls from India were more sensitive to the need to hide negative emotions than were English girls at the same age (Joshi and MacLean 1994), but English preschoolers show display rules for masking negative emotions earlier than Italian children (Manstead 1995).

Knowledge about emotions can have ramifications for children's social development. For example, children who have substantial knowledge about the emotions that usually accompany given situations (such as fear during a nightmare) are better liked by their peers (Denham et al. 1990). The reason may be that these children are more likely to respond appropriately to the emotional expressions of their age-mates.

Social Development

Peer interaction. Children's peer relationships are an important part of early childhood. In the company of others, youngsters become individuals in their own right, gaining insight into their own personalities, observing what effects their behaviors have on others, and refining their self-concepts through social interactions with peers. Peers, in fact, provide the child with direct feedback about how well she or he is doing in the academic, social, and emotional realms, information that can significantly influence the child's self-esteem. Preschool children have sharp increases in their attachment to peers, and their social relationships become closer, more frequent, and more sustained. It is in this period of age that children start to prefer same-sex peer groups and to choose same-sex best friends.

This tendency persists and intensifies through the years of middle childhood, although it is more pronounced in boys than girls (Berndt and Ladd 1989). Preferences for same-sex interactions or gender segregation have also been confirmed in several cultures (Leaper 1994). As children become older, they are more willing to participate in joint efforts, coordinate their activities more effectively, and often collaborate successfully in solving problems.

Ethnic and racial identity. The preschool period is also the period in which children's ethnic and racial identities emerge. That is, they acquire "an enduring, fundamental aspect of the self that includes a sense of membership in an ethnic group and the attitudes and feelings associated with that membership" (Phinney 1996, p. 922). Already, four-year-olds are aware of group ethnic and racial differences, and they also become aware of their own ethnicity and form judgments about it. Children's attitudes toward their own and other people's ethnicity depend on both the attitudes of their adult caregivers and their understanding of the power and the wealth of their own group in relations to others (see Jackson, McCullough, and Gurin 1997).

Moral Development

Moral understanding in childhood is a rich and diverse phenomenon not completely described by any single theory. When young children are asked to reason about their moral understanding, they display moral judgments that are considerably more advanced than predicted by Jean Piaget's ([1932] 1965) and Lawrence Kohlberg's (1976) theories. Preschoolers even have a beginning grasp of justice in that they distinguish moral rules from social conventions. During early childhood and later

in middle childhood, children's notions of how to divide up resources fairly become more differentiated and adapted to the requirements of situations. Four-year-olds recognize the importance of sharing, but their reasons for doing so often seem contradictory and self-serving. When asked why they gave some of their toys to a playmate, preschoolers typically say something like, "I let her have some, but most are for me because I'm older." Only later, around five or six years of age, do children start to express more mature notions of distributive justice and prosocial behavior, in that children begin to divide rewards according to an equality principle, with all children receiving the same share, whatever their input (Damon 1988; Eisenberg et al. 1991).

Cross-cultural research on moral development in early childhood stresses the importance of the effects of culture beliefs on moral development. For example, the developmental trend in moral thinking that was detected in India was different from the developmental trend detected in the United States (Shweder et al. 1990). With age, Indian children saw more and more issues as matters of universal moral principle, whereas U.S. children saw fewer issues in the same light and more as a matters of arbitrary social convention that can legitimately differ from society to society. Richard Shweder and his colleagues (1990) also questioned whether all children are able to distinguish between moral rules and social-conventional rules from an early age. They argued that the concept of social-conventional rules was simply not meaningful to Indians of any age. The general issue of cultural variations in thinking about moral rules and social convention is still in dispute. The reason might be that most of the relevant cross-cultural data have been collected from adolescents and adults, making it risky to draw conclusions about the role of cultural factors in such reasoning during early and middle childhood.

What kind of parenting could foster the child's moral maturity? Childrearing studies consistently imply that use of *inductive discipline* promotes moral maturity. Inductive discipline is a nonpunitive form of discipline in which an adult explains why a child's behavior is wrong and should be changed by emphasizing its effects on others. On the contrary, *power assertion* (use of superior power to modify the child's behavior) is often associated with moral immaturity. However, Grazyna

Kochanska (1997) proposed that the most effective kind of parenting on foster children's internalization of moral rules depends on the child's temperament (see van Haaften, Wren, and Tellings 1999).

Research has also shown that children themselves prefer inductive discipline to other approaches, and they view this approach as the right way to deal with transgressions, and they may be motivated to accept discipline from an adult whose world view matches their own (Siegal and Cowen 1984).

Language Development

During the preschool period language accomplishments include learning 10,000 words or more. Accounting for how children manage to learn words as quickly and accurately as they do is the main arena where different theoretical orientations clash in the study of lexical development. Proposals consonant with a *nativist view of language development* suggest that children know something about how words work before they learn any words. One counterproposal claims that children can find all the information they need for word learning in the social context in which words are encountered, whereas another argues that ordinary processes of attention and memory explain word learning.

One interesting account for children's word learning is that children make basic assumptions that help them to learn new words (Woodward and Markman 1998). Children do not have to consider all of the many possible meanings each time they hear a new word, but they enter word-learning situations with several assumptions about how the lexicon works. They assume, for example, that words refer to whole objects (rather than to their parts), that each object has only one label, and that a word has several meanings.

Between the ages of three and six, children also show marked growth in their understanding of basic grammatical forms. Once childen begin combining two or more words, they show evidence of syntactic awareness and later, when they master the auxiliary verb, they learn to form negatives, questions, and the use of passive voice.

As the preschool years end, children use most of the grammatical structures of their native language competently. Children of this age, however, often over-regularize, or apply grammatical rules

where they do not fit (e.g., "I knowed him"). Therefore, these kinds of mistakes do not reflect a grammatical defect, but instead indicate that children apply grammatical rules creatively, since they do not hear mature speakers use these over-regularized forms (Marcus et al. 1992).

Compared with toddlers, the pragmatic quality of preschoolers' language is more diverse. Reciprocal turn-taking and a greater range of expressions to convey messages now accompany preschoolers' speech. More complex styles of interaction between speaker and listener are also evident, such as initiating and terminating conversations. Preschoolers also know that when listeners move away they have to raise their voices in order to be heard. All these outpourings indicate that, in addition to their awareness of grammatical rules (and the cognitive capacities to grasp these rules), preschoolers are better at understanding the social implications of language use (Turner and Helms 1995).

Although three-year-olds can be considered language-using human beings, their language development is obviously incomplete. All aspects of language continue to develop during childhood. Moreover, as children begin to acquire the specialized skills they will need to cope with an adult life in their culture, deliberate teaching may begin to play a conspicuous role in language development.

Parent-Child Relationships

Parental socialization. Parents differ along two broad childrearing dimensions: *acceptance/ responsiveness* and *demand/control* (Maccoby and Martin 1983) When considered together, these dimensions yield four patterns of parenting. In general, accepting and demanding (or *authoritative*) parents who appeal to reason in order to enforce their demands tend to raise highly competent, well-adjusted children. Children of less accepting but more demanding (or *authoritarian*) parents and accepting but undemanding (or *permissive*) parents display less favorable developmental outcomes, and children of unaccepting, unresponsive, and undemanding (or *uninvolved*) parents are often deficient in virtually all aspects of psychological functioning (Baumrind 1971).

In recent years, it has become clear that this last style of parenting is the least successful parenting style. Research has demonstrated that by age three, children of uninvolved parents are already relatively high in aggression and such externalizing behaviors as temper tantrums (Miller, Woody-Ramsey, and Aloise 1991). Furthermore, they tend to perform poorly in school later in childhood, and often become hostile, selfish, and rebellious adolescents.

Robert Le Vine (1988) studied childrearing practices in many cultures and proposed that parents follow three major goals. The most important goal for parents is their children's *physical survival.* It is not until the safety and health of their children appear secure that parents can focus on the other two goals: the *economic goal,* to ensure that their children acquire the skills and the other resources needed to be economically productive adults, and the *cultural goal,* to ensure that their children acquire the basic cultural values of the group. In order to achieve these two goals, a family will try to establish stable daily routines that ensure a workable fit between the family's resources and its local ecology. Although these three basic parenting goals are universal and all families seek to create a set of activities to ensure that they are achieved, the manner in which parents go about achieving them vary dramatically, depending on local economic, social, and cultural circumstances.

An interesting example of how differences in family life shape the development of children especially during early childhood comes from the study by David MacPhee, Janet Fritz, and Jan Miller-Heyl (1996). They observe that Hispanic and Native-American parents are more inclined than European-American parents to maintain close ties to a variety of kin and insist that their children display proper, calm, and polite behavior and a strong respect for others, as opposed to independence, competitiveness, and pursuit of individual goals. Asian and Asian-American parents also tend to stress interpersonal harmony and self-discipline, whereas research with African-American families (although it is difficult to summarize the diversity of childrearing practices that characterize this ethnic group) indicates that urban African-American mothers (particularly if they are younger, single, and less educated) demand strict obedience from their children and are inclined to use coercive forms of discipline (Ogbu 1994).

In sum, parents from different cultures, subcultures, and social classes have different values, concerns, and beliefs on life that influence their childrearing practices. Yet, parents from all cultural backgrounds emphasize the characteristics that contribute to success as they know it in their own ecological niches, and it is inappropriate to conclude that one particular style of parenting is somehow better or more competent than all others (Cole and Cole 2001).

See also: CHILDHOOD; DEVELOPMENT: COGNITIVE; DEVELOPMENT: EMOTIONAL; DEVELOPMENT: MORAL; DEVELOPMENT: SELF; OPPOSITIONALITY; PEER INFLUENCE: PLAY; SEPARATION-INDIVIDUATION

Bibliography

Avis, J., and Harris, P. L. (1991). "Belief-Desire Reasoning among Baka Children: Evidence for a Universal Conception of Mind." *Child Development* 62:460–467.

Baumrind, D. (1971). "Current Patterns of Parental Authority." *Developmental Psychology Monographs* 4(1).

Berger, K. (2001). *The Developing Person through the Life Span.* New York: Worth.

Berndt, T. J., and Ladd, G. V. (1989). *Peer Relationships in Child Development.* New York: Wiley.

Cole, M., and Cole, S. (2001). *The Development of Children.* New York: Freeman.

Damon, W. (1988). *The Moral Child.* New York: Free Press.

Denham, S. A.; McKinley, M.; Couchoud, E. A.; and Holt, R. (1990). "Emotional and Behavioral Predictors of Preschool Ratings." *Child Development* 61:1145–1152.

Dunn, J. (1994). "Experience and Understanding of Emotions, Relationships, and Membership in a Particular Culture." In *The Nature of Emotion: The Fundamental Question,* ed. P. Ekman and R. J. Davidson. New York: Oxford University Press.

Eisenberg, N.; Miller, P. A.; Shell, R.; McNalley, C.; and Shea, C. (1991). "Prosocial Development in Adolescence: A Longitudinal Study." *Developmental Psychology* 27:849–857.

Flavell, J. H.; Zhang, X.-D.; Zou, H.; Dong, Q.; and Qi, S. (1983). "A Comparison of the Appearance-Reality Distinction in the People's Republic of China and the United States." *Cognitive Psychology* 15:459–466.

Frye, D., and Moore, C. (1991). *Children's Theory of Mind: Mental States and Social Understanding.* Hillsdale, NJ: Lawrence Erlbaum Associates.

Gardner, D.; Harris, P. L.; Ohomoto, M.; and Hamasaki, T. (1988). "Japanese Children's Understanding of the Distinction Between Real and Apparent Emotion." *International Journal of Behavioral Development* 11:203–218.

Kochanska, G. (1997). "Multiple Pathways to Conscience for Children with Different Temperaments: From Toddlerhood to Age 5." *Developmental Psychology* 33:228–240.

Kohlberg, L. (1976). "Moral Stages and Moralization: The Cognitive Developmental Approach." In *Moral Development and Behavior. Theory, Research and Social Issues,* ed. T. Lickona. New York: Holt.

Jackson, J. S.; McCullough, W. R.; and Gurin, G. (1997). "Family Socialization Environment, and Identity Development in Black Americans." In *Black Families,* 3rd edition, ed. H. P. McAdoo. Thousand Oaks, CA: Sage.

Joshi, M. S., and MacLean, M. (1994). "Indian and English Children's Understanding of the Distinction between Real and Apparent Emotion." *Child Development* 65(5):1372–1384.

Leaper, C., ed. (1994). *Childhood Gender Segregation: Causes and Consequences.* New Directions for Child Development, No. 65. San Francisco: Jossey-Bass.

Le Vine, R. (1988). "Human Parental Care: Universal Goals, Cultural Strategies, Individual Behavior." In *Parental Behavior in Diverse Societies: New Directions for Child Development,* Social and Behavioral Sciences Series, No. 40, ed. R. A. Le Vine; P. M. Miller; and M. M. West. San Francisco: Jossey-Bass.

Lewis, C., and Mitchell, P. (1994). *Children's Early Understanding of Mind: Origins and Development.* Hillsdale, NJ: Lawrence Erlbaum Associates.

Maccoby, E. E., and Martin, J. A. (1983). "Socialization in the Context of the Family: Parent-Child Interaction." In *Handbook of Child Psychology,* Vol. 4: *Socialization, Personality, and Social Development,* ed. E. M. Hetherington. New York: Wiley.

MacPhee, D.; Fritz, J.; and Miller-Heyl, J. (1996). "Ethnic Variations in Personal Social Networks and Parenting." *Child Development* 67:3278–3295.

Manstead, A. S. R. (1995). "Children's Understanding of Emotion." In *Everyday Conceptions of Emotion: An Introduction to the Psychology, Anthropology, and Linguistic of Emotions,* ed. J. A. Russell and J. M. Fernandez-Dols. Boston: Kluwer Academic.

Marcus, G. F.; Pinker, S.; Ullman, M.; Hollander, M.; Rosen, T. J.; and Xu, F. (1992). "Overregularization in Language Acquisition." Monographs for the Society for Research in Child Development, No. 57(4).

Miller, P. H.; Woody-Ramsey, J.; and Aloise, P. A. (1991). "The Role of Strategy Effortfulness in Strategy Effectiveness." *Developmental Psychology* 27:738–745.

Ogbu, J. U. (1994). "From Cultural Differences to Differences in Cultural Frames of Reference." In *Cross-Cultural Roots of Minority Child Development,* ed. P. M. Greenfield and R. R. Cocking. Hillsdale, NJ: Lawrence Erlbaum Associates.

Phinney, J. S. (1996). "When We Talk About American Ethnic Groups, What Do We Mean?" *American Psychologist* 51(9):918–927.

Piaget, J. (1929). *The Child's Conception of the World.* London: Routledge and Kegan Paul.

Piaget, J. ([1932] 1965). *The Moral Judgment of the Child.* Reprint, New York: Free Press.

Saarni, C. (1999). *The Development of Emotional Competence.* New York: Guilford Press.

Shweder, R. A.; Mahapatra, M.; and Miller, J. G. (1990). "Culture and Moral Development." In *Cultural Psychology. Essays on Comparative Human Development,* ed. J. W. Stigler, R. A. Shweder, and G. Herdt. Cambridge: Cambridge University Press.

Siegal, M., and Cowen, J. (1984). "Appraisals of Intervention: The Mother's versus the Culprit's Behavior as Determinants of Children's Evaluations of Discipline Techniques." *Child Development* 55:1760–1766.

Thompson, R. A. (1998). "Early Sociopersonality Development." In *Handbook of Child Psychology,* 5th edition, Vol. 3: *Social, Emotional, and Personality Development,* ed. N. Eisenberg. New York: Wiley.

Turner, J. S., and Helms, D. B. (1995). *Lifespan Development.* Orlando, FL: Harcourt Brace.

van Haaften, W.; Wren, T.; and Tellings, A., eds. (1999). *Moral Sensibilities and Education,* Vol. 1: *The Preschool Child.* London: Concorde Publishing.

Vinden, P. (1996). "Junín Quechua Children's Understanding of Mind." *Child Development* 67:1707–1716.

Wellman, H. (1990). *Children's Theories of Mind.* Cambridge, MA: MIT Press.

Woodward, A. L., and Markman, E. M. (1998). "Early Word Learning." In *Handbook of Child Psychology,* 5th edition, Vol. 2: *Cognition, Perception, and Language,* ed. W. Damon, D. Kuhn, and R. S. Siegler. New York: Wiley.

M. G. CARELLI
M. CUSINATO

TODDLERHOOD

During the second and the third year of life the child makes a slow but important shift from a dependent infant to an independent individual. The toddler can move around easily, communicate more clearly, and has a sense of identity as a separate person with specific characteristics. The child can also interact more fully and successfully with playmates, be empathic toward other people, and show early signs of moral development. However, increased independence and newfound skills are not accompanied by impulse control. Toddlerhood is the period of the *terrible twos*. That is, the no-saying, newly oppositional toddlers now want to do things for themselves. Parents experience many conflicts with children at this age because they must limit the child, not only to teach impulse control, but also for the child's own survival (Bee 1998).

Cognitive Development

In their second year toddlers find new ways to achieve their goals, first by actively experimenting with objects and actions, and then by manipulating mental images of objects and behaviors. They can pretend, remember what they did days before, and repeat the same action.

In Jean Piaget's terms (Piaget and Inhelder 1969), after the child has completed the sensorimotor stage and acquired the symbolic function (i.e., the capability to mentally represent reality), he or she steps into a qualitatively different phase of cognitive development, called the preoperational stage (two to six years). The child's cognitive adaptation is faster, more efficient, mobile, and socially sharable. The transition from the sensorimotor to the pre-operational period brings problems as well as advances. Piaget concluded that children of this age are egocentric (self-centered) and captured by appearances. Subsequent research suggests, however, that toddlers (and preschoolers) are less egocentric than Piaget originally thought, but have problems in distinguishing between appearance and reality. Research on children's ability to take others' perspectives shows that even two or three-year-olds can understand that other people experience things differently from them. For example, they can adapt speech or play to the demands of their companions. They play differently with older or younger playmates and they talk differently to younger or handicapped children.

John Flavell and his collaborators (Flavell et al. 1992) examined children's understanding of appearance and reality by presenting objects under colored lights to disguise their original colors or putting masks on animals to make them look like other animals. Their main finding was that two- and three-year-olds consistently judge things by their appearances. More broadly, toddlers show a form of logic that Piaget considered impossible at this stage, but still they do not experience the world with so general a set of rules as older children do. Their thinking is often dictated by their own views rather than by reality.

During toddlerhood the child's representational capacity is transformed in symbolic play activities. By the age of two, children invent new uses of objects: A cup can become a hat, a ball can represent a piece of food. Children are now capable of symbolism; they can either create or accept an arbitrary relationship between an object and an idea. This is probably a uniquely human quality. Animals have not been observed to engage in pretend play without prior training (Newcombe 1996).

An important change occurs late in the second year, during which children begin to replace themselves with toys as the active agents in play. They may put a telephone beside a doll's head rather than their own. Between twenty-four and thirty-six months children begin to engage in cooperative social pretend play, such as bus driver versus passenger, store owner versus customer. Nevertheless, toddlers still do not play games with rules and their play episodes last only a few minutes.

Early Self-Awareness

During toddlerhood children make important steps toward self-recognition. Between eighteen and twenty-four months children begin to express self-awareness, a capacity to perceive their own characteristics, states, and abilities. Research with mirrors, videotapes, and photographs indicates reliable self-recognition by about the age of two. Early signs of self-awareness can be observed in other behaviors as well, such as the determined rejection of help and insistence on doing things for himself or herself, or in the new attitude the child takes toward toys ("mine"). Much of the famous *terrible twos* can be understood as an outgrowth of self-awareness.

One important characteristic of toddlers' self-concept is the tendency to focus on his or her own visible characteristics rather than on more enduring inner qualities. This pattern parallels with cognitive

Children reach toddlerhood around the second and the third year of life. At this stage they are no longer dependent infants but independent individuals. Toddlers can move around easily and communicate more clearly; however, they are not yet in control of their impulses and must have limits set by their parents. WALTER HODGES/CORBIS

development in that children's attention tends to be focused on the external appearance of objects rather than on their enduring properties.

The development of self-awareness has important consequences on children's emotional and social development. A toddler is now able to experience self-conscious emotions, such as embarrassment, and becomes more socially skilled, more outgoing, and better able to cooperate with a playmate in order to achieve a shared goal (Brownell and Carriger 1990).

Empathy and Moral Sense

Another important consequence of the beginning of self-awareness is the emergence of *empathy,* that is, the ability to infer the emotional state of another person. Toward the end of the second year toddlers show an increased tendency to hug or kiss someone who has been hurt, or to give a victim a toy or food (Zahn-Waxler and Radke-Yarrow 1990).

Around the second birthday children begin to evaluate actions and events as good or bad. They are amused by violations of adult rules and by events that will provoke disgust or disapproval in others (e.g., refusing to get dressed or eating on the floor).

The age at which this appreciation of right and wrong behavior appears seems to be similar in children from different cultures and families. Several studies have found that even three-year-olds from a variety of cultures can distinguish among *moral, social,* and *personal rules* (Turiel 1998). For example, they respond differently to violations of moral rules (e.g., hurting another child), of social conventions (e.g., wearing pajamas to school), or of personal rules (e.g., forgetting to thank someone for a gift).

There are cultural variations in the boundaries between moral and conventional rules, as well as differences within a culture on what might be considered as conventional behavior and what is a matter of personal choice. It will take children many years to acquire their respective cultures'

In their second year toddlers can pretend, remember what they did days before, and repeat the same action. They also start to replace themselves with toys as the active agent in play. REFLECTION PHOTOLIBRARY/CORBIS

normative separation and deciding in which situations certain rules should be applied (for a review, see Eckensberger and Zimba 1997).

Language Development

In the middle of their second year children's speaking vocabulary is about fifty words and they begin to express simple relations between words or concepts. In English these relations are generally communicated by word order: The sentence "Simon hit Sofia" means something quite different from "Sofia hit Simon." Thus, children acquiring languages that emphasize word order begin to express relations by putting words together in the correct order. The development of two-word sentences is followed by the emergence of short telegraphic sentences consisting mainly of nouns and verbs. They resemble a telegram, but despite grammatical omissions of articles, the words necessary to give the sentence meaning are included.

Besides, there are other important linguistic gains. The average vocabulary of a three-year-old is nearly 900 words and children's knowledge of syntax, semantics, and word meanings increases daily as they use language more and more as a vehicle to express their thoughts and feelings (Warren and McCloskey 1997). By the age of three, the pragmatic aspects of language (its use in social situations) improve, and toddlers become more effective participants in conversations, more skilled at adapting their verbalizations to the response of those around them, and begin to take into account the listener's needs. For example, children as young as two and a half years show that they can take the listener into account by modifying what they say to include information important to the listener. They also use simpler language when they talk to younger children than when they talk to adults, showing they are aware that younger children's language ability is more primitive than their own (Tomasello and Mannle 1995; see also Hoff 2001).

Emotional Development

During toddlerhood children's emerging linguistic skills and their cognitive growth affect the way in which they express emotions. Children can now not only communicate their feelings by verbalizing but also discuss the conditions causing a specific emotion and the actions that followed as a consequence. They can express new complex emotions, such as pride, shame, guilt, and more varied forms of joy and fear. By the age of two many children begin to show emotions that reflect a more complex understanding of social relationships. Guilt, shame, and envy are emotions that require understanding of another person's perspective and also consciousness about the self and one's relations to others. Toddlers also show visible signs of jealousy. The child might hit a sibling that a parent has just kissed or wedge herself between mother and father when they are hugging. As the child's cognitive capabilities, moral awareness, and social understanding grow, he can express more complex emotions and more elaborate and controlled forms of the basic emotions.

Cultural Influences on Children's Development

According to Piaget, cognitive structures undergo generalized transformations as children mature and acquire experience. By contrast, the *cultural-context view* (Cole and Cole 2001; Rogoff 1990; Laboratory of Comparative Human Cognition 1983) has children developing context-specific abilities that are tied to the content and structure of events in which they participate. Parents have a powerful role in the cultural-context approach because they select and shape the environments in which children grow up through their own cultural beliefs, ways of earning a living, and social traditions.

Barbara Rogoff (1990) refers to *guided participation* to describe the ways adults and children collaborate in routine problem-solving activities with the adult at first directing the learning experience and then gradually transferring control and responsibility to the child. Through guided participation children receive help in adapting their understanding to new situations, in structuring their problem-solving attempts, and eventually in achieving mastery.

According to the cultural-context view, development during early childhood is uneven. The content and structure of new events in which young children participate will depend on the contexts provided by their culture and on the roles they are expected to play within those contexts. Cultures seem to influence the unevenness of children's development in some important ways (Feldman 1994). Examples of this include emphasizing activities that promote widely held cultural values, regulating the difficulty of the child's role, and arranging the occurrence and nonoccurrence of specific activities. A three-year-old growing up among the Bushmen of the Kalahari Desert is unlikely to learn about taking baths or pouring water into a glass; a child growing up in Paris is unlikely to be skilled at tracking animals or finding water-bearing roots in the desert.

Another important way in which culture affects development is by determining the frequency of basic activities. Children growing up in a Mexican village famous for its pottery may work with clay every day, whereas children living in a nearby town known for its weaving may rarely encounter clay. Likewise, children in Bali may be skilled dancers by the age of four and Swedish children are likely to become good skiers. In each case adults arrange for children to practice activities that often promote the values of the community. The study of these values reveals important information about the kinds of adult skills and knowledge that children will acquire.

Parent-Child Relationships

Attachment. By the end of the second year, the process of attachment goes through the phase of a *reciprocal relationship formation*. Rapid growth in representation and language permits toddlers to understand some factors that influence their parents' coming and going and to predict their return.

As a result, separation protests decline. Now children start to negotiate with the caregivers, using requests and persuasion to alter their goals, rather than crawling after and clinging to them.

A variety of factors affect the development of attachment. Infants deprived of affectional ties with one or more adults show lasting emotional and social problems. Sensitive responsive caregiving promotes secure attachment, whereas insensitive caregiving is linked to attachment insecurity. Even temperamentally irritable and fearful infants are likely to become securely attached if parents adapt their caregiving to the babies' needs. Some family conditions, including stress, instability, and parents' own history of attachment experiences influence the security of the infant-caregiver bond (Berk 1994).

Family environment. The growth of self-awareness, symbolic ability, and sense of morality in the second and third year might seem to be clearly valuable developments. Nevertheless, for many parents of toddlers the changes of these years make this special period of children's life into the aforementioned *terrible twos*. In fact, as infants develop into children with definite ideas and values of their own, these desires increasingly conflict with those of the adults around them and can lead to problems in caretaking. Areas of potential conflicts at this age can be toilet training (with great cross-cultural variation in when it is considered appropriate), standards of cleanliness, violations of daily routines (times to go bed), or limitation of aggressiveness. Parents, however, cannot simply wait for their children to mature, but they must care for their toddlers every day to protect them from physical harm and foster in them a sense of responsibility and morality, while at the same time not inhibiting their developing autonomy.

Effective caregiving and beneficial ways of socializing toddlers can be obtained by being sensitive to their behaviors and needs; by serving as warm models and reinforcing children's mature behavior; by using reasoning, explanation, and inductive discipline to promote morality and self-control; and by attributing children's failures to lack of effort rather than low ability. As children begin to exhibit behavior that parents want to change, parents need to think carefully about what behaviors they want to socialize. Then they can use verbal disapproval and provide reasons for restrictions. The effect of any of these childrearing practices depends, however, on their fit with the sociocultural context in which they occur.

The family's ability to support the child's development in these years is affected not only by the knowledge and the skills parents bring to the process, but also by the amount of outside stress they are experiencing and the quality of support they have in their personal lives (Crockenberg and Litman 1990). In particular, mothers who are experiencing high levels of stress are more likely to be punitive and negative toward their children, with resulting increases in the child's defiant and noncompliant behavior (Webster-Stratton and Hammond 1988). Depressed mothers are also likely to be negative toward their children, as are mothers from poverty-level families, who may well have experienced the same parents' attitude in their own childhood. Thus, toddlers, like children of every age, are affected by broader social forces outside the family as well as by the family interaction itself.

See also: ATTACHMENT: PARENT-CHILD RELATIONSHIPS; CHILDHOOD; DEVELOPMENT: COGNITIVE; DEVELOPMENT: EMOTIONAL; DEVELOPMENT: MORAL; DEVELOPMENT: SELF; FAILURE TO THRIVE; OPPOSITIONALITY; PLAY; SEPARATION-INDIVIDUATION

Bibliography

Bee, H. (1998). *Lifespan Development*. New York: Longman

Berk, L. E. (1994). *Child Development*. Boston: Allyn and Bacon.

Brownell, C. A., and Carriger, M. S. (1990). "Changes in Cooperation and Self/Other Differentiation during the Second Year." *Child Development* 61:1164–1174.

Cole, M. and Cole, S. (2001). *The Development of Children*. New York: Freeman.

Crockenberg, S. B., and Litman, C. (1990). "Autonomy as Competence in 2-Year-Olds: Maternal Correlates of Child Defiance, Compliance, and Self-Assertion." *Developmental Psychology* 26:961–971.

Eckensberger, L., and Zimba, R. (1997). "The Development of Moral Judgment." In *Basic Processes and Human Development*, Vol. 2: *Cross-Cultural Psychology*, ed. J. W. Berry, P. R. Dasen, and T. S. Saraswathi. Boston: Allyn and Bacon.

Feldman, D. H. (1994). *Beyond Universal in Cognitive Development*. Norwood, NJ: Ablex.

Flavell, J. H.; Lindberg, N. A.; Green, F. L.; and Flavell, E. R. (1992). "The Development of Children's Understanding of the Appearance-Reality Distinction between How People Look and What They Are Really Like." *Merrill-Palmer Quarterly* 38:513–524.

Hoff, E. (2001). *Language Development*. Pacific Grove, CA: Brooks/Cole.

Laboratory of Comparative Human Cognition. (1983). "Culture and Cognitive Development." In *History, Theory, and Methods,* Vol. 1: *Handbook of Child Psychology,* ed. P. Mussen. New York: Wiley.

Newcombe, N. (1996). *Child Development: Change over Time*. New York: HarperCollins.

Rogoff, B. (1990). *Apprenticeship in Thinking: Cognitive Development in Social Context*. Oxford: Oxford University Press.

Tomasello, M., and Mannle, S. (1985). "Pragmatics of Siblings Speech to One-Year-Olds." *Child Development* 56:911–917.

Turiel, E. (1998). "The Development of Morality." In *Social, Emotional, and Personality Development,* Vol. 3: *Handbook of Child Psychology,* 5th edition, ed. W. Damon and N. Eisenberg. New York: Wiley.

Warren, A., and McCloskey, L. (1997). "Language in Social Contexts." In *The Development of Language,* ed. B. Gleason. Boston: Allyn and Bacon.

Webster-Stratton, C., and Hammond, M. (1988). "Maternal Depression and Its Relationship to Life Stress, Perceptions of Child Behavior Problems, Parenting Behaviors and Child Conduct Problems." *Journal of Abnormal Child Psychology* 16:299–315.

Zahn-Waxler, C., and Radke-Yarrow, M. (1990). "The Origin of Empathetic Concern." *Motivation and Emotion* 14:107–130.

M. CUSINATO
M. G. CARELLI

CHILDLESSNESS

Childlessness is one aspect of the diversity inherent in contemporary experience of marriage and the family. With this greater diversity, once-common pressures for childbearing have given way to greater social acceptance of remaining single or married without children. Nonetheless, childlessness is a concern, partly because of its implications for the maintenance of societies and partly because of its unwanted consequences for individuals. Rising levels of childlessness are contributing to falling birth rates and strengthening prospects of prolonged population decline in many industrialized countries. For some people, conditions of employment can make it difficult to combine having children with the pursuit of an income or a vocation. A long-term consequence, in later life, is that the childless have fewer resources for family interaction and support.

In industrialized countries, childlessness was more prevalent at the start of the twentieth century than at the end of the twentieth century. It was, however, less conspicuous because it occurred in conjunction with a large family system: That some had four or more children partly offset the childlessness of others, keeping birth rates relatively high. In the present situation, and one reason why the effects of childlessness are now more apparent, is that smaller families are more prevalent, with pronounced preferences for two children; relatively few couples have four or more. Childlessness can now make the difference between maintaining population numbers and precipitating long-term decline.

Trends

Statistics on trends in childlessness over time suggest three main features: high levels of childlessness for women born in the 1900s, declining levels for women born between about 1910 and 1949, followed by an increase among those born after 1950 (Figure 1). The changes reflect the impact of different social circumstances during their reproductive spans. Adding thirty to the birth year indicates the time when a female birth cohort, composed of women born in a given period, would have been in the midst of their potential childbearing years.

The peak figures for women born in the 1900s were related to the effects of the Great Depression on family formation, which led to delays in childbearing that some never made up, especially since World War II followed closely. Although figures varied among countries, 20 to 25 percent childless

were typical peaks from which the subsequent decline in childlessness ensued.

The decline, among women born in the next four decades, reduced the prevalence of childlessness to between 10 and 15 percent, the lowest figures being for women born in the 1940s. The change was associated with economic and social conditions that fostered rises in the proportions marrying and having children, most notably in countries, such as the United States, that experienced protracted baby booms for fifteen or more years after World War II. Thus, the cohorts that became the parents of the baby boom generation had the lowest proportions of childless. The period of the decline in childlessness, like the boom in marriage and childbearing with which it was associated, was exceptional and relatively short-lived.

The childbearing years of the cohorts born between 1910 and 1949 largely preceded the changes that became particularly evident in the 1980s, toward greater social acceptance of family diversity, and weakening social expectations that individuals should marry and become parents (van de Kaa 1987; Lesthaeghe 1998). A return to higher levels of childlessness has been occurring among women born since the start of the 1950s. The trend is commonly associated with lower proportions marrying and with birth rates falling below replacement level, that is, below the level needed to maintain population numbers. Sharp increases in childlessness have been evident in the United States, England and Wales, Australia, Denmark, and Sweden. Some countries, such as France and Italy, have experienced a more delayed revival of childlessness (van de Kaa 1997; Toulemon 1996). Estimates of childlessness for cohorts still in the reproductive ages are necessarily tentative, but social researchers generally agree that the resurgence is an ongoing trend, with figures around 20 percent forecast for cohorts currently of reproductive age (Hakim 2001; Merlo and Rowland in press).

Explanations

The lowest-known proportion childless among ever-married women is less than 3 percent for a Hutterite religious community in North America with virtually universal early marriage of women (Veevers 1972). Low figures occur where a population has high proportions married in their early twenties and does not use family planning or

FIGURE 1

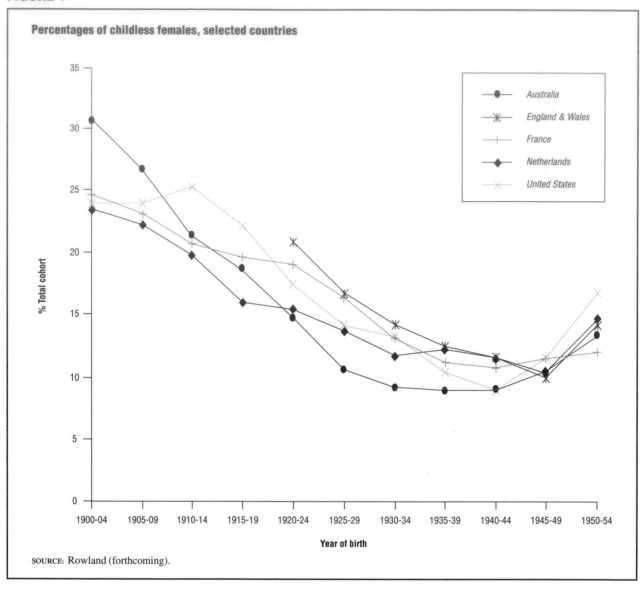

Percentages of childless females, selected countries

Legend:
- Australia
- England & Wales
- France
- Netherlands
- United States

(Y-axis: % Total cohort, 0 to 35)
(X-axis: Year of birth — 1900-04, 1905-09, 1910-14, 1915-19, 1920-24, 1925-29, 1930-34, 1935-39, 1940-44, 1945-49, 1950-54)

SOURCE: Rowland (forthcoming).

abortion to delay the first birth. Conversely, high proportions of childless are related to late marriage, low proportions marrying, and use of birth prevention.

The early peak in childlessness, for women born in the 1900s, was associated particularly with childless marriages, rather than a fall in the proportions marrying. The Great Depression and World War II had more impact on childbearing than on marriage, but couples who postponed having children until better times risked remaining permanently childless if they delayed too long. Staying childless within marriage did not depend on innovations in methods of family limitation, but on early and widespread use of methods already

known. Gigi Santow (1995) considered that *coitus interruptus* was "instrumental" in the trend to lower birth rates in Western countries and that it was in common use in all European countries during the early decades of the twentieth century. Sexual abstinence and abortion were also important, and low coital frequency may have been as well (Santow 1995; Szreter 1995). The passing of the effects of economic depression and war later facilitated a decline in married childlessness to relatively low figures, especially among the cohorts that produced the baby boom after World War II.

Changes in the proportions of people who marry have also shaped trends in childlessness. A major twentieth century development was *the marriage revolution*—a trend toward earlier and more universal marriage in Western societies, associated with a weakening of economic constraints. For example, in France, 11 percent of women born in 1900 had never been married by their fiftieth birthdays, compared with 7 percent of women born in 1940 (Toulemon 1996). A similar fall, to somewhat lower minimum figures, occurred in the United States (Haines 1996). The marriage revolution reduced the proportions of single and childless people and contributed to social expectations, peaking in the 1950s and 1960s, that most people would marry and become parents.

The subsequent resurgence of childlessness occurred in the context of the end of the marriage revolution, bringing a decline in the proportions marrying and a rise in age at marriage. The increasing educational attainments of women reinforced the trend toward delayed marriage, as well as supporting roles and value systems that represent alternatives to motherhood. Later marriage decreases the time during which pregnancy can occur, brings better knowledge of contraception, and strengthens the likelihood of a commitment to a childless lifestyle (de Jong and Sell 1977). Later marriage also increases the likelihood of low fecundity and difficulties in achieving a viable pregnancy. The revival of childlessness was further associated with the availability of more efficient methods of family limitation, especially the contraceptive pill and wider recourse to safe methods of sterilization and abortion.

For cohorts born since the 1950s, the distinction between married and unmarried childlessness has become less clear because consensual unions have attained greater acceptance in many countries, where higher proportions of children have been born outside formal marriages. Some authors perceive a global transformation of the matrimonial system in which relationships are merely the expression of individual choices, without societal regulation or concern.

Social scientists, however, are still debating the relative importance of voluntary and involuntary factors in the upturn in levels of childlessness, although individual self-fulfillment and freedom of choice have been seen as important (Poston and Kramer 1983; Carmichael 1995; Lesthaeghe 1998). In the United States, Dudley Poston and Erin Gotard (1977, p. 212) attributed the early part of the rise in childlessness mainly to voluntary factors "linked to broader changes in the fabric of society regarding fertility control, contraceptive technology, female work preferences and patterns, and sexual and family norms." They saw as a key trend the equalization between the sexes of opportunities for nonfamilial roles. Other commentators, however, consider the workplace insufficiently supportive of women who would like to combine employment and motherhood: equality of opportunity in employment does not necessarily entail adequate support for childbearing and parenting. Others commenting on the rise of childlessness emphasize the long-term consequences of delaying family formation, given that many women do not wish to have a child until they are in their thirties, when the likelihood of fertility problems is greater.

Overall, there has probably always been a mixture of voluntary and involuntary factors in childlessness. It cannot be assumed that in the past marriage and family formation were universally desired, or that in the present, all are able to achieve their particular marital and reproductive goals. Nor is there an absolute distinction between voluntary and involuntary outcomes, especially since childlessness often results from delaying childbearing, rather than from a single decision never to have children (Poston and Trent 1982; Morgan 1991).

In West German opinion polls since 1953, less than 5 percent of women said that they did not want to have children (Schwarz 1986), but this is far fewer than the actual proportions remaining childless. Similar surveys in other European countries mostly found that only 2 to 5 percent of young women did not want any children (Coleman 1996). Respondents may wish to give the appearance of conforming to traditional family norms, but postponements strengthen preferences for a lifestyle without children.

Overall, the rising prevalence of childlessness is one aspect of the diversity of life-cycle experience among people of reproductive age. It arises from a combination of varied phenomena including: the decline of social pressures to marry and bear children, inability to find a partner, lack of interest in finding a partner, insufficient commitment in relationships, concern about the durability of relationships, concern about the prospects for children in insecure environments, financial problems and constraints, difficulties in combining parenting and employment, dislike of children, postponement of childbearing, declining fecundity at older ages of family formation, and pursuit of careers and material consumption.

Consequences

Childlessness has varied consequences through its effects on societies and on the lifestyles and life chances of individuals. The childless lifestyle enhances life satisfaction for some individuals, while diminishing it for others, for whom parenthood was a personal goal. For societies, childlessness is a factor in low birth rates and population decline, with which are associated diminishing labor force entries and rising proportions in older ages. Childlessness is therefore a consideration for policy makers, both because of its demographic impact and because of its effects on the lives of individuals. The latter become most apparent in the older ages, where childlessness means that family resources for support of the disabled or frail are less assured.

Studies of the advantages and disadvantages of childlessness in later life suggest that well-being is not necessarily dependent on children, because the childless can meet their expressive (emotional) needs through greater contact with other relatives, friends, and neighbors, as well as with organizations such as clubs and churches. However, the childless in poor health appear to have a higher risk of social isolation or of admission to aged care institutions (Bachrach 1980; Rowland 1998). This implies that the support networks of the childless elderly are less effective in providing instrumental (practical) support, at least when the need is continuing. Although the majority of the elderly do not necessarily see family care as the best alternative (Rempel 1985), without the prospect of periodic help from children, or their assistance as a last resort, the childless must be more reliant on formal services or institutional care.

Thus, as cohorts with high proportions childless reach the older ages, family-centered approaches to aged care become less effective. In the late twentieth century, many of the aged in industrialized countries had few close relatives, which brought to the fore questions about their access to support. The decline of childlessness among later cohorts is now reducing the prevalence of such problems. However, by the 2020s, similar concerns about the adequacy of personal resources will confront the 1950s cohorts, as childlessness continues to shape their destiny. The proportions childless are unlikely to fall below 10 percent in any of the more developed countries for which data are available. Indeed, Catherine Hakim (2001, p. 51) forecasts "a stable plateau in most rich modern societies" of 20 percent childless.

See also: BIRTH CONTROL: CONTRACEPTIVE METHODS; BIRTH CONTROL: SOCIOCULTURAL AND HISTORICAL ASPECTS; FAMILY PLANNING; FAMILY POLICY; FERTILITY; LATER LIFE FAMILIES; SINGLES/NEVER MARRIED PERSONS

Bibliography

Bachrach, C. A. (1980). "Childlessness and Social Isolation among the Elderly." *Journal of Marriage and the Family* 42:627–637.

Bloom, D. E., and Pebley, A. R. (1982). "Voluntary Childlessness: A Review of the Evidence and Implications." *Population Research and Policy Review* 1(3):203–224.

Carmichael, G. A. (1995). "Consensual Partnering in the More Developed Countries (review article)." *Journal of the Australian Population Association* 12(1):51–86.

Coleman, D., ed. (1996). *Europe's Population in the 1990s.* Oxford, UK: Oxford University Press.

De Jong, G. F., and Sell, R. R. (1977). "Changes in Childlessness in the United States: A Demographic Path Analysis." *Population Studies* 31(1):129–141.

Haines, M. R. (1996). "Long-term Marriage Patterns in the United States from Colonial Times to the Present." *The History of the Family* 1(1):15–39.

Hakim, C. (2001). *Work-Lifestyle Choices in the 21st Century: Preference Theory.* New York: Oxford University Press.

Lesthaeghe, R. (1998). "On Theory Development: Applications to the Study of Family Formation." *Population and Development Review* 24(1):1–14.

May, E. T. (1995). *Barren in the Promised Land: Childless Americans and the Pursuit of Happiness.* New York: Basic Books.

Merlo, R, and Rowland, D. (2000). "The Prevalence of Childlessness in Australia." *People and Places* 8(2):21–32.

Morgan, S. P. (1991). "Late Nineteenth and Early Twentieth-Century Childlessness." *American Journal of Sociology* 97(3):779–807.

Poston, D. L., and Gotard, E. (1977). "Trends in Childlessness in the United States (1919–1975)." *Social Biology* 24(3):212–224.

Poston, D. L., and Kramer, K. B. (1983). "Voluntary and Involuntary Childlessness in the United States (1955–1973)." *Social Biology* 30(3):290–306.

Poston, D. L., and Trent, K. (1982). "International Variability in Childlessness: A Descriptive and Analytical Study." *Journal of Family Issues* 3(4):473–491.

Rempel, J. (1985). "Childless Elderly: What Are They Missing?" *Journal of Marriage and the Family* 47:343–348.

Rowland, D. T. (1998). "Consequences of Childlessness in Later Life." *Australasian Journal on Ageing* 17(1):24–28.

Rowland, D. T. (in press). "Historical Trends in Childlessness." In *Aging Without Children: A Cross-National Handbook on Childlessness in Late Life,* ed. P. A. Dykstra. Westport, CT: Greenwood Press.

Santow, G. (1995). "*Coitus Interruptus* and the Control of Natural Fertility." *Population Studies* 49(1).19–43.

Schwarz, K. (1986). "Childlessness in Germany: Past and Present." In *Lifestyles, Contraception, and Parenthood: Proceedings of a Workshop,* ed. H. Moors and J. Schoorl. The Hague: Netherlands Interdisciplinary Demographic Institute.

Szreter, S. (1996). *Fertility, Class, and Gender in Britain, 1860–1940.* Cambridge, UK: Cambridge University Press.

Toulemon, L. (1996). "Very Few Couples Remain Voluntarily Childless." *Population: An English Selection* 8:1–28.

van de Kaa, D. J. (1987). "Europe's Second Demographic Transition." *Population Bulletin* 42(1):1–59.

Veevers, J. E. (1972). "Factors in the Incidence of Childlessness in Canada: An Analysis of Census Data." *Social Biology* 19:266–274.

D. T. ROWLAND

CHILDREN OF ALCOHOLICS

Children of Alcoholics (COAs) is a general term used to describe individuals with one or more alcoholic parents. Although the ramifications of living with an addicted, alcoholic parent are variable, nearly all children from alcoholic families are at risk for behavioral and emotional difficulties (Christensen and Bilenberg 2000), and live with scars—psychological or physical—as a result of parental alcoholism (Seixas and Youcha 1985). From prenatal influences leading to learning and memory problems (Coles and Platzman 1993) to vulnerabilities in behavioral control and aggression in adulthood (Jacob and Windle 2000), a significant number of COAs exhibit psychological and/or interpersonal difficulties. In fact, COAs can be differentiated from nondistressed and psychiatric comparison groups in regard to such factors as personality characteristics, depressive symptomatology, and educational attainments, as well as patterns of alcohol and drug use (Jacob et al. 1999).

Effects of parental alcoholism, then, unfortunately can lead to untoward psychological effects as well as difficulties with adult relationships. Leon I. Puttler, Robert A. Zucker, Hiram E. Fitzgerald, and C. Raymond Bingham (1998) noted that both male and female COAs are at risk for myriad difficulties. At the same time, developmental trajectories can differ widely, depending upon both the parent's alcoholism as well as individual resilience. As a result, psychiatrists, psychologists, family therapists, and counselors commonly consider an array of family dynamics when examining the effects of parental alcoholism.

Family Dynamics and Developmental Influences

There is no doubt that living in the presence of an alcoholic parent yields negative impacts (Christensen and Bilenberg 2000; Crespi 1990; Steinglass 1987). Parental alcoholism can instill a legacy which affects the development of both individual family members and patterns carried forward from one generation to the next (Rosellini and Worden 1985; Seixas and Youcha 1985). Still, what are the specific developmental implications of living within a family stained by alcoholism?

Developmental implications of an alcohol-focused family. Much of what is known about the developmental implications of growing up within an alcohol-focused family system (i.e., a family adjusting and reacting to an alcoholic parent) comes from research comparing children (and adult children) of alcoholic parents to the children of nonalcoholic parents. The research conclusively indicates that children from alcoholic family systems are more prone to develop life-long psychological and/or behavioral problems than children from nonalcohol-focused family systems (e.g., Black 1981; Crespi 1985, 1990; Jacob et al. 1999; Woititz

1985, 1983). Thus, children of alcoholics are often thought to be casualties of parental drinking, with such generalized problems as impaired school performance, low self-esteem, role confusion, impulsiveness, and depression. In addition, partially as a product of the behavioral consequences associated with living within a dysfunctional alcoholic system, children of alcoholics are at-risk for abuse, eating disorders, conduct disorders, alcoholism, communication problems, relational deficits, and problems with intimacy (Whipple, Fitzgerald, and Zucker 1995; Chassin, Rogosch, and Barrera 1991; Jacob, Krahn, and Leonard 1991; West and Prinz 1987). Moreover, families of alcoholics tend to be less organized, less cohesive, and marked by increased levels of conflict than nonalcoholic families.

The developmental problems resulting from growing up in an alcohol-focused family system are further supported by the longitudinal research on COAs. In a 33-year study of children of alcoholics, for instance, Robert E. Drake and George E. Vaillant (1988) noted that sons of alcoholic fathers were less competent in such tasks as schooling and interpersonal relationships, were more likely to be delinquent, and were more likely to become alcohol dependent than sons of nonalcoholics.

In spite of the fact that much of the extant research has used relatively small comparative samples, the widespread problems associated with familial alcoholism cannot be discounted. Thus, Janet G. Woititz (1983) identifies thirteen long-term after-effects of alcoholic parenting:

(1) Adult children of alcoholics guess at what normal behavior is.

(2) Adult children of alcoholics have difficulty following a project through from beginning to end.

(3) Adult children of alcoholics lie when it would be just as easy to tell the truth.

(4) Adult children of alcoholics judge themselves without mercy.

(5) Adult children of alcoholics have difficulty having fun.

(6) Adult children of alcoholics take themselves very seriously.

(7) Adult children of alcoholics have difficulty with intimate relationships.

(8) Adult children of alcoholics overreact to changes over which they have no control.

(9) Adult children of alcoholics constantly seek approval and affirmation.

(10) Adult children of alcoholics usually feel that they are different from other people.

(11) Adult children of alcoholics are super-responsible or super-irresponsible.

(12) Adult children of alcoholics are extremely loyal, even in the face of evidence that their loyalty is undeserved.

(13) Adult children of alcoholics are impulsive. They tend to lock themselves into a course of action without giving serious consideration to alternative behaviors or possible consequences. This impulsivity leads to confusion, self-loathing, and loss of control over their environment. In addition, they spend an excessive amount of energy cleaning up the mess.

Family dynamics within the alcohol-focused family system. As noted above, the alcohol-focused family system is associated with developmental problems. Although common sense would suggest that parental alcoholism would not be a positive influence, and whereas all children are not impacted equally, there is striking evidence that COAs have felt that their families were not "real" families and that the family environment was adversely impacted by an alcoholic parent (Wilson and Orford 1978). In addition, the research makes it clear that children within alcohol-focused systems often occupy roles that limit their autonomy, flexibility, and overall adjustment.

Building a conceptual framework, Edward M. Scott (1970) identified an assortment of roles often assumed by children of alcoholics. Each of Scott's identified roles reflects unresolved themes that hamper happiness and well-being. Those he categorizes as *babes in the woods,* for instance, retain many childlike and immature emotional reactions throughout adulthood. Likewise, Scott's *bedroom adult* reflects a person who finds adulthood through sexuality, while actually being hampered from psychological maturity and autonomy because of unresolved familial issues stemming from alcoholic influences. Elsewhere, Tony D. Crespi (1990), drawing on a detailed case analysis as a foundational framework, described the concept of *tool children* to illuminate a devastating categorization of roles in COAs, using the conceptualization of children as tools for parental needs. From *sexual magnets* used to gratify inappropriate adult needs to *garbage children* treated as so much discarded garbage, the model of tool children reflects the negative consequences which result when children are used in overly restrictive ways. Unfortunately, a tool that breaks when used inappropriately may be replaced; children cannot.

While different researchers use different terms for different roles, the concept of narrowly restricted behavioral roles is noteworthy for COAs. In effect, children in alcoholic families rarely learn the combinations of roles characteristic of healthy adult personalities and instead become locked into narrow roles based upon what they need to do to survive. Such roles (e.g., Wegschscheder-Cruse 1989) can include *the enabler, the hero, the scapegoat, the lost child,* or *the mascot.* As a result, COAs do not develop flexible behavioral ways of coping with stress and learn to focus on overly narrow ways. As the alcoholic becomes the focus of family adjustment, family members begin to act and react to alcoholic-induced and -effected behavior, rather than reacting in healthy unimpaired ways.

While this only partially captures the complex dynamics of an alcoholic family, it highlights how the developmental adjustment of adulthood is impacted by an alcoholic parent. While the effects of parental alcoholism can vary depending upon a child's developmental stage (Harter 2000), there is growing evidence that parental alcoholism impacts development across the lifespan. A sampling of developmental research conducted on COAs at different ages and stages of development reveals that pre-school and young children have demonstrated behavior problems, vulnerabilities to aggressive and delinquent behavior, and difficulties in such areas as academic achievement and cognitive functioning (Puttler et al. 1998); adolescents have demonstrated negative academic performances in English and math, as well as negative psychological and substance abuse outcomes (McGrath, Watson, and Chassin 1999; West and Prinz 1987); depression has been noted as elevated in college samples (Sher et al. 1991); and increased marital conflict, decreased family cohesion, and role distress has been reported in a middle-aged sample (Domenico and Windle 1993).

Ironically, in spite of individual efforts to separate and reject the family, the legacy of an alcoholic parent can assert influence and control over a wide array of life events, as well as a life course. COAs are at greater risk of possessing psychological and behavioral difficulties. H. Bygholm Christensen and Niels Bilenberg (2000) found that COAs had more than twice the risk as non-COAs for depression and social behavioral disorders and enhanced risk for alcoholism.

Conclusion

In short, dysfunctional alcoholic families have the potential to vividly restrict the individuation process. Extant research underscores the importance for children from alcoholic dysfunctional families to learn strategies for enhancing separateness from parental influences. In other words, children need to be encouraged to accept their parents' illness and to understand that they are not responsible either for the illness or for helping the parents to resolve their personal problems. Only in this way will children be able to constructively individuate from the family, explore their own identity options, and maintain constructive relationships with the parents at the same time.

See also: ACADEMIC ACHIEVEMENT; CHILD ABUSE: PHYSICAL ABUSE AND NEGLECT; CODEPENDENCY; CONDUCT DISORDER; DEPRESSION: ADULTS; DEPRESSION: CHILDREN AND ADOLESCENTS; DEVELOPMENT: COGNITIVE; DEVELOPMENT: EMOTIONAL; DEVELOPMENT: SELF; DEVELOPMENTAL PSYCHOPATHOLOGY; FAMILY DIAGNOSIS/DSM-IV; HEALTH AND FAMILIES; JUVENILE DELINQUENCY; RUNAWAY YOUTHS; SEPARATION-INDIVIDUATION; SUBSTANCE ABUSE

Bibliography

Black, C. (1981). *It Will Never Happen to Me.* New York: Ballantine Books.

Chassin, L.; Rogosch, F.; and Barrera, M. (1991). "Substance Use and Symptomatology Among Adolescent Children of Alcoholics." *Journal of Abnormal Psychology* 100:449–463.

Christensen, H. B., and Bilenberg, N. (2000). "Behavioral and Emotional Problems in Children of Alcoholic Mothers and Fathers." *European Child and Adolescent Psychiatry* 9:219–226.

Coles, C. D., and Platzman, K. A. (1993). "Behavioral Development in Children Prenatally Exposed to Drugs and Alcohol." *International Journal of Addictions* 28:1393–1433.

Crespi, T. D. (1990). *Becoming an Adult Child of an Alcoholic.* Springfield, IL: Charles C. Thomas.

Crespi, T. D. (1995). "Adult Children of Alcoholics: The Family Praxis." *Family Therapy* 22:81–95.

Domenico, D., and Windle, M. (1993). "Intrapersonal and Interpersonal Functioning Among Middle-Aged Female Adult Children of Alcoholics." *Journal of Consulting and Clinical Psychology* 61:659–666.

Drake, R. E., and Vaillant, G. E. (1988). "Predicting Alcoholism and Personality Disorder in a 33-Year Longitudinal Study of Children of Alcoholics." *British Journal of Addition* 83:799–807.

Harter, S. L. (2000). "Psychosocial Adjustment of Adult Children of Alcoholics: A Review of the Recent Empirical Literature." *Clinical Psychology Review* 20:311–337.

Jacob, T.; Krahn, G.; and Leonard, K. (1991). "Parent-Child Interactions in Families with Alcoholic Fathers." *Journal of Consulting and Clinical Psychology* 59:176–181.

Jacob, T., and Windle, M. (2000). "Young Adult Children of Alcoholic, Depressed and Nondistressed Parents." *Journal of Studies on Alcohol* 61:836–844.

Jacob, T.; Windle, M.; Seilhamer, R. A.; and Bost, J. (1999). "Adult Children of Alcoholics: Drinking, Psychiatric, and Psychosocial Status." *Psychology of Addictive Behaviors* 13:3–21.

McGrath, C. E.; Watson, A. L.; and Chassin, L. (1999). "Academic Achievement in Adolescent Children of Alcoholics." *Journal of Studies on Alcohol* 60:18–26.

Puttler, L. I.; Zucker, R. A.; Fitzgerald, H. E.; and Bingham, C. R. (1998). "Behavioral Outcomes Among Children of Alcoholics during the Early and Middle Childhood Years: Familial Subtype Variations." *Alcoholism: Clinical and Experimental Research* 22:1962–1972.

Rosellini, G., and Worden, M. (1985). *Of Course You're Angry.* San Francisco: Harper and Row.

Scott, E. M. (1970). *Struggles in an Alcoholic Family.* Springfield, IL: Charles C. Thomas.

Seixas, J. S., and Youcha, G. (1985). *Children of Alcoholics: A Survivor's Manual.* New York: Crown Publishers.

Sher, K. J.; Walitzer, K. S.; Wood, P. K.; and Brent, E. E. (1991). "Characteristics of Children of Alcoholics: Putative Risk Factors, Substance Use and Abuse, and Psychopathogy." *Journal of Abnormal Psychology* 100:427–448.

Steinglass, P. (1987). *The Alcoholic Family.* New York: Basic Books.

Wegscheider-Cruse, S. (1989). *Another Chance: Hope and Health for the Alcoholic Family.* Palo Alto, CA: Science and Behavior Books.

West, M., and Prinz, R. (1987). "Parental Alcoholism and Childhood Psychopathology." *Psychological Bulletin* 102:204–218.

Whipple, E.; Fitzgerald, H.; and Zucker, R. (1995). "Parent-Child Interactions in Alcoholic and Non-Alcoholic Families." *American Journal of Orthopsychiatry* 65:153–159.

Wilson, C., and Orford, J. (1978). "Children of Alcoholics: Report of a Preliminary Study and Comments on the Literature." *Journal of Studies on Alcohol* 39:121–142.

Woititz, J. G. (1983). *Adult Children of Alcoholics.* Pompano Beach, FL: Health Communications.

Woititz, J. G. (1985). *Struggle for Intimacy.* Pompano Beach, FL: Health Communications.

Ziegler-Driscoll, G. (1979). "The Similarities in Families of Drug Dependents and Alcoholics." In *Family Therapy of Drug and Alcohol Abuse,* ed. E. Kaufman and P. N. Kaufmann. New York: Gardner Press.

TONY D. CRESPI

CHILDREN'S RIGHTS

A country can be judged by countless measures, but for many people the most significant are its treatment of children under eighteen years of age and the legal protection that society affords them. Most people profess to love children: Is this merely an abstraction, or are political and social environments truly child-centered? Are children accorded the rights, dignity, and benefits worthy of their status as citizens and human beings, or does their legal incapacity result in their needless subjection to abuse, exploitation, and other dangers? Does society permit, to the detriment of children, the unrestricted exercise of parental prerogative and the neglect of elected officials who realize that "children don't vote"?

These questions have increasingly been the focus of debate around the world. The *children's rights movement,* begun in the early part of the last century, has been an effort by government organizations, advocacy groups, academics, lawyers, lawmakers, and judges to construct a system of laws and policies that enhance and protect the lives of children.

For some the cause of children's rights has wrongfully been viewed as simply a war of youth liberation or overcoming adult oppression of young people. However, freedom from parental authority, control, and discipline has never been a major theme of serious children's rights advocates. Most groups have focused on child victims of abuse and neglect and how government agencies can better protect them. The most active advocates for children are not engaged in a drive to secure children's independence from adult supervision, but rather are addressing such issues as improving a country's system of enforcing child support obligations, preventing child sexual exploitation, and helping assure that children receive adequate education and health care.

Historical Roots of the Children's Rights Movement

The assumption that children either could or should have rights of any type is a relatively new idea. For most of history children were largely consigned to the status of parental property or chattel (primarily the father's chattel). Absolute parental control of the child, unfettered by the state, was in part a reflection of the agrarian society and the family itself as a work unit. Even where a child became orphaned or was so severely mistreated by parents or guardians that courts sentenced the abusers to prison, the child would often be indentured into the service of a new parent-master. This concept of children having an economic value was often matched with even sterner religious views, in which children were seen as inherently evil and needing a strict, punitive upbringing.

This view of children began to change in the West due to a variety of reasons. First, a more child-centered concept of human rights and family life began to emerge from the European Renaissance in the late fifteenth and early sixteenth century. John Locke (1632–1704) espoused the contractual nature of marriage and wrote of the value of self-determination. In the Enlightenment period in the eighteenth century a strong emphasis was placed

on expression of individual freedom and one's rights. And during the American Revolution sentiments were raised supporting abolition of all types of tyranny, including tyranny of parents over children. All of this set the stage for a new way of thinking about childhood and the rights of children.

With the Industrial Revolution in the nineteenth century, structural changes were made in the nature of work and the family that further affected how children were raised and how their role in the family was construed. For the first time, the spheres of home and work were separated. The family was no longer the main economic unit and the period of childhood socialization was lengthened. During this time there was also a level of children's rights activity unmatched before or since. *Child saving* became a central theme of social reformers who wanted a public policy shift from punishment to education and rehabilitation. Many private, public, and especially progressive religious organizations became involved in efforts to create institutions—orphanages, houses of refuge, and reform schools—for abandoned, destitute, delinquent, wayward, and vagrant youths. Societies for the prevention of cruelty to children were established. The first child labor and compulsory schooling laws were enacted, and just before the turn of the twentieth century, new concepts of child protection were institutionalized.

In all of this there was a divide between those who focused mainly on nurturance and protection of children and those who focused more on children's rights to participation and self-expression. In the traditional *nurturance model*, adults were seen as the main determiners of what is in the best interest of the child. In the more *rights-oriented model*, greater decisional freedom for children was encouraged.

At the heart of this is a debate over the limits of parental authority versus child liberty. Lawrence Wrightsman (1994) suggests that a basic tension still exists between the circumstances in which the state should be permitted to take action for the child against the parents and the idea of the sanctity of family privacy and parental control. Even as late as the early twentieth century most children in the world had no legal status separate from their parents. The view that the best interests of the child were protected by parents was reflected in U.S. law in the early 1900s. For instance, the 1923

U.S. Supreme Court decision in *Meyer* v. *Nebraska* enunciated the fundamental legal right of parents to establish a home and bring up children, including dictating their education. In that case, the Court struck down a state law prohibiting foreign-language education in all primary schools. The Court held that the community's interest in children—resulting in the dictating of educational policy—could not prevail over parents' rights to control their child (and thus the child's education).

In 1967, the U.S. Supreme Court issued a decision that marked a new era in the relationship between children and the legal system. In the case of *In re Gault,* nullifying a juvenile delinquency adjudication and sentence that had been given by a juvenile court in which the affected child was not afforded the right to counsel, the Supreme Court rejected the unrestricted authority of the "benevolent" juvenile court system that permitted children to be incarcerated without the legal protections afforded adults. *Gault* breathed new life into the phrase *children's rights.*

Within a few years writings on children's rights in the United States and around the world began to multiply. One of the most important of these articles was "Children under the Law" (Rodham 1973), which thoroughly explored the implications of legal issues that were then quite new to systems of jurisprudence.

Universal Standards on the Rights of Children

In 1959, the United Nations approved a modest but much-cited ten-point Declaration of the Rights of the Child. In the early 1970s, writers John Holt and Richard Farson both promulgated bills of rights for children, as did New York attorneys Henry Foster and Doris Jonas Freed.

To mark the twentieth anniversary of the UN Declaration of the Rights of the Child, the United Nations proclaimed 1979 the International Year of the Child and embarked on a decade-long project to place into international treaty form the values contained in the declaration. What emerged in 1989, the Convention on the Rights of the Child, is a comprehensive compilation of rights of children—including civil-political, economic-social-cultural, and humanitarian—for all nations of the world to use as a common agreement on the minimum rights that governments should guarantee to children. The Convention represented a turning point in how children are viewed. It shifted the emphasis from simply protecting children and serving their needs to respecting their individual rights. The basic rights outlined in the Convention are presented in Table 1.

Prior to this, there had been more than eighty international legal instruments developed over a sixty-year period that in some way addressed the special status of children. However, the new convention is the ultimate articulation of children's rights in the sense that when nations ratify it they become bound by its provisions. The many articles of the convention stress the importance of actions being in the best interests of the child; recognize the child's evolving capacities; provide protection to the child from abuse, neglect, and exploitation; address the child's civil rights and rights in the juvenile justice system; affect the child's ability to be heard and represented meaningfully in official actions; focus on the child's right to an adequate education, standard of living, health and rehabilitative care, mental health, adoption, and foster care services; place importance on the child's access to diverse intellectual, artistic, and recreational resources; and protect children from involvement in armed conflict.

By 2001, the Convention had been ratified by all but two member nations of the UN, including almost all the world's democracies. The two member states that have not ratified the treaty are Somalia and the United States. In February 1995 the United States signed the Convention and then passed to the Senate Foreign Relations Committee for consideration. Consent for ratification has been delayed in the Senate because of a lengthy legal and constitutional review process and concerns by some over the Convention's social impact. Those opposed to ratification suggested that the Convention would weaken U.S. national and state sovereignty, and would lessen the authority of parents by allowing international bodies such as the UN to dictate how children in the United States should be raised. Roger Levesque (1996) argued that the Convention would be divergent with current U.S. jurisprudence and social policy and would represent a radical new view of children and families. Others asserted that the Convention is sufficiently protective of U.S. federal and state law and that it does emphasize the importance of family authority.

TABLE 1

Rights covered in the UN Convention on the Rights of the Child

Family environment
Rights to live with parents; rights to be reunited if separated from parents; rights to be provided with alternative care if necessary

Basic health and welfare
Rights of disabled children; rights to health and healthcare; rights to social security, rights to childcare; and rights to an adequate standard of living

Education and cultural activities
Rights to education; rights to play; rights to leisure and participation in cultural life and the arts

Civic rights and freedom
Rights to a name and nationality; rights to access to information; rights to freedom of expression, of thought, and of association; right not to be subjected to torture

Special protections
Rights of refugees, rights of children caught in conflict, rights of children in juvenile justice system; rights of children deprived of their liberty or suffering economic, sexual, or other exploitation

---

Although by 2001 the Convention had been officially ratified by 191 nations, at that time few countries had developed concrete plans for its implementation. This has caused some to worry that the Convention will have more symbolic than practical impact. The treaty has spurred the construction of a variety of other children's rights documents around the world. For instance, in 1990 Africa signed the African Charter on the Rights and Welfare of Children. This document covers the same domain of rights as the Convention on the Rights of the Child but adds some specific articles that deal with local African concerns such as protections against child trafficking and prohibitions against apartheid. The African Charter was officially ratified by sixteen African states in 1999. In 1990 the Riyadh Guidelines were also signed. These guidelines emphasize the importance of an active voice for children in decision making. A variety of legal and institutional reforms concerning children's rights have also been put in place since the passage of the Convention in areas as diverse as Sri Lanka, Rwanda, South America, and Europe. For instance, in 1988 Brazil passed the Statute on the Child and Adolescent that promoted children's rights to protection, freedom from harm, and participation in society. In October of 1996, Jamaica and sixteen other countries in the Caribbean areas signed a Commitment to Action to improve national capacities to support children.

Status of Children Worldwide

Despite this progress, there are still many concerns about the status of children worldwide. According to the International Child Saving Alliance and a report by UNICEF, in 1999 650 million children still lived in poverty; 12 million children under age five died every year, many of preventable illnesses; 130 million children, especially girls, had no schooling; 160 million children were malnourished; 250 million children were involved in some type of child labor, often in unsanitary and harsh conditions; and over 300,000 children were estimated to be fighting in armed conflicts throughout the world. Added to this is the fact that, although there has been an increase in global wealth, the gap between the rich and the poor of the world is widening.

These statistics suggest that many children are still not enjoying the rights to basic health and welfare guaranteed in the Convention. Additionally, the Convention has been criticized by some as being culturally narrow and as promoting mainly Western ways of thinking about children and families. For instance, in 1994 Joan Miller asserted that cultures could be divided into those that are primarily rights-based versus those that are more duty-based. In rights-based cultures, individual freedom and personal preference is emphasized whereas in duty-based cultures, which include many Asian societies, fulfilling social obligations to others is more important. Some writers, such as Virginia Murphy-Berman (1996), argue that these types of cultural differences are reflected in variations in how children and families are viewed worldwide. For instance, there are variations worldwide in (1) what is seen as the appropriate distribution of power between parents and children in families, including what type of decision-making voice is allowed to children; (2) the degree to which children are encouraged to act on the basis of individual preference versus adhere to social norms and customs; (3) the scope of duty and responsibility family members have for themselves, their immediate and extended families, and their society; and (4) the importance of individual freedom versus family and group loyalties. Murphy-Berman and others suggest that, because of its emphasis on equality of relationships, individual rights, choice, and freedom of expression, the Convention is Western in tone. Other commentators, such as Gary Melton (1996), assert that the

Convention is culturally inclusive because it protects the child's rights to a "family environment" and not a specific type of family structure.

Issues for the Future

Globalization will bring about powerful new linkages among people and nations through law, technology, the media, and the marketplace. An important question is how these new linkages will affect the lives of families and children across the world. The last decade of the twentieth century witnessed an unprecedented increase in the level of international cooperation around the issue of children's rights. The status of children and their social, intellectual, and physical welfare came to be a topic of great worldwide concern, and calls were raised for the creation of clear universal guidelines to ensure that children's rights were protected around the globe. The challenge is how to draft international documents that create binding standards for children but are sufficiently sensitive to variations in local cultural values and customs. Accommodating cultural diversity within broad global frameworks will continue to challenge decision makers as they struggle to formulate policies that enhance the dignity of children worldwide.

See also: ADOPTION; CHILD ABUSE: PHYSICAL ABUSE AND NEGLECT; CHILD ABUSE: PSYCHOLOGICAL MALTREATMENT; CHILD ABUSE: SEXUAL ABUSE; CHILD CUSTODY; CHILDHOOD; FAMILY LAW; FAMILY POLICY; ORPHANS; SPANKING

Bibliography

Children's Legal Rights. (1993). *CQ Researcher* (April 23):337–360.

International Save the Children's Alliance. (1999). "Children's Rights: Reality or Rhetoric." London: Author.

Levesque, R. J. (1996). "International Children's Rights: Can They Make a Difference in American Family Policy?" *American Psychologist* 51:1251–1256.

Melton, G. B. (1996). "The Child's Right to a Family Environment: Why Children's Rights and Family Values are Compatible." *American Psychologist* 51:1234–1238.

Miller, J. G. (1994). "Cultural Diversity in the Morality of Caring: Individually Oriented versus Duty-Based Moral Codes." *Cross-Cultural Research* 28:3–39.

Murphy-Berman, V.; Levesque, H.; and Berman, J. (1996). "U.N. Convention on the Rights of the Child: A Cross-Cultural View." *American Psychologist* 51:1257–1261.

Rodham, H. (1973). "Children under the Law." *Harvard Educational Review* 43:487–514.

Special Symposium Issue on the Rights of Children. (1993). *Family Law Quarterly* 27.

UNICEF. (2000). *The State of the World's Children*. New York: Author.

Woodhouse, B. B. (1993). "Hatching the Egg: A Child-Centered Perspective on Parents' Rights." *Cardozo Law Review* 14:1747–1865.

Wrightsman, L.; Nietzel, M.; and Fortune, W. (1994). *Psychology and the Legal System*. Pacific Grove, CA: Brooks/Cole.

Cases

Gault. In re 387 U.S. 1 (1967).

Meyer v. *Nebraska* 262 U.S. 390 (1923).

VIRGINIA MURPHY-BERMAN
HOWARD A. DAVIDSON

CHILD SUPPORT

See CHILD CUSTODY; CHILDREN'S RIGHTS; FAMILY LAW; FAMILY POLICY; SINGLE-PARENT FAMILIES.

CHINA

High respect for family is a special feature of Chinese civilization. The family is deemed the basic unit of Chinese society. An individual's actions are mostly geared towards the requirements of the family. This fundamental system has remained for about three thousand years without major change (approximately since the Chou dynasty, 1027–256 B.C.E. to the early twentieth century). Although it has been considered relatively stable, the Chinese family system is not resistant to change. The end of the imperial era in 1911 and the following industrialization and modernization brought about an extensive and dramatic change to this enduring system. Even when, in 1949, civil war separated the Chinese regime into two independent governments (the People's Republic of China under the

Chinese Communist Party and the Republic of China, Taiwan, under the nationalist Kuomintang), the changes in Chinese family continued to take place. Nevertheless, there is a striking continuity over time. Much of the tradition is still apparent in contemporary Chinese society, and especially so in Chinese communities outside the People's Republic of China (PRC).

Regulations of Family Relationships

Confucianism is the dominant philosophy and doctrine of proper ethics and conduct of the Chinese people. It is nearly synonymous with traditional Chinese civilization. Over the centuries, Confucians have developed an ideology and social system designed to realize their conception of the good society, a harmonious and hierarchical social order in which everyone knows and adheres to their proper stations (Stacey 1983). According to Confucianism, the family must first be put in order, and only then can the state be ruled. A well-ordered family is thus the microcosm and the basic unit of sociopolitical order. With the great importance of the family order emphasized by Confucius and his disciples, the relationships among family members are regulated by the pecking order that results from generation, age, and gender.

Generation, age, and gender (beifen-nianling-xingbie) *hierarchy.* Confucianism provides a protocol for proper family life. Therefore, the hierarchy of generation-age-gender defines an individual's status, role, privileges, duties, and liabilities within the family order accordingly. Family members know precisely where they stand in the family by referring to this order: to whom each owes respect and obedience. Position in the family is more important than personal idiosyncrasies: people of the elder generation are superior to those of the younger; within each generation, the elder are normally superior to the younger; men are absolutely superior to women (Baker 1979). Everyone in the family owes obedience to the eldest male because he is superior in generation, age, and gender.

For Chinese, increasing age is accompanied by higher status. Even when it is impossible to increase the material comforts of the aged, there is no denying the respect and deference shown to them. Neither the wealthy nor the poor would abandon the elderly, nor does the thought arise (Levy 1971).

In traditional Chinese culture, the world is created by the interaction of *yin,* meaning tender, passive, inferior, and referring to female, and *yang,* meaning tough, active, superior, and referring to male. Therefore, women were appointed to a dependent status; they were secondary to men (Lang 1968). Surnames, being considered highly important, were passed on through the male lines. Only male children were counted as descent group members and had rights to the family's property. Females were not eligible to inherit the family estate, even their husbands', nor did they have primary position in any single crucial ceremonial role.

Female children were considered a bad economic and emotional investment, particularly in poor families. Their names were seldom proclaimed, for once they were married and became members of the husband's family, they were known by their husbands' surnames or their own surnames prefixed by their husbands'. Throughout their whole lives, Chinese women were expected to conform to *Three Obediences* (*san-tsong*): obedience to their fathers before marriage, to their husbands after marriage, and to their sons after their husbands die.

Although generation is definitely superior to age in hierarchy, it is not always the case that age is superior to gender. The heavy emphasis on male superiority in Chinese society may sometimes override the age consideration. For instance, a younger brother can easily see that he owes obedience to his older brother, yet, he may feel that he is superior to his older sister-in-law because of his gender. As generation-age-gender works to coordinate individuals' rights and obligations in the family, the essence of the order in family is expressed through filial piety that is considered the foundation of all kinds of virtue.

Filial piety (xiao). Filial piety is the basis of order in Chinese family. The father-son relationship is the elementary and the most important one in the family and all other relationships in the family system are regarded as extensions of or supplementary to it. Filial piety refers to the kind of superior-inferior relationship inherent in the father-son relationship. As it often appears, filial piety means children, especially sons, must please, support, and subordinate to their parents (Hsu 1971).

The obligations of children toward their parents are far more emphasized than those of parents toward children. As it is stated in the *Xiao Jing* (Classic of Filial Piety written some three thousand years ago), "the first principle of filial piety is that you dare not injure your body, limbs, hair or skin, which you receive from your parents." This principle establishes how a filial child practices filial piety in its rigorous form. In addition to duty and obedience children owed to their parents, parents' names are taboo since using it is considered a serious offence toward one's parents. To avoid using the name of one's father, a filial child would deliberately mispronounce or miswrite the word, or even refuse an official title that is similar to the name of his father or grandfather in ancient time (Ch'u 1965).

Since the relationship between father and son is indisputably most important, the major duty of a man is, thus, to his parents and only second to the state. With the emphasis on filial piety, a son could even be absolved from responsibility for reporting the infractions of his father in the Imperial China, except in the case of treason. In the mean time, sexual love can also be pressed into the service of filial piety, which is incumbent upon any man to continue his male line. Mencius (a great Chinese philosopher second only to Confucius) said that of the three unfilial acts, failure to produce an heir is the worst. It is so because the whole continuum of ancestors and unborn descendants die with him. Children who die young are considered to have committed an unfilial act by the mere fact of dying before their parents do. They are not qualified as potential ancestors (Freedman 1970).

It is believed in Chinese society that an individual exists by virtue of his ancestors. His descendants, then, exist only through him. To worship an individual's ancestors, thus, manifests the importance of the continuum of descent.

Ancestor worship (ji-zu).   The cult of the ancestors is no mere supernatural cult. It lays stress on those moral aspects of the family that tend towards unity and good order. A young and incapable son is fed, clothed, and housed by his parents. As he grows up, he begins to take the same care of his parents. A parent's death merely alters the form of the duty. The transfer of goods from this world to the next is achieved primarily by burning symbolic paper models. Food, on the other hand, can be offered directly. As the annual Grave-sweeping (*qing-ming*) festival in early April arrives, it is the duty of the living descendants to weed and clean up the grave-sites of the ancestors. The ceremony not only serves to keep family solidarity alive; it also enhances the authority of the family head. In the case of a daughter, the reciprocity is performed to her husband's parents.

It is believed that the ancestor's real power begins when he dies. At that moment, he is transformed into a spirit of powers. The spirit ancestors depend on their descendants for food and a comfortable life after death, in the form of sacrifices. The descendants, meanwhile, need the supernatural support in return for the sacrifices and service (Creel 1937).

Kinship (qing-qi-guan-xi).   Kinship is one of the most important principles of social organization in Chinese society. Almost all interactions among individuals are based on their relationships in the social network built by kinship. The term *"kin"* (*qing-qi*) in Chinese is defined as those relatives for whom one wears mourning. Kin are divided into three groups: paternal relatives, maternal relatives, and the relatives of one's wife. The length of mourning depends on the closeness of relationship and varies from three years for one's father or mother to three months for distant cousins (Lang 1968). Because an orderly relationship of the individual and his kin is of great importance, the Chinese have a very elaborate kinship terminology system to properly address the person with whom they interact. All relatives have their specific titles: father's elder brother (*bo-fu*), second maternal aunt (*er-yi*), third younger paternal uncle's wife (*san-shen*), and so on.

Extensions of the conception of family include the *lineage* (*zong-zu*) and *clan* (*shih-zu*). Same surname, common origins, shared ancestors, and worship of a founding ancestor all are common conditions for the foundation of lineages and clans (Wu 1985). Law and customs insist on mutual help among members of the lineage and the clan. Moreover, the Chinese make a great deal of social organization along the surname line. Surnames, considered very important in the family domain, are always put before personal names.

In Chinese society, a family (*jia*) can be vast yet ambiguous, even extended beyond the scope of the lineage and the clan. Because the family has been proven effective as an organizational force, the adoption of its values and institutions has become attractive in non-kinship situations. "My own people" (*zi-jia-ren*) is thus used to include anyone whom you want to drag into your own circle, and it is used to indicate intimacy with that person. The scope of *zi-jia-ren* can be expanded or contracted according to the specific time and place. Compared with the outsider, *zi-jia-ren* always enjoys favoritism (Fei 1992). This explains why Chinese seek connections in higher places and do things for the sake of relationships. However, responsibility and obligations are also expected according to closeness.

Tradition—Persistence and Transition

Several key features of the Chinese family system according to family life-cycle have existed in Chinese societies for thousands of years. Some of them are still valid in modern Chinese societies, whereas others are changing.

Family structure. The large, complex family has been viewed as the typical form of the Chinese family. In this type of family, parents commonly lived with more than one married son and their families, or two or more married brothers lived with or without their parents in the same unit. However, under the effects of the material conditions, demographic factors, and cultural ideals, the predominant pattern was co-residence of parents with only one married son and his family. That is, *three-generation-stem-family (san-dai-tong-tang)* was generally the traditional, typical, and prevalent form of family (Levy 1971).

However, the nuclear family has become the predominant household composition in both Taiwan and contemporary China, with the effects of industrialization, modernization. In addition, China is also affected by the socioeconomic policies of the Communist Party. The stem family is still common in rural China and in Taiwan. A special temporary form of stem family called *meal rotation (lwen-hwo-tou)* is typical in Taiwan. In meal rotation, married sons take turns providing meals and residence for their parents according to a fixed rotation schedule (Hsieh, 1985). This long lasting family structure facilitates mutual care of the young and the old.

Mate selection. With the influence of Confucianism, romantic love between husband and wife was considered detrimental to the supremacy of filial piety between the parent-son relationships. Courtship, in ancient China, was for men to seek concubines or mistresses; it had no place in conventional marriage. Given the emphasis on family importance, one's future mate was decided by one's parents or grandparents, and not by the young couple themselves. Because marital relations were part of one's filial duty to parents, the choice was more important for parents taking a daughter-in-law to continue the family line and to help out with the household chores than for the son taking a wife (Baker 1979). The arranged marriage could ensure that criteria of strength, skill, and conscientiousness were used in the choice rather than criteria of beauty. Personal affection and free choice based on love were considered not only unnecessary but also harmful. The Chinese believed that real affection grew up in marriage, be it romantic or not. Should personal gratification not exist, the couple was still together to continue the family, not to like each other.

The Chinese also emphasized the importance for decent young people not mingle or fall in love until they were married. However, parents never fully succeeded in keeping boys and girls apart or in eliminating love from their life. Premarital sex was forbidden for both genders, but the rule was more strictly enforced for girls than for boys. Young men's sexual experimentation was more likely with prostitutes or household servant girls (Levy 1971).

Although most parents and the society itself still consider premarital sex unacceptable, boys and girls mingle freely in both Taiwan and China. Attractions between one another are prevalent. Despite the moral prohibition, more and more young people think premarital sex is acceptable especially when two people are in love. However, more young boys than girls believe so. Survey researchers have found that it is not unusual for young people to engage in premarital sex. For example, among college students in Taipei (the capital of Taiwan), 37.5% of male students and 26.7% of female students have had premarital sex (Yen, Lin and Chang 1998). Among university students in Beijing (the capital of China), on the other hand, 15% of males and 13% of females have admitted doing so (Li et al. 1999).

Along with freer association between the two genders and the pursuit of romantic love among the youth, the Civil Code of 1930 proposed by the Kuomintang and the Marriage Law of 1950 and 1980 by the Chinese Communist Party have weakened parental control in mate selection. Young people in Taiwan and China alike are more likely to choose their own mate with parents' approval, or under parental arrangement with the children's consent (Yi and Hsung 1994; Riley 1994). The thousand-year-old parent-run system has been transformed into a joint parent-child system. An increasingly child-run pattern is also quite common.

Marriage. Marrying outside the same surname group was demanded by law as well as the custom in ancient China. The husband-wife relationship was strictly held to be supplementary and subordinate to the parents-son relationship. Love was irrelevant. A filial son would devote everything to his parents at the expense of his marital and other relationships. If there were a quarrel between his wife and his parents, he would have no alternative but to side with his parents, even to the extent of divorcing his wife. Marriage was for the purpose of providing heirs for the family and continuing the father-son line, so the husband/wife tie was not one of affection but of duty. Should affection develop, display of it before other family member was disapproved of socially. No upright man showed signs of intimacy in public, not even with his wife. It was regarded as licentious for female to display their personal charms (Hsu 1971).

Division of labor in the household was primarily based on gender. The men dominated the public sector and work in the fields or elsewhere outside the home. The women occupied the domestic sector, by managing the household and providing service for its members. Regarding decision-making in the household, the husband enjoyed absolute power.

Traditionally, Chinese girls married early—as soon as possible after puberty. Marriage brought about drastic changes in women's lives but not so in men's. Once a woman married, she had to leave her natal home and live with her husband's family. A frequent meeting with members from natal family was improper. The first duties for a woman were to her husband's parents, and secondly was she responsible to her husband. Unfortunately, tension and conflict between mothers- and daughters-in-law was frequent. The power, however, always lay with the mother-in-law due to her superiority of generation and age and the emphasis on filial piety.

Regardless of her hard work for her husband's family, a daughter-in-law was seldom counted as zi-jia-ren, nor could she enjoy favoritism, especially if she had no son. As an outsider, without a son to secure her status, a woman was doomed to powerlessness. The head of the family might demand that his son take a concubine, and the wife could only cooperate (Leslie and Korman 1989).

The Marriage Laws of 1950 and 1980 in China and the revisions of Civil Code in Taiwan have helped to raise the status of Chinese women. The average age at marriage has been rising for both men and women. Once married, women do not change their surnames. They also have full inheritance rights with men. Mandatory formal education and participating in paid labor market altogether increase wives' power to achieve a more egalitarian style of decision-making and domestic division of labor. This phenomenon is more predominant in cities than in rural areas, and is more common in China than in Taiwan.

Despite the significant progress, the persistence of tradition still restricts women to inferior status. Wives' full-time paid employment does not guarantee that their husbands will help with household chores. Many young couples begin their marriages by living with the husband's instead of the wife's parents. The mother-in-law/daughter-in-law relationship remains difficult. Visiting the natal home still frequently causes conflict between these two women (Kung 1999).

Child socialization. The differential treatment of the child on the basis of gender began at birth. The birth of a son was greeted joyfully. Daughters, in contrast, were usually deemed liabilities. They experienced a much greater risk of being sold out to act as servants, concubines, or prostitutes. Infanticide often happened.

The Chinese were tender and affectionate toward small children. Discipline was held to a minimum (Levy 1971). Through story-telling, for example, young children learned to obey their parents and older siblings, and, more importantly, to devote themselves to be filial. At the age of three or four, some restrictions began, as did segregation by gender. Boys were under their fathers' direct supervision. Girls were inducted into women's tasks. Education for girls was considered unnecessary and even harmful.

A daughter was trained for marriage, to be a good wife, nurturing mother, and a diligent daughter-in-law. The best training for marriage was illustrated in the *Four Attributes*—proper virtue, speech, carriage, and work (Mann 1991). Should the daughter turn out to be a poor wife or an unfit daughter-in-law, criticism would be directed to her mother as the person responsible for her training in the domestic arts.

Foot-binding, started from early childhood, also confined women to home and made them safer, less mobile property. In 1902 the Ching empress and in 1912 the president of the Republic of China respectively issued edicts that outlawed footbinding. However, the practice did not end until the end of the Sino-Japanese War, Second (1945) (Gao 1995).

Because of the Family-Planning program in Taiwan and One-Child Policy in China, respectively, far fewer children are born in contemporary Chinese families. Daughters are cherished as are sons. Gender segregation no longer exists. Daughters can also enjoy equal rights, but sons are still preferred particularly in the rural areas. Female infanticide still happens occasionally and even has increased in China since the One-Child Policy era began in the 1970s and 1980s.

Extensive school attendance and nonfamily employment have set the youth free from absolute parental authority and much family responsibility. Teenage subcultures have emerged as well. Although the relationship between parents and children has become a more equal and relaxed one, Chinese parents still emphasize training and discipline in addition to care taking (Chao 1994).

Divorce and remarriage. Divorce in imperial China was very rare. Husbands could initiate a divorce on any one of the following seven grounds: (1) failing to have a son, (2) adultery, (3) disobedience to parents-in-law, (4) gossiping, (5) theft, (6) jealousy and ill-will, or (7) incurable disease. These are so called *Seven Outs* (*qi-chu*). Divorce also happened by mutual agreement, but actually required the consent of the heads of the families. Finally, divorce could be initiated by order of the authorities. In each case the welfare of the family was emphasized, not the interests of the couple (Lang 1968). Marriage was infrequently dissolved on the wife's initiative. The poor could not afford divorce and remarriage. The wealthy regarded it as shameful; the taking of concubines thus became a common alternative.

The Chinese considered it sad and tragic for women to be divorced and frowned upon them. They were not entitled to inherit any property, nor

Shoes for bound feet shown next to a coffee cup for size comparison. Foot-binding confined women to home and made them safer, less mobile property. HSIANG-MING KUNG

would other families consider them suitable marriage prospects. They could only go back to their families, but their repudiation brought shame on themselves and their families as well. Their alternatives were suicide, begging, prostitution or becoming nuns.

Revisions of the marriage laws in both Taiwan and China alike grant modern Chinese women equal rights on divorce, child custody, and remarriage. Most divorces nowadays result from mutual consent or from insistence by either party, although for women to be divorced due to failure to produce a son still happens occasioinally. The divorce rates in Chinese societies have been increasing (Thornton and Lin 1994). Although marriage laws have been changed, divorced women are still more discriminated against than are divorced men. For example, the court may appoint a guardian in the interest of the children; and court rulings generally favor the father.

Old age and widowhood. The elderly, as the closest living contacts with ancestors, traditionally received humble respect and esteem from younger family members and had first claim on the family's resources. This was the most secure and comfortable period for men and women alike. Filial piety ensured that the old father still preserved the privilege of venting his anger upon any member of the family, even though his authority in the fields might lessen as he aged. His wife, having produced a male heir, was partner to her husband rather than an outsider in maintaining the family. If not pleased, she had the authority to ask her son to divorce his wife. However, due to her gender, her power was never as complete as her husband's.

The life of widows in traditional China was no less miserable than that of divorced women. Although widowers could remarry without restraint, the pressure of public opinion ever since Sung dynasty (A.D. 960–1279) prevented widows from remarrying. The remarriage of widows was discouraged, and their husbands' families could actually block a remarriage. Nor could the widow take property with her into a remarriage. The only way a widow could retain a position of honor was to stay as the elderly mother in her late husband's home. This way, her family could procure an honorific arch after her death (Yao 1983). A widow's well-being was less valuable than the family's fame.

The decline in fertility and increase in life expectancy both contribute to the growth in the aging population for Taiwan and China. Modern industrial life has weakened the superior status of the aged. The power of filial norms that call for children to live with their elderly parents has declined (Yeh 1997, Xiao 1999). Many aged persons are in danger of being left without financial support. The situation is even worse for aged women because they experience double jeopardy on age and gender grounds. Those elderly parents who still live with their adult son usually have to help with house keeping, child caring, and they sometimes suffer from the grimaces of the younger generation. Elderly abuse is no longer a rare phenomenon. Regardless of revisions of the inheritance laws that guarantee the inheritance rights of widows as well as the elimination of the value of widowhood chastity, remarriage for widows, especially those with grown children, continues to be considered disgraceful. In fact, widowed as well as divorced women in Taiwan experience the highest distress level compared with men and women across all marital statuses (Kung 1997).

See also: ANCESTOR WORSHIP; ASIAN-AMERICAN FAMILIES; BUDDHISM; CONFUCIANISM; ETHNIC VARIATION/ETHNICITY

Bibliography

Baker, H. (1979). *Chinese Family and Kinship.* London, UK: Macmillan Press Ltd.

Chao, R. K. (1994). "Beyond Parental Control and Authoritarian Parenting Style: Understanding Chinese Parenting Through the Cultural Notion of Training." *Child Development* 65:1111–1119.

Ch'u, T. T. (1965). *Law and Society in Traditional China.* Paris: Mouton.

Creel, H. G. (1937). *The Birth of China: a Sudy of the Formative Period of Chinese Civilization.* New York: F. Ungar Pub. Co.

Fei , X. T. (1992). *From The Soil* (G. G. Hamilton & Z. Wang Trans.). Berkeley, CA: University of California. Press (original work, *Xiangtu Zhongguo,* published 1947).

Freedman, M. (1970). "Ritual Aspects of Chinese Kinship and Marriage." In *Family and Kinship in Chinese Society,* ed. M. Freedman. Stanford, CA: Stanford University Press.

Gao, H.X. (1995). *The History of Footbinding.* Shanghai, China: Shanghai Wen-Yi Publishing Company (in Chinese).

Hsieh, J. C. (1985). "Meal Rotation." In *The Chinese Family and Its Ritual Behavior,* ed. J. C. Hsieh and Y. C. Chuang. Taipei, Taiwan: Institution of Ethnology, Academia Sinica.

Hsu, F. L. K. (1971). *Under the Ancestors' Shadow: Kinship, Personality, and Social Mobility in China.* Stanford, CA.: Stanford University Press.

Kung, H. M. (1997). "The Effect of Gender, Marriage, and Family on Psychological Distress: A Case Study of Taiwan's Changing Society." In *Taiwanese Society in 1990s: Taiwan Social Change Survey Symposium Series II,* ed. L.Y. Chang, Y.H. Lu, and F.C. Wang. Taipei, Taiwan: Academia Sinica.

Kung, H. M. (1999). "Intergenerational Interaction between Mothers- and Daughters-in-law: A Qualitative Study." *Research in Applied Psychology* 4:57–96 (in Chinese).

Lang, O. (1968). *Chinese Family and Society.* Hamden: Archon Books.

Leslie, G.R and S. K. Korman (1989). *The Family In Social Context,* 7th edition. New York: Oxford University Press.

Levy, M. J., Jr. (1971). *The Family Revolution in Modern China.* New York: Octagon Books.

Li, A., L. Li, Y. Zhang, and A. Wang (1999). " A Survey on STDs/AIDS Knowledge, Perception and Sexual Behavior Among University Students in Beijing." *China Public Health* V. 15, No. 6:545–546 (in Chinese).

Mann, S. (1991). "Grooming a Daughter for Marriage: Brides and Wives in the Mid-Ch'ing Period." In *Marriage and Inequality in Chinese Society,* ed. R. S. Watson and P. B. Ebrey. CA: University of California Press.

Riley, N. E. (1994). "Interwoven Lives: Parents, Marriage, and Guanxi in China." *Journal of Marriage and the Family* 56:791–803.

Stacey, J. (1983). *Patriarchy and Socialist Revolution in China.* CA: University of California Press.

Thornton, A. and H. S. Lin (1994). *Social Change and the Family in Taiwan*. Chicago: The University of Chicago Press.

Wu, David Y. H. (1985). "The Conditions of Development and Decline of Chinese Lineages and the Formation of Ethnic Groups." In *The Chinese Family and Its Ritual Behavior*, ed. J. C. Hsieh and Y. C. Chuang. Taipei, Taiwan: Institute of ethnology, Academia Sinica.

Xiao, P. (1999). "A Study of the Change of Family Concept and Family Relation in Mainland China of 1990's." *Research in Applied Psychology* 4:175–203 (in Chinese).

Yao, E. S. L. (1983). *Chinese Women: Past & Present*. Mesquite, TX: Ide House, Inc.

Yeh, K. H. (1997). "Living Arrangements of Elderly Parents in Taiwan: A Psychological Perspective." *Bulletin of the Institute of Ethnology* 82:121–168.

Yen, H., Y. C. Lin, and L. Chang (1998). "Exploration of Adolescent Premarital Sex Behavior and Climate." *Formosan Journal of Sexology* 4(2):1–14 (in Chinese).

Yi, C. C. and R. M. Hsung (1994). "The Social Networks of Mate Selecting and Marital Relationship." In *The Social Image of Taiwan: Social Science Approaches*, ed. C. C. Yi. Taipei, Taiwan: Academia Sinica (in Chinese).

HSIANG-MING KUNG

CHRISTIANITY

See ANABAPTISTS (AMISH, MENNONITE); CATHOLICISM; EVANGELICAL CHRISTIANITY; INTERFAITH MARRIAGE; MORMONISM; PROTESTANTISM; RELIGION

CHRONIC ILLNESS

Patterns of health, sickness, and death differ dramatically among countries based on levels of economic development, health policies, and medical technologies. By the mid-1900s, people living in *developed* (industrialized) countries experienced a sharp decline in their incidence of acute, infectious illness and an increase in rates of chronic illness. The National Commission on Chronic Illness defines a chronic illness as having one or more of the following characteristics: It is long-term or permanent; it leaves a residual disability; its causes, natural course, and treatment are ambiguous; it is degenerative; it requires special training of the patient for rehabilitation; and it requires a long period of supervision. Examples of chronic illness include *asthma, allergies, heart disease, diabetes, hypertension, stroke, cancer, cystic fibrosis, sickle-cell disease, varicose veins, arthritis, cirrhosis of the liver, renal disease,* and *mental illness*. As these examples suggest, chronic illnesses range in severity from those that are relatively mild and can be controlled by medical therapies and changes in health behaviors to those that are severe, degenerative, and terminal, causing disability and creating the need for long-term, extensive medical care. Chronic illnesses, now the leading cause of death in industrialized countries, often develop gradually due to a combination of environmental, genetic, or social factors. In many cases, the specific cause of a chronic illness cannot be determined, and its diagnosis and treatment can be difficult. This shift in the disease burden from acute to chronic illness has several important consequences. First, it accentuates global disparities in health and well-being, as most people living in less-developed countries have shorter life spans and high rates of death from acute, parasitic, infectious, and/or poverty-related illnesses. Second, chronic illness challenges the assumptions of modern medicine which, based on the "germ theory" of disease, has focused on finding cures for short-term illnesses with clear causes. Finally, the rise of chronic illness has increased the role of families in providing care for their sick and/or disabled members and caused governments to reassess their health policies.

Sickness in Historical Context

Sickness and death historically were caused mostly by poor nutrition, inadequate housing, unsanitary living conditions, poverty, warfare and—as population density and urbanization grew—exposure to bacteria, parasites, and communicable diseases. These conditions gave rise to acute illnesses such as *influenza, scarlet fever, whooping cough, polio, pneumonia,* and *tuberculosis*. In most cases, acute illnesses occur suddenly and are characterized by a sharp increase in discomfort and pain due to an inflammation, and are of short duration. Whether endemic or epidemic, these illnesses contributed heavily to the high mortality rates and short life spans among persons living in pre-industrial societies. Notable among acute, communicable diseases was the *bubonic plague,* which caused more than 20 million deaths in Europe between 1340 and 1750 (Cockerham 2001). Prior to the 1900s, acute health conditions rarely could be treated successfully by medical therapies, so they were self-limiting, as they led to either spontaneous recovery or to death within a fairly short period of time. Access to doctors was limited, as were effective medical therapies, so families usually took care of their own sick members; however, the duration of that care tended to be relatively short. By the 1700s, however, industrialization, modernization, new medical technologies, and public health measures were transforming the lives of people living in many Western countries. These forces eventually restructured the workplace, produced a system of monopoly capitalism based on class and wealth, and created a global economy dominated by a handful of industrialized nations. One result of this uneven level of economic development has been substantial disparities in wealth and health among populations living in developed countries and those living in less developed, or *developing* countries.

In its early stages, industrialization resulted in a rapid deterioration in the living standards and working conditions of most people living in Western countries. Traditional families and economic systems were disrupted as populations migrated into urban areas in pursuit of employment. The lack of clean water and sanitation, the spread of environmental toxins, population concentration, malnutrition, and the nature of industrial work increased sickness and death from contagious diseases. Gradually, public health measures and improvements in diet, housing, water supplies, and sanitation reduced the spread of deadly diseases in these countries. However, as their economic and military dominance grew, industrialized countries rapidly gained control over many underdeveloped countries. Through colonialism and the exploitation of material and human resources, these countries lost control of their economies and suffered dramatic increases in infectious diseases and death. Today, level of economic development has become a major predictor of patterns of health, illness, and death: People living in developed countries usually have better health profiles and longer life spans than those living in developing countries. Life expectancy at birth now ranges from a high of more than eighty years of age in developed countries to less than fifty years in some developing countries (Population Reference Bureau 1998).

This gap in life expectancy is largely due to the fact that people in developing countries are still disproportionately affected by acute, infectious, and/or parasitic illnesses that lead to early death. Only about 1 percent of people in developed countries die from infectious and parasitic diseases, compared to 43 percent of those in less developed nations (Weitz 2001).

People in developed countries have experienced the "epidemiological transition"—a shift in the disease burden from high rates of death from acute, parasitic, infectious diseases, and short life expectancy to longer life expectancy and high rates of chronic diseases. The first phase of the transition consisted of improvements in hygiene, sanitation, living conditions, and nutrition, which curtailed the spread of contagious disease. Many less developed societies (e.g., Sri Lanka, Cuba, Costa Rica, Kerala, and China) have substantially increased life expectancies through these measures, and by providing greater education, independence, and family planning resources to women (Caldwell 1993; Hertzman and Siddiqi 2000). The second phase in the transition was the rise of scientific medicine. Medical inventions and discoveries during the mid-1800s, especially in Germany and Austria, led scientists and physicians to reformulate the problem of disease and focus on medical intervention to heal diseases. Rudolf Virchow's discovery of cellular pathology was a major breakthrough, as was Robert Koch's and Louis Pasteur's confirmed the link between bacteria and illnesses (Cockerham 2001). At that time tuberculosis, known as the "white plague," was still the leading cause of sickness and death in Europe and the United States. Koch isolated the germ that caused tuberculosis and Pasteur, proving that many diseases were caused by the spread of bacteria, advanced the use of vaccinations to prevent diseases.

Advances in medical science, the development of more accurate diagnostic technologies, and use of antiseptic surgery, gave birth to modern scientific medicine. The germ theory of sickness became the basis of medical practice and the medical approach to dealing with disease. Scientific medicine's success at reducing infectious disease generated great enthusiasm that a cure for virtually all diseases would eventually be found. Pursuit of the "magic bullets" of medicine, or drugs that would "miraculously" heal diseases, became the focus on medical science. Control over contagious diseases and the germ theory of sickness gave rise to a specific conceptualization of health and illness described as the medical model of disease. The medical model of disease assumes there is a sharp and clear distinction between illness and health, based on the belief that sickness can be readily detected by diagnostic tests and confirmed by physicians. Because it is based on acute, infectious diseases, this model also assumes that diseases have specific causes and clearly distinguishing characteristics, and that they can be healed by medical therapies (Mishler 1981).

The development of modern medicine, combined with an expansion of industrialization and specialization, directly affected families in Western nations. Families in agricultural societies were typically large and multi-functional entities that emphasized economic self-sufficiency through the productive labor of all family members. Industrialization, however, moved economic production from homes to factories, excluded women from the workforce, and created the ideology of the breadwinner-homemaker family as best suited to the needs of the industrial economy. One of the most important changes was the loss of family functions. Families were redefined as specialized institutions with two important functions: raising children and meeting the emotional needs of its members. The modern nuclear family was seen as too small and emotionally bonded to effectively care for their sick members, and it was admonished to leave medical care in the hands of professionals. Talcott Parsons, a leading sociologist of the 1950s, argued that the use of physicians and hospital care was functional for families in that it protected them from the disruptive aspects of illness and helped motivate the sick person to get well (Parsons and Fox 1952). Parsons's family theory was consistent with his concept of the sick role, which described the social expectations governing the behavior of sick persons. Essentially, sick people were seen as exempt from their usual social responsibilities but obliged to try to get well, specifically by seeking competent medical advice and complying with medical treatments. The sick-role concept reinforced the medical model by assuming that illness was a temporary departure from health that was best handled by doctors and health care institutions. By the 1960s, however, these theories were being challenged by the growing prevalence of long-term, chronic health conditions.

The Rise of Chronic Illness

Control over acute, infectious illnesses has led to longer life spans for many populations, but also growing rates of chronic illness. Chronic illnesses, however, are not randomly distributed in populations. Although level of economic development is a major predictor of health and life span, patterns of sickness and death also vary within countries based on factors such as social class, age, gender, and race. Wealthy and middle-class people in all countries have better health profiles and longer life spans than those who are less affluent (Fosu and Subedi 1996; Reid 1998) and, in both developed and developing countries, high levels of economic inequality predict higher rates of early death (Lobmayer and Wilkinson 2000). The bulk of the disease burdens falls to the poor and lower classes in all countries, as they are most likely to experience malnutrition, poor living and working conditions, and stressful lives. *Acquired immunodeficiency syndrome* (AIDS) is a chronic illness that has reached epidemic proportions in parts of Africa, and poverty among some groups in the United States has been associated with a resurgence of acute, infectious illness. Age is also a crucial variable in the distribution of chronic illnesses, as longer life spans help account for the prevalence of chronic conditions. In most developed countries, the number of elderly (over age sixty-five) people has grown tremendously. Among the elderly, a few chronic illnesses, specifically *stroke, cancer,* and *heart disease,* are the leading causes of death, whereas *arthritis* and *diabetes* cause most sickness (Weitz 2001). This pattern is reversed for children, however, who are affected by more than two hundred different chronic conditions and disabilities (Ireys and Katz 1997). At least partially because they live longer, women in developed countries have higher rates of chronic illness than do men, although they are less likely than men to have life-threatening chronic illnesses. Finally, race-ethnicity affects health and access to health care, with marginalized racial groups experiencing more sickness and early death than dominant racial groups. Much of the racial difference is due to higher levels of stress and poverty, and less access to health care (LaVeist 1993; Williams 1990). As Wagar Ihsan-Ullah Ahmad (2000) notes, when racial minorities seek health care they are more likely to have their citizenship rights questioned, face language barriers, be blamed for their own health problems, and receive inadequate medical care (Ahmad 2000; LaVeist 1993).

The proliferation of chronic illness challenges the medical model of illness and the current organization and focus of medical care. The medical model of illness has traditionally focused on discovering the link between specific illnesses and their biological agents (e.g., "germs"). Chronic illnesses, however, are rarely the result of a specific pathogen. In many instances the symptoms and course of chronic conditions are variable and ambiguous, so getting an accurate diagnosis can be a long and difficult process. Persons with chronic illnesses often ignore the illness, self-medicate, and/or unconsciously adapt to the symptoms of the disease, especially if they are relatively mild (Charmaz 1991). Most symptoms of illness are treated without the assistance of medical experts: It is usually only when symptoms become persistent, disruptive, visible, and difficult to explain that physician care is sought (Mechanic 1995). Even after medical attention is sought, the gradual and sporadic appearance of symptoms or the unusual nature of the disease may make an accurate and early diagnosis difficult (Hill 1994). In the end, the patients may be diagnosed with diseases they have never heard of. As one patient pointed out:

> After being sick, or knowing there was something wrong for nearly 17 years, I got a diagnosis of Progressive Systemic Sclerosis, which I had never heard of before. But I was so excited, I was so thrilled for this man to be telling me I had this disease! It was stupid, you know—to have an answer. It didn't matter that it is a potentially fatal disease. None of that stuff mattered! (Thorne 1993, p. 26)

The medical model of illness also has been primarily oriented towards an acute curative model of care that emphasizes emergency treatment and the use of advanced technologies (Thorne 1993). Chronic illnesses, however, are often long-term, incurable, and only rarely can they be prevented by direct medical interventions. The causes of chronic illnesses are often complex and/or ambiguous: Some, such as *sickle-cell anemia* (found mostly among Africans and African Americans) and *Tay-Sachs disease* (found among Jews of East European descent) have a genetic component. Others are tied to lifestyle factors or a combination of genetic and environmental factors. Sedentary lifestyles, tobacco and drug use, poverty, and exposure to environmental toxins all affect the likelihood of acquiring a chronic illness. The focus of care for most chronic conditions is managing the illness rather than healing it, yet patients often find no consistent relationship between adhering to medical advice and regimens and the course of the disease. Persons with sickle-cell disease, for example, are often advised to avoid physically rigorous activities, but as one victim pointed out:

> I remember getting a [pain] crisis and I weren't doing nothing strenuous, and I weren't in the cold, and I wasn't doing nothing to bring it on. Basically I sat down and done nothing and I was still ill so I just couldn't do nothing to prevent it. That's what was making me so fed up with it. I mean, I don't know, what else are you supposed to do? (Atkin and Ahmad 2000, p. 51)

Because neither patient nor doctor experiences the gratification of a complete recovery, chronic illnesses have been described as medical failures. Patient compliance becomes a major issue because many medical therapies are expensive, inconvenient, and only marginally effective. The most salient feature of chronic illness is its permanency.

Living with Chronic Illness

There is considerable variability among chronic conditions in their severity, symptoms, and the extent to which they impose limitations on their victims. Some are relatively mild "lived-with" conditions that require lifestyle changes and/or compliance with medical regimens, whereas others are severe, life-threatening, and/or degenerative. In either case, the first step in living with chronic illness is emotional acceptance of the diagnosis and its implications. The diagnosis of chronic illness can generate intense emotional distress in patients and their families. Parents of chronically ill and/or disabled children often experience shame and guilt, and these feelings are exacerbated if they feel responsible for the condition. Their emotional distress is often manifested as feelings of extreme vulnerability, helplessness, and uncertainty over the future (Cohen 1993). As the mother of a fifteen-year old diabetic son said: "I was completely devastated, I was—just really couldn't believe it, like the rug had been pulled out from under me" (Williams 2000, p. 262). In most cases, these feelings wane as individuals accept the diagnosis and begin to cope with its implications. Some research, however, challenges the notion that people move through a series of stages that culminate in emotional acceptance of the illness. Parents may experience chronic sorrow, a "continuous sense of sadness that does not exhibit stages such as shock, anger, and guilt" (Shannon 1996, p. 322). Others deny the diagnosis for an indefinite period of time—often years. For example, a study of families with children who have sickle-cell disease found that mothers denied the diagnosis for a number of reasons—fear that it was racially motivated, the belief that their children were not like others who had the disease, and because they did not want to face the reproductive implications of passing the disease on to future children (Hill 1994). Although denial is typically seen as maladaptive, some research has indicated that denial can have beneficial effects, such as reducing psychological distress and allowing people to continue to participate in important roles and activities (Handron 1993).

Depending on the nature and severity of the condition, living with a chronic illness can prove extremely challenging. Psychologically, people with chronic illnesses experience a number of fears, for example, the fear of keeping their body and self-esteem intact, of losing love, relationships, and the approval of others, and of pain and discomfort (Miller 2000). Constant, recurrent, and/or unpredictable episodes of pain often cause feelings of loss of control. This pain can be constant and all-consuming, making symptom management and participation in everyday activities difficult. Peter E. S. Freund and Meredith B. McGuire (1991) have noted that chronic pain can jeopardize social relationships and lead to isolation, as it often invokes invalidating responses from others. The pain experienced by chronically ill persons often has no organic basis and cannot be verified medically, so others may doubt its existence. This can lead to loss of social relationships with others, as the empathy and support of friends and relatives begins to wear thin. Chronically ill people also have to contend with medical treatments and their side-effects, inexplicable remissions and exacerbations of the disease, and changes in lifestyles, activities, roles, and relationships. Some changes are relatively minor; however, others are substantial and

are often experienced as a series of losses—of freedom, of hobbies, of employment, of physical appearance and abilities, and even of friendships. Many cause a loss of control over the body, which can lead to stigma and devaluation. In describing living with a chronic respiratory illness, characterized by lack of energy and breathlessness, Clare Williams (1993) sees the illness as causing "dwindling social and recreational lives; social isolation; problems of social interaction, stigma, legitimacy and the tolerance of others towards the condition; the threat or reality of 'dependency' . . . and problems pertaining to family life" (p. 130).

Chronic illness is accompanied by a great deal of uncertainty, since even with the best medical care, its course and severity can vary from patient to patient. Mothers of children with sickle-cell anemia experienced considerable uncertainty over how the disease would affect their children, especially when the diagnosis was made prior to the manifestation of symptoms (Hill 1994). Rose Weitz (1990) interviewed persons who have AIDS and found uncertainty to be a major theme. People living with AIDS experience a number of uncertainties: uncertainty about the meaning of illness symptoms, why they had become ill, their ability to function the next day, whether they would be able to live or die with dignity, and whether their health regimens would prolong their lives or heal the disease. Because self-image is integrally tied to the body and a sense of having control over it, the self-image can be dramatically altered by chronic illness.

Family Caregiving

Although modern family and medical ideologies of the mid-1900s argued the wisdom of greater reliance on physicians and medical institutions, the emergence of chronic illness has led to a reassertion of the importance of families in caring for the sick. Modern medical interventions and technologies that have extended the lives of chronically ill persons without affecting complete recovery have increased the responsibility of families for caring for the sick. Many chronic illnesses that once signaled early death (e.g., kidney failure) or institutionalization (e.g., mental illness) can now be managed by medical therapies administered in the home. Moreover, the escalating costs of health care in most countries has led to restrictions on access to physicians and medical facilities and fosters an interest in self-care and family care. Providing

A young girl helps her friend with a blood sugar test. Both children have diabetes. Informal support from friends and family reduces stress and may ameliorate the physical symptoms of chronic illness. A/P WIDE WORLD PHOTOS

long-term care for chronically ill or disabled family members can disrupt the normal functions of families, and it almost always causes stress. Examining caregiving within the context of stress theory, Carol S. Aneshensel, Leonard Pearlin, and Roberleigh Schuler (1993) make a distinction between primary stressors, caused by performing the work required to care for the sick family members, and secondary stressors, problems that emerge in social roles and relationships as a result of caregiving. This distinction highlights the fact that caregiving work is not only stressful because it requires the performance of difficult physical and emotional tasks—for example, supervising, monitoring, encouraging, medicating, lifting, bathing, and feeding—but also because of secondary stressors: marital discord, social isolation, economic strains, and family dysfunction.

Family caregiving for children can start from birth and last indefinitely, especially if the illness or disability prolongs their dependency. Research indicates that about 20 percent of all U.S. children have a chronic illness or disability, and 10 percent have problems that create caregiving demands, including millions who are disabled (Butler,

Rosenbaum, and Palfrey 1987; Sexson and Madan-Swain 1993). The amount of caregiving work performed by family members ranges from fairly minimal to extensive, depending on the nature of the illness. Many children have "lived-with" diseases such as *asthma, epilepsy,* or *diabetes* that cause episodic health crises, but can often be managed on a daily basis through special diets, medications, and changes in activities. Asthma, the most common childhood chronic illness in the United States, affects five million children and is a growing cause of sickness and death (Bleil et al. 2000). Asthma is episodic in nature, causing periodic bouts of breathlessness, wheezing, and coughing. A study of teenagers with asthma by Williams (2000) describes the caregiving role of mothers as "alert assistants" who monitor and supervise their children's compliance with medical treatments and manage medical crises. On the other hand, illnesses like *kidney disease, cystic fibrosis,* and *spina bifida* can be progressive and cause constant pain and impairment.

A great deal of research has focused on children with cystic fibrosis, the most common lethal genetic disease in the United States with an incidence of 1:200 white births (Solomon and Breton 1999). Cystic fibrosis, a progressive disease that leads to early death, requires extensive caregiving work, including "oral medications and special diets, aerosol therapy and bronchial drainage (prescribed two to four times a day, requiring about an hour each time), exercise, and mist tent therapy at night" (Patterson 1985). Providing such extensive care for their children can place a strain on interactions between parents and their sick children. C. Ruth Solomon and Jean-Jacques Breton (1999) observed parents of young children (ages one to two) with cystic fibrosis over a twelve-month period and found that, compared to parents of healthy children, they were more controlling, more serious, and less encouraging in their interactions with their children. Medical therapies are complex, difficult to learn, and can occupy so much time that they become the center of family life. They may also be risky and interfere with normal parental behavior, which ordinarily centers on being nurturing and supportive. One study of pediatric ambulatory dialysis found that parents have difficulty reconciling parenting with the administration of medical regimens:

> Parents are asked to monitor the child's physical state intensely. They are also told not to allow the child's medical problems to become the main family focus. Parents are instructed that an error in the sterile technique could result in their child's serious illness, yet staff is also concerned that parents should not experience excessive anxiety. Parents are asked to function as both medic and parent, and yet it is also expected that the child will be able to progress through the normal stages of separation and individuation (LePontis, Moel, and Cohn 1987, p. 83).

In addition to the work and anxiety entailed in carrying out medical tasks, parents must also address the psychological and emotional needs of the child with chronic illness or disability. Although most children with physical disabilities do not develop mental health problems, they are much more likely to do so than healthy children because of greater social isolation, alienation, and poor school performance (Patterson and Geber 1991; Solomon and Breton 1999). Chronically ill children living in dysfunctional families exhibit much higher rates of psychiatric disorder than those living in well-functioning families (Bleil et al. 2000). Both parents and medical experts endeavor to prevent these problems by encouraging normal life experiences and bolstering coping skills, self-esteem, and confidence of children who are chronically ill. Parents must also try to maintain a sense of balance in meeting the needs of their ill and healthy children.

Longer life spans and an aging population have also made elder care a major responsibility of families. The United Nations (1993) reports that the populations of North America, Europe, Asia, and Latin America are aging at approximately equal rates and that by 2025 those age sixty-five and over will number more than 822 million—or about 10 percent of the global population. The bulk of caregiving work performed today is for the elderly, as chronic conditions, disability, and impaired health increase with age. *Heart disease, cancer, stroke, arthritis,* and *dementia* cause most chronic illnesses and disability among the elderly. Eighty percent of the noninstitutionalized elderly have one or more chronic health problems (Freund and McGuire 1991; Wagner 1999). Caregiving for elderly often starts out gradually, with family members assisting elders in paying bills, maintaining their homes, shopping, visiting doctors, or other daily living tasks. In many cases, caregiving work expands and becomes more emotionally and physically exhausting as health declines. When the health status of an elderly person dramatically declines, family members usually rally in support by providing care for their loved one. However, there is a tendency for that support to wane over time and for one primary caregiver to be selected by default: usually based on being female, living nearby, and being unemployed (Aneshensel, Pearlin, and Schuler 1993). As few elderly people have young children, most caregiving work falls to those who are middle-aged or elderly. The quality of the relationship between caregiver and care receiver is an important factor in caregiver burden. Caregiving can solidify emotional bonds in close relationships; on the other hand, it may cause long-standing family disagreements to reemerge.

Much research has focused on caregiving for elderly people with dementia, a long-term, degenerative disease that can require extensive and exhaustive care work. Dementia is defined as "disorders involving impairments of memory, intelligence, judgment, and neuropsychology, which are sufficient to inhibit carrying out social activities or work" (Aneshensel et al. 1995, p. 7). Mild levels of dementia affect more than 60 percent of the elderly and, according to Aneshensel and her associates, 4 to 7 percent of the elderly in North America and Europe have moderate to severe levels of dementia. *Alzheimer's disease* is the most common type of dementia, and caring for its victims can be highly stressful and lead to family dysfunction. In the early stages, family caregivers may recognize that there is a health problem and respond by providing minimal types of assistance. Aneshensel, Pearlin, and Schuler (1993) found that the average caregiver for patients with Alzheimer's disease had been providing care for more than three years before a doctor was consulted. The tendency of individuals with Alzheimer's disease to deteriorate cognitively and physically causes unique caregiving problems. Studies have suggested that cognitive impairment increases strain because it creates an ambiguity in the family boundary: The patient's failure to recognize or emotionally respond to the caregiver creates confusion over whether the patient is in or out of the family system (Boss, Caron, and Horbal 1988). Whatever the strains, caregiving for elderly people is often time-bounded, as serious, degenerative disease among elderly people often leads to death or institutional care.

The notion of "family" caregiving obscures the fact that women do most of the caregiving work. Gender norms that prescribe nurturing and domestic roles for women naturally assign women the responsibility for caring for sick family members at home (Gerstel and Gallagher 1993). In some cultures male caregivers are denigrated: For example, a study of caregiving in South Asian communities found that men who took on the role of caregiver—especially those who quit their jobs to do so—were stigmatized and seen as unworthy of respect (Katbamna, Baker, Ahmad, Bhakta, and Parker 2001). There is also a gender division in the type of work that men and women perform and in their styles of caregiving. Men perform more instrumental tasks for relatives with disability or illness, such as lawn maintenance, lifting, and assisting with financial matters. They also have a more activity-oriented, managerial, and emotionally detached style of caregiving and, when they are the primary caregiver, they receive more help from others in carrying out their tasks (Boss, Caron, and Horbal 1988; Ungerson 1987). Women view caregiving as a duty and obligation and have styles that are more expressive and supportive. They provide more personal service than do men, receive less assistance from others in performing their work, but do have more sources of emotional support. The gendered nature of caregiving work means that the lives of women are more affected than those of men. Caregiving substantially increases the amount of work they perform in the family and may undermine opportunities for employment and other activities.

More recent studies have begun to examine an additional impact of gender on chronic illness: How the sex of the chronically ill or disabled person affects caregiving. For example, in countries where female modesty and chastity are strongly emphasized, caring for sexually mature women can be more difficult than caring for their male counterparts (Katbamna, Baker, Ahmad, Bhakta, and Parker 2001). Parents' caregiving for chronically ill children may also be shaped by gender norms and expectations. Being sick, dependent, or frail is seen as more of a violation of traditional gender norms for men than for women; as Kathy Charmaz (1995, p. 268) has noted, "illness can reduce a man's status in masculine hierarchies, shift his power relations with women, and raise his self-doubts about masculinity." Some research finds that parents see sick sons as more impaired by the illness and less capable of self-care, and that they devote more time and energy to providing care for them (Hill and Zimmerman 1995). Williams (2000) found that boys are more likely than girls to hide their chronic illness, which makes compliance with medical regimens difficult. One mother described her diabetic 15-year old son refusing to do insulin injections at school:

> He won't do them [blood sugars] at school now, he absolutely refuses, he won't even do an injection at school. He's on three injections a day and the hospital would like him to go on to four but he won't do it in front of his friends, and he doesn't like the fact that he is diabetic in that respect, he wants to be normal. (Williams 2000, p. 261)

Studies of family caregiving have often focused on caring as burdensome and disruptive to families, especially women, and as a threat to family stability. However, researchers have begun to emphasize the subjective and experiential aspects of caregiving that arise from the meanings assigned to the work (Fisher and Tronto 1990; Traustadottir 1991). Although caregiver work needs to be recognized, it need not be seen as inherently burdensome or unworthy: Rather, caring can be empowering as it enhances the quality of life for chronically ill and/or disabled persons. This may be especially true when there is a close and reciprocal relationship between caregivers and those they care for. Kathleen Theide Call and her colleagues (1999) use a social exchange perspective to point out that dependent and chronically ill people who receive care often reciprocate in a number of ways, and feel uncomfortable when they cannot do so. They found that caregiving is less burdensome when the care receiver is deemed as worthy and the caregiver is a part of the immediate family. The majority of care receivers have not relinquished all their family roles, relationships, and life activities, but rather they continue to participate in and make vital contributions to their families and communities (Parker 1993). As one researcher points out, "People do not become less human, less interesting, or less deserving just because they have unresolvable or disabling conditions. Rather, they continue to learn, to adapt, and to live their lives as well as they can manage. In other words, they seek a state of health that represents their best effort within the specific challenges of the disease" (Thorne 1993, p. 2).

Stress, Social Support, and Coping

Although providing care for chronically ill and/or disabled family members is inherently stressful, several factors mediate the impact of that stress. Family structure, economic resources, social support, and coping resources and strategies all have an impact on the caregiving experience. Family structure may mediate the impact of caregiving for African Americans, who reportedly experience less stress and burden than other racial groups. One study explains this by noting that African Americans rely on a more diverse group of caregivers, including extended family members and close friends (Tripp-Reimer 1997). Economic resources can also influence caregiving work. Patricia G. Archbold (1983) found that affluent caregivers were care managers who used a variety of institutional resources to coordinate their parents' care, whereas low-income women were direct care providers who performed the heavy physical work of nursing care and personal service. Stress is also reduced by the availability of social support; in fact, social support may also ameliorate the physical symptoms of illness and enhance survival. Many types of social support have been examined, but the three most basic types are emotional support, which fosters feelings of comfort; cognitive support, which entails providing information, knowledge, and advice; and material support, the offer of goods and materials (Jacobsen 1986). Most people expect informal support from their friends and family members, and find such support available and adequate. However, there is a tendency for informal sources of support to be available during acute stages of the illness, such as the diagnosis or terminal stage, but to wane when the illness continues over an extended period of time.

Formal sources of social support are available on a more consistent basis and provide the advantage of talking with experts or people experiencing similar problems. Hospitals, schools, and state and private institutions offer support groups for people with various chronic conditions. These groups provide education about the illness or disability and information about resources available in meeting the daily needs of families. A central theme in support groups is empowerment, which refers to providing chronically ill people and their caregivers with the maximum amount of control over their own lives. Sarah Rosenfield (1992) reported that community resources can enhance the subjective quality of life for persons with chronic illnesses. Evaluating services available for the chronically mentally ill, she found that programs that increase economic resources through vocational training and financial support also increase the status, sense of mastery, and life satisfaction of clients. Findings such as these have led to a growth in the organization of support groups which focus on building family strengths and providing counseling and referral services.

In addition to using social and community resources that enhance coping, chronically ill persons and their families engage in a number of coping activities that mitigate the impact of the illness. Coping has been defined as the things people do to avoid or minimize the stress that would otherwise result from problematic conditions of life (Pearlin and Aneshensel 1986), and coping involves both having resources and using various coping strategies. Coping resources are the psychological and material assets available to individuals and their families in responding to stressful situations. Coping strategies, on the other hand, are the actual behaviors or responses people use in dealing with stressful events. At the individual level, coping resources include one's education, income, self-esteem, sense of mastery, and psychological hardiness, all of which affect one's ability to deal effectively with life strains. Early studies identified integration and adaptability as key family resources (Hill 1954), and other studies have built on this theme. Integration refers to having strong ties of affection, pride in family tradition, and a history of sharing in activities. Adaptability means having flexible social roles, sharing responsibility for performing tasks, and communicating openly. Coping is enhanced when the family does not blame itself for the illness, feels confident in its ability to manage the situation, and continues to be sensitive and responsive to the needs of all family members. Communication and emotional expressiveness, role relationships, available caregivers, and financial resources are all important resources in managing illnesses.

A variety of coping strategies have been identified among persons who experience life strains, including prayer, stoicism, physical activity, denial, withdrawal, and ignoring the problem. The two most common strategies for coping with long-term chronic illness and its debilitating effects, however, are normalization and the attribution of meaning. After the initial impact of the diagnosis of chronic illness wanes, family members are eager to resume their normal lives. Whatever the level of physical or mental impairment caused by the illness, most people do not want the illness to threaten the self-identities, social roles, or activities that they value, or to become the dominant factor in their interactions with others. To avoid this, they attempt to normalize the situation by minimizing the illness and conveying the impression of normalcy to others. One normalizing strategy is to describe behaviors associated with the illness, such as pain, crying, fatigue, forgetfulness, diet changes, and drug therapies, as things that all people experience or engage in from time to time. Parents often make sure that their ill or disabled children participate in as many normal school and household activities as necessary. In some cases chronically ill people invest a great deal of energy in their efforts to manage the impressions and responses of others; they may disguise symptoms, avoid embarrassing situations, or control the information available to others.

The attribution of meaning, a coping strategy that refers to defining the illness in a positive manner, is also an effort to maintain a certain balance in family life. Parents and other family members often view the illness as increasing family cohesion, their patience, and their faith in God or as leading them to develop more meaningful goals and values. Parents may also redefine the expectations they have for their child with chronic illness or disability in a way conducive to maintaining a positive self-image. In a study focusing on preventing mental health problems among children with chronic illness, Joan M. Patterson and Gayle Geber (1991) point out that meanings are at the core of determining whether a disability leads to a handicap, which is a discrepancy between role expectations and actual role performance. The process of definition allows people with chronic illness and their families to endow the illness with meaning.

Although scientific medicine has made progress in treating and managing chronic illnesses, there is little hope that medical interventions will completely eradicate these illnesses. Moreover, the growing elderly population, the prevalence of chronic conditions, the proliferation of medical technologies, and the expectation of virtually unlimited access to medical care has placed severe strains on the health care systems of developed countries. As a result, health authorities are now emphasizing preventive care, healthy lifestyles (e.g., dietary changes, stress reduction, and exercise) as the key to preventing chronic illness, and patients are relying on a broader range healing options such as herbal therapies, acupuncture, and massages. Rather than continuing to focus on finding biophysical/technological cures for every disease, some argue that our attention should be directed toward improvements in primary care and a focus on caring rather than curing. Caring has been defined as "a positive emotional and supportive response . . . to affirm our commitment to their well-being, our willingness to identify with them in their pain and suffering, and our desire to do what we can to relieve their situation" (Callahan 1990, p. 111).

See also: ACQUIRED IMMUNODEFICIENCY SYNDROME
   (AIDS); ALZHEIMER'S DISEASE; ANXIETY
   DISORDERS; ATTENTION DEFICIT/HYPERACTIVITY

DISORDER (ADHD); CAREGIVING; DEATH AND
DYING; DEPRESSION: ADULTS; DEPRESSION:
CHILDREN AND ADOLESCENTS; DEMENTIA;
DISABILITIES; GRIEF, LOSS, AND BEREAVEMENT;
HEALTH AND FAMILIES; HOMELESS FAMILIES;
HOSPICE; INDUSTRIALIZATION; LEARNING
DISORDERS; POVERTY; RESPITE CARE: ADULT;
RESPITE CARE: CHILD; SCHIZOPHRENIA; STRESS;
SUBSTANCE ABUSE; SUBSTITUTE CAREGIVERS

Bibliography

Ahmad, W. I. U. (2000). *Ethnicity, Disability and Chronic Illness.* Buckingham, UK: Open University Press.

Aneshensel, C. A.; Pearlin, L. I.; Mullan, J. T.; Zarit, S. H.; and Whitlatch, C. J. (1995). *Profiles in Caregiving: The Unexpected Career.* San Diego, CA: Academic Press.

Aneshensel, C. S.; Pearlin, L. I.; and Schuler, R. H. (1993). "Stress, Role Captivity, and the Cessation of Caregiving." *Journal of Health and Social Behavior* 34:54–70.

Archbold, P. G. (1983). "Impact of Parent-Caring on Women." *Family Relations* 32:39–45.

Atkin, K., and Ahmad, W. I. U. (2000). "Living With Sickle Cell Disorder: How Young People Negotiate Their Care and Treatment." In *Ethnicity, Disability and Chronic Illness,* ed. W. I. U. Ahmad. Buckingham, UK: Open University Press.

Blcil, M. A., Ramesh, S., Miller, B. D., and Wood, B. L. (2000). "The Influence of Parent-Child Relatedness on Depressive Symptoms in Children with Asthma: Tests of Moderator and Mediator Models." *Journal of Pediatric Psychology* 25:481–491.

Boss, P.; Caron, W.; and Horbal, J. (1988). "Alzheimer's Disease and Ambiguous Loss." In *Chronic Illness and Disability,* ed. C. S. Chilman, E. W. Nunnally, and F. M. Cox. Newbury Park, CA: Sage Publications.

Caldwell, J. C. (1993). "Health Transition: The Cultural, Social and Behavioral Determinants of Health in the Third World." *Social Science and Medicine* 36:125–135.

Call, K. T.; Finch, M. A.; Huck, S. M.; and Kane, R. A. (1999). "Caregiver Burden from a Social Exchange Perspective: Caring for Older People after Hospital Discharge." *Journal of Marriage and the Family* 61:688–699.

Callahan, D. (1990). "The Primacy of Caring: Choosing Health-Care Priorities." *Commonweal,* February 23, 107–112.

Carter, B. D.; Urey, J. R.; and Eid, N. S. (1992). "The Chronically Ill Child and Family Stress: Family Developmental Perspectives on Cystic Fibrosis." *Psychosomatics* 33:397–403.

Charmaz, K. (1991). *Good Days, Bad Days: The Self in Chronic Illness and Time.* New Brunswick, NJ: Rutgers University Press.

Charmaz, K. (1995). "Identity Dilemmas of Chronically Ill Men." In *Men's Health and Illness–Gender, Power and the Body,* ed. D. Sabo and D. Gordon. London: Sage Publications.

Cockerham, W. C. (2001). *Medical Sociology,* 8th edition. Upper Saddle River, NJ: Prentice Hall.

Cohen, M. H. (1993). "The Unknown and the Unknowable: Managing Sustained Uncertainty." *Western Journal of Nursing Research* 15:77–96.

Corbin, J. M., and Strauss, A. (1988). *Unending Work and Care: Managing Chronic Illness in the Home.* San Francisco: Jossey-Bass.

Fisher, B., and Tronto, J. (1990). "Toward a Feminist Theory of Caring." In *Circles of Care: Work and Identity in Women's Lives,* ed. E. K. Abel and M. K. Nelson. Albany: State University of New York Press.

Fosu, G. B., and Subedi, J. (1996). "The Demographic, Cultural, and Behavioral Contexts of Maternal and Child Health in Developing Countries." In *Society, Health, and Disease: Transcultural Perspectives,* ed. J. Subedi and E. B. Gallagher. Upper Saddle River, NJ: Prentice Hall.

Freund, P. E. S., and McGuire, M. D. (1991). *Health, Illness, and the Social Body: A Critical Sociology.* Englewood Cliffs, NJ: Prentice Hall.

Gerstel, N., and Gallagher, S. K. (1993). "Kinkeeping and Distress: Gender, Recipients of Care, and Work-Family Conflict." *Journal of Marriage and the Family* 55:598–607.

Hamlett, K. W., Pelligrini, D. S., and Karz, K. S. (1992). "Childhood Chronic Illness as a Family Stressor." *Journal of Pediatric Psychology* 17:33–47.

Handron, D. S. (1993). "Denial and Serious Chronic Illness: A Personal Perspective." *Perspectives in Psychiatric Care* 29:29–33.

Hertzman, C., and Siddiqi, A. (2000). "Health and Rapid Economic Change in the Twentieth Century." *Social Science and Medicine* 51:809–819.

Hill, R. (1954). "Social Stresses on the Family." *Social Casework* 39:139–156.

Hill, S. (1994). *Managing Sickle-Cell Disease in Low-Income Families.* Philadelphia: Temple University Press.

Hill, S., and Zimmerman, M. (1995). "Valiant Girls and Vulnerable Boys: The Impact of Gender and Race on Mothers' Caregiving for Chronically-Ill Children." *Journal of Marriage and the Family* 57:43–53.

Hymovich, D. P., and Hagopian, G. A. (1992). *Chronic Illness in Children and Adults: A Psychosocial Approach*. Philadelphia: Saunders.

Ireys, H. T., and Katz, S. (1997). "The Demography of Disability and Chronic Illness Among Children." In *Mosby's Resource Guide to Children with Disabilities and Chronic Illness,* ed. H. M. Wallace, R. F. Biehl, J. C. MacQueen, and J. A. Blackman. St. Louis, MO: Mosby.

Jacobsen, D. E. (1986). "Types and Timing of Social Support." *Journal of Health and Social Behavior* 27:250–264.

Katbamna, S.; Baker, R.; Ahmad, W.; Bhakta, P.; and Parker, G. (2001). "Development of Guidelines to Improved Support of South Asian Carers by Primary Health Care Teams." *Quality Health Care* 10(3):166–172.

Kromer, M. E.; Prihoda, T. J.; Hidalgo, H. A.; and Wood, P. R. (2000). "Assessing Quality of Life in Mexican-American Children with Asthma: Impact on Family and Functional Status." *Journal of Pediatric Psychology* 25:415–426.

LaVeist, T. A. (1993). "Segregation, Poverty, and Empowerment: Health Consequences for African Americans." *Milbank Quarterly* 71:41–64.

LePontis, J.; Moel, D. I.; and Cohn, R. A. (1987). "Family Adjustment to Pediatric Ambulatory Dialysis." *American Journal of Orthopsychiatry* 51:78–83.

Lobmayer, P., and Wilkinson, R. (2000). "Income, Inequality and Mortality in 14 Developed Countries." *Sociology of Health and Illness* 22:401–414.

Mechanic, D. (1995). "Sociological Dimensions of Illness Behavior." *Social Problems* 41:1207–1216.

Miller, J. F. (2000). *Coping with Chronic Illness: Overcoming Powerlessness,* 3rd edition. Philadelphia: F. A. Davis Company.

Mishler, E. G. (1981). "Critical Perspectives on the Biomedical Model." In *Social Contexts of Health, Illness, and Patient Care,* ed. E. G. Mishler, L. A. Singham, S. T. Hauser, R. Liem, S. D. Osherson, and N. E. Waxler. Cambridge, UK: Cambridge University Press.

Moen, P.; Robison, J.; and Dempster-McClain, D. (1995). "Caregiving and Women's Well-Being: A Life Course Approach." *Journal of Health and Social Behavior* 36:259–273.

National Commission on Chronic Illness. (1956). *Chronic Illness in the United States: Care of the Long-Term Patient,* Vol. II. Cambridge, MA: Harvard University Press.

Parker, G. (1993). *With This Body: Caring and Disability in Marriage*. Buckingham, UK: Open University Press.

Parsons, T., and Fox, R. (1952). "Illness, Therapy, and the Modern Urban American Family." *Journal of Social Issues* 13:31–44.

Patterson, J. M. (1985). "Critical Factors Affecting Family Compliance with Home Treatment for Children with Cystic Fibrosis." *Family Relations* 34:79–88.

Patterson, J. M. (1988). "Chronic Illness in Children and the Impact on Families." In *Chronic Illness and Disability,* ed. C. S. Chilman, E. W. Nunnally, and F. M. Cox. Newbury Park, CA: Sage Publications.

Patterson, J. M., and Geber, G. (1991). "Preventing Mental Health Problems in Children with Chronic Illness or Disability: Parent to Parent Conference." *Children's Health Care* 20:150–161.

Pearlin, L. I., and Aneshensel, C. S. (1986). "Coping and Social Supports: Their Functions and Applications." In *Applications of Social Science to Clinical Medicine and Health Policy,* ed. L. Aiken and D. Mechanic. New Brunswick, NJ: Rutgers University Press.

Population Reference Bureau. (1998). *World Population Data Sheet*. Washington, DC: Author.

Reid, I. (1998). *Social Class Differences in Britain*. Cambridge, UK: Polity Press

Rosenfield, S. (1992). "Factors Contributing to the Subjective Quality of Life of the Chronic Mentally Ill." *Journal of Health and Social Behavior* 33:299–315.

Seaburn, D. B.; Lorenz, A.; and Kaplan, D. (1992). "The Transgenerational Development of Chronic Illness Meanings." *Family Systems Medicine* 10:385–394.

Sexson, S. B., and Madan-Swain, A. (1993). "School Reentry for the Child with Chronic Illness." *Journal of Learning Disabilities* 26:115–125.

Shannon, C. (1996). "Dealing With Stress: Families and Chronic Illness." In *Handbook of Stress, Medicine, and Health,* ed. C. L. Cooper. New York: CRC Press.

Sloper, P. (2000). "Predictors of Distress in Parents of Children with Cancer: A Prospective Study." *Journal of Pediatric Psychology* 25:79–91

Solomon, C. R., and Breton, J. J. (1999). "Early Warning Signals in Relationships Between Parents and Young Children with Cystic Fibrosis." *Children's Health Care* 28:221–240.

Traustadottir, R. (1991). "Mothers Who Care: Gender, Disability, and Family Life." *Journal of Family Issues* 12:211–228.

Tripp-Reimer, T. (1997). "Ethnicity, Aging, and Chronic Illness." In *Chronic Illness and the Older Adult,* ed. E. A. Swanson and T. Tripp-Reimer. New York: Springer.

Turner-Henson, A.; Holaday, B.; and Swan, J. H. (1992). "When Parenting Becomes Caregiving: Caring for the Chronically Ill Child." *Family and Community Health* 15:19–30.

Ungerson, C. (1987). *Policy is Personal: Sex, Gender, and Informal Care.* New York: Tavistock.

United Nations (1993). *World Population Trends and Prospects: The 1992 Revision.* New York: Author.

Voydanoff, P., and Donnelly, B. W. (1999). "Multiple Roles and Psychological Distress: The Intersection of the Paid Worker, Spouse, and Parent Roles with the Role of Adult Child." *Journal of Marriage and the Family* 61:725–738.

Wagner, E. H. (1999). "Care of Older People With Chronic Illness." In *New Ways to Care For Older People,* ed. E. Calkins, C. Boult, E. H. Wagner, and J. T. Pacala. New York: Springer.

Weitz, R. (1990). "Uncertainty and the Lives of Persons with AIDS." In *The Sociology of Health and Sickness,* 3rd edition, ed. P. Conrad and R. Kern. New York: St. Martin's.

Weitz, R. (2001). *The Sociology of Health, Illness, and Health Care: A Critical Approach.* Belmont, CA: Wadsworth.

Williams, C. (2000). "Alert Assistants in Managing Chronic Illness: The Case of Mothers and Teenage Sons." *Sociology of Health and Illness* 22:254–272.

Williams, D. (1990). "Socioeconomic Differentials in Health: A Review and Redirection." *Social Psychology Quarterly* 53:81–99.

Williams, S. J. (1993). *Chronic Respiratory Illness.* London: Routledge.

SHIRLEY A. HILL

CIRCUMCISION

Circumcision is the practice of surgically removing parts of a person's genitalia, usually involving skin covering the clitoris or glans of the penis. This surgery is most commonly performed on children: either newborn infants or adolescents. The practices, meanings, and implications attached to this activity vary greatly by region, religion, and gender. Because the implications and types of procedures differ immensely across gender lines, it is important to consider male and female circumcision separately. However, great controversy surrounds the practice of circumcision of both genders. The controversies center on the health implications, effects on sexuality, natural states of bodies, social acceptance, religious rites, and proper treatment of children. These issues become especially compelling in the context of globalization, secularization, and competing views of health.

Male Circumcision

Male circumcision entails the removal of the penis foreskin, the flap of skin that covers the penile glans. (Male circumcision does not usually include such practices as piercings of the penis or scrotum, penile implants, gender modifications, or an Aboriginal Australian tradition of *splitting* the penis.) Male circumcision is most widely practiced among Jewish, Islamic, African, and North American populations. It is uncommon in Asia, South America, Central America, and most of Europe (American Academy of Pediatrics 1999). Approximately 60 percent of males in the United States are circumcised, compared to only 6 percent of males in the United Kingdom (Smith 1998). An estimated 1.2 million newborn males are circumcised annually within the United States (American Academy of Pediatrics 1999). For both cultural and medical reasons, the percentage of newborn infants being circumcised in the United States has been decreasing since the mid-twentieth century.

The surgery is usually performed on children ranging from newborns to adolescents. In secular and Christian North American culture, no explicit ceremony surrounds the operation, which physicians perform in clinical settings as elective procedures. Increasingly, physicians administer local anesthesia during the procedure. Complication rates range between 0.2 percent and 0.6 percent and include such problems as postoperative bleeding and unintended surgical damage to the penis (American Academy of Pediatrics 1999). Circumcision is occasionally performed on uncircumcised adult males when the foreskin becomes infected and adheres to the glans.

The claimed medical advantages of circumcision include decreases in occurrences of penile

A Jewish community participates in the circumcision ceremony known as "bris." DAVID H. WELLS/CORBIS

cancer, local infections, urinary tract infections in the first year of life, and STD/HIV infection later in life. The medical disadvantages described include the chance of postoperative bleeding, pain during the operation, and loss of sexual sensitivity. For claimed advantages and disadvantages both, great controversy surrounds the veracity and magnitude.

Among other populations, circumcision is tied to religion. A Jewish circumcision ceremony is called a *brit milah* or *bris* and is performed on the eighth day after birth by a *mohel*. An Islamic circumcision ceremony is referred to as *khitan*. In Islam this practice is supported by Sunnah teachings, as opposed to teachings directly from the Qur'an. Traditional African ceremonies vary greatly among cultural groups, with circumcision being performed as part of a coming-of-age ritual at puberty. In these circumstances, traditionally trained males from within the community perform the surgery.

Several common themes run through the cultural and religious reasons for circumcision. Ceremonially, circumcision marks membership in a particular group of people, a shedding of femaleness in order to become fully male, and at times an agreement with, or pledge to, a deity. The circumcised penis is understood as being a *cleaner* state of a male both in a ceremonial and physical sense. Beyond this is an aesthetic argument that the circumcised penis is more attractive and *natural* looking than an uncircumcised penis, even though all healthy males are born with a foreskin.

Although carried out infrequently, there are procedures that aid circumcised adults in redeveloping parts of the foreskin. These include various methods of stretching the foreskin not removed during the original circumcision. Circumcised males may undergo this procedure to become fully *intact* and *unmutilated* or to regain sexual sensitivity of the glans.

Male Issues

In North American medicine, the trend is to offer circumcision only as an elective procedure, rather than a standard practice as was the tradition. The primary debates revolve around issues of cleanliness, health benefits, social inclusion, infliction of pain on infants, *mutilation,* and cultural or religious identity. The widespread continued support for male circumcision in the United States relies on the potential health benefits of the surgery. The stance of the American Academy of Pediatrics is to give parents information about the advantages and disadvantages so that they may make an informed decision (1999). The traditional medical benefits are not as significant as physicians once thought, although well-documented studies do show some prophylactic benefit from the procedure. In the face of a decline in circumcisions, a greater emphasis is being placed on good hygiene for those who are uncircumcised.

A debate continues concerning whether routine circumcision is cost-effective. To achieve a statistically significant drop in cases of urinary tract infection or penile cancer, a large number of males must be circumcised; the rates of both diseases are low. For instance, the rate of penile cancer increases from 0.00001 percent to 0.00009 percent for uncircumcised males (American Academy of Pediatrics 1999). Although this is a statistically significant increase, penile cancer is still rare in the uncircumcised population. The percentage of risk as well as the actual rarity of occurrence should be weighed when evaluating the importance of the procedure.

The final issues center on a worldview of fundamental rights, a natural state as good, and social inclusion. Anticircumcision groups use the descriptors of mutilation and amputation for male circumcision. They label it as abuse. The language invokes *rights* and *autonomy,* as well as the constitution of a *valued* body. Using this language, the unaltered and *natural* state is the one that should be highly prized, and circumcision moves the male away from that. Further, the child has a right to make decisions about long-term health care. By performing the operation before the child reaches an age of assent or consent, we remove this possibility.

The flip side to this debate is that parents have the right to decide what is best for their children. Even if the health benefits may be slight, religious ceremony and social inclusion weigh importantly when the risks are relatively low. Also, geriatric health care issues arise when considering the implications of keeping the penis clean for an uncircumcised elderly male who can no longer carry out basic self-cleaning tasks (Frank et al. 2000).

Female Circumcision

The term *female circumcision* has a greater range of meanings and implications than does male circumcision. It refers to anything from the removal of the clitoral hood, the small flap of skin covering the clitoris, to the removal of the labia and clitoris, as well as to the stitching shut of the vulva. Opponents of the practice often refer to female circumcision as *female genital mutilation* (FGM). (Female circumcision does not usually refer to such practices as consensual piercing of the labia and clitoris or gender modifications) Ceremonially, female circumcision is performed only in populations in Middle and Northern sections of Africa, parts of the Middle East, and parts of Malaysia. Worldwide, more than 100 million women have been circumcised. (Hosken 1994). It is estimated that at least 95 percent of the women in Somalia, Djibouti, and Egypt are circumcised (Gruenbaum 2001). Circumcision is traditionally performed in more than thirty countries, at least twenty-eight of which are in Africa. At the same time, given contemporary emigration patterns, circumcised women are found among immigrant populations in countries of Europe and North America. When performed on adolescents, the operation accompanies traditional instruction about womanhood. Although there appears to be no textual support for female circumcision in Islamic holy writings, the geographic areas of practice are primarily Islamic.

Nonceremonial genital modification was briefly practiced in Western medicine as a medical treatment. Western physicians recommended the practice of removing the clitoris as a treatment for women with certain nervous and sexual problems in the nineteenth and early twentieth century (Hosken 1994). This was bolstered by a belief that masturbation could cause insanity. The practice did not continue, and genital modification was never adopted as a religious ceremony or as a routine operation for females in Western culture.

Ceremonial female circumcision is variously thought to remove the maleness from the female by removing a undeveloped penis, the clitoris, to assure chastity among wives and young women, to purify and cleanse, and to make a woman more beautiful and sexually attractive to men. In places where this is most widely practiced, women must be circumcised before they can be married.

There are at least three categories of female circumcision: Sunna, Excision, and Infibulation. Sunna circumcision refers to the practice of letting a small amount of blood from the clitoral hood or removing sections of the clitoral hood. This is not a widely practiced type of circumcision and is confined primarily to sections of Malaysia. Sunna circumcision is the closest analogue to male circumcision, although the delicate nature of the operation increases chances of surgical error.

Excision is the practice of removing, that is, excising, a portion of the genitalia. This ranges from the removal of the clitoris to the removal of the clitoris, labia major, and labia minor. The medicalized term of *clitorectomy* is used in the historic medical literature to refer to the removal of the clitoris alone.

Infibulation involves the excision of the clitoris, labia major, and labia minor, and the stitching shut of the vulva with only a small hole left for urination and menses. This is also referred to as pharonic circumcision because of a traditional attribution of this practice as being imposed on the female Jewish population by ancient Egyptian Pharaohs. Infibulation is the most radical procedure and carries the most significant medical implications. The procedure is most common in populations from Somalia, Ethiopia, Sudan, and Egypt. The procedure leaves a girl with a smooth, nondescript genital area that is considered by some to be aesthetically pleasing. However, it also leaves a girl with significant health problems, such as chronic urinary infections, menstrual difficulties, sexual dysfunction, and difficulties when giving birth.

Female Issues

A fundamental difference between male and female circumcisions is that female circumcision does not have the potential for medical benefit. Both excision and infibulation carry very significant negative health consequences. All types of female circumcision rely on cultural and religious reasoning. Opponents greatly resist naming this practice *circumcision* because using the term may diminish the seriousness of the practices of infibulation and excision. Health organizations, Islamic

groups, women's groups, and Western governments continue to press for the abolition of these practices. They have used various strategies to try to achieve this. For example, the Kenyan Family Planning Association has proposed alternate ceremonies that would be accompanied by the traditional educational information given when an adolescent is circumcised. This strategy helps make proponents of change seem to respect tradition and culture while changing an unhealthy aspect of a particular tradition.

Some of the issues that surround female circumcision are similar to those related to male circumcision: pain, the risk of infection, alteration of a *natural* state, and the status of children. Female circumcision, however, carries more serious implications, which include significant chance of damage to the clitoris during surgery (in the Sunna form), loss of sexual pleasure, patriarchal control, birthing complications, increased infections throughout life, refugee status in developed countries, and loss of mobility (in the infibulation form). Support for maintaining the practice relies on arguments from tradition and religion, and from the concern that daughters will not make fit wives if they are not circumcised. However, as women become more educated and empowered within these societies, practices of female circumcision are being modified.

In Western countries, questions are raised as to whether female circumcisions should be offered in clinical settings when parents who have emigrated request it. This would be done to avoid complications brought about when unskilled people perform the surgery in nonsterile environments; however, this would seem to go against a principle of basic Western medicine—to do no harm to patients. Some suggest the practice is a type of child abuse or persecution such that young, uncircumcised girls should be granted refugee status. These issues are being continuously challenged and debated in legislatures and medical governing associations.

See also: Family Planning; Family Rituals; Islam; Judaism; Religion; Sexuality; Sexuality Education

Bibliography

American Academy of Pediatrics. (1999). "Circumcision Policy Statement." *Pediatrics* (March) 103:686–693.

Denniston, G., and Milos, M., eds. (1997). *Sexual Mutilations: A Human Tragedy*. New York: Plenum Press.

Frank, R. et al. (2000). "A Trade-off Analysis of Routine Newborn Circumcision / Reply." *Pediatrics* (October) 106:954.

Gollaher, D. (2000). *Circumcision: A History of the World's Most Controversial Surgery*. New York: Basic Books.

Gruenbaum, E. (2001). *The Female Circumcision Controversy: An Anthropological Perspective*. Philadelphia: University of Pennsylvania Press.

Hosken, F. (1994). *The Hosken Report: Genital and Sexual Mutilation of Females*, 4th edition. Lexington, MA: Women's International Network News.

Hicks, E. (1993). *Infibulation: Female Mutilation in Islamic Northeastern Africa*. New Brunswick: Transaction Publishers.

Igwegbe A., and Egbuonu, I. (2000). "The Prevalence and Practice of Female Genital Mutilation in Nnewi, Nigeria: The Impact of Education." *Journal of Obstetrics and Gynecology* (September) 20:520–522.

Magied, A. A., and Omram, M. (1999). "The Uncircumcised Female is an Ideal State of Circumcision—A Case Study from Sudan." *Ahfad Journal* (December) 16:2–15.

Preiser, G., et. al. (2000). "Circumcision—The Debate Goes On / In Reply." *Pediatrics* (March) 105:681–684.

Toubia, N. (1994). "Female Circumcision as a Public Health Issue." *The New England Journal of Medicine*. 331:712–716.

Other Resources

Smith, Jacqueline. (1998). "Male Circumcision and the Rights of the Child." In *To Baehr in Our Minds: Essays in Human Rights from the Heart of the Netherlands,* ed. M. Bulterman, A. Hendriks; and J. Smith. Utrecht: SIM. Available from http://www.nocirc.org.

United Nations High Commissioner for Human Rights. (1989). "Convention on the Rights of the Child." Available from http://www.unhchr.ch.

World Health Organization. "Female Genital Mutilation." Available from http://www.who.int/frh-whd/.

PAUL J. FORD

CLAN

A *clan*—alternatively called a *sib* or *gens*—is a kind of kin group whose members claim a shared identity and certain rights based upon descent from a common ancestor. Clans are usually found in societies with descent systems based on only one lineage—descent is figured only through the male line (producing *patriclans*) or female line (producing *matriclans*). They have, however, also been reported from some societies with cognatic descent systems, in which descent may be traced through alternating generations, via either male or female connections. Clans usually contain a number of lineages; that is, groups whose members trace descent from a common ancestor through *known* genealogical links. Clan members will often rank internal lineages according to their seniority, with the lineages believed to be closest in direct descent from the clan's founder ranked highest. Such rankings are reached through consensus because clan members usually do not know or need to know the actual genealogical connections between the earliest remembered ancestors of each lineage and the apical, or first known, founder of the clan as a whole. In short, the clan is an extension of the lineage: it is a corporate kin group whose members define themselves by reference to their *believed,* but not demonstrated, common descent from a historically remote ancestral founder (Holly 1994).

The clan systems of different societies vary tremendously in terms of typical size and patterns of residence. In some small-scale cultures, all members of a clan may reside together to form a single community. More often, however, the lineages that make up a clan, which tend to be the land-holding units, reside in several locations. This was the case in precontact times for the Tsimshean nation on the north coast of British Columbia prior to contact, for instance, where a typical village included lineages belonging to two or more of the four clans named for the eagle, raven, wolf, and killer whale (Garfield 1939).

Clan membership in pre-Revolutionary southeastern China was notably extensive. All married men with their wives belonged to a *tsu,* a landholding patrilineage that worshipped together in a temple in which was stored the names of all members of the descent group, past and present. As a *tsu* expanded, members moved to new territories and set up new temples. A copy of the original genealogy would be stored there and a new one begun. As the original *tsu* expanded and dispersed, members continued to regard all those bearing the same surname as members of one exogamous clan (that is, a group of relatives from which one cannot choose a spouse). In rural China, the *tsu* lineage remained the key unit of kinship (Freedman 1958). As Chinese migrated to North America, however, they drew on wider clan identities to form mutual help associations. In a similar way, people of Scottish descent who are now dispersed across the globe maintain ties to their homeland by identifying with one or another of the Highland clans, each represented by distinctive tartans.

Clans thus provide members with a sense of identity. The founding ancestor often provides a key symbol for the group. Stories may be told of his or her exploits, and the name may be venerated. Members of clans in many small-scale cultures attribute a sacred quality to founding ancestors. In Aboriginal Australia, Melanesia, and Native North America, clan members often associate their founding ancestor with various natural phenomena—plants, animals, places, and so forth. These *totems* in turn stand as emblems of group identity and are treated with reverence. They are often associated with particular territories and landforms that the ancestor is believed to have created. They should not be eaten or damaged, and they often form key symbols in clan rituals (Lévi-Strauss 1963).

Clans form a common type of "corporate kin group" with legal and political functions in many cultures in which kinship forms a prominent element of social organization (Keesing 1975). Clans tend to be exogamous in small-scale cultures (and even some very large ones, as observed with traditional rural China). Because marriages must take place across clan lines, clan elders often play a key role in arranging marriages and associated exchanges. Although rights to land and other tangible assets tend to rest with lineages, members of clans may be drawn in to resolve disputes over inheritance. Clan members may appeal to clan solidarity to deal with special circumstances including organizing ceremonial exchanges, defending themselves against enemies or launching their own attacks on others, forming special work parties when a large project needs to be accomplished, and protecting common interests as when, for instance, individual members seek to sell lands to foreigners or undertake some other controversial measure such as inviting in foreign missionaries.

See also: KINSHIP

Bibliography

Freedman, M. (1958). *Lineage Organization in Southeastern China*. London: Athlone Press.

Garfield, V. E. (1939). "Tsimshian Clan and Society." *University of Washington Publications in Anthropology* 7:167–340.

Holy, L. (1996). *Anthropological Perspectives on Kinship*. London: Pluto Press.

Keesing, R. M. (1975). *Kin Groups and Social Structure*. New York: Holt, Rinehart and Winston.

Lévi-Strauss, C. (1963). *Totemism*. Boston: Beacon Press.

JOHN BARKER

CODEPENDENCY

The concept of codependency in the family system emerged from the study and treatment of alcoholism (Gorski and Miller 1984). In the alcoholic family system, codependency may be defined as a particular family relationship pattern in which the alcoholic is married to a spouse who, despite being a non-drinker, serves as a helper or facilitator to the alcoholic's problem behavior (Scaturo and McPeak 1998). The spouse, therefore, plays a role in the ongoing chemically dependent behavior of the alcoholic. The spouse's behavior may, unintentionally, foster the maintenance of the drinking problem by *enabling* the drinking pattern to continue. For example, the codependent spouse may make "sick calls" to the alcoholic's workplace following drinking episodes, thereby delaying the problem from coming to the foreground. Thus, the spouse is said to be a "co-dependent" of the alcoholic's chemically dependent behavior.

Codependency and the Family System: Related Terms and Synonyms

The notion of codependency is predicated upon and encompasses earlier ideas about family functioning. These concepts have included the notions of *family homeostasis, interlocking family pathology, the over-adequate/inadequate marital functioning, the one-up/one-down marital relationship, the marital quid pro quo,* and *marital complementarity.* A brief discussion of these concepts will be helpful in clarifying and understanding the nature and scope of codependency.

Family homeostasis (Jackson 1957) refers to the observation of significant changes in other family members in response to the behavior changes that take place in an identified patient undergoing some form of psychotherapy. For example, the mother of a boy in therapy for low self-esteem may not be entirely pleased by his recent success in winning an achievement award (Jackson 1957). In such an instance, the mother may rely on her son's low self-image and neediness to enhance her own feelings of usefulness and self-esteem, in which case the mother's subtle discouraging behavior may serve to maintain the boy's problem of poor self-esteem rather than to improve it. Family therapists, who anticipate the family's interdependent needs, are generally prepared for such an upset in the mother in response to such desired gains in treatment by the identified patient (in this instance, her son with low self-esteem). The family, and its interaction patterns, is a homeostatic system that remains in a constant state of balance with respect to one another.

One reason for this homeostatic mechanism in family functioning is that people tend to seek out marital partners whose neurotic needs and emotional issues fit with their own. This observation, which has been termed also the *interlocking pathology* (Ackerman 1958) in family relationships, is based upon a psychodynamic view of the family. This perspective highlights the interdependence and reciprocal effects of disturbed behavior among the various members of a family, rather than focusing on the emotional distress or internal conflicts of a single family member who is seen exclusively as "the patient." Ackerman (1958) asserted that an individual's personality should be assessed not in isolation, but within the social and emotional context of the entire family group.

A codependent marital relationship has been termed by various family therapists as *over-adequate versus inadequate functioning* of each of the spouses (Bowen 1960). This configuration has been described similarly as a *one-up versus one-down* marital relationship (Haley 1963). *One-up* denotes a dominant position (i.e., the one who is "in charge") in the family hierarchy, while *one-down* denotes an inferior position (i.e., the one who is being "taken care of") in the power arrangements within the family (Simon, Stierlin, and Wynne 1985). Murray Bowen (1960) points out

that these functional positions are, in actuality, only family "facades" rather than representative of the actual abilities of each of the spouses, each one appearing to occupy reciprocal positions in the family relative to the other. Thus, the *over-adequate* spouse presents a picture of an unrealistic facade of strength in the marriage. Likewise, the *inadequate* spouse presents a picture of helplessness in relation to the other. In actuality, spouses who have been married for any appreciable length of time usually have comparable emotional strength and maturity (Goldenberg and Goldenberg 1980). The codependent spouse, therefore, occupies the "appearance" of being over-adequate in relation to the inadequate position of the alcoholic spouse.

The above-noted ideas about family systems, upon which the popular concept of codependency is based, are clinical terms that have emerged from the field of family psychotherapy. As a result, codependency and its related concepts are a way of describing various kinds of *family dysfunction* or problem families in which there is some sort of mental health concern. However, degrees of psychopathology, or abnormal behavior, typically exist upon some continuum from the "severely pathological" (e.g., psychotic behavior or suicidality in a given family member) on one end versus relatively "normative social behavior" on the other, with various forms of human behavior falling somewhere in between these two poles. Thus, codependency as a dysfunctional form of family interaction is likely to fall on the pathological end of the continuum. However, this basic pattern of family behavior, in less extreme forms, can be seen in families at the normative end of the continuum, as well.

The concept of marital *complementarity* (Bateson 1972) has been used to describe dyadic (i.e., two-person) relationship patterns in which an individual's behavior and coping strategies differ from that of their spouse, but the two styles or patterns of behavior fit together in a dynamic equilibrium or active balance with one another (Simon, Stierlin, and Wynne 1985). In addition, the notion of complementary needs among potential spouses has been cited as an important factor in selecting a mate (Winch 1958). Likewise, Don D. Jackson (1965) has applied the legal term, *quid pro quo,* in the sphere of marriage to describe the type of "bargain," or complementarity, to which couples typically arrive in an agreement to marry. Literally translated from Latin as "something for something," marital quid pro quo implies that arrangements in the marriage generally function best over the long run if a suitable agreement that is genuinely collaborative in nature can be reached by the spouses. For example, to run relatively smoothly, agreements typically need to be made in the "division of family labor," which takes into account the sum total of the labor (both income-producing, as well as maintenance of home life) with sufficient fairness and acknowledgement of the contributions made by both. Only when this division of family functions becomes polarized and taken to the extreme (e.g., breadwinner *versus* homemaker roles), does such a quid pro quo risk rigidity, misunderstanding, and proneness to family pathology. Codependency is one such form of polarized marital role behavior (e.g., the "helper" versus the "sick" role) that signifies pathological complementarity and family dysfunction.

Codependency: Popular Definition and Usage

Melody Beattie (1987) popularized the concept of codependency in self-help literature (Starker 1990). She defined codependency for the lay reader: "A codependent person is one who has let another person's behavior affect him or her, and who is obsessed with controlling that person's behavior" (Beattie 1987, p. 36). She notes that the expression has been used as "alcohol treatment center jargon" and "professional slang," and acknowledged that the term, as it was used, had a "fuzzy definition."

The popularization of the term *codependency* has had both positive and negative consequences for the fields of psychotherapy and family therapy. On the positive side of the ledger, the self-help literature in general, and the popular usage of the term codependency in particular, have been helpful in raising public awareness of the complex interrelationships which take place within alcoholic families. They have provided, in relatively simple and understandable terms, an appreciation of the role that everyone assumes in a family where a severe psychological disorder such as alcoholism occurs. For example, wives may "cover" for their alcoholic husbands' inability to keep up with the everyday demands of the home and workplace due to their excessive drinking. Children may take on age-inappropriate tasks, such as making sure that the house is locked at night because the alcoholic

parents are too inebriated to do so (this is known as the *parentification* of children in the family therapy literature [Haley 1976]). In essence, no one in an alcoholic family is immune from the devastating effects which alcohol has upon them, and the contribution to the maintenance of an alcohol problem that others in the family may inadvertently take on. Indeed, enhancing a general understanding of these complex family behaviors is no small contribution to the realm of public education.

However, the widespread usage of the term *codependency* frequently has resulted in misunderstanding and misuse of the expression by the general public, as well as some imprecision by professional mental health practitioners in clinic settings. With regard to the lay public, Barbara Fiese and Douglas Scaturo (1995) conducted group discussions with adult children of alcoholics (ACOAs) in an effort to understand the difficulties that they confront in parenting their own children, given their own problematic upbringings. In these group discussions, there was a frequent misuse of professional jargon by the ACOAs that often led to misunderstandings of the complex and painful life experiences that the group members were trying to convey to one another. The circuitous use of jargon seemed to prevent group members from communicating with one another in clear, commonly understood language. The use and misuse of such jargon also appeared to short-circuit group discussion by promoting a presumed commonality of family life experience that may or may not have been accurate. Group members responded to the jargon used by others prematurely—without waiting to discover whether actual life experiences were comparable between them. Overall, the use of professional jargon by these lay people appeared to diminish the degree of coherence in their discussions.

Even more problematic is that the widespread generality of the concept's usage has contributed to some degree of imprecision by practicing psychotherapists. The treatment of codependent family dynamics is considerably more complex than the lay concept of codependency might suggest. Scaturo and his colleagues (2000) have discussed several complexities in the family treatment of codependency that require a precise understanding and knowledge of the concept. The first involves the proper therapeutic confrontation of codependent behavior by the psychotherapist in family therapy with this dimension. Briefly, the confrontation of the codependent spouse's contribution to the chemically dependent behavior of the alcoholic involves the complex therapeutic task of "(a) acknowledging and validating the well-intended nature of the codependent's responses, and (b) assisting the codependent spouse in finding new ways of being useful in the family in order not to deprive them of their helping role within the family" (Scaturo et al. 2000, p. 68). A second issue involves making the proper therapeutic distinction between codependency and the "normal" nurturant behavior of a parent or spouse. In short, codependent patients in treatment may engage in inappropriate self-criticism and characterize ordinary and necessary care-taking behaviors in family life as unhealthy "codependency," and it is the therapist's responsibility to assist them in making proper distinctions. Thus, how mental health care professionals understand the concept of codependency has implications for the treatment of these family dynamics as well as how these concepts are understood by codependent patients and their families in treatment.

Codependency in Other Psychological and Family Problems

Codependent family dynamics have been observed in areas of psychological difficulty other than in families with chemical dependency. For example, Scaturo and his colleagues (Scaturo and Hardoby 1988; Scaturo and Hayman 1992) have observed codependent relationships, discussed in terms of "interlocking pathology" (Ackerman 1958), in families of military veterans suffering from Posttraumatic Stress Disorder (PTSD) following traumatic combat experiences in war. PTSD is a psychiatric disorder in which someone who has been exposed to a psychologically traumatic experience, such as combat, experiences an array of disabling symptoms, including intrusive distressing recollections of the experience or recurrent traumatic nightmares, an avoidance of anything that might be associated with the trauma, a numbing of emotional responsiveness to significant others, and a hypervigilance or an exaggerated startle response to the over-anticipation of danger (American Psychiatric Association 1994). In marriages prior to the wartime traumatization, the spouses of combat veterans seem to experience a genuine change in the character of the person that they knew before the

war, and returning to an emotionally intimate relationship required a substantial adjustment of mutual expectations. However, in relationships that began after the trauma, something much more like codependency, or interlocking pathology, becomes part of the couple's relationship. The posttraumatic disability is already a known quantity to both parties at the outset of their relationship. The "helper" and "sick" roles are already established as a part of the mutual attraction to one another, and the codependency of the "helper" is an integral part of the relationship's development. The same observation is applicable to forms of traumatic experience other than military trauma, such as the survivors of rape.

Similarly, the psychiatric maladies of panic disorder and agoraphobia are another such example of where the "helper" versus "sick" roles play a part in coping with what ultimately becomes a family problem (Scaturo 1994). Panic attacks are brief periods of intense fear without a clear precipitant (i.e., objective threat) with various psychophysiological symptoms of disabling severity, including heart palpitations, trembling, abdominal distress, and possible fears of dying (American Psychiatric Association 1994). When the fear, or anxiety, is accompanied by fear of being outside one's home, being in a crowd or public place, and such situations are avoided and travel restricted, then agoraphobia may be said to go along with the panic disorder. Again, if the syndrome of panic disorder is a known quantity at the outset of marital relationship, a codependent situation in which clearly defined "helper" and "sick" roles may be easily established. Such a codependent marital dynamic may be one of the reasons that what has been termed "spouse-assisted behavior therapy" (Scaturo 1994)—in which the spouse is included in the anxiety patient's treatment—has been demonstrated to have superior effectiveness over the use of individual behavior therapy with the patient alone (Barlow, O'Brien, and Last 1984; Cerney et al. 1987).

Summary

Codependency has been defined as an alcoholic family dynamic in which the alcoholic is married to a spouse who, despite him- or herself not being chemically dependent, serves as a helper in, and inadvertent contributor to, the maintenance of the alcoholic's problem drinking. The notion of codependency was predicated upon related concepts in family systems theory that have included family homeostasis, interlocking family pathology, over-adequate/inadequate marital functioning, the one-up/one-down marital relationship, the marital quid pro quo, and marital complementarity. The popularization of the term *codependency* among the general public through the self-help literature has had both positive and negative consequences for the practice of psychotherapy. On the one hand, the popular usage of the term has been helpful in raising public awareness regarding the complex interrelationships that transpire within alcoholic families. On the other hand, the widespread usage of the term often has resulted in misunderstanding and misuse of the concept by the general public, as well as some imprecision in its usage by mental health professionals. For example, psychologically healthy and normally nurturing behaviors on the part of a parent or spouse frequently may be misconstrued as pathologically codependent behavior when the complexity, functions, or ramifications of this concept are not fully understood. Finally, although codependent family dynamics were initially observed in chemically dependent families, they have also been observed clinically in families with other kinds of psychological and behavioral difficulties. Examples include families of military veterans suffering from war-related post-traumatic stress disorder and families with a member suffering from panic disorder and agoraphobia. Families in which a member exhibits psychological or behavioral problems are likely to be vulnerable to codependent family dynamics, as well.

See also: ANXIETY DISORDERS; CHILDREN OF ALCOHOLICS; FAMILY SYSTEMS THEORY; MARITAL QUALITY; POSTTRAUMATIC STRESS DISORDER (PTSD); SUBSTANCE ABUSE; THERAPY: COUPLE RELATIONSHIPS; THERAPY: FAMILY RELATIONSHIPS

Bibliography

Ackerman, N. W. (1958). "Interlocking Pathology in Family Relationships." In *Changing Concepts in Psychoanalytic Medicine,* ed. S. Rado and G. Daniels. New York: Grune and Stratton.

American Psychiatric Association. (1994). *Diagnostic and Statistical Manual of Mental Disorders,* 2nd edition. Washington, DC: Author.

Barlow, D. H.; O'Brien, G. T.; and Last, C. G. (1984). "Couples Treatment of Agoraphobia." *Behavior Therapy* 15:41–58.

Bateson, G. (1972). *Steps to an Ecology of Mind.* New York: Ballantine Books.

Beattie, M. (1987). *Codependent No More.* New York: Ballantine Books.

Bowen, M. (1960). "A Family Concept of Schizophrenia." In *The Etiology of Schizophrenia,* ed. D. D. Jackson. New York: Basic Books.

Cerny, J. A.; Barlow, D. H.; Craske, M. G.; and Himadi, W. G. (1987). "Couples Treatment of Agoraphobia: A Two-Year Follow-Up." *Behavior Therapy* 18:401–415.

Fiese, B. H., and Scaturo, D. J. (1995). "The Use of Self-Help Terminology in Focus-Group Discussions with Adult Children of Alcoholics: Implications for Research and Clinical Practice." *Family Therapy* 22(1):1–8.

Goldenberg, I., and Goldenberg, H. (1980). *Family Therapy: An Overview.* Monterey, CA: Brooks/Cole.

Gorski, T. T., and Miller, M. (1984). "Co-Alcoholic Relapse: Family Factors and Warning Signs." In *Co-Dependency, An Emerging Issue.* Pompano Beach, FL: The U.S. Journal of Drug and Alcohol Dependency and Health Communications.

Haley, J. (1963). *Strategies of Psychotherapy.* New York: Grune and Stratton.

Haley, J. (1976). *Problem-Solving Therapy.* San Francisco: Jossey-Bass.

Jackson, D. D. (1957). "The Question of Family Homeostasis." *Psychiatric Quarterly, Supplement* 31:79–90.

Jackson, D. D. (1965). "Family Rules: Marital Quid Pro Quo." *Archives of General Psychiatry* 12:589–594.

Scaturo, D. J. (1994). "Integrative Psychotherapy for Panic Disorder and Agoraphobia in Clinical Practice." *Journal of Integrative Psychotherapy* 4(3):253–272.

Scaturo, D. J., and Hardoby, W. J. (1988). "Psychotherapy with Traumatized Vietnam Combatants: An Overview of Individual, Group, and Family Treatment Modalities." *Military Medicine* 153:262–269.

Scaturo, D. J., and Hayman, P. M. (1992). "The Impact of Combat Trauma Across the Family Life Cycle." *Journal of Traumatic Stress* 5(2):273–288.

Scaturo, D. J., and McPeak, W. R. (1998). "Clinical Dilemmas in Contemporary Psychotherapy: The Search for Clinical Wisdom." *Psychotherapy* 35(1):1–12.

Scaturo, D. J.; Hayes, T.; Sagula, D.; and Walter, T. (2000). "The Concept of Codependency and Its Context

Within Family Systems Theory." *Family Therapy* 27(2):63–70.

Simon, F. B.; Stierlin, H.; and Wynne, L. C. (1985). *The Language of Family Therapy: A Systemic Vocabulary and Sourcebook*. New York: Family Process Press.

Starker, S. (1990). "Self-Help Books: Ubiquitous Agents of Health Care." *Medical Psychotherapy* 3:187–194.

Winch, R. F. (1958). *Mate Selection: A Study of Complementary Needs*. New York: Harper.

DOUGLAS J. SCATURO

COHABITATION

Cohabitation, sometimes called *consensual union* or *de facto marriage,* refers to unmarried heterosexual couples living together in an intimate relationship. Cohabitation as such is not a new phenomenon. It has, however, developed into a novel family form in contrast with conventional marriage. Part of this change is associated with the absolute rise in cohabitational relationships. Since the 1970s, many countries, particularly those in North America and Europe, have experienced rapid growth in their cohabitation rates. Although these numbers generally remain small relative to families composed of married couples, the absolute numbers of cohabiting couples have increased dramatically. Cohabitation was obscure and even taboo throughout the nineteenth century and until the 1970s. Nonmarital unions have become common because the meaning of the family has been altered by individualistic social values that have progressively matured since the late 1940s. As postwar trends illustrate, marriage is no longer the sanctified, permanent institution it once was. The proliferation of divorce, remarriage, stepfamilies, and single parenthood has transformed the institution of the family. With these structural changes, attitudes toward nonmarital unions have become increasingly permissive.

Because cohabitation involves a shared household between intimate partners, it has characteristics in common with marriage. Similarities include pooled economic resources, a gender division of labor in the household, and sexual exclusivity. However, even though the day-to-day interaction between cohabiting couples parallels that of married couples in several ways, important distinctions remain. While some argue that cohabitation has become a variant of marriage, the available evidence does not support this position. Kingsley Davis (1985) points out that if cohabitation were simply a variant of marriage then its increased prevalence vis-à-vis marriage would lack significance. Sociologists treat cohabitation as a distinct occurrence not just because it has displaced marriage, but also because it represents a structural change in family relationships.

Cohabitational relationships are distinct from marital ones in several crucial ways. Although these differences have become less pronounced with the increase in cohabitation (and could thus eventually vanish), the following characteristics define the essential boundaries between cohabitation and marriage.

(1) *Age.* People in cohabitational relationships tend to be younger than people in marital relationships. This supports the argument that cohabitation is often an antecedent to marriage. The majority of cohabitational relationships dissolve because the couples involved get married;

(2) *Fertility.* Children are less likely to be born into cohabitational relationships than they are into marital relationships;

(3) *Stability.* Cohabitational relationships are short-lived compared to marital relationships. In Canada, only about 12 percent of cohabitations are expected to last ten years. By comparison, 90 percent of first marriages are expected to last this long (Wu 2000). The majority of cohabitational relationships terminate within three years. Although many of these relationships end because of marriage, the lack of longevity in cohabitations as such illustrates that these relationships have yet to develop into a normative variant of marriage;

(4) *Social acceptance.* Even with its numerical growth and spread throughout society, cohabitation is not as socially acceptable as marriage. Cohabitation is socially tolerated in part because it is expected that cohabiting partners will eventually become married. Indeed, according to U.S. data, about three-quarters of never married cohabitors had definite plans for marriage or believed they

would eventually marry their partner (Bumpass, Sweet, and Cherlin 1991). The youthful profile of cohabitation shows that marriage is still the preferred choice of union for most couples. If cohabitation were a variant of marriage, it would have a larger prevalence in older cohorts. Although many people have chosen to delay marriage, most have not rejected it completely. A major reason cohabitations have lower fertility than marriage is because couples tend to abandon cohabitation when children are in the immediate future (Manning and Smock 1995). In most countries, marriage is perceived as the most secure and legitimate union when children are involved;

(5) *State recognition.* Unlike marriage, cohabitation is not sanctioned by the state, and persons in nonmarital unions do not necessarily acquire specific legal rights and obligations through their union. Without a formal ceremony and legal documentation, a couple is not married even if they have lived together for many years. However, after a set period of time (usually one or two years), cohabiting couples are recognized as *common-law* partners in some countries. In such instances, common-law partners can have similar rights and obligations as they would in a legal marriage. Common-law marriage can parallel legal marriage in terms of child support and custody, spousal maintenance, income tax, unemployment insurance, medical and dental benefits, and pensions. The degree to which cohabitors are treated like legally married couples usually corresponds to the degree nonmarital unions are socially accepted. But even where cohabitors do have rights, these are often unknown to cohabitors and more complicated to exercise than they are for married persons. In many cases, the rights that cohabiting couples possess have been established by court decisions rather than by state law, as they are for married couples. Perhaps the most crucial legal distinction between these unions is the absence of shared property rights in common-law relationships. Married couples acquire shared property rights upon establishing their union, but cohabiting couples must do so through the courts. In sum, no uniform and guaranteed set of rights applies to cohabitation. This deficiency shows that in most countries, cohabitation is not yet perceived as a legitimate variant to marriage from the perspective of the state.

Trends and Patterns

Although sociologists treat cohabitation as a novel phenomenon, it is generally recognized that it has existed long enough to predate marriage. Until the mid-eighteenth century, the difference between marriage and cohabitation was unclear in many countries. In England, for example, the distinction between these unions remained fluid until Lord Hardwicke codified marriage in 1753. However, common-law marriage remained popular well after the passage of Hardwicke's Marriage Act. The lack of officials to oversee formal marriages and jurisdictional nuances kept marriage and cohabitation indistinct (Holland 1998; Seff 1995). Marriage really developed into the institution as we understand it today in the nineteenth century. During this period, marriage transformed from a more or less religious practice to one commonly formalized under civil law, and thus became the norm. But this should not be taken out of context. As Winifred Holland (1990) remarks, the family has always been a flexible organization and has responded to changing social circumstances in a dynamic manner, and marriage became the norm for specific historical reasons. Hence, it is incorrect to suggest that cohabitation is "deviant" behavior because this implies that marriage has *always* been the norm.

Although cohabitation has existed for a very long time, modern trends in cohabitation are qualitatively different from those of the past. The significance rests in the fact that cohabitation has increased in a context where conventional marriage is a clearly defined and dominant social institution. What sets contemporary patterns of cohabitation apart from historical patterns is not simply numerical preponderance. Cohabitation after the 1960s has special importance because it indicates a clear shift in normative behavior related to how families are formed and perceived. Although common-law unions were not unusual or contrary to social values before the nineteenth century, the same cannot be said about cohabitation in contemporary times. The lack of distinction between marital and nonmarital union in England before the nineteenth century meant that cohabitation was not abnormal behavior. By contrast, today's nonmarital families represent a clear break from social convention.

Prevalence. One of the most salient facts about cohabitation is how much more prevalent it has become since the 1970s. In the United States, there were 523,000 households with two unrelated adults of opposite sex in 1970, compared with 1,589,000 in 1980—a 300 percent increase in just one decade (Spanier 1985). U.S. survey data on marital status and living arrangements indicate that cohabitation grew by 12 percent per annum between 1970 and 1980 (Davis 1985). This trend continued in the following decades. In 1990, there were 2.9 million cohabiting couples in the United States (Seltzer 2000), and the U.S. Bureau of the Census recorded over 4.2 million cohabiting households in March 1998.

Although these figures account for small percentages of the total pool of marital and nonmarital households, the increase in the number of people who have *ever* cohabited shows that cohabitation is a much more prevalent social trend than the proportional figures reveal. According to U.S. estimates of cohabitation, almost half of the population in their late twenties to early thirties had at some time been in a cohabitational relationship (Bumpass and Sweet 1989). Larry Bumpass and James Sweet's data also show that cohabitation has rapidly become an important antecedent to marriage. Of first marriages in the 1965–74 cohort, 9 percent of married respondents reported that they had cohabited with their future spouse. In the 1975–79 cohort, 26 percent had cohabited with their future spouse, and in the 1980–84 cohort, 34 percent had cohabited. In the 1990–94 cohort, almost 60 percent of all marriages formed had begun as nonmarital unions (Bumpass and Lu 2000).

In Canada, remarkable increases can be charted since 1981, the year in which the Canadian census began to record data on cohabitation. Over the period 1981–96, the number of cohabiting households increased from 356,600 to 920,640. Today, one in seven families is composed of unmarried couples in comparison to one in seventeen only fifteen years ago. As a percentage of all unions, cohabitations accounted for 13.7 percent in the mid-nineties, a significant difference over the 6.3 percent recorded in the early eighties. In the early 1970s, over 16 percent of all first unions were

Cohabitation involves a shared household between intimate partners and thus has characteristics in common with marriage. Although division of labor according to gender prevails, women may look for partners who are willing to share domestic work in what they perceive as a "trial marriage." SCOTT ROPER/CORBIS

cohabitational relationships. By the late 1980s, more than 51 percent of Canadian first unions were cohabitational relationships (Wu 2000).

Similar patterns have been observed in many European countries. In Sweden, which has the highest prevalence of nonmarital union in the world, cohabitation has been the norm since the 1970s. For Swedes, cohabitation is nearly a universal experience—for example, 96 percent of married Swedish women had previously been in a cohabitational relationship by the late 1970s (Hoem and Hoem 1988). In France, about 65 percent of all first unions were cohabitational by the early 1980s, more than double the level of one decade earlier (Leridon 1990). In 1994, the percentage of unmarried cohabiting couples was about 10 percent of all family units in Denmark, 13 percent in Finland, and 9 percent in Iceland (Yearbook of Nordic Statistics 1996). In England, cohabitation before marriage grew from one in four in the 1960s to about seven in ten in the early 1990s (Kiernan and Estaugh 1993). Data show that these trends prevail throughout Western Europe. In rough correspondence with declining marriage rates, the Eurobarometer Surveys conducted in 1996 show a preference for cohabitation among youth. For women between the ages of twenty-five and twenty-nine, for example, 40 percent of first unions were cohabitations in Austria, 37 percent in Switzerland, and 46 percent in West Germany (Kiernan 2000).

Differentials. In a study of U.S. and Dutch couples, Geertje Wiersma (1983) points out that contemporary patterns of cohabitation are unique because they developed in circumstances characterized by individual choice. Previous patterns emerged mainly because of social prerogative or constituted an imperative, and because of this, cohabitation tended to be isolated to particular segments of society (e.g., the poor classes). Having come about in a context of free choice, contemporary cohabitation is not restricted to any subdivision of society. However, although cohabitation occurs across social categories, important differentials exist that affect its prevalence. Not all people have the same propensity to cohabit. Rates of cohabitation are influenced by factors such as age, gender, marital status, education, employment status, religion, and others. Certain people are selected into cohabitational relationships, or, in other words, cohabitors tend to be certain types, even though cohabitation has spread throughout society. Researchers have isolated numerous factors that determine the selection process. Among the many traits that affect who cohabits, the basic differences are characterized by age, gender, race, socioeconomic status, and personal attitude.

First, age is certainly the most important factor. Although cohabitation is found in every adult birth cohort, cohabitors are primarily selected from younger groups. U.S. census data shows that 38 percent of all cohabitors were between the ages of twenty-five and thirty-four and another 20 percent were between the ages of thirty-five and forty-four. At the other end, very few were in cohabitational relationships in the over-sixty-four group. This group accounted for only 4 percent of all households with two unmarried, unrelated adults (U.S. Bureau of the Census 1998). Comparable trends are visible in other countries. In England, the General Household Survey from 1989 recorded that more than 47 percent of cohabiting men and more than 39 percent of cohabiting women were between the ages of twenty-five and thirty-four. In sharp contrast, only about 7 percent of cohabiting men and 8 percent of cohabiting women were between the ages of forty-five and fifty-four (Kiernan and Estaugh 1993). In Canada, cohabitation is also rare in the older age cohorts. About 13 percent of cohabitations in 1996 were between the ages of forty-five and fifty-four, compared to 31 percent between the ages of twenty-five and thirty-four and 20 percent ranging from thirty-five to forty-four. However, like all cohorts, the older ones have become increasingly more likely to enter cohabitational relationships. In 1981, only a little over 4 percent of cohabitations involved those between the ages of forty-five and fifty-four, which means that the 1996 figure represents a threefold increase (Wu 2000).

Second, a greater proportion of men cohabit than do women. One would expect the numbers to be equal in this regard since every cohabitation includes one man and one woman. However, the higher prevalence of men is not calculated in terms of absolute numbers—it is a ratio of cohabiting men to the total male population. For example, the rate of cohabitation for Canadian men in 1996 was slightly more than 17 percent. For Canadian women the rate was about 15.5 percent. Evidence suggests that this trend has deepened over time. Men tend to marry women younger than themselves, and therefore enter marriage at later ages than do women. Men are thus selected into cohabitation at a greater rate than women because being unmarried longer places them at a greater risk of being drawn into a cohabitational relationship (Wu 2000).

Socioeconomic status is a third factor that affects who cohabits. Although cohabitation first came to scholarly attention because of the living arrangements of 1960s college students, these persons were the imitators, not the innovators (Cherlin 1992). It was been widely observed that lower education levels and poorer employment status positively affect the propensity to cohabit (Cherlin 1992; Raley 2000; Seltzer 2000; Smock and Manning 1997). Researchers argue that economic security is a key factor for the formation of marriages (e.g., Oppenheimer 1994). People from poorer backgrounds often delay marriage because of insufficient economic resources. This makes them more likely to form cohabitational relationships than well-educated people. U.S. evidence shows that of nineteen to forty-four-year-old women who have ever cohabited, the probability for high school dropouts was 60 percent versus 37 percent for college graduates (Bumpass and Lu 1999).

Fourth, many cohabitors are self-selected because of their personal attitudes toward nonmarital unions. Because cohabitation occurs against the norm, cohabitors are partially rejecting the society's dominant value system. Those people who enter cohabitational relationships tend to perceive social rules in flexible terms. On the other hand, people with traditional perceptions of the family and religious backgrounds that prohibit premarital unions are unlikely to enter into cohabitation because of their conservative values (Axinn and Thornton 1993).

Reasons for Cohabitation

Many observers have assumed that the trend toward cohabitation and later marriage signifies a breakdown of the traditional family. However, this standpoint rests on a limited understanding of family relationships. The notion of the traditional family is mostly a discursive construction, and, as such, it ultimately fails to comprehend the historical complexities of family relationships. For example, as Andrew Cherlin (1992) points out, the pattern of later marriage is anomalous only in comparison to the 1940 to 1960 marriage pattern. The men and women born between 1920 and 1945 married at earlier ages than any other cohort in the twentieth century.

The average age of first marriage in late twentieth century actually suggests a return to the pattern that prevailed at the turn of the century. Evidence given by Catherine Fitch and Steven Ruggles (2000) shows that, in 1890, the median age at marriage of white U.S. men was twenty-six and twenty-two for white U.S. women. From this long-term peak, the decline between 1890 and 1930 (which was especially large for men) was followed by a sudden, acute drop dating from about 1940 to 1960. By 1960, the average age of marriage for men was twenty-two and less than twenty for women. These ages have rapidly increased since the 1970s. By 1980, the average ages at marriage

were about twenty-four and twenty-two, respectively; by 1990, about twenty-six and twenty-four. The key point here is that the timing of marriage can widely fluctuate in the long term. Such vicissitudes are not necessarily caused by the so-called breakdown of the family, but are usually symptomatic of specific historical conditions.

The notion that cohabitation somehow represents a collapse of the traditional family is inaccurate considering the historical prevalence of nonmarital union and broad shifts in the timing of marriage. Indeed, the intensification of cohabitation is associated with factors integral to the institutionalization of the nuclear family in the 1950s. According to Cherlin (1992), the pattern of early marriage prevalent in the late 1940s and the 1950s was partially caused by peace and prosperity, both of which released a social demand for marriage that had been suppressed by the Great Depression and World War II.

In the United States, the proliferation of the nuclear family was encouraged by government-guaranteed mortgages, of which millions of families took advantage to purchase single-family houses outside of the cities. The postwar economic boom created a large, stable market of high-paying (family-wage) employment for men, and this made the nuclear family more or less self-sufficient. This period emphasized home and family life, which partly accounts for the baby boom, which followed the marriage boom. Many of the values associated with these trends were projected (and disseminated) through the popular media. Television programs such as *Leave it to Beaver* centered on Mr. and Mrs. Cleaver and their children and had little to do with grandparents, uncles, and aunts. The new focus on the nuclear family signified a disintegration of extended kin networks. The postwar retreat into the nuclear family marked the progressive development of individualism because it was a step away from group-oriented family life. As the bonds between individuals and wider kin networks weakened and even dissolved, people gradually began to seek meaning through more self-oriented goals and values, particularly those realized through spousal relationships (Cherlin 1992).

Cherlin (1992) remarks that there was no reason for individualism to stop at the nuclear family since personal fulfillment and family obligations could often conflict. Moreover, the general economic expansion, which made the nuclear family secure, also created a large job market for women. More and more women began either to delay marriage or to balance paid employment and family responsibilities because of high demand for their labor in the service sector. Women's new-found financial independence and the spread of more individual-centered values eventually contributed to the instability of marriage. Changes in social standards meant that people no longer felt as obligated to remain in unhappy marriages. Financial independence meant that they did not have to. Besides increasing the divorce rate, changes in postwar economics and ideas caused the rise in delayed marriage and cohabitation.

Gary Becker (1981) argues that a couple marries because they realize economic benefits from each other's specialized skills. These skills (which are rooted in the gender division of labor) created economic interdependence between men and women, and marriage became the institution that reproduced their economic security. According to Becker, the single most important factor underlying social transformation related to lower fertility, divorce, and cohabitation has been the rise in the earning power of women. An essential change in the gender division of labor has followed women's increased participation in the waged labor force. This change has reduced the economic advantages and necessity of marriage, and consequently, divorce rates have increased and marriage rates have decreased. The reduced benefits of marriage and the specter of marital instability have made nonmarriage more attractive. Reduction in the expected economic gains from marriage has made men and women more hesitant to enter marital unions, but a shared household still offers economic advantages. Cohabitations make good sense because they capitalize on the benefits of a shared household without the economic risks associated with marriage.

Valerie Oppenheimer (1994) explains patterns of cohabitation from another economic perspective. She suggests that rather than being a result of women's growing economic independence, the decline in marriage more closely relates to the deterioration of men's position in the labor market. Oppenheimer's theory holds considerable explanatory value because periods of early marriage have typically paralleled periods with strong labor markets. Oppenheimer argues that because marriage timing usually corresponds to men's ability to establish an independent household, reduction in

their earning power temporarily prices them out of the marriage market. However, even though economic costs delay marriage, they do not affect the desirability of union as such, and because of its lesser costs, cohabitation has emerged as an important alternative to marital union.

Apart from economic explanations, changes in social norms bound up in the rise of individualism also explain the increase in cohabitation. Perhaps more than anything else, it is this shift in thinking that separates contemporary cohabitation from past. For the most part, trends in historical cohabitation were associated with the ambiguity between legal and common-law marriage, or with the availability of officials to formalize marriages. By contrast, contemporary cohabitation behavior is a conscious choice, one that expresses the tension that has developed between personal goals and social norms. In this respect, cohabitation has increased because marriage can often decrease or disrupt individual goal attainment.

Meanings of Cohabitation

First, in most instances, cohabitation serves as a transitional stage between single and married life. Cohabitation is perceived as a trial marriage that is meant to assess the viability of the partnership in the long term. In this sense, cohabitation is a pragmatic option because of its potential to weed out bad matches before marriage, with the putative intention being less chance of divorce. As noted above, the majority of cohabiting couples expect to transform their cohabitation into marriage, and most do. For example, cohabitation has rapidly become an antecedent to marriage in Britain. About 6 percent of British first marriages from 1965 to 1969 were preceded by cohabitation; in contrast, about 58 percent were preceded by cohabitation from 1985 to 1988. This trend has been more pronounced for remarriages. In the 1960s, about one-quarter of all remarriages were preceded by cohabitation compared to more than two-thirds by the late 1980s (Kiernan and Estaugh 1993).

Second, cohabitation is also an alternative to marriage. In some cases, this means a renouncement of marriage. For most couples, however, cohabitation is not a rejection of marriage, but an alternative union that expresses the reality that marriage is not the defining characteristic of their family lives (Seltzer 2000). Cohabitation exists as an alternative when marriage is not immediately desirable, practical, or possible. Cohabitation requires comparatively less economic and social commitment, and it is generally regarded as more flexible and egalitarian than marriage. Hence, cohabitation is attractive to people who have personal goals that might be disrupted by marriage, or by people who cannot form a marriage for financial or legal reasons.

Third, some observers argue that cohabitation is an alternative to being single. Ronald Rindfuss and Audrey VandenHeuvel (1990) suggest that, although cohabitation is similar to marriage in some ways, it is also appropriate to compare it to single life. From this point of view, cohabitation occupies an intermediate position between singlehood and marriage. Although cohabiters obviously embrace some of the characteristics of marriage, such as shared household and sexual intimacy, in terms of fertility, nonfamilial activities, and homeownership, their behavior has more in common with single people than the married. Hence, Rindfuss and VandenHeuvel argue that cohabitation is not necessarily a premarital phase or an alternative to marriage, but can be an intensification of the dating experience.

Consequences of Cohabitation

Marital stability. Because cohabitation performs the function of a trial marriage, we would intuitively expect marriages preceded by cohabitation to be more stable than those not preceded by cohabitation. However, studies have shown that cohabitation negatively influences the quality and longevity of marriages (Axinn and Thornton 1992; Balakrishnan et al. 1987; Bennett, Blanc, and Bloom 1988). The higher incidence of divorce among former cohabitors has two basic explanations. First, the *selection* hypothesis suggests that same characteristics that make certain people most likely to enter cohabitation also make them most likely to divorce. People who cohabit before marriage generally have individualistic attitudes that make them less committed to marital union in the first place and more likely to seek divorce in response to marital problems. The *experience* hypothesis suggests that premarital union conditions cohabitors to accept divorce more readily. The cohabitation experience changes people's perspective on marriage and divorce because it emphasizes individual needs and demonstrates that there are alternatives to marriage.

Gender equality. Although the gender division of labor prevails within cohabitation, cohabiting couples may choose to organize this more equitably than is characteristic of marriage. Judith Seltzer (2000) notes that because cohabitation is often perceived as a trial marriage, women may select men who are willing to share domestic work. The desire for a fairer distribution of housework is pronounced for cohabiting women because many of them have paid employment outside of the home. However, although cohabitors profess more liberal gender attitudes, the reality is a different matter. According to Scott South and Glenna Spitze (1994), cohabitation and marriage do not differ significantly in terms of the gender division of labor. Cohabiting women do thirty-one hours of housework per week compared to thirty-seven hours for married women, and cohabiting men do nineteen hours per week compared to eighteen hours for married men.

Children. One of the essential purposes of marriage is procreation. If cohabitation is to develop into a viable alternative to marriage, then it must become a good environment for children to be born and raised. U.S. census data show that children are a significant presence in cohabitations. As of March 1998, approximately 35 percent of cohabitational households included children under fifteen (U.S. Bureau of the Census). Pamela Smock (2000) observes that an estimated 40 percent of children will live in a cohabitational household sometime during their childhood, which stresses the importance of understanding the effects that cohabitations have on children. Smock identifies two major issues facing these children. First, in general, cohabiting households have fewer economic resources than married households. Second, children in cohabiting households are likely to experience family instability because many cohabitational relationships terminate. Both of these matters have serious implications for the well-being of children who experience parental cohabitation.

Conclusion

Although cohabitation has existed throughout history, modern trends are especially important because they are part of a broader pattern of social transformation affecting the family. The institution of marriage remains the dominant form of family living, but the rapid increase in cohabitation suggests this could change. In the broad sweep of history, marriage has been dominant for a relatively short period. From this point of view, family institutions express the needs and values of society at a given time. As such, we must take care to perceive marriage in these terms. Marriage is not necessarily a permanent institution, nor is it the best form of family organization. The dominance of marriage over the past two centuries should not be taken as evidence that other forms of family living are immoral or illegitimate. If the decline in marriage rates and increase in cohabitation rates tell us one thing, it is that the family is a flexible institution. Given that the meaning of the family has shifted throughout history, it is simply inappropriate to rule out the possibility that nonmarital union will become the norm.

See also: DATING; FAMILY ROLES; INFIDELITY; MARRIAGE, DEFINITION OF; MATE SELECTION; NONMARITAL CHILDBEARING; RESOURCE MANAGEMENT; SEXUALITY; SINGLES/NEVER MARRIED PERSONS; SOCIOECONOMIC STATUS; WORK AND FAMILY

Bibliography

Axinn, W. G., and Thornton, A. (1992). "The Relationship Between Cohabitation and Divorce: Selectivity or Causal Influence?" *Demography* 29:357–374.

Axinn, W. G., and Thornton, A. (1993). "Mothers, Children, and Cohabitation: The Intergenerational Effects of Attitudes and Behaviour." *American Sociological Review* 58:233–246.

Balakrishnan, T. R.; Rao, K. V.; Lapierre-Adamcyk, E.; and Kròtki, K. J. (1987). "A Hazard Model Analysis of the Covariates of Marriage Dissolution in Canada." *Demography* 24:395–406.

Becker, G. (1981). *A Treatise on the Family.* Cambridge: Harvard University Press.

Bennett, N. G.; Blanc, A. K.; and Bloom, D. E. (1988). "Commitment and the Modern Union: Assessing the Link Between Premarital Cohabitation and Subsequent Marital Stability." *American Sociological Review* 53:127–138.

Bumpass, L. L., and Lu, H-H. (2000). "Trends in Cohabitation and Implications for Children's Family Contexts in the United States." *Population Studies* 54:29–41.

Bumpass, L. L., and Sweet, J. A. (1989). "National Estimates of Cohabitation." *Demography* 26:615–625.

Bumpass, L. L.; Sweet, J. A.; and Cherlin, A. J. (1991). "The Role of Cohabitation in Declining Rates of Marriage." *Journal of Marriage and the Family* 53:913–927.

Cherlin, A. J. (1992). *Marriage, Divorce, Remarriage.* Revised and Enlarged Edition. Cambridge, MA: Harvard University Press.

Davis, K. (1985). "The Future of Marriage." In *Contemporary Marriage: Comparative Perspectives on a Changing Institution,* ed. K. Davis. New York: Russell Sage Foundation.

Fitch, C. A., and Ruggles, S. (2000). "Historical Trends in Marriage Formation: The United States 1850-1990." In *The Ties That Bind: Perspectives on Marriage and Cohabitation,* ed. L. J. Waite. New York: Aldine de Gruyter.

Hoem, B., and Hoem, J. E. (1988). "The Swedish Family: Aspects of Contemporary Developments." *Journal of Family Issues* 9:397–424.

Holland, W. H. (1998). "Introduction." In *Cohabitation: The Law in Canada,* ed. W. H. Holland and B. E. Stalbecker-Pountney. Toronto: Carswell.

Kiernan, K. E. (2000). "European Perspectives on Union Formation." In *The Ties That Bind: Perspectives on Marriage and Cohabitation,* ed. L. J. Waite. New York: Aldine de Gruyter.

Kiernan, K. E., and Estaugh, V. (1993). *Cohabitation: Extra-marital Childbearing and Social Policy.* London: Family Policy Studies Centre.

Leridon, H. (1990). "Cohabitation, Marriage, and Separation: An Analysis of Life Histories of French Cohorts from 1968 to 1985." *Population Studies* 44:127–144.

Manning, W. D., and Smock, P. J. (1995). "Why Marry? Race and the Transition to Marriage among Cohabitors." *Demography* 32:509–520.

Nordic Statistical Secretariat, ed. (1996). *Yearbook of Nordic Statistics 1996.* Copenhagen: Nordic Council of Ministers.

Oppenheimer, V. (1994). "Women's Rising Employment and the Future of the Family in Industrial Societies." *Population and Development Review* 20:293–342.

Raley, R. K. (2000). "Recent Trends and Differentials in Marriage and Cohabitation: The United States." In *The Ties That Bind: Perspectives on Marriage and Cohabitation,* ed. L. J. Waite. New York: Aldine de Gruyter.

Rindfuss, R. R., and VandenHeuvel, A. (1990). "Cohabitation: A Precursor to Marriage or an Alternative to Being Single?" *Population and Development Review* 16:703–726.

Seff, M. (1995). "Cohabitation and the Law." In *Families and Law, ed.* L. J. McIntyre and M. B. Sussman. New York: The Hawthorn Press.

Seltzer, J. A. (2000). "Families Formed Outside of Marriage." *Journal of Marriage and the Family* 62:1247–1268.

Smock, P. J. (2000). "Cohabitation in the United States: An Appraisal of Research Themes, Findings, and Implications." *Annual Review of Sociology* 26:1–20.

Smock, P. J., and Manning, W. D. (1997). "Cohabiting Partners' Economic Circumstances and Marriage." *Demography* 34:331–341.

South, S. J., and Spitze, G. (1994). "Housework in Marital and Nonmarital Households." *American Sociological Review* 59:327–347.

Spanier, G. B. (1985). "Cohabitation in the 1980s: Recent Changes in the United States." In *Contemporary Marriage: Comparative Perspectives on a Changing Institution,* ed. K. Davis. New York: Russell Sage Foundation.

U.S. Bureau of the Census. (1998). "Marital Status and Living Arrangements: March 1998 (Update)." Series P-20, Number 514. Washington, DC: U.S. Government Printing Office.

Wiersma, G. E. (1983). *Cohabitation, An Alternative to Marriage? A Cross-National Study.* Boston: Martinus Nijhoff Publishers.

Wu, Z. (2000). *Cohabitation: An Alternative Form of Family Living.* Toronto: Oxford University Press.

ZHENG WU
CHRISTOPH M. SCHIMMELE

COLIC

For most parents, a human baby's crying is a particularly evocative signal, which compels them to seek and resolve the cause. Some babies, though, cry for prolonged amounts of time without apparent reason in the first three months after they are born, worrying their parents and leading many to seek expert help. In Western societies, this puzzling phenomenon has come to be known as *colic*. From a scientific viewpoint, both this word and the nature of the phenomenon that underlies it remain a source of controversy.

Defining and Measuring Colic

Part of the confusion in this area arises because the word *colic* has historical and etymological connotations. It comes from the Greek word *kolikos,* the adjectival form of *kolon* (the intestine), so that it is often used not just to refer to the behavior—crying—but to infer the presumed cause: gastrointestinal disturbance and pain. The eminent English pediatrician Ronald Illingworth, for instance, referred in 1985 to "pain that is obviously of intestinal origin" (p. 981). In fact, whether or not most babies who cry in this way have indigestion, and whether they are in pain, are both uncertain.

The second source of confusion is that, for obvious reasons, the clinical phenomenon is parental complaint about infant crying, rather than infant crying itself. Not surprisingly, factors such as parental inexperience have been found to increase the likelihood of clinical referral, throwing the spotlight onto parental, rather than infant, characteristics. This has raised issues about individual parents' vulnerability and tolerance, and about the extent to which colic as a distinct condition might be a Western, socially constructed, phenomenon.

One way to resolve this confusion is to define colic strictly in terms of a specific amount of infant crying. Morris Wessel and colleagues' (1954) *Rule of Threes* ("Fussing or crying lasting for a total of more than three hours per day and occurring on more than three days in any one week," p. 425) has been used in this way. From a research point of view, the advantage is that infants can be identified for study in a standard way. The disadvantage is that the definition is arbitrary; it is unlikely to help parents to be told that their baby does not have colic because he or she fails to meet this research criterion. Moreover, it implies the need to measure crying for a week without intervening, which many parents are reluctant to do.

Rather than employing a single definition, a workable alternative is to define colic broadly as prolonged, unexplained crying in a healthy one- to three-month-old baby, and the impact of this on parents. Information about the infant and parental parts of this phenomenon, within and between cultures, can then be sought in a systematic way. The alternative—of abandoning and replacing the word *colic*—has also been proposed, but it is so ingrained that this seems unlikely to work in practice.

Infant Crying and Its Impact in Western Cultures

Ronald Barr, Ian St. James-Roberts, and Maureen Keefe (2001) brought together our knowledge of infant crying and its impact on Western parents and clinical services. The principal findings can be summarized as follows:

(1) In general, Western infants cry about twice as much in the first three months as they do at later ages, with the amount of crying peaking at around five weeks of age (the *infant crying peak*). Around two hours of fussing and crying in twenty-four hours has been reported in U.S., Canadian, and English samples. Rather less has been reported in other European countries, but the reason for this is not yet clear. Infant crying at this age also clusters in the evening (the *evening crying peak*);

(2) As well as its greater amount, infant crying in the first three months has distinct qualitative features, which help to explain its impact on parents. These include the existence of bouts which occur unexpectedly and are prolonged, relatively intense to listen to, and difficult to soothe effectively;

(3) Parental complaints to clinicians about infant crying problems also peak during the first three months, while infants identified in this way share the same features as other infants, but often to a more extreme degree. This has led to the view that many infants identified as problem criers—and hence labelled as *colic cases*—are at the extreme end of the normal distribution of crying at this age, rather than having a clinical condition;

(4) Crying in the early months is a *graded signal,* which signals the degree of an infant's distress, but not precisely what is causing the crying (Gustafson, Wood, and Green 2000). It was previously believed that babies had different cry "types" (e.g., hunger, anger, pain) that allowed a sensitive parent to detect the causes of crying and to intervene to stop it. The unfortunate implication was that a baby who cried a lot had incompetent parents. Instead, it has become clear that "reading" the cause of crying from its sound is at best difficult and, in everyday circumstances, often impossible during the first three months. At this age, babies may cry intensely but the cry itself does not tell you what the problem is;

(5) Most babies grow out of their crying as they get older. Providing their parents can cope,

follow-up studies have found that the infants are normal in their cognitive, social and emotional development, and sleep. However, a small minority do have long-term problems (Papousek and von Hofacker 1998). It is not yet clear whether these infants are different in what causes their crying, or in how their parents respond to and care for their babies over the long term.

(6) Women who are prone to depression can have their depression triggered by an objectively irritable newborn (Murray et al. 1996). This emphasizes the need to consider infant crying and colic in terms of parental and family vulnerability, rather than solely as an infant phenomenon.

Infant Crying and Its Impact in Non-Western Cultures

In his 1985 review, Illingworth identified a Punjabi word for infant colic, noting that it was recognized in India, where it was considered to be due to the evening gods. In contrast, many anecdotal accounts have suggested that babies in non-Western cultures hardly cry at all, and attribute this to the almost continuous holding, frequent breastfeeding, and rapid response to babies' cries in such cultures (referred to as *proximal care*). Overall, the empirical evidence from non-Western cultures is not adequate to resolve this issue. There is clear evidence of a difference in amounts infants cry in-between African cultures which employ proximal, compared to more *distal care* (Hewlett et al. 2000). However, the study involved infants over three months of age, by which age colic is usually over, and crying has reduced, in Western infants. Other studies have certainly indicated that non-Western infants cry less in the first three months (Barr et al. 1991; Lee 2000), but this finding requires clarification and it is uncertain whether it reflects care differences or other factors. Attempts to introduce aspects of proximal care, such as *supplementary carrying,* into Western families have not produced reliable benefits (St. James-Roberts et al. 1995).

Since infants often do stop crying when responded to, it is reasonable to suppose that proximal care is associated with somewhat reduced crying, but whether or not it prevents the bouts of prolonged, unexplained, and "unsoothable" crying in one- to three-month-old infants that trouble Western parents is not yet known.

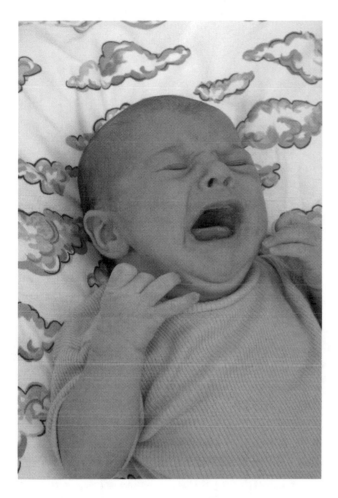

Some babies in their first three months cry for prolonged amounts of time without apparent reason. In Western societies this phenomenon has come to be known as colic.
LAURA DWIGHT/CORBIS

The Causes of Colic

Although most babies identified as colic cases probably have nothing wrong with them, organic disorders, including food intolerances, can give rise to crying in occasional cases. The best evidence-based estimate is that organic diseases as a whole are responsible for no more than 10 percent of cases where unexplained crying in one- to three-month-old infants is the presenting complaint (Gormally 2001).

There is growing evidence that intolerance of certain foods, especially cow's milk protein, can cause crying in some young babies. The mechanism is not certain, but it appears to be possible for the proteins to be passed via breast-feeding as well as bottle-fed milk or formula. However, reviews by a research pediatrician (Gormally 2001) and pediatric gastroenterologist (Treem 2001) have both concluded that food intolerance of this sort is rare. William Treem estimates that about 2 percent of infants overall are allergic to cow's milk protein, while only 1 in 10 infants taken to clinicians with problem crying have food intolerance. Only around 5 percent of infants diagnosed as having colic have *gastroesophageal reflux* (gastric acid refluxed into the esophagus). Treem also emphasizes that infants with feed-intolerance or gastrointestinal disorders can often be easily identified, by symptoms such as vomiting and diarrhea, blood in their stools, or a strong family history of atopy, asthma, or eczema.

A second possible cause of colic sometimes proposed is inadequate parenting. As noted above, it remains possible that Western approaches to baby-care as a whole may contribute to infant crying, although there is insufficient evidence to establish if this is the case. In principle, too, parental neglect can cause a baby to cry. However, recent evidence has made clear that many—probably most—Western babies who cry a lot do so in spite of highly sensitive and responsive parental care. Indeed, their parents have usually made extraordinary efforts to resolve the crying. The implication is that there is something about these babies that makes them cry despite care that does not cause crying in most babies.

The search for what this might be has focused on the so-called *neurobehavioral shift* believed to occur at around two months of age, whereby control over behavior moves from subcortical brain systems to the cerebral cortex. Evidence of this shift can be seen in the disappearance of newborn infant reflexes, such as the grasping reflex, and in the emergence of social smiling and more sophisticated perceptual and cognitive abilities. During this transition period, neurological regulation of behavior is believed to be poor, leading infants to be more or less overreactive, or poor at damping-down their crying once they have started (that is, at *self-soothing*). Several studies have found evidence that infants who cry a lot are highly reactive when undressed and challenged by handling and standard tests (e.g., White et al. 2000). The goal now is to understand the neurological and developmental processes involved, so that the reasons for the differences in reactivity between babies becomes clear. By understanding the types of stimulation which most provoke reactive behavior, it may also be possible to assist parents in how to minimize it.

Managing Crying in One-
to Three-Month-Old Infants

Many parents are accurate in their judgments of crying, but some may be influenced by their anxiety or expectations. Because the presenting complaint is usually parental concern about infant crying, accurate assessment of the crying is the first goal. Behavior diaries kept prospectively by parents are the method of choice, with detailed questionnaires and interviews being used where diaries are impossible. The resulting information can assist diagnosis and may provide parents with reassurance and insight.

Many parents link their baby's crying to digestive disturbances and are likely to want to change their method of infant feeding. As noted earlier, such disturbances are rare—evidence suggests no more than 2 percent of infants overall, and 10 percent of infants who are presented with crying problems, have gastrointestinal disorders, and these cases can usually be identified by their symptoms. Siobhán Gormally (2001) adds other symptoms of organic disorders for parents and physician to look out for, including a high pitched cry, lack of a time-of-day peak, failure to thrive or weight loss, a positive family history of migraine, maternal drug ingestion, and persistence of symptoms past four months of age. She stresses the importance of infant skin, eye, skeletal, neurological, gastrointestinal, and cardiovascular assessments, highlighting the need for parents to involve physicians in the decision process.

Where infants lack these symptoms, and are otherwise healthy and putting on weight normally, there is no evidence-based reason for assuming that their crying has a gastrointestinal cause, or for treating it with a change of feeding method or diet. In practice, clinicians differ in how readily they recommend a dietary change as a treatment for persistent crying. Where this is contemplated, the disadvantages need to be balanced against the possible gains. One is that breast-feeding is beneficial for young babies, whereas excluding cow's milk protein from a lactating mother's diet is likely to be trying for her and her family. A second is that research trials using dietary change to treat crying have seldom produced clear-cut advantages. Typically, some infants have improved somewhat, but continue to cry above normal levels, whereas other infants have not benefited at all. Other pitfalls include a high *placebo rate*–where babies seem to improve initially following any change—and the danger that an infant will be considered generally *allergic* or *fragile* by parents.

The alternative to dietary change is to use *behavior management strategies* to support parents and to help them to minimize the crying until it resolves. This approach follows from the evidence, cited earlier, that some parents are especially vulnerable to persistent infant crying, highlighting the need to consider this as a family, rather than infant, problem. Elements of this approach can include:

- Viewing the first three months of infancy as a developmental transition, which all babies go through more or less smoothly.

- Reassuring parents that it is normal to find crying aversive and discussing the dangers of abuse and *shaken baby syndrome*.

- Examining the notion that crying means that there is something *wrong* with a baby of this age and introducing alternatives—such as the possibility that it signals a reactive or vigorous baby.

- Discussing ways of containing and minimizing the crying, and highlighting positive features of the baby.

- Considering the availability of supports and the development of strategies which allow parents to cope, take time out and "recharge their batteries."

- Empowering parents and reframing the first three months as a challenge to be overcome, with positive consequences for themselves and their relationships with their babies.

Also implicit in this approach is the need for health services to find means of identifying and supporting the most vulnerable families, and to continue to monitor the infant, at least until the crying problems have resolved.

See also: CHILDCARE; CHILDHOOD, STAGES OF: INFANCY

Bibliography

Barr, R. G.; Konner, M.; Baseman, R.; and Adamson, L. (1991) "Crying in Kung San Infants: A Test of the Cultural Specificity Hypothesis." *Developmental Medicine and Child Neurology* 33:601–610.

Barr, R. G.; St. James-Roberts, I.; and Keefe, M. R., eds. (2001). *New Evidence on Early Infant Crying: Its Origins, Nature and Management.* Skillman, NJ: Johnson and Johnson Pediatric Institute Round Table Series.

Gormally, S. (2001) "Clinical Clues to Organic Etiologies in Infants with Colic." In *New Evidence on Early Infant Crying: Its Origins, Nature and Management,* edited by R. G. Barr, I. St. James-Roberts, and M. R. Keefe. Skillman, NJ: Johnson and Johnson Pediatric Institute Round Table Series.

Gustafson, G. E.; Wood, R. M.; and Green J. A. (2000). "Can We Hear the Causes of Infant Crying?" In *Crying as a Sign, a Symptom, and a Signal,* ed. R. G. Barr, B. Hopkins, and J. A. Green. London: MacKeith Press.

Hewlett, B. S.; Lamb, M.; Leyendecker B.; and Scholmerich, A. (2000). "Internal Working Models, Trust, and Sharing Among Foragers." *Current Anthropology* 41:287–297.

Illingworth, R. S. (1985). "Infantile Colic Revisited." *Archives of Disease in Childhood* 60:981–985.

Lee, K. (2000). "Crying Patterns of Korean Infants in Institutions." *Child: Care, Health and Development* 26:217–228.

Murray, L.; Stanley, C.; Hooper, R.; King, F.; and Fiori-Cowley, A. (1996). "The Role of Infant Factors in Postnatal Depression and Mother-Infant Interaction." *Developmental Medicine and Child Neurology* 38:109–119.

Papousek, M., and von Hofacker, N. (1998). "Persistent Crying in Early Infancy: A Non-Trivial Condition of Risk for the Developing Mother-Infant Relationship." *Child: Care, Health and Development* 24:395–424.

St. James-Roberts, I.; Hurry, J.; Bowyer, J.; and Barr, R. G. (1995). "Supplementary Carrying Compared with Advice to Increase Responsive Parenting as Interventions to Prevent Persistent Infant Crying." *Pediatrics* 95:381–388.

Treem, W. R. (2001). "Assessing Crying Complaints: The Interaction with Gastroesophageal Reflex and Cow's Milk Protein Intolerance." In *New Evidence on Early Infant Crying. Its Origins, Nature and Management,* edited by R. G. Barr, I. St. James-Roberts, and M. R. Keefe. Skillman, NJ: Johnson and Johnson Pediatric Institute Round Table Series.

Wessel, M. A.; Cobb, J. C.; Jackson, E. B.; Harris, G. S.; and Detwiler, A. C. (1954). "Paroxysmal Fussing in Infancy, Sometimes called 'Colic.'" *Pediatrics* 14:421–433.

White, B. P.; Gunnar, M. R.; Larson, M. C.; Donzella, B.; and Barr, R. G. (2000). "Behavioral and Physiological Responsivity, Sleep, and Patterns of Daily Cortisol Production in Infants with and without Colic." *Child Development* 71:862–877.

IAN ST. JAMES-ROBERTS

COLOMBIA

See LATIN AMERICA

COMMITMENT

See COMMUTER MARRIAGES; FAMILY LOYALTY; FAMILY STRENGTHS; FORGIVENESS; FRIENDSHIP; INFIDELITY; INTENTIONAL COMMUNITIES; INTIMACY; LOVE; MARITAL QUALITY; MARITAL TYPOLOGIES; POWER; MARITAL RELATIONSHIPS; RELIGION; SOCIAL EXCHANGE THEORY; STRESS; TRUST

COMMON-LAW MARRIAGE

See COHABITATION; MARRIAGE, DEFINITION OF

COMMUNICATION

COUPLE RELATIONSHIPS *Tara M. Emmers-Sommer*
FAMILY RELATIONSHIPS *Kathleen M. Galvin*

COUPLE RELATIONSHIPS

Individuals often treat their significant others more poorly than they do strangers (Birchler, Weiss, and Vincent 1975; Miller 1997). Figures suggest that the divorce rate hovers between 50 and 60 percent in the United States for all first marriages and 27 percent for all marriages in Australia (Americans for Divorce Reform). Although the divorce rate in the United States is higher than in other countries, divorce is not uncommon elsewhere. The Japanese Ministry of Health, Labour and Welfare reported that in 2002, 2.1 percent of Japanese had been divorced at least once. This is in comparison to the 4.3 percent they reported for the total U.S. population. They also reported that the divorce rate in Germany was 2.5 percent of the total population; in France 2.0 percent; in the United Kingdom 2.7 percent; and in Sweden 2.4 percent. Italy was credited as having the lowest divorce rate in Western culture (0.6% of the total population).

Indeed, many a gap seems to exist between an individual's relational ideal and eventual relational reality. As much of the scholarship suggests, problematic communication patterns can contribute to relational demise (Gottman 1994).

Much of the popular literature suggests that men and women are different and that these differences manifest themselves through the sexes' different communication and relationship needs (Gray 1992). Some of the scholarly research, however, suggests that men and women are not very different in their communication or relationship needs (Canary and Emmers-Sommer 1997). Although some differences do exist, so do several similarities.

When considering couple communication in close relationships, a variety of things are relevant and of interest. First, what gender differences (if any) are recognizable in couple communication patterns? Second, how do couple-type identification and gender-role adherence play a part in how individuals communicate with their partners? Finally, how do aspects of gender-role adherence and couple-type identification relate to (dis)satisfactory couple communication? It should be noted that most of the relevant research has been done in Western cultures, with most of it conducted in the United States.

Couple-Type Identification and Gender-Role Adherence

Often, the terms *sex* difference and *gender* difference are used interchangeably. This collapsing of terms is somewhat in error. Specifically, sex differences refer to biological differences between men and women. Gender differences, on the other hand, refer to social expectations and stereotypes attributed to men and women by virtue of the biological sex. Similarly, the terms *man* and *woman* should be used when referring to sex differences and *masculine* and *feminine* are the applicable terms when referring to gender differences. Finally, although the concepts of sex and gender are different, gender is implicitly influenced by sex (Canary and Emmers-Sommer 1997).

Gender Differences and Similarities in Couple Communication

Much of the literature in popular culture leads one to believe that men and women are truly quite different in terms of their emotional experiences and their communication of those experiences. According to John Gray (1992), author of *Men are from Mars; Women are from Venus,* men and women differ in their experience of emotions and their communication of them. Gray, however, is not an academic, and his work is not based on empirical research.

Indeed, much of the empirical scholarship on sex and gender differences indicates quite the

Empirical studies on sex and gender differences indicate that men and women are more similar than they are different in terms of communicating in their close, personal relationships. PAUL BARTON/CORBIS

opposite. Specifically, it shows that men and women are more similar than they are different in terms of communicating in their close, personal relationships (Canary and Emmers-Sommer 1997). Although some differences do exist, they are not substantial enough to declare that the sexes or genders are significantly different. Many of the so-called differences in the sex and gender literature are related more to flaws in the studies themselves, such as errors in recollection in self-report studies, or individuals' reports that are affected by *social desirability*. Specifically, social desirability refers to an individual reporting what he or she thinks others would find acceptable, rather than what actually may be the truth. Within the context of gender differences, this would account for men and women reporting what they stereotypically believe men and women *should* do from a social expectation standpoint versus what they actually do.

Research on communication in close, personal relationships suggests that men and women are more similar than they are different. Nevertheless, some differences do exist between men and women. Many of the differences surface within the contexts of conflict or household chores. For example, in their extensive examination of the sex and gender literature, Dan Canary and Tara Emmers-Sommer (1997) offered the following conclusions regarding sex and gender differences. First, women, compared to men, express a greater range of emotions, such as sadness, fear, love, happiness, and anger. Women are also more inclined than men to disclose personal information, such as their personal opinion or details of their personal history. Compared to men, women are more likely to use touch to convey feelings of closeness; these feelings could be sexual in nature, but not necessarily. Interestingly, women are more likely to exercise power strategies than men. Compared to men, women are more likely to engage in manipulative behaviors and to exercise negative and confrontational conflict behaviors. Finally, women are more likely than men to enact self-disclosure behaviors, engage in loyalty toward their partner and relationship, and enact task-sharing in an effort to maintain their relationship. The authors also found that women, even in dual-career couples, tend to do the lion's share of the household chores and childrearing duties. Thus, some differences do exist between men and women; however, the extensive literature on sex and gender differences indicates that the differences are far outweighed by the similarities.

Interestingly, however, some of the subtle differences that do exist contribute in a noteworthy fashion to how men and women manage their relationships, particularly issues of contention and conflict. According to John Gottman (1994), both sex (physiological) and gender (sociological) differences are exhibited in couple conflict. Similarly, men's and women's adherence to particular gender role and relational ideologies relates to their responses during conflict.

Couple-Types

The distinction between sex and gender differences is important in communication research. For example, gender differences, rather than sex differences, play an important role in defining couple-types. Mary Anne Fitzpatrick (1988) argued that a variety of couple-types exist and that each couple-type's attitudes and beliefs toward their partner and relationship hold particular implications for their responses to conflict. It is important to consider the variety of couple-types that exist for several reasons. First, embedded within the couple-types are demonstrations of adherence to gender roles. Second, couple-type relates to how spouses respond in conflict situations, which, third, holds implications for couple communication patterns and for the satisfaction/dissatisfaction of the relationship.

Traditional couple-types. Men and women who are *traditionals* are highly interdependent and emphasize doing things together versus autonomously. Traditionals hold traditional gender role beliefs (e.g., the woman takes the husband's last name when married) and hold the stability of the relationship in high esteem. Traditionals use positive communication behaviors during conflict (e.g., discuss issues keeping the relationship in mind, not using threats), tend not to argue over petty issues, but do openly engage about salient issues (Fitzpatrick 1988).

Independent couple-types. *Independents* value both connection and personal autonomy. They actively discuss many aspects of their relationship and hold nontraditional beliefs about relationships (i.e., do not espouse the belief that the "man is in charge") (Fitzpatrick 1988). Independents actively engage in conflict over minor and major issues, argue for personal positions, and offer reasons for accepting their positions rather than rely on a one-up/one-down solution by virtue of gender (Witteman and Fitzpatrick 1986).

Separate couple-types. *Separates,* unlike independents or traditionals, are not interdependent and avoid interaction, particularly conflict. Separates are likely to withdraw or give in during early stages of conflict because active engagement in conflict involves interaction and a degree of interdependence. However, when separates do engage in conflict, the interaction can be quite hostile (Fitzpatrick 1988).

Mixed couple-types. Approximately half of couple-types do not neatly fall into a specific category such that both husband and wife are traditionals, independents, or separates. Rather, many couples represent a meshing of two different types. The most common mixed couple-type is the separate husband and the traditional wife (Fitzpatrick 1988). Several implications for this couple-type exist in terms of gender role adherence, engagement in conflict, and effects on the satisfaction of the relationship.

The research suggests that certain communication patterns can be constructive to a relationship's preservation, whereas other communication patterns can be destructive to a relationship's maintenance.

Communication Patterns and Couple (Dis)satisfaction

Gottman and colleagues (Gottman 1994; Gottman and Levenson 1988) have offered specific couple communication patterns that contribute to both satisfactory and dissatisfactory couple relationships, with a specific focus on the close, personal relationship of marriage. (It is important to note that most or all of this research has been conducted in the United States.) In fact, Gottman is able to predict divorce accurately 94 percent of the time. Gottman has found that the behaviors of criticism, defensiveness, contempt, and withdrawal hold the most impact in influencing a close relationship negatively. Although men and women can exercise all of these behaviors, it is of particular harm when the man in the relationship withdraws from conversation about important issues of contention. This particular behavioral pattern is indicative, for example, of a mixed couple-type in which the husband is a separate and the wife is a traditional.

Overall, Gottman (1994) offered several observations regarding what delineated a satisfied relationship from a dissatisfied one. First, dissatisfied couples more often engage in destructive communication patterns than satisfied couples. Specifically, dissatisfied couples are more likely to engage in criticism, defensiveness, contempt, and withdrawal. Many of these behaviors can also be conveyed nonverbally. For example, a partner stiffening up to convey defensiveness, rolling his or her eyes to convey contempt, or withdrawing and staring off into space to convey withdrawal. Of the four behaviors, Gottman (1994) argued that the behaviors of contempt and defensiveness are the most corrosive and that the man's withdrawal from conflict is the strongest predictor of divorce. In addition to emotional harm, these behaviors can also contribute to physiological distress. Second, husbands are more likely to withdraw from conflict in dissatisfied marriages and less likely to do so in satisfied marriages. That is, husbands are more likely to self-disclose their feelings to their wives in happy marriages. This suggests that one cannot assume that men are emotionally distant from everyone, as the common stereotype would indicate, and nondisclosive. Indeed, the mediating factor might be the state of the relationship. Research also suggests that women have a greater repertoire of individuals to disclose to than men do and are more inclined to disclose regardless of marital satisfaction, whereas some men only disclose to their wife. For those men in unhappy marriages, their feelings are often revealed to no one. Overall, much of the research suggests these aforementioned patterns (Canary and Emmers-Sommer 1997; Gottman 1994; House 1981). Third, men and

women function differently in the face of negative affect. Specifically, the research suggests that women function more aptly in high conflict situations than men. Within the context of satisfied marriages, both husbands and wives engage in de-escalation behaviors (i.e., reducing the conflict) during low-level conflict. Women engage in de-escalation behaviors during high conflict as well, whereas men find it difficult regardless of their marital satisfaction. Within dissatisfied marriages, neither the husband nor wife engages in conflict de-escalation behaviors (Gottman 1979, 1994). Fourth, research suggests that destructive communication during conflict affects men more adversely from a physiological standpoint than women. Gottman (1994) concluded that men and women may differ in their responses to negative communication such that men react more quickly to negative affect and that their recovery from the episode is slower than that of women. These reactions to negative communication are evidenced through means such as elevated adrenal excretions and blood pressure. Interestingly, Gottman (1994) noted that while women's health appears to be superior to men's within these contexts, men seem to benefit from marriage more than women do. Fifth, Gottman (1994) argued that a five-to-one ratio is necessary for a stable relationship; specifically, that five positive communications are necessary to balance one negative communication. Further, negative communications that involve the four destructive behaviors mentioned earlier (criticism, defensiveness, contempt, and withdrawal) are particularly harmful to the relationship. In response to these destructive behaviors, Gottman (1994) suggests that partners engage in the behaviors of soothing, nondefensive listening, and validating.

Sixth, in addition to certain communication behaviors and patterns, dissatisfied or distressed couples are often distinguished from satisfied or nondistressed couples in terms of how their conflict behaviors collectively produce cycles. Specifically, dissatisfied couples often find themselves in what Gottman (1994) termed "negativity cycles." Such cycles involve one partner offering a complaint and that complaint is met with the partner's countercomplaint, which is met with another countercomplaint, and so forth. Gottman found that satisfied and dissatisfied couples were distinguished, in part, by the couples' ability to remove themselves from the complaint/countercomplaint pattern. Whereas a satisfied couple might take only a few passes at the destructive complaint/countercomplaint cycle, dissatisfied couples kept hashing out the complaints, forcing themselves into a deeper and deeper negativity spiral. Finally, distressed couples are more inclined to form negative attributions toward the partner during conflict and attribute behavior to internal factors, whereas nondistressed couples were more likely to attribute behavior to external factors. For example, if John and Jane are a distressed couple, they are more likely to attribute blame to one another, whereas if they are a nondistressed couple, they are more likely to attribute behaviors to the situation at hand.

Conclusion

Numerous conclusions can be gleaned from the aforementioned findings. First, it is important to note that the findings reviewed here are not exhaustive. Second, it is important to emphasize that the majority of the research presented here focuses on marital couples. Third, and as noted earlier, it must be kept in mind that some of the past gender and sex research might be somewhat in error as reliability and validity issues exist. Fourth, it is necessary to note that the majority of the research presented here was conducted in the United States. Surely, some cultural differences exist in relational ideologies and communication patterns. Nevertheless, certain noteworthy patterns do exist in the research findings that speak to sex and gender differences and similarities as well as what couple communication patterns contribute to satisfied and dissatisfied relationships.

What is particularly salient about work done on couple communication patterns is that awareness is being increased about demonstrable patterns that work and do not work in close, personal relationships. Indeed, how individuals communicate in their close personal relationships holds direct implications for individuals' personal and relational well-being. Of value in the extant research on couple communication patterns and relational satisfaction is that noticeable learned patterns can be unlearned by partners in dissatisfied and distressed relationships if the desire exists to better the relationship.

See also: AFFECTION; ATTRACTION; COMMUNICATION: FAMILY RELATIONSHIPS; COMMUTER MARRIAGES; CONFLICT: COUPLE RELATIONSHIPS; DATING; DECISION MAKING: DIALECTICAL THEORY; FAMILY ROLES; INFIDELITY; INTIMACY; MARITAL QUALITY; NAGGING AND COMPLAINING; PROBLEM SOLVING; RELATIONSHIP DISSOLUTION; RELATIONSHIP INITIATION; RELATIONSHIP MAINTENANCE; RELATIONSHIP METAPHORS; RELATIONSHIP THEORIES—SELF-OTHER RELATIONSHIP; RENEWAL OF WEDDING VOWS; SELF-DISCLOSURE; SEXUAL COMMUNICATION: COUPLE RELATIONSHIPS; SOCIAL NETWORKS; THERAPY: COUPLE RELATIONSHIPS; TRANSITION TO PARENTHOOD

Bibliography

Birchler, G. R., Weiss, R. L., and Vincent, J. P. (1975). "Multimethod Analysis of Social Reinforcement Exchange Between Maritally Distressed and Nondistressed Spouse and Stranger Dyads." *Journal of Personality and Social Psychology* 31:349–360.

Canary, D. J., and Emmers-Sommer, T. M. (1997). *Sex and Gender Differences in Personal Relationships.* New York: Guilford Press.

Fitzpatrick, M. A. (1988). *Between Husbands and Wives: Communication in Marriage.* Newbury Park, CA: Sage.

Gottman, J. M. (1994). *What Predicts Divorce?* Hillsdale, NJ: Lawrence Erlbaum Associates.

Gottman, J. M. (1979). *Marital Interaction: Experimental Investigations.* New York: Academic Press.

Gottman, J. M., and Levenson, R. W. (1988). "The Social Psychophysiology of Marriage." In *Perspectives on Marital Interaction,* ed. P. Noller and M. A. Fitzpatrick. Philadelphia: Multilingual Masters.

Gray, J. (1992). *Men are from Mars, Women are from Venus.* New York: Harper Collins.

House, J. S. (1981). *Work, Stress, and Social Support.* Reading, MA: Addison-Wesley.

Miller, R. S. (1997). "We Always Hurt the Ones We Love: Aversive Interactions in Close Relationships." In *Aversive Interpersonal Behaviors,* ed. R. W. Kowalski. New York: Plenum Press.

Witteman, H., and Fitzpatrick, M. A. (1986). "Compliance-gaining in Marital Interaction: Power Bases, Processes, and Outcomes." *Communication Monographs* 53:130–143.

Other Resources

Americans for Divorce Reform. "Divorce Statistics Collection." Available from http://www.divorcereform.org/stats.html.

Japanese Ministry of Health, Labour and Welfare. "Vital Statistics. Divorces (1983–2000)." Japan Information Network web site. Available from http://www. jinjapan.org/stat/stats/02VIT32.html.

TARA M. EMMERS-SOMMER

FAMILY RELATIONSHIPS

Families and communication have a symbiotic relationship. Family communication encompasses the multiple ways family members interact, which reflect the relational ties as well as the communication processes that create each unique family system. Communication patterns serve to reflect, as well as construct, family reality.

It is through talk that family members define their identities and negotiate their relationships with each other and the rest of the world. Each family is defined through its communication, verbal and nonverbal, rather than just through biological and legal kinship. Communication serves as a process by which family members differentiate themselves from non-family members; some families include units constructed only through choice and interaction, such as partners, long-term friends, and other fictive kin (Whitchurch and Dickson 1999). Given the increasing complexities of family forms created through means such as multiple remarriage, chosen partnerships, and single parenting, communication patterns have taken on increasing significance in examining family dynamics. Studying relationships has taken a "decided communication turn with a growing recognition of the formative, constitutive nature of communicative processes, and perhaps this is nowhere as notable as in the study of marriage and family relationships" (Rogers 2001, p. 25).

Multigenerational and cultural communication patterns affect family interactions. Each generation teaches the next how to manage issues such as intimacy, conflict, gender roles, and handling stress. Family members are affected by family-of-origin influences—or the patterns of previous generations—even as they create their own patterns that will influence future generations. Such patterns do not determine but, unless consciously altered, affect interaction in the next generations.

Many families reflect significant cultural communication patterns that affect everything from family identity to values and interaction styles. For

A family gathers in front of a store in Mount Hagen, Papua New Guinea. Through communication, family members negotiate their relationships with each other and the rest of the world. OTTO LANG/CORBIS

example, families of Chinese, Ugandan, or Irish heritage hold different beliefs about who *is* family; they may also relate differently to family members or outsiders based on their ancestry. Family ethnicity sets norms for communication that influence those of succeeding generations (McGoldrick 1993). When people from very different families of origin or cultural backgrounds create a family, considerable discussion and negotiation is needed to construct a functioning system.

Meaning-Making

A primary family task is *meaning-making*. Communication is the process by which family members create meanings, share them with the rest of the world, and eventually develop their own relational culture or shared reality. Indicators of family meaning include language patterns, stories, rituals, and rules.

Family meanings are developed as members interpret behaviors through communication. Comments such as "I was only kidding when I said that" or "Yelling is just a way of getting rid of stress" serve to create a shared reality. Nicknames, nonverbal codes, inside jokes, shared references, and unique terminology separate members from non-members.

Stories, common sources of family meanings, bring the past into the present, constructing a common history and convey messages to present generations about what is valued. Narratives distill unique family experiences while answering members' questions such as, how did this family come to be? Will the family stand behind its members? What does it mean to be a [family name]? In addition, the performance of family stories—who tells and who hears the story, and how stories are told—contributes to meanings. For example, storytelling research identifies three couple types through their performative style: *connected couples* tell stories that include dialogue overlaps and mutual confirmation; *functional separate couples* demonstrate respect, validation, and support while telling individual stories; *dysfunctional couples* exhibit contradictions and disagreement (Dickson 1995).

Rituals serve to develop and reflect a family's sense of itself. A family ritual is "a symbolic form of communication that, owing to the satisfaction that family members experience through the repetition, is acted out in a systematic fashion over time" (Wolin and Bennett 1984, p. 401). Marital rituals include time for togetherness, idiosyncratic actions, intimacy expressions, or daily routines which serve to maintain the relationship and signal coupleness to the outside world (Bruess and Pearson 1995). Family rituals develop around vacations, dinnertime, or bedtime, as well as celebrations of holidays, birthdays, or cultural events.

Certain patterns, based on "shoulds" and "oughts," evolve into family rules that serve to coordinate meanings among family members. Families develop communication rules: shared understandings of what communication means and what behaviors are appropriate in various situations (Wood 1997). Rules may be explicitly stated ("Do not swear") or implicitly emerge through multiple interactions ("Don't tell Mom about anything Dad's new wife bought us"). Family communication rules tell members what can be talked about, in what ways, and who is allowed to hear the talk. Frequently rules serve to protect secrets and establish and maintain family boundaries; families with an alcoholic member typically adhere to the communication rule "Don't talk about Dad's drinking."

Partnerships and family dyads are maintained as members manage competing needs and obligations, coordinate their activities, introduce pleasure into their relationship, and build a place in which to nurture the relationships. Dialectical theory, which addresses contradictions and oppositions, is useful in examining these predictable relational tensions. Communication scholars identify a range of possible dialectical tensions including (1) autonomy-connection, or the desire to be independent while wishing to integrate with another person; (2) openness-closeness, or the desire to be expressive and disclosive and to be closed and private; and (3) predictability-novelty or the desire for sameness and constancy while also desiring stimulation and change. (Baxter 1990; Baxter and Montgomery 1996). Partners may each feel similar pressure to be independent and connected; a parent and teenager may wish to be close and have an open relationship, but also to protect areas of privacy. One stepfamily dialectical dilemma involves managing the voluntary marital relationship and the involuntary stepparent-stepchild relationship (Cissna, Cox, and Bochner 1990). The tensions are ongoing, and partners and family members work to manage them strategically over the life of their relationship.

Intimacy

Couple and family intimacy reflects many similarities. Marital intimacy involves the following characteristics: (1) a close, familiar, and usually affectionate or loving personal relationship; (2) a detailed and deep knowledge and understanding from close personal connection or familiar experience; and (3) sexual relations (Feldman 1979).

With the exception of sexual relations, these characteristics may be applied to all family relationships, understanding that intimacy is much different between partners than between children and parents or young siblings due to their developmental stages.

Talk, including confirmation and positivity, self-disclosure, and sexual communication, contributes to intimacy development. Its function varies with the unique multigenerational familial system, its ethnic heritage, and the maturity of its members.

Talk provides symbolic evidence of the connections among communicators while strengthening those connections. For example, time spent in debriefing conversations, when couples inform each other about events, thoughts, and emotions they experienced while apart, is positively associated with relational satisfaction (Vangelisti and Banski l993). Confirmation messages recognize another person's existence, respond relevantly to the other's communication, accept the other's way of experiencing life, and suggest a willingness to become involved with the other. Positivity includes displaying interest, affection, caring, acceptance, empathy, and joy. Based on a review of his research with hundreds of couples, John Gottman (1994b) maintains that stable couples exhibit in a 5:1 positivity to negativity ratio. (Negativity consists of criticism, contempt, defensiveness, withdrawal, loneliness, and isolation.) These kinds of talk lay the connecting groundwork for long-term, intimate familial ties.

Self-disclosure, or voluntarily sharing personal and private information with another, serves to deepen relationships. Disclosure about self is complex and difficult, and involves risk on the part of the discloser and a willingness to accept such disclosure on the part of the other. High mutual self-disclosure is usually associated with voluntary adult relationships, such as couples or extended family, and is characterized by trust, confirmation, and affection, and is influenced by ethnic and family of origin patterns. Discussions between parents and younger children, given differences in developmental stages, seldom include mutual disclosure. High levels of self-disclosure of negative feelings about the other may occur at points in familial relationships resulting in conflict and anger. In most families, boundary management is an ongoing processes. Family members must continuously decide which feelings and thoughts they are willing to share: the cost is personal vulnerability. Relational boundary management is achieved by developing, using, and coordinating rules and managing relational turbulence when boundaries are invaded (Petronio 2000). Some cautions about unrestrained self-disclosure need to be considered, since it can be destructive or manipulative (Wilder and Collins 1994). Selective, rather than total, self-disclosure contributes to intimacy development in partner and parent-child relationships.

Sexuality is linked directly to communication at both the partner and family level. Sexual attitudes and behavior may be viewed as a topic of communication, a form of communication, and a contributing factor to relational intimacy and satisfaction. Family sex communication includes ". . . a composite of a few direct, sometimes forceful, verbal messages; a lot of indirect verbal messages; a background mosaic of innumerable nonverbal messages" (Warren 1992, p. 130). How a family encourages or discourages talk about issues such as pregnancy, birth control, masturbation, menstrual cycles, the initial sexual encounters of adolescents, and the sexual intimacy of the parents is related to communication and sexuality rules (Yerby, Buerkel-Rothfuss, and Bochner 1990).

Family approaches to sexuality range along a continuum from sexually neglectful to sexually healthy to sexually abusive (Maddock 1989). In some "sexually neglectful" families, sex is seldom mentioned or it is discussed so abstractly that a direct connection is not made between the topic and the personal experience of family members. Sexually abusive families are typically closed and emotionally inexpressive with boundary confusion between members and generations. Sexually healthy families are characterized by respect for both genders, developmentally appropriate boundaries, effective and flexible communication patterns that support intimacy, and a shared system of culturally relevant sexual values and meanings.

Each partner's background influences sexual encounters, as does the partner's sexual identity. Couples establish their own patterns of sexual activity early in the relationship, and these patterns typically continue throughout the relationship (Specher and McKinney 1994). Open communication becomes critical, since a good sexual relationship depends on what is satisfying to each partner. A couple that cannot communicate effectively about many areas of their life will have difficulty developing effective communication about their sexual life because "Communication in the bedroom starts in other rooms" (Schwartz 1994, p. 74).

Conflict

Family conflict patterns become repetitive and predictable. A stage model for analyzing the frequently recurring family conflict patterns lists prior conditions, frustration awareness, active conflict, solution or non-solution, follow-up, and resolution stage (Galvin and Brommel 2000). Gottman (1994a) classifies three couple types according to their styles of conflict interactions: validating, volatile, and conflict avoiders. Whereas validating partners respect one another's point of view on a variety of topics and strive toward compromise, volatile partners are emotionally expressive, comfortable with disagreement, and highly persuasive. Conflict avoiders abhor negative messages and strive to lessen potential conflicts by placating or deferring to one another. All three groups of stable couples exhibited a 5:1 positivity to negativity ratio.

Sometimes family conflict escalates to abuse. Abusive couples exhibit significantly more reciprocity in verbally aggressive exchanges than do distressed, non-abusive control groups (Sabourin, Infante, and Rudd 1990). For the majority of couples that use verbal aggression, conflict does not lead to physical aggression although some physically aggressive couples view verbal aggression as a catalyst for their physical acts (Roloff 1996).

Parent-parent and parent-child abuse become a part of role relationships; in physically combative families such behaviors occur frequently enough for children, husbands, wives, or lovers to become accustomed to it. Family aggression relates to gender and age: boys receive more verbal aggression than girls and both experience more of it after age six (Vissing and Baily 1996). Non-abusive mothers introduce more topics into discussions, give more verbal and nonverbal instructions, and use more signs of verbal and nonverbal affection. Non-abusive parents use more time-outs, privilege denials, and explanation of consequences to discipline their children (Wilson and Whipple 1995).

Technology and Families

Technological developments are impacting family communication patterns. Technology, particularly the Internet, is altering hierarchical communication structures in many families as youngsters gain information and skills which many parents do not possess. The Internet weakens parental supervision of media use; parents report concerns of child safety, such as Internet strangers, and concerns about content such as pornography, violence, and hate speech (Wartella and Jennings 2001). Working parents and working partners are increasingly technology-dependent as family members use e-mail, cell phones, and other new media to stay in touch. Non-custodial parents often maintain relationships with children via e-mail as do parents or partners who travel frequently.

More family members are creating family websites and family listservs, researching family history, sharing photos, and rekindling Internet relationships with long-lost relatives. Whereas e-mail has increased communication among some family members, it is used as a substitute for face-to-face conversation among others. Many siblings stay in touch more frequently with e-mail than with telephones. There appear to be some gender differences in the use of electronic messages to maintain family ties (PEW Internet and American Life Project 2000)—women are more likely to use the Internet to rekindle relationships with relatives who have been out of contact for a long time. Because teens frequently teach other family members how to use the Internet, it creates a generational reversal which may enhance parent-child relationships or exacerbate conflicts (PEW Internet and American Life Project 2001).

Enrichment

Communication strategies are valuable as family members aim for increased satisfaction, commitment, and stability. Many people enter marriage and parenthood naïvely assuming that this wonderful relationship will endure indefinitely without much effort. Yet significant amounts of thought, time, and energy need to be invested to sustain a well-functioning family.

Sometimes family members make relational changes on their own through discussing, listening, and trying new behaviors; frequently this is insufficient to effect desired changes (Galvin and Brommel 2000). Couples or family members may participate in enrichment programs designed to improve communication; others decide to enter marital or family therapy when family life is painful.

The study of family communication is developing rapidly. Recent research has focussed on race and ethnicity (Socha and Diggs 1999; Gudykunst and Lee 2001), gay and lesbian families (West and Turner 1995), and work/family interface issues (Golden 2000). Given the complexity and power of communication patterns, and their impact on current and future generations, the importance of this research cannot be underestimated.

See also: COMMUNICATION: COUPLE RELATIONSHIPS; COMPUTERS AND FAMILY; CONFLICT: COUPLE RELATIONSHIPS; CONFLICT: FAMILY RELATIONSHIPS; CONFLICT: PARENT-CHILD RELATIONSHIPS;

DECISION MAKING; DISABILITIES; FAMILY AND RELATIONAL RULES; FAMILY BUSINESS; FAMILY LIFE EDUCATION; FAMILY STORIES AND MYTHS; FAMILY STRENGTHS; FAVORITISM/DIFFERENTIAL TREATMENT; FOOD; INTIMACY; NAGGING AND COMPLAINING; POWER: FAMILY RELATIONSHIPS; PROBLEM SOLVING; RELATIONSHIP MAINTENANCE; SELF-DISCLOSURE; SEXUAL COMMUNICATION: PARENT-CHILD RELATIONSHIPS; SIBLING RELATIONSHIPS; STEPFAMILIES; TRANSITION TO PARENTHOOD

Bibliography

Baxter, L. A. (1990). "Dialectical Contradictions in Relationship Development." *Journal of Social and Personal Relationships* 7:69–88.

Baxter, L. A., and Montgomery, B. M. (1996). *Relating: Dialogues and Dialectics*. New York: Guilford Press.

Bruess, C. J. S., and Pearson, J. C. (1997). "Interpersonal Rituals in Marriage and Adult Friendship." *Communication Monographs* 64:25–46.

Cissna, K. K.; Cox, D. E.; and Bochner, A. P. (1990). "The Dialectic of Marital and Parental Relationships Within the Stepfamily." *Communication Monographs* 57:45–61.

Dickson, F. C. (1995). "The Best is Yet to Be: Research on Long-Lasting Marriages." In *Under-Studied Relationships,* eds. J. T. Wood and S. Duck. Thousand Oaks, CA: Sage Publishing.

Feldman, L. B. (1979). "Marital Conflict and Marital Intimacy: An Integrative Psychodynamic Behavioral Systemic Model." *Family Process* 18:69–78.

Galvin, K. M., and Brommel, B. J. (2000). *Family Communication: Cohesion and Change,* 5th edition. New York: Longman.

Gottman, J. M. (1994a). *What Predicts Divorce*. Hillsdale, NJ: Erlbaum.

Gottman, J. M. (1994b). *Why Marriages Succeed or Fail*. New York: Simon and Schuster.

Gudykunst, W. B., and Lee, C. M. (2001). "An Agenda for Studying Ethnicity and Family Communication." *Journal of Family Communication* 1:75–86.

Maddock, J. (1989). "Healthy Family Sexuality: Positive Principles for Educators and Clinicians." *Family Relations* 38:130–136.

McGoldrick, M. (1993). "Ethnicity, Cultural Diversity and Normality." In *Normal Family Processes,* 2nd edition., ed. F. Walsh. New York: Guilford Press.

Petronio, S. (2000). "The Boundaries of Privacy: Praxis of Everyday Life." In *The Secrets of Private Disclosures,* ed. S. Petronio. Mahwah, NJ: Erlbaum.

Rogers, L. E. (2001). "Relational Communication in the Context of Family." *Journal of Family Communication* 1:25–36.

Roloff, M. (1996). "The Catalyst Hypothesis: Condition Under Which Coercive Communication Leads to Physical Aggression." In *Family Violence from a Communication Perspective,* ed. D. Cahn and S. Floyd. Thousand Oaks, CA: Sage Publications.

Socha, T. J., and Diggs, R., eds. (1999). *Communication, Race and Family: Exploring Communication in Black, White, and Biracial Families*. Mahwah, NJ: Erlbaum.

Specher, S., and McKinney, K. (1994). "Sexuality in Close Relationships." In *Perspectives in Close Relationships,* ed. A. Weber and J. Harvey. Needham Heights, MA: Allyn & Bacon.

Vangelisti, A. L., and Banski, M. A. (1993). "Couples Debriefing Conversations, The Impact of Gender, Occupation and Demographic Characteristics." *Family Relations* 14:149–157.

Vissing, Y., and Baily, W. (1996). " Parent-to-Child Verbal Aggression." In *Family Violence from a Communication Perspective,* ed. D. Cahn and S. Floyd. Thousand Oaks, CA: Sage Publications

Warren, C. (1992). "Perspectives on International Sex Practices and American Family Sex Communication Relevant to Teenage Sexual Behavior in the United States." *Health Communication* 4:121–136.

Warren, C. (1995). "Parent-Child Communication about Sex." In *Parents, Children and Communication: Frontiers of Theory and Research,* ed. T. J. Socha and G. H. Stamp. Mahwah, NJ: Erlbaum.

Wartella, E., and Jennings, N. (2001). "New Members of the Family: The Digital Revolution in the Home." *Journal of Family Communication* 1:59–70.

West, R., and Turner, L. H. (1995). "Communication in Lesbian and Gay Families: Developing a Descriptive Base." In *Parents, Children, and Communication,* ed. T. Socha and G. Stamp. Mahwah, NJ: Erlbaum.

Whitchurch, G., and Dickson, F. C. (1999). "Family Communication." In *Handbook of Marriage and the Family,* 2nd edition., ed. S. K. Steinmetz and G. W. Peterson. New York: Plenum Press.

Wilder, C., and Collins, S. (1994). "Patterns of Interactional Paradoxes." In *The Dark Side of Interpersonal Communication,* ed. W. R. Cupach and B. H. Spitzberg. Mahwah, NJ: Erlbaum.

Wilson, S. R., and Whipple, E. E. (1995). "Communication, Discipline, and Physical Child Abuse." In *Parents, Children, and Communication: Frontiers in Theory and Research,* ed. T. Socha and G. Stamp. Hillsdale, NJ: Erlbaum.

Wolin, S. J. and Bennett, L. A. (1984). "Family Rituals." *Family Process* 23:401–420.

Wood, J. T. (1997). *Gendered Lives: Communication, Gender, and Culture,* 2nd edition. Belmont, CA: Wadsworth.

Yerby, J.; Buerkel-Rothfuss, N. L.; and Bochner, A. (1990). *Understanding Family Communication.* Scottsdale, AZ: Gorsuch Scarisbrick.

Other Resources

Golden, A., ed. (2000). "Communication Perspective on Work and Family." *Electronic Journal of Communication* 10:3–4. Available from http://www.cios.org/www/ejc/v10n3400.htm.

PEW Internet and American Life Project. (2000). "Tracking Online Life: How Women Use the Internet to Cultivate Relationships with Family and Friends." Available from http://www.pewinternet.org.

PEW Internet and American Life Project. (2001). "Teenage Life Online: The Rise of the Instant-Message Generation and the Internet's Impact on Friendships and Family Relationships." Available from http://www.pewinternet.org.

KATHLEEN M. GALVIN

COMMUTER MARRIAGES

Commuter marriage is a voluntary arrangement where dual-career couples maintain two residences in different geographic locations and are separated at least three nights per week for a minimum of three months (Gerstel and Gross 1982; Orton and Crossman 1983). Dual-career families (Rapoport and Rapoport 1976) are those where both heads of the household pursue careers, and their work requires a high degree of commitment and special training, with a continuous developmental character involving increasing degrees of responsibility.

Although researchers (Kirschner and Walum 1978) have acknowledged that living apart is not unusual for some occupations such as politicians, entertainers, or salespeople, as well as certain circumstances (e.g., war, immigration, imprisonment, and seasonal work), historically it is the male who

has left the family for a period of time. In contrast, commuter marriages came about because both spouses have career goals that cannot be met in the same geographic location. Hence, increasingly we observe women's mobility from the family for work-related reasons. A commuter marriage is a work solution compromise allowing both spouses to pursue their careers, while maintaining their marriage relationship. Often the commuter arrangement is considered temporary until the couple achieves career goals that enable them to relocate together (Farris 1978).

The primary factors contributing to the occurrence of commuter marriages are: the number of women in the workforce, the number of dual-career couples, and the number of women seeking careers requiring specialized training, all of which are increasing (Anderson 1992). Further, it has been suggested that tighter job markets that force people to relocate, greater equality within marriage that places more attention on wives' careers, and society's increasing emphasis on individualism also add to the increased incidence of commuter marriages.

Demographics of Commuter Marriages

Demographers have speculated that annually 700,000 to one million American couples have adopted a commuting lifestyle (Johnson 1987). By 1995, according to labor statistics, both partners in 61 percent of married couples worked, in contrast to 53.5 percent in 1990, 46.3 percent in 1980, and only 38.1 percent in 1970 (U.S. Bureau of the Census 1996). Additionally, in 1998 the U.S. Census Bureau indicated that 2.4 million Americans said they were married, but that their spouses did not live at home, a 21 percent reported increase over the previous four years. Further, these people did not consider themselves separated, implying a troubled marriage. Although the above figures include military couples that may spend long periods of time apart, these data suggest that the number of commuter marriages in the United States continues to increase (Kiefer 2000). Although no known research has been reported on commuter marriages in other countries, one could surmise that other industrialized countries with married dual-career couples may also be experiencing this lifestyle arrangement.

The handful of U.S. studies conducted on commuter marriages suggest the following profile: (1) a large majority of these spouses are well-educated—over 90 percent have completed at least some graduate work; (2) almost all are professionals or executives with a high proportion in academics; (3) their median family income is between $30,000 and $40,000; (4) the mean age of the individuals is mid-to-late thirties with a range of 25 to 55 years; (5) 40 to 50 percent have children; and (6) more than half have been married for nine years or longer (Anderson and Spruill 1993; Bunker et al. 1992).

In regard to couples' commuting characteristics, there is much more variation. The period of time couples have maintained separate residences ranges from three months to fourteen years. Spouses travel from a range of forty to twenty-seven hundred miles and reunite as often as every weekend to as seldom as a few days a month (Gerstel and Gross 1984). One home is usually considered the primary residence and the other a sort of satellite home. Typically the place the couple reunites is considered the primary residence.

According to Elaine Anderson (1992), 47 percent of men and 29 percent of women did all the commuting, or traveled more frequently, whereas 25 percent report splitting the travel equally. Factors affecting the decision of who does most of the commuting in descending order of frequency are: flexibility of time, one home considered the home base, friend network, children at home, and community commitment. Further, Karen Patterson-Stewart, Anita Jackson, and Ronald Brown (2000) reported from a sample of African-American commuter marriages that loss of community, which limits one's ability to engage in nonwork-related activities, clearly was salient to these couples. Typically, 49 percent of the couples (Anderson 1992) report the wife suggested the idea of commuting, 24 percent said the husband instigated the idea, 19 percent replied both equally, and 8 percent said an employer offered commuting as an option. Likewise, data suggest women are more comfortable with the commuting relationship than men.

There is some disagreement in the literature concerning the effect of commuting on the division of household labor. Initially, researchers found that each newly commuting spouse develops competence in domestic tasks their spouse had previously performed. More recently, Elaine Anderson and Jane Spruill (1993) found that couples report a traditional gendered division of their household labor regardless of having more than one residence.

Commuter couples have been described as determined, capable, independent, resourceful, and self-reliant people who have confidence in their own judgment and who are not concerned with contradicting societal norms of marriage. Couples often face employers' doubts about whether or not the commuter would be "giving his/her best performance when living out of a separate household . . . [and/or] thought a commuter marriage would result in either a divorce or a decision to leave the company" (Taylor and Lounsbury 1988, p. 418). However, Anderson and Spruill (1993) report only 9 percent of commuter marriages terminated in divorce. Further, John Orton and Sharyn Crossman (1983) found extramarital affairs and the contemplation of divorce were relevant for only a minority of those in commuter marriages, and for those for whom these were issues, the commuting lifestyle had not jeopardized the marriage relationship.

Benefits for Commuter Marriage Couples

Clearly, the commuter lifestyle can bring some benefits to the marriage relationship. Trust and commitment tend to be rated as high for couples that successfully negotiate a commuter marriage (Maines 1993). In addition, cooperation and enhanced communication skills, along with "flexibility, common interests, interdependence, and a desire for self-actualization" are also reported (Winfield 1985, p. 174). Couples in later stages of family development who have achieved financial stability and who perceive well-being in their marriage have also been associated with more satisfactory commuting.

The individuals in the commuter marriage also may benefit from this lifestyle. Research suggests this lifestyle brings increased autonomy, achievement, and feelings of satisfaction for the individual as well as enhanced self-esteem and confidence (Chang and Browder-Wood 1996; Groves and Horm-Wingerd 1991). There is a greater ability to pursue one's career without some of the everyday family constraints, as well as an opportunity for developing one's self-identity and self-gratification.

Further, the commuting lifestyle affords individuals the possibility of greater concentration and more time at work by separating work and family responsibilities (Bunker and Vanderslice 1982). Catherine Chang and Amy Browder-Wood (1996) reported that female commuters experienced less psychological and physical difficulties if they could successfully resolve role conflicts, whereas males reported improved relationships with their children and feeling more effective in the parenting role. Finally, Patterson-Stewart and colleagues (2000) reported that commuters from racial minorities indicated that this lifestyle allowed them to counter employment limitations, prior assumptions that people might have about their abilities, and negative racial stereotypes and oppression. However, in spite of the myriad benefits, commuter marriages still face numerous obstacles.

Challenges Faced by Commuter Marriage Couples

Harriett Gross (1980) suggested there are two types of couples in commuter marriages, *adjusting* and *established*. Adjusting couples tend to be younger in age, are confronting separation earlier in their marriage, and have few, if any, children. In contrast, established couples are older and further along in their marriages, and their children are typically older and often have moved out of the house. Thus, the established couples tend to find the commuter marriage less stressful in comparison to adjusting couples. Trust seems to be a bigger issue for the younger adjusting couple, whereas maintaining excitement in the relationship may be an issue for the established couple.

Clearly, the financial costs of a commuter marriage can be significant. In addition to increased phone bills and travel costs, there is the burden of maintaining two households. The necessity of attending to all work or home activities in a relatively short period of time can become a source of strain. Finally, couples report the emotional costs of separation and the lack of emotional support and companionship, as well as feelings of loneliness, isolation, tension, frustration, and even depression (Chang and Browder-Wood 1996). In particular, younger adjusting couples report fearing they will grow apart and jeopardize their marriage. Commuting couples can lose their "intimacy of routine" or daily intimacy that "helps produce the ordered world typically entailed in a marital relationship" (Gerstel and Gross 1982, p. 81). Commuting couples have less time together; thus they feel more pressure when together to make all reunions special. Such unrealistic expectations can lead to disappointment. Commuting couples also experience a reduction in sexual intercourse, perhaps due to fatigue, pressure, and readjustment.

In commuter relationships where the children are in college, the children report they were not affected by their parents' commuting (Patterson-Stewart, Jackson, and Brown 2000). In contrast, where children are still living at home, the children report more concern that the commuter parent seems uninvolved in their lives. Friends of commuter marriage couples report they admire the trust in their friends' relationship, but worry about the strain that commuting can bring to a relationship. They also report missing their friends' companionship.

There appear to be four factors that add stress and strain to the commuter marriage and lead to dissatisfaction with the arrangement. First, Anderson (1992) suggests stress from the commute can be exacerbated if the spouses do not enjoy spending time alone. Second, having particularly young children seems more problematic regarding the logistics of managing the household tasks and child care (Anderson and Spruill 1993). Third, those typically younger couples, with fewer years of marriage, and without the stability or security necessarily of either a long-term relationship or career may feel more strain (Orton and Crossman 1983). Finally, not only do couples that are separated by longer distances incur more monetary costs and energy outlay to reunite; they undoubtedly have less frequent, less regular, and shorter reunions. Therefore, suggestions for helping these couples cope with this lifestyle are warranted.

Coping Strategies for Commuter Marriage Couples

In order to maximize a couple's capacity to cope with the commuting lifestyle, intervention should begin at the decision-making stage, with a discussion of how to integrate work and family. Issues to consider for a commuter marriage are: (1) how financially stable the family is (i.e., will the commute produce undue financial burden?); (2) what stage of the family life cycle the family is at; (3) how much time individuals have spent by themselves, and how they react to alone time; (4) how systematic the couple is in making decisions; and (5) what kind of time frame for reassessing whether or not the lifestyle is working has been developed?

Coping with commuter marriage is significantly supported if the couple can more easily afford the increased financial costs of the lifestyle (Farris 1978; Gerstel and Gross 1982; Anderson 1992). Additionally, if spouses have no children at home, are older, have been married longer, and have at least one established career, commuting seems to be easier. Those spouses who can tolerate periods of separation and enjoy spending time alone also seem to adjust to and cope with the lifestyle most easily. Finally, using a more systematic or planned decision style helps many couples to express higher satisfaction with their decision to commute and their adapting to the commuting lifestyle. However, it is important to recognize that entering into a commuter marriage is a decision that couples make. Reevaluating the implemented decision to assess its effectiveness also is critical for enhancing family well-being.

See also: COMMUNICATION: COUPLE RELATIONSHIPS; HOME; RELATIONSHIP MAINTENANCE; TRUST; WORK AND FAMILY

Bibliography

Anderson, E. A. (1992). "Decision-Making Style: Impact on Satisfaction of the Commuter Couples' Lifestyle." *Journal of Family and Economic Issues* 13:1–21.

Anderson, E. A., and Spruill, J. W. (1993). "The Dual-Career Commuter Family: A Lifestyle on the Move." *Marriage and Family Review* 19:131–147.

Bunker, B. B., and Vanderslice, V. J. (1982). "Tradeoffs: Individual Gains and Relational Losses of Commuting Couples." Paper presented at the annual meeting, American Psychological Association, Washington, DC, August.

Bunker, B. B.; Zubek, J. M.; Vanderslice, V. J.; and Rice, R. W. (1992). "Quality of Life in Dual-Career Families: Commuting versus Single-Residence Couples." *Journal of Marriage and the Family* 54:399–407.

Chang, C. Y., and Browder-Wood, A. M. (1996). "Dual-Career Commuter Marriages: Balancing Commitments to Self, Spouse, Family and Work." Paper presented at the National Conference, American Counseling Association, Pittsburgh, PA, April.

Farris, A. (1978). "Commuting." In *Working Couples,* ed. R. Rapoport and R. N. Rapoport. London: Routledge and Kegan Paul.

Gerstel, N., and Gross, H. E. (1982). "Commuter Marriages: A Review." *Marriage and Family Review* 5:71–93.

Gerstel, N., and Gross, H. E. (1984). *Commuter Marriage.* New York: Guilford.

Gross, H. E. (1980). "Dual-Career Couples Who Live Apart: Two Types." *Journal of Marriage and Family* 42:567–576.

Groves, M. M., and Horm-Wingerd, D. M. (1991). "Commuter Marriages: Personal, Family and Career Issues." *Sociology and Social Research* 75:212–217.

Johnson, S. E. (1987). "Weaving the Threads: Equalizing Professional and Personal Demands Faced by Commuting Career Couples." *Journal of the National Association of Women Deans and Counselors* 50:3–10.

Kiefer, F. (2000). "Commuter Marriages Test More Americans." *Christian Science Monitor* 92:1.

Kirschner, B., and Walum, L. (1978). "Two-Location Families: Married Singles." *Alternative Lifestyles* 1:513–525.

Maines, J. (1993). "Long-Distance Romances." *American Demographics* 15:47.

Orton, J., and Crossman, S. M. (1983). "Long Distance Marriage: Cause of Marital Disruption or a Solution to Unequal Dual-Career Development?" In *Family, Self, and Society,* ed. D. B. Gutknecht. Lanham, MD: University Press of America.

Patterson-Stewart, K. E.; Jackson, A. P.; and Brown, R. P. (2000). "African Americans in Dual-Career Commuter Marriages: An Investigation of their Experiences." *Family Journal—Counseling Therapy for Couples and Families* 8:22–47.

Rapoport, R., and Rapoport, R. N. (1976). *Dual-Career Families Re-Examined.* New York: Harper and Row.

Taylor, A. S., and Lounsbury, J. W. (1988). "Dual-Career Couples and Geographic Transfer: Executives' Reactions to Commuter Marriage and Attitudes toward the Move." *Human Relations* 41:405–424.

U.S. Bureau of the Census. (1996). *Current Population Reports, Series P60: Income Statistics,* Branch/HHES Division, U.S. Government Printing Office, Washington, DC.

Winfield, F. E. (1985). *Commuter Marriage: Living Together, Apart.* New York: Columbia University Press.

ELAINE A. ANDERSON

COMPARATIVE ANALYSIS

The comparative method has taken many forms since Augustus Comte first employed the concept in 1853 in his foundational *Cours de philosophie positive.* Subsequently a variety of comparative methods have emerged in the social sciences with different goals, units of comparison, and types of data that reflect a variety of theoretical assumptions and interests. Comparison has formed the core of anthropology, sociology and other social sciences, to the extent that Emile Durkheim (1938) viewed all sociological analysis as necessarily comparative. Comparative methods have been employed for both quantitative and qualitative studies of such diverse phenomena as language, political organization, economic relations, religion, myth, kinship, marriage, and the family.

Three strategies are used in comparative methodologies: illustrative comparison, complete or universe comparison, and sampled-based comparisons (Sarana 1975). They are distinguished by the units of comparison (including cultures, societies, regions, or communities) and the particular items or features used to compare the units. Societies as units can be compared by examining items or traits such as institutions or practices. Illustrative comparison is the most common form of comparative analysis and has been employed extensively by theorists from diverse camps. Items are used as examples to explain or exemplify phenomena found in different units. They are chosen for their illustrative value and not systematically selected to be statistically representative. Illustrative comparisons are used in historical reconstructions, and to support interpretations or general assertions. Ethnographic case studies are commonly justified as the source for illustrative comparisons.

The second strategy is complete or universe comparison, in which all elements of the domain within the study, defined geographically (e.g., global or regional) or topically (e.g., analytical concepts or institutions), form the units of comparison. Comprehensive regional ethnographic surveys and analyses of particular topics, such as the national population health indicators of the World Health Organization reports, employ this approach.

Finally, sampled comparison strategically delimits part of the whole, with the goal of selecting data that are statistically representative of the variations within the whole and are intended as the basis for statistical generalizations. While studies of this type abound in sociology and human geography, they are much less common in anthropology. Within anthropology, the most widely known example is the George Murdock's Human Relations Area Files.

General Strategies of Comparative Methods

Comparative methods have been used for three types of goals: the construction of inferential histories, the development of typologies, and the explication of generalized processes (Peel 1987). Theories based on inferential histories dominated the formation of the social sciences until the early twentieth century, while the development of typologies and analyses of processes are now the predominate comparative strategies.

Natural histories of society. During the late nineteenth and early twentieth centuries scholars compared institutions and practices from many societies to construct evolutionary accounts of the origin of civilization, culture, and society. Contemporary *primitive* societies gave these theorists evidence of earlier social forms. Following the natural sciences' histories of geological formations and biological evolution, widely influential theorists, including Comte, Friedrich Engles (1965 [1846]), Lewis Henry Morgan (1870, 1877), Karl Marx, Herbert Spencer (1898), Max Mueller (1909), James Frazer (1907), and Edward Tylor (1889, 1903), each constructed an historical narrative that traced the emergence of human civilization from ancient, primitive societies into complex and sophisticated civilizations of Europe. They proposed a variety of developmental stages, with characteristic types of social organization, economic activity, and religious practices, that all societies necessarily passed though during their evolution. They shared the belief that the nuclear family was the precursor of more complex forms of social relations such as the clan, tribe, city, and nation-state.

Multi-linear evolutionist and diffusionist theories. A second wave of historical comparativists followed in the early twentieth century. Rather than constructing a single history of human culture or civilization, these scholars attempted to explain the emergence of particular cultures and the historical diffusion of cultural traits. Commonalities and differences among cultures were explained as either independent inventions of social forms, artifacts, and beliefs, or taken to have diffused from a single point of origin. The several different schools of diffusionists preferred to believe that invention was infrequent, so consequently they developed comparative methods to infer relationships among cultural traits and infer their sources. British anthropologists Alfred Haddon (1895) and W. H. R. Rivers (1914) came to the conclusion, based on their research in Melanesia, that social change was the product of migration and culture contact. Taken further, G. Elliott Smith (1928) and W. J. Perry (1923) contended that Egypt was the root of Western European civilization and that culture diffused to ancient Europe as the result of culture contact and migration. A similar approach was developed in Germany and Austria under the tutelage of Fritz Graebner (1903) and Wilhelm Schmidt, who postulated the existence of *Kulturekreise,* culture centers, presumably in central Asia, from which archetypical cultural items were spread.

The German diffusionists' methodology and conclusions were inspired by the comparative method that linguists including William Jones (1799), Franz Bopp (1967 [1816]), and Jakob Grimm (1967 [1893]) used to identify historically related Romance and Germanic language families. These linguists inferred the previous existence of a common mother-language, Proto-Indo-European, from the systemic variation in sound systems among these languages and Sanskrit.

Criticisms of the historical comparative methods concern the units of analysis used for comparison including similarity and diversity among the societies studied, the comparability of the data used, and the kinds of generalizations that are possible given the nature of the data. Furthermore the inferential histories paid little heed to the contextual factors that molded the particular institutions that they examined.

The historical comparativists and the diffusionists' comparative methods and research suffered several weaknesses. They were unable to adequately respond to Francis Galton's criticism in the discussion that followed Tylor's address to the Royal Anthropological Institute (Tylor 1899) that, if data were gathered from neighboring groups, it would be impossible to determine if similarities resulted from a common history or arose independently from common functions. Questions were also raised about the ability to establish social rules based on historically contingent phenomena. In addition, the inferences they made were based on data that was often gathered unsystematically. Most significantly these theories seemed increasingly less credible as researchers had greater contact with people in the societies they attempted to explain. Diffusionist theories lost currency after World War II with the rise of theories designed to identify social laws rather than cultural origins. Though the diffusionists' theories were largely discredited as inadequately supported by historical data, the explorer Thor Heyerdahl (1952) kept them alive with his attempts to demonstrate the possibility of ancient transoceanic migrations.

Comparison and social laws. Three different approaches to comparative studies superceded the inferential histories of the evolutionists and diffusionists and established the parameters for anthropological and sociological comparison for the twentieth-century. The German-American anthropologist Franz Boas ([1896] 1940) decried the "conjectural history" of the diffusionists' comparative method, in favor of comprehensive ethnographic descriptions that might reveal the "uniform laws that govern the human mind" (p. 271). Boas directed the efforts of the American Bureau of Ethnology to document the many cultures and languages of the native peoples of North America. His goal was to identify and classify the external (environmental) and internal (psychological) factors that shape the expression of these fundamental features of humans societies.

Durkheim's sociology echoed the analytical distinction between structure and process in Comte's positivist method. His goal was to identify structural forms or morphological units and their subtypes. He created a descriptive-analytic typology with analytical units that were examined synchronically for contextual variations. The goals of his sociological analysis were to identify social crucial facts that are elemental in every society and combined in different numbers and combinations into particular social species. He contended that "societies are only different combinations of the same original society" (Durkheim 1938, p. 86). In his studies of religion and social organization, he drew upon examples from Europe, North American native peoples, and Australia to identify elementary structures and their elaborations. Durkheim's study of *social morphology* laid the foundation for both British structure-functionalism in anthropology and Continental structuralist sociology and anthropology.

The failures of the conjectural histories of the diffusionists spurred a new and different approach to comparative studies in anthropology based primarily on Durkheim's social morphology and comparative sociology. British anthropologists A. R.

Radcliffe-Brown (1951), Fred Eggan (1954), and Edward Evans-Pritchard (1963) severely criticized the historical comparativists and responded by developing more systematic, controlled comparisons that focused on systems of kinship, marriage and family.

Max Weber (1968) took a less positivist approach to social analysis and based his comparative method on the formulation of *ideal types*. He began with the recognition that the researcher plays an important role in framing research questions, identifying units of analysis, and selecting items for comparison. Rather than assuming an objective separation of the researcher and data, he constructed ideal types, or analytical models that did not confuse the researcher's conceptualization of the phenomena with the phenomena itself. These types enabled him to investigate the phenomena from an acknowledged starting point and interrogate other aspects of the object during analysis. He employed ideal types in his comparative studies of the relationship between economy and religion in Protestant Northern and Catholic southern Europe, the differences between charismatic and bureaucratic forms of leadership in Europe and China, and religious practices in Europe, China, and India.

Clifford Geertz (1963, 1968) used ethnographic cases as real types for comparisons of social organization, economic systems, and educational systems, and paved the way for comparisons in interpretative anthropology and cultural studies.

A third response to the inadequacies of the historical comparative methods was to develop sample-based comparisons with ethnographic databases. George Murdock's Human Relations Area Files and accompanying Ethnographic Atlas were the most extensive attempt to identify cross-cultural correlations and make statistical generalizations (Murdock 1963; Murdock and Yale University Institute of Human Relations 1982). To this end, he cataloged existing ethnographic data from 10 percent of the world's cultures identified by the late 1930s. Murdock's approach floundered due to the difficulties of making correlations, identified by Galton, and its dependence upon existing data, gathered by others who did not use comparable research strategies or common definitions of phenomena.

Comparisons of processes. Comparative studies of social process have returned to some topics previously examined by classical evolutionists and the diffusionists, but with much more constraint and caution. Research on social and economic change, migration, and cultural contact have attempted to return a historical dimension to structural analyses. Edmund Leach's (1954) study of the dynamics of ethnic and political relations in highland Burma paved the way for the more complex formulations in the French sociologist Pierre Bourdieu's (1977) theory of social practice, and in Ulf Hannerz's (1992) analysis of creolization, or the synthesis of new cultural forms, under the pressures of culture contact and globalization.

Comparative Methods in the Study of Kinship, the Family, and Marriage

Kinship and family relations were early subjects of comparison and debate in the social sciences. Studies of kinship and the family have formed the core of British social anthropology and have dominated North American and European anthropology throughout the twentieth century. Family and kinship were central to the nineteenth- and early twentieth-century debates about the origins and evolution of society. Henry Maine (1861 [1911]), James McLennan (1865, 1886), and Johann Bachofen (1967 [1861]) examined forms of family and marriage. Maine compared Greek, Roman, and more contemporary British and continental family law. Bachofen, confusing matrilineality as matriarchy, argued that social authority originally developed from mothers' roles in primitive families that were transformed during cultural development into male authority in patriarchies. McLennan traced social evolution though changes in forms of marriage, from primitive promiscuity though marriage by capture and eventually the monogamous marital relationships of Victorian England.

L. H. Morgan, a U.S. lawyer, is considered the father of kinship studies in anthropology, however. He described the legal or jural dimensions of family and kinship among the Iroquois of the state of New York, and compared their family and clan structures with those of European societies and Australian Aborigines (who have figured significantly in comparative studies of kinship) (Morgan 1870, 1963 [1877]). From his analysis of kinship, Morgan developed a theory of evolution in which the division of labor within the family was the basis for the development of more complex forms of social organization including the nation-state. Another enduring contribution was to distinguish between kin terms used to describe and classify individuals. This opened the door to the use of kin terms as the basis for comparisons of kinship terms as cultural systems of classification.

Morgan's evolutionary schema had a marked impact upon another social theorist, Karl Marx. Though Marx initially replaced Morgan's focus on the family with private property in his social and economic analysis, Marx and Frederick Engels returned to the centrality of the family in their discussion of the origin of private property (Engels 1988 [1884]). Studies of kinship and the family took second place in diffusionist theories to explanations of the transmission of material culture, particularly technology and religious beliefs.

During the later half the twentieth century, comparative studies of kinship dominated anthropology. They were of three types, each closely aligned with the theories of Boas, Durkheim, and Weber, and concerned with social structure rather than history. The first is the controlled case study approach recommended by Radcliffe-Brown and Forde (1950) and Evans-Pritchard (1963). These comparative studies of social forms focused on kinship and marriage and the structural relationships among kin groups. They compared societies' rules concerning the rights and obligations that established group membership, inheritance, and succession. They described them with terms they believed were universal features of kinship and family: descent, generation, gender, collaterality (or siblingship), and marital relations. Their units of study were the nuclear family, the lineage, and the clan. They reduced the variability among their comparative units by concentrating their research on regions of Africa with patrilineally and matrilineally based societies. Social organizations were classified by the rules of group membership, inheritance patterns, laws of succession, and patterns of prohibited and preferred marriage and post marital residence.

British structural-functionalist analyses concentrated attention on kinship to the expense of the family, many contending that lineage and clan relations were the logical and psychological extension of ties among nuclear family members. These anthropological analyses of the structures of family and kinship relations were similar to the functionalist analyses of families and family structures that developed sociology. Comparative sociologists examined the functions and structural attributes of families, household composition, and family dynamics as did anthropological studies of the time. In addition they considered more emotional and psychological issues such as love (Goode 1959). Comparisons by sociologists focused on variations across time and national, ethnic, and class lines, rather than across cultures.

Claude Levi-Strauss developed another method based on the comparison of structural principles. His structuralist treatment of kinship and marriage (referred to as alliance theory) examined the nature of relationships among groups, rather then focusing upon groups' rules of composition. Levi-Straus's seminal *Elementary Structures of Kinship* 1969) began by examining the significance of incest rules and rules of group exogamy (the practice of marrying outside of one's group) that used marriage as a means of both delineating group boundaries (in terms of those whom one may or may not marry) and establishing alliances. From this starting point, he compared the complex patterns of marriage-based alliances among a number of Australian aboriginal groups and societies in Southeast Asia and India, to compare the various conceptual elaborations of the principles of marriage exchange and alliance.

During the 1960s and 1970s comparative studies declined, in part due to methodological and epistemological debates that questioned the concepts employed in comparative research. Studies of kinship and the family were at the heart of these debates. Questions were raised about the nature of analytical definitions and the use of Western European concepts such as descent, marriage, and kinship as analytical constructs for the description and analysis of systems in other cultures (Needham 1971). Examination of other cultures' theories of conception and paternity even called into question the very nature of kinship and its recognition as a universal phenomena. David Schneider (1968) contended that kinship systems were culturally constructed idioms of social relations. Nevertheless, comparative studies of kinship terminologies continued to use Western concepts such as descent as analytical concepts in comparisons of kinship semantics and the cognitive classifications of kin (Tyler 1969). Consequently, Leach (1966) raised serious doubts about the value of the typologies developed to describe the kinship systems. These questions further undermined the already weak reception for statistical studies such as those of Murdock.

Networks and Process. Anthropologists also became increasing concerned about variation within the kinds of social units that they had previously used in comparisons. Case studies that were the staple of the method of controlled comparison of British structure-functionalists and Levi-Straussian structuralism treated families, clans, societies, and cultures as closed systems. Migration by members of formerly isolated societies forced researchers to face growing diversity and the disjunction of features—language, common history, religious beliefs and practice—that had coincided in geographically bound populations. Studies of networks and their structures attempted to overcome the restrictions of geographically defined analytical units (Sanjek 1978). The development of network theory and formal models such as directed graphs provided researchers with new ways to describe and compare families structures and systems of kinship and marriage (Hage and Harary 1996), kin terms, (Schweizer and White 1998), and ties between household and family members and their communities (Wellman and Berkowitz 1997).

Not only were classical comparative studies called into question on epistemological grounds, their adequacy in representing kinship and family systems was attacked for their substantive limitations grounds. Earlier studies had focused on the legal and political aspects of kinship that were dominated by men. Feminist critics argued that they generally ignored women and the domestic sphere, thereby undermining the adequacy of earlier conventional studies. This criticism reinvigorated comparative studies of the family, women's roles, socialization, and gender relations (Yanagisako 1979) that found antecedents in the early comparative work of Boas's student, Margaret Mead (Mead [1935] 2001; Mead and Malinowski [1930] 2001). The reconsideration of the role of women, the family, and socialization also coincided with Bourdieu's attention to the processes of social reproduction (Bourdieu and Passeron 1977).

Conclusion

Comparative analyses remain an essential aspect of anthropology and other social sciences, just as Durkheim asserted (1938). With the growth of literacy and political activism, the peoples who anthropologists had studied and described have challenged professional social scientists' place as ethnographers. At the same time, anthropologists, sociologists, and cultural geographers' comparative analyses take on greater academic significance and practical value (Sperber 1985).

Bibliography

Bachofen, J. J. (1967 [1861]). *Myth, Religion, and Mother Right: Selected Writings of J. J. Bachofen.* Princeton, NJ: Princeton University Press.

Boas, F. (1940 [1896]). *Race, Language and Culture.* New York: Macmillan.

Bopp, F. (1967 [1816]). "On the Conjugational System of the Sanskrit Language: In Comparison with That of Greek, Latin, Persian and the Germanic Languages." In *A Reader in Nineteenth Century Historical Indo-European Linguistics,* ed. W. P. Lehmann. Bloomington: Indiana University Press.

Bourdieu, P. (1977). *Outline of a Theory of Practice.* Cambridge, UK: Cambridge University Press.

Bourdieu, P., and Passeron, P. (1977). *Reproduction in Education, Society, and Culture.* London: Sage.

Comte, A. (1853). *Positive Philosophy of Auguste Comte.* London: J. Chapman.

Durkheim, E. (1938). *The Rules of Sociological Method,* 8th edition. Glencoe: The Free Press.

Eggan, F. (1954). "Social Anthropology and the Method of Controlled Comparison." *American Anthropologist* 56:643–763.

Engles, F. (1988 [1884]). *The Origin of the Family, Private Property, and the State.* 1st edition. New York: Pathfinder Press.

Engels, F., and Leacock, E. B. (1972). *The Origin of the Family, Private Property, and the State, in the Light of the Researches of Lewis H. Morgan.* 1st edition. New York: International Publishers.

Evans-Pritchard, E. E. (1963). *The Comparative Method in Social Anthropology.* London: University of London, Athlone Press.

Frazer, J. G. (1907). *The Golden Bough: A Study in Magic and Religion.* 3rd edition. London and New York: Macmillan.

Geertz, C. (1963). *Peddlers and Princes: Social Change and Economic Modernization in Two Indonesian Towns.* Chicago: University of Chicago Press.

Geertz, C. (1968). *Islam Observed: Religious Development in Morocco and Indonesia.* New Haven, CT: Yale University Press.

Goode, W. J. (1959). "The Sociology of the Family: Horizons in Family Theory." In *Sociology Today; Problems and Prospects,* ed. R. K. Merton, L. Broom and L. Cottrell. New York: Basic Books.

Graebner, F. (1903). "Kulturekreise Und Kultureschichten in Ozeania." *Zeitschrift fur Ethnologie* 37:28–53.

Grimm, J. (1967 [1893]). "Germanic Grammar." In *A Reader in Nineteenth Century Historical Indo-European Linguistics,* ed. W. P. Lehmann. Bloomington: Indiana University Press.

Haddon, A. C. (1895). *Evolution in Art: As Illustrated by the Life-Histories of Designs.* London: W. Scott.

Hage, P., and Harary, F. (1996). *Island Networks: Communication, Kinship, and Classification Structures in Oceania.* Cambridge, UK: Cambridge University Press.

Hannerz, U. (1992). *Cultural Complexity: Studies in the Social Organization of Meaning.* New York: Columbia University Press.

Heyerdahl, T. (1952). *American Indians in the Pacific: The Theory behind the Kon-Tiki Expedition.* London: Allen and Unwin.

Holý, L. (1987). *Comparative Anthropology.* Oxford, UK, and New York: Blackwell.

Jones. W. (1799). *Works of Sir William Jones.* London: G. G. and J. Robinson.

Leach, E. R. (1954). *Political Systems of Highland Burma: A Study of Kachin Social Structure.* London: London School of Economics and Political Science.

Leach, E. R. (1966). *Rethinking Anthropology.* London: Athlone Press.

Lehmann, W. P. (1967). *A Reader in Nineteenth Century Historical Indo-European Linguistics.* Bloomington: Indiana University Press.

Levi-Strauss, C. (1969). *Elementary Structures of Kinship,* rev. edition. Boston: Beacon Press.

McLennan, J. F. (1865). *Primitive Marriage.* Edinburgh: Adam and Charles Black.

McLennan, J. F. (1886). *Studies in Ancient History: Comprising a Reprint of Primitive Marriage.* London and New York: Macmillan.

Maine, H. S. (1911 [1861]) *Ancient Law, Its Connection with the Early History of Society and Its Relation to Modern Ideas.* London: Murray.

Mead, M. ([1935] 2001). *Sex and Temperament in Three Primitive Societies.* New York: HarperCollins.

Mead, M., and B. Malinowski. ([1930] 2001). *Growing Up in New Guinea: A Comparative Study of Primitive Education.* New York: HarperCollins.

Morgan, L. H. (1870). *Systems of Consanguinity and Affinity of the Human Family.* Washington, DC: Smithsonian Institution.

Morgan, L. H. (1963). *Ancient Society; or, Researches in the Lines of Human Progress from Savagery through Barbarism to Civilization.* Cleveland, OH: World Pub. Co.

Müller, F. M. (1909 [1856]). *Comparative Mythology.* London: G. Routledge and Sons.

Murdock, G. P. (1963). *Outline of World Cultures.* 3rd rev. edition. New Haven, CT: Human Relations Area Files.

Murdock, G. P., and Yale University Institute of Human Relations. (1982). *Outline of Cultural Materials.* 5th rev. edition. New Haven, CT: Human Relations Area Files.

Needham, R. (1971). Introduction to *Rethinking Kinship and Marriage.* London: Tavistock.

Peel, J. D. Y. (1987). "History, Culture and the Comparative Method." In *Comparative Anthropology,* edited by L. Holý. Oxford, UK and New York: Blackwell.

Perry, W. J. (1923). *The Children of the Sun.* London: Metheun.

Radcliffe-Brown, A. R. (1951). The comparative Method in Social Anthropology. *Journal of the Royal Anthropological Institute* 81:15–22.

Radcliffe-Brown, A. R., and C. D. Forde. (1950). *African Systems of Kinship and Marriage.* London and New York: Published for the International African Institute by the Oxford University Press.

Rivers, W. H. R. (1914). *The History of Melanesian Society.* Cambridge, UK: University Press.

Sanjek, R. (1978). "What Is Network Analysis, and What Is It Good For?" *Annual Review of Anthropology* 1:588–597.

Sarana, G. (1975). *Methodology of Anthropological Comparisons.* Tucson: University of Arizona Press.

Schneider, D. M. (1968). *American Kinship: A Cultural Account.* Englewood Cliffs, NJ: Prentice-Hall.

Schweizer, T., and D. R. White. (1998). *Kinship, Networks, and Exchange.* New York: Cambridge University Press.

Smelser, N. J. (1976). *Comparative Methods in the Social Sciences.* Englewood Cliffs, NJ: Prentice-Hall.

Smith, G. E. (1928). *in the Beginning: The Origin of Civilization.* New York: Morrow.

Spencer, H. (2002 [1898]). *The Principles of Sociology.* New Brunswick, NJ: Transaction Publishers.

Sperber, D. (1985). *On Anthropological Knowledge: Three Essays.* Cambridge, UK: Cambridge University Press.

Tyler, S., ed. (1969). *Cognitive Anthropology.* New York: Holt, Rinehart and Winston.

Tylor, S. E. B. (1889). "On a Method of Investigating the Development of Institutions: Applied to Laws of Marriage and Descent." *Journal of the Royal Anthropolocial Institute* 18:245–269.

Tylor, S. E. B. (1903). *Primitive Culture: Researches into the Development of Mythology, Philosophy, Religion, Language, Art, and Custom.* 4th revised edition. London: J. Murray.

Weber, M. (1968). *Economy and Society: An Outline of Interpretive Sociology.* New York: Bedminster Press.

Wellman, B., and Berkowitz, S. D.. (1997). *Social Structures : A Network Approach.* Greenwich, CT: JAI Press.

Yanagisako, S. J. (1979). "Family and Household: The Analysis of Domestic Groups." *Annual Review of Anthropology* 8:161–205.

WILLIAM H. MCKELLIN

COMPUTERS AND FAMILY

The emergence of new technologies in the home, such as microwave ovens and food processors, has continued at an unprecedented rate over the last several decades. Perhaps none of these new technologies is as fraught with questions about its impact on the family as home computers and the Internet. For example, in the developed world, it is commonly estimated that 60 percent of homes have at least one computer. Questions such as "Do home computers bring families together or isolate individuals from the family?", "What effect does computer use have on child development?", and "Who has and controls access to the family computer and Internet?" are being heard more frequently. The potential effects and use of computers in education, communication, home management, recreation, and home businesses have received attention. As David Watt and James White (1999) point out, the measure of the impact depends on the unit of analysis—individual or family group—and the age or stage of development of the individual or family. Thus, a home computer for business purposes might assist the mother of a newborn to stay at home with her child and complete breastfeeding, but the effect would be quite different for the mother with adolescent children. Similarly, a computer game that might be educa-

tional for an individual at one age could well have detrimental effects on concentration at another age.

Education. Most research (e.g., Haddon and Skinner 1991) has supported the educational benefits of children's early access and use of home computers for acquiring knowledge (e.g., Attwell and Battle 1999). Children can learn at their own pace, and research tends to support the view that their learning is faster and better than with some traditional forms of education (Bracey 1982). However, computer learning via games continues to be a disputed area. Research tends to report a stronger positive effect for learning among boys than girls and indicates that upper socioeconomic groups make the most of this technology for their children's learning (Attwell and Battle 1999). There is some concern among researchers that this technology will assist the upper socioeconomic groups the most, generating what is sometimes called the *Sesame Street effect* (see Attwell and Battle 1999). As children get older, questions of the desirability of certain types of knowledge (i.e., parental and institutional censorship) arise, especially in regard to access to the Internet and its many pornographic sites on the World Wide Web (WWW, or simply *the web*) with sexual content. Techniques of parental and institutional control have not yet been rigorously studied, perhaps in part because appropriate research techniques are only now emerging. Older children and adults clearly benefit from computer-assisted learning as part of high school, college, and university curriculum (e.g., Willie 1992; Rowe, Baker, and Mottram 1993), as well as distance education programs. In addition, family computer access may assist family members with the management of illnesses (Johnson, Ravert, and Everton 2001) and may be useful in dealing with problems associated with aging (e.g., Schnelle et al. 1995).

Communication. In many ways, computers can bring family members into closer contact. E-mail and the Internet provide diverse and relatively inexpensive forms of communication for family members to interact with other members. At the most basic level this might be written communication, exchange of family photos as files, or interactive "chats" in real time. On the other hand, the computer may isolate an individual—often a male—from the other family members within the household (Orleans and Laney 2000). In this context, the home computer would have a potential negative effect on family communication (Watt and White 1999).

Home management. Programs for household financial management, banking, and income tax are available (e.g., Carroll and Broadhead 1996). There are numerous programs and sources available for assisting in the interactional aspects of the family, for everything from parenting to marital advice, and these are available both as software and on the web. In addition, many commercial interests—from banking to groceries—offer on-line delivery of goods and services to the household. New technology (see Bluetooth 2001) will allow for the computer to monitor systems (e.g., lights, refrigerators, and alarms) throughout the household as well as performing routine maintenance and chores (such as ordering groceries). The advent of this technology has the potential to move families toward a more integrated and cybernetically controlled form of home management. At this time it is too early to predict the degree of acceptance and popularity such technology will have.

Recreation. Although most families intend to use home computers for educational purposes, it has been found that the major use is for recreation, especially games (Venkatesh and Vitalari 1987). It might have been possible, during the 1980s, to make a clear delineation between games and education. It has become, however, somewhat more difficult to clearly separate the recreational from the educational because many games have attendant educational outcomes, such as the development of problem-solving skills.

Home offices. As early as 1985, some experts were predicting that by the turn of the century 25 to 30 percent of paid work would be conducted from the home (Wakefield 1985). It was predicted that women with children would be particularly likely to take advantage of the opportunity to work at home (Cetron 1984). It is difficult to assess the accuracy of these predictions because computers and the Internet, as well as hand-held devices and cell phones, have spread work sites to areas other than homes (e.g., hotels), and many white collar workers no longer encapsulate their *work* in a specific time frame (e.g., the traditional "9 to 5" work day). As a result, all one can say is that more work is performed outside of the traditional office than was the case in the 1980s.

Families use home computers for a wide variety of purposes, such as communication, household management, entertainment, and school work. JOE CARLSON/CORBIS

There are several factors that complicate the analysis of the impact of computers on families. First, the technology that is available changes very rapidly; as a result, predictions of potential impacts are extremely difficult. Second, families and individuals at different stages of the life course interact with this technology in different ways (Watt and White 1999). For example, family concerns about pornographic materials on the Internet are most likely when at least one adolescent is in the household. Third, impacts must be conceptualized as potentially different for various age cohorts and historical periods. As children have access and gain computer literacy at earlier ages, effects will undoubtedly change by cohort. Finally, the cultural setting undoubtedly changes the type of impact computers have on families. Indeed, a highly prized educational program in one culture might be viewed as immoral or degenerate in another. Most of the research has focused on impacts in the developed world, but the World Wide Web is ubiquitous. The paucity of research on the family and computers is most pronounced in less-developed countries. For example, it is not known if the salutary educational outcomes reported (e.g., Attwell and Battle 1999) will be consistently encountered in less-developed countries with different value systems. As a result, meaningful empirical research and measurement will continue to be difficult though important.

See also: COMMUNICATION: FAMILY RELATIONSHIPS; FAMILY LITERACY; GLOBAL CITIZENSHIP; HOME; HOUSEWORK; LEISURE; TELEVISION AND FAMILY; TIME USE; WORK AND FAMILY

Bibliography

Attwell, P., and Battle, J. (1999). "Home Computers and School Performance." *Information Society* 15:1–10.

Becker, H. J. (2000). "Who's Wired and Who's Not: Children's Access to and Use of Computer Technology." *Future Child* 10:44–57.

Bracey, G. W. (1982). "Computers in Education: What the Research Shows." *Electronic Learning* 2:51–55.

Carroll, J., and Broadhead, R. (1996). *Canadian Money Management Online.* Scarborough, Ontario: Prentice Hall Canada.

Cetron, M. (1984). *Jobs of the Future: The 500 Best Jobs—Where They Will Be and How to Get Them.* New York: McGraw-Hill.

Haddon, L., and Skinner, D. (1991). "The Enigma of the Micro: Lessons from the British Home Computer Boom." *Social Science Computer Review* 9:435–451.

Johnson, K. B.; Ravert, R. D.; and Everton A. (2001). "Hopkins Teen Central: Assessment of an Internet-Based Support System for Children with Cystic Fibrosis." *Pediatrics* 107:U54–U61.

Orleans, M., and Laney, M. C. (2000). "Children's Computer Use in the Home: Isolation or Sociation?" *Social Science Computer Review* 18:56–72.

Rowe, P. H.; Baker, R.; and Mottram, D. R. (1993). "Pharmlex: A Computer Based Training Program on Pharmacy Law." *Computer Education* 20:163–167.

Schnelle, J. F.; McNees, P.; Crooks, V.; and Ouslander, J. G. (1995). "The Use of a Computer-Based Model to Implement an Incontinence Program." *Gerontologist* 35:656–665.

Subrahmanyam, K.; Greenfield, P.; and Kraut, R. (2001). "The Impact of Computer Use on Children's and Adolescent's Development." *Journal of Applied Developmental Psychology* 22:7–30.

Venkatesh, A., and Vitalari, N. (1987). "A Post-Adoption Analysis of Computing in the Home." *Journal of Economic Psychology* 8:1961–1980.

Wakefield, R. A. (1985). "Home Computers and Family Empowerment." *Marriage and Family Review* 8:71–88.

Watt, D., and White, J. M. (1999). "Computers and Family Life: A Family Development Perspective." *Journal of Comparative Family Studies* 30:1–15.

Willie, S. (1992). "Takeaway Learning Resources for Information Technology Courses." *IFIP Transactions A— Computer Science And Technology* 13:73–79.

Other Resource

Bluetooth (2001). "The Official Bluetooth Website." Available from http://www.bluetooth.com.

JAMES M. WHITE

CONDUCT DISORDER

Conduct disorder (CD) refers to a broad spectrum of potentially enduring behaviors that violate social norms. The behaviors and symptoms of CD vary, with diagnostic criteria clustered into one of four

FIGURE 1

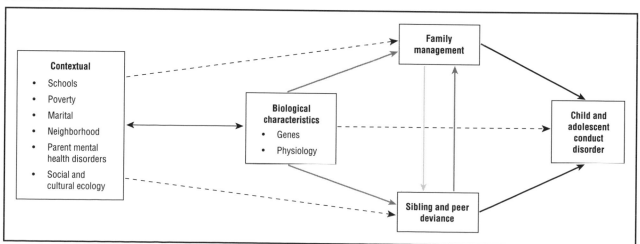

broad categories: (a) aggressive behavior; (b) nonaggressive misbehavior; (c) deceitfulness or theft; and (d) a serious infraction of established rules.

Aggressive conduct is that which threatens or causes physical harm to people or animals and typically involves acts such as initiating fights, bullying, intimidating, overt aggression, and physical cruelty. *Nonaggressive conduct* is characterized by vandalism or intentional destruction of property. Common manifestations of *deceitfulness* include stealing, persistent lying, and fraudulent behavior. Lastly, *rule violation* entails deeds that defy or circumvent social convention. The severity of observed behaviors is rated as mild, moderate, or severe, depending upon the number and seriousness of acts committed and the extent to which others are harmed.

Reported rates of the disorder have increased over several decades, with 6 to 16 percent of males and 2 to 9 percent of females under the age of 18 fulfilling diagnostic criteria (American Psychiatric Association 1994). These results are generally consistent across cultures. Epidemiological data indicate that the prevalence rates for CD are generally greater for males than females. However, some researchers are concerned that the current diagnostic protocol overemphasizes behaviors that are more typical of male than female problem behavior.

To receive a diagnosis of CD, three or more behaviors in any of the four categories must occur within the last twelve months, with at least one of these behaviors persisting during the previous six months. Noncompliance with adults (parents, teachers, or both) typically marks the beginning of a behavior pattern that often culminates in the youth engaging in acts consistent with CD. In general, the early onset of problem behavior in multiple settings and variability of observed problem behavior are associated with more serious psychosocial disruption, escalation to more serious problem behaviors in adolescence (Loeber and Dishion 1983), and ultimately, continuity of adjustment problems into adulthood (e.g., antisocial personality disorder, chronic offending, substance use, marital problems, employment difficulties).

Children and adolescents diagnosed with CD also tend to suffer from elevated rates of hyperactivity and emotional difficulties. Many individuals with behavior problems experience clinical levels of *attention deficit hyperactivity disorder* (ADHD),

depression, and anxiety. Research suggests that youth with both ADHD and CD experience high levels of peer rejection, academic problems, psychosocial hardship, conflict with parents, and parental psychopathology (see Angold and Costello 2001, for a review). The prognosis for persons with both ADHD and behavioral maladjustment also tends to be worse than for those with either diagnosis alone. Combined with depression, CD is generally a marker for more severe psychosocial disruption and heightens the risk for suicide and other adjustment problems in young adulthood. Children with CD often do not simply outgrow their problem behavior (Robins 1966).

A Model of Conduct Problems

Given the magnitude and breadth of difficulties experienced by children fitting the CD diagnosis, coupled with the costs of adolescent problem behavior to families, community, and society, there have been hundreds of studies of CD. Findings from carefully controlled intervention research combined with those of longitudinal investigations provide the best evidence of causality and offer suggestions regarding promising intervention strategies. Figure 1 summarizes a model that synthesizes the results of a several longitudinal and intervention studies.

A crucial issue that emerges from research on child and adolescent socialization is that the development of a behavioral repertoire is determined by a variety of interrelated factors. Multidirectional transactions between child genes, family environment, and the broader social and cultural ecology create a history of experience through which antisocial behavior is successively manifested and reinforced. Figure 1 illustrates this complexity, with bold arrows indicating effects demonstrated in both longitudinal and experimental intervention research.

Biological Factors

Certain neuropsychological indicators (influences in the brain that are linked to psychological functioning) are linked with aggression. Aggression and impulsiveness are associated with structural abnormalities related to thought processing and inhibition of behavior. Deficits in certain neurochemicals, including serotonin and norepinephrine, are also linked to behavior problems. Reductions in the functioning of the autonomic nervous system, which is responsible for the regulation of bodily processes, is also linked to chronic conduct problems. In particular, low-resting heart rate and low-skin conductance are frequently present in individuals with persistent behavior problems. These deficits and resultant reductions in behavioral inhibition are characteristic of both CD and ADHD.

Contemporary theories accentuate a dynamic interplay between biological and environmental factors and propose that most of the effects of a person's biological constitution on CD are mediated through disrupted parenting and peer environments (Deater-Deckard and Bullock, in press). There is some evidence that child-onset CD, characterized by antisocial behavior and hyperactivity, may have stronger biological underpinnings than later-onset CD. Exploration of reciprocal transactions between genes and the environment suggests that children may evoke reactions from parents and others that contribute to antisocial behavior (Rutter et al. 1997).

Individual differences in infant temperament are also directly implicated in behavioral development, with mothers' ratings of children's difficult and hyperpersistent temperament at six months predicting later teacher ratings of conduct difficulties. Studies of adoptees at genetic risk for conduct problems also indicate that genetically compromised children are more likely to experience harsh, negative parenting in their adoptive families, compared to children without a liability for problem behavior (Ge et al. 1996).

Some theorists propose that individuals actively select environments and relationships consistent with their genetic disposition (Scarr and McCartney 1983), with antisocial youth selecting peers who reinforce deviance. Although little research focuses on the biological characteristics that contribute to the influence of deviant peers in early adolescence, the ability of individuals to regulate their behavior and emotions seems to be a promising candidate. Many other biologically oriented constructs have been proposed, but none have clarified whether such constructs are causally unique or simply by-products of being raised in a harsh family environment from an early age.

Family Management

Parenting behavior is also mediated by genetic influence. Individuals prone to aggression,

impulsiveness, and antisocial acts are more inclined to create harmful rearing environments characterized by harsh parenting, hostile relationships, and little supervision. Inconsistent harsh discipline, insufficient monitoring, coercive parenting, and child abuse and neglect have long been associated with child-conduct problems and adult criminal behavior.

Parental behaviors directed to one or more siblings may further contribute to the development of deviance. A recent investigation of differential parenting and adjustment revealed that parent-directed behaviors toward each sibling were strongly correlated with individual levels of adolescent problem behavior. Youths with a negatively treated sibling had better outcomes, suggesting that harsh behavior directed toward a fellow sibling may serve a protective function (O'Connor, Hetherington, and Reiss 1998). These findings suggest that children's interpretation of the dynamics of their rearing environment influences the manner in which they respond to future parent attempts to socialize.

Parent behavior may vary greatly for individuals of different ethnic or cultural backgrounds. Physical discipline is known to exert a differential impact on outcomes for European-American children in contrast to their African-American counterparts (Deater-Deckard et al. 1996). A recent report suggests that physical discipline is associated with higher scores of conduct problems only among European-American children. It is hypothesized that physical discipline may be perceived as being more normative and less destructive or deviant by African-American children. Thus, the effectiveness of particular parenting techniques may be mediated by cultural factors and universal statements regarding parenting behavior are ill advised.

Peer Deviance

As development progresses, children become more involved in choosing and shaping their environments. In particular, adolescents are more active in shaping the constituency of their peer environment, and unfortunately may select settings with greater prevalence of problem behavior and substance use. Parent involvement and monitoring of adolescent activities can be an important counteractive force in the drift to deviant peers.

Evidence is compelling that the peer group can cause escalations in drug use, delinquency, and violent behavior in adolescence (Dishion, Spracklen, and Andrews 1996). Problem behavior becomes a mechanism for making friends and eventually in selecting relationship partners with similar values. When peers encourage deviance, youngsters may become especially difficult to monitor and display more resistance to parenting efforts.

Contextual Influences

An *ecological framework* for understanding development promotes research linking contextual influences with basic socialization processes in the emergence of competence and dysfunction (Bronfenbrenner 1989). Child relationships with teachers and other school officials, as well as influences that arise from factors including poverty and social disadvantage, all interact to create an intricate developmental tapestry that potentially supports maladaptive behavior.

Contextual conditions that can affect the development of antisocial behavior include divorce, marital transitions, poverty, and unemployment. Consistent with an ecological emphasis, it seems that these factors influence CD by disrupting family and peer environments. In a classic study, Glen Elder, Tri Van Nguyen, and Avshalom Caspi (1985) showed that poverty associated with the Great Depression disrupted parent-child interactions and was a factor in behavior problems in children.

For some children, the climate at school is reminiscent of their own family context in that relationships with teachers and peers can be experienced as conflictual, coercive, and embedded in spirals of negative interactions. This elevates the likelihood of child disengagement from the learning process. Academic failure is well documented to be strongly linked to aggressive, impulsive, antisocial behavior and criminality. In addition, studies of school environments suggest that classroom aggression may also influence the development of conduct problems. A study of first grade children revealed that individually aggressive boys in highly aggressive classes are at increased risk of being rated aggressive by sixth grade teachers (Kellam et al. 1998), confirming that experiences across multiple domains influence the development of conduct problems.

Cross-Cultural Research

Comprehensive reviews of the literature on the development of antisocial behavior and conduct problems suggest that prevalence and incidence is highest among children and adolescents within the United States (Dishion, French, and Patterson 1995). However, several longitudinal studies have been conducted outside of the United States that are integral to the development of theory, for example, in London (West and Farrington 1977), Finland (Pulkkinen 1996), Norway (Olweus 1979), New Zealand (Fergusson and Horwood 2002), and Sweden (Stattin and Magnusson 1991). Although prevalence rates vary, the major models of etiology, symptom clustering, stability, and longitudinal course over the lifetime show a high level of convergence across international contexts.

Implications for Treatment

The pioneering work of Gerald Patterson, Rex Forehand, and Bob Wahler brought *family management* to the fore as a critical component of systematic parent-training programs. These programs often produced observable changes in parenting strategies, which, in turn, positively affected child behavior. Interventions that improve school organization and support teachers' proactive behavior management also show promise in preventing antisocial behaviors at school, which are highly relevant to CD.

In general, interventions that encourage adults to manage the family context, promote prosocial classroom norms, and foster proactive supervision of school behavior generate reductions in antisocial behavior. Reviewers of the treatment literature on CD concur that interventions emphasizing family management practices are among the most effective strategies to date (Kazdin 1993).

Intervention research also addresses the power of the peer group in contributing to CD. Random assignment studies show that treatments that combine youth into groups lead to escalations in drug use, increased problem behavior at school, and long-term negativity. In one study, assignment of high-risk children to summer camps was associated with a ten-fold increase in risk for thirty-year negative outcomes (Dishion, McCord, and Poulin 1999). Treatment strategies that combine high-risk youth run the risk of exacerbating the problem behavior, with less-supervised intervention groups being more likely to produce *iatrogenic* or negative effects. This finding is disturbing, given that aggregating high-risk youth into treatment groups is a frequently employed therapeutic approach. Reviews of the literature also indicate that 29 percent of reported outcome analyses yield negative effects for youth with behavior problems (Lipsey 1992). Given that most evaluations of interventions with negative effects are unpublished, this is likely an underestimate of iatrogenic treatment effects, particularly for youth with CD.

Intervention Process

Clearly, professional skills are critical to the success of interventions, especially those that target parenting practices (Patterson 1985). Parents and other adults can develop negative attributions and expectations toward children with CD. Those issues must be sensitively addressed before interventions can move forward. Therapist skills in supporting and validating negative parenting experiences, while simultaneously encouraging proactive behavior management strategies, are especially important.

An exemplary parenting intervention designed to address conduct issues in young children utilizes videotaped modeling and collaborative group process to encourage change in parenting (Webster-Stratton 1990). For adolescents with more serious CD symptoms, Scott Henggeler and colleagues (1998) conducted parenting interventions in the home, expanding the array of issues addressed to include contextual, peer, and other systemic barriers to change. Thus, youth with extreme CD symptoms that warrant removal from the home may be effectively treated within a family-centered model.

Mark Eddy and Patti Chamberlain (2000) report that training foster parents in proactive behavior management skills and monitoring reduces serious delinquent behavior, compared to invoking group-home interventions. Though conduct problems may appear to be intractable, interventions that engage parents and buttress their efforts to improve family management skills can be effective in mitigating antisocial behavior.

Conclusion

Research regarding the origins of CD suggests that environmental and biological risk factors are primarily mediated through parenting and peer environments. Intervention research confirms the importance of promoting family management, attending to peer dynamics, and addressing self-regulation to reduce problem behavior in youth with CD.

Successful interventions are those that are flexible in delivery, promote a collaborative process with related individuals, and involve proactive behavior management. The prevalence of conduct disorder within a family can profoundly affect individual and collective functioning and initiate a cycle of frustration, negativity, and escalating behavior problems. It is important to engage families in processes that will mitigate the development of CD symptoms and promote positive and sustainable change in both parent and child behavior.

See also: ATTENTION DEFICIT HYPERACTIVITY DISORDER (ADHD); CHILD ABUSE: PHYSICAL ABUSE AND NEGLECT; CHILD ABUSE: PSYCHOLOGICAL MALTREATMENT; CHILD ABUSE: SEXUAL ABUSE; CHILDHOOD, STAGES OF: ADOLESCENCE; CHILDREN OF ALCOHOLICS; DEPRESSION: CHILDREN AND ADOLESCENTS; DEVELOPMENT: MORAL; DEVELOPMENTAL PSYCHOPATHOLOGY; DISCIPLINE; DIVORCE: EFFECTS ON CHILDREN; FAMILY DIAGNOSIS/DSM-IV; INTERPARENTAL CONFLICT—EFFECTS ON CHILDREN; INTERPARENTAL VIOLENCE—EFFECTS ON CHILDREN; JUVENILE DELINQUENCY; OPPOSITIONALITY; PARENTING EDUCATION; PARENTING STYLES; PEER INFLUENCE; RUNAWAY YOUTHS; SPANKING; SUBSTANCE ABUSE; SUBSTITUTE CAREGIVERS; TEMPERAMENT

Bibliography

American Psychiatric Association. (1994). *Diagnostic and Statistical Manual of Mental Disorders,* 4th edition. Washington, DC: Author.

Angold, A., and Costello, E. J. (2001). "The Epidemiology of Disorders of Conduct: Nosological Issues and Comorbidity." In *Conduct Disorders in Childhood and Adolescence,* ed. J. Hill and B. Maughan. Cambridge, UK: Cambridge University Press.

Bronfenbrenner, U. (1979). "Contexts of Child Rearing: Problems and Prospects." *American Psychologist* 34(10):844–850.

Deater-Deckard, K., and Bullock, B. M. (in press) "Gene-Environment Transactions and Family Process: Implications for Clinical Research and Practice." In *Children and Parents: Recent Research and Its Clinical Applications,* ed. R. Gupta and D. Gupta. London: Whurr.

Deater-Deckard, K.; Dodge, K. A.; Bates, J. E.; and Pettit, G. S. (1996). "Physical Discipline among African American and European American Mothers: Links to

Children's Externalizing Behaviors." *Developmental Psychology* 32(6):1065–1072.

Dishion, T. J.; French, D. C.; and Patterson, G. R. (1995). "The Development and Ecology of Antisocial Behavior." In *Developmental Psychopathology*, Vol. 2: *Risk, Disorder, and Adaptation,* ed. D. Cicchetti and D. J Cohen. New York: Wiley.

Dishion, T. J.; McCord, J.; and Poulin, F. (1999). "When Interventions Harm: Peer Groups and Problem Behavior." *American Psychologist* 54:755–764.

Dishion, T. J.; Spracklen, K. M.; Andrews, D. W.; and Patterson, G. R. (1996). "Deviancy Training in Male Adolescents Friendships." *Behavior Therapy* 27:373–390.

Eddy, J. M., and Chamberlain, P. (2000). "Family Management and Deviant Peer Association as Mediators of the Impact of Treatment Condition on Youth Antisocial Behavior." *Journal of Child Clinical Psychology* 5:857–863.

Elder, G. H.; Van Nguyen, T.; and Caspi, A. (1985). "Linking Family Hardship to Children's Lives." *Child Development* 56:361–375.

Fergusson, D. M., and Horwood, L. J. (2002). "Male and Female Offending Trajectories." *Development and Psychopathology* 14:159–177.

Ge, X.; Conger, R. D.; Cadoret, R. J.; Neiderhiser, J. M.; Yates, W.; Troughton, E.; and Stewart, M. A. (1996). "The Developmental Interface between Nature and Nurture: A Mutual Influence Model of Child Antisocial Behavior and Parent Behaviors." *Developmental Psychology* 32(4):574–589.

Henggeler, S. W.; Schoenwald, S. K.; Borduin, C. M.; Rowland, M. D.; and Cunningham, P. B. (1998). *Multisystemic Treatment of Antisocial Behavior in Children and Adolescents.* New York: Guilford.

Kazdin, A. E. (1993). "Treatment of Conduct Disorder: Progress and Directions in Psychotherapy Research." *Development and Psychopathology* 5:277–310.

Kellam, S. G.; Ling, X.; Merisca, R.; Brown, C. H.; and Ialongo, N. (1998). "The Effect of the Level of Aggression in the First Grade Classroom on the Course and Malleability of Aggressive Behavior into Middle School." *Development and Psychopathology* 10:165–185.

Lipsey, M. W. (1992). "Juvenile Delinquency Treatment: A Meta-Analytic Inquiry into the Variability of Effects." In *Meta-Analysis for Explanation: A Casebook,* ed. T. D. Cook, H. Cooper, D. S.

Cordray, H. Hartmann, L. V. Hedges, R. J. Light, T. A. Lewis, and F. Mosteller. New York: Russell Sage Foundation Press.

Loeber, R., and Dishion, T. J. (1983). "Early Predictors of Male Delinquency: A Review." *Psychological Bulletin* 94:68–99.

O'Connor, T. G.; Hetherington, E. M.; and Reiss, D. (1998). "Family Systems and Adolescent Development: Shared and Nonshared Risk and Protective Factors in Nondivorced and Remarried Families." *Development and Psychopathology* 10:353–375.

Olweus, D. (1979). "Stability of Aggressive Reaction Patterns in Males: A Review." *Psychological Bulletin* 86: 852–875.

Patterson, G. R. (1985). "Beyond Technology: The Next Stage in the Development of a Parent Training Technology." In *Handbook of Family Psychology and Therapy,* Vol. 2, ed. L. Abate. Homewood, IL: Dorsey.

Pulkkinen, L. (1996). "Proactive and Reactive Aggression in Early Adolescence As Precursors to Anti- and Prosocial Behavior in Young Adults." *Aggressive Behavior* 22:241–257.

Robins, L. N. (1966). *Deviant Children Grow Up: A Sociological and Psychiatric Study of Sociopathic Personality.* Baltimore, MD: Williams and Williams.

Rutter, M.; Dunn, J.; Plomin, R.; Simonoff, E.; Pickles, A.; Maughan, B.; Ormel, J.; Meyer, J.; and Eaves, L. (1997). "Integrating Nature and Nurture: Implications of Person-Environment Correlations and Interactions for Developmental Psychopathology." *Development and Psychopathology* 9:335–364.

Scarr, S., and McCartney, K. (1983). "How People Make Their Own Environments: A Theory of Genotype Environment Effects." *Child Development* 54(2): 424–435.

Stattin, H., and Magnusson, D. (1991). "Stability and Change in Criminal Behaviour Up to Age 30." *British Journal of Criminology* 31:327–346.

Webster-Stratton, C. (1990). "Long-Term Follow-Up of Families with Young Conduct Problem Children: From Preschool to Grade School." *Journal of Clinical Child Psychology* 19:144–149.

West, D. J., and Farrington, D. P. (1977). *The Delinquent Way of Life.* London: Heinemann.

BERNADETTE MARIE BULLOCK
THOMAS J. DISHION

CONFLICT

COUPLE RELATIONSHIPS *William R. Cupach, Daniel J. Canary*

FAMILY RELATIONSHIPS *Sam Vuchinich*

PARENT-CHILD RELATIONSHIPS *Susan J. Messman*

COUPLE RELATIONSHIPS

Conflict is natural and inevitable in marriages and other close relationships. Ironically, one's experience of interpersonal conflict is often highest with one's spouse, compared to other long-term relationships (Argyle and Furnham 1983). Marital relationships are particularly prone to conflict because spouses develop a great deal of shared intimacy and interdependence. These qualities make the partners more vulnerable to one another. At the same time, cohesion strengthens the relationship such that partners can better withstand criticism from one another and the relationship can survive partner disagreements.

The term *conflict* often conjures up perceptions of hostile disputes and dysfunctional relationships. However, research has shown that the mere existence of conflict is not necessarily bad. In fact, some conflict produces positive outcomes. Conflict allows relational partners to express important feelings and to devise creative solutions to problems. Further, successfully managed conflict can strengthen relational bonds and increase relational cohesion and solidarity. Marital conflict also contributes to the social development of children.

The most frequent topics of conflict in marital relationships include communication, finances, children, sex, housework, jealousy, and in-laws (Gottman 1979; Mead et al. 1990). Sometimes what appears on the surface to be a simple issue can reflect deeper relational struggles about power and intimacy (e.g., disagreements about how much time to spend together versus with other people). Persistent conflict about such relational issues has the greatest impact on relationship satisfaction (Kurdek 1994).

The intensity and seriousness of conflicts varies widely both within and between couples. Some oppositions are merely mild disagreements or complaints. They receive minimal attention and

produce short-lived effects. Other conflicts represent ongoing struggles about personally significant issues that produce intense personal anxiety and relational tension. Conflicts that are recurrent and stable over time are most problematic for relational stability (Lloyd 1990), although relational harm can be mitigated when partners communicate relationally confirming messages during continued conflicts (Johnson and Roloff 2000).

Determining how much conflict is typical or normal between spouses is difficult, although there are estimates (McGonagle, Kessler, and Schilling 1992). Indeed, averages of the number of disagreements across marriages are probably not meaningful because different types of marriages exhibit different amounts of conflict (Fitzpatrick 1988; Gottman 1994; Raush et al. 1974). Some couples construct a relational culture where they argue frequently; others experience disagreements infrequently and develop a norm to disagree only on issues of importance. Developmental patterns, however, can be consistent. For example, older spouses who have been married for a longer period of time engage in fewer overt disagreements compared to younger newlyweds (Zietlow and Sillars 1988). Yet, the mere frequency of disagreements reveals very little about the overall health or stability of marital relationships. More important is the seriousness of disputes, and the manner in which they are managed (e.g., Gottman 1994).

Perhaps the most important feature of conflict management concerns its constructiveness or destructiveness (Deutsch 1973). *Constructive conflict* tends to be cooperative, pro-social, and relationship-preserving in nature. Constructive behaviors are relatively positive in emotional tone. *Destructive conflict* is competitive, antisocial, and relationship-damaging in nature. Destructive behaviors exhibit negativity, disagreeableness, and sometimes hostility.

Research has demonstrated that constructive and destructive conflict behaviors are connected to the quality and stability of marriage. This connection is probably reciprocal—conflict behaviors both influence and are affected by one's relationship satisfaction over time (Fletcher and Thomas 2000). Methods for confronting or avoiding conflict influence the extent to which spouses are satisfied in their marriage, and ultimately affect the likelihood of separation and divorce. At the same time, spouses' degree of happiness or unhappiness in a marriage affects how they communicate during their conflicts.

A rather sizeable body of research has shown that conflict behaviors effectively discriminate between distressed and nondistressed married couples. Distressed couples are those in which partners report they are unhappy with their marriage. In addition, they typically have sought marital counseling. The findings from this research yield three robust conclusions (Gottman 1994; Schaap, Buunk, and Kerkstra 1988). First, distressed couples engage in more negativity during conflict interactions. Negativity includes demands, threats, attacks, criticisms, put-downs, belligerence, contempt, rejection, defensiveness, and hostility. Second, distressed marriages demonstrate less positivity, such as showing approval, using humor, making statements that validate partner and the relationship, and seeking to understand partner's point of view. In fact, John Gottman (1994) reports that stable marriages consistently exhibit about five times more positive behaviors than negative behaviors in conflict. Third, negative behaviors in distressed marriages are more likely to be reciprocated and become absorbing. Distressed spouses are more likely to get caught up in lengthy *sequences* of negative behaviors that are difficult to break out of. Such sequences occur, for example, when one partner makes a complaint, and the other partner responds with a counter-complaint; or one spouse attacks and the other defends; or one partner attacks and the other withdraws.

Compared to dissatisfied couples, satisfied couples are more likely to exhibit patterns of accommodation (Rusbult et al. 1991). *Accommodation* occurs when one partner inhibits the tendency to respond in-kind to a partner's destructive conflict behavior. In other words, in the face of a negative sequence of events, one partner takes responsibility to nudge the discussion back onto a constructive course. Thus, although even happy couples can enact negative conflict behaviors, they are less inclined to get locked into sequences of reciprocated negative actions.

Based upon more than two decades of extensive observation of marital interaction, Gottman (1994) has proposed a theory of behavioral patterns that predict divorce. Behaviors during conflict that erode satisfaction in a marriage also jeopardize the long-term stability of marriage. Gottman refers to the most significant of these behaviors as the *Four Horsemen of the Apocalypse*. Couples at greater risk for divorce repeatedly engage in complaining and criticizing, which leads to contempt, which produces defensiveness, which results in stonewalling.

Complaints allow marital partners to express dissatisfaction or disapproval. When a complaint takes the form of a personal attack, in other words, when it communicates disapproval of the character or personality of the recipient, it is regarded as criticism. Because criticism conveys devaluation of the relationship, it is typically hurtful to the recipient (Leary et al. 1998). Criticism can be accompanied by the expression of contempt, and it can elicit contempt from the criticized person. Messages showing contempt communicate blatant disrespect, as well as disdain and bitter scorn.

Defensiveness is common in conflict as one attempts to protect his or her own interests. Naturally it is heightened when one is the recipient of messages showing contempt. Defensive responses include denying responsibility for reproachful actions, making excuses for untoward behavior, and responding to complaints with counter-complaints. A whining tone often accompanies defensive remarks.

Stonewalling manifests itself in emotional withdrawal from conflict interaction. Stonewallers exhibit silence, repress verbal and nonverbal feedback, and generally attempt to show a complete lack of expressiveness. Although individuals who stonewall sometimes claim they are simply displaying calmness, rationality, and objectivity, their actions actually communicate smugness, disapproval, and icy distancing, according to Gottman (1994).

Criticism, contempt, defensiveness, and stonewalling can be exhibited in stable relationships as well as unstable ones. These behaviors are particularly problematic for relationships when they are (1) habitual, (2) reciprocated, and (3) insufficiently counterbalanced with positive behaviors.

Several factors have been proposed to account for the connection between relationship quality (e.g., marital satisfaction) and the constructive or destructive nature of conflict interactions. Among the more prominent accounts are (1) the causal and responsibility attributions that partners make about each other's behavior; (2) the perceived competence of conflict communication and; (3) the perceived face threat that attends conflict interactions. Attributions consist of the explanations that partners hold regarding the causality and responsibility of each other's behavior. Distressed couples tend to make negative and relationship-damaging attributions more than non-distressed couples; in other words, individuals who are unhappy with their relationship tend to attribute blame and causality to their partner for relationship problems (Bradbury and Fincham 1990). Specifically, individuals in distressed relationships tend to attribute that their partner's contribution to relationship problems is global rather than issue-specific, stable rather than fleeting, and due to their partner's personality rather than contextual circumstances. Moreover, those experiencing less relational satisfaction perceive that their partner's problematic behavior is intentional, blameworthy, and selfishly motivated. Such negative attributions are also associated with destructive conflict behaviors (Fincham and Bradbury 1992; Sillars 1980). As attributions become more negative, they contribute to a climate whereby the individual feels emotionally overwhelmed by the partner's negativity, which leads to a further decline in relational satisfaction. Thus, distressed couples get caught up in a regressive spiral such that declines in satisfaction lead to increasingly negative attributions, which lead to and derive from destructive conflict behaviors, which in turn, further diminish satisfaction over time. The greater the frequency and duration of these perceptions over time, the more likely that marital partners experience distance and isolation in the marriage and move toward divorce (Gottman 1994).

Similar to attributions, perceptions of communication competence and communication satisfaction filter the association between relational quality and conflict behavior (Canary and Cupach 1988; Canary, Cupach, and Serpe 2001; Spitzberg, Canary, and Cupach 1994). Specifically, when one enacts constructive conflict tactics, one's partner is generally more satisfied with conflict interaction and the partner sees one as communicatively competent. Destructive behaviors, on the other hand, are associated with one's partner's communication dissatisfaction and with partner perceptions that one is communicatively incompetent. Feelings of communication satisfaction and perceptions of a partner's communication competence are associated, in turn, with relational qualities such as satisfaction, trust, control mutuality, liking, and loving. Thus, more communication satisfaction and greater perceptions of partner competence contribute to improved relational qualities including higher levels of relational satisfaction and trust.

Another reason that negative conflict behaviors erode relationships is because they are face threatening. *Face* refers to the positive social value that one claims in social interaction, and that one assumes will be validated by others involved in the interaction (Goffman 1967). Generally people desire to be accepted, valued, and respected by important others (Brown and Levinson 1987). Partners cooperatively support one another's face by expressing affiliation and respect, and by avoiding affronts to each other's face.

By its very nature, conflict interaction threatens the face of each partner. Insofar as conflict conveys disapproval about something connected to the relational partner, the partner's face is threatened. In close interpersonal relationships such as marriage, one's face becomes inextricably tied to the relationship. When one criticizes a relational partner, the partner infers that his or her status in the relationship has been called into question (Cupach and Metts 1994).

The degree of face threat perceived in conflict depends upon the manner in which partners communicate. Messages that are seen as unfair, impolite, or disrespectful aggravate face threat. A complaint accompanied by a hostile or sarcastic tone, for example, not only communicates disapproval of an idea or a behavior, but also conveys disapproval of the partner. Individuals who perceive such disapproval experience hurt and feel devalued as a relational partner; in other words, they believe that the partner "does not regard his or her relationship with the person to be as important, close, or valuable as the person desires" (Leary et al. 1998, p. 1225). As a consequence, she or he may distance himself or herself to insulate against further hurt and face threat (Vangelisti and Young 2000).

Constructive behaviors are relationship-preserving, in part, because they tend to mitigate perceived face threat. Softening complaints by communicating diplomatically and by showing expressions of positive regard saves face for partners and reassures them that their standing in the relationship remains solid and intact, despite the expression of disagreement or discontent. Mark Leary and Carrie Springer provide the following example: "You know I adore you honey, but I can't stand it when (fill in the blank)" (2001, p. 160).

Consequences of poor conflict management extend beyond the survival of the marriage. Increasingly, research suggests that negative conflict interactions can hurt one's health. For example, one research team found that negative conflict behaviors adversely affect blood pressure and immune systems (Kiecolt-Glaser et al. 1993). Although the long-term effects of conflict interaction on health are unknown, this research suggests that negative conflict behavior in one discussion can harm physical well-being for at least a day. If negative conflict occurs routinely, it appears that one's health would be adversely affected over time.

On-going hostilities between spouses can also adversely affect their children. Although separation and divorce are often blamed for child adjustment problems, the inability to constructively manage conflict between them is much more important (Amato and Keith 1991; Emery 1982, 1992). Hostile marital conflict adversely affects children by lowering their self-esteem, diminishing achievement in school, and increasing the likelihood of depression and antisocial behavior (Gottman 1994; Jenkins and Smith 1991; Montemayor 1983). Moreover, young children learn their own methods of managing conflict by observing their parents (Minuchin 1992). To the extent that parents are incompetent at managing differences, their children are at risk for being similarly incompetent at managing conflict as grown-ups in their own families. The damaging effects of divorce on a child can be somewhat nullified if parents constructively manage their relational problems and breakups, and if parents provide positive support and do not use the child as a resource for winning the conflict.

Despite the paucity of available data regarding differences in marital conflict across cultures, there is sufficient research to speculate that different cultures exhibit different preferences for the manner in which conflict is managed. Relying on the cultural dimensions of individualism-collectivism and high versus low context, Stella Ting-Toomey (1988) proposes that individuals from different cultures privilege different forms of conflict communication. Ting-Toomey argues that members of individualistic, low-context cultures pursue maintenance of own face and rely on autonomy-preserving strategies, whereas members of collectivistic cultures tend to preserve mutual and other face and rely on approval-seeking strategies. Studies across several cultures provide preliminary support for Ting-Toomey's (1988) theory. Members of individualistic cultures tend to be more self-oriented, competitive, and direct, whereas members of collectivistic cultures tend to be more indirect, obliging, and avoiding in conflict situations (Ohbuchi and Takahashi 1994; Ting-Toomey et al. 1991; Trubisky, Ting-Toomey, and Lin 1991). Although people from individualistic cultures appear to be more direct than people from collectivistic cultures, all people appear to prefer the use of constructive conflict messages before they resort to competitive, destructive messages (Kim and Leung 2000). More empirical work needs to be conducted to explore cross-cultural differences in marital conflict specifically.

See also: ATTACHMENT: COUPLE RELATIONSHIPS; COMMUNICATION: COUPLE RELATIONSHIPS; COMMUNICATION: FAMILY RELATIONSHIPS; CONFLICT: FAMILY RELATIONSHIPS; CONFLICT: PARENT-CHILD RELATIONSHIPS; COPARENTING; DECISION MAKING; DIALECTICAL THEORY; DIVORCE MEDIATION; EQUITY; FORGIVENESS; INTERPARENTAL CONFLICT—EFFECTS ON CHILDREN; INTERPARENTAL VIOLENCE—EFFECTS ON CHILDREN; JEALOUSY; MARITAL QUALITY; MARITAL TYPOLOGIES; NAGGING AND COMPLAINING; POWER: MARITAL RELATIONSHIPS; PROBLEM SOLVING; RELATIONSHIP DISSOLUTION; REMARRIAGE; SELF-DISCLOSURE; SEXUAL DYSFUNCTION; SPOUSE ABUSE: PREVALENCE; SPOUSE ABUSE: THEORETICAL EXPLANATIONS; STEPFAMILIES; STRESS; THERAPY: COUPLE RELATIONSHIPS; TRANSITION TO PARENTHOOD; TRIANGULATION

Bibliography

Amato, P. R., and Keith, B. (1991). "Parental Divorce and the Well-Being of Children: A Meta-Analysis." *Psychological Bulletin* 110:26–46.

Argyle, M., and Furnham, A. (1983). "Sources of Satisfaction and Conflict in Long-Term Relationships." *Journal of Marriage and the Family* 45:481–493.

Bradbury, T. N., and Fincham, F. D. (1990). "Attributions in Marriage: Review and Critique." *Psychological Bulletin* 107:3–33.

Brown, P., and Levinson, S. (1987). *Politeness: Some Universals in Language Usage.* Cambridge, UK: Cambridge University Press.

Canary, D. J., and Cupach, W. R. (1988). "Relational and Episodic Characteristics Associated with Conflict Tactics." *Journal of Social and Personal Relationships* 5:305–325.

Canary, D. J.; Cupach, W. R.; and Serpe, R. T. (2001). "A Competence-Based Approach to Examining Interpersonal Conflict." *Communication Research* 28:79–104.

Cupach, W. R., and Metts, S. (1994). *Facework.* Thousand Oaks, CA: Sage Publications.

Deutsch, M. (1973). *The Resolution of Conflict: Constructive and Destructive Processes.* New Haven, CT: Yale University Press.

Emery, R. E. (1982). "Interparental Conflict and the Children of Discord and Divorce." *Psychological Bulletin* 92:310–330.

Emery, R. E. (1992). "Family Conflicts and Their Developmental Implications: A Conceptual Analysis of Meanings for the Structure of Relationships." In *Conflict in Child and Adolescent Development,* ed. C. U. Shantz and W. W. Hartup. Cambridge, UK: Cambridge University Press.

Fincham, F. D., and Bradbury, T. N. (1992). "Assessing Attributions in Marriage: The Relationship Attribution Measure." *Journal of Personality and Social Psychology* 62:457–468.

Fitzpatrick, M. A. (1988). "Negotiation, Problem Solving and Conflict in Various Types of Marriages." In *Perspectives on Marital Interaction,* ed. P. Noller and M. A. Fitzpatrick. Philadelphia: Multilingual Matters.

Fletcher, G. J. O., and Thomas, G. (2000). "Behavior and On-Line Cognition in Marital Interaction." *Personal Relationships* 7:111–130.

Goffman, E. (1967). *Interaction Ritual: Essays on Face-to-Face Behavior.* New York: Pantheon Books.

Gottman, J. M. (1979). *Marital Interaction: Experimental Investigations.* New York: Academic Press.

Gottman, J. M. (1994). *What Predicts Divorce? The Relationship between Marital Processes and Marital Outcomes.* Hillsdale, NJ: Erlbaum.

Jenkins, J. M., and Smith, M. A. (1991). "Marital Disharmony and Children's Behavior Problems: Aspects of a Poor Marriage that Affect Children Adversely." *Journal of Child Psychology and Psychiatry and Allied Disciplines* 32:793–810.

Johnson, K. L., and Roloff, M. E. (2000). "Correlates of the Perceived Resolvability and Relational Consequences of Serial Arguing in Dating Relationships: Argumentative Features and the Use of Coping Strategies." *Journal of Social and Personal Relationships* 17:676–686.

Kiecolt-Glaser, J. K.; Malarkey, W. B.; Chee, M. A.; Newton, T.; Cacioppo, J. T.; Mao, H. Y.; and Glaser, R. (1993). "Negative Behavior During Marital Conflict is Associated with Immunological Down-Regulation." *Psychosomatic Medicine* 55:395–409.

Kim, M. S., and Leung, T. (2000). "A Multicultural View of Conflict Management Styles: Review and Critical Synthesis." In *Communication Yearbook 23,* ed. M. E. Roloff. Thousand Oaks, CA: Sage Publications.

Kurdek, L. A. (1994). "Areas of Conflict for Gay, Lesbian, and Heterosexual Couples: What Couples Argue About Influences Relationship Satisfaction." *Journal of Marriage and the Family* 56:923–934.

Leary, M. R., and Springer, C. A. (2001). "Hurt Feelings: The Neglected Emotion." In *Behaving Badly: Aversive Interpersonal Behaviors,* ed. R. Kowalski. Washington, DC: American Psychological Association.

Leary, M. R.; Springer, C.; Negel, L.; Ansell, E.; and Evans, K. (1998). "The Causes, Phenomenology, and Consequences of Hurt Feelings." *Journal of Personality and Social Psychology* 74:1225–1237.

Lloyd, S. A. (1990). "A Behavioral Self-Report Technique for Assessing Conflict in Close Relationships." *Journal of Social and Personal Relationships* 7:265–272.

McGonagle, K. A.; Kessler, R. C.; and Schilling, E. A. (1992). "The Frequency and Determinants of Marital Disagreements in a Community Sample." *Journal of Social and Personal Relationships* 9:507–524.

Mead, D. E.; Vatcher, G. M.; Wyne, B. A.; and Roberts, S. L. (1990). "The Comprehensive Areas of Change Questionnaire: Assessing Marital Couples' Presenting Complaints." *American Journal of Family Therapy* 18:65–79.

Minuchin, P. (1992). "Conflict and Child Maltreatment." In *Conflict in Child and Adolescent Development,* ed. C. U. Shantz and W. W. Hartup. Cambridge, UK: Cambridge University Press.

Montemayor, R. (1983). "Parents and Adolescents in Conflict. All Forms Some of the Time and Some Forms Most of the Time." *Journal of Early Adolescence* 3:83–103.

Ohbuchi, K., and Takahashi, Y. (1994). "Cultural Styles of Conflict Management in Japanese and Americans: Passivity, Covertness and Effectiveness of Strategies." *Journal of Applied Social Psychology* 24:1345–1366.

Raush, H. L.; Barry, W. A.; Hertel, R. J.; and Swain, M. A. (1974). *Communication, Conflict, and Marriage*. San Francisco: Jossey-Bass.

Rusbult, C. E.; Verette, J.; Whitney, G. A.; Slovik, L. F.; and Lipkus, I. (1991). "Accommodation Processes in Close Relationships: Theory and Preliminary Empirical Evidence." *Journal of Personality and Social Psychology* 60:53–78.

Schaap, C.; Buunk, B.; and Kerkstra, A. (1988). "Marital Conflict Resolution." In *Perspectives on Marital Interaction,* ed. P. Noller and M. A. Fitzpatrick. Philadelphia: Multilingual Matters.

Sillars, A. L. (1980). "The Sequential and Distributional Structure of Conflict Interactions as a Function of Attributions Concerning the Locus of Responsibility and Stability of Conflicts." In *Communication Yearbook 4,* ed. D. Nimmo. New Brunswick, NJ: Transaction.

Spitzberg, B. H.; Canary, D. J.; and Cupach, W. R. (1994). "A Competence-Based Approach to the Study of Interpersonal Conflict." In *Conflict in Personal Relationships,* ed. D. D. Cahn. Hillsdale, NJ: Erlbaum.

Ting-Toomey, S. (1988). "Intercultural Conflict Styles: A Face Negotiation Theory." In *Theories in Intercultural Communication,* ed. Y. Y. Kim and W. B. Gudykunst. Newbury Park, CA: Sage Publications.

Ting-Toomey, S.; Gao, G.; Trubisky, P.; Yang, Z.; Kim, H. S.; Lin, S.-L.; and Nishida, T. (1991). "Culture, Face Maintenance, and Styles of Handling Interpersonal Conflict: A Study in Five Cultures." *International Journal of Conflict Management* 2:275–296.

Trubisky, P.; Ting-Toomey, S.; and Lin, S. (1991). "The Influence of Individualism-Collectivism and Self-Monitoring on Conflict Styles." *International Journal of Intercultural Relations* 15:65–84.

Vangelisti, A. L., and Young, S. L. (2000). "When Words Hurt: The Effects of Perceived Intentionality on Interpersonal Relationships." *Journal of Social and Personal Relationships* 17:393–424.

Zietlow, P. H., and Sillars, A. L. (1988). "Life-Stage Differences in Communication During Marital Conflicts." *Journal of Social and Personal Relationships* 5:223–245.

WILLIAM R. CUPACH
DANIEL J. CANARY

FAMILY RELATIONSHIPS

Family conflict refers to active opposition between family members. Because of the nature of family relationships, it can take a wide variety of forms, including verbal, physical, sexual, financial, or psychological. Conflicts may involve different combinations of family members. Most research has focused on dyadic marital conflict and parent-child conflict. But other types are significant, such as sibling conflict, coalitions, and feuds between different parts of extended families.

As in any kind of human group, some conflict in families is normal and serves useful social functions. But in excess, certain forms of family conflict can be damaging and even dangerous. Family conflict that is not managed effectively can be a symptom or contributing factor to serious negative outcomes for individuals or families as a whole (Vuchinich 1999). These include marital difficulties leading to divorce, domestic violence, ineffective parenting, antisocial child behavior, child psychopathology, and child abuse. As a result there has been continuing professional interest in how to regulate it. This work has resulted in useful findings and practices in a variety of treatment and prevention programs involving families. These include couple therapy, family therapy, parent training, peer mediation programs, and individual problem solving training for troubled children.

Unique Characteristics

Three characteristics distinguish family conflict from other types: intensity, complexity, and the duration of relationships. First, relationships between family members are typically the closest, most emotionally intense of any in the human experience (Bowlby 1982). The bonds between adult partners, between parents and children, or between siblings involve the highest level of attachment, affection, and commitment. There is typically daily contact for many years that bonds individuals together. When serious problems emerge in these relationships, the intense positive emotional investment can be transformed into intense negative emotion. A betrayal of a relationship, such as an extramarital affair or child sexual abuse, can produce hate as intense as the love that existed prior to the betrayal. It is well known that a high percentage of murders are committed within family groups. Family conflicts are typically more intense than conflict in other groups. This intensity means that managing conflicts may be more difficult in families, and that their consequences can be more damaging.

The second distinguishing feature of family conflicts, complexity, is especially important for understanding their sometimes-baffling characteristics. Why do battered wives stay with their husbands? Why do most abused children want to stay with the abusive parent rather than be placed elsewhere? One answer is that positive emotional bonds outweigh the pain involved with the conflicts (e.g., Wallace 1996). These are examples of the most pertinent type of complexity in family relationships—ambivalence. The person is loved, but they do things that produce hate as well. The web of family relationships includes dimensions such as love, respect, friendship, hate, resentment, jealousy, rivalry, and disapproval. Several of these dimensions are typically present in any given family relationship. Frequent family conflict may not be a problem if there are even more frequent displays of bonding behaviors. The course of conflict often depends on which dimensions are active in a relationship. Recognizing the multiple dimensions of conflict is a prerequisite for helping families deal more effectively with their problems.

The third distinguishing feature of family conflict is the duration of the relationships, the duration of some conflicts, and the long-term effects of dysfunctional conflict patterns. Family relationships last a lifetime (White 2001). A person's parents and siblings will always be their parents and siblings. Thus serious conflictual relationships within families can continue for longer periods. Such extended exposure increases the risk of harm from the conflict. It is possible to escape such relationships through running away from home, divorce, or estrangement from family ties. But even after contact has been stopped, there are residual psychological effects from the conflict.

Work on family conflict has led to some important findings relevant to prevention and treatment. One is that the form of the conflict is as important as how much of it occurs. Some families have a lot of conflict but still function well. This is possible because conflicts are embedded in the context of other behaviors. One significant factor is whether or not the conflicts are resolved (Cummings and Davies 1994). High rates of conflict may not be

damaging if most of the episodes are resolved. Another key factor is how much positive behavior is exchanged when the family is not fighting. John Gottman (1995) has reported that if there are five positive behaviors for each negative behavior, then relationships are still healthy. As a result of such findings, family conflict is not always considered to be a problematic pattern. However, if conflict occurs in forms that are physically or psychologically damaging, then intervention is necessary.

Family conflict often involves more than two individuals. A third family member can be drawn into dyadic conflict to take sides in disputes. Multiple members may join forces and work as a team to win or settle disagreements. Such coalitions may be short-lived or become a permanent part of family life. They are common and can be beneficial. For example, parents typically side with each other in disputes with their children. This helps parents maintain order and is especially useful in large families.

Coalitions add a complex dimension to dispute dynamics and strategy. Skill in forming alliances can be especially valuable to individuals with little power. As with other features of conflict, coalitions can be carried to extremes. *Scapegoating*, a recurrent, excessive alliance between parents against a child or children, is known to be damaging to development. Certain coalitions disrupt healthy family functioning. An on-going strong alliance between one parent and a child against the other parent can threaten the interparental relationship.

Conflict Style

Conflict style influences the kinds of disputes families have. It refers to specific tactics and behavioral routines individuals or families typically use when conflicts occur. Individuals have conflict styles of their own (Sternberg and Dobson 1987). These develop through repeated exposure to conflict situations in the family of origin. The combination of individual styles and the family system results in a family style of conflict. For example, one family member may dominate in all disputes and forcefully settle all conflicts. This is a *power assertive style* that is based on the power relations that are part of the family system. Another style involves endless bickering in which any kind of settlement or resolution is rare. Such an irrational style often creates a negative family climate that erodes positive family bonds. A family may avoid any kind of conflict at the first sign of trouble. Conflict may be seen as being too stressful or simply inappropriate among family members. Such an *avoidant style* often includes covert conflict in which secretive actions lead to negative consequences for opponents (Buehler et al. 1998). A *constructive conflict style* is an especially important type because it openly addresses the complaints of family members and moves toward rational changes that eliminate the problem. Several other conflict styles have been identified and research in this area continues. Furthermore, it should be noted that each family is unique and thus will have unique elements in its conflict style. But most families tend to use one of the main styles identified above.

Family conflict styles are learned in childhood. Years of exposure to the same patterns indoctrinate the child with the family's conflict style (e.g., Patterson, Reid, and Dishion 1992). The parents or primary caregivers usually establish the style for the children. Years of participation in the conflict style allow the child to learn the intricacies of using the style to protect or extend their interests. Acquiring a conflict style defines the orientation one brings to any dispute situation. For example, a child in a family with a power assertive style will tend to see any disagreement as a zero-sum game. There must be one winner and one loser. One dominates, the other submits. One must strive to use whatever power one has to defeat the opponent, who is striving to defeat you. Learning a conflict style thus includes assumptions about how interpersonal relationships should be conducted. Conflict styles learned in the family are used by children as they interact with peers and others outside of the family context. This can create difficulties in developing relationships with peers. For example, a child who is an aggressive power-assertive bully in the family may have difficulties making friends with peers who reject that style of interaction.

The concept of conflict style has been useful because it clarifies the assessment of problematic interaction patterns in families. In addition it provides a framework for improving conflict management in families. Some family conflict styles tend to interfere with healthy functioning. Power assertive, irrational, and avoidant styles can be especially troublesome. Getting troubled families with such styles to use elements of the constructive conflict style can improve conflict management and problems related to it. Considerable success has been achieved with conflict management training as a component in individual, couple, and family therapy (Vuchinich 1999). However, conflict style is only one part of the family system. As a result, conflict patterns may be resistant to change unless other elements of the family system are also changed. It is important to acknowledge this fact during efforts to improve conflict management in troubled families.

Sibling Conflict

Sibling rivalry has long been recognized as a key element in family conflict. The concept assumes that parents or primary caregivers have a limited amount of affection to give to their children (Neborsky 1997). Children therefore tend to compete for the parental affection, which they want and need. Through that competition, siblings can develop ambivalence toward each other. Siblings have affection for each other, but also some enmity. If parents provide sufficient affection for both siblings, the rivalry dissipates. But if they do not, then the rivalry can be a primary feature of sibling and family relationships through adulthood. In such cases siblings strive to out-do each other to win the approval of a parent or caregiver. Often the siblings are not consciously aware that their striving is based on sibling rivalry. Harmless sibling rivalry is common in most families. But in some cases it fuels long-term destructive conflict between siblings.

The negative impact of excessive sibling rivalry can be seen from a developmental perspective (Brody et al. 1992). Rivalry can erode the positive interaction dynamics that usually occurs between young siblings. Siblings can help each other learn to walk, talk, share, and show support. Intense rivalry interrupts these processes. In addition, a conflictual relationship with a sibling can be the template for relationships with peers outside the family. Troubled peer relations in childhood are known to be a precursor of negative outcomes later on.

The key to avoiding problems with sibling rivalry is providing all children in the family with adequate emotional support. Most parents try to treat their children equally. This is an important goal because recent research has shown that differential parental treatment of siblings is linked to adjustment problems (Feinberg and Hetherington 2001).

Although equal treatment is a worthy goal, achieving it is an ongoing challenge. This is especially true when the differences in the sibling age are large. For example, it is difficult to determine what is equal parental treatment if one child is a teenager and another a preschooler. Stepfamilies and blended families further complicate equal treatment.

Conflict in the Extended Family

Extended kin are those more than one generation distant in blood lines, and may include relations created through marriage, adoption, or other social mechanisms. Most frequently, bonds with extended kin are less strong than those with nuclear family members (parents, children, siblings). As a consequence, conflicts with extended kin are usually less intense than those with nuclear family members. But when extended kin have religious, legal, economic, or ethical concerns about specific marital or parenting behaviors, the potential for more serious conflict is present. There is great variation in the organization of extended kinship relations across human cultures. There is little sustained research on conflict involving extended kin outside of the United States.

Grandparents can disagree with the way their grandchildren are parented (e.g., Cherlin and Furstenberg 1986). This can be a result of generational changes in parenting practices or problematic relationships between parent and grandparent. In-laws often disagree on a variety of marital and parenting issues. This is normal given that a marriage is a merger between two different family systems. These conflicts can become severe if there are also ethnic, cultural, or religious differences involved.

U.S. society usually gives the biological parents the right to make major decisions about their children in terms of parenting style, cultural orientation, and religion. But a high rate of divorce complicates matters in many cases. For example, immediately after divorce, noncustodial parents and grandparents often disagree with the way the children are parented by the biological parent and stepparent. Grandparents may be denied visitation rights. Such circumstances create an ongoing potential for extended family conflict. But the geographical distance that is typical between extended family members, and the U.S. cultural emphasis on the priority of the nuclear family, mitigates most extended family conflicts.

Conclusion

Family conflicts are usually experienced as unpleasant events, unless some resolution occurs. There is often reluctance to talk about personal disputes. But some families can benefit from changing their conflict style. Such change requires open discussions and sustained effort. But it can improve family functioning. When conflict is severe, there may be deeper family issues involved besides conflict style and communication. In such cases, addressing conflict dynamics can be a beginning point in dealing with more complex family problems.

See also: COMMUNICATION: FAMILY RELATIONSHIPS; CONFLICT: COUPLE RELATIONSHIPS; CONFLICT: PARENT-CHILD RELATIONSHIPS; DECISION MAKING; DEVELOPMENTAL PSYCHOPATHOLOGY; FAMILY AND RELATIONAL RULES; FAMILY BUSINESS; FORGIVENESS; INTERPARENTAL CONFLICT—EFFECTS ON CHILDREN; INTERPARENTAL VIOLENCE—EFFECTS ON CHILDREN; JUVENILE DELINQUENCY; NAGGING AND COMPLAINING; PROBLEM SOLVING; SELF-DISCLOSURE; SIBLING RELATIONSHIPS; SPANKING; SPOUSE ABUSE: PREVALENCE; SPOUSE ABUSE: THEORETICAL EXPLANATIONS; THEORETICAL EXPLANATIONS; STEPFAMILIES; STRESS; THERAPY: PARENT-CHILD RELATIONSHIPS; TRIANGULATION

Bibliography

Bowlby, J. (1982). *Attachment and Loss,* 2nd edition. New York: Basic Books.

Brody, G. H.; Stoneman, Z.; McCoy, J. K.; and Forehand, R. (1992). "Contemporaneous and Longitudinal Association of Sibling Conflict with Family Relationship Assessments and Family Discussions about Sibling Problems." *Child Development* 63:391–400.

Buehler, C.; Krishnakumar, A.; Stone, G.; Anthony, C.; Pemberton, S.; Gerard, J.; and Barber, B. K. (1998). "Interpersonal Conflict Styles and Youth Problem Behaviors: A Two-Sample Replication Study." *Journal of Marriage and the Family* 60:119–132.

Cherlin, A., and Furstenberg, F. (1986). *The New American Grandparent.* New York: Basic Books.

Cummings, E. M., and Davies, P. T. (1994). *Children and Marital Conflict: The Impact of Family Dispute and Resolution.* New York: Guilford Press.

Gottman, J. M. (1995). *Why Marriages Succeed or Fail.* New York: Simon & Schuster.

Feinberg, M., and Hetherington, E. M. (2001). "Differential Parenting as a Within-Family Variable." *Journal of Family Psychology* 15:22–37.

Neborsky, Robert J. (1997). "Sibling Rivalry: The Role of the Sibling in the Unconscious." In *New Directions in Integrative Treatment, Vol. 2: The Handbook of Infant, Child, and Adolescent Psychotherapy,* ed. B. S. Mark and J. A. Incorvaia. Northvale, NJ: Aronson.

Patterson, G. R.; Reid, J. B.; and Dishion, T. J. (1992). *Antisocial Boys.* Eugene, OR: Castalia.

Sternberg, R. J., and Dobson, D. M. (1987). "Resolving Interpersonal Conflicts: An Analysis of Stylistic Consistency." *Journal of Personality and Social Psychology* 52:794–812.

Vuchinich, S. (1999). *Problem Solving in Families: Research and Practice.* Thousand Oaks, CA: Sage.

Wallace, H. (1996). *Family Violence: Legal, Medical and Social Perspectives.* Boston: Allyn and Bacon.

White, L. (2001). "Sibling Relationships over the Life Course: A Panel Analysis." *Journal of Marriage and the Family* 63:555–568.

SAM VUCHINICH

PARENT-CHILD RELATIONSHIPS

Living with others increases the opportunity for all types of interaction, especially conflict. Struggles between parents and their children are common manifestations of family life. In fact, families may have more conflict that other social groups. Prior theory and research regarding Western, individualist cultures suggests that as such contact and interdependence between people increases, conflict becomes more likely and more frequent (Braiker and Kelley 1979). However, in Eastern collectivist cultures, the increase in conflict may not result in such situations due to a preference for nonconfrontation (Chua and Gudykunst 1987). However, virtually no research examines how family communication in conflict differs based upon culture. Some reasons for this paucity of research are discussed in the conclusion. This entry focuses on research describing the nature of parent-child conflict from a Western perspective.

As with marital relationships, an average amount of conflict between parents and children is difficult to determine, although there are estimates (e.g., Montemayor 1986). The frequency of conflict appears to be linked with child development. For example, the highest number of conflicts—mother-child interactions—occurred with two-year-olds versus children who were eighteen months or three years old (Dunn and Munn 1987). Among adolescents, conflict interactions tend to increase until about the age of fifteen, and then subside in later adolescence. Parent-child conflict is probably related to parental development as well, though research is currently less definitive in this area.

Beyond conflict frequency, one of the most rudimentary features of conflict management is whether an issue is engaged or avoided. Engagement involves overt, verbal confrontation. Avoidance can take many forms, including withholding complaints, evading discussion of sensitive issues, and defensively withdrawing from a conflict discussion. Different families establish different norms regarding the frequency with which conflicts are engaged or avoided.

Another important dimension of conflict management concerns its positivity or negativity (Sillars and Wilmot 1994). Some behaviors are relatively positive in sentiment and affective tone, such as conciliatory statements, supportive comments that validate the other's point of view, attempts to understand the other's position, and so on. Negative behaviors are disagreeable, inflammatory, and sometimes hostile. Examples include demands, threats, insults, and defensiveness. Distressed families exhibit more negative conflict behaviors, greater reciprocation of negative emotions and behaviors, and a lower proportion of positive behaviors compared to non-distressed families (e.g., Montemayor 1986).

An important feature of parent-child relationships that may affect the negativity of conflicts is that the relationships are not voluntary. In other words, children do not pick their parents. Like marriage partners, parents and their offspring develop considerable intimacy. More so than spouses, however, parents and their children are "bound" in a family relationship, which can serve to intensify serious conflicts between them, and family disputes often represent underlying relational struggles regarding power or intimacy (Emery 1992).

Regardless of the "involuntary" nature of parent-child relationships, family conflict has the potential to positively impact children. Specifically, childhood conflict interactions can contribute positively to personal and social development. Moreover, parents can develop their negotiation skills in conflicts with their children. To garner such positive rewards from conflict interactions, family members need two basic skills for conflict management: flexibility versus rigidity and the ability to manage conflict without escalating the severity of the problem.

Clearly, the study of these general features of parent-child conflict contributes to understanding the experience. Additionally, one important theme consistently emerges in discussions of these general features: development. Focusing on how parent-child conflict evolves as children (and parents) age provides a more thorough picture of the phenomenon. The following sections survey the research findings regarding parent-child conflict based upon the general age group of the children.

Conflict with Young Children

Much of the research on parent-child conflict has focused on conflicts between toddlers and their parents. Although conflict may be especially prevalent during the "terrible twos" phase, conflict with parents becomes a significant feature of family interactions beginning at eighteen months (Dunn and Munn 1985) and continuing over the life span. Importantly, both parents' and children's conflict behaviors evolve over time.

For example, before children reach the age of sixteen months, mothers are more likely to use distraction or simple labels such as "naughty" or "nice" during conflict episodes. As the child ages, mothers are more likely to reference social rules, use bargaining, and provide justifications to the child during conflict episodes (Dunn and Munn 1985). Learning from these experiences with their mothers, children begin to develop their own abilities to use reasoning and justifications as early as age three.

Most of the research on parent-child conflict focuses on interactions between mothers and children. The mother most frequently acts as the primary caregiver. As such, mothers participate much more in parent-child conflicts than do fathers (Vuchinich 1987). Specifically, children oppose mothers more often than they oppose fathers. This greater number of interactions for mothers may

mean that mothers exert more influence over children's development of conflict management behaviors. Additionally, fathers achieve child compliance slightly more frequently than do mothers (Lytton 1979). Moreover, children rarely follow a father's simple "no" with a bold opposition, but they would boldly oppose a mother's "no."

Traditional perspectives on parent-child conflict have considered conflict as parental discipline and/or parental attempts at compliance-gaining with their children. Research focused on observing conflict interactions between mothers and their small children illustrates some keys to successful parental compliance gaining. First, when a parent's behavior is synchronous (i.e., staying on topic) with what the child just stated (child's immediately preceding talk turn), children are more likely to comply with parental requests (Rocissano, Slade, and Lynch 1987). In addition, these same researchers argued that parental flexibility during interactions with toddlers leads to more child compliance. In general, parental positivity and flexibility before and during interactions has been consistently linked with child compliance.

Although much of the early parent-child conflict research focused on parental control and child noncompliance, more recent research has emphasized the *bidirectionality* of parent-child conflict (e.g., Eisenberg 1992; Patterson 1982). Bidirectionality means that just as parents' behaviors influence children, children's behaviors influence parents. For example, Gerald Patterson's theory of coercive control suggests that parents adapt their conflict management behaviors to children's coercive behaviors (e.g., hitting, yelling, and ignoring the parent) rather the reverse. This bidirectional approach to parent-child conflict broadens the focus from just compliance-gaining to a wider variety of conflict topics.

For instance, conflict between parents and toddlers in the two- to four-year-old range largely reflects the child's attempt to gain social control. Consequently, disagreements about rights of possession are particularly salient for children in this age group (Hay and Ross 1982). Other common conflict issues involve caretaking, manners, destructive/hurtful actions, rules of the house, physical space, and independence.

Between the ages of four and seven, children become less concerned with possessions and the rightful use of objects, and more concerned with controlling the actions of others (Shantz 1987). For instance, five-year-olds can become quite distressed when the mother will not play in a preferred manner. Such struggles to gain the compliance of others are integral to the child's development of interpersonal competence. The child learns that cooperating with others is an important part of control and achieving one's own instrumental goals. Engaging in conflict facilitates children's acquisition of social perspective-taking skills (Selman 1980).

Conflict with Adolescents

By the time children reach adolescence, their communication with others has gained greater sophistication across contexts. In conflict situations, they no longer express unrestrained hostility as a small child does. In addition, they exhibit greater flexibility in conflicts with their parents. Nonetheless, adolescents still express more hostility and show more rigidity than do adults. Even with their increased maturity, adolescents are still developing their conflict management skills. For example, when observing interactions between mothers and teenagers, researchers have found that mothers more consistently respond to their child in a flexible and positive manner regardless of the child's comment (Fletcher et al. 1996). However, the researchers also found that, unlike the mothers, the teenagers tended to parallel the mothers' comments in terms of following a negative comment with a negative reply.

Given the broad range of what qualifies as a teenager, adolescence consists of multiple stages rather than one. Traditional perspectives hold that due to parallel hormonal and physiological changes during puberty, conflict behavior first increases from the early stages of adolescence to the middle stages and then decreases again by late adolescence. However, other researchers have found that conflict simply decreases from early to late adolescence with no peak during middle adolescence. In attempting to resolve this controversy, researchers have found that conflict increases in hostile and coercive families but decreases in warm and supportive families (Rueter and Conger 1995) .

Mothers and fathers take on different roles during conflict than they had with their younger children. In particular, adolescent boys begin to act more assertive and forceful with their mothers but not their fathers. Mothers complement their sons' behavior by being less dominant, whereas fathers become more dominant (Paikoff and Brooks-Gunn 1991). Even though both mothers' and children's behaviors change, mothers still experience more conflicts with their adolescent children than do fathers.

The topics of conflict evolve as the child matures. Whereas younger children are concerned with gaining social control, adolescents attempt to gain personal control. Adolescents and parents often disagree about the extent to which parental control and supervision over the adolescent are legitimate. Specifically, parents and adolescents have conflict about such routine, day-to-day issues as responsibility for chores, doing schoolwork, observing a curfew, and respecting the adolescent's right to privacy. Interestingly, the issues of parent-adolescent conflict persist across generations. Thus, today's "rebellious" adolescents mature into tomorrow's "controlling" parents (Montemayor 1983).

Although conflict between parents and teens may be inevitable, effective conflict management does not always occur. The potential costs of poorly managed parent-adolescent conflict are great. For example, adolescents may become "ungovernable," use drugs, and/or run away from home. Certain communication behaviors during conflict have been linked with such teenage misbehaviors (Alexander 1973). Specifically, the researcher found that when parents and adolescents *do not* reciprocate each other's supportive communication behaviors (e.g., showing empathy and equality) and *do* reciprocate each other's defensive behaviors (e.g., showing indifference and superiority) the child appears more likely to engage in delinquent behaviors.

Conflict with Adult Children

Although conflicts between parents and children persist after the child becomes an adult, little research examines these relationships. The frequency of conflicts likely drops off significantly for most parents and their adult children. However, with some level of maintained contact and interdependence, conflicts likely remain a fundamental aspect of the parent-child relationship. For example, young adults have been found to experience psychological adjustment and identity problems when they perceive that their families have a great deal of conflict (Nelson et al. 1993). Just as personal development continues past adolescence, the impact of conflict with significant others on that development continues.

Karen Fingerman's (1996) research illustrates that conflicts with parents continue even as the child reaches middle age and the parent becomes elderly. Again, development appears to play an important in role in understanding difficulties between middle-aged daughters and their elderly mothers. Due to their different stages in life, the mothers and daughters hold differing opinions regarding the salience of the relationship. In addition, mothers and daughters tend to disagree regarding the mother's needs. These studies illustrate both that parent-child conflict endures and that the link between development and conflict persists.

Conclusion

Although conflict may be inevitable in families, the consequences of parent-child conflict tend to be positive rather than negative. For example, oppositions between parents (usually mothers) and their small children are usually brief in duration and not emotionally charged. Although such conflicts can test the patience of both child and parent, they do not seriously affect the relationship between parent and child. In addition, while conflict interactions between parents and adolescents can be more intense and dramatic, only 5 to 10 percent of families with adolescents experience detrimental effects on parent-child relationships (Paikoff and Brooks-Gunn 1991).

Considerable research depicts the processes surrounding conflict between parents and their young children and conflict between parents and their adolescent children. However, more research is needed to understand the nature of conflict between parents and their adult children. In addition, the research into parent-child conflict has not sufficiently examined the influence of culture on conflict management. It seems likely that the topics of conflict between mothers and toddlers as well as between teenagers and their parents may be universal.

However, the management of conflict between parents and children likely varies by culture (Ting-Toomey 1988). Unfortunately, researchers have not explored conflict management differences due to cultural norms in parent-child interactions. Moreover, such investigations of cultural differences appear problematic for two reasons. First, the concepts of individualism and collectivism may oversimplify cultural differences. Although a nation might be defined as collectivist or individualist, the individuals that make up that country likely vary widely in their behavior (Kim and Leung 2000). For example, a family living in the highly individualistic United States may nevertheless value nonconfrontation in conflict and may exhibit a strong tendency toward collectivist culture communication behaviors.

Second, virtually every investigation of conflict management differences due to culture has utilized various conflict style scales (Kim and Leung 2000). Obviously, survey methods do not work well with young children. Moreover, the conceptualization that underlies such scales appears problematic for effective comparisons across cultures. Specifically, Min-Sun Kim and Truman Leung (2000) argued that the dimensions (concern for self and concern for other) that underlie the various styles of conflict management do not have the same meaning in conflict situations across cultures. For example, U.S. society values assertiveness in conflict and perceives avoidance behaviors as showing a lack of concern for others. However, in Chinese society, avoidance of confrontation is perceived as showing high concern for others. Future research needs to resolve such methodological and conceptual issues to examine how culture likely plays an important role in the development of conflict management behaviors from early childhood.

See also: COMMUNICATION: FAMILY RELATIONSHIPS; CONFLICT: COUPLE RELATIONSHIPS; CONFLICT: FAMILY RELATIONSHIPS; DECISION MAKING; DEVELOPMENTAL PSYCHOPATHOLOGY; DISCIPLINE; DIVORCE: EFFECTS ON PARENTS; FAMILY BUSINESS; FATHERHOOD; FILIAL RESPONSIBILITY; FORGIVENESS; MOTHERHOOD; NAGGING AND COMPLAINING; OPPOSITIONALITY; PARENTING EDUCATION; PARENTING STYLES; PROBLEM SOLVING; SELF-DISCLOSURE; SPANKING; STEPFAMILIES; STRESS; THERAPY: PARENT-CHILD RELATIONSHIPS; TRIANGULATION

Bibliography

Alexander, J. F. (1973). "Defensive and Supportive Communication in Normal and Deviant Families." *Journal of Consulting and Clinical Psychology* 40:223–231.

Braiker, H. B., and Kelley, H. H. (1979). "Conflict in the Development of Close Relationships." In *Social Exchange in Developing Relationships,* ed. R. L. Burgess and T. L. Huston. New York: Academic Press.

Chua, E., and Gudykunst, W. B. (1987). "Conflict Resolution Styles in Low- and High-Context Cultures." *Communication Research Reports* 5:32–37.

Dunn, J., and Munn, P. (1985). "Becoming a Family Member: Family Conflict and the Development of Social Understanding." *Child Development* 56:480–492.

Dunn, J., and Munn, P. (1987). "Development of Justification in Disputes with Another Sibling." *Developmental Psychology* 23:791–798.

Eisenberg, A. R. (1992). "Conflicts between Mothers and Their Young Children." *Merrill-Palmer Quarterly* 38:21–43.

Emery, R. E. (1992). "Family Conflicts and Their Developmental Implications: A Conceptual Analysis of Meanings for the Structure of Relationships." In *Conflict in Child and Adolescent Development,* ed. C. U. Shantz and W. W. Hartup. Cambridge, UK: Cambridge University Press.

Fingerman, K. L. (1996). "Sources of Tension in the Aging Mother and Adult Daughter Relationship." *Psychology and Aging* 11:591–606.

Fletcher, K. E.; Fischer, M.; Barkley, R. A.; and Smallish, L. (1996). "A Sequential Analysis of the Mother-Adolescent Interactions of ADHD, ADHD/ODD, and Normal Teenagers during Neutral and Conflict Discussions." *Journal of Abnormal Child Psychology* 24:271–297.

Hay, D. F., and Ross, H. S. (1982). "The Social Nature of Early Conflict." *Child Development* 53:105–113.

Kim, M., and Leung, T. (2000). "A Multicultural View of Conflict Management Styles: Review and Critical Synthesis." *Communication Yearbook* 23:227–269.

Lytton, H. (1979). "Disciplinary Encounters Between Young Boys and Their Mothers and Fathers: Is There a Contingency System?" *Developmental Psychology* 15:256–268.

Montemayor, R. (1983). "Parents and Adolescents in Conflict: All Forms Some of the Time and Some Forms Most of the Time." *Journal of Early Adolescence* 3:83–103.

Montemayor, R. (1986). "Family Variation in Parent-Adolescent Storm and Stress." *Journal of Adolescent Research* 1:15–31.

Nelson, W. L.; Hughes, H. M.; Handal, P.; Katz, B.; and Searight, H. R. (1993). "The Relationship of Family Structure and Family Conflict to Adjustment in Young Adult College Students." *Adolescence* 28:29–40.

Paikoff, R. L., and Brooks-Gunn, J. (1991) "Do Parent-Child Relationships Change during Puberty?" *Psychological Bulletin* 110:47–66.

Patterson, G. R. (1982). *Coercive Family Processes.* Eugene, OR: Castalia.

Rocissano, L.; Slade, A.; and Lynch, V. (1987). "Dyadic Synchrony and Toddler Compliance." *Developmental Psychology* 23:698–704.

Rueter, M. A., and Conger, R. D. (1995). "Antecedents of Parent-Adolescent Disagreements." *Journal of Marriage and the Family* 57:435–448.

Selman, R. L. (1980). *The Growth of Interpersonal Understanding: Developmental and Clinical Analyses.* New York: Academic Press.

Shantz, C. U. (1987). "Conflicts between Children." *Child Development* 58:283–305.

Sillars, A. L., and Wilmot, W. W. (1994). "Communication Strategies in Conflict and Mediation." In *Strategic Interpersonal Communication,* ed. J. A. Daly and J. M. Wiemann. Hillsdale, NJ: Lawrence Erlbaum Associates.

Ting-Toomey, S. (1988). "Intercultural Conflict Styles: A Face Negotiation Theory." In *Theories in Intercultural Communication,* ed. Y. Y. Kim and W. B. Gudykunst. Newbury Park, CA: Sage Publications.

Vuchinich, S. (1987). "Starting and Stopping Spontaneous Family Conflicts." *Journal of Marriage and Family* 49:591–601.

SUSAN J. MESSMAN

CONFUCIANISM

Confucianism is a philosophy with a religious function. It is named after Confucius, whose teachings on ethical behavior have been adopted as a national development model in Chinese history. Currently, Confucianism has a strong influence in China, Korea, Taiwan, and the countries of Southeast Asia, as well as influencing people of Far Eastern descent living around the world. An increasing number of Western people are able to appreciate Confucianism through international contacts and literature.

Confucianism consists of some elements of traditional Chinese religion, such as reverence toward Heaven and the worship of ancestors. It does not assert the existence of a deity, although it recognizes and promotes synchronization with *Tien* (Heaven, Ultimate, Tao) in harmonious relationships with others and environments. Most Chinese view Confucianism as a philosophy or a practical way to reach an ideal world rather than as a religion.

History of Confucianism

Confucius (551–479 B.C.E.) is renowned as a philosopher and educator, but little attention is given to his roles as researcher, statesman, change agent, social planner, social innovator, enabler, and spiritual advocate. He is said to have spent nearly thirty years touring various states in China, advising local rulers of social reforms but receiving no real opportunities to actualize his political and social vision. It is widely believed that during his old age, Confucius edited several ancient works that later formed the basic canon of Chinese scholarship, such as *The Book of Odes (Shi-Ching)*. The method that he developed offers a means to transform individuals, families, communities, and nations into a harmonious universal society.

Since the second-century B.C.E., Confucianism has strongly influenced Chinese political, and ultimately social and intellectual, behaviors. When the Chinese came into contact with Indian Buddhism around the first century C.E., the programmatic side of Confucianism responded, and they developed a spiritual discipline called Ch'an (meditation), which Japan adopted around 1200 C.E. as Zen. Zen is thus a unique blend of the philosophies and idiosyncrasies of four different cultures: the typical way of Japanese life, Buddhism of India, the Taoists' love of nature, and the pragmatism of the Confucian mentality.

Since the eleventh century, Buddhism and Taoism have been better known for their increasingly religious content rather than as schools of philosophies. They forced Confucians to find metaphysical and epistemological foundations for their ethics. Chinese scholars have incorporated Western concepts and methods into their studies. The Western and Eastern cultures have been integrated and resulted in some eclectic new systems of thought. This integration led to three major eclectic schools in modern Chinese philosophy. The first is the school of comprehensive synthesis, which takes any philosophical view it finds useful and profound, and offers insights into cosmic existence and human nature. The second is the school of contemporary neo-Confucian synthesis, which emphasizes the idealist school of inquiry into the "mind." The third is the Chinese scholastic synthesis school, the principal concept of which is benevolence, through which a person is capable of endless development.

The different strands of thought within Confucianism notwithstanding, the overall vision is to revitalize the human virtue of *Te* (an ethical code of loving and caring). Confucianism seeks to enable people to assume responsibilities to carry out the dual aim of cultivating the individual self and contributing to the attainment of an ideal, harmonious society.

Confucian Worldview

Confucians believe that *Tai Chi* is the Ultimate, an integrated energy of *Yin* and *Yang,* which is evolved from *Wu Chi* (void energy) and can be transformed into various forms. The ultimate source of all energy and knowledge is called *Tao,* which is a continuum without boundaries in time and space, infinite, formless, and luminous (I-Ching).

In Confucian philosophy, the system of Yin and Yang was conceived as a way of explaining the universe. It is a purely relativist system; any one thing is either Yin or Yang in relation to some other object or phenomena, and all things can be described only in relation to each other. The Yin and Yang are the negative and positive principles of universal force and are pictorially represented by the symbol of Tai Chi. The Yin and Yang together constitute the Tao, the eternal principle of heaven and earth, the origin of all things human and divine. The Tao produced the Chi (*Qi,* energy or life force). Human nature was good; however, negative and endless human desires may lead to systems become unbalanced, which can produce problematic situations.

In contemporary terms, the Yin-Yang theoretical worldview can be defined as a school of transformation that is research-oriented and employs an approach that is multidimensional, cross-cultural, multilevel, multimodal, multisystemic, and comprehensive. It is a way of life or an art of living that aims to synchronize the systems of the universe to achieve both individual and collective fulfillment.

Four major principles describe changes in the interrelationships within environmental systems.

The symbol of Tai Chi pictorially represents the Yin and Yang, the negative and positive principles of universal force.

These principles of change historically are used to empower the individual and family:

(1) Change is easy because the Tao as its source exists in everything and every moment in daily life;

(2) Change is a transforming process due to the dynamics of Yin and Yang. Any change in part of Yin or Yang will lead to a change in the system and its related systems;

(3) Change has the notion of constancy—the change itself is unchanging. Thus, one should constantly search for the truth and engage in lifelong transformation;

(4) The best transformations are those that promote growth and development of the individual and the whole at the same time.

In summary, any systems' solution to conflict and goals for development aim to integrate love (*Jen*), justice, freedom, and faithfulness (the image of Tao) in the dynamics. It is a situational approach to fulfill human needs (love). Justice is seen as perfectly equal treatment. Freedom is practiced by participation in negotiation and compromise with flexibility of new patterns and behavior. The stability, repeatability, and accountability of leadership revealed by the natural laws reach faithfulness. The core image of the Tao is integrated in the dynamics of conflict resolution. Role equity and role change, therefore, are the core implication of the Yin-Yang theory. Reaching Yin-Yang balance,

family well-being, and an ideal world commonwealth are all aspects of Confucius practice.

Confucian Meditation and Family Integration

The Confucian transformation model (Chung 1992a, 2001) starts with individual meditation; goes through personal enhancement, self-discipline, personality integrity, family integration, and state governance; and reaches the excellence of universal commonwealth. Individual meditation starts with learning to rest the energy (*chu chu*), in order to be stabilized (*ting*), be still and calm (*ching*), reach peace (*an*), and be mindful (*li*). A mindful energy is ready to learn the truth and reveal the virtue (*te*) (Confucius 1971; Liu, K. 1985). An example of Confucian meditative *qigong* is sitting still to free the ego and get in touch with the real self. It aims to internalize and calm the energy (*qi*) to calm the mind, body, and spirit. It aims to reach a peaceful state so that the practitioner becomes a thoughtful person towards the self and others. It is a process of mind, body, and spiritual training with the aim of regaining control of the self/mind and preparing for further training and development for *Tien jen* unification (micro and macro self-unification).

Confucians called this meditation *Chou Won*. *Chou* means sit. *Won* means to forget (the self). It is a process of synthesizing with Tao by "letting go and allowing God to work," similar to Christian concepts. It is an essential means of detaching the ego and reaching mental freedom. It is important because it teaches self-awareness, self-enhancement, self-discipline, and self-actualization, as well as how to find the truth and create social change. This is a cornerstone of Confucian transformation technology.

These mental processes aim to revitalize the internal virtue (te—moral consciousness through mindfulness or Tao's image) that leads to the insight of real self and awareness of universal energy interconnection. This meditation is training the individual to become a highly self-disciplined sage who integrates various social developmental strategies for large-scale social applications. This simple meditation method aims to integrate mind, body, and spirit for holistic healing with three main functional goals: disease prevention, healing, and human capacity development. Historically, it serves as an empowerment tool for the Confucians and their family members by teaching them stress management, personal enhancement, family integration, and career development.

Confucian Family Teaching

Many forms of wisdom have been developed after years of practice. The following are some examples of family teaching derived from Confucian classics.

> *Family life:* "When a parent behaves like a parent, a child like a child, an elder like an elder, a youth like a youth, a husband like a husband, and a wife like a wife, then the conduct of the household is correct. Make the home correct, and the country will be stable" (I-Ching, People in the home).
>
> *Good deeds of family:* "Family with good deeds will enjoy abundance" (I-Ching, Earth).
>
> *Holistic life:* "Let the will be set on the path of duty. Let every attainment in what is good be firmly grasped. Let perfect virtue be accorded with. Let relaxation and enjoyment be found in the polite arts" (Confucian Analects, Confucius 1971 [500 B.C.E.]).
>
> *Modeling:* "When I walk along with two others, they may serve as my teachers. I will select their good qualities and follow them, their bad qualities and avoid them" (Confucian Analects, Confucius 1971 [500 B.C.E.]).
>
> *The Great Learning:* "What the Great Learning teaches, is—to illustrious virtue; to renovate the people; and to rest in the highest excellence" (The Great Learning).

Stages and Rituals of Life Transformation

Confucius considered life as a process of transformation that moves through different developmental stages, with each stage having its own task and process. Confucius reviewed his own life journey and suggested the following stages of life (Confucian Analects, Confucius 1971 [500 B.C.E.]; Cheng, Y. 1988). Confucians created various rituals of *Li* (a proper behavior in a certain situation) that demands certain behaviors to fulfill the expected performance. Li ranges from a bow to an elder, taking off shoes before entering the house, being silent and respectful to elders, bringing a gift to the host, and writing thank-you notes to a helper. Society

considers a serious violation of Li as a violation of the law (Confucian Analects, Confucius 1971 [500 B.C.E.]). The original purpose of Li is to help the individual to express proper ways of building and maintaining caring relationships.

Birth as a creative life form. Confucianism considers the individual as a link in the chain of existence from the past to the future. Everyone should have descendents to continue the family tree. To have no children is considered the most unforgivable thing in life. Having a child, particularly a boy, is very important to carry on the family name.

Therefore, when a new life is born to the family, by the end of one month, the family will give a party for the extended family and friends to announce and celebrate the arrival of the new family member. It is the family's responsibility to take care of the mother's needs to reward her production and contribution to the family. Her family status will be increased accordingly. In the future, the person is given a birthday party anywhere from every year to every ten years, according to the extended family's desire. Egg is served as a symbol of life, and the noodle serves as a symbol of longevity, thus, the longer the better. Many parents also offer different gifts to the child during the party to test his or her talents or areas of interest with reference to future education.

At home, children are taught to honor the ethical code (Li), such as honoring parents, loving brothers and sisters, respecting elders, trusting friends, and retaining loyalty to the family and the nation. It means that life is a creative force because it is connected with the Ultimate. Based on virtue, children are taught to make friends by studying with others who are interested in learning similar subjects. Parents are encouraged to appreciate the strengths of a less favored child and look at the weaknesses of the favored one to avoid any prejudice.

Young adulthood. At fifteen years of age, a child reaches young adulthood and starts to dress differently (Adulthood Li). The social symbols of adulthood are given with expectation that the individuals will perform their roles adequately with the help of family members and others. They participate in social activities and assume related responsibilities, which extend the ethical code of obedience to society. Self-searching, self-awareness, self-acceptance, identity development, acceptance of others, and systematic synchronicity with the environment are expected to take place.

Age of independence. At age thirty, with life established, a person should become an independent professional and have his or her own family and career established. A journey of self-searching is done between the ages of sixteen and thirty. During this stage, it is important to outwardly express one's inner qualities to understand and develop the self.

A wedding ceremony (Wedding Li) is given by both families to announce the establishment of the new couple. During the wedding ceremony, both bride and groom have to pay their honor to Heaven, Earth, their ancestors (at the symbolic shrine in the family hall), and their parents, with family and friends as witnesses. The third day after the wedding, another wedding party is held with the bride's family.

Age of mental maturity. At age forty, a person should have matured and acquired a defined self, no longer struggling in a trial-and-error fashion. As Confucius says, "When a person at forty is the object of dislike, he will always continue what he is" (Confucian Analects, Confucius 1971 [500 B.C.E.]).

Age of spiritual maturity. At age fifty, a person should be spiritually reconnected with the Ultimate and be synchronized with it. A matured person should know the answers to the questions: "Where did I come from?" "What is the purpose of my life?" and "Who am I?" During this stage, a person should be synchronizing life energies with the systems' needs according to mission and vision. Real life is only beginning, not ending.

Age of acceptance. At age sixty, a person is ready to take a spiritual journey that is the only way that he or she may actualize the self spiritually. Spiritual maturity will facilitate the acceptance of diversity and differences within the family or community and guide the community in leadership.

Age of unification. After the age of seventy, one can purify his or her mind and free the self from negative thoughts. The real self becomes outwardly apparent after it reconnects with the Ultimate and accepts the self and others. During this stage, retirement and detachment from worldly situations may be beneficial.

Funeral service. Confucians respect the end of the life by giving a sincere funeral service (Funeral Li/rite) to honor the dead and promote the social morality (Confucian Analects, Confucius 1971 [500 B.C.E.]). The name of the dead will be added to the shrine of the family hall as a part of the dead (*Yin*) family.

Honor the ancestors. Confucians promote ancestor worship by burning paper money and offering food to respect the lives of the dead on April fifth. This ritual respects ancestors and educates younger generations. It becomes a community asset of honoring the self as well as the family.

Teacher's day. This is an elaborate ceremony to honor Confucius at Taipei's Confucian Temple on Confucius's birthday, September 28. His birthday has been dedicated to honor all teachers as a teachers' day, which is a national holiday in Taiwan. Confucian music and dance are performed to honor Confucius and all teachers. The best gift to the teacher or helper may be a successful outcome of one's project, or letters of appreciation.

Family life and structural relations. The Confucian role approach (Chung 1993b, 1994) is based on the assumption that lawlessness and social problems are due to uncultivated individuals, a lack of morals in the social structure, and lack of adequate relationships. Confucius defined five social relationships on which Chinese and other Asian social structures and relationships are based. Various Asians still feel, profoundly, his influence in these areas in their daily life.

In societies that have been influenced by Confucius, the traditional social structure is based on five fundamental interpersonal relationships: superior-subordinate, parent-child, husband-wife, brothers, and friends (Chung 1992b). These relationships are arranged in a hierarchy based on the members' respective position and status. For example, the first superior-subordinate relationship requires loyalty to the government or one's superior on the job. In return, the employer takes care of the employees' needs. Second, the parent-child relationship requires filial piety; children should obey, honor, and respect their parents, and parents should love their children. The husband-wife relationship prescribes that the wife submit to the husband and the husband love the wife. Young brothers should respect the older brother, while the elders should love the young ones. Among friends, righteousness and trust are the rule.

Confucianism prescribes family relationships and indicates the degree of intimacy and obligations. Anyone who is within this network is considered part of the family. Otherwise, he or she is an outsider. As a member of the family, one enjoys membership privileges such as trust, intimacy, and sharing. Confucians promote universal brotherhood and sisterhood by respecting others and observing propriety (Confucian Analects, Confucius 1971 [500 B.C.E.]).

Concept of Religion and Spirituality

According to Confucians, spiritual development comes after physical, emotional, and mental development. One must first learn to know oneself and to respect and honor oneself as one goes about daily business. As Confucius said, "If you don't know how to live as a person, how can you serve the spirit?" (Confucian Analects, Confucius 1971 [500 B.C.E.]). Confucius avoided talking about extraordinary things, feats of strength (violence), disorder, and religious gods (Confucian Analects, Confucius 1971 [500 B.C.E.]). Confucianism stresses being spiritual, but not religious.

Concept of Jen as loving relationship. Jen is a proper relationship between two parties, a loving and caring relationship to reach humanity. Meditation is considered a cornerstone to search for self, find truth, and achieve individual and collective goals.

Concept of harmony. A central feature of Confucianism is harmony between people and their environment, Nature, or Tao. The Tao Chi (Yin-Yang diagram) is an example of the value of harmony with the environment. It is also applied to the concept of health for energy (*qi/chi*), balance for disease prevention, healing, and the development of human potential. Meditation is a way of managing energy that is applied to reach physical, emotional, mental, and spiritual harmony for individual holistic health.

This core value of Confucianism has had positive and negative effects on Chinese history; it became quite detrimental to women and children. Contemporary Confucians prescribe family conflict resolution to remedy this. The younger generations are not allowed to express their opinions before their elders. According to social standards, women and children who were abused are still expected to be submissive. Social workers and helping professionals must understand the hidden cultural dynamics to deal with the root philosophies and beliefs as they try to help people.

Family conflict resolution. Based on the Yin Yang theory from the Tai Chi diagram, contemporary Confucians such as Douglas K. Chung (1993a) prescribe the family conflict resolution model. It is an example of innovation of Confucianism in redefining the image of Tao through daily practice. In the model, any systems' solutions to conflict resolutions and goals for development aim to integrate love (Jen), justice, freedom, and fidelity (the image of Tao) in the dynamics. The approach aims to fulfill human needs (love). Justice is seen by the end of the cycle under perfectly equal treatment. Freedom is practiced by volunteer choice and participation in negotiation and compromise—the flexibility of mean line and possibility of forming new systems. Faithfulness is reached by the stability, repeatability, and accountability of leadership and/or revealed by the natural laws. Role equity and role change, therefore, are the core implication of the Yin-Yang Theory.

Conclusion

The Confucian life model includes seven developmental stages. Theories, values, and skills derive from *Taology,* the Confucian worldview. Rituals and practices show that Confucianism's cultural roots still affect daily family life. The Confucian healing and developmental model, part of the ecological-systems perspective for a global generalist practice, outlines healing and developmental concepts in a comprehensive and holistic approach to achieve a great vision of commonwealth of the world (Chung 2001).

See also: ANCESTOR WORSHIP; ASIAN-AMERICAN FAMILIES; CHINA; JAPAN; KOREA; RELIGION; VIETNAM

Bibliography

Brandon, D. (1976). *Zen in the Art of Helping.* Boston: Routledge and Kegan Paul.

Cheng, Y. (1988). *I Ching The Tao of Organization,* trans. T. Cleary. Boston: Shambhala.

Chou, R. J. (1995). "Confucianism and the Concept of Yang-sheng in Ancient China." *Journal of Wen Shu Hsueh Po* 42:105–152.

Chung, D. (1988). "Transformation Model for Cross-Cultural Social Work Practice." Paper presented to the Continuing Professional Education Sessions of the 1988 NACSW Training Conference, San Antonio, Texas.

Chung, D. (1989). "A Cultural Competent Social Work Practice for Asian Americans." Paper presented at the 1989 NASW Annual Conference in San Francisco.

Chung, D. (1990). "Social transformation model for cross-cultural generalist social work practice." Paper presented to the Council on Social Work Education 1990 Annual Program Meeting, Reno, Nevada.

Chung, D. (1992a). "Confucian Model of Social Transformation." In *Social Work Practice with Asian Americans,* ed. R. Biswas, D. Chung, K. Murase, and F. Ross-Sheriff. Newbury Park, CA: Sage.

Chung, D. (1992b). "Asian Cultural Commonalities: A Comparison with Mainstream American Culture." In *Social Work Practice with Asian Americans,* ed. R. Biswas, D. Chung, K. Murase, and F. Ross-Sheriff. Newbury Park, CA: Sage.

Chung, D. (1993a). "Chung Model of Family Conflict Management." Paper presented at the Second International Symposium on Families: East and West, August 22–24, 1993, University of Indianapolis.

Chung, D. (1993b). "Using Confucian Role Approach and Yin-Yang Theory to Understand and Help South-East Asian Refugee Families in Cultural Transition." Paper presented at the Second International Symposium on Families East and West, August 22–24, 1993, University of Indianapolis.

Chung, D. (1994). "Overcoming Poverty by Confucian Role Approach and Yin Yang Theory" Paper presented at the fortieth Annual Program Meeting, Council of Social Work Education, Atlanta, Georgia, March 5–8, 1994.

Chung, D. (2001). "Confucian Healing and Development Model." In *Spiritualities and Social Work Practice,* ed. M. Van Hook. New York: Cole.

Confucius. (1971). *Confucian Analects, the Great Learning and the Doctrine of the Mean,* trans. J. Legge. New York: Dover. (Originally published circa 500 B.C.E.).

Confucius. (1967). *Li Chi,* trans. J. Legge. New York: University Books. (Originally published circa 500 B.C.E.).

Eden, D. (1999). *Energy Medicine: Balance Your Body's Energies for Optimum Health, Joy, and Vitality.* New York: Penguin Putnam.

Germain, C. B., ed. (1979). "Ecology and Social Work." (In German). *Social Work Practice: People and Environments.* New York: Columbia University Press.

Germain, C. B., and Gitterman, A. (1980). *The Life Model of Social Work Practice.* New York: Columbia University Press.

Getzels, J. W., and Guba, E. G. (1954). "Role, Role Conflict, and Effectiveness: An Empirical Study." *American Sociological Review.* 19(1):164–175.

Harrison, W. D. (1989). "Social Work and the Search for Postindustrial Community." *Social Work* 34(1):73–75.

Humphreys, C. (1971). *A Western Approach to Zen.* London: Allen & Unwin.

I Ching. (1988). Trans. C. F. Bayaes. London: Routledge and Kegan Paul. Original authors: Fu Hsi (3000 B.C.E.); King Wen and the Duke of Chou (11th century B.C.E.); Confucius (500 B.C.E.).

I-Ching The Tao of Organization. (1988). Trans. T. Cleary. Boston: Shambhala. (Original work published 1000 B.C.E.).

I-Ching Mandalas A Program of Study for The Book of Changes. (1989). Trans. T. Cleary, Boston: Shambhala. (Original work published 1000 B.C.E.).

Kahn, R. L.; Wolfe, D. M.; Quinn, R. P.; and Snoek, J. D. (1964). *Organizational Stress: Studies in Role Conflict and Ambiguity.* New York: John Wiley and Sons.

Kapleau, P., ed. (1966). *The Three Pillars of Zen.* New York: Harper and Row.

Lee, Liou Chio, ed. (1982). "Mental Fasting." In *Shien Shui Mou Shiun (Selected Articles among Qigongology).* Taipei, Taiwan: Truth, Goodness, and Beauty Publisher. (Original work published about 2,500 years ago under "Mental Fasting" in *Chuang Tzu.*).

Liao, Kou, (1993). *Tsu-yang Chih-tao.* Taipei: Ming-wen Shu-chu.

Liu, S. C. (1985). *A New View of the Chinese Philosophy.* Taipei, Taiwan: World Book.

Ou-i, Chih-hsu. (1987). *The Buddhist I Ching,* trans. T. Cleary. Boston: Shambhala.

Rose, K., and Yu Huan, Z. (1999). *Who Can Ride the Dragon? An Exploration of the Cultural Roots of Traditional Chinese Medicine.* Miami: Paradigm Publications.

Tseng, Shu Chiang, ed. (1990). "Confucianism as Main Stream of Chinese Management Style." In *Chinese Management Perspective.* Taipei, Taiwan: Kuei Kuang.

Van de Vliert, E. (1981). "A Three-Step Theory of Role Conflict Resolution." *Journal of Social Psychology,* 113:77–83.

DOUGLAS K. CHUNG

COPARENTING

The term *coparenting* refers to the support that adults provide for one another in the raising of children for whom they share responsibility (McHale 1995). Joint parenting of children has been the norm in families cross-nationally since the earliest human societies, with children's grandmothers or other female family members (rather than fathers) most often the ones sharing everyday parenting responsibilities with children's biological mothers. Surprisingly, most of what is known about coparenting is due to studies of shared parenting in nuclear family systems headed by a mother/wife and father/husband. Perhaps more surprisingly, it was not until the late 1970s and early 1980s when clinically oriented family researchers first began grappling with the correlates and consequences of shared parenting in divorced families that a field of coparenting studies even came to exist at all. Early work on coparenting in families of divorce was followed about a decade later by initial reports of interadult parenting dynamics in families that had not undergone the divorce process (Belsky, Crnic, and Gable 1995; McHale 1995)—and from this point on the field of empirical coparenting studies has taken firm root.

According to the family theorist and therapist Salvador Minuchin, effectively functioning coparenting partnerships are those which assure that children are receiving adequate care, control, and nurturance, as defined by prevailing cultural mores. Effective functioning in the family's *executive subsystem* (Minuchin 1974) also provides children with a sense of predictability, stability, and security in the family (McHale 1997). To provide such predictability and stability, however, it is important that coparenting partners support one another and be "on the same page" with respect to family rules, practices, and discipline. Rebecca Cohen and Sidney Weissman (1984) maintain that supportive coparenting partnerships are only made possible when parenting adults acknowledge, respect, and value the roles and tasks of the partner.

Unfortunately, many parents who may parent alone successfully find it difficult to coordinate successfully with coparenting partners (McHale 1997). Gayla Margolin and her colleagues capture this distinction in noting that "a parent may display excellent child management skills and a high level of emotional responsiveness *to a child* but still be disparaging *of the other partner* to the child" (Margolin, Gordis, and John 2001, p. 5, emphasis added). This distinction between parenting and coparenting practices is an important one; equally important is a similar distinction between marital and coparenting relations (Belsky, Crnic, and Gable 1995; McHale 1995). Coparenting relationships exist even when marital relationships dissolve (Cowan and McHale 1996), and coparenting relations often involve blood or fictive kin who are not married partners at all. Supporting these important conceptual distinctions, studies substantiate that coparenting processes explain variability in children's behavior not accounted for by marital or parenting indicators (Belsky, Putnam, and Crnic 1996; McHale, Johnson, and Sinclair 1999; McHale and Rasmussen 1998; McHale, Rao, and Krasnow 2000a).

Typologies of Coparenting

Coparenting partnerships exist in all kinds of families. Although most published studies have investigated coparenting dynamics in families headed by heterosexual married or divorced European-American couples, this circumstance is gradually beginning to change. Growing literatures exist on coparenting in mother-grandmother-headed families, step-families, and families headed by gay and lesbian partners (see McHale et al. 2002a, for a more detailed review). However, most empirical typologies of coparenting that have appeared in the literature describe coparenting dynamics in nuclear middle-class families.

Coparenting dynamics have been characterized along dimensions such as whether the children's father is actively engaged as a parent or not (Johnson 2001; Ogata and Miyashita 2000); whether the coparenting process itself between parenting partners (whomever they may be) is supportive or oppositional (Belsky, Putnam, and Crnic 1996; McHale 1995; Schoppe, Mangelsdorf, and Frosch 2001); whether the family's interactive process allows engagement and enjoyment among all family members (parenting partners included) or whether it is intensively child-focused (McHale et al. 2001b); and whether there is daily, meaningful caregiving involvement by grandparents, extended family, or fictive kin (McHale et al. 2002a).

Although attempts to describe families along multiple coparenting dimensions are relatively uncommon, findings have identified families where the parenting partners are connected and effectively "on the same page"; families where the coparents are nonsupportive and antagonistic; and families where the coparents are disconnected from one another (and where, often, one parent is also disconnected from the child; McHale 1997; McHale et al. 2000b). Beyond these essential types, certain studies hint at other family types, including families whose focus is principally on the child with little positive connection between the adults (McHale et al. 2002b), and families where regular coparenting disputes are balanced by high family warmth and support (McHale 1997; McHale, Kuersten, and Lauretti 1996). Of course, sampling issues in studies of coparenting must always be carefully scrutinized. As James McHale and his colleagues (2002b) caution, statistical techniques can only detect family types actually represented in the researcher's sample; they cannot describe types of families whom, for whatever reason, have not found their way into research studies.

Coparenting and Children's Adjustment

Numerous studies have linked coparenting indicators to children's socioemotional and academic adjustment. *Supportive* and *harmonious* coparenting relationships are tied to preschoolers' social (McHale, Johnson, and Sinclair 1999; McHale, Kuersten, and Lauretti 1996; Schoppe, Mangelsdorf, and Frosch 2001) and academic competence (McHale, Rao, and Krasnow 2000a). Among older children, supportive coparenting has also been linked to well-developed self-regulatory abilities (Abidin and Brunner 1995; Brody, Flor, and Neubaum 1998). By contrast, *unsupportive* or *discordant* coparenting has been associated with adjustment difficulties in children. For example, *competitive* and *conflictual* coparenting is linked with poor self-regulation and disinhibition among toddlers (Belsky, Putnam, and Crnic 1996), and with *acting out* and internalizing behavior among both preschoolers (McHale and Rasmussen 1998) and school-age boys (McConnell and Kerig 2002).

As has been true with most coparenting research, studies substantiating associations between coparenting and child adjustment have typically involved samples of predominantly Caucasian, middle-class families. To date, only limited data are available on coparenting in non-Anglo cultural or ethnic groups. Nonetheless, those few studies that have engaged African-American or Asian families have suggested similar patterns of linkage between quality of coparenting and children's well-being. For instance, Gene Brody's studies with rural, African-American families show that supportive, nonconflictual coparenting is associated with adolescents' self-regulation and, in turn, with their academic performance (Brody, Stoneman, and Flor 1995). Research on urban Chinese families suggests that mothers who report more collaborative coparenting rate their preschoolers as more successful academically, while conflictful coparenting is linked to problems with acting out and anxiety (McHale, Rao, and Krasnow 2000a). Among Japanese families, involvement in daily child-related activities by fathers has been linked to greater child empathy (Ogata and Miyashita 2000).

Notwithstanding these intriguing results, much remains to be learned about the relationship between coparenting and children's development in populations besides European-American ones. To advance this field, researchers will need to shed Western notions of mothers and fathers as the functional coparenting partners to include other caregivers such as grandparents, older children, and extended family members. The evidence is clear that such individuals play pivotal caregiving roles in families within Vietnamese (Kibria 1993), Asian-Indian and Malaysian (Roopnarine, Lu, and Ahmeduzzaman 1989), Native-American, Hispanic-American (Coll, Meyer, and Brillon 1995), and other cultures.

Some exemplary studies have already been conducted. For example, Brody's work illustrates that African-American mothers who receive parenting support from grandmothers are more likely to engage in *no-nonsense parenting* (control, restraint, and punishment combined with affection); such parenting, in turn, aids children's self-regulation, academic, and social competence (Brody, Stoneman, and Flor 1995). At the same time, however, mothers are less involved in children's schooling when grandmother-mother co-caregiving conflict is high. Benefits of intergenerational support are also suggested by research with British Hindu and Muslim families. In one study children living in extended family environments with a co-caregiving grandmother showed better adjustment than children living in nuclear families (Sonuga-Barke and Mistry 2000). However, the presence of extended family co-caregivers may promote child adjustment only to the extent that such family members support, rather than undermine, the children's parents.

Factors Contributing to Supportive or Antagonistic Coparenting Partnerships

Numerous studies of coparenting dynamics in two-parent families have indicated the importance of the marital partnership in supporting cohesive, respectful coparenting relations. Marital-coparenting linkages have been established both concurrently (Belsky, Crnic, and Gable 1995; McHale 1995), and longitudinally (Lewis, Cox, and Owen 1989; Lindahl, Clements, and Markman 1998; McHale and Rasmussen 1998). Data also indicate, perhaps not surprisingly, that features of parents' personalities likewise affect the developing coparental partnership (McHale and Fivaz-Depeursinge 1999). For example, personal attributes such as whether parents remain calm and unfettered, or retaliate when criticized by others, or whether they experience threat and jealousy when those they love also bond strongly with others besides them, may directly affect how they negotiate the challenges of shared parenting. Second, personal strengths or resources (such as self-restraint or flexibility) possessed by one or both parents may help to protect or *buffer* the coparental relationship from the potentially negative effects of marital discontent. For example, difficult though it may be, a flexible, resilient parent may consciously squelch active anger they are feeling toward the marital partner in order to support that partner's parenting ministrations, in the child's best interests.

Other motives can be important, too. Parents who grew up in families characterized by divisive coparenting relationships may be motivated to rectify this state of affairs in their new families. Unfortunately, as McHale has argued, if two parents each work fervently to create a different, better climate in their new family, but have different visions for how they would like those new and better families to function, they may unwittingly set into motion the same state of affairs in the new family as existed in the old one (Cowan and McHale 1996;

McHale, Kuersten, and Lauretti 1996; McHale and Fivaz-Depeursinge 1999).

Coparenting Interventions

Because studies of the determinants and consequences of coparenting coordination are a relatively recent phenomenon, efforts to alter or forestall the development of coparental difficulties are rare. However, one exemplary program of research has been concerned with strengthening coparental partnerships in two-parent families with young children. Philip and Carolyn Cowan, whose creative interventions with couples during the transition to parenthood had shown some salutary effects on early coparenting mutuality (including enhancement of fathers' psychological involvement with babies and mothers' satisfaction with division of family labor), described an innovative couples group intervention specifically concerned with coparenting dilemmas of families with preschool-aged children.

Preliminary results from this intervention study indicated that participation in a sixteen-week couples group dealing with how family strains affect coparenting had far-reaching effects for both parents and children. Among the benefits of this intervention were greater marital satisfaction, more effective father-child interaction, and significant improvements for children on a number of academic and social adjustment indicators (Cowan and Cowan 1997).

See also: CONFLICT: COUPLE RELATIONSHIPS; DISCIPLINE; FAMILY LIFE EDUCATION; FATHERHOOD; INTERPARENTAL CONFLICT—EFFECTS ON CHILDREN; MARITAL QUALITY; MOTHERHOOD; PARENTING EDUCATION; PARENTING STYLES; SPANKING; SUBSTITUTE CAREGIVERS; THERAPY: COUPLE RELATIONSHIPS; TRANSITION TO PARENTHOOD; TRIANGULATION

Bibliography

Abidin, R. R., and Brunner, J. F. (1995). "Development of a Parenting Alliance Inventory." *Journal of Clinical Child Psychology* 24:31–40.

Belsky, J.; Crnic, K.; and Gable, S. (1995). "The Determinants of Coparenting in Families with Toddler Boys: Spousal Differences and Daily Hassles." *Child Development* 66:629–642.

Belsky, J.; Putnam, S.; and Crnic, K. (1996). "Coparenting, Parenting, and Early Emotional Development." In

Understanding How Family-Level Dynamics Affect Children's Development: Studies of Two-Parent Families. New Directions for Child Development, No. 74, ed. J. P. McHale and P. A. Cowan. San Francisco: Jossey-Bass.

Brody, G.; Flor, D.; and Neubaum, E. (1998). "Coparenting Processes and Child Competence among Rural African-American Families." In *Families, Risk, and Competence,* ed. M. Lewis and C. Feiring. Mahwah, NJ: Lawrence Erlbaum Associates.

Brody, G. H.; Stoneman, Z.; and Flor, D. (1995). "Linking Family Processes and Academic Competence among Rural African American Youths." *Journal of Marriage and the Family* 57:567–579.

Cohen, R. S., and Weissman, S. H. (1984). "The Parenting Alliance." In *Parenthood: A Psychodynamic Perspective,* ed. R. S. Cohen, B. J. Cohler, and S. H. Weissman. New York: Guilford.

Coll, C. T.; Meyer, E. C.; and Brillon, L. (1995). "Ethnic and Minority Parenting." In *Handbook of Parenting,* Vol. 2, ed. M. Bornstein. Mahwah, NJ: Lawrence Erlbaum Associates.

Cowan, C. P., and Cowan, P. A. (1997). "Working with Couples during Stressful Transitions." In *The Family on the Threshold of the Twenty-first Century: Trends and Implications,* ed. S. Dreman. Mahwah, NJ: Lawrence Erlbaum Associates.

Cowan, P. A., and McHale, J. P. (1996). "Coparenting in a Family Context: Emerging Achievements, Current Dilemmas, and Future Directions." In *Understanding How Family-Level Dynamics Affect Children's Development: Studies of Two-Parent Families. New Directions for Child Development,* No. 74, ed. J. P. McHale and P. A. Cowan. San Francisco: Jossey-Bass.

Johnson, W. E. (2001). "Paternal Involvement among Unwed Fathers." *Children and Youth Services Review* 23:513–536.

Kibria, N. (1993). *Family Tightrope: The Changing Lives of Vietnamese Americans.* Princeton: Princeton University Press.

Lewis, J.; Owen, M.; and Cox, M. (1988). "The Transition to Parenthood, III: Incorporation of the Child into the Family." *Family Process* 27:411–421.

Lindahl, K.; Clements, M.; and Markman, H. (1998). "The Development of Marriage: A 9-Year Perspective." In *The Developmental Course of Marital Dysfunction,* ed. T. Bradbury. New York: Cambridge University Press.

Margolin, G.; Gordis, E. B.; and John, R. S. (2001). "Coparenting: A Link between Marital Conflict and Parenting in Two-Parent Families." *Journal of Family Psychology* 15:3–21.

McConnell, M. C., and Kerig, P. K. (2002). "Assessing Coparenting in Families of School Age Children: Validation of the Coparenting and Family Rating System." *Canadian Journal of Behavioural Science* 34:56–70.

McHale, J. (1995). "Coparenting and Triadic Interactions during Infancy: The Roles of Marital Distress and Child Gender." *Developmental Psychology* 31:985–996.

McHale, J. (1997) "Overt and Covert Coparenting Processes in the Family." *Family Process* 36:183–210.

McHale, J., and Fivaz-Depeursinge, E. (1999). "Understanding Triadic and Family Group Process during Infancy and Early Childhood." *Clinical Child and Family Psychology Review* 2:107–127.

McHale, J.; Khazan, I.; Erera, P.; Rotman, T.; DeCourcey, W.; and McConnell, M. (2002a). "Coparenting in Diverse Family Systems." In *Handbook of Parenting,* 2nd edition, ed. M. Bornstein. Mahwah, NJ: Lawrence Erlbaum Associates.

McHale, J.; Kuersten, R.; and Lauretti, A. (1996). "New Directions in the Study of Family-Level Dynamics during Infancy and Early Childhood." In *Understanding How Family-Level Dynamics Affect Children's Development: Studies of Two-Parent Families. New Directions for Child Development,* No. 74, ed. J. McHale and P. Cowan. San Francisco: Jossey-Bass.

McHale, J.; Kuersten-Hogan, R.; Lauretti, A.; and Rasmussen, J. (2000b). "Parental Reports of Coparenting and Observed Coparenting Behavior during the Toddler Period." *Journal of Family Psychology* 14: 220–237.

McHale, J.; Lauretti, A.; Talbot, J.; and Pouquette, C. (2002b). "Retrospect and Prospect in the Psychological Study of Coparenting and Family Group Process." In *Retrospect and Prospect in the Psychological Study of Families,* ed. J. McHale and W. Grolnick. Mahwah, NJ: Lawrence Erlbaum Associates.

McHale, J.; Rao, N.; and Krasnow, A. (2000a). "Constructing Family Climates: Chinese Mothers' Reports of Their Coparenting Behavior and Preschoolers' Adaptation." *International Journal of Behavioral Development* 24:111–118.

McHale, J. P.; Johnson, D.; and Sinclair, R. (1999). "Family Dynamics, Preschoolers' Family Representations, and Preschool Peer Relationships." *Early Education and Development* 10:373–401.

McHale, J. P., and Rasmussen, J. L. (1998). "Coparental and Family Group-Level Dynamics during Infancy:

Early Family Precursors of Child and Family Functioning during Preschool." *Development and Psychopathology* 10:39–59.

Minuchin, S. (1974). *Families and Family Therapy*. Cambridge, MA: Harvard University Press.

Ogata, K., and Miyashita, K. (2000). "Exploring Links between Father's Participation in Family Chores, Child's Empathy, Family Function, and Father's Identity Development." *Japanese Journal of Family Psychology* 14:15–27.

Roopnarine, J. L.; Lu, M. W.; and Ahmeduzzaman, M. (1989). "Parental Reports of Early Patterns of Caregiving, Play and Discipline in India and Malaysia." *Early Child Development and Care* 30:109–120.

Schoppe, S. J.; Mangelsdorf, S. C.; and Frosch, C. (2001). "Coparenting, Family Process, and Family Structure: Implications for Preschoolers' Externalizing Behavior Problems." *Journal of Family Psychology* 15:526–545.

Sonuga-Barke, E., and Mistry, M. (2000). "The Effect of Extended Family Living on the Mental Health of Three Generations within Two Asian Communities." *British Journal of Clinical Psychology* 39:129–141.

MELANIE C. MCCONNELL
EASTER DAWN VO
JAMES P. MCHALE

COPING

See CHRONIC ILLNESS; DISABILITIES; FAMILY STRENGTHS; GRIEF, LOSS, AND BEREAVEMENT; INTERPARENTAL CONFLICT—EFFECTS ON CHILDREN; LONELINESS; RELIGION; SPOUSE ABUSE: THEORETICAL EXPLANATIONS; STRESS; WIDOWHOOD

COUSINS

English-speakers classify up to four distinct groups of relatives as *cousins*. The children of a set of brothers and sisters form the primary category: they are *first cousins* to each other. More distantly related kin of one's own generation (*collateral kin*) form the second category. The grandchildren of your grandparents' siblings are your *second cousins*; the great-grandchildren of your great-grandparents' siblings are your *third cousins*; and so forth. (To put this in another way, children of

first cousins stand as second cousins to each other while grandchildren stand as third cousins). The third and potentially broadest category includes the children of aunts, uncles, and cousins who belong to a different generation from one's self. The child of your second cousin, for instance, is technically your *second cousin-once-removed,* as you are to her (the terms are reciprocal). Finally, some English-speakers refer to the cousins of spouses and other in-laws as *cousin,* although these people are not technically kin. It is important to note that people do not use these categories consistently, especially with more distant kin.

The categorical expansiveness of *cousin* in English and other European languages rests on a distinction between the nuclear family and more distant kin. This kind of kinship terminology system is technically known as *Eskimo* and is also found in small hunter-gatherer groups that lack strong descent groups. Other societies classify kin differently. *Hawaiian* terminology, found in Polynesia and many West African cultures, provides the simplest variation. All relatives are classified according to generation. There is no distinct term for *cousin* in the English sense. Collateral relatives are referred to by the same terms as *brother* and *sister* (Keesing 1975).

Most societies with unilineal descent systems make a finer distinction between *cross* and *parallel* relatives. Parallel cousins include the children of one's father's brothers and mother's sisters. In general, one refers to parallel cousins by the same terms as one's own siblings and to their parents as *father* and *mother*. Cross-cousins include the children of one's father's sisters and mother's brothers. They receive a special term, as do their parents and children, indicating their separation from the immediate family. A range of societies in the Americas, Oceania, and southern Asia prefer marriage between cross-cousins. This kind of marriage forms strong and lasting alliances between the groups exchanging spouses, even when, as is often the case, the marriage is between classificatory cross-cousins—that is, people who share at best a distant genealogical relationship but who refer to each other as cross-cousins (Lévi-Straus 1969). A few Middle Eastern societies prefer marriages between parallel cousins, a pattern that enforces marriage within a descent group (Holy 1996).

Cousins often enjoy warm relationships, even in societies with weak extended family systems.

Societies differ in the degree to which closely related cousins are regarded as immediate family and thus subject to the incest taboo. The U.S. rock-and-roll star Jerry Lee Lewis was widely condemned in 1958 for marrying a second cousin (and criticized also because she was only thirteen at the time). On the other hand, such respected figures as Charles Darwin and Queen Victoria married first cousins. Most U.S. states ban or place severe restrictions on first cousin marriages, but such marriages are legal in Canada and Europe (Ottenheimer 1996).

See also: AUNT; KINSHIP; SIBLING RELATIONSHIPS; UNCLE

Bibliography

Holy, L. (1996). *Anthropological Perspectives on Kinship.* London: Pluto Press.

Keesing, R. M. (1975). *Kin Groups and Social Structure.* New York: Holt, Rinehart, and Winston.

Lévi-Straus, C. (1969). *The Elementary Structures of Kinship.* London: Eyre and Spottiswood.

Ottenheimer, M. (1996). *Forbidden Relatives: The American Myth of Cousin Marriage.* Urbana: University of Illinois Press.

JOHN BARKER

CUBA

See ETHNIC VARIATION/ETHNICITY; HISPANIC-AMERICAN FAMILIES

CZECH REPUBLIC

The Czech Republic is a landlocked country measuring 78,866 square kilometers, lying in the central part of Europe. It was established in 1993 after Czechoslovakia split into the Czech Republic and Slovakia. The Czech Republic has 10.2 million inhabitants, 94.2 percent of which are Czech by nationality. The country's borders neighbor Germany, Poland, Austria, and Slovakia. The Czech Republic is a democratic state and a member of NATO and is preparing for entry into the European Union.

With respect to marriage and the family, Czech society has always been strongly influenced by political and cultural changes. These experiences are shared among the entire social strata and generations, and are reflected in individual value orientations and attitudes towards the family as an institution. Marriage and—especially—the family have always been respected as structures that help mitigate the effects of difficult political and economic conditions and changes.

Marriage

In the Czech Republic, marriage is a legal bond between any two adult individuals of the opposite sex who are not close relatives. The cultural and historical foundation of marriage lies in Roman family law and later Christian marriage doctrines, strictly defining its monogamous character and the inseparability of the bond. The individual and free choice of partner is most characteristic of marriage today, motivated by an emotional relationship—love—and accompanied by the legal possibility of divorce. In addition, since 1998 future marriage partners have been able to settle legal and property aspects of the relationship in a premarital agreement.

Marriage enables partners to start a family, as a specifically intimate form of partnership between a man and a woman. In the early twenty-first century, other forms (e.g., marriage between homosexual partners, open polygamy, or polyandry) were not legally permissible. Since 1992 it has been possible to marry in either a civic or a church ceremony. The conditions for entering into a marriage are legally set and stipulate that an individual may not enter into a marriage with a person who is already married, or with a parent, child, brother, or sister, and require that a person be of legal marrying age (eighteen years), although a court may grant exceptions. A marriage may be terminated in a manner stipulated in the legal code—in other words, through the death of a spouse or through divorce.

Family

Family status. In the Czech Republic the family is considered in both the private and the public sphere as an irreplaceable structure ascribed with the highest values and significance. Biological reproduction—having children and raising them—and the related participation in the demographic renewal of society, is still viewed as the basic function of the family. In early twenty-first century

Czech society, however, the majority of the population views the family as one of the basic institutions of social stability and one closely linked to other institutions in society. The laws governing the processes involved in starting and maintaining a family stem from the civil code of the year 1811, amended over the course of the twentieth century with new family laws.

Demographic features. In a country with a population of 10.2 million people (as of the year 2000), there are over 2.5 million families representing a broad range of types of family cohabitation in which a number of factors play a role: age, family composition, the number of family members, the preference of a certain type of household, location, income and property, religion, and lifestyle attitudes. The actual way in which families are formed and experienced is affected by living conditions and by cultural and social norms. The demographic structure of the family is influenced by the fact that on average 8 percent of married couples remain childless, and that the number of children born to and living in incomplete families is increasing (Maříková 2000). Alongside the *traditional* forms of families—the nuclear and the incomplete family, and the deeply rooted model of the two-child family—deep and extensive changes—both societal and resulting from the transformation since the fall of the communist regime—have generated new forms of family structure and cohabitation, especially the form of "premarital unmarried cohabitation on a trial basis" (Maříková 2000, p. 34, and Rychtaříková 2001, pp. 46–52). The number of children born outside marriage during the past decade has increased by almost 22 percent (Statistical Yearbook of the Czech Republic 2001). Women lead 70 percent of all forms of incomplete families in the Czech Republic (Večerník and Matějů 1999). Divorce, which was legalized after World War I, increased sharply in frequency particularly during the 1970s and the first half of the 1980s, and has made a significant contribution to the increase in the number of incomplete families. The erosion of the nuclear family was however also sustained by secondary processes, which became evident only after the *divorce ceiling* had been reached (on average 32,000 cases a year during the past fifteen years [Statistical Yearbook of the Czech Republic 2001]). These processes led to an increase in the number of individuals who had been affected by divorce as

children and were unprepared for the responsibilities of family life and maintaining strong family ties. In the 1990s significant demographic/social changes occurred in the structure and dynamics of family, marriage, and reproductive behavior among the Czech population, which can be characterized as new trends and indicate a qualitative social change. In particular, the following changes are worth nothing:

- The average age of men and women entering into marriage increased rapidly (the male average grew in the years 1989–1997 from 24.6 to 27.7 and the female average from 21.8 to 25.4).

- The marriage rate declined (5.4 per 1,000 inhabitants, roughly half the figure for the 1970s).

- The birth rate declined (the aggregate birth rate of 1.14 in the year 2000 is among the lowest in Europe, and the Czech Republic has now recorded the lowest number of children born since the year 1918).

- The average age of parents increased (in the years 1990–1997 from 24.8 to 26.4), including first-time parents (from 22.5 to 24.0).

- There has been a significant decline in the number of families having a second child, and a shift from the originally dominant two-child model of the Czech family towards single-child families.

- There has been a significant decline in the abortion rate (in the years 1991–1998 the number of abortions decreased from 103,000 to 41,000).

Political and social influences. Secularization has influenced at least 70 percent of the Czech population. Of the remaining 30 percent of the population with a religious orientation, there are many that are not actively practicing (Sčítání 2002). Secularization is accompanied by a more liberal view of premarital sex, a broad acceptance of abortion, and a weakening of attitudes that contribute to the maintenance of tradition and the rituals associated with family life. This reality has come to be reflected in everyday language. Some terms formerly used to refer to family relatives have almost been forgotten, such as godmother, godfather, and godchild. Although in the Czech population traditional and liberal views on family issues continue to co-exist, over the course of the socialist period (1948–1989) some inner control mechanisms that regulate the area of family ties were weakened or fell apart. Relationships between neighbors disintegrated owing to the consequences of migration processes necessitated by socialist industrialization. Attempts to solve housing issues through the construction of massive, anonymous panel housing estates led to the accelerated atomization of the nuclear family. State and political interference during the socialist period and the paternalistic social policy prior to 1989 led to the long-term deformation of the essence of family structures and values. From the perspective of the Czech family since the 1970s the key areas of interference were: (1) the unprecedented intervention of social engineering in population policy; (2) the deformed ties stemming from the redistribution of income and the state assumption of some responsibilities of the family and the individual; and (3) the current failure of the state in these areas. In terms of culture and norms, however, Czech society overcame the impact of the two worst totalitarian regimes of the twentieth century—the Nazis (1938–1945) and the Bolshevics (1948–1988).

Economic and social conditions of the Czech family. At the beginning of the twenty-first century the Czech family faces the growing influence of increasing social and economic inequalities in family living standards. The impact of the economic transformation in the post-socialist era most affects young families with a larger number of children, incomplete families with children not provided for, families with a single income, or those entirely dependent on social support from the state.

The family and women. Significant questions regarding the function and profile of the contemporary Czech family concern (1) the position of women in the family; (2) the position of the man/father; (3) the division of labor in the family; and (4) the influence of social stereotypes on the division of male and female roles. Women make up 44 percent of the workforce in the Czech Republic, and the application of strategies founded on the models of *part-time employment* or *housewives* are marginal phenomena (Maříková 2000). The educational structure of the female population is comparable with the male population in terms of

achieving higher levels of education. In the early years of the twenty-first century, however, women had not achieved the same opportunities in the labor market as men, and their average income was roughly a third lower than that of men. Even so, it is the woman's income that determines the living standard of a family, as Czech families have long depended on two incomes. In everyday family and household labor, a residue of the patriarchal-traditional division of labor between the sexes persists, and woman/mother continues to bear the heavy burden, including the *second shift*. This pattern is less obvious in partnership relations, decision making in the family, and control over the family budget, where particularly among the younger generation an egalitarian model has asserted itself (Čermáková 2000).

Other family patterns. Other distinct family patterns and behavior can be seen, particularly in the ethno-culturally distinct *Roma* population living in the Czech Republic, which has long demonstrated different behavior in relation to marriage and the family (e.g., a high birth rate, low divorce rate, or the set position of Roma women in the patriarchal family). After the division of Czechoslovakia in 1992, the issue of mixed marriages and families comprised of Czechs and Slovaks became more important, although the phenomenon itself was common and characterized by similar patterns and behavior.

Future Trends

Future trends can be characterized as a return to the European patterns of family behavior, with some specific determinants related both to the long-term forced paternalistic-socialist trajectories and habits, and to the economic and social consequences of the social transformation.

The decreasing marriage rate and plummeting birth rate are among the processes that were earlier predicted and for which Czech society was not prepared. The population explosion of the 1970s was used as a determining factor for future development, as were prognoses concerning the Czech population and family development (Večerník 1999). However, in the 1990s other alternatives asserted themselves in the institution of marriage and in the family. The individual, improvised search for alternatives to former, eroded models of marriage

A grandfather takes his granddaughters on an excursion in Prague. In a country that has gone through difficult political and economic conditions and changes, family is respected as an institution that helps people cope.
WOLFGANG KAEHLER/CORBIS

Czech society is moving towards models of marriage and family characteristic of advanced democratic European societies, including changes in the interpersonal ties within the family or in the relationship of the family to the state. Analogous situations can be found in a number of Western European societies (though usually occurring there in their early phase in the 1960s and 1970s). Both the observed demographic changes and sociological research indicate that even in the Czech case a "deep change in the cultural factor is occurring, i.e. in the thought of Czech women, men and couples. This involves a shift in the value system towards the pluralizing of values (tolerating divorce, abortion and homosexuality), a search for individual lifestyles and personal identity." (Rychtaříková, Pikálková, and Hamplová 2001). For the Czech Republic, this trend represents a historically new model, but one that is becoming deeply rooted in society. Theoretically, the process is defined as the second demographic transition (Rychtaříková 2001). In the case of the Czech Republic it is assumed that this is a delayed process, characterized by specific cultural features. The trends shaping family behavior in the Czech Republic in early twenty-first century are:

- A tendency to copy the trends of Western Europe—putting off marriage until later, having children at a later age, a high divorce rate;

- The above-mentioned trend exists alongside a strong preference for legal marriages if there are children, and a strong emphasis on the institution of the traditional family; and

- Important roles played by the high employment rate among women, the lack of apartments, and the weak purchasing power of Czech currency.

Research on the Family and Demographic Trends in the Czech Republic

Sociologists and demographers have been extremely active in the Czech Republic since 1990s. Because they are directly affected by the economic problems of the transformation period, both marriage and the family are frequently studied, often as preparation for legislation affecting the family, employment, and childcare. Researchers are also giving significant attention to

and the family gave rise to experimentation. Over one-half of the young population now try unmarried cohabitation prior to entering into a marriage, and this has become the most widespread and the most preferred variant of partnership life among young people. However, only 10 percent of those in this particular group consider this type of partnership a part of their long-term life strategy (Rychtaříková 2001). However, the life strategies of many young people, which have changed the demographic structure of Czech society, are founded on more complicated motives than political change or economic difficulties. Twenty-first century such issues as of the possible legalization of homosexual partnerships, domestic violence, and gender inequalities in the family.

See also: SLOVAKIA

Bibliography

Čermáková, M. (1997). *Rodina a měnící se gender role—sociální analýza české rodiny* (Family and changing gender roles—social analysis of the Czech family). Praha: Working Papers SoÚ AV.

Čermáková, M.; Hašková, H.; Křížková, A.; Linková, M.; Maříková, H.; and Musilová, M. (2000). *Relations and Changes of Gender Differences in the Czech Society in the 90s.* Praha: Institute of Sociology of Academy of Science of the Czech Republic.

Fialová, L.; Hamplová, D.; Kučera, M.; and Vymětalová, S. (2000). *Představy mladých lidí o manželství a rodičovství* (Ideas of young people about marriage and parenthood). Praha: Sociologické nakladatelství.

Kroupa, A., and Mácha, M., eds. (1999). *Zpráva o lidském rozvoji Česká republika 1999* (Report on human development: Czech Republic 1999). Praha: VÚPSV.

Lenderová, M. (1999). *K hříchu a k modlitbě* (Towards a sin and prayer). Praha: Mladá fronta.

Maříková, H., ed. (2000). *Proměny současné české rodiny (Rodina-gender-stratifikace)* (Changes of current Czech family [family-gender-stratification]). Praha: Sociologické nakladatelství.

Maříková H., Petrusek M., and Vodáková A., eds. (1996). *Velký sociologický slovník* (The great lexicon of sociology). Parts 1 and 2. Praha: Karolinum

Matoušek, O. (1993). *Rodina jako sociální instituce a sít'* (Family as social institution and social network). Praha: Sociologické nakladatelství.

Možný, I. (1983). *Rodina vysokoškolsky vzdělaných manželu* (Two-career families). Brno: UJEP.

Možný, I. (1990). *Moderní rodina (mýty a skutečnost)* (Modern Family [Myths and Reality]). Brno: Blok.

Možný, I. (1999). *Sociologie rodiny* (Sociology of Family). Praha: Sociologické nakladatelství.

Rychtaříková, J.; Pikálková, S.; and Hamplová, D. (2001). *Diferenciace reprodukčního a rodinného chování v evropských populacích* (Differentiation of reproductive and family behavior in the European populations). Praha: Sociologické texty SoÚ AV ČR.

Sčítání lidu, domů a bytů 2001—Základní informace z defnitivnich výsledků (Population and housing census—Basic figures from complete final results). (2002). Praha: Český statistický úřad.

Statistical Yearbook of the Czech Republic. (2001). Praha: Český statistický úřad.

Večerník, J., and Matějů, P. eds. (1999). *Ten Years of Rebuilding Capitalismus: Czech Society after 1989.* Praha: Academia.

MARIE ČERMÁKOVÁ

D

DATE RAPE

See RAPE

DATING

Dating, from casual to serious, is likely to involve romance and sexual activity, which distinguishes it from social outings between people who consider themselves merely friends (Newman 1999). It is related to two broader processes—*courtship* and *mate selection*. Historically, the term courtship has been applied to situations where the intent to marry was explicit and referred to the socializing between young adults on the path to marriage (Rothman 1984). The term *mate selection* refers to how we choose someone to marry and involves structural and social factors such as the nature of the "marriage market" (the persons from among whom we select our partners), and considerations such as age, race, class, education, religion, and cultural ideas (Schwartz and Scott 1955). The vast majority of daters are unmarried, and most studies of dating have used samples of college students who are more diverse than in the past, and are more like the general population than a group of social elites.

In contemporary North American society, "dating is the recognized means by which most people move from being single to being coupled" (Newman 1999, p. 176). However, it is not necessarily

the route to couplehood in all societies. David Newman draws a distinction between individualist cultures (e.g., western Europe, the United States, Canada, and Australia) and collectivist cultures (e.g., China, Vietnam, and Japan), pointing out that because the former allow free choice of potential spouses, they are more likely to include dating than are collectivist cultures.

In collectivist cultures such as China, young people (especially in the larger cities) may "go out" together, but this is probably courtship rather than dating, because their coupling has been pre-arranged and the goal of marriage is fixed. Another example is India where marriages are still arranged by families or trusted go-betweens. When young people are chosen for each other, it is not considered necessary that they know each other well before marriage and love is scarcely a consideration. When a meeting is arranged, following an exchange of photographs and a resume, it is not a meeting that may be followed by dates. Rather, it is a meeting to answer the question, "Am I going to marry this person?" Thus, dating, as Westerners understand it, is not applicable. Letters and flowers may be exchanged, but the couple may not spend much, if any, time together. Love is expected to grow after marriage. Faith in religion and in the wisdom of those who arranged the pairing is the basis for this system. The system prevails among Muslims in America as well as in India (Ettenborough 1998).

A third non-western example is Japan. Only about 10 percent of matings are prearranged, and others may avail themselves of "dating parties,"

A couple walks together in Yokohama, Japan. In Japan only about 10 percent of mate selections are prearranged.
MICHAEL S. YAMASHITA/CORBIS

members-only bars (where men pay steep fees and women merely register), or cell-phone dating network services (French 2001). China suffers from a huge lack of marriageable women (men outnumber women nearly two to one) and this gap will become more severe "as the first wave of people born under China's 'one-child policy' hits the marriage market. In the near future . . . countless young men may have little or no chance of landing a wife" (Chu 2001). One result is the abduction of women by "fixers" who sell them to men as wives. Under these circumstances, which have already affected thousands of Chinese women, there is neither dating nor courtship.

In marked contrast, dating in Western societies is for the most part similar to the North American pattern, which began only in the last century. Starting around 1900, the selection of dating partners began to become more autonomous (less under family supervision) than before in the United States. This was partly due to the rise of city life versus the previous predominantly rural background of most Americans, and to the related expanded employment opportunities for both sexes in the cities. Choices were less affected by considerations such as wealth (i.e., the ability to support a family) than by personal qualities such as character. Then, from about 1920 to World War II, a system of dating evolved in which there was considerable "playing the field" to demonstrate one's popularity (called *casual dating*), which might gradually become more exclusive (called *going*

steady). Going steady might in turn result in an engagement or in marriage.

By the 1950s, a youth culture had developed in which dating started at earlier ages than before (e.g., among pre-teens). Moreover, the sexual exploration (ranging from kissing to sexual intercourse) which had previously been part of the last stage of courtship (engagement), now often occurred earlier, even among very young couples.

The "youth revolution" of the 1960s was partly about the right of unmarried people to express themselves sexually and partly about the widespread rejection of the belief that a woman's value lay in her virtue (virginity). The revolution was a struggle for power, freedom, equality, and autonomy, but the gains in freedom undermined the old rules; that is, courtship, and dating within it, began to lose coherence as the *what, why,* and even *how* became less clear (Bailey 1988).

Today, self-help books proliferate in response to that lack of clarity; for example, *Dating for Dummies* (Browne 1996), *The Rules* (Fein and Schneider 1995), and *Mars and Venus on a Date* (Gray 1998). Some of these guides are highly traditional, counseling that daters should behave in accordance with pre-1960s gender roles. Some are semi-egalitarian and semi-traditional. Still others, intended primarily for women (such as Lerner's *The Dance of Anger,* 1997) are egalitarian, rejecting the man-superior/woman-subordinate traditional view. Curiously, scholars who have studied dating behavior report that both men and women who claim to be egalitarian behave in traditional ways on dates (Laner and Ventrone 1998; 2000).

Competitiveness

Some aspects of dating are competitive in nature (i.e., a win/lose relationship in which each partner tries to get her or his own way). Researcher Mary Laner (1986, 1989) points out that competitive behaviors can be of three kinds: pleasant, unpleasant, or abusive/aggressive. Pleasant competitive behaviors consist of such tactics as using charm or diplomacy to get one's way (i.e., to win). Unpleasant competitiveness includes tactics such as using sarcasm or deceit to get one's way. Finally, abusive/aggressive tactics include displays of anger, the use of insults, and various forms of violence. Laner (1989) reports that although daters prefer cooperative (egalitarian) behaviors and attitudes, dating is rife with both pleasant and unpleasant competitive behaviors. Pleasant tactics are virtually undetectable. Unpleasant tactics, however, are associated with the likelihood of violence between the partners (such as hitting and grabbing). When asked whether such relationships are violent, fewer men and women say yes than those who identify conflict or disagreements as causing problems. The tactics themselves, however (such as slapping and punching) are reported surprisingly often by these same daters (Laner 1990). Evidently, the power struggle behind the competitiveness remains unrecognized.

Another competitive aspect of dating can be seen in the way men and women deal with potential rivals. Researchers David Buss and Lisa Dedden (1990) report that daters attempt to manipulate others' impressions of them by derogating ("putting down") suspected competitors. Men do this by making derogatory remarks about other men's strength, financial resources, and goals: all traditional masculine characteristics. Women, in contrast, put down potential competitors by derogating their attractiveness and sexual activity (calling them promiscuous), and by questioning their fidelity (e.g., "she cheats on her boyfriend"). Buss and Dedden point out that the tactics men use are more likely to be successful in keeping competitors at bay than those used by women.

Dating has been likened to a market in which the buyer must be wary and in which there is not necessarily truth in advertising. Persons compete, given their own assets, for the most status-conferring date. Willard Waller and Reuben Hill (1951) warned many years ago about the potential for exploitation in both casual and serious dating. Indeed, critics of traditional dating have decried it as a sexist bargaining system in which men are exploited for money and women for sexual favors. The superficiality of dating, its commercialization, the deceit involved, and the high levels of anxiety it can provoke are additional drawbacks. Since status differentials still characterize men and women (although women have gained status in recent years), dating may be seen as a contest in which a struggle for power and control between partners is part of "the game."

Sexuality

The sexual aspect of dating has affected how women and men judge one another's desirability.

Susan Sprecher and Kathleen McKinney summarize these attitudes: "a moderate level of sexual experience in a potential partner is more desirable than either extensive sexual experience or no experience at all" (1996, p. 41). Further, they report, men's and women's standards differ somewhat—men want a dating partner with more experience than women want. Studies like theirs are among those based on never-married college students. However, dating following separation or divorce differs from premarital dating in that it may involve a more liberal sexual ethic, be less leisurely, and may include additional considerations such as arrangements for child care.

Delights and Discontents

When daters are asked what's good about dating, they identify the following topics (Laner 1995):

(1) Companionship and communication;

(2) Friendship;

(3) Intimacy;

(4) Freedom of choice;

(5) Good times and having fun;

(6) Love and romance;

(7) Feelings of security;

(8) A sense of specialness;

(9) Learning about another person;

(10) Sharing (mutuality);

(11) An opportunity for personal growth; and

(12) An opportunity for sexual contact.

When asked about problems associated with dating, all of the same topics are identified. Thus, they each have their good and bad aspects. The list shown here appears in sequence—that is, companionship and communication were most often mentioned and sexual contact was least often mentioned. Yet, in terms of problems associated with dating, "a large number of questions were raised about several sexual dilemmas. They focused on problems relating to infidelity, and to differences between men and women regarding sexual attitudes, feelings, and behaviors" (Laner 1995, p. 182).

Communication and Deception

It is interesting that communication is at the top of the list of good things about dating and also high on the list of problematic aspects. A study of taboo topics among unmarried couples reveals that several areas of potential conversation are avoided by partners, primarily for fear of destroying the relationship. The more romantically involved the couple (versus merely platonic friends), the larger the number of topics to be avoided. Avoided areas include almost any that might induce conflict, as well as talk about past partners, and revelations about one's self that could be seen in a negative light (Baxter and Wilmot 1985).

Another aspect of communication that makes dating problematic has to do with deception. Sandra Metts (1989) asked almost four hundred college students about their relationships and 92 percent admitted that they had been deceptive at least once with a dating partner. Lying was most frequently used form of deception (versus distorting or omitting the truth). Metts reports that a plurality of the reasons for lying amounted to blaming one's partner—specifically, "to avoid hurting the partner."

Making Initial Contact

At the beginning of the dating process, we must first be aware of one another and then make a successful contact that results in *going out* or *hanging out*—the latter a less formal form of dating—or even *hooking up* (which is extremely limited, usually indicating a one-night date in which sexual activity is anticipated).

Who makes the initial contact? It is traditionally assumed to be the man. However, when Monica Moore (1985) and her colleagues observed women sitting alone in singles bars, they recorded some fifty-two kinds of flirting behavior that resulted in male contact within fifteen seconds of the behavior. These included smiling, skirt hiking, primping, pouting, and hair-flipping. According to Moore, women who signal the most often are also those who are most often approached by men.

Chris Kleinke, Frederick Meeker, and Richard Staneski (1986) categorized the opening lines that men and women use when meeting a potential date into three types: cute/flippant, innocuous (harmless), and direct. For lines used by men, the least preferred were the cute/flippant lines ("I'm easy, are you?"). For lines used by women, however, men liked both the cute/flippant and the direct lines ("Since we're both eating alone, would you like to join me?"). Women liked the innocuous

lines ("Does the #5 bus stop here?") but men didn't. Women who use cute/flippant lines may be setting themselves up for unpleasant situations since many such lines have a sexual connotation. Since virtually no one liked men's cute/flippant lines, their persistence is curious. It may be due to a lack of social skills, reinforcement of such lines by television shows and movies, or fear of rejection.

Dating Scripts

Suzanna Rose and Irene Frieze (1989), who have studied men's and women's *scripts* for first dates, point out that the behaviors expected of men form the more rigid script. For this reason alone, men may dread asking women out or making mistakes, thus anticipating rejection more than they otherwise might. As noted earlier, men were traditionally expected to be the initiators, the planners, and the decision makers about dates. Women primarily reacted to men's actions. In Rose and Frieze's study, men and women disagreed about only two of forty-seven script items (twenty-seven for men, twenty for women) which suggests that the expectations for each sex are well known by members of both sexes. It also means that first-date behavior is highly predictable and, as also noted earlier, tends to follow traditional lines from beginning to end (i.e., man calls for woman at her home; man attempts a good-night kiss).

Why is it that dates are so highly scripted especially in individualistic cultures like that of the United States, which appear to value openness, naturalness, and spontaneity? First, scripts help daters to make a good first impression (without which there would be no second date). Second, they ease whatever awkwardness daters may feel in view of the fact that they are probably relative strangers.

Following first dates, what motivates daters to continue to go out together? Bert Adams (1979) has identified some of the conditions under which the relationship is likely to continue: (1) if significant others react favorably to the relationship; (2) if the partners react favorably to one another's self-disclosure; (3) if the partners have good rapport; (4) if the partners agree on values; (5) if the partners are at about the same level of physical attractiveness and have similar personalities; (6) if the partners are role compatible (e.g., both traditional or both egalitarian); (7) if the partners can empathize with one another; and (8) if the partners define each other as "right" or even as "the best I can get."

Variations and Changes

Not all traditionalist societies subscribe to arranged marriages in which there is no parallel to "free choice" dating systems. In some (e.g., Borneo, and among the Tepoztlan of Mexico), young men initiate relationships themselves (Ramu 1989). However, contacts that follow are, as in China, not dating but courtship. Among second generation immigrants to the West from collectivist societies, customs may be changing—more or less rapidly depending on the culture of origin and certain other factors such as education. Muslim Arab Americans, for instance, see western dating practices as threatening to several requirements of their patrilineal families. However, their boys are given more latitude to date than are their girls, and in general, group dating is preferred (DeGenova 1997).

In individualist societies, certain aspects of dating are changing. Forms of meeting and getting acquainted now include "video dating services, introduction services, computer bulletin boards, and 900 party line services" (Strong et al. 2001, p. 229)—often called *cyberdating*. What their effect will be is not clear, but certain changes can already be seen. For instance, in face-to-face meetings, physical appearance is the initial basis of attraction while in cyberdating, face-to-face contact is replaced by conversational skill as the basis for the initial impression. The consequence of this and other changes, however, is as yet unknown.

See also: ATTRACTION; COHABITATION; COMMUNICATION: COUPLE RELATIONSHIPS; LOVE; MATE SELECTION; RELATIONSHIP INITIATION; RELATIONSHIP MAINTENANCE; SEXUAL COMMUNICATION: COUPLE RELATIONSHIPS; SEXUALITY; SINGLES/NEVER MARRIED PERSONS; SOCIAL NETWORKS

Bibliography

Adams, B. N. (1979). "Mate Selection in the United States: A Theoretical Summarization." In *Contemporary Theories About the Family,* ed. W. R. Burr, R. Hill, F. I. Nye, and I. L. Reiss. New York: Free Press

Bailey, B. L. (1988). *From Front Porch to Back Seat: Courtship in Twentieth Century America.* Baltimore, MD: Johns Hopkins University Press.

Baxter, L. A., and Wilmot, W. W. (1985). "Taboo Topics in Close Relationships." *Journal of Social and Personal Relationships* 2(3):253–269.

Browne, J. (1996). *Dating for Dummies.* Foster City, CA: IDG Books.

Buss, D. M. and Dedden, L. A. (1990). "Derogation of Competitors." *Journal of Social and Personal Relationships* 7:395–422.

Chu, H. (2001). "China's Marriage Crisis." *Los Angeles Times,* March 3.

DeGenova, M. K. (1997). *Families in Cultural Context.* Mountain View, CA: Mayfield.

Ettenborough, K. (1998). "Muslim Courtship a Family Affair." *Arizona Republic,* June 6.

Fein, E., and Schneider, S. (1995). *The Rules: Time-Tested Secrets for Capturing the Heart of Mr. Right.* New York: Warner Books.

French, H. W. (2001). "Japan's Lonely Look for Love in New Ways." *New York Times,* February 18.

Gray, J. (1998). *Mars and Venus on a Date.* New York: HarperCollins.

Kleinke, C. L.; Meeker, F. B.; and Staneski, R. A. (1986). "Preference for Opening Lines: Comparing Ratings by Men and Women." *Sex Roles* 15:585–600.

Laner, M. R. (1986). "Competition in Courtship." *Family Relations* 35(2):275–279.

Laner, M. R. (1989). "Competitive vs. Noncompetitive Styles: Which is Most Valued in Courtship?" *Sex Roles* 20(3/4):163–170.

Laner, M. R. (1990). "Violence or its Precipitators: Which is More Likely to be Identified as a Dating Problem?" *Deviant Behavior* 11(4):319–329.

Laner, M. R. (1995). *Dating: Delights, Discontents, and Dilemmas.* Salem, WI: Sheffield.

Laner, M. R., and Ventrone, N. A. (1998). "Egalitarian Daters/Traditionalist Dates." *Journal of Family Issues* 19 (4):468–474.

Laner, M. R., and Ventrone N. A. (2000). "Dating Scripts Revisited." *Journal of Family Issues* 21(4):488–500.

Lerner, H. ([1985] 1997). *The Dance of Anger: A Woman's Guide to Changing the Patterns of Intimate Relationships.* New York: HarperCollins.

McCornack, S. A., and Parks, M. R. (1990). "What Women Know That Men Don't: Sex Differences in Determining the Truth Behind Deceptive Messages." *Journals of Social and Personal Relationships* 7:107–118.

Metts, S. (1989). "An Exploratory Investigation of Deception in Close Relationships." *Journal of Social and Personal Relationships* 6(2):159–179.

Moore, M. M. (1985). "Nonverbal Courtship Patterns in Women: Context and Consequences." *Ethology and Sociobiology* 6(2):237–247.

Newman, D. M. (1999). *Sociology of Families.* Thousand Oaks, CA: Pine Forge Press.

Ramu, G. N. (1989). "Patterns of Mate Selection." In *Family and Marriage: Cross Cultural Perspectives,* ed. K. Ishwaran. Toronto: Wall and Thompson.

Rose, S., and Frieze, I. H. (1989). "Young Singles' Scripts for a First Dates." *Gender and Society* 3(2):258–268.

Rothman, E. K. (1984). *Hands and Hearts: A History of Courtship in America.* New York: Basic Books.

Schwartz, M. A., and Scott, B. M. (1995). "Mate Selection: Finding and Meeting Partners." In *Diversity and Change in Families,* ed. M. R. Rank and E. L. Kain. Englewood Cliffs, NJ: Prentice Hall.

Sprecher, S., and McKinney, K. (1995). *Sexuality.* Newbury Park, CA: Sage.

Strong, B.; DeVault, D.; Sayad, B. W.; and Cohen, T. F. (2000). *The Marriage and Family Experience,* 8th edition. Belmont, CA: Wadsworth.

Waller, W., and Hill, R. (1951). *The Family: A Dynamic Interpretation,* rev. edition. New York: Dryden.

MARY RIEGE LANER

DAY CARE

See RESPITE CARE: ADULT; RESPITE CARE: CHILD

DEATH AND DYING

Death is something that all human beings can expect to experience. But just as there are variations in when life is seen to begin, so too are there variations in when death is seen to occur. In Western cultures, death is assumed to occur when a person irreversibly stops breathing, their heart stops, and there is no evidence of brain activity (Frederick 2001), but this definition is not necessarily held by other cultures.

Death is a social construction, which means that it is defined by using words, concepts, and ways of thinking available in the culture (Kastenbaum 1998). Because this meaning is socially constructed, death can mean different things to different people, and the meaning can change over time

for each person. Marilyn Webb (1997) writes about the cultural mix that is the United States:

> American families in fact have widely different views on such crucial issues as the nature of death, necessary rituals, expectations of an afterlife, whether folk medicines or faith healers need to be involved in the medical process, whether or not the patient should even be told of a poor prognosis whether the patient or the family should be the primary decision maker, and who in the family should make decisions. (p. 214–215)

When one looks around the world, one can see evidence of differences in interpretations of death and dying and appropriate behavior in their regard. Death may be seen differently in other cultures, with questions not just about when and how death occurs, but what death is. As an example, persons who would be considered unconscious by Western physicians, would be seen as dead by people living on Vanatinai, a small island near Papua New Guinea, leaving the possibility that they could die over and over (Lepowsky 1985). Clearly, there are social and cultural constraints that act upon beliefs, attitudes, standards, and behavior with regard to death and dying.

Death Systems

Death systems (Kastenbaum 1998) are *"the interpersonal, sociophysical and symbolic network, through which an individual's relationship to mortality is mediated by his or her society"* (p. 59, emphasis in original). In one sense, we face death as individuals; in another, we face it as a part of a society and a culture. As indicated above, there is no single, consistent, cross-cultural view of death and how we are to respond to it. *Death systems* help the members of a particular group to know what death is and how to respond. A death system includes cognitive, emotional, and behavioral components and teaches the members of a group how to think, feel, and behave regarding death. Even when social groups share basic beliefs, such as religious beliefs, death systems will differ among groups, as Kathryn Braun and Rhea Nichols (1997) described in their study of four Asian-American cultures, and with groups over time, as Patricia Swift (1989) saw in the evolving death system of Zimbabwe.

At this funeral in China, attendants carry luggage that will accompany the dead person to the afterworld. Funerals and religious rites can help family members cope with death, and often reflect the family's death system—rules about how to think, feel, and act regarding death. KEREN SU/CORBIS

Although death systems are most clearly seen in large cultural groups, the family, with its unique shared past, present, and assumed future, also maintains a death system. Its assumptions about who can and should participate in such things as a *death watch,* who should attend a *funeral,* what they should wear, and how they should behave are all elements of a family's death system. The family, as an intimate system, acts as a filter for information from the broader culture. Beliefs about what death means, if there is an afterlife and what it is like, may come from the broader culture, but these beliefs are mediated by the family's death system.

Family Relationships and Death

"There is no more emotionally connected system than the family, if for no other reason than because no one can ever truly leave it" (Rosen 1998, p. 17). Families are a collection of individuals, with a unique shared history and unique responsibilities to each other. Indeed, the understanding of *family* in its most expansive sense, includes all

generations: those living, those dead, and those yet to be born (Rosen 1998). We may choose to sever ties by ending contact, or terminating legal responsibilities, but in truth, can never truly sever relationship ties. Family ties may be voluntary or involuntary, wanted or unwanted, central to our thoughts or held to the side, and they often extend beyond death.

For any system to operate, it needs certain functions to take place and roles to be played (Rosen 1998). Each family has its own unique structure, functions, relationships, roles and role responsibilities, and interaction patterns (Rando 1984). Family members often carry out many roles in the family, and the more central these roles are to the family's ongoing operation, the more disruptive is the loss of the person who carried them out.

Families also maintain a certain balance and achieve a predictability in normal day-to-day life (Rosen 1998). This can be challenging without the loss of a family member, because families must deal with normative change that comes from such simple things as normal aging of family members and the evolving character of relationships within the family (Doka 1993). When a crisis like a death occurs, the family is thrown into disorder. The stability that has been established in the family is disrupted and, in order to continue to function, the family must somehow regain some sort of stability and shift the various responsibilities among the remaining family members. Death is what Reuben Hill (1949) referred to as a *crisis of dismemberment,* an apt term for the loss of a part of the *family body.* This form of crisis occurs when a family member is lost to the family and his or her various role responsibilities must be shifted to at least one other family member.

The family's ability to adapt to a terminal illness or a death is affected by a variety of factors (Murray 2000): the timing of the illness or the death in the life cycle, the nature of the death itself, and the degree to which the loss is acknowledged—that is, the degree to which it is disenfranchised (Doka 1989), stigmatized, or both. In addition, if families have concurrent stressors, if the person is central to the family's operations, or if there was conflict with the person who is dying or has died, the family will be more vulnerable at this time. Families with a variety of resources within and outside the family as well as openness, flexibility, and cohesiveness are better able to handle the various stressors related to the death (Murray 2000).

The Dying Process—Moving Toward a Death

There is disagreement as to when dying begins. In a sense, dying begins at birth. As Colin Murray Parkes, Pittu Laungani and Bill Young (1997) note, "Life [is] an incurable disease which always ends fatally" (p. 7). Typically, though, dying is considered as starting at a point close to the end of one's life when a life-threatening illness or condition develops. A variety of approaches can be taken: dying can be seen as beginning when the facts are recognized by the physician, when the facts are communicated to the patient, when the patient realizes or accepts the facts, or when nothing more can be done to preserve life (Kastenbaum 1998). Kenneth Doka (1995–96) broke the process of dying into three phases: the *acute,* the *chronic,* and the *terminal* phases of dying, in which the individual initially is given the diagnosis, then lives with the disease and then, finally, succumbs to death.

Like the dying person, the family goes through their own dying process. Families who are faced with the potentiality of the death of a family member generally will follow a pattern of changes, according to Elliott Rosen (1998):

Preparatory phase. In this phase, fear and denial are common. The family may be highly disorganized and the illness is highly disruptive to normal family operation. The family turns inward and is protective of itself and of its members. Anxiety may be higher at this time than at any other point in the dying process.

Living with the disease/condition. This phase can be quite long, and the family may settle into their new roles within the family. Supporters may become comfortable in their caregiving role and adjust to the idea of death. This is an important adjustment, because a great deal of the care for the terminally ill is provided by family members (Mezey, Miller, and Linton-Nelson 1999). Other roles may shift throughout this phase, including those of the terminally ill person. The family may close itself off from others. The family may be less disorganized during this phase, but the reorganization may not be healthy if, for example, the family isolates themselves and refuses offers of help. Anxiety is related to finances, resource availability, and caregiving. As Doka (1998) notes, this phase "is often a period of continued stress, punctuated by points of crisis" (p. 163).

Final acceptance. Usually the shortest phase, death is accepted and family members may say goodbye, although not all family members are equally willing to accept the death. The family is again disorganized and in shock, and roles no longer work as they did in the last phase. The family may become anxious of how others will think of them and view them, which can cause the family to move to extremes, becoming closer or moving further apart.

Throughout this process of moving toward the biological death of the family member, some or all family members may see the dying person to be socially dead (Sudnow 1967). In this, the dying person is seen to be "already dead" with the result that they may then become more and more isolated, as others move on with their lives and visit less and less frequently.

In a model similar to Rosen's, Doka (1993) includes a fourth phase, which he calls *recovery,* where the family resumes and reorders family roles and expectations. This may take place relatively smoothly, or may be complicated by the reluctance of some family members to give up the roles they held during the illness.

The Family After Death

Froma Walsh and Monica McGoldrick (1991) proposed that in order to successfully adapt to the loss of their family member, the family must do the following:

Recognize the loss as real. Family members must acknowledge the loss as real while each family member shares his or her grief. In order to do this, family members must share emotions and thoughts with each other. Grief is an isolating experience; a sense of acceptance among members would be promoted by displays of tolerance of differences in behavior by family members.

Reorganize and reinvest in the family system. As indicated above, the family system is destabilized by the loss; yet for it to continue to function, order and control must be reclaimed. Family members must reconstruct what family means to them and the roles and related tasks of the person who has died must be reassigned or given up. Family life may seem chaotic at this time and there may be battles over how the family will be reorganized. Differences in grieving may contribute to a feeling of being out-of-synch among family members. To get in-synch, families must reframe, that is, relabel their differences as strengths rather than weaknesses. The family must reinvest itself in normal developmental evolution. Tasks that are carried out as a matter of course in families must again be carried out in the family. This reclaiming of a normal life may be seen by some as abandonment of the deceased loved one. Trying to avoid mention of the deceased may inhibit communication, contributing to a sense of secretiveness in the family. Family members should let each other hold onto the memory until releasing them feels voluntary.

According to Walsh and McGoldrick, open communication is essential to completion of these tasks. This process may be slow, as each family member has strong needs and limited resources after a loss. Family members, who are already more emotional, may not recognize each other's different grief styles as legitimate. Rituals like funerals, religious rites, even family holiday rituals, can be used to facilitate the process of recognition, reorganization, and reinvestment in the family.

See also: ACQUIRED IMMUNODEFICIENCY SYNDROME (AIDS); CHRONIC ILLNESS; DISABILITIES; ELDERS; EUTHANASIA; GRIEF, LOSS, AND BEREAVEMENT; LATER LIFE FAMILIES; HEALTH AND FAMILIES; HOSPICE; INFANTICIDE; STRESS; SUDDEN INFANT DEATH SYNDROME (SIDS); SUICIDE; WAR/POLITICAL VIOLENCE; WIDOWHOOD

Bibliography

Braun, K. L., and Nichols, R. (1997). "Death and Dying in Four Asian American Cultures: A Descriptive Study." *Death Studies* 21:327–360.

Doka, K. J., ed. (1989). *Disenfranchised Grief.* Lexington, MA: Lexington Books.

Doka, K. J. (1993). *Living with Life-Threatening Illness: A Guide for Patients, Their Families and Caregivers.* New York: Lexington Books.

Doka, K. J. (1995–96). "Coping with Life-threatening Illness: A Task Model." *Omega: Journal of Death and Dying* 32:111–122.

Hill, R. (1949). *Families under Stress; Adjustment to the Crises of War Separation and Reunion.* New York: Harper.

Kastenbaum, R. J. (1998). *Death, Society, and Human Experience,* 6th edition. Boston: Allyn and Bacon.

Lepowsky, M. (1985). "Gender, Aging and Dying in an Egalitarian Society." In *Aging and Its Transformations—Moving Toward Death in Pacific Societies,* ed. D. R. Counts and D. A. Counts. Lanham, MD: University Press of America.

Mezey, M.; Miller, L. L.; and Linton-Nelson, L. (1999). "Caring for Caregivers of Frail Elders at the End of Life." *Generations* 23:44–51.

Murray, C. I. (2000). "Coping with Death, Dying, and Grief in Families." In *Families and Change: Coping with Stressful Events and Transitions,* ed. P. C. McKenry and S. J. Price. Thousand Oaks, CA: Sage.

Parkes, C. M.; Laungani, P.; and Young, B. (1997). Introduction to *Death and Bereavement Across Cultures,* ed. C. M. Parkes, P. Laungani, and B. Young. London: Routledge.

Rando, T. (1984). *Grief, Dying and Death: Clinical Interventions for Caregivers.* Champaign, IL: Research Press.

Rosen, E. J. (1998). *Families Facing Death: A Guide for Healthcare Professionals and Volunteers.* San Francisco: Jossey-Bass.

Sudnow, D. (1967). *Passing On: The Social Organization of Dying.* Englewood Cliffs, NJ: Prentice Hall.

Swift, P. (1989). "Support for the Dying and Bereaved in Zimbabwe: Traditional and New Approaches." *Journal of Social Development in Africa* 4:25–45.

Walsh, F., and McGoldrick, M. (1991). "Loss and the Family: A Systemic Perspective." In *Living Beyond Loss: Death in the Family,* ed. F. Walsh and M. McGoldrick. New York: Norton.

Webb, M. (1997). *The Good Death: The New American Search to Reshape the End of Life.* New York: Bantam Books.

Other Resource

Frederick, C. J. (2001). "Death and Dying." *Microsoft Encarta Online Encyclopedia, 2001.* Available from http://encarta.msn.com.

KATHLEEN R. GILBERT

DECISION MAKING

Decision making is a term used to describe the process by which families make choices, determine judgments, and come to conclusions that guide behaviors. That the process is called family decision-making implies that it requires more than one member's input and agreement (Scanzoni and Polonko 1980). The family decision-making process is a communication activity—it rests on the making and expression of meaning. The communication may be explicit (as when families sit down and discuss a prospective decision) or implicit (as when families choose an option based on their past decisions or some other unspoken rationale). Families are confronted with a myriad of decisions, including the purchase of products, the selection of educational practices, the choice of recreational activities, the use of disciplinary practices, and the deployment of limited resources. Decision making is an unavoidable, daily process.

Family decision making is a process that can be filled with tension, extremely pleasant and rewarding, both, or somewhere in between. In the decision-making process, families can address the differences among members (Galvin and Brommel 2000) and negotiate their needs for closeness and independence (Baxter and Montgomery 1996). Further, as James Atkinson and Timothy Stephen (1990) observed, decision making is inextricably bound to values. In decision making "values are communicated within the family group and [they] will become part of a family's assumptive foundation as its members coordinate future action" (Atkinson and Stephen, p. 5). Thus, family decision-making spans many family goals and practices.

Family Decision-Making Processes

Decisions within families may be classified into several types: instrumental, affective, social, economic, and technical. Instrumental decisions are those which rest on functional issues such as providing money, shelter, and food for the family members (Epstein, Bishop, and Baldwin 1982). Affective decisions deal with choices related to feelings and emotions. Decisions such as whether to get married are affective. Social decisions (Noller and Fitzpatrick 1993) are those related to the values, roles, and goals of the family, such as decisions about whether one parent will stay at home while the children are preschool age. Economic decisions focus on choices about using and gathering family resources. Whether an eighteen-year-old child should get a job and contribute to the family income is an economic decision. Technical decisions relate to all the subdecisions that have to be made to carry out a main decision. For instance, if a family decides that one member will quit work and go to college, then a variety of technical decisions must be made to enact that decision (Noller and Fitzpatrick 1993).

Families use a variety of processes for actually reaching a decision. Many families have a habitual process that they use regularly whenever they need to make a decision. Other families vary in the way they approach decision making depending on the type of decision, their mood, and their stage of development. Researchers often discuss five possible processes that families use in reaching decisions. These include appeals to authority and status, rules, values, use of discussion and consensus, and de facto decisions.

Authority and Status

This approach allows family decisions to occur as a result of the will of the person in the family with the most status and/or authority. For example, in some traditional families, decision making may be vested in the father. The other members of the family are thus guided by what he says is right. If a family is discussing where they should go for a family summer vacation, for instance, and the father decides that a camping trip is the best decision, the rest of the family concurs because of his authority. This method of decision making works for a family as long as all the members agree about who has the most status and authority. If the family members do not agree that the father has the authority to make decisions, they may engage in serious conflict rather than allowing the father to make a decision for them.

Further, the authority approach may be more complex than the previous discussion implies. Many families may have divided family decision-making domains. In so doing, they designate certain types of decisions as the province of one member and other types that belong to other family members. For example, many households divide the labor and then delegate authority based on who is in charge of a particular area. If a husband is in charge of maintaining the family finances, he may have authority over major buying decisions. However, he may have no authority over issues concerning the children; for instance, the decision about bedtimes might be out of his jurisdiction. In this process, everyone in the family might have authority over some decision-making concerns.

Some families grant authority and status to members based on expertise. Thus, if an adolescent knows a great deal about computers and the Internet or about automobiles, the adolescent may be the one who decides about major expenditures such as what type of computer to buy for the family, what Internet provider to use, or which car to purchase.

Finally, the complexity involved in understanding decision making by authority is revealed in examining the communication process involved in making decisions. As Kay Palan and Robert Wilkes (1997) observe, the interactions between adolescents and parents often influence the decision outcome even though a parent may seem to make the final decision. Palan and Wilkes found that teenagers used a wide variety of strategies that allowed them to influence decisions in their families.

Rules

Many families use rules to ease decision making. Rules in general create structures that help families to function. Some specific rules may provide guidance for decisions about dividing family resources. For instance, if a family is confronted with an inheritance without specific assignments, as in a will that states generally that the possessions should be divided among the children, a system of rules can be useful in dividing the estate. A system of rules for this situation could be as follows: heirs would alternate in choosing something they wished to keep. If someone else wanted what had been chosen they could offer to trade, but the first person has the right of refusal. This process guides decision making by providing a system to which all of the family agrees. Sometimes parents use rules like this when they instruct one child to divide a treat like a pie and then allow the second child first choice among those portions.

Rules may also structure decision-making discussions. For example, some families maintain rules about equal participation in a decision-making conversation. They will not come to a decision until all family members involved have an approximately equal say about the topic. Some families have a rule specifying that each member of the family has to say something before a decision can be reached. Other families have rules setting time limits for the process and a decision has to be reached when the time has lapsed.

Values

Decisions based on values are exercised in families that have strongly articulated principles. These principles may be explicitly stated or indirectly communicated, perhaps through family stories or other meaning-making practices. Some of these principles may derive from organized religion, a commitment to social justice, racial equality, or some other cherished value. For example, when parents are deciding about schooling for their children, some may choose religious education or may choose to homeschool, based on a dedication to their values. Additionally, families may choose to give volunteer time, donate money, or take in foster children as a result of their value system.

Discussion and Consensus

Decisions founded in discussion and consensus are related to decisions based on values. Families that use discussion and consensus as their mode of reaching a decision are committed to the principle of democratic process. It is important to these families that all members have a voice and that members feel that they contributed to the eventual decision. Families utilizing discussion and consensus often convene family meetings to discuss a potential decision. If a family wanted to adopt this process, they would call a family meeting and let everyone have a voice in discussing the decision to be made. The process of consensus necessitates that the family would continue discussing the decision until all the members were satisfied with the eventual decision.

A family follows this decision-making process when they talk about their separate positions on a decision and continue talking until they reach an acceptable compromise. This type of decision-making process works best when the family is comfortable with power sharing.

De Facto

This type of decision occurs when the family fails to actively engage in a specific process, and the decision gets made by default. For example, when Todd and Ellen want to buy a new car, they discuss the decision. They find a car at a price they can afford, but they cannot absolutely agree to buy it. While they wait, trying to decide about the purchase, the car is sold, and they cannot find another that suits them at the right price. In another example, Roberto is trying to decide about taking a new job and moving his family to another state. He is unsure about whether this is a good idea, both personally and professionally. Further, he receives conflicting input from his family about the decision. If he lets the deadline pass for acting on the job offer, the decision is, in effect, made without the family actually stating that they have decided not to move. De facto decisions allow family members to escape responsibility for the repercussions of a decision since no one actively supports the course of action taken.

Conclusion

Some families discuss their processes and have an overt, preferred mode for decision making. Other families simply fall into one or another process without thinking about it much. Additionally, many families may say they prefer to reach a decision through a discussion of all the members, yet the power relations in the family are such that discussion only confirms what the father, for example, wants as the decision. In this manner, the family may preserve an illusion of openness while actually using an authoritarian process for coming to a decision. Barbara J. Risman and Danette Johnson-Summerford (2001) talk about *manifest power* and *latent power*. Manifest power is present in decision making by authority because it involves enforcing one's will against others. Latent power, sometimes called unobtrusive power, exists when the "needs and wishes of the more powerful are anticipated and met" (p. 230). When families profess a democratic style of decision making, but really acquiesce to the will of an authority figure, latent power is being exercised. Families make countless decisions using power relations and these various processes: authority, rules, values, discussion, and de facto. Often the process engaged in by the family reveals more about them and affects them more profoundly than the outcome.

See also: COMMUNICATION: COUPLE RELATIONSHIPS; COMMUNICATION: FAMILY RELATIONSHIPS; CONFLICT: COUPLE RELATIONSHIPS; CONFLICT: FAMILY RELATIONSHIPS; CONFLICT: PARENT-CHILD RELATIONSHIPS; EQUITY; FAMILY BUSINESS; FAMILY LIFE EDUCATION; HEALTH AND FAMILIES; HOSPICE; NAGGING AND COMPLAINING; POWER: FAMILY RELATIONSHIPS; POWER: MARITAL RELATIONSHIPS; PROBLEM SOLVING; RESOURCE MANAGEMENT; SEXUAL COMMUNICATION: COUPLE RELATIONSHIPS

Bibliography

Atkinson, J., and Stephen, T. (1990). "Reconceptualizing Family Decision-Making: A Model of the Role of Outside Influences." Paper presented at the annual meeting of the Speech Communication Association, Chicago, IL.

Baxter, L. A., and Montgomery, B. M. (1996). *Relating: Dialogues and Dialectics*. New York: Guilford Press.

Epstein, N. B.; Bishop, D. S.; and Baldwin, L. M. (1982). "McMaster Model of Family Functioning." In *Normal Family Processes*, ed. F. Walsh. New York: Guilford Press.

Galvin, K. M., and Brommel, B. J. (2000). *Family Communication: Cohesion and Change*, 5th edition. New York: Longman.

Noller, P., and Fitzpatrick, M. A. (1993). *Communication in Family Relationships*. Englewood Cliffs, NJ: Prentice-Hall.

Palan, K. M., and Wilkes, R. E. (1997). "Adolescent-Parent Interaction in Family Decision Making." *Journal of Consumer Research* 24:159–169.

Risman, B. J., and Johnson-Summerford, D. (2001). "Doing it Fairly: A Study of Post-Gender Marriages." In *Men and Masculinity*, ed. T. F. Cohen. Belmont, CA: Wadsworth.

Scanzoni, J., and Polonko, K. (1980). "A Conceptual Approach to Explicit Marital Negotiation." *Journal of Marriage and the Family* 42:31–44.

LYNN H. TURNER

DEMENTIA

Dementia (from the Latin *de mens*—from the mind) is not a specific disease itself, but rather a group of psychological and behavioral symptoms associated with a variety of diseases and conditions that affect the brain (Rabins, Lyketsos, and Steele 1999). Generally, dementia is characterized as the loss or impairment of mental abilities. With dementia, these cognitive losses (e.g., in reasoning, memory, and thinking) are severe enough to interfere with a person's daily life. Additionally, such losses are noticeable in a person who is awake and alert—the term *dementia* does not apply to cognitive problems caused by drowsiness, intoxication or simple inattention (American Psychiatric Association 1994).

Although often associated with later life, the symptoms of dementia can affect people of any age. Before age sixty-five, however, the incidence of dementia is low—affecting one-half to 1 percent of the population (Rabins et al. 1999). As people get older, the risk of dementia rises. While variation in measurement across countries makes it difficult to determine the world-wide prevalence of dementia, it is estimated that dementia affects less than 10 percent of the sixty-five-and-over population globally (Ikels 1998). In the United States, approximately 5 to 8 percent of people over the age of sixty-five suffer from dementia (Tinker 2000). For the oldest old (age seventy-five and over), the risk of dementia is much greater. Approximately 18 to 20 percent of those over the age of seventy-five have dementia and between 35 to 40 percent of people eighty-five years of age or older are affected (Ikels 1998; Rabins et al. 1999; Tinker 2000).

Signs and Symptoms

As a diagnostic category, dementia is comprised of several symptoms of which the most notable is memory loss. Additional symptoms include impairment of judgment (including social appropriateness), abstract reasoning, sense of time, speech and communication, and physical coordination. Changes in emotional responses may also be seen (American Psychiatric Association 1994). Since dementia results from many different diseases, an individual's symptoms may progress at varying rates and in different ways. Additionally, losses in dementia can be uneven, with one ability (e.g., comprehension) being lost before another (e.g., reading) (Rabins et al. 1999).

In the early stages of dementia, it may be hard to distinguish "normal" behavior (such as forgetfulness) from pathological (or illness based) changes. Since a person rarely uses their full capacities for daily functioning, a person in the early stages of dementia may be able to compensate for some of their losses by developing a variety of coping strategies (Mace and Rabins 1999). While some of these strategies (e.g., leaving oneself notes) can be helpful for a while, others may lead to additional behavioral and psychological symptoms that can add to the person's confusion and pose significant challenges for their caregivers.

An example of this may be seen in regard to impairments in a person's emotional responses. Often such changes are characterized by a lack of emotional involvement. On the other hand, persons with dementia might also demonstrate heightened emotional responses. Such reactions, where a person may become excessively upset or combative over something they might have earlier perceived as trivial, are referred to as *catastrophic reactions* (Mace and Rabins 1999). Sometimes catastrophic reactions can be confused with obstinacy when they are really a response to too much stimulation. A person may cry or even strike out to cover up their confusion or frustration. Such reactions can be particularly trying for caregivers. Recognizing and removing the triggers for such outbursts (e.g., by removing an offending noise or breaking down a confusing task into simpler steps) may help to reduce their occurrence.

Another example of behavioral symptoms may be seen in the strategies used for communication.

—397—

Two distinct communication challenges for persons with dementia are making themselves understood and understanding others. With regard to being understood, common communication issues include word substitution; incomplete or incoherent thoughts; making up information to fill in the gaps (*confabulation*); and frequent repetition of a response (*perseveration*). In regard to understanding others, it is important to note that reading and understanding are not the same skill. Thus, a person may be able to read words but not understand the content. Also, persons with dementia may only catch part of what is being said, and thus fill in (often inaccurately) the rest on their own. This can lead to confusion and frustration for all involved (Small, Geldart, and Gutman 2000).

Types and Causes of Dementia

There are close to 100 different diseases associated with the clinical symptoms of dementia. While the causes of some are known (e.g., traumatic injury, stroke, brain tumors, infection, vitamin deficiencies, and nervous system toxicity from substances such as alcohol, cocaine, opiates, marijuana, inhalants, and heavy metals), the causes of many dementia producing diseases are still being sought. Ongoing research continues to advance our understanding of these disorders. This is particularly true of the most common dementia producing disorder, *Alzheimer's disease,* which accounts for approximately 50 to 70 percent of all cases of dementia in old age (or about 3–5% of the U.S. population over the age of 65) (Rabins et al. 1999). First described in 1907, Alzheimer's disease is a degenerative brain disorder characterized by amyloid plaques and neurofibrillary tangles in the brain. Early stages of Alzheimer's disease include memory problems, followed by impairments in language and the ability to do daily tasks. In later stages, impairments in memory, communication, and physical ability become quite severe. While some progress has been made in slowing memory losses in the early stages of Alzheimer's disease, treatments to prevent or cure the disease are not yet available (National Institute on Aging and National Institute on Health 1999).

Another leading cause of dementia, *cerebrovascular disease,* is associated with vascular dementia (also referred to as *multi-infarct dementia*) (Ringholz 2000). Sometimes mistaken for Alzheimer's disease, vascular dementia may appear to have a more sudden or step-wise onset than Alzheimer's disease. Also, in contrast to Alzheimer's disease and most of the other dementia-producing diseases discussed here, the progression of vascular dementia may be slowed or stopped by addressing the underlying cause of the damage (e.g., strokes or other brain damage due to cerebrovascular disease) (Rabins et al. 1999; Ringholz 2000).

Also often mistaken for Alzheimer's disease, *Lewy body disease* is receiving increased attention as a significant cause of dementia in later life (Brown 1999). First described as a distinct disorder in the mid-1990s, Lewy body disease is an irreversible degenerative disorder associated with protein deposits in the brain called *Lewy bodies.* Symptoms vary depending on where the deposits are located, but typically include problems with motor coordination similar to those seen in *Parkinson's disease* (McKeith and Burn 2000). In early stages, forgetfulness, walking instability, and depression may be seen. In the middle stages, cognitive impairments seem to fluctuate but become more frequent at night. The final stage is characterized by rapid cognitive decline, delusions, and hallucinations.

In addition to the most widely known disorders described above, there are a number of less common dementia producing diseases. For example, *frontotemporal degeneration* is a group of dementia-producing disorders in which there is degeneration in the frontal and temporal lobes of the brain. Frontotemporal degeneration has been known by a number of different names, including *frontal lobe dementia* and *Pick's disease.* Frontotemporal degeneration usually begins with changes in personality and behaviors such as the ability to follow social rules and think abstractly. Prevalence of frontotemporal dementia is thought to be fairly low (up to 3% of all patients with dementia). Since it is associated with an earlier onset (around age fifty-four), it may account for closer to 10 percent of those who die with dementia before age seventy (Rabins et al. 1999).

Huntington's disease (formerly known as *Huntington's Chorea*), is a rare, inherited degenerative disorder which can produce slurred speech and problems with physical movement in addition to the progressive symptoms of dementia. When the gene for Huntington's disease is inherited, there is almost certain that the disease will occur. Onset of the disease is variable, ranging from age two to age seventy, although it is mostly a disease of adulthood (average onset is in the late thirties to forties). Due to the physical disturbances, early stages of Huntington's disease may be mistaken for alcoholism (Rabins et al. 1999; Siemers 2001).

Prion dementias represent an even more rare group of diseases. Known as *spongiform encephalopathy* because of the characteristic degeneration of the neurons and a spongy appearance of the brain's gray matter, prion dementia was first described in 1921. Although *Bovine Spongiform Encephalopathy* (BSE), also known as "mad cow disease," is the most widely known form of the disease, two additional forms of spongiform encephalopathy (*Creutzfeld-Jakob disease* and *Gerstman-Straussler-Scheinker syndrome*) are associated with dementia in humans. With spongiform encephalopathy, the progression of symptoms is rapid and change can occur over weeks. Prion dementia is very rare—literally one in a million (Nguyen and Rickman 1997).

In addition to the disorders described above, several forms of dementia have been associated with outside agents. Some involve exposure to toxins such as alcohol or heavy metals (e.g., lead, arsenic, or mercury). Others are associated with infectious agents such as syphilis and *human immunodeficiency virus* (HIV). The growing body of research on HIV/AIDS (*acquired immunodeficiency syndrome*) suggests that AIDS dementia complex (also known as *HIV-associated dementia*) may affect up to 60 percent of patients with AIDS before their death (Brew 1999; Rabins et. al 1999).

Diagnosing Dementia

Diagnosing the specific diseases that cause dementia can be difficult because of the number of potential causes, overlapping symptoms, and current technological limitations. Many diseases can not yet be definitively diagnosed without an autopsy. Declining abilities of the patient, and fear of what might lie ahead may also delay diagnosis. Many other highly treatable disorders (e.g., depression, malnutrition, drug reactions, or thyroid problems), however, can mimic the symptoms of dementia. Thus, a complete and thorough evaluation is important in order to understand the nature of a person's illness; whether the condition can be treated and or reversed; the extent of the impairment; the areas in which a person may still function successfully; whether the person has other health problems that need treatment; the social and psychological needs and resources of the patient and family; and the changes which might be expected in the future (Mace and Rabins 1999).

Impact of Dementia

Dementia poses considerable medical, social, and economic concerns as it impacts individuals, families, and health-care systems throughout the world (National Institute on Aging and National Institutes of Health 1999; O'Shea and O'Reilly 2000). Not surprisingly, increasing attention and resources have been directed toward the medical aspects of dementia—with the goal of better understanding the various causes, treatments, and possible cures for the diseases that produce dementia's debilitating symptoms.

Greater attention is being directed as well toward the concerns of families of persons with dementia. Previously known as the "hidden victims," family caregivers gained considerable attention throughout the 1980s and 1990s. With the majority of persons with dementia being cared for in the community, it has been suggested that the coping mechanisms and resources of families may be severely tested (Dunkin and Anderson-Hanley 1998; O'Shea and O'Reilly 2000). During the prolonged care period characteristic of Alzheimer's disease and other demential conditions, caregivers face the potential for social isolation; financial drain; and physical duress (Clyburn et al. 2000). Women are particularly vulnerable, as they make up the majority of care providers (Gwyther 2000).

With the development and expansion of programs including support groups, respite care, adult day care, and a growing number of specialized care facilities, assistance for families is increasingly available. Use of such assistance, however, varies widely depending upon availability, cost, quality, and simply knowing that these resources exist. Family expectations and guilt can also play a role in their use, as do cultural attitudes about both dementia and caregiving obligations (Ikels 1998; Yamamoto-Mitani et al. 2000). Additionally, the use of such services does not necessarily alleviate the strains of caregiving. The decision to use outside services can pose its own challenges, and, especially in the case of moving a person with dementia into a care facility, the decision-making process is often a stressful and contentious one. Even after institutionalization, much of the family's experience of caregiving burden may remain (Levesque, Ducharme, and LaChance 2000).

In addition to the medical and caregiving aspects of dementia, new interest is being directed toward the social needs of persons with dementia. Some advancements have focused on developing supportive environments for persons with dementia (Day, Carreon, and Stump 2000). Others have focused on behavior management (Kaplan and Hoffman 1998) and modes of effective communication and interpersonal interaction (Feil 1993; Zgola 1999). Very little attention, however, has focused on understanding the personal and emotional experiences of having dementia. One exception is Diana Friel McGowin's (1993) account of her experiences with Alzheimer's disease. Another is the call to mental health professionals for person-centered therapies for persons with dementia (Cheston and Bender 1999).

As the population of older adults—and thus the number of persons affected by dementia—increases, it is expected that the subjective experiences of persons with dementia will garner even greater interest. Overall, our knowledge and understanding of the diseases that produce dementia is expanding at a rapid rate. To those affected by dementia, however, these advances can not come soon enough.

See also: ACQUIRED IMMUNODEFICIENCY SYNDROME (AIDS); ALZHEIMER'S DISEASE; CAREGIVING: FORMAL; CAREGIVING: INFORMAL; CHRONIC ILLNESS; DISABILITIES; ELDER ABUSE; ELDERS; HEALTH AND FAMILIES; HOSPICE; RESPITE CARE: ADULT

Bibliography

American Psychiatric Association (1994). *Diagnostic and Statistical Manual of Mental Disorders,* 4th edition. Washington, DC: American Psychiatric Association.

Brew, B. (1999). "AIDS Dementia Complex." *Neurologic Clinics* 17(4):861–881.

Brown, D. F. (1999). "Lewy Body Dementia." *Annals of Medicine* 31(3):188–196.

Cheston, R., and Bender, M. (1999). *Understanding Dementia: The Man with the Worried Eyes.* Philadelphia: Jessica Kingsley.

Clyburn, L.; Stones, M.; Hadjistavropoulos, T.; and Tuokko, H. (2000). "Predicting Caregiver Burden and Depression in Alzheimer's Disease." *Journal of Gerontology: Social Sciences* 55B(1):S2–13.

Day, K.; Carreon, D.; and Stump, C. (2000). "The Therapeutic Design of Environments for People with Dementia: A Review of the Empirical Literature." *The Gerontologist* 40(4):397–416.

Dunkin, J., and Anderson-Hanley, C. (1998). "Dementia Caregiving Burden: A Review of the Literature and Guidelines for Assessment and Intervention." *Neurology* 51(1):S53–S60.

Feil, N. (1993). *The Validation Breakthrough: Simple Techniques for Communicating with People with "Alzheimer's-Type Dementia."* Baltimore, MD: Health Professions.

Gwyther, L. (2000). "Family Issues in Dementia: Finding a New Normal." *Neurologic Clinics* 18(4):993–1010.

Ikels, C. (1998). "The Experience of Dementia in China." *Culture, Medicine and Psychiatry* 22(4):257–283.

Kaplan, M., and Hoffman, S., eds. (1998). *Behaviors in Dementia: Best Practices for Successful Management.* Baltimore, MD: Health Professions Press.

Levesque, L.; Ducharme, F.; and Lachance, L. (2000). "A One-Year Follow-Up Study of Family Caregivers of Institutionalized Elders with Dementia." *American Journal of Alzheimer's Disease* 15(4):229–238.

Mace, N., and Rabins, P. (1999). *The 36-Hour Day: A Family Guide to Caring for Persons with Alzheimer's Disease, Related Dementing Illness and Memory Loss in Later Life,* 3rd edition. Baltimore, MD: Johns Hopkins University Press.

McGowin, D. F. (1993). *Living in the Labyrinth: A Personal Journey through the Maze of Alzheimer's.* New York: Delacorte.

McKeith, I., and Burn, D. (2000). "Spectrum of Parkinson's Disease, Parkinson's Dementia, and Lewy Body Dementia." *Neurologic Clinics* 18(4):865–883.

National Institute on Aging, and National Institute on Health (1999). *Progress Report on Alzheimer's Disease, 1999.* Silver Spring, MD: Alzheimer's Disease Education and Referral Center.

Nguyen, S., and Rickman, L. (1997). "Understanding Creutzfeldt-Jakob Disease." *Journal of Gerontological Nursing* 23(11):22–27.

O'Shea, E., and O'Reilly, S. (2000). "The Economic and Social Costs of Dementia in Ireland." *International Journal of Geriatric Psychiatry* 15:208–218.

Rabins, P.; Lyketsos, C.; and Steele, C. (1999). *Practical Dementia Care.* New York: Oxford University Press.

Ringholz, G. (2000). "Diagnosis and Treatment of Vascular Dementia." *Topics in Stroke Rehabilitation* 7(3):38–46.

Siemers, E. (2001). "Huntington Disease." *Archives of Neurology* 58(2):308–310.

Small, J.; Geldart, K.; and Gutman, G. (2000). "Communication between Individuals with Dementia and their Caregivers During Activities of Daily Living." *American Journal of Alzheimer's Disease and Other Dementias* 15(5):200–209.

Tinker, A. (2000). "Population Aspects of the Dementias." *International Journal of Geriatric Psychiatry* 15:753–757.

Yamamoto-Mitani, N.; Tamura, M.; Deguchi, Y.; Ito, K.; and Sugishita, C. (2000). "The Attitudes of Japanese Family Caregivers Toward the Elderly with Dementia." *International Journal of Nursing Studies* 37:415–417.

Zgola, J. (1999). *Care that Works: A Relationship Approach to Persons with Dementia.* Baltimore, MD: Johns Hopkins University Press.

RONA J. KARASIK

DENMARK

See GERMANY; GREENLAND; SCANDINAVIA

DEPRESSION

ADULTS *Ian H. Gotlib, Karen L. Kasch*

CHILDREN AND ADOLESCENTS *Judith Semon Dubas, Anne C. Petersen*

ADULTS

Major depression is a syndrome that affects 15 to 20 percent of the population. It is among the most prevalent of all psychiatric disorders. Moreover, twice as many women than men comprise the 15 to 20 percent of the population who will experience a clinically significant episode of depression at some point in their lives. *Major Depressive Disorder,* the diagnostic label for a clinically significant episode of depression, is characterized by at least a two-week period of persistent sad mood or a loss of interest or pleasure in daily activities, and four or more additional symptoms, such as marked changes in weight or appetite, sleep disturbance, restlessness or slowing of thoughts and movements, fatigue, feelings of guilt or worthlessness, concentration difficulties, and thoughts of suicide. Although there are clearly difficulties in attempting to study depression in different cultures (Tsai and Chentsova-Dutton 2002), the prevalence of depression varies widely across the world. In general, Asian countries, such as Japan and Taiwan, have the lowest documented lifetime prevalence rates of depression (both approximately 1.5%); poorer countries like Chile have the highest rates (27%); the United States and other Western countries have intermediate lifetime prevalence rates of depression (Tsai and Chentsova-Dutton 2002). It is interesting to note that studies have shown that Mexicans born in Mexico have lower rates of depression, while those born in the United States have rates the same as non-Hispanic whites (Golding, Karno, and Rutter 1990; Golding and Burnam 1990). In general, the more acculturated Mexican-Americans are, the less likely they are to experience depression. However, those with more acculturative stress (e.g., coping with a move from being high status in Mexico to being lower status in the United States) tend to experience more depression than those with less acculturative stress (Hovey 2000).

The relatively high rates of depression have led the World Health Organization Global Burden of Disease Study to rank this disorder as the single most burdensome disease in the world in terms of total disability-adjusted life years (Murray and Lopez 1996). More importantly, depression not only has a high prevalence rate, but also has a high rate of recurrence. Over 75 percent of depressed patients have more than one depressive episode (Boland and Keller 2002), often developing a relapse of depression within two years of recovery from a depressive episode. This high recurrence rate in depression suggests that there are specific factors that increase people's risk for developing repeated episodes of this disorder. In attempting to understand this elevated risk for depression, investigators have examined genetic and biological factors, and psychological and environmental characteristics, that may lead individuals to experience depressive episodes.

Some forms of depression have a strong genetic influence. Depression has been shown to run in biological families; indeed, having a biological

Although there is no conclusive evidence that a specific, single gene for depression exists, vulnerability to depression seems to be inherited. An identical twin with a depressed twin is 67 percent more likely to be depressed.
DENNIS DEGNAN/CORBIS

relative with a history of depression increases a person's risk for developing an episode of depression. Furthermore, twin research has consistently and reliably demonstrated that major depression is a heritable condition (e.g., Kendler and Aggen 2001). Research using broad definitions of depression suggests that men and women have different heritabilities for depression, with genetic factors proving more etiologically important for women than for men (Kendler and Aggen 2001). Gaining a better understanding of this difference in heritabilities may help to elucidate the reasons underlying the higher rates of depression in women than in men.

Although genetic factors are important, they do not fully explain the etiology of depression. For example, there are sets of identical (monozygotic) twins in which one is affected with depression and the other never becomes depressed. Because monozygotic twins have identical genetic makeups, these differences must be due to factors that the twins do not share. Some of these factors are biological (but not genetic). There is abundant evidence that biology can affect mood. For example, thyroid problems can often mimic depression and cause weight changes, sad mood, and other symptoms of depression. Similarly, investigators have demonstrated some drugs or medications (e.g., reserpine) can induce a depression-like syndrome, whereas other medications (e.g., antidepressants) are effective in alleviating depressed mood. These

medications generally affect the neurotransmitters implicated in depression. Biological factors can also affect the risk for depression. For instance, obstetrical complications seem to increase the risk of developing depression later in life (Fan and Eaton 2000; Preti et al. 2000). In addition, because in virtually every culture women are at greater risk for depression than are men (cf. Nolen-Hoeksema 1990), it is likely that something about the biology of being female, such as hormonal functioning, may make depression more likely to occur.

There are also psychosocial influences in the development of depression. Some research suggests, for example, that a childhood history of abuse or neglect can put an adult at greater risk for depression (e.g., Bifulco, Brown, and Adler 1991). Moreover, there is evidence that a history of abuse may be related to suicidal thoughts and behavior both in patients and nonpatients, above and beyond the effects of having a diagnosis of depression (Read et al. 2001; Molnar, Berkman, and Buka 2001). Furthermore, social support (e.g., from friends or family) can mitigate depression, whereas a lack of support may increase the severity or length of a depressive episode (George et al. 1989; Goering, Lancee, and Freeman 1992). Finally, there appears to be a robust link between stressful life events (e.g., divorce, bankruptcy) and the onset of major depression, suggesting that such events may play a role in the etiology of some major depressive episodes (Stueve, Dohrenwend, and Skodol 1998). Recent studies have examined the impact of befriending as an intervention for women with chronic depression, and have found that the addition of such social support had a positive impact on the depression, further bolstering the importance of social support in depression (Harris, Brown, and Robinson 1999).

Temperamental factors have been found to increase people's risk for developing depression. For instance, there is a great deal of evidence linking neuroticism to depression (e.g., Duggan et al. 1995; Kendler et al. 1993). In fact, high levels of neuroticism have been found not only to be associated with current depression, but also to persist in people following recovery from their depressions. Some investigators have drawn on these data to suggest that neuroticism may be present prior to the first onset of depression, and may represent a vulnerability marker or risk factor for developing depression (Duggan et al. 1995).

Finally, there may be specific patterns of thinking that elevate people's risk for the development of depression. Research has demonstrated that certain cognitions or cognitive styles are strongly related to depression. For example, according to the reformulated *learned helplessness model* (Abramson, Seligman, and Teasdale 1978), people who believe that negative events result from stable, global, and internal factors are more likely to become depressed than are individuals who do not hold these views. For instance, if a person believes that he failed a math test because he is bad at math, rather than attributing the failure to the difficulty of the test or his having had a bad day, then he is attributing his failure to an internal factor. If he then says that he is bad at school more generally and has always been, then he is making stable and global attributions as well, putting him, according to this model, at increased risk for becoming depressed. Similarly, Aaron Beck (1976) has posited that individuals who attend to negative stimuli more readily than to positive stimuli, and who have dysfunctional beliefs about loss and failure (e.g. that others never fail, or that they should never fail), are also likely to become depressed. Although these negative cognitive styles may be longstanding and appear to be a part of someone's personality, it is still unclear whether these cognitive patterns cause depression, are a consequence of depression, or have a more complex relationship to this disorder (Gotlib and Abramson 1999).

Depression and Interpersonal Relationships

Depression in adults can often have a negative impact on interpersonal relationships. Depressed people evaluate their social skills negatively, reporting that they do not enjoy, and are not very adept at, socializing (Davis 1982; Lewinsohn et al. 1980). Independent observers have documented that depressed people have fewer social skills than nondepressed individuals (Segrin 2000). The relationships of depressed people are often characterized by low intimacy, poor communication, and withdrawal, characteristics that may lead to rejections and disappointments. Indeed, depression in individuals can lead others around them to feel irritability, anger, and fatigue; depressed people have been found to exhibit a high level of dependency on others, or to withdraw from others, both of which can put a strain on interpersonal relationships.

Late-twentieth-century research indicates that depression also adversely affects the quality of relationships with spouses and children. For example, investigators have found the interactions of married couples in which one spouse is depressed to be characterized by less cooperation and more angry exchanges than is the case among couples in which neither spouse is depressed (Davila 2001; Goldman and Haaga 1995). Not surprisingly, depression in marriage has been shown to be strongly associated with distress and disruptions in marital relationships; indeed, the rate of divorce among individuals who have experienced clinical depression is significantly higher than is the case among nondepressed individuals (e.g., Wade and Cairney 2000).

Given the high level of marital distress and discord associated with depression, it is not surprising to learn that the children of depressed parents have themselves been found to exhibit greater emotional and somatic symptomatology, and to have more school, behavioral, and social problems, than have children of nondepressed parents. Children of depressed parents have also been found to be at elevated risk for developing psychopathology (see Gotlib and Goodman 1999, for a review of these literatures). Several lines of research have emerged trying to understand the mechanisms underlying the elevated levels of psychopathology among children of depressed parents (Goodman and Gotlib 1999). Whereas a number of investigators have examined the genetic transmission of risk for depression from parent to child (e.g., Wallace, Schneider, and McGuffin 2002), other researchers have focused on aspects of the relationships between depressed parents and their children. For example, when they are depressed, adults are less effective at disciplining their children and are more likely to exhibit frustration and anger or withdraw and behave in a rejecting manner when they cannot achieve their desired outcomes with their children. Children of depressed parents may also model their parent's behavior and either act out and exhibit anger, or become isolated and withdrawn. They may feel unloved and find that they only get attention when they misbehave, which will tend to increase the amount of misbehavior. Depressed parents may come to rely to heavily on their children to perform tasks that they have become unable to carry out. Depressed parents may also rely too heavily on their children for emotional support when their marital relationship becomes strained. In this context, a depressed parent may share information that a child is unable to handle emotionally, such as thoughts of suicide or hopelessness.

Treatment of Depression

Depression is a treatable disorder. Because there are a variety of methods for treating depression, people who experience depression have several choices with respect to the type of treatment they choose to undertake. Treatments that focus on the depressed individual alone include pharmacotherapy (e.g., antidepressant medication) and psychotherapy (e.g., cognitive therapy, behavior therapy, or social skills training). Depressed people who are married may choose from these individual approaches to treatment, or they may undertake marital or family therapy for depression. Regardless of which form of treatment a depressed person chooses, it is important that the treatment has been demonstrated empirically to be effective in reducing depressive symptoms.

Although it may seem counterintuitive to treat marital problems in order to alleviate depression, there is evidence in support of the efficacy of this type of treatment, particularly in distressed marriages. Indeed, there are several different forms of marital and family therapy that are effective in the treatment of depression. For example, in maritally distressed couples, marital therapy has been found to be effective in treating depression in the context of marriage. K. Daniel O'Leary, Lawrence Riso, and Steven Beach (1990) asked wives in distressed marriages to identify which came first, the marital problems or their depression. In couples who reported that marital discord preceded the onset of depression, the wives reported that the marital distress was an important cause of their depression. This raised the possibility that marital therapy would be a way of targeting the perceived causes for depression. In fact, studies have demonstrated that marital therapy is as effective as individual cognitive-behavioral therapy in alleviating depressive symptoms of spouses in distressed marriages. Moreover, patients receiving marital therapy have been found to report higher marital satisfaction than do patients receiving cognitive-behavior therapy (Jacobson et al. 1991; O'Leary and Beach 1990). Steven Beach, Mark Whisman, and K.

Daniel O'Leary (1994) suggest that behavioral marital therapy is an effective intervention for a specific subgroup of married depressed patients.

Interpersonal therapy (IPT) for depression usually takes approximately twelve weeks and also focuses on the current marital distress. Although IPT bears some relationship to psychodynamic treatments that preceded it, its focus is different. Instead of dealing with past conflicts and unconscious material, this treatment emphasizes current problems and concerns. This form of treatment was adapted in the late twentieth century to work with geriatric populations by including certain kinds of concrete help in the treatment (e.g., obtaining transportation for the patient to attend sessions), flexibility in the length of sessions, and acknowledging the different life circumstances of older adults that may make some solutions less feasible or desirable (e.g., divorce after a long marriage; see Gotlib and Schraedley 2000 for a review of IPT for depression).

Another form of treatment for depression that has an interpersonal focus is *behavioral family therapy*. Like interpersonal therapy, behavioral treatment focuses on current problems. Behavioral treatment emphasizes concrete and specific behavior changes, along with skills training as needed. Early in the treatment, families in which a member is depressed are educated about depression's symptoms and consequences. The therapist underscores both the legitimacy of the disorder and the importance of treatment compliance, both for the person suffering from depression and for the family. In addition, families are taught better communication skills, including how to compromise, negotiate, manage anger, constructively express feelings, and listen empathically. Families are also provided with problem-solving skills training, and learn to concretely define their goals and generate more solutions to achieve those goals.

Finally, *cognitive-behavioral family therapy* has also been found to be effective in the treatment of depression. As with behavioral treatment, cognitive-behavioral family therapy also offers skills training in communication and problem solving as needed. In addition, the therapist models appropriate behavior: for example, parental discipline as part of skills training in parenting. Here, too, the focus is on current problems and concerns. Although cognitive-behavioral treatment is similar to behavioral therapy in its emphasis on current behavior and training of skills, this form of treatment is based on the notion that people's thoughts about events and actions lead them to make specific attributions about the event or action. This process may lead them to have overly negative expectations of their relationships and interpersonal interactions. Individuals with these negative cognitive schemas are also believed to filter their experience through the lens of their expectations, perceiving more of their interactions as negative than is actually the case. One of the therapist's primary tasks is to help the family identify attributions and the irrational beliefs that underlie them. The therapist demonstrates to the family how these thoughts and beliefs can affect their behavior and the behavior of those with whom they come into contact. Once the therapist has elucidated the relationship between the cognitions and behavior, cognitive restructuring can begin. *Cognitive restructuring* involves the therapist helping the family to understand the irrationality of the original maladaptive cognitions. According to cognitive-behavioral theory, by changing people's attitudes and beliefs, cognitive restructuring leads to behavior change.

Depression and Culture

Depression is a heterogeneous condition that may call for different types of treatment depending on the specific marital context in which the depressed person lives. Depression also occurs, of course, in many different cultural contexts. As with any disorder, depression can interact with culture and values; consequently, treatments need to be culturally sensitive and aware. Moreover, these different values mean that specific treatments or recommendations may be more useful and effective in some groups and, in fact, may even be contraindicated in others. For example, in African-American families, there is generally less of an emphasis on culturally defined gender roles than is the case in Caucasian families. Employment for women from African-American families has been found to be helpful to these women and their families, whereas employment showed fewer benefits for Caucasian women and their families, at least among older adults (Cochran, Brown, and MacGregor 1999). Therefore, clinicians may find that helping African-American women gain access to employment opportunities would be a useful intervention, whereas Caucasian women may receive fewer benefits from such help.

In Asian cultures, in which there is a greater focus on the interdependence of family members and connection with other people within the larger culture, depression may manifest in different ways than in the West and may therefore respond to different types of treatment. Because of Asians' greater cultural emphasis on social connection, what are viewed as symptoms of depression in the West may be interpreted more as interpersonal difficulties in these cultures. In addition, Asians may focus more on somatic difficulties than on emotional symptoms, perhaps in part because they make fewer mind/body distinctions in their culture than do Westerners. Therefore, "depression" in those cultures may be expressed and experienced more through physical than emotional symptoms. This may also be related to the fact that emotional problems are typically viewed as more stigmatizing in Asian cultures than they are in the West. Because of this greater stigma, Western treatments of discussing feelings and troubles are often contraindicated with Asian patients because this may exacerbate emotional pain and the shame, rather than alleviating suffering. Finally, Asians generally experience greater family and social connections and support than do people in Western cultures. This seems to be somewhat protective against depression and rates of depression in Asian countries such as Japan, China, and Taiwan are lower than in the Western world.

Latin/Hispanic cultures also place a greater emphasis on family than do many other Western cultures. Although the social support from family is protective, poverty and lack of resources continue to plague many Latino communities. Latino families living in the United States may find themselves relatively isolated from American culture and opportunities and, consequently, at greater risk for depression and other difficulties. Given the findings that lower acculturation is associated with more depression (e.g., Hovey 2000), it would seem important to aid less assimilated families in accessing resources and finding ways to become acculturated while maintaining their original cultural identity. In addition, it is crucial that clinicians attempt to remove the linguistic, cultural, and practical barriers to treatment faced by many minority populations. Finally, clinicians need to be sufficiently culturally knowledgeable to understand certain symptoms in context. For example, in Puerto Rican culture, dissociative states may be a normal part of spiritual practice, though these states would generally be considered psychopathological in mainstream U.S. culture (Tsai et al. 2001). Clinicians who can recognize culturally normative practices and differentiate them from pathology, and who develop culturally appropriate treatments, will be the most likely to be successful in alleviating their patients' distress.

See also: CHILDREN OF ALCOHOLICS; CHRONIC ILLNESS; DEPRESSION: CHILDREN AND ADOLESCENTS; DEVELOPMENT: SELF; DEVELOPMENTAL PSYCHOPATHOLOGY; GRIEF, LOSS, AND BEREAVEMENT; HEALTH AND FAMILIES; POSTPARTUM DEPRESSION; POWER: MARITAL RELATIONSHIPS; SELF-ESTEEM; STRESS; SUICIDE; THERAPY: COUPLE RELATIONSHIPS

Bibliography

Abramson, L. Y.; Seligman, M. E. P.; and Teasdale, J. D. (1978). "Learned Helplessness in Humans: Critique and Reformulation." *Journal of Abnormal Psychology* 87:49–74.

Beach, S. R. H.; Whisman, M. A.; and O'Leary, K. D. (1994). "Marital Therapy for Depression: Theoretical Foundation, Current Status, and Future Directions." *Behavior Therapy* 25:345–371.

Beck, A. T. (1976). *Cognitive Therapy and the Emotional Disorders.* New York: International Universities Press.

Bifulco, A.; Brown, G. W.; and Adler, Z. (1991). "Early Sexual Abuse and Clinical Depression in Adult Life." *British Journal of Psychiatry* 159:115–122.

Boland, R. J., and Keller, M. B. (2002). "Course and Outcome of Depression." In *Handbook of Depression,* ed. I. H. Gotlib and C. L. Hammen. New York: Guilford Press.

Cochran, D. L.; Brown, D. R.; and MacGregor, K. C. (1999). "Racial Differences in the Multiple Social Roles of Older Women: Implications for Depressive Symptoms." *Gerontologist* 39:465–472.

Davila, J. (2001). "Paths to Unhappiness: The Overlapping Courses of Depression and Romantic Dysfunction." In *Marital and Family Processes in Depression: A Scientific Foundation for Clinical Practice,* ed. S. R. H. Beach. Washington, DC: American Psychological Association.

Davis, S. (1982). "Cognitive Processes in Depression." *Journal of Clinical Psychology* 38:125–129.

Duggan, C.; Sham, P.; Lee, A.; Minne, C.; and Murray, R. (1995). "Neuroticism: A Vulnerability Marker for Depression Evidence from a Family Study." *Journal of Affective Disorders* 35:139–143.

Fan, A. P., and Eaton, W. W. (2000). "The Influence of Perinatal Complications and Early Social Environment on Mental Health and Status Attainment in Adulthood: The Baltimore NCPP Follow-Up, 1960–1994." *British Journal of Psychiatry* 178 (Supplement 40):S78–S83.

George, L. K.; Blazer, D. G.; Hughes, D. C.; and Fowler, N. (1989). "Social Support and the Outcome of Major Depression." *British Journal of Psychiatry* 154:478–485.

Goering, P. N.; Lancee, W. J.; and Freeman, S. J. J. (1992). "Marital Support and Recovery from Depression." *British Journal of Psychiatry* 160:76–82.

Golding J. M., and Burnam M. A. (1990). "Immigration, Stress, and Depressive Symptoms in a Mexican-American Community." *Journal of Nervous and Mental Disease* 178:161–171

Golding J. M.; Karno, M.; and Rutter C. M. (1990). "Symptoms of Major Depression among Mexican-Americans and Non-Hispanic Whites." *American Journal of Psychiatry* 147:861–866.

Goldman, L., and Haaga D. A. F. (1995). "Depression and the Experience and Expression of Anger in Marital and Other Relationships." *Journal of Nervous and Mental Disease* 183:505–509.

Goodman, S. H., and Gotlib, I. H. (1999). "Risk for Psychopathology in the Children of Depressed Mothers: A Developmental Model for Understanding Mechanisms of Transmission." *Psychological Review* 106:458–490.

Gotlib, I. H., and Abramson, L. Y. (1999). "Attributional Theories of Emotion." In *Handbook of Cognition and Emotion,* ed. T. Dalgleish and M. J. Power. Chichester, UK: John Wiley.

Gotlib, I. H., and Goodman, S. H. (1999). "Children of Parents with Depression." In *Developmental Issues in the Clinical Treatment of Children,* ed. W. K. Silverman and T. H. Ollendick. Boston: Allyn and Bacon.

Gotlib, I. H., and Schraedley, P. K. (2000). "Interpersonal Psychotherapy." In *Handbook of Psychological Change: Psychotherapy Processes and Practices for the 21st Century,* ed. C. R. Snyder and R. E. Ingram. New York: Wiley.

Harris, T.; Brown, G. W.; and Robinson, R. (1999). "Befriending as an Intervention for Chronic Depression among Women in an Inner City: 1: Randomised Controlled Trial." *British Journal of Psychiatry* 174:219–224.

Hovey, J. (2000). "Acculturative Stress, Depression, and Suicidal Ideation in Mexican Immigrants." *Cultural Diversity and Ethnic Minority Psychology* 6:134–151.

Jacobsen, N. S.; Dobson, K.; Fruzzetti, A. E.; Schmaling, K. B.; and Salusky, S. (1991). "Marital Therapy as a Treatment for Depression." *Journal of Consulting & Clinical Psychology* 59(4):547–557.

Kendler, K. S., and Aggen, S. H. (2001). "Time, Memory, and the Heritability of Major Depression." *Psychological Medicine* 31:923–928.

Kendler, K. S.; Gardner, C. O.; Neale, M. C.; and Prescott, C. A. (2001). "Genetic Risk Factors for Major Depression in Men and Women: Similar or Different Heritabilities and Same or Partly Distinct Genes?" *Psychological Medicine* 31:605–616.

Kendler, K. S.; Kessler, R. C.; Neale, M. C.; Heath, A. C.; and Eaves, L. J. (1993). "The Prediction of Major Depression in Women: Toward an Integrated Etiologic Model." *American Journal of Psychiatry* 150:1139–1148.

Lewinsohn, P. M.; Mischel, W.; Chaplin, W.; and Barton, R. (1980). "Social Competence and Depression: Tthe Role of Illusory Self-Perceptions." *Journal of Abnormal Psychology* 89:203–212.

Molnar, B. E.; Berkman, L. F.; and Buka, S. L. (2001). "Psychopathology, Childhood Sexual Abuse and Other Childhood Adversities: Relative Links to Subsequent Suicidal Behaviour in the U.S." *Psychological Medicine* 31:965–977.

Murray, C. J. L., and Lopez, A. D., eds. (1996). *The Global Burden of Disease: A Comprehensive Assessment of Mortality and Disability from Diseases, Injuries, and Risk Factors in 1990 and Projected to 2020.* Cambridge, MA: Harvard University Press.

Nolen-Hoeksema, S. (1990). *Sex Differences in Depression.* Stanford, CA: Stanford University Press.

O'Leary, K. D., and Beach, S. R. H. (1990). "Marital Therapy: A Viable Treatment for Depression and Marital Discord." *American Journal of Psychiatry* 147:183–186.

Preti, A.; Cardascia, L.; Zen, T.; Pellizzari, P.; Marchetti, M.; Favaretto, G.; and Miotto, P. (2000). "Obstetric Complications in Patients with Depression: A Population-Based Case-Control Study." *Journal of Affective Disorders* 61:101–106.

Read, J.; Agar, K.; Barker-Collo, S.; Davies, E.; and Moskowitz, A. (2001). "Assessing Suicidality in Adults: Integrating Childhood Trauma as a Major Risk Factor." *Professional Psychology* 32:367–372.

Segrin, C. (2000). "Social Skills Deficits Associated with Depression." *Clinical Psychology Review* 20:379–403.

Stueve, A.; Dohrenwend, B. P.; and Skodol, A. E. (1998). "Relationships between Stressful Life Events and Episodes of Major Depression and Nonaffective Psychotic Disorders: Selected Results from a New York Risk Factor Study." In *Adversity, Stress, and Psychopathology,* ed. B. P. Dohrenwend. New York: Oxford University Press.

Tsai, J. L.; Butcher, J. N.; Muñoz, R. F.; and Vitousek, K. (2001). "Culture, Ethnicity, and Psychopathology." In *Comprehensive Handbook of Psychopathology,* 3rd edition, ed. P. B. Sutker and H. E. Adams. New York: Plenum.

Tsai, J. L., and Chentsova-Dutton, Y. (2002). "Understanding Depression across Cultures." In *Handbook of Depression,* ed. I. H. Gotlib and C. L. Hammen. New York: Guilford Press.

Wade, T. J., and Cairney, J. (2000). "Major Depressive Disorder and Marital Transition among Mothers: Results from a National Panel Study." *Journal of Nervous and Mental Disease* 188:741–750.

Wallace, J.; Schneider, T.; and McGuffin, P. (2002). "The Genetics of Depression." In *Handbook of Depression,* ed. I. H. Gotlib and C. L. Hammen. New York: Guilford Press.

IAN H. GOTLIB
KAREN L. KASCH

CHILDREN AND ADOLESCENTS

The sadness that characterizes depression is similar at all ages but is most upsetting to adults when observed in children. Depression is characterized by feelings of sadness, fatigue, and a general lack of enthusiasm about life. It can be of short or long duration, of low or high intensity, and can occur at any stage of development. Up until the 1970s there was considerable disagreement about whether depression could occur before the onset of formal operational thought, a cognitive ability that emerges in adolescence. Later debates have shifted to determining the specific age at which children are able to identify and label feelings related to depression, and recent findings suggest that by five or six years of age children are capable of doing so

(Ialongo, Edelsohn, and Kellam 2001). The use of parent reports has allowed for the identification of depressive disorders among preschoolers, and additional work has focused on identifying young children who are at risk for depression because they have one or more relatives with a mood disorder (Cicchetti and Toth 1998).

Depression Classifications

The classification and investigation of depression typically focuses on: depressed mood, depressive syndromes, or clinical depression (or depressive disorders). Each approach reflects differences in assumptions concerning the nature of depression and denotes different levels of depressive phenomena (Petersen et al. 1993; Cicchetti and Toth 1998).

Depressed mood. Research on depressed mood has focused on depression as a symptom denoted by feelings of sadness, unhappiness, or the blues lasting for an unspecified period of time. It is differentiated from normal sadness by the absence of positive affect, a loss of emotional involvement with other persons, objects, and activities, and negative thoughts about oneself and the future (Fombonne 1995). Self-report measures are most often used with older children and adolescents; parent and/or teacher reports are typically used for younger children.

Depressed mood occurs in about one-third of all youth at any point in time, and ranges from 15 to 45 percent among adolescent samples. Results from the few studies that have charted depressed mood across the adolescent years suggest that it peaks around the ages of fourteen and fifteen and then attenuates slightly (Petersen, Sarigiani, and Kennedy 1991). Reliable gender differences do not exist until adolescence, when girls are more likely to experience depressed mood than boys.

Depressive syndromes. Depressive syndromes involve sets of symptoms that have been shown to occur together. Behavior problem checklists, completed either by children/adolescents or parents/teachers, are the main source of identification. These checklists usually include either severity or frequency ratings and consist of items such as sadness, moodiness, sleep disturbances, feelings of worthlessness, guilt, and loneliness. Most research examining depressive syndromes has used a cutoff score corresponding to the ninety-fifth percentile

in nationally representative samples. In comparing the mean scores on the Anxious/Depressed Syndrome of the Child Behavior Checklist across twelve cultures (ages ranged from six to seventeen years), Alfons Crijnen and colleagues (1999) found Germany, the Netherlands, Sweden, and Thailand to be lower on average, whereas Greece, Israel, Puerto Rico, and the United States were above average, with Australia, Jamaica, Belgium, and China being average. Girls obtained higher scores than boys across all cultures.

Clinical depression. Clinical depression is more severe and lasts longer than depressive mood or syndromes and has a major impact on daily living. Clinical depression is identified by categorical diagnoses, such as those described in the *Diagnostic and Statistical Manual of Mental Disorders* (DSM-IV) (American Psychiatric Association 1994) or the *International Classification of Diseases* (ICD-10) (World Health Organization 1996). Most often these diagnoses are made through individual interviews with a clinical psychologist. According to the DSM-IV, two forms of depression have been identified: *Major Depressive Disorder* (MDD) and *Dysthymic Disorder* (DD).

The diagnosis of MDD requires the presence of at least five of nine symptoms during the same two-week period, with one of the symptoms being depressed mood (dysphoria) for most of the day nearly every day or loss of interest and pleasure (Kolvin and Sadowski 2001). Irritable mood in children and adolescents may be substituted for depressed mood. The other possible symptoms include: significant weight change (in children, the failure to make expected weight gains), insomnia or hypersomnia, psychomotor agitation or retardation, fatigue or loss of energy, feelings of worthlessness or inappropriate guilt, diminished ability to concentrate or indecisiveness, and recurrent thoughts of death, suicidal ideation, or suicide attempt. The symptoms are not due to direct psychological effects of a substance, a general medical condition, or bereavement. An episode of MDD in children lasts, on average, about eleven months, with recovery generally taking about seven to nine months (Kovacs and Sherill 2001). Estimates of the point prevalence of MDD range from 0.4 to 2.5 percent for children and from 0.4 to 8.3 percent for adolescents (Birmaher et al. 1996; Verhulst et al. 1997). The estimated lifetime prevalence of MDD for adolescents is 15 to 20 percent, a rate comparable to that for adults (Harrington, Rutter, and Fombonne 1996).

The diagnosis of DD requires the experience of depressed mood for most of the day, for most days for at least two years (Kolvin and Sadowski 2001). For children and adolescents irritable mood and a duration of at least one year are allowed as alternative criteria. Two of six additional symptoms (poor appetite or overeating, insomnia or hypersomnia, low energy or fatigue, poor self-esteem, difficulty concentrating or making decisions, and feelings of hopelessness) are also required.

There appears to be a trend for both an increased rate of depression across generations, and an earlier onset of major depressive disorder, with more onsets occurring during adolescence than previously (Fombonne 1995). A recent review of the gender differences in rate of clinical depression concluded that prior to puberty boys are anywhere from two to five times more likely to exhibit depression than are girls, whereas after age thirteen this difference shifts to girls with depression occurring at least twice as frequently in girls and women as in boys and men (Angold and Costello 2001)

Additional co occurring problems with depression. Studies on both community and clinical samples report that anywhere from 7 to 51 percent of depressed children and adolescents have multiple psychiatric disorders, with anxiety and conduct or disruptive behavior disorders as the most common co-occurring disorders (Kovacs and Sherrill 2001). Anxiety disorders often precede depressive conditions. Eating disorders and drug and alcohol use often co-occur with depressive symptoms. Adolescents with affective disorders have a higher than normal risk of suicide.

Causes

There is no single cause for depression and any single risk factor rarely results in depressive outcomes. Rather, the structure of biological, psychological, and social systems over an individual's development need to be considered (Cicchetti and Toth 1998).

Heredity. Although there is no conclusive evidence that there exists a specific, single gene for depression, there is evidence that some families have an inherited vulnerability to depression. Close relatives of depressed people have a 15 percent chance of inheriting major depression. An identical twin with a depressed twin is 67 percent more likely to be depressed. A child having one depressed parent is six times more likely to develop depression than a child without a depressed parent and the risk for a child to develop depression increases to 40 percent if both parents are depressed. The parents and extended family members of depressed children are not only more likely to exhibit a higher incidence of depression but also found to have higher levels of anxiety, substance abuse, and antisocial behavior (Cicchetti and Toth 1998). Although this association is partially a result of heredity, the environment that family members share also contributes to depressive symptoms (Rende et al. 1993). The fact that many depressed children promptly recover when hospitalized, even when no other treatments are administered, lends additional credence to the role the family may play in a child's depression (Cicchetti and Toth 1998). Additionally, relapse of depression after being released from in-patient psychiatric care is confined primarily to children who return home to an environment characterized by high emotional overinvolvement, criticism, and hostility (Asarnow et al. 1993).

Parental depression. As noted above, children having one or two clinically depressed parents are more vulnerable to developing depression than children without a depressed parent. In addition, more severe and chronic parental depression is associated with greater impairment in children (Goodyer 2001). Several possible mechanisms for the increased vulnerability to depression for children of depressed parents, besides direct hereditary transmission of depression, have been proposed. Most research in this regard has focused on mothers and how they interact with their children, although more recent work is including fathers. A parent struggling with his or her own depression may not be able to provide adequate responsiveness and care to children as the depression may interfere with the ability to react flexibly and creatively to the normative challenges that parenting entails (Kaslow, Deering, and Racusin 1994). Children of depressed mothers are at greater risk for an insecure attachment and for disruptions in emotional regulation (Cicchetti and Toth 1998; McCauley, Pavlidis, and Kendell 2001), which, in turn, increases a child's vulnerability for depression. Compared to nondepressed mothers, depressed mothers are more likely to use withdrawal, conflict avoidance, or overcontrolling strategies rather than negotiation to cope with child noncompliance (McCauley, Pavlidis, and Kendell 2001). Depressed mothers and fathers tend to be more hostile and irritable when interacting with their children, and the marital relationship itself often is characterized as dysfunctional and conflictive. Moreover, families with a depressed parent experience increased and persistent stressors, further taxing a parent's ability to cope constructively. Hence, not only is child nurturance disrupted but also a depressed parent serves as a role model for depressive thinking (McCauley, Pavlidis, and Kendell 2001). Moreover, the child becomes increasingly exposed to stressful life events that are not under his or her control, further increasing vulnerability to feelings of helplessness, hopelessness, and depression. Thus, children of depressed parents are at increased hereditary risk for depression, are more likely to experience disruptions in both physical and emotional relations with parents, have parental role models for depressive thinking, and are more likely to experience stressful life events and conflict. Together these findings underscore how children of depressed parents are exposed to a variety of risk factors that increase their vulnerability for depression.

Family context. Compared to families of nondepressed children, families of depressed youth have higher levels of marital and parent-child conflict, low levels of family cohesion, and diminished overall social support. Regardless of ethnicity, social class, or parents' marital status, parents who are accepting, firm, and democratic have adolescents who report less depression (Steinberg et al. 1991; Herman-Stahl and Petersen 1996). Longitudinal studies have also demonstrated that adolescents with warm family relations are less likely to become depressed several years later (Petersen, Sarigiani, and Kennedy 1991).

Dante Cicchetti and Sheree Toth (1998) propose that a vulnerability to depression may begin in infancy if there is an insecure attachment to primary caretakers. Infants who are insecurely attached are more likely to have less than optimal emotional regulation and expression, and as these infants grow into young children significant others are perceived as unavailable or rejecting while the self is perceived as unlovable. These perceptions may contribute to a proneness to self-processes that have been linked to depression (e.g., low self-esteem, helplessness, hopelessness, and negative attributional biases). When combined with additional environmental stressors these self-processes may contribute to a modification of hormonal and brain processes that further increase vulnerability.

Brain and hormonal processes. Research on biological disregulation during depression focuses on the hypothalamic-endocrine and neurotransmitter systems. As noted in the Surgeon General's report on mental health (1999), some of the primary symptoms of depression, such as changes in sleep patterns and appetite, are related to functions of the hypothalamus. The hypothalamus, in turn, is closely linked to the pituitary gland. Increased rates of circulating cortisol and hypo- and hyperthyroidism, each associated with pituitary function, are established features of adult depression. Research on the hypothalamic-endocrine link involved in childhood and adolescent depression focuses on the hypothalamic-pituitary-adrenal (HPA), hypothalamic-pituitary-gonadal (HPG), and hypothalamic-pituitary-somatotropic (HPS) axes, all of which are related to growth processes and pubertal change (Brooks-Gunn, Auth, Petersen, and Compas 2001). In each of these axes the hypothalamus secretes a releasing hormone that triggers the pituitary to release a stimulating hormone, which, in turn, then stimulates the secretion of an additional hormone by the particular gland in question (adrenal, gonadal, thyroid). This hormone is then released into circulation, inhibiting the hypothalamus and pituitary to produce more releasing and stimulating hormones (Brooks-Gunn et al. 2001). Variations from normal patterns of coritsol and dehydroepiandrosterone (both from the HPA axis), prolactin (from the HPG), and growth hormone (from the HPS axis), have been observed among depressed children and adolescents (Dahl et al. 2000; Schulz and Remschmidt 2001).

At the neurotransmitter level, differences in serotogenic, cholinergic, noradrenic, and dopaminergic systems have all been associated with depression (Brooks-Gunn et al. 2001; Sokolov and Kutcher 2001). Whereas early research focused on deficiencies or excesses in neurotransmitter substances, current research now focuses on the functioning of the neurotransmitter systems with respect to the storage, release, reuptake, and responsiveness (Sokolov and Kutcher

2001). New research is examining the interaction between the hypothalamic-endocrine and neurotransmitter systems. However, as noted by Jeanne Brooks-Gunn and her colleagues (2001), less certain is whether changes and deficits in these systems are causes, correlates, or a result of depression. Nevertheless, once a depressive episode occurs, biological disregulation follows, further influencing behavior, thought, mood, and physiological patterns.

Cognitive factors. Attributional bias and coping skills are the two main cognitive factors investigated with respect to understanding depression. Considerable research has focused on the *pessimistic attributional biases* that are prevalent among depressed adults. A person with this bias readily assumes personal blame for negative events, expects that one bad experience will be followed by another, and that this pattern will endure permanently. Individuals who think this way have a tendency to cope with situations more passively and ineffectively than those without this bias. Among children, this attributional style is related to depression after the age of eight years; prior to this, childhood depression is primarily linked to negative life events (Nolen-Hoeksma, Girgus, and Seligman 1991).

Adaptive coping skills are important in order to regulate negative emotions when unpleasant and challenging events occur. Problem-focused coping refers to how an individual responds to the demands of a stressful situation in terms of active efforts to do something about the problem. Emotion-focused coping, in contrast, refers to the individual's attempts to control the emotion experienced. One form of emotion-focused coping is *rumination*: the tendency to focus repetitively on feelings of depression and their possible causes without taking any actions to relieve them. Another form is *avoidant coping*: the tendency to withdraw from or avoid stressors or to deny their existence. Emotion-focused coping such as rumination and avoidant coping have been linked to depression in adults, adolescents, and children (Herman-Stahl and Petersen 1999; Nolen-Hoeksma 1998).

Gender Differences

Most theories concerning gender differences have focused on explaining the female preponderance during adolescence and adulthood. Males and females appear to have different coping styles: males distract themselves, whereas females ruminate on their depressed mood and therefore amplify it (Nolen-Hoeksma 1998). Most young adolescents are faced with significant changes in every aspect of their lives: pubertal development, cognitive maturation, school transition, and increased performance pressures in academics. For many adolescents these events are stressful. Girls experience more challenges during adolescence compared to boys, including more negative life events, simultaneous changes in pubertal development and school transitions, making them more vulnerable to depression (Petersen, Sarigiani, and Kennedy 1991). Not only are differences in challenges and coping important but the hormonal changes that accompany pubertal development may also make girls more vulnerable (Angold, Costello, and Worthman 1998). Thus, it now appears that a combination of factors, including less effective coping styles, more challenges, and hormonal changes, may help to explain the gender differences in depression during adolescence.

Treatment

Treatments for depression in children and adolescents generally include three forms: pharmacological, psychotherapy, and a combination of the two. Unlike studies on adults, methodologically sound investigations on the relative effectiveness of each type of therapy on youth are only just beginning to be conducted. Thus, most findings are based on a few studies and therefore need to be interpreted cautiously.

Pharmacological. The drugs most commonly used for treating depression in children and adolescents are available in three major types: the monoamine oxidase inhibitors (including phenelzine and tranylcypromine), the tricyclic antidepressants (including lofepramine, imipramine, and nortriptyline) the recently developed selective serotonin and serotonin-noradrenergic re-uptake inhibitors (including fluoxetine, paroxetine and venlafaxine) (Schulz and Remschmidt 2001). Although virtually all medications found to be effective for adult depression have been tested with children, systematic studies with clear results are rare, and superiority of antidepressant medication over placebos for children and adolescents has not been reliably demonstrated (Kovacs and Sherrill 2001; Schulz and Remschmidt 2001). Therefore, antidepressant medications should only be prescribed for children and adolescents when: symptoms are so severe that they prevent effective psychotherapy; symptoms fail to respond to psychotherapy; and the depression is either chronic/recurrent, non-rapid bipolar, or psychotic (Schulz and Remschmidt 2001). Selective re-uptake inhibitors are the initial antidepressant of choice, although the presence of other symptoms such as impulsivity, suicide, or attention deficit hyperactivity disorder (ADHD) may require alternative medications (Schulz and Remschmidt 2001).

Psychotherapy. Studies of psychosocial interventions for depression among youngsters have traditionally included clinically diagnosed children, children classified as having a depressive syndrome, or youngsters deemed at risk for depression based on elevated scores on depressive symptom checklists. Controlled psychotherapy trials on clinically depressed youth typically include short-term *cognitive behavioral therapy* (CBT) delivered in individual or group format (Kovacs and Sherrill 2001). Cognitive behavioral therapy is based on the premise that depressed individuals have distortions in thinking concerning themselves, the world, and their future. Thus, therapy focuses on changing or preventing these distortions (*cognitive restructuring*), and also includes training in social skills, assertiveness, relaxation, and coping skills. Of the seven clinical studies reported to date, 35 to 90 percent of the youths recovered, with higher rates of success for experimental therapies than the control conditions (Kovacs and Sherrill 2001). Although only two studies included a parent component as part of the treatment condition, including the parent component did not improve outcomes. Interventions targeted at nonclinical but at-risk youth identified in school settings have had even more favorable results. Seven of eight studies reported decreases in depressed mood and syndromes. One demonstrated long-term effects of the intervention in reducing the likelihood for developing clinical levels of depression. These promising results highlight the beneficial effects of early identification and prevention efforts. Additional studies are needed to clarify how parents and other family members may be included in treatment programs.

According to Maria Kovacs and Joel Sherrill (2001), clinically referred depressed youth usually experience a disruption to the parent-child relationship. Because depressed children and adolescents are either unwilling or unable to verbalize their affective experience, parents, in turn, may withhold emotional support, guidance, and expressions of affection. Based on their work and that of others, Kovacs and Sherrill suggest that the most appropriate treatment of depressed juveniles should include structured, goal-directed, or problem-solving oriented interventions that focus on symptom reduction, enhancement of self-esteem, and social/interpersonal skill development. In addition, involvement of the parents or primary caretakers is essential and should occur at two levels. First, parents should be assessed to determine if they themselves suffer from a form of emotional or mental disorder. Those who are positively identified should receive treatment. Second, parents should be engaged as agents of change in treatment of their own children, including some sessions explicitly focused on the depressed child's needs and concerns.

See also: ATTACHMENT: PARENT-CHILD RELATIONSHIPS; CHILD ABUSE: PHYSICAL ABUSE AND NEGLECT; CHILD ABUSE: PSYCHOLOGICAL MALTREATMENT; CHILD ABUSE: SEXUAL ABUSE; CHILDHOOD, STAGES OF: ADOLESCENCE; CHILDREN OF ALCOHOLICS; CHRONIC ILLNESS; CONDUCT DISORDER; DEPRESSION: ADULTS; DEVELOPMENT: SELF; DEVELOPMENTAL PSYCHOPATHOLOGY; GRIEF, LOSS, AND BEREAVEMENT; EATING DISORDERS; HEALTH AND FAMILIES; INTERPARENTAL CONFLICT— EFFECTS ON CHILDREN; INTERPARENTAL VIOLENCE—EFFECTS ON CHILDREN; SELF-ESTEEM; STRESS; SUICIDE

Bibliography

American Psychiatric Association. (1994). *Diagnostic and Statistical Manual for Mental Disorders,* 4th edition (DSM-IV). Washington, DC: American Psychiatric Press.

Angold, A., and Costello, E. J. (2001). "The Epidemiology of Depression in Children and Adolescents." In *The Depressed Child and Adolescent,* 2nd edition, ed. I. M. Goodyer. Cambridge, UK: Cambridge University Press.

Angold, A.; Costello, E. J.; and Worthman, C. M. (1998). "Puberty and Depression: The Role of Age, Pubertal Status and Pubertal Timing." *Psychological Medicine* 28:51–61.

Asarnow, J. R.; Goldstein, M. J.; Tompson, M.; and Guthrie, D. (1993). "One-Year Outcomes of Depressive Disorders in Child Psychiatric In-Patients: Evaluation of the Prognostic Power of a Brief Measure of

Expressed Emotion." *Journal of Child Psychology and Psychiatry and the Allied Disciplines* 34:129–137.

Birmaher, B.; Ryan, N. D.; Williamson, D. E.; Brent, D. A.; and Kaufman, J. (1996). "Childhood and Adolescent Depression: A Review of the Past 10 Years: Part II." *Journal of the American Academy of Child and Adolescent Psychiatry* 35:1575–1583.

Brooks-Gunn, J.; Auth, J. J.; Petersen, A. C.; and Compas, B. E. (2001). "Physiological Processes and the Development of Childhood and Adolescent Depression." In *The Depressed Child and Adolescent,* 2nd edition, ed. I. M. Goodyer. Cambridge, UK: Cambridge University Press.

Cicchetti, D., and Toth, S. L. (1998). "The Development of Depression in Children and Adolescents." *American Psychologist* 53:221–241.

Crijnen, A. A. M.; Achenbach, T. M.; and Verhulst, F. C. (1999). "Problems Reported by Parents of Children in Multiple Cultures: The Child Behavior Checklist Syndrome Constructs." *American Journal of Psychiatry* 156(4):569–574.

Dahl, R. E.; Birmaher, B.; Williamson, D. E.; Dorn, L.; Perel, J.; Kaufman, J.; Brent, D. A.; Axelson, D. A.; and Ryan, D. (2000). "Low Growth Hormone-Releasing Hormone in Child Depression." *Biological Psychiatry* 48:981–988.

Fombonne, E. (1995). "Depressive Disorders: Time Trends and Possible Explanatory Mechanisms." In *Psychological Disorders in Young People: Time Trends and Their Causes,* ed. M. Rutter and D. J. Smith. New York: Wiley.

Goodyer, I. M. (2001). "Life Events: Their Nature and Effects." In *The Depressed Child and Adolescent,* 2nd edition, ed. I. M. Goodyer. Cambridge, UK: Cambridge University Press.

Harrington, R. C.; Rutter, M.; and Fombonne, E. (1996). "Developmental Pathways in Depression: Multiple Meanings, Antecedents, and Endpoints." *Developments in Psychopathology* 8:601–616.

Herman-Stahl, M., and Petersen, A. C. (1996). "The Protective Role of Coping and Social Resources for Depressive Symptoms among Young Adolescents." *Journal of Youth and Adolescence* 25(6):733–753.

Ialongo, N. S.; Edelsohn, G.; and Kellam, S. G. (2001). "A Further Look at the Prognostic Power of Young Children's Reports of Depressed Mood and Feelings." *Child Development* 72:736–747.

Kaslow, N. J.; Deering, C. G.; and Racusin, G. R. (1994). "Depressed Children and Their Families." *Clinical Psychology Review* 14:39–59.

Kolvin, I., and Sadowski, H. (2001). "Childhood Depression: Clinical Phenomenology and Classification." In *The Depressed Child and Adolescent,* 2nd edition, ed. I. M. Goodyer. Cambridge, UK: Cambridge University Press.

Kovacs, M., and Sherill, J. T. (2001). "The Psychotherapeutic Management of Major Depressive and Dysthymic Disorders in Childhood and Adolescence: Issues and Prospects." In *The Depressed Child and Adolescent,* 2nd edition, ed. I. M. Goodyer. Cambridge, UK: Cambridge University Press.

McCauley, E.; Pavlidis, K.; and Kendell, K. (2001). "Developmental Precursors of Depression: the Child and the Social Environment." In *The Depressed Child and Adolescent,* 2nd edition, ed. I. M. Goodyer. Cambridge, UK: Cambridge University Press.

Nolen-Hoeksma, S. (1998). "Ruminative Coping with Depression." In *Motivation and Self-Regulation across the Life Span,* ed. J. Heckhausen and C. S. Dweck. Cambridge, UK: Cambridge University Press.

Nolen-Hoeksma, S.; Girgus, J. S.; and Seligman, M. E. P. (1991). "Sex Differences in Depression and Explanatory Style in Children." *Journal of Youth and Adolescence* 20:233–245.

Petersen, A. C.; Compas, B. E.; Brooks-Gunn, J.; Stemmler, M.; Ey, S.; and Grant, K. E. (1993). "Depression in Adolescence." *American Psychologist* 48:155–168.

Petersen, A. C.; Sarigiani, P. A.; and Kennedy, R. E. (1991). "Adolescent Depression: Why More Girls?" *Journal of Youth and Adolescence* 20:247–271.

Rende, R. D.; Plomin, R.; Reiss, D.; and Hetherington, E. M. (1993). "Genetic and Environmental Influences on Depressive Symptomatology in Adolescence: Individual Differences and Extreme Scores." *Journal of Child Psychology and Psychiatry* 34:1387–1398.

Schulz, E., and Remschmidt, H. (2001). "Psychopharmacology of Depressive States in Childhood and Adolescence." In *The Depressed Child and Adolescent,* 2nd edition, ed. I. M. Goodyer. Cambridge, UK: Cambridge University Press.

Sokolov, S. and Kutcher, S. (2001). "Adolescent Depression: Neuroendocrine Aspects." In *The Depressed Child and Adolescent,* 2nd edition, ed. I. M. Goodyer. Cambridge, UK: Cambridge University Press.

Steinberg, L.; Mounts, N. S.; Lambourn, S. D.; and Dornbusch, S. M. (1991). "Authoritative Parenting and Adolescent Adjustment across Various Ecological Niches." *Journal of Research on Adolescence* 1(1):19–36.

Verhulst, F. C.; van der Ende, J. M. S.; Ferdinand, R. F.; and Kasius, M. C. (1997). "The Prevalence of DSM-III-R Diagnoses in a National Sample of Dutch Adolescents." *Archives of General Psychiatry* 54:329–336.

World Health Organization. (1996). *Multiaxial Classification of Child and Adolescent Psychiatric Disorders*. New York: Cambridge University Press.

Other Resource

Shalala, D. E. (2001). "Mental Health: A Report of the Surgeon General." Available from http://www.surgeongeneral.gov/library/mentalhealth.

JUDITH SEMON DUBAS
ANNE C. PETERSEN

DEVELOPMENT

COGNITIVE *Usha Goswami*

EMOTIONAL *Susanne A. Denham, Anita Kochanoff, Karen Neal, Teresa Mason, Hideko Hamada*

MORAL *Silvia Koller, Angela M.B. Biaggio*

SELF *Susan Harter, Lisa Kiang*

COGNITIVE

The ages of birth to ten are a peak period of sensitivity for learning. During much of this time, a child's brain actually consumes twice as much glucose as an adult's. The infant brain doubles in size during the first year of life. At birth, each neuron in the cerebral cortex has around 2,500 synapses. By the age of two to three years, each neuron has 15,000 synapses. This massive growth in connectivity is matched by terrific pruning. As the brain adapts itself to its surroundings and becomes more specialized, old connections are pruned away. This is the main mechanism by which cognitive development fits itself to the social and cultural environment of the child. Yet although the plasticity of the developing child's brain is remarkable, equally remarkable is the similarity in cognitive development that is found across cultures and social contexts.

Piaget's Theory of Cognitive Development

Cognitive-developmental psychology traditionally coped with cross-cultural similarity by positing culture-general theories of knowledge development. The most famous of these theories was that proposed by Jean Piaget. Piaget suggested that reasoning in all kinds of cognitive domains (e.g., moral reasoning, physical reasoning, and logical reasoning) progressed through a series of universal stages that transcended culture and context. For Piaget, children progressed through three levels of knowing or of mental organization (Smith 2002). These were infancy (during which knowledge was based on action—the *sensorimotor period*), childhood (based on representational thought—the attainment of *concrete operations*), and adolescence (based on formal understanding—the attainment of *formal operations*). Piaget stressed that the levels in his theory were levels of knowledge, not levels of the child. He also suggested that the stages were not age-related, although he did provide indicative ages at which they occurred (sensorimotor, birth to two years; preoperational, two to seven years; concrete operations, seven to eleven years; formal operations, adolescence onwards). Nevertheless, he is usually characterized as a stage theoretician, and has been much criticized accordingly. Even quite young children can be shown to possess cognitive abilities that, according to Piaget's stage theory, they should not have at a given stage. For example, three-year-old children can reason by analogy, characterized by Piaget as a formal operation (see Goswami 1998). Other criticisms concern Piaget's assumptions that early thought is not representational, and that language plays a peripheral role in cognitive development.

Vygotsky's Theory of Cognitive Development

Lev Vygotsky differed from Piaget in that the role of social context and culture in children's cognition was a central part of his theory (Rowe and Wertsch 2002). Rather than seeing the development of knowledge as transcending culture and context, Vygotsky argued that an understanding of how knowledge develops requires an understanding of the social and historical origins of knowledge and of changes in that knowledge. He also proposed a central role for language in cognitive development. Vygotsky argued that human knowledge originates in socially meaningful activity and is shaped by language. Processes that originate in the social world are transferred to the inner *mental world* (*inner speech*), and shape the development of

Through play, children develop cognitive understanding of the minds of others. ROBERT J. HUFFMAN/FIELD MARK
PUBLICATIONS

higher cognitive processes such as problem-solving. A key part of this transfer lies in the child's mastery of the symbolic or artificial stimuli (*signs*) characteristic of the child's culture, such as language. Part of the development of children's thinking therefore requires *apprenticeship* into culturally specific cognitive and social practices. According to Vygotsky, cognitive development does not happen just in the head of the child. Rather, it is a process of learning to operate with physical, symbolic, and cognitive tools in ways that in themselves change cognitive processes. The difference between a child's individual performance and that child's performance when guided by experts is metaphorically described by Vygotsky's *zone of proximal development* (ZPD). The ZPD was described by Vygotsky (1978) as "the distance between the actual developmental level as determined by independent problem solving and the level of potential development as determined through problem solving under adult guidance or in collaboration with more capable peers" (p. 86).

This notion of an enhanced level of mental functioning when an expert guides an apprentice has been influential in education and in the study of learning disability.

Information Processing Theories of Cognitive Development

Later theories of cognitive development have been based on a computer metaphor. The idea that the brain is like a computer, able to take certain inputs, convert them into representations, and use these representations to compute certain outputs, led to new theoretical models for cognitive development called information-processing and connectionist models. *Neo-Piagetian information processing theories* explained cognitive development in terms of two fundamental components: the child's assumed available memory storage and the level of complexity at which the child was assumed to be capable of processing information (e.g., Case 1992; Halford 1993). *Connectionist models* are learning systems, and are loosely based on principles of neural information processing. They are intended to employ the same *style* of computation as the brain (they do not model exactly what is understood about neural circuits and the computational primitives/representations in the cortex and elsewhere in the brain that are extracted from environmental input). Connectionist models have proved particularly useful for their insights into possible causes of atypical development. For example, small changes in learning algorithms (routines) can model either reading development or dyslexia. This suggests that very small differences in a basic aspect of cognitive processing can lead eventually to quite noticeable differences in developmental outcome. Connectionist models also force the theorist to be more aware of the effects of incremental and context-dependent piecemeal learning for the child's development: every input to a connectionist system makes a difference to final learning, and theorists must be aware that every aspect of a child's environment will contribute to cognitive development.

Latest Perspectives on Cognitive Development

According to the latest conceptualizations of cognitive development, the infant begins the process of knowledge acquisition with a set of core principles that guide and constrain future cognitive development (e.g., Gopnik, Meltzoff, and Kuhl 1999; Goswami 2002). These core principles are either innate, or are given by simple perceptual information such as a sensitivity to contingency (events that appear contingent on one another). Experience of the physical and social worlds allows infants to enrich and revise these initial expectations, and even to replace them with new understandings. Knowledge acquisition is guided by the core constraints, and also by the ways in which surrounding adults behave—the social, emotional, and cultural contexts within which learning takes place. The kinds of innate or early-developing core principles postulated include physical principles like solidity and continuity of objects (e.g., that one object can only be in one place at a time) (Spelke et al. 1992), expecting words to refer to commonalities among objects (e.g., words label shared categories, functions, or perceptual aspects of objects) (Waxman 2002), and a basic animate/inanimate distinction (e.g., living versus nonliving

(Gelman 1990). In contrast to traditional theories, therefore, current cognitive developmental psychology does not characterize the newborn as incapable of distinguishing self from other, incapable of forming representations, or incapable of retaining memories. Rather, newborns are characterized as active learners, equipped with certain innate expectations that, although quite primitive, enable them to benefit hugely from experience. The extent of this benefit depends on powerful learning mechanisms, such as the absorption of statistical regularities in the environment (e.g., in early perceptual tuning to the sounds of one's native language); making relational mappings, as in mapping the actions of other people onto the actions of one's own body (*infant imitation*); mapping the responses of another person to one's own emotional states; and *explanation-based learning*: noticing causal regularities in environmental information and seeking explanations for them, as in noticing that objects sometimes fall unexpectedly, and that this tends to occur when they are insufficiently supported (see Goswami 2002). Following are two examples of how the social, emotional and cultural contexts within which learning takes place affects cognitive development within this newer theoretical framework.

Social Cognition

Infants are innately interested in, and attentive to, people. Even newborn babies can imitate facial expressions, and older infants prefer to imitate people rather than machines (Meltzoff 1995). Joint attention skills develop by about nine months, and infants probably have a basic notion of agency by the end of the first year. Infants' conscious awareness of their own emotional states and of how they are related to the actions of their caregivers also develops during the first year of life. Although an understanding of *representational* mental states (e.g., thoughts, beliefs, knowledge, ideas, or false beliefs) develops more slowly, a basic understanding of desires and emotions is present relatively early (by around two years). This early focus on other people means that parents and caretakers have an enormously important role to play in cognitive development.

As an illustration, take *pretending,* an early example of the child's symbolic capacity. Children across the world play pretend games, and pretending is important both for the development of the cognitive understanding of the minds of others (Lillard 2002) and for the development of social cognition more generally. Pretence activities focused on objects and props typically begin during the second year of life, and sociodramatic pretending with caretakers and peers typically emerges at around three to four years. Cultural contexts affect children's choice of pretend play topics. For example, the pretend play of U.S. preschoolers shows greater enactment of fantasy themes than the pretend play of Taiwanese children, whereas Taiwanese children spend a lot more time playing games about social routines and "proper" conduct (Haight et al. 1999). Parental attitudes and parental engagement also affect the frequency of pretend play, with more pretend play found in cultures where it is actively encouraged. Thus parents and caretakers act, usually quite unconsciously, in ways that promote and influence cognitive change.

A second illustration comes from research into children's understanding of mental states (*theory of mind*). A basic division between the mental (thoughts, ideas, beliefs) and the physical (substantive, objective objects) is present from early in childhood (Wellman 2002). As they seek causes and explanations for the actions of others, children gradually develop an understanding of mental states such as beliefs, knowledge, and false beliefs. For example, an understanding of false belief, with a consequent understanding of deception and intentional lying, develops at around four years. One important source of individual differences in the development of theory of mind is parent-child and family relationships. Children with brothers and sisters, particularly those with older siblings, typically show earlier psychological understanding, for example passing false belief tasks at earlier ages than children without siblings (e.g., Youngblade and Dunn 1995). Children whose families openly discuss emotions and feelings also show earlier developments in psychological understanding, particularly if the family discussions analyze the causes of emotions. The ways in which we talk to our children and the things that we talk to them about both play key roles in cognitive development.

The Development of Logical Reasoning

Research into the development of logical reasoning was for a long time dominated by Piaget's idea that development consisted of the child's gradual discovery of formal rules and principles such as transitivity and deductive logic. These formal principles were thought to be *domain-general* (applying across all fields of learning) and *content-independent* (applying irrespective of the material concerned), and were assumed to operate in their purest form in totally unfamiliar domains. The existing state of the child's conceptual system was therefore ignored. Late twentieth-century research has demonstrated that difficulties in logical reasoning are not usually determined by the intrinsic logical structure of the task. Rather, they are determined by the content or mode of presentation of the problem itself. This can be shown both across cultures and within different social contexts.

For example, it was believed that young children and adults from less Westernized cultures suffered from an *empirical bias* in logical (syllogistic) reasoning. If given a classical logical deduction such as "All Kpelle men are rice farmers. Mr. Smith is not a rice farmer. Is he a Kpelle man?", West African Kpelle tribespeople seemed unable to answer correctly (Scribner 1977). They said that they did not know the man in question and thus could not verify whether he was a Kpelle man or not. Young children given similar logical problems showed a similar "empirical bias." They seemed unable to reason about unfamiliar or incongruent information simply by applying deductive logic. However, Maria Dias and Paul Harris (1988; 1990) showed that even preschoolers could reason about incongruent premises if the reasoning task was presented in a "fantasy" mode. When the experimenter pretended that she was on another planet and used a "make-believe" intonation, even four-year-olds could solve syllogisms such as "All cats bark. Rex is a cat. Does Rex bark?" Dias and Harris concluded that young children were capable of deductive reasoning, as long as logical problems were presented in a context that clearly marked for the child that the situation was make-believe.

As another example, take performance on a classic Piagetian task, conservation. The conservation task is a measure of children's understanding of the *principle of invariance*: quantities do not alter unless something is added or taken away. In the conservation task, a child is shown two identical quantities, such as two rows of five beads arranged in 1:1 correspondence, or two glasses of liquid filled to exactly the same level. An adult experimenter then alters the appearance of one of these quantities while the child is watching. For example, the adult could pour the liquid in one of the glasses into a shorter, wider beaker, or could spread out the beads in one of the rows so that the row looked longer. Piaget showed that in these circumstances, children younger than around seven years told the experimenter that there was now less water in the wider beaker, or that there were more beads in the spread-out row. Again, however, social context plays a role in determining children's performance in this task. For example, when a "naughty teddy" alters the beads in one of the rows instead of an important adult, children as young as four and five years show conservation (McGarrigle and Donaldson 1975). Also, children who grow up in cultures that provide extensive experience with changes in appearance that do not alter quantity show earlier conservation. For example, the children of potters in certain rural societies show very early conservation of mass (Price-Williams, Gordon, and Ramirez 1969). Again, rather than being independent of culture and context, children's logical abilities are to some extent determined by both.

Conclusion

Late twentieth-century theoretical frameworks in cognitive developmental psychology have emphasized the importance of *explanation-based learning* models of cognitive development. Children are conceptualized as seeking to explain the world around them in terms of the collateral and background information that is available to them. The child's access to such information will vary with individual experience, parental and family practices, educational and cultural practices, and with socio-historical context. Knowledge acquisition is thought guided by certain core constraints, and also by the ways in which surrounding adults behave—unconsciously transmitting social, emotional, and cultural norms within which learning takes place. The fact that children across the world seem to develop remarkably similar cognitive frameworks suggests that the learning mechanisms in the brain are actually fairly heavily constrained, and that environmental inputs across different cultures and social contexts share considerably more similarities than differences.

See also: ACADEMIC ACHIEVEMENT; CHILDHOOD; CHILDHOOD, STAGES OF: INFANCY; CHILDHOOD, STAGES OF: MIDDLE CHILDHOOD; CHILDHOOD, STAGES OF: PRESCHOOL; CHILDHOOD, STAGES OF: TODDLERHOOD; CHILDREN OF ALCOHOLICS; DEVELOPMENT: EMOTIONAL; DEVELOPMENT: MORAL; DEVELOPMENT: SELF; FAILURE TO THRIVE; GIFTED AND TALENTED CHILDREN; INTERPARENTAL VIOLENCE—EFFECTS ON CHILDREN; LEARNING DISORDERS; PLAY; SIBLING RELATIONSHIPS; SCHOOL; SUBSTITUTE CAREGIVERS

Bibliography

Case, R. (1985). *Intellectual Development: Birth to Adulthood*. New York: Academic Press.

Dias, M. G., and Harris, P. L. (1988). "The Effect of Make-Believe Play on Deductive Reasoning." *British Journal of Developmental Psychology* 6:207–221.

Dias, M. G., and Harris, P. L. (1990). "The Influence of the Imagination on Reasoning by Young Children." *British Journal of Developmental Psychology* 8:305–318.

Gelman, R. (1990). "First Principles Organize Attention to and Learning about Relevant Data: Number and the Animate-Inanimate Distinction as Examples." *Cognitive Science* 14:79–106.

Gopnik, A.; Meltzoff, A. N.; and Kuhl, P. K. (1999). *How Babies Think*. London: Weidenfeld and Nicholson.

Goswami, U. (1998). *Cognition in Children*. Hove, UK: Psychology Press.

Goswami, U. (2002). *Blackwell's Handbook of Childhood Cognitive Development*. Oxford: Blackwells.

Haight, W. L.; Wang, X.-L.; Fung, H. H.-T.; Williams, K.; and Mintz, J. (1999). "Universal, Developmental, and Variable Aspects of Young Children's Play: A Cross-Cultural Comparison of Pretending at Home." *Child Development* 70:1477–1488.

Halford, G. S. (1993). *Children's Understanding: The Development of Mental Models*. Hillsdale, NJ: Lawrence Erlbaum Associates.

Lillard, A. (2002). "Pretend Play and Cognitive Development." In *Blackwell's Handbook of Childhood Cognitive Development*, ed. U. Goswami. Oxford: Blackwells.

McGarrigle, J., and Donaldson, M. (1975). "Conservation Accidents." *Cognition* 3:341–350.

Meltzoff, A. N. (1995). "Understanding the Intentions of Others: Re-Enactment of Intended Acts by 18-Month-Old Children." *Developmental Psychology* 31:838–850.

Price-Williams, D.; Gordon, W.; and Ramirez, M. (1969). "Skill and Conservation: A Study of Pottery-Making Children." *Developmental Psychology* 1:769.

Rowe, S. M., and Wertsch, J. V. (2002). "Vygotsky's Model of Cognitive Development." In *Blackwell's Handbook of Childhood Cognitive Development,* ed. U. Goswami. Oxford: Blackwells.

Scribner, S. (1977). "Modes of Thinking and Ways of Speaking: Culture and Logic Reconsidered." In *Thinking: Readings in Cognitive Science,* ed. P. N. Johnson-Laird and P. C. Wason. Cambridge, UK: Cambridge University Press.

Smith, L. (2002). "Piaget's Model." In *Blackwell's Handbook of Childhood Cognitive Development,* ed. U. Goswami. Oxford: Blackwells.

Spelke, E. S.; Breitlinger, K.; Macomber, J.; and Jacobson, K. (1992). "Origins of Knowledge." *Psychological Review* 99:605–632.

Vygotsky, L. S. (1978). *Mind in Society: The Development of Higher Psychological Processes,* ed. M. Cole, V. John-Steiner, S. Scribner, and E. Souberman. Cambridge, MA: Harvard University Press.

Waxman, S. R. (2002). "Early Word Learning and Conceptual Development." In *Blackwell's Handbook of Childhood Cognitive Development,* ed. U. Goswami. Oxford: Blackwells.

Wellman, H. M. (2002). "Understanding the Psychological World: Developing a Theory of Mind." In *Blackwell's Handbook of Childhood Cognitive Development,* ed. U. Goswami. Oxford: Blackwells.

Youngblade, L. M., and Dunn, J. (1995). "Individual Differences in Young Children's Pretend Play with Mother and Sibling: Links to Relationships and Understanding of Other People's Feelings and Beliefs." *Child Development* 66:1472–1492.

USHA GOSWAMI

EMOTIONAL

Broadly stated, aspects of lifespan *emotional development* include emotional expression and experience, understanding emotions of self and others, and emotion regulation. As such, emotional development is central to children's ability to interact and form relationships with others. Much of the variation in children's emotional development derives from experiences within the family.

Theories of Emotion

Several perspectives help explain the role of emotion in development. Some theorists emphasize that emotions occur during events involving self and environment, but that events must be cognitively appraised before an emotion is experienced; this appraisal occurs with reference to one's goals (Frijda, Kuipers, and ter Schure 1989; Lazarus 1991). The *social constructivist* approach (e.g., Saarni 1999) also highlights appraisal, but focuses on emotions as social products based on cultural beliefs. In contrast, *Differential Emotions Theory* asserts that different emotions are already present at birth (Izard 1991). Keith Oatley and Jennifer Jenkins (1996) assimilate these divergent views, holding that emotions derive from a universal biological core, but also contain an appraisal/semantic component that is largely a product of social construction.

Emotional Competence

Both Susanne Denham (1998) and Carolyn Saarni (1990, 1999) have written about children's emotional competence; they agree that, although there are no overarching stages for emotional development, children become increasingly sophisticated in their expression and experience, understanding, and regulation of emotions. These early foundations of emotional competence contribute to mental health throughout the lifespan.

Socialization of emotional competence. Because emotions are inherently social, skills of emotional competence are vividly played out during interaction and within relationships with others. As noted by Joseph Campos and Karen Barrett (1984), emotions provide useful information for self and others. This entry focuses on the emotional transactions between parent and child and on parents' contributions to emotional competence.

Amy Halberstadt (1991) has highlighted three possible mechanisms of parents' socialization of emotional competence: modeling, reactions to children's emotions, and teaching about emotions. The theories of psychologists like Sylvan Tomkins (1963, 1991), as well as empirical findings from late twentieth-century research (e.g., Denham, Cook and Zoller 1992; Denham and Kochanoff, in press; Denham et al. 1997; Denham, Zoller, and Couchoud 1994; Dunn, Brown, and Beardsall 1991; Eisenberg, Cumberland, and Spinrad 1998; Eisenberg and Fabes 1994; Eisenberg, Fabes, and Murphy 1996; Eisenberg et al. 1999), predict that parents' positive emotional expression and experience, accepting and helpful reactions to children's emotions, and emphasis on teaching about emotions in the family, contribute to young children's more sophisticated emotional competence.

Over and above these mechanisms for the socialization of emotion, cultural issues are paramount (e.g., Kitayama and Markus 1994; Lutz 1994; Markus and Kitayama 1994; Matsumoto 1994; Matsumoto et al. 1988; Saarni 1998; Shiraev and Levy 2001). Parents socialize their children based on specific cultural values and norms, but cross-cultural similarities and differences remain to be delineated. In both Japan and the United States, people often agree on the antecedents and evaluative components of emotional experience, and even on some primitive aspects of appraisal (e.g., "I was scared of the loud noise; that didn't feel good; it seemed certain that something bad was about to happen; I had to decide how to cope"). Nevertheless, they differ markedly on some of the more advanced aspects of appraisal, including control of and responsibility for emotion. In the United States, people might state, "I have to show this emotion," or even "I am not responsible for this emotion," whereas the Japanese might say "I should not show this emotion" and "I am responsible for this emotion" (Mauro, Sato, and Tucker 1992; Nakamura, Buck, and Kenny 1990). Given these differences, the goals of emotion socialization surely differ across the two cultures.

Regarding modeling, children observe parents' ever-present emotions, and incorporate this learning into their expressive behavior. Parents' expressiveness also teaches children which emotions are acceptable in which contexts. Their emotional displays tell children about the emotional significance of differing events, behaviors that may accompany differing emotions, and others' likely reactions. A mostly positive emotional family climate makes learning about emotions accessible to children (e.g., Garner, Jones, and Miner 1994). Thus, parents' expressiveness is associated with children's understanding of emotions as well as their expressiveness (Denham and Grout 1992, 1993; Denham, Zoller, and Couchoud 1994).

However, several factors suggest possible negative contributions of parents' expressiveness to children's emotional competence. Parents' frequent and intense negative emotions may disturb children, making emotional learning more difficult. Further, parents whose expressiveness is generally limited impart little information about emotions to their children (Denham, Zoller, and Couchoud 1994).

Parents may cultivate some emotional expressions, but not others. Western cultures urge children to separate self from others and express themselves, but many non-Western cultures view people as fundamentally connected, with the goal of socialization attunement or alignment of one's actions and reactions with that of others'. Thus, in Japan, the public display of emotions is mostly discouraged because it is seen as disruptive, leading us to expect Japanese parents to model mostly low intensity emotions (Ujiie 1997).

Moreover, there is a qualitative difference in the emotions modeled. Valued emotions accompanying interdependence—friendliness, affiliation, calmness, smoothness, and connectedness—would be most available for observation by Japanese children. In contrast, anger, regarded as extremely negative in Japan because it disturbs interdependence, would be modeled less (Ujiie 1997). Research on these culturally unique aspects of socialization of emotions, however, is still largely lacking.

Parents' contingent reactions to children's emotional displays are also linked to children's emotionally competent expression, experience, understanding, and regulation of emotions (Denham, Zoller, Couchoud 1994; Denham et al. 1997; Eisenberg and Fabes 1994; Eisenberg, Fabes, and Murphy 1996; Eisenberg et al. 1999). Contingent reactions include behavioral and emotional encouragement or discouragement of specific emotions. Parents who dismiss emotions may actively punish children for showing emotions, or they may want to be helpful, but ignore their child's emotions in an effort to "make it better." Children who experience negative reactions are distressed by their parents' reactions as well as the events that originally elicited emotion.

Positive reactions, such as tolerance or comforting, convey a very different message—that emotions are manageable, even useful. Good emotion coaches, at least in the United States, accept children's experiences of emotion and their expression of emotions that do not harm others; they empathize with and validate emotions. In fact, emotional moments may be opportunities for parent-child intimacy (Gottman, Katz, and Hooven 1997).

Japanese parents' reactions to children's emotions differ from U.S. parents', although not at every age or in every situation. In general, U.S. parents

Children observe parents' emotions and incorporate this learning into their expressive behavior. Parents' emotional displays tell children about the significance of events, behaviors that may accompany emotions, and others' likely reactions.
OWEN FRANKEN/CORBIS

see expression of emotions as legitimate and part of healthy self-assertion. Japanese mothers also respond positively to their infants and young children's emotions (Kanaya, Nakamura, and Miyake 1989), but gradually emphasize, more than U.S. parents, parenting goals of *inhibitory self-regulation* and *acquisition of good manners*. Thus, for children older than about three years, Japanese mothers react most positively to children's suppression of emotion and demonstration of empathy. Compared to U.S. parents, they especially discourage negative emotional expression (Kojima 2000).

Socializers' tendencies to discuss emotions, if nested within a warm parent-child relationship, assist the child acquiring emotional competence (Kochanoff 2001). Parents directly teach their children about emotions, explaining its relation to an observed event or expression, directing attention to salient emotional cues, and helping children understand and manage their own responses.

Parents who are aware of emotions and talk about them in a differentiated manner (e.g., clarifying and explaining, rather than "preaching") assist their children in experiencing and regulating their own emotions. Children of such parents gradually formulate a coherent body of knowledge about emotional expressions, situations, and causes (Denham, Cook, and Zoller 1992; Denham, Zoller, and Couchoud 1994).

Late twentieth-century research suggests that Japanese mothers also talk to their preschoolers about emotions (e.g., Clancy, 1999; Sonoda and Muto 1996). They use emotion language for similar reasons as U.S. mothers; what differs is the content of their conversations, which focus on aspects of emotion relevant for Japanese culture.

Thus, positive elements of emotion socialization seem clear. Moreover, there is some evidence that parents' support of one another also helps to ensure such positive elements (Denham and Kochanoff, in press). However, do beneficial aspects of parents' socialization of emotion differ across children's ages, or across parents? Although more research is needed in this area, it is predicted that these socializing techniques would occur across development and parents, albeit with different emphasized emotions, and different aspects yielding positive child outcomes. In part, however, these questions require an elucidation of children's changing skills of emotional competence.

Expression and experience of emotions. An important element of emotional competence is emotional expressiveness, the sending of affective messages. Emotions must be expressed in keeping with the child's goals, and in accordance with the social context; goals of self and others must be coordinated. Thus, emotional competence includes *expressing emotions* in a way that is advantageous to moment-to-moment interaction and relationships over time (Halberstadt, Denham, and Dunsmore 2001).

First, emotionally competent individuals are aware that an affective message needs to be sent in a given context. But what affective message should be sent, for interaction to proceed smoothly? Children slowly learn which expressions of emotion facilitate specific goals. Second, children also come to determine the appropriate affective message, one that works in the setting or with a specific playmate. Third, children must also learn how to send the affective message convincingly. Method, intensity, and timing of an affective message are crucial to its meaning, and eventual success or failure.

After preschool, children learn that their goals are not always met by freely showing their most intense feelings. For example, grade-schoolers regulate anger in anticipation of the negative consequences they expect in specific situations or from specific persons (e.g., Zeman and Shipman 1996). Along with the *cool rule* mandating more muted emotions within most social settings, older children's emotional messages become more complex, with the use of more blended signals, and better-differentiated expressions of social emotions.

These general tenets of competent experience and expression of emotion may be universal, but children from different cultures differ in the emotions they express. For example, Japanese preschoolers show less anger and distress in conflict situations than U.S. children, even though the two groups' prosocial and conflict *behaviors* do not differ (Zahn-Waxler et al. 1996). These differences fit the Japanese taboo on publicly displayed negative emotions.

Japanese toddlers and preschoolers' expressiveness is not always different from that of their U.S. peers'. For example, they express empathy in response to others' distress. Even this similarity, however, may arise from differing cultural imperatives. Japanese youngsters are encouraged to feel as one with their group, whereas Western children are encouraged to feel the state of another as part of their increasingly autonomous regulation of emotional states. The import of these subtle differences needs further exploration.

Understanding emotions. Emotion knowledge predicts later social functioning, such as social acceptance by peers. By preschool, most children can infer basic emotions from expressions or situations, and understand their consequences. Preschoolers gradually come to differentiate among the negative emotions, and become increasingly capable of using emotional language. Furthermore, young children begin to identify other peoples' emotions, even when they may differ from their own (Denham, 1986; Fabes et al. 1988; Fabes et al. 1991).

Grade-schoolers become more aware of emotional experience, including multiple emotions, and realize that inner and outer emotional states may differ. By middle school, children comprehend the time course of emotions, display rules associated with emotional situations, and moral emotions. They now have an adult-like sense of how different events elicit different emotions in different people, and that enduring personality traits may impact individualized emotional reactions (Gnepp 1989; Olthof, Ferguson, and Luiten 1989).

These general tenets of competent emotion knowledge seem similar for Japanese children. For example, even two-year-olds use some emotion language; by the end of preschool, their understanding of culturally appropriate emotion language is acute (Clancy 1999; Matsuo 1997). They begin to understand dissemblance of emotion (Sawada 1997). As in U.S. research, however, there is a relative dearth of research on older children.

Emotion regulation. Emotion regulation is necessary when the presence or absence of emotional expression and experience interferes with a person's goals. Negative or positive emotions can need regulating, when they threaten to overwhelm or need to be amplified. Children learn to retain or enhance those emotions that are relevant and helpful, to attenuate those that are relevant but not helpful, and to dampen those that are irrelevant. These skills help them to experience a greater sense of well-being and maintain satisfying relationships with others (Thompson 1994).

Early in preschool, much of this emotion regulation is biobehavioral (e.g., thumb sucking), and much is supported by adults. Important cognitive foundations of emotion regulation contribute to the developmental changes observed in emotional competence from preschool to adolescence. Preschoolers gradually begin to use independent coping strategies for emotion regulation, and grade-schoolers refine these strategies—problem solving, support-seeking, distancing, internalizing, externalizing, distraction, reframing/redefining, cognitive "blunting" (i.e., convincing oneself that one's distress is minimal), and denial.

Older children are uniquely aware of the multiple strategies at their command, and know which are adaptive in specific situations. They also use more cognitive and problem-solving, and fewer support-seeking, strategies. Adolescents appraise the controllability of emotional experiences, shift thoughts intentionally, and reframe situations to reach new solutions (Saarni 1997).

Japanese children, as noted above, are initially very close to their mothers, who assist them in emotion regulation even more than Western mothers. Some researchers have noted, however, that once emotionally distressed, Japanese children find it harder to regain their equilibrium (Kojima 2000). It could be that extended maternal coregulation, coupled with stricter cultural display rules, make it more difficult for these children to self-regulate once distressed. More research is needed to follow up on these findings.

Applications

How can parents become skilled at the emotion socialization techniques appropriate to their culture? In the United States, many intervention programs exist to show parents how to foster children's social-emotional outcomes (Cowan and Cowan 1998). Most focus on parents helping children already showing difficult behavior, delineating remedial steps toward children's self-control and social skills (e.g., Webster-Stratton 1994). Other programs focus on more proactive parenting techniques (e.g., Shure 1993). In none of these programs, however, are emotion socialization techniques central (Greenberg, Kusche, and Mihalic 1998; Olds et al. 1998). Thus, even the best parenting programs generally fail to address emotion socialization directly.

However, parental instruction on emotional competence could be especially promising as a preventive approach. A few programs highlight such techniques—including those of Maurice Elias, Steven Tobias, and Brian Friedlander (1999), John Gottman (1997), and Lawrence Shapiro (1997)—emphasizing the importance of emotion-friendly family climate and parents' specific roles as emotion socializers for young children. Specific attention to the necessity of emotional competence and to the emotion socialization techniques most likely to contribute to it, in families and daycare and schools, is recommended (e.g., Denham and Burton 1996).

Conclusion

Research has delineated considerable information about children's emotional competence and how it is fostered. Nevertheless, much remains to be learned. More detail is necessary about emotional competence, its socialization, and its contribution to social success and well-being, after preschool (O'Neil and Parke 2000). Finally, the field needs to be broadened to include emotional competence and its socialization in non-Western cultures.

See also: ATTACHMENT: PARENT-CHILD RELATIONSHIPS; CHILDHOOD; CHILDHOOD, STAGES OF: INFANCY; CHILDHOOD, STAGES OF: MIDDLE CHILDHOOD; CHILDHOOD, STAGES OF: PRESCHOOL; CHILDHOOD, STAGES OF: TODDLERHOOD; CHILDREN OF ALCOHOLICS; DEVELOPMENT: COGNITIVE; DEVELOPMENT: MORAL; DEVELOPMENT: SELF; DEVELOPMENTAL PSYCHOPATHOLOGY; FAILURE TO

THRIVE; GIFTED AND TALENTED CHILDREN; INTERPARENTAL VIOLENCE—EFFECTS ON CHILDREN; SIBLING RELATIONSHIPS; SUBSTITUTE CAREGIVERS

Bibliography

Campos, J. J., and Barrett, K. C. (1984). "Toward a New Understanding of Emotions and Their Development." In *Emotions, Cognition, and Behavior,* ed. C. E. Izard, J. Kagan, and R. B. Zajonc. Cambridge, UK: Cambridge University Press.

Clancy, P. M. (1999). "The Socialization of Affect in Japanese Mother-Child Conversation." *Journal of Pragmatics* 31:1397–1421.

Cowan, P. A., and Cowan, C. P. (1998). "Parenting Interventions: A Family Systems Perspective." In *Handbook of Child Psychology,* Vol. 4: *Child Psychology in Practice,* ed. I. E. Siegal and K. A. Renninger. New York: Wiley.

Denham, S. A. (1986). "Social Cognition, Social Behavior, and Emotion in Preschoolers: Contextual Validation." *Child Development* 57:194–201.

Denham, S. A. (1998). *Emotional Development in Young Children.* New York: Guilford.

Denham, S. A., and Burton, R. (1996). "Social-Emotional Interventions for At-Risk Preschoolers." *Journal of School Psychology* 34:225–245.

Denham, S. A.; Cook, M. C.; and Zoller, D. (1992). "'Baby Looks *Very* Sad': Discussions about Emotions between Mother and Preschooler." *British Journal of Developmental Psychology* 10:301–315.

Denham, S. A., and Grout, L. (1992). "Mothers' Emotional Expressiveness and Coping: Topography and Relations with Preschoolers' Social-Emotional Competence." *Genetic, Social, and General Psychology Monographs* 118:75–101.

Denham, S. A., and Grout, L. (1993). "Socialization of Emotion: Pathway to Preschoolers' Emotional and Social Competence." *Journal of Nonverbal Behavior* 17:205–227.

Denham, S. A., and Kochanoff, A. T. (in press). "Parental Contributions to Preschoolers' Understanding of Emotion." *Marriage and Family Review.*

Denham, S. A.; Mitchell-Copeland, J.; Strandberg, K.; Auerbach, S.; and Blair, K. (1997). "Parental Contributions to Preschoolers' Emotional Competence: Direct and Indirect Effects." *Motivation and Emotion* 21:65–86.

Denham, S. A.; Zoller, D.; and Couchoud, E. A. (1994). "Socialization of Preschoolers' Understanding of Emotion." *Developmental Psychology* 30:928–936.

Dunn, J.; Brown, J. R.; and Beardsall, L. (1991). "Family Talk about Feeling States and Children's Later Understanding of Others' Emotions." *Developmental Psychology* 27:448–455.

Eisenberg, N.; Cumberland, A.; and Spinrad, T. L. (1998). "Parental Socialization of Emotion." *Psychological Inquiry* 9:241–273.

Eisenberg, N., and Fabes, R. A. (1994). "Mothers' Reactions to Children's Negative Emotions: Relations to Children's Temperament and Anger Behavior." *Merrill-Palmer Quarterly* 40:138–156.

Eisenberg, N.; Fabes, R. A.; and Murphy, B. C. (1996). "Parents' Reactions to Children's Negative Emotions: Relations to Children's Social Competence and Comforting Behavior." *Child Development* 67:2227–2247.

Eisenberg, N.; Fabes, R. A.; Shepard, S. A.; Guthrie, I.; Murphy, B. C.; and Reiser, M. (1999). "Parental Reactions to Children's Negative Emotions: Longitudinal Relations to Quality of Children's Social Functioning." *Child Development* 70:513–534.

Elias, M. J.; Tobias, S. E.; and Friedlander, B. S. (1999). *Emotionally Intelligent Parenting.* New York: Harmony Books.

Fabes, R. A.; Eisenberg, N.; McCormick, S. E.; and Wilson, M. S. (1988). "Preschoolers' Attributions of the Situational Determinants of Others' Naturally Occurring Emotions." *Developmental Psychology* 24:376–385.

Fabes, R. A.; Eisenberg, N.; Nyman, M.; and Michealieu, Q. (1991). "Young Children's Appraisal of Others' Spontaneous Emotional Reactions." *Developmental Psychology* 27:858–866.

Frijda, N. H.; Kuipers, P.; and ter Schure, E. (1989). "Relations among Emotion, Appraisal, and Emotional Action Readiness." *Journal of Personality and Social Psychology* 57:212–228.

Garner, P. W.; Jones, D. C.; and Miner, J. L. (1994). "Social Competence among Low-Income Preschoolers: Emotion Socialization Practices and Social Cognitive Correlates." *Child Development* 65:622–637.

Gnepp, J. (1989). "Children's Use of Personal Information to Understand Other People's Feelings." In *Children's Understanding of Emotion,* ed. P. Harris and C. Saarni. Cambridge, UK: Cambridge University Press.

Gottman, J. M. (1997). *Raising an Emotionally Intelligent Child.* New York: Simon and Schuster.

Gottman, J. M.; Katz, L. F.; and Hooven, C. (1997). *Meta-Emotion: How Families Communicate Emotionally.* Mahwah, NJ: Lawrence Erlbaum Associates.

Greenberg, M. T.; Kusché, C.; and Mihalic, S. F. (1998). *Promoting Alternative Thinking Strategies (PATHS),* Blueprints for Violence Prevention, Book 10. Boulder, CO: Center for the Study and Prevention of Violence.

Halberstadt, A. G. (1991). "Socialization of Expressiveness: Family Influences in Particular and a Model in General." In *Fundamentals of Emotional Expressiveness,* ed. R. S. Feldman and S. Rimé. Cambridge, UK: Cambridge University Press.

Halberstadt, A. G.; Denham, S. A.; and Dunsmore, J. (2001). "Affective Social Competence." *Social Development* 10:79–119.

Izard, C. E. (1991). *The Psychology of Emotions.* New York: Plenum.

Kanaya, Y.; Nakamura, C.; and Miyake, K. (1989). "Cross-Cultural Study of Expressive Behavior of Mothers in Response to Their 5-Month-Old Infants' Different Emotion Expression." *Research and Clinical Center for Child Development* 11:25–31.

Kitayama, S., and Markus, H. R. (1994). "Introduction to Cultural Psychology and Emotion Research." In *Emotion and Culture: Empirical Studies of Mutual Influence,* ed. S. Kitayama and H. R. Markus. Washington, DC: American Psychological Association.

Kochanoff, A. T. (2001). "Parental Disciplinary Styles, Parental Elaborativeness and Attachment: Links to Preschoolers' Emotion Knowledge." Ph.D. diss., George Mason University, Fairfax, Virginia.

Kojima, Y. (2000). "Maternal Regulation of Sibling Interactions in the Preschool Years: Observational Study of Japanese Families." *Child Development* 71:1640–1647.

Lazarus, R. S. (1991). *Emotion and Adaptation.* New York: Oxford University Press.

Lutz, C. (1994). "Cultural Patterns and Individual Differences in the Child's Emotional Meaning System." In *Emotion and Culture: Empirical Studies of Mutual Influence,* ed. S. Kitayama and H. R. Markus. Washington, DC: American Psychological Association.

Markus, H. R., and Kitayama, S. (1994). "The Cultural Construction of Self and Emotion: Implications for Social Behavior." In *Emotion and Culture: Empirical Studies of Mutual Influence,* ed. S. Kitayama and H. R. Markus. Washington, DC: American Psychological Association.

Matsumoto, D. (1994). *People: Psychology from a Cultural Perspective.* Pacific Grove, CA: Brooks/Cole.

Matsumoto, D.; Kudoh, T.; Scherer, K.; and Walbott, H. (1988). "Antecedents of and Reactions to Emotions in the United States and Japan." *Journal of Cross-Cultural Psychology* 19:267–286.

Matsuo, K. (1997). "Young Children's Comprehension of Figurative Language which Describe Emotions." *Japanese Journal of Developmental Psychology* 8:165–175.

Mauro, R.; Sato, K.; and Tucker, J. (1992). "The Role of Appraisal in Human Emotions: A Cross-Cultural Study." *Journal of Personality and Social Psychology* 62:301–318.

Nakamura, M.; Buck, R.; and Kenny, D. A. (1990). "Relative Contributions of Expression Behavior and Contextual Information to the Judgment of the Emotional State of Another." *Journal of Personality and Social Psychology* 59:1032–1039.

Oatley, K., and Jenkins, J. M. (1996). *Understanding Emotions: In Psychology, Psychiatry, and Social Science.* Cambridge, MA: Blackwell.

Olds, D.; Hill, P.; Mihalic, S.; and O'Brien, R. (1998). *Prenatal and Infancy Home Visitation by Nurses,* Blueprints for Violence Prevention, Book 7. Boulder, CO: Center for the Study and Prevention of Violence.

Olthof, T.; Ferguson, T. J.; and Luiten, A. (1989). "Personal Responsibility Antecedents of Anger and Blame Reactions in Children." *Child Development* 60:1328–1336.

O'Neil, R., and Parke, R. D. (2000). "Family-Peer Relationships: The Role of Emotion Regulation, Cognitive Understanding, and Attentional Processes As Mediating Processes." In *Family and Peers: Linking Two Social Worlds,* ed. K. Kerns, J. Contreras, and A. M. Neal-Barnett. Westport, CT: Praeger.

Saarni, C. (1990). "Emotional Competence." In *Nebraska Symposium: Socioemotional Development,* ed. R. Thompson. Lincoln: University of Nebraska Press.

Saarni, C. (1997). "Coping with Aversive Feelings." *Motivation and Emotion* 21:45–63.

Saarni, C. (1998). "Issues of Cultural Meaningfulness in Emotional Development." *Developmental Psychology* 34:647–652.

Saarni, C. (1999). *The Development of Emotional Competence.* New York: Guilford.

Sawada, T. (1997). "Development of Children's Understanding of Emotional Dissemblance in Another Person." *Japanese Journal of Educational Psychology* 45:50–59.

Shapiro, L. E. (1997. *How to Raise a Child with a High E.Q.* New York: HarperCollins.

Shiraev, E., and Levy, D. (2001). *Introduction to Cross-Cultural Psychology: Critical Thinking and Contemporary Applications.* Needham Heights, MA: Allyn and Bacon.

Shure, M. B. (1993). *Interpersonal Problem Solving and Prevention: A Comprehensive Report of Research and Training.* #MH-40801. Washington, DC: National Institute of Mental Health.

Sonoda, N., and Muto, T. (1996). "References to Internal States in Mother-Child Interactions: Effect of Different Settings and Maternal Individual Differences." *Japanese Journal of Developmental Psychology* 7:159–169.

Thompson, R. A. (1994). "Emotional Regulation: A Theme in Search of Definition." In *The Development of Emotion Regulation: Biological and Behavioral Considerations,* ed. N. A. Fox. Monographs of the Society for Research in Child Development, No. 59.

Tomkins, S. S. (1963). *Affect, Imagery, and Consciousness,* Vols. 1 and 2. New York: Springer.

Tomkins, S. S. (1991). *Affect, Imagery, and Consciousness,* Vol. 3: *The Negative Affects: Anger and Fear.* New York: Springer.

Ujiie, T. (1997). "How Do Japanese Mothers Treat Children's Negativism?" *Journal of Applied Developmental Psychology* 18:467–483.

Webster-Stratton, C. (1994). "Advancing Videotape Parent Training: A Comparison Study." *Journal of Consulting and Clinical Psychology* 62:583–593.

Zahn-Waxler, C.; Friedman, R. J.; Cole, P. M.; Mizuta, I.; and Hiruma, N. (1996). "Japanese and United States Preschool Children's Responses to Conflict and Distress." *Child Development* 67:2462–2477.

Zeman, J., and Shipman, K. (1996). "Children's Expression of Negative Affect: Reasons and Methods." *Developmental Psychology* 32:842–849.

SUSANNE DENHAM
ANITA KOCHANOFF
KAREN NEAL
TERESA MASON
HIDEKO HAMADA

MORAL

Moral development is a topic of great interest to psychology, philosophy, sociology, and education. How does an infant—born without moral principles—gradually become a person who respects others and can live in society? This question is studied in the context of socialization.

Earlier Theoretical Models: Psychoanalysis and Behaviorism

Theories have approached morality differently. Sigmund Freud (1856–1939) described *Oedipus complex* to explain the origins of moral conscience, called the *superego.* The Oedipus complex occurs when a child loves the opposite sex parent and, in order to avoid the anxiety and fear of punishment that this causes, the child identifies with the same sex parent. The child incorporates the same sex parent's prohibitions, starting with "Do not love (sexually) your parent."

For behaviorist theorists, such as Robert R. Sears, Robert Grinder, and Albert Bandura (1982), conscience or morality was considered analogous to the phenomenon of resistance to extinction. H. Hartshorne and M. A. May, at the end of the 1920s, were pioneers in this line of research. Later, Robert Sears, Eleanor Maccoby, and Harry Levin (1957) and other researchers studied the influence of maternal and paternal disciplines upon development of the conscience. These studies found that warm and affectionate parents, who reason with their children rather than punish them physically, are more successful in having their children assimilate the moral values of the culture. Cognitive behaviorists have added other dimensions to this process, such as *expectancies* (what the child expects is going to happen), *incentive value* (how much the child wants something), *hypothesis testing* ("If I do this, then that will happen"), and *self-efficacy* (one's capacity and confidence on doing something) (Bandura 1977, 1978). In the psychoanalytic and behaviorist models, morality seems to be something that comes from outside, from society, which is internalized.

Cognitive Models

Jean Piaget (1896–1980) and Lawrence Kohlberg's (1928–1987) theories considered the role of the human being as agent in the moral process. These scholars focused on *moral judgment*: on the knowledge of right and wrong. In the latter decades of the twentieth century, the cognitive approach took over the study of morality, with few studies conducted on moral behavior or feelings. Both Piaget and Kohlberg were influenced by the philosopher Immanuel Kant (1724–1804) and by sociologist Emile Durkheim (1858–1917). From Kant, with the notion of *categorical imperative* came the idea of universal moral principles, and from Durkheim came the importance of social and collective factors.

Piaget's model. In Piaget's constructivist perspective, he speaks of the interaction between cognitive structures, or stages of development, which are biologically determined, and environmental stimulation. He is most famous for his work on with the identification of universal stages through which thinking evolves in an invariant sequence (i.e., in the same order for all persons of all cultures) (Piaget and Inhelder, 1967).

In *The Moral Judgment of the Child* (1932), Piaget argues that moral judgment evolves through stages that are roughly parallel to the stages of cognitive development. He observed children behavior and attitudes in games of marbles. He identified stages in the development of rules, and the children's attitudes regarding rules. The first stage consists of *sensorimotor* (sense organs and motor development) exercises: the child plays with the marbles, for example, with no notion of rules. In this stage, vision and touch are practiced. In the second stage, called egocentric: the child follows his/her own rules, while trying to imitate others' rules. Paradoxically, the child has great respect for the rules, says they cannot be changed, but does not follow them. If one asks four- or five-year-olds, for example, who created the rules of the game of marbles, they might say God, Santa Claus, or "my father," all other authority figures. During this stage the child considers material losses as more serious than intentions. Piaget used pairs of short stories to test this, for example: Peter rushed into the kitchen and accidentally broke twelve glasses that were on a tray behind the door. Johnny got mad because his mother did not let him play outside, picked up a glass on a tray, and threw it on the floor in order to break it. Which of the two boys deserve more punishment, Peter or Johnny? The younger child says it is worse for a child to break a dozen glasses accidentally than one glass on purpose, because twelve glasses will cost more to replace than one glass. In the third stage, *beginning cooperation,* the child begins to cooperate, follow rules, and understand the importance of *intentionality.* It is only in the fourth stage, however, that the child is able to codify rules and understand that game rules are arbitrary and can be changed if all players agree beforehand. Conceptions about justice also evolve from retribution and vengeance (in the young

Games such as hopscotch may challenge children in developing and shaping morals. These children may consider the fairness of the rules, who made them up, and whether or not to follow them. JENNIE WOODCOCK; REFLECTIONS PHOTOLIBRARY/CORBIS

child) to the notion of reform of the culprit and reparation, or making up for wrong doing (in the older child). *Immanent justice* (punishment by nature) also diminishes. *Heteronomy* (norms imposed by external forces) is substituted by *autonomy* (making decisions depending on one's own conscience).

Kohlberg's cognitive model. Lawrence Kohlberg (1958) based his theories on Piaget's ideas. Unlike Piaget, however, Kohlberg presents a more precise conceptualization and discrimination of the stages, and the dimension of heteronomy-autonomy that underlie the stages. His method allows for quantified scores of maturity of moral judgment. The six stages proposed by Kohlberg are subsumed in three levels: *preconventional* (stages one and two), *conventional* (stages three and four), and *postconventional* (stages five and six). In order to understand the meaning of the stages, it is important first to understand the meaning of levels.

The preconventional level is characteristic of younger children, some adolescents, and many criminals. There is not yet any sense of real morality, or any internalization of values. The conventional level is typical of the majority of adolescents and adults in U.S. society (Colby and Kohlberg 1984), and probably all Western societies and even non-Western societies as well (Snarey 1985). At the postconventional level individuals have come to question the morality of the status quo and are able to change laws and cultural rules. Approximately 5 percent of adults reach the postconventional level, usually after age twenty or twenty-five.

At stage one, the orientation is toward punishment and obedience; at stage two, morality is geared toward pleasure and satisfaction of one's own needs; at stage three, morality centers on pleasing others and fulfilling conventional roles; at stage four, the emphasis is on law and order; at stage five, the person tries to change unfair laws through democratic channels; and at stage six individual conscience prevails.

Kohlberg interviewed children and adolescents of ages ten, thirteen, and sixteen years, and identified levels and stages of moral development, proposing moral dilemmas such as one about a husband who steals medicine to save his dying wife when all efforts to get money to pay for the expensive drug failed. Another dilemma has to do with a boy who wanted to go camping, and his father promises he may go if he saves money from his newspaper delivery job. Then the father requests the money for himself, in order to go on a fishing trip. Answers to dilemmas are analyzed and the researcher classifies a person's response into one of the six stages. It is not the content (to steal or not to steal, or to give the money to the father or not to give it) that determines a person's stage of moral judgment, but the reasoning behind it. If a person says the husband should not steal it because he could be caught and go to jail, this person is responding at stage one. If one says he should steal the money to look good before his friends, or only if he loves his wife, this person would be responding at stage three. If, in response to the first dilemma, one says stealing is against the law, so the husband should not steal the money, this person is responding at stage four. Valuing human life over the pharmacist's profit situates the respondent at stage five or six. In the second dilemma, appeals to the father's authority and the duty of a son to obey him places a response at stage one, whereas speaking of the importance of fulfilling a promise places a person at a higher stage. Details about the scoring procedure appear in the Manual for scoring the Kohlberg Moral Judgment Interview, which is a guide to evaluating at which stage of moral development a person's responses are at (Colby and Kohlberg 1984).

Many moral education programs in schools are based on Kohlberg's theory, consisting of group discussion of moral dilemmas, as initially proposed by Moshe Blatt and Kohlberg (1975). These debates or discussions create cognitive conflict when a participant is faced with someone's responses, which may be in a higher stage than his/her own. This usually increases level of moral maturity. Kohlberg started involving whole schools, including any teachers, students, or faculty that wanted to participate, in discussing real-life moral dilemmas of the participants' school situation, a technique referred to as *just community*, which has been proven very valuable (Power, Higgins, and Kohlberg 1989).

Kohlberg claims that there is a core of moral values that are universal, in other words, the sequence of stages is invariant, and the same for every person of each culture. As a result, certain moral values, such as the respect for human life, and not causing harm to others, are upheld in all cultures. John Snarey's (1985) review of the literature supports this notion. He analyzed more that forty studies conducted in twenty-seven different cultures, which support Kohlberg's claim for universality, although the higher stages (five and six) did not appear in all cultures. However, Richard Shweder and his colleagues (1991) argue for the role of culture, based on their research in India (Shweder, Mahapatra, and Miller 1987): they did not find distinctions between conventional and moral transgressions. Jonathan Haidt, Silvia Koller, and Maria da Graça Dias (1993) corroborated those findings in their research with Brazilian children. Contrary to this relativistic view of morality, some neo-Kohlbergians, such as Elliot Turiel (1983) and Larry Nucci (1981), distinguish between moral and conventional domains, and present evidence that even preschool children distinguish between the severity of transgressions of each domain. Carol Gilligan (1982) argues that women's morality is different from, but not inferior to, male morality. Women emphasize the justice of care, whereas males stress justice, which is the central concept in Kohlberg's theory.

Prosocial Behavior

Comparatively few researchers have examined similarities and differences in the positive sides of morality. There have been few examinations of the dilemmas in which one person's needs or desires conflict with those others in need in a context in which the role of prohibitions (e.g., formal laws or rules), authorities' dictates, and formal obligations. However, children and adolescents often are faced with the decision to help others at cost to themselves. Those decisions have been the focus of prosocial moral reasoning research that emphasizes reasoning about moral dilemmas in which one's needs or desires conflict with those of others in need (Eisenberg 1986).

The development of prosocial moral reasoning is consistent with Kohlbergian justice-oriented developmental stages. The similarity is due to the role of cognition as a necessary, but not sufficient factor, for reasoning about moral dilemmas. Nancy Eisenberg and her colleagues (Eisenberg et al. 1995; Eisenberg et al. 1991) have found a developmental progression from hedonistic and needs-oriented, to approval-oriented and stereotypic (norm-related), to, finally, empathic and internalized, modes of prosocial moral reasoning during childhood and adolescence. However, in contrast to prohibition-oriented moral reasoning, older children and adolescents express both cognitively sophisticated types of prosocial moral reasoning as well as the less sophisticated types (Eisenberg et al. 1995). Based on socialization theory (Gilligan 1982; Maccoby and Jacklin 1974), individual and group (e.g., cultural, national, and gender) differences in prosocial moral reasoning may be most evident in late adolescence when differences in moral reasoning due to cognitive development are reduced, and socialization processes are consolidated. Thus, by late adolescence (e.g., for college students), prior and current educational experiences, and cultural socialization processes are expected to become increasingly important to individuals' reasoning in moral situations. Consistent with cognitive developmental theory, researchers frequently have found that the sophistication of moral judgment increases during adolescence, presumably due in part to an increase in perspective taking and reflective abstraction skills (Colby et al. 1983; Eisenberg 1986; Rest 1983; Selman 1980).

The processes involved in prosocial moral reasoning and in prosocial behavior (as reported by Carlo et al. 1996; and Eisenberg, Zhou, and Koller 2001) appear to be similar for children and adolescents of different cultures (North American middle-class adolescents compared to low and high socioeconomic status Brazilian adolescents).

For most people, life is continual change: moral character changes as cognitive and emotional developmental processes (from hedonistic or egocentric behaviors to self-reflexive perspective taking and internalized norm-related or other-related judgments and behaviors) combine and as individuals face new social and familial roles and contexts (Mason and Gibbs 1993; Rest and Narvaez 1991). There are increases in personal and social responsibilities that parallel the developmental changes that occur during the life cycle. Each change provides new opportunities for having a greater impact on personal development, society, and others. Although the aforementioned changes are common to many people during the life cycle, ecological theorists (e.g., Bronfenbrenner 1979) suggest that different culture-specific socialization experiences lead to specific developmental outcomes. Socialization experiences, including social norms, expectations, and educational experiences, may indeed be different for individuals from different cultures depending on the beliefs, attitudes, and behaviors deemed desirable for success in that society. These culture-specific experiences may lead to different patterns of thinking about moral and prosocial issues.

See also: CHILDHOOD; CHILDHOOD, STAGES OF: INFANCY; CHILDHOOD, STAGES OF: MIDDLE CHILDHOOD; CHILDHOOD, STAGES OF: PRESCHOOL; CHILDHOOD, STAGES OF: TODDLERHOOD; CONDUCT DISORDER; DEVELOPMENT: COGNITIVE; DEVELOPMENT: EMOTIONAL; DEVELOPMENT: SELF; DEVELOPMENTAL PSYCHOPATHOLOGY; DISCIPLINE; GIFTED AND TALENTED CHILDREN; PARENTING STYLES; PLAY

Bibliography

Bandura, A. (1977). *Social Learning Theory*. Englewood-Cliffs, NJ: Prentice-Hall.

Bandura, A. (1978). "The Self System in Reciprocal Determinism." *American Psychologist* 33:344–358.

Bandura, A. (1982). "Self-Efficacy Mechanism in Human Agency." *American Psychologist* 37:122–147.

Blatt, M., and Kohlberg, L. (1975). "The Effects of Classroom Moral Discussion upon Children's Level of Moral Judgment." *Journal of Moral Education* 4:129–161.

Bronfenbrenner, U. (1979). *The Ecology of Human Behavior*. Cambridge, MA: Harvard University Press.

Carlo, G.; Koller, S. H.; Eisenberg, N.; Da Silva, M.; and Frohlich, C. (1996). "A Cross National Study of the Relations among Prosocial Moral Reasoning, Gender Role Orientations, and Prosocial Behaviors." *Developmental Psychology* 32:231–240.

Colby, A., and Kohlberg, L. (1984). "Invariant Sequence, and Internal Consistency in Moral Judgment Stages." In *Morality, Moral Behavior, and Moral Development,* ed. W. Kurtines and J. Gewirtz. New York: Wiley.

Colby, A., and Kohlberg, L. (1987). *The Measurement of Moral Judgment.* Cambridge, UK: Cambridge University Press.

Colby, A.; Kohlberg, L.; Gibbs, J.; and Lieberman, M. (1983). *A Longitudinal Study of Moral Judgment.* Monographs of the Society for Research in Child Development, no. 48 (1–2, serial 200).

Eisenberg, N. (1986). *Altruistic Emotion, Cognition and Behavior.* Hillsdale, NJ: Lawrence Erlbaum Associates.

Eisenberg, N.; Carlo, G.; Murphy, B.; and Van Court, P. (1995). "Prosocial Development in Late Adolescence: A Longitudinal Study." *Child Development* 66:1179–1197.

Eisenberg, N.; Miller, P. A.; Shell, R.; McNalley, S.; and Shea, C. (1991). "Prosocial Development in Adolescence: A Longitudinal Study." *Developmental Psychology* 27:849–857.

Eisenberg, N.; Zhou, Q.; and Koller, S. H. (2001). "Brazilian Adolescents' Prosocial Moral Judgment and Behavior: Relations to Sympathy, Perspective Taking, Gender Role Orientation, and Demographic Characteristics." *Child Development* 72:518–534.

Gilligan, C. (1982). *In a Different Voice: Psychological Theory and Women's Development.* Cambridge, MA: Harvard University Press.

Grinder, R. E. (1962). "Parental child-rearing practices, conscience, and resistance to temptation of sixth-grade children." *Child Development* 33:803–820.

Haidt, J.; Koller, S. H.; and Dias, M. G. B. B. (1993). "Affect, Culture and Moral Judgment, or Is It Wrong to Eat Your Dog?" *Journal of Personality and Social Psychology* 65:613–628.

Hawthorne, H. and May, M. A. (1928-1930). *Studies in the Nature of Character,* Vols. 1–3. New York: Macmillan.

Kohlberg, L. (1958). "The Development of Modes of Thinking and Choices in the Years from 10 to 16." Ph.D. diss., University of Chicago.

Kohlberg, L. (1963). "The Development of Children's Orientation toward a Moral Order: I. Sequence in the Development of Moral Thought." *Vita Humana* 6:11–13.

Maccoby, E. E., and Jacklin, C. N. (1974). *The Psychology of Sex Differences.* Stanford, CA: Stanford University Press.

Mason, M. G., and Gibbs, J. C. (1993). "Social Perspective Taking and Moral Judgment Among College Students." *Journal of Adolescent Research* 8:109–123.

Nucci, L. (1981). "Conceptions of Personal Issues: A Domain Distinct from Moral or Societal Concepts." *Child Development* 52:114–121.

Piaget, J. (1932). *The Moral Judgment of the Child.* London: Kegan Paul.

Piaget, J. (1967). *The Child's Conception of Space.* New York: Macmillan.

Power, F. C.; Higgins, A.; and Kohlberg, L. (1989). *Lawrence Kohlberg's Approach to Moral Education.* Cambridge, MA: Harvard University Press.

Rest, J. (1983). "Morality." In *Cognitive Development,* Vol. 3 of *Handbook of Child Psychology,* ed. P. Mussen, J. H. Flavell, and E. Markman. New York: Wiley.

Rest, J., and Narvaez, D. (1991). "The College Experience and Moral Development." In *Handbook of Moral Behavior and Development,* Vol. 2: *Research,* ed. W. M. Kurtines and J. L. Gewirtz. Hillsdale, NJ: Lawrence Erlbaum Associates.

Sears, R. R. (1957) "Identification as a Form of Behavioral Development." In *The Concept of Development,* ed. D. B. Harris. Minneapolis: University of Minnesota Press.

Sears, R. R.; Maccoby, E.; and Levin, H. (1957). *Patterns of Child Rearing.* New York: Harper & Row.

Selman, R. (1980). *The Growth of Interpersonal Understanding.* New York: Academic Press.

Shweder, R. (1991). *Thinking through Cultures: Explorations in Cultural Psychology.* Cambridge, MA: Harvard University Press.

Shweder, R.; Mahapatra, M.; and Miller, J. (1987). "Culture and Moral Development." In *The Emergence of Morality in Young Children,* ed. J. Kagan, and S. Lamb. Chicago: University of Chicago Press.

Snarey, J. (1985). "The Cross-Cultural Universality of Socio-Moral Development: A Critical Review of Kohlbergian Research." *Psychological Bulletin* 97:202–232.

Turiel, E. (1983). *The Development of Social Knowledge.* Cambridge, UK: Cambridge University Press.

SILVIA H. KOLLER
ANGELA M. B. BIAGGIO

SELF

Children's self-evaluations fall into two categories: evaluations of their competence or adequacy in particular life domains (for example, scholastic competence, physical appearance), and evaluations of their overall worth as a person, which is referred to in this entry as *self-esteem.* An analysis of the effects of parental variables on children's self-evaluations and personality development is timely given claims (see Harris 1998) that parents have little influence on their children's psychological development other than their genetic contribution. There is considerable research to the contrary, which is not to negate the role of genetics. What is needed is a balanced perspective on the nature-nurture controversy, namely, an appreciation of both genetic contributions and the critical role of parent-child interactions beginning in infancy and continuing through adolescence and beyond. Two theories have dominated the study of the effects of parent-child interactions on children's self-representations: William James' (1890) formulation on the determinants of one's level of global self-esteem—that is, the overall evaluation of one's worth as a person (see Harter 1999a)—and Charles Horton Cooley's (1902) theory of the looking-glass self.

James' Theory of the Determinants of Self-Esteem

For James (1890), self-esteem results not from a summary evaluation of one's successes or failures, but rather from an assessment of one's sense of adequacy or competence in areas one deems important. For children, such domains include scholastic competence, athletic competence, peer likability, physical appearance, and behavioral conduct. Thus, if children feel adequate in those domains judged important and are able to discount the importance of domains in which they feel that they have limitations, then they will have high global self-esteem. Those who continue to assign importance to areas in which they perceive weaknesses will report low self-esteem.

The primary contribution of parents to this process lies in the origins of children's judgments of importance. Children naturally come to accept their parents' definition of the importance of success in given domains, particularly in early childhood where parental values and authority are highly respected. Parents who give high importance to academic success, for example, will convey this attitude, directly or indirectly, and their children will come to view the academic arena as extremely important. However, if a particular child has a palpable weakness (for example, a learning disability, a low IQ, or temperamental traits that interfere with the ability to attend to and concentrate on schoolwork), then this child will not be successful. This, in

turn creates a discrepancy between high importance and low success, the very formula that leads to low self-esteem from a Jamesian perspective. Conversely, if the child's abilities and talents are convergent with parental values, then there will not be a discrepancy between importance values and the child's success in various domains, and the child will have high self-esteem. Thus, parents' values can directly affect the self-esteem of their children.

Cooley's Theory of the Looking Glass Self

For Cooley (1902), significant others, notably parents in childhood, constitute social mirrors into which a child gazes to detect parental opinions of the self. These opinions of others are then, in turn, incorporated into a child's sense of self, namely an evaluation of his or her worth as a person. Thus, if parents approve of the self, these positive attitudes are adopted in the form of high self-esteem as well as a sense of adequacy in the specific areas where there is parental feedback (e.g., scholastic competence, athletic competence, behavioral conduct, appearance). Conversely, if parents manifest their disapproval of child's worth or capabilities, the child will devalue the self and experience low self-esteem. Thus, for Cooley, the self is very much a social construction. Numerous studies have documented the fact that approval from significant others is a powerful contributor to a child's sense of self (Harter 1999a).

The manner in which approval from parents is communicated to children is more complex than mere direct verbal feedback (see Harter 1999a). Negative parental opinions can be communicated through a lack of positive feedback. Another family member may also serve as a source of information about parental appraisals. In addition, through observing how parents evaluate others (e.g., siblings), children can gain indirect information about how parents evaluate the self. Thus, if a sibling receives praise but the target child does not, negative self-evaluations can result.

The looking-glass self represents a dynamic process that occurs over the formative years of development. Ideally, children will come to internalize positive approval such that ultimately they are no longer totally dependent upon the opinions of others. That is, they become able to evaluate their own worth, successes, and failures in the absence of either direct feedback or indirect communication. However, there are potential liabilities when the self is developed in the crucible of family interactions (see Harter 1999b). The first and most obvious are liabilities associated with the internalization of unfavorable evaluations of the self by others. The incorporation of disapproving opinions of parents will lead, in turn, to perceptions of personal inadequacy and low self-esteem.

There are liabilities associated with the failure to internalize standards and evaluative judgments of parents, standards and judgments that one should come to own and that can serve as the basis for one's sense of self-worth and as guides in regulating one's behavior. If one is constantly drawn to the social looking glass, if one persists in primarily basing one's sense of self-worth on the appraisals of others, a constellation of negative correlates will arise. Research by Susan Harter, Clare Stocker, and Nancy Robinson (1996) revealed several related liabilities among young adolescents who, rather than internalizing parental opinions of the self, continued to base their self-esteem on the external views of others. First, these adolescents reported significantly greater preoccupation with approval of peers than did those who had internalized the opinions of others. Second, teachers' ratings confirmed the researchers' expectations that those still gazing into the social mirror were more socially distracted in the classroom, devoting less energy to their scholastic activities, given their greater preoccupation with peer approval. Third, the adolescents in the study reported more perceived fluctuations in peer approval. Fourth, they reported greater fluctuations in self-esteem, which is understandable since by definition they were basing their self-esteem on the perceived approval of others. Fifth, they reported lower levels of peer approval, perhaps because in their preoccupation with approval, they engaged in behaviors that did not garner this type of peer support. They may have tried too hard to obtain peer approval or may have employed inappropriate strategies, and in so doing may have annoyed or alienated their classmates. Finally, given that these adolescents, who by definition based their self-esteem on approval, reported lower peer approval, they reported lower self-esteem.

Aspects of early parent-child interactions may prevent the internalization process from developing. If children receive inconsistent feedback—for example, fluctuations between approval and disapproval from parents—it may be difficult for them to internalize a coherent evaluation of the self. Alternatively, receiving support that is conditional upon meeting unrealistic demands of parents may also prevent the internalization of feelings of self-approval. Conditionality can be contrasted to *unconditional positive regard* (Rogers 1951) in which parents provide general approval for their child. Adolescents do not find conditional support to be personally supportive (Harter 1999a). Rather, it identifies contingencies (e.g., "If you are successful, I will approve of you," "If you do exactly as I say, I will love you"). Thus, an early history of such conditional approval, as well as fluctuating feedback, does not provide the kind of validating support that can be internalized as approval of the self, nor does it provide a consistent pattern of disapproval that can be internalized as lack of acceptance of the self.

An Attachment Theory Perspective on the Self

From an attachment theory perspective, representations and evaluations of oneself can only be considered with the context of the caregiver-child relationship. Thus, as John Bowlby (1969) contended, children who experiences parents as emotionally available, loving, and supportive of their mastery efforts will construct a working model of the self as lovable and competent. In contrast, children who experience attachment figures as rejecting, emotionally unavailable, insensitive and nonsupportive, or inconsistent will construct a working model of the self that is unlovable, incompetent, and generally unworthy (see Bretherton 1991; Sroufe 1990; Verschureren, Buyck, and Marcoen 2001). In addition, those who are securely attached will report more realistic or balanced self-concepts, reporting on both positive and negative characteristics, although typically more positive attributes are cited (see Cassidy 1990; Easterbrooks & Abeles, 2000). That is, securely attached children have more *access* to both positive and negative self-attributes than do insecurely attached children, who often present an unrealistically positive account of their strengths in an attempt to mask underlying feelings of unworthiness.

Moreover, Lisa Kiang (2001) found that childhood attachment has a long-term effect on self-esteem in the college years. Kiang found that one type of insecure attachment (avoidance) led to the psychological correlates of eating disordered behavior (feelings of ineffectiveness, perfectionism, interpersonal distrust, maturity fears). These psychological symptoms, in turn, took their toll on self-esteem. Thus, patterns of early parent-child interactions can have far-reaching implications for later development, including maladaptive eating practices and low self-esteem.

Cross-Cultural Issues

Attention has shifted to whether attachment dynamics are universal across cultures or are more culture-specific (see Rothbaum, Weisz, Pott, Miyake, and Morelli 2000; Van Ijzendoorn and Sagi 1999). The most thoughtful conclusion is that for evolutionary reasons, the attachment system does have universal characteristics that are designed for infants' survival during a period when they are vulnerable and therefore highly dependent upon parents. That said, how parental sensitivity is specifically defined should also logically vary from culture to culture, depending upon societal values. Whatever these variations, sensitive parenting should lead to securely-attached behavior that, in turn, should lead to positive self-evaluations in culturally-relevant domains as well as to positive self-esteem. However, cultural variations dictate that one develop different instruments to assess self-evaluations in different cultures.

For example, it is noteworthy that those who have taken Western self-perception measures to various Asian cultures (Korea, China, Taiwan, Hong Kong, Japan) have found that the item content may not be relevant and that the question format, which pulls for social comparison, is not appropriate given that social comparison is frowned upon (see Harter 1999a). Thus, researchers need to take a more culture-specific look at what the self means in different cultures, how salient or important it is in different cultures, and with what outcomes it may be associated.

Conclusion

Parent-child behavior within the context of the family has a profound effect on numerous aspects of self-development. Various parental behaviors influence the level of a child's self esteem, domain-specific self-concepts, accuracy of self-evaluations, and preoccupation with approval which can have debilitating effects on the self. Each of these, in turn, has mental health implications since children's self-perceptions are highly related to their

mood, namely the extent to which they are cheerful or depressed (see Harter 1999a). Any thoughtful approach to issues involving the self will require a sensitive inquiry into cross-cultural issues. As the world becomes more interconnected and more global, sensitivity to cultural differences and similarities is integral to the understanding of self-development.

See also: ATTACHMENT: PARENT-CHILD RELATIONSHIPS; BOUNDARY DISSOLUTION; CHILDHOOD, STAGES OF: ADOLESCENCE; CHILDHOOD; CHILDHOOD, STAGES OF: INFANCY; CHILDHOOD, STAGES OF: MIDDLE CHILDHOOD; CHILDHOOD, STAGES OF: PRESCHOOL; CHILDHOOD, STAGES OF: TODDLERHOOD; CHILDREN OF ALCOHOLICS; DEPRESSION: ADULTS; DEPRESSION: CHILDREN AND ADOLESCENTS; DEVELOPMENT: COGNITIVE; DEVELOPMENT: EMOTIONAL; DEVELOPMENT, MORAL; DEVELOPMENTAL PSYCHOPATHOLOGY; FAMILY LIFE EDUCATION; FAVORITISM/DIFFERENTIAL TREATMENT; ONLY CHILDREN; PARENTING STYLES; SELF-ESTEEM; SEPARATION-INDIVIDUATION; SIBLING RELATIONSHIPS

Bibliography

Bowlby, J. (1969). *Attachment and Loss,* Vol. 1: *Attachment.* New York: Basic Books.

Bretherton, I. (1991). "Pouring New Wine into Old Bottles: The Social Self as Internal Working Model." In *Self Processes and Development: The Minnesota Symposia on Child Development,* Vol. 23, ed. M. R. Gunnar and L. A. Sroufe. Hillsdale, NJ: Erlbaum.

Cassidy, J. (1990). "Theoretical and Methodological Considerations in the Study of Attachment and the Self in Young Children." In *Attachment in the Preschool Years: Theory, Research, and Intervention,* ed. M. T. Greenberg, D. Cicchetti, and E. M. Cummings. Chicago: University of Chicago Press.

Cooley, C. H. (1902). *Human Nature and the Social Order.* New York: Scribner.

Easterbrooks, M. A., and Abeles, R. (2000). "Windows to the Self in 8-Year Olds: Bridges to Attachment Representation and Behavioral Adjustment." *Attachment and Human Development* 2:85–106.

Harris, J. R. (1998). *The Nurture Assumption: Why Children Turn Out the Way They Do. Parents Matter Less Than You Think.* New York: The Free Press.

Harter, S. (1999a). *The Construction of the Self: A Developmental Perspective.* New York: Guilford Press.

Harter, S. (1999b). "Symbolic Interactionism Revisited: Potential Liabilities for the Self Constructed in the Crucible of Interpersonal Relationships." *Merrill-Palmer Quarterly* 45:677–703.

Harter, S.; Stocker, C.; and Robinson, N. (1996). "The Perceived Directionality of the Link between Approval and Self-Worth: The Liabilities of a Looking Glass Self Orientation among Young Adolescents." *Journal of Research on Adolescence* 6:285–308.

James, W. (1890). *Principles of Psychology.* Chicago: Encyclopedia Britannica.

Kiang, L. (2001). "Attachment and Sociocultural Values of Appearance: An Integrated Model of Eating Disorder Symptomatology." Unpublished Master's thesis. Colorado: University of Denver.

Rogers, C. R. (1951). *Client-Centered Therapy.* Boston: Houghton Mifflin.

Rothbaum, F.; Weisz, J.; Pott, M.; Miyake, K.; and Morelli, G. (2000). "Attachment and Culture: Security in the United States and Japan." *American Psychologist* 55:1093–1104.

Sroufe, A. (1990). "An Organizational Perspective on the Self." In *The Self in Transition: Infancy to childhood,* ed. D. Cicchetti and M. Beeghly. Chicago: University of Chicago Press.

Van Ijzendoorn, M. H., and Sagi, A. (1999). "Cross-Cultural Patterns of Attachment: Universal and Contextual Dimensions." In *Handbook of Attachment: Theory, Research, and Clinical Applications,* ed. J. Cassidy and P. Shaver. New York: Guilford.

Verschueren, K.; Buyck, P.; and Marcoen, A. (2001). "Self-Representations and Socioemotional Competence in Young Children: A 3-Year Longitudinal Study." *Developmental Psychology* 37:126–134.

SUSAN HARTER
LISA KIANG

DEVELOPMENTAL DISABILITIES

The term *developmental disabilities* was introduced in the United States in the late 1960s as a term to refer to the disabilities of mental retardation, epilepsy, and cerebral palsy. Parent leaders Elizabeth Boggs and Ilse Helsel advocated for the term in an effort to unify the political efforts of what was then the National Association of Retarded Children and United Cerebral Palsy Association (Pelka 1997). It is a term specific to the United States and, within the United States, specific to legislation meant to focus on individuals whose disability was manifested before age twenty-one. However, although the term does not appear in legislation that mandates any specific services, such as education or health care, it has had the effect that Boggs and Helse intended of unifying groups that were created for specific conditions in the common cause of pursuing rights and opportunities for individuals whose disability occurred in childhood. In 1970, the Developmental Disabilities Services and Facilities Construction Amendment was passed, thus codifying a legislative definition of developmental disabilities. In 1990, the Developmental Disabilities Assistance and Bill of Rights Act incorporated the following definition of developmental disability: "a severe, chronic disability of a person 5 years of age or older" that is "attributable to a mental or physical impairment or a combination of mental or physical impairments" and is "evident before the person attains age 22." A developmental disability is "likely to continue indefinitely" and "results in substantial functional limitations in three or more major life activities including self care, language, learning, mobility, self direction, capacity for independent living, and economic self sufficiency." The use of the term developmental disabilities and the legislative entitlement to education and social security supports and the mandate for accessible physical environments is unique to the United States. Other Western countries have progressive service models but do not have the universal guarantees found in the United States.

Causes of Developmental Disabilities

Developmental disabilities, including *mental retardation, autism,* and *cerebral palsy,* are imprecise terms in relation to the underlying etiology and the severity of impairments and disabilities each imposes. *Mental retardation,* for example, has various underlying causes, including chromosomal abnormalities such as *Down's Syndrome* and *Fragile X.* Other causes include inborn errors of metabolism (Phenylketonuria, or P.K.U.), environmental toxins (e.g., lead), prenatal infections (rubella, Cytomegolic inclusion virus, or CMV, and HIV/AIDs), maternal ingestion of alcohol during pregnancy

(Fetal Alcohol Syndrome/Effects, or FAS/FAE), postnatal infections (e.g., meningitis) and trauma (e.g., stroke or head injury).

As mapping of the *human genome* proceeds, the interactions between individual genotypes and environmental conditions are becoming ever more specifically defined. Thus, although conventional wisdom attributed much of individual variation to genetic influences, few of these traits are transmitted in a direct manner. The mapping of the human genome will provide the basis for much greater certainty regarding the interactions between genotype and specific environments that result in specific phenotypes. Although such information will undoubtedly improve treatment options eventually, before that benefit is realized such findings will also increase the frequency of families learning the source of the underlying genomic variation in terms of family pedigree. This knowledge can be expected to be a point of considerable stress both for individuals and marital relationships.

How Do Different Countries Treat People with Developmental Disabilities?

How a country treats its citizens with developmental disabilities varies widely, and no generalizations are possible. In his cross-cultural anthropologic work on traditional cultures in the 1960s, Robert Edgerton found wide variation, with some traditional cultures being fully inclusive of people with developmental disabilities and some traditional cultures rejecting and isolating people with developmental disabilities. Scandinavian countries are credited with providing the intellectual capital and practical innovations that have revolutionized the treatment of people with developmental disabilities throughout the world (Nirje, as cited in Dybwad 1969). This movement in English-speaking countries was characterized as *normalization* (Kugel and Wolfensberger 1969). Wolf Wolfensberger (1969) and Gunner Dybwad (1969) are widely credited as the key instrumental forces in bringing this concept to the United States and using the concept to change services in English-speaking countries. Although the United States is unique in the breadth of its legislation and policies in support to people with developmental disabilities, the advocacy movement for creating opportunities for self-determination and independence for people with developmental disabilities is truly international (Keith and Schalock 2000).

Impact on the Marital Relationship and the Family

Historically, there have been a number of myths and stereotypes about the impact of a child with a developmental disability upon the marital relationship and the family. Many factors may mediate the impact upon individuals, the marriage, and the family. A major factor can be the underlying etiology of the developmental disability and whether there was anything done or not done—such as maternal consumption of alcohol—that resulted in the disability. If the course of the developmental disability is known and related to known factors in either parents' genetic inheritance or related to action taken (or not taken) by either parent, the diagnosis of a developmental disability presents a situation where the marital relationship may be threatened by both blame and guilt. How and whether the relationship survives such a threat may be influenced by a number of factors, including the parents' individual beliefs, the beliefs and roles played by extended family members, cultural beliefs, extended family, the community and societal supports available to the family, and the family's material well-being.

An individual parent's reaction to a diagnosis is going to have cognitive, emotional, and—possibly—spiritual components, and these components may not be consistent with each other or over time. When discussion of parents' reaction to a diagnosis of mental retardation first began to be reported, it was characterized as *grief* and *chronic sorrow* (Solnit and Stark 1961; Olshansky 1962). These characterizations persisted despite cautions that they were obtained from nonrepresentative populations and were viewed through a perspective that saw such disabilities as the most devastating of circumstances for a family (Wolfensberger 1967). Terms such as *denial, chronic sorrow,* and *overprotection,* used descriptively, became explanations for parental behavior that was invariably viewed in a negative light (Hartley and Robinson 1987). Ray Barsch characterized this no-win situation:

> If the parent is militantly aggressive in seeking to obtain therapeutic services for his child, he may be accused of not realistically accepting his child's limitations. If he does not concern himself with efforts to improve or obtain services, he may be accused of apathetic rejection of his child. If he questions too much, he has a "reaction formation" and may be over-solicitous. If

At the Kennedy-Kriger Institute for Handicapped Children in Baltimore, Maryland, an instructor educates disabled students. The legislative right to education and other services for people with developmental disabilities is unique to the United States. RICHARD T. NOWITZ/CORBIS

he questions too little, he is branded as disinterested and insensitive. (1968, p. 8)

Although the emphasis on *family-centered care* includes an acceptance of the variety of parental and family reactions to a diagnosis as legitimate, families still report feeling that they are being judged in their reactions to and methods of coping with a diagnosis of developmental disability or mental retardation.

One of the factors that may mediate a family's reaction to a child with a disability is society's acceptance of disability. Part of the community that historically has not been accepting of developmental disabilities is the medical community. The standard advice given to families when a child's disability was identified at birth or in the first several months of life was that the child should be "institutionalized" and that the family should "get on with their lives." Whether or not the family followed this advice, a critical issue in adjustment was whether there was agreement between the

parents—and in many cases support of the decision on the part of the grandparents—regarding whatever decision was made. With the passage of the Developmental Disabilities Act in 1970, the development of increased community supports, and decisions to close institutions, the frequency of institutional placements of young children with developmental disabilities decreased dramatically.

Impact on Siblings

A generalization used to justify a recommendation of institutionalization of a child with a developmental disability has been the assumption that such a child will have a negative impact on other children in the family. The negative impact is assumed to come from the time and material resources the care of the child with a developmental disability demands and from the stigma of the disability itself. Alternatively, those whose ideology rejects institutionalization offer the generalization that having a sibling with a disability will make the sibling a better person. Examples may be found to support both generalizations and this speaks to the importance of not making such generalizations but rather seeking to find the conditions that will help all family members successfully accomplish life tasks of coping and responding, using successful problem solving strategies.

Impact on the Family's Material Well-Being

Despite the progress that has been made on behalf of people with developmental disabilities and their families, there is still a significant negative financial impact for the majority of families that have a child with a developmental disability. *Family Voices,* a grassroots parent advocacy organization, recently documented the impact on families' financial well-being. Care of a child at home in the current environment of piecemeal funding and lack of qualified personnel means that, in many cases, in two parent families one parent cannot join the workforce, or family members who do work must work reduced hours due to lack of other providers, or working family members must stay below a certain income so as to not risk losing benefits.

In sum, all the factors that influence any couple's adjustment to and commitment to a marriage can be expected to play a role in the adjustment of a couple and family to the diagnosis of a child with a disability (Farber 1960; Robinson, Rosenberg, and Beckman 1988; Wikler 1986).

Effect on Romantic Relationships

It was only in the last three decades of the twentieth century that persons with developmental disabilities began to assume a place in society as fully participating members. One aspect of that participation is the development of romantic relationships. One of the myths regarding mental retardation or developmental disabilities is that persons with such disabilities do not have typical romantic feelings. There is nothing about the nature of cognitive disabilities that has direct implications for expression of sexuality (Krajicek 1982). Up until the mid-twentieth century many states had legislation that made it illegal for people with mental retardation to marry. In some states, legislation required sterilization of the mentally retarded. Legislation, beginning with the reauthorization of the Developmental Disabilities Act and Bill of Rights (1975), Section 504 of the Rehabilitation Act (1973), and the Americans with Disabilities Act (1990) has made such state level prohibitions illegal. People with developmental disabilities are now living in the community, getting married, and having children. Although services and supports have been expanded, parents who have developmental disabilities experience a significant prejudice concerning their ability to parent. Although there has been documentation of neglect and abuse by parents with cognitive impairments, it also has been documented that, with both formal and informal supports, parents with cognitive disabilities can provide appropriate parenting. Advocacy movements specific to parenting, such as *People First* and *Through the Looking Glass,* have done a great deal to support parents with disabilities. However, unfortunately all too often parents may lose custody of a child due to the a priori assumption that a developmental disability is incompatible with a capacity to successfully parent (Edgerton 1988; Edgerton, Bollinger, and Herr 1984; Rosenberg and McTate 1982, Schilling et al. 1982).

Conclusion

The second half of the twentieth century has witnessed revolutionary changes in philosophy, values, and attitudes toward and rights of persons with developmental disabilities. The period of 1950 to 2000 can be characterized as being devoted to securing the civil rights of individuals with developmental disabilities and their families. The movement—a collaboration of parents, professionals, and self-advocates—has emphasized acceptance of people as people in their own right with whatever limitations are part of that disability. The emphasis on securing rights occurred in a context that, for the most part, discounted efforts regarding search for treatment that would ameliorate a disability as evidence of a lack of acceptance of the person with a disability.

See also: DISABILITIES; HEALTH AND FAMILIES; RESPITE CARE: CHILD

Bibliography

American Association on Mental Retardation. (1992). *Mental Retardation: Definition, Classification, and Systems of Supports,* 9th edition. Washington, DC: American Association on Mental Retardation.

Barsch, R. H. (1968). *The Parent of the Handicapped Child: The Study of Child Rearing Practices.* Springfield, IL: Charles C. Thomas.

Dybwad, G. (1969). "Action Implications, U.S.A. Today." In *Changing Patterns in Residential Services for the Mentally Retarded,* ed. R. B. Kugel and W. Wolfensberger. Washington, DC: President's Committee on Mental Retardation.

Edgerton, R. B. (1988). "Community Adaptation of People with Mental Retardation." In *Understanding Mental Retardation: Research Accomplishment and New Frontiers,* ed. J. F. Kavanagh. Baltimore, MD: Brookes.

Edgerton, R. B.; Bollinger, M.; and Herr, B. (1984). "The Cloak of Competence: After Two Decades." *American Journal of Mental Deficiency* 88:345–351.

Farber, B. (1960). "Family Organization and Crisis: Maintenance of Integration in Families with a Severely Mentally Retarded Child." *Monographs of the Society for Research in Child Development* 25 (1).

Hartley, R., and Robinson, C. (1987). "Mental Retardation." In *Mental Health-Psychiatric Nursing (A Continuum of Care),* ed. J. Norris, M. Kunes-Connell, S. Stockard, P. M. Ehrhart, and G. R. Newton. New York: Wiley.

Keith, D. K., and Schalock, R. (2000). *Cross-Cultural Perspectives on Quality of Life.* Washington, DC: American Association on Mental Retardation.

Krajicek, M. J. (1982). "Developmental Disability and Human Sexuality." *Nursing Clinics of North America* 86:223–234.

Kugel, R. B., and Wolfensberger, W. (1969). *Changing Patterns in Residential Services for the Mentally Retarded.* Washington, DC: President's Committee on Mental Retardation.

Olshansky, S. (1962). "Chronic Sorrow: A Response to Having a Mentally Defective Child." *Social Casework* 43:191–194.

Pelka, F. (1997). *The ABC-CLIO Companion to the Disability Rights Movement.* Santa Barbara, CA: ABC-CLIO.

Robinson, C.; Rosenberg, S. A.; and Beckman, P. J. (1988). "Parent Involvement in Early Childhood Special Education." In *Early Childhood Special Education: Birth to Three,* ed. J. B. Jordan, P. L. Hutinger, J. J. Gallagher, and M. B. Karnes. Reston, VA: Council for Exceptional Children and Division for Early Childhood.

Rosenberg, S. A., and McTate, G. (1982). "Intellectually Handicapped Mothers: Problems and Prospects." *Children Today* 2:14–26.

Schilling, R.; Schinke, S.; Blythe, B.; and Barth, R. (1982). "Child Maltreatment and Mentally Retarded Parents: Is There a Relationship?" *Mental Retardation* 20: 201–209.

Solnit, A., and Stark, M. (1961). "Mourning and the Birth of a Defective Child." *Journal for the Psychoanalytic Study of the Child* 16:523–537.

Wikler, L. M. (1986). "Family Stress Theory and Research on Families of Children with Mental Retardation." In *Families of Handicapped Persons: Research, Programs, and Policy Issues,* ed. J. J. Gallagher and P. M. Vietze. Baltimore, MD: Brookes.

Wolfensberger, W. (1967). "Counseling the Parents of the Retarded." In *Mental Retardation: Appraisal, Education, and Rehabilitation,* ed. A. A. Baumeister. Chicago, IL: Aldine-Atherton, Inc.

Wolfensberger, W. (1969). "The Origin and Nature of Our Institutional Models." In *Changing Patterns in Residential Services for the Mentally Retarded,* ed. R. B. Kugel and W. Wolfensberger. Washington, DC: President's Committee on Mental Retardation.

Other Resource

Family Voices: Family and Friends Speaking on Behalf of Children with Special Health Care Needs. (2002). Available from http://www.familyvoice.org.

CORDELIA ROBINSON

DEVELOPMENTAL PSYCHOPATHOLOGY

Developmental psychopathology is an approach or field of study designed to better understand the complexities of human development. Its primary goal is to chart the diverse pathways individuals take in the development of psychological difficulties (e.g., aggression, depression, substance use) and normal or optimal psychological health (e.g., self-esteem, scholastic success, moral development). Several key questions guide developmental psychopathology. First, how are individuals similar to and different from each other in the healthy and maladaptive paths they take as they grow older? Second, what accounts for why individuals experience differences in psychological functioning over time? For example, what characteristics within (e.g., genes, personality, perceptions of relationships) and outside (e.g., family relationships, neighborhoods) the individual are responsible for similarities and differences in psychological development over time? Third, what consequences do people's histories of experiences, coping, and adjustment have on their subsequent mental health? Because developmental psychopathology, as an approach, is concerned with answering a broad set of questions, it can be usefully applied to a number of specialty areas in psychology, biology, and sociology.

Risk and Resilience

Understanding why some children develop disorders or maladaptation whereas other children develop normally necessitates considering a host of factors that may undermine or foster healthy adjustment. The search for these factors is guided, in part, by the notion that interdependency exists among parts in any system, that is, the principle of *holism*. Thus, in any system or unit of study, parts must be examined in the fabric of the larger context of the system. For example, the way parents interact with children is a key factor that affects children's development.

However, the impact of parenting practices on children is affected by other characteristics in the larger ecological context, including child or parent characteristics (e.g., temperament, personality), the quality of family relationships, and parameters in the community (e.g., neighborhood, schools, peer relations) and culture. Consequently, the effects and meaning of parenting practices must be examined in the context of the larger setting or ecology. For example, the effects of various parenting practices on children vary across different ethnic groups. Thus, although strict parental discipline styles increase children's risk for psychological difficulties (e.g., anxiety, depression, submissiveness, poor self-confidence) among white families, the same discipline styles pose little or no risk for children in Asian or African U.S. families (Chao 1994; Deater-Deckard et al. 1996; Steinberg, Dornbusch, and Brown 1992). A possible explanation for these findings is that the same parenting practices take on different meanings in families with different cultural backgrounds. For example, strict control may be interpreted as a sign of involved, caring, and effective parenting within certain ethnic and cultural groups (Chao 1994; Baumrind 1997).

Thus, child development is best understood as embedded in a variety of social and ecological contexts, including community, cultural, and ethnic contexts of child development (Bronfenbrenner 1979). By extension, both normal and abnormal development are regarded as a cumulative result of multiple influences originating in the child, family, and larger community or cultural setting.

The Complexity of Risk Processes

By definition, *risk factors* increase the likelihood of experiencing psychological difficulties. Family risk factors include child maltreatment, parental rejection, lax supervision, inconsistent or harsh discipline practices, parental conflict, unsupportive family relations, and parental mental illness and substance use. However, exposure to even the most harmful risk factors does not doom all or even most children to a life of psychological problems. Also, children exposed to the same risk factor may have a range of healthy and maladaptive psychological outcomes. For example, although parental depression is one of the most robust risk factors, children of depressed parents exhibit a wide range of adaptive and maladaptive outcomes (e.g., depression, anxiety, aggression, academic problems) (Cummings and Davies 1994). Moreover, exposure to parental mental illness does not affect children in a psychological vacuum. Instead, parental psychopathology (e.g., depression, alcoholism) often co-occurs with other risk factors: familial (e.g., parenting impairments, marital discord, poor parent-child relations); sociocultural (e.g., poverty, community isolation); and biological (e.g., transmission of risk through the operation of genes, birth complications, temperament). These risk factors may contribute to the caustic effects of growing up in depressive or alcoholic families. Consequently, to better understand the development of psychological problems, developmental psychopathologists advocate moving beyond simply identifying individual risk factors that increase the likelihood of disorder to answer more complex questions of: When, how, and why do only some children exposed to risk develop problems?

Mediating mechanisms. The search for mediators answers the question of "how" and "why" risk conditions lead to maladaptive outcomes. *Mediators* are the processes or mechanisms that explain or account for why family characteristics increase children's risk for psychopathology. Returning to the example of parental depression, a primary goal of a developmental psychopathologist would be to identify the mechanisms by which parental depression leads to child behavior problems. For example, parental depression is associated with increases in parental conflict and poor parenting practices. The stressfulness of experiencing parental conflict and poor parenting practices, in turn, may directly compromise children's mental health. It is also important to understand the mechanisms that underlie or account for the effects of mediating processes. For example, although the focus on parental conflict and poor parenting practices provide part of the answer to why parental depression is a risk factor, we are still not at the level of specifying the response processes in children that ultimately lead to disorder. For example, the stressfulness of parental conflict and poor parenting practices may negatively affect the way children function and cope in various settings (e.g., family, school) on a day-to-day basis. These daily difficulties in functioning in certain settings may eventually grow into disorders that are stable across time and setting.

Moderating conditions. The search for *moderators* in models of risk answers questions of "who" is a greatest risk and "when" is the risk greatest. Thus, the assumption is that the likelihood that a risk factor leads to disorder varies across different individuals (i.e., who is at greater risk) and conditions (i.e., when is the risk greatest). Answering the question of who is at greatest risk involves searching for attributes of the person (e.g., gender, temperament, personality) that might amplify or increase the likelihood that they will experience a disorder when exposed to risk. For example, parental discord is especially likely to increase psychological problems for children who have difficult, rather than easy, temperaments (Davies and Windle 2001). Attributes outside the person (i.e., family, school, community, peers) may also intensify the effects of the risk factor. For example, Michael Rutter and colleagues (1976) found that the risk for psychopathology in children exposed to any one of six family risk factors (e.g., family discord, maternal psychiatric disorder, family dissolution) was comparable to risk for children who experienced no risk factors. However, experiencing two or three risk factors increased the incidence of children's psychiatric problems threefold.

Resilience and the Role of Protective Factors

Even when multiple risk factors are present, many, if not most, children at risk develop along normal, adaptive trajectories. Developmental psychopathologists use the term *resilience* to refer to children who develop competently and adapt successfully to life's challenges under adverse conditions (Cummings, Davies, and Campbell 2000). Resilience, by definition, cannot occur without some appreciable risk. Thus, a primary challenge is to distinguish between two general groups of competent children: (a) the relatively "normal" children, who experience minimal or no adverse conditions, and (b) the resilient children, who developed relatively normally in the face of considerable risk (Garmezy 1985; Luthar 1993). For example, it cannot be assumed that children of depressed parents who experience healthy development are resilient. Some of these children may, in fact, experience benign contexts of development characterized by parental warmth, consistent discipline, safe and supportive neighborhoods, and high quality schools. Thus, the competence of some of these children may result from the absence of risk rather than the presence of resilience.

Developmental psychopathologists are also sensitive to the notion that resilience is best characterized as consisting of multiple dimensions or features that may change over time. Thus, resilient outcomes are not simply "traits" that individuals have and carry with them across time and setting. These individuals are, by no means, regarded as "invincible" or "invulnerable" to adversity. Rather, resilient children may experience bouts of considerable problems over time or within certain domains of functioning. For example, children may experience normal functioning in one domain of adjustment (e.g., academic achievement) while experiencing difficulties in another domain of functioning (e.g., loneliness, anxiety).

Developmental psychopathologists further emphasize that how resilience is defined may change across contexts and people. For instance, among white, middle-class groups of children, peer ratings of popularity and social competence have been associated with greater academic competence (e.g., better grades) and behavioral competence (e.g., low levels of aggression). In contrast, high-risk inner-city adolescents who were popular among their peers displayed higher levels of conduct (e.g., aggression) and academic problems. In this same group of children, academic competence came at a cost of experiencing lower peer popularity, social isolation, and anxiety problems. Thus, for developmental psychopathologists, identifying who is "resilient" is no simple matter. Resilience is regarded as a complex process that may vary across context (e.g., subculture or culture), domain of functioning (e.g., academic, social, emotional), and the developmental stage of individuals (e.g., children versus adolescents).

Once people who meet the criteria for exhibiting resilience are identified, the next step is to search for the *protective factors* that account for their healthy outcomes. Protective factors, which are also called *buffers,* are moderators that dilute or counteract the negative effects of risk factors. Like risk factors, protective factors can be characteristics of the individual (e.g., personality) or larger ecological setting (e.g., family, school, peers). For example, child intelligence appears to offset the negative effects of interparental conflict on children (Katz and Gottman 1997). Likewise, various family characteristics and relationships (e.g., parental warmth, good sibling relations) appear to act as buffers that help shield children from the risk posed by parental conflict (Cummings and Davies 2002).

The Transactional Nature of Risk and Protective Factors

An assumption of developmental psychopathology is that humans are active agents in influencing their own development. Thus, children are not simply at the mercy of the family that raises them. Rather, the family is part of a transactional, developmental process that not only influences child development, but is also influenced by child development over time. For example, in explaining the development of childhood aggression, the *early starter hypothesis* stresses that the development of childhood aggression is set in motion by an escalating, reciprocal spiral of negativity and distress in the parent-child relationship rather than in the parent or child alone (Patterson and Yoerger 1997). In this reciprocal process involving an inconsistent parent and difficult child, the parent first responds to child misbehavior with aversive, hostile behavior. In reaction, the child, in turn, maintains or escalates the negative behavior. Sometime during this escalating cycle of negativity, the inconsistent parent eventually displays neutral or positive behavior toward

the child as a means of escaping the aversive interaction. However, in the course of surrendering and ending the negative disciplinary bout, the parent inadvertently reinforces or encourages the intensification of child misbehavior. This process may eventually evolve into more persistent behavior problems. Thus, the development of mental health and disorder is an ever-changing product of the mutual, reciprocal influences between the child and his or her family and ecological setting.

Risk and Resilience From a Developmental Perspective

Embedding the "psychopathology" component (i.e., risk and protection) within the "developmental" component in developmental psychopathology requires understanding resilience and maladaptation within broader windows of time instead of a single snapshot at a particular point in the life span. The value of examining risk and resilience from a developmental perspective is supported by three key themes in developmental psychopathology: (a) the dynamic nature of risk and resilience, (b) stage-salient or developmental tasks, and (c) the multiplicity of developmental pathways.

The Dynamic Nature of Risk and Resilience

Developmental psychopathologists stress that the nature of risk and resilience may vary considerably over parts of the life span. First, risk and protective factors differ in terms of their duration and patterning over time. For example, the degree of risk to children of depressed parents depends on their history of exposure to parental depression (e.g., length, frequency), with lengthier and more frequent bouts markedly increasing children's risk for disorder (e.g., Campbell, Cohn, and Meyers 1995). Thus, in understanding why some children develop disorders and others do not, it may be useful to distinguish between transient (e.g.., short-term, temporary conditions) and enduring (e.g., conditions persisting over significant parts of the life span) risk and protective factors (Cicchetti and Toth 1995)

Second, disorders often follow the course of several stages, including *onset, maintenance* (i.e., continuation of symptoms), *remission* (i.e., temporary alleviation of symptoms), *recurrence* (i.e., redevelopment of symptoms) and *termination.* Each of these stages of maladaptation may be associated with different sets of factors, causes, and consequences. For example, family conflict may play a causal role in the *onset* of children's conduct problems, but peers and teachers may *maintain* or further *intensify* the problems even in the face of marked reductions in family conflict (Fincham, Grych, and Osborne 1994).

Third, individuals may vary in how susceptible they are to risk factors across different parts of the life span. Thus, some models of developmental psychopathology have stressed that children may be most vulnerable to parental depression during the periods of infancy and adolescence (e.g., Cummings and Davies 1994; Gelfand and Teti 1990). However, since age and developmental periods are rather crude markers for the actual processes that increase vulnerability, this information cannot tell us why certain age groups are especially likely to develop disorders in the face of risk. On the one hand, age differences in risk may result from differences in experiences with risk. For example, adolescents of depressed parents may be especially likely to develop disorders because, on average, they have been exposed to depression for a longer period of time than younger children. On the other hand, age differences may also result from the operation of *sensitive periods,* in which specific risk factors have especially strong influences on individuals within certain periods of the life span (Cicchetti 1993). Thus, the stress of living with a depressed parent may more easily overwhelm adolescents than children because they (a) are more sensitive to family distress; (b) face more developmental challenges (e.g., career decisions, independence from parents, establishment of dating relationships); and (c) must cope with especially an especially large number of stressful events (e.g., establishment of romantic relationships) (Davies and Windle 1997).

Developmental or Stage-Salient Tasks

Developmental psychopathologists commonly view development as a series of biological, psychological, and social challenges that become especially important or salient during a certain period of the life span and remain important throughout the individual's lifetime (Cicchetti 1993). Thus, each developmental period (e.g., infancy, toddlerhood, preschool, school-age, early adolescence) is accompanied by important developmental tasks. For example, during infancy, babies are faced with the challenges of managing biological functions (e.g., eating and sleeping routines, distress and arousal) and forming emotionally meaningful relationships, especially with parents. The transition to toddlerhood is characterized by a new set of challenges, including effectively exploring the social and physical worlds, achieving a sense of mastery and autonomy in the face of new problems and tasks, and acquiring a sense of right and wrong.

Although the quality of family relationships plays an important role in the children's achievement of developmental tasks, the relationship between the family and children's developmental tasks is best viewed as *reciprocal* or *bidirectional.* In reflecting the influence of parents on children, infants are more likely to form strong, trusting relationships with caregivers when their caregivers are sensitive and responsive to their signals (e.g., accurately diagnosing the source of infant distress and taking action to help manage the distress; carefully timing and pacing interactions with infants). Conversely, in reflecting children's effects on parents, challenges that arise in each developmental period during childhood create new challenges for parenting. Thus, as children reach the toddler years, their emerging sense of autonomy, individuality, and motivation to explore the world generate a new set of challenges for parents centered on developing effective, consistent methods of supervising and disciplining their toddlers and implementing clear, realistic expectations for the child (Cummings, Davies, and Campbell 2000).

Stage-salient tasks in the earlier developmental periods serve as building blocks or tools for successfully overcoming future developmental challenges. For example, developing trusting emotional relationships with sensitive, responsive primary caregivers is accompanied by relatively favorable thoughts and expectancies about the self and larger social world. The resulting self-confidence and social interest may, in turn, increase children's chances of successfully exploring the world and developing a sense of mastery and autonomy. The opposite also applies: Failing to resolve developmental tasks in healthy ways (e.g., insecure, untrusting relations with parents) reduces children's chances of successfully dealing with developmental tasks later in life. Consequently, the study of adaptation and maladaptation is defined by children's history of success in managing and coping with developmental tasks.

Multiple Developmental Pathways

Resolving earlier developmental tasks does not guarantee that children will successfully overcome later challenges. By extension, children who experience difficulties with earlier developmental challenges are not destined to develop problems in coping with tasks later in life. Change is always possible. Thus, although many children who begin their lives along healthy developmental paths may continue to traverse along healthy paths, some of these children will also evidence discontinuity in their development. In other words, they will experience difficulties in adapting to subsequent developmental challenges despite having the advantage of experiencing healthy development in earlier developmental periods. Similarly, even though many children who suffer from problems early in life will continue to experience difficulties later in life, many of them will be able to "grow out" of their problems by successfully handling later developmental challenges. So, children who begin on the same path may end up in very different places later in life. Still other children who begin life on different developmental paths may end up resembling each other later in life. Development, then, is characterized by many different starts and stops and multiple directions toward competence and disorder.

A key assumption is that change and diversity in developmental paths is, in large part, predictable or understandable when it is evaluated in the larger context of each child's current and past experiences with risk and protective factors. For example, changes in the balance among exposure to risk and protective factors in the family may account in part for why some children develop disorders or difficulties after experiencing earlier histories of adaptive functioning, whereas other children are able to eventually develop normally after experiencing earlier difficulties. Thus, the emergence of later problems may result from increases in exposure to family risk factors (e.g., poor parental supervision, family instability or divorce, high parental conflict, parent depression) and decreases in the accessibility of protective factors (e.g., positive parent-child relationships, supportive family relations). Similarly, children who eventually reclaim healthy trajectories may have been able to benefit from greater access to family resources or protective factors (e.g., development of a positive relationship with a new caregiver), especially relative to their exposure to forms of family risk (e.g., decreases in conflict between primary caregiver and former romantic partner).

Conclusion

In conclusion, the developmental psychopathology perspective views adjustment and development as a dynamic, cumulative result of the reciprocal influences between child, family, and ecological characteristics across time. In studying family relationships, the developmental psychopathology approach highlights: (a) the complex, interdependent relations among different family characteristics and relationships; (b) the role ecological characteristics play in altering or affecting family relations (e.g., culture or subculture, peer relations, school); and (c) the multiple, developmental pathways taken by individuals and families across the life span.

See also: ANXIETY DISORDERS; ATTACHMENT: PARENT-CHILD RELATIONSHIPS; ATTENTION DEFICIT/HYPERACTIVITY DISORDER (ADHD); CHILDREN OF ALCOHOLICS; CONDUCT DISORDER; CONFLICT: PARENT-CHILD RELATIONSHIPS; CONFLICT: FAMILY RELATIONSHIPS; DEPRESSION: ADULTS; DEPRESSION: CHILDREN AND ADOLESCENTS; DEVELOPMENT: EMOTIONAL; DEVELOPMENT: MORAL; DEVELOPMENT: SELF; DISABILITIES; FAMILY DIAGNOSIS/DSM IV; FAMILY SYSTEMS THEORY; INTERPARENTAL CONFLICT—EFFECTS ON CHILDREN; INTERPARENTAL VIOLENCE—EFFECTS ON CHILDREN; MUNCHAUSEN SYNDROME BY PROXY; OPPOSITIONALITY; POSTTRAUMATIC STRESS DISORDER; SCHIZOPHRENIA; SCHOOL PHOBIA AND SCHOOL REFUSAL; SELF-ESTEEM; SEPARATION ANXIETY; SHYNESS; SUBSTANCE ABUSE; TEMPERAMENT

Bibliography

Baumrind, D. (1997). "Necessary Distinctions." *Psychological Inquiry* 8:176–182.

Bronfenbrenner, U. (1979). *The Ecology of Human Development: Experiments by Nature and Design.* Cambridge, MA: Harvard University Press.

Campbell, S. B.; Cohn, J. F.; and Meyers, T. (1995). "Depression in First-Time Mothers: Mother-Infant Interaction and Depression Chronicity." *Developmental Psychology* 31:349–357.

Chao, R. K. (1994). "Beyond Parental Control and Authoritarian Parenting Style: Understanding Chinese Parenting through the Cultural Notion of Training." *Child Development* 65:1,111–1,119.

Cicchetti, D. (1993). "Fractures in the Crystal: Developmental Psychopathology and the Emergence of the Self." *Developmental Review* 11:271–287.

Cicchetti, D., and Toth, S. L. (1995). "A Developmental Psychopathology Perspective on Child Abuse and Neglect." *Journal of the American Academy of Child and Adolescent Psychiatry* 34:541–565.

Cummings, E. M., and Davies, P. T. (1994). "Maternal Depression and Child Development." *Journal of Child Psychology and Psychiatry* 35:73–112.

Cummings, E. M., and Davies, P. T. (2002). "Effects of Marital Conflict on Children: Recent Advances and Emerging Themes in Process-Oriented Research." *Journal of Child Psychology and Psychiatry* 43:31–63.

Cummings, E. M.; Davies, P. T.; and Campbell, S. B. (2000). *Developmental Psychopathology and Family Process: Theory, Research, and Clinical Implications.* New York: Guilford.

Davies, P. T., and Windle, M. (1997). "Gender-Specific Pathways Between Maternal Depressive Symptoms, Family Discord, and Adolescent Adjustment." *Developmental Psychology* 33:657–668.

Davies, P. T., and Windle, M. (2001). "Interparental Discord and Adolescent Adjustment Trajectories: The Potentiating and Protective Role of Intrapersonal Attributes." *Child Development* 72:1,163–1,178.

Deater-Deckard, K.; Dodge, K. A.; Bates, J. E.; and Pettit, G. S. (1996). "Physical Discipline Among African American and European American Mothers: Links to Children's Externalizing Behaviors." *Developmental Psychology* 32:1,065–1,072.

Fincham, F. D.; Grych, J. H.; and Osborne, L. N. (1994). "Does Marital Conflict Cause Child Maladjustment: Directions and Challenges for Longitudinal Research." *Journal of Family Psychology* 8:128–140.

Garmezy, N. (1985). "Stress-Resilient Children: the Search for Protective Factors." In *Recent Research in Developmental Psychopathology,* ed. J.E. Stevenson. Oxford: Pergamon.

Gelfand, D. M., and Teti, D. M. (1990). "The Effects of Maternal Depression on Children." *Clinical Psychology Review* 10:329–353.

Katz, L. F., and Gottman, J. M. (1997). "Buffering Children from Marital Conflict and Dissolution." *Journal of Clinical Child Psychology* 26:157–171.

Luthar, S. S. (1993). "Annotation: Methodological and Conceptual Issues in Research on Childhood Resilience." *Journal of Child Psychology and Psychiatry* 34:441–453.

Patterson, G. R., and Yoerger, K. (1997). "A Developmental Model for Late-Onset Delinquency." *Nebraska Symposium on Motivation* 44:119–177.

Rutter, M.; Tizard, J.; Yule, M.; Graham, P.; and Whitmore, K. (1976). "Research Report: Isle of Wight Studies 1964–1974." *Psychological Medicine* 6:313–332.

Steinberg, L.; Dornbusch, S. M.; and Brown, B. B. (1992). "Ethnic Differences in Adolescent Achievement: An Ecological Perspective." *American Psychologist* 47:723–739.

PATRICK T. DAVIES
E. MARK CUMMINGS
SUSAN B. CAMPBELL

DIALECTICAL THEORY

The fundamental assumption of social dialectical theorists is that all relationships—friendships, romantic relationships, family relationships—are interwoven with multiple contradictions. Social dialectics is not a single theory but a family of theories (Montgomery and Baxter 1998). Like any family, the various dialectical approaches share some features in common yet differ in others. This entry emphasizes the common features.

Relating as a Process of Contradiction

The central concept of dialectical theorists is the *contradiction*. A contradiction is the dynamic interplay between unified opposites. Three terms are important in understanding this definition: *opposites, unified,* and *dynamic interplay.*

Central to the notion of opposition is mutual negation: Semantically, opposites are the antonyms of one another and function to nullify, cancel, undo, or otherwise undermine one another. Barbara Montgomery (1993) has identified three kinds of oppositions: (1) oppositions that are mutually exclusive and exhaustive (e.g., openness versus non-openness); (2) oppositions that are mutual exclusive but not exhaustive (e.g., connection versus autonomy); and (3) oppositions that are complementary (e.g., dominance versus submissiveness).

Opposites are unified if they are in some way interdependent. Interdependence can take two basic forms, which Irwin Altman and his colleagues (1981) referred to as the *unity of identity* and *interactive unity*. The unity of identity is semantic or definitional unity. For example, we understand what "night" means only because we have a concept of "day." With interactive unity, the opposing phenomena are united in practice or in function as part of the same interacting system. For example, marriages require both similarities and differences between the partners. Partners must be similar to some extent in order to establish and sustain a common bond. However, partners must also be different from each other in order to sustain autonomous identities.

Contradictory phenomena are yoked together at the same time that they negate one another. This simultaneous "both-and" dynamic produces an ongoing dialectical tension or interplay between opposites. To dialectical theorists, dialectical tensions keep the relating process vibrant and alive, as parties navigate the unity of opposites in an ongoing manner. Therefore, contradictions are not a sign of trouble for a relationship, but are inherent in the process of relating.

Leslie Baxter and her colleagues (Baxter 1993; Baxter and Montgomery 1996; Werner and Baxter 1994) have described three clusters of contradictions that have been identified by several dialectical scholars: the *dialectic of integration-separation,* the *dialectic of expression-nonexpression,* and the *dialectic of stability-change.* The dialectic of integration-separation is a family of related contradictions, all of which share the family resemblance of necessitating both partner integration and partner separation in relationships. A relationship is a union of two distinct individuals. Without union or integration, a relationship ceases to exist. But in the absence of separate individuals, there is nothing to integrate. Relating partners, therefore, face the ongoing challenge of negotiating the united opposition of integration and separation. Several different terms have been used to capture contradictions that can be located in this integration-separation cluster including: connection versus autonomy, interdependence versus independence, integration versus differentiation, intimacy versus autonomy, intimacy versus identity, the communal versus the individual, intimacy versus detachment,

involved versus uninvolved, the freedom to be dependent versus the freedom to be independent, intimacy versus freedom, and stability versus self-identity (Werner and Baxter 1994). Although some of these labels are mere synonyms of one another, the variation in terms often captures subtle, situation-specific differences in the interplay of integration and separation. The negotiation of integration-separation can be experienced by relationship parties at the mundane level of how much time to spend together versus how much time to spend alone or in activities with others. It can also be experienced as a dilemma of rights and obligations; for example, the right to have one's own needs fulfilled versus the obligation to be responsive to the needs of the other person. This dialectic could also be experienced as a dilemma of identity: sustaining a distinct "I" at the same time that a "we" identity is constructed. In short, the dialectic of integration-separation can be experienced in many ways by relating partners.

The dialectic of expression-nonexpression refers to a cluster of contradictions that revolve around the united opposition of candor and discretion. Relationship intimacy is built on a scaffold of openness, honesty, and complete disclosure. Yet, at the same time, intimacy also involves respect for each person's right to privacy and the obligation to protect one's partner from the hurt or embarrassment that can result from insufficient discretion. The dialectic of expression-nonexpression requires an ongoing negotiation of revelation and concealment, both in interactions between the two partners and in their interactions with others outside the relationship.

The dialectic of expression-nonexpression can be experienced in many different ways by relationship parties (Baxter and Montgomery 1996). For example, parties can frame the dialectic as a matter of individual rights: the right to privacy and the right to freedom of expression (Rawlins 1983). Alternatively, parties might frame the dialectic around issues of protection, in which the decision to disclose or not revolves around a desire to protect oneself from hurt or embarrassment versus a desire to protect the partner from hurt (Dindia 1998).

Finally, the dialectic of stability versus change refers to a family of contradictions that revolve around the unified opposition of predictability, certainty, routinization, and stability, on the one hand,

and unpredictability, uncertainty, spontaneity, and change, on the other hand. Relationships require both stability and change to establish and sustain their well-being (Bochner and Eisenberg 1987). Leslie Baxter and Barbara Montgomery (1996) use the metaphor of jazz in discussing the dialectic of stability-change in relationships. Jazz artists follow a basic melody which functions as the predictable center of a given artistic performance. This backdrop of certainty enables wildly spontaneous and unpredictable musical departures. Similarly, relationship parties tack back and forth between the stable "givens" of their relationship and unpredictable "new" demands and experiences.

This discussion of commonly identified contradictions does not exhaust the list of possible unified oppositions that face relationship pairs, but it provides an introduction to at least some of the dialectical tensions that friends, romantic partners, marital couples, and families face as they conduct their everyday relating (Brown, Werner, and Altman 1998; Conville 1991; Rawlins 1992).

Contradictions and Change

Social dialectical scholars agree that the dynamic interplay of unified opposites results in ongoing and inevitable change for relationship partners. Although the ongoing tension of oppositions can be negotiated in temporary moments or periods in which all oppositions are responded to at the same time, it is much more common to see an ongoing pattern in which one pole is temporarily responded to at a cost of negating the other pole. The communicative actions that parties enact at a given moment change how a contradiction is experienced at a later point in time. For example, if parties embrace spontaneity and abandon planning, this will create pressure at some point for greater certainty and predictability in their lives.

The most common conception of this change process among dialectical scholars is a helical model, in which responsiveness to one dialectical pole, or opposite, creates pressure to attend to the opposite dialectical pole (Conville 1991). Over time, a relationship pair cycles back and forth between responsiveness to the opposing demands. For example, a parent and child may cycle back and forth between autonomy and interconnection throughout their lives. However, each time a pair cycles back, it is never exactly to the same place

they were before—the parties have acquired additional experiences and perspectives. Thus, relating is like a helix.

Over time, the very meaning of a given contradiction is likely to shift. For example, Daena Goldsmith (1990) found that among romantic couples, issues of connection versus autonomy took on different meanings depending on where a couple was in their relationship's development.

Several dialectical scholars (e.g., Baxter and Erbert 1999; Conville 1991; Pawlowski 1998) have argued that relationship change is an erratic, up-and-down motion propelled by pivotal turning point events. *Turning points* are often moments of heightened dialectical struggle that are negotiated by the parties with varying degrees of effectiveness, thereby resulting in a negative or a positive effect on the relationship. Existing research suggests that not all contradictions are equally important in turning-point relationship change. The integration-separation dialectic consistently appears as the most significant family of contradictions (Baxter 1990; Baxter and Erbert 1999; Pawlowski 1998). Further, the salience of various contradictions appears to vary depending on whether the change takes place early or later in a relationship's development (Baxter 1990; Pawlowski 1998).

Arthur VanLear (1998) has argued that dialectical change can function more modestly than the major moments of change captured in turning points of relationship development. In examining the cycles of openness and non-openness behavior in relationship pairs, VanLear found that cycles can vary in amplitude, with large or small swings between dialectical poles. Turning points capture only the dialectical cycles that are large in amplitude. In addition, he found that shorter cycles of change can be nested within longer cycles of change. For example, as part of a general upswing in openness, smaller cycles of candor and discretion can be identified.

Communication and Contradictions

Dialectical contradictions are constituted in the communicative practices of relationship parties. It is through communication that contradictions are given a social life. How parties constitute a given contradiction at Time 1 affects how that contradiction will be experienced at Time 2. Several kinds of communicative practices have been identified in existing dialectical work (Baxter and Montgomery 1996).

Because of the helical pattern that frequently characterizes dialectical change, it is not surprising that researchers have found two dominant communication practices in the negotiation of contradiction. In enacting *spiraling inversion,* relationship parties tack back and forth through time, alternating an emphasis first on one dialectical pole and then on the other dialectical pole. For example, a long-distance marital couple trying to negotiate the dialectic of integration and separation could alternate their week-ends between those spent together and those spent apart. In enacting *segmentation,* relationship parties negotiate by topic or activity domain, agreeing that in domain *A* one dialectical pole will be emphasized whereas in domain *B* the other dialectical pole will be emphasized. The long-distance couple may decide that Monday through Friday are the days in which their individual lives will take priority, whereas Saturday and Sunday are the days in which their relationship will take priority. Both spiraling inversion and segmentation allow a relationship pair to move back and forth between oppositions, but in different ways.

Although it is less common for relationship parties to be responsive to both dialectical poles simultaneously, three communication practices have been identified to accomplish this both/and simultaneity. When parties enact *balance,* they basically strive for a compromise response; that is, a response in which both dialectical poles are fulfilled but only partially. For example, family members struggling with the dialectic of expression-nonexpression might compromise by revealing partial, not full, truths to one another. Such a compromise would be neither fully open nor fully closed but somewhere in the middle.

The next practice, *integration,* involves a complete instead of a partial response to both dialectical poles at the same time. Given that the poles negate each other, this practice is a complex one. Several dialectical scholars have argued that communication rituals exemplify integration practices (e.g., Braithwaite, Baxter, and Harper 1998). Rituals hold both sides of a contradiction at once through their multiple layers of symbolism. For example, the marriage ritual at once celebrates the uniqueness of the particular marital couple at the same time that it celebrates the conventions and traditions of marriage as an institution.

The third practice, *recalibration,* occurs when a relationship pair is able to symbolically reconstruct a contradiction such that the dialectical demands are no longer experienced as oppositional. For example, a marital pair might take a break from their marriage—separate vacations, for example—in order to enhance closeness. Such a transformation of the integration-separation dialectic would produce a paradoxical recalibration in which separation enhanced integration rather than negating it.

Common to all five of these dialectical practices—spiraling inversion, segmentation, balance, integration, and recalibration—is an appreciation of the dialectical nature of relating. However, Baxter and Montgomery (1996) also have described two communicative practices that they regard as less functional in negotiating the dialectics of relating. In communicative *denial,* relationship parties attempt to extinguish one opposition of a given dialectic, ignoring its existence by wishing it away. A pair may say that they are "totally open" with one another, but such a declaration belies the importance of discretion. In enacting *disorientation,* parties construct contradiction as a totally negative problem which overwhelms them and brings them to a nihilistic state of despair. A disoriented partner might say something like "Why bother to make the marriage work, anyway? No matter what you do, you'll be unhappy."

Conclusion

A social dialectical perspective has been employed in understanding a wide range of relationship types, including platonic friendships, polygamous families, abusive families, stepfamilies, friendships among coworkers, marital couples, romantic pairs, couple relationships with their social network, the relationships between parents and their adolescent children, the post-divorce relationship between ex-spouses, and families who face a dying member.

Dialectical researchers have used a variety of methods studying contradictions. Some scholars have used in-depth interviews in which relationship parties are asked simply to talk about the details of their relationship without explicit attention focused on contradictions; these interviews are subsequently analyzed by the researcher for evidence of contradiction. Other scholars have used in-depth interviewing to probe relationship parties explicitly about their awareness of, and reactions to, contradictions. Sometimes, dialectically oriented researchers have employed narrative analysis of stories of relating told by participants. Other dialectically oriented researchers have employed traditional survey methods to solicit parties' perceptions of the extent to which they experience dialectical tensions. Field-based ethnography has also been employed by dialectically oriented researchers. Finally, some dialectical researchers have coded the communicative behaviors of interacting partners for dialectical oppositions. Clearly, there is no single way to study the contradictions of relating.

Social-dialectics theories are not traditional deductive, axiomatic theories that attempt to explain cause-and-effect relations in the world, nor are they suitable for traditional hypothesis-testing. Social-dialectics theories instead typify what Jonathan Turner calls descriptive/sensitizing theories; that is, "loosely assembled congeries of concepts intended only to sensitize and orient researchers to certain critical processes" (1986, p. 11). Thus, the evaluative question to ask about social-dialectics theories is not whether their explanations are correct but whether they are useful in rendering relationships intelligible.

See also: COMMUNICATION: COUPLE RELATIONSHIPS; CONFLICT: COUPLE RELATIONSHIPS; FAMILY THEORY; NAGGING AND COMPLAINING; RELATIONSHIP INITIATION; RELATIONSHIP MAINTENANCE; RELATIONSHIP THEORIES: SELF-OTHER RELATIONSHIP; RENEWAL OF WEDDING VOWS; TRANSITION TO PARENTHOOD

Bibliography

Altman, I.; Vinsel, A.; and Brown, B. (1981). "Dialectic Conceptions in Social Psychology: An Application to Social Penetration and Privacy Regulation." In *Advances in Experimental Social Psychology,* Vol. 14, ed. L. Berkowitz. New York: Academic Press.

Baxter, L. A. (1990). "Dialectical Contradictions in Relationship Development." *Journal of Social and Personal Relationships* 7:69–88.

Baxter, L. A. (1993). "The Social Side of Personal Relationships: A Dialectical Analysis." In *Social Context and Relationships,* ed. S. Duck. Newbury Park, CA: Sage Publications.

Baxter, L. A., and Erbert, L. A. (1999). "Perceptions of Dialectical Contradictions in Turning Points of Development in Heterosexual Romantic Relationships." *Journal of Social and Personal Relationships* 16:547–569.

Baxter, L. A., and Montgomery, B. M. (1996). *Relating: Dialogues & Dialectics.* New York: Guilford Press.

Bochner, A. P., and Eisenberg, E. (1987). "Family Process: System Perspectives." In *Handbook of Communication Science,* ed. C. R. Berger and S. Chaffee. Newbury Park, CA: Sage Publications.

Braithwaite, D. O.; Baxter, L. A.; and Harper, A. M. (1998). "The Role of Rituals in the Management of the Dialectical Tension of 'Old' and 'New' in Blended Families." *Communication Studies* 49:101–120.

Brown, B. B.; Werner, C. M.; and Altman, I. (1998). "Choice Points for Dialecticians: A Dialectical-Transactional Perspective on Close Relationships." In *Dialectical Approaches to Studying Personal Relationships,* ed. B. M. Montgomery and L. A. Baxter. Mahwah, NJ: Erlbaum.

Conville, R. L. (1991). *Relational Transitions.* Westport, CT: Praeger Publishers.

Dindia, K. (1998). "'Going Into and Coming Out of the Closet': The Dialectics of Stigma Disclosure." In *Dialectical Approaches to Studying Personal Relationships,* ed. B. M. Montgomery and L. A. Baxter. Mahwah, NJ: Erlbaum.

Goldsmith, D. (1990). "A Dialectical Perspective on the Expression of Autonomy and Connection in Romantic Relationships." *Western Journal of Communication* 54:537–556.

Montgomery, B. M. (1993). "Relationship Maintenance Versus Relationship Change: A Dialectical Dilemma." *Journal of Social and Personal Relationships* 10:205–224.

Montgomery, B. M., and Baxter, L. A., eds. (1998). *Dialectical Approaches to Studying Personal Relationships.* Mahwah, NJ: Erlbaum.

Pawlowski, D. R. (1998). "Dialectical Tensions in Marital Partners' Accounts of Their Relationships." *Communication Quarterly* 46:396–416.

Rawlins, W. K. (1983). "Openness as Problematic in Ongoing Friendships: Two Conversational Dilemmas." *Communication Monographs* 50:1–13.

Rawlins, W. K. (1992). *Friendship Matters: Communication, Dialectics, and the Life Course.* New York: Aldine de Gruyter.

Turner, J. H. (1986). *The Structure of Sociological Theory,* 4th edition. Chicago: Dorsey Press.

VanLear, C. A. (1998). "Dialectic Empiricism: Science and Relationship Metaphors." In *Dialectical Approaches to Studying Personal Relationships,* ed. B. M. Montgomery and L. A. Baxter. Mahwah, NJ: Erlbaum.

Werner, C. M., and Baxter, L. A. (1994). "Temporal Qualities of Relationships: Organismic, Transactional and Dialectical Views." In *Handbook of Interpersonal Communication,* 2nd edition, ed. M. L. Knapp and G. R. Miller. Newbury Park, CA: Sage Publications.

LESLIE A. BAXTER

DISABILITIES

Disability does not just happen to an individual; it happens to the whole family. Disability affects families in many different ways, depending on the type of disability, the age of the person, and the type of family. Disability does not go away like acute illness does. It is always there; it is chronic. It changes the life course of the family as a unit and often changes the life course of some family members. Reciprocally, how the family responds to the disability and its challenges affects the life course and development of the person with the disability. Some families cope and adapt very well; they even become stronger by learning to live with disability. Other families struggle and experience more problems when they are not able to discover the resources they need to manage. These two perspectives—the impact of disability on the family and the family's response to the disability—are part of a continuous cycle of effects. These effects are diagrammed in Figure 1.

This way of thinking about the reciprocal effects of the disability on the family and the family on the person with disability is called a family systems perspective (Patterson 1991a). This perspective has become increasingly important for those who develop policies and design programs and interventions to support persons with disability and their families to have a full and complete life (Dunst et al. 1993; Singer and Powers 1993; Turnbull and Turnbull 1986). From this perspective it is no longer enough to focus only on the person with the disability. Rather, the goals of programs and interventions are to support and empower the families of persons with disabilities so they all can adapt successfully and have a high quality of life (Dunst, Trivette, and Deal 1988).

Definition and Prevalence

Disabilities have become a major health-related issue for an increasing number of people in the United States. Based on data from the 1988 National Health Interview Survey, it is estimated that 35 million Americans have a disability (Pope and Tarlov 1991). Furthermore, the overall prevalence of disabilities has been increasing in the United

FIGURE 1

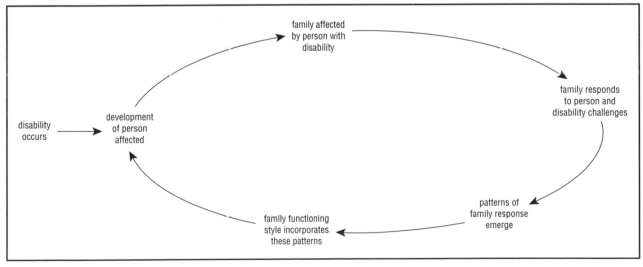

The impact of disability on the family and the family's response to the disability are part of a continuous cycle of effects.

States, primarily because of biomedical advances that are able to keep people alive longer. This is the case for all ages across the lifespan, from very premature infants to the elderly. However, maintaining life does not always mean cure. Many more individuals live with the residue of what cannot be cured; they live with chronic conditions, and many chronic conditions create disability or gradually lead to disability over time. By definition, disability is the inability to engage in any substantial gainful activity by reason of some medically determined physical or mental impairment that can be expected to last or has lasted for a continuous period of not less than twelve months. Disability is the gap between a person's capabilities and what the environment expects a person to be able to perform in personal, familial, and social roles (Pope and Tarlov 1991). When estimates of the prevalence of disabilities are made, primary social roles are defined as follows: "playing" for children under five years; "going to school" for children ages five to seventeen; "working or keeping house" for adults ages eighteen to sixty-nine; and "living independently" for adults over seventy.

The main causes of activity limitation leading to disability are mobility impairments (38%); chronic diseases (32%); sensory impairments (8%); and intellectual impairments, including mental retardation (7%) (LaPlante 1988). Both the prevalence and the severity of disabilities increase with age. The percent of each age group with a disability is 2 percent of children under five years, 8 percent of children ages five to seventeen years, 10 percent of adults eighteen to forty-four years, 23 percent of adults forty-five to sixty-four years, 36 percent of adults sixty-five to sixty-nine years, and 38 percent of adults over seventy (National Center for Health Statistics 1989). For children under eighteen years, intellectual limitations and chronic diseases are the major causes. Above eighteen years, mobility impairments are the primary cause. For those between eighteen and forty-four years of age, accidents and injuries are a major contributing factor to mobility impairment; among older ages, mobility impairment is more the result of chronic disease, such as arthritis.

Not all chronic conditions are associated with disability. Some chronic conditions cause no limitations. For those that do, the degree of limitation varies from minor to being unable to perform a major activity, such as working. For those conditions associated with disability, families increasingly have taken over a major role in providing assistance and care for their members who are disabled (Chilman, Nunnally, and Cox 1988). Very few families can expect to go through their life course without caring for at least one member with a disability. In many instances, however, the onset and severity of disability can be prevented or postponed, especially those related to chronic diseases. This is influenced by the person's lifestyle, access to regular medical care, and willingness to take an active role in managing his or her health condition. The family, of course, is a critical social context influencing how an individual responds to a chronic condition, as well as how an individual responds to physical, intellectual, and sensory impairment. In this way the family can have a major impact on the course of chronic conditions, if and when disability emerges, and how severe the disability is.

Impact of Disabilities on Families

Disability places a set of extra demands or challenges on the family system; most of these demands last for a long time (Murphy 1982). Many of these challenges cut across disability type, age of the person with the disability, and type of family in which the person lives. There is the financial burden associated with getting health, education, and social services; buying or renting equipment and devices; making accommodations to the home; transportation; and medications and special food. For many of these financial items, the person or family may be eligible for payment or reimbursement from an insurance company and/or a publicly funded program such as Medicaid or Supplemental Security Income. However, knowing what services and programs one is eligible for and then working with a bureaucracy to certify that eligibility (often repeatedly) is another major challenge faced by families. Coordination of services among different providers (such as a physician, physical therapist, occupational therapist, dietician, social worker, teacher, and counselor) who often are not aware of what the other is doing and may provide discrepant information is another challenge faced by families (Sloper and Turner 1992). While care coordination or case management is often the stated goal of service programs, there are many flaws in implementation. Families experience the burden of this lack of coordination.

A mother and young daughter communicate through sign language. Families find ways to cope with the demands that having a disability adds to family life. CUSTOM MEDICAL STOCK PHOTO, INC.

The day-to-day strain of providing care and assistance leads to exhaustion and fatigue, taxing the physical and emotional energy of family members. There are a whole set of issues that create emotional strain, including worry, guilt, anxiety, anger, and uncertainty about the cause of the disability, about the future, about the needs of other family members, about whether one is providing enough assistance, and so on. Grieving over the loss of function of the person with the disability is experienced at the time of onset, and often repeatedly at other stages in the person's life.

Family life is changed, often in major ways. Care-taking responsibilities may lead to changed or abandoned career plans. Female family members are more likely to take on caregiving roles and thus give up or change their work roles. This is also influenced by the fact that males are able to earn more money for work in society. When the added financial burden of disability is considered, this is the most efficient way for families to divide role responsibilities.

New alliances and loyalties between family members sometimes emerge, with some members feeling excluded and others being overly drawn in. For example, the primary caregiver may become overly involved with the person with disability. This has been noted particularly with regard to mothers of children with disabilities. In these families, fathers often are underinvolved with the child and instead immerse themselves in work

or leisure activities. This pattern usually is associated with more marital conflict. It is important to note, however, that there does not appear to be a greater incidence of divorce among families who have a child with a disability, although there may exist more marital tension (Hirst 1991; Sabbeth and Leventhal 1984).

The disability can consume a disproportionate share of a family's resources of time, energy, and money, so that other individual and family needs go unmet. Families often talk about living "one day at a time." The family's lifestyle and leisure activities are altered. A family's dreams and plans for the future may be given up. Social roles are disrupted because often there is not enough time, money, or energy to devote to them (Singhi et al. 1990).

Friends, neighbors, and people in the community may react negatively to the disability by avoidance, disparaging remarks or looks, or overt efforts to exclude people with disabilities and their families. Despite the passage of the Americans with Disabilities Act in 1990, many communities still lack programs, facilities, and resources that allow for the full inclusion of persons with disabilities. Families often report that the person with the disability is not a major burden for them. The burden comes from dealing with people in the community whose attitudes and behaviors are judgmental, stigmatizing, and rejecting of the disabled individual and his or her family (Knoll 1992; Turnbull et al. 1993). Family members report that these negative attitudes and behaviors often are characteristic of their friends, relatives, and service providers as well as strangers (Patterson and Leonard 1994).

Overall, stress from these added demands of disability in family life can negatively affect the health and functioning of family members (Patterson 1988; Varni and Wallander 1988). Numerous studies report that there is all increased risk of psychological and behavioral symptoms in the family members of persons with disabilities (Cadman et al. 1987; Singer and Powers 1993; Vance, Fazan, and Satterwhite 1980). However, even though disability increases the risk for these problems, most adults and children who have a member with a disability do not show psychological or behavioral problems. They have found ways to cope with this added stress in their lives. Increasingly, the literature on families and disabilities emphasizes this adaptive capacity of families. It has been called family resilience (Patterson 1991b; Singer and Powers 1993; Turnbull et al. 1993). Many families actually report that the presence of disability has strengthened them as a family—they become closer, more accepting of others, have deeper faith, discover new friends, develop greater respect for life, improve their sense of mastery, and so on.

While there are many commonalities regarding the impact of disabilities on families, other factors lead to variability in the impact of disability on the family. Included in these factors are the type of disability, which member of the family gets the disability, and the age of onset of the disability.

Disabilities vary along several dimensions, including the degree and type of incapacitation (sensory, motor, or cognitive); the degree of visibility of the disability; whether the course of the condition is constant, relapsing, or progressive; the prognosis or life expectancy of the person; the amount of pain or other symptoms experienced; and the amount of care or treatment required. John Rolland (1994) has outlined a typology of chronic conditions based on some of these factors and has described the psychosocial impact on families based on these factors. His argument, and that of several others (Perrin et al. 1993; Stein et al. 1993), is that the variability in the psychosocial impact of chronic conditions is related more to characteristics of the condition than to the diagnosis per se.

Consider the course of the condition. When it is progressive (such as degenerative arthritis or dementia), the symptomatic person may become increasingly less functional. The family is faced with increasing caretaking demands, uncertainty about the degree of dependency and what living arrangement is best, as well as grieving continuous loss. These families need to readjust continuously to the increasing strain and must be willing to find and utilize outside resources. If a condition has a relapsing course (such as epilepsy or cancer in remission), the ongoing care may be less, but a family needs to be able to reorganize itself quickly and mobilize resources when the condition flares up. They must be able to move from normalcy to crisis alert rapidly. An accumulation of these dramatic transitions can exhaust a family. Disabilities with a constant course (such as a spinal cord injury) require major reorganization of the family at the outset and then perseverance and stamina for a long time. While these families can plan, knowing what

is ahead, limited community resources to help them may lead to exhaustion.

Disabilities where mental ability is limited seem to be more difficult for families to cope with (Breslau 1993; Cole and Reiss 1993; Holroyd and Guthrie 1986). This may be due to greater dependency requiring more vigilance by family members, or because it limits the person's ability to take on responsible roles, and perhaps limits the possibilities for independent living. If the mental impairment is severe, it may create an extra kind of strain for families because the person is physically present in the family but mentally absent. This kind of incongruence between physical presence and psychological presence has been called boundary ambiguity (Boss 1993). Boundary ambiguity means that it is not entirely clear to family members whether the person (with the disability in this case) is part of the family or not because the person is there in some ways but not in others. Generally, families experience more distress when situations are ambiguous or unclear because they do not know what to expect and may have a harder time planning the roles of other family members to accommodate this uncertainty.

In addition to cognitive impairment, other characteristics of disabilities can create ambiguity and uncertainty for families. For example, an uncertain life expectancy makes it difficult to plan future life roles, to anticipate costs of care, or to make decisions about the best living arrangements for adults requiring assistance in the activities of daily living. For example, from 1970 to 1991, survival for children with cystic fibrosis increased 700 percent, to a life expectancy of twenty-six years in the United States (Fitzsimmons 1991). These young adults now face difficult family decisions, such as whether to marry and whether to have children. In more extreme cases related to severe medical conditions, persons may have their lives extended by using advances in biomedical science and technology. When this happens, families can be faced with very difficult decisions about what techniques and equipment should be used, for how long, with what expected gains, at what cost, and so on. Society is facing new issues in biomedical ethics, but there is no social consensus about how aggressively to intervene and under what circumstances. Family members who bear the emotional burden of these decisions do not always agree on a course of action and, furthermore, may be blocked by hospitals and courts from carrying out a particular course of action. While these kinds of cases may not yet be widespread, they have sparked intense debate and raised the consciousness of many families about issues they may face.

In addition to type of impairment, there is variability in the severity of impairment. The degree to which a person with disability is limited in doing activities or functions of daily living (e.g., walking, feeding oneself, and toileting) can be assessed and is called functional status. The lower the person's functional status, the more assistance he or she will need from other people and/or from equipment and devices. Family members are a primary source of this needed assistance (Biegel, Sales, and Schulz 1991; Stone and Kemper 1989). Providing this assistance can create a burden for family caregivers, which may result in physical or psychological symptoms of poor health. For example, parents, especially mothers, experience more depression when their children with disabilities have lower functional status (Patterson, Leonard, and Titus 1992; Singer et al. 1993). For elderly caregivers, physical strain may be a limiting factor in how much and for how long assistance can be provided for the disabled individual (Blackburn 1988).

The age of the person when the disability emerges is associated with different impacts on the family and on the family's life course, as well as on the course of development for the person with disability (Eisenberg, Sutkin, and Jansen 1984). When conditions emerge in late adulthood, in some ways this is normative and more expectable. Psychologically it is usually less disruptive to the family. When disability occurs earlier in a person's life, this is out of phase with what is considered normative, and the impact on the course of development for the person and the family is greater. More adjustments have to be made and for longer periods of time.

When the condition is present from birth, the child's life and identity are shaped around the disability. In some ways it may be easier for a child and his or her family to adjust to never having certain functional abilities than to a sudden loss of abilities later. For example, a child with spina bifida from birth will adapt differently than a child who suddenly becomes a paraplegic in adolescence due to an injury.

The age of the parents when a child's disability is diagnosed is also an important consideration in how the family responds. For example, teenage parents are at greater risk for experiencing poor adaptation because their own developmental needs are still prominent, and they are less likely to have the maturity and resources to cope with the added demands of the child. For older parents there is greater risk of having a child with certain disabilities, such as Down syndrome. Older parents may lack the stamina for the extra burden of care required, and they may fear their own mortality and be concerned about who will care for their child when they die.

The course of the child's physical, psychological, and social development will forever be altered by the chronic condition. Since development proceeds sequentially, and since relative success at mastering the tasks of one stage is a prerequisite for facing the challenges of the next stage, one could anticipate that the earlier the onset, the greater the adverse impact on development (Eisenberg, Sutkin, and Jansen 1984).

There are many ways in which the accomplishment of development tasks is complicated for persons with disabilities. This, in turn, has an effect on their families as well as on which family roles can be assumed by the person with disability (Perrin and Gerrity 1984). For example, in infancy, disability may frighten parents, or the infant may be unresponsive to their nurturing efforts such that attachment and bonding necessary for the development of trust are compromised. The parent may feel inadequate as a caregiver, and parenting competence is undermined. For a toddler, active exploration of the social environment, needed to develop a sense of autonomy and self-control, may be restricted because of the child's motor, sensory, or cognitive deficits. Parents, fearing injury or more damage to their young child, may restrict their child's efforts to explore and learn, or they may overindulge the child out of sympathy or guilt. If other people react negatively to the child's disability, parents may try to compensate by being overly protective or overly solicitous. These parent behaviors further compromise the child's development of autonomy and self-control.

As children with disabilities move into school environments where they interact with teachers and peers, they may experience difficulties mastering tasks and developing social skills and competencies. Although schools are mandated to provide special education programs for children in the least restrictive environment and to maximize integration, there is still considerable variability in how effectively schools do this. Barriers include inadequate financing for special education; inadequately trained school personnel; and, very often, attitudinal barriers of other children and staff that compromise full inclusion for students with disabilities. Parents of children with disabilities may experience a whole set of added challenges in assuring their children's educational rights. In some instances, conflict with schools and other service providers can become a major source of strain for families (Walker and Singer 1993). In other cases, school programs are a major resource for families.

Developmental tasks of adolescence—developing an identity and developing greater autonomy—are particularly difficult when the adolescent has a disability. Part of this process for most adolescents generally involves some risk-taking behaviors, such as smoking and drinking. Adolescents with disabilities take risks too, sometimes defying treatment and procedures related to their condition, such as skipping medications or changing a prescribed diet. Issues related to sexuality may be particularly difficult because the person with disability has fears about his or her desirability to a partner, sexual performance, and worries about ever getting married or having children (Coupey and Cohen 1984). There is some evidence that girls may be at greater risk for pregnancy because of their desire to disavow their disability and prove their normalcy (Holmes 1986). Teens with mental impairment may be subjected to sexual exploitation by others.

When disability has its onset in young adulthood, the person's personal, family, and vocational plans for the future may be altered significantly. If the young adult has a partner where there is a long-term commitment, this relationship may be in jeopardy, particularly if the ability to enact adult roles as a sexual partner, parent, financial provider, or leisure partner are affected (Ireys and Burr 1984). When a couple has just begun to plan a future based on the assumption that both partners would be fully functional, they may find the adjustment to the disability too great to handle. The development of a relationship with a significant other *after* the disability is already present is more likely to lead to positive adjustment. Young adulthood is that critical transition from one's family of origin to creating a new family unit with a partner

and possibly children. When disability occurs at this stage, the young adult's parents may become the primary caregivers, encouraging or bringing the young person home again. The risk is that the developmental course for the young adult and his or her parents may never get back on track. This is influenced in part by the extent to which there are independent living options for persons with disabilities to make use of in the community.

When the onset of disability occurs to adults in their middle years, it is often associated with major disruption to career and family roles. Those roles are affected for the person with the disability as well as for other family members who have come to depend on him or her to fulfill those roles. Some kind of family reorganization of roles, rules, and routines is usually required. If the person has been employed, he or she may have to give up work and career entirely or perhaps make dramatic changes in amount and type of work. The family may face a major loss of income as well as a loss in health and other employee benefits. If the person is a parent, childrearing responsibilities may be altered significantly. The adult may have to switch from being the nurturer to being the nurtured. This may leave a major void in the family for someone to fill the nurturing role. If the person is a spouse, the dynamics of this relationship will change as one person is unable to perform as independently as before. The partner with the disability may be treated like another child. The sexual relationship may change, plans for having more children may be abandoned, lifestyle and leisure may be altered. Some spouses feel that their marital contract has been violated, and they are unwilling to make the necessary adjustments. Children of a middle-aged adult with a disability also experience role shifts. Their own dependency and nurturing needs may be neglected. They may be expected to take on some adult roles, such as caring for younger children, doing household chores, or maybe even providing some income. How well the family's efforts at reorganization work depends ultimately on the family's ability to accommodate age-appropriate developmental needs. In families where there is more flexibility among the adults in assuming the different family roles, adjustment is likely to be better.

The onset of disability in old age is more expectable as bodily functions deteriorate. This decline in physical function is often associated with more depression. An older person may live for many years needing assistance in daily living, and the choices of where to get that assistance are not always easily made. Spouses may be unable to meet the extra caretaking needs indefinitely as their own health and stamina decline (Blackburn 1988). Adult children are often in a position of deciding where their elderly parent or parents should live when they can no longer care for themselves. Having their parents move in with them or having them move to a nursing home or seniors' residence are the most common options. However, each of these choices carries with it emotional, financial, and social costs to the elderly person as well as to his or her adult children. This responsibility for elderly parents is not always shared among adult children. Adult daughters are more likely than adult sons to be involved in providing direct care for their elderly parents (Brody 1985). The many decisions and responsibilities can be sources of tension, conflict, and resentment among extended family members. This period of disability in old age can go on for a very long time, given the medical capability to sustain life. While the practice is still not widespread, more elderly people are preparing a living will, which is a legal document preventing extraordinary means from being used to prolong their lives.

Family Response to Disabilities

How do families respond to the challenges of disabilities? Some of the more common responses will be discussed, although it is important to emphasize that there are many different ways by which families can successfully adapt. Response to disability can be divided into three phases: crisis, chronic, and terminal (Rolland 1994).

The initial response of most families to the sudden onset of disability is to pull together and rally around the person affected and provide support to each other (Steinglass et al. 1982). Some or all family members may suspend their daily routines for a period of time as they focus on the immediate crisis. They gather more information about the condition, its course, treatment options, and where to get services. Often there are new behaviors to be learned, including how to provide care and treatment to the person with the disability, how to interact with health care and other service providers, and how to access needed information. There is also a whole set of emotional issues that confronts family members, including grief over the loss of abilities; worry about the future and the costs; feelings of guilt, blame, or responsibility; and trying to find a cause and a meaning for this event. Families are more variable in how they deal with these emotional challenges. Some avoid them altogether and stay focused on gathering information and learning new behaviors. Other families are split, with some members having intense emotional reactions and others avoiding them. Even though there is the expectation that family members should provide support to each other in times of crisis, this is often unrealistic when members are out of sync with each other and each person needs so much. This is a place where health care providers could be more helpful to families—both in validating their strong emotional reactions and in providing support or finding other resources, as well as in recognizing and not judging family members who have different responses. This is a very vulnerable time for most families, and those who make the diagnosis and provide the initial care are powerful in influencing how the family responds. In many ways their early response sets the stage for how the family will adapt to the disability over the long run (Rolland 1994).

Following this crisis phase, there is the chronic phase of living with a disability. This phase varies in length depending on the condition, but it is essentially the "long haul," when the family settles into living with the disability. The ultimate challenge to the family is to meet the disability-related needs and simultaneously to meet the needs of the family and its members of having a normal life. A metaphor used to describe this challenge is "finding a place for the disability in the family, but keeping the disability in its place" (Gonzalez, Steinglass, and Reiss 1989).

The terminal phase is when the inevitability of death is clear. Of course, not all conditions signal a terminal phase, but for those that do, the patient and family are faced with a set of choices about how directly they wish to face death and saying good-bye. Families vary in their responses at this phase as well. In some cases, it is an occasion of healing and of celebration of what the person's life has meant for a family. In other cases, it can be a tremendous relief and an escape from a burden that was resented and never acknowledged. Family members who respond in this way usually need healing after the death. In still other families, the death creates a void in the family's lifestyle that may never be filled because the person's disability was the cornerstone around which family life was organized.

How the family organizes itself for the chronic phase of a disability is particularly important in understanding how the course of development for the person, the disability, and the family will evolve (see Figure 1, lower left quadrant). The central issue seems to be the degree to which the condition takes over family life and becomes the centerpiece around which all other activities are organized. David Reiss, Peter Steinglass, and George Howe (1993) have emphasized that a family's identity can be subsumed within and around the disability: "We are an 'asthmatic family.'" Important aspects of family life such as routines, rituals, leisure activities, and friends may be changed or given up to accommodate the disability-related needs. One person's needs take precedence over the needs of the whole family system to mature and for other members to progress along their developmental course. This "skew toward the disability" can evolve into a larger pattern of family responses (Gonzalez, Steinglass, and Reiss 1989). There is the tendency for family members to hold back from discussing any strong negative feelings they may have about their situation. It is as though they have no right to feel angry or resentful since, after all, they are not the one with the disability. This can lead to general repression of feelings in the family—an emotional shutdown. The overall climate in the family may frequently be tense, as though "walking on eggshells." When no one wants to upset the balance, there is a tendency to try to maintain control by becoming rigid and fixed in daily routine and activity. The flexibility that is generally adaptive for families may be given up. If families get to this point, they usually are resistant to help from the outside, including advice from friends and relatives. They tend to become socially isolated. Families can stay locked in this pattern for a very long time. A crisis related to the chronic condition or even related to another family member may be the occasion for such a pattern to change (since crisis, by definition, disrupts the status quo) and could put the family in contact with professional or informal resources that could help them. This particular pattern of family response, which is based on clinicians' experiences working with families coping with disability, has been elaborated to illustrate one way in which a family's response patterns could be problematic for the person with the disability and for the family unit. However, there are many other ways by which families respond.

There is a growing body of research that emphasizes the many positive ways by which families adapt to disability. Several aspects of family functioning patterns have been associated with good adjustment in the person with the disability and in other family members. This approach emphasizes resilience, or the ability of families to discover resources and overcome challenges. Nine aspects of resilient family process have been described based on the findings from numerous studies of successful family coping with disabilities (Patterson 1991b).

Balancing the condition with other family needs. Because there is a tendency to let the disability dominate daily life, many families learn to meet the normative developmental needs of the person with the disability as well as their disability needs (Cappelli et al. 1989). They plan for and take time for other family needs as well as those associated with the chronic condition (Beavers et al. 1986; Spinetta et al. 1988). They also try to maintain their normal family routines and rituals as a way to preserve their identity and lifestyle (Newbrough, Simpkins, and Maurer 1985; Steinglass and Horan 1987).

Maintaining clear family boundaries. A boundary is that psychological line that sets a system, such as a family, apart from its context. While families need to develop connections to the service delivery system to meet the needs of the person with a disability, they also need to maintain their own integrity and sense of control over their lives and not allow themselves to be overdirected by what professionals want them to do. In this way the family maintains its external boundary and improves the likelihood that the family will stay intact. Inside the family, it is usually best for family functioning when the parents work together to manage the family. This is called a generational boundary. When it is clear, children know that parents are in charge, and they function better (Beavers et al. 1986; Foster and Berger 1985). It reduces the likelihood of overinvolvement of one parent with the child, and it helps to maintain marital quality (Cappelli et al. 1989).

Developing communication competence. When disability is present, there are often more decisions to be made and more problems to be solved. Many families living with disability become more effective in learning to work through these issues (Newbrough, Simpkins, and Maurer 1985). Because there are so many intense feelings associated with living with disability, families do better over the long run when they are able to express feelings openly and respectfully, even when the feelings are negative and seem unjustified (Daniels et al. 1987; Kupst and Schulman 1988).

Attributing positive meanings to the situation. In addition to being able to talk openly, families who are able to think positively about their situation and develop positive attitudes manage better (Austin and McDermott 1988; Cowen et al. 1985; Krause and Seltzer 1993). Family members often acknowledge the positive contributions that the person with disability brings to family life (Behr and Murphy 1993) and how they have developed a new outlook on life that has more meaning (Frey, Greenberg, and Fewell 1989; Venters 1981).

Maintaining family flexibility. Flexibility is one of those family resources that benefits all families, particularly when chronic demands are present and when day-to-day life is not predictable. Being able to shift gears, change expectations, alter roles and rules, and try new things all contribute to better outcomes (Watson, Henggeler, and Whelan 1990).

Maintaining a commitment to the family unit. Of all the family resources studied, cohesion, or the bonds of unity and commitment linking family members, is probably the single most important protective factor that has consistently been reported in well-functioning families when a member has a chronic condition (Daniels et al. 1987; Kazak 1989; Spinetta et al. 1988; Thompson et al. 1992; Varni and Setoguchi 1993). These families cooperate with and support each other in their efforts to manage the disability. One member does not have a disproportionate burden of caregiving. A sense of teamwork prevails. Good family relationships provide a buffer from the stress of caregiving (Evans, Bishop, and Ousley 1992).

Engaging in active coping efforts. Many different aspects of coping have been studied relating to families' responses to chronic conditions. Those families who actively seek information and services (Donovan 1988), who actively work to solve problems and express feelings (Timko, Stovel, and Moos 1992), and who balance their personal, family, and illness needs (Patterson et al. 1993) show better adaptation than do families who engage in passive resignation.

Maintaining social integration. The ability to maintain supportive relationships with people in the community is another important protective factor for the family (Frey, Greenberg, and Fewell 1989; Kazak 1989; Jessop, Riessman, and Stein 1988). It is also a resource that often is threatened by the presence of disability in the family. There may be less time for maintaining social connections, and in some cases, friends and relatives are not supportive in their responses and old networks are abandoned. Support from other families who have a member with a chronic condition has become a major resource to many families, as evidenced in the many parent-to-parent support programs (Santelli et al. 1993).

Developing relationships with professionals. In addition to informal support from friends and relatives, the quality of the relationships that families have with professionals who provide services to the member with a disability becomes another protective factor for them (Walker and Singer 1993). Family members, of course, are only half of these dyads and cannot solely determine the quality of the relationship. Taking time to share information, working together to make decisions about care, respecting differences, avoiding attempts to control the other, and sharing risks associated with outcomes are factors that contribute to satisfaction on both sides (Chesler and Barbarin 1987).

Programs and Interventions

The unit of care and support when a person has a disability should be the family or caregiving system, not just the individual (McDaniel, Hepworth, and Doherty 1992). As already noted, the family is both affected by the disability and is a major source of capabilities for responding to it. Within the United States, there is a strong emphasis on family support initiatives as a way to improve the quality of life for people with disabilities (Dunst et al. 1993). Family support has been articulated in the philosophy of the Maternal and Child Health Bureau with regard to children with special health needs: Care should be family-centered, community-based, coordinated, comprehensive, and culturally competent (Hutchins and McPherson 1991).

Family support is also being implemented in early intervention programs for children with disabilities. Federal legislation has mandated states to develop systems of care that integrate health, education, and social services for these children and their families. One component of this legislation calls for an individual family service plan (McGonigel and Garland 1988). There is a meeting of family members and professionals serving the child to develop a comprehensive plan for meeting the needs of the child and the family. Families have a key role in identifying the needs and in identifying their strengths. The intent of the legislation is that parents should be included as an equal partner and full collaborator in deciding about and managing their child's care.

At the heart of the family support movement is the concept of family empowerment, which is defined as enabling an individual or family to increase their abilities to meet needs and goals and maintain their autonomy and integrity (Patterson and Geber 1991). Rather than the helper doing everything for the person being helped, thus maintaining dependency, a process is begun whereby the help-seeker discovers and builds on his or her own strengths, leading to a greater sense of mastery and control over his or her life.

Professionals who provide services to persons with disabilities and their families are being challenged to use this orientation when working with families. Training programs have curricula for developing these skills in new professionals. The emphasis is on the *process* of providing services and not just the *outcomes*. Empowerment involves believing in and building on the inherent strengths of families; respecting their values and beliefs; validating their perceptions and experiences as real; creating opportunities for family members to acquire knowledge and skills so they feel more competent; mobilizing the family to find and use sources of informal support in the community; and developing a service plan together and sharing responsibility for it (Dunst et al. 1993; Knoll 1992).

Coordination is another important way by which service delivery can be improved for persons with disabilities. Many persons need a multiplicity of services, and often they do not know what they are eligible for or where to find it. Case management or care coordination is needed to provide this information, to create linkages among these providers, and to assure that families are given complete and congruent information (Sloper and Turner 1992). In some instances, families are able to function as their own case managers, but this requires a high level of knowledge as well as skill in dealing with a bureaucratic system. Furthermore, it consumes a lot of time that many family members would prefer to devote to meeting other family needs. High-quality care coordination can reduce costs, relieve family stress, and improve the quality of life for persons with disabilities.

Another strategy to facilitate family coping and adaptation is linking persons with disabilities and their families together in support programs. There are many support groups for specific conditions (epilepsy, spina bifida, etc.) across the country that meet regularly to provide information and emotional support to those living with disability. In other instances, someone who has lived with the disability for a long time is paired with someone newly diagnosed (Santelli et al. 1993). These informal connections (in contrast to professional therapy services) are particularly effective because people feel they are not alone and are not abnormal in their struggles. There is the opportunity both to give and to receive support, which benefits both sides.

While family members are the primary source for providing care and assistance to a person with a disability, many families are unable to do this for an extended period of time without help from other community sources (Nosek 1993). Many persons with disability now use personal assistance services on a regular basis, which relieves the family of these tasks and allows them to interact with the person with a disability in more normative ways. In addition, personal assistants contribute to an adult's ability to make independent choices about where he or she will live. It makes it possible to transition from the family home and to live as an adult in the community.

Respite care is another community resource that can give families a break from caretaking and prevent total burnout and exhaustion (Folden and Coffman 1993). Respite care is usually provided on an as-needed basis, in contrast to personal assistants, who are usually available every day. When these kinds of resources are available to support families in their caregiving efforts, the families are better able to keep the persons with disability at home, and they do not have to turn to institutional placement.

Many different types of interventions have been developed by psychologists, social workers, and other mental health professionals for families who have members with disabilities (Singer and Powers 1993). These psychoeducational interventions are designed with a variety of goals in mind. They may be designed to support families in dealing with their emotional responses or to teach skills and strategies for managing difficult behavior. Programs may teach techniques for managing stress more effectively, or they may teach family members how to interact with professional providers of services. Some programs target one individual in the family, such as the primary caregiver; in other instances the whole family is the unit of intervention (Gonzalez, Steinglass, and Reiss 1989). Many families with members with disabilities are reluctant to use psychological resources because they cannot find time to go or they may interpret use as a judgment that they are not competent. Generally, persons from lower socioeconomic groups are more likely to view therapy as stigmatizing and so do not participate. Given the evidence that disability increases stress in families and increases the chance that someone will experience psychological or behavioral problems, programs and services to help families cope could prevent many of these secondary problems.

With increasing numbers of persons experiencing disability in the United States and with the reality that families are their primary source of care, it is important that public policies are designed so that families are given the support they need to fulfill this important role. Most families want to provide assistance to their members. However, community resources are also needed to augment their contributions. This kind of family-community collaboration will ultimately contribute to the best quality of life for persons with disabilities, members of their families, and the people in their communities.

See also: ALZHEIMER'S DISEASE; ANXIETY DISORDERS; BOUNDARY AMBIGUITY; CAREGIVING: FORMAL; CAREGIVING: INFORMAL; CHILDCARE; CHRONIC ILLNESS; COMMUNICATION: FAMILY RELATIONSHIPS; DEATH AND DYING; DEMENTIA; DEVELOPMENTAL DISABILITIES; DEVELOPMENTAL PSYCHOPATHOLOGY; ELDERS; FAMILY ROLES; FAMILY STRENGTHS; FAMILY SYSTEM THEORY; GRIEF, LOSS, AND BEREAVEMENT; HEALTH AND FAMILIES; RESPITE CARE: ADULT; RESPITE CARE: CHILD; SCHOOL; STRESS

Bibliography

Albrecht, G.; Seelman, K.; and Bury, M. (2001). *Handbook of Disability Studies.* Thousand Oaks, CA: Sage Publications.

Austin, J., and McDermott, N. (1988). "Parental Attitude and Coping Behavior in Families of Children with Epilepsy." *Journal of Neuroscience Nursing* 20:174–179.

Baxter, C.; Cummins, R.; and Polak, S. (1995). "A Longitudinal Study of Parental Stress and Support: From Diagnosis of Disability to Leaving School." *International Journal of Disability, Development, and Education* 42:125–136.

Beavers, J.; Hampson R.; Hulgus, Y.; and Beavers, W. (1986). "Coping in Families with a Retarded Child." *Family Process* 25:365–378.

Behr, S., and Murphy, D. (1993). "Research Progress and Promise: The Role Perceptions in Cognitive Adaptation to Disability." In *Cognitive Coping, Families, and Disability,* ed. A. Turnbull, J. Patterson, S. Behr, D. Murphy, J. Marquis, and M. Blue-Banning. Baltimore: Paul H. Brookes.

Biegel, D.; Sales, E.; and Schulz, R. (1991). *Family Caregiving in Chronic Illness.* Newbury Park, CA: Sage Publications.

Blackburn, J. (1988). "Chronic Health Problems of the Elderly." In *Chronic Illness and Disability,* ed. C. Chilman, E. Nunnally, and F. Cox. Newbury Park, CA: Sage Publications.

Boss, P. (1993). "The Reconstruction of Family Life with Alzheimer's Disease: Generating Theory to Lower Family Stress from Ambiguous Loss." In *Sourcebook of Family Theories and Methods: A Contextual Approach,* ed. P. Boss, W. Doherty, R. LaRossa, W. Schumm, and S. Steinmetz. New York: Plenum.

Breslau, N. (1993). "Psychiatric Sequelae of Brain Dysfunction in Children: The Role of Family Environment." In *How Do Families Cope with Chronic Illness?,* ed. R. Cole and D. Reiss. Hillsdale, NJ: Lawrence Erlbaum.

Brody, E. (1985). "Parent Care as a Normative Family Stress." *Gerontologist* 25:19–29.

Cadman, D.; Boyle, M.; Szatmari, P.; and Offord, D. (1987). "Chronic Illness, Disability, and Mental and Social Well-Being: Findings of the Ontario Child Health Study." *Pediatrics* 79:805–812.

Cappelli, M.; McGrath, P.; MacDonald, N.; Katsanis, J.; and Lascelles, M. (1989). "Parental Care and Overprotection of Children with Cystic Fibrosis." *British Journal of Medical Psychology* 62:281–289.

Chesler, M., and Barbarin, O. (1987). *Childhood Cancer and the Family: Meeting the Challenge of Stress and Support*. New York: Brunner/Mazel.

Chilman, C.; Nunnally, E.; and Cox, F., eds. (1988). *Chronic Illness and Disability*. Newbury Park, CA: Sage Publications.

Cohen, M. (1999). "Families Coping with Childhood Chronic Illness: A Research Review." *Families, Systems, and Health* 17:149–164.

Cole, R., and Reiss, D. (1993). *How Do Families Cope with Chronic Illness?* Hillsdale, NJ: Lawrence Erlbaum.

Coupey, S. M., and Cohen, M. I. (1984). "Special Considerations for the Health Care of Adolescents with Chronic Illnesses." *Pediatric Clinics of North America* 31:211–219.

Cowen, L.; Corey, M.; Keenan, N.; Simmons, R.; Arndt, E.; and Levison, H. (1985). "Family Adaptation and Psychosocial Adjustment to Cystic Fibrosis in the Preschool Child." *Social Science and Medicine* 20:553–560.

Daniels, D.; Moos, R.; Billings, A.; and Miller, J. (1987). "Psychosocial Risk and Resistance Factors Among Children with Chronic Illness, Healthy Siblings, and Healthy Controls." *Journal of Abnormal Child Psychology* 15:295–308.

Donovan, A. (1988). "Family Stress and Ways of Coping with Adolescents Who Have Handicaps: Maternal Perceptions." *American Journal of Mental Retardation* 92:502–509.

Dunst, C.; Trivette, C.; and Deal, A. (1988). *Enabling and Empowering Families: Principles and Guidelines for Practice*. Cambridge, MA: Brookline Books.

Dunst, C.; Trivette, C.; Starnes, A.; Hamby, D.; and Gordon, N. (1993). *Building and Evaluating Family Support Initiatives*. Baltimore: Paul H. Brookes.

Dyson, L. (1993). "Response to the Presence of a Child with Disabilities: Parental Stress and Family Functioning over Time." *American Journal on Mental Retardation* 98:207–218.

Eisenberg, M. G.; Sutkin, L. C.; and Jansen, M. A:, eds. (1984). *Chronic Illness and Disability Through the Lifespan: Effects on Self and Family*. New York: Springer-Verlag.

Evans, R.; Bishop, D.; and Ousley, R. (1992). "Providing Care to Persons with Physical Disability: Effect on Family Caregivers." *American Journal of Physical Medicine and Rehabilitation* 71:140–144.

Fitzsimmons, S. C. (1991). *Cystic Fibrosis Foundation Patient Registry Pulmonary Data 1990*. Bethesda, MD: Cystic Fibrosis Foundation.

Folden, S., and Coffman, S. (1993). "Respite Care for Families of Children with Disabilities." *Journal of Pediatric Health Care* 7:103–110.

Foster, M., and Berger, M. (1985). "Research with Families with Handicapped Children: A Multilevel Systemic Perspective." In *The Handbook of Family Psychology and Therapy*, Vol. II, ed. L. L'Abate. Homewood, IL: Dorsey Press.

Frey, K.; Greenberg, M.; and Fewel, R. (1989). "Stress and Coping Among Parents of Handicapped Children: A Multidimensional Approach." *American Journal of Mental Retardation* 94:240–249.

Gonzalez, S.; Steinglass, P.; and Reiss, D. (1989). "Putting the Illness in Its Place: Discussion Groups for Families with Chronic Medical Illnesses." *Family Process* 28:69–87.

Hirst, M. (1991). "Dissolution and Reconstitution of Families with a Disabled Young Person." *Developmental Medicine and Child Neurology* 33:1073–1079.

Hodapp, R.M. (1998). *Development and Disabilities: Intellectual, Sensory and Motor Impairments*. New York: Cambridge University Press.

Holmes, D. M. (1986). "The Person and Diabetes in Psychosocial Context." *Diabetes Care* 9:194–206.

Holroyd, J., and Guthrie, D. (1986). "Family Stress with Chronic Childhood Illness: Cystic Fibrosis, Neuromuscular Disease, and Renal Disease." *Journal of Clinical Psychology* 42:552–561.

Hornby, G. (1992). "A Review of Fathers' Accounts of Their Experiences of Parenting Children with Disabilities." *Disability, Handicap, and Society* 7:363–374.

Hutchins, V., and McPherson, M. (1991). "National Agenda for Children with Special Health Needs." *American Psychologist* 46:141–143.

Ireys, H., and Burr, C. (1984). "Apart and A Part: Family Issues for Young Adults with Chronic Illness and Disability." In *Chronic Illness and Disability Through the Life Span: Effects on Self and Family*, ed. M. G. Eisenberg, L. C. Sutkin, and M. A. Jansen. New York: Springer-Verlag.

Jessop, D.; Riessman, C.; and Stein, R. (1988). "Chronic Childhood Illness and Maternal Mental Health." *Journal of Developmental and Behavioral Pediatrics* 9:147–156.

Kazak, A: (1989). "Family Functioning in Families with Older Institutionalized Retarded Offspring." *Journal of Autism and Developmental Disorders* 19:501–509.

Knoll, J. (1992). "Being a Family: The Experience of Raising a Child with a Disability or Chronic Illness."

Monographs of the American Association on Mental Retardation 18:9–56.

Krause, M., and Seltzer, M. (1993). "Coping Strategies Among Older Mothers of Adults with Retardation: A Lifespan Developmental Perspective." In *Cognitive Coping, Families, and Disability,* ed. A: Turnbull, J. Patterson, S. Behr, D. Murphy, J. Marquis, and M. Blue-Banning. Baltimore: Paul H. Brookes.

Kupst, M., and Schulman, J. (1988). "Long-Term Coping with Pediatric Leukemia: A Six-Year Follow-Up Study." *Journal of Pediatric Psychology* 13:7–22.

LaPlante, M. P. (1988). *Data on Disability from the National Health Interview Survey, 1983–1985: An InfoUse Report*. Washington, DC: National Institute on Disability and Rehabilitation Research.

Lopez, S. (1998). "Maternal Reactions to Children with Mental Retardation." In *Handbook of Mental Retardation and Development,* ed J. Burack, R. Hodapp, and E. Zigler. New York: Cambridge University Press.

Marshak, L.; Seligman, M.; and Prezant, F. (1999). *Disability and the Family Life Cycle*. New York: Basic Books.

McDaniel, S.; Hepworth, J.; and Doherty, W. (1992). *Medical Family Therapy*. New York. Basic Books.

McGonigel, M., and Garland, C. (1988). "The Individualized Family Service Plan and the Early Intervention Team: Team and Family Issues and Recommended Practices." *Infants and Young Children* 1:10–21.

Murphy, M. A. (1982). "The Family with a Handicapped Child: A Review of the Literature." *Developmental and Behavioral Pediatrics* 3:73–82.

National Center for Health Statistics. (1989). "Current Estimates from the National Health Interview Survey, 1988." *Vital and Health Statistics*. Series 10, no. 166, PHS 89–1501. Washington, DC: U.S. Government Printing Office.

Newbrough, J.; Simpkins, C.; and Maurer, M. (1985). "A Family Development Approach to Studying Factors in the Management and Control of Childhood Diabetes." *Diabetes Care* 8:83–92.

Nosek, M. (1993). "Personal Assistance: Its Effect on the Long-Term Health of a Rehabilitation Hospital Population." *Archives of Physical Medicine and Rehabilitation* 74:127–132.

Patterson, J. (1988). "Chronic Illness in Children and the Impact: on Families." In *Chronic Illness and Disability,* ed. C. Chilman, E. Nunnally, and F. Cox. Newbury Park, CA: Sage Publications.

Patterson, J. (1991a). "A Family Systems Perspective for Working with Youth with Disability." *Pediatrician* 18:129–141.

Patterson, J. (1991b). "Family Resilience to the Challenge of a Child's Disability." *Pediatric Annals* 20:491–496.

Patterson, J.; Budd, J.; Goetz, D.; and Warwick, W. (1993). "Family Correlates of a Ten-Year Pulmonary Health Trend in Cystic Fibrosis." *Pediatrics* 91:383–389.

Patterson, J., and Geber, G. (1991). "Preventing Mental Health Problems in Children with Chronic Illness or Disability." *Children's Health Care* 20:150–161.

Patterson, J., and Leonard, B. (1994). "Caregiving and Children." In *Family Caregiving Across the Lifespan,* ed. E. Kahana, D. Biegel, and M. Wykle. Newbury Park, CA: Sage Publications.

Patterson, J.; Leonard, B.; and Titus, J. (1992). "Home Care for Medically Fragile Children: Impact on Family Health and Well-Being." *Developmental and Behavioral Pediatrics* 13:248–255.

Perrin, E., and Gerrity, P. S. (1984). "Development of Children with a Chronic Illness." *Pediatric Clinics of North America* 31.19–31.

Perrin, E.; Newacheck, P.; Pless, I; Drotar, D.; Gortmaker, S.; Leventhal, J.; Perrin, J.; Stein, R.; Walker, D.; and Weitzman, M. (1993). "Issues Involved in the Definition and Classification of Chronic Health Conditions." *Pediatrics* 91:787–793.

Pope, A., and Tarlov, A., eds. (1991). *Disability in America: Toward a National Agenda for Prevention*. Washington, DC: National Academy Press.

Reiss, D.; Steinglass, P.; and Howe, G. (1993). "The Family's Reorganization Around Illness." In *How Do Families Cope with Chronic Illness?,* ed. R. Cole and D. Reiss. Hillsdale, NJ: Lawrence Erlbaum.

Rolland, J. (1994). *Families, Illness, and Disability: An Integrative Treatment Model*. New York: Basic Books.

Sabbeth, B., and Leventhal, J. (1984). "Marital Adjustment to Chronic Childhood Illness: A Critique of the Literature." *Pediatrics* 73:762–768.

Santelli, B.; Turnbull, A.; Lerner, E.; and Marquis, J. (1993). "Parent-to-Parent Programs." In *Families, Disability, and Empowerment,* ed. G. Singer and L. Powers. Baltimore: Paul H. Brookes.

Singer. G.; Irvin, L.; Irvine, B.; Hawkins, N.; Hegreness, J.; and Jackson, R. (1993). "Helping Families Adapt Positively to Disability." In *Families, Disability, and Empowerment,* ed. G. Singer and L. Powers. Baltimore: Paul H. Brookes.

Singer, G., and Powers, L., eds. (1993). *Families, Disability, and Empowerment*. Baltimore: Paul H. Brookes.

Singhi, P.; Goyal, L.; Pershad, D.; Singhi, S.; and Walia, B. (1990). "Psychosocial Problems in Families of Disabled Children." *British Journal of Medical Psychology* 63: 173–182.

Sloper, P., and Turner, S. (1992). "Service Needs of Families of Children with Severe Physical Disability." *Child: Care, Health, and Development* 18:259–282.

Spinetta, J.; Murphy, J.; Vik, P.; and Day, J. (1988). "Long-Term Adjustment in Families of Children with Cancer." *Journal of Psychosocial Oncology* 6:179–191.

Stainton, T., and Besser, H. (1998). "The Positive Impact of Children with an Intellectual Disability on the Family." *Journal of Intellectual & Developmental Disability* 23:57–70.

Stein, R. E. K.; Bauman, L. J.; Westbrook, L. E.; Coupey, S. M.; and Ireys, H. T. (1993). "Framework for Identifying Children Who Have Chronic Conditions: The Case for a New Definition." *The Journal of Pediatrics* 122:342–347.

Steinglass, P., and Horan, M. (1987). "Families and Chronic Medical Illness." *Journal of Psychotherapy and the Family* 3:127–142.

Steinglass, P.; Temple, S.; Lisman, S.; and Reiss, D. (1982). "Coping with Spinal Cord Injury: The Family Perspective." *General Hospital Psychiatry* 4:259–264.

Stone, R., and Kemper, P. (1989). "Spouses and Children of Disabled Elders: How Large a Constituency for Long-Term Care Reform?" *Milbank Quarterly* 67:485–506.

Stoneman, Z., and Berman, P., eds. (1993). *The Effects of Mental Retardation, Disability, and Illness on Sibling Relationships: Research Issues and Challenges*. Baltimore: Brookes.

Taanila, A.; Kokkonen, J.; and Jarvelin, M. (1996). "The Long-term Effects of Children's Early-Onset Disability on Marital Relationships." *Developmental Medicine and Child Neurology* 38:567–577.

Thompson, R.; Gustafson, K.; Hamlett, K.; and Spock, A. (1992). "Stress, Coping, and Family Functioning in the Psychological Adjustment of Mothers of Children and Adolescents with Cystic Fibrosis." *Journal of Pediatric Psychology* 17:573–585.

Turnbull, A.; Patterson, J.; Behr, S.; Murphy, D.; Marquis, J.; and Blue-Banning, M., eds. (1993). *Cognitive Coping, Families, and Disability*. Baltimore: Paul H. Brookes.

Turnbull, A. P., and Turnbull, H. R. (1986). *Families, Professionals, and Exceptionalities: A Special Partnership*. Columbus, OH: Charles E. Merrill.

Vance, J.; Fazan, L.; and Satterwhite, B. (1980). "Effects of Nephrotic Syndrome on the Family: A Controlled Study." *Pediatrics* 65:948–956.

Varni, J., and Setoguchi, Y. (1993). "Effects of Parental Adjustment on the Adaptation of Children with Congenital or Acquired Limb Deficiencies." *Developmental and Behavioral Pediatrics* 14:13–20.

Varni, J., and Wallender, J. (1988). "Pediatric Chronic Disabilities: Hemophilia and Spina Bifida as Examples." In *Handbook of Pediatric Psychology*, ed. D. Routh. New York: Guilford.

Venters, M. (1981). "Familial Coping with Chronic and Severe Childhood Illness: The Case of Cystic Fibrosis." *Social Science and Medicine* 15A:948–956.

Walker, B., and Singer, G. (1993). "Improving Collaborative Communication Between Professionals and Parents." In *Families, Disability, and Empowerment*, ed. G. Singer and L. Powers. Baltimore: Paul H. Brookes.

Watson, S.; Henggeler, S.; and Whelan, J. (1990). "Family Functioning and the Social Adaptation of Hearing-Impaired Youths." *Journal of Abnormal Child Psychology* 18:143–163.

Yau, M., and Li-Tsang, C. (1999). "Adjustment and Adaptation in Parents of Children with Developmental Disability in Two-Parent Families: A Review of the Characteristics and Attributes." *British Journal of Developmental Disabilities* 45:38–51.

JOÄN M. PATTERSON (1995)
BIBLIOGRAPHY REVISED BY JAMES J. PONZETTI, JR.

DISCIPLINE

For many parents, the word *discipline* refers to punishment intended to decrease child misbehavior. In truth, the word is derived from *disciplinare*, referring to a system of teaching or instruction (Howard 1996). Although few would dispute the value of teaching children, the topic of parental discipline has long been controversial, even among experts. In the leading parenting book of the 1930s, *Psychological Care of Infant and Child* (1928), John B. Watson argued that mothers should avoid being nurturant with their children. Parental nurturance and common sense made a comeback with Benjamin Spock's *Common Sense Book of Baby and Child Care* (1946). Discipline advice has changed from Watson's strict discipline to the permissiveness of the 1950s and 1960s to mixed messages (Forehand and McKinney 1993).

Two complementary perspectives of childrearing and parental discipline have been offered. The first perspective considers the kinds of parental discipline associated with moral thoughts and actions in normally developing children (e.g., Grusec and Kuczysnki 1997). The second perspective has focused on helping parents reduce disruptive behavior in clinically referred children, such as noncompliance, temper tantrums, defiance, and aggression (Briesmeister and Schaefer 1998; Serketich and Dumas 1996). The two perspectives complement each other concerning the goals of discipline, foundations for discipline, and proactive strategies for preventing discipline problems.

Goals of Discipline

Cognitive developmental psychologists have emphasized moral internalization and autonomy as important goals. *Moral internalization* is the process whereby children adopt a set of values as their own. *Autonomy* refers to children's growing ability to act independently. Developmental psychologists thus focus more on optimal development, such as prosocial behavior, and see problems when children comply too much with parents (Kuczynski and Hildebrandt 1997).

The goals of parent trainers using the second perspective, in contrast, have been to improve child compliance from deviant to normal rates while decreasing problem behaviors such as antisocial aggression (Roberts and Powers 1990). Note that an intermediate level of compliance is considered optimal from both perspectives. Some have criticized behavioral clinicians for their emphasis on child compliance (Houlihan et al. 1992; Kuczynski and Hildebrandt 1997). Noncompliance, however, is the most frequent complaint about clinically referred children (Forehand and McMahon 1981). Defiant noncompliance is a major risk factor for poor moral internalization as well as increased aggression, delinquency, and academic underachievement (Kochanska and Aksan 1995; Loeber and Schmaling 1985; Patterson, Reid, and Dishion 1992).

Foundations for Discipline

Cognitive developmental psychologists and behavioral parent trainers agree that the overall quality of the parent-child relationship is crucial for discipline. The relationship quality influences children's behavior directly as well as indirectly, by means of making disciplinary responses more effective.

Parental nurturance is the most crucial part of a good parent-child relationship. Disciplinary responses are more effective when parents consistently communicate love toward the child. Positive involvement, verbal and nonverbal expressions of love and concern, praise and encouragement for appropriate behavior, and calm responses to conflict all enhance moral development (Chamberlain and Patterson 1995; Kochanska and Thompson 1997; Pettit, Bates, and Dodge 1997, Rothbaum and Weisz 1994). Responding sensitively to child cues and encouraging child-directed play are two ways to express nurturance. Responding sensitively to an infant's cues makes a secure attachment to the parents more likely. A secure attachment, in turn, is associated with many aspects of appropriate development (Erickson, Sroufe, and Egeland 1985).

The more parents play with preschoolers, the fewer behavior problems appear later on (Pettit and Bates 1989). Frances Gardner (1994) found that conduct-problem children were less involved with their mothers in joint activity and constructive play. They watched more television, and they spent more time doing "nothing." Their mothers initiated fewer positive interactions and were less responsive to their children's initiatives.

Consistent with these findings, most behavioral parent training programs teach parents to initiate child-directed play times (Forehand 1993). Therapists coach parents to follow the child's lead; to describe, imitate, and praise the child's appropriate behavior; to mimic appropriate child talk; and to ignore minor misbehavior. They also train parents to avoid criticizing, instructing, or questioning during child-directed play (Hembree-Kigin and McNeil 1995). Cooperating with children's initiatives at such times has been shown to enhance their cooperating with parents at other times (Parpal and Maccoby 1985).

Proactive Discipline

Proactive discipline builds on a foundation of nurturance with specific strategies to promote appropriate behavior and to prevent inappropriate behavior. When mothers use proactive strategies as well as just reacting to misbehavior, their children behave more appropriately (Gardner et al. 1999). Cognitive developmental psychologists and behavioral parent trainers have emphasized different kinds of proactive discipline skills.

George Holden (1985) studied specific proactive strategies for two-year-old children during shopping trips. Mothers shopped when the store was not busy and when the child was not hungry or tired. Among other things they instructed the child ahead of time, kept the child occupied, and diverted attention away from tempting items.

Proactive strategies can be taught. For example, Matthews Sanders and Mark Dadds (1982) trained parents to plan daily activities, which reduced deviant child behavior in most families. Another strategy states that parents can reward a disliked activity (e.g., cleaning one's room) with a desired activity (e.g., playing outdoors).

Child behavior can also be improved simply by improving parental instructions or requests (Green, Forehand, and McMahon 1979; Roberts et al. 1978). Child cooperation is more likely when parental instructions are direct and specific, and designate a one-step task that the child is capable of (Hembree-Kigin and McNeil 1995; Houlihan 1994). Instructions are also more effective if phrased positively (do versus don't) and followed by a five-second pause (Houlihan and Jones 1990; Patterson 1982).

"Catching them being good" is another important aspect of proactive discipline. Parents of well-behaved children tend to recognize and praise appropriate behavior more than do parents of disruptive children (Grusec and Goodnow 1994). Every time a parent misses an opportunity to catch a child being good, they miss a chance to teach that child appropriate behavior (Christophersen 1988). As a result, parental attention to misbehavior may be more rewarding to children than being ignored when they are behaving appropriately (Shriver and Allen 1996).

Prime opportunities to learn new abilities were called the "zone of proximal development" by Lev Vygotsky (Vygotsky [1934] 1987). He noted that new abilities are learned one step at a time. Parents can facilitate children's learning by first demonstrating a new skill, asking leading questions, introducing the first parts of the new skill, and then giving the children more independence in performing the skill. Such skillful coaching by parents may enhance children's social skills and thereby their popularity.

Monitoring children's activities is another important proactive strategy. Supervision tends to prevent delinquency and drug abuse while enhancing popularity and scholastic achievement (Chamberlain and Patterson 1995). Monitoring takes different forms depending on the child's age. During the preteenage years, the important dimensions of monitoring include parental involvement and responsiveness. Later, knowing an adolescent's whereabouts and activities becomes a more important aspect of monitoring, reflecting an appropriate balance between parental influence and the teenager's growing independence.

Discipline Responses

In an ideal world a positive parent-child relationship and proactive discipline would be enough to prevent all misbehavior. Unfortunately, only about 6 percent of even well-educated families accomplish this by the time the child is 4 years old (Baumrind 1971). Opinions differ greatly as to how the other 94 percent should respond to misbehavior.

Cognitive developmental psychologists recommend *disciplinary reasoning,* while avoiding negative consequences as much as possible (Grusec and Kuczysnki 1997). In contrast, behavioral parent trainers recommend the opposite in applying consistent consequences such as a time-out or privilege removal while minimizing verbal discipline (Briesmeister and Schaefer 1998).

The cognitive developmental recommendation comes from studies showing that parents of well-behaved children rely more on reasoning, whereas the parents of poorly behaved children rely more on punishment of various kinds (Grusec and Goodnow 1994). In contrast, behavioral parent trainers criticize this approach, and feel that parents who rely too much on reasoning risk giving children more attention when they misbehave than when they behave appropriately (Blum et al. 1995). Contingent use of negative consequences—such as a time-out—is a crucial component for training these parents to manage their children's behavior more effectively.

Attribution theory provides a popular explanation of why parents of well-behaved children rely

Behavioral parent trainers recommend applying consistent consequences for misbehavior such as a time-out or privilege removal while minimizing verbal discipline. LAURA DWIGHT/CORBIS

more on milder disciplinary responses. If appropriate behavior occurs without forceful parental influences, then children are more likely to attribute their behavior to their own internal motivations (e.g., "I want to behave appropriately"), thereby enhancing their internalization of those moral standards (Lepper 1983). Attribution theory assumes, however, that parents can make their children behave appropriately without being obvious about it. Cognitive developmentalists have not explained how mild disciplinary responses—such as reasoning—acquire their effectiveness in producing appropriate behavior. Nonetheless, they often recommend that parents use mild disciplinary tactics, such as reasoning, while avoiding negative consequences as much as possible (Kochanska and Thompson 1997; Pettit, Bates, and Dodge 1997). Mothers of two- and three-year-old children who followed that advice, however, witnessed an increased rate of disruptive behavior during the preschool years, while their peers' rates decreased

(Larzelere et al. 1998). In contrast, the largest decrease in disruptive behavior occurred when mothers used frequent reasoning, but backed reasoning with negative consequences at least 10 percent of the time.

This finding may result from two factors. First, reasoning is more effective at decreasing the recurrence of misbehavior when combined with a negative consequence (Larzelere et al. 1996). Second, reasoning becomes more effective by itself after it has been combined with a negative consequence such as a time-out or privilege removal (Larzelere et al. 1998). By making reasoning more effective by itself, this process fulfills a prerequisite for attributions to enhance moral internalization when children start making adult-like attributions around six years of age.

Consistent with this, several studies have found that reasoning is more effective at an intermediate intensity than if used matter-of-factly. The intermediate intensity could be achieved by verbal firmness or by an accompanying negative consequence (Larzelere and Merenda 1994). When used in these ways, reasoning has consistently been an effective disciplinary response, whereas matter-of-fact reasoning is only average in its effectiveness. Thus, both reasoning and negative consequences have appropriate roles in optimal discipline. Combining reasoning with consequences when necessary stands in contrast to a sole preference for one to the exclusion of the other, which is sometimes recommended by cognitive developmental psychologists or behavioral parent trainers.

Consistent use of negative consequences is particularly crucial for children with severe behavior problems. After working extensively with antisocial children, Gerald Patterson (1982) concluded that the most important component of treatment is to teach their parents how to use nonphysical negative consequences more effectively. He was referring to time-outs, privilege removal, and grounding.

The most effective parent-training programs teach parents to use a specific time-out procedure as a consequence for critical misbehaviors (Barkley 1997; Hembree-Kigin and McNeil 1995). Although the effectiveness of time-outs for reducing misbehavior is well-documented in a variety of settings and behaviors, it can be difficult for parents to implement appropriately (Shriver and Allen 1996). Typical guidelines for time-outs include: (1) start with only a few types of misbehavior; (2) make sure children understand what is expected of them; (3) use one, and only one, warning; (4) take the child immediately to the time-out location, such as a chair in a safe, boring place; (5) set a timer for a maximum of five minutes; and (6) require the child to follow the original instruction upon completion of the time-out (Danforth 1998). Some behavioral parent trainers replace Guideline #5 with a requirement for sitting quietly at least momentarily. The quiet requirement is then gradually increased to one to five minutes (Shriver and Allen 1996).

Children sometimes refuse to follow the time-out procedure when it is first used. Practicing the entire procedure before can be helpful. Many children, however, require a backup to enforce time-out compliance (Danforth 1998; Hembree-Kigin and McNeil 1995). The most effective backups have been either two swats with an open hand to the buttocks (for children from two to six years of age) or putting the child in a room with the door closed for one minute (Roberts and Powers 1990). Withdrawing privileges or adding chores are preferable backup strategies for older children (Forgatch and Patterson 1989). If a child does not comply with the time-out procedure after six successive backup repetitions, then parents should consider an alternative back-up tactic or seek help from a mental health professional experienced in behavioral parent training (Roberts and Powers 1990).

Privilege removal or *grounding* has been demonstrated to be effective in reducing misbehavior (Pazulinec, Meyerrose, and Sajwaj 1983), but other studies have found that parents rarely use them (Ritchie 1999). In one interesting variation of grounding, Edward Christophersen (1988) required an older child to complete a specified job in order to terminate the grounding. Then the child can work productively toward ending the grounding rather than manipulating the parents.

Overcorrection is an innovative disciplinary tactic that encompasses two different procedures, restitution and positive practice (Axelrod, Brantner, and Meddock 1978). *Restitution* requires the child to restore the situation as it was prior to the misbehavior. *Positive practice* involves repetitive practice of an appropriate behavior to replace the problem behavior. Overcorrection has been used successfully to teach academic and toileting skills, and to reduce aggressive behavior (Azrin, Sneed, and Foxx 1973; Lenz, Singh, and Hewett 1991; Matson et al. 1979). For example, Christina Adams and Mary Lou Kelley (1992) found that a brief restitution (apology) and positive practice (doing or saying something nice) significantly reduced sibling aggression. They concluded that overcorrection and time-outs were equivalent in efficacy, but parents rated overcorrection as more acceptable.

Restraint and *distraction* are often used with young preschoolers. They are usually effective in putting an immediate stop to the misbehavior. They are also reasonably effective in delaying recurrences of similar misbehavior when combined with reasoning (Larzelere and Merenda 1994). However, backing up reasoning with restraint or distraction does not enhance subsequent reasoning in preschoolers as clearly as do nonphysical consequences (Larzelere 2001).

Conditional Sequence of Responses

A *conditional sequence approach* is one of the few attempts to combine cognitive developmental and parent-training recommendations for disciplinary responses (Larzelere 2001). First, a sound foundation should be established with parental nurturance and proactive strategies. A parent's goal should then be to establish reasoning as an effective discipline response by itself during the preschool years. Negative consequences should be used primarily to enforce verbal corrections and rationales as effective discipline responses, beginning at least by two years of age.

For example, a possible sequence of discipline responses to a preschooler's misbehavior might consist of the following steps: (1) getting the child's attention; (2) issuing a verbal directive; (3) presenting an age-appropriate rationale; (4) one warning of a time-out; (5) using a time-out; (6) one warning of a backup for the time-out; and (7) using the backup (e.g., two-swat spank or brief room isolation; Roberts and Powers 1990). For targeted or severe misbehaviors, the sequence would be followed until compliance or a mutually acceptable negotiation. Less severe misbehaviors (e.g., irritations) might be ignored rather than overusing this sequence of disciplinary tactics. Research has shown that the later steps in this sequence improve the effectiveness of the earlier steps by themselves in later discipline encounters (Larzelere et al. 1998; Roberts and Powers 1990). Once the earlier steps become effective, the later steps are rarely needed.

There are several considerations relevant to the effectiveness of this sequence of disciplinary responses. First, the sequence needs to be used flexibly, adapting it to the situation and the child. Second, parents should avoid overusing negative consequences, because they can become less effective the more frequently they are used. Parents who reserve negative consequences for more important misbehaviors tend to get better results than those who overuse them for minor misbehaviors. Third, children sometimes need to be allowed to negotiate what they do in an appropriate way. For example, a child might ask politely to take five minutes to complete an activity before getting ready for bed. Fourth, parents need to be sober and in control of their emotions. Unpredictable, explosive disciplinary responses are consistently associated with detrimental child outcomes

(Chamberlain and Patterson 1995; Straus and Mouradian 1998). Finally, if spanking is used (e.g., as a backup for time-outs with two- to six-year-olds), it should never leave marks other than temporary redness. Its use is empirically supported primarily as a backup for milder disciplinary tactics such as time-out with two- to six-year-old children by loving parents in control of their emotions (Larzelere 2000).

Conclusion

Parental discipline is a complex responsibility. Those parents who are successful develop an appropriate foundation for discipline, provide good strategies for proactive discipline, and use effective but nonabusive disciplinary responses.

Successful parents also find their own authoritative balance of love and limits, avoiding the extremes of overly permissive or overly punitive discipline. Yet a range of authoritative approaches all work well. Somewhat strict parenting works reasonably well as long as it is clearly motivated by love and concern. Fairly permissive parenting also works as long as parents can enforce important limits with reasonable methods when needed.

See also: ATTACHMENT: PARENT-CHILD RELATIONSHIPS; CHILD ABUSE: PHYSICAL ABUSE AND NEGLECT; CHILDCARE; CHILDHOOD; CONDUCT DISORDERS; CONFLICT: PARENT-CHILD RELATIONSHIPS; COPARENTING; DEVELOPMENT: MORAL; FAMILY AND RELATIONAL RULES; FORGIVENESS; JUVENILE DELINQUENCY; OPPOSITIONALITY; PARENTING EDUCATION; PARENTING STYLES; RELIGION; SPANKING; STEPFAMILIES; TEMPERAMENT; THERAPY: PARENT-CHILD RELATIONSHIPS

Bibliography

Adams, C. D., and Kelley, M. L. (1992). "Managing Sibling Aggression: Overcorrection as an Alternative to Time-Out." *Behavior Therapy* 23(4):707–717.

Axelrod, S.; Brantner, J. P.; and Meddock, T. D. (1978). "Overcorrection: A Review and Critical Analysis." *Journal of Special Education* 12(4):367–392.

Azrin, N. H.; Sneed, T. J.; and Foxx, R. M. (1973). "Dry Bed: A Rapid Method of Eliminating Bedwetting (Enuresis) of the Retarded." *Behaviour Research and Therapy* 11(4):427–434.

Barkley, R. A. (1997). *Defiant Children: A Clinician's Manual for Assessment and Parent Training,* 2nd edition. New York: Guilford.

Baumrind, D. (1971). "Harmonious Parents and Their Preschool Children." *Developmental Psychology* 4: 99–102.

Blum, N. J.; Williams, G. E.; Friman, P. C.; and Christophersen, E. R. (1995). "Disciplining Young Children: The Role of Verbal Instructions and Reasoning." *Pediatrics* 96:336–341.

Briesmeister, J. M., and Schaefer, C. E. (1998). *Handbook of Parent Training*. New York: Wiley

Chamberlain, P., and Patterson, G. R. (1995). "Discipline and Child Compliance in Parenting." In *Handbook of Parenting,* Vol 4: *Applied and Practical Parenting,* ed. M. H. Bornstein. Mahwah, NJ: Lawrence Erlbaum Associates.

Christophersen, E. R. (1988). *Little People: Guidelines for Common Sense Child Rearing,* 3rd edition. Kansas City, MO: Westport.

Danforth, J. S. (1998). "The Behavior Management Flow Chart: A Component Analysis of Behavior Management Strategies." *Clinical Psychology Review* 18: 229–257.

Erickson, M. F.; Sroufe, L. A.; and Egeland, B. (1985). "The Relationship between Quality of Attachment and Behavior Problems in Preschool in a High-Risk Sample." *Monographs of the Society for Research in Child Development* 50(1–2):147–166.

Forehand, R. (1993). "Twenty Years of Research on Parenting: Does It have Practical Implications for Clinicians Working with Parents and Children?" *Clinical Psychologist* 46(4):169–176.

Forehand, R., and McKinney, B. (1993). "Historical Overview of Child Discipline in the United States: Implications for Mental Health Clinicians and Researchers." *Journal of Child and Family Studies* 2(3): 221–228.

Forehand, R. L., and McMahon, F. J. (1981). *Helping the Noncompliant Child*. New York: Guilford.

Forgatch, M., and Patterson, G. (1989). *Parents and Adolescents: Living Together.* Eugene, OR: Castalia.

Gardner, F. E.; Sonuga-Barke, E. J.; and Sayal, K. (1999). "Parents Anticipating Misbehaviour: An Observational Study of Strategies Parents Use to Prevent Conflict with Behaviour Problem Children." *Journal of Child Psychology and Psychiatry and Allied Disciplines* 40(8):1185–1196.

Gardner, F. E. M. (1994). "The Quality of Joint Activity Between Mothers and Their Children with Behavior Problems." *Journal of Child Psychology and Psychiatry and Allied Disciplines* 35:935–948.

Green, K. D.; Forehand, R.; and McMahon, R. J. (1979). "Parental Manipulation of Compliance and Noncompliance in Normal and Deviant Children." *Behavior Modification* 3:245–266.

Grusec, J., and Kuczysnki, L., eds. (1997). *Parenting and Children's Internalization of Values.* New York: Wiley.

Grusec, J. E., and Goodnow, J. J. (1994). "Impact of Parental Discipline Methods on the Child's Internalization of Values: A Reconceptualization of Current Points of View." *Developmental Psychology* 30:4–19.

Hembree-Kigin, T. L., and McNeil, C. B. (1995). *Parent-Child Interaction Therapy*. New York: Plenum.

Holden, G. W. (1985). "How Parents Create a Social Environment Via Proactive Behavior." In *Children within Environments: Toward a Psychology of Accident Prevention,* ed. T. Garling and J. Valsinger. New York: Plenum.

Houlihan, D. (1994). "Assessing Childhood Noncompliance: Subtle Differences in One-Step Commands and Their Effects on Response Topography." *Child and Family Behavior Therapy* 16:9–20.

Houlihan, D., and Jones, R. N. (1990). "Exploring the Reinforcement of Compliance with 'Do' and 'Don't' Requests and the Side Effects: A Partial Replication and Extension." *Psychological Reports* 67:439–448.

Houlihan, D.; Sloane, H. N.; Jones, R. N.; and Patten, C. (1992). "A Review of Behavioral Conceptualizations and Treatments of Child Noncompliance." *Education and Treatment of Children* 15(1):56–77.

Howard, B. J. (1996). "Advising Parents on Discipline: What Works." *Pediatrics* 98:809–815.

Kochanska, G., and Aksan, N. (1995). "Mother-Child Mutually Positive Affect, the Quality of Child Compliance to Requests and Prohibitions, and Maternal Control As Correlates of Early Internalization." *Child Development* 66:236–254.

Kochanska, G., and Thompson, R. A. (1997). "The Emergence and Development of Conscience in Toddlerhood and Early Childhood." In *Parenting and Children's Internalization of Values,* ed. J. E. Grusec and L. Kuczynski. New York: Wiley.

Kuczynski, L., and Hildebrandt, N. (1997). "Models of Conformity and Resistance in Socialization Theory." In *Parenting and Children's Internalization of Values,* ed. J. E. Grusec and L. Kuczynski. New York: Wiley.

Larzelere, R. E. (2000). "Child Outcomes of Nonabusive and Customary Physical Punishment by Parents: An

Updated Literature Review." *Clinical Child and Family Psychology Review* 3(4):199–221.

Larzelere, R. E. (2001). "Combining Love and Limits in Authoritative Parenting." In *Parenthood in America,* ed. J. C. Westman. Madison: University of Wisconsin Press.

Larzelere, R. E., and Merenda, J. A. (1994). "The Effectiveness of Parental Discipline for Toddler Misbehavior at Different Levels of Child Distress." *Family Relations* 43:480–488.

Larzelere, R. E.; Sather, P. R.; Schneider, W. N.; Larson, D. B.; and Pike, P. L. (1998). "Punishment Enhances Reasoning's Effectiveness as a Disciplinary Response to Toddlers." *Journal of Marriage and the Family* 60: 388–403.

Larzelere, R. E.; Schneider, W. N.; Larson, D. B.; and Pike, P. L. (1996). "The Effects of Discipline Responses in Delaying Toddler Misbehavior Recurrences." *Child and Family Behavior Therapy* 18:35–57.

Lenz, M.; Singh, N. N.; and Hewett, A. E. (1991). "Overcorrection As an Academic Remediation Procedure: A Review and Reappraisal." *Behavior Modification* 15(1):64–73.

Lepper, M. R. (1983). "Social-Control Processes and the Internalization of Social Values: An Attributional Perspective." In *Social Cognition and Social Development: A Sociocultural Perspective,* ed. E. T. Higgins, D. N. Ruble, and W. W. Hartup. Cambridge: Cambridge University Press.

Loeber, R., and Schmaling, K. B. (1985). "Empirical Evidence for Overt and Covert Patterns of Antisocial Conduct Problems: A Meta-Analysis." *Journal of Abnormal Child Psychology* 13:337–352.

Matson, J. L.; Horne, A. M.; Ollendick, D. G.; and Ollendick, T. H. (1979). "Overcorrection: A Further Evaluation of Restitution and Positive Practice." *Journal of Behavior Therapy and Experimental Psychiatry* 10(4): 295–298.

Parpal, M., and Maccoby, E. (1985). "Maternal Responsiveness and Subsequent Child Compliance." *Child Development* 56:1326–1344.

Patterson, G. R. (1982). *Coercive Family Process.* Eugene, OR: Castalia.

Patterson, G. R.; Reid, J. B.; and Dishion, T. J. (1992). *Antisocial Boys.* Eugene, OR: Castalia.

Pazulinec, R.; Meyerrose, M.; and Sajwaj, T., eds. (1983). *Punishment via Response Cost.* New York: Academic Press.

Pettit, G. S., and Bates, J. E. (1989). "Family Interaction Patterns and Children's Behavior Problems from Infancy to Four Years." *Developmental Psychology* 25:413–420.

Pettit, G. S.; Bates, J. E.; and Dodge, K. A. (1997). "Supportive Parenting, Ecological Context, and Children's Adustment: A Seven-Year Longitudinal Study." *Child Development* 68(5):908–923.

Ritchie, K. L. (1999). "Maternal Behaviors and Cognitions during Discipline Episodes: A Comparison of Power Bouts and Single Acts of Noncompliance." *Developmental Psychology* 35:580–589.

Roberts, M. W.; McMahon, R. J.; Forehand, R.; and Humphreys, L. (1978). "The Effect of Parental Instruction-Giving on Child Compliance." *Behavior Therapy* 9:793–798.

Roberts, M. W., and Powers, S. W. (1990). "Adjusting Chair Timeout Enforcement Procedures for Oppositional Children." *Behavior Therapy* 21:257–271.

Rothbaum, F., and Weisz, J. R. (1994). "Parental Caregiving and Child Externalizing Behavior in Nonclinical Samples: A Meta-Analysis." *Psychological Bulletin* 116:55–74.

Sanders, M. R., and Dadds, M. R. (1982). "Effects of Planned Activities and Child Management Procedures in Parent-Training: An Analysis of Setting Generality." *Behavior Therapy* 13:452–461.

Serketich, W. J., and Dumas, J. E. (1996). "The Effectiveness of Behavioral Parent Training to Modify Antisocial Behavior in Children: A Metaanalysis." *Behavior Therapy* 27:171–186.

Shriver, M. D., and Allen, K. D. (1996). The Time-Out Grid: A Guide to Effective Discipline. *School Psychology Quarterly* 11(1):67–75.

Spock, B. (1946). *The Common Sense Book of Baby and Child Care.* New York: Duell, Sloan and Pearce.

Straus, M. A., and Mouradian, V. E. (1998). "Impulsive Corporal Punishment by Mothers and Antisocial Behavior and Impulsiveness of Children." *Behavioral Sciences and the Law* 16:353–374.

Vygotsky, L. S. [1934] (1987). "Thinking and Speech." In *The Collected Works of L. S. Vygotsky,* Vol. 1: *Problems of General Psychology,* ed. R. W. Rieber and A. S. Carton. Reprint, New York: Plenum.

Watson, J. B. (1928). *Psychological Care of Infant and Child.* New York: Norton.

ROBERT E. LARZELERE
BRETT R. KUHN

DIVISION OF LABOR

Families provide love and support to adults and children, but homes are also workplaces, and households are important parts of the larger economy. Even when families do not directly produce or market goods and services, they keep the economy running by supporting and maintaining adult workers, buying and consuming products, and reproducing the workforce by having babies and socializing children. These domestic activities require labor. The total amount of time and effort put into feeding, clothing, and caring for family members rivals that spent in all other forms of work.

Every home is a combination of hotel, restaurant, laundry, and often childcare and entertainment center. The mundane work that goes into these activities is usually invisible to the people who benefit from it, especially children and husbands, who are the equivalent of nonpaying customers. Cleaning and cooking obviously require work, but even fun activities like parties or holiday gatherings require planning, preparation, service, clean-up, and other behind-the-scenes effort. Women perform most of this family labor, even though men do the same sorts of things outside the home for pay as chefs, waiters, or janitors. Although people tend to think of domestic activities as "naturally" being women's work, there is enormous variation in who does what both inside and outside the home. Every society has restrictions on what kinds of work men and women do, but there is no global content to these roles, and studies show that divisions of labor are influenced by specific environmental and social conditions. Activities often associated with women, such as nurturance, domestic chores, and childcare, are sometimes performed by men, and activities often associated with men, such as warfare, hunting, and politics, are sometimes performed by women. Thus, although gender is often used to divide labor, there is no universal set of tasks that can be defined as "women's work" or "men's work."

Historical Trends

During the late 1800s, belief in separate work spheres for men and women gained popularity in the United States. Before the nineteenth century, men, women, and children tended to work side-by-side in family-based agricultural production, often doing different chores, but cooperating in the mutual enterprise of running a farm or family business. After the rise of industrialization, most men entered the paid labor force and worked away from home. A romantic ideal of separate spheres emerged to justify the economic arrangement of women staying home while men left home to earn wages. Women came to be seen as pure, innocent, and loving, traits that made them ideally suited to the "private" sphere of home and family. The "cult of true womanhood" that became popular at this time elevated mothering to a revered status and treated homemaking as a full-time profession. Men who were previously expected to be intimately involved in raising children and running the home were now considered temperamentally unsuited for such duties, and were expected to find their true calling in the impersonal "public" sphere of work. Men's occupational achievement outside the home took on moral overtones and men came to be seen as fulfilling their family and civic duty by being a "good provider." This simplified account of the historical emergence of separate spheres ignores the partial and uneven pace of industrialization, the continual employment of working-class and minority women, and the many families that deviated from the ideal, but it underscores the importance of cultural myths in creating a rigid division of family labor (Coontz 1992).

Household work has changed. Before the twentieth century, running the typical household was more physically demanding; most houses lacked running water, electricity, central heating, and flush toilets. Without modern conveniences, people had to do everything by hand, and household tasks were arduous and time consuming. In the nineteenth century, most middle- and upper-class households in the United States, England, and Europe also included servants, so live-in maids, cooks, and housekeepers did much of this work. In the twentieth century, indoor plumbing and electricity became widely available and the invention and distribution of labor-saving appliances changed the nature of housework. By mid-century, the suburbs had multiplied, home ownership had become the norm, and the number of household servants had dropped dramatically.

In spite of the introduction of modern conveniences, the total amount of time that U.S. women spent on housework was about the same in 1960 as it was in 1920, because standards of comfort rose during this period for most families (Cowan 1983). When laundry was done by hand, people changed clothes less often, unless they had servants to do the washing. With the advent of the washing machine, the average housewife began to wash clothes more often, and people began to change clothes more frequently. Similarly, standards for personal hygiene, diet, and house cleanliness increased as conveniences such as hot running water, refrigerators, and vacuum cleaners became available. Although women's total housework time changed little, there were shifts in the types of tasks performed, with food preparation and meal clean-up consuming somewhat less time, but shopping, direct childcare, and household management taking up more.

Paid labor has also changed. The most striking change has been the increased presence of women in the workforce in almost all regions of the world. Over the course of the twentieth century, women's labor force participation has risen from under 20 percent to over 60 percent. In the United States, since the 1970s, manufacturing jobs (traditionally filled by men) have increasingly been replaced by service-sector jobs (traditionally filled by women). Associated with this shift, income for U.S. men peaked in 1974 and has fluctuated since that time, while women's income has risen steadily. The U.S. labor market, however, remains segregated by gender, with women's salaries remaining consistently and significantly lower than men's. In 1999, median annual earnings for women working full-time year-round were only 72.2 percent of men's annual earnings (U.S. Department of Labor 1999). The persistent gender wage gap can be at least partially explained by women's traditional obligation to care for home and family.

The international workplace has also changed. Between 1969 and 1994, women's labor force participation has risen in all developed countries. With the exception of Japan, all countries with available data show men's labor force participation rates to be decreasing (Jacobsen 1999). Moreover, women throughout the world have become progressively more likely to be employed during their reproductive years, although they continue to face difficulties combining family work with employment. Internationally, working mothers often report that they receive unequal treatment by employers (United Nations 2000).

Contemporary Divisions of Labor

Before the 1970s, most family researchers accepted the ideal of separate spheres and assumed that wives would do the housework and childcare, and that husbands would limit their family contributions to being a good provider. As more women entered the paid labor force, and as women's issues gained prominence, studies of household labor became more common. Researchers began asking questions about the relative performance of housework in families. Depending on the method and sample used, researchers arrived at different estimates of the amount of time men and women spent on various tasks. Interpreting the results from these studies can be difficult because of methodological limitations; nevertheless, these studies provide us with rough estimates of who does what in North American families.

The few household labor studies that included men before the 1970s found that wives did virtually all of the repetitive inside chores associated with cooking and cleaning whereas husbands spent most of their household work time doing repairs, paying bills, or performing outside chores like mowing the lawn or taking out the trash. If U.S. men contributed to other forms of routine housework, it was usually in the area of meal preparation, where husbands averaged just over one hour each week compared to an average of over eight hours per week for wives (Robinson 1988). Even when cooking, however, husbands tended to limit their contributions to gender stereotyped tasks like barbecuing on the weekend, rather than contributing substantially to the preparation of daily meals. In the mid-1960s, husbands contributed less than a tenth of the time spent in cleaning up after meals or washing dishes in the average household, and only about a twentieth of the time spent doing housecleaning. Married men were extremely unlikely to do laundry or iron clothes, averaging about five hours per *year* in the 1960s, compared to over five hours per *week* for married women. Overall, husbands contributed only about two hours per week to the combined tasks of cooking, meal clean-up, housecleaning, and laundry, compared to an average of almost twenty-five hours per week for wives (Robinson 1988).

Later housework studies have found that women—especially employed women—are doing less housework than before and that men are

Households and the activities that take place in homes require labor. Gender is often used to divide labor; however, there is no universal set of tasks defined as "women's" work or "men's" work. MICHAEL KELLER/CORBIS

doing somewhat more. Nevertheless, the average married woman in the United States did about three times as much cooking, cleaning, laundry, and other routine housework in the 1990s as the average married man. Household work continues to be divided according to gender, with women performing the vast majority of the repetitive indoor housework tasks and men performing occasional outdoor tasks (Coltrane 2000).

Despite continuing gender segregation in household labor, norms and behaviors are being renegotiated. U.S. men are increasingly likely to report enjoying cooking and cleaning, and almost half of married women say they want their husbands to do more housework (Robinson and Godbey 1997). This attitude shift reflects women's frustrations with being overburdened by housework, especially when they work outside the home (Hochschild 1989).

Psychological distress is greatest among wives whose husbands do little to assist with household chores. Not only do women spend many more hours on household labor than men, but they also tend to do the least pleasant tasks, most of which are relentless, obligatory, and performed in isolation. The lonely and never-ending aspects of women's housework contribute to increased depression for U.S. housewives. Men's household chores, in contrast, have tended to be infrequent or optional, and they concentrate their efforts on relatively fun activities like playing with the children or cooking (Coltrane 2000; Thompson and Walker 1989).

Studies have also consistently found that mothers spend more time than fathers in feeding, supervising, and caring for children, although men have increased their time with children, especially in conventional gender-typed activities like physical play (Parke 1996). However, effective parenting also includes providing encouragement, meeting emotional needs, anticipating problems, facilitating social and intellectual learning, and enforcing discipline, activities for which mothers are primarily responsible. Even if couples share housework before they have children, they often shift to a more conventional gender-based allocation of chores when they become parents (Cowan and Cowan 2000).

Getting married increases women's domestic labor, whereas it decreases men's. Still, most wives consider their divisions of household labor to be fair. According to surveys conducted through the 1990s, most wives expected only moderate amounts of help with housework. Women rarely seek or receive help with behind-the-scenes family work, such as overseeing childcare, managing emotions and tension, sustaining conversations, or maintaining contact with kin. Many women (and some men) derive considerable satisfaction and self-worth from caring for loved ones and enjoy autonomy in these activities. Women feel less entitled to domestic services than do most men, and view husbands' help as a gift that requires appreciation. Some women who demand equal sharing of domestic tasks find that it threatens the harmony of the family relationships they work so hard to foster (DeVault 1991; Hochschild 1989).

Although men are putting in more hours on housework tasks, responsibility for noticing when tasks should be performed or setting standards for their performance are still most often assumed by wives. Women in the 1990s tended to carry the burden of managing the household as well as putting in more hours and performing the most unpleasant tasks. In line with this division of responsibility for management of household affairs, most couples continue to characterize husbands' contributions to housework or childcare as "helping" their wives (Coltrane 1996).

Children and other family members also perform various household tasks. In some households, their domestic contributions are sorely needed; they are required to participate for practical and financial reasons. In other households, children are expected to assume responsibility for household chores as part of their training and socialization, or because it expresses a commitment to the family. For children, as for adults, household tasks are divided by gender, with girls putting in more hours and performing more of the cooking and cleaning. Children's housework is typically conceived of as helping the mother, and young people's contributions tend to substitute for the father's (Goodnow 1988).

Caring for elder relatives has also become pertinent globally as whole populations age due to increased longevity and reduced fertility rates. Because women tend to live longer than men, they predominate as beneficiaries of care. Women also tend to be the providers of elder care, particularly if the beneficiary is a parent. A majority of these women caregivers are employed or want to re-enter the labor force. Elder care can have both positive and negative effects on the psychological and social stress of caregivers. While employer elder care programs can moderate some stress, only about one-quarter of major corporations offer such programs in the United States (Spitze and Loscocco 1999). In some northern European countries, the state takes on much of the responsibility for elder care, as it does for childcare, but in many other countries families are assumed to be solely responsible (Phillips 1998).

The unbalanced division of household labor continues to be reflected in the dynamics of paid labor. In the global workforce, occupations remain segregated by gender, and women are still paid much less than men doing the same or similar jobs. Although many countries have incorporated the principle of equal pay for equal work into their labor legislation, and gender differences in pay vary between countries and occupations, in no country do women earn as much as men (United Nations 2000).

Not only are women discouraged from entering predominantly male occupations, but when they do, they tend to get the least desirable jobs. Moreover, studies in the United States have found that segregation at the job level may actually exceed that at the occupational level (Bielby and Baron 1986). Research in different countries reflects similar occupational segregation, which is unrelated to women's participation in the labor force or to the level of economic development.

Moreover, to the extent that occupational segregation is decreasing, it reflects men's movement into predominantly female occupations rather than the other way around. A glass ceiling still tends to limit women's rise to top administrative and managerial positions in all regions of the world (United Nations 2000).

Theoretical Explanations

Various theories have been advanced to explain why men monopolize higher paid positions and why women perform most unpaid household labor. Such theories also predict the conditions under which divisions of labor might change. The theories can be grouped into four general categories according to the primary causal processes thought to govern the sexual division of labor: nature, culture, economy, and gender inequality.

Nature. Biological and religious arguments suggest that women are physically or spiritually predisposed to take care of children and husbands; housework is assumed to follow naturally from the nurturance of family members. Similarly, functionalist theories suggest that the larger society needs women to perform expressive roles in the family while men perform instrumental roles connecting the family to outside institutions. However, feminist critiques claim that these theories have flawed logic and methods, and cite historical and cross-cultural variation to show that divisions of labor are socially constructed (Thorne and Yalom 1992); only women can bear and nurse children, but the gender of the people who cook or clean is neither fixed nor preordained.

Culture. Theories that consider the division of labor to be culturally fashioned tend to emphasize the importance of socialization and ideology. Historical analyses of the ideal of separate spheres fall into this category, as do cultural explanations that rely on rituals, customs, myths, and language to explain divisions of labor. Socialization theories suggest that children and adults acquire beliefs about appropriate roles for men and women, and that they fashion their own family behaviors according to these gender scripts (Bem 1993). Some sociocultural and psychological theories suggest that exclusive mothering encourages girls to develop personalities dependent on emotional connection, which, in turn, propels women into domestic roles. Boys also grow up in the care of mothers, but in order to establish a masculine identity, they reject things feminine, including nurturance and domestic work (Chodorow 1978).

The basic idea in most cultural theories is that values and ideals shape people's motivations and cause them to perform gender-typed activities. Empirical tests of hypotheses derived from these theories yield mixed results. Some researchers conclude that abstract beliefs about what men and women "ought" to do are relatively inconsequential for actual behavior, whereas others conclude that there is a consistent, though sometimes small, increase in sharing when men and women believe that housework or childcare should be shared (Coltrane 2000).

Economy. Theories that consider the division of labor by gender to be a practical response to economic conditions are diverse and plentiful. New home economics theories suggest that women do the housework and men monopolize paid work because labor specialization maximizes the efficiency of the entire family unit. Women are assumed to have "tastes" for doing housework, and their commitments to childbearing and child rearing are seen as limiting their movement into the marketplace (Becker 1981). Resource theories similarly assume that spouses make cost-benefit calculations about housework and paid work using external indicators such as education and income. Family work is treated as something to be avoided, and women end up doing more of it because their time is worth less on the economic market and because they have less marital power due to lower earnings and education.

Educational differences between spouses are rarely associated with divisions of labor, and men with more education often report doing *more* housework, rather than less, as resource theories predict. Similarly, total family earnings have little effect on how much housework men do, though middle-class men talk more about the importance of sharing than working-class men. Some studies show that spouses with more equal incomes—usually in the working class—share more household labor, but women still do more than men when they have similar jobs. Thus, relative earning power is important, but there is no simple trade-off of wage work for housework (Gerson 1993; Thompson and Walker 1989). Most studies find that the number of hours spouses are employed is more important to the division of household labor than simple earnings. Time demands and time availability—labeled by researchers as practical considerations, demand-response capability, or situational constraints—undergird most peoples' decisions about allocating housework and childcare.

Gender inequality. The final set of theories also focuses on economic power, but more emphasis is placed on conflict and gender inequality. Women are compelled to perform household labor because economic market inequities keep women's wages below those of men, effectively forcing women to be men's domestic servants. Unlike the new home economics, these theories do not assume a unity of husband's and wife's interests, and unlike many resource theories, they do not posit all individuals as utility maximizers with equal chances in a hypothetical free market. Other versions of theories in this tradition suggest that social institutions like marriage, the legal system, the media, and the educational system also help to perpetuate an unequal division of labor in which women are forced to perform a "second shift" of domestic labor when they hold paying jobs (Chafetz 1990; Hochschild 1989). Some versions draw on the same insights, but focus on the ways that the performance of housework serves to demarcate men from women, keep women dependent on men, and construct the meaning of gender in everyday interaction (Berk 1985; Coltrane 1996).

Household labor theories are often complementary or overlapping. The theories in the last three categories suggest that a more equal division of household labor could exist if more women move into the paid labor market; if men's and women's educations, incomes, and work schedules converge; if cultural images portray parenting as a shared endeavor; if governments and businesses promote sharing through programs and policies; and if more children are exposed to egalitarian practices and ideals. Related trends (e.g., continued high levels of cohabitation, divorce and remarriage, along with postponement of marriage and parenthood) also imply that more sharing of household labor is probable in the future (Coltrane and Collins 2001). Changes are likely to be modest, however, as many of the conditions that brought about the unequal division of labor still exist. As long as men monopolize the best jobs, get paid more, and receive more promotions than women, they are unlikely to assume more responsibility for housework. Even if women gain more economic power, until cultural and economic forces promote more gender equality, changes in the division of labor will be small.

See also: CAREGIVING: INFORMAL; CHILDCARE; DUAL-EARNER FAMILIES; EQUITY; FAMILY ROLES; FOOD; GENDER; HOME ECONOMICS; HOUSEWORK; HUSBAND; INDUSTRIALIZATION; LEISURE; MARITAL QUALITY; POWER: MARITAL RELATIONSHIPS; RESOURCE MANAGEMENT; TIME USE; WIFE; WORK AND FAMILY

Bibliography

Becker, G. S. (1981). *A Treatise on the Family.* Cambridge, MA: Harvard University Press.

Bem, S. L. (1993). *The Lenses of Gender: Transforming the Debate on Sexual Inequality.* New Haven, CT: Yale University Press.

Berk, S. F. (1985). *The Gender Factory: The Apportionment of Work in American Households.* New York: Plenum.

Bielby, W. T., and Baron, J. N. (1986). "Men and Women at Work: Sex Segregation and Statistical Discrimination." *American Journal of Sociology* 91:759–799.

Chafetz, J. S. (1990). *Gender Equity: An Integrated Theory of Stability and Change.* Newbury Park, CA: Sage Publications.

Chodorow, N. (1978). *The Reproduction of Mothering.* Berkeley: University of California Press.

Coltrane, S. (1996). *Family Man: Fatherhood, Housework, and Gender Equity.* New York: Oxford University Press.

Coltrane, S. (2000). "Research on Household Labor: Modeling and Measuring the Social Embeddedness of Routine Family Work." *Journal of Marriage and the Family* 62:1208–1233.

Coltrane, S., and Collins, R. (2001). *Sociology of Marriage and the Family: Gender, Love, and Property.* Belmont, CA: Wadsworth.

Coontz, S. (1992). *The Way We Never Were: American Families and the Nostalgia Trap.* New York: Basic Books.

Cowan, C. P., and Cowan, P. A. (2000). *When Partners Become Parents: The Big Life Change for Couples.* New York: Basic Books.

Cowan, R. S. (1983). *More Work for Mother.* New York: Basic Books.

DeVault, M. L. (1991). *Feeding the Family: The Social Organization of Caring as Gendered Work.* Chicago: University of Chicago Press.

Gerson, K. (1993). *No Man's Land: Men's Changing Commitments to Family and Work.* New York: Basic Books.

Goodnow, J. (1988). "Children's Household Work: Its Nature and Functions." *Psychological Bulletin* 103:5–26.

Hochschild, A. R. *The Second Shift: Working Parents and the Revolution at Home.* New York: Viking.

Jacobsen, J. P. (1999). "Labor Force Participation." *Quarterly Review of Economics and Finance* 39:597–610.

Parke, R. D. (1996). *Fatherhood.* Cambridge, MA: Harvard University Press.

Phillips, J. (1998). "Paid Work and Care of Older People: A UK Perspective." In *Women, Work, and the Family in Europe,* ed. E. Drew, R. Emerek, and E. Mahon. London: Routledge.

Robinson, J. (1988). "Who's Doing the Housework?" *American Demographics* 10:24–28, 63.

Robinson, J., and Godbey, G. (1997). *Time for Life.* University Park: Pennsylvania State University Press.

Spitze, G., and Loscocco, K. (1999). "Women's Position in the Household." *Quarterly Review of Economics and Finance* 39:647–661.

Thompson, L., and Walker, A. J. (1989). "Gender in Families." *Journal of Marriage and the Family* 51 (1989):845–871.

Thorne, B., with Yalom, M. (1992). *Rethinking the Family: Some Feminist Questions.* New York: Longman.

United Nations. (2000). *The World's Women 2000: Trends and Statistics.* New York: United Nations.

Other Resource

United States Department of Labor Women's Bureau. (1999). "Earnings Differences Between Women and Men." Available from http://www.dol.gov/dol/wb/public/wb_pubs/wagegap2000.htm.

SCOTT COLTRANE
MICHELE ADAMS

DIVORCE

EFFECTS ON CHILDREN *David H. Demo, Andrew J. Supple*

EFFECTS ON COUPLES *Kari Henley, Kay Pasley*

EFFECTS ON PARENTS *Colleen L. Johnson*

EFFECTS ON CHILDREN

Two of the strongest and most widely held beliefs about contemporary family life are that marriage should be a lifelong commitment and that parental divorce has serious negative effects on children. Because of the conviction with which these values are held, many people are alarmed by the high divorce rate in the United States and in many other industrialized nations. Across industrialized nations, the divorce rate is by far the highest in the United States, where about half of all first marriages formed in the 1990s will end in divorce, and more than one million children experience parental divorce each year (U.S. Bureau of the Census 1998). While the divorce rate in the United States is 4.33 per 1,000 population, the comparable rates in the United Kingdom, Sweden, Canada, Germany, France, Japan, and Italy are 2.91, 2.42, 2.41, 2.14, 2.01, 1.65, and .47, respectively (United Nations 2000). Although marital dissolution is an important social issue in many countries, research on its effects on children has largely been conducted in the United States.

In the United States, dramatic changes in children's living arrangements have occurred across all racial, ethnic, and socioeconomic categories. From 1970 to 1998, the percentage of white children living with two parents (including stepparents) fell from 90 percent to 74 percent; for African-American children, the percentage declined from 60 percent to 36 percent; and for Hispanic children, the percentage decreased from 78 percent to 64 percent (Teachman, Tedrow, and Crowder 2000).

With so many children and adolescents experiencing their parents' divorce and living in single-parent families and stepfamilies, it is important to understand how parental divorce affects children. During the 1980s and 1990s, a considerable amount of social scientific scholarship was devoted to considering whether or not divorce negatively affects the lives of children. Social scientific and psychological evidence regarding the influence of divorce on children is also used in formulating social policies and laws regarding marriage and divorce. In the 1990s alone, more than 9,000 studies on divorce were conducted in the United States across a variety of disciplines, including sociology, family studies, developmental psychology, clinical psychology, family therapy, social work, social policy, and law (Amato 2000).

With so much attention being devoted to the topic across such diverse fields, and with divorce being both deeply personal and controversial, it is perhaps not surprising that there are different interpretations of the consequences of divorce for children. Although there are scientific data to suggest that divorce has negative effects on children, scholars are not in complete agreement regarding how strong the effects are, whether or not negative effects are due to divorce as an event or a process, and whether or not divorce may actually be good for children in some situations. Three prevailing themes are supported by the bulk of research evidence: (1) divorce is better understood as a process rather than a discrete life event; (2) the consequences of divorce for children are not as severe nor as longlasting as popularly assumed; and (3) there is a substantial degree of variation in how individual children and adolescents respond to divorce. This last point suggests that divorce undoubtedly has some negative effects for some children, particularly in certain situations. What is not clear, however, is whether the negative effects of divorce are due to family circumstances prior to the divorce, or after divorce.

Divorce as a Process

One instructive means of thinking about divorce is to consider divorce not as a single event that influences people's lives, but rather as a process. This conceptualization of divorce suggests that the manner in which divorce ultimately affects children involves a confluence of factors and processes that occur early in the divorce, as well as processes occurring after the divorce. Moreover, this line of reasoning suggests that many negative effects for children in divorced families may be due to exposure to traumatic experiences and processes that have nothing to do with divorce per se. That is, children whose parents divorce witness negative family interaction prior to a divorce and also experience many life transitions and strained familial relationships after divorce. This view of divorce as a process has been corroborated in a review of studies conducted in the United Kingdom, New Zealand, and Australia (Rodgers and Pryor 1998).

Marriages that end in divorce typically begin a process of unraveling, estrangement, or emotional separation years before the actual legal divorce is obtained. During the course of the marriage, one or both of the marital partners begins to feel alienated from the other. Conflicts with each other and with the children intensify, become more frequent, and often go unresolved. Feelings of bitterness, helplessness, and anger escalate as the spouses weigh the costs and benefits of continuing the marriage versus separating. Gay C. Kitson's (1992) influential study of marital breakdown describes a distressing process characterized by emotional distance, dissatisfaction, and frequent thoughts and discussions about whether and how to separate. Many unhappy couples explore marital counseling, extramarital relationships, and trial separations, with marital happiness fluctuating upward and downward from day to day and year to year as the marital relationship and marital roles are renegotiated.

These predivorce changes in the family often negatively influence the psychological states of parents; parental stress, anxiety, and depression, in turn, inhibit effective parenting. Paul R. Amato and Alan Booth (1996) conducted a rare longitudinal study on a national sample and documented problems in parent-child relationships as early as eight to twelve years prior to parental divorce. Other studies observe that, before parental divorce, U.S. and U.K. children and adolescents suffer due to high levels of marital discord, ineffective and inconsistent parenting, diminished parental wellbeing, and reduced parent-child affection (Demo and Cox 2000; Rodgers and Pryor 1998). Taken together, these studies suggest that the alterations in family functioning that occur during a predivorce process lead to children witnessing their parents fighting, parents' emotional and psychological states deteriorating, and diminishing levels of parental warmth, affection, and supervision. It is important to note that these changing family dynamics contribute to children experiencing behavior problems prior to parental divorce, and that children's behavior problems, in turn, strain marital relationships, undermine parental well-being, and increase the chances of parental divorce (Acock and Demo 1994; Cherlin et al. 1991). Consequently, some researchers would argue that the negative effects of divorce on children begin *well before* an actual divorce occurs.

For both parents and children, the most difficult and stressful phase of the divorce process is usually the period leading up to and immediately following parental separation and divorce. The uncoupling process takes on several dimensions at this stage, as divorcing parents confront legal challenges and expenses, make their intentions public

to family and friends, and redefine their roles as residential and nonresidential parents.

In addition, the process of unraveling and family dissolution continues, coupled with numerous potentially life-altering transitions for children. Following divorce, children live in many different family forms, but the most common pattern is they live with their mothers and have less contact with their fathers. In the United States, five of every six single-parent households are headed by a mother (U.S. Bureau of the Census 1998). As a result, a common alteration that children are forced to make is an adjustment to life without their father at home. Most children share time between the mother's household and the father's household, and families are creative in finding ways for children to maintain meaningful relationships with both parents. For example, children change residences to accommodate changes in their relationships with their parents, changes in parental employment, remarriage, and stepfamily formation (Maccoby and Mnookin 1992). Still, most children suffer from declining father involvement after divorce. National surveys indicate that more than one-fourth of children living in single-mother families never saw their fathers in the previous year, slightly more than one-fourth saw their fathers at least weekly, and among those children who maintain regular contact with their fathers, less than one-third had opportunities to spend significant amounts of time with them. There is evidence, however, that frequent father-child interaction and close relationships are more common in African-American families. Postdivorce father involvement is also higher among fathers who had very close relationships with their children prior to divorce, fathers who live near their children, and fathers who have joint custody (Arditti and Keith 1993; Mott 1990). These studies provide further evidence to suggest that characteristics of families prior to and after divorce ultimately influence the adjustment and well-being of children.

Individual Variation

Substantial research evidence shows that, on average, children who have experienced parental divorce score somewhat lower than children in first-marriage families on measures of social development, emotional well-being, self-concept, academic performance, educational attainment, and physical health (Amato 2000; Furstenberg and

Kiernan 2001). This conclusion is based on group comparisons that consistently show small differences between the average adjustment level of children in first-marriage families and the average level for children whose parents have divorced. Equally important, but less well understood, is that children and adolescents in divorced families vary widely in their adjustment (Demo and Acock 1996). That is, many children exhibit delinquent behavior, difficulties with peers, and low self-esteem following their parents' divorce, while many others adjust readily, enjoy popularity with friends, and think highly of themselves. A useful way of thinking about this is that children's adjustment within any particular family structure (e.g., first-marriage families, divorced families, stepfamilies) varies along a continuum from very poor adjustment to very positive adjustment, with many children and adolescents faring better postdivorce than their counterparts living in first-marriage families. This latter point raises the possibility that in some cases, parental divorce may have *positive* effects on children. Children most likely to benefit from parental divorce include those who endured years of frequent and intense marital conflict (Amato and Booth 1997; Hanson 1999), and those who develop very close, mutually supportive, and satisfying relationships with single parents (Arditti 1999). These studies support the notion that pre- and postdivorce family environments (i.e., highly conflicted prior; supportive after) have great potential to assist in understanding how children will adjust to life after their parents' divorce.

The preponderance of scientific evidence thus suggests that popular impressions, media images, and stereotypes greatly exaggerate the effects of divorce on children. On average, there are small differences in emotional and social adjustment between children of divorce and children in intact families, and in some instances, parental divorce has a positive effect on children. Most children and adolescents experience short-term emotional, behavioral, and academic difficulties, which usually peak at the point in the divorce process when their parents physically separate and engage in legal battles related to divorce. These problems tend to subside with time, however. Children tend to be resilient, adapt well to most changes in their family roles and life situations, and exhibit normal adjustment (Emery and Forehand 1994). Still, a minority remains vulnerable. Following divorce,

approximately 20 to 25 percent of children in divorced families experience long-term adjustment problems, compared to roughly 10 percent of children in first-marriage families (Hetherington and Stanley-Hagan 2000).

The children and adolescents who appear to be most vulnerable socially and emotionally are those who experience multiple transitions in parenting arrangements throughout their childhood. Research indicates that children who experience no changes in family structure (e.g., children who live continuously with both biological parents, or those who live their entire childhood with a single parent) have higher levels of adjustment (Demo and Acock 1996; Najman et al. 1997). As the number of parenting transitions increases, children's adjustment generally decreases, albeit modestly. Thus, children whose parents divorce (one transition) have somewhat lower adjustment; those who experience divorce and subsequent remarriage of their residential parent (two transitions) exhibit lower adjustment than those in the one transition group; and children who experience two or more parental divorces and/or remarriages have the lowest adjustment and most behavioral problems (Capaldi and Patterson 1991). Studies conducted in the United Kingdom, New Zealand, and Australia corroborate these findings (Rodgers and Pryor 1998). Again, there is wide variation among children who experience multiple family transitions, but the evidence suggests that each change in parenting arrangements represents a risk factor, thus increasing the likelihood that a child will react negatively to their postdivorce environment.

Interventions to Alleviate the Negative Effects of Divorce on Children

Overall, research suggests that family relationships and economic circumstances prior to and following divorce have considerable potential to influence child adjustment. Consequently, there are ample opportunities for intervention efforts that may offset some of these negative processes.

Given that a large proportion of U.S. children will experience divorce, an important research and public policy objective is the development of strategies to assist children during the divorce process. Although in some instances divorce may have positive effects for children (as in the case where exposure to intense and frequent fighting between parents is reduced), in many other situations, changing parent-child relationships, life transitions, and economic strains that accompany divorce present challenges to children's well-being. Social science research has successfully identified key factors accompanying divorce that negatively affect children, thus illuminating potential areas for intervention. That is, programs and policies can be developed to address the factors that ultimately compromise children's well-being during the divorce process.

Many states require divorcing parents to complete either a divorce mediation or parent education program (Emery 1995; Grych and Fincham 1992). These programs are designed to increase parents' understanding of the difficulties that their children may face during the divorce process. Parents are taught, for example, how to manage their conflict, avoid treating children like pawns in disputes, and to appreciate the importance of maintaining positive relationships with their children. Studies have shown that following a divorce, parents may find it difficult to maintain optimal parenting behaviors, such as monitoring their children's activities, providing warmth and support, and keeping consistent rules. Consequently, if programs for parents can intervene and educate divorced parents to the importance of maintaining positive parenting during stressful transitions, some negative effects on children may be mitigated.

Other possible areas for intervention include policies and programs that recognize the economic strain that divorcing parents, and especially the custodial mother, often face post-divorce. Studies have shown that custodial mothers often face dramatic economic losses following divorce, leading to feelings of stress that adversely affect parenting. Researchers have postulated that divorce is disruptive for children largely because the custodial parent faces a significant amount of economic stress in the time period immediately following the divorce (Furstenberg 1990). Economic loss may trigger multiple transitions for the child (e.g., moving, changing schools, taking in other household members), adversely affecting child well-being. Social policies should address the economic strain experienced by divorcing parents and recognize its potential to adversely affect family relationships.

Another important step toward reducing the negative effects of divorce on children involves the de-stigmatization of divorce. Given our cultural emphasis on the sanctimony of marriage and our cultural disapproval of divorce, many children suffer psychologically because they perceive that their family experiences are dysfunctional. Societal mores and cultural beliefs strongly devalue divorced families. Such families (in their many forms) are judged to be inferior to the traditional nuclear family headed by a male breadwinner and female mother and homemaker who live together from marriage until death, and who produce and rear children in an intact family environment. The popular North American culture, Hollywood movies, television sitcoms and talk shows, and best-selling books on how to survive divorce perpetuate these images and sensationalize the negative experiences of parents and children living in postdivorce families. In European countries, there is great concern about rising divorce rates, but divorce may be seen as more acceptable, at least in Sweden (Wadsby and Svedin 1996). Consequently, most U.S. children who experience parental divorce face the challenge of adjusting to new family arrangements and life situations in a society that has negative perceptions and stigmas associated with divorced families. Another way to allay negative feelings related to divorce, then, would be to counsel children regarding the normative process of divorce, to let them know that they are not alone as children of divorce, and to educate them regarding the healthy functioning of many divorced families. Finally, scholars in the United States, United Kingdom, and Australia have suggested that social service personnel and officials of the courts could be trained to be supportive of divorcing parents and their children as a means to strengthen family relationships and reduce feelings of stigma.

See also: CHILD CUSTODY; CONDUCT DISORDER; DIVORCE: EFFECTS ON COUPLES; DIVORCE: EFFECTS ON PARENTS; DIVORCE MEDIATION; GRIEF, LOSS, AND BEREAVEMENT; INTERGENERATIONAL RELATIONS; INTERPARENTAL CONFLICT—EFFECTS ON CHILDREN; INTERPARENTAL VIOLENCE—EFFECTS ON CHILDREN; JUVENILE DELINQUENCY; PARENTING EDUCATION; RELIGION; REMARRIAGE; SELF-ESTEEM; SINGLE-PARENT FAMILIES; STEPFAMILIES; STRESS

Bibliography
Acock, A. C., and Demo, D. H. (1994). *Family Diversity and Well-Being*. Thousand Oaks, CA: Sage.

Amato, P. R. (2000). "The Consequences of Divorce for Adults and Children." *Journal of Marriage and the Family* 62:1269–1287.

Amato, P. R., and Booth, A. (1996). "A Prospective Study of Divorce and Parent-child Relationships." *Journal of Marriage and the Family* 58:356–365.

Amato, P. R., and Booth, A. (1997). *A Generation at Risk: Growing Up in an Era of Family Upheaval.* Cambridge, MA: Harvard University Press.

Arditti, J. A. (1999). "Rethinking Family Relationships between Divorced Mothers and their Children: Capitalizing on Family Strengths." *Family Relations* 48:109–119.

Arditti, J. A., and Keith, T. Z. (1993). "Visitation Frequency, Child Support Payment, and the Father-child Relationship Postdivorce." *Journal of Marriage and the Family* 55:699–712.

Capaldi, D. M., and Patterson, G. R. (1991). "Relations of Parental Transitions to Boys' Adjustment Problems: I. A Linear Hypothesis; II. Mothers at Risk for Transitions and Unskilled Parenting." *Developmental Psychology* 27:489–504.

Cherlin, A. J.; Furstenberg, F. F., Jr.; Chase-Lansdale, L P.; Kiernan, K. E.; Robins, P. K.; Morrison, D. R.; and Teitler, J. O. (1991). "Longitudinal Effects of Divorce in Great Britain and the United States." *Science* 252:1386–1389.

Demo, D. H., and Acock, A. C. (1996). "Family Structure, Family Process, and Adolescent Well-being." *Journal of Research on Adolescence* 6:457–488.

Demo, D. H., and Cox, M. (2000). "Families with Young Children: A Review of Research in the 1990s." *Journal of Marriage and the Family* 62:876–895.

Emery, R. E. (1995). "Divorce Mediation: Negotiating Agreements and Renegotiating Relationships." *Family Relations* 44:377–383.

Emery, R. E., and Forehand, R. (1994). "Parental Divorce and Children's Well-being: A Focus on Resilience." In *Stress, Risk, and Resilience in Children and Adolescents,* ed. R. J. Haggerty, L. R. Sherrod, N. Garmezy, and M. Rutter. Cambridge: Cambridge University Press.

Furstenberg, F. F. (1990). "Coming of Age in a Changing Family System." In *At the Threshold: The Developing Adolescent,* ed. S. Feldman and G. Elliot. Cambridge, MA: Harvard University Press.

Furstenberg, F. F., and Kiernan, K. E. (2001). "Delayed Parental Divorce: How Much Do Children Benefit?" *Journal of Marriage and Family* 63:446–457.

Grych, J. H., and Fincham, F. (1992). "Interventions for Children of Divorce: Toward Greater Integration of Research and Action." *Psychological Bulletin* 111:434–454.

Hanson, T. L. (1999). "Does Parental Conflict Explain Why Divorce Is Negatively Associated with Child Welfare?" *Social Forces* 77:1283–1316.

Hetherington, E. M., and Stanley-Hagan, M. (2000). "Diversity among Stepfamilies." In *Handbook of Family Diversity,* ed. D. H. Demo, K. R. Allen, and M. A. Fine. New York: Oxford University Press.

Kitson, G. C. (1992). *Portrait of Divorce: Adjustment to Marital Breakdown.* New York: Guilford.

Maccoby, E. E., and Mnookin, R. H. (1992). *Dividing the Child: Social and Legal Dilemmas of Custody.* Cambridge, MA: Harvard University Press.

Mott, F. L. (1990). "When Is a Father Really Gone? Paternal-child Contact in Father-Absent Homes." *Demography* 27:499–517.

Najman, J. M.; Behrens, B. C.; Andersen, M.; Bor, W.; O'Callaghan, M.; and Williams, G. M. (1997). "Impact of Family Type and Family Quality on Child Behavior Problems: A Longitudinal Study." *Journal of the American Academy of Child and Adolescent Psychiatry* 36:1357–1365.

Rodgers, B., and Pryor, J. (1998). *Divorce and Separation: The Outcomes for Children.* York, UK: Joseph Rowntree Foundation.

Teachman, J. D.; Tedrow, L. M.; and Crowder, K. D. (2000). "The Changing Demography of America's Families." *Journal of Marriage and the Family* 62:1234–1246.

United Nations. (2000). *1998 United Nations Demographic Yearbook.*

U.S. Bureau of the Census. (1998). *Statistical Abstract of the United States,* 118th edition. Washington, DC: U.S. Government Printing Office.

Wadsby, M., and Svedin, C. G. (1996). "Academic Achievement in Children of Divorce." *Journal of School Psychology* 34:325–336.

DAVID H. DEMO
ANDREW J. SUPPLE

EFFECTS ON COUPLES

Compared internationally, the United States has the highest divorce rate by a large margin—one and a half times that of the United Kingdom, approximately twice that of Japan, Germany, France, and

Sweden, and more than seven times that of Italy. Although estimates vary, approximately half of all first-marriages and 60 percent of remarriages in the United States end in divorce. In the mid-nineteenth century approximately 5 percent of first marriages ended in divorce, so this dramatic increase in divorce has implications for all family members. Those family members most studied are children; yet the decision to end a marriage and the experiences that follow also affect the divorcing adults.

Explaining Adjustment to Divorce: Theoretical Perspectives

Numerous theoretical perspectives have been used to explain how adults adjust to divorce, including *feminist theories, social exchange theory, family systems theory, social learning theory,* and *sociobiological theories.* However, many researchers apply *family stress theory* to offer two general models of adult adjustment. The *crisis model* suggests that divorce poses a crisis for divorcing adults that results in temporary declines in well-being, but from which most individuals ultimately recover. The *chronic strain model* depicts divorce as setting a number of other stressful events into motion (e.g., moving to a new neighborhood, ongoing conflict between the former spouses, economic hardship) that send divorced individuals into a downward spiral from which they never fully recover. Research supports both models to some degree. In a review of research from the 1990s regarding the consequences of divorce, Paul Amato (2000) found that the crisis model best described the postdivorce experiences of some individuals, and the chronic strain model best described the experiences of others. He concluded that both models contained some truth, and that the determination of which model more accurately depicted postdivorce adjustment largely depended upon characteristics of the individuals studied (e.g., education, age, self-esteem), as well as the context in which the divorce occurred (e.g., social support networks, child custody status).

Adult Adjustment

Divorce affects the couple economically, mentally, emotionally, and physically. Divorce also influences the current and future relationships of the couple. Despite the predominant belief that only negative outcomes exist (*deficit perspective*), divorce also benefits some individuals. Best viewed

as a process rather than a discrete event, divorce influences individuals before the divorce occurs, immediately following the divorce, and years later.

Economic outcomes. Because of the political and policy implications of the economic situation associated with divorce, much attention has focused on its economic impact. In the United States, Canada, and most other countries, women generally experience a decline in their economic situation following divorce, whereas men undergo lesser declines or slight increases in their economic status. It is important to note that differences in both the magnitude of these changes and the disparity between men and women's postdivorce economic outcomes have been debated (see Braver and O'Connell 1998, for a discussion of U.S. findings). However, research shows that German men fare better than U.S. men after divorce, and German women fare worse than U.S. women (Burkhauser et al. 1991). Similarly, Indian women generally fare worse economically than their U.S. counterparts, whereas Indian men experience little or no economic disruption following divorce (Amato 1994). Therefore, although magnitudes may differ, the same postdivorce economic pattern appears to occur cross-culturally.

Because divorce divides resources that originally went to one household, an immediate decline in the standard of living for both spouses results. How severe and how long the decline lasts affects couples' postdivorce adjustment due to the economic hardship imposed. It also is important to understand individuals' perceptions of the degree of economic hardship, as these perceptions affect adjustment more than objective measures of their economic situation. For example, Hongyu Wang and Paul Amato (2000) explained that an objective decline in standard of living may be viewed positively, if the more limited income also is accompanied by a gain in control over the income.

Mental and emotional outcomes. Studies demonstrate that divorced individuals exhibit higher levels of depression and anxiety than do individuals who are married, and those divorced also tend to have poorer self-concepts and exhibit more symptoms of psychological distress (compared with those who are married). Those with a history of two or more divorces report significantly more depression than either those with one divorce or those who are not divorced (Kurdek 1991), suggesting the cumulative nature of stress from divorce. Research findings are similar in other countries, as Amato (1994) found that two-thirds of divorced women in India suffer severe emotional problems. Further, Sheila Cotten (1999) noted that the common practice of categorizing divorced and widowed individuals into a single group underestimates the actual depression levels of divorced individuals, because widows often exhibit lower levels of depression and psychological distress. Consistent with the crisis model of divorce adjustment, depressive symptoms appear to peak shortly after the divorce and then gradually decline for most.

Physical outcomes. Divorced individuals also have more health problems and higher mortality rates than married or other nondivorced persons. Divorced adults exhibit more risk-taking behaviors (e.g., elevated rates of drugs and alcohol use/abuse). Particularly among those recently divorced, there is an increased risk for illness, likely due to poorer immune system functioning from the stress associated with divorce. (Kitson and Morgan 1990).

Relationship outcomes. Relationships and social networks are influenced in various ways by divorce. Divorced individuals generally experience more social isolation and have smaller social networks than do married individuals. This is explained in terms of them having less in common with married friends following divorce. Moreover, friendships can become divided between the couple like other the marital assets, as friends may choose sides.

In countries where divorce is still stigmatized, social isolation is more extreme. For example, in Japan divorced women experience discrimination in employment opportunities and future marital opportunities due to the *impurity* that divorce introduces into their family registry, and the effect of this impurity spills over to their children (Bryant 1992; Yuko 1998). Similarly, women in India are isolated following divorce, largely due to the principle of *pativratya* (i.e., that a woman should devote herself completely to her husband's needs, sacrificing her own if necessary). When a marriage ends, the assumption of fault resides with the wife. Also, family structure in India follows patriarchal lines, with many households consisting of a man, his wife, his sons, and the sons' wives and children. Following divorce, Indian men retain both their household and the support of their extended families, whereas Indian women leave the family household and become isolated from the entire family. Because remarriage is not common in India, women are likely experience further social isolation (Amato 1994).

Coparental relationships also are affected by divorce, which has a significant impact on children. Although coparental interactions in marriage are generally cooperative and supportive (Jain, Belsky, and Crnic 1996), coparenting after divorce is likely to be less cooperative and more conflicted. Although the amount of conflict does not appear to be detrimental to adjustment, coparental relationships that are high in hostility are harmful to the parties and are detrimental to their postdivorce adjustment (Ahrons 1994; Buehler and Trotter 1990).

Most divorced individuals ultimately remarry and usually do so within four years (Coleman, Ganong, and Fine 2000). Remarriage rates (like divorce rates) are higher in the United States than anywhere else; however, the trends are similar cross-culturally. However, remarriages are less stable than first marriages, a finding that is generally attributed to the fact that those having experience with divorce are more likely to see divorce as a viable option in remarriage. Therefore, divorce appears to influence future marital relationships, making them less stable and more vulnerable to dissolution.

Positive outcomes. Most studies to date have looked for, and found, primarily negative outcomes from divorce. The few studies that have investigated the potential benefits of divorce show that, particularly for women, divorce can be a positive experience (Amato 2000). If the marriage was highly conflictual, ending the marriage can relieve stress in all family members. Also, an individual's sense of having successfully survived divorce is associated with increased self-confidence and efficacy, particularly for women.

Factors Influencing Adjustment

Numerous factors affect the ways in which couples adjust to divorce. These include both *personal factors* (those that reside within or are inherent to individuals) and *contextual factors* (those that reside outside individuals).

Personal factors. Several personal characteristics influence adjustment to divorce, such as demographic characteristics (i.e., age, education level, employment, and socioeconomic status). For example, some studies found that older individuals have more difficulty adjusting, due to their limited postdivorce options (e.g., employment, remarriage) (Kitson and Morgan 1990). Other studies found better adjustment among older divorced individuals, because they had fewer coparenting issues and conflicts due to children being older. Higher education, higher socioeconomic status, and being employed are consistently associated with better postdivorce adjustment among adults. It is likely that employment contributes positively to adjustment because more sources of social support are available and less economic hardship is experienced.

Individuals' levels of preseparation psychological functioning also affect divorce adjustment (Hetherington, Law, and O'Connor 1997; Tschann, Johnston, and Wallerstein 1989). Adults who have better coping skills and higher levels of emotional stability and psychological functioning before the divorce are generally more well-adjusted afterwards. Individuals who have a higher sense of self-mastery and self-esteem also experience higher levels of well-being following divorce.

Whether the individual initiated the divorce is another factor affecting adjustment. Spouses typically do not emotionally leave the marriage simultaneously and, therefore, may experience different trajectories in their adjustment. The person who initiates the divorce often mourns the loss of the marriage before the legal divorce takes place; however, noninitiators can experience surprise when the request for a divorce surfaces, and they then begin to consider the end of the marriage—when the initiator is already on the road to recovery.

Similarly, individuals' beliefs about divorce can affect their postdivorce adjustment. Those with more nontraditional views about marriage and who look at divorce more favorably exhibit better adjustment than do those who hold more traditional views about marriage and believe that divorce is unacceptable.

The degree of attachment to the former spouse also can affect adjustment. Research shows that cooperative postdivorce relationships are both possible and healthy for the couple, and particularly for parents (Ahrons 1994). However, when one or both spouses remain preoccupied with their former spouse (with feelings of either love or hate), postdivorce adjustment is hindered. It is interesting to note that Carol Masheter (1997) found that unhealthy (preoccupied) postdivorce attachment was more important to postdivorce well-being than was the amount of hostility in the postdivorce relationship.

Contextual factors. There are a number of contextual factors that affect postdivorce adjustment, such as the amount of social support both perceived and received by divorced individuals. Those who are less socially involved and more socially isolated following divorce generally have a more difficult time adjusting. Some research has proposed that the benefit of social involvement stems from the link between social involvement and attachment to the former spouse (Tschann, Johnston, and Wallerstein 1989). Higher levels of social involvement generally are associated with lessened attachment to the former spouse, and as noted, less attachment facilitates healthy postdivorce adjustment. However, Wang and Amato (2000) suggested that some social support comes with a price, including feelings of guilt, dependence on others, or criticism from the giver of the support, particularly if the support comes from kin. The differing influences of support are found in studies of other countries as well, as Frode Thuen and O. J. Eikeland (1998) found similar results among Norwegian divorced couples.

The most influential form of social support comes in the form of new relationships. Research consistently shows that new romantic relationships, both dating relationships and remarriages, are associated with better postdivorce adjustment for both men and women (Hetherington, Law, and O'Connor 1997).

Children, especially when older, also can serve as sources of social support for divorcing parents. This is particularly true of women, because they commonly retain custody of children. However, children also can be a source of postdivorce stress, as the added complications of maintaining the coparental relationship can result in stress for the divorcing parents. Further, reduced contact and influence by noncustodial parents (usually fathers) can be a source of stress for custodial parents, as the latter parent believes that they must go it alone (Arendell 1995). For noncustodial fathers, reduced contact is associated with higher levels of depression and poorer postdivorce adjustment.

Cultural factors. Adjustment is affected by the amount of stigma associated with divorce, the opportunities available (socially and economically) for divorced individuals, and differing legal contexts. As noted, divorce is associated with more social stigma in certain countries (e.g., India, Japan) and social opportunities in such countries generally are more limited. Divorced women in India have difficulty finding other single mothers with whom to develop a support network. They generally are reluctant to seek friendships with Indian men out of a concern that their efforts at friendship might be misinterpreted; employment and remarriage rates for Indian women are lower than those of U.S. women. Divorced individuals (particularly women) who reside in countries where divorce is less common and more stigmatized generally fare worse than individuals residing in countries where divorce is more common and less stigmatized (e.g., the United States).

The differing legal contexts of divorce can be influential to adult adjustment. Mark Fine and David Fine (1994) noted that most countries in Western Europe (with the exception of Ireland, which did not allow divorce until 2000) have moved from fault-based, punitive divorce laws to *no-fault divorce* laws, making divorces less painful to obtain. Such changes have had ramifications for divorce outcomes, most notably financial settlements. Since the 1960s, property settlements have become more egalitarian and awards of alimony have dramatically decreased, with the goal being to promote self-sufficiency for both divorcing spouses. For example, France has a system in which spousal support is rarely ordered; however, in the few rare cases that support is granted, a lump-sum payment is made at the time of the divorce, so continuing contact (and presumably, continuing conflict) between former spouses is minimized. Sweden has adopted an even more extreme view of postdivorce self-sufficiency, virtually eliminating spousal support altogether and declaring pensions to be individual property and therefore not divisible in the divorce settlement.

Although cross-culturally property settlements have become more egalitarian, in Australia these property settlements are largely determined by the future needs of the children. The future needs of spouses typically are not considered, and settlements also ignore any nonfinancial contributions of either party (e.g., stay-at-home mothers) when dividing marital assets (Sheehan and Hughes 2000). Similar neglect of nonfinancial investments during marriage occurs in Tanzania, where legal decisions through the 1980s predominantly have held that domestic contributions should not be considered in the division of marital property (Mtengeti-Migiro 1990). Thus, legal practices often ignore the contributions of women to marriage, reducing their postdivorce awards. Yet, the prevailing mood has been one of promoting self-sufficiency following divorce. This contradiction between behavior and mood, in turn, can result in a more difficult adjustment process, particularly for women.

Methodological Issues in Divorce Research

To date, most research regarding divorce and its impact on adults has assumed a *deficit perspective*—divorce is bad and has a negative effect on families. This perspective is reflected in the questions asked, the outcomes investigated, results showing negative outcomes, and the interpretation of these results. As noted, cross-cultural studies that investigate the potentially positive effects of divorce find that divorce can increase self-confidence, self-efficacy, well-being, and relief from a bad marriage for some. Therefore, future research should aim to further explore the range of influences of divorce on adults.

Because there is wide variation among divorced individuals in their postdivorce adjustment, simple comparisons between divorced and nondivorced individuals should be undertaken with caution. Just as divorce is best conceptualized as a process, adjustment to divorce also is a process, and studies show that the amount of time since divorce affects adjustment. However, many studies fail to examine time, ignoring the heterogeneity of the adjustment of divorced couples. Future research should investigate the multiple factors that aid or hinder adjustment, and should consider variations in the trajectory of the adjustment process among divorcing couples.

Despite variations in the structure and function of families in different countries, divorce is experienced by an increasing number of families. Data from the National Center for Health Statistics indicate that the annual number of divorces in the United States alone has climbed from 158,000 in 1921 to 1,163,000 in 1997, an increase of more than 700 percent (Norton and Miller 1992; *Monthly*

Vital Statistics 1999). In addition, it should be noted that the latter figure underestimated of the actual number of divorces in the United States, as it failed to include divorce figures from all fifty states. Given the magnitude of its occurrence, divorce and its impact on divorcing couples continues to be an area worthy of investigation. Because of the policy and political implications, greater care is warranted in examining the complexity inherent in this process.

See also: DIVORCE: EFFECTS ON CHILDREN; DIVORCE: EFFECTS ON PARENTS; DIVORCE MEDIATION; FAMILY LAW; GRIEF, LOSS, AND BEREAVEMENT; LATER LIFE FAMILIES; LONELINESS; MARITAL QUALITY; RELATIONSHIP DISSOLUTION; STRESS

Bibliography

Ahrons, C. (1994). *The Good Divorce.* New York: Harper Collins.

Amato, P. R. (1994). "The Impact of Divorce on Men and Women in India and the United States." *Journal of Comparative Family Studies* 25:207–221.

Amato, P. R. (2000). "The Consequences of Divorce for Adults and Children." *Journal of Marriage and the Family* 62:1269–1287.

Arendell, T. (1995). *Fathers and Divorce.* Thousand Oaks, CA: Sage.

Braver, S. L., and O'Connell, D. (1998). *Divorced Dads: Shattering the Myths.* New York: Putnam.

Bryant, T. L. (1992). "'Responsible' Husbands, 'Recalcitrant' Wives, Retributive Judges: Judicial Management of Contested Divorce in Japan." *Journal of Japanese Studies* 18:407–443.

Buehler, C., and Trotter, B. (1990). "Nonresidential and Residential Parents' Perceptions of the Former Spouse Relationship and Children's Social Competence following Marital Separation: Theory and Programmed Intervention." *Family Relations* 39:395–404.

Burkhauser, R. V.; Duncan, G. J.; Hauser, R.; and Berntsen, R. (1991). "Wife or Frau, Women Do Worse: A Comparison of Men and Women in the United States and Germany after Marital Dissolution." *Demography* 28:353–360.

Catlett, B. S., and McKenry, P. C. (1996). "Implications of Feminist Scholarship for the Study of Women's Postdivorce Economic Disadvantage." *Family Relations* 45:91–97.

Cole, C. L., and Cole, A. L. (1999). "Essays for Practitioners: Boundary Ambiguities that Bind Former Spouses Together after the Children Leave Home in Post-Divorce Families." *Family Relations* 48:271–272.

Coleman, M.; Ganong, L.; and Fine, M. (2000). "Reinvestigating Remarriage: Another Decade of Progress." *Journal of Marriage and the Family* 62:1288–1307.

Cotten, S. R. (1999). "Marital Status and Mental Health Revisited: Examining the Importance of Risk Factors and Resources." *Family Relations* 48:225–233.

Emery, R. E., and Dillon, P. (1994). "Conceptualizing the Divorce Process: Renegotiating Boundaries of Intimacy and Power in the Divorced Family System." *Family Relations* 43:374–379.

Fine, M. A., and Demo, D. H. (2000). "Divorce: Societal Ill or Normative Transition?" In *Families as Relationships,* ed. R. M. Milardo and S. Duck. New York: Wiley.

Fine, M. A., and Fine, D. R. (1994). "An Examination and Evaluation of Recent Changes in Divorce Laws in Five Western Countries: The Critical Role of Values." *Journal of Marriage and the Family* 56:249–263.

Finnie, R. (1993). "Women, Men, and the Economic Consequences of Divorce: Evidence from Canadian Longitudinal Data." *Canadian Review of Sociology and Anthropology* 30:205–241.

Hetherington, E. M.; Law, T. C.; and O'Connor, T. G. (1997). "Divorce: Challenges, Changes, and New Chances." In *Family in Transition,* ed. A. S. Skolnick and J. H. Skolnick. New York: Longman.

Jain, A.; Belsky, J.; and Crnic, K. (1996). "Beyond Fathering Behaviors: Types of Dads." *Journal of Family Psychology* 10:431–442.

Kitson, G. C., and Morgan, L. A. (1990). "The Multiple Consequences of Divorce: A Decade Review." *Journal of Marriage and the Family* 52:913–924.

Kurdek, L. A. (1991). "The Relations between Reported Well Being and Divorce History, Availability of a Proximate Adult, and Gender." *Journal of Marriage and the Family* 53:71–78.

Lorenz, F. O.; Simons, R. L.; Conger, R. D.; Elder, G. H., Jr.; Johnson, C.; and Chao, W. (1997). "Married and Recently Divorced Mothers' Stressful Events and Distress: Tracing Change across Time." *Journal of Marriage and the Family* 59:219–232.

Masheter, C. (1997). "Healthy and Unhealthy Friendship and Hostility between Ex-Spouses." *Journal of Marriage and the Family* 59:463–475.

Mtengeti-Migiro, R. (1990). "The Division of Matrimonial Property in Tanzania." *Journal of Modern African Studies* 28:521–526.

Monthly Vital Statistics. (1999). 47 (July 6): 1–4.

Norton, A. J., and Miller, L. F. (1992). "Marriage, Divorce, and Remarriage in the 1990's." *U.S. Bureau of the Census, Current Population Reports* P23–180. Washington, DC: Government Printing Office.

Peterson, R. R. (1996). "A Re-Evaluation of the Economic Consequences of Divorce." *American Sociological Review* 61:528–536.

Sheehan, G., and Hughes, J. (2000). "The Division of Matrimonial Property in Australia." *Family Matters* (Autumn):28–33.

Smyth, B.; Sheehan, G.; and Fehlberg, B. (2001). "Post-Divorce Parenting Patterns." *Family Matters* (Winter): 61–63.

Teachman, J. D.; Tedrow, L. M.; and Crowder, K. D. (2000). "The Changing Demography of Today's Families." *Journal of Marriage and the Family* 62:1234–1346.

Thuen, F., and Eikeland, O. J. (1998). "Social Support Among Males and Females After Marital Disruption." *Psychology, Health and Medicine* 3:315–326.

Tschann, J. M.; Johnston, J. R.; and Wallerstein, J. S. (1989). "Resources, Stressors, and Attachment as Predictors of Adult Adjustment after Divorce: A Longitudinal Study." *Journal of Marriage and the Family* 51:1033–1046.

Wang, H., and Amato, P. R. (2000). "Predictors of Divorce Adjustment: Stressors, Resources, and Definitions." *Journal of Marriage and the Family* 62:655–668.

Yuko, K. (1998). "Breaking Up Still Hard to Do." *Japan Quarterly* 45:84–89.

KARI HENLEY
KAY PASLEY

EFFECTS ON PARENTS

Half of the parents sixty years and older with ever-married children have experienced a child's divorce, thus divorce is a common event for a large proportion of people in middle age and old age (Spitze et al. 1994). Nevertheless, studies of divorce's effects upon parents has been overshadowed by the large literature on its effects upon children of the divorcing parents. When studies of the parents of divorced individuals are reported, parents are usually depicted in the context of being a grandparent, a role that is derived from and regulated by their child. This research concentrates upon the parents and adult children who have minor children. Whereas most research on the effects of divorce focuses on the adaptation of children of divorce, there has been increasing interest in the effects an adult child's divorce may have on members of the extended family.

Research Perspectives

The effects of divorce on parents are most frequently studied from a resource perspective by focusing on the exchanges taking place between parents and their divorcing children (Spitze et al. 1994). The studies are based upon the assumption that as children's marriages dissolve, they will turn to their parents for help (Johnson 1988a). An alternate situation may occur, however, particularly for older parents who are in need of help. A child going through a divorce may not be readily available to offer support to them because of the demands and stressors of the divorce process.

Other researchers maintain that conceptions of continuity provide an alternative but less common perspective on the adult children and their parents (Rossi and Rossi 1990). This focus assumes that divorce has no discernable effects on the relationship between the adult child and his or her parents. Advocates of this perspective propose that there may be some changes in the level of contacts and supports, but there is no evidence of changes in the level of closeness and contact (Umberson 1992).

When minor children are present, the continuity perspective is difficult to sustain as marriages dissolve. One spouse, usually the husband, leaves the household, and in the process, the quality of parenting changes as one parent is performing the role previously performed by two people. This situation can have major repercussions not only on the former nuclear family but also on grandparents and the wider kinship group. The custodial parent's extended family becomes the primary sphere of activity, as members of the ex-spouse's kinship group become more distant.

The Post-Divorce Parent-Child Relationship

Researchers on the relationship between parent and adult child have diverse views. On one hand, those in human development tend to take a positive view of intergenerational relationships by emphasizing the strong bonds of affection and solidarity between generations. In such an environment, when a child is going through the divorce process, a parent is a potential source of help and one who can ease the strains inherent during this major change in family life. On the other hand, other researchers (Hess and Waring 1978) speak of the inherent tensions and constraints between parent and adult child in normal times which may become magnified during the divorce process. The contradictory research findings between love and attachment versus tensions and conflict may reflect the major changes occurring during the divorce process and the reorganization of a child's family.

The divorce of a child can be a major event (in terms of stress) not only for divorcing partners, but also their parents, particularly if grandchildren are present. These major changes occur during the divorce process in a social limbo in which there are few guidelines on how to behave: even whether one should act pleased or relieved. The cultural context adds to the relatively normless environment of the divorce process. Mainstream Western values endorse the rights of the individual to be independent and self-reliant. Although a child's independence is extolled, some form of dependence may develop as a divorcing child turns to parents for help. In keeping with the adult child's right to independence, parents usually adhere to the norm of noninterference in their child's life, a value stance that must be discarded as parents take a more active helping role in their child's household.

As the child's household becomes more public and subject to parental scrutiny, the greater the parents' involvement, the more they observe what is going on in what was once a private household (Johnson 1988a, 1988b). Thus, both parents and divorcing children are placed in an ambivalent situation. If minor children are involved, grandparents are expected to help. Although such demands are more often placed upon the maternal grandparents, most maternal and paternal grandparents resist assuming a parental role, yet they recognize their responsibility to help. A common theme often expressed is: "If I do some things for them, I may have to do it all. If I don't help, I may lose them." This parental reluctance has rarely been discussed in the literature. One exception is Karl Pillemer and Jill Suitor's (1991) article "Will I Ever Escape My Child's Problem?," one of the few reports on the underside of the parent-adult child relationship.

Parents' Responses to Children's Needs

Because of custody relationships, sons and daughters face markedly different situations that have repercussions on their relationship with parents. The parent-son relationship and the parent-daughter have markedly different functions. Because custody is generally granted to the mother, her parents are usually a major source of support. In the process, they have no problem gaining access to the grandchildren. These parents may have to extend not only financial assistance but also emotional support to compensate for the loss of one parent in the household (Johnson 1988b; Hamon 1995).

In contrast, men's parents usually must gain access to the grandchildren through a former daughter-in-law, to whom they are no longer legally related after a divorce (Johnson 1988b). Some paternal grandparents explicitly retain a strong relationship with a former daughter-in-law sometimes at the expense of their relationship with their son. If needed, paternal grandparents can also compensate for a son's deficiencies as a parent, or they may strengthen their son's attentiveness to his children.

Divorce is a dynamic series of events as households dissolve, affinal kin (relatives by marriage) are no longer related, and new kin are added with remarriage. The individuals involved must construct new roles, redefine relationships, and restructure their lives. The relationship between parents and children is particularly interesting, because children assume a new life style that may be at odds with their parents' values. Because most parents try to maintain a noninterfering stance, their child usually must take the initiative in seeking help. Most parents may be responsive to the needs of their child and grandchildren, but they resist having to act as a parent in terms of disciplining and fulfilling day-to-day instrumental care.

Intergenerational Exchanges

Age and gender are factors that influence the relationship between parent and adult child. In later life, those with adult children found that divorce had a sizable effect on the parent-child relationship in terms of relationship qualities and contact (Johnson 1988b). The negative effects were stronger between father and child than between mother and child. If divorced fathers shared a residence with their child, they were less likely to be depressed than the non-resident fathers (Shapiro and Lambert 1999; Schone and Pezzin 1999). The age of the ever-divorced father had negative effects on caregiving and economic ties between parent and child. Likewise, Teresa Cooney and Peter Uhlenberg's (1990) study showed that divorced men experienced long-term negative effects on the frequency of contact between older men and their children, and children were less likely to be considered as potential caregivers. The gender of the divorcing child has also been studied: for example, daughters received more help from their parents than sons (Johnson 1988a).

Divorce can affect kinship networks positively as both divorcing men and women rely on kin for practical aid. Males turn to kin in the early stages of the divorce process, whereas women seek long-term assistance. Leigh Leslie and Katherine Grady (1985) found that one year after a divorce, social networks of divorcing individuals become more homogeneous with increased numbers of supportive kin.

A qualitative study of fifty divorces in middle-class suburbs (Johnson 1988a, 1988b) found that the relationship between parent and child varied by the organizational emphasis during the structural reorganization of the post-divorce family networks. First, those divorcing parents, who placed an emphasis upon the privacy of an abbreviated nuclear family, were relatively remote from parents, and they were likely to remarry over a three-year period. Second, others emphasized the generational bond and the solidarity with their parents. They usually received support from parents. Third, those who remarried tended to form loose-knit networks that incorporated former relatives of divorce and remarriage. These respondents tended to maintain distant but cordial relationships with their parents.

Surrogate Parenting

Major strains on the parent-child relationship after divorce comes in those situations when these adult children are no longer able to perform the parent role. There has been heightened interest in a recent phenomenon of grandparents assuming the role of surrogate parents. Such arrangements are vulnerable, because of economic problems and difficulty accessing entitlements. A North Carolina survey of 25,000 households found that of the grandparents who were sole surrogate parents of grandchildren, 42 percent lived in poverty and another 15 percent were "near poor" (Shone and Pizzin 1999). Despite the interest in this family arrangement, demographers find that surrogate parenting is rare in the United States. For example, in ongoing research on 160 African-American families, no one was currently a surrogate parent at the time of the interview, and only a few had been in the past.

Conclusion

The research literature on divorce's effects on aging parents is not large, and most reports focus on supports between generations rather than relationship qualities and how they change over time. Nevertheless, the existing literature indicates that divorce is a stressful process that affects divorcing individuals and their children as well as their parents. The divorce process has a stressful beginning, but over a year's time, the situation—for most—stabilized: most parents provided assistance to children when needed; the stressors on the older people had diminished.

See also: CONFLICT: PARENT-CHILD RELATIONSHIPS; DIVORCE: EFFECTS ON CHILDREN; DIVORCE: EFFECTS ON COUPLES; DIVORCE MEDIATION; ELDERS; IN-LAW RELATIONSHIPS; INTERGENERATIONAL RELATIONS; GRANDPARENTHOOD; GRANDPARENTS' RIGHTS; GRIEF, LOSS, AND BEREAVEMENT; STRESS

Bibliography

Cooney, T. M., and Uhlenberg, P. (1990). "The Role of Divorce in Men's Relationship with Their Adult Children." *Journal of Marriage and the Family* 52:677–688.

Hamon, R. R. (1995). "Parents as Resources When Adult Children Divorce." *Journal of Divorce and Remarriage* 23:171–183.

Hess, B., and Waring, J. (1978). "Parent and Child in Later Life: Rethinking the Relationship." In *Child Influences on Marital and Family Interactions,* ed. R. Lerner. New York: Academic Press.

Johnson, C. L. (1988a). "Post-Divorce Reorganization of the Relationship between Divorcing Children and Their Parents." *Journal of Marriage and the Family* 50:221–231

Johnson, C. L. (1988b). *Ex Familia: Grandparents, Parents, and Children Adjust to Divorce.* New Brunswick, NJ: Rutgers University Press.

Leslie, L. A., and Grady, K. (1985). "Changes in Mothers' Social Networks and Social Supports following Divorce." *Journal of Marriage and the Family* 47:663–673.

Pillemer, K., and Suitor, J. J. (1991). "Will I Ever Escape My Child's Problems? Effects of Children's Problems on Elderly Parents." *Journal of Marriage and the Family* 53:585–594.

Rossi, A. S., and Rossi, P. H. (1990). *Of Human Bonding: Parent-Child Relationship Across the Life Course.* New York: Aldine de Gruyter.

Shone, S., and Pezzin, L. E. (1999). "Parental Marital Disruption and Intergenerational Transfers." *Demography* 36:287–297.

Shapiro, A., and Lambert, J. D. (1999). "Longitudinal Effects on the Quality of the Father-Child Relationship and the Father's Psychological Well-Being." *Journal of Marriage and the Family* 61:387–408.

Spitze, G.; Logan, J. R.; Deane, G.; and Zerger, S. (1994). "Adult Child's Divorce and Intergenerational Relationships." *Journal of Marriage and the Family* 56:279–293.

Umberson, D. (1992). "Relationships between Adult Children and Their Parents: Psychological Consequences for Both Generations." *Journal of Marriage and the Family* 54.664–685.

COLLEEN L. JOHNSON

DIVORCE MEDIATION

Society, and the cultures that comprise it, change through time. The increasing prevalence of divorce is one example of change that societies and cultures experience. Data gathered on divorce in the United States indicate that approximately 50 percent of couples marrying can expect to divorce sometime in their lifetime (Coulson 1996). The divorce experience affects the parties divorcing, friends, extended family, and children. At the beginning of the twenty-first century numerous authors emphasized the effects of divorce and parental conflict on children (e.g., Coulson 1996; Twaite and Luchow 1996). Effects can vary from a decrease in self-esteem and increase in behavioral

problems as older siblings are asked to be responsible for younger siblings or children being used as messengers or spies (e.g., report on parent's dating behavior). These are only a few examples of how divorce and continuing conflict may affect children. Efforts to mitigate the effects of divorce may include informal support systems such as friends, family, religion, or more formal support systems such as mental health professionals, the legal system and, in the last twenty-six years, divorce mediation. *Divorce mediation*, as a helping process, was formally created in 1975 (Emery 1995; Helm, Boyd, and Longwill 1992). Only after no-fault divorces emerged in the 1970s was the no-fault dispute resolution process of mediation possible. Divorce mediation (hereafter referred to as mediation) was originally conceptualized as an alternative conflict resolution strategy to litigation.

Many questions have arisen in mediation's short history, such as what mediation is, should be, its effectiveness, who should perform it and the training requirements of mediators. This entry will discuss mediation processes, common themes, and variations and trends, as well as the perceived advantages and disadvantages of mediation, including when necessary, commonly used, and contraindicated. Research conducted on mediation, including the assessment of these advantages and disadvantages, will follow with an examination of international perspectives on mediation as well as cross-cultural issues.

Divorce Mediation Process

Though mediation has only formally existed for approximately twenty-five years (Helm, Boyd, Longwill 1992) the process of mediation has been around for centuries. Ancient Chinese used mediation as the primary means for conflict resolution. This ancient process involved a neutral third person helping parties to resolve disputes. This, in its simplest form, is the essence of mediation today; a settlement process emphasizing informed decision making and mutually acceptable agreements between disputants. Mediation can provide an alternative to the adversarial approach of the legal system. It is goal-focused and time-limited; targeting the issues to be resolved (Beck and Sales 2001; Gentry 1997). Common issues addressed are division of property, spousal support, child support, custody, and visitation (Emery 1995; Schwebel et al. 1994). Mediators assist parties to communicate clearly, clarify their disagreements, determine intentions, interests, and consider settlement options; all for the sake of a fair, mutually agreeable decision. The mediation process can take place, broadly speaking, in either public or private-sector settings.

The context of mediation can be broadly understood to take place either in public or private settings. Mediation that is *court-referred*, or offered through the court system with mediators contracted through the court system, are examples of *public-sector mediation*. When the disputants choose, or are referred to, a mediator who has no contractual arrangement with the court system, they are involved in a private mediation setting. Mediators working in private settings can come from professions such as law, mental health counseling, family counseling/therapy, social work, or psychology. The general process of mediation is similar across both settings.

Initial meetings with mediators typically involve a description of the mediation process. Some information may be gathered regarding disputants' perspectives on separation and divorce, plans to communicate with family and friends about the divorce, and child support. If the couple chooses to pursue mediation a contract between the couple and a mediator is commonly signed (see Coulson 1996, for one example of a contract). Once a contract is signed initial meetings commonly include the following steps: (1) orientation and introduction; (2) information gathering to facilitate goal setting; (3) framing issues and developing options for mutual agreement; (4) reaching an initial settlement and drafting a tentative agreement for discussion with attorneys (and possible families); and (5) finalizing the agreement in court.

The divorce mediator (hereafter referred to as *mediator*) has the immediate task of creating an appropriate, respectful, working atmosphere where the mediator's neutrality is unmistakable (Schwebel et al. 1994). The mediator is faced with working with two people who have chosen to separate and divorce. The range and intensity of emotion can be great. Of paramount importance for the mediator is the instillation of hope; an opportunity to approach that which seems unapproachable: agreement. Though mediation can take place in public or private settings, be voluntary or involuntary, similarities exist regarding the initial tasks of the mediator. Beyond these similarities, numerous

differences are possible given the array of mediation models.

Models of Mediation

Models of mediation can be conceptualized as being grounded in one of the four generally recognized mediation models (Beck and Sales 2001; Schwebel et al. 1994): *legal model* (Coogler 1978), *labor management model* (Haynes 1981), *therapeutic model,* and the *communication and information model* (Black and Joffe, 1978). The legal model (Coogler 1978), also referred to as *structured mediation,* is firmly controlled by the ground rules for mediation set forth by the mediator. Couples are seen together and discuss the issues of division of property, spousal support, child support, custody, and visitation, in this order. Discussion of these issues takes place over five two-hour sessions with the parties following a decision-making process clearly outlined by the mediator. The role of mediator is one of strict neutrality in which child advocacy and education of parents about children's needs is not encouraged. Both parties must use the same advisory lawyer who draws up a contract based on the decisions made in mediation. If failure occurs, referral to an arbiter is made.

The *labor management model* (LMM) (Haynes 1981) presupposes that mediation involves a bargaining process between parties with comparable levels of power, skill, and knowledge who can act in their own self-interest (Schwebel et al. 1994). Agreements must be viewed as adequate across eight criteria: (1) full disclosure of economic assets; (2) equitable division of assets; (3) no victims; (4) open and direct channels of communication between parents; (5) protected parental roles; (6) assumed access to children for both parents; (7) an explicit process for making future decisions; and (8) assured access to important relatives for the child or children. Mediators may meet individually with both parties to help prepare for negotiations. The mediator's role is active and directive, but shaped by the individual's needs. Knowledge of both legal and psychological issues related to divorce is essential for the mediator adopting this model. The approach is flexible and attends to the needs of the child or children.

The *therapeutic model* of divorce mediation is informed by the therapeutic theory chosen. Traditional conceptualizations of this model assumes participants cannot engage in effective communication and problem-solving until unresolved emotional and relational issues are addressed (Beck and Sales 2001). Unresolved emotional issues may require individual meetings with the mediator prior to any effort to produce a mutually acceptable agreement. Given the emphasis on relational issues and emotional impasses, the therapeutic model typically involves a greater number of sessions than other models (Schwebel et al. 1994). The mediator is active, directive, and child-focused, with the goal of facilitating a healthy family system. Attorneys have a more limited role in this model and typically are asked to review the agreement written up by the mediator. Agreements in the therapeutic model tend to emphasize cooperative language. If an agreement is unacceptable, parties can pursue other means to construct a workable agreement.

The appearance of the therapeutic model of mediation is dependent upon the therapeutic theory utilized. For example, Wayne Regina (2000) has grounded the mediation process in Bowen *systems theory*. Thus, mediation would focus on disputants' patterns of managing anxiety (i.e., *triangulation*), their ability to separate from emotion and process their emotional experience in mediation (i.e., *differentiation*). In contrast, John Winslade and Allison Cotter (1997) use *narrative theory* in conducting mediation. The focus is on the stories disputants tell of themselves that keep them from achieving agreement. Bowen systems theory and narrative theory are merely two examples of how a theory of therapy from the individual or family counseling/therapy contexts can be utilized to meet the objectives of mediation. See Beck, C. J. A. and Sales (2001) for further discussion of other therapeutic models of mediation.

The last general model is referred to as the *communication and information model*. This interdisciplinary model assumes that mutually agreeable agreements are attainable if the necessary information is freely available and exchanged (Black and Joffe 1978). Specialists from both the legal and mental health fields work together providing legal advice, resources in problem solving, drafts of the agreement, and focuses on specific details of the settlement (Beck and Sales 2001; Helm, Boyd, and Longwill 1992). An educational component is present, as parents are educated on the needs of their children and communication skills to assist in problem solving.

Across models variance is possible merely by the mediator's professional and personal background. For example, Bruce Phillips (1999) stresses the importance of active-listening skills as not simply a means to understand disputants' concerns but as a means to facilitate the change process. Carl Schneider (2000) stresses disputants' successful apologizing to maximize movement through the mediation process. Other concepts currently receiving attention in the literature include the importance of emotions for both mediator and disputants (Lund 2000; Retzinger and Scheff 2000) and theories power and feminism (Ellis and Wight 1998).

An emphasis on children's needs and their participation in the mediation process is one variation of mediation process that has received more detailed attention in the literature. Though educating parents about their children's needs is an aspect of all mediation models discussed above (except the legal mediation model), many researchers (Beck and Biank 1997a; Beck and Biank 1997b; Kelly 1996; McIntosh 2000) suggest mediators attend more to the needs of children. Wallerstein (1995, as cited in Beck and Biank 1997) views children as "hidden clients" as discussion of children's needs are not an emphasis of the mediation process. Focusing on children's needs occurs by helping parents assess the needs of their children as well as mediators conducting individual assessments with children. Allowing children to speak directly to a mediator may provide information that is more accurate than parent assessment, given the duress parents are under during divorce (Cohen, Dattner, and Luxenburg 1999; Johnston and Campbell 1988). This variation to the mediation process runs counter to the traditionally defined role of mediator (Beck and Biank 1997b), yet this role has its own variations.

Mediator's Role

Traditional theoretical formulations of the mediator's role are being reexamined. The traditional view of mediator was that of a neutral, honest facilitator of couples' decision-making processes (Emery 1994), with neutrality being the hallmark of mediator role. Neutrality has been defined as "scrupulously giving each disputant equal attention and doing exactly what is needed by each disputant" (Cohen, Dattner, and Luxenburg 1999, p. 342), being impartial and showing equidistance (Beck and Sales 2001; Cohen, Dattner, and Luxenburg 1999). *Impartiality* involves creating and maintaining an unbiased relationship with the disputants. *Equidistance* refers to the mediator's ability to have each disputant tell their position (i.e., balance the conversation so each has equal power in session). Connie J. A. Beck and Bruce D. Sales (2001) found numerous mediation researchers advocating against adopting an impartial stance as mediator. Cohen, Dattner, and Luxenburg (1999) have argued that mediators need to attend more to children's needs and assume a child advocacy role (Menin 2000). Those mediators whose training is in, for example, counseling, psychology, and social work, versus law can more easily adopt such an advocacy role (Cohen, Dattner, and Luxenburg 1999). Given that mediators are a diversely trained group, it is not surprising that some argue for clarity of training, standards, and mediator assessment (Bagshaw 1999; Bronson 2000). Ultimately the process of mediation, across all countries, needs improvement through professional standards (Bagshaw 1999).

Advantages of Mediation

The evolution of mediation process, theory, and the mediator's role seeks to better meet the purported advantages of the mediation process over litigation. General benefits argued to be unavailable through litigation include: the opportunity for each disputant to (1) air their concerns and be heard; (2) be assisted by a neutral third party; (3) and do so in a nonadversarial context (Beck and Sales 2001). Increased efficiency is one specific advantage purported by mediation supporters (Twaite et al. 1998). Supporters of mediation generally see mediation as avoiding the adversarial context that has the potential to increase the length and cost of reaching a settlement. A second advantage is increased accessibility to assistance in the divorce process. As mediation tends to be cheaper than litigation, those disputants who cannot afford a lawyer can afford to engage in the mediation process. Third, it has been argued that litigated settlements tend to be based on legal precedents versus addressing the unique needs of each disputant (Twaite et al. 1998). Mediation seeks to hear, understand, and address the unique

situations and needs of disputants; creating settlements that are more personally relevant. The increased privacy that comes from mediation versus litigation is also seen as more related to the interests of the disputants. A fourth specific benefit of mediation is its greater potential than litigation for self-empowerment. Disputants in mediation experience greater self-efficacy and control as they play a more active role in mediation and have the opportunity to air their concerns and be heard in ways not available through litigation (this benefit forms the central goal of an emerging mediation model [Bush and Folger 1994]).

Joan Kelly's (1996) seminal research review article examining divorce mediation research conducted between 1986 and 1996 found robust support for the positive effect mediation has on settlement rates. Settlement rates ranged from 50 to 85 percent across studies, countries, and mediation contexts. Beck and Sales (2001), in their review of research conducted since 1996, found similar settlement rates for those disputants going through mediation. Kelly (1996) also reported that most studies indicate higher compliance rates and less relitigation for disputants using mediation versus litigation. Beck and Sales (2001) support Kelly's report but point out long-term compliance is not clearly evident, primarily due to methodological issues of the studies conducted to date. Mediation has been found (Beck and Sales 2001; Kelly, 1996) to reduce conflict and cooperation between disputants in most studies though the effects are small and short-lived, which supports the common belief that the effects of divorce for disputants and their families last long into the future. Research on the appropriateness of mediation shows that the field is still lacking knowledge on the effect of personality styles on mediation outcome (Kelly 1996). Despite substantial support for divorce mediation disadvantages do exist.

Disadvantages of Mediation

Detractors to mediation do exist (Twaite et al. 1998). Detractors' claims can be framed against the above-description of advantages. Viewing mediation as more efficient seems advantageous, yet, expediting the decision-making process may potentially threaten fairness. The litigation process, with its lawyers protecting client interests and disclosure rules ensuring full disclosure of information, can be seen to ensure fairness more than the informal and variable process of mediation. Regarding the espoused benefits of increased accessibility with mediation, it has been argued that the decreased cost of mediation is related to the fact that lawyers charge higher fees due to their greater level of expertise and legal status. As lawyers can better predict settlement outcome if a case goes to court, proponents of litigation contend that lawyers can thus provide better input to their clients. Moreover, the claims of Robert Bush and Joseph Folger (1994) for the potential for increased self-empowerment and growth have been critiqued on the basis of an erroneous assumption: equal power between disputants. James Twaite and his colleagues (1998) summarize the view of many detractors of mediation on this issue. Detractors believe the potential for inequitable settlement for women with the mediator's role of neutrality being inadequate to contain a dominant, or more powerful, disputant. Jessica Pearson (1997), speaking from a feminist perspective, believes mediation decriminalizes domestic violence by offering a conciliatory approach that does not hold the abuser accountable for his or her actions. Additionally, placing the abused and the abuser in the same room for mediation leads to obvious safety issues. Kelly (1996) and Pearson (1997) communicate the complex nature of researching this issue. Both conclude that mediation has been beneficial when domestic violence is a variable but only under certain conditions and only after adequate assessment.

International and Cultural Perspectives on Mediation

Divorce mediation is an international means of conflict resolution. For example, divorce mediation studies have been conducted in Australia (McIntosh 2000), England (Dingwall, Greatbatch, and Ruggerone 1998) Norway (Tjersland 1999), and Scotland (Mackay and Brown 1999). These studies all address aspects of mediation that also challenge mediators in the United States. The impact of custody decisions on children's mental health, the structure and effectiveness of mandatory divorce mediation, mediator competence, the influence of gender on the mediation process, and mediation models are issues equally relevant on an international level. However, perspectives on mediation unique to a given country are also present. For example, in Australia concern has been given to the relevance of Western-based models of mediation.

In Scotland, where the legal system is separate from the UK-based umbrella organization, overseeing mediation in Scotland challenges the coordination of services. Studies have focused on cultural issues (e.g., value incongruence between mediation models and mediation participants of Asian descent) and the lack of relevant research on mediation with specific ethnic populations (e.g., Hispanic, African-American, Asian) (Molina 1999; Wong 1995). International research requires development on methodological as well as on cultural fronts (Beck and Sales 2001).

New mediation models are also being developed internationally. Canada, for example, has seen the development and increased use of what has been referred to as *collaborative divorce* or *collaborative family practice* (Sacks 2000). In short, these models discard the adversarial stance of most mediation models in favor of a model that emphasizes win-win solutions, a *both/and perspective* on parties' interests, difference in perceptions over right or wrong perceptions, empathic responses over defensive or aggressive ones, curiosity and compassion over judgment and blame, both parties against a problem over both parties against one another, and empowerment over domination. These premises are highlighted in a process that involves an interdisciplinary team. Such teams may be comprised of the relevant parties, lawyers, a divorce coach (i.e., facilitating understanding of and movement through the divorce process), a child specialist (i.e., speaking as a voice for the needs of children involved), and a financial specialist (i.e., providing budgetary and financial assistance). The collaborative model is well received in Canada as it has been experienced as healthier than other models (MacDonald 2000). At the beginning of the twenty-first century, those involved in divorce mediation are beginning to emphasize the creation of healthy relationships and not simply a resolution of some conflict as the outcome of divorce mediation.

See also: CHILD CUSTODY; CONFLICT: COUPLE RELATIONSHIPS; DIVORCE: EFFECTS ON CHILDREN; DIVORCE: EFFECTS ON COUPLES; DIVORCE: EFFECTS ON PARENTS; RELATIONSHIP DISSOLUTION

Bibliography
Bagshaw, D. (1999). "Developing Mediation Standards: An Australian Experience." *Mediation Quarterly* 16: 389–406.

Beck, C. J. A., and Sales, B. D. (2001). *Family Mediation: Facts, Myths, and Future Prospects*. Washington, DC: American Psychological Association.

Beck, P., and Biank, N. (1997a). "Enhancing Therapeutic Intervention during Divorce." *Journal of Analytic Social Work* 4:63–81.

Beck, P., and Biank, N. (1997b). "Broadening the Scope of Mediation to Meet the Needs of Children." *Mediation Quarterly* 14:179–199.

Black, M., and Joffee, W. (1978). "A Lawyer/Therapist Team Approach to Divorce." *Concilliation and Courts Review* 16:1–5.

Bronson, S. (2000). "Improving Mediator Competence through Self-Assessment." *Mediation Quarterly* 18:171–179.

Bush, R. A. B., and Folger, J. P. (1994). *The Promise of Mediation: Responding to Conflict through Empowerment and Recognition*. San Francisco: Jossey-Bass.

Cohen, O., Dattner, N., and Luxenburg, A. (1999). "The Limits of the Mediator's Neutrality." *Mediation Quarterly,* 16:341–348.

Coogler, O. J. (1979). "Divorce Mediation: A Means of Facilitating Divorce and Adjustment." *Family Coordinator,* 28:255–259.

Coulson, R. (1996). *Family Mediation*. San Francisco: Jossey-Bass.

Dingwall, R.; Greatbatch, D.; and Ruggerone, L. (1998). "Gender and Interaction in Divorce Mediation." *Mediation Quarterly* 15:277–287.

Ellis, D. and Wight, L. (1998) "Theorizing Power in Divorce Negotiations: Implications for Practice." *Mediation Quarterly* 15:227–244.

Emery, R. E. (1994). "Mediation: Negotiating Agreements and Renegotiating Relationships." *Family Relations* 44:377–383.

Haynes, J. M. (1981). *Mediation*. New York: Springer.

Helm, B.; Boyd, L. W.; and Longwill, C. K. (1992). "Professional Interdependence in Divorce Practices: The Psychotherapist and the Mediator." *Famiy and Conciliation Courts Review* 30:385–396.

Johnston, J. R., and Campbell, L. E. G. (1988). *Impasses of Divorce: The Dynamics and Resolution of Family Conflict*. New York: Free Press.

Kelly, J. (1996). "A Decade of Mediation Research: Some Answers and Questions." *Family and Conciliation Courts Review* 34:373–385.

Lund, M. E. (2000). "A Focus on Emotion in Mediation Training." *Family and Conciliation Courts Review,* 38 (1):62–68.

McIntosh, J. (2000). "Child-Inclusive Divorce Mediation: Report on a Qualitative Research Study." *Mediation Quarterly* 18:55–69.

Mackay, R. E., and Brown, A. J. (1999). "Practice Issues in Community Mediation." *Mediation Quarterly* 17:181–195.

Menin, B. (2000). "The Party of the Last Part: Ethical and Process Implications for Children in Mediation." *Mediation Quarterly* 17:281–293.

Molina, O. (1999). "The Effects of Divorce on African American Working Women." *Journal of Divorce and Remarriage* 32:1–15.

Pearson, J. (1997). "Mediating When Domestic Violence Is a Factor: Policies and Practices in Court-Based Mediation Programs." *Mediation Quarterly* 14:319–335.

Phillips, B. (1999). "Reformulating Dispute Narratives through Active Listening." *Mediation Quarterly* 17:161–168.

Regina, W. (2000). "Bowen Systems Theory and Mediation." *Mediation Quarterly* 18:1–11.

Retzinger, S., and Scheff, T. (2000). "Emotion, Alienation, and Narratives: Resolving Intractable Conflict." *Mediation Quarterly* 18 (1):71–85.

Schneider, C. D. (2000). "What It Means to Be Sorry: The Power of Apology in Mediation." *Mediation Quarterly* 17:265–279.

Schwebel, A. I., Gately, D. W., Renner, M. A., and Milburn, T. W. (1994). "Divorce Mediation: Four Models and Their Assumptions about Change in Parties' Positions." *Mediation Quarterly* 11:211–227.

Tjersland, O. A. (1999). "Evaluation of Mediation and Parental Cooperation Based on Observations and Interviews with the Clients of a Mediation Project." *Mediation Quarterly* 16:407–423.

Twaite, J. A., Keiser, S., and Luchow, A. "Divorce Mediation: Promises, Criticisms, Achievements, and Current Challenges." *Journal of Psychiatry and Law* 26:353–381

Twaite, J. A., and Luchow, A. (1996). "Custodial Arrangments and Parental Conflict following Divorce: The Impact on Children's Adjustment." *Journal of Psychiatry and the Law* 24:53–75.

Winslade, J., and Cotter, A. (1997). "Moving from Problem Solving to Narrative Approaches in

Mediation." In *Narrative Therapy in Practice: The Archaeology of Hope,* ed. G. Monk, J. Winslade, K. Crocket, and D. Epston. San Francisco: Jossey-Bass.

Wong, R. R. (1995). "Divorce Mediation among Asian Americans: Bargaining in the Shadow of Diversity." *Mediation Quarterly* 33:110–128.

Other Resources

MacDonald, J. C. (2000). "Collaborative Family Practice: A New Approach." *Joel Miller's Family Law Centre.* Available at: www.familylawcentre.com/macdonald.html.

Sacks, M. (2000). "Collaborative Divorce and Separation." Available at: www.collaborativedivorce.ca/intro.html.

DAVID M. KLEIST

DOMESTIC VIOLENCE

See ELDER ABUSE; INTERPARENTAL VIOLENCE—EFFECTS ON CHILDREN; RAPE; SPOUSE ABUSE: PREVALENCE; SPOUSE ABUSE: THEORETICAL EXPLANATIONS

DOWRY

A *dowry* is a type of payment or gift of property that accompanies a bride upon marriage. The custom has been most common in settled agricultural societies where it may form an important part of the financial arrangements for a marriage. The types of property included in a dowry vary tremendously depending on the economic circumstances of the families involved and the customary expectations of the society. A woman's dowry might include personal possessions (such as clothing and jewels), money, servants, or land. Societies vary in regarding a dowry as the property of the bride, her husband, or her husband's family. Where the custom exists, women frequently receive dowries in lieu of a right of inheritance from their father's estates (Goody and Tambiah 1973).

The custom of giving dowries may perform several positive functions. First, as with other common forms of marital exchange such as bride-wealth (also called *bride-price*), a dowry affirms an alliance between two families united by marriage. Second, a dowry may provide a bride with some protection against an abusive husband. Should she leave her husband, a woman's family may demand that all or part of her dowry be returned. Third, a young couple may use the dowry to set up their own household. Finally, a woman may need to rely upon her dowry for support should her husband die and she has no rights to inheritance. These are by no means universal functions. They are contingent on the ways that people conceive of the dowry and, especially, on whether the wife controls all or part of it.

Dowry often has a marked political dimension. In medieval Europe, noble families down on their fortunes often sought to marry their sons to women from rich families whose dowries would thus enhance their own financial situations. By the same token, a newly wealthy family could improve its social standing by using rich dowries to form marital alliances with those of a higher class. In northern India, marrying daughters upwards, using the enticement of dowries, has long provided one of the chief means for families to raise their status (by very small increments) within the rigidly hierarchical caste system, a process technically known as *hypergamy*. In general, the custom of dowry imposes a financial burden upon families with daughters that can be especially heavy when the family has few or no sons who might themselves attract wives with dowries.

Dowry had disappeared from most of Europe by the beginning of the twentieth century, but remains a common practice in south Asia. In India it has become a matter of some controversy and a subject for legal reform because of a large number of incidents in which women have been harassed and even murdered by their in-laws in attempts to extort richer dowries. Debate continues as to whether *dowry deaths* should be understood as a byproduct of the custom itself or as the result of modern conditions that have undermined the traditional connections between families brought together in marriage while inflating the cash value of dowries (Menski 1999).

See also: BRIDE-PRICE; KINSHIP; MARRIAGE CEREMONIES; MATE SELECTION; WIFE

Bibliography

Goody, J. and Tambiah, S. J. (1973). *Bridewealth and Dowry.* Cambridge, UK: Cambridge University Press.

Menski, W., ed. (1999). *South Asians and the Dowry Problem*. Stoke-on-Trent, Stratfordshire, UK: Trentham Books.

JOHN BARKER

DUAL-EARNER FAMILIES

The language of *dual-earner families* developed in research on families in industrialized societies. The term was needed to describe what was then a new family form that arose when women who had once worked inside the home, doing everything from nurturing work to family farming to producing goods such as candles and clothes, moved into a cash economy and took paid jobs. Questions that emerged from women's paid employment ranged from the effect of women's income on their power within marriage to who would take care of the children at home. These questions only make sense, however, in societies in which most couples live in nuclear families, a cash economy predominates, and both spouses leave the family setting in order to earn money to provide for their household.

Asia and the Middle East

In general, few Asian nuclear households can actually be considered dual-earner families. When married women work for pay, it is usually because their husbands are working in marginal jobs, and the family needs the extra income to survive (Kim 1997; Saso 1990). Research in Asia suggests that the majority of women value being a housewife, as this status coincides with wealth. This value fits well with the traditional beliefs about women in Asia, where women's loyalty is presumed to be solely to their husbands and children (Kim 1997; Lewis et al. 1992; Saso 1990). When women work for pay because husbands are unable to support the family solely, it is not expected that this would significantly change the balance of power or the division of labor. When asked, these employed women say that they should be in charge of the home, and their husbands should not necessarily share the work in the house. Stigma exists against wives who work for money; they are often accused of neglecting their husbands and children. Some evidence suggests that an increasing number of women in dual-earner families feel the burden is unfair (Kim 1997; Saso 1990).

Local governments in some Japanese and Singaporean cities provide day nurseries for poor families, at times with most of the cost absorbed (Lewis et al. 1992; Saso 1990). Commentators continually call for more part-time work for mothers and flexibility in mothers' work schedules rather than for increased participation of husbands and fathers in household work and childcare (Saso 1990). Research on dual-earner Singaporean families shows that, as elsewhere, fathers spend considerably less time with their children and on housework than do mothers (Lewis et al. 1992). Also as elsewhere, the greater his participation in childcare, the more the husband is likely to support his wife's employment (Wang 1992).

In the 1980s, many middle-class to lower middle-class Middle Eastern women became part of dual-earner families against their husbands' wishes because of dire economic need. Many men in Arabic societies would prefer to take two or three jobs to keep wives out of paid labor. Although the husbands may disapprove, the women report their positive economic contribution to the household as well as the financial security for their family for the long term. Many Middle Eastern Arabic women work in spite of the prevailing ideology supporting patriarchal families, which promotes selflessness for women in their marriages, men's sole providership, and husbands as head of the family. When spouses both work for pay despite believing in an ideology that supports male dominance, female selflessness, and women's role as restricted to family life, both wives and husbands experience internal distress. Since the mid-1980s, however, the number of Middle Eastern dual-earner families has been on the decline (Ghorayshi 1996; Redclift and Sinclair 1991).

Due to inflation, it is difficult in urban India for a couple to lead comfortable lives unless both spouses work; this family type is increasing because of economic necessity, rather than egalitarian ideals. Dual-earner lifestyles generally benefit women, but stress their husbands (Andrade; Postma; and Abraham 1999). Several researchers have found that employed and unemployed women in India did not differ in measures of psychological well-being (Mukhopadhyay, Dewanji, and Majumder 1993). Dual-earner wives reported greater freedom in certain parts of their lives, though their husbands still controlled financial matters. Employed wives still reported doing five times as much household work as their husbands did (Ramu 1989) and do not hold significantly less traditional attitudes than other women.

Between 1966 and 1989, the proportion of dual-earner families among married couples in Israel increased from 26 percent to 47 percent. Israeli cultural beliefs focus on motherhood as not simply a family role, but a role in providing additional citizens for the nation. The cultural assumption is that a woman will combine family and work, in that order (Lewis et al. 1992). Israeli women receive a double message as they are educated toward modern achievement-oriented values but also taught to have strong family-oriented norms and be responsible for household labor. Women, but not men, are expected to take time off from work for family needs. Both spouses in dual-earner families were found to report a higher quality of marital life and psychological well-being when compared to families where the husband is the only employed spouse (Frankel 1997).

Latin America

Mexico is the only Latin American country where research in the English language has been published, and therefore where the proportion of and experiences of wives participating in the cash economy can be assessed. Rural women in large numbers began working in the maquiladora industry in Mexico as it emerged in the mid-1960s. The typical household structure changed from a breadwinner-homemaker to an assortment of household structures, including female-breadwinner married couples, extended family households where individuals pool their incomes, and single person households (Cravey 1998). Some research suggests that in urban areas of Mexico, married women are not engaging in paid work until their children are old enough to care for themselves (Selby, Murphy, and Lorenzen 1990). Dual-earner wives in Mexico have noted that their marital relationships suffer as a result of their employment because it becomes more difficult to find time to spend alone with their husbands (Frankel 1997). Where married women are employed, there is a subtle change in the balance of power in the home (Cravey 1998). Women in dual-earner families generally have nontraditional beliefs about the division of labor in the home, but rarely have enough power to put their beliefs into practice (Frankel 1997).

Eastern Europe and Russia

When Eastern Europe and Russia were socialist, paid employment was both a right and an obligation of all adults; dual-earner families were the normative type of family. Since the transition to a market economy in these areas, governmental ideology has often used women's home obligations to justify their removal from jobs, and the unemployment rates of women have markedly increased (Arber and Gilbert 1992; Lewis et al. 1992; Lobodzinska 1995). There is no evidence that women want to define themselves as homemakers; they are unemployed and searching for ways to earn income. The dual-earner family continues to be the modal family type in most post-Soviet societies. The majority of Russian and East European women regard themselves as either the primary or cobreadwinner of their family (Lobodzinska 1995).

As elsewhere, dual burdens have been conceptualized in Eastern Europe as women's burden. Women in dual-earner families have always been expected to work for pay after childbirth and to maintain the home and family, while men are only expected to work for pay (Arber and Gilbert 1992; Lewis et al. 1992). During the socialist era, this dual burden was less weighty than in capitalist societies because of the widespread availability of childcare facilities and governmental subsidies including maternity leave and health care. Although communist countries varied some in the extent to which such policies existed, the normative requirement that women work in paid labor helped to justify a wide-ranging set of services. This has been discontinued in the post-communist era, and women are finding the double-burden very heavy (Gal and Kligman 2000; Vannoy et al. 1999).

Western and Southern Europe

Research has found that the majority of married French women maintained full-time employment after childbirth (Arber and Gilbert 1992). Dual-earner families have increased in number since the early 1980s in Great Britain, but dual-earner families where both partners are employed full-time are still in the minority there (Crompton 1997; Hatt

1997). Women in Great Britain, especially those with a spouse in full-time employment, are likely to work part-time (Hatt 1997).

Germany is unique in Western Europe in that this democratic, capitalist country is the result of the unification of one democratic and one communist country in 1989. Many women from the former East Germany expect to be employed, even if their husbands could afford to support their family on their salaries. While many former East German families continue to be dual-earner families, after unification, women have been forced into lower status jobs, removing their place as economic equals in their marriages (Lobodzinska 1995). In the former East Germany, the government subsidized childcare facilities, aiding most dual-earner families; since unification, the focus has been on mothers caring for their children rather than the state providing care (Lobodzinska 1995). While dual-earner families were normative in the former East Germany, West German women have always struggled more in combining work and family roles. Former West German mothers who delegate childcare and work as a part of a dual-earner family sometimes experience guilt regarding meeting society's expectations that they be full-time mothers (Frankel 1997).

Dual-earner families are supported through public policy in Norway, Sweden, Finland, and the Netherlands. Living arrangements supportive of dual-earner families, housing that is close to workplaces, and a multitude of childcare arrangements are all supported through governmental policy (Fortuijn 1996; Lewis et al. 1992; Sundström 1999). Additionally, tax policy in Sweden provides incentives for dual-earner families rather than penalizing them. A large proportion of dual-earner families in many of these countries follow the pattern of the husband working full-time and the wife working *long part-time,* which is employment between twenty and thirty-five hours per week. In Sweden, long part-time work carries the same benefits and job security provisions as full-time work (Lewis et al. 1992; Sundström 1999). This long part-time work, although available to all parents, is used mostly by women. Perhaps because of this, women in Sweden are less successful in the workforce (as in pay equality and holding top positions) than in the United States, where employed women are more likely to work full-time (Rosenfeld and

Kalleberg 1990). Even within Nordic countries, attitude surveys find that most men do not fully support an equal division of household labor, or spend equal hours in family work. Among Nordic countries, the Dutch are relatively conservative regarding dual-earners in the family, although they do not feel that children in dual-earner families are disadvantaged compared to children in single-earner families (Scott 1999).

While many women in the predominantly Catholic countries of Southern Europe want to work for pay, expect to work for many years of their lives, and value the independence of employment, relatively few married women actually engage in market work while their children are young. Many of the dual-earner families change to this status after the children are in school (Bimbi 1989; López 1998). Government policies encourage women to stay home with very young children. Italy provides generous maternity policies and widespread preschool coverage for children over the age of three (Scott 1999). The Italian government favors the dual-earner family through the income tax system, as the proportional net income added by a second earner is treated more generously than the main income (Shaver and Bradshaw 1995). Spain provides differential publicly funded childcare services by age of the child; 2 percent of the childcare services for children under the age of three are publicly funded, while 84 percent of the childcare services for children ages three to six are publicly funded (López 1998). In countries within Southern Europe, the division of labor in dual-earner couples is less gendered than in families in which the husband is the sole support because men do slightly more housework and spend more time with their children than do husbands of housewives (Bimbi 1989). Nevertheless, the work of rearing children and running a household remains primarily with women.

United States, Canada, and Australia

In the United States, most women expect to remain in the labor force for their adult lives, with only brief interruptions for childbearing (Coltrane and Collins 2001). Although most marriages with young children involve two paid spouses, somewhere between one-third and one-half of these have one spouse, usually the wife, who works less than a full forty-hour week. The evidence is contradictory as to whether part-time dual-earner couples or couples where both spouses work between thirty-nine and forty-five hours per week are the happiest with their work/family roles (Moen and Yu 1999; White 1999). However, most dual-earner families cope well and are personally satisfied with their lives (Lewis and Cooper 1988). Although many women in dual-earner families find that their spouses support their employment, employment may also be a source of conflict in male-dominated relationships. The husband's job and his attitude toward contributing to the wife's career success is a significant predictor of how well the wife negotiates her roles as well as how she feels about her job and her life as a wife (Gill and Hibbins 1996; Poole and Langan-Fox 1997).

The evidence is also contradictory evidence on whether the time that men spend doing housework is affected by the amount of time their wives spend on paid labor. Some studies suggest that husbands in dual-earner families do increase their participation in housework and childcare, albeit only slightly. Wives' longer employment hours are linked to their lower proportional share of childcare and lower absolute levels of household work (Almeida, Maggs, and Galambos 1993). Wives in dual-earner families who work full-time and who earn more than 50 percent of the family income do less housework than if they earned less than 50 percent of the family income (McFarlane, Beaujot, and Haddad 2000). Wives seem to need to earn as much as their husband, as well as to work as many hours, in order to change the power dynamics successfully enough to increase the husbands' contribution to household labor (Crompton 1997).

Family dynamics are changing as marital roles change. Although many dual-earner fathers still do not spend as much time on their family role as do dual-earner mothers, those who do find many rewards that at times offset the negative effects (e.g., increased stress, stagnated earnings) (Frankel 1997). Fathers who become involved in general childcare find it easier to balance work/family stress than fathers who are less involved in childcare (Berry and Rao 1997). Girls raised in dual-earner families hold less stereotypic views of women and men as well as what typical women and men are like and are able to do than those reared in father as single-earner families (Lewis et al. 1992). Full-time dual-earner families expect more housework from their daughters but little from their sons compared to other family types; part-time dual earner families expect the least amount of chore time from their children overall (Benin and Edwards 1990).

Conclusion

Tax policies and the provision of governmental grants generally determine whether mothers work full-time outside of the home. Those countries where policies provide benefits to full-time dual-earner families have a higher proportion of married mothers working full-time than do countries where policies penalize more than one full-time employed worker in a home (Crompton 1997; Moss 1988; Scott 1999).

Further, it is clear is that wives' income production does not, by itself, transform male-dominated marriages into egalitarian ones. Women's ability to earn their own incomes, and to survive economically outside marriages, seems to be a necessary but not sufficient condition for equality within marriage. Cultural beliefs continue to matter tremendously. In a patriarchal kinship network, if women enter paid labor because their men are underemployed or unemployed, they simply carry two jobs, the double burden, and do not necessarily challenge, at least in the short run, the submissiveness presumed to be a part of the wife role. Only societies in which women entering and remaining in the paid labor is part of a gender revolution, in which there is a cultural belief in individual rights, for women as well as men, is women's labor force participation part of a larger social change toward equality between the sexes. Only in the context of social change toward gender equality more generally is there a movement toward equality in marriage when women work for pay.

See also: CHILDCARE; DIVISION OF LABOR; EQUITY; FAMILY ROLES; FATHERHOOD; HOUSEWORK; MARITAL QUALITY; MOTHERHOOD; POWER: MARITAL RELATIONSHIPS; TIME USE; WORK AND FAMILY

Bibliography

Almeida, D. M.; Maggs, J. L.; and Galambos, N. L. (1993) "Wives' Employment Hours and Spousal Participation in Family Work." *Journal of Family Psychology* 7: 233–244.

Andrade, C.; Postma, K.; and Abraham, K. (1999) "Influence of Women's Work Status on the Well-Being of

Indian Couples." *International Journal of Social Psychiatry* 45:65–75.

Arber, S., and Gilbert, N., eds. (1992). *Women and Working Lives: Divisions and Change.* New York: St. Martin's Press.

Behrend, H. (1995) "East German Women—Chief Losers in German Unification." In *Family, Women, and Employment in Central-Eastern Europe,* ed. B. Lobodzinska. Westport, CT: Greenwood Press.

Benin, M. H. and Edwards, D. A. (1990) "Adolescents' Chores: The Difference between Dual- and Single-Earner Families." *Journal of Marriage and the Family* 52:361–373.

Berry, J. O. and Rao, J. M. (1997) "Balancing Employment and Fatherhood: A Systems Perspective." *Journal of Family Issues* 18:386–402.

Bimbi, F. (1989) "'The Double Presence': A Complex Model of Italian Women's Labor." In *Cross-Cultural Perspectives on Families, Work, and Change,* ed. K. Boh, G. Sgretta, and M.B. Sussman. Binghamton, NY: Haworth Press.

Cravey, A. J. (1998) *Women and Work in Mexico's Maquiladoras.* New York: Rowman and Littlefield Publishers.

Crompton, R. (1997) *Women and Work in Modern Britain.* New York: Oxford University Press.

Fortuijn, J. D. (1996) "City and Suburb: Contexts for Dutch Women's Work and Daily Lives." In *Women of the European Union: The Politics of Work and Daily Life,* ed. M. D. García-Ramon and J. Monk. New York: Routledge.

Frankel, J., ed. (1997). *Families of Employed Mothers.* New York: Garland.

Gal, S., and Kligman, G., eds. (2000) *Reproducing Gender: Politics, Publics and Everyday Life after Socialism.* Princeton, NJ: Princeton University Press.

Ghorayshi, P. (1996) "Women, Paid-Work and the Family: In the Islamic Republic of Iran." *Journal of Comparative Family Studies* 27:453–466.

Gill, G. K. and Hibbins, R. (1996) "Wives' Encounters: Family Work Stress and Leisure in Two-Job Families." *International Journal of Sociology of the Family* 26:43–54.

Hatt, S. (1997) *Gender, Work and Labor Markets.* New York: St. Martin's Press.

Kim, S. (1997) *Class Struggle or Family Struggle? The Lives of Women Factory Workers in South Korea.* Cambridge, UK: Cambridge University Press.

Lewis, S. N. C., and Cooper, C. L. (1988). "Stress in Dual-Earner Families." *Women and Work* 3:139–168.

Lewis, S. N. C.; Izraeli, D. N.; and Hootsmans, H., eds. (1992). *Dual-Earner Families: International Perspectives.* Newbury Park, CA: Sage.

Lobodzinska, B., ed. (1995). *Family, Women, and Employment in Central-Eastern Europe.* Westport, CT: Greenwood.

López, M. J. G. (1998) "Do Modern Welfare States Foster Democratic Family Arrangements? Comparative Case Studies of Britain and Spain." *South European Society and Politics* 3:98–123.

McFarlane, S.; Beaujot, R.; and Haddad, T. (2000) "Time Constraints and Relative Resources as Determinants of the Sexual Division of Domestic Work." *Canadian Journal of Sociology* 25:61–82.

Moen, P., and Yu, Y. (1999) "Having it All: Overall Work/Life Success in Two-Earner Families." *Research in the Sociology of Work* 7:109–139.

Mukhopadyay, S.; Dewanji, A.; and Majumder, P. P. (1993) "Working status and anxiety levels of urban educated women in Calcutta." *International Journal of Social Psychiatry* 39:200–207.

Poole, M. E., and Langan-Fox, J. (1997) *Australian Women and Careers: Psychological and Contextual Influences Over the Life Course.* New York: Cambridge University Press.

Ramu, G. N. (1989) *Women, Work and Marriage in Urban India: A Study of Dual- and Single-Earner Couples.* New York: Sage.

Redclift, N., and Sinclair, M. T., eds. (1991). *Working Women: International Perspectives on Labour and Gender Ideology.* New York: Routledge.

Rosenfeld, R. A., and Kalleberg, A. L. (1990) "A Cross-National Comparison of the Gender Gap in Income." *American Journal of Sociology* 96:69–106.

Saso, M. (1990) *Women in the Japanese Workplace.* London: Hilary Shipman.

Scott, J. (1999) "European Attitudes Towards Maternal Employment." *International Journal of Sociology and Social Policy* 9/10/11:144–177.

Selby, H. A., Murphy, A. D., and Lorenzen, S. A. (with I. Cabrera, A. Castañeda, and I. Ruiz Love). (1990) *The Mexican Urban Household: Organizing for Self-Defense.* Austin: University of Texas Press.

Shaver, S. and Bradshaw, J. (1995) "The Recognition of Wifely Labour by Welfare States." *Social Policy and Administration* 29:10–25.

Sundström, E. (1999) "Should Mothers Work? Age and Attitudes in Germany, Italy, and Sweden." *International Journal of Social Welfare* 8: 193–205.

Vannoy, D.; Rimashevskaya, N.; Cubbins, L.; Malysheva, M.; Meshterkina, E.; and Pisklakova, M. (1999) *Marriages in Russia: Couples during the Economic Transition*. Westport, CT: Praeger.

Wang, L. R. (1992) *The Investigation of the Needs of Employed Mothers and Children in Taipei*. Taipei City Government: Bureau of Social Affairs.

White, J. M. (1999) "Work-Family Stage and Satisfaction with Work-Family Balance." *Journal of Comparative Family Studies* 30:163–175.

SHANNON N. DAVIS
BARBARA J. RISMAN

ISBN 0-02-865673-3

90000